THE OFFICIAL® PRICE GUIDE TO Antique & Modern Firearms

BY
THE HOUSE OF COLLECTIBLES

We have compiled the information contained herein through a *patented computerized process* which relies primarily on a nationwide sampling of information provided by noteworthy collectible experts, auction houses and specialized dealers. This unique retrieval system enables us to provide the reader with the most current and accurate information available.

EDITOR
THOMAS E. HUDGEONS III

SIXTH EDITION
THE HOUSE OF COLLECTIBLES
NEW YORK, NEW YORK 10022

PHOTOGRAPHIC RECOGNITION

Cover Photograph: Photographer — Marc Hudgeons, Orlando, FL 32809;
Courtesy of: Praeger's Gun Shop, Orlando, FL 32074.

IMPORTANT NOTICE. The format of **THE OFFICIAL PRICE GUIDE SERIES,** published by **THE HOUSE OF COLLECTIBLES,** is based on the following proprietary features: **ALL FACTS AND PRICES ARE COMPILED THRU A COMPUTERIZED PROCESS** which relies on a nationwide sampling of information obtained from noteworthy experts, auction houses, and specialized dealers. **DETAILED "INDEXED" FORMAT** enables quick retrieval of information for positive identification. **ENCAPSULATED HISTORIES** precede each category to acquaint the collector with the specific traits that are peculiar to that area of collecting. **VALUABLE COLLECTING INFORMATION** is provided for both the novice as well as the seasoned collector: How to begin a collection; How to buy, sell, and trade; Care and storage techniques; Tips on restoration; Grading guidelines; Lists of periodicals, clubs, museums, auction houses, dealers, etc. **AN AVERAGE PRICE RANGE** takes geographic location and condition into consideration when reporting collector value. **A SPECIAL THIRD PRICE COLUMN** enables the collector to compare the current market values with last year's average selling price indicating which items have increased in value. **INVENTORY CHECKLIST SYSTEM** is provided for cataloging a collection. **EACH TITLE IS ANNUALLY UPDATED** to provide the most accurate information available in the rapidly changing collector's marketplace.

All of the information, including valuations, in this book has been compiled from the most reliable sources, and every effort has been made to eliminate errors and questionable data. Nevertheless the possibility of error, in a work of such immense scope, always exists. The publisher will not be held responsible for losses which may occur in the purchase, sale, or other transaction of items because of information contained herein. Readers who feel they have discovered errors are invited to **WRITE** and inform us, so they may be corrected in subsequent editions. Those seeking further information on the topics covered in this book are advised to refer to the complete line of Official Price Guides published by The House of Collectibles.

Published by: The House of Collectibles
201 East 50th Street
New York, New York 10022

Distributed by Ballantine Books, a division of Random House, Inc., New York and simultaneously in Canada by Random House of Canada Limited, Toronto.

Printed in the United States of America

Library of Congress Catalog Card Number: 80-81290

ISBN: 0-87637-287-6 / Paperback

10 9 8 7 6 5 4 3

TABLE OF CONTENTS

NOTE TO READERS

MARKET REVIEW

The major development in the firearms market since publication of our last edition was U.S. relaxation of import restrictions. This occurred in October, 1984. While the full effects have yet to be felt, some noticeable changes in values have already taken place. The greater ease with which firearms can now be imported into the U.S. will create, in the coming months, abundant supplies of guns that were previously difficult to get in this country. Military models from Germany, Italy, South America and elsewhere are now being imported in large numbers, with a corresponding decline in market value. It is believed the military models will continue to comprise the largest category of imports, at least for the next several years. This could mean an eventual decline in price to a virtual fraction of the pre-October, 1984, levels.

The rewritten laws apply exclusively to arms manufactured at least twenty five years ago. Hence the value of currently or recently produced foreign guns are not likely to change. The laws were designed to cover secondhand and obsolete models which are not in direct competition against guns made by U.S. companies. In a sense it could be termed a "collector law(s)," but collectors are far from universally enthusiastic about it. The beginning gun collector will certainly appreciate the lower prices, as will veteran hobbyists who want to add specific foreign models to their collections. However, the collectors who already own foreign guns for which they paid pre-October, 1984, prices are now in a position of watching their investments decline. Nor can this be regarded as a temporary decline, such as occurs during times of economic slumps. It is likely to be permanent, as the quantities of guns imported into the country are not apt to be exported. They will always be with us, and for all practical purposes one must assume that the old price levels will not return.

At this point it is too early to say how low the prices will go. In the final analysis some models, and possibly all the models of some manufacturers, may be hit much harder than others. This all depends on the stockpiles that exist in foreign countries and the eagerness of foreign dealers to export them. At first, of course, the situation greatly favored foreign exporters. They could ship their guns to this country and receive a much higher price for them than at home. With prices then declining in the U.S., the margin of profit became smaller. If prices dip really low, it is probable that many foreign dealers will have nothing to gain by exportation, and a stabilization will be brought about.

Various intangibles are involved which make predictions impossible. For one thing, the reduced prices on so many foreign arms may encourage their purchase by persons who would not otherwise have bought them. If the number of buyers increases, this in itself could provide some measure of price stabilization. For another, the very strong hobbyist interest in certain foreign military guns, such as those of Nazi Germany, could be sufficient to prevent a drastic price decline. There are undoubtedly many collectors who will rush to buy Nazi guns at a 20% or 25% savings. Then again, the foreign dealers have a healthy market for guns of that type in their homeland, and may not export them in wholesale numbers.

The basically common guns of World Wars I and II are likely to suffer the greatest value declines. Guns classified as antiques should not be hurt in the least, but many of the "curio" graded guns will be. Collectors should keep in mind that the model year for a gun is not necessarily the year of manufacture. During World War I, a number of foreign countries were using rifles with model years in the 1880s and 1890s, even though the war was fought from 1914 to 1918. They were not using "old" guns but guns which had remained in production for several decades. This was also true, though to a lesser degree, in World War II.

Elsewhere in the firearms market, commemoratives had a generally off year, most of them slipping in value from 5% to around 15%. Non-commemorative limited editions did considerably better on the whole, either holding steady or even gaining. This development seems to vindicate those who had long warned of a saturation of commemorative guns on the market. Commemoratives have been issued in increasing numbers since the mid 1970s, sparked by the success of the many Bicentennial models. With the secondary market on commemoratives going soft, a decrease in the number issued may follow. This could, however, be merely a temporary situation. Even with their value declines, it should be noted, most commemoratives did no worse than return to their late 1982/early 1983 value levels. They simply lost the increases gained thereafter. Most commemoratives are still selling for more than their original factory prices.

FACTORS THAT DETERMINE VALUE

CONDITION

With the passage of time everything deteriorates and guns are no exception. Use, abuse, wear and aging all adversely affect the price of guns to a varying degree, and in the case of collectible guns the difference in price can be very significant. Because of the importance of describing the condition of a gun the N.R.A. devised a set of guidelines to standardize firearms grading. The prices listed in this guide are for guns in N.R.A. Very Good and N.R.A. Excellent condition *(Antiques are N.R.A. Antique Very Good to Antique Fine),* and you can easily adjust those prices to determine the value of your gun if it does not fall into either of those categories. But strict grading of condition following N.R.A. guidelines is essential.

Antique firearms in excellent to new condition add 25% to 100% to the "excellent" price depending on scarcity and demand. For antiques in good condition, deduct 30% to 35% from "very good."

Modern firearms in good condition deduct 20% to 25% from "very good"; fair condition, deduct 45% to 55%. Arms in "perfect" to "new" add 30% to 75% depending on collectability.

Any collectible firearm, no matter how poor the condition (so long as it hasn't been crushed or melted), should fetch 20% to 30% of the "very good" price. As the saying goes, "old guns never die, they just get reblued".

N.R.A. CONDITION GUIDELINES

NEW: not previously sold at retail, in same condition as current factory production.

NEW-DISCONTINUED: Same as New, but discontinued model.

The following definitions will apply to all secondhand articles:

PERFECT: In new condition in every respect.

EXCELLENT: New condition, used but little, no noticeable marring of wood or metal, bluing perfect (except at muzzle or sharp edges).

VERY GOOD: In perfect working condition, no appreciable wear on working surfaces, no corrosion or pitting, only minor surface dents or scratches.

GOOD: In safe working condition minor wear on working surfaces, no broken parts, no corrosion or pitting that will interfere with proper functioning.

FAIR: In safe working condition, but well worn, perhaps requiring replacement of minor parts or adjustments, which should be indicated in advertisement, no rust, but may have corrosion pits which do not render article unsafe or inoperable.

Another set of standards applies to "antique" arms as follows:

FACTORY NEW: 100% original finish and parts, everything perfect.

EXCELLENT: All parts and 80%-100% finish original; all letters, numerals, designs sharp; unmarred wood, fine bore.

FINE: All parts and over 30% finish original; all letters, numerals, designs sharp; only minor wood marks, good bore.

VERY GOOD: Up to 30% original finish, all original parts; metal surfaces smooth, with all edges sharp; clear letters, numerals, designs, wood slightly scratched or bruised; bore on collector items disregarded.

GOOD: Only minor replacement parts; metal smoothly rusted or lightly pitted in places; cleaned or reblued; principal letters, numerals, designs legible; wood refinished, scratched, bruised, or with minor cracks repaired; mechanism in good working order.

FAIR: Some major parts replaced; minor replacements; metal may be lightly pitted all over, vigorously cleaned or reblued, edges partly rounded; wood scratched, bruised, cracked or repaired; mechanism in working order.

ORNAMENTATION

Engraving

It's hard to generalize about art, and that is what engraving is. You must examine a number of examples to learn to judge the quality of the work.

Crude engraving: sparse, add about 25%; medium coverage, add 50% to 75%; full coverage add 100% to 125%.

High quality engraving: sparse, add 50% to 100%; medium coverage, add 150% to 200%; full coverage, add 300% up.

Ornate, high quality work with gold inlays, etc., add 400% up.

Wood carving and marquetry (stock inlays)

This is also in the realm of art, and you should try to look at as many specimens as possible to compare craftsmanship.

Carvings: simple, add $10 to $40 each depending on the quality of execution; complex, add $60 to $150. Full coverage, good quality, add $125 up. Remember that a poor carving (such as crude initials) will detract from the value.

Inlays: simple, add $10 to $25 each; ornate, add $50 up. Exotic materials, such as ivory or mother-of-pearl, can double the value of the inlay. The value of wire inlays depends as much on the coverage as the execution.

Note: N.R.A. Grading Standards reprinted with the permission of the N.R.A.

Simple wire inlays using brass or German silver should start at $40 each, tripling if silver is used, and multiplying by 10 if gold is used. Initial shields that are unmarked and not standard equipment on the gun add $15; $25 for sterling silver; $100 for 14k gold.

Heat carving, stampings, and woodburnings are becoming increasingly common and should not be confused with real carving. These should add about $25 if done well.

Custom checkering

As with carving, craftsmanship is paramount. A poorly done checkering job will lower the value of a gun. Nicely executed patterns on a long gun, add $35 to $50. Fine, complex patterns with wide coverage, add $60 up.

Gold damascening:

The is the art of applying gold leaf or gold plate in a fancy pattern, usually in conjunction with engraving, and should not be confused with gold inlay. Simple patterns, add $60 to $85; fancy patterns, add $265 to $395.

LOCATION OF SALE

As this guide lists average national prices, several regional factors must be considered.

Antiques: If a particular arm was made in your area, or saw wide service there, there should be more interest in it. This increased market demand will run prices 10% to 15% higher than listed. The reverse is also true.

Modern: Much depends on the type of area you live in. In wide-open places where long-range shooting is possible, high-powered rifles may bring 10% over value listed, whereas shotguns will be 15% less. In wooded areas the reverse will occur. In high crime areas, handguns for home protection will bring premiums. Trap and skeet generally stay constant. Wherever you are, judge the type of hobby shooting most prevalent, and the types of guns used for it will follow the above pattern.

SPECIAL MARKINGS AND COMMEMORATIVES

Standard firearms of most all companies have at some time been ordered or issued with special markings, special features, or as commemoratives. The important consideration in this section is that all deviations from the norm be factory original.

Special markings

Governments, law enforcement agencies, and stores have ordered the factory to put special marks on guns, and the main requirement in adding value to a gun with these marks is that the gun itself be collectable. The percentage additions shown reflect "common" variations. Rare marks on already very scarce guns may run five to ten times that percentage; however, caution is advisable since this particular market is limited and highly specialized, and as always with rare items, when you get out of your field it's best to consult an expert.

Police or agency markings in lieu of regular marks (not overstamps or extra stamps), add 25% to 50%; trade marks of stores in exotic locales (Rhodesia, etc.), add 50% to 75%; foreign military marks, add 50% to 75%.

Mismarked guns: No stamps, upside-down stamps, wrong markings, etc., add 100% up depending on the collectability of the gun itself.

Special features: This section applies to custom modifications done by the factory and not listed under a particular manufacturer elsewhere in this guide.

Special sights, add 10% to 15%; special metal finish (nickel, etc.), add 10%

to 15%; extra-fancy wood on long guns, add 15% to 25%; special barrel lengths, add 20% to 30%.

Commemoratives

One very important question to ask yourself: Is this gun a standard mass-produced item with just an extra stamp or applied token, or is it actually from a limited production and different from standard in style and embellishment? If your gun falls into the first category, appreciation will be quite slow; if the latter, than the value will rise sharply for the first two or three years, thereafter leveling off to a little better than the inflation rate.

HISTORIC RELICS

Documentation is the key word in connecting an old gun with a historic event or famous person. Saying "it used to belong to grandpa and he was so and so" just isn't enough. To be absolutely certain of a weapon's ownership or use, records contemporary with its use must be available. They can be factory records showing the gun's disposition, wills, diaries, etc. Lacking that, if there is strong evidence of ownership such as a name engraved and some documentation showing that the person could have owned it, then it should be labeled "probably." "Grandpa" testimony without supporting evidence can be labeled "possibly." The value of a historic relic transcends the worth of the gun, and depends on the fame (or infamy) of the owner, the artistic value, the location of the sale, and the intangible "mood" of the public as to what period of history is "in."

LEGAL CLASSIFICATIONS OF FIREARMS

There are four classifications of firearms used by the Bureau of Alcohol, Tobacco, and Firearms of the Treasury Department.

Antique: Any firearm manufactured in or before 1898, and replicas that do not fire rim-fire or center-fire cartridges readily available in commercial trade. Antiques are exempt from federal regulation.

Modern: Firearms manufactured after 1898, excluding Replica Antiques, and with special regulations for Class III arms.

Curios and Relics: Certain modern firearms that can be sent interstate to licensed collectors.

Class III Arms: This includes machine guns, silencers, short (under 18") shotguns, short (under 16") rifles, modern smoothbore handguns, and modern arms with a rifled bore diameter greater than .50".

All of the above may be legally owned, notwithstanding federal regulations and local restrictions in a few areas. For further information, contact your local office of the Bureau of Alcohol, Tobacco, and Firearms.

A SPECIAL NOTE ABOUT LEGAL CLASSIFICATIONS

Curios: This is a subdivision of "modern" and pertains to arms that may be sent interstate to licensed collectors. However, there is a great deal of confusion as to what constitutes a "curio". The B.A.T.F. issues a yearly list of arms so classified, which is constantly changing and, by virtue of time and space limitations, is incomplete.

Since this guide followed the curio list in force at the time of writing, far more arms are "curios" than are described as such.

The following is the federal guideline to use to determine if a specific firearm or cartridge is a "curio". It must:

1. have been manufactured at least 50 years prior to the current date, but not including replicas there of, or

2. be certified by the curator of a municipal, state, or federal museum that exhibits firearms to be curios or relics of museum interest; or

3. derive a substantial part of its monetary value from the fact that it is novel, rare, or bizarre, or from the fact of its association with some historical figure, period, or event.

Collectors wishing to obtain a curio or relic determination from ATF on a specific firearm or round of ammunition should submit a letter to the Chief of the Firearms Technology Branch, Bureau of Alcohol, Tobacco, and Firearms, Washington, D.C. 20226. The letter should include a complete physical description of the firearm or ammunition, stating the reasons that the collector believes that the firearm or ammunition in question merits such classification, and supporting data concerning the history of the firearm or ammunition, including production figures, if available, and market value.

Antiques: Many arms listed in this guide were produced between dates overlapping the "antique" determination date. In cases where experts have given a recognized serial number cutoff for "antiques" I have tried to include it. In other instances where arms have no numbers, or where no number is generally recognized as the magic one, I have classified them as modern and leave it to a specialist to make an individual determination.

HOW TO BUY AND SELL FIREARMS

BUYING COLLECTORS GUNS

Where to buy

Reliable estimates place the number of guns in private hands in the U.S. at over 100 million! Quite a lot, but if you've picked out the special items you wish to collect and started looking you've probably noticed that you can generally find everything but what you need. So where do you go to find them? There are several sources.

Mail Order. Even though the Gun Control Act of 1968 prohibited the mailing of firearms to individuals, the mail order gun business is alive and well. However, the method is a little different because of the laws and the nature of the business. According to U.S. law only federally licensed gun dealers may ship and receive modern firearms, but many dealers for a small fee will be happy to receive the gun you've ordered and transfer it to you. Another alternative for the collector is to apply for a collector's license from the Bureau of Alcohol, Tobacco and Firearms. This license allows the collector to receive and send interstate shipments of modern firearms that are classified as curios to another licensee. For more information about licenses contact your local office of the B.A.T.F.

Mail order done properly is legal and fairly simple and, most importantly, an excellent way to build your collection and to take advantage of prices that may be more competitive than in your local area. Most specialist mail order dealers are very reputable, and many offer an inspection period so that you may return the gun in the same condition as it arrived if you're not satisfied. Almost all of the dealers of collectable guns advertise, and many have regular lists of guns offered for sale that you can subscribe to for a nominal rate Many gun magazines and collector newsletters have classified sections that provide good leads, but an excellent starting point would be Shotgun News (P.O. Box 669, Hastings, Nebr. 68901).

Gun Shows. There are a great many gun shows held in all parts of the U.S. with good frequency. They provide an opportunity to examine a large number of collectable guns at one place, and a chance to bargain with the owners for a better price. Gun show listings can be found in magazines such as Gun Report (P.O. Box 111, Aledo, Ill. 61231)

Gun Shops. Gun stores and pawn shops offer an exciting chance to find a collector's item at a good price because they may not have a market to sell some of the more interesting items. As a result they sometimes buy low and sell low in order to turn their inventory.

Private Individuals. This categorv includes non-gun shops as well as individuals, and this is the area where real caution must be exercised. Although bargains may be found, many times people have an inflated idea of the value of their gun, and very often the article for sale is misidentified. Remember, knowledge is power!

Pitfalls

Refinished Guns. A refinished gun can be beautiful. Unfortunately it also drastically reduces the value of a collector's item, so it's valuable to know how to spot refinishing. Most of the time when a gun is reblued or replated it must be heavily polished to remove small pits. A good craftsman will keep all of the edges sharp, will preserve the lettering, and will avoid "ripple" (waves polished into the gun in places where the metal should be flat). Poor craftsmen will remove lettering, round edges, and in general remove too much metal. The finish on a good job will be even and bright, on a poor job it will look splotchy and uneven. If you suspect that a gun has been refinished look for these signs: the lettering will have "drag-out marks" (one edge of the letter will be furrowed from polishing); the quality of finish doesn't match the original factory job; parts have been finished to a different color than original. Remember, most factories did an excellent job of finishing.

Upgrades. Upgrading is taking a normal gun that is in decent condition and engraving or otherwise embellishing it so that it is more valuable. In many cases a good upgrade comes within 60% to 70% of the value of the factory original if the job is well done. But beware of guns that people try to pass off as original. The best defense is education. If you're interested in high grade guns try to examine as many known originals as you can to get a feel for that factory's style and quality, or enlist the aid of an expert to help you.

Fakes. Counterfeits, it seems, have always been with us, and as with any item of value, low cost reproductions have been made and passed along as the real thing. There are all kinds of reproductions, from the crude kitchen table conversion with the uneven lettering stamps to the ultra-sophisticated copy made with some original parts. Fakes include complete reproductions of antique guns to ⅛" police stamps on World War II German pistols. Once again knowledge is everything. Learn all you can before buying, and on valuable items buy from someone you can trust. Most dealers of collectable guns are extremely honest, and it's very rare to hear of a dealer intentionally trying to sell a fake.

Condition Descriptions. The N.R.A. guidelines are not always used by dealers and collectors when describing their guns. Many times there will be descriptions such as "95% blue" or "near mint," which while they sound good sometimes mask a multitude of sins. Just because someone uses either vague descriptions or their own grading does not necessarily mean that they're trying to hide something. Sometimes people get entrenched in their ways and you have to learn their system. But it does pay to ask a few questions to make sure that everything is functioning as it should be, and that all of the parts are there. Accurate percentage descriptions are an acquired skill and when used in conjuction with a good description can give an accurate picture, but be sure that you have complete information.

SELLING COLLECTOR GUNS

As important as buying is the ability to sell what you have, and there are many ways to do this. The major things to consider when you sell is how fast do you want to sell your guns and how much do you want for them. The two are not necessarily mutually exclusive, but usually if you want top price you have to compete with the dealer and it takes time. Always remember that guns are cashable items and the choice of what you are willing to take for them is yours and will be based on your salesmanship.

Where to sell

Gun Stores. The local gun dealer generally cannot pay you a top price on a collectable gun unless he has a good market for it. Even then he must make a profit. But this is a good source to sell your guns quickly.

Specialist and Mail Order Dealers. Many times these dealers will pay somewhat higher prices and work on a slimmer margin because they have built up customer lists over the years and may have a guaranteed resale of your gun.

Your Own Ad. This may be the way to get the most for your guns, but it also takes the longest and requires the cooperation of a gun licensee for shipping. There is usually a four to eight week time lag between the time you place an ad and the time it is in print and the publication distributed. Additionally, you also have the cost of the ad to consider as well as the cost of packaging and shipping.

Gun Shows. This can provide not only a place to sell your guns but a great meeting ground for fellow collectors. Of course your salesmanship is of prime importance to get your best price, but you will meet people with similar interests who may be very interested in buying what you have.

Auctions. This can sometimes be a risky venture. In an unreserved auction the highest bid wins, and if there is a bad crowd your guns could go for very little, and to add insult to injury you will have to pay a commission. In a reserved auction you are allowed to set a reasonable bottom figure, and if the gun does not reach that amount you get it back. However, you will generally have to pay a small commission to have it returned on reserve. But the other side of the coin is that people sometimes get carried away at an auction, and many times guns fetch a much higher price than what is expected. With auctions you have to be lucky.

Recordkeeping

U.S. law is very specific about a firearms licensee's recordkeeping responsibilities, but although the private individual is not required to, he should also keep records. Suggested information to keep for your own use would include the name and address of the person you acquired the gun from and the date, the make, model, caliber, type, and serial number of your gun, and when you sell it the name and address of the buyer and the date you sold it. It would also be handy to keep a record of the price you paid.

THE NATIONAL RIFLE ASSOCIATION OF AMERICA

The right to private ownership of firearms, a right so obviously vital to gun collectors as well as sportsmen, has been the primary cause championed by the National Rifle Association of Washington, D.C. This historic organization, now more than a century old and numbering well over 3 million members, has also made vast contributions toward the study, technology, history, and safe use of firearms. Nearly all U.S. gun dealers, and a large proportion of collectors, are members of the NRA, and have derived numerous benefits from membership.

Most readers of this book are, undoubtedly, already familiar with the NRA. But a work on firearms collecting could hardly be complete without a few words on the organization, and (at the end of this brief article) information on becoming a member.

While the firearms hobbyist has his choice of many organizations to join, membership in the nationwide NRA seems almost basic for anyone interested in gun collecting. The NRA's strength, supplied by its ever-increasing roster of members, insures a strong voice for the hobby. Whether the collector cares to realize it or not, there are individuals, including some in government — who would strangle the hobby by outlawing the possession, sale, or trade of ALL firearms.....or who would support such stringent restrictions on firearms ownership that gun collection would, for all practical purposes, come to an end. This is a battle that is never officially over. The tide can be kept in the collector's favor ONLY by interested parties making themselves known and counted. And the fact that the NRA membership has increased more dramatically in recent years, than ever in the past, is solid evidence that the future will be bright for gun enthusiasts.

The National Rifle Association has many goals and serves multitudes of purposes. The public hears, occasionally of it's activities in lobbying against gun control legislation. Seldom does the news media report the numerous other NRA functions. Among these is its continuing efforts to promote better understanding of the safe use and care of all types of firearms, in conjunction with this goal, the NRA holds many seminars on gun-use instruction, as well as field meets and other training activities for firearms owners. It believes — and the belief is an historic one, a long tradition of the organization — that citizens well-trained in the use of firearms will be better citizens, and will be more capable of contributing to the defense of themselves, their community, and the nation. The NRA is also very active in conservation programs, to preserve endangered species and to encourage hunting only when and where the hunter presents no danger to the ecology.

THE HISTORY

The NRA is now more than 114 years old, having been chartered (originally by the State of New York) in 1871. It was born as a direct outgrowth of the Civil War. Of the many lessons that came from the war's battlefields, one was imprinted indelibly on the minds of officers; the majority of infantry soldiers were simply unskilled in the use of firearms. Even the rudimentary rules of gun use were foreign to them. In part the military was to blame. It devoted more attention to parade

Dr. Alonzo H. Garcelon
President

G. Ray Arnett
Executive Vice President

marching and drills than to firearms instruction. If Uncle Sam could not be counted on to do the job, it was then the responsibility of concerned citizens to promote firearms training. In 1871, the New York National Guard comprised a number of such concerned citizens. They were all ex-Union veterans and had seen at first hand, the severity of the problem in combat. So in September of that year an ambitious group of 15 of them collected to establish an organization — the first of its kind in the country. It would strive to instill pride in proper gun handling, and marksmanship, to increase the level of firearms knowledge among U.S. citizens, and in this way, better prepare Americans for military service in the event of war. It was a lofty ideal, but history showed it was unachievable. A hundred years earlier, the American colonists were highly skilled in firearms use because the necessity to hunt and protect one's property left little choice in the matter. There was no doubt that proper education could once again hone the shooting skills of the average citizen.

It was decided to model the organization after Britain's National Rifle Association, so the name National Rifle Association of America was chosen. A leader with military background and national recognition was a necessity; one was found in the person of General Ambrose Burnside who had served in the Civil War. On November 17, 1871, the charter was formally granted. But the new organization faced stiff challenges. The "media" of that time consisted almost wholly of newspapers, and newspaper accounts of the young NRA brought no groundswell of membership. There were the inevitable difficulties with funding, which limited the number of tournaments and other activities; and the hazards faced by changes in the government's administration, since some Presidents were more supportive of the NRA than others.

Though times occasionally looked bleak, the organization pushed forward, spread its message, and succeeded in surviving. Finally the country was awakened to the truth of the NRA's warnings about ill-prepared soldiers, when the Spanish-American War broke out in the late 1890's. This conflict brought immediate attention to the NRA, and when the war ended things began changing. In 1903 the government established its National Board for the Promotion of Rifle Practice, and NRA training activities were greatly increased. Thanks to the NRA, which grew impressively in the years from 1903 to 1916, the country was far better prepared for entry into World War I than it could otherwise have been. Many of the enlisted men had received NRA training. This was doubly so 25 years later, when America went into World War II. In the meantime, the NRA was also at work with law enforcement agencies, on federal and local levels, to promote more efficient firearms use by police officers. The firearms collector, if he takes an interest in memorabilia, has certainly seen and perhaps owned some of the NRA award medals. These handsome medals took the place of large-size trophies of earlier years, and were eagerly competed for in NRA-sanctioned events. A number of types exist, for competition among civilians and law enforcement agents.

After World War II, the NRA inaugurated the first hunter safety program, designed to eliminate hunting accidents arising from ignorance of firearms use and/or poor marksmanship. Then in 1975 came the epochal establishment of the NRA Institute for Legislative Action, to protect the right of law-abiding citizens to own firearms.

The three millionth member was added to the NRA membership rolls in 1985 — a striking record of growth for an organization that began with little more than guts, hope and 15 far-sighted members 114 years earlier.

THE NRA INSTITUTE FOR LEGISLATIVE ACTION

The NRA's Institute for Legislative Action performs many functions. It monitors all gun-related bills put before Congress, to study their fairness and seek change when necessary. It likewise keeps careful watch on court rulings in all parts of the country, in cases involving the right to own and bear arms or similar questions. When rulings are made contrary to the NRA's position, it often assigns an attorney and allocates funds for the preparation of appeals, and to date has been very successful in this phase of its operations.

NRA FIELD SERVICES

The NRA Field Services are designed primarily for furthering the goals of the organization's founders and promoting a better understanding of firearms use among private citizens. Officers of the Field Services work closely with those of the Institute for Legislative Action in a number of interrelated areas. One of the primary arms of the NRA Field Services is its Volunteer Resources Department, which recruits and trains volunteer members. The Range Development Department, also a branch of Field Services, is active in inspecting target-shooting ranges at various firearms clubs. One of the goals of the NRA, through its Field Services, is to arrive at a level of standardization in rifle and pistol tournaments so that each tournament is held under similar conditions and with corresponding rules and regulations. This, of course, is an aid to the shooter and a springboard to developing increased skill, rather than having to adapt to different rules and conditions at each tournament. Shooting tournaments are growing at such a rapid rate that the NRA has had to greatly expand its staff to keep pace with the demand for skilled range and tournament supervision. The Field Services are also involved with selection of suitable sites for tournament and practice ranges; design of ranges for maximum efficiency and safety; and legal assistance on all aspects of range establishment and operation. This is vital because the laws of individual states sometimes differ and a range operator must be fully informed of the local applicable laws.

In 1981, the NRA reached an all-time high in the number of its affiliated range clubs, with 12,560. Also, in 1981, the Field Services appointed separate State Association Coordinators for the range clubs in each State, thereby providing an individual with local knowledge to work directly with the clubs in his state and act as a kind of liason between them and the NRA.

One of the chief aspects of Field Services is the NRA Range Loan Program, which has so far supplied more than $400,000 to local clubs for the establishment or renovation of their range shooting facilities.

NRA PUBLIC EDUCATION

The NRA Public Education department is the link between the NRA and the general public — "general public" meaning persons who are not members of the NRA nor who are even gun owners or hunting enthusiasts. Its purpose is to explain the position of NRA members and sportsmen in general, on various affairs, to the public. This is of course of great significance because the general public elects the country's legislators and, in a roundabout way, makes its laws. Whenever an issue arises involving the ownership of firearms or anything to concern hunters and gun hobbyists, the Public Education branch of the NRA prepares its view and disseminates it to the news media. Usually, the matters involved in legal questions or other complex subjects need to be put into plain language for the public to better understand. This is seldom done by the news media itself, which contains many elements opposed to the principles of the NRA. Unfortunately some segments of the public have formed very false conclusions about gun owners and hunters, and about the motives of the NRA. They assume that hunters are automatically bad for the ecology and that firearms ownership among private citizens breeds criminal activity. One project of the NRA Public Education department has been an advertising campaign in various national magazines, picturing the hunter and gun hobbyist as he really is; just an average citizen like the "general public" and not someone to be feared or shunned.

But the Public Education activities go deeper than this. They involve the development of such tools as the Shooting Sports Library Kit, designed to be placed into public and school libraries and containing various publications on the positive aspects of hunting, shooting, and gun ownership. The NRA strongly believes that gun education, like other forms of education, is most effective when begun early, and that the rudiments of gun knowledge should be taught to even very young children.

NRA'S OTHER OPERATIONS

The other operations of the National Rifle Association comprise; Membership Services; Competitions; Hunter Services; Junior Programs; Education and Training; Law Enforcement Services, and NRA Publications. All of these interrelated activities bring the NRA's activities and purposes close to the public. Among the Membership Benefits are of course the well-known *American Rifleman* and *American Hunter* magazines which are sent automatically to NRA members. The most widely read and authorative publications of their kind, they carry articles on all aspects of hunting, shooting, gun care, and related topics, authored by experts in their fields; and also the latest reports on news of interest to hunters and gun hobbyists in the way of pending legislation, improvements in gun design, inauguration of new clubs and so on.

One of the highlights of the NRA is its sponsorship of shooting tournaments, which has been a vital function of the organization since its earliest pioneer days. The number of events and the total of competitors has constantly increased over the years, reaching unprecedented heights in 1984 (the most recent year for which statistics are available). In 1984 the NRA's famous National Matches were participated in by 3,838 contestants, and attended by more than 6,000 spectators. They were held at Camp Perry, Ohio. The NRA is likewise active in sponsoring collegiate shooting competitions, and in 1981 organized the first National Collegiate Pistol Championships at Massachusetts Institute of Technology.

The NRA's Youth Programs include National Junior Olympic Shooting Camps, State Junior Olympic Shooting Camps, National Junior Smallbore Camp, Junior Rifle and Pistol Clubs, Junior Gun Collecting Activities, 4-H State Shooting Sports Programs, and a variety of programs in partnership with the Boy Scouts of America. In addition to rifle and pistol shooting for youth, the NRA also sponsors air-gun shooting matches.

MEMBERSHIP

Membership in the NRA is both inexpensive and rewarding for anyone interested in firearms. Membership places one in league with all the leading sportsmen and gun hobbyists of the country, and adds further weight to the NRA's ability to carry out its programs and objectives.

NRA	
1 Year	$ 15
3 Years	$ 40
5 Years	$ 60
Life	$300

NRA SENIOR (65 and over)	
1 Year	$ 10
Life	$150

NRA ASSOCIATE (spouse) (without magazine)	
1 Year	$ 10
Life	$100

NRA JUNIOR (Under 20)	
1 Year	$ 5
(without magazine)	
1 Year	$ 12
Life	$150

Foreign: Canada add $2.00; Other countries add $3.00 postage per year.

GLOSSARY

ACP. Abbreviation for Automatic Colt Pistol, applied to ammunition designed originally or adopted by Colt.

ACTION. That part of a firearm made up of the breech and the parts designed to fire and cycle cartridges.

ADJUSTABLE CHOKE. Device attached to the muzzle of a shotgun enabling a change of choke by a rotational adjustment or by changing tubes.

ANTIQUE. A legal classification that in the U.S. is applied to weapons manufactured in or before 1898, and replicas that don't fire fixed ammunition.

ARSENAL. Military installation that stores and usually upgrades and modifies military weapons, and sometimes also applies to governmental weapon manufacturing facilities.

AUTOMATIC. Action type that ejects a spent cartridge and brings a fresh cartridge into firing position without manual intervention and has the capability of firing more than one shot with each pull of the trigger.

AUTOMATIC EJECTOR. Cases are ejected from the firearm when the action is opened without any manual intervention.

AUTOMATIC REVOLVER. Firearm action which resembles a conventional revolver except that on firing the cylinder is rotated and the hammer recocked by the recoil energy of the firing cartridge.

AUTOMATIC SAFETY. A block that prevents firing which is applied by the gun every time the action is cycled.

AYDT ACTION. A singleshot action utilizing a curved breechblock and a hinged section below the forward part of the chamber. The breechblock moves downward in an arc when pressure is applied to the finger lever.

BACKSTRAP. Rearmost part of the grip portion of a handgun frame.

BACK LOCK. Self-contained hammer, sear, and spring mounted on a single plate with the exposed hammer on the forward part of the plate, set into the side of a gun.

BARREL. Tube through which the bullet or shot passes on firing.

BARREL BAND. Metal band that secures the barrel to the forend.

BARRELED ACTION. The assembled barrel and complete action.

BARREL LINER. Thin steel tube usually permanently inserted into the barrel to either change the caliber, restore the gun, or to make the gun more functional when the barrel is formed from softer material.

BAYONET LUG. Metal projection at the end of the barrel for attaching a bayonet.

BAYONET. A knife or spike designed to be attached to a firearm.

BEAD SIGHT. Usually a round bead on the forward top of the barrel to aid in aiming (pointing) without the aid of a rear sight.

BEAVERTAIL FOREND. A wide, hand-filling forestock on long guns.

BENCHREST RIFLE. A heavy rifle designed for accurate shooting supported on a bench.

BIPOD. A two legged support attached to the forend of a rifle.

BLOWBACK ACTION. Automatic and semi-automatic action in which the breechblock is held forward only by spring pressure and cycles from the rearward gas thrust of the fired cartridge.

BLOW FORWARD ACTION. Automatic and semi-automatic action which has a fixed breechblock and in which spring pressure secures a barrel that reciprocates and cycles the action from the pressure of expanding gasses when a cartridge is fired.

BLUE. An artificial oxidation process that yeilds some rust protection and leaves steel surfaces with a blue-black color.

BLUNDERBUSS. A smoothbore weapon with a very flared muzzle.

BOLT ACTION. A manual action cycled by moving a reciprocating breechbolt.

BORE. The inside of a barrel; the diameter of a barrel.

BOX LOCK. Generally a break top action which contains the hammer, sear, springs and trigger in an integral unit directly behind the breech.

BREAK TOP. Action which exposes the breech by unlocking and the barrel(s) tipping downward, rotating on a point just forward of the breech.

BREECH. Rear end of the barrel; that part of the action that contacts the rear of the cartridge.

BREECHBOLT. The part of the action that secures the cartridge in the chamber.

BULL BARREL. A heavy barrel, usually with no taper.

BUTT. The rearmost portion of a stock.

BUTT PLATE. A plate fastened to the rear of the butt.

CALIBER. Bore diameter usually measured land to land in decimals of an inch or in millimeters.

CARBINE. A short, lightweight rifle.

CARTRIDGE. A self contained unit of ammunition.

CASE HARDENED. A surface hardening on that firearms is usually done so as to leave a broad spectrum of colors on the metal.

CENTER FIRE. Cartridge that contains a primer in the center of the base of the case.

CHAMBER. Portion of the gun in which the cartridge is placed.

CHECKERING. Geometric carving in the shape of parallel lines that cross to form diamonds, and used for both beauty and to provide a better handgrip.

CHEEKPIECE. A raised portion of the stock where the shooter's cheek touches the butt.

CHOKE. A muzzle constriction on shotguns which is used to control the pattern of shot.

CLIP. A detachable box that holds feeds ammunition into the gun by spring pressure.

COMBINATION GUN. A multi-barreled weapon that has a rifle barrel and a shotgun barrel.

CONDITION. The state of newness or wear of a gun. See the introduction for a complete description.

CONVERSION. The rebuilding of a military arm into a sporting arm; converting the arm to use a different cartridge;changing the general configuration of a gun.

CURIO. Curios and Relics are a legal subclassification of modern arms. See the complete defination in the introduction.

CUT-OFF. A device that can stop the flow of ammunition from the magazine.

CYLINDER. The rotating container with cartridge chambers in a revolver.

DAMASCENE. An overlay of metal, usually gold leaf, sometimes combined with light engraving and used for decoration.

DAMASCENING. Also called Engine Turning or Jeweling, this is an ornamental polishing consisting of repeated and overlapping circles.

DAMASCUS. A metal formed usually by twisting strands of iron and steel and repeatedly hammer-welding them.

DERINGER. A small percussion pistol developed by Henry Deringer.

DERRINGER. A copy of the Deringer, now meaning any very small manually operated pistol.

DOUBLE ACTION. The ability to both cock and fire a gun by the single pull of a trigger.

DOUBLE-BARREL. A gun having two barrels.

DOUBLE TRIGGER. A gun having two triggers, each usually firing a different trigger.

DRILLING. A three-barreled gun usually consisting of two shotgun barrels and one rifle barrel.

DUMMY SIDEPLATES. Metal plates usually used for decorative purposes and on the sides of boxlock actions to simulate sidelocks.

DUST COVER. Usually a sliding or turning piece of sheet metal used to keep foreign matter out of the action.

EJECTOR. Metal stud or rod that forcibly knocks cases out of the chamber.

ENGRAVING. Metal carving for decoration.

EXPRESS SIGHTS. The rear open rifle sight that has folding leafs for different elevations.

EXTRACTOR. The metal part that lifts the case out of the chamber.

FALLING BLOCK. Singleshot action type in which the breechblock moves vertically, propelled by a finger lever.

FIELD GRADE. Usually the standard grade of gun with little or no embellishment.

FINGER GROOVE. A groove cut into the forend of a long gun to aid in gripping.

FINISH. Materials used to coat the wood or the treatment of the metal parts.

FIXED SIGHTS. Non-adjustable sights.

FLASH HIDER. A device that reduces the amount of muzzle flash.

FLINTLOCK. Muzzle-loading action type that utilizes a hammer holding a flint that strikes a spring-loaded frizzen/pan cover to produce ignition.

FLOBERT. Singleshot action for low power cartridges employing a hammer and rotating breechblock.

FLUTED BARREL. A barrel with longitudinal grooves cut into it for decoration and for strength.

FOLDING GUN. Usually a break-top shotgun that pivots until folded in half.

FOREND. The forward part of a long gun's stock forward of the breech and under the barrel.

FRAME. The metal part of the gun that contains the action.

FREE PISTOL. A handgun designed for certain types of target shooting.

FREE RIFLE. A rifle designed for certain types of target shooting.

FRIZZEN. The part of the flintlock or snaphaunce lock that is hit by the flint to produce sparks.

FURNITURE. Metal parts except for the action and barrel.

GALLERY GUN. A gun designed to fire .22 Shorts for use in shooting galleries.

GAS OPERATED. Automatic or semi-automatic action type using vented gasses from the fired cartridge to cycle the action.

GAUGE. A unit of shotgun bore measurement derived from the number of lead balls of that diameter to a pound.

GERMAN SILVER. Also known as nickel silver, consisting of copper, nickel and zinc, used for gun decorations.

GRIP. The portion of the gun to the rear of the trigger that is held by the firing hand.

GRIPFRAME. On handguns that portion of the frame that is held by the hand.

GRIPS. On handguns the stocks.

GRIP SAFETY. A mechanical block that is released when the gun is held by hand in the firing position.

GRIPSTRAP. The exposed metal portion of the gripframe to the front or rear of the grips.

HAMMER. The part of the mechanism that hits and imparts thrust to the firing pin.

HAMMERLESS. A term applied to both striker-actuated guns and guns with hammers hidden within the action.

HAMMER SHROUD. A device that covers the sides of a hammer, while leaving the top exposed.

HANDGUARD. On rifles the forestock above the barrel and forward of the breech.

HANDGUN. A firearm designed to be held and fired with one hand.

HEAT CARVING. Decorative patterns in wood formed either by heat or the combination of heat and pressure.

HOLSTER STOCK. A holster usually made of wood, or wood and leather, that attaches to a handgun for use as a shoulderstock.

HOODED SIGHT. A front sight with a protective cover over it.

INLAY. Decoration made by inlaying patterns on metal or wood.

IRON SIGHTS. Open sights, usually with a rear sight adjustable for elevation, and a front sight adjustable for windage by drifting it.

KENTUCKY RIFLE. A style of gun developed around 1770 in Pennslyvania, and produced first in flintlock and later in percussion varieties.

KNURLING. Checkering on metal.

LANYARD RING. A ring used to secure the gun by a lanyard to the shooter so it won't be lost if dropped.

LEVER ACTION. Usually a repeating type of action with a reciprocating breechblock powered by a finger lever.

LIP-FIRE. An early type of rimfire cartridge.

LOCK. The part of the action that carries the firing mechanism.

LONG GUN. A term used to describe rifles and shotguns.

MAGAZINE. In repeating arms a storage device that feeds cartridges into the breech.

MAGNUM. Usually refers to arms or cartridges that more powerful than normal, or of higher pressure.

MANNLICHER. In common usage does not refer to the man or his guns but to a type of rifle stock in which the forestock extends to the end of the muzzle.

MANUAL SAFETY. A block which prevents discharge that must be engaged and disengaged manually.

MARTINI ACTION. A singleshot action that utilizes a rear pivoting breechblock with a striker operated by finger lever.

MATCH RIFLE. A rifle specifically designed for target shooting.

MATCHLOCK. A muzzle loading arm that uses "Slow Match" to ignite a priming charge.

MATTE FINISH. A dull finish that does not reflect light.

MAUSER ACTION. A type of reciprocating turn-bolt action.

MIQUELET LOCK. A flintlock action that has an exposed sear on the outside of the lockplate.

MODERN. A legal term applied to cartridge firearms manufactured after 1898. Also see the introduction.

MONTE CARLO. A raised portion on the top of the buttstock that elevates the cheek over the level of the buttplate.

MUSKET. A long military style gun with a long forend.

MUZZLE. The most forward end of the barrel.

MUZZLE BRAKE. A device to capture powder gasses at the end of the muzzle to reduce recoil and barrel climb.

MUZZLE LOADER. A black powder arm that is loaded through the muzzle.

NIPPLE. The hollow projection that the percussion cap is fitted to.

OCTAGON BARREL. A barrel with the outside ground into an octagonal shape.

OFF-HAND RIFLE. A target rifle designed to be held, not rested.

OPEN SIGHTS. Iron Sights.

OVER-UNDER. Barrel mounting on double barreled guns with the barrels superposed over one another.

PALM REST. Hand support on the forend of an off-hand match rifle.

PAN. The place on flintlock and earlier arms in which the priming powder is placed.

PARKERIZED. A matte, phosphated finish that is highly rust resistant and usually placed on military arms.

PATCH BOX. A container inletted into the butt of a muzzle loading long gun.

PEEP SIGHT. A circular rear sight with a small hole in the center to aim through.

PEPPERBOX. A revolving pistol with multiple rotating barrels.

PERCUSSION ARM. A muzzle loader that uses a percussion cap placed over a nipple to ignite the powder charge.

PERCUSSION CAP. A small disc that contains a fulminating chemical to ignite a powder charge.

PINFIRE. A type of cartridge with an exposed side pin that detonates the primer when strick.

PISTOL. A non-revolving handgun.

PISTOL GRIP. The grip on a pistol.

PLAINS RIFLE. Percussion rifle design of the mid-1800's developed in St. Louis.

POCKET REVOLVER. A small revolver.

PORT. An opening into the action for ejected cases to pass through; an opening for gasses to flow through.

PROOF. The testing of a gun to see if it stands the stress of firing.

PUMP ACTION. Slide Action.

RAMP SIGHT. A front sight mounted on a ramp.

RAMROD. A rod used to push the charge down the barrel of a muzzle loader.

RECEIVER. The part of the frame that houses the bolt or breechblock

RECOIL. The rearward push of the gun when fired.

RECOIL OPERATED. An automatic or semi-automatic action that is cycled by the recoil from the fired cartridge.

RECOIL PAD. A rubber pad at the end of the butt to absorb recoil.

REPEATER. Capable of firing more that one round of ammunition; having a magazine.

REVOLVER. A firearm with a revolving cylinder containing multiple chambers.

RIFLE. A long gun with a rifled barrel,

RIFLING. Grooves cut into the bore to impart a spin to a bullet.

RIMFIRE. Cartridges containing the priming compound in the rim.

ROLLING BLOCK. Action with a pivoting breechblock that rotates ahead of the hammer, and which is locked by the hammer.

SADDLE RING. A ring on the side of rifles to attach a lanyard to.

SAFETY. A mechanical block that prevents the gun from firing.

SAWED-OFF SHOTGUN. A legal term describing a shotgun with barrels shorter than 16"; a Class 3 weapon.

SCHNABEL FOREND. A downcurving projection at the end of a forestock.

SCHUETZEN RIFLE. A type of fancy singleshot target rifle used for off-hand matches.

SCOPE. Telescopic sights.

SCOPE BASES. The mounts that attaches scopes to guns.

SEAR. That part of the action that engages the striker or hammer, and allows them to fall when released by the trigger.

SEMI-AUTOMATIC. Action type that ejects the spent case and cycles a new round into the chamber with the energy of the fired round, and only fires one shot with each pull of the trigger.

SET TRIGGER. A trigger that can be "cocked" so that the final pull is very light.

SHOTGUN. A smoothbore gun designed to fire small shot pellets.

SIDE-BY-SIDE. A double barreled gun with the barrels mounted next to each other.

SIDEHAMMER. A gun having the hammer mounted on the side rather than in the center.

SIDE LEVER. A gun with the action operating lever on the side of the action.

SIDEPLATE. A plate that covers the action, or that the action is mounted on.

SIDELOCK. An action that is contained on the inside of a plate mounted directly behind the breech.

SIGHT. A device that allows precise aim.

SIGHT COVER. Protective covering placed around a sight to prevent damage from jarring.

SIGHT RADIUS. The distance between the front and rear sight.

SILENCER. A device that reduces the noise of firing.

SINGLE ACTION. An action type that requires manual cocking for each shot.

SINGLESHOT. A gun capable of firing only one shot; having no magazine.

SKELETON BUTTPLATE. A buttplate with the center section removed to let the wood show through.

SLEEVE. Either a barrel liner or a tube placed on the outside of target barrel to stiffen it.

SKELETON STOCK. A buttstock, generally of wood or plastic, with the center removed to lighten the weight.

SLIDE. The reciprocating part of a semi-automatic pistol containing the breechblock.

SLIDE ACTION. A repeating action with a reciprocating forestock connected to the breechbolt.

SLING. A carrying strap on a long gun.

SLUG GUN. A shotgun designed to shoot lead slugs rather than pellets.

SNAPHAUNCE. An early form of flintlock with a manual frizzen.

SOLID FRAME. A non-takedown gun; a revolver that does not have a hinged frame.

SOLID RIB. A raised sighting plane on a barrel.

SPLINTER FOREND. A small wood forend under the barrel.

SPORTERIZED. A conversion of military arms to sporting type.

SPUR TRIGGER. A trigger with no guard, but protected by a sheath.

STIPPLING. An area roughened by center-punching for improved grip.

STOCK. The non-metal portion of the gun which is actually held.

STRIKER. A spring activated firing pin held in place by a sear which when released has enough energy to fire a primer.

SWIVELS. The metal loop that the sling is attached to.

TAKEDOWN. Capable of coming apart easily.

TARGET. Designed for target shooting.

TARGET STOCK. A stock designed for target shooting.

THUMBHOLE STOCK. A stock with a hole for the thumb to wrap around in the pistol grip.

THUMB REST. A ledge on the side of target grips for the thumb to rest on.

TIP-UP. A revolver with a frame hinged at the upper rear portion; a single shot pistol that has a break-top action.

TOE. The area on the bottom of the buttplate and the bottom rear of the stock.

TOGGLE ACTION. A semi-automatic action with a toggle joint that locks the breechblock.

TOP BREAK. Another term for tip-up, meaning that the barrel assembly swivels down on a hinge pin to expose the action.

TOP LEVER. An action actuated or opened with a lever on top.

TOP STRAP. The portion of a revolver above the cylinder.

TOUCH HOLE. The hole into the chamber area on muzzle loaders through which the priming flash ignites the charge.

TRIGGER. The exterior sear release.

TRIGGER, DOUBLE PULL. Two stage trigger in which the slack must be taken up before the sear can be released.

TRIGGER GUARD. A band usually of metal that encircles the trigger preventing accidental discharge.

TRIGGER PULL. The amount of force required to release the sear.

TRIGGER SHOE. An accessory fitted to the trigger to provide a wide gripping surface.

TRIGGER STOP. A device to prevent trigger overtravel.

TRY-GUN. A long gun with a completely adjustable stock for measuring the proper fit of a custom gun.

TUBE FEED. A magazine with cartridges loaded behind one another instead of stacked.

TWIST BARREL. A gun with superposed barrels that are manually turned to bring a fresh charge into play; damascus steel barrel.

UNDER LEVER. An action actuated or opened by a lever underneath the action.

UNDERHAMMER. An action with the hammer on the bottom of the frame.

VARMINT RIFLE. A heavy barreled small caliber hunting rifle designed for accuracy.

VENT RIB. A raised sighting plane on barrels with air vents between it and the barrel.

VIERLING. A combination weapon with four barrels.

WATER TABLE. The flat part of the action forward of the standing breech on break open actions.

WHEEL-LOCK. A muzzle loading action that used a spring operated spinning wheel to ignite sparks.

WITNESS MARK. A line place on assembled parts to show proper line-up between the two.

WILDCAT. A non-standard cartridge.

ZWILLING. A double-barrel long gun with one smooth bore barrel and one rifled barrel.

SHOTGUN GAUGES

The gauge of a shotgun or any smoothbore was standardized in the last half of the nineteenth century in England by the Gun Barrel Proof Act of 1868. Until that time the general rule of thumb among gunmakers was the formula that gauge was the number of round lead balls of a given bore diameter in a pound. This still holds true with the exception of the obsolete letter gauges, and .410 gauge which is the actual bore diameter.

Gauge	Diameter	Gauge	Diameter
A	2.000″	22	.596″
B	1.938″	23	.587″
C	1.875″	24	.579″
D	1.813″	25	.571″
E	1.750″	26	.563″
F	1.688″	27	.556″
1	1.669″	28	.550″
H	1.625″	29	.543″
J	1.563″	30	.537″
K	1.500″	31	.531″
L	1.438″	32	.526″
M	1.375″	33	.520″
2	1.325″	34	.515″
O	1.313″	35	.510″
P	1.250″	36	.506″
3	1.157″	37	.501″
4	1.052″	38	.497″
5	.976″	39	.492″
6	.919″	40	.488″
7	.873″	41	.484″
8	.835″	42	.480″
9	.803″	43	.476″
10	.775″	44	.473″
11	.751″	45	.469″
12	.729″	46	.466″
13	.710″	47	.463″
14	.693″	48	.459″
15	.677″	49	.456″
16	.662″	50	.453″
17	.649″		
18	.637″		
19	.626″	.410	.410″
20	.615″		
21	.605″		

AMMUNITION INTERCHANGEABILITY

Many calibers (or cartridges) are known by more than one name and there are some that, while having different case sizes, can fit in an arm chambered for another caliber. Other cartridges may have a one-way interchangeability because of power. Caution must always be used when interchanging ammunition for gaps as small as several thousandths of an inch between the cartridge case and the limits of the chamber can destroy a gun and injure the shooter.

.22 W.R.F.
.22 Remington Special
.22 Win. M-1890

.25 Stevens Short R.F. in
.25 Stevens, but not the reverse

.25-20 Marlin
.25-20 Remington
.25-20 W.C.F.
.25-20 Win.

.25 Automatic
.25 A.C.P.
6.35mm Browning
6.35mm Automatic Pistol

.30-30 Marlin
.30-30 Savage
.30-30 W.C.F.
.30-30 Win.

.32 Short R.F. in
.32 Long R.F., but not the reverse

.32 Short Colt in
.32 Long Colt, but not the reverse (not to be used in .32 S&W or .32 S&W Long)

.32 A.C.P.
.32 Colt Automatic
7.65mm Automatic Pistol
7.65mm Browning

.32 S&W in
.32 S&W Long, but not the reverse

.32 Colt New Police
.32 Colt Police Positive
.32 S&W Long

.32-20 Colt
.32-20 Marlin
.32-20 Win.
.32-20 W.C.F.
.32-20 Win. & Marlin
.32 Marlin
.32 Rem.
.32 Win.
.32 W.C.F.
(Hi Speed are for rifles only)

.38 S&W
.38 Colt New Police

.38 Short Colt in
.38 Long Colt, but not the reverse. Both can be used in .38 Special.

.38 Colt Special
.38 S&W Special
.38 Targetmaster
.38-44 Special
(Hi Speed or Plus P cartridges are not to be used in light frame guns. Check with the manufacturer.)

.38 Marlin
.38 Rem.
.38 W.C.F.
.38 Win.
.38-40 Win.

.38 Automatic (A.C.P.) in
.38 Super but not the reverse.

.380 Automatic
.380 A.C.P.
9mm Browning Short
9mm Corto
9mm Kurz

.380 Automatic
.380 A.C.P.
9mm Browning Short
9mm Corto
9mm Kurz

9mm Luger
9mm Parabellum
(9x19mm is Plus P)

.44 S&W Russian in
.44 Special, but not the reverse

.44 S&W Special in
.44 Magnum, but not the reverse

.44 Marlin
.44 Rem.
.44 Win.
.44 W.C.F.
.44-40 Win.

.45-70 Government
.45-70 Marlin
.45-70 Win.
.45-70-405

HOW TO USE THIS GUIDE

There are three price columns found next to each listing. The first two columns show the retail selling price for each piece in very good to excellent condition. The third column is last year's value in excellent condition. It shows which items have decreased or increased in value over the previous year. The prices reflect the geographical differences in the market and were determined by averaging the prices of actual sales across the country. They should be used only as a guideline.

For the sake of simplicity the following organization has been adopted for this book:

1.Manufacturer, importer, or brand name
2.Type of gun
3.Type of action
4.Model
5.Caliber or gauge

To find your gun in this guide first look under the name of the manufacturer, importer, or brand name, then look under the subdivision "type of gun" (i.e., rifle, handgun, etc.). For instance if you want to find a "General Hood Centennial" Colt Scout .22 l.r.r.f. single action revolver, look for:

COLT; Handgun, Revolver; General Hood Centennial, .22 l.r.r.f.

If nothing is known about the origin of a particular gun, an approximation of the value can be determined by checking the categories of: "type of action" (wheel lock, percussion, cartridge weapon, etc.), "Unknown Maker". To further aid in evaluating guns of unknown origin look under "Firearms, Custom Made", "Plains Rifles", "Scheutzen Rifles", and "Kentucky Rifles and Pistols".

In some cases there is a general listing for a manufacturer or a specific model of gun with the instructions "add" a given value. These additions should be made for all guns in the listed category that have the modification mentioned.

	V.G.	Exc.	Prior Year Exc. Value

A & R SALES
South El Monte, Calif. Current.

HANDGUN, SEMI-AUTOMATIC

	V.G.	Exc.	Prior Year Exc. Value
☐ **Government**, .45 ACP, Lightweight, Clip Fed "Parts Gun" *Modern*	185.00	275.00	245.00

RIFLE, SEMI-AUTOMATIC

	V.G.	Exc.	Prior Year Exc. Value
☐ **Mark IV Sporter**, .308 Win., Clip Fed, Version of M-14, Adjustable Sights, *Modern*	345.00	475.00	450.00

ABBEY, GEORGE T.
Chicago, Ill. 1858-1875.

RIFLE, PERCUSSION

	V.G.	Exc.	Prior Year Exc. Value
☐ **.44**, Octagon Barrel, Brass Furniture, *Antique*	400.00	575.00	525.00
☐ **.44**, Double Barrel, Over-Under, Brass Furniture, *Antique*	700.00	1,050.00	950.00

ABBEY, J.F. & CO.
Chicago, Ill. 1871-1875. Also made by Abbey & Foster.

RIFLE, PERCUSSION

	V.G.	Exc.	Prior Year Exc. Value
☐ **Various Calibers**, *Antique*	300.00	450.00	400.00

☐ **SHOTGUN, PERCUSSION**

	V.G.	Exc.	Prior Year Exc. Value
☐ **Various Gauges**, *Antique*	350.00	500.00	475.00

ABILENE
See Mossberg

ACHA
Domingo Acha y Cia., Ermua, Spain 1927-1937.

HANDGUN, SEMI-AUTOMATIC

	V.G.	Exc.	Prior Year Exc. Value
☐ **Ruby M1916**, .32 ACP, Clip Fed, *Curio*	90.00	145.00	135.00

ACME
Made by Hopkins & Allen, Sold by Merwin & Hulbert, c. 1880.

HANDGUN, REVOLVER

	V.G.	Exc.	Prior Year Exc. Value
☐ **.22 Short R.F.**, 7 Shot, Spur Trigger, Solid Frame, Single Action, *Antique*	95.00	165.00	165.00
☐ **.32 Short R.F.**, 5 Shot, Spur Trigger, Solid Frame, Single Action, *Antique*	95.00	175.00	175.00

ACME ARMS
Maker unknown, sold by J. Stevens Arms Co., c. 1880.

HANDGUN, REVOLVER

	V.G.	Exc.	Prior Year Exc. Value
☐ **.22 Short R.F.**, 7 Shot, Spur Trigger, Solid Frame, Single Action, *Antique*	95.00	160.00	160.00
☐ **.32 Short R.F.**, 5 Shot, Spur Trigger, Solid Frame, Single Action, *Antique*	95.00	175.00	175.00

SHOTGUN, DOUBLE BARREL, SIDE-BY-SIDE

	V.G.	Exc.	Prior Year Exc. Value
☐ **12 Gauge**, Damascus Barrel, *Antique*	95.00	190.00	185.00

	V.G.	Exc.	Prior Year Exc. Value

ACME HAMMERLESS

Made by Hopkins & Allen for Hulbert Bros. 1893.

HANDGUN, REVOLVER

	V.G.	Exc.	Prior Year Exc. Value
☐ **.32 S & W**, 5 Shot, Top Break, Hammerless, Double Action, 2½" Barrel, *Antique*	75.00	135.00	125.00
☐ **.38 S & W**, 5 Shot, Top Break, Hammerless, Double Action, 3" Barrel, *Antique*	75.00	135.00	125.00

ACRA

Tradename used by Reinhard Fajen of Warsaw, Mo., c. 1970.

RIFLE, BOLT ACTION

	V.G.	Exc.	Prior Year Exc. Value
☐ **RA**, Various Calibers, Santa Barbara Barreled Action, Checkered Stock, *Modern*	140.00	225.00	215.00
☐ **S24**, Various Calibers, Santa Barbara Barreled Action, Fancy Checkering, *Modern*	160.00	245.00	235.00
☐ **M18**, Various Calibers, Santa Barbara Barreled Action, Mannlicher Checkered Stock, *Modern*	190.00	300.00	295.00

ACTION

Modesto Santos; Eibar, Spain.

HANDGUN, SEMI-AUTOMATIC

	V.G.	Exc.	Prior Year Exc. Value
☐ **Model 1920**, .25 ACP, Clip Fed, *Curio*	90.00	175.00	160.00
☐ **#2**, .32 ACP, Clip Fed, *Curio*	150.00	235.00	225.00

ADAMS

Made by Deane, Adams, & Deane, London, England.

HANDGUN, PERCUSSION

	V.G.	Exc.	Prior Year Exc. Value
☐ **.38 M1851**, Revolver, Double Action, 4½" Barrel, *Antique*	575.00	975.00	875.00
☐ **.38 M1851**, Revolver, Double Action, 4½" Barrel, Cased with Accessories, *Antique*	775.00	1,200.00	1,000.00
☐ **.44 M1851**, Revolver, Double Action, 6" Barrel, *Antique*	435.00	750.00	650.00
☐ **.44 M1851**, Revolver, Double Action, 6" Barrel, Cased with Accessories, *Antique*	450.00	775.00	675.00
☐ **.500 M1851**, Dragoon, Revolver, Double Action, 8" Barrel, *Antique*	425.00	800.00	700.00
☐ **.500 M1851 Dragoon**, Revolver, Double Action, 8" Barrel, Cased with Accessories, *Antique*	650.00	1,100.00	950.00
☐ **.54 Beaumont-Adams**, Revolver, Double Action, 5½" Barrel, *Antique*	525.00	825.00	750.00
☐ **.54 Beaumont-Adams**, Revolver, Double Action, 5½" Barrel, Cased with Accessories, *Antique*	750.00	1,400.00	1,200.00

RIFLE, PERCUSSION

	V.G.	Exc.	Prior Year Exc. Value
☐ **.50 Sporting Rifle**, Revolver, Double Action, 20" Barrel, *Antique*	525.00	800.00	750.00

ADAMS, JOSEPH

Birmingham, England 1767-1813.

RIFLE, FLINTLOCK

	V.G.	Exc.	Prior Year Exc. Value
☐ **.65 Officers Model Brown Bess**, Musket, Military, *Antique*	925.00	1,600.00	1,450.00

	V.G.	Exc.	Prior Year Exc. Value

ADAMY GEBRUDER
Suhl, Germany 1921-1939.

SHOTGUN, DOUBLE BARREL, OVER-UNDER

	V.G.	Exc.	Prior Year Exc. Value
☐ **16 Ga.**, Automatic Ejector, Double Trigger, Engraved, Cased, *Modern*	1,250.00	1,900.00	1,850.00

ADIRONDACK ARMS CO.
Plattsburg, N.Y. 1870-1874. Purchased by Winchester 1874.

RIFLE, LEVER ACTION

	V.G.	Exc.	Prior Year Exc. Value
☐ **Robinson 1875 Patent**, Various Rimfires, Octagon Barrel, Open Rear Sight, *Antique*	775.00	1,425.00	1,350.00
☐ **Robinson Patent**, Various Calibers, Octagon Barrel, *Antique*	725.00	1,325.00	1,275.00

ADLER
Engelbrecht & Wolff; Zella St. Blasii, Germany 1904-1906.

HANDGUN, SEMI-AUTOMATIC

	V.G.	Exc.	Prior Year Exc. Value
☐ **7.25 Adler**, Clip Fed, *Curio*	1,600.00	2,500.00	2,650.00

AERTS, JAN
Maastricht, Holland, c. 1650.

HANDGUN, FLINTLOCK

	V.G.	Exc.	Prior Year Exc. Value
☐ **Ornate Pair**, Very Long Ebony Full Stock, Silver Inlay, High Quality, *Antique*		70,000.00+	67,500.00+

AETNA
Made by Harrington & Richardson, c. 1876.

HANDGUN, REVOLVER

	V.G.	Exc.	Prior Year Exc. Value
☐ **.22 Short R.F.**, 7 Shot, Spur Trigger, Solid Frame, Single Action, *Antique*	85.00	150.00	150.00
☐ **Aetna**, .32 Short R.F., 5 Shot, Spur Trigger, Solid Frame, Single Action, *Antique*	90.00	165.00	165.00
☐ **Aetna 2**, .32 Short R.F., 5 Shot, Spur Trigger, Solid Frame, Single Action, *Antique*	90.00	165.00	165.00
☐ **Aetna 2½**, .32 Short R.F., 5 Shot, Spur Trigger, Solid Frame, Single Action, *Antique*	90.00	165.00	165.00

AETNA ARMS CO.
N.Y.C., c. 1880.

HANDGUN, REVOLVER

	V.G.	Exc.	Prior Year Exc. Value
☐ **.22 Short R.F.**, 7 Shot, Spur Trigger, Tip-Up Barrel, *Antique*	245.00	375.00	350.00
☐ **.32 Short R.F.**, 5 Shot, Spur Trigger, Tip-Up Barrel, *Antique*	265.00	400.00	380.00

AFFERBACH, WILLIAM
Philadelphia, Pa. 1860-1866.

HANDGUN, PERCUSSION

	V.G.	Exc.	Prior Year Exc. Value
☐ **.40 Derringer**, Full Stock, *Antique*	450.00	675.00	650.00

	V.G.	Exc.	Prior Year Exc. Value

AGAWAM ARMS
Agawam, Mass., c. 1970.

RIFLE, SINGLESHOT

	V.G.	Exc.	Prior Year Exc. Value
☐ **Model M-68**, .22 L.R.R.F., Lever Action, Open Sights, *Modern*	30.00	55.00	50.00
☐ **Model M-68M**, .22 W.M.R., Lever Action, Open Sights, *Modern*	40.00	70.00	65.00

AJAX ARMY
Maker Unknown, Sold By E.C. Meacham Co., c. 1880.

HANDGUN, REVOLVER

	V.G.	Exc.	Prior Year Exc. Value
☐ **.44 Short R.F.**, 5 Shot, Spur Trigger, Solid Frame, Single Action, *Antique*	175.00	275.00	275.00

AKRILL, E.
Probably St. Etienne, France, c. 1810.

RIFLE, FLINTLOCK

	V.G.	Exc.	Prior Year Exc. Value
☐ **.69**, Smoothbore, Octagon Barrel, Damascus Barrel, Breech Loader, Plain, *Antique*	950.00	2,100.00	1,975.00

ALAMO
Tradename used by Stoeger Arms, c. 1958.

HANDGUN, REVOLVER

	V.G.	Exc.	Prior Year Exc. Value
☐ **Alamo**, .22 L.R.R.F., Double Action, Ribbed Barrel, *Modern*	20.00	35.00	35.00

ALASKA
Made by Hood Firearms, Sold by E.C. Meacham Co. 1880.

HANDGUN, REVOLVER

	V.G.	Exc.	Prior Year Exc. Value
☐ **.22 Short R.F.**, 7 Shot, Spur Trigger, Solid Frame, Single Action, *Antique*	95.00	160.00	160.00

ALASKAN
Skinner's Sportman's Supply, Juneau, Alaska, c. 1970.

RIFLE, BOLT ACTION

	V.G.	Exc.	Prior Year Exc. Value
☐ **Standard**, Various Calibers, Checkered Stock, Sling Swivels, *Modern*	185.00	285.00	275.00
☐ **Magnum**, Various Calibers, Checkered Stock, Recoil Pad, Sling Swivels, *Modern*	220.00	300.00	295.00
☐ **Carbine**, Various Calibers, Checkered Stock, Sling Swivels, *Modern*	220.00	300.00	290.00

ALBRECHT, ANDREW
Lancaster, Pa. 1779-1782. See Kentucky Rifles and Pistols.

ALBRIGHT, HENRY
Lancaster, Pa. 1740-1745. See Kentucky Rifles and Pistols.

ALDENDERFER, M.
Lancaster, Pa. 1763-1784. See Kentucky Rifles and Pistols.

	V.G.	Exc.	Prior Year Exc. Value

ALERT
Made by Hood Firearms Co., c. 1874.

HANDGUN, REVOLVER

	V.G.	Exc.	Prior Year Exc. Value
☐ **.22 Short R.F.**, 7 Shot, Spur Trigger, Solid Frame, Single Action, *Antique*	90.00	160.00	160.00

ALEXIA
Made by Hopkins & Allen, c. 1880.

HANDGUN, REVOLVER

	V.G.	Exc.	Prior Year Exc. Value
☐ **.22 Short R.F.**, 7 Shot, Spur Trigger, Solid Frame, Single Action, *Antique*	90.00	160.00	160.00
☐ **.32 Short R.F.**, 5 Shot, Spur Trigger, Solid Frame, Single Action, *Antique*	95.00	170.00	170.00
☐ **.38 Short R.F.**, 5 Shot, Spur Trigger, Solid Frame, Single Action, *Antique*	95.00	180.00	180.00
☐ **.41 Short R.F.**, 5 Shot, Spur Trigger, Solid Frame, Single Action, *Antique*	140.00	250.00	250.00

ALEXIS
Made by Hood Firearms Co., Sold by Turner & Ross Co. Boston, Mass.

HANDGUN, REVOLVER

	V.G.	Exc.	Prior Year Exc. Value
☐ **.22 Short R.F.**, 7 Shot, Spur Trigger, Solid Frame, Single Action, *Antique*	90.00	160.00	160.00

ALFA
Armero Especialistas Reunidas, Eibar, Spain, c. 1920.

HANDGUN, REVOLVER

	V.G.	Exc.	Prior Year Exc. Value
☐ **Colt Police Positive Type**, .38, Double Action, Blue, *Curio*	65.00	125.00	120.00
☐ **S. & W. M & P Type**, .38, Double Action, 6 Shot, Blue, *Curio*	65.00	125.00	120.00
☐ **S. & W. #2 Type**, Various Calibers, Double Action, Blue, Break-Top, *Curio*	90.00	150.00	140.00

ALFA
Adolf Frank, Hamburg, Germany, c. 1900.

HANDGUN, MANUAL REPEATER

	V.G.	Exc.	Prior Year Exc. Value
☐ **"Reform" Type**, .230 C.F., Four-barreled Repeater, Engraved, *Curio*	145.00	240.00	190.00

HANDGUN, SEMI-AUTOMATIC

	V.G.	Exc.	Prior Year Exc. Value
☐ **Pocket**, .25 ACP, Clip Fed, Blue, *Curio*	90.00	140.00	125.00

RIFLE, PERCUSSION

	V.G.	Exc.	Prior Year Exc. Value
☐ **Back-lock**, Various Calibers, Imitation Damascus Barrel, *Antique*	50.00	90.00	80.00
☐ **Back-lock**, Various Calibers, Carved, Inlaid Stock, Imitation Damascus Barrel, *Antique*	85.00	150.00	140.00

SHOTGUN, PERCUSSION

	V.G.	Exc.	Prior Year Exc. Value
☐ **Double Barrel**, Various Gauges, Back-lock, Double Triggers, Damascus Barrels, *Antique*	65.00	120.00	110.00
☐ **Double Barrel**, Various Gauges, Back-lock, Double Triggers, Damascus Barrels, Carved Stock, Engraved, *Antique*	120.00	200.00	190.00

	V.G.	Exc.	Prior Year Exc. Value
SHOTGUN, DOUBLE BARREL, SIDE-BY-SIDE			
☐ **Greener Boxlock**, Various Gauges, Checkered Stock, Double Triggers, *Curio*	125.00	200.00	180.00
☐ **Greener Boxlock**, Various Gauges, Checkered Stock, Double Triggers, Engraved, *Curio*	170.00	260.00	245.00
SHOTGUN, SINGLESHOT			
☐ **Roux Underlever**, Various Gauges, Tip-Down Barrel, No Forestock, *Curio*	35.00	55.00	55.00
☐ **Nuss Underlever**, Various Gauges, Tip-Down Barrel, No Forestock, *Curio*	35.00	55.00	55.00
☐ **Sidebutton**, Various Gauges, Tip-Down Barrel, No Forestock, *Curio*	30.00	50.00	50.00

ALKARTASUNA

Spain Made by Alkartasuna Fabrica De Armas 1910-1922.

	V.G.	Exc.	Prior Year Exc. Value
HANDGUN, SEMI-AUTOMATIC			
☐ **Alkar 1924**, .25 ACP, Cartridge Counter, Grips, Clip Fed, *Curio*	250.00	400.00	375.00
☐ **Pocket**, .32 ACP, Clip Fed, Long Grip, *Curio*	120.00	190.00	175.00
☐ **Pocket**, .32 ACP, Clip Fed, Short Grip, *Curio*	110.00	170.00	150.00
☐ **Vest Pocket**, .25 ACP, Clip Fed, Cartridge Counter, *Modern*	125.00	195.00	170.00
☐ **Vest Pocket**, .25 ACP, Clip Fed, *Modern*	95.00	165.00	150.00

ALLEGHENY WORKS

Allegheny, Pa. 1836-1875. See Kentucky Rifles and Pistols.

ALLEN

Made by Hopkins & Allen, c. 1880.

	V.G.	Exc.	Prior Year Exc. Value
HANDGUN, REVOLVER			
☐ **22 Short R.F.**, 7 Shot, Spur Trigger, Solid Frame, Single Action, *Antique*	90.00	160.00	160.00

ALLEN

Tradename used by McKeown's Guns of Pekin, Ill., c. 1970.

	V.G.	Exc.	Prior Year Exc. Value
SHOTGUN, DOUBLE BARREL, OVER-UNDER			
☐ **MCK 68**, 12 Ga., Vent Rib, Double Triggers, Plain, *Modern*	200.00	300.00	290.00
☐ **Olympic 68**, 12 Ga., Vent Rib, Single Selective Trigger, Automatic Ejectors, Checkered Stock, Engraved, *Modern*	300.00	450.00	445.00
☐ **S201**, Various Gauges, Vent Rib, Double Triggers, Checkered Stock, Light Engraving, *Modern*	250.00	395.00	385.00
☐ **S201 Deluxe**, Various Gauges, Vent Rib, Single Trigger, Automatic Ejectors, Checkered Stock, Engraved, *Modern*	325.00	475.00	470.00

ALLEN & THURBER

Grafton, Mass. 1837-1842, Norwich, Conn. 1842-1847.

	V.G.	Exc.	Prior Year Exc. Value
HANDGUN, PERCUSSION			
☐ **.28 (Grafton) Pepperbox**, 6 Shot, 3" Barrel, *Antique*	625.00	1,300.00	1,250.00

	V.G.	Exc.	Prior Year Exc. Value
☐ **.28 (Norwich) Pepperbox**, 6 Shot, Bar Hammer, 3″ Barrel, *Antique*	295.00	600.00	575.00
☐ **.28 (Norwich) Pepperbox**, 6 Shot, Hammerless, 3″ Barrel, *Antique*	345.00	695.00	675.00
☐ **.28, Singleshot**, Bar Hammer, Various Barrel Lengths, Half-Octagon Barrel, *Antique*	125.00	275.00	265.00
☐ **.31 (Grafton) Pepperbox**, 6 Shot, 3″ Barrel, *Antique*	485.00	975.00	950.00
☐ **.31 (Norwich) Pepperbox**, 6 Shot, Bar Hammer, 3″ Barrel, *Antique*	285.00	625.00	600.00
☐ **.31 (Norwich) Pepperbox**, 6 Shot, Hammerless, 3″ Barrel, *Antique*	365.00	750.00	700.00
☐ **.31, Singleshot**, Tube Hammer, Various Barrel Lengths, Half-Octagon Barrel, *Antique*	565.00	995.00	950.00
☐ **.31, Singleshot**, Under Hammer, Various Barrel Lengths, Half-Octagon Barrel, *Antique*	285.00	675.00	650.00
☐ **.31, Singleshot**, Under Hammer, Various Barrel Lengths, Saw-Handle Grip, Half-Octagon Barrel, *Antique*	260.00	490.00	475.00
☐ **.31, "In-Line" Singleshot**, Center Hammer, Various Barrel Lengths, Half-Octagon Barrel, *Antique*	160.00	300.00	290.00
☐ **.34, Singleshot**, Side Hammer, Various Barrel Lengths, Half-Octagon Barrel, *Antique*	185.00	495.00	475.00
☐ **.36 (Grafton) Pepperbox**, 6″ Barrel, *Antique*	750.00	1,350.00	1,250.00
☐ **.36 (Norwich) Pepperbox**, 6 Shot, Bar Hammer, 6″ Barrel, *Antique*	425.00	775.00	750.00
☐ **.36 (Norwich) Pepperbox**, 6 Shot, Ring Trigger, 6″ Barrel, *Antique*	590.00	1,125.00	1,050.00
☐ **.36, Singleshot**, Bar Hammer, Various Barrel Lengths, Half-Octagon Barrel, *Antique*	130.00	300.00	290.00
☐ **.36, Singleshot**, Center Hammer, Various Barrel Lengths, Half-Octagon Barrel, *Antique*	160.00	320.00	290.00
☐ **.41, Singleshot**, Side Hammer, Various Barrel Lengths, Half-Octagon Barrel, *Antique*	190.00	475.00	450.00

ALLEN & THURBER

Worcester, Mass. 1855-1856.

COMBINATION WEAPON, PERCUSSION

	V.G.	Exc.	Prior Year Exc. Value
☐ **Over-Under,** Various Calibers, Rifle and Shotgun Barrels, *Antique*	675.00	1600.00	1550.00

HANDGUN, PERCUSSION

	V.G.	Exc.	Prior Year Exc. Value
☐ **.28, Pepperbox,** Bar-Hammer, Various Barrel Lengths, 5 Shot, *Antique*	225.00	450.00	425.00
☐ **.30, Pepperbox,** Ring Hammerless, 6 Shot, *Antique*	425.00	775.00	550.00
☐ **.31, Pepperbox,** Bar Hammer, 5 Shot, Various Barrel Lengths, *Antique*	275.00	495.00	475.00
☐ **.31, Pepperbox,** Thumb Hammer, 5 Shot, Various Barrel Lengths, *Antique*	325.00	600.00	575.00
☐ **.34, Pepperbox,** Bar Hammer, Various Barrel Lengths, 4 Shot, *Antique*	270.00	550.00	525.00

	V.G.	Exc.	Prior Year Exc. Value
☐ **.36, Target Pistol,** 12″ Octagon Barrel, Adjustable Sights, Detachable Shoulder Stock, *Antique* ...	950.00	2100.00	2150.00
RIFLE, PERCUSSION			
☐ **.43, Singleshot,** Sporting Rifle, *Antique*	480.00	775.00	750.00

ALLEN & WHEELOCK

Worcester, Mass. 1856-1865.

	V.G.	Exc.	Prior Year Exc. Value
HANDGUN, PERCUSSION			
☐ **.25, Pepperbox,** 4″ Barrel, 5 Shot, *Antique*	250.00	475.00	450.00
☐ **.36, Pepperbox,** 6″ Barrel, 6 Shot, *Antique*	475.00	900.00	900.00
☐ **.28, Revolver,** Side Hammer, Octagon Barrel, 3″ Barrel, 5 Shot, *Antique*	175.00	425.00	400.00
☐ **.31, Revolver,** Bar Hammer, Octagon Barrel, 2¼″ Barrel, 5 Shot, *Antique*	160.00	310.00	300.00
☐ **.34, Revolver,** Bar Hammer, Octagon Barrel, 4″ Barrel, 5 Shot, *Antique*	230.00	420.00	400.00
☐ **.34, Revolver,** Bar Hammer, Octagon Barrel, 4″ Barrel, 5 Shot, *Antique*	230.00	420.00	400.00
☐ **.31, Revolver,** Side Hammer, Octagon Barrel, 3″ Barrel, 5 Shot, *Antique*	170.00	400.00	390.00
☐ **.36, Revolver,** Center Hammer, Octagon Barrel, 3″ Barrel, 6 Shot, Spur Trigger, *Antique*	190.00	465.00	450.00
☐ **.36, Revolver,** Side Hammer, Octagon Barrel, 6″ Barrel, 6 Shot, *Antique*	400.00	900.00	900.00
☐ **.36, Revolver,** Center Hammer, Octagon Barrel, 7½″ Barrel, 6 Shot, *Antique*	500.00	1100.00	975.00
☐ **.44, Revolver,** Center Hammer, Half-Octagon Barrel, 7½″ Barrel, 6 Shot, *Antique*	450.00	975.00	945.00
HANDGUN, REVOLVER			
☐ **.22 Short R.F.,** 7 Shot, Side Hammer, Solid Frame, *Antique*	135.00	290.00	275.00
☐ **.25 L.F.,** 7 Shot, Side Hammer, Solid Frame, *Antique*	300.00	475.00	450.00
☐ **.32 L.F.,** 6 Shot, Side Hammer, Solid Frame, *Antique*	350.00	625.00	600.00
☐ **.32 Short R.F.,** 6 Shot, Side Hammer, Solid Frame, *Antique*	140.00	290.00	275.00
☐ **.36 L.F.,** 6 Shot, Side Hammer, Solid Frame, *Antique*	410.00	675.00	650.00
☐ **.38 Short R.F.,** 6 Shot, Side Hammer, Solid Frame, *Antique*	140.00	310.00	295.00
☐ **.44 L.F.,** 6 Shot, Side Hammer, Solid Frame, *Antique*	575.00	1100.00	1000.00
☐ **.44 Short R.F.,** 6 Shot, Side Hammer, Solid Frame, *Antique*	190.00	375.00	350.00
HANDGUN, SINGLESHOT			
☐ **.22 Short R.F.,** Derringer, Spur Trigger, *Antique* .	160.00	300.00	285.00
☐ **.22 Short R.F.,** Large Frame, Spur Trigger, *Antique*	160.00	265.00	250.00
☐ **.32 Short R.F.,** Derringer, Spur Trigger, *Antique* .	315.00	600.00	575.00
☐ **.32 Short R.F.,** Large Frame, Spur Trigger, *Antique*	130.00	260.00	245.00
☐ **.41 Short R.F.,** Derringer, Spur Trigger, *Antique* .	265.00	500.00	475.00

RIFLE, PERCUSSION

☐ **.36 Allen Patent,** Carbine, Tap Breech Loader, *Antique* 475.00 850.00 800.00

☐ **.36 Allen Patent,** Tap Breech Loader, Sporting Rifle, *Antique* 410.00 835.00 800.00

☐ **.38 Sidehammer,** Plains Rifle, Iron Mounted, Walnut Stock, *Antique* 305.00 535.00 500.00

☐ **.44 Center Hammer,** Octagon Barrel, Iron Frame, *Antique* 310.00 630.00 600.00

☐ **.44 Revolver,** Carbine, 6 Shot, *Antique* 4400.00 10250.00 9950.00

RIFLE, REVOLVING

☐ **.44 L.F.,** Walnut Stock, 6 Shot, *Antique* 4175.00 7175.00 6950.00

RIFLE, SINGLESHOT

☐ **.22 R.F.,** Falling Block, Sporting Rifle, *Antique* .. 300.00 520.00 475.00

☐ **.38 R.F.,** Falling Block, Sporting Rifle, *Antique* .. 275.00 410.00 395.00

☐ **.62 Allen R.F.,** Falling Block, Sporting Rifle, *Antique* 275.00 450.00 435.00

☐ **.64 Allen R.F.,** Falling Block, Sporting Rifle, *Antique* 275.00 450.00 435.00

SHOTGUN, PERCUSSION

☐ **12 Ga. Double,** Hammers, Light Engraving, *Antique* 290.00 450.00 395.00

SHOTGUN, DOUBLE BARREL, SIDE-BY-SIDE

☐ **12 Ga.,** Checkered Stock, Hammers, Double Triggers, *Antique* 225.00 425.00 400.00

ALLEN, C.B.

Springfield, Mass. 1836-1841. Also See U.S. Military.

HANDGUN, PERCUSSION

☐ **.36 Cochran Turret,** 7 Shot, 4¾" Barrel, *Antique* .6350.00 9000.00 8500.00

☐ **.40 Cochran Turret,** 7 Shot, 5" Barrel, *Antique* . .7500.00 9950.00 9500.00

☐ **.35 Elgin Cutlass,** Octagon Barrel, with Built-in Knife, Smoothbore, *Antique* 3750.00 5500.00 5250.00

☐ **.54 Elgin Cutlass,** Octagon Barrel, with Built-in Knife, Smoothbore, *Antique* 6600.00 13000.00 9950.00

RIFLE, PERCUSSION

☐ **.40 Cochran Turret,** 7 Shot, Octagon Barrel, *Antique* 5750.00 8500.00 8250.00

☐ **.40 Cochran Turret,** 9 Shot, Octagon Barrel, *Antique* 5750.00 8500.00 8250.00

ALLEN, ETHAN

Grafton, Mass. 1835-1837, E. Allen & Co. Worcester, Mass. 1865-1871.

HANDGUN, PERCUSSION

☐ **Various Calibers**, Various Barrel Lengths, Under Hammer, Singleshot, Saw Handle Grip, *Antique* 265.00 475.00 450.00

☐ **.31, Singleshot**, Under Hammer, Half-Octagon Barrel, *Antique* 295.00 625.00 600.00

☐ **.31, Pepperbox**, 6 Shot, 3" Barrel, *Antique* 495.00 950.00 900.00

☐ **.36, Pepperbox**, 6 Shot, 5" Barrel, *Antique* 675.00 1,200.00 1,150.00

HANDGUN, REVOLVER

☐ **.22 Short R.F.**, 7 Shot, Side Hammer, Sheath Trigger, *Antique* 125.00 250.00 250.00

☐ **.32 Short R.F.**, 6 Shot, Side Hammer, Sheath Trigger, *Antique* 125.00 250.00 250.00

	V.G.	Exc.	Prior Year Exc. Value
HANDGUN, SINGLESHOT			
☐ **Derringer**, .32 Short R.F., Side-Swing Barrel, Round Barrel, *Antique*	325.00	600.00	550.00
☐ **Derringer**, .32 Short R.F., Side-Swing Barrel, Half-Octagon Barrel, *Antique*	160.00	240.00	225.00
☐ **Derringer**, .41 Short R.F., Side-Swing Barrel, Half-Octagon Barrel, *Antique*	275.00	485.00	450.00
☐ **Derringer**, .41 Short R.F., Side-Swing Barrel, Round Barrel, *Antique*	165.00	295.00	275.00
☐ **Derringer**, .41 Short R.F., Side-Swing Barrel, Octagon Barrel, *Antique*	165.00	295.00	275.00
RIFLE, SINGLESHOT			
☐ **Various Rimfires**, Sporting Rifle, *Antique*	375.00	500.00	475.00

ALLEN, SILAS

Shrewsbury, Mass. 1796-1843. See Kentucky Rifles and Pistols.

ALLIES

Berasaluze Areitio-Arutena y Cia., Eibar, Spain, c. 1920.

	V.G.	Exc.	Prior Year Exc. Value
HANDGUN, SEMI-AUTOMATIC			
☐ **Model 1924**, .25 ACP, Clip Fed, *Curio*	100.00	175.00	160.00
☐ **Pocket**, .32 ACP, Clip Fed, *Curio*	100.00	180.00	165.00
☐ **Vest Pocket**, .25 ACP, Clip Fed, *Curio*	90.00	150.00	140.00
☐ **Vest Pocket**, .32 ACP, Clip Fed, Short Grip, *Curio*	100.00	165.00	150.00

ALL RIGHT FIREARMS CO.

Lawrence, Mass., c. 1876.

	V.G.	Exc.	Prior Year Exc. Value
HANDGUN, REVOLVER			
☐ **Little All Right Palm Pistol**, .22 Short R.F., Squeeze Trigger, 5 Shot, *Antique*	450.00	775.00	725.00

ALPINE INDUSTRIES

Los Angeles, Calif. 1962-1965.

	V.G.	Exc.	Prior Year Exc. Value
RIFLE, SEMI-AUTOMATIC			
☐ **M-1 Carbine**, .30 Carbine, Clip Fed, Military Style, *Modern*	165.00	275.00	250.00

ALSOP, C.R.

Middleton, Conn. 1858-1866.

	V.G.	Exc.	Prior Year Exc. Value
HANDGUN, PERCUSSION			
☐ **.36 Navy**, 5 Shot, Octagon Barrel, Spur Trigger, Top Hammer, Safety, *Antique*	950.00	1,850.00	1,700.00
☐ **.36 Navy**, 5 Shot, Octagon Barrel, Spur Trigger, Top Hammer, No Safety, *Antique*	695.00	1,350.00	1,250.00
☐ **.36 Pocket**, 5 Shot, Octagon Barrel, Spur Trigger, *Antique*	375.00	675.00	650.00

AMERICA

Made by Bliss & Goodyear, c. 1878.

	V.G.	Exc.	Prior Year Exc. Value
HANDGUN, REVOLVER			
☐ **.22 Short R.F.**, 7 Shot, Spur Trigger, Solid Frame, Single Action, *Antique*	95.00	160.00	160.00

AMERICA

Made by Norwich Falls Pistol Co., c. 1880.

	V.G.	Exc.	Prior Year Exc. Value
HANDGUN, REVOLVER			
☐ **.32 Long R.F.**, Double Action, Solid Frame, *Modern*	65.00	120.00	115.00

AMERICAN ARMS CO.

Boston, Mass. 1861-1897, Milwaukee, Wisc. 1897-1901. Purchased by Marlin 1901.

	V.G.	Exc.	Prior Year Exc. Value
HANDGUN, DOUBLE BARREL, OVER-UNDER			
☐ **Wheeler Pat.**, .22 Short R.F., 32 Short R.F., Brass Frame, Spur Trigger, *Antique*	500.00	725.00	700.00
☐ **Wheeler Pat**, .32 Short R.F., Brass Frame, Spur Trigger, *Antique*	350.00	525.00	475.00
☐ **Wheeler Pat**, .41 Short R.F., Brass Frame, Spur Trigger, *Antique*	425.00	725.00	690.00
HANDGUN, REVOLVER			
☐ **.38 S & W**, 5 Shot, Double Action, Top Break, *Antique*	80.00	140.00	140.00
☐ **.38 S & W**, 5 Shot, Single Action, Top Break, Spur Trigger, *Antique*	95.00	150.00	150.00
☐ **.32 S & W**, 5 Shot, Double Action, Top Break, Hammerless, *Antique*	100.00	175.00	175.00
SHOTGUN, DOUBLE BARREL, SIDE-BY-SIDE			
☐ **12 Ga.**, Semi-Hammerless, Checkered Stock, *Antique*	275.00	475.00	450.00
☐ **Whitmore Patent**, 10 Ga., 2⅞", Hammerless, Checkered Stock, *Antique*	275.00	475.00	450.00
☐ **Whitmore Patent**, 12 Ga., Hammerless, Checkered Stock, *Antique*	350.00	550.00	500.00
SHOTGUN, SINGLESHOT			
☐ **12 Ga.**, Semi-Hammerless, Checkered Stock, *Antique*	150.00	260.00	250.00

AMERICAN ARMS & AMMUNITION CO.

Miami, Florida, c. 1979. Successors to Norton Armament Corp. (Norarmco).

	V.G.	Exc.	Prior Year Exc. Value
HANDGUN, SEMI-AUTOMATIC			
☐ **TP-70**, .22 L.R.R.F., Double Action, Stainless, Clip Fed, *Modern*	160.00	275.00	225.00
☐ **TP-70**, .25 ACP, Double Action, Stainless, Clip Fed, *Modern*	145.00	235.00	200.00

AMERICAN ARMS INTERNATIONAL

Salt Lake City, Utah, Current.

	V.G.	Exc.	Prior Year Exc. Value
AUTOMATIC WEAPON, SUBMACHINE GUN			
☐ **American 180**, .22 L.R.R.F., 177 Round Drum Magazine, Peep Sights, *Class 3*	275.00	400.00	375.00

☐ **Laser-Lok** Sight System, *Add* **$350.00-$450.00**
☐ **Extra Magazine**, *Add* **$50.00-$75.00**

Allen & Thurbur Ring Hammerless Pepperbox, .30 Caliber

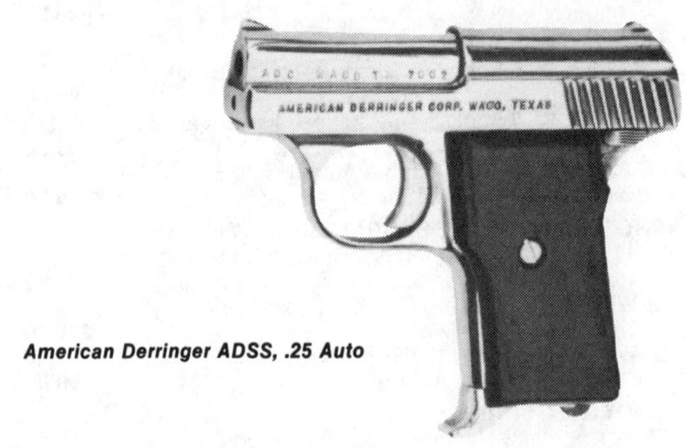

American Derringer ADSS, .25 Auto

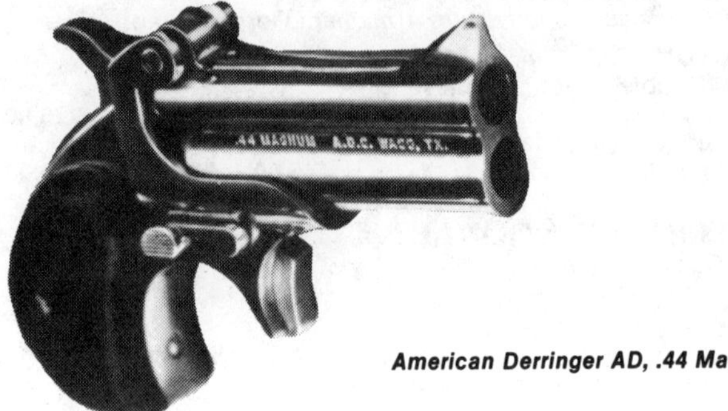

American Derringer AD, .44 Magnum

	V.G.	Exc.	Prior Year Exc. Value
RIFLE, SEMI-AUTOMATIC			
☐ **American 180**, .22 L.R.R.F., 177 Round Drum Magazine, Peep Sights, *Modern*	275.00	400.00	375.00
☐ **Laser-Lok** Sight System, *Add* **$350.00-$450.00**			
☐ **Extra Magazine**, *Add* **$50.00-$75.00**			

AMERICAN BARLOCK WONDER

Made by Crescent for Sears-Roebuck & Co.

	V.G.	Exc.	Prior Year Exc. Value
SHOTGUN, DOUBLE BARREL, SIDE-BY-SIDE			
☐ **Various Gauges**, Outside Hammers, Damascus Barrel, *Modern*	100.00	185.00	175.00
☐ **Various Gauges**, Hammerless, Steel Barrel, *Modern*	135.00	220.00	200.00
☐ **Various Gauges**, Hammerless, Damascus Barrel, *Modern*	100.00	185.00	175.00
☐ **Various Gauges**, Outside Hammers, Steel Barrel, *Modern*	125.00	195.00	190.00
SHOTGUN, SINGLESHOT			
☐ **Various Gauges**, Hammer, Steel Barrel, *Modern*	55.00	90.00	85.00

AMERICAN BOY

Made by Bliss & Goodyear for Townley Hdw. Co.

	V.G.	Exc.	Prior Year Exc. Value
HANDGUN, REVOLVER			
☐ **.32 Short R.F.**, Single Action, Solid Frame, Spur Trigger, 7 Shot, *Antique*	85.00	150.00	150.00

AMERICAN BULLDOG

Made by Johnson, Bye & Co., Worcester, Mass. 1882-1900.

	V.G.	Exc.	Prior Year Exc. Value
HANDGUN, REVOLVER			
☐ **.22 Short R.F.**, 7 Shot, Spur Trigger, Solid Frame, Single Action, *Antique*	95.00	175.00	175.00
☐ **.32 S & W**, 5 Shot, Spur Trigger, Solid Frame, Single Action, *Modern*	90.00	150.00	150.00
☐ **.32 Short R.F.**, 5 Shot, Spur Trigger, Solid Frame, Single Action, *Antique*	95.00	175.00	175.00
☐ **.38 S & W**, 5 Shot, Spur Trigger, Solid Frame, Single Action, *Modern*	90.00	155.00	155.00
☐ **.38 Short R.F.**, 5 Shot, Spur Trigger, Solid Frame, Single Action, *Antique*	95.00	180.00	180.00
☐ **.41 Short C.F.**, 5 Shot, Spur Trigger, Solid Frame, Single Action, *Antique*	100.00	195.00	195.00

AMERICAN CHAMPION

	V.G.	Exc.	Prior Year Exc. Value
SHOTGUN, SINGLESHOT			
☐ **M1899**, 12 Gauge, Plain, *Modern*	65.00	125.00	125.00

AMERICAN DERRINGER CORP.

Waco, Texes 1979 to date.

	V.G.	Exc.	Prior Year Exc. Value
HANDGUN, DOUBLE BARREL, OVER-UNDER			
☐ **Model AD**, .32 S & W Long, Remington Style Derringer, Stainless Steel, Spur Trigger, Hammer, *Modern*	110.00	145.00	140.00

	V.G.	Exc.	Prior Year Exc. Value
☐ **Model AD**, .38 Spec., Remington Style Derringer, Stainless Steel, Spur Trigger, Hammer, *Modern*	110.00	150.00	145.00
☐ **Model AD**, .357 Mag., Remington Style Derringer, Stainless Steel, Spur Trigger, Hammer, *Modern*	120.00	155.00	150.00
☐ **Model AD**, .41 Mag., Remington Style Derringer, Stainless Steel, Spur Trigger, Hammer, *Modern*	180.00	275.00	260.00
☐ **Model AD**, .44 Mag., Remington Style Derringer, Stainless Steel, Spur Trigger, Hammer, *Modern*	180.00	275.00	260.00
☐ **Model AD**, .45 A.C.P., Remington Style Derringer, Stainless Steel, Spur Trigger, Hammer, *Modern*	130.00	185.00	160.00
☐ **Model AD**, .45 Win. Mag., Remington Style Derringer, Stainless Steel, Spur Trigger, Hammer, *Modern*	225.00	350.00	300.00
☐ **Model ADL**, Various Calibers, Remington Style Derringer, Stainless Steel, Lightweight, Spur Trigger, Hammer, *Modern*	100.00	140.00	130.00

HANDGUN, SINGLESHOT

	V.G.	Exc.	Prior Year Exc. Value
☐ **Model ADS**, Various Calibers, Remington Style Derringer, Stainless Steel, Spur Trigger, Hammer, *Modern*	125.00	160.00	150.00

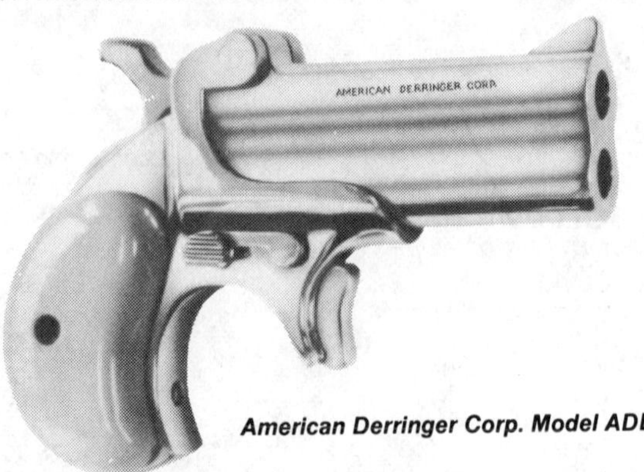

American Derringer Corp. Model ADL

HANDGUN, SEMI-AUTOMATIC

	V.G.	Exc.	Prior Year Exc. Value
☐ **Model ADSS**, .25 ACP, Clip Fed, Stainless Steel, *Modern*	55.00	85.00	80.00
☐ **Model ADBS**, .25 ACP, Clip Fed, Blue, *Modern*	45.00	65.00	60.00
☐ **Model ADM**, .250 Mag., Clip Fed, Stainless Steel, *Modern*	75.00	115.00	100.00
☐ **Model ADMB**, .250 Mag., Clip Fed, Blue, *Modern*	60.00	95.00	90.00

AMERICAN FIREARMS CO.

San Antonio, Texas 1966-1974.

HANDGUN, SEMI-AUTOMATIC

	V.G.	Exc.	Prior Year Exc. Value
☐ **.22 L.R.R.F.**, Clip Fed, Stainless Steel, *Modern*	75.00	130.00	125.00
☐ **.25 ACP**, Clip Fed, Blue, *Modern*	55.00	100.00	95.00
☐ **.25 ACP**, Clip Fed, Stainless Steel, *Modern*	70.00	120.00	115.00
☐ **.32 ACP**, Clip Fed, Stainless Steel, *Modern*	65.00	145.00	145.00
☐ **.380 ACP**, Clip Fed, Stainless Steel, *Modern*	120.00	195.00	195.00

AMERICAN EAGLE

Made by Hopkins & Allen 1870-1898.

	V.G.	Exc.	Prior Year Exc. Value
HANDGUN, REVOLVER			
☐ **.22 Short R.F.**, 7 Shot, Spur Trigger, Solid Frame, Single Action, *Antique*	95.00	175.00	175.00
☐ **.32 Short R.F.**, 5 Shot, Spur Trigger, Solid Frame, Single Action, *Antique*	95.00	195.00	195.00

AMERICAN GUN CO.

Made by Crescent Firearms Co. Sold by H. & D. Folsom Co.

	V.G.	Exc.	Prior Year Exc. Value
HANDGUN, REVOLVER			
☐ **.32 S & W**, 5 Shot, Double Action, Top Break, *Modern*	60.00	125.00	125.00
☐ **.32 S & W**, 5 Shot, Double Action, Top Break, *Modern*	60.00	125.00	125.00
SHOTGUN, DOUBLE BARREL, SIDE-BY-SIDE			
☐ **Various Gauges**, Outside Hammers, Damascus Barrel, *Modern*	100.00	175.00	175.00
☐ **Various Gauges**, Hammerless, Steel Barrel, *Modern*	135.00	220.00	200.00
☐ **Various Gauges**, Hammerless, Damascus Barrel, *Modern*	100.00	175.00	175.00
☐ **Various Gauges**, Outside Hammers, Steel Barrel, *Modern*	125.00	200.00	190.00
SHOTGUN, SINGLESHOT			
☐ **Various Gauges**, Hammer, Steel Barrel, *Modern*	55.00	85.00	85.00

AMERICAN STANDARD TOOL CO.

Newark, N.J. 1865-1870, Successor to Manhattan Firearms Co.

	V.G.	Exc.	Prior Year Exc. Value
HANDGUN, PERCUSSION			
☐ **Hero**, .34, Screw Barrel, Center Hammer, Spur Trigger, *Antique*	90.00	190.00	175.00
HANDGUN, REVOLVER			
☐ **.22 Short R.F.**, 7 Shot, Spur Trigger, Tip-Up, *Antique*	240.00	375.00	350.00

AMERICUS

Made by Hopkins & Allen 1870-1900.

	V.G.	Exc.	Prior Year Exc. Value
HANDGUN, REVOLVER			
☐ **.22 Short R.F.**, 7 Shot, Spur Trigger, Solid Frame, Single Action, *Antique*	95.00	170.00	170.00
☐ **.32 Short R.F.**, 5 Shot, Spur Trigger, Solid Frame, Single Action, *Antique*	95.00	180.00	180.00

AMSDEN, B.W.

Saratoga Springs, N.Y. 1852.

	V.G.	Exc.	Prior Year Exc. Value
COMBINATION WEAPON, PERCUSSION			
☐ **.40-16 Ga.**, Double Barrel, Rifled, *Antique*	750.00	995.00	975.00
RIFLE, PERCUSSION			
☐ **.40**, Octagon Barrel, Set Trigger, Rifled, *Antique*	450.00	700.00	675.00

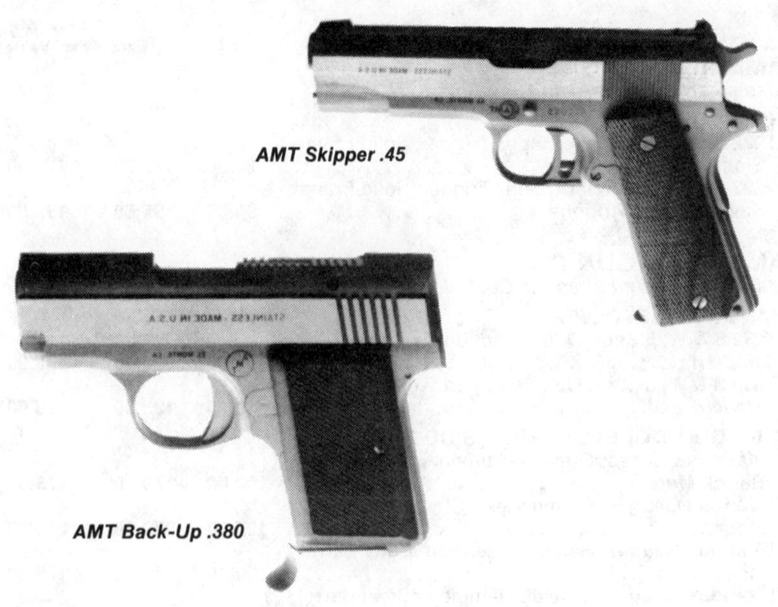

AMT Skipper .45

AMT Back-Up .380

	V.G.	Exc.	Prior Year Exc. Value

AMT

Arcadia Machine & Tool, since 1976 in Arcadia, Calif.

HANDGUN, SEMI-AUTOMATIC

	V.G.	Exc.	Prior Year Exc. Value
☐ **Back Up**, .22 L.R.R.F., Stainless Steel, Clip Fed, *Modern*	225.00	250.00	175.00
☐ **Back Up**, .380 ACP, AMT, Stainless Steel, Clip Fed, *Modern*	225.00	250.00	172.00
☐ **Back Up**, .380 ACP, TDE, Stainless Steel, Clip Fed, *Modern*	175.00	250.00	225.00
☐ **Back Up**, .380 ACP, OMC, Stainless Steel, Clip Fed, *Modern*	140.00	180.00	165.00
☐ **Combat Skipper**, .45 ACP, Stainless Steel, Clip Fed, Fixed Sights, *Modern*	225.00	350.00	350.00
☐ **Government**, .45 ACP, Stainless Steel, Clip Fed, Fixed Sights, *Modern*	215.00	310.00	300.00
☐ **Hardballer**, .45 ACP, Stainless Steel, Clip Fed, Adjustable Sights, *Modern*	275.00	400.00	400.00
☐ **Lightning**, .22 L.R., Stainless Steel, 5″ Bull Barrel, Adjustable Sights	262.00	280.00	—
☐ As Above, Fixed Sights	230.00	250.00	—
☐ As Above, 6½″ Bull Barrel, Adjustable Sights	262.00	280.00	—
☐ As Above, Fixed Sights	230.00	250.00	—
☐ **Lightning**, .22 L.R., Stainless Steel, 6½″ Tapered Barrel, Adjustable Sights	262.00	280.00	—
☐ As Above, Fixed Sights	230.00	250.00	—
☐ **Longslide**, .45 ACP, Stainless Steel, Clip Fed, Adjustable Sights, *Modern*	350.00	500.00	500.00
☐ **Parts Gun**, .45 ACP, made with Stainless Steel Frame, *Modern*	170.00	275.00	250.00

	V.G.	Exc.	Prior Year Exc. Value
☐ **Skipper**, .45 ACP, Stainless Steel, Clip Fed, Adjustable Sights, *Modern*	250.00	375.00	375.00

ANDRUS & OSBORNE
Canton, Conn. 1847-1850, moved to Southbridge, Mass. 1850-1851.

HANDGUN, PERCUSSION

	V.G.	Exc.	Prior Year Exc. Value
☐ **.36 Underhammer**, Boot Pistol, Half-Octagon Barrel, *Antique*	145.00	275.00	245.00

ANGSTADT, A. & J.
Berks County, Pa. 1792-1808. See Kentucky Rifles and U.S. Military.

ANGSTADT, PETER
Lancaster County, Pa. 1770-1777. See Kentucky Rifles and Pistols.

ANGUSH, JAMES
Lancaster County, Pa. 1771. See Kentucky Rifles and Pistols.

ANNELY, L.
London, England 1650-1700.

HANDGUN, FLINTLOCK

	V.G.	Exc.	Prior Year Exc. Value
☐ **.62**, Holster Pistol, Brass Mounting, *Antique*	500.00	995.00	950.00

ANSCHUTZ, E.
Philadelphia, Pa., c. 1860.

RIFLE, PERCUSSION

	V.G.	Exc.	Prior Year Exc. Value
☐ **.36 Schutzen Rifle**, Octagon Barrel, Target, *Antique*	1,450.00	2,250.00	1,950.00

Anschutz, J.G. Revolver

ANSCHUTZ, J.G.
Zella Mehlis, Germany 1922-1938, 1945 to date in Ulm, West Germany. Also see Savage Arms Co. for rifle listings.

HANDGUN, REVOLVER

	V.G.	Exc.	Prior Year Exc. Value
☐ **J.G.A.**, 7mm C.F., Folding Trigger, Pocket Revolver, *Curio*	120.00	195.00	175.00

ANSCHUTZ, UDO
Zella Mehlis, Germany 1927-1939.

HANDGUN, SINGLESHOT

	V.G.	Exc.	Prior Year Exc. Value
☐ **Record-Match M1933**, .22 L.R.R.F., Free Pistol, Martini Action, Fancy Stocks, Target Sights, *Modern*	385.00	700.00	650.00

Arminex - Trifire Standard

Arminex - Trifire Target

	V.G.	Exc.	Prior Year Exc. Value
☐ **Record-Match M210**, .22 L.R.R.F., Free Pistol, Martini Action, Fancy Stocks, Target Sights, Light Engraving, *Modern*	575.00	900.00	850.00

ANSTADT, JACOB
Kurztown, Pa. 1815-1817. See Kentucky Rifles and Pistols.

APACHE
Fab. de Armas Garantazadas, Spain, c. 1920.

HANDGUN, REVOLVER

	V.G.	Exc.	Prior Year Exc. Value
☐ **Colt Police Positive Type**, .38, Double Action, 6 Shots, *Curio*	70.00	120.00	110.00

APACHE
Tempe, Ariz., c. 1970.

RIFLE, SEMI-AUTOMATIC

	V.G.	Exc.	Prior Year Exc. Value
☐ **Thompson Replica**, .45 ACP, Clip Fed, *Class 3*	95.00	165.00	150.00

APACHE
Made by Ojanguren y Vidosa; Eibar, Spain.

HANDGUN, SEMI-AUTOMATIC

	V.G.	Exc.	Prior Year Exc. Value
☐ **.25 ACP**, Clip Fed, *Modern*	80.00	135.00	125.00

APAOLOZO HERMANOS
Zumorraga, Spain, c. 1925.

HANDGUN, REVOLVER

	V.G.	Exc.	Prior Year Exc. Value
☐ **Colt Police Positive Type**, .38 Spec., Double Action, *Curio*	70.00	120.00	110.00

APEX RIFLE CO.
Sun Valley, Calif., c. 1952.

RIFLE, BOLT ACTION

	V.G.	Exc.	Prior Year Exc. Value
☐ **Bantam Light Sporter**, Various Calibers, 7 Lbs., Monte Kennedy Stock, Standard Grade, No Sights, *Modern*	350.00	495.00	475.00
☐ **Apex Eight**, Various Calibers, 8 Lbs., Monte Kennedy Stock, Standard Grade, No Sights, *Modern*	300.00	450.00	425.00
☐ **Reliable Nine**, Various Calibers, 9 Lbs., Monte Kennedy Stock, Standard Grade, No Sights, *Modern*	300.00	450.00	425.00
☐ **Varmint & Target**, Various Calibers, Monte Kennedy Target Stock, Heavy Barrel, No Sights, *Modern*	350.00	525.00	500.00
☐ **Bench Rester**, Various Calibers, Monte Kennedy Laminated Stock with Rails, Bull Barrel, Canjar Trigger, *Modern*	450.00	675.00	650.00

ARAMBERRI
Spain

	V.G.	Exc.	Prior Year Exc. Value
SHOTGUN, DOUBLE BARREL, SIDE-BY-SIDE			
☐ **Boxlock**, 12 Gauge, Single Trigger, Checkered Stock, Vent Rib, *Modern*	135.00	195.00	190.00

ARGENTINE MILITARY

	V.G.	Exc.	Prior Year Exc. Value
AUTOMATIC WEAPON, ASSAULT RIFLE			
☐ **FN-FAL,** .308 Win., Clip Fed, *Class 3*	1200.00	1600.00	1650.00
AUTOMATIC WEAPON, SUBMACHINE GUN			
☐ **C-3,** .45 ACP, *Class 3*	250.00	395.00	375.00
☐ **C-4 Hafdasa,** .45 ACP, *Class 3*	200.00	375.00	350.00
☐ **M E M S,** 9mm Luger, *Class 3*	475.00	675.00	650.00
☐ **M1943,** .45 ACP, *Class 3*	225.00	375.00	350.00
☐ **M1946,** .45 ACP, *Class 3*	225.00	375.00	350.00
☐ **P A M,** 9mm Luger, *Class 3*	350.00	675.00	650.00
☐ **Star M D,** 9mm Luger, *Class 3*	475.00	775.00	750.00
HANDGUN, REVOLVER			
☐ **Colt M 1985,** Double Trigger, Solid Frame, Swing-out Cylinder, Military, *Modern*	115.00	180.00	185.00
HANDGUN, SEMI-AUTOMATIC			
☐ **Ballester-Molina,** .45 ACP, Clip Fed, *Modern*	190.00	295.00	275.00
☐ **Ballester-Rigaud,** .45 ACP, Clip Fed, *Modern*	215.00	335.00	300.00
☐ **Mannlicher M1905,** 7.63 Mannlicher, *Curio*	130.00	260.00	325.00
☐ **Modelo 1916 (Colt 1911),** .45 ACP, Clip Fed, *Modern*	185.00	380.00	475.00
☐ **Modelo 1927 (Colt 1911A1),** .45 ACP, Clip Fed, *Modern*	220.00	420.00	525.00

Argentine M1905

	V.G.	Exc.	Prior Year Exc. Value
RIFLE, BOLT ACTION			
☐ **M 1908/09,** 7.65 Argentine, Carbine, Open Rear Sight, Full-Stocked Military, *Modern*	100.00	160.00	200.00
☐ **M 1891,** 7.65 Argentine, Rifle, Full Stocked Military, *Modern*	50.00	90.00	150.00
☐ **M 1891,** 7.65 Argentine, Carbine, Open Rear Sight, Full Stocked Military, *Modern*	60.00	100.00	150.00

	V.G.	Exc.	Prior Year Exc. Value
☐ **M1909,** 7.65 Argentine, Rifle, Full Stocked Military, *Modern*	62.00	105.00	130.00

RIFLE, SINGLESHOT

☐ **M1879,** .43 Mauser, Rolling Block, *Antique*	250.00	375.00	325.00

ARISTOCRAT

Made by Hopkins & Allen for Suplee Biddle Hardware 1870-1900.

HANDGUN, REVOLVER

☐ **.22 Short R.F.**, 7 Shot, Spur Trigger, Solid Frame, Single Action, *Antique*	95.00	160.00	160.00
☐ **.32 Short R.F.**, 5 Shot, Spur Trigger, Solid Frame, Single Action, *Antique*	90.00	175.00	175.00

ARISTOCRAT

Made by Stevens Arms.

SHOTGUN, DOUBLE BARREL, SIDE-BY-SIDE

☐ **M 315**, Various Gauges, Hammerless, Steel Barrel, *Modern*	95.00	165.00	160.00

ARIZAGA, GASPAR

Eibar, Spain.

HANDGUN, SEMI-AUTOMATIC

☐ **.32 ACP**, Clip Fed, *Modern*	95.00	150.00	145.00

ARMALITE

Costa Mesa, Calif.

AUTOMATIC WEAPON, ASSAULT RIFLE

☐ **AR-10 .308 Win.**, Clip Fed, Commercial, *Class 3*	2,500.00	3,500.00	3,250.00
☐ **AR-18 .223 Rem.**, Clip Fed, Commercial, *Class 3*	500.00	675.00	625.00
☐ **AR-18 .223 Rem.**, Clip Fed, Folding Stock, *Class 3*	600.00	900.00	800.00

RIFLE, SEMI-AUTOMATIC

☐ **AR-180 .223 Rem.**, Clip Fed, Folding Stock, *Modern*	275.00	450.00	475.00
☐ **AR-7 Explorer**, .22 L.R.R.F., Clip Fed, *Modern*	50.00	80.00	85.00
☐ **AR-7 Explorer Custom**, .22 L.R.R.F., Checkered Stock, Clip Fed, *Modern*	60.00	100.00	100.00

SHOTGUN, SEMI-AUTOMATIC

☐ **AR-17**, 12 Ga., Lightweight, *Modern*	400.00	650.00	600.00

ARMI JAGER

Turin, Italy. Imported by E.M.F.

HANDGUN, REVOLVER

☐ **Dakota**, .22 L.R.R.F., Single Action, Western Style, Various Barrel Lengths, *Modern*	85.00	140.00	135.00
☐ **Dakota**, .22 L.R.R.F. and .22 W.M.R., Single Action, Western Style, Various Barrel Lengths, *Modern*	110.00	170.00	165.00
☐ **Dakota**, Various Calibers, Single Action, Western Style, Various Barrel Lengths, *Modern*	125.00	170.00	150.00

	V.G.	Exc.	Prior Year Exc. Value
☐ **Dakota**, Various Calibers, Single Action, Western Style, Buntline Barrel Lengths, *Modern*	135.00	195.00	165.00
☐ **Dakota**, Various Calibers, Single Action, Western Style, Engraved, Various Barrel Lengths, *Modern*	200.00	300.00	200.00
☐ **Dakota Sheriff**, Various Calibers, Single Action, Western Style, 3½" Barrel, *Modern*	110.00	180.00	150.00
☐ **Dakota Target**, Various Calibers, Single Action, Western Style, Adjustable Sights, Various Barrel Lengths, *Modern*	140.00	200.00	170.00
RIFLE, SEMI-AUTOMATIC			
☐ **AP-74 Standard**, .22 L.R.R.F., Military Style, Plastic Stock, *Modern*	60.00	100.00	90.00
☐ **AP-74 Standard**, .32 ACP, Military Style, Plastic Stock, *Modern*	65.00	110.00	100.00
☐ **AP-74**, .22 L.R.R.F., Military Style, Wood Stock, *Modern*	65.00	100.00	95.00
☐ **AP-74**, .32 ACP, Military Style, Wood Stock, *Modern*	70.00	120.00	110.00
☐ **AP-74 Commando**, .22 L.R.R.F., Military Style, Wood Stock, *Modern*	70.00	120.00	110.00

ARMINEX LTD.

Scottsdale, Ariz. since 1982.

HANDGUN, SEMI-AUTOMATIC

	V.G.	Exc.	Prior Year Exc. Value
☐ **Trifire**, .45 A.C.P., 9mm Luger, or .38 Super, Blue or Nickel, Clip Fed, Hammer, Adjustable Sights, *Modern*	220.00	300.00	—
☐ **Trifire Presentation**, .45 A.C.P., 9mm Luger, or .38 Super, Cased, Blue or Nickel, Clip Fed, Hammer, Adjustable Sights, *Modern*	250.00	335.00	—

ARMINIUS

Herman Weihrauch Sportwaffenfabrik, Mellrichstadt/ Bayern, West Germany before 1968; for Current Models, See F.I.E.

HANDGUN, REVOLVER

	V.G.	Exc.	Prior Year Exc. Value
☐ **HW-3**, .22 L.R.R.F., *Modern*	20.00	35.00	35.00
☐ **HW-3**, .32 S & W Long, *Modern*	25.00	45.00	45.00
☐ **HW-5**, .22 L.R.R.F., *Modern*	20.00	35.00	35.00
☐ **HW-5**, .32 S & W Long, *Modern*	25.00	40.00	40.00
☐ **HW-7**, .22 L.R.R.F., *Modern*	20.00	35.00	35.00
☐ **HW-9**, .22 L.R.R.F., Adjustable Sights, *Modern*	35.00	55.00	55.00

ARMINIUS

Friederich Pickert, Zella-Mehlis, Germany 1922-1939.

HANDGUN, REVOLVER

	V.G.	Exc.	Prior Year Exc. Value
☐ **Model 1**, .22 L.R.R.F., Hammerless, *Modern*	85.00	140.00	130.00
☐ **Model 2**, .22 L.R.R.F., Hammer, *Modern*	85.00	140.00	130.00
☐ **Model 3**, .25 ACP, Hammerless, Folding Trigger, *Modern*	85.00	140.00	130.00
☐ **Model 4**, 5.5 Velo Dog, Hammerless, Folding Trigger, *Modern*	85.00	140.00	130.00
☐ **Model 5/1**, 7.5mm Swiss, Hammer, *Modern*	95.00	165.00	160.00

	V.G.	Exc.	Prior Year Exc. Value
☐ **Model 5/2**, 7.62 Nagant, Hammer, *Modern*	85.00	155.00	150.00
☐ **Model 7**, .320 Revolver, Hammer, *Modern*	75.00	130.00	120.00
☐ **Model 8**, .320 Revolver, Hammerless, Folding Trigger, *Modern*	75.00	130.00	120.00
☐ **Model 9**, .32 ACP, Hammer, *Modern*	85.00	140.00	135.00
☐ **Model 10**, .32 ACP, Hammerless, Folding Trigger, *Modern*	85.00	140.00	130.00
☐ **Model 13**, .380 Revolver, Hammer, *Modern*	85.00	140.00	130.00
☐ **Model 14**, .380 Revolver, Hammerless, *Modern*	85.00	140.00	130.00
HANDGUN, SINGLESHOT			
☐ **TP 1**, .22 L.R.R.F., Target Pistol, Hammer, *Modern*	195.00	375.00	350.00
☐ **TP 2**, .22 L.R.R.F., Hammerless, Set Triggers, *Modern*	195.00	375.00	350.00

ARMSPORT

Current Importers, Miami, Fla.

	V.G.	Exc.	Prior Year Exc. Value
HANDGUN, FLINTLOCK			
☐ **Kentucky**, .45, Reproduction, *Antique*	45.00	80.00	75.00
HANDGUN, PERCUSSION			
☐ **New Remington Army**, .44, Stainless Steel, Brass Trigger Guard, Reproduction, *Antique*	80.00	125.00	125.00
☐ **New Remington Army**, .44, Blue, Brass Trigger Guard, Reproduction, *Antique*	60.00	95.00	90.00
☐ **Whitney**, .36, Solid Frame, Brass Trigger Guard, Reproduction, *Antique*	60.00	95.00	90.00
☐ **Spiller & Burr**, .36, Solid Frame, Brass Frame, Reproduction, *Antique*	45.00	70.00	65.00
☐ **1851 Colt Navy**, .36, Brass Frame, Reproduction, *Antique*	45.00	75.00	70.00
☐ **1851 Colt Navy**, .44, Brass Frame, Reproduction, *Antique*	45.00	75.00	70.00
☐ **1851 Colt Navy**, .36, Steel Frame, Reproduction, *Antique*	55.00	90.00	85.00
☐ **1851 Colt Navy**, .44, Steel Frame, Reproduction, *Antique*	55.00	90.00	85.00
☐ **1860 Colt Army**, .44, Brass Frame, Reproduction, *Antique*	50.00	85.00	80.00
☐ **1860 Colt Army**, .44, Steel Frame, Reproduction, *Antique*	60.00	95.00	95.00
☐ **New Hartford Police**, .36, Reproduction, *Antique*	45.00	85.00	80.00
☐ **1847 Colt Walker**, .44, Reproduction, *Antique*	75.00	120.00	115.00
☐ **Corsair**, .44, Double Barrel, Reproduction, *Antique*	50.00	85.00	80.00
☐ **Kentucky**, .45 or .50, Reproduction, *Antique*	45.00	75.00	70.00
☐ **Patriot**, .45, Target Sights, Set Triggers, Reproduction, *Antique*	60.00	100.00	100.00
RIFLE, BOLT ACTION			
☐ **Tikka**, Various Calibers, Open Sights, Checkered Stock, Clip Fed, *Modern*	275.00	395.00	375.00

	V.G.	Exc.	Prior Year Exc. Value
RIFLE, LEVER ACTION			
☐ **Premier 1873 Winchester**, Various Calibers, Rifle, Engraved, Reproduction, *Modern*	700.00	950.00	900.00
☐ **Premier 1873 Winchester**, Various Calibers, Carbine, Engraved, Reproduction, *Modern*	600.00	800.00	775.00
RIFLE, FLINTLOCK			
☐ **Kentucky**, .45, Reproduction, *Antique*	100.00	145.00	145.00
☐ **Deluxe Kentucky**, .45, Reproduction, *Antique*	150.00	200.00	200.00
☐ **Hawkin**, .45, Reproduction, *Antique*	120.00	160.00	160.00
☐ **Deluxe Hawkin**, .50, Reproduction, *Antique*	130.00	170.00	170.00
RIFLE, PERCUSSION			
☐ **Kentucky**, .45 or .50, Reproduction, *Antique*	95.00	140.00	140.00
☐ **Deluxe Kentucky**, .45, Reproduction, *Antique*	130.00	185.00	185.00
☐ **Hawkin**, Various Calibers, Reproduction, *Antique*	110.00	150.00	150.00
☐ **Deluxe Hawkin**, Various Calibers, Reproduction, *Antique*	120.00	160.00	160.00
COMBINATION WEAPON, OVER-UNDER			
☐ **Tikka Turkey Gun**, 12 Ga. and .222 Rem., Vent Rib, Sling Swivels, Muzzle Break, Checkered Stock, *Modern*	425.00	600.00	575.00
RIFLE, DOUBLE BARREL, SIDE-BY-SIDE			
☐ **Emperor**, Various Calibers, Holland and Holland Type Sidelock, Engraved, Checkered Stock, Extra Barrels, Cased, *Modern*	8,000.00	9,950.00	9,500.00
☐ **Emperor Deluxe**, Various Calibers, Holland and Holland Sidelock, Fancy Engraving, Checkered Stock, Extra Barrels, *Modern*	9,500.00	15,000.00	14,500.00
RIFLE, DOUBLE BARREL, OVER-UNDER			
☐ **Emperor**, Various Calibers, Checkered Stock, Engraved, Extra Barrels, Cased, *Modern*	6,000.00	7,750.00	7,500.00
☐ **Express**, Various Calibers, Checkered Stock, Engraved, *Modern*	1,500.00	2,350.00	2,250.00
SHOTGUN, PERCUSSION			
☐ **Hook Breech**, Double Barrel, Side-by-Side, 10 and 12 Gauges, Reproduction, *Antique*	150.00	225.00	225.00
SHOTGUN, DOUBLE BARREL, SIDE-BY-SIDE			
☐ **Goose Gun**, 10 Ga. 3½" Mag., Checkered Stock, *Modern*	350.00	465.00	450.00
☐ **Side-by-Side**, 12 and 20 Gauges, Checkered Stock, *Modern*	300.00	420.00	400.00
☐ **Express**, 12 and 20 Gauges, Holland and Holland Type Sidelock, Engraved, Checkered Stock, *Modern*	2,000.00	2,850.00	2,750.00
☐ **Western Double**, 12 Ga. Mag. 3", Outside Hammers Double Trigger, *Modern*	275.00	395.00	375.00
SHOTGUN, DOUBLE BARREL, OVER-UNDER			
☐ **Premier**, 12 Ga., Skeet Grade, Checkered Stock, Engraved, *Modern*	1,000.00	1,400.00	1,350.00
☐ **Model 2500**, 12 and 20 Ga., Checkered Stock, Adjustable Choke, Single Selective Trigger, *Modern*	400.00	550.00	525.00

	V.G.	Exc.	Prior Year Exc. Value
SHOTGUN, SINGLESHOT			
☐ **Monotrap**, 12 Ga., Two Barrel Set, Checkered Stock, *Modern*	**1,500.00**	**2,100.00**	**2,000.00**
☐ **Monotrap**, 12 Ga., Checkered Stock, *Modern*	**1,000.00**	**1,450.00**	**1,350.00**

ARMSTRONG, JOHN

Gettysburg, Pa. 1813-1817. Also See Kentucky Rifles and Pistols.

ARRIOLA HERMANOS

Eibar, Spain, c. 1930.

	V.G.	Exc.	Prior Year Exc. Value
HANDGUN, REVOLVER			
☐ **Colt Police Positive Copy**, .38 Spec., Double Action, *Modern*	**65.00**	**115.00**	**110.00**

ARRIZABALAGA, HIJOS DE CALIXTO

Eibar, Spain, c. 1915.

	V.G.	Exc.	Prior Year Exc. Value
HANDGUN, SEMI-AUTOMATIC			
☐ **Ruby Type**, .32 ACP, Clip Fed, Blue, *Curio*	**85.00**	**150.00**	**145.00**

ASCASO, FRANCISCO

Tarassa, Spain, c. 1937.

	V.G.	Exc.	Prior Year Exc. Value
HANDGUN, SEMI-AUTOMATIC			
☐ **Astra 400 Copy**, 9mm, Clip Fed, Military Type, *Curio*	**625.00**	**975.00**	**950.00**

ASHEVILLE ARMORY

Asheville, N.C. 1861-1864.

	V.G.	Exc.	Prior Year Exc. Value
RIFLE, PERCUSSION			
☐ **.58 Enfield Type**, Rifled, Brass Furniture, Military, *Antique*	**1,300.00**	**2,150.00**	**1,950.00**

ASTRA

Founded in 1908 as Unceta y Esperanza in Eibar, Spain. In 1913 moved to Guernica, Spain and the name was reversed to Esperanza y Unceta; name changed again in 1926 to Unceta y Cia.; name changed again in 1953 to Astra-Unceta y Cia.

	V.G.	Exc.	Prior Year Exc. Value
AUTOMATIC WEAPON, MACHINE-PISTOL			
☐ **Model 901**, 7.63 Mauser, Holster Stock, *Class 3*	**750.00**	**1,300.00**	**1,250.00**
☐ **Model 902**, 7.63 Mauser, Holster Stock, *Class 3*	**750.00**	**1,300.00**	**1,250.00**
☐ **Model 903**, 7.63 Mauser, Holster Stock, *Class 3*	**750.00**	**1,300.00**	**1,250.00**
☐ **Model F**, 9mm Bayard Long, Holster Stock, *Class 3*	**750.00**	**1,300.00**	**1,250.00**
HANDGUN, REVOLVER			
☐ **Model 41**, .41 Magnum, Blue, *Modern*	**300.00**	**350.00**	—
☐ **Model 45**, .45 Colt, Blue, *Modern*	**300.00**	**350.00**	—
☐ **250**, .22 L.R.R.F., Double Action, Small Frame, *Modern*	**80.00**	**140.00**	**135.00**
☐ **250**, .22 W.M.R., Double Action, Small Frame, *Modern*	**80.00**	**140.00**	**135.00**
☐ **250**, .32 S & W Long, Double Action, Small Frame, *Modern*	**70.00**	**140.00**	**130.00**
☐ **250**, .38 Special, Double Action, Small Frame, *Modern*	**85.00**	**150.00**	**140.00**

Astra Model 900

Astra M1911 .32

Astra Cub

Astra Model 200 with Long Clip

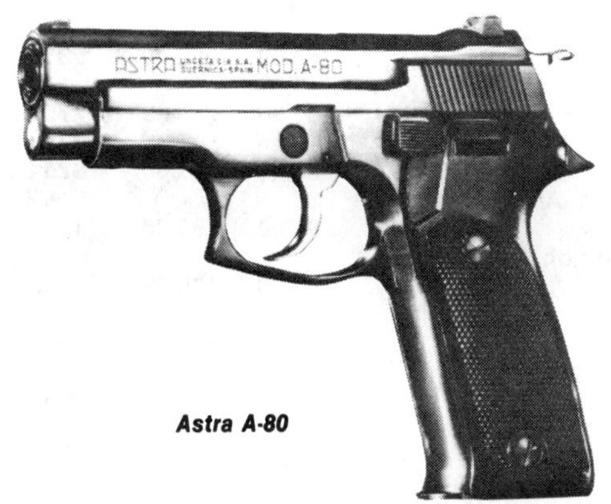

Astra A-80

Astra Constable

	V.G.	Exc.	Prior Year Exc. Value
☐ **357 Magnum**, .357 Magnum, Double Action, Adjustable Sights, *Modern*	**150.00**	**250.00**	**235.00**
☐ **357 Magnum**, .357 Magnum, Double Action, Adjustable Sights, Stainless Steel, *Modern*	**185.00**	**285.00**	**275.00**
☐ **44 Magnum**, .44 Magnum, Double Action, Adjustable Sights, *Modern*	**200.00**	**335.00**	**325.00**
☐ **960**, .38 Special, Double Action, Adjustable Sights, *Modern*	**95.00**	**165.00**	**160.00**
☐ **Cadix**, .22 L.R.R.F., Double Action, Adjustable Sights, *Modern*	**80.00**	**140.00**	**140.00**
☐ **Cadix**, .22 W.M.R., Double Action, Adjustable Sights, *Modern*	**90.00**	**150.00**	**150.00**
☐ **Cadix**, .32 S & W Long, Double Action, Adjustable Sights, *Modern*	**80.00**	**130.00**	**130.00**
☐ **Cadix**, .38 Special, Double Action, Adjustable Sights, *Modern*	**95.00**	**160.00**	**155.00**
☐ **Inox**, .38 Special, Stainless Steel, Double Action, Small Frame, *Modern*	**120.00**	**190.00**	**185.00**
☐ **Match**, .38 Special, Double Action, Adjustable Sights, *Modern*	**100.00**	**165.00**	**165.00**
HANDGUN, SEMI-AUTOMATIC			
☐ **Chrome Plating**, *Add* **$25.00-$45.00**			
☐ **Light Engraving**, *Add* **$60.00-$110.00**			
☐ **A-50**, Various Calibers, Blue, Single Action, *Modern*	**145.00**	**220.00**	**—**
☐ **A-80**, Various Calibers, Double Action, Blue, Large Magazine, *Modern*	**225.00**	**385.00**	**375.00**
☐ **A-80**, Various Calibers, Double Action, Chrome Large Magazine, *Modern*	**225.00**	**400.00**	**390.00**
☐ **Constable**, Various Calibers, Blue, *Modern*	**165.00**	**250.00**	**240.00**
☐ **Constable Pocket**, Various Calibers, Blue, *Modern*	**165.00**	**250.00**	**245.00**
☐ **Constable Sport**, Various Calibers, Blue, *Modern*	**165.00**	**270.00**	**240.00**
☐ **Constable Target**, .22 L.R.R.F., Blue, *Modern*	**200.00**	**325.00**	**300.00**
☐ **Model 100**, .32 ACP, *Curio*	**120.00**	**165.00**	**150.00**
☐ **Model 100 Special**, .32 ACP, 9 Shot, *Curio*	**125.00**	**185.00**	**175.00**
☐ **Model 1000**, .32 ACP, 12 Shot, *Modern*	**125.00**	**200.00**	
☐ **Model 1911**, .32 ACP, *Curio*	**135.00**	**225.00**	**235.00**
☐ **Model 1915**, .32 ACP, *Curio*	**100.00**	**170.00**	**165.00**
☐ **Model 1916**, .32 ACP, *Curio*	**120.00**	**190.00**	**185.00**
☐ **Model 1924**, .25 ACP, *Curio*	**115.00**	**165.00**	**160.00**
☐ **Model 200 Firecat**, .25 ACP, Early Model, Concave Indicator Cut, *Modern*	**120.00**	**165.00**	**155.00**
☐ **Model 200 Firecat**, .25 ACP, Late Model, Rear Indicator, *Modern*	**90.00**	**145.00**	**135.00**
☐ **Model 200 Firecat**, .25 ACP, Late Model, Long Clip, *Modern*	**100.00**	**150.00**	**145.00**
☐ **Model 2000 Camper**, .22 Short R.F., *Modern*	**110.00**	**170.00**	**160.00**
☐ **Model 2000 Cub**, .22 Short R.F., *Modern*	**95.00**	**150.00**	**150.00**
☐ **Model 2000 Cub**, .25 ACP, *Modern*	**95.00**	**145.00**	**150.00**
☐ **Model 2000 Camper or Cub**, Conversion Kit Only,	**60.00**	**90.00**	**80.00**
☐ **Model 300**, .32 ACP, Clip Fed, *Modern*	**135.00**	**220.00**	**210.00**
☐ **Model 300**, .32 ACP, Nazi-Proofed, Clip Fed, *Curio*	**350.00**	**475.00**	**450.00**
☐ **Model 300**, .380 ACP, Clip Fed, *Modern*	**145.00**	**235.00**	**225.00**
☐ **Model 300**, .32 ACP, Nazi-Proofed, Clip Fed, *Curio*	**350.00**	**475.00**	**450.00**

Astra TS-22

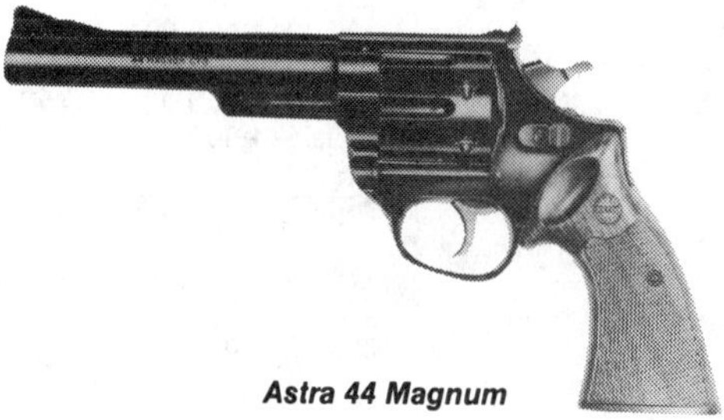

Astra 44 Magnum

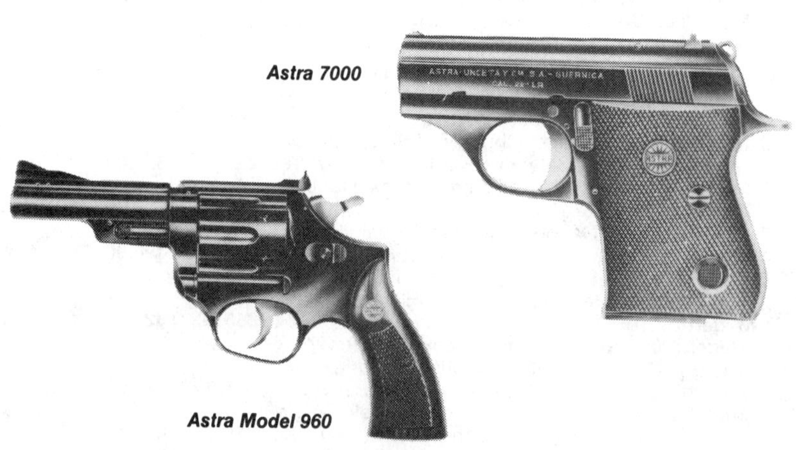

Astra 7000

Astra Model 960

	V.G.	Exc.	Prior Year Exc. Value
☐ **Model 3000 (Late)**, .380 ACP, Clip Fed, *Modern*	100.00	155.00	150.00
☐ **Model 400**, .32 ACP, *Modern*	470.00	695.00	650.00
☐ **Model 400**, 9mm Bayard Long, Nazi-Proofed, Clip Fed, *Curio*	475.00	650.00	600.00
☐ **Model 400**, 9mm Bayard Long, *Modern*	225.00	345.00	300.00
☐ **Model 4000 Falcon**, Conversion Unit Only	65.00	100.00	95.00
☐ **Model 4000 Falcon**, .22 L.R.R.F., Clip Fed, *Modern*	150.00	220.00	200.00
☐ **Model 4000 Falcon**, .32 ACP, Clip Fed, *Modern*	140.00	200.00	190.00
☐ **Model 4000 Falcon**, .380 ACP, Clip Fed, *Modern*	140.00	200.00	190.00
☐ **Model 600**, .32 ACP, Clip Fed, *Modern*	165.00	250.00	225.00
☐ **Model 600**, 9mm Luger, Nazi-Proofed, Clip Fed, *Curio*	270.00	400.00	375.00
☐ **Model 600**, 9mm Luger, Clip Fed, *Modern*	190.00	270.00	250.00
☐ **Model 700**, .32 ACP, Clip Fed, *Curio*	480.00	675.00	650.00
☐ **Model 700 Special**, .32 ACP, 12 Shots, Clip Fed, *Modern*	450.00	625.00	600.00
☐ **Model 7000**, .22 L.R.R.F., Clip Fed, *Modern*	115.00	165.00	150.00
☐ **Model 800 Condor**, .380 ACP, Clip Fed, *Modern*	125.00	185.00	175.00
☐ **Model 900**, 7.63 Mauser, Holster Stock, *Modern*	900.00	1,475.00	1,350.00
☐ **Model 900**, 9mm Luger, *Modern*	995.00	1,650.00	1,550.00
☐ **Model 902**, 9mm Bayard Long, Holster Stock, *Curio*	1,250.00	1,900.00	1,750.00
☐ **Model 903E**, .38 Super, *Modern*	1,200.00	1,900.00	1,750.00
☐ **Model 903E**, 7.63 Mauser, Holster Stock, *Modern*	925.00	1,450.00	1,250.00
☐ **Model 903E**, 9mm Bayard Long, *Modern*	950.00	1,500.00	1,250.00
☐ **Model 5000 Sport (Constable)**, .22 L.R.R.F. Target Pistol, Clip Fed, *Modern*	175.00	275.00	275.00
☐ **Model TS-22**, .22 L.R.R.F. Target Pistol, Single Action, Clip Fed, *Modern*	200.00	325.00	320.00
RIFLE, SEMI-AUTOMATIC			
☐ **Model 1000**, .32 ACP, Clip Fed, *Modern*	315.00	435.00	425.00
☐ **Model 3000 (Early)**, .32 ACP, *Modern*	110.00	170.00	165.00
☐ **Model 3000 (Late)**, .22 L.R.R.F., *Modern*	95.00	150.00	145.00
☐ **Model 3000 (Late)**, .32 ACP, *Modern*	105.00	160.00	150.00
☐ **Model 800 Condor**, 9mm Luger, *Curio*	450.00	625.00	595.00
☐ **Model 902**, 7.63 Mauser, *Modern*	1,100.00	1,700.00	1,500.00
SHOTGUN, DOUBLE BARREL, OVER-UNDER			
☐ **Model 650**, 12 Gauge, Checkered Stock, Double Triggers, Vent Rib, *Modern*	190.00	285.00	275.00
☐ **Model 650E**, 12 Gauge, Checkered Stock, Double Triggers, Vent Rib, Selective Ejectors, *Modern*	225.00	385.00	375.00
☐ **Model 750**, 12 Gauge, Checkered Stock, Double Triggers, Vent Rib, *Modern*	225.00	385.00	375.00
☐ **Model 750E**, 12 Gauge, Checkered Stock, Single Trigger, Vent Rib, Selective Ejectors, *Modern*	325.00	490.00	475.00
☐ **Model 750 Skeet**, 12 Gauge, Checkered Stock, Single Trigger, Vent Rib, Selective Ejectors, *Modern*	355.00	525.00	500.00
☐ **Model 750 Trap**, 12 Gauge, Checkered Stock, Single Trigger, Vent Rib, Selective Ejectors, *Modern*	355.00	525.00	500.00
☐ **Model ID-13**, 12 Gauge, Checkered Stock, Single Trigger, Selective Ejectors, Vent Rib, *Modern*	315.00	465.00	450.00

	V.G.	Exc.	Prior Year Exc. Value
SHOTGUN, DOUBLE BARREL, SIDE-BY-SIDE			
☐ **Model 811**, 10 Gauge Magnum, Checkered Stock, Double Triggers, *Modern*	195.00	300.00	295.00
☐ **Model 805**, Various Gauges, Checkered Stock, Double Triggers, *Modern*	160.00	265.00	250.00
SHOTGUN, SINGLESHOT			
☐ **Cyclops**, Various Gauges, Checkered Stock, *Modern*	55.00	90.00	85.00

ATIS

Ponte S. Marco, Italy.

	V.G.	Exc.	Prior Year Exc. Value
SHOTGUN, SEMI-AUTOMATIC			
☐ **12 Ga.**, Lightweight, Vent Rib, *Modern*	165.00	240.00	225.00
☐ **12 Ga.**, Lightweight, Vent Rib, Left-Hand, *Modern*	220.00	290.00	275.00

ATLAS

Domingo Acha y Cia., Ermua, Spain, c. 1920.

	V.G.	Exc.	Prior Year Exc. Value
HANDGUN, SEMI-AUTOMATIC			
☐ **Vest Pocket**, .25 ACP, Clip Fed, *Modern*	85.00	130.00	120.00

ATLAS ARMS

Chicago, Ill. from about 1962 to 1972.

	V.G.	Exc.	Prior Year Exc. Value
HANDGUN, DOUBLE BARREL, OVER-UNDER			
☐ **Derringer**, .22 L.R.R.F., Remington Style, *Modern*	30.00	55.00	50.00
☐ **Derringer**, .38 Spec., Remington Style, *Modern*	45.00	65.00	65.00
SHOTGUN, DOUBLE BARREL, SIDE-BY-SIDE			
☐ **Model 145**, Various Gauges, Boxlock, Vent Rib, Engraved, Hammerless, Checkered Stock, *Modern*	325.00	440.00	425.00
☐ **Model 200**, Various Gauges, Boxlock, Double Triggers, Hammerless, Checkered Stock, *Modern*	165.00	260.00	245.00
☐ **Model 204**, Various Gauges, Boxlock, Single Trigger, Hammerless, Checkered Stock, *Modern*	225.00	300.00	295.00
☐ **Model 206**, Various Gauges, Boxlock, Single Trigger, Automatic Ejector, Hammerless, Checkered Stock, *Modern*	250.00	335.00	325.00
☐ **Model 208**, Various Gauges, Boxlock, Double Triggers, Vent Rib, Recoil Pad, *Modern*	225.00	300.00	295.00
☐ **Model 500**, Various Gauges, Boxlock, Double Triggers, Vent Rib, Recoil Pad, *Modern*	225.00	300.00	295.00
SHOTGUN, SINGLESHOT			
☐ **Trap Gun**, 12 Gauge, Automatic Ejector, Engraved, Checkered Stock, *Modern*	375.00	490.00	475.00
☐ **Insuperable 101**, Various Gauges, Vent Rib, Engraved, Checkered Stock, *Modern*	55.00	90.00	85.00
SHOTGUN, DOUBLE BARREL, OVER-UNDER			
☐ **Model 65**, Various Gauges, Boxlock, Double Triggers, Vent Rib, *Modern*	225.00	340.00	325.00

	V.G.	Exc.	Prior Year Exc. Value
☐ **Model 65-ST**, Various Gauges, Boxlock, Single Trigger, Vent Rib, *Modern*	240.00	375.00	365.00
☐ **Model 87**, Various Gauges, Merkel Type Sidelock, Single Trigger, Vent Rib, Engraved, *Modern*	325.00	435.00	425.00
☐ **Model 150**, Various Gauges, Boxlock, Single Trigger, Vent Rib, *Modern*	235.00	375.00	365.00
☐ **Model 150**, Various Gauges, Boxlock, Single Trigger, Vent Rib, Automatic Ejectors, *Modern*	285.00	400.00	395.00
☐ **Model 160**, Various Gauges, Boxlock, Single Trigger, Vent Rib, Automatic Ejectors, *Modern*	325.00	435.00	425.00
☐ **Model 180**, Various Gauges, Boxlock, Single Trigger, Vent Rib, Automatic Ejectors, Light Engraving, *Modern*	375.00	490.00	475.00
☐ **Model 750**, Various Gauges, Merkel Type Sidelock, Single Trigger, Vent Rib, Engraved, *Modern*	325.00	435.00	425.00
☐ **Model 750**, Various Gauges, Merkel Type Sidelock, Single Trigger, Vent Rib, Engraved, Automatic Ejectors, *Modern*	375.00	525.00	495.00
☐ **Grand Prix**, 12 or 20 Gauge, Merkel Type Sidelock, Single Selective Trigger, Fancy Engraving, Automatic Ejectors, *Modern*	750.00	1,150.00	1,100.00

ATKIN, HENRY E. & CO.

London, England 1874-1900.

SHOTGUN, DOUBLE BARREL, SIDE-BY-SIDE

☐ **Raleigh**, 12 Gauge, Sidelock, Double Triggers, Checkered Stock, Engraved, Automatic Ejectors, "Purdey" Barrels, *Modern*	5,250.00	8,500.00	8,000.00

AUBREY

Made by Meridan Arms Co., sold by Sears-Roebuck 1900-1930.

HANDGUN, REVOLVER

☐ **.32 S & W**, 5 Shot, Double Action, Top Break, *Modern*	55.00	95.00	95.00
☐ **.38 S & W**, 5 Shot, Double Action, Top Break, *Modern*	55.00	95.00	95.00

AUDAX

Trade name of Manufacture D'Armes Des Pyrenees, Hendaye, France, marketed by La Cartoucherie Francaise, Paris 1931-1939.

HANDGUN, SEMI-AUTOMATIC

☐ **.25 ACP**, Clip Fed, Magazine Disconnect, Grip Safety, *Modern*	80.00	140.00	135.00
☐ **.32 ACP**, Clip Fed, Magazine Disconnect, Blue, *Modern*	85.00	150.00	150.00

AUSTRALIAN MILITARY

RIFLE, BOLT ACTION

☐ **Mk. III,** .303 British, Clip Fed, WW I Issue, *Curio*	105.00	165.00	245.00
☐ **Mk. III,** .303 British, Clip Fed, WW II Issue, *Curio*	95.00	150.00	215.00

	V.G.	Exc.	Prior Year Exc. Value
RIFLE, SINGLESHOT			
☐ **Martini,** .32/40, Small Action, *Curio*	135.00	210.00	350.00

AUSTRIAN MILITARY

	V.G.	Exc.	Prior Year Exc. Value
AUTOMATIC WEAPON, ASSAULT RIFLE			
☐ **FN FAL,** .308 Win., *Class 3*	1250.00	1700.00	1700.00
AUTOMATIC WEAPON, SUBMACHINE GUN			
☐ **MP Solothurn 34,** 9mm Mauser, Clip Fed, *Class 3*	975.00	1500.00	1500.00
☐ **MP 34,** 9mm Luger, *Class 3,*	625.00	875.00	875.00
HANDGUN, FLINTLOCK			
☐ **.64 Dragoon,** with Shoulder Stock, Singleshot, *Antique*	500.00	800.00	800.00
HANDGUN, PERCUSSION			
☐ **.64 Dragoon,** with Shoulder Stock, Singleshot, *Antique*	350.00	600.00	600.00
HANDGUN, REVOLVER			
☐ **M1898 Rast Gasser,** 8mm Rast-Gasser, *Curio*	150.00	260.00	340.00
HANDGUN, SEMI-AUTOMATIC			
☐ **M1907 Roth Steyr,** 8mm Roth-Steyr, *Curio*	150.00	280.00	365.00
☐ **M1908 Steyr,** 8mm Roth-Steyr, *Curio*	130.00	240.00	325.00
☐ **M1911 Steyr Hahn,** 9mm Steyr, *Curio*	180.00	290.00	425.00
☐ **M1912 Steyr Hahn,** 9mm Steyr, *Curio*	130.00	235.00	300.00
☐ **Mannlicher 1901,** 7.63 Mannlicher, *Curio*	160.00	260.00	400.00
☐ **Mannlicher 1905,** 7.63 Mannlicher, *Curio*	145.00	250.00	325.00
HANDGUN, SINGLESHOT			
☐ **Werder Lightning,** 11mm, *Antique*	375.00	550.00	550.00
RIFLE, BOLT ACTION			
☐ **M1883 Schulhof,** 11.15 x 58R Werndl, 8 Shot, *Antique*	375.00	550.00	550.00
☐ **M1885 Steyr,** 11.15 x 58R Werndl, Straight-Pull, *Antique*	275.00	425.00	425.00
☐ **M1886 Steyr,** 11.15 x 58R Werndl, Straight-Pull Bolt, *Antique*	80.00	150.00	150.00
☐ **M1888,** 8 x 50R Mannlicher, *Antique*	85.00	150.00	150.00
☐ **M1888/90,** 8 x 50R Mannlicher, *Antique*	75.00	125.00	125.00
☐ **M1890,** 8 x 50R Mannlicher, Carbine, *Antique*	80.00	125.00	125.00
☐ **M1895,** 8 x 50R Mannlicher, Carbine, *Modern,*	50.00	85.00	125.00
☐ **M1895,** 8 x 50R Mannlicher, *Curio*	45.00	80.00	120.00
☐ **M1895 Stutzen,** 8 x 50R Mannlicher, *Curio*	55.00	120.00	175.00

AUTO MAG

Started in Pasadena, Calif. about 1968, and moved to North Hollywood, Calif. when purchased by T D E in 1971. Marketed by T D E, Jurras Associates, and High Standard.

	V.G.	Exc.	Prior Year Exc. Value
HANDGUN, SEMI-AUTOMATIC			
☐ **Shoulder Stock Only**, For Various Models And Calibers, *Class 3*	250.00	375.00	350.00
☐ **First Model (Pasadena)**, .357 AMP, Clip Fed, Stainless Steel, Hammer, Adjustable Sights, Cased, *Modern*	995.00	1,650.00	1,450.00

Austrian Military M1907 Roth Steyr

Auto Mag Model 180

	V.G.	Exc.	Prior Year Exc. Value
☐ **First Model (Pasadena)**, .44 AMP, Clip Fed, Stainless Steel, Hammer, Adjustable Sights, Cased, *Modern*	950.00	1,450.00	1,250.00
☐ **Model 160**, .357 AMP, Clip Fed, Stainless Steel, Hammer, Adjustable Sights, Cased, *Modern*	875.00	1,250.00	975.00
☐ **Model 170**, .41 JMP, Clip Fed, Stainless Steel, Hammer, Adjustable Sights, Cased, *Modern*	900.00	1,400.00	1,150.00
☐ **Model 180**, .44 AMP, Clip Fed, Stainless Steel, Hammer, Adjustable Sights, Cased, *Modern*	725.00	1,050.00	950.00
☐ **Model 260**, .357 AMP, Clip Fed, Stainless Steel, Hammer, Adjustable Sights, Cased, *Modern*	775.00	1,100.00	950.00
☐ **Model 280**, .44 AMP, Clip Fed, Stainless Steel, Hammer, Adjustable Sights, Cased, *Modern*	700.00	995.00	900.00
☐ **Alaskan Model**, .44 AMP, Clip Fed, Stainless Steel, Hammer, Adjustable Sights, Cased, *Modern*	1,700.00	2,500.00	2,250.00
☐ **High Standard**, .44 AMP, Clip Fed, Stainless Steel, Hammer, Adjustable Sights, Cased, *Modern*	850.00	1,250.00	1,100.00
☐ **Jurras Custom Model 200**, .44 AMP, Clip Fed, Stainless Steel, Hammer, Adjustable Sights, Cased, *Modern*	2,750.00	3,875.00	3,450.00

AUTOMATIC

Made by Hopkins & Allen, c. 1900.

HANDGUN, REVOLVER

	V.G.	Exc.	Prior Year Exc. Value
☐ **.32 S & W**, 5 Shot, Top Break, Hammerless, Double Action, *Modern*	60.00	95.00	95.00
☐ **.38 S & W**, 5 Shot, Top Break, Hammerless, Double Action, *Modern*	60.00	95.00	95.00

AUTOMATIC HAMMERLESS

Made by Iver Johnson, c. 1900.

	V.G.	Exc.	Prior Year Exc. Value
HANDGUN, REVOLVER			
☐ **.22 L.R.R.F.**, 7 Shot, Double Action, Top Break, Hammerless, *Modern*	55.00	90.00	95.00
☐ **.32 S & W**, 5 Shot, Top Break, Hammerless, Double Action, *Modern*	60.00	100.00	110.00
☐ **.38 S & W**, 5 Shot, Top Break, Hammerless, Double Action, *Modern*	60.00	100.00	110.00

AUTOMATIC PISTOL

Spain, Maker Unknown.

	V.G.	Exc.	Prior Year Exc. Value
HANDGUN, SEMI-AUTOMATIC			
☐ **Pocket**, .32 ACP, Clip Fed, *Modern*	60.00	100.00	95.00

AUTOMATIC POLICE

See Forehand & Wadsworth.

AUTO-ORDNANCE CORP.

See Thompson.

AUTO-POINTER

Made by Yamamoto Mfg. Co., Imported by Sloans.

	V.G.	Exc.	Prior Year Exc. Value
SHOTGUN, SEMI-AUTOMATIC			
☐ **12 and 20 Gauges**, Tube Feed, Checkered Stock, *Modern*	180.00	295.00	280.00

AUTOSTAND

Made for ManuFrance by Mre. d'Armes des Pyrenees.

	V.G.	Exc.	Prior Year Exc. Value
HANDGUN, SINGLESHOT			
☐ **E-1 (Unique)**, .22 L.R.R.F., Target Pistol, Adjustable Sights, *Modern*	65.00	95.00	90.00

AVENGER

	V.G.	Exc.	Prior Year Exc. Value
HANDGUN, REVOLVER			
☐ **.32 Long R.F.**, 5 Shot, Single Action, Spur Trigger, *Antique*	90.00	140.00	140.00

AVION

Azpiri y Cia., Eibar, Spain, c. 1915.

	V.G.	Exc.	Prior Year Exc. Value
HANDGUN, SEMI-AUTOMATIC			
☐ **Vest Pocket**, .25 ACP, Clip Fed, *Curio*	70.00	120.00	110.00

A Y A

Aguirre y Aranzabal, Spain. Now Imported by Ventura.

	V.G.	Exc.	Prior Year Exc. Value
SHOTGUN, DOUBLE BARREL, OVER-UNDER			
☐ **Model 37 Super**, Various Gauges, Single Selective Trigger, Automatic Ejector, Fancy Engraving, Sidelock, *Modern*	1,250.00	1,850.00	1,750.00

	V.G.	Exc.	Prior Year Exc. Value
SHOTGUN, DOUBLE BARREL, SIDE-BY-SIDE			
☐ **Bolero**, Various Gauges, Single Trigger, Checkered Stock, *Modern*	175.00	250.00	240.00
☐ **Matador**, Various Gauges, Single Selective Trigger, Checkered Stock, Selective Ejector, *Modern*	225.00	350.00	335.00
☐ **Matador II**, Various Gauges, Single Selective Trigger, Checkered Stock, Selective Ejector, Vent Rib, *Modern*	275.00	425.00	390.00
☐ **Model 1**, Various Gauges, Automatic Ejector, Sidelock, Fancy Checkering, Engraved, Lightweight, *Modern*	950.00	1,700.00	1,650.00
☐ **Model 117**, 12 Gauge, Sidelock, Single Selective Trigger, Engraved, Checkered Stock, *Modern*	475.00	725.00	700.00
☐ **Model 2**, Various Gauges, Automatic Ejector, Sidelock, Engraved, Checkered Stock, Double Trigger, *Modern*	475.00	725.00	700.00
☐ **Model 53E**, 12 and 20 Gauges, Sidelock, Single Selective Trigger, Fancy Checkering, Fancy Engraving, *Modern*	800.00	1,400.00	1,350.00
☐ **Model 56**, 12 and 20 Gauges, Sidelock, Raised Matted Rib, Fancy Checkering, Fancy Engraving, *Modern*	950.00	1,850.00	1,850.00
☐ **Model 76**, 12 and 20 Gauges, Automatic Ejector, Single Selective Trigger, Engraved, Checkered Stock, *Modern*	275.00	440.00	425.00
☐ **Model 76**, .410 Gauge, Double Triggers, Engraved, Checkered Stock, *Modern*	190.00	325.00	300.00
☐ **Model 400**, Various Gauges, Single Trigger, Checkered Stock, *Modern*	175.00	250.00	240.00
☐ **Model 400E**, Various Gauges, Single Selective Trigger, Checkered Stock, Selective Ejector, *Modern*	225.00	350.00	335.00
☐ **Model XXV/SL**, 12 Ga., Sidelock, Automatic Ejector, Engraved Checkered Stock, *Modern*	575.00	800.00	775.00

AZANZA Y ARRIZABALAGA

Eibar, Spain, c. 1916.

	V.G.	Exc.	Prior Year Exc. Value
HANDGUN, SEMI-AUTOMATIC			
☐ **M1916**, .32 ACP, Clip Fed, Long Grip, *Modern*	85.00	145.00	135.00

AZUL

Eulegio Aristegui, Eibar, Spain, c. 1930.

	V.G.	Exc.	Prior Year Exc. Value
HANDGUN, SUBMACHINE GUN			
☐ **Super Azul MM31**, 7.63mm Mauser, Selective Fire, Box Magazine, *Class 3*	750.00	1,300.00	1,250.00
HANDGUN, SEMI-AUTOMATIC			
☐ **Azul**, 7.63mm Mauser, Copy of Broomhandle Mauser, *Modern*	500.00	875.00	800.00
☐ **Azul**, .25 ACP, Clip Fed, Hammerless, *Modern*	80.00	125.00	115.00
☐ **Azul**, .32 ACP, Clip Fed, Hammerless, *Modern*	85.00	135.00	125.00
☐ **Azul**, .32 ACP, Clip Fed, Hammer, *Modern*	95.00	150.00	145.00

	V.G.	Exc.	Prior Year Exc. Value

BABCOCK
Maker Unknown c. 1880.

HANDGUN, REVOLVER

	V.G.	Exc.	Prior Year Exc. Value
☐ **.32 Short R.F.**, 5 Shot, Spur Trigger, Solid Frame, Single Action, *Antique*	90.00	160.00	160.00

BABY BULLDOG

HANDGUN, REVOLVER

	V.G.	Exc.	Prior Year Exc. Value
☐ **.22 L.R.R.F.**, Double Action, Hammerless, Folding Trigger, *Modern*	85.00	135.00	130.00
☐ **.32 Short R.F.**, Double Action, Hammerless, Folding Trigger, *Modern*	80.00	125.00	120.00

BABY RUSSIAN
Made by American Arms Co. c. 1890.

	V.G.	Exc.	Prior Year Exc. Value
☐ **.38 S & W**, 5 Shot, Single Action, Spur Trigger, Top Break, *Curio*	125.00	200.00	195.00

BACKHOUSE, RICHARD
Easton, Pa. 1774-1781. See Kentucky Rifles.

BACKUP
See T D E, and A M T.

BACON ARMS CO.
Norwich, Conn. 1858-1891. Also known as Bacon & Co. and Bacon Mfg. Co.

HANDGUN, PERCUSSION

	V.G.	Exc.	Prior Year Exc. Value
☐ **.34**, Boot Gun, Underhammer, Half-Octagon Barrel, *Antique*	195.00	325.00	295.00
☐ **6 Shot,** Fluted Barrel, Pepperbox, Underhammer, Pocket Pistol, *Antique*	575.00	800.00	750.00

HANDGUN, REVOLVER

	V.G.	Exc.	Prior Year Exc. Value
☐ **.22 Short R.F.,** 7 Shot, Spur Trigger, Solid Frame, Single Action, *Antique*	115.00	195.00	185.00
☐ **.32 Short R.F.,** 5 Shot, Spur Trigger, Solid Frame, Single Action, *Antique*	110.00	190.00	170.00
☐ **.32 Short R.F.,** 6 Shot, Solid Frame, Spur Trigger, Single Action, *Antique*	160.00	295.00	285.00
☐ **.32 Short R.F.,** 6 Shot, Solid Frame, Single Action with Trigger Guard, *Antique*	140.00	275.00	260.00
☐ **"Navy," .38 Long R.F.,** 6 Shot, 7½" Barrel, Solid Frame, Spur Trigger, Single Action, *Antique*	200.00	385.00	385.00

HANDGUN, SINGLESHOT

	V.G.	Exc.	Prior Year Exc. Value
☐ **Derringer,** .32 R.F., Spur Trigger, Side-Swing Barrel, *Antique*	170.00	345.00	320.00
☐ **SS Percussion,** .31 Cal., Ring Trigger, *Antique*	155.00	270.00	—

BAIKAL
Made in U.S.S.R., imported by Commercial Trading Imports.

SHOTGUN, DOUBLE BARREL, OVER-UNDER

	V.G.	Exc.	Prior Year Exc. Value
☐ **MC-5-105**, 20 Gauge, Boxlock, Engraved, Checkered Stock, Double Triggers, Solid Rib, Cased, *Modern*	550.00	800.00	800.00

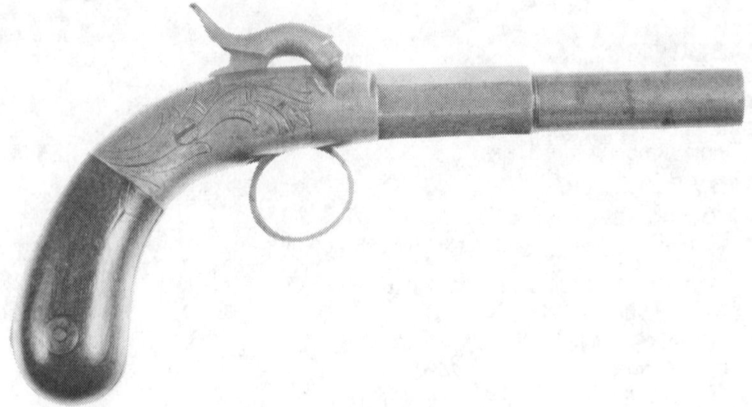

Bacon Ring Trigger, Single Shot, .31 Caliber

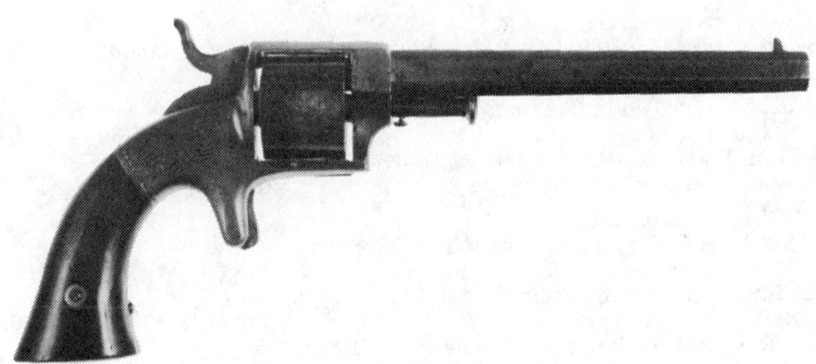

Bacon Navy Six Shot, .38 Caliber

	V.G.	Exc.	Prior Year Exc. Value
☐ **MC-6-105**, 12 Gauge, Boxlock, Engraved, Checkered Stock, Double Triggers, Solid Rib, Cased, *Modern*	750.00	1,275.00	1,250.00
☐ **MC-7-105**, 12 or 20 Gauge, Boxlock, Engraved, Checkered Stock, Single Triggers, Selective Ejector, Solid Rib, Cased, *Modern*	1,400.00	2,200.00	2,150.00
☐ **MC-8-105**, 12 Gauge, Trap or Skeet, Boxlock, Engraved, Checkered Stock, Single Trigger, Solid Rib, Cased, *Modern*	1,250.00	1,900.00	1,850.00
☐ **MC-109**, 12 Gauge, Sidelock, Engraved, Checkered Stock, Single Selective Trigger, Selective Ejectors, Vent Rib, Cased, *Modern*	2,750.00	4,000.00	4,000.00
☐ **IJ-27E1C**, 12 or 20 Gauge, Boxlock, Engraved, Checkered Stock, Single Selective Trigger, Selective Ejectors, Vent Rib, *Modern*	225.00	375.00	350.00
☐ **IJ-27E1C Silver**, 12 or 20 Gauge, Boxlock, Engraved, Checkered Stock, Single Selective Trigger, Selective Ejectors, Vent Rib, *Modern*	300.00	450.00	425.00
☐ **IJ-27E1C Super**, 12 or 20 Gauge, Boxlock, Engraved, Checkered Stock, Single Selective Trigger, Selective Ejectors, Vent Rib, *Modern*	390.00	595.00	575.00
☐ **TOZ-34E**, 12 or 28 Gauge, Boxlock, Engraved, Checkered Stock, Double Triggers, Vent Rib, *Modern*	335.00	495.00	475.00
SHOTGUN, DOUBLE BARREL, SIDE-BY-SIDE			
☐ **MC-110**, 12 or 20 Gauge, Boxlock, Engraved, Checkered Stock, Double Triggers, Solid Rib, Cased, *Modern*	1,500.00	2,300.00	2,250.00
☐ **MC-111**, 12 Gauge, Sidelock, Engraved, Checkered Stock, Single Selective Trigger, Selective Ejectors, Cased, *Modern*	2,750.00	4,000.00	4,000.00
☐ **IJ-58MAE**, 12 or 20 Gauge, Boxlock, Engraved, Checkered Stock, Double Triggers, *Modern*	125.00	220.00	200.00
SHOTGUN, SINGLESHOT			
☐ **IJ-18E**, 12 or 20 Gauge, Checkered Stock, *Modern*	35.00	55.00	55.00

BAKER GUN & FORGING CO.

Batavia, N.Y. 1886-1919, Purchased by Folsom in 1919.

	V.G.	Exc.	Prior Year Exc. Value
RIFLE, SEMI-AUTOMATIC			
☐ **Batavia**, .22 Short, Clip Fed, *Modern*	265.00	425.00	395.00
SHOTGUN, DOUBLE BARREL, SIDE-BY-SIDE			
Single Trigger, Add **$90.00-165.00**			
Deduct **50%** for Damascus Barrels			
Automatic Ejectors, Add **$110.00-225.00**			
☐ **Batavia Leader**, Various Gauges, Sidelock, Double Trigger, Checkered Stock, *Modern*	290.00	450.00	425.00
☐ **Batavia Leader Special**, Various Gauges, Sidelock, Double Trigger, Checkered Stock, Automatic Ejector, *Modern*	365.00	560.00	535.00
☐ **Black Beauty**, Various Gauges, Sidelock, Double Trigger, Checkered Stock, *Modern*	390.00	645.00	595.00
☐ **Black Beauty Special**, Various Gauges, Sidelock, Double Trigger, Checkered Stock, Automatic Ejector, *Modern*	495.00	725.00	675.00

	V.G.	Exc.	Prior Year Exc. Value
☐ **Deluxe ($1,000 Grade)**, Various Gauges, Sidelock, Fancy Wood, Fancy Engraving, Fancy Checkering, Automatic Ejector, *Modern*	9,000.00	14,000.00	13,250.00
☐ **Deluxe ($300 Grade)**, Various Gauges, Sidelock, Fancy Wood, Fancy Engraving, Fancy Checkering, Automatic Ejector, *Modern*	2,975.00	4,450.00	4,200.00
☐ **Expert**, Various Gauges, Sidelock, Fancy Wood, Fancy Engraving, Fancy Checkering, Automatic Ejector, *Modern*	2,200.00	3,150.00	2,950.00
☐ **Grade A**, Various Gauges, Sidelock, Hammerless, Engraved, Damascus Barrel, *Modern*	190.00	325.00	295.00
☐ **Grade B**, Various Gauges, Sidelock, Hammerless, Engraved, Damascus Barrels, *Modern*	180.00	310.00	280.00
☐ **Grade C Batavia**, Various Gauges, Boxlock, Hammerless, Engraved, Damascus Barrels, *Modern*	155.00	245.00	225.00
☐ **Grade H Deluxe**, Various Gauges, Sidelock, Fancy Engraving, *Modern*	2,650.00	3,600.00	3,450.00
☐ **Grade L Pigeon**, Various Gauges, Sidelock, Fancy Engraving, *Modern*	1,350.00	2,100.00	1,950.00
☐ **Grade N Krupp Trap**, 12 Ga., Sidelock, Engraved, *Modern*	850.00	1,350.00	1,250.00
☐ **Grade R**, Various Gauges, Sidelock, Light Engraving, *Modern*	395.00	660.00	625.00
☐ **Grade S**, Various Gauges, Sidelock, Light Engraving, *Modern*	375.00	560.00	525.00
Model 1896, 10 and 12 Gauges, Hammers, *Modern*	175.00	265.00	250.00
☐ **Model 1897**, Various Gauges, Hammers, *Modern*	175.00	265.00	250.00
☐ **New Baker Model**, 10 and 12 Gauges, Hammers, *Modern*	165.00	250.00	225.00
☐ **Paragon**, Various Gauges, Sidelock, Double Trigger, Engraved, Fancy Checkering, *Modern*	750.00	1,150.00	1,000.00
☐ **Paragon**, Various Gauges, Sidelock, Double Trigger, Engraved, Fancy Checkering, Automatic Ejector, *Modern*	850.00	1,475.00	1,350.00
☐ **Paragon Special**, 12 Ga., Sidelock, Fancy Wood, Fancy Engraving, *Modern*	975.00	1,700.00	1,600.00
SHOTGUN, SINGLESHOT			
☐ **Elite**, 12 Ga., Vent Rib, Fancy Engraving, *Modern*	750.00	1,200.00	1,100.00
☐ **Sterling**, 12 Ga., Vent Rib, Light Engraving, *Modern*	535.00	750.00	700.00
☐ **Superba, 12 Ga.**, Trap Grade, Fancy Wood, Fancy Engraving, Fancy Checkering, Automatic Ejector, *Antique*	1,900.00	2,725.00	2,600.00

BAKER GUN CO.

Made in Belgium for H & D Folsom Arms Co.

	V.G.	Exc.	Prior Year Exc. Value
SHOTGUN, DOUBLE BARREL, SIDE-BY-SIDE			
☐ **Various Gauges**, Outside Hammers, Damascus Barrel, *Antique*	80.00	160.00	150.00
☐ **Various Gauges**, Hammerless, Steel Barrel, *Antique*	110.00	190.00	175.00

	V.G.	Exc.	Prior Year Exc. Value
☐ **Various Gauges**, Hammerless, Damascus Barrel, *Antique*	80.00	160.00	150.00
☐ **Various Gauges**, Outside Hammers, Steel Barrel, *Antique*	95.00	185.00	175.00

SHOTGUN, SINGLESHOT

	V.G.	Exc.	Prior Year Exc. Value
☐ **Various Gauges**, Hammer, Steel Barrel, *Antique*	45.00	75.00	75.00

BAKER, EZEKIEL

London, England 1784-1825

HANDGUN, PERCUSSION

	V.G.	Exc.	Prior Year Exc. Value
☐ **.58**, Holster Pistol, Round Barrel, Light Ornamentation, *Antique*	475.00	675.00	625.00

BAKER, JOHN

Providence, Pa. 1768-1775. See Kentucky Rifles.

BAKER, W.H. & CO.

Marathon, N.Y. 1870, Syracuse, N.Y. 1878-1886.

COMBINATION WEAPON, DRILLING

	V.G.	Exc.	Prior Year Exc. Value
☐ **Hammer Drilling**, Various Gauges, Damascus Barrels, Front Trigger Break, *Antique*	400.00	675.00	650.00

RIFLE, PERCUSSION

	V.G.	Exc.	Prior Year Exc. Value
☐ **.60**, Brass Furniture, Scope Mounted, Target, Octagon Barrel, *Antique*	1,800.00	2,500.00	2,400.00

SHOTGUN, DOUBLE BARREL, SIDE-BY-SIDE

	V.G.	Exc.	Prior Year Exc. Value
☐ **Hammer Double**, 10 and 12 Gauges, Damascus Barrels, Front Trigger Break, *Antique*	200.00	350.00	325.00

BALL & WILLIAMS

Worcester, Mass. 1861-1866.

RIFLE, SINGLESHOT

	V.G.	Exc.	Prior Year Exc. Value
☐ **Ballard**, .44 Long R.F., Military, Carbine, Falling Block, *Antique*	550.00	750.00	725.00
☐ **Ballard**, .46 Long R.F., Kentucky Rifle, Falling Block, *Antique*	700.00	900.00	850.00
☐ **Ballard**, Various Rimfires, Falling Block, Sporting Rifle, *Antique*	375.00	550.00	500.00
☐ **Ballard**, Various Rimfires, Military, Falling Block, *Antique*	650.00	925.00	875.00
☐ **Merwin & Bray**, .54 Ballard R.F., Military, Carbine, Falling Block, *Antique*	575.00	875.00	825.00
☐ **Merwin & Bray**, Various Rimfires, Falling Block, Sporting Rifle, *Antique*	475.00	700.00	650.00

BALLARD RIFLE

Made by Ball & Williams 1861-1866, Merrimack Arms & Mfg. Co. 1866-1869, Brown Mfg. Co. 1869-1873, J.M. Marlin from 1875.

RIFLE, SINGLESHOT

	V.G.	Exc.	Prior Year Exc. Value
☐ **#1½ Hunter (Marlin)**, .40-65 Ballard Everlasting, Falling Block, Sporting Rifle, Open Rear Sight, *Antique*	575.00	825.00	800.00

	V.G.	Exc.	Prior Year Exc. Value
☐ **#1 Hunter (Marlin),** .44 Long R F/C F, Falling Block, Sporting Rifle, Recoil Pad, *Antique*	580.00	825.00	800.00
☐ **#2 (Marlin),** .44-40 WCF, Falling Block, Sporting Rifle, Open Rear Sight, *Antique*	615.00	900.00	875.00
☐ **#2 (Marlin),** Various Calibers, Falling Block, Sporting Rifle, Recoil Pad, Early Model, *Antique*	565.00	825.00	800.00
☐ **#3½ (Marlin),** .40-65 Ballard Everlasting, Falling Block, Target Rifle, Target Sights, Octagon Barrel, *Antique*	825.00	1100.00	1050.00
☐ **#3 Gallery (Marlin),** .22 Short R.F., Falling Block, Target Rifle, Early Model, *Antique*	390.00	630.00	600.00
☐ **#4½ (Marlin),** .40-65 Ballard Everlasting, Falling Block, Mid-Range Target Rifle, Checkered Stock, *Antique*	775.00	1100.00	1050.00
☐ **#4½ (Marlin),** .45-70 Government, Falling Block, Sporting Rifle, *Antique*	735.00	1050.00	1000.00
☐ **#4½ (Marlin),** Various Calibers, Falling Block, Sporting Rifle, *Antique*	690.00	935.00	900.00
☐ **#4½ (Marlin),** Various Calibers, Falling Block, Mid-Range Target Rifle, Target Sights, Fancy Wood, *Antique*	925.00	1600.00	1575.00
☐ **#4 Perfection (Marlin),** Various Calibers, Falling Block, Target Rifle, Target Sights, Set Trigger, Early Model, *Antique*	590.00	875.00	850.00
☐ **#5 Pacific (Marlin),** .45-70 Government, Falling Block, Target Rifle, Open Rear Sight, Set Trigger, Octagon Barrel, *Antique*	615.00	1000.00	975.00
☐ **#5 Pacific (Marlin),** Various Calibers, Falling Block, Target Rifle, Open Rear Sight, Set Trigger, Octagon Barrel, *Antique*	520.00	850.00	825.00
☐ **#6½ (Marlin),** .40-65 Ballard Everlasting, Falling Block, Off-Hand Target Rifle, Target Sights, Set Trigger, *Antique*	870.00	1375.00	1350.00
☐ **#6½ (Marlin),** Various Calibers, Falling Block, Mid-Range Target Rifle, *Antique*	925.00	1500.00	1450.00
☐ **#6 Pacific (Marlin),** Various Calibers, Falling Block, Schutzen Rifle, Target Sights, Fancy Wood, Set Trigger, *Antique*	1390.00	2150.00	2100.00
☐ **#7 A-1 (Marlin),** .44-75 Ballard Everlasting, Falling Block, Creedmore Long Range, Target Sights, Fancy Wood, Set Trigger, *Antique*	2000.00	2875.00	2800.00
☐ **#7 A (Marlin),** .44-100 Ballard Everlasting, Falling Block, Long Range Target Rifle, Target Sights, Set Trigger, *Antique*	800.00	1375.00	1350.00
☐ **#7 A-1 (Marlin),** .44-100 Ballard Everlasting, Falling Block, Long Range Target Rifle, Target Sights, Set Trigger, Fancy Wood, *Antique*	1225.00	1950.00	1900.00
☐ **#7 A-1 Extra Deluxe,** .44-100 Ballard Everlasting, Falling Block, Long Range Target Rifle, Target Sights, Set Trigger, Fancy Wood, *Antique*	1850.00	2500.00	2475.00
☐ **1½ Hunter (Marlin),** .45-70 Government, Falling Block, Sporting Rifle, Open Rear Sight, *Antique*	625.00	925.00	900.00
☐ **1¾ Far West (Marlin),** .40-65 Ballard Everlasting, Falling Block, Sporting Rifle, Open Rear Sight, Set Trigger, *Antique*	600.00	850.00	825.00

	V.G.	Exc.	Prior Year Exc. Value
☐ **1¾ Far West (Marlin),** .45-70 Government, Falling Block, Sporting Rifle, Open Rear Sight, Set Trigger, *Antique*	650.00	950.00	925.00
☐ **5½ Montana (Marlin),** .45-100 Sharps, Falling Block, Sporting Rifle, Octagon Barrel, *Antique*	825.00	1385.00	1350.00
☐ **#8 (Marlin),** .44-75 Ballard Everlasting, Falling Block, Creedmore Long Range, Target Sights, Pistol-Grip Stock, Set Trigger, *Antique*	465.00	800.00	775.00
☐ **#9 (Marlin),** .44-75 Ballard Everlasting, Falling Block, Creedmore Long Range, Target Sights, Set Trigger, *Antique*	535.00	930.00	900.00
☐ **(Ball & Williams),** .44 Long R.F., Military, Carbine, Falling Block, *Antique*	590.00	780.00	765.00
☐ **(Ball & Williams),** .46 Long R.F., Kentucky Rifle, Falling Block, *Antique*	740.00	950.00	925.00
☐ **(Ball & Williams),** .54 Ballard R.F., Military, Carbine, Falling Block, *Antique*	600.00	875.00	850.00
☐ **(Ball & Williams),** Various Rimfires, Falling Block, Sporting Rifle, *Antique*	400.00	590.00	575.00
☐ **(Ball & Williams),** Various Rimfires, Military, Falling Block, *Antique*	690.00	975.00	950.00
☐ **Brown Mfg. Co.,** .44 Long R.F., Falling Block, Mid-Range Target Rifle, *Antique*	785.00	1100.00	1075.00
☐ **Hunter,** .44 Long R F/C F, Falling Block, Sporting Rifle, Recoil Pad, *Antique*	510.00	675.00	650.00
☐ **Merrimack Arms,** .44 Long R.F., Falling Block, Carbine, *Antique*	590.00	825.00	800.00
☐ **Merrimack Arms,** .46 Long R.F., Falling Block, Military, *Antique*	690.00	930.00	900.00
☐ **Merrimack Arms,** .56-52 Spencer R.F., Falling Block, Carbine, *Antique*	590.00	845.00	820.00
☐ **Merrimack Arms,** Various Rimfires, Falling Block, Sporting Rifle, *Antique*	590.00	825.00	800.00
☐ **Merwin & Bray,** Various Rimfires, Falling Block, Sporting Rifle, *Antique*	485.00	710.00	685.00

BALLARD & CO.

Worcester, Mass 1861-1871. Also see U.S. Military.

RIFLE, SINGLESHOT

	V.G.	Exc.	Prior Year Exc. Value
☐ **#2 (Marlin)**, Various Calibers, Falling Block, Sporting Rifle, *Antique*	600.00	875.00	825.00
☐ **#3 Gallery (Marlin)**, Various Calibers, Falling Block, Target Rifle, *Antique*	575.00	775.00	725.00
☐ **#3 Gallery (Marlin)**, Various Rimfires, Falling Block, Target Rifle, *Antique*	375.00	585.00	550.00
☐ **#3-F Gallery (Marlin)**, .22 Long R.F., Falling Block, Target Rifle, Fancy Wood, *Antique*	650.00	850.00	825.00
☐ **#4 Perfection (Marlin)**, Various Calibers, Falling Block, Target Rifle, Target Sights, Set Trigger, Octagon Barrel, *Antique*	575.00	850.00	800.00

BANG-UP

Made by Hopkins & Allen, c. 1880.

	V.G.	Exc.	Prior Year Exc. Value
HANDGUN, REVOLVER			
☐ **.22 Short R.F.**, 7 Shot, Spur Trigger, Solid Frame, Single Action, *Antique*	90.00	160.00	160.00

BANISTER, T.

England, c. 1700.

	V.G.	Exc.	Prior Year Exc. Value
HANDGUN, FLINTLOCK			
☐ **Pocket Pistol**, Screw Barrel, Steel Mounts, Engraved, High Quality, *Antique*	995.00	1,775.00	1,650.00

BARKER, F.A.

Fayettesville, N.C. 1860-1864. See Confederate Military.

BARKER, T.

Made by Crescent; Also Made in Belgium.

	V.G.	Exc.	Prior Year Exc. Value
SHOTGUN, DOUBLE BARREL, SIDE-BY-SIDE			
☐ **Various Gauges**, Outside Hammers, Damascus Barrel, *Modern*	80.00	150.00	150.00
☐ **Various Gauges**, Hammerless, Steel Barrel, *Modern*	95.00	185.00	175.00
☐ **Various Gauges**, Hammerless, Damascus Barrel, *Modern*	75.00	150.00	150.00
☐ **Various Gauges**, Outside Hammers, Steel Barrel, *Modern*	95.00	185.00	175.00
SHOTGUN, SINGLESHOT			
☐ **Various Gauges**, Hammer, Steel Barrel, *Modern*	45.00	75.00	75.00

BARLOW, J.

Moscow, Ind. 1836-1840. See Kentucky Rifles.

BARNETT & SON

London, England 1750-1832.

	V.G.	Exc.	Prior Year Exc. Value
RIFLE, FLINTLOCK			
☐ **.75, 3rd. Model Brown Bess**, Musket, Military, *Antique*	950.00	1,675.00	1,550.00

BARNETT, J. & SONS

London, England 1835-1875.

	V.G.	Exc.	Prior Year Exc. Value
RIFLE, PERCUSSION			
☐ **.577, C.W. Enfield**, Rifled, Musket, Military, *Antique*	425.00	700.00	675.00

BARRETT, J.

Wythesville, Va. 1857-1865. See Confederate Military.

BAUER FIREARMS (FRASER ARMS CO.)

Fraser, Mich.

	V.G.	Exc.	Prior Year Exc. Value
COMBINATION WEAPON, OVER-UNDER			
☐ **Rabbit**, .22/.410, Metal Frame, Survival Gun, *Modern*	45.00	70.00	70.00

	V.G.	Exc.	Prior Year Exc. Value
HANDGUN, SEMI-AUTOMATIC			
☐ **25-Bicentennial**, .25 ACP, Clip Fed, Pocket Pistol, Stainless Steel, Hammerless, Engraved, *Modern*	170.00	230.00	225.00
☐ **25-SS**, .25 ACP, Clip Fed, Pocket Pistol, Stainless Steel, Hammerless, *Modern*	65.00	100.00	95.00

BAUER, GEORGE

Lancaster, Pa. 1770-1781. See Kentucky Rifles.

BAY STATE ARMS CO.

Uxbridge & Worcester, Mass. 1873-1874.

	V.G.	Exc.	Prior Year Exc. Value
RIFLE, SINGLESHOT			
☐ **.32 Long R.F.**, Dropping Block, *Antique*	115.00	190.00	175.00
☐ **Various Calibers**, Target Rifle, *Antique*	575.00	850.00	825.00
SHOTGUN, SINGLESHOT			
☐ **Davenport Patent**, 12 Ga., *Antique*	195.00	285.00	275.00

BAYARD

Belgium. Made by Anciens Etablissments Pieper, c. 1900. Also see Bergmann and Danish Military.

	V.G.	Exc.	Prior Year Exc. Value
HANDGUN, SEMI-AUTOMATIC			
☐ **Bergmann/Bayard 1910,** 9mm Bayard, Clip Fed, Blue, Commercial, *Curio*	410.00	635.00	750.00
☐ **Bergmann/Bayard 1910,** 9mm Bayard, Clip Fed, Blue, Commercial, with Holster/Stock, *Curio*	530.00	825.00	950.00
☐ **Model 1908 (1912) Pocket,** .25 ACP, Blue, Clip Fed, *Modern*	120.00	190.00	220.00
☐ **Model 1908 (1912) Pocket,** .25 ACP, Nickel, Clip Fed, *Modern*	125.00	200.00	235.00
☐ **Model 1908 (1910) Pocket,** .32 ACP, Blue, Clip Fed, German Military, *Modern*	120.00	190.00	275.00
☐ **Model 1908 (1910) Pocket,** .32 ACP, Blue, Clip Fed, *Modern*	125.00	210.00	250.00
☐ **Model 1908 (1910) Pocket,** .32 ACP, Nickel, Clip Fed, *Modern*	130.00	215.00	260.00
☐ **Model 1908 (1911) Pocket,** .380 ACP, Blue, Clip Fed, *Modern*	160.00	280.00	350.00
☐ **Model 1908 (1911) Pocket,** .380 ACP, Nickel, Clip Fed, *Modern*	150.00	300.00	375.00
☐ **Model 1923 Pocket, Early,** .25 ACP, Blue, Clip Fed, With Magazine Safety, *Modern*	125.00	200.00	235.00
☐ **Model 1923 Pocket, Standard,** .25 ACP, Blue, Clip Fed, No Magazine Safety, *Modern*	110.00	170.00	200.00
☐ **Model 1923 Pocket, Early,** .32 ACP, Blue, Clip Fed, With Magazine Safety, *Modern*	130.00	220.00	265.00
☐ **Model 1923 Pocket, Standard,** .32 ACP, Blue, Clip Fed, No Magazine Safety, *Modern*	115.00	200.00	235.00
☐ **Model 1923 Pocket, Early,** .380 ACP, Blue, Clip Fed, With Magazine Safety, *Modern*	145.00	260.00	320.00
☐ **Model 1923 Pocket, Standard,** .380 ACP, Blue, Clip Fed, No Magazine Safety, *Modern*	130.00	225.00	275.00
☐ **Model 1930 Pocket,** .25 ACP, Blue, Clip Fed, *Modern*	105.00	175.00	210.00

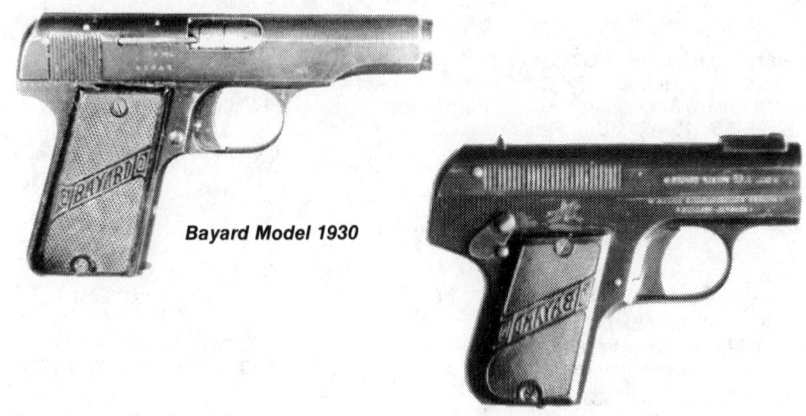

Bayard Model 1930

Bayard Model 1908 (1910) .32 ACP

	V.G.	Exc.	Prior Year Exc. Value
☐ **Model 1930 Pocket,** .32 ACP, Blue, Clip Fed, *Modern*	110.00	180.00	225.00
☐ **Model 1930 Pocket,** .380 ACP, Blue, Clip Fed, *Modern*	130.00	220.00	290.00
HANDGUN, REVOLVER			
☐ **S & W Style,** .32 S&W Long, Double Action, *Modern*	45.00	90.00	125.00
☐ **S & W Style,** .38 S&W, Double Action, *Modern*	45.00	95.00	135.00
RIFLE, SINGLESHOT			
☐ **Boy's Rifle,** .22 L.R.R.F., Plain, Takedown, *Modern*	30.00	55.00	55.00
☐ **Half-Auto Carbine,** .22 Short, Plain, *Curio*	35.00	60.00	70.00
☐ **Half-Auto Carbine,** .22 Short, Checkered Stock, *Curio*	40.00	70.00	90.00
SHOTGUN, DOUBLE BARREL, SIDE-BY-SIDE			
☐ **Hammerless,** 12 Gauge, Double Triggers, Light Engraving, Boxlock, Steel Barrels, *Curio*	110.00	175.00	225.00
☐ **Hammer,** 12 Gauge, Double Triggers, Light Engraving, Boxlock, Damascus Barrels, *Curio*	65.00	135.00	150.00
☐ **Hammer,** 12 Gauge, Double Triggers, Light Engraving, Boxlock, Steel Barrels, *Curio*	75.00	145.00	175.00
☐ **Hammer,** 12 Gauge, Double Triggers, Fancy Engraving, Boxlock, Steel Barrels, *Curio*	125.00	210.00	295.00

BEATTIE, JAMES

London, England 1835-1865.

HANDGUN, PERCUSSION

	V.G.	Exc.	Prior Year Exc. Value
☐ **.40 Six Shot**, Revolver, Octagon Barrel, Fancy Wood, Fancy Engraving, Cased with Accessories, *Antique*	2,975.00	3,900.00	3,750.00

BECK, GIDEON

Lancaster, Pa. 1780-1788. See Kentucky Rifles and Pistols.

	V.G.	Exc.	Prior Year Exc. Value

BECK, JOHN
Lancaster, Pa. 1772-1777. See Kentucky Rifles and Pistols.

BECK, ISAAC
Miffinberg, Pa. 1830-1840.

RIFLE, PERCUSSION

	V.G.	Exc.	Prior Year Exc. Value
☐ **.47**, Octagon Barrel, Brass Furniture, *Antique*	775.00	1,275.00	1,150.00

BEEMAN PRECISION FIREARMS
San Raphael, Calif., Importers.

HANDGUN, SEMI-AUTOMATIC

	V.G.	Exc.	Prior Year Exc. Value
☐ **Agner M80**, .22 L.R.R.F., Clip Fed, Bright or Black Chrome Plating, Adjustable Target Grips, Adjustable Trigger, *Modern*	575.00	800.00	—
☐ **FAS Model 601**, .22 Short R.F., Clip Fed, Target Grip, Rapid Fire Target Pistol, *Modern*	435.00	600.00	—
☐ **FAS Model 602**, .22 L.R.R.F., Clip Fed, Target Grip, Match Pistol, *Modern*	550.00	775.00	—
☐ **FAS Model 603**, .32 S&W Wadcutter, Clip Fed, Target Grip, Match Pistol, *Modern*	500.00	725.00	—
☐ **Unique Model 69**, .22 L.R.R.F., Clip Fed, Adjustable Target Grips, Match Pistol, *Modern*	400.00	550.00	—
☐ **Unique Model 823-U**, .22 Short R.F., Clip Fed, Adjustable Target Grips, Rapid Fire Match Pistol, *Modern*	450.00	600.00	—

HANDGUN, PERCUSSION

	V.G.	Exc.	Prior Year Exc. Value
☐ **PB Aristocrat**, .36 or .44, Single Set Trigger, Fluted Stock, Reproduction, *Antique*	165.00	225.00	—
☐ **Hege-Siber, French**, .33, Checkered Stock, Engraved, Gold Inlays, Cased, Reproduction, *Antique*	775.00	1,100.00	—
☐ **Hege-Siber, English**, .33, Checkered Stock, Light Engraving, Cased, Reproduction, *Antique*	435.00	600.00	—

RIFLE, BOLT ACTION

	V.G.	Exc.	Prior Year Exc. Value
☐ **Feinwerkbau 2000 Match**, .22 L.R.R.F., Single Shot, Adjustable Trigger, Adjustable Target Stock, *Modern*	400.00	575.00	—
☐ **Feinwerkbau 2000 Mini**, .22 L.R.R.F., Single Shot, Adjustable Trigger, Adjustable Target Stock, *Modern*	375.00	535.00	—
☐ **Feinwerkbau 2000 Running Target**, .22 L.R.R.F., Single Shot, Adjustable Trigger, Adjustable Target Stock, *Modern*	475.00	650.00	—
☐ **Feinwerkbau 2000 Universal**, .22 L.R.R.F., Single Shot, Adjustable Trigger, Adjustable Target Stock, *Modern*	435.00	600.00	—
☐ **Feinwerkbau Free Rifle**, .22 L.R.R.F., Single Shot, Adjustable Electric Trigger, Adjustable Target Stock, Counterweights, Hook Buttplate, *Modern*	750.00	1,100.00	—
☐ **Krico Model 302**, .22 L.R.R.F., Clip Fed, Checkered Stock, Open Sights, *Modern*	225.00	300.00	—
☐ **Krico Model 304**, .22 L.R.R.F., Clip Fed, Checkered Stock, Mannlicher Stock, Set Triggers, Open Sights, *Modern*	275.00	375.00	—

Beeman Agner M80

Beeman FAS Model 601

Beeman Unique Model 69

Beeman Fabarm Gamma

Beeman Feinwerkbau 2000 Match

Beeman Krico Model 650

	V.G.	Exc.	Prior Year Exc. Value
☐ **Krico Model 340**, .22 L.R.R.F., Metallic Silhouette Match Rifle, Clip Fed, Checkered Stock, Target Stock, *Modern*	325.00	430.00	—
☐ **Krico Model 340**, .22 L.R.R.F., Mini-Sniper Match Rifle, Clip Fed, Checkered Stock, Target Stock, *Modern*	350.00	475.00	—
☐ **Krico Model 400**, .22 Hornet, Clip Fed. Checkered Stock, Open Sights, *Modern*	325.00	425.00	—
☐ **Krico Model 420**, .22 Hornet, Clip Fed, Checkered Stock, Set Triggers, Mannlicher Stock, Open Sights, Sling Swivels, *Modern*	350.00	465.00	—
☐ **Krico Model 600**, Various Calibers, Clip Fed, Checkered Stock, Open Sights, Sling Swivels, Recoil Pad, *Modern*	450.00	635.00	—
☐ **Krico Model 620**, Various Calibers, Clip Fed, Checkered Stock, Set Triggers, Mannlicher Stock, Open Sights, Sling Swivels, *Modern*	465.00	650.00	—
☐ **Krico Model 640**, Various Calibers, Deluxe Varmint Rifle, Clip Fed, Checkered Stock, Target Stock, *Modern*	450.00	630.00	—
☐ **Krico Model 650**, Various Calibers, Sniper/Match Rifle, Clip Fed, Checkered Stock, Target Stock, *Modern*	575.00	800.00	—
☐ **Krico Model 700**, Various Calibers, Clip Fed, Checkered Stock, Open Sights, Sling Swivels, Recoil Pad, *Modern*	450.00	635.00	—
☐ **Krico Model 720**, Various Calibers, Clip Fed, Checkered Stock, Set Triggers, Mannlicher Stock, Open Sights, Sling Swivels, *Modern*	465.00	650.00	—
☐ **Weihrauch HW60**, .22 L.R.R.F., Singleshot Target Rifle, Target Sights, Target Stock, Heavy Barrel, *Modern*	265.00	390.00	375.00

SHOTGUN, DOUBLE BARREL, OVER-UNDER

	V.G.	Exc.	Prior Year Exc. Value
☐ **Fabarm Gamma**, 12 Gauge, Trap/Field Model, Single Selective Trigger, Checkered Stock, Vent Rib, *Modern*	325.00	450.00	—
☐ **Fabarm Gamma**, 12 Gauge, Skeet Model, Single Selective Trigger, Checkered Stock, Vent Rib, *Modern*	325.00	450.00	—
☐ **Fabarm Gamma**, 12 Gauge, Trap/Skeet Combo, 2 Barrels, Single Selective Trigger, Checkered Stock, Vent Rib, *Modern*	500.00	700.00	—

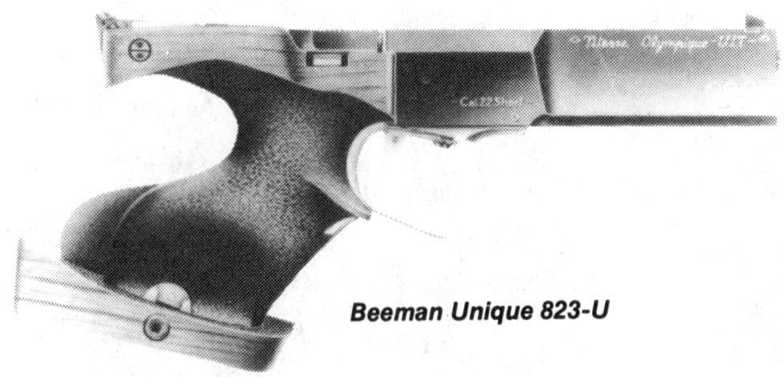

Beeman Unique 823-U

	V.G.	Exc.	Prior Year Exc. Value

BEERSTECHER, FREDERICK
Lewisburg, Pa. 1849-1860.

HANDGUN, PERCUSSION

	V.G.	Exc.	Prior Year Exc. Value
☐ **.40**, Double Shot, Superimposed Loading, Derringer Style, *Antique*	2,300.00	4,500.00	4,350.00

BEHOLLA
Made by Becker & Hollander, Suhl, Germany c. 1910. Also made under this patent were the Stenda, Leonhardt, and Menta.

HANDGUN, SEMI-AUTOMATIC

	V.G.	Exc.	Prior Year Exc. Value
☐ **.32 ACP,** Clip Fed, Commercial, Blue, Hard Rubber Grips, *Curio*	170.00	265.00	265.00
☐ **.32 ACP,** Clip Fed, Military, Blue, Hard Rubber Grips, *Curio*	100.00	160.00	235.00
☐ **.32 ACP,** Clip Fed, Commercial, Blue, Wood Grips, *Curio*	160.00	250.00	250.00
☐ **.32 ACP,** Clip Fed, Military, Blue, Wood Grips, *Curio*	90.00	145.00	220.00

BELGIAN MILITARY
Also see Browning, FN.

RIFLE, BOLT ACTION

	V.G.	Exc.	Prior Year Exc. Value
☐ **M 1924,** Various Calibers, Military, *Curio*	70.00	115.00	200.00
☐ **M 1930,** Various Calibers, Military, *Curio*	70.00	115.00	200.00
☐ **M 1934/30,** Various Calibers, Military, *Curio*	70.00	115.00	200.00
☐ **M 1950,** .30-06 Springfield, Military, *Modern*	100.00	150.00	265.00
☐ **M 1889 Mauser,** Military, *Curio*	50.00	75.00	130.00
☐ **M 1889 Mauser,** Carbine, Military, *Curio*	52.00	80.00	140.00
☐ **M 1935 Mauser,** Military, *Modern*	55.00	87.00	165.00
☐ **M 1936 Mauser,** Military, *Modern*	52.00	80.00	145.00

RIFLE, SEMI-AUTOMATIC

	V.G.	Exc.	Prior Year Exc. Value
☐ **M 1949,** .30-06 Springfield, Military, *Modern*	250.00	375.00	650.00
☐ **M 1949,** Various Calibers, Military, *Modern*	200.00	310.00	500.00

BELL, JOHN
Carlisle, Pa. c. 1800. See Kentucky Rifles and Pistols.

BELLMORE GUN CO.
Made by Crescent, c. 1900.

SHOTGUN, DOUBLE BARREL, SIDE-BY-SIDE

	V.G.	Exc.	Prior Year Exc. Value
☐ **Various Gauges**, Outside Hammers, Damascus Barrel, *Modern*	80.00	150.00	150.00
☐ **Various Gauges**, Hammerless, Steel Barrel, *Modern*	95.00	185.00	175.00
☐ **Various Gauges**, Hammerless, Damascus Barrel, *Modern*	75.00	150.00	150.00
☐ **Various Gauges**, Outside Hammers, Steel Barrel, *Modern*	90.00	185.00	175.00

SHOTGUN, SINGLESHOT

	V.G.	Exc.	Prior Year Exc. Value
☐ **Various Gauges**, Hammer, Steel Barrel, *Modern*	45.00	75.00	75.00

BENELLI

Made in Italy, imported by H & K Inc. and Sile.

	V.G.	Exc.	Prior Year Exc. Value
HANDGUN, SEMI-AUTOMATIC			
☐ **B 76**, 9mm Luger, Clip Fed, Blue, *Modern*	185.00	275.00	265.00
RIFLE, SEMI-AUTOMATIC			
☐ **Model 940**, .30-06 Springfield, Clip Fed, Open Sights, Recoil Pad, Sling Swivels, *Modern*	300.00	400.00	—
SHOTGUN, SEMI-AUTOMATIC			
☐ **Model SL 121V**, 12 Gauge, Slug Gun, Open Sights, Checkered Stock, Recoil Pad, *Modern*	240.00	375.00	375.00
☐ **Model SL 121MI**, 12 Gauge, Police, Open Sights, Checkered Stock, Recoil Pad, *Modern*	250.00	380.00	380.00
☐ **Model SL 201**, 20 Gauge, Checkered Stock, Plain Barrel, *Modern*	225.00	345.00	345.00
☐ **Model 123V**, 12 Gauge, Standard Model, Checkered Stock, Vent Rib, *Modern*	225.00	345.00	345.00
☐ **Model 123V Deluxe**, 12 Gauge, Engraved Model, Checkered Stock, Vent Rib, *Modern*	300.00	450.00	450.00
☐ **Special Trap**, 12 Gauge, White Receiver, Checkered Stock, Vent Rib, *Modern*	375.00	550.00	550.00
☐ **Special Skeet**, 12 Gauge, White Receiver, Checkered Stock, Vent Rib, *Modern*	400.00	575.00	575.00

BENFER, AMOS

Beaverstown, Pa. c. 1810. See Kentucky Rifles and Pistols.

BERETTA, GIOVANNI

Brescia, Italy, c. 1700

	V.G.	Exc.	Prior Year Exc. Value
HANDGUN, SNAPHAUNCE			
☐ **Belt Pistol**, Engraved, Carved, Light Ornamentation, *Antique*	2,875.00	3,900.00	3,750.00

BERETTA

Pietro Beretta; Gardone V.T., Italy. Company history extends back to 1680.

	V.G.	Exc.	Prior Year Exc. Value
AUTOMATIC WEAPON, ASSAULT RIFLE			
☐ **Model 70**, .223 Rem., Clip Fed, Plastic Stock, *Class 3*	600.00	875.00	950.00
☐ **Model BM59**, .308 Win., Clip Fed, Bipod, *Class 3*	650.00	950.00	975.00
☐ **BM59 Garand Conversion**, .308 Win., Clip Fed, Bipod, *Class 3*	950.00	1,400.00	1,450.00
☐ **Model SC70L**, .223 Rem., Clip Fed, Folding Stock, *Class 3*	575.00	775.00	800.00
☐ **Model SC70S**, .223 Rem., Clip Fed, Folding Stock, Short Barreled Rifle, *Class 3*	575.00	775.00	800.00
AUTOMATIC WEAPON, SUBMACHINE GUN			
☐ **Model 12**, 9mm Luger, Clip Fed, Folding Stock, *Class 3*	350.00	525.00	500.00
☐ **Model 38/49**, 9mm Luger, Clip Fed, Wood Stock, *Class 3*	350.00	525.00	500.00
☐ **Model MP38/44**, 9mm Luger, Clip Fed, Military, *Class 3*	725.00	975.00	975.00
☐ **Model MP38A**, 9mm Luger, Clip Fed, Military, Wood Stock, *Class 3*	625.00	900.00	900.00

Beretta Model 1935 .32 ACP

Beretta Bantam

Beretta Model 1915/19 .32 ACP

	V.G.	Exc.	Prior Year Exc. Value
☐ **Model MP38A**, 9mm Luger, Clip Fed, Commercial, Wood Stock, *Class 3*	850.00	1,150.00	1,175.00
HANDGUN, SEMI-AUTOMATIC			
☐ **1915,** .32 ACP, Clip Fed, Military, *Modern*	110.00	145.00	280.00
☐ **1915,** .380 ACP, Clip Fed, Military, *Modern*	140.00	190.00	375.00
☐ **1915/1919,** .32 ACP, Clip Fed, Military, *Modern*	115.00	150.00	275.00
☐ **1919 V P,** .25 ACP, Clip Fed, *Modern*	95.00	175.00	175.00
☐ **Cougar,** .380 ACP, Clip Fed, *Modern*	125.00	200.00	200.00
☐ **Jaguar,** .22 L.R.R.F., Clip Fed, *Modern*	95.00	175.00	175.00
☐ **Jetfire,** .25 ACP, Clip Fed, Blue, *Modern*	75.00	130.00	125.00
☐ **Jetfire,** .25 ACP, Clip Fed, Nickel, *Modern*	80.00	135.00	130.00
☐ **Minx,** .22 Short, Clip Fed, Blue, *Modern*	75.00	130.00	125.00
☐ **Minx,** .22 Short, Clip Fed, Nickel, *Modern*	80.00	135.00	130.00
☐ **Model 100,** .32 ACP, Clip Fed, *Modern*	95.00	165.00	160.00

	V.G.	Exc.	Prior Year Exc. Value
☐ **Model 101,** .22 L.R.R.F., Clip Fed, Adjustable Sights, *Modern*	110.00	175.00	175.00
☐ **Model 1923,** 9mm Luger, Clip Fed, Military, *Modern*	140.00	225.00	350.00
☐ **Model 1923,** 9mm Luger, Clip Fed, Military, with Detachable Shoulder Stock, *Curio*	400.00	550.00	850.00
☐ **Model 1931 Navy,** .32 ACP, Clip Fed, Military, *Modern*	120.00	170.00	290.00
☐ **Model 1934,** .380 ACP, Clip Fed, Military, *Modern*	65.00	105.00	185.00
☐ **Model 1934,** .380 ACP, Clip Fed, Commercial, *Modern*	140.00	235.00	225.00
☐ **Model 1935,** .32 ACP, Clip Fed, Commercial, *Modern*	115.00	200.00	195.00
☐ **Model 1935,** .32 ACP, Clip Fed, Military, *Modern*	65.00	100.00	170.00
☐ **Model 318,** .25 ACP, Clip Fed, *Modern*	110.00	180.00	175.00
☐ **Model 418,** .25 ACP, Clip Fed, *Modern*	110.00	175.00	175.00
☐ **Model 420,** .25 ACP, Clip Fed, Chrome, Light Engraving, *Modern*	185.00	285.00	295.00
☐ **Model 421,** .25 ACP, Clip Fed, Gold Plated, Fancy Engraving, *Modern*	270.00	395.00	395.00
☐ **Model 70S,** .380 ACP, Clip Fed, *Modern*	125.00	215.00	210.00
☐ **Model 70T,** .32 ACP, Clip Fed, Adjustable Sights, *Modern*	115.00	195.00	195.00
☐ **Model 76,** .22 L.R.R.F., Clip Fed, Adjustable Sights, *Modern*	185.00	275.00	275.00
☐ **Model 81,** .32 ACP, Clip Fed, Double Action, *Modern*	200.00	320.00	315.00
☐ **Model 82,** .32 ACP, Clip Fed, Double Action, *Modern*	200.00	300.00	300.00
☐ **Model 84,** .380 ACP, Clip Fed, Double Action, *Modern*	200.00	300.00	300.00
☐ **Model 85,** .380 ACP, Clip Fed, Double Action, *Modern*	215.00	315.00	315.00
☐ **Model 84 Tercentennial,** .380 ACP, Clip Fed, Double Action, Engraved, Cased, *Modern*	750.00	1250.00	1250.00
☐ **Model 90,** .32 ACP, Clip Fed, Double Trigger, *Modern*	195.00	275.00	275.00
☐ **Model 92,** 9mm Luger, 13 Shot Clip Fed, Double Action, *Modern*	325.00	440.00	445.00
☐ **Model 92,** 9mm Luger, 15 Shot Clip Fed, Double Action, *Modern*	340.00	450.00	460.00
☐ **Model 948,** .22 L.R.R.F., Clip Fed, Lightweight *Modern*	85.00	140.00	135.00
☐ **Model 949 Olympic,** .22 L.R.R.F., Clip Fed, Target Pistol, *Modern*	225.00	335.00	330.00
☐ **Model 949 Olympic,** .22 Short R.F., Clip Fed, Target Pistol, *Modern*	225.00	330.00	330.00
☐ **Model 950 Minx,** .22 Short R.F., Clip Fed, 2″ Barrel, *Modern*	90.00	140.00	135.00
☐ **Model 950B Minx,** .22 Short R.F., Clip Fed, 4″ Barrel, *Modern*	90.00	140.00	140.00
☐ **Model 951 Brigadier,** 9mm Luger, Clip Fed, Commercial, *Modern*	225.00	315.00	325.00

	V.G.	Exc.	Prior Year Exc. Value
☐ **Model 951 Egyptian,** 9mm Luger, Clip Fed, Military, *Curio*	250.00	365.00	690.00
☐ **Model 951 Israeli,** 9mm Luger, Clip Fed, Military, *Curio*	250.00	365.00	695.00
☐ **Puma,** .32 ACP, Clip Fed, *Modern*	115.00	195.00	195.00
RIFLE, SEMI-AUTOMATIC			
☐ **Olympia,** .22 L.R.R.F., Clip Fed, Tangent Sights, Checkered Stock, *Modern*	125.00	200.00	195.00
☐ **Silver Gyrfalcon,** .22 L.R.R.F., Checkered Stock, *Modern*	115.00	195.00	190.00
☐ **Super Sport,** .22 L.R.R.F., Fancy Checkering, Clip Fed, *Modern*	135.00	220.00	215.00
SHOTGUN, DOUBLE BARREL, OVER-UNDER			
☐ **Golden Snipe,** 12 and 20 Gauges, Single Trigger, Automatic Ejector, Engraved, Fancy Checkering, *Modern*	350.00	460.00	450.00
☐ **Golden Snipe,** 12 and 20 Gauges, Single Selective Trigger, Automatic Ejector, Engraved, Fancy Checkering, *Modern*	475.00	650.00	625.00
☐ **Golden Snipe Deluxe,** 12 and 20 Gauges, Single Selective Trigger, Automatic Ejector, Fancy Engraving, Fancy Checkering, *Modern*	490.00	700.00	700.00
☐ **Model ASEL,** 12 and 20 Gauges, Single Trigger, Checkered Stock, *Modern*	695.00	920.00	900.00
☐ **Model BL 1,** 12 Ga., Field Grade, Double Trigger, Checkered Stock, *Modern*	275.00	375.00	365.00
☐ **Model BL 2,** 12 Ga., Field Grade, Single Selective Trigger, Checkered Stock, *Modern*	325.00	450.00	445.00
☐ **Model BL 3,** 12 Ga., Trap Grade, Single Selective Trigger, Checkered Stock, Light Engraving, Vent Rib, *Modern*	400.00	520.00	515.00
☐ **Model BL 3,** Various Gauges, Skeet Grade, Single Selective Trigger, Checkered Stock, Light Engraving, Vent Rib, *Modern*	400.00	525.00	510.00
☐ **Model BL 3,** Various Gauges, Field Grade, Single Selective Trigger, Checkered Stock, Light Engraving, Vent Rib, *Modern*	400.00	525.00	510.00
☐ **Model BL 4,** 12 Ga., Trap Grade, Single Selective Trigger, Selective Ejector, Engraved, Vent Rib, *Modern*	550.00	720.00	700.00
☐ **Model BL 4,** Various Gauges, Skeet Grade, Single Selective Trigger, Selective Ejector, Engraved, Vent Rib, *Modern*	550.00	720.00	700.00
☐ **Model BL 4,** Various Gauges, Field Grade, Single Selective Trigger, Selective Ejector, Engraved, Vent Rib, *Modern*	475.00	650.00	650.00
☐ **Model BL 5,** 12 Ga., Trap Grade, Single Selective Trigger, Selective Ejector, Fancy Engraving, Vent Rib, *Modern*	745.00	995.00	975.00
☐ **Model BL 5,** Various Gauges, Skeet Grade, Single Selective Trigger, Selective Ejector, Fancy Engraving, Vent Rib, *Modern*	745.00	995.00	975.00
☐ **Model BL 5,** Various Gauges, Field Grade, Single Selective Trigger, Selective Ejector, Fancy Engraving, Vent Rib, *Modern*	675.00	925.00	900.00

	V.G.	Exc.	Prior Year Exc. Value
☐ **Model BL 6**, 12 Ga., Trap Grade, Single Selective Trigger, Selective Ejector, Fancy Engraving, Vent Rib, *Modern*	995.00	1,400.00	1,375.00
☐ **Model BL 6**, Various Gauges, Field Grade, Single Selective Trigger, Selective Ejector, Fancy Engraving, Vent Rib, *Modern*	925.00	1,350.00	1,300.00
☐ **Model BL 6**, Various Gauges, Skeet Grade, Single Selective Trigger, Selective Ejector, Fancy Engraving, Vent Rib, *Modern*	995.00	1,375.00	1,350.00
☐ **Model S02**, 12 Ga., Sidelock, Selective Ejector, Single Trigger, Checkered Stock, Engraved, *Modern*	1,650.00	2,250.00	2,200.00
☐ **Model S03**, 12 Ga., Sidelock, Automatic Ejector, Single Selective Trigger, Fancy Engraving, Fancy Wood, *Modern*	2,550.00	3,500.00	3,400.00
☐ **Model S03 EELL**, 12 Ga., Sidelock, Automatic Ejector, Single Selective Trigger, Fancy Engraving, Fancy Wood, *Modern*	3,975.00	5,800.00	5,750.00
☐ **Model S03 EL**, 12 Ga. Sidelock, Automatic Ejector, Single Selective Trigger, Fancy Engraving, Fancy Wood, *Modern*	2,850.00	4,000.00	3,950.00
☐ **Model S04**, 12 Ga., Sidelock, Automatic Ejector, Single Trigger, Fancy Engraving, Fancy Wood, *Modern*	2,550.00	3,700.00	3,600.00
☐ **Model S05**, 12 Ga., Sidelock, Selective Ejector, Single Trigger, Fancy Engraving, Fancy Checkering, *Modern*	3,750.00	5,200.00	5,000.00
☐ **Model S55B**, 12 and 20 Gauges, Single Selective Trigger, Automatic Ejector, Vent Rib, Checkered Stock, *Modern*	415.00	575.00	550.00
☐ **Model S56E**, 12 and 20 Gauges, Single Selective Trigger, Automatic Ejector, Engraved, Checkered Stock, *Modern*	435.00	600.00	585.00
☐ **Model S58**, 12 Ga., Trap Grade, Automatic Ejector, Single Selective Trigger, Engraved, Checkered Stock, *Modern*	545.00	695.00	675.00
☐ **Model S58**, 12 and 20 Gauges, Skeet Grade, Automatic Ejector, Single Selective Trigger, Engraved, Checkered Stock, Light Engraving, *Modern*	565.00	725.00	700.00
☐ **Silver Snipe**, 12 and 20 Gauges, Single Trigger, Checkered Stock, Light Engraving, *Modern*	300.00	425.00	415.00
☐ **Silver Snipe**, 12 and 20 Gauges, Single Selective Trigger, Checkered Stock, Light Engraving, *Modern*	325.00	450.00	445.00
☐ **Silver Snipe**, 12 and 20 Gauges, Single Trigger, Checkered Stock, Light Engraving, Vent Rib, *Modern*	300.00	420.00	415.00
☐ **Silver Snipe**, 12 and 20 Gauges, Single Selective Trigger, Light Engraving, Vent Rib, *Modern*	545.00	735.00	725.00
☐ **Model 680**, 12 Gauge, Skeet Grade, Automatic Ejector, Single Selective Trigger, Engraved, Checkered Stock, Light Engraving, *Modern*	550.00	865.00	850.00
☐ **Model 680**, 12 Gauge, Trap Grade, Automatic Ejector, Single Selective Trigger, Checkered Stock, Light Engraving, *Modern*	550.00	865.00	850.00

	V.G.	Exc.	Prior Year Exc. Value
☐ **Model 680**, 12 Gauge, Mono Trap Grade, Automatic Ejector, Single Trigger, Checkered Stock, Light Engraving, *Modern*	550.00	875.00	850.00
☐ **Model 686**, 12 Gauge, Field Grade, Automatic Ejector, Single Selective Trigger, Checkered Stock, Light Engraving, *Modern*	450.00	650.00	625.00
☐ **Model 687EL**, 12 Gauge, Skeet Grade, Automatic Ejector, Single Selective Trigger, Checkered Stock, Fancy Engraving, *Modern*	950.00	1,450.00	1,450.00

SHOTGUN, DOUBLE BARREL, SIDE-BY-SIDE

	V.G.	Exc.	Prior Year Exc. Value
☐ **Model 409PB**, Various Gauges, Double Trigger, Light Engraving, Checkered Stock, *Modern*	365.00	465.00	450.00
☐ **Model 410 Early**, 10 Ga. 3½", Double Trigger, Engraved, Checkered Stock, *Modern*	450.00	500.00	590.00
☐ **Model 410 Late**, 10 Ga. 3½", *Modern*	700.00	850.00	835.00
☐ **Model 410E**, Various Gauges, Double Trigger, Engraved, Checkered Stock, Automatic Ejector, *Modern*	465.00	650.00	625.00
☐ **Model 411E**, Various Gauges, Double Trigger, Engraved, Fancy Checkering, Automatic Ejector, *Modern*	645.00	960.00	925.00
☐ **Model 424**, 12 and 20 Gauges, Double Trigger, Light Engraving, Checkered Stock, *Modern*	400.00	570.00	550.00
☐ **Model 426E**, 12 and 20 Gauges, Single Selective Trigger, Automatic Ejector, Engraved, Checkered Stock, *Modern*	615.00	790.00	775.00
☐ **Model GR 2**, 12 and 20 Gauges, Double Trigger, Checkered Stock, Light Engraving, *Modern*	295.00	450.00	450.00
☐ **Model GR 3**, 12 and 20 Gauges, Single Selective Trigger, Checkered Stock, Light Engraving, *Modern*	350.00	525.00	515.00
☐ **Model GR 4**, 12 Ga., Single Selective Trigger, Selective Ejector, Checkered Stock, Engraved, *Modern*	425.00	600.00	595.00
☐ **Silver Hawk**, 10 Ga. 3½", Double Trigger, Magnum, *Modern*	410.00	575.00	565.00
☐ **Silver Hawk**, 12 Ga., Mag. 3", Double Trigger, Magnum, *Modern*	350.00	475.00	465.00
☐ **Silver Hawk**, 12 Ga. Mag. 3", Magnum, *Modern*	400.00	515.00	510.00
☐ **Silver Hawk**, Various Gauges, Double Trigger, Lightweight, *Modern*	300.00	425.00	415.00
☐ **Silver Hawk**, Various Gauges, Single Trigger, Lightweight, *Modern*	345.00	475.00	475.00

SHOTGUN, SEMI-AUTOMATIC

	V.G.	Exc.	Prior Year Exc. Value
☐ **Gold Lark**, 12 Ga., Vent Rib, Light Engraving, Checkered Stock, *Modern*	185.00	300.00	295.00
☐ **Model A301**, 12 Ga., Slug, Open Rear Sight, *Modern*	245.00	365.00	350.00
☐ **Model A301**, 12 Ga., Trap Grade, Vent Rib, *Modern*	265.00	400.00	385.00
☐ **Model A301**, 12 and 20 Gauges, Field Grade, Vent Rib, *Modern*	240.00	375.00	365.00
☐ **Model A301**, 12 and 20 Gauges, Skeet Grade, Vent Rib, *Modern*	240.00	375.00	365.00

	V.G.	Exc.	Prior Year Exc. Value
☐ **Model A301**, 12 Ga., Mag. 3", Field Grade, Vent Rib, *Modern*	**295.00**	**400.00**	**395.00**
☐ **Model A302**, 12 Ga., Slug, Open Rear Sight, *Modern*	**245.00**	**365.00**	**350.00**
☐ **Model A302**, 12 Ga., Trap Grade, Vent Rib, *Modern*	**265.00**	**400.00**	**385.00**
☐ **Model A302**, 12 and 20 Gauges, Field Grade, Vent Rib, *Modern*	**240.00**	**375.00**	**365.00**
☐ **Model A302**, 12 and 20 Gauges, Skeet Grade, Vent Rib, *Modern*	**240.00**	**375.00**	**365.00**
☐ **Model A302**, 12 Ga., Mag. 3", Field Grade, Vent Rib, *Modern*	**295.00**	**400.00**	**395.00**
☐ **Model AL 1**, 12 and 20 Gauges, Checkered Stock, *Modern*	**170.00**	**290.00**	**280.00**
☐ **Model AL 2**, 12 Ga., Vent Rib, Trap Grade, Checkered Stock, *Modern*	**225.00**	**310.00**	**295.00**
☐ **Model AL 2**, 12 and 20 Gauges, Vent Rib, Checkered Stock, *Modern*	**190.00**	**275.00**	**265.00**
☐ **Model AL 2**, 12 and 20 Gauges, Vent Rib, Skeet Grade, Checkered Stock, *Modern*	**220.00**	**310.00**	**295.00**
☐ **Model AL 3**, 12 Ga., Vent Rib, Checkered Stock, Light Engraving, Trap Grade, *Modern*	**270.00**	**375.00**	**365.00**
☐ **Model AL 3**, 12 and 20 Gauges, Vent Rib, Checkered Stock, Light Engraving, *Modern*	**240.00**	**360.00**	**345.00**
☐ **Model AL3**, 12 and 20 Gauges, Vent Rib, Checkered Stock, Light Engraving, Skeet Grade, *Modern*	**245.00**	**350.00**	**335.00**
☐ **Model AL 3**, 12 Ga. Mag. 3", Vent Rib, Checkered Stock, Light Engraving, *Modern*	**270.00**	**385.00**	**375.00**
☐ **Ruby Lark**, 12 Ga., Vent Rib, Fancy Engraving, Fancy Checkering, *Modern*	**270.00**	**395.00**	**380.00**
☐ **Silver Lark**, 12 Ga., Checkered Stock, *Modern*	**135.00**	**220.00**	**210.00**
SHOTGUN, SINGLESHOT			
☐ **Companion FS 1**, Various Gauges, Folding Gun, *Modern*	**75.00**	**125.00**	**120.00**
☐ **Model Mark II**, 12 Ga., Trap Grade, Vent Rib, Light Engraving, Checkered Stock, Monte Carlo Stock, *Modern*	**265.00**	**420.00**	**395.00**
☐ **Model TR 1**, 12 Ga., Trap Grade, Vent Rib, Light Engraving, Checkered Stock, Monte Carlo Stock, *Modern*	**165.00**	**265.00**	**250.00**
SHOTGUN, SLIDE ACTION			
☐ **Gold Pigeon**, 12 Ga., Vent Rib, Checkered Stock, Engraved, *Modern*	**160.00**	**250.00**	**245.00**
☐ **Gold Pigeon**, 12 Ga., Vent Rib, Fancy Engraving, Fancy Checkering, *Modern*	**270.00**	**385.00**	**375.00**
☐ **Model SL 2**, 12 Ga., Vent Rib, Checkered Stock, *Modern*	**165.00**	**260.00**	**250.00**
☐ **Ruby Pigeon**, 12 Ga., Vent Rib, Fancy Engraving, Fancy Checkering, *Modern*	**385.00**	**540.00**	**525.00**
☐ **Silver Pigeon**, 12 Ga., Light Engraving, Checkered Stock, *Modern*	**125.00**	**210.00**	**200.00**

BERGMANN

Gaggenau, Germany 1892-1944; Company Renamed Bergmann Erben 1931.

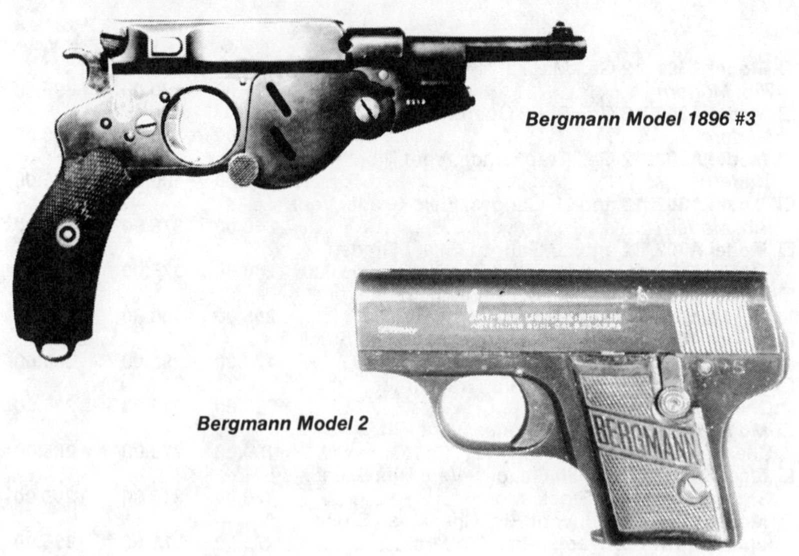

Bergmann Model 1896 #3

Bergmann Model 2

	V.G.	Exc.	Prior Year Exc. Value
HANDGUN, SEMI-AUTOMATIC			
☐ **Model 1894,** 5mm, Blow Back, Clip Fed, *Antique*	10500.00	19500.00	18500.00
☐ **Model 1894,** 8mm, Blow Back, Clip Fed, *Antique*	6500.00	9750.00	9150.00
☐ **Model 1896** #2, 5mm, Small Frame, Clip Fed, *Curio*	920.00	1500.00	1650.00
☐ **Model 1896 #3,** 6.5mm, Clip Fed, *Curio*	1150.00	2000.00	2150.00
☐ **Model 1896 #4,** 8mm, Military, Clip Fed, *Curio*	1300.00	2300.00	2600.00
☐ **Model 1897 #5,** 7.8mm, Clip Fed, *Curio*	1625.00	2400.00	2775.00
☐ **Simplex,** 8mm, Clip Fed, *Curio*	530.00	950.00	1100.00
☐ **Bergmann Mars,** 9mmB, Clip Fed, *Curio*	2000.00	3000.00	3200.00
☐ **Bergmann/Bayard,** Model 1908, 9mmB, Clip Fed, *Curio*	560.00	890.00	950.00
☐ **Bergmann/Bayard,** Model 1910, 9mmB, Clip Fed, *Curio*	615.00	940.00	995.00
☐ **Bergmann/Bayard,** Model 1910/21, 9mmB, Clip Fed, *Curio*	470.00	750.00	795.00
☐ **Model 2,** .25 ACP, Clip Fed, *Modern*	180.00	300.00	325.00
☐ **Model 2A,** .25 ACP, Einhand, Clip Fed, *Modern*	230.00	350.00	365.00
☐ **Model 3,** .25 ACP, Long Grip, Clip Fed, *Modern*	180.00	300.00	320.00
☐ **Model 3A,** .25 ACP, Einhand, Long Grip, Clip Fed, *Modern*	235.00	360.00	400.00
☐ **Erben Special,** .32 ACP, Clip Fed, *Modern*	220.00	335.00	385.00
☐ **Erben Model I,** .25 ACP, Clip Fed, *Modern*	165.00	270.00	300.00
☐ **Erben Model II,** .25 ACP, Clip Fed, *Modern*	190.00	320.00	345.00
RIFLE, SEMI-AUTOMATIC			
☐ **Model 1897,** Karabiner, 7.8mm, Long Barrel, Detachable Stock, *Modern*	3575.00	5600.00	5600.00

	V.G.	Exc.	Prior Year Exc. Value

BERLIN, ABRAHAM

Caston, Pa. 1773-1786. See Kentucky Rifles and Pistols.

BERNARDON-MARTIN

St. Etienne, France 1906-1912.

HANDGUN, SEMI-AUTOMATIC

	V.G.	Exc.	Prior Year Exc. Value
☐ **Automatique Francais**, .32 ACP, Clip Fed, *Curio*	200.00	295.00	275.00

BERNARDELLI

Vincenzo Bernardelli, Gardon V.T., Italy.

HANDGUN, SEMI-AUTOMATIC

	V.G.	Exc.	Prior Year Exc. Value
☐ **M1956**, 9mm Luger, Clip Fed, *Curio*	875.00	1,450.00	1,350.00
☐ **Model 100**, .22 L.R.R.F., Clip Fed, Blue, Target Pistol, *Modern*	200.00	280.00	265.00
☐ **Model 60**, .22 L.R.R.F., Clip Fed, Blue, *Modern*	95.00	160.00	150.00
☐ **Model 60**, .22 L.R.R.F., Clip Fed, Blue, 8″ Barrel, Detachable Front Sight, Adjustable Sights, *Modern*	200.00	325.00	300.00
☐ **Model 60**, .32 ACP, Clip Fed, Blue, *Modern*	110.00	170.00	155.00
☐ **Model 60**, .380 ACP, Clip Fed, Blue, *Modern*	120.00	190.00	175.00
☐ **Model 80**, .22 L.R.R.F., Clip Fed, Blue, *Modern*	115.00	180.00	170.00
☐ **Model 80**, .22 L.R.R.F., Clip Fed, Blue, 6″ Barrel, *Modern*	115.00	190.00	175.00
☐ **Model 80**, .32 ACP, Clip Fed, Blue, *Modern*	110.00	180.00	170.00
☐ **Model 80**, .380 ACP, Clip Fed, Blue, *Modern*	120.00	190.00	180.00
☐ **Model V P**, .22 L.R.R.F., Clip Fed, Blue, *Modern*	130.00	195.00	195.00
☐ **Model V P**, .25 ACP, Clip Fed, Blue, *Modern*	95.00	170.00	165.00
☐ **Standard**, .22 L.R.R.F., Clip Fed, Blue, *Modern*	95.00	170.00	165.00
☐ **Standard**, .22 L.R.R.F., Clip Fed, Blue, 6″ Barrel, Detachable Front Sight, *Modern*	140.00	215.00	195.00
☐ **Standard**, .22 L.R.R.F., Clip Fed, Blue, 8″ Barrel, Detachable Front Sight, *Modern*	160.00	265.00	250.00
☐ **Standard**, .22 L.R.R.F., Clip Fed, Blue, 10″ Barrel, Detachable Front Sight, *Modern*	250.00	375.00	350.00
☐ **Standard**, .32 ACP, Original 17 Shot Clip only, Add **$35.00-$60.00**			
☐ **Standard**, .32 ACP, Clip Fed, Blue, *Modern*	135.00	190.00	185.00
☐ **Standard**, .32 ACP, Clip Fed, Blue, 6″ Barrel, Detachable Front Sight, *Modern*	185.00	275.00	265.00

Bernardelli Standard .32, 8″ Barrel

	V.G.	Exc.	Prior Year Exc. Value
☐ **Standard**, .32 ACP, Clip Fed, Blue, 8″ Barrel, Detachable Front Sight, *Modern*	250.00	385.00	365.00
☐ **Standard**, .32 ACP, Clip Fed, Blue, 10″ Barrel, Detachable Front Sight, *Modern*	295.00	425.00	395.00
☐ **Standard**, .380 ACP, Clip Fed, Blue, *Modern*	140.00	225.00	210.00
☐ **Standard**, 9mm Luger, Clip Fed, Blue, *Modern*	265.00	425.00	400.00
HANDGUN, REVOLVER			
☐ **Standard**, .22 L.R.R.F. or .32 S&W Long, Double Action, Blue, *Modern*	160.00	260.00	260.00
☐ **Target**, .22 L.R.R.F., Double Action, Blue, Target Sights, *Modern*	175.00	280.00	280.00
☐ **Target**, .22 L.R.R.F., Double Action, Engraved, Chrome Plated, , Target Sights, *Modern*	300.00	400.00	400.00
RIFLE, DOUBLE BARREL, OVER-UNDER			
☐ **Various Calibers**, Checkered Stock, Engraved, *Modern*	725.00	1,050.00	995.00
SHOTGUN, DOUBLE BARREL, SIDE-BY-SIDE			
☐ **Brescia**, 12 and 20 Gauges, Checkered Stock, Hammer, *Modern*	450.00	600.00	595.00
☐ **Elio**, 12 Ga., Checkered Stock, Light Engraving, Lightweight Selective Ejector, *Modern*	600.00	775.00	775.00
☐ **Game Cock**, 12 and 20 Gauges, Checkered Stock, Double Trigger, *Modern*	475.00	675.00	675.00
☐ **Game Cock Premier**, 12 and 20 Gauges, Checkered Stock, Single Trigger, Selective Ejector, *Modern*	600.00	845.00	825.00
☐ **Holland**, Various Gauges, Sidelock, Engraved, Checkered Stock, Automatic Ejector, *Modern*	1.600.00	2,950.00	2,875.00
☐ **Holland Deluxe**, Various Gauges, Sidelock, Fancy Engraving, Fancy Checkering, Automatic Ejector, *Modern*	1,950.00	3,650.00	3,500.00
☐ **Holland Presentation**, Various Gauges, Sidelock, Fancy Engraving, Fancy Checkering, Automatic Ejector, *Modern*	2,650.00	4,100.00	3,950.00
☐ **Italia**, 12 and 20 Gauges, Checkered Stock, Hammer, Light Engraving, *Modern*	485.00	725.00	700.00
☐ **Roma #3**, Various Gauges, Engraved, Checkered Stock, Automatic Ejector, *Modern*	425.00	670.00	650.00
☐ **Roma #4**, Various Gauges, Fancy Engraving, Fancy Checkering, Automatic Ejector, *Modern*	550.00	800.00	795.00
☐ **Roma #6**, Various Gauges, Fancy Engraving, Fancy Checkering, Automatic Ejector, *Modern*	700.00	925.00	900.00
☐ **St. Uberto F.S.**, 12 and 16 Gauges, Checkered Stock, Double Trigger, Automatic Ejector, *Modern*	475.00	695.00	675.00
☐ **Wesley Richards**, Various Gauges, Checkered Stock, Light Engraving, Double Trigger, *Modern*	995.00	1,800.00	1,750.00
☐ **Wesley Richards**, Various Gauges, Fancy Checkering, Fancy Engraving, Single Trigger, Selective Ejector, Vent Rib, *Modern*	2,375.00	3,450.00	3,350.00

BERSA

Baraldo S.A.C.I. Argentina.

	V.G.	Exc.	Prior Year Exc. Value
HANDGUN, SEMI-AUTOMATIC			
☐ **Model 62**, .22 L.R.R.F., Clip Fed, Blue, *Modern*	65.00	100.00	100.00

	V.G.	Exc.	Prior Year Exc. Value
☐ **Model 97**, .380 A.C.P., Clip Fed, Blue, *Modern*	95.00	140.00	140.00
☐ **Model 622**, .22 L.R.R.F., Clip Fed, Blue, *Modern*	80.00	125.00	125.00
☐ **Model 644**, .22 L.R.R.F., Clip Fed, Blue, *Modern*	80.00	130.00	130.00

BERTUZZI

Gardone V.T., Italy; Imported by Ventura.

SHOTGUN, DOUBLE BARREL, OVER-UNDER

☐ **Zeus**, 12 Ga., Sidelock, Automatic Ejector, Single Selective Trigger, Fancy Checkering, Fancy Engraving, *Modern*	2,150.00	2,850.00	2,750.00
☐ **Zeus Extra Lusso**, 12 Ga., Sidelock, Automatic Ejector, Single Selective Trigger, Fancy Checkering, Fancy Engraving, *Modern*	4,250.00	5,250.00	5,150.00

BICYCLE

Bicycle by Harrington & Richardson c. 1895.

HANDGUN, REVOLVER

☐ **.22 L.R.R.F.**, Top Break, Double Action, *Modern*	60.00	100.00	95.00
☐ **.32 S & W**, 5 Shot, Double Action, Top Break, *Modern*	60.00	95.00	95.00

BICYCLE

French, Maker Unknown.

HANDGUN, SINGLESHOT

☐ **.22 L.R.R.F.**, Auto Styling, *Modern*	225.00	365.00	345.00

BIG BONANZA

Made by Bacon Arms Co. c. 1880.

HANDGUN, REVOLVER

☐ **.22 Short R.F.**, 7 Shot, Spur Trigger, Solid Frame, Single Action, *Antique*	90.00	160.00	160.00

BIG HORN ARMS CO.

Watertown, S.D.

HANDGUN, SINGLESHOT

☐ **Target Pistol**, .22 Short, Plastic Stock, Vent Rib, *Modern*	85.00	145.00	135.00

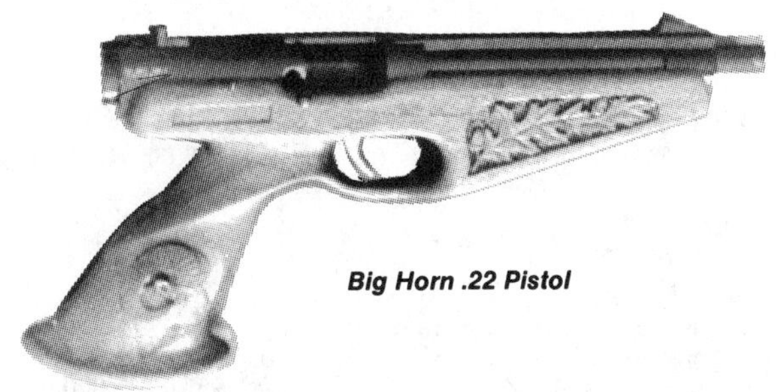

Big Horn .22 Pistol

	V.G.	Exc.	Prior Year Exc. Value
SHOTGUN, SINGLESHOT			
☐ **12 Ga. Short**, Plastic Stock, *Modern*	55.00	100.00	95.00

BILLINGHURST, WILLIAM

Rochester, N.Y. 1843-80

	V.G.	Exc.	Prior Year Exc. Value
HANDGUN, PERCUSSION			
☐ **Buggy Pistol**, Various Calibers, Detachable Stock, Heavy Barrel, *Antique*	700.00	1,300.00	1,250.00
RIFLE, PERCUSSION			
☐ **.36**, Revolver, 7 Shot, Octagon Barrel, *Antique*	1,950.00	2,650.00	2,550.00
☐ **.40**, Revolver, 7 Shot, Octagon Barrel, *Antique*	1,650.00	2,350.00	2,200.00
RIFLE, PILL LOCK			
☐ **.40**, 7 Shot, Octagon Barrel, *Antique*	1,950.00	2,700.00	2,600.00
☐ **.40**, Carbine, 7 Shot, Octagon Barrel, *Antique*	1,950.00	2,750.00	2,600.00

BISBEE, D.H.

Norway, Me. 1835-1860.

	V.G.	Exc.	Prior Year Exc. Value
RIFLE, PERCUSSION			
☐ **.44**, Octagon Barrel, Silver Inlay, *Antique*	1,500.00	2,150.00	2,000.00

BISON

Imported from Germany by Jana International c. 1971.

	V.G.	Exc.	Prior Year Exc. Value
HANDGUN, REVOLVER			
☐ **.22 LR/.22 WMR Combo**, Adjustable Sights, Western Style, Single Action, *Modern*	25.00	45.00	45.00
☐ **.22 L.R.R.F.**, Adjustable Sights, Western Style, Single Action, *Modern*	25.00	40.00	40.00

BITTERLICH, FRANK J.

Nashville, Tenn. from about 1855 until about 1867.

	V.G.	Exc.	Prior Year Exc. Value
HANDGUN, PERCUSSION			
☐ **Derringer**, .40, Plain, *Antique*	500.00	950.00	925.00

BITTNER, GUSTAV

Vejprty, Bohemia, Austria-Hungary c. 1893.

	V.G.	Exc.	Prior Year Exc. Value
HANDGUN, MANUAL REPEATER			
☐ **Model 1893**, 7.7mm Bittner, Box Magazine, Checkered Stocks, *Antique*	1,550.00	2,600.00	2,450.00

BLAKE, ANN

London, England c. 1812.

	V.G.	Exc.	Prior Year Exc. Value
HANDGUN, FLINTLOCK			
☐ **Holster Pistol**, .62, Walnut Stock, *Antique*	425.00	725.00	695.00

BLANCH, JOHN A.

London, England 1809-1835.

	V.G.	Exc.	Prior Year Exc. Value
HANDGUN, PERCUSSION			
☐ **.68 Pair**, Double Barrel, Side by Side, Officer's Belt Pistol, Engraved, Silver Inlay, Steel Furniture, Cased with Accessories, *Antique*	3,950.00	5,000.00	4,800.00

	V.G.	Exc.	Prior Year Exc. Value
☐ **Pair**, Pocket Pistol, Converted from Flintlock, High Quality, Cased with Accessories, *Antique*	**1,975.00**	**2,900.00**	**2,750.00**

BLAND, T. & SONS

London & Birmingham, England from 1876.

SHOTGUN, DOUBLE BARREL, SIDE-BY-SIDE

	V.G.	Exc.	Prior Year Exc. Value
☐ **12 Ga.**, Boxlock, Adjustable Choke, Color Case Hardened Frame, Engraved, *Modern*	**1,350.00**	**2,000.00**	**1,900.00**

BLANGLE, JOSEPH

Gratz, Styria, Austria, c. 1670

RIFLE, WHEEL-LOCK

	V.G.	Exc.	Prior Year Exc. Value
☐ **Brass Furniture**, Engraved, Silver Inlay, Light Ornamentation, Full-Stocked, *Antique*	**4,750.00**	**7,100.00**	**6,800.00**

BLEIBERG

London, England c. 1690.

HANDGUN, FLINTLOCK

	V.G.	Exc.	Prior Year Exc. Value
☐ **Holster Pistol**, Engraved, Silver Inlay, High Quality, *Antique*	**6,550.00**	**9,400.00**	**9,250.00**

BLICKENSDOERFER & SCHILLING

St. Louis, Mo. 1871-1875.

RIFLE, PERCUSSION

	V.G.	Exc.	Prior Year Exc. Value
☐ **.48**, Octagon Barrel, Fancy Wood, Brass Furniture, *Antique*	**850.00**	**1,300.00**	**1,250.00**

BLOODHOUND

Made by Hopkins & Allen c. 1880.

HANDGUN, REVOLVER

	V.G.	Exc.	Prior Year Exc. Value
☐ **.22 Short R.F.**, 7 Shot, Spur Trigger, Solid Frame, Single Action, *Antique*	**85.00**	**150.00**	**150.00**

BLUE JACKET

Made by Hopkins & Allen c. 1880.

HANDGUN, REVOLVER

	V.G.	Exc.	Prior Year Exc. Value
☐ **Model 1**, .22 Short R.F., 7 Shot, Spur Trigger, Solid Frame, Single Action, *Antique*	**85.00**	**150.00**	**150.00**
☐ **Model 2**, .32 Short R.F., 5 Shot, Spur Trigger, Solid Frame, Single Action, *Antique*	**85.00**	**160.00**	**160.00**

BLUE WHISTLER

Made by Hopkins & Allen c. 1880.

HANDGUN, REVOLVER

	V.G.	Exc.	Prior Year Exc. Value
☐ **.32 Short R.F.**, 5 Shot, Spur Trigger, Solid Frame, Single Action, *Antique*	**85.00**	**160.00**	**160.00**

BLUMENFELD

Memphis, Tenn. c. 1970

	V.G.	Exc.	Prior Year Exc. Value
SHOTGUN, SEMI-AUTOMATIC			
☐ **Volunteer Pointer**, 12 Gauge, Checkered Stock, *Modern*	120.00	200.00	195.00
SHOTGUN, DOUBLE BARREL, SIDE-BY-SIDE			
☐ **Arizaga**, 20 Gauge, Double Triggers, Checkered Stock, *Modern*	100.00	180.00	175.00

BLUNT, ORISON & SIMS

N.Y.C. 1837-1865.

	V.G.	Exc.	Prior Year Exc. Value
HANDGUN, PERCUSSION			
☐ **Boot Pistol**, Various Calibers, Bar Hammer, *Antique*	150.00	245.00	220.00
☐ **Boot Pistol**, Various Calibers, Side Hammer, *Antique*	175.00	285.00	270.00
☐ **Boot Pistol**, Various Calibers, Side Hammer, Ramrod, *Antique*	175.00	285.00	270.00
☐ **Boot Pistol**, Various Calibers, Ring Trigger, *Antique*	155.00	265.00	250.00
☐ **Boot Pistol**, Various Calibers, Underhammer, *Antique*	150.00	240.00	220.00
☐ **Pocket Pepperbox**, Various Calibers, Ring Trigger, *Antique*	195.00	345.00	320.00
☐ **Belt Pepperbox**, Various Calibers, Ring Trigger, *Antique*	200.00	335.00	320.00
☐ **Dragoon Pepperbox**, Various Calibers, Ring Trigger, *Antique*	325.00	600.00	575.00
RIFLE, PERCUSSION			
☐ **.37**, Octagon Barrel, Brass Furniture, *Antique*	500.00	675.00	650.00

BOITO

Brazil.

	V.G.	Exc.	Prior Year Exc. Value
HANDGUN, SINGLESHOT			
☐ **.44 C.F.**, Break-Open, Hammer, Blue, *Modern*	65.00	95.00	90.00
SHOTGUN, DOUBLE BARREL, OVER-UNDER			
☐ **O/U**, 12 or 20 Gauge, Checkered Stock, *Modern*	95.00	160.00	155.00
SHOTGUN, DOUBLE BARREL, SIDE-BY-SIDE			
☐ **S/S**, 12 or 20 Gauge, Checkered Stock, *Modern*	85.00	135.00	130.00
SHOTGUN, SINGLESHOT			
☐ **SS**, 12 or 20 Gauge, Checkered Stock, *Modern*	30.00	45.00	40.00

BONANZA

Made by Bacon Arms Co.

	V.G.	Exc.	Prior Year Exc. Value
HANDGUN, REVOLVER			
☐ **Model 1½**, .22 Short R.F., 7 Shot, Spur Trigger, Solid Frame, Single Action, *Antique*	85.00	160.00	160.00

BOND, EDWARD

London, England 1800-1830.

	V.G.	Exc.	Prior Year Exc. Value
HANDGUN, FLINTLOCK			
☐ **.68**, Pair Officers' Type, Holster Pistol, Brass Furniture, Plain, *Antique*	1,975.00	2,850.00	2,750.00

	V.G.	Exc.	Prior Year Exc. Value

BOND, WM.
London, England 1798-1812.

HANDGUN, FLINTLOCK

	V.G.	Exc.	Prior Year Exc. Value
☐ **Pair**, Folding Bayonet, Belt Pistol, Box Lock, Cannon Barrel, Brass Frame and Barrel, Cased with Accessories, *Antique*	4,400.00	5,900.00	5,750.00

BONEHILL, C.G.
Birmingham, England c. 1880.

SHOTGUN, DOUBLE BARREL, OVER-UNDER

	V.G.	Exc.	Prior Year Exc. Value
☐ **.450 N.E. 3¼"**, Under-Lever, Recoil Pad, Plain, *Modern*	775.00	1,300.00	1,250.00

BONIWITZ, JAMES
Lebanon, Pa. c. 1775. See Kentucky Rifles.

BOOWLES, R.
London, England c. 1690

HANDGUN, FLINTLOCK

	V.G.	Exc.	Prior Year Exc. Value
☐ **Holster Pistol**, Engraved, Iron Mounts, Medium Quality, *Antique*	750.00	1,375.00	1,250.00

BOSS & CO. LTD.
London, England 1832 To Date

SHOTGUN, DOUBLE BARREL, OVER-UNDER

	V.G.	Exc.	Prior Year Exc. Value
☐ **12. Ga.**, Single Selective Trigger, Straight Grip, Vent Rib, Trap Grade, Cased, *Modern*	13,500.00	17,000.00	18,000.00
☐ **16 Ga.**, Double Trigger, Plain, *Modern*	4,850.00	6,250.00	6,500.00
☐ **20 Ga.**, Single Selective Trigger, Vent Rib, High Quality, *Modern*	15,500.00	20,000.00	21,000.00

SHOTGUN, DOUBLE BARREL, SIDE-BY-SIDE

	V.G.	Exc.	Prior Year Exc. Value
☐ **12 Ga.**, Vent Rib, Fancy Wood, Fancy Checkering, Fancy Engraving, *Modern*	4,500.00	5,750.00	6,000.00
☐ **Pair**, 12 Ga., Straight Grip, Plain, Cased, *Modern*	8,000.00	11,500.00	12,000.00

BOSTON BULLDOG
Made by Iver Johnson, sold by J.P. Lovell & Sons, Boston, Mass.

HANDGUN, REVOLVER

	V.G.	Exc.	Prior Year Exc. Value
☐ **.22 Short R.F.**, 7 Shot, Double Action, Solid Frame, *Modern*	50.00	85.00	85.00
☐ **.32 S & W**, 5 Shot, Double Action, Solid Frame, *Modern*	50.00	85.00	80.00
☐ **.32 Short R.F.**, 5 Shot, Double Action, Solid Frame, *Modern*	50.00	75.00	75.00
☐ **.38 S & W**, 5 Shot, Double Action, Solid Frame, *Modern*	50.00	85.00	80.00
☐ **.38 Short R.F.**, 5 Shot, Double Action, Solid Frame, *Modern*	45.00	80.00	75.00

BOSWORTH
Lancaster, Pa. 1760-1775. See Kentucky Rifles.

	V.G.	Exc.	Prior Year Exc. Value
BOYINGTON, JOHN			
S. Coventry, Conn. 1841-1847.			
RIFLE, PERCUSSION			
☐ **.50**, Octagon Barrel, Brass Furniture, *Antique* ...	600.00	900.00	850.00
BOY'S CHOICE			
Made by Hood Firearms Co. c. 1875.			
HANDGUN, REVOLVER			
☐ **.22 Short R.F.**, 7 Shot, Spur Trigger, Solid Frame, Single Action, *Antique*	95.00	165.00	160.00
BREDA			
Brescia, Italy, Diana Import Co., Current			
SHOTGUN, DOUBLE BARREL, OVER-UNDER			
☐ **.410 Ga.**, Light Engraving, Checkered Stock, *Modern*	325.00	460.00	450.00
SHOTGUN, SEMI-AUTOMATIC			
☐ **"Magnum"**, 12 Ga., Mag. 3", Checkered Stock, Vent Rib, Lightweight, *Modern*	300.00	400.00	395.00
☐ **Grade 1**, 12 Ga., Checkered Stock, Vent Rib, Lightweight, Engraved, *Modern*	350.00	465.00	450.00
☐ **Grade 2**, 12 Ga., Fancy Checkering, Vent Rib, Lightweight, Fancy Engraving, *Modern*	445.00	585.00	575.00
☐ **Grade 3**, 12 Ga., Fancy Checkering, Vent Rib, Lightweight, Fancy Engraving, *Modern*	520.00	675.00	650.00
☐ **Standard**, 12 Ga., Checkered Stock, Plain Barrel, Lightweight, *Modern*	185.00	265.00	250.00
☐ **Standard**, 12 Ga., Checkered Stock, Vent Rib, Lightweight *Modern*	195.00	275.00	265.00
B.R.F.			
Successor to Pretoria Arms Factory, South Africa, about 1957.			
HANDGUN, SEMI-AUTOMATIC			
☐ **"Junior"**, .25 ACP, Clip Fed, Blue, *Modern*	225.00	325.00	300.00
☐ **"Junior"**, .25 ACP, Clip Fed, Blue, Rough Ground Slide, *Modern*	175.00	225.00	200.00
☐ **"Junior"**, .25 ACP, Clip Fed, Blue, Raised Sight Rib, *Modern*	240.00	325.00	300.00
☐ **"Junior"**, .25 ACP, Clip Fed, Blue, Low Slide, *Modern*	200.00	275.00	250.00
☐ **"Junior"**, .25 ACP, Clip Fed, Blue, PAF Logo on Slide, *Modern*	250.00	350.00	320.00
☐ **"Junior"**, .25 ACP, Clip Fed, Factory Chrome Plated, *Modern*	325.00	425.00	400.00
☐ **"Junior"**, for Cocking Indicator, Add **$75-$125**			
BRIGGS, WILLIAM			
Norristown, Pa. 1848-1875.			
SHOTGUN, PERCUSSION			
☐ **12 Ga.**, Underhammer, *Antique*	250.00	345.00	325.00

	V.G.	Exc.	Prior Year Exc. Value

BRITARMS
Aylesbury, England

HANDGUN, SEMI-AUTOMATIC

	V.G.	Exc.	Prior Year Exc. Value
☐ **M2000 Mk.II**, .22 L.R.R.F., Clip Fed, Target Pistol, *Modern*	575.00	825.00	850.00

BRITISH BULLDOG
Made by Forehand & Wadsworth.

HANDGUN, REVOLVER

	V.G.	Exc.	Prior Year Exc. Value
☐ **.32 S & W**, 7 Shot, Double Action, Solid Frame, *Antique*	50.00	90.00	85.00
☐ **.38 S & W**, 6 Shot, Double Action, Solid Frame, *Antique*	50.00	90.00	85.00
☐ **.44 S & W**, 5 Shot, Double Action, Solid Frame, *Antique*	65.00	130.00	125.00

BRITISH BULLDOG
Made by Forehand & Wadsworth.

HANDGUN, REVOLVER

	V.G.	Exc.	Prior Year Exc. Value
☐ **.32 S & W**, 5 Shot, Double Action, Solid Frame, *Modern*	50.00	90.00	85.00
☐ **.38 S & W**, 5 Shot, Double Action, Solid Frame, *Modern*	50.00	90.00	85.00
☐ **.44 S & W**, 5 Shot, Double Action, Solid Frame, *Modern*	65.00	130.00	125.00

BRITISH MILITARY

AUTOMATIC WEAPON, ASSAULT RIFLE

	V.G.	Exc.	Prior Year Exc. Value
☐ **Sterling-AR18S,** .223 Rem., Clip Fed, Short Rifle, *Class 3*	790.00	1375.00	1350.00

AUTOMATIC WEAPON, HEAVY MACHINE GUN

	V.G.	Exc.	Prior Year Exc. Value
☐ **M1906 Marlin,** .303 British, Belt Fed, Tripod, Potato Digger, Military, *Class 3*	1500.00	2300.00	2250.00
☐ **Vickers Mk I,** .303 British, Belt Fed, Tripod, *Class 3*	4925.00	6400.00	6250.00

AUTOMATIC WEAPON, LIGHT MACHINE GUN

	V.G.	Exc.	Prior Year Exc. Value
☐ **Bren Mk II,** .303 British, Clip Fed, Bipod, *Class 3*	4600.00	6875.00	6750.00
☐ **Hotchkiss Mk I*,** .303 British, all Metal, Tripod, *Class 3*	1475.00	1950.00	1900.00
☐ **Lewis Gun,** .303 British, Drum Magazine, Bipod, *Class 3*	1475.00	2250.00	2200.00

AUTOMATIC WEAPON, SUBMACHINE GUN

	V.G.	Exc.	Prior Year Exc. Value
☐ **Lanchester Mk I*,** 9mm Luger, Wood Stock, Clip Fed, Military, *Class 3*	600.00	875.00	850.00
☐ **Lanchester Mk I*,** 9mm Luger, Wood Stock, Dewat, Clip Fed, Military, *Class 3*	320.00	435.00	420.00
☐ **Sten Mk II,** 9mm Luger, all Metal, Clip Fed, Military, *Class 3*	490.00	730.00	720.00
☐ **Sten Mk II S,** 9mm Luger, Clip Fed, all Metal, Military, Silencer, *Class 3*	740.00	1350.00	1300.00
☐ **Sten Mk III,** 9mm Luger, Clip Fed, all Metal, Military, *Class 3*	575.00	825.00	800.00

British Military #1 MK III

British Military Webley MK I No. 2 .455

	V.G.	Exc.	Prior Year Exc. Value
☐ **Sterling L2A3,** 9mm, Clip Fed, all Metal, Military, *Class 3*	670.00	1225.00	1200.00
☐ **Sterling L3A1,** 9mm, Clip Fed, all Metal, Military, Silencer, *Class 3*	835.00	1450.00	1400.00
☐ **Thompson M1928,** .45 ACP, Clip Fed, with Compensator, Lyman Sights, Finned Barrel, *Class 3*	2850.00	3950.00	3850.00
HANDGUN, FLINTLOCK			
☐ **.58,** New Land M1796 Tower, Long Tapered Round Barrel, Belt Hook, Brass Furniture, *Antique*	1350.00	2100.00	1900.00
☐ **.67,** George III Tower, Calvary Pistol, Military, Tapered Round Barrel, Brass Furniture, *Antique*	1000.00	1500.00	1350.00
☐ **.80,** Modified M1796 Spooner, Holster Pistol, Plain Brass Furniture, *Antique*	1150.00	1900.00	1600.00
HANDGUN, REVOLVER			
☐ **#2 Mk I,** .38 S & W, Military, Top Break, *Curio*	50.00	90.00	160.00
☐ **#2 Mk I R.A.F.,** .38 S & W, Military, Top Break, *Curio*	60.00	110.00	175.00
☐ **S & W M38/200,** .38 S & W, Solid Frame, Swing-Out Cylinder, Double Action, Military, *Curio*	65.00	115.00	185.00
☐ **Webley Mk I,** .455 Revolver Mk I, Top Break, Round Butt, Military, *Antique*	210.00	335.00	290.00
☐ **Webley Mk I*,** .455 Revolver Mk I, Top Break, Round Butt, Military, *Antique*	200.00	310.00	255.00
☐ **Webley Mk I**,** .455 Revolver Mk I, Top Break, Round Butt, Military, *Curio*	70.00	120.00	215.00

	V.G.	Exc.	Prior Year Exc. Value
☐ **Webley Mk II,** .455 Revolver Mk I, Top Break, Round Butt, Military, *Curio*	100.00	185.00	245.00
☐ **Webley Mk II*,** .455 Revolver Mk I, Top Break, Round Butt, Military, *Curio*	85.00	150.00	220.00
☐ **Webley Mk II**,** .455 Revolver Mk I, Top Break, Round Butt, Military, *Curio*	80.00	140.00	200.00
☐ **Webley Mk III,** .455 Revolver Mk I, Top Break, Round Butt, Military, *Curio*	100.00	200.00	270.00
☐ **Webley Mk IV,** .455 Revolver Mk I, Top Break, Round Butt, Military, *Curio*	90.00	170.00	230.00
☐ **Webley Mk V,** .455 Revolver Mk I, Top Break, Round Butt, Military, *Curio*	105.00	195.00	250.00
☐ **Webley Mk VI,** .455 Revolver Mk I, Top Break, Square Butt, Military, *Curio*	90.00	165.00	220.00
HANDGUN, SEMI-AUTOMATIC			
☐ **Webley Mk.I,** .455 Webley Auto, Clip Fed, *Curio*	120.00	230.00	320.00
☐ **Webley Mk.I No. 2 R.A.F.,** .455 Webley Auto, Clip Fed, Cut for Shoulder Stock, *Curio*	385.00	625.00	950.00
☐ **Webley Mk.I No. 2 R.A.F.,** .455 Webley Auto, Clip Fed, with Shoulder Stock, *Curio*	500.00	900.00	1250.00
☐ **M1911A1 Colt,** .455 Webley Auto., Clip Fed, Military, *Curio*	230.00	385.00	535.00
HANDGUN, SINGLESHOT			
☐ **Welrod,** .32 ACP, Bolt Action, Silenced, *Class 3*	420.00	575.00	575.00
RIFLE, BOLT ACTION			
☐ **Lee Metford Mk I,** .303 British, Clip Fed, Carbine, *Curio*	85.00	150.00	245.00
☐ **Lee Metford Mk I,** .303 British, Clip Fed, *Curio*	80.00	140.00	210.00
☐ **Lee Metford MK I*,** .303 British, Clip Fed, Carbine, *Curio*	75.00	135.00	200.00
☐ **Lee Metford MK II,** .303 British, Clip Fed, *Curio*	70.00	135.00	200.00
☐ **Lee Metford MK II*,** .303 British, Clip Fed, *Curio*	85.00	145.00	235.00
☐ **M1896 Lee Metford,** .303 British, Clip Fed, Military, Carbine, *Curio*	60.00	100.00	175.00
☐ **Pattern 14 (U.S.),** .303 British, *Curio*	75.00	150.00	225.00
☐ **SMLE #1 MK I,** .303 British, Military, *Curio*	75.00	145.00	220.00
☐ **SMLE #1 MK III,** .303 British, Military, *Curio*	60.00	125.00	185.00
☐ **SMLE #1 Mk III*,** .303 British, Tangent Sights, Military, Ishapore, *Curio*	55.00	90.00	160.00
☐ **SMLE #1 MK III*,** .303 British, Military, *Curio*	50.00	95.00	165.00
☐ **SMLE #2 MK IV,** .22 L.R.R.F., Singleshot, Training Rifle, *Curio*	70.00	120.00	195.00
☐ **SMLE #3 Mk I* (1914 Enfield),** .303 British, Military, *Curio*	60.00	105.00	175.00
☐ **SMLE #4 MK I*,** .303 British, Military, Lightweight, *Curio*	60.00	105.00	175.00
☐ **SMLE #4 Sniper,** .303 British, Military, Scope Mounted, *Curio*	230.00	365.00	525.00
☐ **SMLE #4 MK I*,** .303 British, Military, Canadian, Lightweight, *Curio*	55.00	100.00	170.00
☐ **SMLE #4 MK I*,** .303 British, Military, New Zealand, Lightweight, *Curio*	75.00	130.00	210.00
☐ **SMLE #4 MK I*,** .303 British, Military, *Curio*	50.00	90.00	160.00
☐ **SMLE #MK V Jungle Carbine,** .303 British, Peep Sights, Military, *Curio*	90.00	160.00	240.00

	V.G.	Exc.	Prior Year Exc. Value
☐ **Santa Fe Jungle Carbine Mk.I MD12011,** .303 British, Peep Sights, No Flash Hider, Commercial, *Modern*	50.00	95.00	145.00
☐ **SMLE #7,** .22 L.R.R.F., Singleshot, Training Rifle, *Curio*	85.00	130.00	210.00
☐ **SMLE #8,** .22 L.R.R.F., Singleshot, Training Rifle, *Curio*	85.00	130.00	210.00
☐ **SMLE #9,** .22 L.R.R.F., Singleshot, Training Rifle, *Curio*	85.00	130.00	210.00
RIFLE, FLINTLOCK			
☐ **.75,** 1st Model Brown Bess, Musket, Brass Furniture, *Antique*	3000.00	4000.00	3700.00
☐ **.75,** 2nd Model Brown Bess, Musket, Military, *Antique*	1550.00	2450.00	2300.00
☐ **.75,** 3rd Model Brown Bess, Musket, Military, *Antique*	1200.00	1900.00	1800.00
RIFLE, PERCUSSION			
☐ **.58 Snider-Enfield,** Military, Musket, *Antique*	410.00	600.00	575.00
☐ **.60 M1856 Tower,** Military, Musket, *Antique*	335.00	500.00	475.00
☐ **.60 M1869 Enfield,** Military, Musket, *Antique*	335.00	500.00	475.00
RIFLE, SINGLESHOT			
☐ **Martini-Henry,** .303 British, Carbine, *Antique*	150.00	250.00	240.00
☐ **Martini-Henry,** .303 British, *Antique*	170.00	275.00	265.00
☐ **Martini-Henry,** .577/.450 Martini-Henry, Carbine, *Antique*	140.00	230.00	225.00
☐ **Martini-Henry,** .577/.450 Martini-Henry, *Antique*	175.00	265.00	255.00
☐ **Martini-Henry,** .577/.450 Martini-Henry, Long Lever, *Antique*	125.00	210.00	200.00
SHOTGUN, SINGLESHOT			
☐ **Martini-Henry,** .12 Gauge Special, Long Lever, *Antique*	100.00	160.00	150.00

BRETTON

St. Etienne, France.

SHOTGUN, DOUBLE BARREL, OVER-UNDER			
☐ **Standard**, 12 Gauge, Dural Frame, Double Triggers, Barrels Can Be Unscrewed, *Modern*	295.00	400.00	375.00
☐ **Deluxe**, 12 Gauge, Engraved, Dural Frame, Double Triggers, Barrels Can Be Unscrewed, *Modern*	375.00	500.00	485.00

BORCHARDT

Made by Ludwig Lowe, Berlin, Germany 1893-1897. In 1897 acquired by D.W.M., superseded by the Luger in 1900.

HANDGUN, SEMI-AUTOMATIC			
☐ **Lowe**, 7.65mm Borchardt, Clip Fed, Blue, Cased with Accessories, *Antique*	5,250.00	9,000.00	8,750.00
☐ **DWM**, 7.65mm Borchardt, Clip Fed, Blue, Cased with Accessories, *Curio*	4,500.00	7,750.00	7,500.00

BRNO

Ceska Zbrojovka, Brno, Czechoslovakia since 1922.

	V.G.	Exc.	Prior Year Exc. Value
RIFLE, BOLT ACTION			
☐ **21 H**, Various Calibers, Sporting Rifle, Express Sights, Cheekpiece, Checkered Stock, Set Trigger, *Modern*	495.00	745.00	725.00
☐ **22 F**, Various Calibers, Sporting Rifle, Express Sights, Mannlicher, Checkered Stock, Set Trigger, *Modern*	520.00	775.00	750.00
☐ **Model I**, .22 L.R.R.F., Sporting Rifle, Express Sights, 5 Shot Clip, Checkered Stock, Set Trigger, *Modern*	240.00	400.00	375.00
☐ **Model II**, .22 L.R.R.F., Sporting Rifle, Express Sights, 5 Shot Clip, Fancy Wood, Set Trigger, *Modern*	245.00	400.00	395.00
☐ **Z-B Mauser**, .22 Hornet, Sporting Rifle, Express Sights, 5 Shot Clip, Checkered Stock, Set Trigger, *Modern*	525.00	775.00	750.00
☐ **ZKB 680 Fox**, .222 Rem., Clip Fed, Checkered Stock, Sling Swivels, *Modern*	225.00	365.00	350.00
☐ **ZKM 452**, .22 L.R.R.F., Clip Fed, Checkered Stock, Tangent Sights, *Modern*	80.00	135.00	130.00
RIFLE, DOUBLE BARREL, OVER-UNDER			
☐ **Super Express**, Various Calibers, Fancy Checkering, Sidelock, Engraved, Double Triggers, *Modern*	465.00	695.00	675.00
☐ **Super Express Grade III**, Various Calibers, Fancy Checkering, Sidelock, Fancy Engraving, Double Triggers, *Modern*	995.00	1,600.00	1,550.00
☐ **Super Express Grade IV**, Various Calibers, Fancy Checkering, Sidelock, Fancy Engraving, Double Triggers, *Modern*	665.00	1,250.00	1,200.00
RIFLE, SEMI-AUTOMATIC			
☐ **ZKM 581**, .22 L.R.R.F., Clip Fed, Checkered Stock, Tangent Sights, *Modern*	120.00	175.00	170.00
SHOTGUN, DOUBLE BARREL, OVER-UNDER			
☐ **Super**, 12 Gauge, Fancy Checkering, Sidelock, Plain, Ejectors, Double Triggers, *Modern*	350.00	695.00	675.00
☐ **Super Grade IV**, 12 Gauge, Fancy Checkering, Sidelock, Engraved, Ejectors, Double Triggers, *Modern*	475.00	865.00	850.00
☐ **Super Grade I**, 12 Gauge, Fancy Checkering, Sidelock, Fancy Engraving, Ejectors, Double Triggers, *Modern*	1,150.00	1,750.00	1,700.00
☐ **ZH 303 Field**, 12 Gauge, Boxlock, Checkered Stock, *Modern*	285.00	450.00	425.00
SHOTGUN, DOUBLE BARREL, SIDE-BY-SIDE			
☐ **ZP 47**, 12 Gauge, Sidelock, Double Triggers, Extractors, Checkered Stock, *Modern*	225.00	335.00	325.00
☐ **ZP 49**, 12 Gauge, Sidelock, Double Triggers, Ejectors, Checkered Stock, *Modern*	325.00	465.00	450.00

BROCKWAY, NORMAN S.

West Brookfield, Mass. 1861-1867, Bellows Falls, Vt. 1867-1900.

	V.G.	Exc.	Prior Year Exc. Value
RIFLE, PERCUSSION			
☐ **Various Calibers**, Target Rifle, *Antique*	1,375.00	2,250.00	2,200.00

	V.G.	Exc.	Prior Year Exc. Value

BRONCO
Imported by Garcia, c. 1970.

COMBINATION WEAPON, OVER-UNDER

	V.G.	Exc.	Prior Year Exc. Value
☐ **.22/.410**, Skeleton Stock, *Modern*	45.00	75.00	70.00

RIFLE, SINGLESHOT

	V.G.	Exc.	Prior Year Exc. Value
☐ **Skeleton Stock**, *Modern*	30.00	55.00	55.00

SHOTGUN, SINGLESHOT

	V.G.	Exc.	Prior Year Exc. Value
☐ **.410 Ga.**, Skeleton Stock, *Modern*	45.00	65.00	60.00

BRONCO
Echave y Arizmendi, Eibar, Spain 1911-1974.

HANDGUN, SEMI—AUTOMATIC

	V.G.	Exc.	Prior Year Exc. Value
☐ **1918 Vest Pocket**, .32 ACP, Clip Fed, *Curio*	90.00	150.00	145.00
☐ **Vest Pocket**, .25 ACP, Clip Fed, *Modern*	85.00	135.00	125.00
☐ **Vest Pocket**, .25 ACP, Clip Fed, Light Engraving, *Modern*	110.00	185.00	175.00

Brooklyn Arms Co. Slocum Revolver

BROOKLYN ARMS CO.
Brooklyn, N.Y. 1863-1867.

HANDGUN, REVOLVER

	V.G.	Exc.	Prior Year Exc. Value
☐ **Slocum Patent**, .32 R.F., 5 Shot Cylinder with Sliding Chambers, Spur Trigger, Single Action, Engraved, *Antique*	240.00	395.00	375.00

BROWN MFG. CO.
Newburyport, Mass. 1869-73. Also see Ballard Rifles.

HANDGUN, SINGLESHOT

	V.G.	Exc.	Prior Year Exc. Value
☐ **Southerner Derringer**, .41 R.F., Side-Swing Barrel, Spur Trigger, Brass Frame, *Antique*	175.00	295.00	275.00

RIFLE, BOLT ACTION

	V.G.	Exc.	Prior Year Exc. Value
☐ **1853 Long Enfield**, .58 U.S. Musket, Converted from Percussion, Brass Furniture, *Antique*	450.00	625.00	595.00
☐ **U.S. M1861 Musket**, .58 U.S. Musket, Converted from Percussion, Brass Furniture, *Antique*	465.00	650.00	625.00

BROWN, JOHN & SONS
Fremont, N.J. 1840-1871.

RIFLE, PERCUSSION

	V.G.	Exc.	Prior Year Exc. Value
☐ **Various Calibers**, Sporting Rifle, *Antique*	700.00	1,300.00	1,200.00

	V.G.	Exc.	Prior Year Exc. Value
☐ **.50**, Target Rifle, Scope Mounted, Set Trigger, *Antique*	1,300.00	2,000.00	1,950.00

BROWN PRECISION CO.

San Jose, Calif. since 1975.

RIFLE, BOLT ACTION

☐ **Sporter**, Various Calibers, Fiberglass Stock, Rem. 700 Action, Sling Swivels, *Modern*	215.00	310.00	300.00

BROWNING

Established 1870 in St. Louis, Mo., now at Morgan, Utah. Also see F.N.

HANDGUN, SEMI-AUTOMATIC

☐ **Various Calibers,** Baby-.380-Hi Power Set, Renaissance, Nickel Plated, Engraved, *Modern*	3650.00	5250.00	5250.00
☐ **380 Auto,** .380 ACP, Clip Fed, Renaissance, Nickel Plated, Engraved, *Modern*	995.00	1650.00	1650.00
☐ **380 Auto,** .380 ACP, Clip Fed, Adjustable Sights, *Modern*	225.00	330.00	350.00
☐ **380 Auto Standard,** .380 ACP, Clip Fed, *Modern*	200.00	250.00	265.00
☐ **Baby,** .25 ACP, Clip Fed, Lightweight, Nickel Plated, *Modern*	385.00	475.00	500.00
☐ **Baby,** .25 ACP, Clip Fed, Renaissance, Nickel Plated, Engraved, *Modern*	975.00	1500.00	1500.00
☐ **Baby Standard,** .25 ACP, Clip Fed, *Modern*	185.00	290.00	290.00
☐ **BDA 380,** .380 ACP, Clip Fed, Double Action, Fixed Sights, *Modern*	195.00	310.00	320.00
☐ **BDA 380,** .380 ACP, Clip Fed, Double Action, Fixed Sights, Nickel, *Modern*	210.00	340.00	340.00
☐ **BDA 38 Super,** .38 Super, Clip Fed, Double Action, Fixed Sights, *Modern*	550.00	800.00	800.00
☐ **BDA 45,** .45 ACP, Clip Fed, Double Action, 7 Shot, *Modern*	345.00	450.00	475.00
☐ **BDA 9,** 9mm Luger, Clip Fed, Double Action, 9 Shot, *Modern*	305.00	400.00	425.00
☐ **Challenger,** .22 L.R.R.F., Clip Fed, Checkered Wood Grips, Adjustable Sights, *Modern*	250.00	350.00	385.00
☐ **Challenger,** .22 L.R.R.F., Clip Fed, Renaissance, Checkered Wood Grips, Fancy Engraving, Nickel Plated, *Modern*	1100.00	1775.00	1775.00
☐ **Challenger,** .22 L.R.R.F., Clip Fed, Checkered Wood Grips, Gold Inlays, Engraved, *Modern*	900.00	1450.00	1450.00
☐ **Challenger II,** .22 L.R.R.F., Clip Fed, Adjustable Sights, *Modern*	120.00	165.00	185.00
☐ **Challenger III,** .22 L.R.R.F., Clip Fed, Adjustable Sights, *Modern*	120.00	165.00	185.00
☐ **Classic Hi Power Pistol,** 9mm, Engraved With Lynx and Bald Eagle, *Modern*	1325.00	1425.00	1425.00
☐ **Gold Classic Hi Power Pistol,** 9mm, Engraved with Lynx and Bald Eagle, *Modern*	2800.00	3000.00	3000.00
☐ **Hi Power,** 9mm, Clip Fed, Pre-War Military, Tangent Sights, *Curio*	650.00	1100.00	1200.00
☐ **Hi Power,** 9mm, Clip Fed, Pre-War Military, Tangent Sights, with Detachable Shoulder Stock, *Curio*	800.00	1250.00	1400.00

	V.G.	Exc.	Prior Year Exc. Value
☐ **Hi Power,** 9mm, Clip Fed, Military, Tangent Sights, *Curio*	380.00	625.00	800.00
☐ **Hi Power,** 9mm, Clip Fed, Military, Tangent Sights, with Detachable Shoulder Stock, *Curio*	530.00	775.00	1000.00
☐ **Hi Power,** 9mm, Clip Fed, Military, *Curio*	300.00	450.00	625.00
☐ **Hi Power,** 9mm, Clip Fed, Military, with Detachable Shoulder Stock, *Curio*	410.00	595.00	825.00
☐ **Hi Power,** 9mm, Clip Fed, Nazi-Marked Military, Tangent Sights, *Curio*	350.00	550.00	600.00
☐ **Hi Power,** 9mm, Clip Fed, Nazi-Marked Military, Tangent Sights, with Detachable Shoulder Stock, *Curio*	550.00	875.00	1075.00
☐ **Hi Power,** 9mm, Clip Fed, Nazi-Marked Military, *Curio*	360.00	500.00	575.00
☐ **Hi Power,** 9mm, Clip Fed, Nazi-Marked Military, with Detachable Shoulder Stock, *Curio*	500.00	650.00	825.00
☐ **Hi Power Estonian,** 9mm, Clip Fed, Military, *Curio*	675.00	1100.00	1500.00
☐ **Hi Power Inglis #1 Mk I,** 9mm, Tangent Sights, Slotted for Shoulder Stock, Military, *Curio*	550.00	835.00	1200.00
☐ **Hi Power Inglis #1 Mk I*,** 9mm, Tangent Sights, Slotted for Shoulder Stock, Military, *Curio*	410.00	680.00	975.00
☐ **Hi Power Inglis #1 Mk I*,** 9mm, Tangent Sights, with Shoulder Stock, Military, *Curio*	570.00	950.00	1400.00
☐ **Hi Power Inglis #2 Mk I,** 9mm, Fixed Sights, Military, *Curio*	370.00	520.00	800.00
☐ **Hi Power Inglis #2 Mk I*,** 9mm, Tangent Sights, Slotted for Shoulder Stock, Military, *Curio*	280.00	430.00	650.00
☐ **Hi Power "FM" Argentine,** 9mm, Clip Fed, Made Under License, Military, *Modern*	325.00	450.00	525.00
☐ **Hi Power Louis XVI,** Fancy Engraving, Nickel Plated, Fixed Sights, Cased, *Modern*	850.00	1175.00	1200.00
☐ **Hi Power Louis XVI,** Fancy Engraving, Nickel Plated, Adjustable Sights, Cased, *Modern*	900.00	1200.00	1225.00
☐ **Hi Power,** 9mm, Clip Fed, Renaissance, Nickel Plated, Engraved, *Modern*	925.00	1500.00	1550.00
☐ **Hi Power,** 9mm, Clip Fed, Renaissance, Nickel Plated, Engraved, Adjustable Sights, *Modern*	975.00	1550.00	1600.00
☐ **Hi Power,** 9mm, Clip Fed, with Lanyard Ring Hammer, Renaissance, Nickel Plated, Engraved, *Modern*	875.00	1600.00	1650.00
☐ **Hi Power,** 9mm, Clip Fed, with Lanyard Ring Hammer, Renaissance, Nickel Plated, Engraved, Tangent Sights, *Modern*	975.00	1650.00	1700.00
☐ **Hi Power Standard,** 9mm, Nickel Plating, *Add* **$35.00-$50.00**			
☐ **Hi Power Standard,** 9mm, Clip Fed, with Lanyard Ring Hammer, *Modern*	345.00	425.00	485.00
☐ **Hi Power Standard,** 9mm, Clip Fed, with Spur Hammer, *Modern*	265.00	380.00	400.00
☐ **Hi Power Standard,** 9mm, Clip Fed, with Spur Hammer, Adjustable Sights, *Modern*	280.00	410.00	435.00
☐ **Hi Power Standard,** 9mm, Clip Fed, with Spur Hammer, with Tangent Sights, *Modern*	475.00	750.00	800.00
☐ **Hi Power Standard,** 9mm, Clip Fed, with Spur Tangent Sights, Slotted for Shoulder Stock, *Modern*	750.00	1100.00	1200.00

Browning M1922

Browning Hi Power 9mm Military

Browning Model 1900

Browning Challenger III

Browning M1903 9mmK

	V.G.	Exc.	Prior Year Exc. Value
☐ **Model 1900,** .32 ACP, Clip Fed, Early Type, No Lanyard Ring, *Curio*	260.00	395.00	395.00
☐ **Model 1900,** .32 ACP, Clip Fed, *Curio*	145.00	250.00	250.00
☐ **Model 1900,** .32 ACP, Clip Fed, Nickel, *Curio*	155.00	285.00	285.00
☐ **Model 1900,** .32 ACP, Clip Fed, Military, *Curio*	180.00	260.00	325.00
☐ **Model 1903,** 9mm Browning Long, Clip Fed, *Curio*	325.00	450.00	450.00
☐ **Model 1903,** 9mm Browning Long, Clip Fed, Light Engraving, *Curio*	800.00	1100.00	1100.00
☐ **Model 1903,** 9mm Browning Long, Clip Fed, Fancy Engraving, *Curio*	1200.00	1600.00	1600.00
☐ **Model 1903,** 9mm Browning Long, Clip Fed, Military, *Curio*	195.00	280.00	365.00
☐ **Model 1903,** 9mm Browning Long, Clip Fed, Cut for Shoulder Stock, Military, *Modern*	260.00	490.00	600.00
☐ **Model 1903,** 9mm Browning Long, Clip Fed, Cut for Shoulder Stock, with Holster Stock, Military, *Modern*	825.00	1300.00	1450.00
☐ **Model 1905,** .25 ACP, Clip Fed, Grip Safety, *Modern*	165.00	260.00	260.00
☐ **Model 1905,** .25 ACP, Clip Fed, Grip Safety, Nickel, *Modern*	315.00	420.00	420.00
☐ **Model 1905,** .25 ACP, Clip Fed, Grip Safety, Russian Contract, Nickel, *Modern*	250.00	375.00	635.00
☐ **Model 1910,** .32 ACP, Clip Fed, Japanese Military, *Curio*	210.00	325.00	525.00
☐ **Model 1910,** .32 ACP, Clip Fed, Peruvian Military, *Curio*	295.00	400.00	700.00
☐ **Model 1910,** .32 ACP, Clip Fed, Syrian Police, *Curio*	250.00	475.00	625.00
☐ **Model 1910,** .32 ACP, Clip Fed, West German Police, *Modern*	200.00	295.00	375.00
☐ **Model 1910,** .32 ACP, Clip Fed, Military, *Curio*	190.00	280.00	325.00
☐ **Model 1910,** .32 ACP, Clip Fed, *Modern*	155.00	215.00	215.00
☐ **Model 1910,** .380 ACP, Clip Fed, *Modern*	170.00	240.00	240.00
☐ **Model 1922,** .32 ACP, Clip Fed, *Modern*	150.00	240.00	240.00
☐ **Model 1922,** .32 ACP, Clip Fed, Nazi-Marked Military, *Modern*	135.00	235.00	260.00
☐ **Model 1922,** .380 ACP, Clip Fed, Military, *Curio*	265.00	390.00	390.00
☐ **Model 1922,** .380 ACP, Clip Fed, Dutch Military, *Curio*	200.00	260.00	275.00
☐ **Model 1922,** .380 ACP, Clip Fed, Turkish Military, *Curio*	245.00	390.00	475.00
☐ **Model 1922,** .380 ACP, Clip Fed, Yugoslavian Military, *Curio*	245.00	390.00	475.00
☐ **Model 1922,** .380 ACP, Clip Fed, *Modern*	150.00	240.00	240.00
☐ **Medalist,** .22 L.R.R.F., Clip Fed, Checkered Wood Target Grips, Wood Forestock, Target Sights, *Modern*	450.00	675.00	675.00
☐ **Medalist,** .22 L.R.R.F., Clip Fed, Renaissance, Checkered Wood Target Grips, Fancy Engraving, Target Sights, *Modern*	2400.00	3200.00	3200.00
☐ **Medalist,** .22 L.R.R.F., Clip Fed, Checkered Wood Target Grips, Wood Forestock, Gold Inlays, Engraved, *Modern*	1800.00	2600.00	2600.00

	V.G.	Exc.	Prior Year Exc. Value
☐ **Medalist International,** .22 L.R.R.F., Clip Fed, Checkered Wood Target Grips, Target Sights, *Modern*	400.00	550.00	550.00
☐ **Medalist International,** .22 L.R.R.F., Clip Fed, Checkered Wood Target Grips, Gold Inlays, Engraved, Target Sights, *Modern*	1750.00	2400.00	2400.00
☐ **Medalist International,** .22 L.R.R.F., Clip Fed, Renaissance, Checkered Wood Target Grips, Fancy Engraving, Target Sights, *Modern*	2300.00	3000.00	3000.00
☐ **Nomad,** .22 L.R.R.F., Clip Fed, Plastic Grips, Adjustable Sights, *Modern*	250.00	375.00	375.00

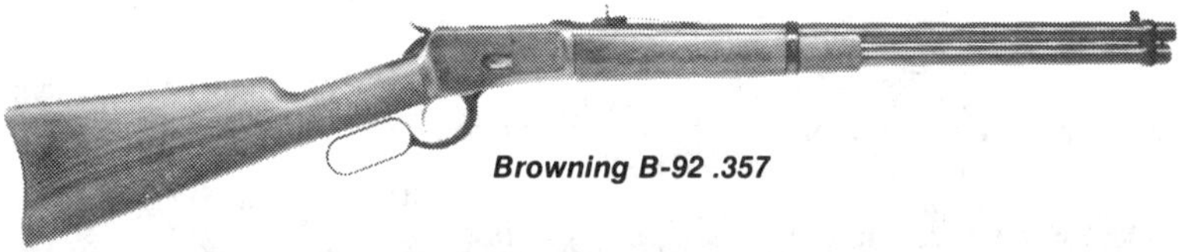

Browning B-92 .357

Browning BAR .22

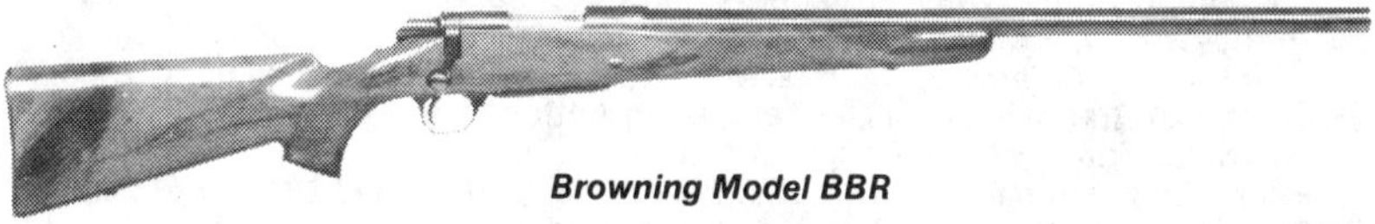

Browning Model BBR

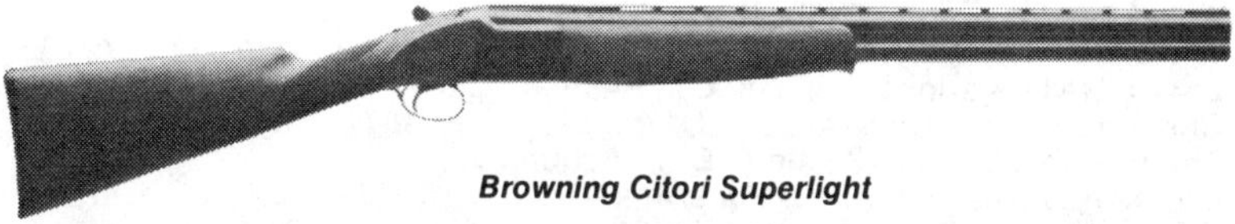

Browning Citori Superlight

Browning B-80

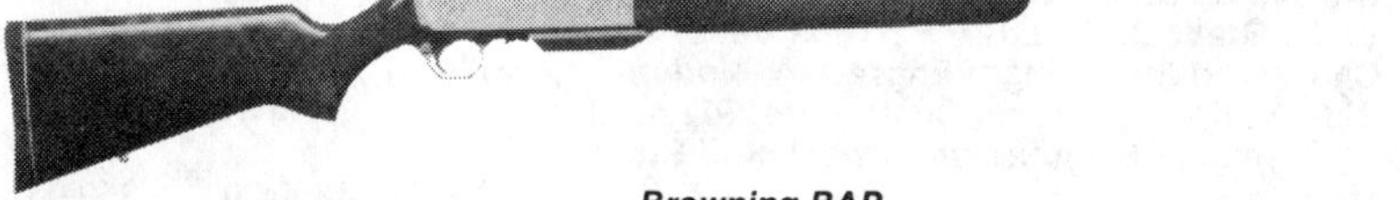

Browning BAR

RIFLE, BOLT ACTION

	V.G.	Exc.	Prior Year Exc. Value
☐ **Model BBR,** Various Calibers, Checkered Stock, *Modern*	300.00	395.00	400.00
☐ **Exhibition Olympian Grade,** Various Calibers, Gold Inlays, Fancy Wood, Fancy Checkering, Engraved, *Modern*	6750.00	8700.00	8750.00
☐ **Medallion Grade,** .458 Win. Mag., Long Action, Fancy Wood, Fancy Checkering, Engraved, Open Rear Sight, *Modern*	975.00	1575.00	1600.00
☐ **Medallion Grade,** Various Calibers, Short Action, Fancy Wood, Fancy Checkering, Engraved, *Modern*	975.00	1475.00	1500.00
☐ **Medallion Grade,** Various Calibers, Long Action, Fancy Wood, Fancy Checkering, Engraved, *Modern*	995.00	1475.00	1500.00
☐ **Medallion Grade,** Various Calibers, Long Action, Magnum, Fancy Wood, Fancy Checkering, Engraved, *Modern*	1075.00	1680.00	1700.00
☐ **Olympian Grade,** .458 Win. Mag., Long Action, Fancy Wood, Fancy Checkering, Engraved, *Modern*	1950.00	2575.00	2600.00
☐ **Olympian Grade,** Various Calibers, Short Action, Fancy Wood, Fancy Checkering, Fancy Engraving, *Modern*	1975.00	2725.00	2750.00
☐ **Olympian Grade,** Various Calibers, Medium Action, Fancy Wood, Fancy Checkering, Fancy Engraving, *Modern*	1700.00	2300.00	2350.00
☐ **Olympian Grade,** Various Calibers, Long Action, Fancy Wood, Fancy Checkering, Fancy Engraving, *Modern*	1825.00	2500.00	2550.00
☐ **Olympian Grade,** Various Calibers, Long Action, Magnum, Fancy Wood, Fancy Checkering, Fancy Engraving, *Modern*	1925.00	2825.00	2850.00
☐ **Safari Grade,** Various Calibers, Short Action, Checkered Stock, *Modern*	375.00	650.00	675.00
☐ **Safari Grade,** Various Calibers, Medium Action, Checkered Stock, *Modern*	465.00	710.00	725.00
☐ **Safari Grade,** Various Calibers, Long Action, Checkered Stock, *Modern*	510.00	815.00	825.00
☐ **Safari Grade,** Various Calibers, Long Action, Magnum, Checkered Stock, *Modern*	600.00	865.00	875.00
☐ **T-Bolt T-1,** .22 L.R.R.F., 5 Shot Clip, Plain, Open Rear Sight, *Modern*	90.00	155.00	160.00
☐ **T-Bolt T-1,** .22 L.R.R.F., 5 Shot Clip, Plain, Open Rear Sight, Left-Hand, *Modern*	115.00	190.00	195.00
☐ **T-Bolt T-2,** .22 L.R.R.F., 5 Shot Clip, Checkered Stock, Fancy Wood, Open Rear Sight, *Modern*	180.00	250.00	260.00

RIFLE, LEVER ACTION

	V.G.	Exc.	Prior Year Exc. Value
☐ **BL-22,** Belgian Manufacture, *Add* **15%-25%**			
☐ **BL-22 Grade 1,** .22 L.R.R.F., Tube Feed, Checkered Stock, *Modern*	145.00	185.00	185.00
☐ **BL-22 Grade 2,** .22 L.R.R.F., Tube Feed, Checkered Stock, Light Engraving, *Modern*	170.00	210.00	210.00
☐ **BLR,** Various Calibers, Center-Fire, Plain, Clip Fed, Belgian Manufacture, Checkered Stock, *Modern*	265.00	350.00	350.00

	V.G.	Exc.	Prior Year Exc. Value
☐ **BLR,** Various Calibers, Center-Fire, Plain, Clip Fed, Checkered Stock, *Modern*	**200.00**	**260.00**	**280.00**
☐ **Model 92,** .357 Mag., Tube Feed, Open Sights, *Modern*	**200.00**	**250.00**	**260.00**
☐ **Model 92,** .44 Mag., Tube Feed, Open Sights, *Modern*	**200.00**	**255.00**	**265.00**
☐ **Model 92 Centennial,** Tube Feed, Open Sights, Commemorative, *Modern*	**235.00**	**335.00**	**350.00**
RIFLE, PERCUSSION			
☐ **J. Browning Mountain Rifle,** Various Calibers, Singleshot, Octagon Barrel, Open Rear Sight, Single Set Trigger, Brass Finish, Reproduction, *Antique*	**225.00**	**350.00**	**325.00**
☐ **J. Browning Mountain Rifle,** Various Calibers, Singleshot, Octagon Barrel, Open Rear Sight, Single Set Trigger, Browned Finish, Reproduction, *Antique*	**225.00**	**350.00**	**325.00**
RIFLE, SEMI-AUTOMATIC			
☐ **Auto-Rifle,** Belgian Mfg., *Add* **20%-30%**			
☐ **Auto-Rifle Grade I,** .22 L.R.R.F., Tube Feed, Takedown, Open Rear Sight, Checkered Stock, *Modern*	**140.00**	**195.00**	**200.00**
☐ **Auto-Rifle Grade I,** .22 Short, Tube Feed, Takedown, Open Rear Sight, Checkered Stock, *Modern*	**140.00**	**205.00**	**210.00**
☐ **Auto-Rifle Grade II,** .22 L.R.R.F., Tube Feed, Takedown, Open Rear Sight, Satin Chrome Receiver, Engraved, *Modern*	**220.00**	**295.00**	**300.00**
☐ **Auto-Rifle Grade III,** .22 L.R.R.F., Takedown, Satin Chrome Receiver, Fancy Wood, Fancy Checkering, Fancy Engraving, Cased, *Modern*	**510.00**	**635.00**	**650.00**
☐ **BAR Grade I,** .22 L.R.R.F., Checkered Stock, *Modern*	**125.00**	**175.00**	**180.00**
☐ **BAR Grade II,** .22 L.R.R.F., Checkered Stock, *Modern*	**125.00**	**250.00**	**265.00**
☐ **BAR,** Various Calibers, Center-Fire, Belgian Mfg., *Add* **15%-25%**			
☐ **BAR,** Various Calibers, Center-Fire, Magnum Calibers, *Add* **10%**			
☐ **BAR Grade 1,** Various Calibers, Center-Fire, Checkered Stock, Plain, *Modern*	**315.00**	**400.00**	**410.00**
☐ **BAR Grade 2,** Various Calibers, Center-Fire, Checkered Stock, Light Engraving, *Modern*	**360.00**	**485.00**	**500.00**
☐ **BAR Grade 3,** Various Calibers, Center-Fire, Fancy Wood, Fancy Checkering, Engraved, *Modern*	**585.00**	**785.00**	**800.00**
☐ **BAR Grade 4,** Various Calibers, Center-Fire, Fancy Wood, Fancy Checkering, Fancy Engraving, *Modern*	**835.00**	**1375.00**	**1400.00**
☐ **BAR Grade 5,** Various Calibers, Center-Fire, Fancy Wood, Fancy Checkering, Fancy Engraving, Gold Inlays, *Modern*	**2225.00**	**2850.00**	**2900.00**
☐ **Classic Light,** 12 Gauge, Engraved With Mallard Ducks, Labrador Retriever and Portrait of John M. Browning, *Modern*	**1175.00**	**1275.00**	**1300.00**

	V.G.	Exc.	Prior Year Exc. Value
☐ **Gold Classic Light,** 12 Gauge, Engraved With Mallard Ducks, Labrador Retriever and Portrait of John M. Browning, *Modern*	6500.00	6700.00	6700.00
RIFLE, SINGLESHOT			
☐ **Model 78,** Various Calibers, Various Barrel Styles, Checkered Stock, *Modern*	270.00	350.00	350.00
☐ **Model 78,** 45-70 Govt., Bicentennial Commemorative, Checkered Stock, *Modern*	1200.00	1900.00	2000.00
RIFLE, DOUBLE BARREL, OVER-UNDER			
☐ **Superposed Continental,** 20 Ga. and 30/06, Engraved, Fancy Wood, Fancy Checkering, *Modern*	2800.00	3550.00	3600.00
☐ **Express Rifle,** 30/06 or .270 Win., Engraved, Fancy Wood, Fancy Checkering, Cased, *Modern*	2150.00	2750.00	2800.00
☐ **Centennial Superposed,** 20 Ga. and 30/06, Engraved, Fancy Checkering, Fancy Wood, Cased, Commemorative, *Modern*	4800.00	7150.00	7400.00
RIFLE, SLIDE ACTION			
☐ **BPR,** .22 L.R.R.F., Grade I, Checkered Stock, *Modern*	120.00	170.00	180.00
☐ **BPR,** .22 Mag., Grade I, Checkered Stock, *Modern*	130.00	185.00	195.00
☐ **BPR,** .22 Mag., Grade II, Checkered Stock, Engraved, *Modern*	175.00	240.00	265.00
SHOTGUN, DOUBLE BARREL, OVER—UNDER			
☐ **Citori,** 12 Ga., Trap Grade, Vent Rib, Checkered Stock, *Modern*	425.00	565.00	575.00
☐ **Citori,** 12 and 20 Gauges, Standard Grade, Vent Rib, Checkered Stock, *Modern*	410.00	540.00	550.00
☐ **Citori,** 12 and 20 Gauges, Skeet Grade, Vent Rib, Checkered Stock, *Modern*	425.00	565.00	575.00
☐ **Citori International,** 12 Ga., Trap Grade, Vent Rib, Checkered Stock, *Modern*	475.00	615.00	625.00
☐ **Citori International,** 12 Ga., Skeet Grade, Vent Rib, Checkered Stock, *Modern*	475.00	615.00	625.00
☐ **Citori Grade II,** Various Gauges, Hunting Model, Engraved, Checkered Stock, Single Selective Trigger, *Modern*	660.00	875.00	885.00
☐ **Citori Grade II,** Trap and Skeet Models, *Add* **10/**			
☐ **Citori Grade V,** Various Gauges, Fancy Engraving, Checkered Stock, Single Selective Trigger, *Modern*	875.00	1380.00	1400.00
☐ **Citori Grade V,** Trap and Skeet Models, *Add* **10/**			
☐ **Classic,** 20 Gauge, 26″ Barrel, Engraved with Bird Dogs, Pheasant and Quail, *Modern*	2400.00	2500.00	2600.00
☐ **Gold Classic,** 20 Gauge, 26″ Barrel, Engraved with Bird Dogs, Pheasant and Quail, *Modern*	8000.00	8500.00	9000.00
☐ **Superposed,** 12 Ga., Broadway Trap Model, Presentation Grade 4, Fancy Engraving, with Sideplates, Gold Inlays, Fancy Checkering, Fancy Wood, *Modern*	5175.00	6500.00	7400.00
☐ **Superposed,** 12 Ga., Lightning Trap Model, Presentation Grade 4, Fancy Engraving, with Sideplates, Gold Inlays, Fancy Checkering, Fancy Wood, *Modern*	5000.00	6250.00	7300.00

	V.G.	Exc.	Prior Year Exc. Value
☐ **Superposed,** 12 Ga., Broadway Trap Model, Presentation Grade 4, Fancy Engraving, with Sideplates, Fancy Checkering, Fancy Wood, *Modern*	4700.00	6200.00	6350.00
☐ **Superposed,** 12 Ga., Lightning Trap Model, Presentation Grade 4, Fancy Engraving, with Sideplates, Fancy Checkering, Fancy Wood, *Modern*	4580.00	5925.00	6200.00
☐ **Superposed,** 12 Ga., Broadway Trap Model, Presentation Grade 3, Fancy Engraving, Gold Inlays, Fancy Checkering, Fancy Wood, *Modern*	4200.00	5450.00	5650.00
☐ **Superposed,** 12 Ga., Lightning Trap Model, Presentation Grade 3, Fancy Engraving, Gold Inlays, Fancy Checkering, Fancy Wood, *Modern*	4150.00	5350.00	5500.00
☐ **Superposed,** 12 Ga., Broadway Trap Model, Presentation Grade 2, Fancy Engraving, Fancy Checkering, Fancy Wood, *Modern*	2700.00	3400.00	3500.00
☐ **Superposed,** 12 Ga., Lightning Trap Model, Presentation Grade 2, Fancy Engraving, Fancy Checkering, Fancy Wood, *Modern*	2600.00	3225.00	3400.00
☐ **Superposed,** 12 Ga., Broadway Trap Model, Presentation Grade 2, Fancy Engraving, Gold Inlays, Fancy Checkering, Fancy Wood, *Modern*	2975.00	3975.00	4200.00
☐ **Superposed,** 12 Ga., Lightning Trap Model, Presentation Grade 2, Fancy Engraving, Gold Inlays, Fancy Checkering, Fancy Wood, *Modern*	2975.00	3975.00	4200.00
☐ **Superposed,** 12 Ga., Broadway Trap Model, Presentation Grade 1, Engraved, Gold Inlays, Fancy Checkering, Fancy Wood, *Modern*	2200.00	2900.00	3100.00
☐ **Superposed,** 12 Ga., Lightning Trap Model, Presentation Grade 1, Engraved, Gold Inlays, Fancy Checkering, Fancy Wood, *Modern*	2150.00	2825.00	3050.00
☐ **Superposed,** 12 Ga., Broadway Trap Model, Presentation Grade 1, Engraved, Fancy Checkering, Fancy Wood, *Modern*	1975.00	2700.00	2800.00
☐ **Superposed,** 12 Ga., Lightning Trap Model, Presentation Grade 1, Engraved, Fancy Checkering, Fancy Wood, *Modern*	1950.00	2650.00	2750.00
☐ **Superposed,** 12 and 20 Gauges, Lightning Skeet Model, Presentation Grade 4, Fancy Engraving, with Sideplates, Gold Inlays, Fancy Checkering, Fancy Wood, *Modern*	4200.00	6900.00	7000.00
☐ **Superposed,** 12 and 20 Gauges, Super-Light Hunting Model, Presentation Grade 4, Extra Barrels, Fancy Engraving, with Sideplates, Gold Inlays, Fancy Checkering, Fancy Wood, *Modern*	6000.00	7500.00	7700.00
☐ **Superposed,** 12 and 20 Gauges, Lightning Hunting Model, Presentation Grade 4, Fancy Engraving, with Sideplates, Gold Inlays, Fancy Checkering, Fancy Wood, Extra Barrels, *Modern*	6000.00	7500.00	7700.00

	V.G.	Exc.	Prior Year Exc. Value
☐ **Superposed,** 12 and 20 Gauges, Lightning Skeet Model, Presentation Grade 4, Fancy Engraving, with Sideplates, Fancy Checkering, Fancy Wood, Extra Barrels, *Modern*	4900.00	7250.00	7300.00
☐ **Superposed,** 12 and 20 Gauges, Super-Light Hunting Model, Presentation Grade 4, Fancy Engraving, with Sideplates, Fancy Checkering, Fancy Wood, Extra Barrels, *Modern*	4675.00	6000.00	7300.00
☐ **Superposed,** 12 and 20 Gauges, Lightning Hunting Model, Presentation Grade 4, Fancy Engraving, with Sideplates, Fancy Checkering, Fancy Wood, Extra Barrels, *Modern*	4675.00	6000.00	7300.00

Browning - Gold Classic Light

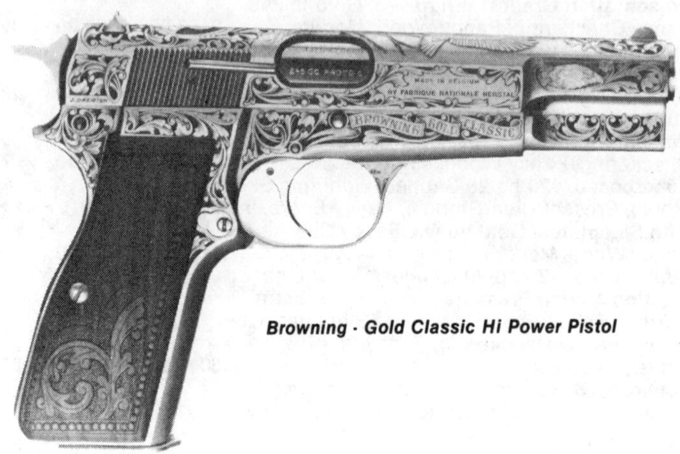

Browning - Gold Classic Hi Power Pistol

	V.G.	Exc.	Prior Year Exc. Value
☐ **Superposed,** 12 and 20 Gauges, Lightning Skeet Model, Presentation Grade 3, Fancy Engraving, Gold Inlays, Fancy Checkering, Fancy Wood, *Modern*	2800.00	3700.00	4850.00
☐ **Superposed,** 12 and 20 Gauges, Super-Light Hunting Model, Presentation Grade 2, Fancy Engraving, Fancy Checkering, Fancy Wood, Extra Barrels, *Modern*	2500.00	3750.00	4500.00
☐ **Superposed,** 12 and 20 Gauges, Lightning Hunting Model, Presentation Grade 2, Fancy Engraving, Fancy Checkering, Fancy Wood, Extra Barrels, *Modern*	2500.00	3750.00	4500.00
☐ **Superposed,** 12 and 20 Gauges, Lightning Skeet Model, Presentation Grade 2, Fancy Engraving, Gold Inlays, Fancy Checkering, Fancy Wood, *Modern*	2650.00	3600.00	4200.00
☐ **Superposed,** 12 and 20 Gauges, Super-Light Hunting Model, Presentation Grade 2, Fancy Engraving, Gold Inlays, Fancy Checkering, Fancy Wood, Extra Barrels, *Modern*	3400.00	4900.00	5500.00
☐ **Superposed,** 12 and 20 Gauges, Lightning Hunting Model, Presentation Grade 2, Fancy Engraving, Gold Inlays, Fancy Checkering, Fancy Wood, Extra Barrels, *Modern*	3400.00	4900.00	5500.00
☐ **Superposed,** 12 and 20 Gauges, Lightning Skeet Model, Presentation Grade 1, Engraved, Gold Inlays, Fancy Checkering, Fancy Wood, *Modern*	2075.00	2975.00	3300.00
☐ **Superposed,** 12 and 20 Gauges, Super-Light Hunting Model, Presentation Grade 1, Engraved, Gold Inlays, Fancy Checkering, Fancy Wood, *Modern*	2025.00	2900.00	3250.00
☐ **Superposed,** 12 and 20 Gauges, Lightning Hunting Model, Presentation Grade 1, Engraved, Gold Inlays, Fancy Checkering, Fancy Wood, *Modern*	1900.00	2850.00	3250.00
☐ **Superposed,** 12 and 20 Gauges, Lightning Skeet Model, Presentation Grade 1, Engraved, Fancy Checkering, Fancy Wood, *Modern*	1875.00	2700.00	2900.00
☐ **Superposed,** 12 and 20 Gauges, Super-Light Hunting Model, Presentation Grade 1, Engraved, Fancy Checkering, Fancy Wood, *Modern*	1875.00	2700.00	2900.00
☐ **Superposed,** 12 and 20 Gauges, Lightning Hunting Model, Presentation Grade 1, Engraved, Fancy Checkering, Fancy Wood, *Modern*	1700.00	2500.00	2800.00
☐ **Superposed,** 28 Ga. or .410 Ga., Lightning Skeet Model, Presentation Grade 4, Fancy Engraving, with Sideplates, Gold Inlays, Fancy Checkering, Fancy Wood, *Modern*	4300.00	5875.00	6750.00
☐ **Superposed,** 28 Ga. or .410 Ga., Lightning Hunting Model, Presentation Grade 4, Fancy Engraving, with Sideplates, Gold Inlays, Fancy Checkering, Fancy Wood, *Modern*	4275.00	5850.00	6700.00
☐ **Superposed,** 28 Ga. or .410 Ga., Lightning Skeet Model, Presentation Grade 4, Fancy Engraving, with Sideplates, Gold Inlays, Fancy Checkering, Fancy Wood, *Modern*	4300.00	5875.00	6750.00

	V.G.	Exc.	Prior Year Exc. Value
☐ **Superposed,** 28 Ga. or .410 Ga., Lightning Hunting Model, Presentation Grade 4, Fancy Engraving, with Sideplates, Gold Inlays, Fancy Checkering, Fancy Wood, *Modern*	4250.00	5800.00	6700.00
☐ **Superposed,** 28 Ga. or .410 Ga., Lightning Skeet Model, Presentation Grade 4, Fancy Engraving, with Sideplates, Fancy Checkering, Fancy Wood, *Modern*	3800.00	4900.00	6000.00
☐ **Superposed,** 28 Ga. or .410 Ga., Lightning Hunting Model, Presentation Grade 4, Fancy Engraving, with Sideplates, Fancy Checkering, Fancy Wood, *Modern*	3800.00	4875.00	5900.00
☐ **Superposed,** 28 Ga. or .410 Ga., Lightning Skeet Model, Presentation Grade 3, Fancy Engraving, Gold Inlays, Fancy Checkering, Fancy Wood, *Modern*	3300.00	4350.00	5150.00
☐ **Superposed,** 28 Ga. or .410 Ga., Lightning Hunting Model, Presentation Grade 3, Fancy Engraving, Gold Inlays, Fancy Checkering, Fancy Wood, *Modern*	3300.00	4350.00	5150.00
☐ **Superposed,** 28 Ga. or .410 Ga., Lightning Skeet Model, Presentation Grade 2, Fancy Engraving, Fancy Checkering, Fancy Wood, *Modern*	2325.00	3150.00	3600.00
☐ **Superposed,** 28 Ga. or .410 Ga., Lightning Hunting Model, Presentation Grade 2, Fancy Engraving, Fancy Checkering, Fancy Wood, *Modern*	2300.00	3175.00	3650.00
☐ **Superposed,** 28 Ga. or .410 Ga., Lightning Skeet Model, Presentation Grade 2, Fancy Engraving, Gold Inlays, Fancy Checkering, Fancy Wood, *Modern*	2775.00	3600.00	4300.00
☐ **Superposed,** 28 Ga. or .410 Ga., Lightning Hunting Model, Presentation Grade 2, Fancy Engraving, Gold Inlays, Fancy Checkering, Fancy Wood, *Modern*	2675.00	3550.00	4300.00
☐ **Superposed,** 28 Ga. or .410 Ga., Lightning Skeet Model, Presentation Grade 1, Engraved, Gold Inlays, Fancy Checkering, Fancy Wood, *Modern*	2150.00	2900.00	3400.00
☐ **Superposed,** 28 Ga. or .410 Ga., Lightning Hunting Model, Presentation Grade 1, Engraved, Gold Inlays, Fancy Checkering, Fancy Wood, *Modern*	2050.00	2825.00	3350.00
☐ **Superposed,** 28 Ga. or .410 Ga., Lightning Skeet Model, Presentation Grade 1, Engraved, Fancy Checkering, Fancy Wood, *Modern*	1750.00	2600.00	3100.00
☐ **Superposed,** 28 Ga. or .410 Ga., Lightning Hunting Model, Presentation Grade 1, Engraved, Fancy Checkering, Fancy Wood, *Modern*	1625.00	2425.00	2900.00
☐ **Superposed,** Various Gauges, Presentation Grade 4, Extra Sets of Barrels, *Add for each:* **$1200.00-$1700.00**			
☐ **Superposed,** Various Gauges, Presentation Grade 3, Extra Sets of Barrels, *Add for each:* **$900.00-$1500.00**			

	V.G.	Exc.	Prior Year Exc. Value
☐ **Superposed,** Various Gauges, Presentation Grade 2, Extra Sets of Barrels, *Add for each:* **$825.00-$1250.00**			
☐ **Superposed,** Various Gauges, Presentation Grade 1, Extra Sets of Barrels, *Add for each:* **$725.00-$1100.00**			
☐ **Superposed,** Pre-1977, Lightning Skeet, *Add* **5%-10%**			
☐ **Superposed,** Pre-1977, Extra Barrel, *Add* **35%-40%**			
☐ **Superposed,** Pre-1977, 4-Barrel, Skeet Set, *Add* **275%-300%**			
☐ **Superposed,** Pre-War, Raised Solid Rib, *Add* **$60.00-$90.00**			
☐ **Superposed,** Pre-1977, Vent Rib, Pre-War, *Add* **10%-15%**			
☐ **Superposed,** Pre-1977, Super-Light Lightning, *Add* **15%-20%**			
☐ **Superposed,** Pre-1977, Lightning Trap Model, *Add* **5%-10%**			
☐ **Superposed,** Pre-1977, Broadway Trap Model, *Add* **8%-13%**			
☐ **Superposed,** For .410 or 28 Gauge, *Add* **15%-25%**			
☐ **Superposed,** For 20 Gauge, *Add* **10%-15%**			
☐ **Superposed,** Various Gauges, Pre-1977, Super Exhibition Grade, Fancy Wood, Fancy Checkering, Fancy Engraving, Gold Inlays, *Modern*	**20000.00**	**27500.00**	**31000.00**
☐ **Superposed,** Various Gauges, Pre-1977, Field Grade, Engraved, Checkered Stock, Vent Rib, Single Selective Trigger, *Modern*	**900.00**	**1250.00**	**1575.00**
☐ **Superposed,** Various Gauges, Pre-1977, Pointer Grade, Fancy Engraving, Fancy Checkering, Single Selective Trigger, *Modern*	**2000.00**	**2500.00**	**2975.00**
☐ **Superposed,** Various Gauges, Pre-1977, Pigeon Grade Hunting Model, Satin Nickel-Plated Frame, Fancy Engraving, Fancy Checkering, Fancy Wood, *Modern*	**1725.00**	**2375.00**	**2600.00**
☐ **Superposed,** Various Gauges, Pre-1977, Diana Grade Hunting Model, Satin Nickel-Plated Frame, Fancy Engraving, Fancy Checkering, Fancy Wood, *Modern*	**2150.00**	**2875.00**	**3300.00**
☐ **Superposed,** Various Gauges, Pre-1977, Midas Grade Hunting Model, Fancy Engraving, Fancy Checkering, Fancy Wood, Gold Inlays, *Modern*	**3100.00**	**4000.00**	**4500.00**
☐ **Superposed,** Various Gauges, Pre-1977, Exhibition Grade, Fancy Engraving, Fancy Checkering, Fancy Wood, Gold Inlays, *Modern*	**6500.00**	**9200.00**	**10750.00**
☐ **Superposed Bicentennial,** Fancy Engraving, Gold Inlays, Fancy Wood, Fancy Checkering, Cased, Commemorative, *Modern*	**6400.00**	**9200.00**	**10650.00**
☐ **Grand Liege,** 12 Ga., Engraved, Single Trigger, Checkered Stock, *Modern*	**500.00**	**675.00**	**750.00**
☐ **Liege,** 12 Ga., Engraved, Single Trigger, Checkered Stock, *Modern*	**350.00**	**475.00**	**575.00**

Browning High Power Standard, Adj. Sights

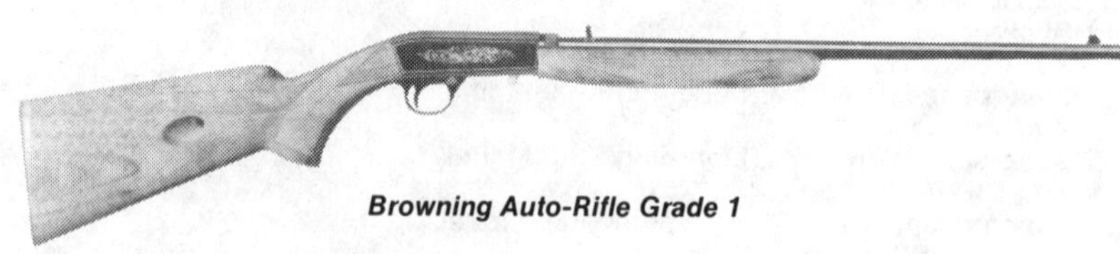

Browning Auto-Rifle Grade 1

	V.G.	Exc.	Prior Year Exc. Value
☐ **ST-100,** 12 Ga., Trap Special, Engraved, Checkered Stock, *Modern*	**1675.00**	**2200.00**	**2650.00**
SHOTGUN, DOUBLE BARREL, SIDE-BY-SIDE			
☐ **B-SS,** 12 and 20 Gauges, Checkered Stock, Field Grade, *Modern*	**330.00**	**435.00**	**460.00**
☐ **B-SS,** 12 and 20 Gauges, Checkered Stock, Sporter Grade, *Modern*	**330.00**	**435.00**	**460.00**
☐ **B-SS,** 12 and 20 Gauges, Checkered Stock, Grade II, Engraved, *Modern*	**550.00**	**675.00**	**745.00**
SHOTGUN, SEMI-AUTOMATIC			
☐ **Auto-5,** For Belgian Make *Add* **15%-25%**			
☐ **Auto-5,** 12 Ga., Trap Grade, Vent Rib, Checkered Stock, *Modern*	**320.00**	**435.00**	**475.00**
☐ **Auto-5,** 12 and 20 Gauges, Magnum, Checkered Stock, Light Engraving, Plain Barrel, *Modern*	**310.00**	**420.00**	**460.00**
☐ **Auto-5,** 12 and 20 Gauges, Skeet Grade, Checkered Stock, Light Engraving, Vent Rib, *Modern*	**315.00**	**445.00**	**475.00**
☐ **Auto-5,** 16 Ga. 2 9/16", Pre-WW2, Checkered Stock, Light Engraving, Plain Barrel, *Modern*	**375.00**	**510.00**	**565.00**
☐ **Auto-5,** 16 Gauge, Sweet Sixteen, Lightweight, Checkered Stock, Light Engraving, Plain Barrel, *Modern*	**390.00**	**520.00**	**565.00**
☐ **Auto-5,** Various Gauges, Lightweight, Checkered Stock, Light Engraving, Plain Barrel, *Modern*	**310.00**	**420.00**	**460.00**
☐ **Auto-5,** Various Gauges, Buck Special, Checkered Stock, Light Engraving, Plain Barrel, *Modern*	**330.00**	**445.00**	**490.00**

	V.G.	Exc.	Prior Year Exc. Value
☐ **Auto-5,** Various Gauges, Vent Rib, *Add* **$35.00-$50.00**			
☐ **Auto-5,** Various Gauges, Raised Solid Rib, *Add* **$30.00-$50.00**			
☐ **Auto-5,** Various Gauges, Diana Grade, Pre-WW2, Plain Barrel, Fancy Engraving, *Modern*	675.00	1000.00	1200.00
☐ **Auto-5,** Various Gauges, Midas Grade, Pre-WW2, Plain Barrel, Fancy Engraving, Gold Inlays, *Modern*	800.00	1275.00	1600.00
☐ **Auto-5,** Various Gauges, Grade V, Plain Barrel, Fancy Engraving, *Modern*	1850.00	2500.00	2900.00
☐ **B-80,** 12 Gauge, Lightweight, Checkered Stock, Vent Rib, *Modern*	290.00	365.00	420.00
☐ **Double-Auto,** 12 Ga., Trap Model, *Add* **10%-15%**			
☐ **Double-Auto,** 12 Gauge, Checkered Stock, Engraved, Plain Barrel, *Modern*	200.00	275.00	325.00
☐ **Double-Auto,** 12 and 20 Gauges, Lightweight, Checkered Stock, Engraved, Plain Barrel, *Modern*	230.00	310.00	365.00
☐ **Double-Auto,** Vent Rib, *Add* **$35.00-$50.00**			
☐ **Double-Auto,** Skeet Model, *Add* **10%-15%**			
☐ **Model 2000,** 12 Ga., Trap Grade, Vent Rib, Tube Feed, Checkered Stock, *Modern*	265.00	350.00	390.00
☐ **Model 2000,** 12 and 20 Gauges, Vent Rib, Tube Feed, Checkered Stock, *Modern*	225.00	310.00	340.00
☐ **Model 2000,** 12 and 20 Gauges, Buck Special, Open Rear Sight, Tube Feed, Checkered Stock, *Modern*	240.00	320.00	350.00
☐ **Model 2000,** 12 and 20 Gauges, Skeet Grade, Vent Rib, Tube Feed, Checkered Stock, *Modern*	265.00	350.00	390.00
☐ **Model 2000 Montreal Olympic,** 12 Ga., Trap Grade, Vent Rib, Engraved, Gold Inlays, Commemorative, Tube Feed, Checkered Stock, *Modern*	1175.00	1750.00	2000.00
SHOTGUN, SINGLESHOT			
☐ **BT-99,** 12 Ga., Trap Grade, Vent Rib, with extra Single Trap Barrel, Checkered Stock, Engraved, *Modern*	425.00	550.00	675.00
☐ **BT-99,** 12 Ga., Pigeon Grade, Checkered Stock, Engraved, Vent Rib, *Modern*	650.00	900.00	1050.00
☐ **BT-99,** 12 Ga., Trap Grade, Vent Rib, Checkered Stock, Engraved, *Modern*	320.00	410.00	450.00
SHOTGUN, SLIDE ACTION			
☐ **BPS,** 12 Ga., Checkered Stock, Vent Rib, *Modern*	175.00	240.00	275.00
☐ **BPS,** 12 Ga., Invector Trap, Checkered Stock, Vent Rib, *Modern*	210.00	275.00	315.00
☐ **BPS,** 12 Ga., Buck Special, Rifle Sights, *Modern*	200.00	260.00	300.00

BRUTUS

Made by Hood Firearms Co. c. 1875-76

HANDGUN, REVOLVER

	V.G.	Exc.	Prior Year Exc. Value
☐ **.22 Short R.F.**, 7 Shot, Spur Trigger, Solid Frame, Single Action, *Antique*	95.00	160.00	165.00

	V.G.	Exc.	Prior Year Exc. Value
BSA			
Birmingham Small Arms, Ltd., Birmingham, England. From 1885			
AUTOMATIC WEAPON, LIGHT MACHINE GUN			
☐ **Lewis Gun**, .303 British, Drum Magazine, Bipod, *Class 3*	1,600.00	2,350.00	2,100.00
RIFLE, BOLT ACTION			
☐ **Model CF-2**, Various Calibers, Sporting Rifle, Checkered Stock, Open Rear Sight, *Modern*	235.00	350.00	345.00
☐ **Model CF-2**, Various Calibers, Sporting Rifle, Checkered Stock, Double Set Triggers, Open Rear Sight, *Modern*	265.00	400.00	385.00
☐ **Imperial**, Various Calibers, Sporting Rifle, Muzzle Brake, Checkered Stock, Open Rear Sight, *Modern*	160.00	265.00	250.00
☐ **Imperial**, Various Calibers, Sporting Rifle, Muzzle Brake, Checkered Stock, Open Rear Sight, Lightweight, *Modern*	185.00	275.00	265.00
☐ **Majestic Deluxe**, .458 Win. Mag., Sporting Rifle, Muzzle Brake, Lightweight, Checkered Stock, Open Rear Sight, *Modern*	215.00	320.00	310.00
☐ **Majestic Deluxe**, Various Calibers, Sporting Rifle, Muzzle Brake, Lightweight, Checkered Stock, Open Rear Sight, *Modern*	175.00	270.00	260.00
☐ **Majestic Deluxe**, Various Calibers, Sporting Rifle, Checkered Stock, Open Rear Sight, *Modern*	165.00	270.00	255.00
☐ **Monarch Deluxe**, Various Calibers, Sporting Rifle, Checkered Stock, Open Rear Sight, *Modern*	185.00	295.00	275.00
☐ **Monarch Deluxe**, Various Calibers, Varmint, Heavy Barrel, Checkered Stock, Open Rear Sight, *Modern*	200.00	295.00	275.00
RIFLE, SINGLESHOT			
☐ **#12 Martini**, .22 L.R.R.F., Target, Target Sights, Checkered Stock, *Modern*	195.00	295.00	275.00
☐ **#12/15 Martini**, .22 L.R.R.F., Target, Target Sights, Target Stock, *Modern*	245.00	340.00	325.00
☐ **#12/15 Martini**, .22 L.R.R.F., Target, Target Sights, Target Stock, Heavy Barrel, *Modern*	250.00	375.00	350.00
☐ **#13 Martini**, .22 Hornet, Sporting Rifle, Checkered Stock, *Modern*	260.00	360.00	345.00
☐ **#13 Martini**, .22 L.R.R.F., Target, Target Sights, Checkered Stock, *Modern*	190.00	265.00	250.00
☐ **#13 Martini**, .22 L.R.R.F., Sporting Rifle, Checkered Stock, *Modern*	180.00	255.00	245.00
☐ **#15 Martini**, .22 L.R.R.F., Target, Target Sights, Target Stock, *Modern*	335.00	430.00	415.00
☐ **Centurian Martini**, .22 L.R.R.F., Target, Target Sights, Target Stock, Target Barrel, *Modern*	245.00	365.00	340.00
☐ **International Martini**, .22 L.R.R.F., Target, Target Sights, Heavy Barrel, Target Stock, *Modern*	250.00	380.00	365.00
☐ **International MK 2 Martini**, .22 L.R.R.F., Target, Target Sights, Target Stock, *Modern*	250.00	400.00	375.00
☐ **International MK 2 Martini**, .22 L.R.R.F., Target, Target Sights, Target Stock, Heavy Barrel, *Modern*	255.00	370.00	355.00

	V.G.	Exc.	Prior Year Exc. Value
☐ **International MK 3 Martini**, .22 L.R.R.F., Target, Target Sights, Target Stock, Heavy Barrel, *Modern*	275.00	395.00	380.00
☐ **Mark V**, .22 L.R.R.F., Heavy Barrel, Target Rifle. Target Sights, Target Stock, *Modern*	325.00	475.00	450.00
☐ **Martini I S U**, .22 L.R.R.F., Target Rifle, Target Sights, Target Stock, *Modern*	325.00	475.00	450.00
RIFLE, SLIDE ACTION			
☐ **.22 L.R.R.F.**, Clip Fed, Takedown, *Modern*	75.00	135.00	130.00
☐ **.22 L.R.R.F.**, Tube Feed, Takedown, *Modern*	85.00	150.00	140.00

BUDDY ARMS

Fort Worth, Tex. during the early 1960's.

	V.G.	Exc.	Prior Year Exc. Value
HANDGUN, DOUBLE BARREL, OVER-UNDER			
☐ **Double Deuce**, .22 L.R.R.F., Remington Derringer Copy, *Modern*	40.00	60.00	60.00

Budischowski TP-70 .25

BUDISCHOWSKY

Made by Norton Armament (Norarmco), Mt. Clemens, Mich. 1973-1977.

	V.G.	Exc.	Prior Year Exc. Value
HANDGUN, SEMI-AUTOMATIC			
☐ **TP-70**, .22 L.R.R.F., Clip Fed, Double Action, Pocket Pistol, Stainless Steel, Hammer, *Modern*	250.00	375.00	350.00
☐ **TP-70**, .25 ACP, Clip Fed, Double Action, Pocket Pistol, Stainless Steel, Hammer, Presentation, Custom Serial Number, *Curio*	975.00	1,500.00	1,500.00
☐ **TP-70**, .25 ACP, Clip Fed, Double Action, Pocket Pistol, Stainless Steel, Hammer, *Modern*	200.00	325.00	300.00

BUFALO

Gabilondo y Cia., Elgoibar, Spain

	V.G.	Exc.	Prior Year Exc. Value
HANDGUN, SEMI-AUTOMATIC			
☐ **Model 1920**, .25 ACP, Clip Fed, *Modern*	80.00	130.00	125.00
☐ **Pocket**, .32 ACP, Clip Fed, *Modern*	80.00	135.00	125.00

BUFFALO ARMS

Tonawanda, N.Y.

	V.G.	Exc.	Prior Year Exc. Value
HANDGUN, DOUBLE BARREL, OVER-UNDER			
☐ **Model 1**, .357 Mag., Hammer, Blue or Nickel, *Modern*	65.00	100.00	95.00

BUFFALO BILL

Maker Unknown, Sold by Homer Fisher Co.

	V.G.	Exc.	Prior Year Exc. Value
HANDGUN, REVOLVER			
☐ **.22 Short R.F.**, 7 Shot, Spur Trigger, Solid Frame, Single Action, *Antique*	90.00	160.00	160.00

BUFFALO STAND

Tradename used by ManuFrance.

	V.G.	Exc.	Prior Year Exc. Value
HANDGUN, SINGLESHOT			
☐ **Bolt Action**, .22 L.R.R.F., Target Pistol, Modern	65.00	120.00	115.00

BUCHEL, ERNST FRIEDRICH

Zella Mehlis, Germany, 1919-1926.

	V.G.	Exc.	Prior Year Exc. Value
☐ **HANDGUN, SINGLESHOT**			
☐ **Luna**, .22 L.R.R.F., Rotary Breech, Free Pistol, Set Triggers, Light Engraving, *Curio*	700.00	1,000.00	925.00
☐ **Practice**, .22 Short R.F., Warnant Action, Hammer, Target Pistol, *Curio*	200.00	295.00	275.00
☐ **Model W.B.**, .22 L.R.R.F., Roux Action, Target Pistol, Hammerless, Tip-Down Barrel, *Curio*	335.00	495.00	450.00
☐ **Tell I**, .22 L.R.R.F., Rotary Breech, Free Pistol, Set Triggers, Light Engraving, *Curio*	700.00	1,000.00	925.00
☐ **Tell II**, .22 L.R.R.F., Rotary Breech, Free Pistol, Set Triggers, Light Engraving, *Curio*	700.00	1,000.00	925.00

BUHAG

Buchsenmacher-Handwerkgenossenschaft M.B.H. of Suhl, East Germany.

	V.G.	Exc.	Prior Year Exc. Value
HANDGUN, SEMI-AUTOMATIC			
☐ **Olympia**, .22 Short R.F., Clip Fed, Target Pistol, *Modern*	360.00	545.00	525.00

BULL DOZER

Made by Norwich Pistol Co., Sold by J. McBride & Co. c. 1875-1883.

	V.G.	Exc.	Prior Year Exc. Value
HANDGUN, REVOLVER			
☐ **.22 Short R.F.**, 7 Shot, Spur Trigger, Solid Frame, Single Action, *Antique*	90.00	165.00	160.00
☐ **.38 Short R.F.**, 5 Shot, Spur Trigger, Solid Frame, Single Action, *Antique*	95.00	180.00	175.00
☐ **.41 Short R.F.**, 5 Shot, Spur Trigger, Solid Frame, Single Action, *Antique*	125.00	200.00	200.00
☐ **.44 Short R.F.**, 5 Shot, Spur Trigger, Solid Frame, Single Action, *Antique*	175.00	260.00	250.00

BULLARD REPEATING ARMS CO.

Springfield, Mass. 1887-1889.

	V.G.	Exc.	Prior Year Exc. Value
RIFLE, LEVER ACTION			
☐ **Military**, Full Stocked, with Bayonet, Open Rear Sight, *Antique*	1,925.00	2,800.00	2,700.00

	V.G.	Exc.	Prior Year Exc. Value
☐ **Military**, Full Stocked, with Bayonet, Open Rear Sight, Carbine, *Antique*	**1,925.00**	**2,800.00**	**2,700.00**
☐ **Various Calibers**, Small Frame, Tube Feed, Round Barrel, Plain, Open Rear Sight, Sporting Rifle, *Antique*	**450.00**	**725.00**	**695.00**
☐ **Various Calibers**, Tube Feed, Round Barrel, Plain, Open Rear Sight, Sporting Rifle, *Antique*	**545.00**	**900.00**	**850.00**

☐ **Various Calibers**, Light Engraving, *Add* **$55.00-$160.00**

☐ **Various Calibers**, Medium Engraving, *Add* **$220.00-$435.00**

☐ **Various Calibers**, Ornate Engraving, *Add* **$775.00-$1,150.00**

☐ **Various Calibers**, Full Nickel Plating, **$55.00-$80.00**

☐ **Various Calibers**, for Fancy Wood, *Add* **$30.00-$50.00**

☐ **Various Calibers**, for Standard Checkering, *Add* **$35.00-$50.00**

☐ **Various Calibers**, Fancy Checkering, *Add* **$75.00-$110.00**

☐ **Various Calibers**, Octagon Barrel, *Add* **$30.00-$55.00**

☐ **Various Calibers**, Half-Octagon Barrel, *Add* **$35.00-$65.00**

☐ **Various Calibers**, Target Sights, *Add* **$125.00-$185.00**

☐ **Various Calibers**, for Lyman Sights, *Add* **$45.00-$75.00**

☐ **Various Calibers**, for Express Sights, *Add* **$110.00-$160.00**

RIFLE, SINGLESHOT

	V.G.	Exc.	Prior Year Exc. Value
☐ **Military**, Full-Stocked, with Bayonet, Open Rear Sight, *Antique*	**975.00**	**1,550.00**	**1,400.00**
☐ **Military**, Full-Stocked, with Bayonet, Open Rear Sight, Carbine, *Antique*	**975.00**	**1,550.00**	**1,400.00**
☐ **Various Calibers**, Schuetzen Target Rifle, Octagon Barrel, Target Sights, Swiss Buttplate, Checkered Stock, *Antique*	**995.00**	**1,975.00**	**1,850.00**
☐ **Various Calibers**, Sporting Rifle, Octagon Barrel, Open Rear Sight, *Antique*	**550.00**	**845.00**	**800.00**
☐ **Various Rimfires**, Target Rifle, Octagon Barrel, Target Sights, Swiss Buttplate, Checkered Stock, *Antique*	**600.00**	**975.00**	**900.00**
☐ **Various Rimfires**, Sporting Rifle, Octagon Barrel, Open Rear Sight, *Antique*	**550.00**	**925.00**	**850.00**

BULLDOG

Made by Forehand & Wadsworth.

HANDGUN, REVOLVER

	V.G.	Exc.	Prior Year Exc. Value
☐ **.32 S & W**, 7 Shot, Double Action, Solid Frame, *Modern*	**60.00**	**100.00**	**95.00**
☐ **.38 S & W**, 6 Shot, Double Action, Solid Frame, *Modern*	**60.00**	**100.00**	**95.00**

	V.G.	Exc.	Prior Year Exc. Value
☐ **.44 S & W**, 5 Shot, Double Action, Solid Frame, *Modern*	**75.00**	**130.00**	**125.00**

BULLS EYE
Maker Unknown c. 1875.

HANDGUN, REVOLVER

	V.G.	Exc.	Prior Year Exc. Value
☐ **.22 Short R.F.**, 7 Shot, Spur Trigger, Solid Frame, Single Action, *Antique*	**90.00**	**155.00**	**150.00**

BULWARK
Beistegui Hermanos, Eibar, Spain.

HANDGUN, SEMI-AUTOMATIC

	V.G.	Exc.	Prior Year Exc. Value
☐ **.25 ACP**, External Hammer, Clip Fed, Blue, *Curio*	**210.00**	**335.00**	**320.00**
☐ **.25 ACP**, Hammerless, Clip Fed, Blue, *Curio*	**85.00**	**150.00**	**140.00**
☐ **.32 ACP**, External Hammer, Clip Fed, Blue, *Curio*	**180.00**	**295.00**	**285.00**
☐ **.32 ACP**, Hammerless, Clip Fed, Blue, *Curio*	**95.00**	**150.00**	**145.00**

BUMFORD
London, England 1730-1760.

HANDGUN, FLINTLOCK

	V.G.	Exc.	Prior Year Exc. Value
☐ **.38**, Pocket Pistol, Boxlock, Queen Anne Style, Screw Barrel, Silver Inlay, *Antique*	**500.00**	**775.00**	**725.00**

BURGESS, ANDREW
Oswego, N.Y. 1874-1887.

RIFLE, LEVER ACTION

	V.G.	Exc.	Prior Year Exc. Value
☐ **Model 1876**, .45-70 Government, Tube Feed, Octagon Barrel, *Antique*	**775.00**	**1,700.00**	**1,600.00**

RIFLE, SLIDE ACTION

	V.G.	Exc.	Prior Year Exc. Value
☐ **Various Calibers**, Folding Gun, With Case, *Antique*	**835.00**	**1,375.00**	**1,250.00**

SHOTGUN, SLIDE ACTION

	V.G.	Exc.	Prior Year Exc. Value
☐ **12 Ga.**, Takedown, Solid Rib, Light Engraving, *Antique*	**200.00**	**395.00**	**375.00**
☐ **12 Ga.**, Folding Gun, With Case, *Antique*	**445.00**	**725.00**	**675.00**

BUSHMASTER
Gwinn Arms Co., Winston-Salem, N.C.

AUTOMATIC WEAPON, MACHINE-PISTOL

	V.G.	Exc.	Prior Year Exc. Value
☐ **.223 Rem.**, Clip Fed, Commercial, *Class 3*	**375.00**	**500.00**	**500.00**

HANDGUN, SEMI-AUTOMATIC

	V.G.	Exc.	Prior Year Exc. Value
☐ **Bushmaster**, .223 Rem., Clip Fed, *Modern*	**225.00**	**330.00**	**325.00**

RIFLE, SEMI-AUTOMATIC

	V.G.	Exc.	Prior Year Exc. Value
☐ **.223 Rem.**, Clip Fed, Wood Stock, *Modern*	**200.00**	**300.00**	**300.00**
☐ **.223 Rem.**, Clip Fed, Folding Stock, *Modern*	**220.00**	**335.00**	**330.00**

BUSOMS
Spain c. 1780.

HANDGUN, MIQUELET-LOCK

	V.G.	Exc.	Prior Year Exc. Value
☐ **.70 Pair**, Belt Pistol, Belt Hook, Engraved, Brass Furniture, *Antique*	**1,850.00**	**2,450.00**	**2,350.00**

	V.G.	Exc.	Prior Year Exc. Value

BUSTINDUI, AUGUSTIN
Toledo, Spain c. 1765.

HANDGUN, MIQUELET-LOCK

	V.G.	Exc.	Prior Year Exc. Value
☐ **Pair**, Locks by Guisasola, Half-Octagon Barrel, *Antique*	3,775.00	5,250.00	4,900.00

BUSTINDIU, JUAN ESTEBAN
Eibar, Spain c. 1775.

HANDGUN, MIQUELET-LOCK

	V.G.	Exc.	Prior Year Exc. Value
☐ **Pair**, Half-Octagon Barrel, Silver Inlay, Light Decoration, *Antique*	2,950.00	4,000.00	3,850.00

C.A.C.
Made by A.I.G. Corp., North Haven, Conn. Distributed by Mossberg.

HANDGUN, SEMI-AUTOMATIC

	V.G.	Exc.	Prior Year Exc. Value
☐ **Combat**, .45 ACP, Clip Fed, Stainless Steel, *Modern*	325.00	440.00	425.00

CADET
Sold by Maltby-Curtis Co.

HANDGUN, REVOLVER

	V.G.	Exc.	Prior Year Exc. Value
☐ **.22 Long R.F.**, 7 Shot, Single Action, Solid Frame, Spur Trigger, *Antique*	85.00	145.00	140.00

CALDERWOOD, WILLIAM
Phila., Pa. 1808-1816. See Kentucky Rifles and Pistols and U.S. Military

CANADIAN MILITARY

HANDGUN, SEMI-AUTOMATIC

	V.G.	Exc.	Prior Year Exc. Value
☐ **Hi Power Inglis #1 Mk I,** 9mm, Tangent Sights, Slotted for Shoulder Stock, Military, *Modern*	695.00	1075.00	995.00
☐ **Hi Power Inglis #1 Mk I*** 9mm, Tangent Sights, Slotted for Shoulder Stock, Military, *Modern*	595.00	965.00	900.00
☐ **Hi Power Inglis #2 Mk I,** 9mm, Fixed Sights, Military, *Modern*	535.00	800.00	750.00
☐ **Hi Power Inglis #2 Mk I***, 9mm, Tangent Sights, Slotted for Shoulder Stock, Military, *Modern*	395.00	625.00	585.00

RIFLE, BOLT ACTION

	V.G.	Exc.	Prior Year Exc. Value
☐ **SMLE #4 Mk.1***, .303 British, Clip Fed, *Curio*	70.00	125.00	175.00
☐ **1907 MK 2 Ross,** .303 British, Full-Stocked, Military, *Modern*	100.00	170.00	220.00
☐ **1910 MK 3 Ross,** .303 British, Full-Stocked, Military, *Modern*	105.00	185.00	240.00

CAPT. JACK
Made by Hopkins & Allen 1871-1875.

HANDGUN, REVOLVER

	V.G.	Exc.	Prior Year Exc. Value
☐ **.22 Short R.F.**, 7 Shot, Spur Trigger, Solid Frame, Single Action, *Antique*	85.00	155.00	150.00

CAROLINE ARMS

Made by Crescent Firearms Co. 1892-1900.

	V.G.	Exc.	Prior Year Exc. Value
SHOTGUN, DOUBLE BARREL, SIDE-BY-SIDE			
☐ **Various Gauges**, Outside Hammers, Damascus Barrel, *Modern*	85.00	155.00	150.00
☐ **Various Gauges**, Hammerless, Steel Barrel, *Modern*	100.00	180.00	175.00
☐ **Various Gauges**, Hammerless, Damascus Barrel, *Modern*	75.00	155.00	150.00
☐ **Various Gauges**, Outside Hammers, Steel Barrel, *Modern*	95.00	180.00	175.00
SHOTGUN, SINGLESHOT			
☐ **Various Gauges**, Hammer, Steel Barrel, *Modern*	45.00	75.00	75.00

CARPENTER, JOHN

Lancaster, Pa. 1771-1790. See Kentucky Rifles.

CARROLL, LAWRENCE

Philadelphia, Pa. 1786-1790. See Kentucky Rifles.

CARTRIDGE FIREARMS

Unknown Makers.

	V.G.	Exc.	Prior Year Exc. Value
HANDGUN, REVOLVER			
☐ **11mm Pinfire**, Lefaucheux Military Style, *Antique*	150.00	235.00	225.00
☐ **11mm Pinfire**, Lefaucheux Military Style, Engraved, *Antique*	225.00	395.00	350.00
☐ **7mm Pinfire**, Pocket Pistol, Folding Trigger, Engraved, *Antique*	80.00	135.00	125.00
☐ **.22 Short**, Small Pocket Pistol, Folding Trigger, *Modern*	60.00	120.00	110.00
☐ **.22 Short**, Small Pocket Pistol, Double Action, *Modern*	50.00	90.00	85.00
☐ **.25 A.C.P.**, Small Pocket Pistol, Folding Trigger, *Modern*	60.00	120.00	110.00
☐ **.25 A.C.P.**, Small Pocket Pistol, Double Action, *Modern*	45.00	90.00	85.00
☐ **Belgian Proofs**, Various Calibers, Top Break, Double Action, Medium Quality, *Modern*	65.00	95.00	90.00
☐ **Belgian Proofs**, Various Calibers, Top Break, Double Action, Engraved, Medium Quality, *Modern*	75.00	125.00	110.00
☐ **Belgian Proofs**, Various Calibers, Top Break, Double Action, Folding Trigger, Medium Quality, *Modern*	60.00	95.00	85.00
☐ **Chinese Copy of Colt Police Positive**, .38 Special, Double Action, Solid Frame, Swing-Out Cylinder, Low Quality, *Modern*	55.00	95.00	95.00
☐ **Chinese Copy of Police Positive**, 9mm Luger, Double Action, Solid Frame, Swing-Out Cylinder, Low Quality, *Modern*	45.00	80.00	80.00
☐ **Copy of Colt SAA**, Various Calibers, Western Style, Single Action, Low Quality, *Modern*	60.00	100.00	100.00
☐ **Copy of Colt SAA**, Various Calibers, Western Style, Single Action, Medium Quality, *Modern*	80.00	130.00	125.00

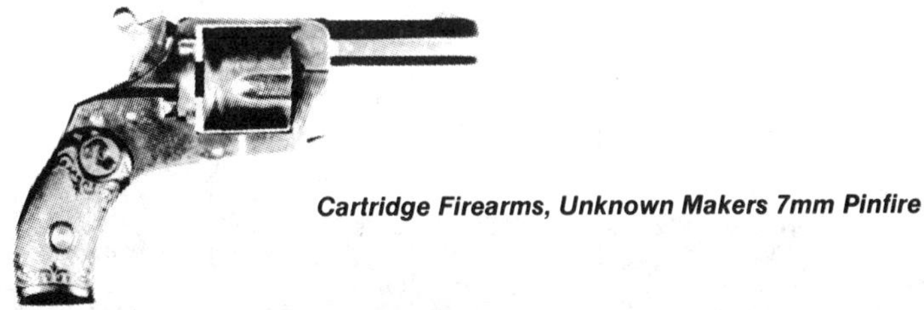

Cartridge Firearms, Unknown Makers 7mm Pinfire

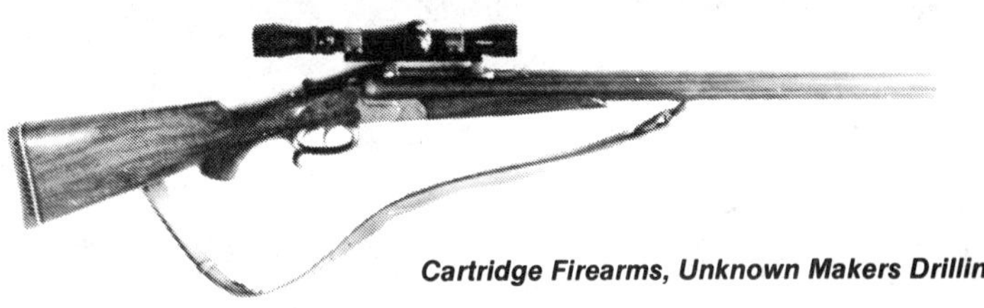

Cartridge Firearms, Unknown Makers Drilling

	V.G.	Exc.	Prior Year Exc. Value
☐ **Chinese Copy of S&W M-10**, .38 Special, Double Action, Solid Frame, Swing-Out Cylinder, Low Quality, *Modern*	50.00	95.00	90.00
☐ **Spanish Copy of S&W M-10**, .38 Special, Double Action, Solid Frame, Swing-Out Cylinder, Low Quality, *Modern*	55.00	95.00	95.00
☐ **Copy of S&W Russian Model**, Various Calibers, Break, Single Action, Low Quality, *Antique*	80.00	140.00	125.00
☐ **Copy of S&W Russian Model**, Various Calibers, Top Break, Single Action, Medium Quality, *Antique*	150.00	245.00	200.00
☐ **Copy of S&W Russian Model**, Various Calibers, Top Break, Single Action, High Quality, *Antique*	365.00	525.00	475.00
☐ **Spanish Copy of S&W M-10**, .32-20 WCF, Double Action, Solid Frame, Swing-Out Cylinder, Low Quality, *Modern*	55.00	85.00	80.00
☐ **Spanish Copy of S&W M-10**, .38 Special, Double Action, Solid Frame, Swing-Out Cylinder, Low Quality, *Modern*	50.00	75.00	70.00
☐ **Various Centerfire Calibers**, Folding Trigger, Open Top Frame, *Modern*	60.00	100.00	100.00
☐ **Various Centerfire Calibers**, Bulldog Style, Double Action, Solid Frame, *Modern*	50.00	90.00	90.00
☐ **Various Centerfire Calibers**, Small Pocket Pistol, Hammerless, Folding Trigger, with Safety, *Modern*	60.00	100.00	100.00
☐ **7.62mm Nagent**, Nagent Style Gas Seal, Solid Frame, Double Action, Modern	85.00	165.00	150.00
☐ **Various Centerfire Calibers**, European Military Style, Double Action, Solid Frame, Modern	85.00	165.00	150.00
☐ **Various Centerfire Calibers**, Warnant Style, Top Break, Double Action, Modern	85.00	155.00	150.00
☐ **Various Centerfire Calibers**, Gasser Style, Solid Frame, Double Action, Modern	85.00	160.00	150.00

	V.G.	Exc.	Prior Year Exc. Value
HANDGUN, SEMI-AUTOMATIC			
Chinese Broomhandle, 7.63 Mauser, Low Quality, Modern	95.00	175.00	160.00
Chinese Copy of FN 1900, Various Calibers, Clip Fed, Low Quality, Modern	60.00	95.00	90.00
Chinese Pocket Pistols, Various Calibers, Clip Fed, Low Quality, Modern	65.00	100.00	95.00
☐ **Copy of Colt M1911**, .45 ACP, Clip Fed, Military, High Quality, *Modern*	190.00	275.00	250.00
☐ **Spanish Pocket Pistols**, .25 ACP, Clip Fed, Low Quality, *Modern*	65.00	100.00	95.00
☐ **Spanish Pocket Pistols**, .32 ACP, Clip Fed, Low Quality, *Modern*	70.00	125.00	115.00
☐ **Spanish Pocket Pistols**, .32 ACP, Clip Fed, Low Quality, Ruby Style, *Modern*	70.00	125.00	115.00
HANDGUN, SINGLESHOT			
☐ **Flobert Style**, Various Configurations, *Modern*	45.00	90.00	85.00
☐ **.22 Short**, Target Pistol, Tip-Up Barrel, Plain, *Modern*	65.00	135.00	120.00
☐ **.22 Short**, Fancy German Target Pistol, Tip-Up Barrel, Engraved, Set Triggers, *Modern*	365.00	550.00	500.00
☐ **.22 R.F.**, Fancy Target Pistol, Hammerless, Set Triggers, *Modern*	265.00	425.00	400.00
RIFLE, BOLT ACTION			
☐ **Various Rimfire Calibers**, Singleshot, Checkered Stock, European, *Modern*	30.00	55.00	50.00
☐ **Various Centerfire Calibers**, Commercial Sporting Rifle, Low Quality, *Modern*	80.00	130.00	125.00
☐ **Arabian Copies**, Various Calibers, Military, Reproduction, Low Quality, *Modern*	55.00	95.00	90.00
RIFLE, SINGLESHOT			
☐ **Various Calibers**, Flobert Style, Checkered Stock, *Modern*	55.00	100.00	95.00
☐ **Various Calibers**, Warnant Style, Checkered Stock, *Modern*	70.00	130.00	125.00
☐ **Belgian Proofs**, .22 Long R.F., Tip-Up, Octagon Barrel, Medium Quality, *Antique*	70.00	100.00	95.00
SHOTGUN, DOUBLE BARREL, SIDE-BY-SIDE			
☐ **Belgian Proofs**, Various Gauges, Damascus Barrel, Low Quality, Outside Hammers, *Modern*	70.00	125.00	120.00
☐ **English Proofs**, Various Gauges, Damascus Barrel, Low Quality, Outside Hammers, *Modern*	80.00	125.00	125.00
☐ **No Proofs**, Various Gauges, Damascus Barrel, Low Quality, Outside Hammers, *Modern*	50.00	100.00	95.00
☐ **Various Gauges**, American, Outside Hammers, Damascus Barrel, *Modern*	80.00	155.00	150.00
☐ **Various Gauges**, American, Hammerless, Steel Barrel, *Modern*	95.00	180.00	175.00
☐ **Various Gauges**, American, Hammerless, Damascus Barrel, *Modern*	75.00	155.00	150.00
☐ **Various Gauges**, American, Outside Hammers, Steel Barrel, *Modern*	95.00	180.00	175.00

	V.G.	Exc.	Prior Year Exc. Value
SHOTGUN, SINGLESHOT			
☐ **Various Gauges**, American, Hammer, Steel Barrel, *Modern*	45.00	80.00	75.00
☐ **Various Gauges**, Warnant Style, Checkered Stock, *Modern*	40.00	75.00	70.00
☐ **"Zulu"**, 12 Ga., Converted from Perc. Musket, Trap Door Action, *Antique*	75.00	130.00	125.00
COMBINATION WEAPON, DRILLING			
☐ **German**, Various Calibers, Light Engraving, *Modern*	475.00	800.00	700.00

CEBRA

Arizmendi, Zulaika y Cia., Eibar, Spain.

	V.G.	Exc.	Prior Year Exc. Value
HANDGUN, SEMI-AUTOMATIC			
☐ **Pocket**, .25 ACP, Clip Fed, Curio	85.00	135.00	125.00

CELTA

Tomas de Urizar y Cia., Eibar, Spain c. 1935.

	V.G.	Exc.	Prior Year Exc. Value
HANDGUN, SEMI-AUTOMATIC			
☐ **Pocket**, .25 ACP, Clip Fed, Curio	85.00	135.00	125.00

CENTENNIAL

Made by Derringer Rifle & Pistol Works 1876.

	V.G.	Exc.	Prior Year Exc. Value
HANDGUN, REVOLVER			
☐ **.22 Short R.F.**, 7 Shot, Spur Trigger, Tip-Up, *Antique*	255.00	390.00	375.00
☐ **.32 Short R.F.**, 5 Shot, Spur Trigger, Solid Frame, Single Action, *Antique*	100.00	180.00	175.00
☐ **.38 Short R.F.**, 5 Shot, Spur Trigger, Solid Frame, Single Action, *Antique*	100.00	185.00	180.00
☐ **Centennial '76**, .38 Long R.F., 5 Shot, Single Action, Spur Trigger, Tip-Up, *Antique*	270.00	365.00	345.00
☐ **Model 2**, .32 R.F., 5 Shot, Single Action, Spur Trigger, Tip-Up, *Antique*	245.00	350.00	340.00

CENTRAL

Made by Stevens Arms.

	V.G.	Exc.	Prior Year Exc. Value
SHOTGUN, DOUBLE BARREL, SIDE-BY-SIDE			
☐ **Model 315**, Various Gauges, Hammerless, Steel Barrel, *Modern*	95.00	170.00	165.00
☐ **Model 215**, 12 and 16 Gauges, Outside Hammers, Steel Barrel, *Modern*	95.00	175.00	160.00
☐ **Model 311**, Various Gauges, Hammerless, Steel Barrel, *Modern*	100.00	185.00	175.00
SHOTGUN, SINGLESHOT			
☐ **Model 94**, Various Gauges, Takedown, Automatic Ejector, Plain Hammer, *Modern*	45.00	70.00	65.00

CENTRAL ARMS CO.

Made by Crescent, For Shapleigh Hardware Co., c.1900.

	V.G.	Exc.	Prior Year Exc. Value
SHOTGUN, DOUBLE BARREL, SIDE-BY-SIDE			
☐ **Various Gauges**, Outside Hammers, Damascus Barrel, *Modern*	85.00	155.00	150.00
☐ **Various Gauges**, Hammerless, Steel Barrel, *Modern*	95.00	180.00	175.00
☐ **Various Gauges**, Hammerless, Damascus Barrel, *Modern*	80.00	155.00	150.00
☐ **Various Gauges**, Outside Hammers, Steel Barrel, *Modern*	95.00	180.00	175.00
SHOTGUN, SINGLESHOT			
☐ **Various Gauges**, Hammer, Steel Barrel, *Modern*	45.00	80.00	75.00

CHALLENGE

Made by Bliss & Goodyear, c. 1878.

HANDGUN, REVOLVER			
☐ **.32 Short R.F.**, 5 Shot, Spur Trigger, Solid Frame, Single Action, *Antique*	90.00	160.00	160.00

CHAMPION

Unknown Maker c. 1870.

HANDGUN, REVOLVER			
☐ **.22 Short R.F.**, 7 Shot, Spur Trigger, Solid Frame, Single Action, *Antique*	90.00	160.00	160.00

CHAMPLIN FIREARMS

Enid, Oklahoma.

RIFLE, BOLT ACTION			
☐ **Basic Rifle**, with Quarter Rib, Express Sights, *Add* **$185.00-$270.00**			
☐ **Basic Rifle**, Fancy Wood, *Add* **$55.00-$90.00**			
☐ **Basic Rifle**, Fancy Checkering, *Add* **$30.00-$45.00**			
☐ **Basic Rifle**, Various Calibers, Adjustable Trigger, Round or Octagon Tapered Barrel, Checkered Stock, *Modern*	1,700.00	2,525.00	2,450.00
SHOTGUN, DOUBLE BARREL, OVER-UNDER			
☐ **12 Ga.**, Extra Barrels, *Add* **$175.00-$250.00**			
☐ **Model 100**, 12 Ga., Field Grade, Checkered Stock, Vent Rib, Single Selective Trigger, Engraved, *Modern*	525.00	850.00	825.00
☐ **Model 100**, 12 Ga., Trap Grade, Checkered Stock, Vent Rib, Single Selective Trigger, Engraved, *Modern*	575.00	925.00	875.00
☐ **Model 100**, 12 Ga., Skeet Grade, Checkered Stock, Vent Rib, Single Selective Trigger, Engraved, *Modern*	570.00	925.00	875.00
☐ **Model 500**, 12 Ga., Field Grade, Checkered Stock, Vent Rib, Single Selective Trigger, Engraved, *Modern*	850.00	1,375.00	1,300.00
☐ **Model 500**, 12 Ga., Skeet Grade, Checkered Stock, Vent Rib, Single Selective Trigger, Engraved, *Modern*	900.00	1,500.00	1,400.00

	V.G.	Exc.	Prior Year Exc. Value
☐ **Model 500**, 12 Ga., Trap Grade, Checkered Stock, Vent Rib, Single Selective Trigger, Engraved, *Modern*	**995.00**	**1,600.00**	**1,525.00**

SHOTGUN, SINGLESHOT

	V.G.	Exc.	Prior Year Exc. Value
☐ **Model SB 100**, 12 Ga., Trap Grade, Checkered Stock, Vent Rib, Single Selective Trigger, Engraved, *Modern*	**575.00**	**875.00**	
☐ **Model SB 500**, 12 Ga., Trap Grade, Checkered Stock, Vent Rib, Single Selective Trigger, Engraved, *Modern*	**875.00**	**1,350.00**	

CHAPUIS

St. Bonnet-le-Chateau, France.

SHOTGUN, DOUBLE BARREL, SIDE-BY-SIDE

	V.G.	Exc.	Prior Year Exc. Value
☐ **Progress RBV, R20**, 12 or 20 Gauge, Automatic Ejectors, Sideplates, Double Triggers, Checkered Stock, *Modern*	**800.00**	**1,200.00**	**1,150.00**
☐ **Progress RG**, 12 or 20 Gauge, Automatic Ejectors, Double Triggers, Checkered Stock, *Modern*	**450.00**	**675.00**	**650.00**
☐ **Progress Slug**, 12 or 20 Gauge, Automatic Ejectors, Slug Barrel, Double Triggers, Checkered Stock, *Modern*	**575.00**	**850.00**	**800.00**

CHARLES DALY

Tradename on guns made in Suhl, Germany prior to WWII, and by Miroku and Breda after WWII.

COMBINATION WEAPON, DRILLING

	V.G.	Exc.	Prior Year Exc. Value
☐ **Diamond**, Various Calibers, Fancy Engraving, Fancy Checkering, *Modern*	**2,950.00**	**4,800.00**	**4,650.00**
☐ **Regent Diamond**, Various Calibers, Fancy Engraving, Fancy Checkering, Fancy Wood, *Modern*	**4,750.00**	**7,000.00**	**6,850.00**
☐ **Superior**, Various Calibers, Engraved, *Modern*	**2,650.00**	**3,500.00**	**3,350.00**

RIFLE, BOLT ACTION

	V.G.	Exc.	Prior Year Exc. Value
☐ **.22 Hornet**, 5 Shot Clip, Checkered Stock, *Modern*	**600.00**	**995.00**	**950.00**

SHOTGUN, DOUBLE BARREL, OVER-UNDER

☐ **For 28 Ga.**, *Add* **10%-15%**

☐ **12 Ga.**, for Wide Vent Rib, *Add* **$25.00-$45.00**

	V.G.	Exc.	Prior Year Exc. Value
☐ **Various Gauges**, Field Grade, Light Engraving, Single Selective Trigger, Automatic Ejector, Post-War, *Modern*	**285.00**	**400.00**	**400.00**
☐ **Commander 100**, Various Gauges, Automatic Ejector, Checkered Stock, Double Trigger, *Modern*	**320.00**	**425.00**	**420.00**
☐ **Commander 100**, Various Gauges, Automatic Ejector, Checkered Stock, Single Trigger, *Modern*	**360.00**	**475.00**	**465.00**
☐ **Commander 200**, Various Gauges, Double Trigger, *Modern*	**470.00**	**600.00**	**595.00**
☐ **Commander 200**, Various Gauges, Automatic Ejector, Checkered Stock, Engraved, Single Trigger, *Modern*	**520.00**	**685.00**	**675.00**

	V.G.	Exc.	Prior Year Exc. Value
☐ **Diamond**, 12 Ga., Trap Grade, Selective Ejector, Single Selective Trigger, Post-War, *Modern*	495.00	750.00	750.00
☐ **Diamond**, 12 and 20 Gauges, Field Grade, Trap Grade, Selective Ejector, Single Selective Trigger, Post-War, *Modern*	525.00	800.00	800.00
☐ **Diamond**, 12 and 20 Gauges, Skeet Grade, Trap Grade, Selective Ejector, Single Selective Trigger, Post-War, *Modern*	525.00	800.00	800.00
☐ **Diamond**, Various Gauges, Double Trigger, Automatic Ejector, Fancy Engraving, Fancy Checkering, *Modern*	3,000.00	5,250.00	5,200.00
☐ **Empire**, Various Gauges, Double Trigger, Automatic Ejector, Checkered Stock, Engraved, *Modern*	2,650.00	4,275.00	4,200.00
☐ **Superior**, 12 Ga., Trap Grade, Automatic Ejector, Single Selective Trigger, Post-War, *Modern*	335.00	465.00	465.00
☐ **Superior**, Various Gauges, Field Grade, Trap Grade, Automatic Ejector, Single Selective Trigger, Post-War, *Modern*	335.00	465.00	465.00
☐ **Superior**, Various Gauges, Skeet Grade, Trap Grade, Automatic Ejector, Single Selective Trigger, Post-War, *Modern*	335.00	465.00	465.00
☐ **Venture**, 12 Ga., Trap Grade, Single Trigger, Monte Carlo Stock, Post-War, *Modern*	260.00	375.00	375.00
☐ **Venture**, 12 and 20 Gauges, Field Grade, Single Trigger, Trap Grade, Post-War, *Modern*	255.00	365.00	365.00
☐ **Venture**, 12 and 20 Gauges, Skeet Grade, Single Trigger, Trap Grade, Post-War, *Modern*	260.00	375.00	375.00
SHOTGUN, DOUBLE BARREL, SIDE-BY-SIDE			
☐ **Diamond**, Various Gauges, Double Trigger, Fancy Engraving, Fancy Checkering, Fancy Wood, Automatic Ejector, *Modern*	2,675.00	4,250.00	4,150.00
☐ **Empire**, Various Gauges, Double Trigger, Engraved, Checkered Stock, Automatic Ejector, *Modern*	1,900.00	2,700.00	2,600.00
☐ **Empire**, Various Gauges, Vent Rib, Single Trigger, Checkered Stock, Engraved, Post-War, *Modern*	235.00	340.00	340.00
☐ **Regent Diamond**, Various Gauges, Double Trigger, Fancy Engraving, Fancy Checkering, Fancy Wood, Automatic Ejector, *Modern*	3,200.00	5,500.00	5,350.00
☐ **Superior**, Various Gauges, Double Trigger, Light Engraving, Checkered Stock, *Modern*	925.00	1,700.00	1,650.00
SHOTGUN, SEMI-AUTOMATIC			
☐ **Novamatic**, 12 Ga., Takedown, Trap Grade, Vent Rib, Checkered Stock, Monte Carlo Stock, *Modern*	175.00	240.00	235.00
☐ **Novamatic**, 12 and 20 Gauges, Takedown, Plain Barrel, Checkered Stock, Lightweight, *Modern*	135.00	190.00	185.00
☐ **Novamatic**, 12 and 20 Gauges, Takedown, Vent Rib, Checkered Stock, Lightweight, *Modern*	150.00	200.00	195.00
☐ **Novamatic**, 12 and 20 Gauges, Takedown, Plain Barrel, Checkered Stock, Lightweight, Interchangeable Choke Tubes, *Modern*	140.00	200.00	190.00

	V.G.	Exc.	Prior Year Exc. Value
☐ **Novamatic**, 12 and 20 Gauges, Takedown, Vent Rib, Checkered Stock, Lightweight, Interchangeable Choke Tubes, *Modern*	160.00	225.00	220.00
☐ **Novamatic**, 12 Ga. Mag. 3", Takedown, Vent Rib, Checkered Stock, Magnum, *Modern*	170.00	230.00	225.00
☐ **Novamatic**, 20 Ga., Takedown, Checkered Stock, Magnum, Lightweight, *Modern*	145.00	215.00	210.00
☐ **Novamatic Super Light**, 12 and 20 Gauges, Takedown, Plain Barrel, Checkered Stock, *Modern*	130.00	200.00	195.00
☐ **Novamatic Super Light**, 12 and 20 Gauges, Takedown, Plain Barrel, Checkered Stock, Interchangeable Choke Tubes, *Modern*	140.00	220.00	215.00
☐ **Novamatic Super Light**, 12 and 20 Gauges, Takedown, Vent Rib, Checkered Stock, *Modern*	150.00	235.00	230.00

SHOTGUN, SINGLESHOT

☐ **Empire**, 12 Ga., Trap Grade, Fancy Engraving, Fancy Wood, Automatic Ejector, *Modern*	3,650.00	4,975.00	4,850.00
☐ **Sextuple Empire**, 12 Ga., Trap Grade, Fancy Checkering, Fancy Engraving, Fancy Wood, Automatic Ejector, *Modern*	4,075.00	5,400.00	5,200.00
☐ **Sextuple Regent Diamond**, 12 Ga., Trap Grade, Fancy Checkering, Fancy Engraving, Fancy Wood, Automatic Ejector, *Modern*	5,350.00	6,950.00	6,750.00
☐ **Superior**, 12 Ga., Trap Grade, Monte Carlo Stock, Selective Ejector, Engraved, Post-War, *Modern*	275.00	385.00	385.00

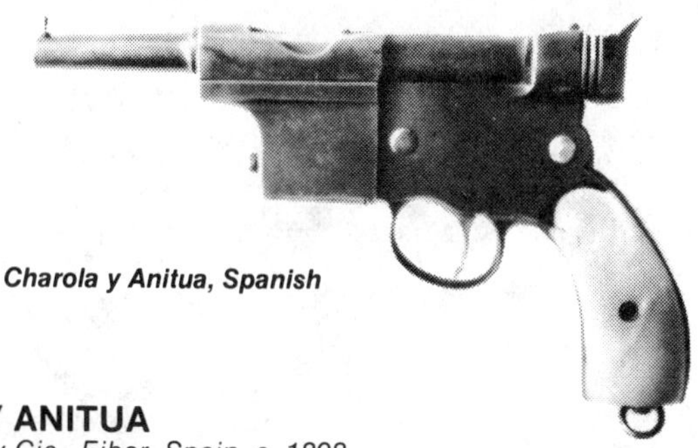

Charola y Anitua, Spanish

CHAROLA Y ANITUA

Garate, Anitua y Cia., Eibar, Spain, c. 1898.

HANDGUN, SEMI-AUTOMATIC

☐ **Charola**, 5mm Clement, Locked Breech, Box Magazine, Belgian Made, *Curio*	425.00	600.00	575.00
☐ **Charola**, 5mm Clement, Locked Breech, Box Magazine, Spanish Made, *Curio*	550.00	845.00	775.00

CHARTER ARMS

Stratford, Conn. since 1965.

HANDGUN, REVOLVER

☐ **Milestone Limited Edition,** .44 Special, Bulldog, Engraved, Silver Plated, Cased with Accessories, *Modern*	835.00	1175.00	1200.00

Charter Arms M40, Double Action Pistol

Charter Arms M79K, .380 Caliber

Charter Arms Police Bulldog

	V.G.	Exc.	Prior Year Exc. Value
☐ **Bulldog Tracker,** .357 Magnum, Double Action, Blue, Adjustable Sights, *Modern*	115.00	160.00	155.00
☐ **Bulldog,** .44 Special, Double Action, Blue, *Modern*	100.00	155.00	150.00
☐ **Bulldog,** .44 Special, Double Action, Nickel Plated, *Modern*	115.00	165.00	160.00
☐ **Bulldog,** .44 Special, Double Action, Stainless, *Modern*	130.00	180.00	175.00
☐ **Off-Duty,** .38 SPL, 5 Shot, 2″ Barrel, Steel Frame, *Modern*	150.00	160.00	160.00
☐ **Off-Duty,** .38 SPL, 5 Shot, 2″ Barrel, Stainless, *Modern*	200.00	250.00	250.00
☐ **Pathfinder,** .22 L.R.R.F., Adjustable Sights, Bulldog Grips, Double Action, *Modern*	105.00	155.00	150.00
☐ **Pathfinder,** .22 L.R.R.F., Adjustable Sights, Bulldog Grips, Double Action, Stainless Steel, *Modern*	145.00	195.00	190.00
☐ **Pathfinder,** .22 L.R.R.F., Adjustable Sights, Square-Butt, Double Action, *Modern*	95.00	145.00	140.00
☐ **Pathfinder,** .22 WMR, Adjustable Sights, Double Action, Bulldog Grips, *Modern*	105.00	150.00	150.00
☐ **Pathfinder,** .22 WMR, Adjustable Sights, Double Action, Square-Butt, *Modern*	100.00	145.00	140.00
☐ **Police Bulldog,** .38 Special, Double Action, Blue, Adjustable Sights, *Modern*	100.00	140.00	135.00
☐ **Police Bulldog,** .32 H&R Magnum, 4″ Bull Barrel, Checkered Grips, Blue, *Modern*	200.00	250.00	250.00
☐ **Police Bulldog,** .38 Special, 4″ Tapered Barrel, Square Grips, Stainless, *Modern*	255.00	275.00	275.00
☐ **Police Bulldog,** .38 Special, 4″ Bull Barrel, Stainless, *Modern*	255.00	275.00	275.00
☐ **Police Bulldog Tracker,** .357 Magnum, 2½″ Barrel, Blue, *Modern*	210.00	250.00	250.00
☐ **Police Bulldog Tracker,** .357 Magnum, 4″ Barrel, Bulldog Grips, Blue, *Modern*	210.00	260.00	260.00
☐ **Police Undercover,** .32 H&R Magnum, 2″ Barrel, Checkered Panel Grips, Blue, *Modern*	190.00	220.00	220.00
☐ **Police Undercover,** .38 Special, 2″ Barrel, Blue, Pocket Hammer, *Modern*	190.00	220.00	220.00
☐ **Police Undercover,** Law Enforcement Version, .38 Special, Five Shot, Neoprene Grips, *Modern*	250.00	280.00	280.00

	V.G.	Exc.	Prior Year Exc. Value
☐ **Target Bulldog,** .357 Magnum, Double Action, Blue, Adjustable Sights, *Modern*	125.00	170.00	165.00
☐ **Target Bulldog,** .44 Special, Double Action, Blue, Adjustable Sights, *Modern*	130.00	175.00	170.00
☐ **Undercover,** .38 Special, Double Action, Blue, *Modern*	95.00	145.00	140.00
☐ **Undercover,** .38 Special, Double Action, Stainless Steel, *Modern*	145.00	185.00	180.00
☐ **Undercover,** .38 Special, Double Action, Blue, Bulldog Grips, *Modern*	100.00	155.00	150.00
☐ **Undercover,** .38 Special, Double Action, Nickel Plated, *Modern*	100.00	145.00	140.00
☐ **Undercoverette,** .32 S & W Long, Double Action, Blue, Bulldog Grips, *Modern*	90.00	135.00	130.00
HANDGUN, SEMI-AUTOMATIC			
☐ **Model 40,** .22 L.R., 8 Shot Mag, Checkered Walnut Gripstock, Stainless, *Modern*	299.00	325.00	325.00
☐ **Model 79K,** .380 Autoloader, 7 Shot Mag, Checkered Gripstock, Stainless, *Modern*	375.00	400.00	400.00
☐ **Model 79K32,** .32 Caliber Autoloader, 7 Shot Mag, Stainless, *Modern*	375.00	450.00	450.00
☐ **Explorer II,** .22 L.R.R.F., Clip Fed, Takedown, *Modern*	53.00	75.00	70.00
☐ **Explorer SII,** .22 L.R.R.F., Clip Fed, Takedown, 6″ and 10″ Optional Barrels, *Modern*	102.00	130.00	130.00
RIFLE, SEMI-AUTOMATIC			
☐ **Explorer,** .22 L.R.R.F., Clip Fed, Takedown, *Modern*	53.00	80.00	75.00

Charter Arms Bulldog "Tracker" .357 Magnum 5-Shot, 4″ Barrel

	V.G.	Exc.	Prior Year Exc. Value
CHASE, WILLIAM			
Pandora, Ohio 1854-1860.			
COMBINATION WEAPON, PERCUSSION			
☐ **Various Calibers**, Double Barrel, *Antique*	750.00	1,275.00	1,200.00
CHEROKEE ARMS CO.			
Made by Crescent, C.M. McClung & Co. Tennessee, c. 1900.			
SHOTGUN, DOUBLE BARREL, SIDE-BY-SIDE			
☐ **Various Gauges**, Outside Hammers, Damascus Barrel, *Modern*	80.00	155.00	150.00
☐ **Various Gauges**, Hammerless, Steel Barrel, *Modern*	95.00	180.00	175.00
☐ **Various Gauges**, Hammerless, Damascus Barrel, *Modern*	75.00	155.00	150.00
☐ **Various Gauges**, Outside Hammers, Steel Barrel, *Modern*	90.00	180.00	175.00
RIFLE, SINGLESHOT			
☐ **Various Gauges**, Hammer, Steel Barrel, *Modern*	45.00	80.00	75.00
CHERRINGTON, THOMAS P.			
Cattawissa, Pa. 1847-1858.			
RIFLE, PILL LOCK			
☐ **.40**, Revolver, Octagon Barrel, *Antique*	1,900.00	2,675.00	2,525.00
CHICAGO ARMS CO.			
Sold by Fred Bifflar Co. Made by Meriden Firearms Co. 1870-1890.			
HANDGUN, REVOLVER			
☐ **.32 S & W**, 5 Shot, Double Action, Top Break, *Modern*	55.00	100.00	95.00
☐ **.38 S & W**, 5 Shot, Double Action, Top Break, *Modern*	55.00	100.00	95.00
☐ **.38 S & W**, Top Break, Hammerless, Double Action, Grip Safety, *Modern*	80.00	130.00	125.00

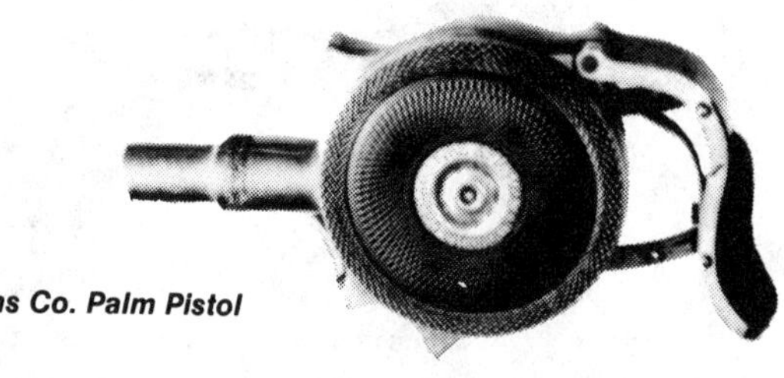

Chicago Fire Arms Co. Palm Pistol

CHICAGO FIRE ARMS CO.			
Chicago, Ill. 1883-1894.			
HANDGUN, PALM PISTOL			
☐ **.32 Extra Short R.F.**, Engraved, *Antique*	550.00	800.00	775.00

	V.G.	Exc.	Prior Year Exc. Value

CHESAPEAKE GUN CO.

Made by Crescent c. 1900.

SHOTGUN, DOUBLE BARREL, SIDE-BY-SIDE

	V.G.	Exc.	Prior Year Exc. Value
☐ **Various Gauges**, Outside Hammers, Damascus Barrel, *Modern*	80.00	155.00	150.00
☐ **Various Gauges**, Hammerless, Steel Barrel, *Modern*	100.00	180.00	175.00
☐ **Various Gauges**, Hammerless, Damascus Barrel, *Modern*	75.00	155.00	150.00
☐ **Various Gauges**, Outside Hammers, Steel Barrel, *Modern*	95.00	180.00	175.00

SHOTGUN, SINGLESHOT

	V.G.	Exc.	Prior Year Exc. Value
☐ **Various Gauges**, Hammer, Steel Barrel, *Modern*	45.00	80.00	75.00

CHICNESTER

Made by Hopkins & Allen, c. 1880.

HANDGUN, REVOLVER

	V.G.	Exc.	Prior Year Exc. Value
☐ **.38 Short R.F.**, 5 Shot, Spur Trigger, Solid Frame, Single Action, *Antique*	100.00	175.00	170.00

CHIEFTAIN

Made by Norwich Pistol Co., c. 1880.

HANDGUN, REVOLVER

	V.G.	Exc.	Prior Year Exc. Value
☐ **.32 Short R.F.**, 5 Shot, Spur Trigger, Solid Frame, Single Action, *Antique*	95.00	160.00	160.00

CHILEAN MILITARY

RIFLE, BOLT ACTION

	V.G.	Exc.	Prior Year Exc. Value
☐ **M1895 Rifle,** 7mm Mauser, Military, *Curio*	45.00	90.00	145.00
☐ **M1895 Short Rifle,** 7mm Mauser, Military, *Curio*	50.00	95.00	155.00
☐ **M1895 Carbine,** 7mm Mauser, Military, *Curio*	48.00	92.00	150.00

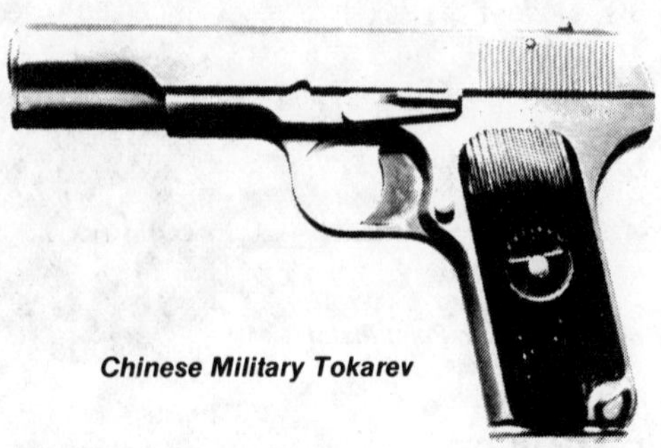

Chinese Military Tokarev

CHINESE MILITARY

AUTOMATIC WEAPON, HEAVY MACHINE GUN

	V.G.	Exc.	Prior Year Exc. Value
☐ **Type 24**, 8mm Mauser, Belt Fed, Tripod, *Class 3*	3,600.00	4,850.00	4,700.00

HANDGUN, SEMI-AUTOMATIC

	V.G.	Exc.	Prior Year Exc. Value
☐ **Makarov**, 9mm Mak., Clip Fed, *Modern*	565.00	875.00	850.00
☐ **Tokarev**, 7.62mm Tokarev, Clip Fed, *Modern*	180.00	275.00	245.00

	V.G.	Exc.	Prior Year Exc. Value
☐ **Walther PPk Type**, .32 A.C.P., Double Action, Blue, Clip Fed, Military, *Modern*	1,075.00	1,700.00	1,650.00
RIFLE, BOLT ACTION			
☐ **Type 53 (Nagent)**, 7.62 x 54R Russian, *Modern*	85.00	155.00	155.00
RIFLE, SEMI-AUTOMATIC			
☐ **SKS**, 7.62 x 39 Russian, Folding Bayonet, Military, *Modern*	260.00	375.00	365.00

CHINESE NATIONALIST MILITARY

	V.G.	Exc.	Prior Year Exc. Value
AUTOMATIC WEAPON, SUBMACHINE GUN			
☐ **Sten MK II,** 9mm Luger, all Metal, Clip Fed, *Class 3*	575.00	825.00	775.00
HANDGUN, SEMI-AUTOMATIC			
☐ **Hi Power,** 9mm Luger, Clip Fed, Military, Tangent Sights, *Curio*	400.00	620.00	750.00
☐ **Hi Power,** 9mm Luger, Clip Fed, Military, Tangent Sight, with Detachable Shoulder Stock, *Curio*	520.00	750.00	995.00
RIFLE, BOLT ACTION			
☐ **Kar 98k Type 79,** 8mm Mauser, *Modern*	80.00	145.00	185.00
☐ **M1871 Mauser,** .43 Mauser, Carbine, *Antique*	100.00	165.00	160.00
☐ **M1888 Hanyang,** 8mm Mauser, 5 Shot, *Curio*	70.00	120.00	155.00
☐ **M98 Mukden,** 8mm Mauser, *Modern*	100.00	180.00	250.00

CHIPMUNK

Medford, Ore. since 1982

	V.G.	Exc.	Prior Year Exc. Value
RIFLE, BOLT ACTION			
☐ **.22 L.R.R.F.**, Single Shot, Manual Cocking, Modern	55.00	80.00	—

CHURCHILL, E.J. & ROBERT

London, England 1892 to Date.

	V.G.	Exc.	Prior Year Exc. Value
RIFLE, BOLT ACTION			
☐ **One of 1,000**, Various Calibers, Checkered Stock, Recoil Pad, Express Sights, Cartridge Trap, *Modern*	700.00	900.00	875.00
☐ **One of 1,000**, Various Calibers, Fancy Checkering, Engraved Express Sights, Cartridge Trap, Cased With Accessories, *Modern*	1,650.00	2,375.00	2,250.00
SHOTGUN, DOUBLE BARREL, SIDE-BY-SIDE			
☐ **Utility Model**, Various Gauges, Boxlock, Double Triggers, Color Case Hardened Frame, Engraved, *Modern*	2,475.00	3,450.00	3,300.00
☐ **Hercules Model XXV**, Various Gauges, Hammerless Sidelock, Engraved, Fancy Checkering, Fancy Wood, Cased, *Modern*	3,950.00	5,400.00	5,200.00
☐ **Field Model**, Various Gauges, Hammerless Sidelock, Fancy Checkering, Automatic Ejectors, Engraved, *Modern*	6,650.00	8,150.00	7,900.00
☐ **Imperial Model XXV**, Various Gauges, Hammerless Sidelock, Fancy Checkering, Automatic Ejectors, Engraved, *Modern*	6,700.00	8,000.00	7,825.00

	V.G.	Exc.	Prior Year Exc. Value
☐ **Premier Quality**, Various Gauges, Hammerless Sidelock, Fancy Checkering, Automatic Ejectors, Engraved, *Modern*	7,750.00	9,100.00	8,800.00
☐ **Regal Model XXV**, Various Gauges, Hammerless Sidelock, Fancy Checkering, Automatic Ejectors, Engraved, *Modern*	3,200.00	4,450.00	4,250.00

☐ **For Single Selective Trigger** *Add* **$375.00-$535.00**

SHOTGUN, DOUBLE BARREL, OVER-UNDER

☐ **Premier Quality**, Various Gauges, Hammerless Sidelock, Fancy Checkering, Automatic Ejectors, Engraved, *Modern*	10,275.00	14,000.00	13,500.00

☐ **Premier Quality**, for Single Selective Trigger, *Add* **$400.00-$535.00**

☐ **Premier Quality**, for Raised Vent Rib, *Add* **$350.00-$520.00**

Chylewski .25 With Locking Screw

CHYLEWSKI, WITOLD

Austria, 1910-1918. Pistols made by S.I.G.

HANDGUN, SEMI-AUTOMATIC

	V.G.	Exc.	Prior Year Exc. Value
☐ **Einhand**, .25 ACP, Clip Fed, Blue, With Locking Screw, *Curio*	550.00	700.00	575.00
☐ **Einhand**, .25 ACP, Clip Fed, Blue, No Locking Screw, *Curio*	625.00	850.00	675.00

CLARK, F.H.

Memphis, Tenn., c. 1860.

HANDGUN, PERCUSSION

	V.G.	Exc.	Prior Year Exc. Value
☐ **Deringer**, .41, German Silver Mountings, *Antique*	495.00	750.00	725.00
☐ **Deringer Copy**, .41, German Silver Mountings, *Antique*	575.00	850.00	835.00

CLARKSON, J.

London, England 1680-1740.

HANDGUN, FLINTLOCK

	V.G.	Exc.	Prior Year Exc. Value
☐ **.32**, Pocket Pistol, Queen Anne Style, Box Lock, Screw Barrel, Silver Furniture, *Antique*	470.00	700.00	675.00

CLASSIC ARMS

Palmer, Mass.

	V.G.	Exc.	Prior Year Exc. Value
HANDGUN, PERCUSSION			
☐ **.36 Duckfoot**, 3 Shot, Brass Frame, Reproduction, *Antique*	25.00	40.00	40.00
☐ **.36 Twister**, 2 Shot, Brass Frame, Reproduction, *Antique*	25.00	40.00	40.00
☐ **.36 Ethan Allen**, Pepperbox, 4 Shot, Brass Frame, Reproduction, *Antique*	25.00	40.00	40.00
☐ **.36 Snake-Eyes**, Double Barrel, Side by Side, Brass Frame, Reproduction, *Antique*	20.00	35.00	35.00
☐ **.44 Ace**, Rifled, Brass Frame, Reproduction, *Antique*	15.00	25.00	25.00

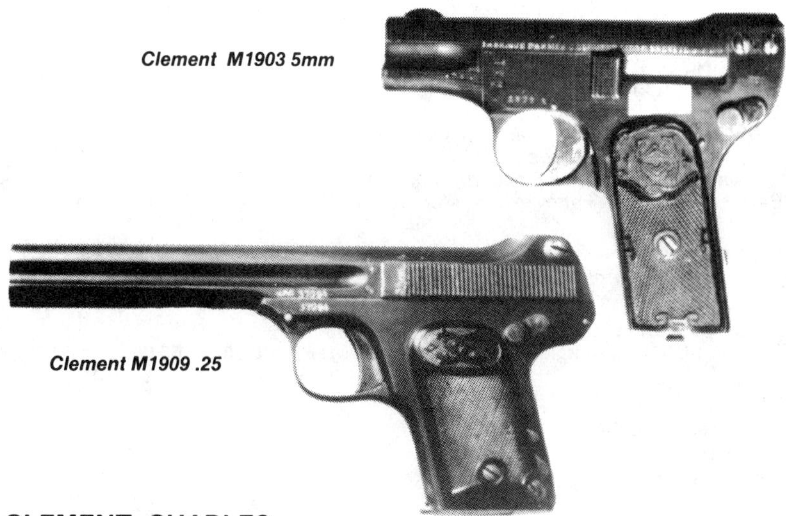

Clement M1903 5mm

Clement M1909 .25

CLEMENT, CHARLES

Liege, Belgium 1886-1914.

	V.G.	Exc.	Prior Year Exc. Value
HANDGUN, SEMI-AUTOMATIC			
☐ **M1903**, 5mm Clement, Clip Fed, Blue, *Curio*	365.00	500.00	485.00
☐ **M1907**, .25 ACP, Clip Fed, Blue, *Curio*	200.00	320.00	290.00
☐ **M1907**, .32 ACP, Clip Fed, Blue, *Curio*	250.00	395.00	370.00
☐ **M1908**, .25 ACP, Clip Fed, Blue, *Curio*	250.00	395.00	370.00
☐ **M1909**, .25 ACP, Clip Fed, Blue, *Curio*	200.00	320.00	290.00
☐ **M1909**, .32 ACP, Clip Fed, Blue, *Curio*	250.00	410.00	370.00
☐ **M1912 Fulgor**, .32 ACP, Clip Fed, Blue, *Curio*	450.00	700.00	675.00
RIFLE, SEMI-AUTOMATIC			
☐ **Clement-Neumann**, .401 Win., Clip Fed, Checkered Stock, Matted Rib, *Curio*	450.00	650.00	625.00
SHOTGUN, DOUBLE BARREL, SIDE-BY-SIDE			
☐ **Various Gauges**, Outside Hammers, Damascus Barrel, *Curio*	110.00	185.00	175.00
☐ **Various Gauges**, Hammerless, Steel Barrel, *Curio*	145.00	220.00	200.00
☐ **Various Gauges**, Hammerless, Damascus Barrel, *Curio*	110.00	185.00	175.00

	V.G.	Exc.	Prior Year Exc. Value

CLEMENT, J.B.
Belgium.

SHOTGUN, DOUBLE BARREL, SIDE-BY-SIDE

	V.G.	Exc.	Prior Year Exc. Value
☐ **Various Gauges**, Hammerless, Steel Barrel, *Modern*	**140.00**	**210.00**	**200.00**
☐ **Various Gauges**, Outside Hammers, Steel Barrel, *Modern*	**130.00**	**200.00**	**190.00**

CLERKE
Santa Monica, Calif.

HANDGUN, REVOLVER

	V.G.	Exc.	Prior Year Exc. Value
☐ **32-200**, .32 S & W, Nickel Plated, *Modern*	**15.00**	**25.00**	**25.00**
☐ **CF200**, .22 L.R.R.F., Nickel Plated, *Modern*	**15.00**	**25.00**	**25.00**

RIFLE, SINGLESHOT

	V.G.	Exc.	Prior Year Exc. Value
☐ **Hi-Wall**, Various Calibers, Fancy Wood, *Modern*	**200.00**	**325.00**	**295.00**
☐ **Hi-Wall Deluxe**, Various Calibers, Octagon Barrel, Fancy Wood, *Modern*	**290.00**	**425.00**	**395.00**
☐ **Hi-Wall Deluxe**, Various Calibers, Octagon Barrel, Set Trigger, Fancy Wood, *Modern*	**325.00**	**465.00**	**435.00**

CLIMAS
Made by Stevens Arms.

SHOTGUN, SINGLESHOT

	V.G.	Exc.	Prior Year Exc. Value
☐ **Model 90**, Various Gauges, Takedown, Automatic Ejector, Plain Hammer, *Modern*	**40.00**	**65.00**	**60.00**

CLIPPER
Maker unknown, c. 1880.

HANDGUN, REVOLVER

	V.G.	Exc.	Prior Year Exc. Value
☐ **.22 Short R.F.**, 7 Shot, Spur Trigger, Solid Frame, Single Action, *Antique*	**90.00**	**155.00**	**150.00**

CODY MANUFACTURING CO.
Chicopee, Mass. 1957-1959.

HANDGUN, REVOLVER

	V.G.	Exc.	Prior Year Exc. Value
☐ **Thunderbird**, .22 R.F., 6 Shot, Double Action, Aluminium with Steel Liners, *Modern*	**115.00**	**180.00**	**175.00**

COGSWELL & HARRISON
London, England 1770 to Date; Branch in Paris 1924-1938.

HANDGUN, REVOLVER

	V.G.	Exc.	Prior Year Exc. Value
☐ **S & W Victory**, .38 Special, Double Action, Swing-Out Cylinder, Refinished and Customized. Rebored from .38 S & W and may be unsafe with .38 Spec., *Modern*	**75.00**	**140.00**	**135.00**

RIFLE, BOLT ACTION

	V.G.	Exc.	Prior Year Exc. Value
☐ **BSA-Lee Speed**, .303 British, Sporting Rifle, Express Sights, Engraved, Checkered Stock, Commercial, *Modern*	**550.00**	**825.00**	**800.00**

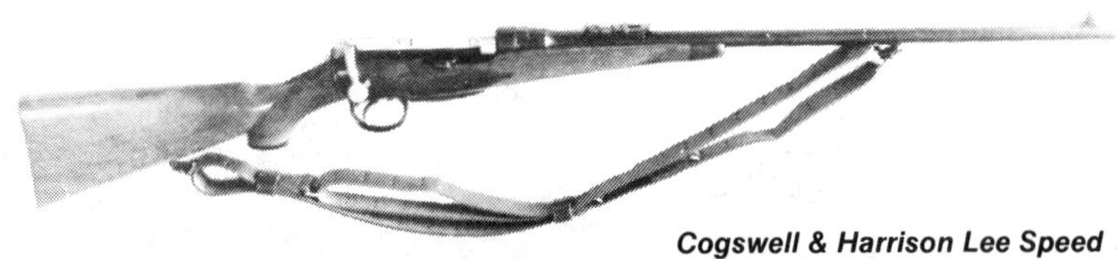

Cogswell & Harrison Lee Speed

	V.G.	Exc.	Prior Year Exc. Value
SHOTGUN, DOUBLE BARREL, SIDE-BY-SIDE			
☐ **Avant Tout (Konor)**, Various Gauges, Box Lock, Automatic Ejector, Fancy Checkering, Fancy Engraving, Double Trigger, *Modern*	2,150.00	3,000.00	2,975.00
☐ **Avant Tout (Konor)**, Various Gauges, Box Lock, Automatic Ejector, Fancy Checkering, Fancy Engraving, Single Trigger, *Modern*	2,400.00	3,350.00	3,275.00
☐ **Avant Tout (Konor)**, Various Gauges, Box Lock, Automatic Ejector, Fancy Checkering, Fancy Engraving, Single Selective Trigger, *Modern*	2,650.00	3,550.00	3,475.00
☐ **Avant Tout (Rex)**, Various Gauges, Box Lock, Automatic Ejector, Checkered Stock, Light Engraving, Double Trigger, *Modern*	1,300.00	2,250.00	2,175.00
☐ **Avant Tout (Rex)**, Various Gauges, Box Lock, Automatic Ejector, Checkered Stock, Light Engraving, Single Trigger, *Modern*	1,450.00	2,450.00	2,375.00
☐ **Avant Tout (Rex)**, Various Gauges, Box Lock, Automatic Ejector, Checkered Stock, Light Engraving, Single Selective Trigger, *Modern*	1,625.00	2,675.00	2,575.00
☐ **Avant Tout (Sandhurst)**, Various Gauges, Box Lock, Automatic Ejector, Fancy Checkering, Engraved, Double Trigger, *Modern*	1,950.00	2,900.00	2,775.00
☐ **Avant Tout (Sandhurst)**, Various Gauges, Box Lock, Automatic Ejector, Fancy Checkering, Engraved, Single Trigger, *Modern*	2,200.00	3,100.00	2,975.00
☐ **Avant Tout (Sandhurst)**, Various Gauges, Box Lock, Automatic Ejector, Fancy Checkering, Engraved, Single Selective Trigger, *Modern*	2,350.00	3,300.00	3,150.00
☐ **Huntic**, Various Gauges, Sidelock, Automatic Ejector, Checkered Stock, Double Trigger, *Modern*	2,450.00	3,600.00	3,450.00
☐ **Huntic**, Various Gauges, Sidelock, Automatic Ejector, Checkered Stock, Single Trigger, *Modern*	2,700.00	3,800.00	3,675.00
☐ **Huntic**, Various Gauges, Sidelock, Automatic Ejector, Checkered Stock, Single Selective Trigger, *Modern*	2,800.00	3,900.00	3,775.00
☐ **Markor**, Various Gauges, Box Lock, Automatic Ejector, Checkered Stock, Double Trigger, *Modern*	1,200.00	2,300.00	2,175.00
☐ **Markor**, Various Gauges, Box Lock, Checkered Stock, Double Trigger, *Modern*	875.00	1,925.00	1,850.00
☐ **Primic**, Various Gauges, Sidelock, Automatic Ejector, Fancy Engraving, Fancy Checkering, Double Trigger, *Modern*	3,300.00	4,575.00	4,450.00

	V.G.	Exc.	Prior Year Exc. Value
☐ **Primic**, Various Gauges, Sidelock, Automatic Ejector, Fancy Engraving, Fancy Checkering, Single Trigger, *Modern*	3,500.00	4,775.00	4,650.00
☐ **Primic**, Various Gauges, Sidelock, Automatic Ejector, Fancy Engraving, Fancy Checkering, Single Selective Trigger, *Modern*	3,550.00	4,800.00	4,675.00
☐ **Victor**, Various Gauges, Sidelock, Automatic Ejector, Engraved, Checkered Stock, Double Trigger, *Modern*	5,200.00	6,700.00	6,575.00
☐ **Victor**, Various Gauges, Sidelock, Automatic Ejector, Engraved, Checkered Stock, Single Trigger, *Modern*	5,550.00	7,000.00	6,850.00
☐ **Victor**, Various Gauges, Sidelock, Automatic Ejector, Engraved, Checkered Stock, Single Selective Trigger, *Modern*	5,600.00	7,000.00	6,875.00

COLON

Antonio Azpiri y Cia. Eibar, Spain 1914-1918.

HANDGUN, SEMI-AUTOMATIC

	V.G.	Exc.	Prior Year Exc. Value
☐ **Pocket**, .25 ACP, Clip Fed, *Curio*	85.00	125.00	120.00

COLON

Made by Orbea Hermanos Eibar, Spain c. 1925.

HANDGUN, REVOLVER

	V.G.	Exc.	Prior Year Exc. Value
☐ **Colt Police Positive Copy**, .32/20, Double Action, Blue, *Curio*	90.00	140.00	135.00

COLONIAL

Fabrique d'Armes de Guerre de Grand Precision, Eibar, Spain.

HANDGUN, SEMI-AUTOMATIC

	V.G.	Exc.	Prior Year Exc. Value
☐ **.25 ACP**, Clip Fed, Blue, *Modern*	80.00	125.00	115.00
☐ **.32 ACP**, Clip Fed, Blue, *Modern*	100.00	150.00	145.00

COLT

Patterson, N.J. 1836-1841. Whitneyville, Conn. 1847-1848. Hartford, Conn. 1848 to Date; London, England 1853-1864. Also see U.S. Military.

AUTOMATIC WEAPON, ASSAULT RIFLE

	V.G.	Exc.	Prior Year Exc. Value
☐ **AR-15,** .223 Rem., Clip Fed, Early Model, *Class 3*	725.00	1250.00	1200.00
☐ **M16-M A C,** .22 L.R.R.F., Clip Fed, Conversion Unit only, *Class 3*	75.00	120.00	115.00
☐ **M16A1,** .223 Rem., Clip Fed, Commercial, *Class 3*	625.00	880.00	865.00
☐ **M1919 BAR,** .30-06 Springfield, Clip Fed, Commercial, Finned Barrel, with Compensator, Curio, *Class 3*	2950.00	3800.00	3750.00

AUTOMATIC WEAPON, HEAVY MACHINE GUN

	V.G.	Exc.	Prior Year Exc. Value
☐ **M1906 Colt,** .30-06 Springfield, Belt Fed, Tripod Potato Digger, Military, *Class 3*	2000.00	2775.00	2650.00
☐ **M2 Browning,** .50 BMG, Belt Fed, Heavy Barrel, Military, *Class 3*	2025.00	2900.00	2800.00
☐ **M2 Browning,** .50 BMG, Belt Fed, Heavy Barrel, Commercial, *Class 3*	3700.00	4750.00	4600.00

	V.G.	Exc.	Prior Year Exc. Value
AUTOMATIC WEAPON, LIGHT MACHINE GUN			
☐ **Benet-Mercie U.S.N. 1912,** .30-06 Springfield, Clip Fed, Dewat, *Class 3*	2800.00	3825.00	3800.00
AUTOMATIC WEAPON, SUBMACHINE GUN			
☐ **XM177E2,** .223 Rem., Clip Fed, Folding Stock, Silencer, Short Rifle, Military, *Class 3*	1600.00	2325.00	2300.00
COMBINATION WEAPON, DRILLING			
☐ **Various Calibers,** Engraved, Fancy Checkering, *Modern*	1700.00	2650.00	2600.00
HANDGUN, PERCUSSION			
☐ **.28 Model 1855 Root,** Full Fluted Cylinder, Side Hammer, Spur Trigger, Revolver, Octagon Barrel, *Antique*	500.00	770.00	740.00
☐ **.28 Model 1855 Root,** Full Fluted Cylinder, Side Hammer, Spur Trigger, Revolver, Round Barrel, *Antique*	525.00	775.00	750.00
☐ **.28 Model 1855 Root,** Round Cylinder, Side Hammer, Spur Trigger, Revolver, Octagon Barrel, *Antique*	430.00	725.00	700.00
☐ **.28 Model 1855 Root,** Round Cylinder, Side Hammer, Spur Trigger, Revolver, Round Barrel, *Antique*	465.00	775.00	750.00
☐ **.28 Model Patterson (Baby),** 5 Shot, Various Barrel Lengths, Octagon Barrel, no Loading Lever, *Antique*	2575.00	3850.00	3800.00
☐ **.28 Model Patterson (Baby),** 5 Shot, Various Barrel Lengths, Octagon Barrel, with Factory Loading Lever, *Antique*	3000.00	4350.00	4250.00
☐ **.31 Model 1848 Revolver,** Baby Dragoon, 5 Shot, Various Barrel Lengths, no Loading Lever, no Capping Groove, *Antique*	2050.00	3175.00	3100.00
☐ **.31 Model 1848 Revolver,** Baby Dragoon, 5 Shot, Various Barrel Lengths, no Loading Lever, Stagecoach Cylinder, *Antique*	1275.00	2450.00	2350.00
☐ **.31 Model 1848 Revolver,** Baby Dragoon, 5 Shot, Various Barrel Lengths, no Loading Lever, *Antique*	1600.00	2850.00	2750.00
☐ **.31 Model 1848 Revolver,** Baby Dragoon, 5 Shot, Various Barrel Lengths, with Loading Lever, *Antique*	1800.00	3100.00	2950.00
☐ **.31 Model 1849 Revolver,** Wells Fargo, 5 Shot, no Loading Lever, Pocket Pistol, *Antique*	1350.00	2025.00	1950.00
☐ **.31 Model 1849 Revolver,** Pocket Pistol, with Loading Lever, 5 Shot, Round-Backed Trigger Guard, Large, 1-Line N.Y. Address, Brass Frame, *Antique*	475.00	680.00	645.00
☐ **.31 Model 1849 Revolver,** Pocket Pistol, with Loading Lever, 5 Shot, Large Round-Backed Trigger Guard, 1-Line Hartford Address, Brass Frame, *Antique*	550.00	800.00	765.00
☐ **.31 Model 1849 Revolver,** Pocket Pistol, with Loading Lever, 5 Shot, Round-Backed Trigger Guard, Large, 1-Line Hartford Address, Iron Frame, *Antique*	565.00	845.00	800.00

	V.G.	Exc.	Prior Year Exc. Value
☐ **.31 Model 1849 Revolver,** Pocket Pistol, with Loading Lever, 5 Shot, Large Round-backed Trigger Guard, 1-Line London Address, Iron Frame, *Antique*	750.00	1050.00	995.00
☐ **.31 Model 1849 Revolver,** Pocket Pistol, with Loading Lever, 5 Shot, Round-Backed Trigger Guard, Small, 2-Line N.Y. Address, Iron Frame, *Antique*	485.00	625.00	600.00
☐ **.31 Model 1849 Revolver,** Pocket Pistol, with Loading Lever, 5 Shot, Round-Backed Trigger Guard, Small, 2-Line N.Y. Address, Brass Frame, *Antique*	485.00	625.00	600.00
☐ **.31 Model 1849 Revolver,** Pocket Pistol, with Loading Lever, 5 Shot, Square-Backed Trigger Guard, Small, 2-Line N.Y. Address, *Antique*	1000.00	1725.00	1600.00
☐ **.31 Model 1849,** For 5″ Barrel, *Add* **10%-15%**			
☐ **.31 Model 1849,** For 6″ Barrel, *Add* **15%-25%**			
☐ **.31 Model 1849,** 6 Shot (Model 1850), *Add* **15%-25%**			
☐ **.31 Baby Dragoon,** Late, Unfluted Cylinder, Reproduction, *Antique*	130.00	210.00	200.00
☐ **.31 Model 1855 Root,** Full Fluted Cylinder, Side Hammer, Spur Trigger, Revolver, Octagon Barrel, *Antique*	570.00	875.00	850.00
☐ **.31 Model 1855 Root,** Full Fluted Cylinder, Side Hammer, Spur Trigger, Revolver, Round Barrel, *Antique*	595.00	875.00	850.00
☐ **.31 Model 1855 Root,** Round Fluted Cylinder, Side Hammer, Spur Trigger, Revolver, Octagon Barrel, *Antique*	595.00	875.00	850.00
☐ **.31 Model 1855 Root,** Round Fluted Cylinder, Side Hammer, Spur Trigger, Revolver, Round Barrel, *Antique*	675.00	1025.00	975.00
☐ **.31 Model 1855,** For 4½″ Barrel, *Add* **10%-15%**			
☐ **.31,** .28 Model 1855, London Markings, *Add* **50%-75%**			
☐ **.31 Model Patterson (Baby),** 5 Shot, Octagon Barrel, Various Barrel Lengths, no Loading Lever, no Capping Groove, *Antique*	2325.00	3925.00	3800.00
☐ **.31 Model Patterson (Baby),** 5 Shot, Octagon Barrel, Various Barrel Lengths, with Factory Loading Lever, *Antique*	2875.00	4350.00	4250.00
☐ **.31,** .34 Model Patterson (Pocket), 5 Shot, Octagon Barrel, Various Barrel Lengths, no Loading Lever, no Capping Groove, *Antique*	2950.00	4375.00	4275.00
☐ **.31 Model Patterson (Pocket),** 5 Shot, Octagon Barrel, Various Barrel Lengths, with Factory Loading Lever, *Antique*	3650.00	5075.00	4900.00
☐ **.31 Model Patterson (Belt),** 5 Shot, Octagon Barrel, Various Barrel Lengths, no Loading Lever, no Capping Groove, Straight Grip, *Antique*	3100.00	4750.00	4600.00
☐ **.31 Model Patterson (Belt),** 5 Shot, Octagon Barrel, Various Barrel Lengths, no Loading Lever, no Capping Groove, Flared Grip, *Antique*	3650.00	5250.00	5100.00
☐ **.31 Model Patterson (Belt),** Factory Loading Lever, *Add* **10%-15%**			

	V.G.	Exc.	Prior Year Exc. Value
☐ **.36 M1851 Grant-Lee Set,** Revolver, Commemorative, Cased Reproduction, *Antique*	750.00	1100.00	1100.00
☐ **.36 M1851 Late,** Revolver, 6 Shot, Reproduction, *Antique*	130.00	230.00	225.00
☐ **.36 M1851 R.E. Lee,** Revolver, Commemorative, Cased Reproduction, *Antique*	230.00	380.00	375.00
☐ **.36 M1851 U.S. Grant,** Revolver, Commemorative, Cased Reproduction, *Antique*	230.00	380.00	375.00
☐ **.36 Model 1851,** Half-Fluted, Rebated Cylinder, *Add* **25%-40%**			
☐ **.36 Model 1851 Navy,** Revolver, with Loading Lever, Square-Backed Trigger Guard, 1st Type, Under #1250, 6 Shot, *Antique*	3000.00	4250.00	3775.00
☐ **.36 Model 1851 Navy,** Revolver, with Loading Lever, Square-Backed Trigger Guard, 2nd Type, #1250 to #3500, 6 Shot, *Antique*	1500.00	2400.00	2300.00
☐ **.36 Model 1851 Navy,** Revolver, with Loading Lever, 6 Shot, Small Round-Backed Guard, Small Loading Cut, *Antique*	800.00	1500.00	1425.00
☐ **.36 Model 1851 Navy,** Revolver, with Loading Lever, 6 Shot, Small Round-Backed Guard, Large Loading Cut, *Antique*	800.00	1500.00	1425.00
☐ **.36 Model 1851 Navy,** Revolver, with Loading Lever, 6 Shot, Round-Backed Trigger Guard, Large Loading Cut, London Address, Iron Frame, *Antique*	825.00	1600.00	1525.00
☐ **.36 Model 1851 Navy,** Revolver, with Loading Lever, 6 Shot, Round-Backed Trigger Guard, Small Loading Cut, London Address, Iron Frame, *Antique*	1075.00	1900.00	1825.00
☐ **.36 Model 1851 Navy,** Revolver, with Loading Lever, 6 Shot, Large Round-Backed Guard, Large Loading Cut, N.Y. Address, *Antique*	590.00	1050.00	995.00
☐ **.36 Model 1851 Navy,** Revolver, with Loading Lever, 6 Shot, Large Round-Backed Guard, Large Loading Cut, Hartford Address, *Antique*	675.00	1250.00	1175.00
☐ **.36 Model 1851 Navy,** Revolver, with Loading Lever, 6 Shot, Large Round-Backed Guard, Cut for Shoulder Stock, Iron Backstrap, *Antique*	2100.00	3350.00	3275.00
☐ **.36 Model 1851 Navy,** Revolver, with Loading Lever, 6 Shot, Large Round-Backed Guard, with Detachable Shoulder Stock, Iron Backstrap, *Antique*	3900.00	6100.00	5900.00
☐ **.36 Model 1862 Navy,** Revolver, New Navy Pocket Pistol 4½" Barrel, Rebated Cylinder, *Antique*	585.00	960.00	925.00
☐ **.36 Model 1862 Navy,** Revolver, New Navy Pocket Pistol 5½" Barrel, Rebated Cylinder, *Antique*	635.00	1020.00	975.00
☐ **.36 Model 1862 Navy,** Revolver, Late New Navy Pocket Pistol 5½" Barrel, Rebated Cylinder, Reproduction, *Antique*	130.00	215.00	200.00
☐ **.36 Model 1862 Navy,** Revolver, New Navy Pocket Pistol 1861, 6½" Barrel, Rebated Cylinder, *Antique*	635.00	975.00	925.00
☐ **.36 Model 1861 Navy,** Revolver, Round Barrel, Military Model, no Cuts for Shoulder Stock, *Antique*	1950.00	3300.00	3100.00

	V.G.	Exc.	Prior Year Exc. Value
☐ **.36 Model 1861 Navy,** Revolver, Round Barrel, Civilian Model, no Cuts for Shoulder Stock, *Antique*	845.00	1500.00	1450.00
☐ **.36 Model 1861 Navy,** Revolver, Late, Round Barrel, Civilian Model, no Cuts for Shoulder Stock, Reproduction, *Antique*	125.00	225.00	225.00
☐ **.36 Model 1861 Navy,** Revolver, Round Barrel, Military, Cut for Shoulder Stock, *Antique*	2325.00	4225.00	4100.00
☐ **.36 Model 1861 Navy,** Revolver, Round Barrel, Military, With Shoulder Stock, *Antique*	3175.00	6850.00	6600.00
☐ **.36 Model 1862 Police,** Revolver, Half-Fluted Rebated Cylinder, *Antique*	550.00	950.00	900.00
☐ **.36 Model 1862 Police,** Revolver, Late, Half-Fluted Rebated Cylinder, Reproduction, *Antique*	130.00	210.00	200.00
☐ **.36 Model 1862 Police,** for Hartford Marks, *Add* 10%-20%			
☐ **.36 Model 1862 Police,** for London Marks, *Add* 10%-20%			
☐ **.36 Model Patterson (Holster),** 5 Shot, Octagon Barrel, Various Barrel Lengths, no Loading Lever, no Capping Groove, *Antique*	6775.00	10250.00	10000.00
☐ **.36 Model Patterson (Holster),** 5 Shot, Octagon Barrel, Various Barrel Lengths, with Factory Loading Lever, *Antique*	9500.00	18000.00	17500.00
☐ **.44 Model 1847,** Revolver, Whitneyville Walker (U.S.M.R.), Square-Backed Trigger Guard, 6 Shot, *Antique*	18250.00	28500.00	28000.00
☐ **.44 Model 1847 Revolver,** Dragoon, (Hartford) Horizontal Loading Lever Latch, 6 Shot, *Antique*	5480.00	10000.00	9975.00
☐ **.44 Model 1847,** Revolver, Dragoon, (Hartford) Vertical Loading Lever Latch, Square-Backed Trigger Guard, 6 Shot, *Antique*	3200.00	5275.00	5100.00
☐ **.44 Dragoon 1st Model,** Revolver, 6 Shot, Civilian, *Antique*	1925.00	4175.00	4050.00
☐ **.44 Dragoon 1st Model,** Revolver, 6 Shot, Military, *Antique*	2125.00	4700.00	4600.00
☐ **.44 Dragoon 1st Model,** Revolver, 6 Shot, Military, Cut for Shoulder Stock, *Antique*	2400.00	5300.00	5125.00
☐ **.44 Dragoon 1st Model,** Revolver, 6 Shot, Military, With Shoulder Stock, *Antique*	4075.00	8075.00	7900.00
☐ **.44 Dragoon 1st Model,** Revolver, 6 Shot, Reproduction, *Antique*	165.00	235.00	235.00
☐ **.44 Dragoon 1st Model,** Revolver, 6 Shot, Fluck Variation, *Antique*	2825.00	4900.00	4700.00
☐ **.44 Dragoon 2nd Model,** Revolver, 6 Shot, Civilian, *Antique*	1625.00	3800.00	3650.00
☐ **.44 Dragoon 2nd Model,** Revolver, 6 Shot, Military, *Antique*	1750.00	3975.00	3875.00
☐ **.44 Dragoon 2nd Model,** Revolver, 6 Shot, Military, Cut for Shoulder Stock, *Antique*	2725.00	5450.00	5200.00
☐ **.44 Dragoon 2nd Model,** Revolver, 6 Shot, Military, With Shoulder Stock, *Antique*	5400.00	9100.00	8900.00
☐ **.44 Dragoon 2nd Model,** Revolver, 6 Shot, Militia, *Antique*	2050.00	4800.00	4650.00

	V.G.	Exc.	Prior Year Exc. Value
☐ **.44 Dragoon 3rd Model,** Revolver, 6 Shot, Civilian, *Antique*	1280.00	3025.00	2875.00
☐ **.44 Dragoon 3rd Model,** Revolver, 6 Shot, Military, *Antique*	1635.00	3250.00	3100.00
☐ **.44 Dragoon 3rd Model,** Revolver, 6 Shot, Military, Cut for Shoulder Stock, *Antique*	2075.00	4000.00	3875.00
☐ **.44 Dragoon 3rd Model,** Revolver, 6 Shot, Military, With Shoulder Stock, *Antique*	3100.00	6100.00	5900.00
☐ **.44 Statehood Dragoon 3rd Model,** Revolver, 6 Shot, Fancy Engraving, Gold Inlays, Ivory Stocks, Commemorative, Reproduction, *Antique*	10875.00	15500.00	15000.00
☐ **.44 Model 1860 Army,** Revolver, Cut for Shoulder Stock, *Antique*	750.00	1250.00	1200.00
☐ **.44 Model 1860 Army,** Revolver, Cut for Shoulder Stock, Four-Screw Frame, *Antique*	890.00	1550.00	1500.00
☐ **.44 Model 1860 Army,** Revolver, Cut for Shoulder Stock, Four-Screw Frame, with Shoulder Stock, *Antique*	2925.00	3925.00	3850.00
☐ **.44 Model 1860 Army,** Revolver, Cut for Shoulder Stock, Four-Screw Frame, Fluted Cylinder, *Antique*	1325.00	2050.00	1950.00
☐ **.44 Model 1860 Army,** Revolver, Cut for Shoulder Stock, Four-Screw Frame, Fluted Cylinder, Hartford Address, *Antique*	1800.00	2550.00	2450.00
☐ **.44 Model 1860 Army,** Revolver, Cut for Shoulder Stock, Four-Screw Frame, Fluted Cylinder, Hartford Address, with Shoulder Stock, *Antique*	3400.00	4785.00	4650.00
☐ **.44 Model 1860 Army,** Revolver, Fluted Cylinder, Reproduction, *Antique*	180.00	260.00	250.00
☐ **.44 Model 1860 Army,** Revolver, Butterfield Overland Express Commemorative, Two Cylinders, Reproduction, *Antique*	460.00	690.00	665.00
☐ **.44 Model 1860 Army,** Revolver, Cut for Shoulder Stock, Civilian Model, *Antique*	725.00	1300.00	1225.00
☐ **.44 Model 1860 Army,** Revolver, Cut for Shoulder Stock, London Markings, *Add* **50%-75%**			

HANDGUN, CARTRIDGE CONVERSIONS

	V.G.	Exc.	Prior Year Exc. Value
☐ **Model 1851 Navy,** .38 R.F. or C.F., Richards-Mason, *Antique*	465.00	765.00	725.00
☐ **Model 1851 Navy,** .36 Thuer, Thuer Style, *Antique*	2100.00	3600.00	3450.00
☐ **Model 1860 Army,** .44 Thuer, Thuer Style, *Antique*	2100.00	3600.00	3450.00
☐ **Model 1860 Army,** .44 Colt, Richards, *Antique*	590.00	900.00	865.00
☐ **Model 1860 Army,** .44 Colt, Richards-Mason, *Antique*	780.00	1275.00	1200.00
☐ **Model 1861 Navy,** .36 Thuer, Thuer Style, *Antique*	2650.00	4800.00	4650.00
☐ **Model 1862 Pocket Navy,** .36 Thuer, Thuer Style, *Antique*	2100.00	3925.00	3800.00
☐ **Model 1862 Pocket Navy,** .38 R.F., no Ejector, Octagon Barrel, *Antique*	375.00	650.00	625.00
☐ **Model 1862 Pocket Navy,** .38 R.F., no Ejector, Round Barrel, *Antique*	330.00	610.00	585.00
☐ **Model 1862 Pocket Navy,** .38 R.F., with Ejector, Round Barrel, *Antique*	490.00	815.00	785.00

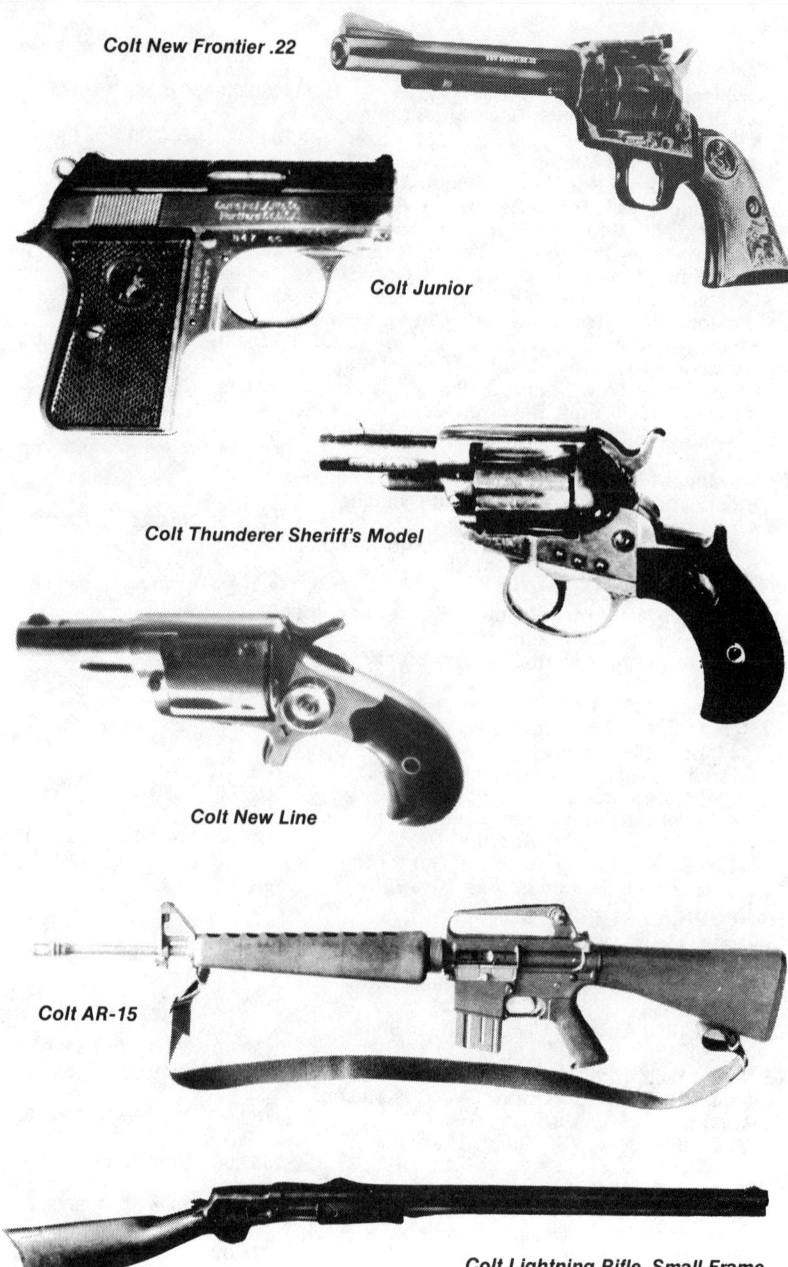

Colt New Frontier .22

Colt Junior

Colt Thunderer Sheriff's Model

Colt New Line

Colt AR-15

Colt Lightning Rifle, Small Frame

	V.G.	Exc.	Prior Year Exc. Value
HANDGUN, REVOLVER			
☐ **For Nickel Plating,** *Add* **$20.00-$30.00**			
☐ **".357 Magnum",** .357 Magnum, 6 Shot, Various Barrel Lengths, Adjustable Sights, Target Hammer, Target Grips, *Modern*	310.00	460.00	440.00
☐ **".357 Magnum",** .357 Magnum, 6 Shot, Various Barrel Lengths, Adjustable Sights, *Modern*	250.00	390.00	385.00
☐ **125th Anniversary,** .45 Colt, Single Action Army, Commemorative, Blue, with Gold Plating, Cased, *Curio*	450.00	715.00	700.00
☐ **Agent,** .38 Special, 6 Shot, Parkerized, 2" Barrel, Lightweight, *Modern*	115.00	155.00	150.00
☐ **Agent,** .38 Special, 6 Shot, Blue, 2" Barrel, Lightweight, *Modern*	145.00	205.00	200.00
☐ **Agent,** .38 Special, 6 Shot, Nickel Plated, 2" Barrel, Lightweight, *Modern*	155.00	225.00	220.00
☐ **Agent Early,** .38 Special, 6 Shot, 2" Barrel, Lightweight, *Modern*	155.00	230.00	225.00
☐ **Alabama Sesquicentennial,** .22 L.R.R.F., Frontier Scout S.A., Commemorative, Gold Plated, with Nickel Plating, 4¾" Barrel, Cased, *Curio*	215.00	295.00	310.00
☐ **Alamo Model,** .22 L.R.R.F., Frontier Scout S.A., Commemorative, Blue, with Gold Plating, 4¾" Barrel, Cased, *Curio*	190.00	275.00	290.00
☐ **Alamo Model,** .22 L.R.R.F., and .45 Colt Set, Frontier Scout and S.A.A., Commemorative, Blue, with Gold Plating, Cased, *Curio*	720.00	1075.00	1150.00
☐ **Alamo Model,** .45 Colt, Single Action Army, Commemorative, Blue, with Gold Plating, 5½" Barrel, Cased, *Curio*	560.00	775.00	825.00
☐ **Abercrombie & Fitch,** .45 Colt, Trailblazer New Frontier S.A., Commemorative, New York, 7½" Barrel, Cased, *Curio*	1375.00	1900.00	1995.00
☐ **Abercrombie & Fitch,** .45 Colt, Trailblazer New Frontier S.A., Commemorative, Chicago, 7½" Barrel, Cased, *Curio*	1400.00	1900.00	1995.00
☐ **Abercrombie & Fitch,** .45 Colt, Trailblazer New Frontier S.A., Commemorative, San Francisco, 7½" Barrel, Cased, *Curio*	1400.00	1900.00	1995.00
☐ **Appomattox Centennial,** .22 L.R.R.F., Frontier Scout S.A., Commemorative, Blue, With Nickel Plating, 4¾" Barrel, Cased, *Curio*	200.00	305.00	290.00
☐ **Appomattox Centennial,** .22 L.R.R.F., and .45 Colt Set, Frontier Scout and S.A.A., Commemorative, Blue, with Nickel Plating, Cased, *Curio*	715.00	1025.00	1100.00
☐ **Appomattox Centennial,** .45 Colt, Single Action Army, Commemorative, Blue, with Nickel Plating, 5½" Barrel, Cased, *Curio*	500.00	775.00	820.00
☐ **Argentine M1895,** .38, Double Action, Solid Frame, Swing-Out Cylinder, Military, *Curio*	120.00	180.00	175.00
☐ **Arizona Ranger,** .22 L.R.R.F., Frontier Scout S.A., Commemorative, Blue, Color Case Hardened Frame, 4¾" Barrel, Cased, *Curio*	200.00	295.00	300.00

	V.G.	Exc.	Prior Year Exc. Value
☐ **Arizona Territorial Centennial,** .22 L.R.R.F., Frontier Scout S.A., Commemorative, Blue, with Gold Plating, 4¾″ Barrel, Cased, *Curio*	220.00	305.00	315.00
☐ **Arizona Territorial Centennial,** .45 Colt, Single Action Army, Commemorative, Blue, with Gold Plating, 4¾″ Barrel, Cased, *Curio*	525.00	810.00	825.00
☐ **Arkansas Territorial Sesquicentennial,** .22 L.R.R.F., Frontier Scout S.A., Commemorative, Blue, 4¾″ Barrel, Cased, *Curio*	180.00	230.00	245.00
☐ **Army Special,** .32-20 WCF, 6 Shot, Various Barrel Lengths, *Curio*	200.00	360.00	340.00
☐ **Army Special,** .38 Special, 6 Shot, Various Barrel Lengths, *Curio*	200.00	310.00	295.00
☐ **Army Special,** .41 Long Colt, 6 Shot, Various Barrel Lengths, *Curio*	165.00	250.00	245.00
☐ **Banker's Special,** .22 L.R.R.F., 6 Shot, 2″ Barrel, *Modern*	525.00	790.00	775.00
☐ **Banker's Special,** Fitzgerald Trigger Guard, *Add* **$150.00-$250.00**			
☐ **Banker's Special,** .38 S & W, 6 Shot, 2″ Barrel, *Modern*	330.00	465.00	450.00
☐ **Battle of Gettysburg Centennial,** .22 L.R.R.F., Frontier Scout S.A., Nickel Plated, Blue, with Gold Plating, 4¾″ Barrel, Cased, *Curio*	225.00	315.00	310.00
☐ **Bicentennial Set,** Python, SAA, Dragoon, Commemorative, Cased, *Curio*	1750.00	2300.00	2350.00
☐ **California Bicentennial,** .22 L.R.R.F., Frontier Scout S.A., Commemorative, Gold Plated, with Nickel Plating, 6″ Barrel, Cased, *Curio*	200.00	300.00	290.00
☐ **California Gold Rush,** .22 L.R.R.F., Frontier Scout S.A., Commemorative, Gold Plated, 4¾″ Barrel, Cased, *Curio*	215.00	320.00	345.00
☐ **California Gold Rush,** .45 Colt, Single Action Army, Commemorative, Gold Plated, 5½″ Barrel, Cased, *Curio*	800.00	1025.00	1100.00
☐ **Carolina Charter Tercentennial,** .22 L.R.R.F., Frontier Scout S.A., Commemorative, Blue, with Gold Plating, 4¾″ Barrel, Cased, *Curio*	265.00	375.00	400.00
☐ **Carolina Charter Tercentennial,** .22 L.R.R.F., and .45 Colt Set, Frontier Scout & S.A.A., Commemorative, Blue, with Gold Plating, 4¾″ Barrel, Cased, *Curio*	675.00	1025.00	1050.00
☐ **Chamizal Treaty,** .22 L.R.R.F., Frontier Scout S.A., Commemorative, Blue, with Gold Plating, 4¾″ Barrel, Cased, *Curio*	200.00	290.00	310.00
☐ **Chamizal Treaty,** .22 L.R.R.F., and .45 Colt Set, Frontier Scout and S.A.A., Commemorative, Blue, with Gold Plating, Cased, *Curio*	1200.00	1850.00	1995.00
☐ **Chamizal Treaty,** .45 Colt, Single Action Army, Commemorative, Blue, with Gold Plating, 5½″ Barrel, Cased, *Curio*	775.00	1100.00	1200.00
☐ **Cherry's 35th Anniversary,** .22 L.R.R.F., and .45 Colt Set, Frontier Scout and S.A.A., Nickel Plated, Gold Plated, 4¾″ Barrel, Cased, *Curio*	880.00	1400.00	1495.00
☐ **Cobra,** .38 Special, Blue, 2″ Barrel, 6 Shot, Lightweight, *Modern*	155.00	230.00	225.00

	V.G.	Exc.	Prior Year Exc. Value
☐ **Cobra,** .38 Special, Nickel Plated, 2″ Barrel, 6 Shot, Lightweight, *Modern*	170.00	245.00	240.00
☐ **Cobra,** .38 Special, 6 Shot, 5″ Barrel, Military, Lightweight, *Modern*	140.00	205.00	200.00
☐ **Cobra Early,** .38 Special, 6 Shot, 2″ Barrel, Lightweight, *Modern*	155.00	235.00	225.00
☐ **Cobra Early,** .38 Special, 6 Shot, 4″ Barrel, Lightweight, *Modern*	160.00	245.00	240.00
☐ **Cobra Early,** .38 Special, 6 Shot, 2″ Barrel, Lightweight, Hammer Shroud, *Modern*	165.00	255.00	255.00
☐ **Cobra Early,** .38 Special, 6 Shot, 4″ Barrel, Lightweight, Hammer Shroud, *Modern*	185.00	265.00	265.00
☐ **Col. Sam Colt Sesquicentennial,** .45 Colt, Single Action Army, Commemorative, Blue, Silver-Plated Gripframe, 7½″ Barrel, Cased, *Curio*	650.00	870.00	925.00
☐ **Col. Sam Colt Sesquicentennial,** .45 Colt, Single Action Army, Commemorative, Deluxe, Blue, Silver-Plated Gripframe, 7½″ Barrel, Cased, *Curio*	1250.00	1825.00	1995.00
☐ **Col. Sam Colt Sesquicentennial,** .45 Colt, Single Action Army, Commemorative, Special Deluxe, Blue, Silver-Plated Gripframe, 7½″ Barrel, Cased, *Curio*	2150.00	2850.00	2950.00
☐ **Colorado Gold Rush,** .22 L.R.R.F., Frontier Scout S.A., Commemorative, Gold Plated, with Nickel Plating, 4¾″ Barrel, Cased, *Curio*	200.00	295.00	310.00
☐ **Columbus Sesquicentennial,** .22 L.R.R.F., Frontier Scout S.A., Commemorative, Gold Plated, 4¾″ Barrel, Cased, *Curio*	415.00	535.00	560.00
☐ **Commando,** .38 Special, 6 Shot, Military, *Curio*	125.00	195.00	190.00
☐ **Commando Special,** .38 Caliber, Snub Nose, Similar To Banker's Special, Matt Finish, *Modern*	254.00	295.00	295.00
☐ **Courier,** .22 L.R.R.F., 6 Shot, 2″ Barrel, Lightweight, *Modern*	500.00	735.00	725.00
☐ **Courier,** .32 S & W Long, 6 Shot, 2″ Barrel, Lightweight, *Modern*	480.00	700.00	675.00
☐ **Dakota Territory,** .22 L.R.R.F., Frontier Scout S.A., Commemorative, Blue, with Gold Plating, 4¾″ Barrel Cased, *Curio*	205.00	300.00	310.00
☐ **Detective Special,** .38 Special, 6 Shot, 4″ Barrel, Heavy Barrel, *Modern*	205.00	305.00	300.00
☐ **Detective Special Early,** .32 S & W, 6 Shot, 2″ Barrel, *Modern*	140.00	195.00	190.00
☐ **Detective Special Early,** .38 S & W, 6 Shot, 2″ Barrel, *Modern*	150.00	200.00	195.00
☐ **Detective Special Early,** .38 Special, 6 Shot, 2″ Barrel, *Modern*	165.00	235.00	225.00
☐ **Detective Special Late,** .38 Special, 6 Shot, 2″ Barrel, Blue, *Modern*	185.00	250.00	240.00
☐ **Detective Special Late,** .38 Special, 6 Shot, 2″ Barrel, Nickel Plated, *Modern*	195.00	280.00	265.00
☐ **Detective Special Late,** .38 Special, 6 Shot, 2″ Barrel, Electroless Nickel Plated, *Modern*	230.00	315.00	300.00
☐ **Diamondback,** .22 L.R.R.F., Blue, Vent Rib, 6 Shot, *Modern*	200.00	295.00	280.00

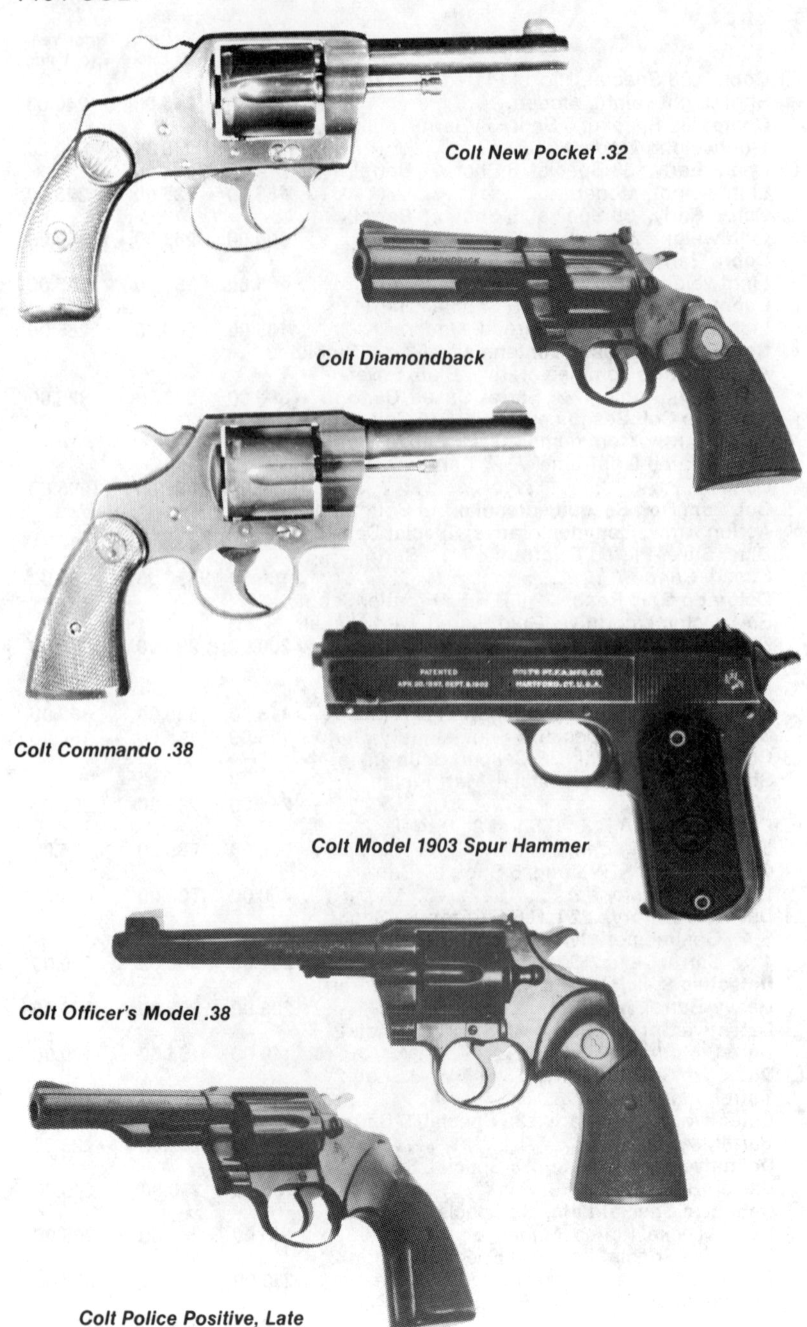

Colt New Pocket .32

Colt Diamondback

Colt Commando .38

Colt Model 1903 Spur Hammer

Colt Officer's Model .38

Colt Police Positive, Late

	V.G.	Exc.	Prior Year Exc. Value
☐ **Diamondback,** .22 L.R.R.F., Electroless Nickel Plated, Vent Rib, 6 Shot, *Modern*	235.00	335.00	330.00
☐ **Diamondback,** .38 Special, Blue, Vent Rib, 6 Shot, *Modern*	185.00	270.00	265.00
☐ **Diamondback,** .38 Special, Electroless Nickel Plated, Vent Rib, 6 Shot, *Modern*	245.00	350.00	345.00
☐ **Diamondback,** .38 Special, Nickel Plated, Vent Rib, 6 Shot, *Modern*	215.00	295.00	290.00
☐ **Florida Sesquicentennial,** .22 L.R.R.F., Frontier Scout S.A., Commemorative, Blue, Color Case, Hardened Frame, 4¾″ Barrel, Cased, *Curio*	200.00	265.00	295.00
☐ **Fort Findlay Sesquicentennial,** .22 L.R.R.F., Frontier Scout S.A., Commemorative, Gold Plated, 4¾″ Barrel, Cased, *Curio*	390.00	500.00	550.00
☐ **Fort Findlay Sesquicentennial Pair,** .22 LR/.22 WMR Combo, Frontier Scout S.A., Commemorative, Gold Plated, 4¾″ Barrel, Cased, *Curio*	1600.00	2200.00	2450.00
☐ **Fort Stephenson Sesquicentennial,** .22 L.R.R.F., Frontier Scout S.A., Nickel Plated, Blue, with Nickel Plating, 4¾″ Barrel, Cased, *Curio*	400.00	520.00	550.00
☐ **Forty-Niner Miner,** .22 L.R.R.F., Frontier Scout S.A., Commemorative, Blue with Gold Plating, 4¾″ Barrel, Cased, *Curio*	190.00	275.00	300.00
☐ **Frontier Scout,** .22 L.R.R.F., Single Action, Western Style, 6 Shot, Various Barrel Lengths, *Modern*	125.00	190.00	185.00
☐ **Frontier Model 1878 Double Action,** Various Calibers, Various Barrel Lengths, with Ejector, *Curio*	335.00	550.00	525.00
☐ **Frontier Model 1878 Double Action,** Sheriff's Model, Various Calibers, Various Barrel Lengths, no Ejector, *Curio*	350.00	570.00	550.00
☐ **Frontier Model 1878 Double Action,** Phillipine Model, .45 Colt, 6″ Barrel, Large Trigger Guard, *Curio*	410.00	725.00	700.00
☐ **Frontier Model 1878,** Serial #'s under 39,000 are *Antique.*			
☐ **Gen. J.H. Morgan Indian Raid,** .22 L.R.R.F., Frontier Scout S.A., Nickel Plated, Blue, with Gold Plating, 4¾″ Barrel, Cased, *Curio*	480.00	710.00	695.00
☐ **Gen. Nathan Bedford Forrest,** .22 L.R.R.F., Frontier Scout S.A., Commemorative, Blue, with Gold Plating, 4¾″ Barrel, Cased, *Curio*	205.00	300.00	310.00
☐ **Gen. Hood Centennial,** .22 L.R.R.F., Frontier Scout S.A., Commemorative, Blue, with Gold Plating, 4¾″ Barrel, Cased, *Curio*	210.00	300.00	310.00
☐ **Gen. Meade Campaign,** .22 L.R.R.F., Frontier Scout S.A., Commemorative, Blue, with Gold Plating, 4¾″ Barrel, Cased, *Curio*	200.00	280.00	300.00
☐ **Gen. Meade Campaign,** .45 Colt, Single Action Army, Commemorative, Blue, with Gold Plating, 5½″ Barrel, Cased, *Curio*	585.00	850.00	895.00
☐ **Golden Spike,** .22 L.R.R.F., Frontier Scout S.A., Commemorative, Blue, with Gold Plating, 6″ Barrel, Cased, *Curio*	200.00	280.00	300.00

	V.G.	Exc.	Prior Year Exc. Value
☐ **H. Cook 1 of 100,** .22 L.R.R.F., and .45 Colt Set, Commemorative, Nickel Plated, Blue Frame, Cased, *Curio*	710.00	1100.00	1150.00
☐ **House Pistol,** .41 Short R.F., Cloverleaf-Cylinder Model 1871, 4 Shot, 3" Barrel, Round Barrel, Spur Trigger, *Antique*	345.00	480.00	465.00
☐ **House Pistol,** .41 Short R.F., Cloverleaf-Cylinder Model 1871, 4 Shot, 1½" Barrel, Round Barrel, Spur Trigger, *Antique*	500.00	690.00	675.00
☐ **House Pistol,** .41 Short R.F., Cloverleaf-Cylinder Model 1871, 4 Shot, 1½" Barrel, Octagon Barrel, Spur Trigger, *Antique*	675.00	925.00	895.00
☐ **House Pistol,** .41 Short R.F., Round Cylinder Model of 1871, 5 Shot, 2⅝" Barrel, Round Barrel, Spur Trigger, *Antique*	375.00	515.00	500.00
☐ **Idaho Territorial Centennial,** .22 L.R.R.F., Frontier Scout S.A., Nickel Plated, Blue, with Nickel Plating, 4¾" Barrel, Cased, *Curio*	290.00	400.00	385.00
☐ **Indiana Sesquicentennial,** .22 L.R.R.F., Frontier Scout S.A., Commemorative, Blue, with Gold Plating, 4¾" Barrel, Cased, *Curio*	210.00	270.00	290.00
☐ **Joaquin Murietta,** .22 L.R.R.F., and .45 Colt Set, Frontier Scout and S.A.A., Commemorative, Blue, with Gold Plating, Cased, *Curio*	820.00	1375.00	1450.00
☐ **Kansas Centennial,** .22 L.R.R.F., Frontier Scout S.A., Commemorative, Gold Plated, Walnut Grips, Cased, *Curio*	210.00	270.00	290.00
☐ **Kansas Cowtown: Abilene,** .22 L.R.R.F., Frontier Scout S.A., Commemorative, Gold Plated, 4¾" Barrel, Cased, *Curio*	200.00	285.00	300.00
☐ **Kansas Cowtown: Coffyville,** .22 L.R.R.F., Frontier Scout S.A., Commemorative, Blue, with Gold Plating, 4¾" Barrel, Cased, *Curio*	200.00	285.00	300.00
☐ **Kansas Cowtown: Dodge City,** .22 L.R.R.F., Frontier Scout S.A., Commemorative, Blue, with Gold Plating, 4¾" Barrel, Cased, *Curio*	200.00	285.00	300.00
☐ **Kansas Cowtown: Wichita,** .22 L.R.R.F., Frontier Scout S.A., Commemorative, Gold Plated, 4¾" Barrel, Cased, *Curio*	200.00	285.00	300.00
☐ **Kansas Fort Hays,** .22 L.R.R.F., Frontier Scout S.A., Commemorative, Blue, with Nickel Plating, 4¾" Barrel, Cased, *Curio*	200.00	285.00	300.00
☐ **Kansas Fort Learned,** .22 L.R.R.F., Frontier Scout S.A., Commemorative, Blue, with Nickel Plating, Cased, *Curio*	205.00	280.00	275.00
☐ **Kansas Fort Riley,** .22 L.R.R.F., Frontier Scout S.A., Commemorative, Blue, with Nickel Plating, 4¾" Barrel, Cased, *Curio*	205.00	280.00	275.00
☐ **Kansas Fort Scott,** .22 L.R.R.F., Frontier Scout S.A., Commemorative, Blue, with Nickel Plating, 4¾" Barrel, Cased, *Curio*	225.00	305.00	300.00
☐ **Kansas: Chisholm Trail,** .22 L.R.R.F., Frontier Scout S.A., Commemorative, Blue, with Nickel Plating, 4¾" Barrel, Cased, *Curio*	205.00	280.00	275.00
☐ **Kansas: Pawnee Trail,** .22 L.R.R.F., Frontier Scout S.A., Commemorative, Blue, with Nickel Plating, 4¾" Barrel, Cased, *Curio*	205.00	280.00	275.00

	V.G.	Exc.	Prior Year Exc. Value
☐ **Kansas: Santa Fe Trail,** .22 L.R.R.F., Frontier Scout S.A., Commemorative, Blue, with Nickel Plating, 4¾" Barrel, Cased, *Curio*	205.00	280.00	275.00
☐ **Kansas: Shawnee Trail,** .22 L.R.R.F., Frontier Scout S.A., Commemorative, Blue, with Nickel Plating, 4¾" Barrel, Cased, *Curio*	205.00	280.00	275.00
☐ **Lawman MK III,** .357 Magnum, Various Barrel Lengths, Blue, 6 Shot, *Modern*	135.00	185.00	180.00
☐ **Lawman MK III,** .357 Magnum, Various Barrel Lengths, Nickel Plated, 6 Shot, *Modern*	140.00	190.00	185.00
☐ **Lawman MK V,** .357 Magnum, Various Barrel Lengths, Blue, 6 Shot, *Modern*	165.00	240.00	235.00
☐ **Lawman MK V,** .357 Magnum, Various Barrel Lengths, Nickel Plated, 6 Shot, *Modern*	180.00	260.00	250.00
☐ **Lawman: Bat Masterson,** .22 L.R.R.F., Frontier Scout S.A., Commemorative, Nickel Plated, 4¾" Barrel, Cased, *Curio*	250.00	335.00	325.00
☐ **Lawman: Bat Masterson,** .45 Colt, Single Action Army, Commemorative, Nickel Plated, 4¾" Barrel, Cased, *Curio*	575.00	865.00	850.00
☐ **Lawman: Pat Garrett,** .22 L.R.R.F., Frontier Scout S.A., Commemorative, Gold Plated, with Nickel Plating, 4¾" Barrel, Cased, *Curio*	250.00	335.00	325.00
☐ **Lawman: Pat Garrett,** .45 Colt, Single Action Army, Commemorative, Gold Plated, with Nickel Plating, 5½" Barrel, Cased, *Curio*	575.00	865.00	850.00
☐ **Lawman: Wild Bill Hickock,** .22 L.R.R.F., Frontier Scout S.A., Commemorative, Blue, with Nickel Plating, 6" Barrel, Cased, *Curio*	250.00	335.00	325.00
☐ **Lawman: Wild Bill Hickock,** .45 Colt, Single Action Army, Commemorative, Blue, with Nickel Plating, 7½" Barrel, Cased, *Curio*	575.00	865.00	850.00
☐ **Lawman: Wyatt Earp,** .22 L.R.R.F., Frontier Scout S.A., Commemorative, Blue, with Nickel Plating, Cased, *Curio*	300.00	410.00	400.00
☐ **Lawman: Wyatt Earp,** .45 Colt, Single Action Army, Commemorative, Blue, with Nickel Plating, 16⅛" Barrel, Cased, *Curio*	925.00	1365.00	1350.00
☐ **Lightning Model 1877,** .38 Colt, 6 Shot, Double Action, Standard Model, *Curio*	245.00	445.00	435.00
☐ **Lightning Model 1877,** .38 Colt, 6 Shot, Double Action, Sheriff's Model, *Curio*	275.00	490.00	460.00
☐ **Lightning Model 1877,** Serial Numbers under 105, 123 are *Antique.*			
☐ **Maine Sesquicentennial,** .22 L.R.R.F., Frontier Scout S.A., Commemorative, Gold Plated, with Nickel Plating, 4¾" Barrel, Cased, *Curio*	210.00	290.00	280.00
☐ **Marshal,** .38 Special, 6 Shot, Round Butt, *Modern*	215.00	300.00	280.00
☐ **Metropolitan MK III,** .38 Special, 4" Barrel, 6 Shot, *Modern*	155.00	240.00	235.00
☐ **Missouri Sesquicentennial,** .22 L.R.R.F., Frontier Scout S.A., Commemorative, Blue, with Gold Plating, 4¾" Barrel, Cased, *Curio*	210.00	285.00	280.00

	V.G.	Exc.	Prior Year Exc. Value
☐ **Missouri Sesquicentennial,** .45 Colt, Single Action Army, Commemorative, Blue, with Gold Plating, 5½″ Barrel, Cased, *Curio*	425.00	650.00	700.00
☐ **Model 1872 Army,** .44 Henry R.F., Open-Top Frontier Single Action, Army Style Gripframe, *Antique*	1775.00	2800.00	2650.00
☐ **Model 1872 Army,** .44 Henry R.F., Open-Top Frontier Single Action, Navy Style Gripframe, *Antique*	1925.00	2950.00	2850.00
☐ **Model 1889,** .38 Long Colt, 6 Shot, Commercial, Various Barrel Lengths, Double Action, Swing-Out Cylinder, *Antique*	230.00	395.00	385.00
☐ **Model 1889,** .41 Long Colt, 6 Shot, Commercial, Various Barrel Lengths, Double Action, Swing-Out Cylinder, *Antique*	190.00	385.00	375.00
☐ **Model 1889 Navy,** .38 Long Colt, 6 Shot, Military, 6″ Barrel, Double Action, Swing-Out Cylinder, *Antique*	290.00	510.00	495.00
☐ **Model 1892 New Army,** .38 Long Colt, 6 Shot, Military, 6″ Barrel, Double Action, Swing-Out Cylinder, *Antique*	180.00	300.00	285.00
☐ **Model 1892 New Navy,** .38 Long Colt, 6 Shot, Military, 6″ Barrel, Double Action, Swing-Out Cylinder, *Antique*	225.00	360.00	340.00
☐ **Model 1892 New Navy,** .38 Long Colt, 6 Shot, Commercial, Various Barrel Lengths, Double Action, Swing-Out Cylinder, *Antique*	145.00	240.00	230.00
☐ **Model 1892 New Navy,** .41 Long Colt, 6 Shot, Commercial, Various Barrel Lengths, Double Action, Swing-Out Cylinder, *Antique*	145.00	245.00	235.00
☐ **Model 1894 New Army,** .38 Long Colt, 6 Shot, Military, 6″ Barrel, Double Action, Swing-Out Cylinder, *Antique*	175.00	285.00	275.00
☐ **Model 1894 New Navy,** .38 Long Colt, 6 Shot, Military, 6″ Barrel, Double Action, Swing-Out Cylinder, *Antique*	205.00	310.00	290.00
☐ **Model 1895 New Army,** .38 Long Colt, 6 Shot, Military, 6″ Barrel, Double Action, Swing-Out Cylinder, *Antique*	160.00	270.00	255.00
☐ **Model 1895 New Navy,** .38 Long Colt, 6 Shot, Military, 6″ Barrel, Double Action, Swing-Out Cylinder, *Antique*	220.00	355.00	340.00
☐ **Model 1896 New Army,** .38 Long Colt, 6 Shot, Military, 6″ Barrel, Double Action, Swing-Out Cylinder, *Curio*	195.00	285.00	275.00
☐ **Model 1896 New Navy,** .38 Long Colt, 6 Shot, Military, 6″ Barrel, Double Action, Swing-Out Cylinder, *Curio*	195.00	285.00	275.00
☐ **Model 1901 New Army,** .38 Long Colt, 6 Shot, Military, 6″ Barrel, Double Action, Swing-Out Cylinder, *Curio*	165.00	245.00	240.00
☐ **Model 1902 Army,** .45 Colt, 6 Shot, Military, 6″ Barrel, Double Action, *Curio*	335.00	515.00	495.00
☐ **Model 1903 New Army,** .38 Long Colt, 6 Shot, Military, 6″ Barrel, Double Action, Swing-Out Cylinder, *Curio*	165.00	245.00	235.00

	V.G.	Exc.	Prior Year Exc. Value
☐ **Model 1903 New Navy,** .32-20 WCF, 6 Shot Commercial, Various Barrel Lnegths, Double Action, Swing-Out Cylinder, *Curio*	215.00	360.00	345.00
☐ **Model 1903 New Navy,** .38 Long Colt, 6 Shot, Commercial, Various Barrel Lengths, Double Action, Swing-Out Cylinder, *Curio*	195.00	305.00	295.00
☐ **Model 1903 New Navy,** .38 Long Colt, 6 Shot, Commercial, Various Barrel Lengths, Double Action, Swing-Out Cylinder, *Curio*	170.00	300.00	290.00
☐ **Model 1905 U.S.M.C.,** .38 Long Colt, 6 Shot, Military, 6″ Barrel, Swing-Out Cylinder, *Curio*	700.00	1350.00	1300.00
☐ **Model 1905 U.S.M.C.,** .38 Long Colt, 6 Shot, Commercial, 6″ Barrel, Swing-Out Cylinder, *Curio*	725.00	1450.00	1400.00
☐ **Model 1909 Army,** .45 Colt, 6 Shot, Military, 5½″ Barrel, *Curio*	300.00	530.00	495.00
☐ **Model 1909 U.S.M.C.,** .45 Colt, 6 Shot, 5½″ Barrel, *Modern*	570.00	900.00	865.00
☐ **Model 1909 U.S.N.,** .45 Colt, 6 Shot, Military, 5½″ Barrel, *Modern*	360.00	610.00	595.00
☐ **Model 1917 Army,** .45 Auto-Rim, 6 Shot, Military, 5½″ Barrel, *Modern*	275.00	415.00	385.00
☐ **Montana Territory Centennial,** .22 L.R.R.F., Frontier Scout S.A., Commemorative, Blue, with Gold Plating, 4¾″ Barrel, Cased, *Curio*	220.00	305.00	300.00
☐ **Montana Territory Centennial,** .45 Colt, Single Action Army, Commemorative, Blue, with Gold Plating, 7½″ Barrel, Cased, *Curio*	575.00	815.00	800.00
☐ **Nebraska Centennial,** .22 L.R.R.F., Frontier Scout S.A., Commemorative, Gold Plated, 4¾″ Barrel, Cased, *Curio*	215.00	285.00	280.00
☐ **Ned Buntline,** .45 Colt, New Frontier Single Action Army, 12″ Barrel, Commemorative, *Modern*	700.00	965.00	950.00
☐ **Nevada Battle Born,** .22 L.R.R.F., Frontier Scout S.A., Commemorative, Blue, with Nickel Plating, 4¾″ Barrel, Cased, *Curio*	235.00	330.00	315.00
☐ **Nevada Battle Born,** .22 L.R.R.F. and .45 Colt Set, Frontier Scout and S.A.A., Commemorative, Blue, with Nickel Plating, Cased, *Curio*	1575.00	2400.00	2200.00
☐ **Nevada Battle Born,** .45 Colt, Single Action Army, Commemorative, Blue, with Nickel Plating, 5½″ Barrel, Cased, *Curio*	865.00	1250.00	1200.00
☐ **Nevada Centennial,** .22 L.R.R.F., Frontier Scout S.A., Commemorative, Blue, with Nickel Plating, 4¾″ Barrel, Cased, *Curio*	215.00	285.00	280.00
☐ **Nevada Centennial,** .22 L.R.R.F. and .45 Colt Set, Frontier Scout and S.A.A., Nickel Plated, Blue, with Nickel Plating, Cased, *Curio*	535.00	800.00	785.00
☐ **Nevada Centennial,** .22 L.R.R.F. and .45 Colt Set, Frontier Scout and S.A.A., Commemorative, Blue, with Nickel Plating, with Extra Engraved Cylinder, Cased, *Curio*	865.00	1315.00	1290.00
☐ **Nevada Centennial,** .45 Colt, Single Action Army, Nickel Plated, Blue, with Nickel Plating, 5½″ Barrel, Cased, *Curio*	715.00	1125.00	1100.00

	V.G.	Exc.	Prior Year Exc. Value
☐ **New Frontier,** .22 L.R.R.F., Various Barrel Lengths, Blue, 6 Shot, Adjustable Sights, *Modern*	145.00	190.00	185.00
☐ **New Frontier,** .22 L.R.R.F., 7½″ Barrel, Blue, 6 Shot, Adjustable Sights, *Modern*	150.00	200.00	195.00
☐ **New Frontier,** .22LR/.22WMR Combo, Various Barrel Lengths, Blue, 6 Shot, Adjustable Sights, *Modern*	155.00	240.00	220.00
☐ **New Frontier,** .22R/.22 WRM Combo, 7½″ Barrel, Blue, 6 Shot, Adjustable Sights, *Modern*	165.00	235.00	230.00
☐ **New Jersey Tercentenary,** .22 L.R.R.F., Frontier Scout S.A., Commemorative, Blue, with Nickel Plating, 4¾″ Barrel, Cased, *Curio*	215.00	295.00	280.00
☐ **New Jersey Tercentenary,** .45 Colt, Single Action Army, Commemorative, Blue, with Nickel Plating, 5½″ Barrel, Cased, *Curio*	615.00	880.00	865.00
☐ **New Line,** .38 Long Colt, Police and Thug Model, with Ejector, 5 Shot, Spur Trigger, Standard, *Antique*	465.00	725.00	700.00
☐ **New Line,** .32 or .41 C.F., Police and Thug Model, with Ejector, 5 Shot, Spur Trigger, *Antique*	600.00	985.00	945.00
☐ **New Line,** .38 Long Colt, House Civilian Model, with Ejector, 5 Shot, Spur Trigger, *Antique*	260.00	410.00	395.00
☐ **New Line,** .38 Long Colt, House Civilian Model, no Ejector, 5 Shot, Spur Trigger, *Antique*	260.00	405.00	390.00
☐ **New Line,** .41 Short C.F., House Civilian Model, with Ejector, 5 Shot, Spur Trigger, *Antique*	285.00	475.00	450.00
☐ **New Line,** .41 Short C.F., House Civilian Model, no Ejector, 5 Shot, Spur Trigger, *Antique*	250.00	410.00	395.00
☐ **New Line Pocket,** Locking Notches on Cylinder Periphery, *Add* **20%-30%**			
☐ **New Line Pocket,** .22 Long R.F., "the Little Colt," 7 Shot, Spur Trigger, *Antique*	195.00	350.00	325.00
☐ **New Line Pocket,** .30 Long R.F., "the Pony Colt," 5 Shot, Spur Trigger, *Antique*	205.00	360.00	340.00
☐ **New Line Pocket,** .32 Long R.F. or .32 Long Colt, for 4″ Barrel, *Add* **100%-150%**			
☐ **New Line Pocket,** .32 Long Colt, "the Ladies Colt," 5 Shot, Spur Trigger, *Antique*	200.00	325.00	300.00
☐ **New Line Pocket,** .32 Long R.F., "the Ladies Colt," 5 Shot, Spur Trigger, *Antique*	190.00	315.00	295.00
☐ **New Line Pocket,** .38 Long Colt, "the Pet Colt," 5 Shot, Spur Trigger, *Antique*	250.00	370.00	350.00
☐ **New Line Pocket,** .38 Long R.F., "the Pet Colt," 5 Shot, Spur Trigger, *Antique*	225.00	315.00	300.00
☐ **New Line Pocket,** .41 Long R.F., "the Big Colt," 5 Shot, Spur Trigger, *Antique*	285.00	405.00	385.00
☐ **New Line Pocket,** .41 Short C.F., "the Big Colt," 5 Shot, Spur Trigger, *Antique*	295.00	420.00	410.00
☐ **New Mexico Golden Anniv.,** .22 L.R.R.F., Frontier Scout S.A., Commemorative, Blue, with Gold Plating, 4¾″ Barrel, Cased, *Curio*	260.00	340.00	325.00
☐ **New Pocket,** .32 Long Colt, 6 Shot, Various Barrel Lengths, *Curio*	200.00	310.00	295.00
☐ **New Pocket,** .32 S & W Long, 6 Shot, Various Barrel Lengths, *Curio*	220.00	325.00	310.00

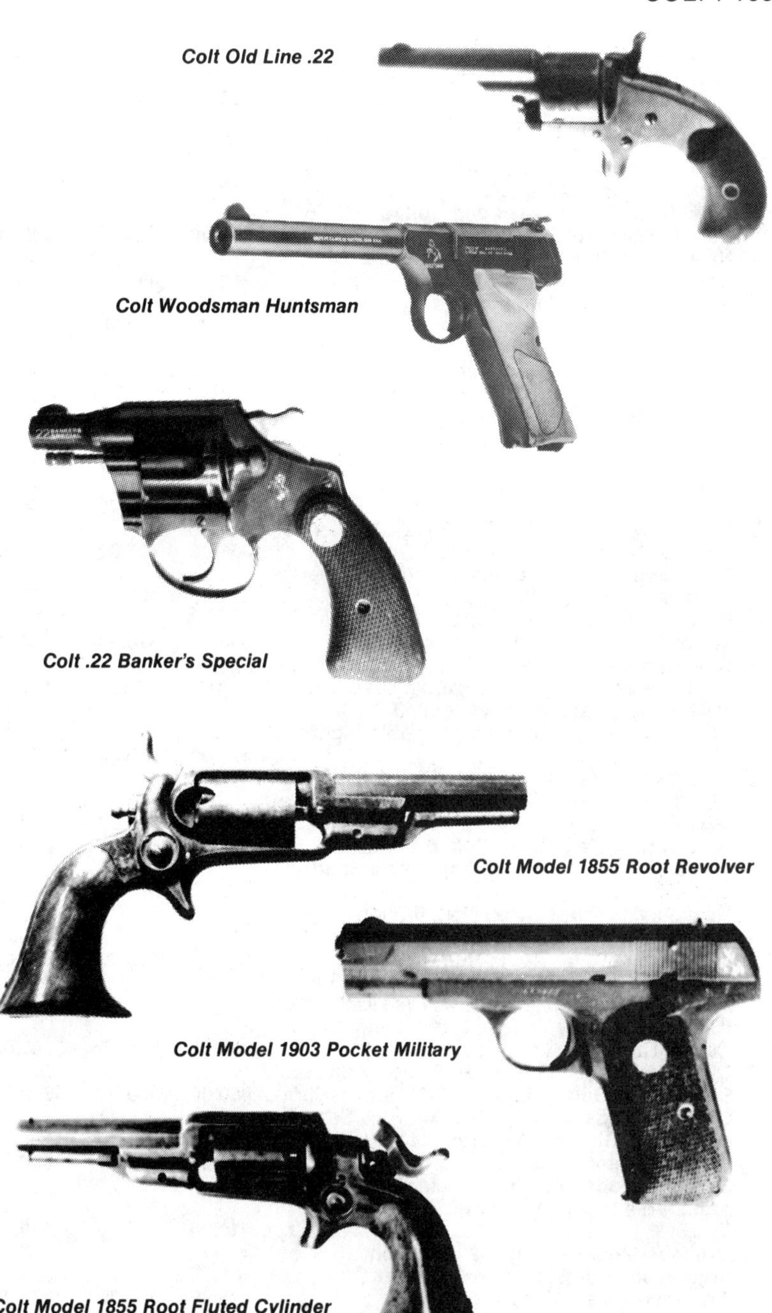

Colt Old Line .22

Colt Woodsman Huntsman

Colt .22 Banker's Special

Colt Model 1855 Root Revolver

Colt Model 1903 Pocket Military

Colt Model 1855 Root Fluted Cylinder

	V.G.	Exc.	Prior Year Exc. Value
☐ **New Police,** .32 Long Colt, 6 Shot, Various Barrel Lengths, *Curio*	185.00	300.00	280.00
☐ **New Police,** Serial Numbers under 7,300 are Antique.			
☐ **New Police,** .32 S & W Long, 6 Shot, Various Barrel Lengths, *Curio*	170.00	270.00	260.00
☐ **New Police Target,** .32 Long Colt, 6 Shot, 6″ Barrel, Adjustable, *Modern*	260.00	400.00	385.00
☐ **New Police Target,** .32 S & W Long, 6 Shot, 6″ Barrel, Adjustable Sights, *Modern*	260.00	400.00	385.00
☐ **New Service,** .357 Magnum, 6 Shot, Commercial, Various Barrel Lengths, *Modern*	375.00	575.00	550.00
☐ **New Service,** .38 Special, 6 Shot, Commercial, Various Barrel Lengths, *Modern*	270.00	410.00	395.00
☐ **New Service,** .38-40 WCF, 6 Shot, Commercial, Various Barrel Lengths, *Modern*	310.00	490.00	465.00
☐ **New Service,** .38-44, 6 Shot, Commercial, Various Barrel Lengths, *Modern*	335.00	525.00	500.00
☐ **New Service,** .44 Special, 6 Shot, Commercial, Various Barrel Lengths, *Modern*	375.00	600.00	545.00
☐ **New Service,** .44-40 WCF, 6 Shot, Commercial, Various Barrel Lengths, *Modern*	355.00	535.00	515.00
☐ **New Service,** .45 Auto-Rim, 6 Shot, Commercial, Various Barrel Lengths, *Modern*	250.00	425.00	400.00
☐ **New Service,** .45 Colt, 6 Shot, Commercial, Various Barrel Lengths, *Modern*	330.00	510.00	485.00
☐ **New Service,** .455 Colt, 6 Shot, Commercial, Various Barrel Lengths, *Modern*	330.00	485.00	465.00
☐ **New Service Target,** .44 Special, 6 Shot, Commercial, 7½″ Barrel, Adjustable Sights, *Modern*	520.00	830.00	795.00
☐ **New Service Target,** .45 Auto-Rim, 6 Shot, Commercial, 7½″ Barrel, Adjustable Sights, *Modern*	495.00	765.00	735.00
☐ **New Service Target,** .45 Colt, 6 Shot, Commercial, 7½″ Barrel, Adjustable Sights, *Modern*	550.00	875.00	840.00
☐ **New Service Target,** .455 Colt, 6 Shot, Commercial, 7½″ Barrel, Adjustable Sights, *Modern*	515.00	860.00	820.00
☐ **NRA Centennial,** .357 Mag. or .45 Colt, Single Action Army, Commemorative, Blue, Color Case, Hardened Frame, Various Barrel Lengths, Cased, *Curio*	490.00	715.00	700.00
☐ **Officer's Model,** .38 Special, 6 Shot, Adjustable Sights, with Detachable Shoulder Stock, *Curio*	960.00	1600.00	1550.00
☐ **Officer's Model Match,** .22 L.R.R.F., 6 Shot, Adjustable Sights, 6″ Barrel, Target Grips, Target Hammer, *Modern*	285.00	410.00	380.00
☐ **Officer's Model Match,** .22 W.M.R., 6 Shot, Adjustable Sights, 6″ Barrel, Target Grips, Target Hammer, *Modern*	510.00	715.00	695.00
☐ **Officer's Model Match,** .32 S&W Long, 6 Shot, Adjustable Sights, 6″ Barrel, Target Grips, Target Hammer, *Modern*	495.00	700.00	675.00

	V.G.	Exc.	Prior Year Exc. Value
☐ **Officer's Model Match,** .38 Special, 6 Shot, Adjustable Sights, 6″ Barrel, Target Grips, Target Hammer, *Modern*	225.00	340.00	320.00
☐ **Officer's Model Special,** .22 L.R.R.F., 6 Shot, Adjustable Sights, 6″ Barrel, Heavy Barrel, *Modern*	205.00	345.00	320.00
☐ **Officer's Model Special,** .38 Special, 6 Shot, Adjustable Sights, 6″ Barrel, Heavy Barrel, *Modern*	230.00	350.00	325.00
☐ **Officer's Model Target,** .22 L.R.R.F., 6 Shot, Adjustable Sights, 6″ Barrel, Second Issue, *Modern*	315.00	450.00	425.00
☐ **Officer's Model Target,** .32 S & W Long, 6 Shot, Adjustable Sights, 6″ Barrel, Second Issue, *Modern*	330.00	475.00	450.00
☐ **Officer's Model Target,** .38 Special, 6 Shot, Adjustable Sights, 6″ Barrel, *Modern*	255.00	425.00	400.00
☐ **Officer's Model Target,** .38 Special, 6 Shot, Adjustable Sights, 6″ Barrel, Second Issue, *Modern*	290.00	470.00	450.00
☐ **Official Police,** .22 L.R.R.F., 6 Shot, Various Barrel Lengths, *Modern*	190.00	275.00	275.00
☐ **Official Police,** .32-20 WCF, 6 Shot, *Modern*	250.00	380.00	365.00
☐ **Official Police,** .38 Special, 6 Shot, *Modern*	150.00	215.00	215.00
☐ **Official Police Mk.III,** .38 Special, 6 Shot, *Modern*	175.00	240.00	235.00
☐ **Official Police,** .41 Long Colt, 6 Shot, *Modern*	180.00	250.00	250.00
☐ **Oklahoma Territory,** .22 L.R.R.F., Frontier Scout S.A., Commemorative, Blue, with Gold Plating, 4¾″ Barrel, Cased, *Curio*	225.00	320.00	310.00
☐ **Old Fort Des Moines,** .22 L.R.R.F., Frontier Scout S.A., Commemorative, Gold Plated, 4¾″ Barrel, Cased, *Curio*	250.00	360.00	350.00
☐ **Old Fort Des Moines,** .22 L.R.R.F. and .45 Colt Set, Frontier Scout S.A. and S.A.A., Commemorative, Gold Plated, Cased, *Curio*	875.00	1275.00	1250.00
☐ **Old Fort Des Moines,** .45 Colt, Single Action Army, Commemorative, Gold Plated, 5½″ Barrel, Cased, *Curio*	595.00	875.00	850.00
☐ **Old Line Pocket,** .22 Short R.F., Open Top, First Model with Ejector, 7 Shot, Spur Trigger, *Antique*	560.00	825.00	800.00
☐ **Old Line Pocket,** .22 Short R.F., Open Top, Second Model, No Ejector, 7 Shot, Spur Trigger, *Antique*	220.00	375.00	350.00
☐ **Oregon Trail,** .22 L.R.R.F., Frontier Scout S.A., Commemorative, Blue, with Gold Plating, 4¾″ Barrel, Cased, *Curio*	200.00	275.00	275.00
☐ **Peacemaker,** .22LR/.22 WMR Combo, Various Barrel Lengths, Blue, 6 Shot, *Modern*	130.00	200.00	190.00
☐ **Peacemaker,** .22 LR/.22 WMR Combo, 7½″ Barrel, Blue, 6 Shot, *Modern*	130.00	205.00	195.00
☐ **Peacemaker Centennial,** .44-40 WCF, Single Action Army, Commemorative, Blue, Color Case, Hardened Frame, 7½″ Barrel, Cased, *Curio*	575.00	780.00	765.00

	V.G.	Exc.	Prior Year Exc. Value
☐ **Peacemaker Centennial,** .44-40 and .45 Colt Set, Single Action Army, Commemorative, Blue, Color Case, Hardened Frame, 7½" Barrel, Cased, *Curio*	1025.00	1500.00	1650.00
☐ **Peacemaker Centennial,** .45 Colt, Single Action Army, Commemorative, Blue, Color Case, Hardened Frame, 7½" Barrel, Cased, *Curio*	560.00	780.00	765.00
☐ **Pocket Positive,** .32 Long Colt, 6 Shot, Various Barrel Lengths, *Modern*	195.00	280.00	265.00
☐ **Pocket Positive,** .32 S & W Long, 6 Shot, Various Barrel Lengths, *Modern*	225.00	310.00	295.00
☐ **Police Positive,** .22 L.R.R.F., 6 Shot, Various Barrel Lengths, *Modern*	165.00	235.00	230.00
☐ **Police Positive,** .22 WRF, 6 Shot, Various Barrel Lengths, *Modern*	195.00	280.00	265.00
☐ **Police Positive,** .32 Long Colt, 6 Shot, Various Barrel Lengths, *Modern*	125.00	185.00	180.00
☐ **Police Positive,** .32 S & W Long, 6 Shot, Various Barrel Lengths, *Modern*	130.00	190.00	185.00
☐ **Police Positive,** .38 S & W, 6 Shot, Various Barrel Lengths, *Modern*	135.00	195.00	190.00
☐ **Police Positive Late,** .38 Special, Blue, 4" Barrel, *Modern*	150.00	205.00	200.00
☐ **Police Positive Late,** .38 Special, Nickel Plated, 4" Barrel, 6 Shot, *Modern*	155.00	230.00	225.00
☐ **Police Positive Special,** .32 S & W Long, 6 Shot, Various Barrel Lengths, *Modern*	135.00	195.00	190.00
☐ **Police Positive Special,** .32-20 WCF, 6 Shot, Various Barrel Lengths, *Modern*	190.00	300.00	290.00
☐ **Police Positive Special,** .38 S & W, 6 Shot, Various Barrel Lengths, *Modern*	120.00	185.00	175.00
☐ **Police Positive Special,** .38 Special, Shot, Various Barrel Lengths, *Modern*	145.00	205.00	200.00
☐ **Police Positive Target,** .22 L.R.R.F., 6 Shot, 6" Barrel, Adjustable Sights, *Modern*	230.00	410.00	395.00
☐ **Police Positive Target,** .22 WRF, 6 Shot, 6" Barrel, Adjustable Sights, *Modern*	245.00	445.00	425.00
☐ **Police Positive Target,** .32 Long Colt, 6 Shot, 6" Barrel, Adjustable Sights, *Modern*	235.00	360.00	340.00
☐ **Police Positive Target,** .32 S & W Long, 6 Shot, 6" Barrel, Adjustable Sights, *Modern*	235.00	360.00	340.00
☐ **Police Positive Target,** .38 S & W Long, 6 Shot, 6" Barrel, Adjustable Sights, *Modern*	225.00	350.00	335.00
☐ **Pony Express Centennial,** .22 L.R.R.F., Frontier Scout S.A., Commemorative, 4¾" Barrel, Gold Plated, Cased, *Curio*	330.00	490.00	475.00
☐ **Pony Express Presentation,** .45 Colt, Single Action Army, Commemorative, Nickel Plated, 7½" Barrel, Cased, *Curio*	735.00	975.00	950.00
☐ **Pony Express Presentation 4 Gun Set,** .45 Colt, Single Action Army, Commemorative, Nickel Plated, 7½" Barrel, Cased, *Curio*	2375.00	3500.00	3850.00
☐ **Python,** .357 Magnum, 2" Barrel, Blue, Vent Rib, Adjustable Sights, 6 Shot, *Modern*	295.00	395.00	380.00
☐ **Python,** .357 Magnum, 4" Barrel, Blue, Vent Rib, 6 Shot, Adjustable Sights, *Modern*	275.00	380.00	370.00

	V.G.	Exc.	Prior Year Exc. Value
☐ **Python,** .357 Magnum, 4″ Barrel, Nickel, Vent Rib, 6 Shot, Adjustable Sights, *Modern*	280.00	400.00	390.00
☐ **Python,** .357 Magnum, 6″ Barrel, Blue, Vent Rib, 6 Shot, Adjustable Sights, *Modern*	280.00	400.00	390.00
☐ **Python,** .357 Magnum, 6″ Barrel, Nickel, Vent Rib, 6 Shot, Adjustable Sights, *Modern*	305.00	425.00	410.00
☐ **Python,** .357 Magnum, 8″ Barrel, Blue, Vent Rib, 6 Shot, Adjustable Sights, *Modern*	305.00	410.00	400.00
☐ **Python,** .357 Magnum, 8″ Barrel, Nickel, Vent Rib, 6 Shot, Adjustable Sights, *Modern*	335.00	445.00	430.00
☐ **Sheriff's Model,** .45 Colt, Single Action Army, Commemorative, Blue, Color Case, Hardened Frame, 3″ Barrel, *Curio*	875.00	1325.00	1450.00
☐ **Sheriff's Model,** .45 Colt, Single Action Army, Commemorative, Nickel Plated, 3″ Barrel, *Curio*	2275.00	3100.00	3350.00
☐ **Shooting Master,** .357 Magnum, 6 Shot, Commercial, 6″ Barrel, Adjustable Sights, *Modern*	525.00	725.00	700.00
☐ **Shooting Master,** .38 Special, 6 Shot, Commercial, 6″ Barrel, Adjustable Sights, *Modern*	460.00	635.00	600.00
☐ **Shooting Master,** .44 Special, 6 Shot, Commercial, 6″ Barrel, Adjustable Sights, *Modern*	530.00	700.00	675.00
☐ **Shooting Master,** .45 Auto-Rim, 6 Shot, Commercial, 6″ Barrel, Adjustable Sights, *Modern*	460.00	600.00	575.00
☐ **Shooting Master,** .45 Colt, 6 Shot, Commercial, 6″ Barrel, Adjustable Sights, *Modern*	500.00	690.00	660.00
☐ **Single Action Army Late,** .357 Magnum, Various Barrel Lengths, Blue, 6 Shot, *Modern*	335.00	445.00	430.00
☐ **Single Action Army Late,** .357 Magnum, 7½″ Barrel, Blue, 6 Shot, *Modern*	3 00.00	405.00	390.00
☐ **Single Action Army Late,** .44 Special, 7½″ Barrel, Blue, 6 Shot, *Modern*	305.00	415.00	400.00
☐ **Single Action Army Late,** .45 Colt, 7½″ Barrel, Blue, 6 Shot, *Modern*	300.00	400.00	385.00
☐ **Single Action Army Late,** .45 Colt, Various Barrel Lengths, Blue, 6 Shot, *Modern*	300.00	405.00	390.00
☐ **Single Action Army Buntline Late,** .45 Colt, 12″ Barrel, Blue, 6 Shot, *Modern*	400.00	515.00	500.00
☐ **Single Action Army Late,** .45 Colt, 7½″ Barrel, Nickel Plated, 6 Shot, *Modern*	310.00	415.00	400.00
☐ **Single Action Army New Frontier,** .357 Magnum, Various Barrel Lengths, Blue, 6 Shot, Adjustable Sights, *Modern*	345.00	450.00	440.00
☐ **Single Action Army New Frontier,** .44 Special, 7½″ Barrel, Blue, 6 Shot, Adjustable Sights, *Modern*	345.00	460.00	450.00
☐ **Single Action Army New Frontier,** .45 Colt, Various Barrel Lengths, Blue, 6 Shot, Adjustable Sights, *Modern*	350.00	460.00	450.00
☐ **Single Action Army Buntline New Frontier,** .45 Colt, 12″ Barrel, Blue, 6 Shot, Adjustable Sights, *Modern*	420.00	615.00	600.00

	V.G.	Exc.	Prior Year Exc. Value
☐ **Single Action Army,** .45 Colt, Standard Cavalry Model # Under 15,000, Screw-Retained Cylinder Pin, Blue, Military, 7½″ Barrel, *Antique*	1675.00	3175.00	2900.00
☐ **Single Action Army,** .45 Colt, Indian Scout Model, #'s Under 30,000, Screw-Retained Cylinder Pin, Nickel Plated, Military, 7½″ Barrel, *Antique*	2025.00	3575.00	3400.00
☐ **Single Action Army,** .45 Colt, Artillery Model, Screw-Retained Cylinder Pin, Military, 5½″ Barrel, *Antique*	1030.00	2100.00	2000.00
☐ **Single Action Army,** Various Calibers, Storekeeper's Model, No Ejector, Short Barrel, Commercial, *Antique*	2000.00	3250.00	3100.00
☐ **Single Action Army,** Various Calibers, Standard Peacemaker, Calibers: .45 Colt, .44-40, .38-40, .41, .32-20, Commercial, *Antique*	700.00	1250.00	1200.00
☐ **Single Action Army,** for Rare Calibers, *Add* **50%-200%**			
☐ **Single Action Army,** Folding Rear Sight, Long Barrel, *Add* **$1975.00-$3000.00**			
☐ **Single Action Army,** Target Model (Flat-Top), *Add* **$975.00-$1900.00**			
☐ **Single Action Army,** 8″ or 9″ Barrel, *Add* **$375.00-$600.00**			
☐ **Single Action Army,** for 12″ Barrel, *Add* **$445.00-$700.00**			
☐ **Single Action Army,** for 16″ Barrel, *Add* **$580.00-$995.00**			
☐ **Single Action Army,** Shoulder Stock, *Add* **$995.00-$1850.00**			
☐ **Single Action Army,** #'s over 182,000 are *Modern,* #'s under 165,000 are Black Powder Only			
☐ **Single Action Army,** Nickel Plating, *Add* **15%-25%**			
☐ **Single Action Army,** Rimfire Calibers, *Add* **100%-125%**			
☐ **Single Action Army,** Long-Fluted Cylinder #'s 330,000 to 331,379, Commercial, *Curio*	1000.00	1700.00	1625.00
☐ **Single Action Bisley,** Various Calibers, Standard Model, Calibers: 32-20, 38-40, 41, 41-40, 45, Target Trigger, *Modern*	610.00	1000.00	975.00
☐ **Single Action Bisley,** Various Calibers, Target Model, (Flat-Top), *Modern*	1025.00	2050.00	1975.00
☐ **Single Action Bisley,** other than Standard Calibers, *Add* **50%-100%**			
☐ **Single Action Bisley,** Non-Standard Barrel Lengths, *Add* **20%-30%**			
Single Action Bisley, No Ejector Housing, *Add* **25%-35%**			
☐ **Second Amendment,** .22 L.R.R.F., Frontier Scout, Cased, *Curio*	235.00	330.00	325.00
☐ **St. Augustine Quadricentennial,** .22 L.R.R.F., Frontier Scout S.A., Commemorative, Blue, with Gold Plating, 4¾″ Barrel, Cased, *Curio*	230.00	330.00	325.00
☐ **St. Louis Bicentennial,** .22 L.R.R.F., Frontier Scout S.A., Commemorative, Blue, with Gold Plating, 4¾″ Barrel, Cased, *Curio*	205.00	300.00	310.00

Colt Viper

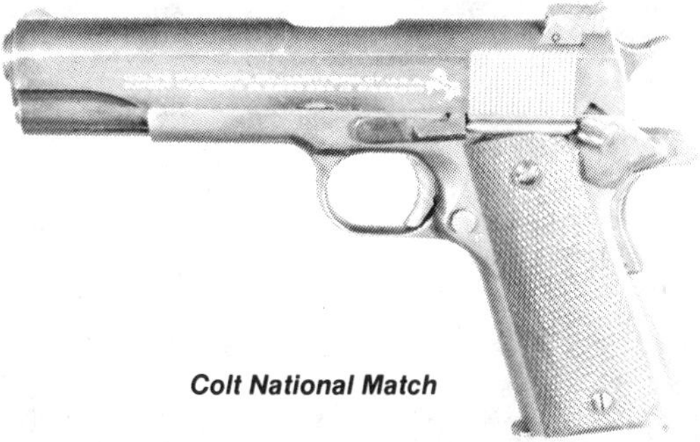

Colt National Match

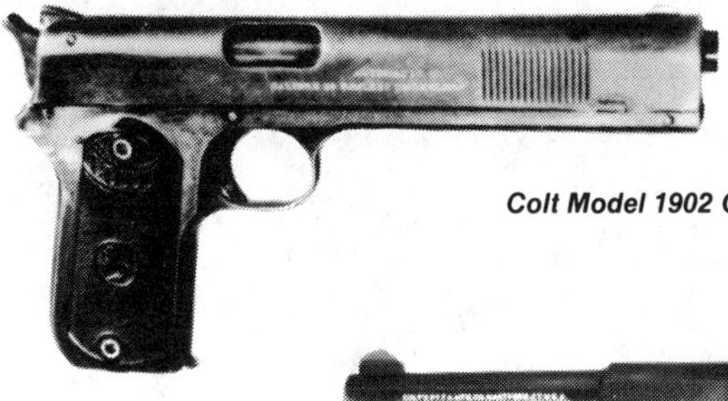

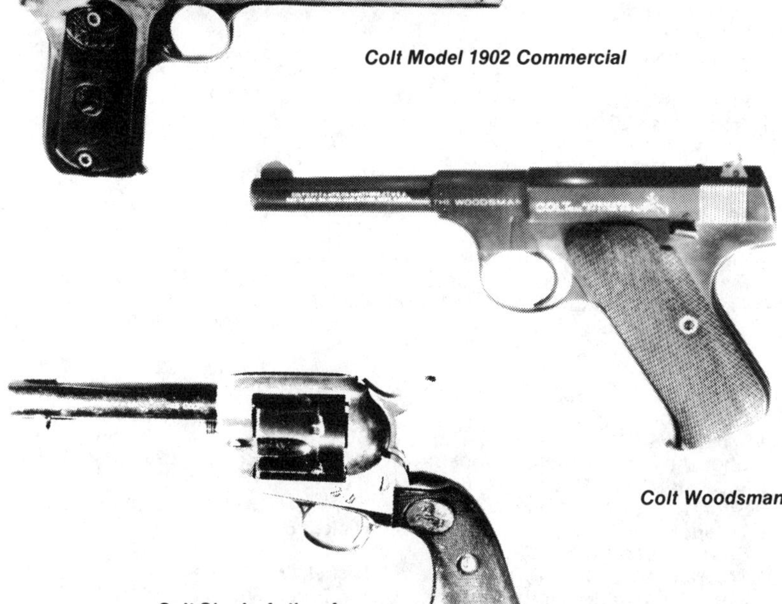

Colt Model 1902 Commercial

Colt Woodsman

Colt Single Action Army

	V.G.	Exc.	Prior Year Exc. Value
☐ **St. Louis Scout,** .22 L.R.R.F. and .45 Colt Set, Frontier Scout and S.A.A., Commemorative, Blue, with Gold Plating, Cased, *Curio*	725.00	1050.00	1100.00
☐ **St. Louis Bicentennial,** .45 Colt, Single Action Army, Commemorative, Blue, with Gold Plating, 5½" Barrel, Cased, *Curio*	510.00	775.00	880.00
☐ **Texas Ranger,** Standard, .45 Colt, Single Action Army, Commemorative, Blue, Color Case Hardened Frame, Cased, *Curio*	900.00	1400.00	1475.00
☐ **Thunderer Model 1877,** .41 Colt, 6 Shots, Double Action, Standard Model, *Modern*	310.00	460.00	435.00
☐ **Thunderer Model 1877,** .41 Colt, 6 Shots, Double Action, Sheriff's Model, *Modern*	315.00	470.00	450.00
☐ **Trooper,** .22 L.R.R.F., 6 Shot, Adjustable Sights, Target Grips, Target Hammer, *Modern*	195.00	310.00	295.00
☐ **Trooper,** .357 Magnum, 6 Shot, 4" Barrel, Adjustable Sights, *Modern*	200.00	305.00	290.00
☐ **Trooper,** .357 Magnum, 6 Shot, Adjustable Sights, Target Grips, Target Hammer, *Modern*	205.00	305.00	295.00
☐ **Trooper,** .38 Special, 6 Shot, 4" Barrel, Adjustable Sights, *Modern*	195.00	295.00	285.00
☐ **Trooper,** .38 Special, 6 Shot, Adjustable Sights, Target Grips, Target Hammer, *Modern*	200.00	295.00	285.00
☐ **Trooper MK III,** .22 L.R.R.F., 4" Barrel, Blue, 6 Shot, Adjustable Sights, *Modern*	145.00	190.00	185.00
☐ **Trooper MK III,** .22 L.R.R.F., 8" Barrel, Blue, 6 Shot, Adjustable Sights, *Modern*	185.00	260.00	250.00
☐ **Trooper MK III,** .22 L.R.R.F., 6" Barrel, 6 Shot, Adjustable Sights, *Modern*	145.00	185.00	180.00
☐ **Trooper MK III,** .357 Magnum, 4" Barrel, Blue, 6 Shot, Adjustable Sights, *Modern*	150.00	180.00	175.00
☐ **Trooper MK III,** .357 Magnum, 4" Barrel, Nickel Plated, 6 Shot, Adjustable Sights, *Modern*	155.00	185.00	180.00
☐ **Trooper MK III,** .357 Magnum, 6" Barrel, 6 Shot, Adjustable Sights, *Modern*	165.00	200.00	195.00
☐ **Trooper MK III,** .357 Magnum, 6" Barrel, Nickel Plated, 6 Shot, Adjustable Sights, *Modern*	165.00	210.00	200.00
☐ **Trooper MK III,** .357 Magnum, 8" Barrel, 6 Shot, Adjustable Sights, *Modern*	165.00	210.00	200.00
☐ **Trooper MK III,** .357 Magnum, 8" Barrel, Nickel Plated, 6 Shot, Adjustable Sights, *Modern*	170.00	215.00	210.00
☐ **Trooper MK IV,** .22 W.M.R., 4" Barrel, Blue, 6 Shot, Adjustable Sights, *Modern*	155.00	220.00	215.00
☐ **Trooper MK IV,** .22 W.M.R., 6" Barrel, 6 Shot, Adjustable Sights, *Modern*	155.00	220.00	215.00
☐ **Trooper MK IV,** .357 Magnum, 6" Barrel, 6 Shot, Adjustable Sights, *Modern*	170.00	235.00	225.00
☐ **Trooper MK V,** .22 L.R.R.F., 4" Barrel, Blue, 6 Shot, Adjustable Sights, *Modern*	165.00	225.00	215.00
☐ **Trooper MK V,** .22 L.R.R.F., 6" Barrel, Blue, 6 Shot, Adjustable Sights, *Modern*	165.00	230.00	220.00
☐ **Trooper MK V,** .22 L.R.R.F., 4" Barrel, Nickel, 6 Shot, Adjustable Sights, *Modern*	175.00	235.00	225.00
☐ **Trooper MK V,** .22 L.R.R.F., 6" Barrel, Nickel, 6 Shot, Adjustable Sights, *Modern*	175.00	235.00	225.00

	V.G.	Exc.	Prior Year Exc. Value
☐ **Trooper MK V,** .357 Magnum, 4″ Barrel, Blue, 6 Shot, Adjustable Sights, *Modern*	160.00	225.00	225.00
☐ **Trooper MK V,** .357 Magnum, 6″ Barrel, Blue, 6 Shot, Adjustable Sights, *Modern*	160.00	225.00	225.00
☐ **Trooper MK V,** .357 Magnum, 4″ Barrel, Nickel, 6 Shot, Adjustable Sights, *Modern*	170.00	240.00	240.00
☐ **Trooper MK V,** .357 Magnum, 6″ Barrel, Nickel, 6 Shot, Adjustable Sights, *Modern*	170.00	245.00	245.00
☐ **Viper,** .38 Special, Nickel Plated, 4″ Barrel, 6 Shot, Lightweight, *Modern*	160.00	225.00	225.00
☐ **Viper,** .38 Special, Blue, 4″ Barrel, 6 Shot, Lightweight, *Modern*	150.00	230.00	215.00
☐ **West Virginia Centennial,** .22 L.R.R.F., Frontier Scout S.A., Commemorative, Blue, with Gold Plating, 4¾″ Barrel, Cased, *Curio*	210.00	295.00	310.00
☐ **West Virginia Centennial,** .45 Colt, Single Action Army, Commemorative, Blue, with Gold Plating, 4¾″ Barrel, Cased, *Curio*	530.00	750.00	800.00
☐ **Wyatt Earp Buntline,** .45 Colt, Single Action Army, Commemorative, Gold Plated, 12″ Barrel, Cased, *Curio*	1175.00	1725.00	1800.00
☐ **Wyoming Diamond Jubilee,** .22 L.R.R.F., Frontier Scout S.A., Commemorative, Blue, with Nickel Plating, 4¾″ Barrel, Cased, *Curio*	215.00	300.00	310.00
HANDGUN, SEMI-AUTOMATIC			
☐ **Ace,** .22 L.R.R.F., Clip Fed, Adjustable Sights, Target Pistol, Blue, *Curio*	535.00	800.00	750.00
☐ **Ace, Mk. IV,** .22 L.R.R.F., Clip Fed, Adjustable Sights, Target Pistol, Blue, *Modern*	255.00	350.00	325.00
☐ **Ace, Mk. IV,** .22 L.R.R.F., Clip Fed, Adjustable Sights, Target Pistol, Nickel Plated, *Modern*	295.00	410.00	385.00
☐ **Ace Signature,** .22 L.R.R.F., Clip Fed, Adjustable Sights, Target Pistol, Etched and Gold Plated, *Modern*	485.00	700.00	675.00
☐ **Ace Service Model,** .22 L.R.R.F., Clip Fed, Adjustable Sights, Target Pistol, *Curio*	720.00	1075.00	1025.00
☐ **Conversion Unit,** .22 L.R.R.F., Clip Fed, Blue, Adjustable Sights, *Modern*	120.00	195.00	185.00
☐ **Conversion Unit, Service Ace,** .22 L.R.R.F., Clip Fed, Blue, Adjustable Sights, *Modern*	900.00	1650.00	1550.00
☐ **Ace 45-22 Conversion Unit,** .45 ACP, Clip Fed, Adjustable Sights, Target Pistol, *Curio*	185.00	295.00	285.00
☐ **Challenger,** .22 L.R.R.F., Clip Fed, *Modern*	155.00	245.00	235.00
☐ **Combat Commander,** .38 Super, Clip Fed, Blue, *Modern*	215.00	305.00	295.00
☐ **Combat Commander,** .45 ACP, Clip Fed, Blue, *Modern*	220.00	305.00	295.00
☐ **Combat Commander,** .45 ACP, Clip Fed, Satin Nickel, *Modern*	235.00	340.00	320.00
☐ **Combat Commander,** 9mm Luger, Clip Fed, Blue, *Modern*	205.00	305.00	295.00
☐ **Commander,** .45 ACP, Clip Fed, Blue, Lightweight, *Modern*	225.00	315.00	300.00
☐ **Gold Cup,** .45 ACP, Clip Fed, Adjustable Sights, Target Pistol, Military Style Stock, *Modern*	340.00	475.00	450.00

	V.G.	Exc.	Prior Year Exc. Value
☐ **Gold Cup MK III,** .38 Special, Clip Fed, Adjustable Sights, Target Pistol, Military Style Stock, *Modern*	390.00	530.00	500.00
☐ **Gold Cup MK IV,** .45 ACP, Clip Fed, Blue, Target Trigger, *Modern*	330.00	450.00	425.00
☐ **Gold Cup Camp Perry,** .45 ACP, Commemorative, Target Pistol, Light Engraving, Cased, *Modern*	520.00	730.00	775.00
☐ **Gold Cup NRA Centennial,** .45 ACP, Commemorative, Target Pistol, Light Engraving, Cased, *Curio*	425.00	580.00	600.00
☐ **Gold Cup D.E.A. Commemorative,** .45 ACP, Clip Fed, Adjustable Sights, Commemorative, Cased, *Modern*	760.00	1125.00	1200.00
☐ **Government,** .45 ACP, Clip Fed, Commercial, *Modern*	280.00	390.00	365.00
☐ **Government John Browning M1911,** .45 ACP, Commemorative, Light Engraving, Cased, *Modern*	715.00	1025.00	1100.00
☐ **Government 1911 English,** .455 Webley Auto., Clip Fed, Military, *Curio*	510.00	760.00	735.00
☐ **Government 1911 English,** .455 Webley Auto., Clip Fed, Military, R.A.F. Markings, *Curio*	675.00	1000.00	950.00
☐ **Government BB 1911A1,** .45 ACP, Clip Fed, *Curio*	375.00	500.00	475.00
☐ **Government M1911,** M1911A1, .45 ACP, *Also See U.S. Military.*			
☐ **Government M1911,** .45 ACP, Clip Fed, Commercial, *Curio*	615.00	865.00	825.00
☐ **Government M1911,** .45 ACP, Clip Fed, Military, *Curio*	630.00	900.00	875.00
☐ **Government M1911A1,** .45 ACP, Clip Fed, Military, *Modern*	390.00	600.00	550.00
☐ **Government M1911A1,** .45 ACP, Clip Fed, Military, with Detachable Shoulder Stock, *Class 3*	1030.00	1900.00	1825.00
☐ **Government MK IV,** .38 Super, Clip Fed, Blue, *Modern*	225.00	350.00	325.00
☐ **Government MK IV,** .45 ACP, Clip Fed, Blue, *Modern*	220.00	345.00	320.00
☐ **Government MK IV,** .45 ACP, Clip Fed, Nickel Plated, *Modern*	250.00	365.00	335.00
☐ **Government MK IV,** 9mm Luger, Clip Fed, Blue, *Modern*	225.00	350.00	320.00
☐ **Government MK IV U.S.M.C. Limited Edition,** .45 ACP, Clip Fed, Cased, Commemorative, *Modern*	540.00	715.00	750.00
☐ **GM Mark IV/80 380 Auto,** .380 Caliber ACP, 7 Round Mag, Composition Gripstock, Blue, *Modern*	318.00	330.00	330.00
☐ As Above, Nickel	349.95	370.00	370.00
☐ As Above, Satin Nickel In Blue	334.95	350.00	350.00
☐ **GM Mark IV/Series 80,** Various Calibers, Checkered Walnut Gripstock, Blue, *Modern*	491.95	500.00	500.00
☐ **GM Mark IV/Series 80 Combat,** Various Calibers, Checkered Walnut Gripstock, Blue, *Modern*	481.95	500.00	500.00
☐ As Above, Satin Nickel	519.95	540.00	540.00

	V.G.	Exc.	Prior Year Exc. Value
☐ As Above, Light Weight	491.95	500.00	500.00
☐ As Above, Stainless Steel	510.00	532.50	—
☐ **Mark IV/80 Combat Commander,** Various Calibers, O Frame, Checkered Walnut Gripstock, Blue, *Modern*	491.95	500.00	500.00
☐ **Mark IV/80 Gold Cup National Match,** .45 ACP, 7 Round Mag, 5″ Barrel, Blue, *Modern*	642.50	660.00	660.00
☐ **Officer's ACP MK IV/80,** .45 ACP, 6 Round Clip, Checkered Walnut Gripstock, Matt Finish, *Modern*	482.50	500.00	500.00
☐ As Above, Satin Nickel	512.95	525.00	525.00
☐ **M 1911A1 (British),** .455 Webley Auto., Clip Fed, Military, *Modern*	515.00	775.00	745.00
☐ **Junior,** .22 Short R.F., Clip Fed, *Modern*	145.00	205.00	195.00
☐ **Junior,** .25 ACP, Clip Fed, *Modern*	120.00	200.00	190.00
☐ **Model 1900,** .38 ACP, Clip Fed, 6″ Barrel, Commercial, Safety Sight, *Curio*	730.00	1350.00	1300.00
☐ **Model 1900,** .38 ACP, Clip Fed, 6″ Barrel, Commercial, Forward Slide Serrations, *Curio*	625.00	950.00	900.00
☐ **Model 1900,** .38 ACP, Clip Fed, 6″ Barrel, Commercial, *Curio*	510.00	700.00	675.00
☐ **Model 1900 U.S. Army,** .38 ACP, Clip Fed, 6″ Barrel, Military, *Curio*	800.00	1550.00	1500.00
☐ **Model 1900 U.S. Navy,** .38 ACP, Clip Fed, 6″ Barrel, Military, *Curio*	675.00	1325.00	1300.00
☐ **Model 1902,** .38 ACP, Clip Fed, 6″ Barrel, Forward Slide Serrations, Commercial, *Curio*	390.00	575.00	550.00
☐ **Model 1902,** .38 ACP, Clip Fed, 6″ Barrel, Commercial, *Curio*	495.00	675.00	650.00
☐ **Model 1902 Military,** .38 ACP, Clip Fed, 6″ Barrel, Forward Slide Serrations, *Curio*	495.00	650.00	625.00
☐ **Model 1902 Military,** .38 ACP, Clip Fed, 6″ Barrel, *Curio*	415.00	575.00	550.00
☐ **Model 1902 Military U.S. Army,** .38 ACP, Clip Fed, 6″ Barrel, *Curio*	925.00	1500.00	1450.00
☐ **Model 1903 Round Hammer,** .38 ACP, Clip Fed, *Curio*	285.00	425.00	400.00
☐ **Model 1903 Spur Hammer,** .38 ACP, Clip Fed, *Curio*	260.00	395.00	375.00
☐ **Model 1903 Hammerless Pocket 1st Type,** .32 ACP, Clip Fed, Barrel Bushing, Commercial, *Curio*	250.00	360.00	345.00
☐ **Model 1903 Hammerless Pocket 2nd Type,** .32 ACP, Clip Fed, Commercial, *Curio*	180.00	285.00	275.00
☐ **Model 1903 Hammerless Pocket 3rd Type,** .32 ACP, Clip Fed, Commercial, Magazine Disconnect, *Modern*	180.00	290.00	280.00
☐ **Model 1903 Hammerless Pocket 1st Type,** .380 ACP, Clip Fed, Barrel Bushing, Commercial, *Curio*	250.00	365.00	345.00
☐ **Model 1903 Hammerless Pocket 2nd Type,** .380 ACP, Clip Fed, Commercial, *Curio*	200.00	320.00	300.00
☐ **Model 1903 Hammerless Pocket 3rd Type,** .380 ACP, Clip Fed, Commercial, Magazine Disconnect, *Modern*	210.00	330.00	310.00
☐ **Model 1903 Hammerless U.S.,** .32 ACP, Clip Fed, Military, Magazine Disconnect, *Curio*	425.00	625.00	550.00

	V.G.	Exc.	Prior Year Exc. Value
☐ **Model 1903 Hammerless U.S.,** .380 ACP, Clip Fed, Military, Magazine Disconnect, *Curio*	390.00	625.00	550.00
☐ **Model 1905,** .45 ACP, Clip Fed, *Curio*	750.00	1250.00	1200.00
☐ **Model 1905,** .45 ACP, Clip Fed, Adjustable Sights, with Detachable Shoulder Stock, *Curio*	2700.00	4150.00	4000.00
☐ **Model 1905/07 U.S.,** .45 ACP, Clip Fed, Blue, Military, *Curio*	1650.00	2250.00	2200.00
☐ **Model 1908 Pocket,** .25 ACP, Clip Fed, Hammerless, *Curio*	200.00	285.00	275.00
☐ **Model 1908 Pocket,** .25 ACP, Clip Fed, Hammerless, Magazine Disconnect, *Modern*	180.00	255.00	250.00
☐ **Model 1908 Pocket,** .25 ACP, Clip Fed, Hammerless, Magazine Disconnect, Military, *Curio*	285.00	430.00	415.00
☐ **National Match,** .45 ACP, Clip Fed, Target Pistol, Adjustable Sights, *Modern*	600.00	860.00	845.00
☐ **National Match,** .45 ACP, Clip Fed, Target Pistol, *Modern*	510.00	745.00	735.00
☐ **Pony,** .380 ACP, Clip Fed, Hammer, *Modern*	875.00	1425.00	1400.00

Colt · Lawman MK V

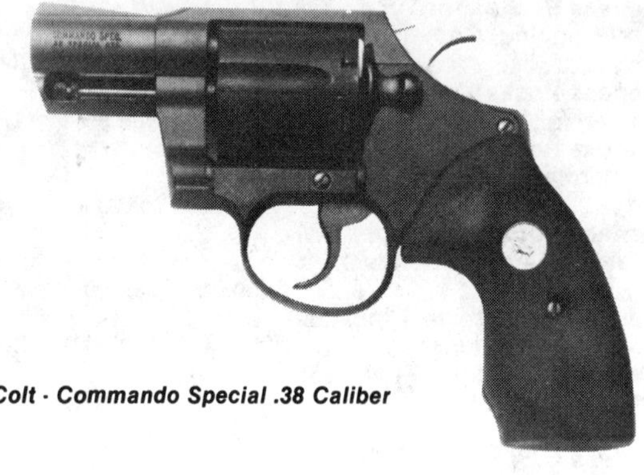

Colt · Commando Special .38 Caliber

	V.G.	Exc.	Prior Year Exc. Value
☐ **Super,** .38 Super, Clip Fed, Commercial, *Modern*	320.00	460.00	440.00
☐ **Super Match,** .38 Super, Clip Fed, Adjustable Sights, Target Pistol, *Modern*	530.00	740.00	720.00
☐ **Super Match,** .38 Super, Clip Fed, Target Pistol, *Modern*	425.00	580.00	565.00
☐ **Super Mexican Police,** .38 Super, Clip Fed, Military, *Modern*	410.00	565.00	545.00
☐ **WWI Battle of 2nd Marne,** .45 ACP, Commemorative, M1911, Light Engraving, Cased, *Curio*	350.00	475.00	500.00
☐ **WWI Battle of 2nd Marne Deluxe,** .45 ACP, Commemorative, M1911, Engraved, Cased, *Curio*	850.00	1275.00	1350.00
☐ **WWI Battle of 2nd Marne Special Deluxe,** .45 ACP, Commemorative, M1911, Fancy Engraving, Cased, *Curio*	1575.00	2275.00	2250.00
☐ **WWI Belleau Wood,** .45 ACP, Commemorative, M1911, Light Engraving, Cased, *Curio*	385.00	510.00	500.00
☐ **WWI Belleau Wood Special Deluxe,** .45 ACP, Commemorative, M1911, Fancy Engraving, Cased, *Curio*	1575.00	2275.00	2250.00
☐ **WWI Belleau Wood Deluxe,** .45 ACP, Commemorative, M1911, Engraved, Cased, *Curio*	820.00	1300.00	1350.00
☐ **WWI Chateau Thierry,** .45 ACP, Commemorative, M1911, Light Engraving, Cased, *Curio*	350.00	475.00	500.00
☐ **WWI Chateau Thierry Deluxe,** .45 ACP, Commemorative, M1911, Engraved, Cased, *Curio*	835.00	1325.00	1375.00
☐ **WWI Chateau Thierry Special Deluxe,** .45 ACP, Commemorative, M1911, Fancy Engraving, Cased, *Curio*	1475.00	2125.00	2250.00
☐ **WWI Meuse-Argonne,** .45 ACP, Commemorative, M1911, Light Engraving, Cased, *Curio*	350.00	470.00	500.00
☐ **WWI Meuse-Argonne Deluxe,** .45 ACP, Commemorative, M1911, Engraved, Cased, *Curio*	800.00	1275.00	1375.00
☐ **WWI Meuse-Argonne Special Deluxe,** .45 ACP, Commemorative, M1911, Fancy Engraving, Cased, *Curio*	1500.00	2175.00	2250.00
☐ **WWII E.T.O.,** .45 ACP, Commemorative, M1911A1, Light Engraving, Cased, *Curio*	360.00	510.00	500.00
☐ **WWII P.T.O.,** .45 ACP, Commemorative, M1911A1, Light Engraving, Cased, *Curio*	360.00	510.00	500.00
☐ **Woodsman,** .22 L.R.R.F., Clip Fed, Adjustable Sights, with Detachable Shoulder Stock, *Curio*	1030.00	1750.00	1675.00
☐ **Woodsman Huntsman,** .22 L.R.R.F., Clip Fed, Blue, Adjustable Sights, *Modern*	190.00	280.00	265.00
☐ **Woodsman Match Target 1st Type,** .22 L.R.R.F., Clip Fed, Extended Target Grips, *Modern*	475.00	700.00	675.00
☐ **Woodsman Match Target 2nd Type,** .22 L.R.R.F., Clip Fed, Blue, Adjustable Sights, *Modern*	240.00	340.00	320.00
☐ **Woodsman N & S,** .22 L.R.R.F., Clip Fed, Adjustable Sights, with Detachable Shoulder Stock, *Curio*	1075.00	1950.00	1900.00

Colt Model 1892 New Navy

Colt Police Positive

Colt Agent

Colt Model 1902 Military

	V.G.	Exc.	Prior Year Exc. Value
☐ **Woodsman Sport 1st. Type,** .22 L.R.R.F., Clip Fed, Adjustable Sights, *Modern*	**305.00**	**430.00**	**415.00**
☐ **Woodsman Sport,** .22 L.R.R.F., Clip Fed, Blue, Adjustable Sights, *Modern*	**235.00**	**350.00**	**335.00**
☐ **Woodsman Target 1st Type,** .22 L.R.R.F., Clip Fed, Adjustable Sights, *Modern*	**205.00**	**335.00**	**325.00**
☐ **Woodsman Target 1st. Type,** .22 L.R.R.F., Clip Fed, Adjustable Sights, with Extra Mainspring Housing, *Modern*	**335.00**	**490.00**	**450.00**
☐ **Woodsman Target 2nd. Type,** .22 L.R.R.F., Clip Fed, Adjustable Sights, *Modern*	**285.00**	**380.00**	**360.00**
☐ **Woodsman Target 3rd. Type,** .22 L.R.R.F., Clip Fed, Blue, Adjustable Sights, *Modern*	**250.00**	**390.00**	**370.00**
☐ **Woodsman Targetsman,** .22 L.R.R.F., Clip Fed, Blue, Adjustable Sights, *Modern*	**180.00**	**275.00**	**250.00**

	V.G.	Exc.	Prior Year Exc. Value
HANDGUN, SINGLESHOT			
☐ **#1 Deringer,** .41 Short R.F., all Metal, Spur Trigger, Light Engraving, *Antique*	610.00	850.00	825.00
☐ **#2 Deringer,** .41 Short R.F., "Address Col. Colt," Wood Grips, Spur Trigger, Light Engraving, *Antique*	635.00	1000.00	975.00
☐ **#2 Deringer,** .41 Short R.F., Wood Grips, Spur Trigger, Light Engraving, *Antique*	445.00	610.00	595.00
☐ **#3 Deringer Thuer,** .41 Short R.F., Wood Grips, Spur Trigger, 1st Issue, Contoured Swell at Pivot, High-Angled Hammer, *Antique*	650.00	1025.00	995.00
☐ **#3 Deringer Thuer,** .41 Short R.F., Wood Grips, Spur Trigger, 2nd Issue, Angled Frame, no Swell, High Angled Hammer, *Antique*	390.00	550.00	525.00
☐ **#3 Deringer Thuer,** .41 Short R.F., Wood Grips, Spur Trigger, 3rd Issue, Straight Thick Frame, High-Angled Hammer, *Antique*	330.00	450.00	425.00
☐ **#3 Deringer Thuer,** .41 Short R.F., Wood Grips, Spur Trigger, London Marked, *Antique*	650.00	860.00	835.00
☐ **#4 Deringer,** .22 Short R.F., Geneseo Anniversary Commemorative, Spur Trigger, *Curio*	325.00	490.00	470.00
☐ **#4 Deringer,** .22 Short R.F., Fort McPherson Commemorative, Spur Trigger, *Curio*	230.00	310.00	300.00
☐ **#4 Deringer,** .22 Short R.F., Spur Trigger, *Modern*	60.00	85.00	80.00
☐ **#4 Deringer,** .22 Short R.F., Spur Trigger, Cased Pair, *Modern*	105.00	170.00	165.00
☐ **#4 Lord Deringer,** .22 Short R.F., Spur Trigger, Cased Pair, *Modern*	100.00	160.00	155.00
☐ **#4 Lady Deringer,** .22 Short R.F., Spur Trigger, Cased Pair, *Modern*	105.00	165.00	160.00
☐ **#4 Lord and Lady Deringers,** .22 Short R.F., Spur Trigger, Cased Pair, *Modern*	100.00	160.00	155.00
☐ **Camp Perry 1st Issue,** .22 L.R.R.F., Adjustable Sights, Target Pistol, *Modern*	650.00	935.00	875.00
☐ **Camp Perry 2nd Issue,** .22 L.R.R.F., Adjustable Sights, Target Pistol, *Modern*	790.00	1300.00	1200.00
☐ **Civil War Centennial,** .22 Short R.F., ⅞ Scale 1860 Army Replica, Commemorative, 6″ Barrel, Blue, Cased, *Curio*	48.00	85.00	90.00
☐ **Civil War Centennial Pair,** .22 Short R.F., ⅞ Scale 1860 Army Replica, Commemorative, 6″ Barrel, Blue, Cased, *Curio*	110.00	170.00	185.00
☐ **Rock Island Arsenal Centennial,** .22 Short R.F., ⅞ Scale 1860 Army Replica, Commemorative, 6″ Barrel, Blue, Cased, *Curio*	90.00	165.00	175.00
RIFLE, BOLT ACTION			
☐ **Colteer 1-22,** .22 L.R.R.F., Singleshot, Plain, *Modern*	45.00	65.00	60.00
☐ **Colteer 1-22,** .22 WMR, Singleshot, Plain, *Modern*	50.00	75.00	70.00
☐ **Coltsman Custom (FN),** Various Calibers, Sporting Rifle, Fancy Wood, Light Engraving, Checkered Stock, Monte Carlo Stock, *Modern*	310.00	435.00	415.00

	V.G.	Exc.	Prior Year Exc. Value
☐ **Coltsman Custom (Sako),** Various Calibers, Sporting Rifle, Fancy Wood, Checkered Stock, Monte Carlo Stock, *Modern*	360.00	480.00	465.00
☐ **Coltsman Deluxe (FN),** Various Calibers, Sporting Rifle, Checkered Stock, Monte Carlo Stock, *Modern*	285.00	385.00	375.00
☐ **Coltsman Deluxe (Sako),** Various Calibers, Sporting Rifle, Checkered Stock, Monte Carlo Stock, *Modern*	310.00	450.00	420.00
☐ **Coltsman Standard (FN),** Various Calibers, Sporting Rifle, Checkered Stock, *Modern*	235.00	330.00	315.00
☐ **Coltsman Standard (Sako),** Various Calibers, Sporting Rifle, Checkered Stock, *Modern*	255.00	390.00	370.00
☐ **Sauer,** Various Calibers, Clip Fed, Checkered Stock, Short Action, *Modern*	550.00	815.00	795.00
☐ **Sauer,** Various Calibers, Clip Fed, Checkered Stock, Magnum, *Modern*	615.00	895.00	860.00
☐ **Sauer,** Various Calibers, Clip Fed, Checkered Stock, *Modern*	565.00	850.00	825.00
☐ **Sauer Grand African,** .458 Win. Mag., Clip Fed, Fancy Wood, *Modern*	660.00	985.00	945.00
☐ **Sauer Grand Alaskan,** .375 H & H Mag., Clip Fed, Checkered Stock, Magnum, *Modern*	630.00	925.00	900.00
RIFLE, SEMI-AUTOMATIC			
☐ **AR-15,** .223 Rem., Clip Fed, *Modern*	345.00	435.00	425.00
☐ **AR-15,** .223 Rem., Clip Fed, Collapsible Stock, *Modern*	375.00	465.00	455.00
☐ **AR-15 A2 Sporter II,** .223 Rem., Pistol Grip, 20″ Barrel, *Modern*	699.95	720.00	720.00
☐ **Colteer 22 Autoloader,** .22 L.R.R.F., Tube Feed, Plain, *Modern*	95.00	140.00	135.00
☐ **Colteer Stagecoach,** .22 L.R.R.F., Tube Feed, Light Engraving, *Modern*	100.00	150.00	145.00
RIFLE, PERCUSSION			
☐ **1st Model Ring Lever,** Various Calibers, 8 or 10 Shot Revolving Cylinder, with Topstrap, *Antique*	4450.00	7250.00	7125.00
☐ **2nd Model Ring Lever,** .44, 8 or 10 Shot Revolving Cylinder, no Topstrap, *Antique*	3875.00	6700.00	6550.00
☐ **Model 1839,** 6 Shot Cylinder, with Hammer, *Antique*	3100.00	4950.00	4850.00
☐ **Model 1855 Sporting Rifle,** .36, 6 Shot Revolving Cylinder, Sidehammer, no Forestock, Spur Triggerguard, *Antique*	1750.00	3400.00	3300.00
☐ **Model 1855 Sporting Rifle,** Various Calibers, 6 Shot Revolving Cylinder, Sidehammer, Halfstock, Scroll Triggerguard, *Antique*	1500.00	2850.00	2750.00
☐ **Model 1855 Sporting Rifle,** Various Calibers, 6 Shot Revolving Cylinder, Sidehammer, Full Stock, Scroll Triggerguard, *Antique*	1700.00	2850.00	2750.00
☐ **Model 1855 Carbine,** Various Calibers, 6 Shot Revolving Cylinder, Sidehammer, no Forestock, *Antique*	1700.00	2850.00	2750.00
☐ **Model 1855 Military Rifle,** Various Calibers, 6 Shot Revolving Cylinder, Sidehammer, Full Stock, U.S. Military, *Antique*	2400.00	4600.00	4450.00

	V.G.	Exc.	Prior Year Exc. Value
☐ **Model 1861 Musket,** .58, Military Contract Musket, *Antique*	575.00	900.00	875.00

RIFLE, SINGLESHOT

☐ **Sharps,** Various Calibers, Fancy Wood, Fancy Checkering, Cased with Accessories, *Modern*	1415.00	2050.00	1975.00

RIFLE, SLIDE ACTION

☐ **Lightning,** .22 R.F., Small Frame (Numbers over 35,300 are Modern), *Antique*	280.00	500.00	485.00
☐ **Lightning,** Various Calibers, Medium Frame (Numbers over 84,000 are Modern), *Antique*	325.00	510.00	495.00
☐ **Lightning Carbine,** Various Calibers, Medium Frame (Numbers over 84,000 are Modern), *Antique*	600.00	875.00	820.00
☐ **Lightning Baby Carbine,** Various Calibers, Medium Frame (Numbers over 84,000 are Modern), *Antique*	700.00	950.00	920.00
☐ **Lightning,** Various Calibers, Large Frame, *Antique*	510.00	690.00	665.00
☐ **Lightning Carbine,** Various Calibers, Large Frame, *Antique*	860.00	1450.00	1400.00
☐ **Lightning Baby Carbine,** Various Calibers, Large Frame, *Antique*	1075.00	1850.00	1800.00

SHOTGUN, DOUBLE BARREL, SIDE-BY-SIDE

☐ **Custom,** 12 and 16 Gauges, Double Trigger, Automatic Ejector, Checkered Stock, Beavertail Forend, Hammerless, *Modern*	260.00	400.00	385.00
☐ **Model 1878 Standard,** Various Gauges, Outside Hammers, Damascus Barrel, *Antique*	410.00	600.00	575.00
☐ **Model 1883 Standard,** Various Gauges, Hammerless, Damascus Barrel, *Antique*	495.00	700.00	675.00

SHOTGUN, SEMI-AUTOMATIC

☐ **Various Gauges,** for Solid Rib, *Add* **$15.00-$25.00**

☐ **Various Gauges,** for Vent Rib, *Add* **$25.00-$35.00**

☐ **Ultra-Light,** 12 and 20 Gauges, Checkered Stock, Takedown, *Modern*	160.00	235.00	220.00
☐ **Ultra-Light Custom,** 12 and 20 Gauges, Checkered Stock, Light Engraving, Takedown, *Modern*	180.00	260.00	250.00
☐ **Ultra-Light Magnum,** 12 and 20 Gauges 3″, Checkered Stock, Takedown, *Modern*	180.00	260.00	250.00
☐ **Ultra-Light Magnum Custom,** 12 and 20 Gauges 3″, Checkered Stock, Light Engraving, Takedown, *Modern*	200.00	280.00	265.00

SHOTGUN, SLIDE ACTION

☐ **Coltsman Custom,** Various Gauges, Takedown, Checkered Stock, Vent Rib, *Modern*	165.00	245.00	235.00
☐ **Coltsman Standard,** Various Gauges, Takedown, Plain, *Modern*	130.00	195.00	185.00

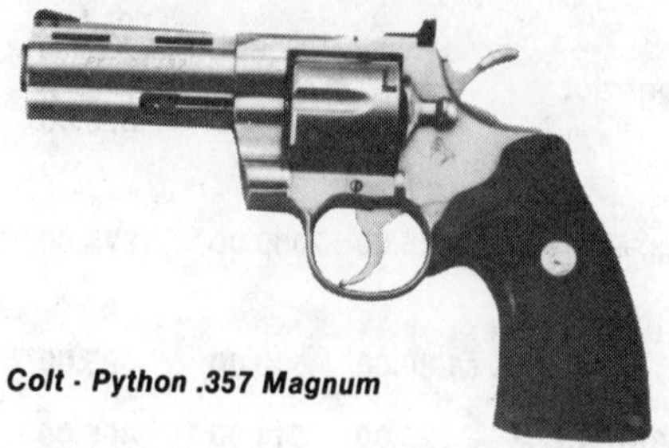

Colt · Python .357 Magnum

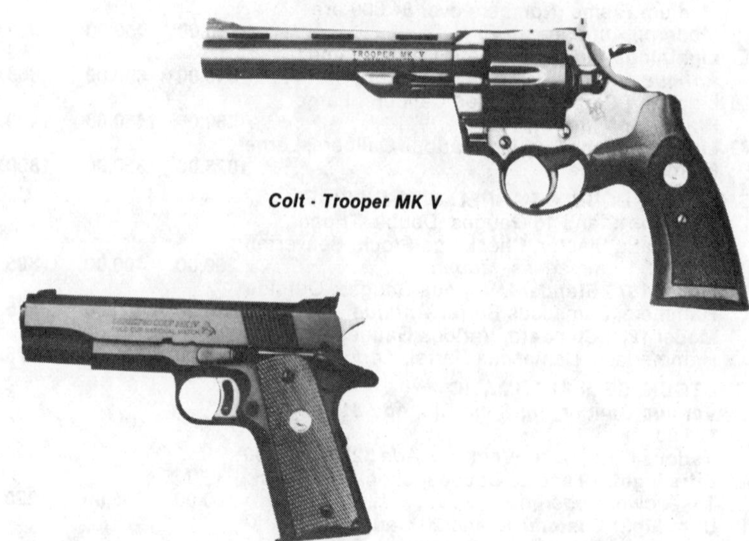

Colt · Trooper MK V

Colt · Mark IV/80 Gold Cup National Match

Colt · GM Mark IV/80 380 Auto

Colt - Mark IV/80 Combat Commander

Colt - GM Mark IV/Series 80 Combat

Colt - Detective Special

Colt - GM Mark IV/Series 80

COLUMBIA ARMORY

Tenn., Maltby & Henley Distributors, c.1890.

HANDGUN, REVOLVER

	V.G.	Exc.	Prior Year Exc. Value
☐ **New Safety**, .22 L.R.R.F., 7 Shot, Double Action, Solid Frame, Grip Safety, *Modern*	70.00	120.00	115.00
☐ **New Safety**, .32 S & W, 5 Shot, Double Action, Solid Frame, Grip Safety, *Modern*	80.00	135.00	135.00
☐ **New Safety**, .38 S & W, 5 Shot, Double Action, Solid Frame, Grip Safety, *Modern*	85.00	145.00	140.00

COLUMBIAN

Made by Foehl & Weeks, Philadelphia, Pa. c. 1890.

HANDGUN, REVOLVER

	V.G.	Exc.	Prior Year Exc. Value
☐ **.32 S & W**, 5 Shot, Double Action, Solid Frame, *Modern*	55.00	95.00	90.00
☐ **.38 S & W**, 5 Shot, Double Action, Solid Frame, *Modern*	55.00	95.00	90.00

COMET

HANDGUN, REVOLVER

	V.G.	Exc.	Prior Year Exc. Value
☐ **.32 Long R.F.**, 7 Shot, Single Action, Spur Trigger, Solid Frame, *Antique*	85.00	150.00	150.00

COMINAZZO OR COMINAZZI

Family of armorers in Brescia, Italy from about 1593 to about 1875.

HANDGUN, FLINTLOCK

	V.G.	Exc.	Prior Year Exc. Value
☐ **.54**, Mid-1600's, Belt Pistol, Brass Furniture, Ornate *Antique*	3,900.00	5,500.00	5,250.00

HANDGUN, WHEEL-LOCK

	V.G.	Exc.	Prior Year Exc. Value
☐ **Ebony Full Stock**, Ivory Pom, Holster Pistol, German Style, Military, Engraved, *Antique*	4,100.00	5,700.00	5,450.00

COMMANDO ARMS

Made by Volunteer Enterprises in Knoxville, Tenn. since 1969.

RIFLE, SEMI-AUTOMATIC

	V.G.	Exc.	Prior Year Exc. Value
☐ **Commando MK III**, .45 ACP, Clip Fed, Horizontal Forend, with Compensator, Carbine, *Modern*	95.00	145.00	135.00
☐ **Commando MK III**, .45 ACP, Clip Fed, Vertical Forend, with Compensator, Carbine, *Modern*	100.00	155.00	145.00
☐ **Commando MK 9**, 9mm Luger, Clip Fed, Horizontal Forend, with Compensator, Carbine, *Modern*	100.00	155.00	145.00
☐ **Commando MK 9**, 9mm Luger, Clip Fed, Vertical Forend, with Compensator, Carbine, *Modern*	115.00	160.00	150.00
☐ **Commando MK 45**, .45 ACP, Clip Fed, Horizontal Forend, with Compensator, Carbine, *Modern*	100.00	155.00	145.00
☐ **Commando MK 45**, .45 ACP, Clip Fed, Vertical Forend, with Compensator, Carbine, *Modern*	115.00	160.00	150.00

COMMANDER

HANDGUN, REVOLVER

	V.G.	Exc.	Prior Year Exc. Value
☐ **.32 Long R.F.**, 7 Shot, Single Action, Spur Trigger Solid Frame, *Antique*	85.00	150.00	145.00

	V.G.	Exc.	Prior Year Exc. Value

COMMERCIAL
See Smith, Otis A.

COMPEER
Made by Crescent for Van Camp Hardware c. 1900.

SHOTGUN, DOUBLE BARREL, SIDE-BY-SIDE

	V.G.	Exc.	Prior Year Exc. Value
☐ **Various Gauges**, Outside Hammers, Damascus Barrel, *Modern*	80.00	155.00	150.00
☐ **Various Gauges**, Hammerless, Steel Barrel, *Modern*	100.00	180.00	175.00
☐ **Various Gauges**, Hammerless, Damascus Barrel, *Modern*	75.00	155.00	150.00
☐ **Various Gauges**, Outside Hammers, Steel Barrel, *Modern*	95.00	180.00	175.00

SHOTGUN, SINGLESHOT

	V.G.	Exc.	Prior Year Exc. Value
☐ **Various Gauges**, Hammer, Steel Barrel, *Modern*	45.00	80.00	75.00

CONE, D.D.
Washington, D.C. c. 1865.

HANDGUN, REVOLVER

	V.G.	Exc.	Prior Year Exc. Value
☐ **.22 Long R.F.**, 7 Shot, Single Action, Spur Trigger, Solid Frame, *Antique*	100.00	180.00	175.00
☐ **.32 Long R.F.**, 6 Shot, Single Action, Spur Trigger, Solid Frame, *Antique*	130.00	215.00	200.00

CONFEDERATE MILITARY

HANDGUN, PERCUSSION

	V.G.	Exc.	Prior Year Exc. Value
☐ **.36 Columbus,** Revolver, Brass Trigger Guard, 6 Shot, *Antique*	4300.00	10250.00	9950.00
☐ **.36 Dance Bros.,** Revolver, Iron Frame, 6 Shot, *Antique*	3700.00	8200.00	7900.00
☐ **.36 Griswald & Gunnison,** Revolver, Brass Frame, 6 Shot, Serial No. is the Only Marking, *Antique*	3075.00	4500.00	4200.00
☐ **.36 Leech & Co.,** Revolver, Brass Grip Frame, 6 Shot, *Antique*	3350.00	4900.00	4500.00
☐ **.36 Leech & Rigdon,** Revolver, Brass Grip Frame, 6 Shot, *Antique*	2180.00	3500.00	3300.00
☐ **.36 Rigdon & Ansley,** Revolver, Brass Grip Frame, 6 Shot, *Antique*	2675.00	4100.00	3975.00
☐ **.36 Shawk & McLanahan,** Revolver, Brass Frame, 6 Shot, *Antique*	4500.00	8950.00	8700.00
☐ **.36 Spiller & Burr,** Revolver, Brass Frame, 6 Shot, *Antique*	2575.00	4075.00	3950.00
☐ **.36 T.W. Cofer,** Revolver, Brass Frame, 6 Shot, *Antique*	8200.00	17500.00	17000.00
☐ **.44 Dance Bros.,** Revolver, Brass Grip Frame, 6 Shot, *Antique*	3450.00	5075.00	4850.00
☐ **.44 Tucker & Sherrod,** Revolver, Copy of Colt Dragoon, Serial Number is the Only Marking, *Antique*	4700.00	9900.00	9650.00
☐ **.54 Palmetto,** Singleshot, Brass Furniture, *Antique*	920.00	1900.00	1800.00
☐ **.58 Fayetteville,** Singleshot, Rifled, *Antique*	1075.00	1950.00	1850.00

	V.G.	Exc.	Prior Year Exc. Value
☐ **.58 Fayetteville,** Singleshot, Rifled, with Shoulder Stock, *Antique*	1750.00	2850.00	2750.00
☐ **.60 Sutherland,** Singleshot, Brass Barrel, Converted from Flintlock, *Antique*	650.00	1025.00	995.00

RIFLE, PERCUSSION

	V.G.	Exc.	Prior Year Exc. Value
☐ **.52,** "P," Tallahassee, Breech Loader, Carbine, *Antique*	2500.00	4450.00	4300.00
☐ **.52,** Tarpley, Breech Loader, Carbine, Brass Breech, *Antique*	3800.00	8600.00	8350.00
☐ **.54,** L.G. Sturdivant, Brass Furniture, Rifled, Serial No. is the Only Marking, *Antique*	1225.00	2100.00	1995.00
☐ **.54,** Wytheville-Hall, Muzzle Loader, Rifled, Brass Frame, *Antique*	1425.00	2375.00	2250.00
☐ **.57,** Texas Enfield, Brass Furniture, *Antique*	2900.00	4600.00	4400.00
☐ **.58,** Musketoon, Brass Furniture, Military, Cook & Brother, *Antique*	1750.00	3100.00	2975.00
☐ **.58,** Military, Carbine, Dickson, Nelson & Co., *Antique*	2000.00	4700.00	4500.00
☐ **.58,** Military, Dickson, Nelson & Co., *Antique*	1775.00	2900.00	2800.00
☐ **.58,** Artillery, Brass Furniture, Military, Cook & Brother, *Antique*	2025.00	3675.00	3500.00
☐ **.58,** D.C. Hodgkins & Co., Iron Mounts, Rifled, Carbine, *Antique*	2075.00	4100.00	3900.00
☐ **.58,** Enfield Type, Brass Furniture, Military, Cook & Brother, *Antique*	1600.00	2850.00	2750.00
☐ **.58,** Enfield Type, Rifled, Brass Furniture, Military, *Antique*	1450.00	2575.00	2450.00
☐ **.58,** Fayetteville, Brass Furniture, 2 Bands, Rifled, *Antique*	1550.00	3150.00	3000.00
☐ **.58,** Georgia, Brass Furniture, Rifled, *Antique*	1475.00	2800.00	2700.00
☐ **.58,** H.C. Lamb & Co., Brass Furniture, 2 Bands, Rifled, *Antique*	2500.00	4450.00	4300.00
☐ **.58,** Palmetto, Musket, *Antique*	1200.00	2300.00	2225.00
☐ **.58,** Richmond, Carbine, *Antique*	1050.00	1950.00	1875.00
☐ **.58,** Richmond, Musket, Rifled, *Antique*	900.00	1750.00	1675.00
☐ **.58,** Tallahassee, Carbine, Brass Furniture, 2 Bands, *Antique*	2825.00	4900.00	4750.00
☐ **.58,** Whitney, Rifled, Musket, *Antique*	420.00	700.00	685.00
☐ **.61,** Whitney Enfield, Rifled, Brass Furniture, *Antique*	420.00	800.00	775.00
☐ **.62,** Richmond Navy, Musketoon, Smoothbore, *Antique*	1025.00	2350.00	2225.00
☐ **.69,** Prussian Musket, Brass Furniture, Military, *Antique*	390.00	600.00	575.00

RIFLE, SINGLESHOT

	V.G.	Exc.	Prior Year Exc. Value
☐ **.50,** S.C. Robinson, Brass Furniture, Breech Loader, Carbine, Imitation Sharps, *Antique*	1050.00	2300.00	2200.00
☐ **.69,** Morse, Smoothbore, Carbine, Breech Loader, *Antique*	1650.00	2850.00	2750.00
☐ **.69,** Morse, Smoothbore, Breech Loader, *Antique*	1050.00	2250.00	2175.00

CONN. ARMS CO.

Norfolk, Conn. 1862-1869.

	V.G.	Exc.	Prior Year Exc. Value
HANDGUN, REVOLVER			
☐ **Wood's Patent**, .28 T.F., Tip-Up Barrel, 6 Shot, Spur Trigger, *Antique*	150.00	310.00	290.00

CONN. ARMS & MFG. CO.

Naubuc, Conn. 1863-1869.

HANDGUN, SINGLESHOT			
☐ **Hammond Patent Bulldog**, .44 R.F., Pivoting Breechblock, Hammer, Spur Trigger, *Antique*	185.00	300.00	275.00
☐ **Hammond Patent Bulldog**, .44 R.F., Pivoting Breechblock, Hammer, Spur Trigger, Very Long Barrel, *Antique*	275.00	445.00	400.00
☐ **Hammond Patent Bull-Dozer**, .44 R.F., Pivoting Breechblock, Hammer, Spur Trigger, *Antique*	200.00	315.00	290.00

CONQUERER

Made by Bacon Arms Co., c. 1880.

HANDGUN, REVOLVER			
☐ **.22 Short R.F.**, 7 Shot, Spur Trigger, Solid Frame, Single Action, *Antique*	85.00	160.00	160.00
☐ **.32 Short R.F.**, 5 Shot, Spur Trigger, Solid Frame, Single Action, *Antique*	85.00	160.00	160.00

CONSTABLE, RICHARD

Philadelphia, Pa. 1817-1851.

HANDGUN, PERCUSSION			
☐ **Dueling Pistols**, Cased Pair, with Accessories, *Antique*	1,800.00	3,500.00	3,450.00
RIFLE, PERCUSSION			
☐ **.44**, Octagon Barrel, Brass Furniture, *Antique*	950.00	1,800.00	1,750.00

CONTENTO

See Ventura Imports.

CONTINENTAL

Made by Jules Bertrand, Liege, Belgium c. 1910.

HANDGUN, SEMI-AUTOMATIC			
☐ **Pocket**, .25 ACP, Clip Fed, *Curio*	160.00	240.00	225.00

CONTINENTAL

Rheinische Waffen u. Munitionsfabrik. Possibly a tradename used by Arizmendi, c. 1910.

HANDGUN, SEMI-AUTOMATIC			
☐ **.25 ACP**, Clip Fed, Blue, *Curio*	90.00	135.00	125.00
☐ **.32 ACP**, Clip Fed, Webley Copy, Blue, *Curio*	120.00	180.00	165.00

CONTINENTAL

Made by Stevens Arms.

RIFLE, BOLT ACTION			
☐ **Model 52**, .22 L.R.R.F., Singleshot, Takedown, *Modern*	35.00	55.00	50.00

	V.G.	Exc.	Prior Year Exc. Value
SHOTGUN, DOUBLE BARREL, SIDE-BY-SIDE			
☐ **Model 315**, Various Gauges, Hammerless, Steel Barrel, *Modern*	110.00	185.00	175.00
☐ **Model 215**, 12 and 16 Gauges, Outside Hammers, Steel Barrel, *Modern*	100.00	175.00	165.00
☐ **Model 311**, Various Gauges, Hammerless, Steel Barrel, *Modern*	135.00	210.00	190.00
SHOTGUN, SINGLESHOT			
☐ **Model 90**, Various Gauges, Takedown, Automatic Ejector, Plain Hammer, *Modern*	40.00	65.00	60.00

CONTINENTAL

Made by Hood Firearms Co., Successors to Continental Arms Co.; Sold by Marshall Wells Co., Duluth, Minn., c. 1870.

	V.G.	Exc.	Prior Year Exc. Value
HANDGUN, REVOLVER			
☐ **.22 Short R.F.**, 7 Shot, Spur Trigger, Solid Frame, Single Action, *Antique*	90.00	165.00	160.00
☐ **.32 Short R.F.**, 5 Shot, Spur Trigger, Solid Frame, Single Action, *Antique*	95.00	175.00	170.00

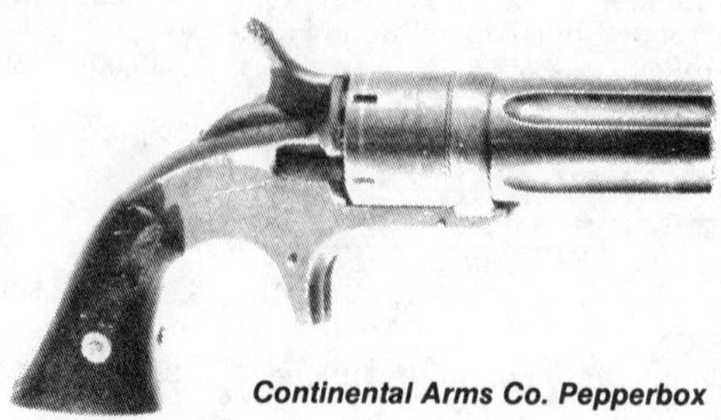

Continental Arms Co. Pepperbox

CONTINENTAL ARMS CO.

Norwich, Conn. 1866-1867.

	V.G.	Exc.	Prior Year Exc. Value
HANDGUN, PEPPERBOX			
☐ **Continental 1**, .22 R.F., 7 Shot, Spur Trigger, Solid Frame, *Antique*	295.00	465.00	425.00
☐ **Continental 2**, .32 R.F., 5 Shot, Spur Trigger, Solid Frame, *Antique*	355.00	570.00	525.00

COONAN ARMS, INC.

St. Paul, Minn. since 1982.

	V.G.	Exc.	Prior Year Exc. Value
HANDGUN, SEMI-AUTOMATIC			
☐ **Model A**, .357 Magnum, Single Action, Stainless, *Modern*	595.00	615.00	—
☐ **Model 357**, .357 Magnum, Pre-Production Model, Serial Numbers Under 1000, Stainless Steel, Clip Fed, Adjustable Sights, *Modern*	500.00	650.00	—
☐ **Model 357**, .357 Magnum, Standard Production Model, Stainless Steel, Clip Fed, Adjustable Sights, *Modern*	300.00	425.00	—

	V.G.	Exc.	Prior Year Exc. Value

COOPER FIREARMS MFG. CO.
Philadelphia, Pa. 1851-1869.

HANDGUN, PERCUSSION

	V.G.	Exc.	Prior Year Exc. Value
☐ **Pocket**, .31, 5 or 6 Shots, Double Action, *Antique*	295.00	475.00	450.00
☐ **Navy**, .31, 5 Shots, Double Action, *Antique*	360.00	585.00	550.00

C.O.P.
M & N Distributers, Torrance, Calif.

HANDGUN, REPEATER

	V.G.	Exc.	Prior Year Exc. Value
☐ **Model SS-1**, .357 Mag., Four Barrels, Stainless Steel, Hammerless, Double Action, *Modern*	145.00	190.00	180.00
☐ **Model Mini**, .22 W.M.R., Four Barrels, Stainless Steel, Hammerless, Double Action, *Modern*	165.00	225.00	220.00
☐ **Model Mini**, .22 L.R.R.F., Four Barrels, Aluminium Frame, Hammerless, Double Action, *Modern*	120.00	155.00	150.00

HANDGUN, SEMI-AUTOMATIC

	V.G.	Exc.	Prior Year Exc. Value
☐ **TP-70 AAI**, .22 L.R.R.F., Double Action, Clip Fed, Stainless Steel, Hammer, *Modern*	120.00	170.00	165.00
☐ **TP-70 AAI**, .25 A.C.P., Double Action, Clip Fed, Stainless Steel, Hammer, *Modern*	115.00	165.00	160.00

COPELAND, F.
Made by Frank Copeland, Worcester, Mass. 1868-1874.

HANDGUN, REVOLVER

	V.G.	Exc.	Prior Year Exc. Value
☐ **.22 Short R.F.**, 7 Shot, Spur Trigger, Solid Frame, Single Action, *Antique*	130.00	200.00	195.00
☐ **.32 Short R.F.**, 5 Shot, Spur Trigger, Solid Frame, Single Action, *Antique*	145.00	225.00	220.00

COQ
Spain, unknown maker, c. 1900.

HANDGUN, SEMI-AUTOMATIC

	V.G.	Exc.	Prior Year Exc. Value
☐ **K-25**, .25 ACP, Clip Fed, *Modern*	75.00	125.00	115.00

CORNFORTH
London, England 1725-1760.

HANDGUN, FLINTLOCK

	V.G.	Exc.	Prior Year Exc. Value
☐ **Pair**, Belt Pistol, Brass Barrel, Brass Furniture, Plain, *Antique*	2,700.00	4,000.00	3,950.00

COSENS, JAMES
Gunmaker in Ordinary to Charles II England, Late 1600's.

HANDGUN, FLINTLOCK

	V.G.	Exc.	Prior Year Exc. Value
☐ **Pair**, Holster Pistol, Silver Furniture, Engraved Silver Inlay, High Quality, *Antique*	9,350.00	16,000.00	15,000.00

COSMI
Made for Abercrombie & Fitch c. 1960.

	V.G.	Exc.	Prior Year Exc. Value
SHOTGUN, SEMI-AUTOMATIC			
☐ **12 or 20 Gauge**, Top Break, Engraved, Checkered Stock, Vent Rib, *Modern*	1,250.00	1,950.00	1,950.00

COSMOPOLITAN ARMS CO.

Hamilton, Ohio 1860-1865. Also see U.S. Military.

	V.G.	Exc.	Prior Year Exc. Value
RIFLE, PERCUSSION			
☐ **.45**, Sporting Rifle, *Antique*	775.00	1,175.00	1,100.00
☐ **.50**, Carbine, *Antique*	650.00	985.00	950.00

COWLES & SON

Cowles & Smith, 1866-1871, Cowles & Son 1871-1876 in Chicopee Falls, Mass.

	V.G.	Exc.	Prior Year Exc. Value
HANDGUN, SINGLESHOT			
☐ **.22 Short R.F.**, Brass Frame, Side Swing Barrel, *Antique*	160.00	240.00	225.00

CRAFT PRODUCTS

	V.G.	Exc.	Prior Year Exc. Value
HANDGUN, SEMI-AUTOMATIC			
☐ **.25 ACP**, Clip Fed, *Modern*	70.00	115.00	110.00

COWELS & SMITH

Chicopee Falls, Mass. 1863-1876. Became Cowels & Son in 1871.

	V.G.	Exc.	Prior Year Exc. Value
HANDGUN, SINGLESHOT			
☐ **.22 R.F.**, Side-Swing Barrel, Hammer, Spur Trigger, *Antique*	135.00	220.00	200.00
☐ **.30 R.F.**, Side-Swing Barrel, Hammer, Spur Trigger, *Antique*	150.00	245.00	220.00

CRESCENT

Made by Norwich Falls Pistol Co., c. 1880.

	V.G.	Exc.	Prior Year Exc. Value
HANDGUN, REVOLVER			
☐ **.32 Short R.F.**, 5 Shot, Spur Trigger, Solid Frame, Single Action, *Antique*	90.00	165.00	160.00

CRESCENT FIRE ARMS CO.

Norwich, Conn., 1892; Purchased by H & D Folsom in 1893, and Absorbed by Stevens Arms & Tool 1926.

	V.G.	Exc.	Prior Year Exc. Value
HANDGUN, SINGLESHOT			
☐ **.410 Ga.**, Top Break, *Class 3*	165.00	275.00	250.00
SHOTGUN, DOUBLE BARREL, SIDE-BY-SIDE			
☐ **Various Gauges**, Outside Hammers, Damascus Barrel, *Modern*	85.00	155.00	150.00
☐ **Various Gauges**, Hammerless, Steel Barrel, *Modern*	110.00	185.00	175.00
☐ **Various Gauges**, Hammerless, Damascus Barrel, *Modern*	80.00	155.00	150.00
☐ **Various Gauges**, Outside Hammers, Steel Barrel, *Modern*	95.00	180.00	175.00
SHOTGUN, SINGLESHOT			
☐ **Various Gauges**, Hammer, Steel Barrel, *Modern*	45.00	80.00	75.00

	V.G.	Exc.	Prior Year Exc. Value

CREEDMORE

Made by Hopkins & Allen, c. 1870.

HANDGUN, REVOLVER

	V.G.	Exc.	Prior Year Exc. Value
☐ **#1**, .22 Short R.F., 7 Shot, Spur Trigger, Solid Frame, Single Action, *Antique*	85.00	160.00	160.00

CRIOLLA

Hispano Argentine Automoviles, Buenos Aires, Argentina, c. 1935.

HANDGUN, SEMI-AUTOMATIC

	V.G.	Exc.	Prior Year Exc. Value
☐ **La Criolla**, .22 L.R.R.F., Colt M1911 Ace Copy, Clip Fed, Blue, *Modern*	245.00	350.00	325.00

CROWN JEWEL

Made by Norwich Falls Pistol Co., c.1880.

HANDGUN, REVOLVER

	V.G.	Exc.	Prior Year Exc. Value
☐ **.32 Short R.F.**, 5 Shot, Spur Trigger, Solid Frame, Single Action, *Antique*	90.00	165.00	160.00

CRUCELEGUI

Spain, Imported by Mandall Shooting Supplies, Scotsdale, Ariz.

SHOTGUN, DOUBLE BARREL, SIDE-BY-SIDE

	V.G.	Exc.	Prior Year Exc. Value
☐ **Model 150**, 12 and 20 Gauges, Outside Hammers, Double Trigger, *Modern*	140.00	190.00	180.00

CRUSO

Made by Stevens Arms.

RIFLE, BOLT ACTION

	V.G.	Exc.	Prior Year Exc. Value
☐ **Model 53**, .22 L.R.R.F., Singleshot, Takedown, *Modern*	35.00	55.00	50.00

SHOTGUN, SINGLESHOT

	V.G.	Exc.	Prior Year Exc. Value
☐ **Model 90**, Various Gauges, Takedown, Automatic Ejector, Plain Hammer, *Modern*	45.00	65.00	60.00

CUMBERLAND ARMS CO.

Made by Crescent for Hibbard-Spencer Bartlett Co., c. 1900.

SHOTGUN, DOUBLE BARREL, SIDE-BY-SIDE

	V.G.	Exc.	Prior Year Exc. Value
☐ **Various Gauges**, Outside Hammers, Damascus Barrel, *Modern*	110.00	185.00	175.00
☐ **Various Gauges**, Hammerless, Steel Barrel, *Modern*	140.00	220.00	200.00
☐ **Various Gauges**, Hammerless, Damascus Barrel, *Modern*	110.00	180.00	175.00
☐ **Various Gauges**, Outside Hammers, Steel Barrel, *Modern*	135.00	195.00	190.00

SHOTGUN, SINGLESHOT

	V.G.	Exc.	Prior Year Exc. Value
☐ **Various Gauges**, Hammer, Steel Barrel, *Modern*	55.00	85.00	85.00

C.V.A. (CONNECTICUT VALLEY ARMS)

Norcross. GA Current (Prices reflect Factory Assembled Guns, not Kits)

	V.G.	Exc.	Prior Year Exc. Value
HANDGUN, FLINTLOCK			
☐ **.50 Hawken,** Brass Furniture, Reproduction, *Antique*	55.00	80.00	80.00
☐ **.45 Kentucky,** Brass Furniture, Reproduction, *Antique, Out of Production, Kit Available*	45.00	60.00	60.00
HANDGUN, PERCUSSION			
☐ **.50 Hawken,** Brass Furniture, Set Triggers, Reproduction, *Antique*	55.00	75.00	75.00
☐ **.45 or .50 Mountain Pistol,** Brass Furniture, Reproduction, *Antique, Out of Production, Kit Available*	55.00	80.00	80.00
☐ **.45 Kentucky,** Brass Furniture, Reproduction, *Antique*	40.00	55.00	55.00
☐ **.45 Tower Pistol,** Brass Furniture, Reproduction, *Antique*	35.00	55.00	55.00
☐ **.45 Colonial Pistol,** Brass Furniture, Reproduction, *Antique*	30.00	45.00	45.00
☐ **.45 Philadelphia Derringer,** Reproduction, *Antique*	25.00	40.00	40.00
☐ **PP258, Pioneer,** .32 Caliber, Octagonal Barrel, Reproduction, *Antique*	70.00	90.00	—
☐ **PP640, Prospector,** .44 Caliber, Single Shot, Reproduction, *Antique*	82.00	100.00	—
HANDGUN, REVOLVER			
☐ **RV600, 1851 Colt Navy,** .36 Caliber, Six Shot, Brass Frame, Reproduction, *Antique*	100.00	125.00	—
☐ **RV610, 1860 Colt Army,** .44 Caliber, Six Shot, Reproduction, *Antique*	158.00	180.00	—
☐ **RV620, 1861 Colt Navy,** .44 Caliber, Steel Frame, Reproduction, *Antique*	156.00	178.00	—
☐ **RV622, 1861 Colt Navy,** .44 Caliber, Brass Frame, Reproduction, *Antique*	100.00	125.00	—
☐ **RV630, 1858 Remington Army,** .44 Caliber, One Piece Frame, Reproduction, *Antique*	164.00	200.00	—
☐ **RV632, 1858 Remington Army,** .44 Caliber, Brass Frame, Reproduction, *Antique*	120.00	145.00	—
☐ **RV650, New Model Pocket Remington,** .31 Caliber, Spur Trigger, Reproduction, *Antique*	81.00	98.00	—
RIFLE, FLINTLOCK			
☐ **.50 Frontier Rifle,** Brass Furniture, Reproduction, *Antique*	95.00	145.00	145.00
☐ **.50 or .54 Hawken Rifle,** Brass Furniture, Reproduction, *Antique*	115.00	170.00	170.00
☐ **.45 or .50 Mountain Rifle,** German Silver Furniture, Reproduction, *Antique, .45 Out of Production*	120.00	180.00	180.00
☐ **.45 Kentucky Rifle,** Brass Furniture, Reproduction, *Antique*	90.00	130.00	130.00
☐ **FR503, Squirrel Rifle,** .32 Caliber, Double Set Triggers, Reproduction, *Antique*	200.00	250.00	—
☐ **FR504, Pennsylvania Long Rifle,** .50 Caliber, Brass Butt Plate, Reproduction, *Antique*	300.00	365.00	—
RIFLE, PERCUSSION			
☐ **.50 or .54 Hawken Rifle,** Brass Furniture, Reproduction, *Antique*	110.00	165.00	165.00

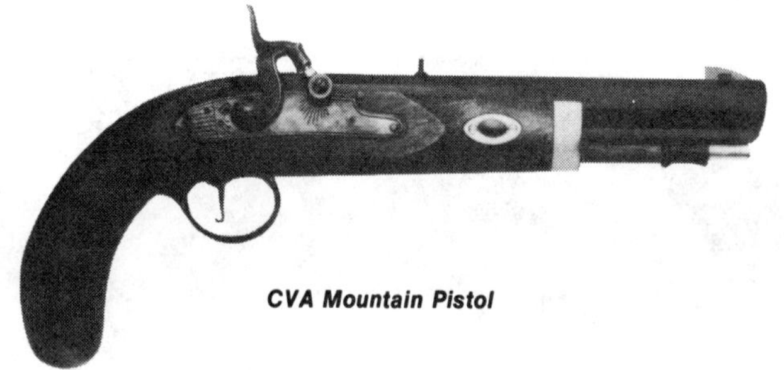

CVA Mountain Pistol

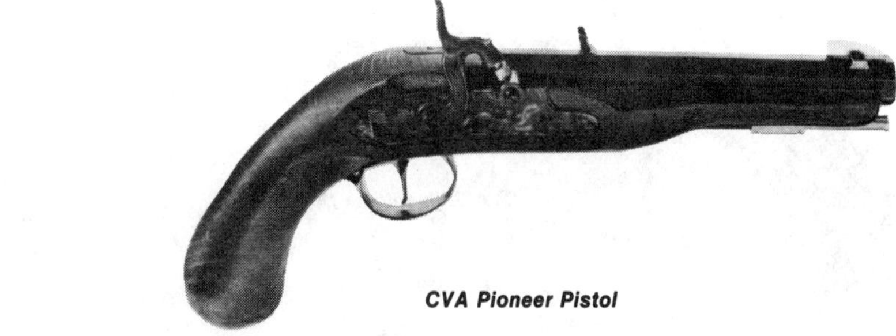

CVA Pioneer Pistol

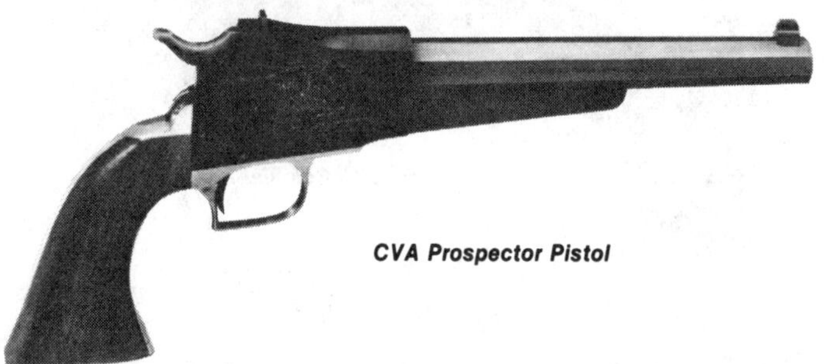

CVA Prospector Pistol

CVA Hawken Pistol

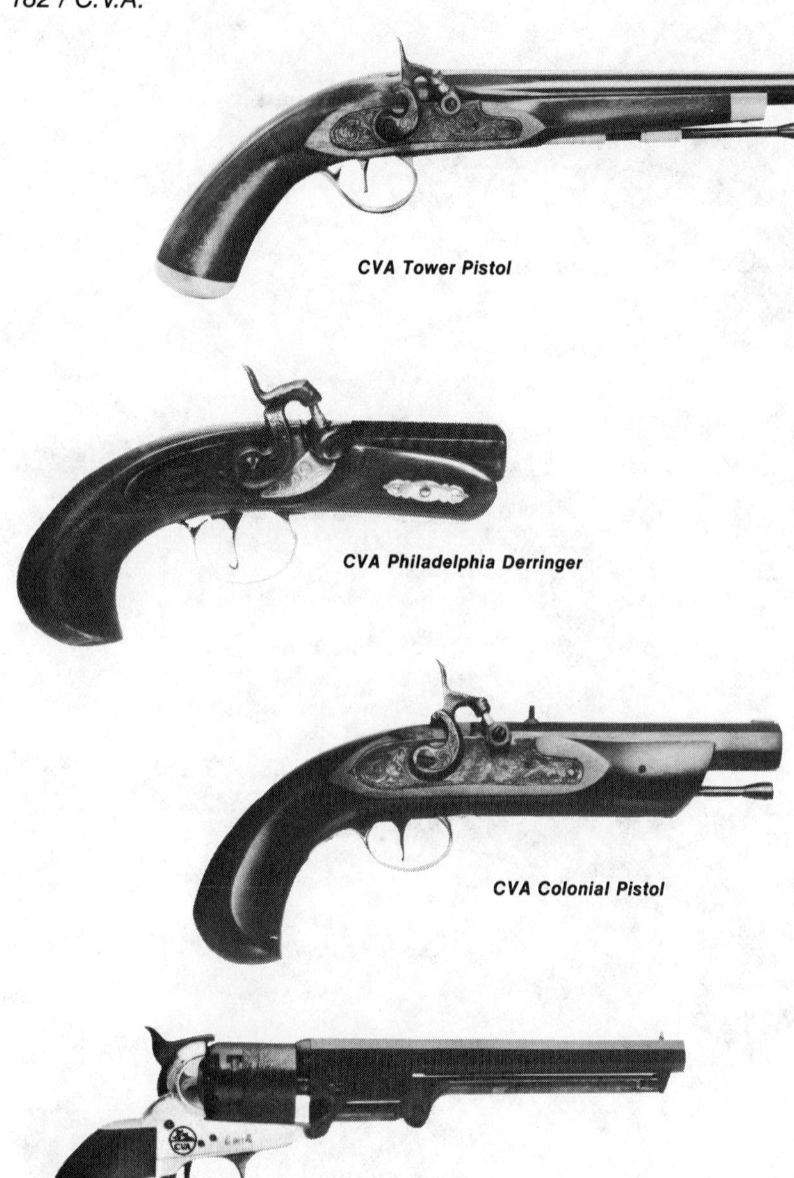

CVA Tower Pistol

CVA Philadelphia Derringer

CVA Colonial Pistol

CVA 1851 Colt Navy

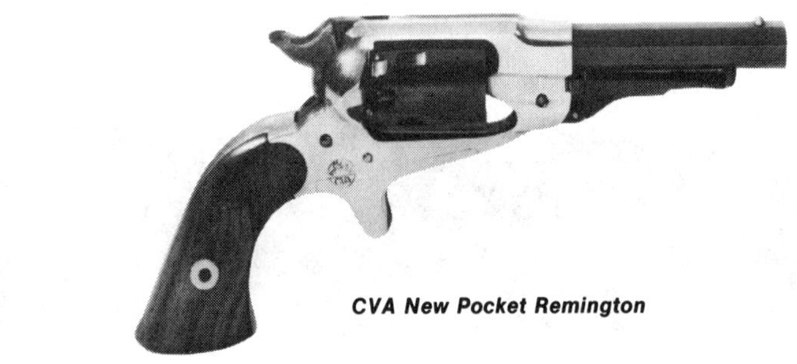

CVA New Pocket Remington

CVA Squirrel Rifle

CVA Pennsylvania Long Rifle

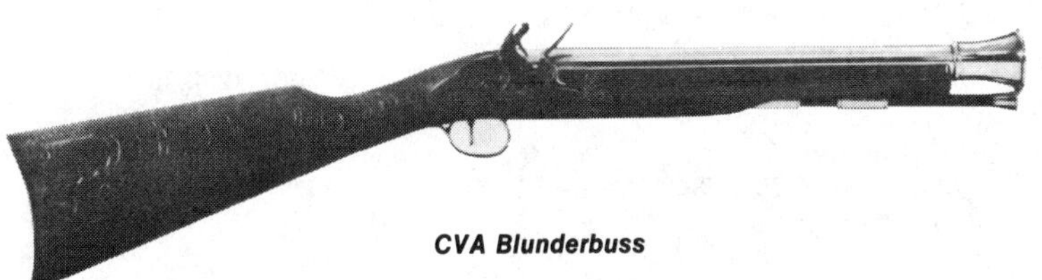

CVA Blunderbuss

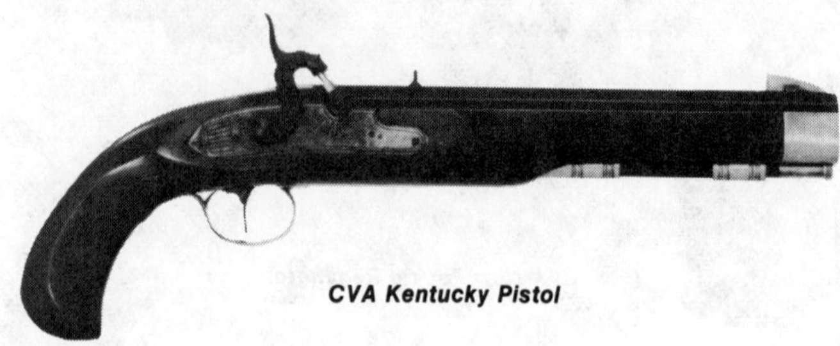

CVA Kentucky Pistol

	V.G.	Exc.	Prior Year Exc. Value
☐ **.45, .50, .54, or .58 Mountain Rifle,** German Silver Furniture, Reproduction, *Antique, .58 Available in Kit Only*	120.00	180.00	180.00
☐ **.45 or .50 Frontier Rifle,** Brass Furniture, Reproduction, *Antique, .45 Available in Kit Only*	90.00	140.00	140.00
☐ **.45 Kentucky Rifle,** Brass Furniture, Reproduction, *Antique*	85.00	130.00	130.00
☐ **.58 Zouave,** Brass Furniture, Reproduction, *Antique, Out of Production*	95.00	155.00	155.00
☐ **PR403, Squirrel Rifle,** .32 Caliber, Right Handed Model, Reproduction, *Antique*	190.00	220.00	—
☐ **PR404, Pennsylvania Long Rifle,** .50 Caliber, Brass Butt Plate, Reproduction, *Antique*	290.00	335.00	—
☐ **PR407, Big Bore Mountain Rifle,** .54 Caliber, Undecorated Stock, Beavertail Cheekpiece, Reproduction, *Antique*	310.00	345.00	—
☐ **PR456, Squirrel Rifle,** .32 Caliber, Left Handed Model, Reproduction, *Antique*	200.00	230.00	—
SHOTGUN, SINGLE BARREL			
☐ **FB557, Blunderbuss,** .69 Caliber, Flintlock, Brass Trigger, Reproduction, *Antique*	250.00	275.00	—
SHOTGUN, DOUBLE BARREL, SIDE-BY-SIDE			
☐ **PS409, .12 Gauge,** Percussion, Muzzleloading, Reproduction, *Antique*	260.00	290.00	—

CZ

Czechoslovakia from 1918 to date. This listing includes both Ceska Zbrojovka Brno and Cesksiovenska Zbrojovka. Also see BRNO.

	V.G.	Exc.	Prior Year Exc. Value
HANDGUN, REVOLVER			
☐ **Grand,** .38 Spec., Double Action, Swing-Out Cylinder, *Modern*	115.00	165.00	160.00
☐ **Grand,** .357 Mag., Double Action, Swing-Out Cylinder, *Modern*	130.00	180.00	175.00
☐ **ZKR 551,** .38 Spec., Single Action, Swing-Out Cylinder, Target Pistol, *Modern*	170.00	250.00	235.00
HANDGUN, SEMI-AUTOMATIC			
☐ **CZ1922,** .25 ACP, Clip Fed, *Curio*	295.00	410.00	375.00
☐ **CZ1922,** .380 ACP, Clip Fed, *Curio*	175.00	265.00	240.00
☐ **CZ1936,** .25 ACP, Clip Fed, *Curio*	125.00	180.00	165.00

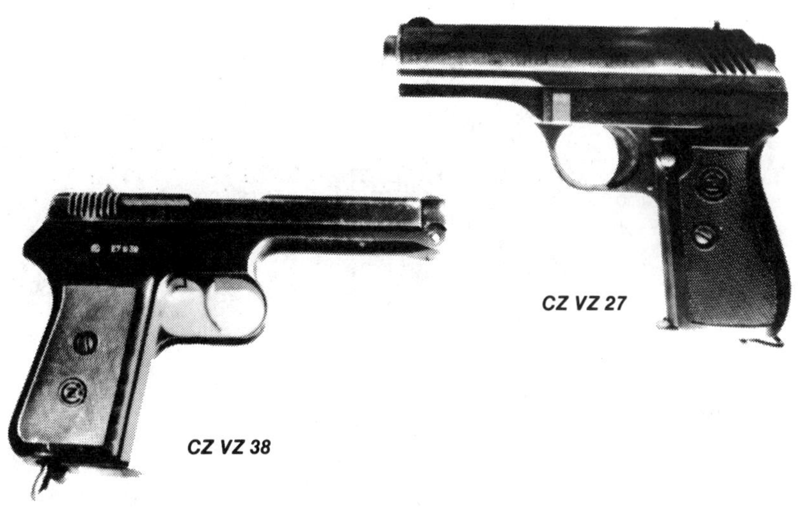
CZ VZ 27

CZ VZ 38

	V.G.	Exc.	Prior Year Exc. Value
☐ **CZ 70**, .32 ACP, CLip Fed, Blue, Double Action, *Modern*	140.00	200.00	190.00
☐ **CZ 75**, 9mm P, Clip Fed, Double Action, Blue, *Modern*	380.00	500.00	450.00
☐ **Duo**, .25 ACP, Clip Fed, *Modern*	110.00	180.00	175.00
☐ **Fox**, .25 ACP, Clip Fed, *Curio*	260.00	365.00	350.00
☐ **M1938**, .380 ACP, Clip Fed, Double Action, *Curio*	130.00	220.00	200.00
☐ **Niva**, .25 ACP, Clip Fed, *Curio*	225.00	310.00	285.00
☐ **PZK**, .25 ACP, Clip Fed, *Modern*	195.00	300.00	275.00
☐ **Vest Pocket CZ 1945**, .25 ACP, Clip Fed, *Modern*	135.00	200.00	185.00
☐ **VZ NB 50 Police**, .32 ACP, Clip Fed, Double Action, *Curio*	240.00	365.00	325.00
☐ **VZ1922**, .380 ACP, Clip Fed, *Curio*	165.00	255.00	240.00
☐ **VZ1924**, .380 ACP, Clip Fed, *Curio*	135.00	215.00	185.00
☐ **VZ1924**, .380 ACP, 10 Shot, Long Grip, Clip Fed, *Curio*	400.00	600.00	500.00
☐ **VZ1924 Navy**, .380 ACP, Clip Fed, Nazi-Proofed, *Curio*	195.00	295.00	275.00
☐ **VZ1938**, .380 ACP, Clip Fed, Double Action, Nazi-Proofed, *Curio*	170.00	295.00	265.00
☐ **VZ1938**, .380 ACP, Clip Fed, Double Action, With Safety, *Curio*	450.00	650.00	600.00
☐ **VZ1938**, .380 ACP, Clip Fed, Double Action, *Curio*	170.00	275.00	250.00
☐ **VZ27**, .22 L.R.R.F., Clip Fed, Nazi-Proofed, *Curio*	575.00	750.00	600.00
☐ **VZ27 Postwar**, .32 ACP, Clip Fed, Commercial, *Curio*	185.00	240.00	200.00
☐ **VZ27 Pre-War**, .32 ACP, Clip Fed, Commercial, *Curio*	165.00	225.00	190.00

	V.G.	Exc.	Prior Year Exc. Value
☐ **VZ27**, .32 ACP, Clip Fed, Barrel Extension for Silencer, *Curio, Class 3*	450.00	625.00	575.00
☐ **VZ27 Communist**, .32 ACP, Clip Fed, *Curio*	195.00	260.00	220.00
☐ **VZ27 Early Luftwaffe**, .32 ACP, Clip Fed, Nazi-Proofed, *Curio*	175.00	250.00	235.00
☐ **VZ27 Late Luftwaffe**, .32 ACP, Clip Fed, Nazi-Proofed, *Curio*	165.00	235.00	225.00
☐ **VZ27 Navy**, .32 ACP, Clip Fed, Nazi-Proofed, *Curio*	175.00	295.00	265.00
☐ **VZ27 Police**, .32 ACP, Clip Fed, Nazi-Proofed, *Curio*	195.00	325.00	250.00
☐ **VZ50**, .32 ACP, Clip Fed, Double Action, Military, *Modern*	175.00	245.00	225.00
☐ **VZ52**, 7.62mm Tokarev, Clip Fed, Double Action, *Curio*	550.00	995.00	950.00
HANDGUN, SINGLESHOT			
☐ **Drulov**, .22 L.R.R.F., Top Break, Target Pistol, Target Sights, *Modern*	320.00	425.00	400.00
☐ **Model P**, .22 L.R.R.F., Top Break, Target Pistol, *Modern*	185.00	265.00	250.00
☐ **Model P**, 6mm Flobert, Top Break, Target Pistol, *Modern*	155.00	235.00	225.00
RIFLE, BOLT ACTION			
☐ **ZKK 602**, Various Magnum Calibers, Checkered Stock, Express Sights, *Modern*	315.00	465.00	450.00
☐ **ZKK 600**, Various Calibers, Checkered Stock, Express Sights, *Modern*	250.00	360.00	350.00
SHOTGUN, DOUBLE BARREL, OVER-UNDER			
☐ **Model 581**, 12 Gauge, Checkered Stock with Cheekpiece, *Modern*	275.00	420.00	400.00

CZAR

Made by Hood Firearms, c. 1876.

	V.G.	Exc.	Prior Year Exc. Value
HANDGUN, REVOLVER			
☐ **.22 Short R.F.**, 7 Shot, Spur Trigger, Solid Frame, Single Action, *Antique*	90.00	165.00	160.00

CZAR

Made by Hopkins & Allen, c. 1880.

	V.G.	Exc.	Prior Year Exc. Value
HANDGUN, REVOLVER			
☐ **.22 Short R.F.**, 7 Shot, Spur Trigger, Solid Frame, Single Action, *Antique*	90.00	165.00	160.00
☐ **.32 Short R.F.**, 5 Shot, Spur Trigger, Solid Frame, Single Action, *Antique*	90.00	170.00	170.00

CZECHOSLAVAKIAN MILITARY

Also see German Military, CZ.

	V.G.	Exc.	Prior Year Exc. Value
AUTOMATIC WEAPON, LIGHT MACHINE GUN			
☐ **ZB-VZ26**, 8mm Mauser, Finned Barrel, Clip Fed, Bipod, *Class 3*	2,750.00	3,700.00	3,500.00

	V.G.	Exc.	Prior Year Exc. Value
RIFLE, BOLT ACTION			
☐ **GEW 33/40,** 8mm Mauser, Military, Nazi-Proofed, Carbine, *Modern*	140.00	215.00	290.00
☐ **Gewehr 24 T,** 8mm Mauser, Military, Nazi-Proofed, *Curio*	130.00	200.00	260.00
☐ **VZ 24,** 8mm Mauser, Military, *Modern*	100.00	160.00	220.00
☐ **VZ 33,** 8mm Mauser, Military, Carbine, *Modern*	100.00	160.00	220.00

DAISY

Made by Bacon Arms Co., c. 1880.

	V.G.	Exc.	Prior Year Exc. Value
HANDGUN, REVOLVER			
☐ **.22 Short R.F.**, 7 Shot, Spur Trigger, Solid Frame, Single Action, *Antique*	85.00	160.00	160.00

DAKIN GUN CO.

San Francisco, Calif., c.1960.

	V.G.	Exc.	Prior Year Exc. Value
SHOTGUN, DOUBLE BARREL, OVER-UNDER			
☐ **Model 170,** Various Gauges, Light Engraving, Checkered Stock, Double Triggers, Vent Rib, *Modern*	275.00	440.00	425.00
SHOTGUN, DOUBLE BARREL, SIDE-BY-SIDE			
☐ **Model 100,** 12 or 20 Gauges, Boxlock, Light Engraving, Double Triggers, *Modern*	155.00	240.00	235.00
☐ **Model 147,** Various Magnum Gauges, Boxlock, Light Engraving, Double Triggers, Vent Rib, *Modern*	180.00	290.00	285.00
☐ **Model 160,** 12 or 20 Gauges, Single Selective Trigger, Ejectors, Vent Rib, *Modern*	230.00	375.00	360.00
☐ **Model 215,** 12 or 20 Gauges, Sidelock, Fancy Engraving, Fancy Wood, Ejectors, Single Selective Trigger, Vent Rib, *Modern*	420.00	745.00	725.00

DALBY, DAVID

Lincolnshire, England, c. 1835.

	V.G.	Exc.	Prior Year Exc. Value
HANDGUN, FLINTLOCK			
☐ **.50**, Pocket Pistol, Box Lock, Screw Barrel, Folding Trigger, Silver Inlay, *Antique*	550.00	835.00	800.00

DALY ARMS CO.

N.Y.C., c. 1890.

	V.G.	Exc.	Prior Year Exc. Value
HANDGUN, REVOLVER			
☐ **.22 Long R.F.**, 6 Shot, Double Action, Ring Trigger, Solid Frame, *Antique*	175.00	250.00	225.00
☐ **Peacemaker**, .32 Short R.F., 5 Shot, Spur Trigger, Solid Frame, Single Action, *Antique*	95.00	170.00	160.00

DAN WESSON ARMS

Monson, Mass. since 1970.

	V.G.	Exc.	Prior Year Exc. Value
HANDGUN, REVOLVER			
☐ **Model 11,** .357 Magnum, Double Action, 3-Barrel Set, Satin Blue, *Modern*	165.00	220.00	215.00

	V.G.	Exc.	Prior Year Exc. Value
☐ **Model 11,** .357 Magnum, Double Action, 3-Barrel Set, Nickel Plated, *Modern*	175.00	240.00	230.00
☐ **Model 11,** .357 Magnum, Various Barrel Lengths, Satin Blue, Double Action, *Modern*	105.00	145.00	140.00
☐ **Model 11,** .357 Magnum, Various Barrel Lengths, Nickel Plated, Double Action, *Modern*	120.00	160.00	155.00
☐ **Model 11,** .38 Special, Various Barrel Lengths, Satin Blue, Double Action, *Modern*	95.00	135.00	130.00
☐ **Model 11,** .38 Special, Various Barrel Lengths, Nickel Plated, Double Action, *Modern*	90.00	130.00	125.00
☐ **Model 12,** .357 Magnum, Double Action, 3-Barrel Set, Satin Blue, Adjustable Sights, *Modern*	170.00	240.00	230.00
☐ **Model 12,** .357 Magnum, Double Action, 3-Barrel Set, Nickel Plated, Adjustable Sights, *Modern*	235.00	350.00	335.00
☐ **Model 12,** .357 Magnum, Various Barrel Lengths, Double Action, Blue, Adjustable Sights, *Modern*	105.00	145.00	140.00
☐ **Model 12,** .357 Magnum, Various Barrel Lengths, Double Action, Nickel Plated, Adjustable Sights, *Modern*	115.00	155.00	150.00
☐ **Model 12,** .38 Special, Various Barrel Lengths, Double Action, Blue, Adjustable Sights, *Modern*	100.00	135.00	130.00
☐ **Model 12,** .38 Special, Various Barrel Lengths, Double Action, Nickel Plated, Adjustable Sights, *Modern*	110.00	150.00	145.00
☐ **Model 14,** .357 Magnum, Double Action, 3-Barrel Set, Satin Blue, *Modern*	215.00	310.00	295.00
☐ **Model 14,** .357 Magnum, Double Action, 3-Barrel Set, Nickel Plated, *Modern*	240.00	340.00	325.00
☐ **Model 14,** .357 Magnum, Various Barrel Lengths, Double Action, Satin Blue, *Modern*	100.00	145.00	140.00
☐ **Model 14,** .357 Magnum, Various Barrel Lengths, Double Action, Nickel Plated, *Modern*	120.00	165.00	160.00
☐ **Model 14,** .38 Special, Various Barrel Lengths, Double Action, Satin Blue, *Modern*	95.00	140.00	135.00
☐ **Model 14,** .38 Special, Various Barrel Lengths, Double Action, Nickel Plated, *Modern*	115.00	160.00	155.00
☐ **Model 14-2,** .357 Magnum, Various Barrel Lengths, Double Action, Satin Blue, *Modern*	100.00	145.00	140.00
☐ **Model 14-2,** .357 Magnum, Double Action, 4-Barrel Set, Blue, *Modern*	235.00	350.00	335.00
☐ **Model 14-2B,** .357 Magnum, Various Barrel Lengths, Double Action, Brite Blue, *Modern*	115.00	155.00	150.00
☐ **Model 14-2B,** .357 Magnum, Double Action, 4-Barrel Set, Brite Blue, *Modern*	260.00	375.00	360.00
☐ **Model 15,** .357 Magnum, Various Barrel Lengths, Double Action, Nickel Plated, Adjustable Sights, *Modern*	120.00	165.00	160.00
☐ **Model 15,** .357 Magnum, Double Action, 3-Barrel Set, Satin Blue, Adjustable Sights, *Modern*	225.00	315.00	300.00
☐ **Model 15,** .357 Magnum, Double Action, 3-Barrel Set, Nickel Plated, Adjustable Sights, *Modern*	250.00	360.00	345.00
☐ **Model 15,** .357 Magnum, Double Action, 3-Barrel Set, Blue, Adjustable Sights, *Modern*	230.00	320.00	310.00
☐ **Model 15,** .357 Magnum, Various Barrel Lengths, Double Action, Satin Blue, Adjustable Sights, *Modern*	115.00	170.00	160.00

	V.G.	Exc.	Prior Year Exc. Value
☐ **Model 15,** .357 Magnum, Various Barrel Lengths, Double Action, Blue, Adjustable Sights, *Modern*	125.00	175.00	170.00
☐ **Model 15,** .38 Special, Various Barrel Lengths, Double Action, Nickel Plated, Adjustable Sights, *Modern*	125.00	170.00	165.00
☐ **Model 15,** .38 Special, Various Barrel Lengths, Double Action, Satin Blue, Adjustable Sights, *Modern*	100.00	150.00	145.00
☐ **Model 15,** .38 Special, Various Barrel Lengths, Double Action, Blue, Adjustable Sights, *Modern*	110.00	155.00	150.00
☐ **Model 15-2,** .357 Magnum or .22 L.R.R.F., Various Barrel Lengths, Double Action, Blue, Adjustable Sights, *Modern*	145.00	195.00	190.00
☐ **Model 15-2,** .357 Magnum or .22 L.R.R.F., Double Action, 4-Barrel Set, Blue, Adjustable Sights, *Modern*	260.00	350.00	335.00
☐ **Model 15-2H,** .357 Magnum or .22 L.R.R.F., Various Barrel Lengths, Double Action, Blue, Adjustable Sights, Heavy Barrel, *Modern*	150.00	215.00	210.00
☐ **Model 15-2H,** .357 Magnum or .22 L.R.R.F., Double Action, 4-Barrel Set, Blue, Adjustable Sights, Heavy Barrel, *Modern*	310.00	400.00	390.00
☐ **Model 15-2V,** .357 Magnum or .22 L.R.R.F., Various Barrel Lengths, Double Action, Blue, Adjustable Sights, Vent Rib, *Modern*	160.00	225.00	220.00
☐ **Model 15-2V,** .357 Magnum or .22 L.R.R.F., Double Action, 4-Barrel Set, Blue, Adjustable Sights, Vent Rib, *Modern*	320.00	435.00	420.00
☐ **Model 15-2VH,** .357 Magnum or .22 L.R.R.F., Various Barrel Lengths, Double Action, Adjustable Sights, Heavy Barrel, Vent Rib, *Modern*	165.00	240.00	230.00
☐ **Model 15-2VH,** .357 Magnum or .22 L.R.R.F., Double Action, 4-Barrel Set, Blue, Adjustable Sights, Heavy Barrel, Vent Rib, *Modern*	340.00	490.00	465.00
☐ **Model 714-2,** .357 Magnum, Various Barrel Lengths, Double Action, Stainless Steel, Fixed Sights, *Modern*	135.00	190.00	185.00
☐ **Model 714-2,** .357 Magnum, Double Action, 4-Barrel Set, Stainless Steel, Fixed Sights, *Modern*	230.00	325.00	315.00
☐ **Model 715-2,** .357 Magnum, Various Barrel Lengths, Double Action, Stainless Steel, Adjustable Sights, *Modern*	170.00	240.00	235.00
☐ **Model 715-2,** .357 Magnum, Double Action, 4-Barrel Set, Stainless Steel, Adjustable Sights, *Modern*	335.00	440.00	420.00
☐ **Model 715-2V,** .357 Magnum, Various Barrel Lengths, Double Action, Stainless Steel, Adjustable Sights, Vent Rib, *Modern*	190.00	270.00	255.00
☐ **Model 715-2V,** .357 Magnum, Double Action, 4-Barrel Set, Stainless Steel, Adjustable Sights, Vent Rib, *Modern*	400.00	510.00	490.00
☐ **Model 715-2VH,** .357 Magnum, Various Barrel Lengths, Double Action, Stainless Steel, Adjustable Sights, Vent Rib, Heavy Barrel, *Modern*	200.00	280.00	270.00

	V.G.	Exc.	Prior Year Exc. Value
☐ **Model 715-2VH,** .357 Magnum, Double Action, 4-Barrel Set, Stainless Steel, Adjustable Sights, Vent Rib, Heavy Barrel, *Modern*	425.00	550.00	535.00
☐ **Model 44-V,** .44 Magnum, Various Barrel Lengths, Double Action, Blue, Adjustable Sights, Vent Rib, *Modern*	215.00	300.00	285.00
☐ **Model 44-V,** .44 Magnum, Double Action, 4-Barrel Set, Blue, Adjustable Sights, Vent Rib, *Modern*	365.00	465.00	450.00
☐ **Model 44-VH,** .44 Magnum, Various Barrel Lengths, Double Action, Adjustable Sights, Heavy Barrel, Vent Rib, *Modern*	235.00	335.00	325.00
☐ **Model 44-VH,** .44 Magnum, Double Action, 4-Barrel Set, Blue, Adjustable Sights, Heavy Barrel, Vent Rib, *Modern*	380.00	500.00	485.00
☐ **Model 744-V,** .44 Magnum, Various Barrel Lengths, Double Action, Stainless, Adjustable Sights, Vent Rib, *Modern*	235.00	330.00	320.00
☐ **Model 744-V,** .44 Magnum, Double Action, 4-Barrel Set, Stainless, Adjustable Sights, Vent Rib, *Modern*	385.00	490.00	475.00
☐ **Model 744-VH,** .44 Magnum, Various Barrel Lengths, Double Action, Adjustable Sights, Stainless, Heavy Barrel, Vent Rib, *Modern*	265.00	365.00	355.00
☐ **Model 744-VH,** .44 Magnum, Double Action, 4-Barrel Set, Stainless, Adjustable Sights, Heavy Barrel, Vent Rib, *Modern*	410.00	530.00	515.00

☐ **Extra Barrel Assemblies,** *Add:*

15″ 15-2 **$75.00-$110.00**; 15-2H **$95.00-$135.00**; 15-2V **$95.00-$135.00**; 15-2VH **$120.00-$160.00**; 715 **$80.00-$120.00**; 715V **$95.00-$140.00**; 715VH **$100.00-$155.00**

12″ 15-2 **$50.00-$80.00**; 15-2H **$75.00-$110.00**; 15-2V **$75.00-$110.00**; 15-2VH **$80.00-$120.00**; 715 **$60.00-$90.00**; 715V **$80.00-$120.00**; 715VH **$95.00-$140.00**

10″ 15-2 **$45.00-$70.00**; 15-2H **$55.00-$85.00**; 15-2V **$55.00-$85.00**; 15-2VH **$70.00-$100.00**; 44-V **$60.00-$100.00**; 44-VH **$80.00-$120.00**; 715 **$45.00-70.00**; 715V **$65.00-$95.00**; 715VH **$75.00-$110.00**; 744-V **$70.00-$115.00**; 744-VH **$90.00-$135.00**

Others 15-2 $20.00-$40.00; 15-2H, **$35.00-$55.00**; 15-2V **$35.00-$55.00**; 15-2VH **$40.00-$70.00**; 44-V **$55.00-$85.00**; 44-VH; 715 **$35.00-$55.00**; 715V $45.00-$65.00; 715VH $50.00-$80.00; 744-V $60.00-$100.00; 44-VH **$70.00-$110.00**

DANISH MILITARY

AUTOMATIC WEAPON, SUBMACHINE GUN

	V.G.	Exc.	Prior Year Exc. Value
☐ **Madsen M50B,** 9mm Luger, Clip Fed, Wood Stock, Military, *Class 3*	650.00	1050.00	995.00

	V.G.	Exc.	Prior Year Exc. Value
HANDGUN, REVOLVER			
☐ **9.1mm Ronge 1891,** Military, Top Break, Hammer-Like Latch, *Antique*	230.00	350.00	335.00
HANDGUN, SEMI-AUTOMATIC			
☐ **M1910,** 9mm B, Made by Pieper, Clip Fed, *Curio*	385.00	620.00	900.00
☐ **M1910/21,** 9mm B, Converted From M1910, Clip Fed, *Curio*	320.00	520.00	725.00
☐ **M1910/21,** 9mm B, Made by Danish Army Arsenal, Clip Fed, *Curio*	435.00	710.00	1025.00
☐ **S.I.G. SG/8 9mm Luger,** Clip Fed, Military, *Modern*	900.00	1375.00	2050.00
RIFLE, BOLT ACTION			
☐ **M98 Mauser,** 6.5 x 57, Haerens Vabenarsenal, *Curio*	200.00	310.00	425.00
☐ **M1889 Krag,** 8 x 54 Krag-Jorgensen, Carbine, *Antique*	400.00	575.00	525.00
RIFLE, SINGLESHOT			
☐ **M1867,** Remington Rolling Block, Full Stock, *Antique*	450.00	650.00	575.00

DANIELS, HENRY & CHARLES

Chester, Conn., 1838-1850.

	V.G.	Exc.	Prior Year Exc. Value
RIFLE, PERCUSSION			
☐ **Turret Rifle**, .40, Underhammer, 8 Shot, Manual Repeater, Octagon Barrel, *Antique*	3,775.00	6,900.00	6,750

DANTON

Made By Gabilondo y Cia.. Elgoibar, Spain, 1925-1933.

	V.G.	Exc.	Prior Year Exc. Value
HANDGUN, SEMI-AUTOMATIC			
☐ **Pocket**, .25 ACP, Clip Fed, *Modern*	95.00	155.00	140.00
☐ **Pocket**, .32 ACP, Clip Fed, *Modern*	105.00	165.00	155.00
☐ **Pocket**, .25 ACP, Grip Safety, Clip Fed, *Modern*	110.00	170.00	155.00
☐ **Pocket**, .32 ACP, Grip Safety. Clip Fed, *Modern*	120.00	175.00	165.00

Danton .25

	V.G.	Exc.	Prior Year Exc. Value

DARDICK
Hamden, Conn., 1954-1962.

HANDGUN, REVOLVER

	V.G.	Exc.	Prior Year Exc. Value
☐ **Series 1100**, .38 Dardick Tround, Double Action, Clip Fed, 3" Barrel, 11 Shot, *Modern*	425.00	580.00	550.00
☐ **Series 1500**, .30, Double Action, Clip Fed, 4¾" Barrel, *Modern*	655.00	890.00	850.00
☐ **Series 1500**, .38 Dardick Tround, Double Action, Clip Fed, 6" Barrel, 15 Shot, *Modern*	410.00	580.00	550.00
☐ **Series 1500**, .22, Double Action, Clip Fed, 2" and 11" Barrels, *Modern*	675.00	940.00	900.00
☐ **For Carbine Conversion Unit .38**, *Add* **$215.00-$325.00**			
☐ **For Carbine Conversion Unit .22**, *Add* **$245.00-$395.00**			

DARNE
St. Etienne, France.

SHOTGUN, DOUBLE BARREL, SIDE-BY-SIDE

	V.G.	Exc.	Prior Year Exc. Value
☐ **Bird Hunter**, Various Gauges, Sliding Breech, Ejectors, Double Triggers, Checkered Stock, *Modern*	540.00	790.00	775.00
☐ **Hors Serie #1**, Various Gauges, Sliding Breech, Ejectors, Fancy Engraving, Checkered Stock, *Modern*	3,550.00	4,475.00	4,350.00
☐ **Magnum**, 12 or 20 Gauges 3", Sliding Breech, Ejectors, Double Triggers, Checkered Stock, *Modern*	875.00	1,450.00	1,400.00
☐ **Pheasant Hunter**, Various Gauges, Sliding Breech, Ejectors, Light Engraving, Checkered Stock, *Modern*	795.00	1,200.00	1,150.00
☐ **Quail Hunter**, Various Gauges, Sliding Breech, Ejectors, Engraved, Checkered Stock, *Modern*	1,300.00	1,865.00	1,800.00

DAVENPORT, W.H.
Providence, R.I. 1880-1883, Norwich, Conn. 1890-1900.

SHOTGUN, DOUBLE BARREL, SIDE-BY-SIDE

	V.G.	Exc.	Prior Year Exc. Value
☐ **8 Ga.**, *Modern*	390.00	545.00	525.00

SHOTGUN, SINGLESHOT

	V.G.	Exc.	Prior Year Exc. Value
☐ **Various Gauges**, Hammer, Steel Barrel, *Modern*	50.00	75.00	75.00

DAVIDSON
Spain Mfg. by Fabrica de Armas, Imported by Davidson Firearms Co., Greensboro, N.C.

SHOTGUN, DOUBLE BARREL, SIDE-BY-SIDE

	V.G.	Exc.	Prior Year Exc. Value
☐ **73 Stagecoach**, 12 or 20 Gauges, Magnum, Checkered Stock, *Modern*	130.00	175.00	170.00
☐ **Model 63B**, 10 Ga. 3½", Magnum, Engraved, Nickel Plated, Checkered Stock, *Modern*	155.00	210.00	200.00
☐ **Model 63B**, 12 and 20 Gauges, Magnum, Engraved, Nickel Plated, Checkered Stock, *Modern*	140.00	185.00	180.00

	V.G.	Exc.	Prior Year Exc. Value
☐ **Model 63B**, Various Gauges, Engraved, Nickel Plated, Checkered Stock, *Modern*	135.00	180.00	175.00
☐ **Model 69 SL**, 12 and 20 Gauges, Sidelock, Light Engraving, Checkered Stock, *Modern*	150.00	225.00	220.00

DAVIS, N.R. & CO.

Freetown, Mass. 1853-1917. Merged with Warner Co. of Norwich, Conn. and became Davis-Warner Arms Co. It was not active between 1920-1922, but in 1930 started again as Crescent-Davis Arms Co., Norwich. This included Crescent Firearms Co. They relocated in Springfield, Mass. 1931-1932 and were taken over in 1932 by Stevens Arms.

RIFLE, PERCUSSION

	V.G.	Exc.	Prior Year Exc. Value
☐ **.45**, Octagon Barrel, *Antique*	400.00	650.00	625.00

SHOTGUN, PERCUSSION

	V.G.	Exc.	Prior Year Exc. Value
☐ **#1 Various Gauges**, Double Barrel, Side by Side Damascus Barrel, Outside Hammers, *Antique*	320.00	475.00	450.00
☐ **#3**, Various Gauges, Double Barrel, Side by Side Damascus Barrel, Outside Hammers, *Antique*	250.00	380.00	365.00

SHOTGUN, DOUBLE BARREL, SIDE-BY-SIDE

	V.G.	Exc.	Prior Year Exc. Value
☐ **Various Gauges**, Outside Hammers, Damascus Barrel, *Modern*	80.00	155.00	150.00
☐ **Various Gauges**, Hammerless, Steel Barrel, *Modern*	100.00	180.00	175.00
☐ **Various Gauges**, Hammerless, Damascus Barrel, *Modern*	75.00	155.00	150.00
☐ **Various Gauges**, Outside Hammers, Steel Barrel, *Modern*	95.00	180.00	175.00

SHOTGUN, SINGLESHOT

	V.G.	Exc.	Prior Year Exc. Value
☐ **Various Gauges**, Hammer, Steel Barrel, *Modern*	45.00	80.00	75.00

DAVIS INDUSTRIES

Current manufacturer in Chino, Calif.

HANDGUN, DOUBLE BARREL, OVER-UNDER

	V.G.	Exc.	Prior Year Exc. Value
☐ **Model D-22**, .22 L.R.R.F., Remington Derringer Style, Chrome, *Modern*	30.00	40.00	—
☐ **Model D-22**, .22 L.R.R.F., Remington Derringer Style, Black Teflon, *Modern*	30.00	40.00	—
☐ **Model D-22**, .25 ACP, Remington Derringer Style, Chrome, *Modern*	30.00	40.00	—
☐ **Model D-22**, .25 ACP, Remington Derringer Style, Black Teflon, *Modern*	30.00	40.00	—

DAY ARMS CO.

San Antonio, Tex.

HANDGUN, SEMI-AUTOMATIC

	V.G.	Exc.	Prior Year Exc. Value
☐ **Conversion Unit Only**, .22 L.R.R.F., For Colt M1911, Clip Fed, *Modern*	95.00	150.00	145.00

DEAD SHOT

L.W. Pond Co.

	V.G.	Exc.	Prior Year Exc. Value
HANDGUN, REVOLVER			
☐ **.22 Long R.F.**, 6 Shot, Single Action, Solid Frame, Spur Trigger, *Antique*	180.00	265.00	250.00

DEBATIR

HANDGUN, SEMI-AUTOMATIC			
☐ **.25 ACP**, Clip Fed, *Modern*	145.00	220.00	195.00
☐ **.32 ACP**, Clip Fed, *Modern*	160.00	255.00	240.00

Debatir .25

DEBERIERE, HENRY

Phila., Pa. 1769-1774, See Kentucky Rifles & Pistols.

DECKER, WILHELM

Zella St. Blasii, Germany, c. 1913.

HANDGUN, REVOLVER			
☐ **Decker**, .25 ACP, Hammerless, 6 Shot, *Curio*	525.00	875.00	850.00
☐ **Mueller Special**, .25 ACP, Hammerless, 6 Shot, *Curio*	625.00	975.00	950.00

DEFENDER

Made by Iver-Johnson, Sold by J.P. Lovell Arms 1875-1895.

HANDGUN, REVOLVER			
☐ **.22 Short R.F.**, 7 Shot, Spur Trigger, Solid Frame, Single Action, *Antique*	95.00	165.00	160.00
☐ **.32 Short R.F.**, 5 Shot, Spur Trigger, Solid Frame, Single Action, *Antique*	95.00	170.00	170.00
☐ **#89**, .22 Short R.F., 7 Shot, Spur Trigger, Solid Frame, Single Action, *Antique*	90.00	160.00	155.00
☐ **#89**, .32 Short R.F., 5 Shot, Spur Trigger, Solid Frame, Single Action, *Antique*	95.00	170.00	165.00

DEFENDER

N. Shore & Co., Chicago, Ill., c.1922

HANDGUN, KNIFE PISTOL			
☐ **#215**, .22 R.F., 3" Over All Length, 1 Blade, *Class 3*	95.00	150.00	140.00

DEFIANCE

Made By Norwich Falls Pistol Co., c. 1880.

	V.G.	Exc.	Prior Year Exc. Value
HANDGUN, REVOLVER			
☐ **.22 Short R.F.**, 7 Shot, Spur Trigger, Solid Frame, Single Action, *Antique*	90.00	155.00	150.00

DEHUFF, ABRAHAM
Lancaster, Pa., c. 1779. See Kentucky rifles & pistols

DEK-DU
Tomas de Urizar y Cia., Eibar, Spain, c. 1910.

	V.G.	Exc.	Prior Year Exc. Value
HANDGUN, REVOLVER			
☐ **Velo Dog**, 5.5mm Velo Dog, 12 Shots, Folding Trigger, *Curio*	110.00	155.00	145.00
☐ **Velo Dog**, .25 ACP, 12 Shots, Folding Trigger, *Curio*	115.00	165.00	150.00

DELPHIAN
Made by Stevens Arms.

	V.G.	Exc.	Prior Year Exc. Value
SHOTGUN, SINGLESHOT			
☐ **Model 90**, Various Gauges, Takedown, Automatic Ejector, Plain Hammer, *Modern*	40.00	65.00	60.00

DELU
Fab. d'Armes Delu & Co.

	V.G.	Exc.	Prior Year Exc. Value
HANDGUN, SEMI-AUTOMATIC			
☐ **.25 ACP**, Clip Fed, *Curio*	145.00	200.00	185.00

DEMRO
Manchester, Conn.

	V.G.	Exc.	Prior Year Exc. Value
HANDGUN, SEMI-AUTOMATIC			
☐ **T.A.C. XF-7 Wasp**, .45 ACP or 9mm Luger, Clip Fed, Modern	285.00	375.00	370.00
RIFLE, SEMI-AUTOMATIC			
☐ **T.A.C. Model 1**, .45 ACP or 9mm Luger, Clip Fed, Modern	225.00	340.00	325.00
☐ **T.A.C. Model 1M**, .45 ACP or 9mm Luger, Clip Fed, Modern	225.00	340.00	325.00
☐ **T.A.C. XF-7 Wasp**, .45 ACP or 9mm Luger, Clip Fed, Folding Stock, Modern	300.00	390.00	380.00

DERR, JOHN
Lancaster, Pa. 1810-1844. See Kentucky Rifles & Pistols.

DERINGER, HENRY, SR.
Richmond, Va. & Philadelphia, Pa. 1768-1814. See Kentucky Rifles & Pistols; U.S. Military.

DERINGER, HENRY, JR.
Philadelphia, Pa. 1806-1868. Also see U.S. Military.

	V.G.	Exc.	Prior Year Exc. Value
HANDGUN, PERCUSSION			
☐ **Pocket**, .41, Back Lock, German Silver Mounts, *Antique*	395.00	750.00	725.00

	V.G.	Exc.	Prior Year Exc. Value
☐ **Medium Pocket**, .41, Back Lock, German Silver Mounts, *Antique*	445.00	795.00	775.00
☐ **Dueller**, .41, Back Lock, German Silver Mounts, Cased Pair, *Antique*	625.00	1,500.00	1,450.00
☐ **Dueller**, .41, Back Lock, Silver Mounts, Cased Pair, *Antique*	995.00	1,975.00	1,950.00
☐ **Dueller**, .41, Back Lock, Gold Mounts, Cased Pair, *Antique*	3,700.00	5,500.00	5,450.00

DERINGER RIFLE AND PISTOL WORKS

Philadelphia, Pa. 1870-1880.

HANDGUN, REVOLVER

	V.G.	Exc.	Prior Year Exc. Value
☐ **Centennial '76**, .38 Long R.F., 5 Shot, Single Action, Spur Trigger, Tip-up, *Antique*	255.00	365.00	350.00
☐ **Model 1**, .22 Short R.F., 7 Shot, Spur Trigger, Tip-up, *Antique*	230.00	340.00	325.00
☐ **Model 2**, .22 Short R.F., 7 Shot, Spur Trigger, Tip-up, *Antique*	220.00	310.00	295.00
☐ **Model 2**, .32 Long R.F., 5 Shot, Single Action, Spur Trigger, Tip-up, *Antique*	220.00	310.00	295.00

DESPATCH

Made by Hopkins & Allen, c. 1875.

HANDGUN, REVOLVER

	V.G.	Exc.	Prior Year Exc. Value
☐ **.22 Short R.F.**, 7 Shot, Spur Trigger, Solid Frame, Single Action, *Antique*	90.00	165.00	160.00

DESTROYER

Made in Spain by Isidro Gaztanaga 1914-1933, reorganized as Gaztanaga, Trocaola y Ibarzabal 1933-1936.

HANDGUN, SEMI-AUTOMATIC

	V.G.	Exc.	Prior Year Exc. Value
☐ **Model 1913**, .25 ACP, Clip Fed, *Modern*	90.00	165.00	150.00
☐ **Destroyer**, .25 ACP, Clip Fed, *Curio*	100.00	170.00	155.00
☐ **Model 1919**, .32 ACP, Clip Fed, *Modern*	100.00	170.00	155.00
☐ **Destroyer**, .32 ACP, Clip Fed, Long Grip, *Curio*	125.00	185.00	170.00
☐ **Super Destroyer**, .32 ACP, Clip Fed, *Modern*	165.00	235.00	220.00

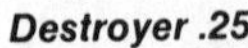

Destroyer .25

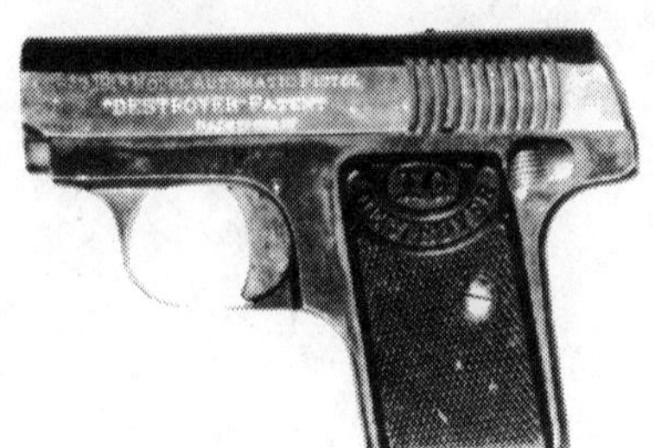

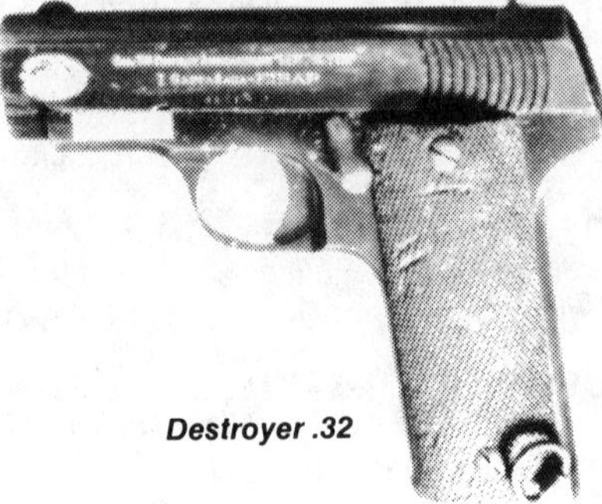

Destroyer .32

	V.G.	Exc.	Prior Year Exc. Value

DESTRUCTOR

Iraola Salaverria, Eibar, Spain.

HANDGUN, SEMI—AUTOMATIC

	V.G.	Exc.	Prior Year Exc. Value
☐ **.25 ACP**, Clip Fed, *Modern*	90.00	150.00	145.00
☐ **.32 ACP**, Clip Fed, *Modern*	100.00	165.00	165.00

DETONICS

Seattle, Washington.

HANDGUN, SEMI-AUTOMATIC

	V.G.	Exc.	Prior Year Exc. Value
☐ **"45" Combat**, .45 ACP, Early Type, Combat Modifications, Clip Fed, Pocket Pistol, Blue, *Modern*	325.00	475.00	370.00
☐ **"45" Combat**, .45 ACP, Early Type, Combat Modifications, Clip Fed, Pocket Pistol, Nickel, *Modern*	400.00	550.00	395.00
☐ **"45" Combat**, .45 ACP, Late Type, Combat Modifications, Clip Fed, Pocket Pistol, Blue, *Modern*	295.00	450.00	370.00
☐ **"45" Combat**, .45 ACP, Late Type, Combat Modifications, Clip Fed, Pocket Pistol, Nickel, *Modern*	325.00	500.00	395.00
☐ **Combat MC-1**, .45 ACP, Combat Modifications, Clip Fed, Pocket Pistol, Matt Blue, *Modern*	300.00	400.00	400.00
☐ **Combat MC-1**, 9mm P., Combat Modifications, Clip Fed, Pocket Pistol, Matt Blue, *Modern*	350.00	440.00	440.00
☐ **Combat MC-1**, .38 Super, Combat Modifications, Clip Fed, Pocket Pistol, Matt Blue, *Modern*	350.00	440.00	440.00
☐ **Combat Master Mk.I**, .45 ACP, Combat Modifications, Clip Fed, Pocket Pistol, Matt Blue, *Modern*	295.00	425.00	395.00
☐ **Combat Master Mk.IV**, .45 ACP, Combat Modifications, Clip Fed, Pocket Pistol, Matt Blue, Adjustable Sights, *Modern*	300.00	410.00	400.00
☐ **Combat Master Mk.V**, .45 ACP, Combat Modifications, Clip Fed, Pocket Pistol, Matt Stainless, *Modern*	330.00	425.00	425.00
☐ **Combat Master Mk.V**, 9mm P., Combat Modifications, Clip Fed, Pocket Pistol, Matt Stainless, *Modern*	350.00	445.00	445.00
☐ **Combat Master Mk.V**, .38 Super, Combat Modifications, Clip Fed, Pocket Pistol, Matt Stainless, *Modern*	350.00	445.00	445.00
☐ **Combat Master Mk.VI**, .45 ACP, Combat Modifications, Clip Fed, Pocket Pistol, Polished Stainless, Adjustable Sights, *Modern*	380.00	475.00	475.00
☐ **Combat Master Mk.VI**, 9mm P., Combat Modifications, Clip Fed, Pocket Pistol, Polished Stainless, Adjustable Sights, *Modern*	385.00	500.00	500.00
☐ **Combat Master Mk.VI**, .38 Super, Combat Modifications, Clip Fed, Pocket Pistol, Polished Stainless, Adjustable Sights, *Modern*	385.00	500.00	500.00
☐ **Combat Master Mk.VI**, .451 Mag., Combat Modifications, Clip Fed, Pocket Pistol, Polished Stainless, Adjustable Sights, *Modern*	450.00	700.00	700.00

	V.G.	Exc.	Prior Year Exc. Value
☐ **Combat Master Mk.IV**, .45 ACP, Combat Modifications, Clip Fed, Pocket Pistol, Matt Blue, Adjustable Sights, *Modern*	**300.00**	**410.00**	**400.00**
☐ **Combat Master Mk.V**, .45 ACP, Combat Modifications, Clip Fed, Pocket Pistol, Matt Stainless, *Modern*	**330.00**	**425.00**	**425.00**
☐ **Combat Master Mk.V**, 9mm P., Combat Modifications, Clip Fed, Pocket Pistol, Matt Stainless, *Modern*	**350.00**	**445.00**	**445.00**
☐ **Combat Master Mk.V**, .38 Super, Combat Modifications, Clip Fed, Pocket Pistol, Matt Stainless, *Modern*	**350.00**	**445.00**	**445.00**
☐ **Combat Master Mk.VI**, .45 ACP, Combat Modifications, Clip Fed, Pocket Pistol, Polished Stainless, Adjustable Sights, *Modern*	**380.00**	**475.00**	**475.00**
☐ **Combat Master Mk.VI**, 9mm P., Combat Modifications, Clip Fed, Pocket Pistol, Polished Stainless, Adjustable Sights, *Modern*	**385.00**	**500.00**	**500.00**
☐ **Combat Master Mk.VI**, .38 Super, Combat Modifications, Clip Fed, Pocket Pistol, Polished Stainless, Adjustable Sights, *Modern*	**385.00**	**500.00**	**500.00**
☐ **Combat Master Mk.VI**, .451 Mag., Combat Modifications, Clip Fed, Pocket Pistol, Polished Stainless, Adjustable Sights, *Modern*	**450.00**	**700.00**	**700.00**
☐ **Combat Master Mk.VII**, .45 ACP, Combat Modifications, Clip Fed, Pocket Pistol, Matt Stainless, No Sights, Lightweight, *Modern*	**380.00**	**490.00**	**490.00**
☐ **Combat Master Mk.VII**, 9mm P., Combat Modifications, Clip Fed, Pocket Pistol, Matt Stainless, No Sights, Lightweight, *Modern*	**400.00**	**525.00**	**525.00**
☐ **Combat Master Mk.VII**, .38 Super, Combat Modifications, Clip Fed, Pocket Pistol, Matt Stainless, No Sights, Lightweight, *Modern*	**400.00**	**525.00**	**525.00**
☐ **Combat Master Mk.VII**, .451 Mag., Combat Modifications, Clip Fed, Pocket Pistol, Matt Stainless, No Sights, Lightweight, *Modern*	**450.00**	**700.00**	**700.00**
☐ **Military Combat OM-3**, .45 ACP, Clip Fed, Pocket Pistol, Matt Stainless, *Modern*	**335.00**	**455.00**	—
☐ **Military Combat OM-3**, 9mm P., Clip Fed, Pocket Pistol, Matt Stainless, *Modern*	**350.00**	**485.00**	—
☐ **Military Combat OM-3**, .38 Super, Clip Fed, Pocket Pistol, Matt Stainless, *Modern*	**350.00**	**485.00**	—
☐ **Scoremaster**, .45 ACP, I.P.S.C. Target Pistol, Target Sights, Stainless Steel, *Modern*	**470.00**	**695.00**	—
☐ **Scoremaster**, .451 Mag., I.P.S.C. Target Pistol, Target Sights, Stainless Steel, *Modern*	**470.00**	**695.00**	—

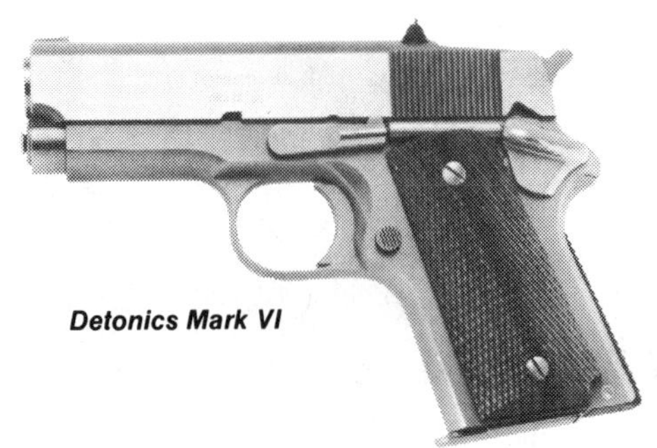
Detonics Mark VI

	V.G.	Exc.	Prior Year Exc. Value
☐ **Combat Master Mk.VII**, .45 ACP, Combat Modifications, Clip Fed, Pocket Pistol, Matt Stainless, No Sights, Lightweight, *Modern*	380.00	490.00	490.00
☐ **Combat Master Mk.VII**, 9mm P., Combat Modifications, Clip Fed, Pocket Pistol, Matt Stainless, No Sights, Lightweight, *Modern*	400.00	525.00	525.00
☐ **Combat Master Mk.VII**, .38 Super, Combat Modifications, Clip Fed, Pocket Pistol, Matt Stainless, No Sights, Lightweight, *Modern*	400.00	525.00	525.00
☐ **Combat Master Mk.VII**, .451 Mag., Combat Modifications, Clip Fed, Pocket Pistol, Matt Stainless, No Sights, Lightweight, *Modern*	450.00	700.00	700.00
☐ **Military Combat OM-3**, .45 ACP, Clip Fed, Pocket Pistol, Matt Stainless, *Modern*	335.00	455.00	—
☐ **Military Combat OM-3**, 9mm P., Clip Fed, Pocket Pistol, Matt Stainless, *Modern*	350.00	485.00	—
☐ **Military Combat OM-3**, .38 Super, Clip Fed, Pocket Pistol, Matt Stainless, *Modern*	350.00	485.00	—
☐ **Scoremaster**, .45 ACP, I.P.S.C. Target Pistol, Target Sights, Stainless Steel, *Modern*	470.00	695.00	—
☐ **Scoremaster**, .451 Mag., I.P.S.C. Target Pistol, Target Sights, Stainless Steel, *Modern*	470.00	695.00	—

DIAMOND

Made by Stevens Arms.

SHOTGUN, SINGLESHOT

	V.G.	Exc.	Prior Year Exc. Value
☐ **Model 89 Dreadnaught**, Various Gauges, Hammer, *Modern*	50.00	70.00	65.00
☐ **Model 90**, Various Gauges, Takedown, Automatic Ejector, Plain Hammer, *Modern*	40.00	65.00	60.00
☐ **Model 95**, 12 and 16 Gauge, Takedown, *Modern*	40.00	60.00	

DIANE

Made by Wilkinson Arms, Covina, Calif.

HANDGUN, SEMI-AUTOMATIC

	V.G.	Exc.	Prior Year Exc. Value
☐ **Standard Model**, .25 ACP, Clip Fed, *Modern*	170.00	275.00	250.00
☐ **Lightweight Model**, .25 ACP, Clip Fed, *Modern*	570.00	825.00	800.00

DEANE, ADAMS & DEANE

See Adams

	V.G.	Exc.	Prior Year Exc. Value

DIANE

Erquiaga, Muguruzu, y Cia., Eibar, Spain, c. 1923.

HANDGUN, SEMI-AUTOMATIC

	V.G.	Exc.	Prior Year Exc. Value
☐ **.25 ACP**, Clip Fed, Blue, *Curio*	180.00	275.00	265.00

DICKINSON, J. & L.

Also E. L. & J. Dickinson, Springfield, Mass. 1863-1880.

HANDGUN, SINGLESHOT

	V.G.	Exc.	Prior Year Exc. Value
☐ **.22 R.F.**, Brass Frame, Pivoting Barrel, Rack Ejector, *Antique*	275.00	390.00	375.00
☐ **.32 R.F.**, Brass Frame, Pivoting Barrel, Rack Ejector, *Antique*	185.00	290.00	275.00

DICKSON

Made in Italy for American Import Co. until 1968.

HANDGUN, SEMI-AUTOMATIC

	V.G.	Exc.	Prior Year Exc. Value
☐ **Detective**, .25 ACP, Clip Fed, *Modern*	85.00	125.00	125.00

DICTATOR

Made by Hopkins & Allen, c. 1880.

HANDGUN, REVOLVER

	V.G.	Exc.	Prior Year Exc. Value
☐ **.22 Short R.F.**, 7 Shot, Spur Trigger, Solid Frame, Single Action, *Antique*	90.00	165.00	160.00
☐ **.32 Short R.F.**, 5 Shot, Spur Trigger, Solid Frame, Single Action, *Antique*	90.00	165.00	160.00
☐ **#2**, .32 Short R.F., 5 Shot, Spur Trigger, Solid Frame, Single Action, *Antique*	90.00	175.00	175.00

DIXIE GUN WORKS

Union City, Tenn.

HANDGUN, FLINTLOCK

	V.G.	Exc.	Prior Year Exc. Value
☐ **Tower**, .67, Brass Furniture, Reproduction, *Antique*	15.00	30.00	30.00

HANDGUN, PERCUSSION

	V.G.	Exc.	Prior Year Exc. Value
☐ **Army**, .44, Revolver, Buntline, Reproduction, *Antique*	55.00	75.00	75.00
☐ **Navy**, .36, Revolver, Buntline, Brass Frame, Reproduction, *Antique*	20.00	40.00	40.00
☐ **Navy**, .36, Revolver, Buntline, Brass Frame, Engraved, Reproduction, *Antique*	25.00	45.00	45.00
☐ **Spiller & Burr**, .36, Revolver, Buntline, Brass Frame, Reproduction, *Antique*	35.00	60.00	60.00
☐ **Wyatt Earp**, .44 Revolver, Buntline, Brass Frame, Reproduction, *Antique*	35.00	55.00	55.00
☐ **Wyatt Earp**, .44 Revolver, Buntline, Brass Frame, With Shoulder Stock, Reproduction, *Antique*	55.00	85.00	85.00

RIFLE, FLINTLOCK

	V.G.	Exc.	Prior Year Exc. Value
☐ **1st. Model Brown Bess**, .75, Military, Reproduction, *Antique*	260.00	365.00	365.00
☐ **2nd. Model Brown Bess**, .74, Military, Reproduction, *Antique*	140.00	215.00	215.00

	V.G.	Exc.	Prior Year Exc. Value
☐ **Coach Guard**, .95, Blunderbuss, Brass Furniture, Reproduction, *Antique*	80.00	125.00	125.00
☐ **Day Rifle**, .45, Double Barrel, Over-under, Swivel Breech, Brass Furniture, Reproduction, *Antique*	265.00	360.00	360.00
☐ **Deluxe Pennsylvania**, .45, Kentucky Rifle, Full-Stocked, Brass Furniture, Light Engraving, Reproduction, *Antique*	190.00	265.00	265.00
☐ **Deluxe Pensylvania**, .45, Kentucky Rifle, Full-Stocked, Brass Furniture, Reproduction, *Antique*	180.00	275.00	275.00
☐ **Kentuckian**, .45, Kentucky Rifle, Full-Stocked, Brass Furniture, Reproduction, *Antique*	85.00	125.00	125.00
☐ **Kentuckian**, .45, Kentucky Rifle, Full-Stocked, Brass Furniture, Reproduction, Carbine, *Antique*	85.00	125.00	125.00
☐ **Musket**, .67 Smoothbore, Reproduction, Carbine, *Antique*	50.00	85.00	85.00
☐ **Squirel Rifle**, .45, Kentucky Rifles, Full-Stocked, Brass Furniture, Reproduction, *Antique*	160.00	215.00	215.00
☐ **York County**, .45, Kentucky Rifle, Full-Stocked, Brass Furniture, Reproduction, *Antique*	90.00	135.00	135.00
RIFLE, LEVER ACTION			
☐ **Win. 73 (Italian)**, .44-40 WCF, Tube Feed, Octagon Barrel, Carbine, *Modern*	175.00	285.00	275.00
☐ **Win 73 (Italian)**, .44-40 WCF, Tube Feed, Octagon Barrel, Color Cased Hardened Frame, Engraved, *Modern*	210.00	320.00	300.00
RIFLE, PERCUSSION			
☐ **Day Rifle**, .45, Double Barrel, Over-under, Swivel Breech, Brass Furniture, Reproduction, *Antique*	160.00	245.00	245.00
☐ **Deluxe Pennsylvania**, .45, Kentucky Rifle, Full-Stocked, Brass Furniture, Reproduction, *Antique*	170.00	240.00	240.00
☐ **Deluxe Pensylvania**, .45, Kentucky Rifle, Full-Stocked, Brass Furniture, Light Engraving, Reproduction, *Antique*	185.00	260.00	260.00
☐ **Dixie Hawkin**, .45, Half-Stocked, Octagon Barrel, Set Trigger, Brass Furniture, Reproduction, *Antique*	110.00	155.00	155.00
☐ **Dixie Hawkin**, .50, Half-Stocked, Octagon Barrel, Set Trigger, Brass Furniture, Reproduction, *Antique*	110.00	155.00	155.00
☐ **Enfield Two-Band**, .577, Musketoon, Military, Reproduction, *Antique*	85.00	150.00	150.00
☐ **Kentuckian**, .45, Kentucky Rifle, Full-Stocked, Brass Furniture, Reproduction, *Antique*	75.00	125.00	125.00
☐ **Kentuckian**, .45, Kentucky Rifle, Full-Stocked, Brass Furniture, Reproduction, Carbine, *Antique*	75.00	125.00	125.00
☐ **Musket**, .66, Smoothbore, Reproduction, *Antique*	45.00	75.00	75.00
☐ **Plainsman**, .45, Half-Stocked, Octagon Barrel, Reproduction, *Antique*	85.00	145.00	145.00

	V.G.	Exc.	Prior Year Exc. Value
☐ **Plainsman**, .50, Half-Stocked, Octagon Barrel, Reproduction, *Antique*	85.00	145.00	145.00
☐ **Squirrel Rifle**, .45, Kentucky Rifle, Full-Stocked, Brass Furniture, Reproduction, *Antique*	145.00	200.00	200.00
☐ **Target**, .45, Half-Stocked, Octagon Barrel, Reproduction, *Antique*	45.00	75.00	75.00
☐ **York County**, .45, Kentucky Rifle, Full-Stocked, Brass Furniture, Reproduction, *Antique*	80.00	125.00	125.00
☐ **Zouave M 1863**, .58, Military, Reproduction, *Antique*	75.00	125.00	125.00

SHOTGUN, FLINTLOCK

	V.G.	Exc.	Prior Year Exc. Value
☐ **Fowling Piece**, 14 Gauge, Single Barrel, Reproduction, *Antique*	50.00	85.00	85.00

SHOTGUN, PERCUSSION

	V.G.	Exc.	Prior Year Exc. Value
☐ **12 Gauge**, Double Barrel, Side by Side, Double Trigger, Reproduction, *Antique*	90.00	135.00	135.00
☐ **28 Gauge**, Single Barrel, Reproduction, *Antique*	25.00	45.00	45.00

DOBSON, T.

London, England, c. 1780.

HANDGUN, FLINTLOCK

	V.G.	Exc.	Prior Year Exc. Value
☐ **.64**, Presentation, Holster Pistol, Gold Inlays, Engraved, Half-Octagon Barrel, High Quality, *Antique*	2,650.00	3,800.00	3,750.00

DOMINO

Made in Italy, Imported by Mandell Shooting Sports. Also see Beeman.

HANDGUN, SEMI-AUTOMATIC

	V.G.	Exc.	Prior Year Exc. Value
☐ **Model O.P. 601**, .22 Short, Target Pistol, Adjustable Sights, Target Grips, *Modern*	450.00	675.00	675.00
☐ **Model O.P. 601**, .22 Short, Target Pistol, Adjustable Sights, Target Grips, *Modern*	450.00	675.00	675.00

DREADNAUGHT

Made by Hopkins & Allen, c. 1880.

HANDGUN, REVOLVER

	V.G.	Exc.	Prior Year Exc. Value
☐ **.22 Short R.F.**, 7 Shot, Spur Trigger, Solid Frame, Single Action, *Antique*	90.00	155.00	150.00
☐ **.32 Short R.F.**, 5 Shot, Spur Trigger, Solid Frame, Single Action, *Antique*	95.00	170.00	170.00

DREYSE

Dreyse Rheinische Metallwaren Machinenfabrik, Sommerda, Germany since 1889. In 1936 merged and became Rheinmetall-Borsig, Dusseldorf, Germany.

HANDGUN, SEMI-AUTOMATIC

	V.G.	Exc.	Prior Year Exc. Value
☐ **M1907**, .32 ACP, Clip Fed, Early Model, *Modern*	145.00	300.00	225.00
☐ **M1907**, .32 ACP, Clip Fed, *Modern*	125.00	200.00	165.00
☐ **M1910**, 9mm Luger, Clip Fed, *Curio*	595.00	840.00	800.00
☐ **Rheinmetall**, .32 ACP, Clip Fed, *Modern*	185.00	325.00	295.00
☐ **Vest Pocket**, .25 ACP, Clip Fed, Early, *Modern*	160.00	230.00	210.00
☐ **Vest Pocket**, .25 ACP, Clip Fed *Modern*	135.00	200.00	195.00

Dreyse Model 1907 Late

Dreyse Model 2

	V.G.	Exc.	Prior Year Exc. Value
RIFLE, SEMI-AUTOMATIC			
☐ **Carbine**, .32 ACP, Clip Fed, Checkered Stock, *Curio*	285.00	435.00	400.00

DRIPPARD, F.
Lancaster, Pa. 1767-1773, See Kentucky Rifles & Pistols.

DRISCOLL, J.B.
Springfield, Mass., c. 1870.

	V.G.	Exc.	Prior Year Exc. Value
HANDGUN, SINGLESHOT			
☐ **.22 R.F.**, Brass Frame, Spur Trigger, *Antique*	165.00	295.00	285.00

DUMARESD, B.
Marseille, France, probably c. 1730.

	V.G.	Exc.	Prior Year Exc. Value
HANDGUN, FLINTLOCK			
☐ **Holster Pistol**, Engraved, Horn Inlays, Ornate, Silver Furniture, *Antique*	995.00	1,975.00	1,950.00

DUBIEL ARMS CO.
Sherman, Tex. since 1975.

	V.G.	Exc.	Prior Year Exc. Value
RIFLE, BOLT ACTION			
☐ **Custom Rifle**, Various Calibers, Various Styles, Fancy Wood, *Modern*	1,200.00	1,750.00	1,750.00

DUMOULIN FRERES ET CIE
Milmort, Belgium since 1849.

	V.G.	Exc.	Prior Year Exc. Value
RIFLE, BOLT ACTION			
☐ **Grade I**, Various Calibers, Fancy Checkering, Engraved, *Modern*	895.00	1,450.00	1,400.00
☐ **Grade II**, Various Calibers, Fancy Checkering, Engraved, Fance Wood, *Modern*	1,375.00	1,975.00	1,975.00
☐ **Grade III**, Various Calibers, Fancy Checkering, Fancy Engraving, Fancy Wood, *Modern*	1,775.00	2,550.00	2,500.00
RIFLE, DOUBLE BARREL, SIDE-BY-SIDE			
☐ **Various Calibers**, Fancy Checkering, Engraved, Fancy Wood, *Modern*	1,675.00	2,250.00	2,200.00

	V.G.	Exc.	Prior Year Exc. Value

DUO

Frantisek Dusek, Opocno, Czechoslovakia 1926-1948. Ceska Zbrojovka from 1948 to date.

HANDGUN, SEMI-AUTOMATIC

	V.G.	Exc.	Prior Year Exc. Value
☐ **.25 ACP**, Clip Fed, *Modern*	100.00	175.00	175.00

DUTCH MILITARY

HANDGUN, REVOLVER

	V.G.	Exc.	Prior Year Exc. Value
☐ **Model 1871 Hemberg,** 9.4mm, Military, *Antique*	105.00	165.00	150.00

RIFLE, BOLT ACTION

	V.G.	Exc.	Prior Year Exc. Value
☐ **Model 95,** 6.5mm Mannlicher, Full Stock, *Curio*	40.00	70.00	100.00
☐ **Model 95,** 6.5mm Mannlicher, Carbine, Full Stock, *Curio*	40.00	70.00	100.00
☐ **Beaumont-Vitale M1871/88,** Military, *Antique*	115.00	185.00	160.00

RIFLE, FLINTLOCK

	V.G.	Exc.	Prior Year Exc. Value
☐ **.70,** Officers Type, Musket, Brass Furniture, *Antique*	825.00	1300.00	1025.00

DUTTON, JOHN S.

Jaffrey, N.H. 1855-1870.

RIFLE, PERCUSSION

	V.G.	Exc.	Prior Year Exc. Value
☐ **.36**, Target Rifle, Swiss Buttplate, Octagon Barrel, Target Sights, *Antique*	800.00	1,500.00	1,400.00

DWM

Deutche Waffen und Munitionsfabrik, Berlin, Germany 1896-1945. Also see Luger and Borchardt.

HANDGUN, SEMI-AUTOMATIC

	V.G.	Exc.	Prior Year Exc. Value
☐ **Pocket**, .32 ACP, Clip Fed, *Curio*	260.00	400.00	375.00

E.A.

Echave y Arizmendi, Eibar, Spain 1911-1975. Also see Echasa and MAB.

HANDGUN, SEMI-AUTOMATIC

	V.G.	Exc.	Prior Year Exc. Value
☐ **1916 Model**, .25 ACP, Clip Fed, *Curio*	75.00	125.00	120.00

E.A.

Eulogio Arostegui, Eibar, Spain, c. 1930.

HANDGUN, SEMI-AUTOMATIC

	V.G.	Exc.	Prior Year Exc. Value
☐ **.25 ACP**, Clip Fed, Blue, Dog Logo on Grips, *Modern*	70.00	120.00	115.00

EAGLE

Made by Iver-Johnson, c. 1879-1886.

HANDGUN, REVOLVER

	V.G.	Exc.	Prior Year Exc. Value
☐ **.22 Short R.F.**, 7 Shot, Spur Trigger, Solid Frame, Single Action, *Antique*	90.00	155.00	150.00
☐ **.32 Short R.F.**, 5 Shot, Spur Trigger, Solid Frame, Single Action, *Antique*	90.00	155.00	150.00
☐ **.38 Short R.F.**, 5 Shot, Spur Trigger, Solid Frame, Single Action, *Antique*	95.00	175.00	175.00

	V.G.	Exc.	Prior Year Exc. Value
☐ **.44 Short R.F.**, 5 Shot, Spur Trigger, Solid Frame, Single Action, *Antique*	**175.00**	**260.00**	**250.00**

EAGLE ARMS CO.

N.Y.C., c.1865.

HANDGUN, REVOLVER

	V.G.	Exc.	Prior Year Exc. Value
☐ **.28 Cup Primed Cartridge,** 6 Shot, Single Action, Spur Trigger, Solid Frame, *Antique*	**185.00**	**345.00**	**325.00**
☐ **.28 Cup Primed Cartridge,** 6 Shot, Single Action, Spur Trigger, Tip-up, *Antique*	**220.00**	**340.00**	**325.00**
☐ **.30 Cup Primed Cartridge,** 5 Shot, Single Action, Spur Trigger, *Antique*	**130.00**	**200.00**	**195.00**
☐ **.30 Cup Primed Cartridge,** 6 Shot, Single Action, Spur Trigger, Solid Frame, *Antique*	**185.00**	**320.00**	**295.00**
☐ **.30 Cup Primed Cartridge,** 6 Shot, Single Action, Spur Trigger, Tip-up, *Antique*	**240.00**	**365.00**	**345.00**
☐ **.42 Cup Primed Cartridge,** 6 Shot, Single Action, Spur Trigger, Solid Frame, *Antique*	**175.00**	**295.00**	**285.00**
☐ **.43 Cup Primed Cartridge,** 6 Shot, Single Action, Spur Trigger, Tip-up, *Antique*	**250.00**	**425.00**	**385.00**

EAGLE GUN CO.

Stratford, Conn., c. 1965.

RIFLE, SEMI-AUTOMATIC

	V.G.	Exc.	Prior Year Exc. Value
☐ **.45 ACP**, Clip Fed, Carbine, *Class 3*	110.00	175.00	175.00
☐ **9mm Luger, Clip Fed, Carbine,** *Class 3*	160.00	225.00	225.00

EARLHOOD

Made by E.L. Dickinson Co. Springfield, Mass. 1870-1880.

HANDGUN, REVOLVER

	V.G.	Exc.	Prior Year Exc. Value
☐ **.32 Short R.F.**, 5 Shot, Spur Trigger, Solid Frame, Single Action, *Antique*	**95.00**	**165.00**	**165.00**

EARLY, AMOS

Dauphin Co. Pa. See Kentucky Rifles.

EARLY, JACOB

Dauphin Co. Pa. See Kentucky Rifles.

EARTHQUAKE

Made by E.L. Dickinson Co. Springfield, Mass. 1870-1880.

HANDGUN, REVOLVER

	V.G.	Exc.	Prior Year Exc. Value
☐ **.32 Short R.F.**, 5 Shot, Spur Trigger, Solid Frame, Single Action, *Antique*	**95.00**	**175.00**	**170.00**

EASTERN ARMS CO.

Made by Meriden Firearms and sold by Sears-Roebuck.

HANDGUN, REVOLVER

	V.G.	Exc.	Prior Year Exc. Value
☐ **.32 S & W**, 5 Shot, Double Action, Top Break, *Modern*	**55.00**	**100.00**	**95.00**
☐ **.38 S & W**, 5 Shot, Double Action, Top Break, *Modern*	**60.00**	**110.00**	**100.00**

	V.G.	Exc.	Prior Year Exc. Value

EASTFIELD
See Smith & Wesson.

EASTERN
Made by Stevens Arms.

SHOTGUN, DOUBLE BARREL, SIDE-BY-SIDE

	V.G.	Exc.	Prior Year Exc. Value
☐ **Model 311**, Various Gauges, Hammerless, Steel Barrel, *Modern*	130.00	185.00	175.00

SHOTGUN, SINGLESHOT

	V.G.	Exc.	Prior Year Exc. Value
☐ **Model 94**, Various Gauges, Takedown, Automatic Ejector, Plain Hammer, *Modern*	40.00	55.00	55.00

Echasa GZ-MAB

ECHASA
Tradename used in the 1950's by Echave, Arizmendi y Cia., Eibar, Spain.

HANDGUN, SEMI-AUTOMATIC

	V.G.	Exc.	Prior Year Exc. Value
☐ **Model GZ MAB**, .22 L.R.R.F., Clip Fed, Hammer *Modern*	90.00	140.00	130.00
☐ **Model GZ MAB**, .25 ACP, Clip Fed, Hammer, *Modern*	110.00	150.00	140.00
☐ **Model GZ MAB**, .32 ACP, Clip Fed, Hammer, *Modern*	115.00	160.00	150.00

ECHABERRIA, ARTURA
Spain, c. 1790.

HANDGUN, MIQUELET-LOCK

	V.G.	Exc.	Prior Year Exc. Value
☐ **Pair**, Holster Pistol, Plain, Brass Furniture, *Antique*	2,900.00	4,350.00	4,200.00

ECLIPSE
Made by Johnson, Bye & Co., c. 1875.

HANDGUN, SINGLESHOT

	V.G.	Exc.	Prior Year Exc. Value
☐ **.25 Short R.F.**, Derringer, Spur Trigger, *Antique*	80.00	125.00	115.00

EDGESON
Lincolnshire, England, 1810-1830.

HANDGUN, FLINTLOCK

	V.G.	Exc.	Prior Year Exc. Value
☐ **.45**, Pair, Box Lock, Screw Barrel, Pocket Pistol, Folding Trigger, Plain *Antique*	975.00	1,700.00	1,650.00

	V.G.	Exc.	Prior Year Exc. Value
EDMONDS, J.			
See Kentucky Rifles.			
EGG, CHARLES			
London, England, c. 1850.			
HANDGUN, PERCUSSION			
☐ **Pepperbox**, .36, 6 Shot, 3½" Barrels, *Antique*	240.00	395.00	370.00
EGG, DURS			
London, England 1770-1840. Also see British Military.			
HANDGUN, FLINTLOCK			
☐ **.50**, Duelling Type, Holster Pistol, Octagon Barrel, Steel Furniture, Light Ornamentation, *Antique*	975.00	1,650.00	1,550.00
HANDGUN, PERCUSSION			
☐ **6 Shot**, Pepperbox, Fluted Barrel, Pocket Pistol, Engraved, *Antique*	995.00	1,750.00	1,600.00
EGYPTIAN MILITARY			
HANDGUN, SEMI-AUTOMATIC			
☐ **Tokagypt M-58,** 9mm Luger, Clip Fed, *Curio*	210.00	345.00	495.00
RIFLE, SEMI-AUTOMATIC			
☐ **Hakim,** .22 L.R.R.F., Training Rifle, Military, *Modern*	220.00	345.00	345.00
☐ **Hakim,** 8mm Mauser, Military, *Modern*	465.00	635.00	635.00
84 GUN CO.			
Eighty Four, Pa., c. 1973.			
RIFLE, BOLT ACTION			
☐ **Classic Rifle**, Various Calibers, Checkered Stock, Standard Grade, *Modern*	210.00	315.00	300.00
☐ **Classic Rifle**, Various Calibers, Checkered Stock, Grade 1, *Modern*	280.00	400.00	400.00
☐ **Classic Rifle**, Various Calibers, Checkered Stock, Grade 2, *Modern*	420.00	600.00	600.00
☐ **Classic Rifle**, Various Calibers, Checkered Stock, Grade 3, *Modern*	835.00	1,300.00	1,300.00
☐ **Classic Rifle**, Various Calibers, Checkered Stock, Grade 4, *Modern*	1,250.00	2,000.00	2,000.00
☐ **Lobo Rifle**, Various Calibers, Checkered Stock, Standard Grade, *Modern*	215.00	320.00	300.00
☐ **Lobo Rifle**, Various Calibers, Checkered Stock, Grade 1, *Modern*	280.00	400.00	400.00
☐ **Lobo Rifle**, Various Calibers, Checkered Stock, Grade 2, *Modern*	420.00	600.00	600.00
☐ **Lobo Rifle**, Various Calibers, Checkered Stock, Grade 3, *Modern*	830.00	1,300.00	1,300.00
☐ **Lobo Rifle**, Various Calibers, Checkered Stock, Grade 4, *Modern*	1,250.00	2,000.00	2,000.00
☐ **Pennsy Rifle**, Various Calibers, Checkered Stock, Standard Grade, *Modern*	220.00	325.00	300.00

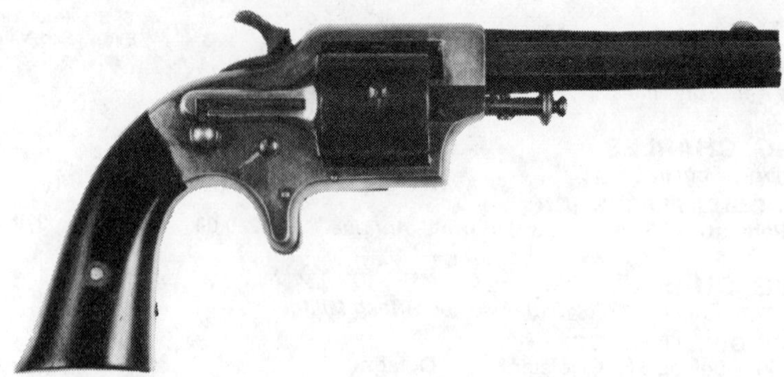

Eagle Arms Plants Patent, .30 Caliber Revolver

Elgin Cutlass Pistol, .54 Caliber

	V.G.	Exc.	Prior Year Exc. Value
☐ **Pennsy Rifle**, Various Calibers, Checkered Stock, Grade 1, *Modern*	280.00	420.00	400.00
☐ **Pennsy Rifle**, Various Calibers, Checkered Stock, Grade 2, *Modern*	420.00	600.00	600.00
☐ **Pennsy Rifle**, Various Calibers, Checkered Stock, Grade 3, *Modern*	825.00	1,325.00	1,300.00
☐ **Pennsy Rifle**, Various Calibers, Checkered Stock, Grade 4, *Modern*	1,250.00	2,000.00	2,000.00

ELECTOR

Made by Hopkins & Allen, c. 1880.

HANDGUN, REVOLVER

☐ **.22 Short R.F.**, 7 Shot, Spur Trigger, Solid Frame, Single Action, *Antique*	95.00	160.00	160.00
☐ **.32 Short R.F.**, 5 Shot, Spur Trigger, Solid Frame, Single Action, *Antique*	95.00	170.00	170.00

ELECTRIC

Made by Forehand & Wadsworth 1871-1880.

HANDGUN, REVOLVER

☐ **.32 Short R.F.**, 5 Shot, Spur Trigger, Solid Frame, Single Action, *Antique*	95.00	160.00	160.00

EL FAISAN

SHOTGUN, DOUBLE BARREL, SIDE-BY-SIDE

☐ **El Faisan**, .410 Gauge, Folding Gun, Double Trigger, Outside Hammers, *Modern*	70.00	110.00	100.00

ELGIN ARMS CO.

Made by Crescent for Fred Bifflar & Co., Chicago, Ill.

SHOTGUN, DOUBLE BARREL, SIDE-BY-SIDE

☐ **Various Gauges**, Outside Hammers, Damascus Barrel, *Modern*	80.00	155.00	150.00
☐ **Various Gauges**, Hammerless, Steel Barrel, *Modern*	115.00	185.00	175.00
☐ **Various Gauges**, Hammerless, Damascus Barrel, *Modern*	80.00	155.00	150.00
☐ **Various Gauges**, Outside Hammers, Steel Barrel, *Modern*	110.00	180.00	175.00

SHOTGUN, SINGLESHOT

☐ **Various Gauges**, Hammer, Steel Barrel, *Modern*	45.00	75.00	75.00

ELLIS, REUBEN

Albany, N.Y. 1808-1829.

RIFLE, FLINTLOCK

☐ **Ellis-Jennings,** .69, Sliding Lock for Multiple Loadings, 4 shot, *Antique*	5,500.00	9,200.00	8,850.00
☐ **Ellis-Jennings,** .69, Sliding Lock for Multiple Loadings, 10 shot, *Antique*	7,950.00	16,250.00	15,500.00

	V.G.	Exc.	Prior Year Exc. Value

EL TIGRE

RIFLE, LEVER ACTION

	V.G.	Exc.	Prior Year Exc. Value
☐ **Copy of Winchester M1892**, .44-40 WCF, Tube Feed, *Modern*	170.00	270.00	255.00

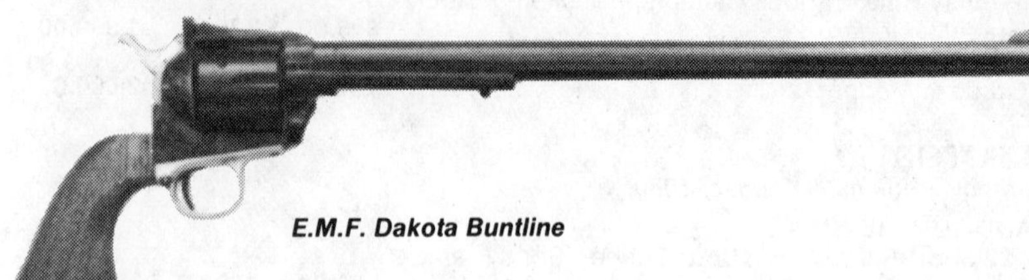

E.M.F. Dakota Buntline

E.M.F.

(Early and Modern Firearms Co., Inc.) Studio City, Calif.

HANDGUN, REVOLVER

	V.G.	Exc.	Prior Year Exc. Value
☐ **California Dragoon**, .44 Magnum, Single Action, Western Style, Engraved, *Modern*	185.00	235.00	225.00
☐ **Dakota**, Various Calibers, Single Action, Western Style, *Modern*	125.00	175.00	155.00
☐ **Dakota**, Various Calibers, Single Action, Western Style, Engraved, *Modern*	165.00	275.00	220.00
☐ **Dakota**, Various Calibers, Single Action, Western Style, Nickel Plated, *Modern*	140.00	210.00	185.00
☐ **Dakota**, Various Calibers, Single Action, Western Style, Nickel Plated, Engraved, *Modern*	195.00	295.00	245.00
☐ **Dakota Buntline**, Various Calibers, 12" Barrel, Single Action, Western Style, *Modern*	140.00	190.00	165.00
☐ **Dakota Buckhorn**, Various Calibers, 16¼" Barrel, Single Action, Western Style, *Modern*	160.00	225.00	180.00
☐ **Dakota Buckhorn**, Various Calibers, 16¼" Barrel, Single Action, Western Style, with Shoulder Stock, *Modern*	190.00	255.00	215.00
☐ **Dakota Sheriff**, Various Calibers, Single Action, Western Style, *Modern*	155.00	225.00	190.00
☐ **Super Dakota**, Various Calibers, Single Action, Western Style, Magnum, *Modern*	150.00	235.00	190.00
☐ **Outlaw 1875**, Various Calibers, Single Action, Remington Style, *Modern*	135.00	190.00	160.00
☐ **Outlaw 1875**, Various Calibers, Single Action, Remington Style, Engraved, *Modern*	190.00	275.00	220.00
☐ **Thermodynamics**, .357 Magnum, Solid Frame, Swing-out Cylinder, Vent Rib, Stainless Steel, *Modern*	130.00	180.00	175.00

HANDGUN, SINGLESHOT

	V.G.	Exc.	Prior Year Exc. Value
☐ **Baron**, .22 Short R.F., Derringer, Gold Frame, Blue Barrel, Wood Grips, *Modern*	30.00	45.00	40.00
☐ **Baron**, Count, Etc., Derringer, if Cased *Add* **$10.00-$15.00**			
☐ **Baroness**, .22 Short R.F., Derringer, Gold Plated, Pearl Grips, *Modern*	35.00	55.00	50.00
☐ **Count**, .22 Short R.F., Derringer, Blue, Wood Grips, *Modern*	30.00	45.00	40.00

	V.G.	Exc.	Prior Year Exc. Value
☐ **Rolling Block**, .357 Magnum, Remington Copy, *Modern*	85.00	135.00	125.00

RIFLE, LEVER ACTION

☐ **1866 Yellowboy**, Various Calibers, Brass Frame, Winchester Copy, *Modern*	185.00	245.00	230.00
☐ **1866 Yellowboy**, Various Calibers, Brass Frame, Winchester Copy, Engraved, *Modern*	230.00	325.00	295.00
☐ **1873 Carbine**, Various Calibers, Winchester Copy, *Modern*	270.00	365.00	350.00
☐ **1873 Rifle**, Various Calibers, Winchester Copy, *Modern*	310.00	400.00	385.00
☐ **1873 Rifle**, Various Calibers, Winchester Copy, Engraved, *Modern*	345.00	500.00	450.00

EM-GE

Gerstenberger & Eberwein, Gussenstadt, West Germany.

HANDGUN, REVOLVER

☐ **Model 220 KS**, .22 L.R.R.F., Double Action, *Modern*	20.00	35.00	35.00
☐ **Model 223**, .22 W.M.R., Double Action, *Modern*	30.00	55.00	55.00
☐ **Target Model 200**, .22 L.R.R.F., Double Action, Target Sights, Vent Rib, *Modern*	35.00	60.00	60.00

EMPIRE

Made by Jacob Rupertus 1858-1888.

HANDGUN, REVOLVER

☐ **.22 Short R.F.**, 7 Shot, Spur Trigger, Solid Frame, Single Action, *Antique*	95.00	160.00	160.00
☐ **.38 Short R.F.**, 5 Shot, Spur Trigger, Solid Frame, Single Action, *Antique*	95.00	195.00	190.00
☐ **.41 Short R.F.**, 5 Shot, Spur Trigger, Solid Frame, Single Action, *Antique*	125.00	225.00	220.00

EMPIRE ARMS

Made by Meriden, and distributed by H. & D. Folsom.

HANDGUN, REVOLVER

☐ **.32 S & W**, 5 Shot, Double Action, Top Break, *Modern*	50.00	100.00	95.00
☐ **.38 S & W**, 5 Shot, Double Action, Top Break, *Modern*	50.00	100.00	95.00

EMPIRE ARMS CO.

Made by Crescent for Sears Roebuck & Co., c. 1900.

SHOTGUN, DOUBLE BARREL, SIDE-BY-SIDE

☐ **Various Gauges**, Outside Hammers, Damascus Barrel, *Modern*	80.00	155.00	150.00
☐ **Various Gauges**, Hammerless, Steel Barrel, *Modern*	115.00	185.00	175.00
☐ **Various Gauges**, Hammerless, Damascus Barrel, *Modern*	80.00	155.00	150.00
☐ **Various Gauges**, Outside Hammers, Steel Barrel, *Modern*	110.00	180.00	175.00

	V.G.	Exc.	Prior Year Exc. Value
SHOTGUN, SINGLESHOT			
☐ **Various Gauges**, Hammer, Steel Barrel, *Modern*	45.00	75.00	75.00

EMPIRE STATE

Made by Meriden Firearms, and distributed by H & D Folsom.

	V.G.	Exc.	Prior Year Exc. Value
HANDGUN, REVOLVER			
☐ **.32 S & W**, 5 Shot, Double Action, Top Break, *Modern*	50.00	95.00	95.00
☐ **.38 S & W**, 5 Shot, Double Action, Top Break, *Modern*	50.00	100.00	95.00

EMPRESS

Made by Jacob Rupertus 1858-1888.

	V.G.	Exc.	Prior Year Exc. Value
HANDGUN, REVOLVER			
☐ **.32 Short R.F.**, 5 Shot, Spur Trigger, Solid Frame, Single Action, *Antique*	100.00	175.00	170.00

ENCORE

Made by Johnson-Bye, also by Hopkins & Allen 1847-1887.

	V.G.	Exc.	Prior Year Exc. Value
HANDGUN, REVOLVER			
☐ **.22 Short R.F.**, 7 Shot, Spur Trigger, Solid Frame, Single Action, *Antique*	95.00	160.00	160.00
☐ **.32 Short R.F.**, 5 Shot, Spur Trigger, Solid Frame, Single Action, A2Antique	100.00	175.00	170.00
☐ **.38 R.F.**, 5 Shot, Spur Trigger, Solid Frame, Single Action, *Antique*	100.00	195.00	190.00

ENDERS OAKLEAF

Made by Crescent for Shapleigh Hardware Co., St. Louis, Mo.

	V.G.	Exc.	Prior Year Exc. Value
SHOTGUN, DOUBLE BARREL, SIDE-BY-SIDE			
☐ **Various Gauges**, Outside Hammers, Damascus Barrel, *Modern*	80.00	155.00	150.00
☐ **Various Gauges**, Hammerless, Steel Barrel, *Modern*	115.00	185.00	175.00
☐ **Various Gauges**, Hammerless, Damascus Barrel, *Modern*	80.00	155.00	150.00
☐ **Various Gauges**, Outside Hammers, Steel Barrel, *Modern*	110.00	180.00	175.00
SHOTGUN, SINGLESHOT			
☐ **Various Gauges**, Hammer, Steel Barrel, *Modern*	45.00	75.00	75.00

ENDERS ROYAL SERVICE

Made by Crescent for Shapleigh Hardware Co., St. Louis, Mo.

	V.G.	Exc.	Prior Year Exc. Value
SHOTGUN, DOUBLE BARREL, SIDE-BY-SIDE			
☐ **Various Gauges**, Outside Hammers, Damascus Barrel, *Modern*	80.00	155.00	150.00
☐ **Various Gauges**, Hammerless, Steel Barrel, *Modern*	115.00	185.00	175.00
☐ **Various Gauges**, Hammerless, Damascus Barrel, *Modern*	80.00	155.00	150.00
☐ **Various Gauges**, Outside Hammers, Steel Barrel, *Modern*	110.00	180.00	175.00

	V.G.	Exc.	Prior Year Exc. Value
SHOTGUN, SINGLESHOT			
☐ **Various Gauges**, Hammer, Steel Barrel, *Modern*	45.00	75.00	75.00

ENTERPRISE

Made by Enterprise Gun Works, Pittsburgh, Pa., c. 1875.

	V.G.	Exc.	Prior Year Exc. Value
HANDGUN, REVOLVER			
☐ **#1**, .22 Short R.F., 7 Shot, Spur Trigger, Solid Frame, Single Action, *Antique*	95.00	175.00	170.00
☐ **#2**, .32 Short R.F., 5 Shot, Spur Trigger, Solid Frame, Single Action, *Antique*	115.00	190.00	185.00
☐ **#3**, .38 Short R.F., 5 Shot, Spur Trigger, Solid Frame, Single Action, *Antique*	125.00	215.00	200.00
☐ **#4**, .41 Short R.F., 5 Shot, Spur Trigger, Solid Frame, Single Action, *Antique*	145.00	250.00	235.00

ERBI

	V.G.	Exc.	Prior Year Exc. Value
SHOTGUN, DOUBLE BARREL, SIDE-BY-SIDE			
☐ **Deluxe Ejector Grade**, 12 and 20 Gauge, Raised Matted Rib, Double Trigger, Checkered Stock, Beavertail Forend, Automatic Ejector, *Modern*	165.00	240.00	230.00
☐ **Field Grade**, 12 and 20 Gauge, Raised Matted Rib, Double Trigger, Checkered Stock, *Modern*	150.00	195.00	185.00

ERIKA

Francois Pfannl, Krems, Austria 1913-1926.

	V.G.	Exc.	Prior Year Exc. Value
HANDGUN, SEMI-AUTOMATIC			
☐ **4.25mm**, Clip Fed, Blue, *Curio*	435.00	650.00	600.00

ERMA

Erfurter Maschinen u. Werkzeugfabrik, Erfurt, Germany prior to WW-II, and after the war became Erma-Werke, Munich-Dachau, West Germany. Imported by Excam, Miami, Fla.

	V.G.	Exc.	Prior Year Exc. Value
AUTOMATIC WEAPON, SUBMACHINE GUN			
☐ **EMP**, 9mm Luger, Clip Fed, *Class 3*	725.00	995.00	975.00
HANDGUN, SEMI-AUTOMATIC			
☐ **EP-22**, .22 L.R.R.F., Clip Fed, *Modern*	95.00	150.00	150.00
☐ **EP-25**, .25 ACP, Clip Fed, *Modern*	90.00	145.00	140.00
☐ **ET-22 Navy**, .22 L.R.R.F., Clip Fed, *Modern*	155.00	235.00	225.00
☐ **ET-22 Navy**, .22 L.R.R.F., Clip Fed, With Conversion Kit, Cased With Accessories, *Modern*	200.00	335.00	325.00
☐ **FB-1**, .25 ACP, Clip, *Modern*	45.00	75.00	75.00
☐ **KGP-68 (Baby)**, .32 ACP, Clip Fed, *Modern*	120.00	165.00	165.00
☐ **KGP-68 (Baby)**, .380 ACP, Clip Fed, *Modern*	125.00	175.00	175.00
☐ **KGP-69**, .22 L.R.R.F., Clip Fed, *Modern*	110.00	150.00	145.00
☐ **LA-22 PO 8**, .22 L.R.R.F., Clip Fed, *Modern*	100.00	160.00	155.00
☐ **RX-22**, .22 L.R.R.F., Double Action, Clip Fed, *Modern*	95.00	145.00	145.00
☐ **Old Model Target**, .22 L.R.R.F., Clip Fed, *Modern*	150.00	225.00	220.00
☐ **New Model Target**, .22 L.R.R.F., Clip Fed, *Modern*	170.00	250.00	240.00

	V.G.	Exc.	Prior Year Exc. Value
HANDGUN, REVOLVER			
☐ **Model 442**, .22 L.R.R.F., Double Action, Swing-Out Cylinder, Blue, *Modern*	95.00	145.00	140.00
☐ **Model 443**, .22 W.M.R., Double Action, Swing-Out Cylinder, Blue, *Modern*	100.00	145.00	145.00
☐ **Model 440**, .38 Spec., Double Action, Swing-Out Cylinder, Stainless, *Modern*	145.00	195.00	190.00
RIFLE, BOLT ACTION			
☐ **M98 Conversion Unit**, .22 L.R.R.F., Clip Fed, Cased, *Modern*	195.00	285.00	260.00
☐ **EG-61**, .22 L.R.R.F., Singleshot, Open Sights, *Modern*	45.00	75.00	75.00
☐ **M1957 KK**, .22 L.R.R.F., Military Style Training Rifle, *Modern*	55.00	90.00	85.00
☐ **Master Target**, .22 L.R.R.F., Checkered Stock, Peep Sights, *Modern*	95.00	150.00	145.00
RIFLE, LEVER ACTION			
☐ **EG-71**, .22 L.R.R.F., Tube Feed, *Modern*	95.00	145.00	140.00
☐ **EG-712**, .22 L.R.R.F., Tube Feed, *Modern*	100.00	155.00	150.00
☐ **EG-712 L**, .22 L.R.R.F., Tube Feed, Octagon Barrel, Nickel Silver Receiver, *Modern*	175.00	240.00	255.00
☐ **EG-73**, .22 W.M.R., Tube Feed, *Modern*	125.00	160.00	170.00
RIFLE, SEMI-AUTOMATIC			
☐ **EM-1**, .22 L.R.R.F., Clip Fed, *Modern*	90.00	140.00	140.00
☐ **EGM-1**, .22 L.R.R.F., Clip Fed, *Modern*	90.00	140.00	140.00
☐ **ESG22**, .22 L.R.R.F., Clip Fed, *Modern*	95.00	150.00	150.00
☐ **ESG22**, .22 W.M.R., Clip Fed, *Modern*	170.00	240.00	245.00

ESSEX

Made by Crescent for Belknap Hardware Co. Louisville, Ky.

	V.G.	Exc.	Prior Year Exc. Value
SHOTGUN, DOUBLE BARREL, SIDE-BY-SIDE			
☐ **Various Gauges**, Outside Hammers, Damascus Barrel, *Modern*	80.00	155.00	150.00
☐ **Various Gauges**, Hammerless, Steel Barrel, *Modern*	115.00	185.00	175.00
☐ **Various Gauges**, Hammerless, Damascus Barrel, *Modern*	80.00	155.00	150.00
☐ **Various Gauges**, Outside Hammers, Steel Barrel, *Modern*	110.00	180.00	175.00
SHOTGUN, SINGLESHOT			
☐ **Various Gauges**, Hammer, Steel Barrel, *Modern*	45.00	75.00	75.00

ESSEX

Made by Stevens Arms.

	V.G.	Exc.	Prior Year Exc. Value
RIFLE, BOLT ACTION			
☐ **Model 50**, .22 L.R.R.F., Singleshot, Takedown, *Modern*	30.00	45.00	40.00
☐ **Model 53**, .22 L.R.R.F., Singleshot, Takedown, *Modern*	30.00	45.00	40.00
☐ **Model 56 Buckhorn**, .22 L.R.R.F., 5 Shot Clip, Open Rear Sight, *Modern*	35.00	55.00	50.00

	V.G.	Exc.	Prior Year Exc. Value
SHOTGUN, DOUBLE BARREL, SIDE-BY-SIDE			
☐ **Model 515**, Various Gauges, Hammerless, *Modern*	95.00	160.00	140.00

ESSEX

Makers of pistol frames in Island Pond, Vt.

	V.G.	Exc.	Prior Year Exc. Value
HANDGUN, SEMI-AUTOMATIC			
☐ **Colt M1911 Copy**, .45 ACP, Parts Gun, *Modern*	185.00	260.00	250.00

ESTEVA, PEDRO

Spain, c. 1740.

	V.G.	Exc.	Prior Year Exc. Value
HANDGUN, FLINTLOCK			
☐ **Pair**, Belt Pistol, Silver Inlay, Silver Furniture, Engraved, Half-Octagon Barrel, *Antique*	6,900.00	9,000.00	8,500.00

EVANS RIFLE MFG. CO.

Mechanic Falls, Maine 1868-1880.

	V.G.	Exc.	Prior Year Exc. Value
RIFLE, LEVER ACTION			
☐ **Old Model**, .44 C.F., Upper Buttstock Only, Tube Feed, Sporting Rifle, *Antique*	635.00	1,050.00	975.00
☐ **New Model**, .44 C.F., Tube Feed, Dust Cover, Sporting Rifle, *Antique*	475.00	800.00	775.00
☐ **New Model**, .44 C.F., Tube Feed, Dust Cover, Military Style, *Antique*	595.00	1,000.00	950.00
☐ **New Model**, .44 C.F., Tube Feed, Dust Cover, Carbine, *Antique*	540.00	850.00	800.00

EVANS, STEPHEN

Valley Forge, Pa. 1742-1797. See Kentucky Rifles and U. S. Military.

EVANS, WILLIAM

London, England 1883-1900.

	V.G.	Exc.	Prior Year Exc. Value
SHOTGUN, DOUBLE BARREL, SIDE-BY-SIDE			
☐ **Pair**, 12 Gauge, Double Trigger, Plain, Cased *Modern*	4,000.00	5,700.00	5,500.00
☐ **Pair**, 12 Gauge, Double Trigger, Straight Grip, Cased, *Modern*	5,000.00	6,700.00	6,500.00

EXCAM

Importers, Hialeah, Fla. Also see Erma and Tanarmi.

	V.G.	Exc.	Prior Year Exc. Value
HANDGUN, DOUBLE BARREL, OVER-UNDER			
☐ **TA-38**, .38 Special, 2 Shot, Derringer, *Modern*	35.00	55.00	55.00
HANDGUN, REVOLVER			
☐ **Buffalo Scout TA-76**, .22LR/.22 WMR Combo, Western Style, Single Action, *Modern*	35.00	55.00	55.00
☐ **Buffalo Scout TA-76**, .22 L.R.R.F., Western Style, Single Action, *Modern*	25.00	45.00	45.00
☐ **Buffalo Scout TA-22**, .22LR/.22 WMR Combo, Western Style, Single Action, Brass Backstrap, *Modern*	40.00	65.00	65.00

	V.G.	Exc.	Prior Year Exc. Value
☐ **Buffalo Scout TA-22**, .22LR/.22 WMR Combo, Western Style, Single Action, Brass Backstrap, Target Sights, *Modern*	45.00	75.00	75.00
☐ **Buffalo Scout TA-22**, .22 L.R.R.F., Western Style, Single Action, Brass Backstrap, *Modern*	30.00	50.00	50.00
☐ **Warrior**, .22 L.R.R.F., Double Action, Blue, Vent Rib, *Modern*	55.00	75.00	70.00
☐ **Warrior**, .22 LR/.22 WMR Combo, Double Action, Blue, Vent Rib, *Modern*	65.00	110.00	100.00
☐ **Warrior**, .38 Spec., Double Action, Blue, Vent Rib, Target Sights, *Modern*	65.00	100.00	100.00
☐ **Warrior**, .357 Mag., Double Action, Blue, Vent Rib, Target Sights, *Modern*	85.00	140.00	135.00

HANDGUN, SEMI-AUTOMATIC

	V.G.	Exc.	Prior Year Exc. Value
☐ **GT-22**, .22 L.R.R.F., Clip Fed, *Modern*	60.00	100.00	95.00
☐ **GT-26**, .25 ACP, Clip Fed, Steel Frame, *Modern*	40.00	55.00	—
☐ **GT-27**, .25 ACP, Clip Fed, *Modern*	30.00	45.00	45.00
☐ **GT-27**, .25 ACP, Clip Fed, Steel Frame, *Modern*	65.00	110.00	100.00
☐ **GT-32**, .32 ACP, Clip Fed, *Modern*	65.00	110.00	95.00
☐ **GT-380**, .380 ACP, Clip Fed, *Modern*	75.00	120.00	110.00
☐ **GT-380**, .25 ACP, Clip Fed, Engraved, *Modern*	95.00	145.00	140.00
☐ **GT-32**, .32 ACP, Clip Fed, 12 Shot, *Modern*	90.00	140.00	135.00
☐ **GT-380**, .380 ACP, Clip Fed, 11 Shot, *Modern*	110.00	155.00	150.00
☐ **RX-22**, .22 L.R.R.F., Clip Fed, *Modern*	75.00	110.00	110.00

EXCELSIOR

Made by Norwich Pistol Co., c. 1880.

HANDGUN, REVOLVER

	V.G.	Exc.	Prior Year Exc. Value
☐ **.32 Short R.F.**, 5 Shot, Spur Trigger, Solid Frame, Single Action, *Antique*	90.00	165.00	160.00

EXCELSIOR

Made in Italy.

SHOTGUN, DOUBLE BARREL, SIDE-BY-SIDE

	V.G.	Exc.	Prior Year Exc. Value
☐ **Super 88**, 12 Ga. Mag. 3", Boxlock, Checkered Stock, *Modern*	240.00	335.00	320.00

EXPRESS

Made by Bacon Arms Co., c. 1880.

HANDGUN, REVOLVER

	V.G.	Exc.	Prior Year Exc. Value
☐ **.22 Short R.F.**, 7 Shot, Spur Trigger, Solid Frame, Single Action, *Antique*	95.00	165.00	160.00

EXPRESS

Tomas de Urizar y Cia., Eibar, Spain, c. 1905-1921.

HANDGUN, SEMI-AUTOMATIC

	V.G.	Exc.	Prior Year Exc. Value
☐ **Type 1**, .25 ACP, Clip Fed, Fixed Ribbed Barrel, *Curio*	175.00	245.00	235.00
☐ **Type 1**, .32 ACP, Clip Fed, 4" Fixed Barrel, *Curio*	165.00	235.00	225.00
☐ **Type 2**, .25 ACP, Clip Fed, Hammerless, Eibar Style, *Curio*	95.00	135.00	125.00

	V.G.	Exc.	Prior Year Exc. Value
☐ **Type 2**, .32 ACP, Clip Fed, Hammerless, Eibar Style, *Curio*	95.00	140.00	135.00
☐ **Type 3**, .25 ACP, Clip Fed, Hammer, Eibar Style, *Curio*	100.00	145.00	140.00
☐ **Type 3**, .32 ACP, Clip Fed, Hammer, Eibar Style, *Curio*	100.00	150.00	145.00

FABRIQUE D'ARMES DE GUERRE

Spain, unknown maker, c. 1900.

HANDGUN, SEMI-AUTOMATIC

	V.G.	Exc.	Prior Year Exc. Value
☐ **Paramount**, .25 ACP, Clip Fed, *Curio*	85.00	135.00	130.00

FABRIQUE D'ARMES DE GUERRE DE GRAND PRECISION

Tradename used by Etxezagarra & Abitua, Eibar, Spain, c. 1920.

HANDGUN, SEMI-AUTOMATIC

	V.G.	Exc.	Prior Year Exc. Value
☐ **Bulwark**, .25 ACP, Clip Fed, *Modern*	90.00	145.00	135.00
☐ **Colonial**, .25 ACP, Clip Fed, *Modern*	95.00	155.00	145.00
☐ **Colonial**, .32 ACP, Clip Fed, *Modern*	125.00	190.00	180.00
☐ **Helvece**, .25 ACP, Clip Fed, *Modern*	85.00	135.00	125.00
☐ **Jupiter**, .32 ACP, Clip Fed, *Modern*	95.00	150.00	145.00
☐ **Libia**, .32 ACP, Clip Fed, *Modern*	120.00	175.00	160.00
☐ **Looking Glass**, .32 ACP, Clip Fed, *Modern*	95.00	155.00	145.00
☐ **Looking Glass**, .32 ACP, Clip Fed, Grip Safety, *Modern*	125.00	185.00	175.00
☐ **Trust**, .25 ACP, Clip Fed, *Modern*	85.00	145.00	140.00

FALCON

HANDGUN, SEMI-AUTOMATIC

	V.G.	Exc.	Prior Year Exc. Value
☐ **.25 ACP**, Clip Fed, Blue, *Modern*	50.00	80.00	80.00

FAMARS

Brescia, Italy.

SHOTGUN, DOUBLE BARREL, SIDE-BY-SIDE

	V.G.	Exc.	Prior Year Exc. Value
☐ **Hammer Gun**, Various Gauges, Automatic Ejector, Fancy Wood, Fancy Engraving, Double Trigger, *Modern*	4,450.00	6,750.00	6,500.00
☐ **Sidelock Gun**, Various Gauges, Automatic Ejector, Double Trigger, Fancy Engraving, Fancy Wood, *Modern*	6,950.00	9,975.00	9,750.00

FARNOT, FRANK

Lancaster, Pa. 1779-1783. See Kentucky Rifles and Pistols.

FARNOT, FREDERICK

Lancaster, Pa. 1779-1782. See Kentucky Rifles and Pistols.

FARROW ARMS CO.

Holyoke, Mass. Established by William Farrow 1878-1885. Became Farrow Arms Co. About 1885 and moved to Mason, Tenn. in 1904, then to Washington, D.C. in 1904 and remained in business until 1917.

	V.G.	Exc.	Prior Year Exc. Value
RIFLE, SINGLESHOT			
☐ **#1**, .30 Long R.F., Target Rifle, Octagon Barrel, Target Sights, Fancy Wood, *Antique*	1,300.00	3,000.00	2,950.00
☐ **#2**, .30 Long R.F., Target Rifle, Octagon Barrel, Target Sights, *Antique*	975.00	2,100.00	2,000.00

FAST

Echave, Arizmendi y Cia., Eibar, Spain.

	V.G.	Exc.	Prior Year Exc. Value
HANDGUN, SEMI-AUTOMATIC			
☐ **Model 221**, .22 L.R.R.F., Clip Fed, Blue, *Modern*	95.00	150.00	145.00
☐ **Model 221**, .22 L.R.R.F., Clip Fed, Chrome, *Modern*	105.00	160.00	150.00
☐ **Model 631**, .25 ACP, Clip Fed, Blue, *Modern*	85.00	140.00	135.00
☐ **Model 631**, .25 ACP, Clip Fed, Chrome, *Modern*	95.00	145.00	140.00
☐ **Model 761**, .32 ACP, Clip Fed, Blue, *Modern*	95.00	160.00	150.00
☐ **Model 761**, .32 ACP, Clip Fed, Chrome, *Modern*	110.00	170.00	155.00
☐ **Model 901**, .380 ACP, Clip Fed, Blue, *Modern*	95.00	165.00	160.00
☐ **Model 901**, .380 ACP, Clip Fed, Chrome, *Modern*	120.00	185.00	180.00

FAULTLESS

Made by Crescent for John M. Smythe Hdw. Co., Chicago, Ill.

	V.G.	Exc.	Prior Year Exc. Value
SHOTGUN, DOUBLE BARREL, SIDE-BY-SIDE			
☐ **Various Gauges**, Outside Hammers, Damascus Barrel, *Modern*	80.00	155.00	150.00
☐ **Various Gauges**, Hammerless, Steel Barrel, *Modern*	115.00	185.00	175.00
☐ **Various Gauges**, Hammerless, Damascus Barrel, *Modern*	80.00	155.00	150.00
☐ **Various Gauges**, Outside Hammers, Steel Barrel, *Modern*	110.00	180.00	175.00
SHOTGUN, SINGLESHOT			
☐ **Various Gauges**, Hammer, Steel Barrel, *Modern*	45.00	75.00	75.00

FAULTLESS GOOSE GUN

Made by Crescent for John M. Smythe Hdw. Co., Chicago, Ill.

	V.G.	Exc.	Prior Year Exc. Value
SHOTGUN, DOUBLE BARREL, SIDE-BY-SIDE			
☐ **Various Gauges**, Outside Hammers, Damascus Barrel, *Modern*	80.00	155.00	150.00
☐ **Various Gauges**, Hammerless, Steel Barrel, *Modern*	115.00	185.00	175.00
☐ **Various Gauges**, Hammerless, Damascus Barrel, *Modern*	80.00	155.00	150.00
☐ **Various Gauges**, Outside Hammers, Steel Barrel, *Modern*	110.00	180.00	175.00
SHOTGUN, SINGLESHOT			
☐ **Various Gauges**, Hammer, Steel Barrel, *Modern*	45.00	75.00	75.00

FAVORITE

Made by Johnson-Bye Co., c. 1874-1884.

	V.G.	Exc.	Prior Year Exc. Value
HANDGUN, REVOLVER			
☐ **#1**, .22 Short R.F., 7 Shot, Spur Trigger, Solid Frame, Single Action, *Antique*	95.00	165.00	160.00

	V.G.	Exc.	Prior Year Exc. Value
☐ **#2**, .32 Short R.F., 5 Shot, Spur Trigger, Solid Frame, Single Action, *Antique*	**95.00**	**170.00**	**170.00**
☐ **#3**, .38 Short R.F., 5 Shot, Spur Trigger, Solid Frame, Single Action, *Antique*	**100.00**	**190.00**	**190.00**
☐ **#4**, .41 Short R.F., 5 Shot, Spur Trigger, Solid Frame, Single Action, *Antique*	**130.00**	**210.00**	**200.00**

FAVORITE NAVY

Made by Johnson-Bye Co., c. 1874-1884.

HANDGUN, REVOLVER

☐ **.44 Short R.F.**, 5 Shot, Spur Trigger, Solid Frame, Single Action, *Antique*	**180.00**	**290.00**	**275.00**

FAY, HENRY C.

Lancaster, Mass., c. 1837.

RIFLE, PERCUSSION

☐ **.58**, Military, *Antique*	**1,500.00**	**2,875.00**	**2,750.00**

FECHT, G. VAN DER

Berlin, Germany, c. 1733.

RIFLE, FLINTLOCK

☐ **Yaeger**, Half-Octagon Barrel, Brass Furniture, Engraved, Carved, *Antique*	**3,550.00**	**4,875.00**	**4,750.00**

FEDERAL ARMS

Made by Meriden Firearms, sold by Sears-Roebuck.

HANDGUN, REVOLVER

☐ **.32 S & W**, 5 Shot, Double Action, Top Break, *Modern*	**45.00**	**95.00**	**95.00**
☐ **.38 S & W**, 5 Shot, Double Action, Top Break, *Modern*	**50.00**	**100.00**	**95.00**

FEMARU

Made by Femaru Fegyver es Gepgyar (Fegyvergyar) Pre-War; Post War Made by Femaru es Szerszamgepgyar, N.V., Budapest, Hungary. Also see Frommer, Hungarian Military.

HANDGUN, SEMI-AUTOMATIC

☐ **M 29**, .380 ACP, Clip Fed, Military, *Curio*	**150.00**	**220.00**	**195.00**
☐ **M 37**, .380 ACP, Clip Fed, Military, *Modern*	**160.00**	**235.00**	**220.00**
☐ **M 37**, .32 ACP, Clip Fed, Nazi-Proofed, *Modern*	**160.00**	**230.00**	**220.00**
☐ **M 37**, .380 ACP, Clip Fed, Nazi-Proofed, *Modern*	**175.00**	**270.00**	**250.00**

	V.G.	Exc.	Prior Year Exc. Value

FENNO
Lancaster, Pa. 1790-1800. See Kentucky Rifles and Pistols.

FERLACH
Genossenschaft der Buchsenmachermeister, Ferlach, Austria.

RIFLE, DOUBLE BARREL, SIDE-BY-SIDE

	V.G.	Exc.	Prior Year Exc. Value
☐ **Standard Grade**, Various Calibers, Boxlock, Engraved, Checkered Stock, Fancy Wood, *Modern*	**2,100.00**	**3,000.00**	**2,900.00**
☐ **Standard Grade**, Various Calibers, Sidelock, Engraved, Checkered Stock, Fancy Wood, *Modern*	**3,700.00**	**4,500.00**	**4,350.00**

FERREE, JACOB
Lancaster, Pa. 1774-1784, see Kentucky Rifles and U.S. Military.

FESIG, CONRAD
Reading, Pa. 1779-1790, see Kentucky Rifles and Pistols.

FIALA
Made for Fiala Arms & Equipment Co. by Blakslee Forging Co., New Haven, Conn.

HANDGUN, MANUAL REPEATER

	V.G.	Exc.	Prior Year Exc. Value
☐ **.22 L.R.R.F.**, Clip Fed, Target Pistol, *Curio*	**250.00**	**395.00**	**370.00**
☐ **.22 L.R.R.F.**, Clip Fed, Target Pistol, With Shoulder Stock, 20" Barrel, 3" Barrel, Cased, *Curio*	**425.00**	**665.00**	**625.00**

F.I.E.
Firearms Import & Export Corp., Miami, Fla.

HANDGUN, DOUBLE BARREL, OVER-UNDER

	V.G.	Exc.	Prior Year Exc. Value
☐ **.38 S & W**, Derringer, *Modern*	**30.00**	**50.00**	**50.00**
☐ **.38 Special**, Derringer, *Modern*	**35.00**	**55.00**	**55.00**

HANDGUN, FLINTLOCK

	V.G.	Exc.	Prior Year Exc. Value
☐ **Kentucky**, .44, Belt Pistol, Reproduction, *Antique*	**35.00**	**50.00**	**50.00**
☐ **Kentucky**, .44, Belt Pistol, Engraved, Reproduction, *Antique*	**40.00**	**55.00**	**55.00**
☐ **Tower**, .69, *Antique*	**15.00**	**30.00**	**28.00**

HANDGUN, PERCUSSION

	V.G.	Exc.	Prior Year Exc. Value
☐ **Baby Dragoon**, .31, Revolver, Reproduction, *Antique*	**25.00**	**40.00**	**40.00**
☐ **Baby Dragoon**, .31, Revolver, Engraved, Reproduction, *Antique*	**30.00**	**45.00**	**45.00**
☐ **Kentucky**, .44, Belt Pistol, Reproduction, *Antique*	**30.00**	**45.00**	**45.00**
☐ **Kentucky**, .44, Belt Pistol, Engraved, Reproduction, *Antique*	**35.00**	**50.00**	**50.00**
☐ **Navy**, .36, Revolver, Reproduction, *Antique*	**25.00**	**35.00**	**35.00**
☐ **Navy**, .36, Revolver, Engraved, Reproduction, *Antique*	**30.00**	**40.00**	**40.00**
☐ **Navy**, .44, Revolver, Reproduction, *Antique*	**25.00**	**40.00**	**40.00**
☐ **Navy**, .44, Revolver, Engraved, Reproduction, *Antique*	**30.00**	**45.00**	**45.00**

	V.G.	Exc.	Prior Year Exc. Value
☐ **Remington**, .36, Revolver, Reproduction, *Antique*	30.00	45.00	45.00
☐ **Remington**, .36, Revolver, Engraved, Reproduction, *Antique*	35.00	55.00	55.00
☐ **Remington**, .44, Revolver, Reproduction, *Antique*	30.00	45.00	45.00
☐ **Remington**, .44, Revolver, Engraved, Reproduction, *Antique*	35.00	55.00	55.00
HANDGUN, REVOLVER			
☐ **Arminius**, .22 L.R.R.F., Double Action, Swing-out Cylinder, Fixed Sights, Chrome, *Modern*	45.00	70.00	65.00
☐ **Arminius**, .22 LR/.22 WMR Combo, Double Action, Swing-out Cylinder, Fixed Sights, Chrome, *Modern*	55.00	90.00	85.00
☐ **Arminius**, .22 LR/.22 WMR Combo, Double Action, Swing-out Cylinder, Adjustable Sights, Chrome, *Modern*	60.00	95.00	90.00
☐ **Arminius**, .22 LR/.22 WMR Combo, Double Action, Swing-out Cylinder, Adjustable Sights, Blue, *Modern*	60.00	90.00	85.00
☐ **Arminius**, .22 LR/.22 WMR Combo, Double Action, Swing-out Cylinder, Adjustable Sights, Blue, Target, *Modern*	50.00	75.00	70.00
☐ **Arminius**, .22 L.R.R.F., Double Action, Swing-out Cylinder, Adjustable Sights, Blue, *Modern*	50.00	70.00	65.00
☐ **Arminius**, .22 L.R.R.F., Double Action, Swing-out Cylinder, Adjustable Sights, Chrome, *Modern*	50.00	80.00	75.00
☐ **Arminius**, .22 L.R.R.F., Double Action, Swing-out Cylinder, Adjustable Sights, Blue, Target, *Modern*	50.00	80.00	75.00
☐ **Arminius**, .22 L.R.R.F., Double Action, Swing-out Cylinder, Adjustable Sights, Chrome, Target, *Modern*	50.00	80.00	75.00
☐ **Arminius**, .32 S & W, Double Action, Swing-out Cylinder, Adjustable Sights, Blue, Target, *Modern*	50.00	80.00	75.00
☐ **Arminius**, .32 S & W, Double Action, Swing-out Cylinder, Adjustable Sights, Chrome, Target, *Modern*	50.00	80.00	75.00
☐ **Arminius**, .357 Magnum, Double Action, Swing-out Cylinder, Adjustable Sights, Chrome, Target, *Modern*	80.00	115.00	110.00
☐ **Arminius**, .357 Magnum, Double Action, Swing-out Cylinder, Adjustable Sights, Blue, Target, *Modern*	80.00	115.00	110.00
☐ **Arminius**, .38 Special, Double Action, Swing-out Cylinder, Adjustable Sights, Blue, Target, *Modern*	60.00	80.00	75.00
☐ **Arminius**, .38 Special, Double Action, Swing-out Cylinder, Adjustable Sights, Chrome, Target, *Modern*	55.00	80.00	75.00
☐ **Arminius**, .38 Special, Double Action, Swing-out Cylinder, Blue, *Modern*	45.00	65.00	60.00
☐ **Arminius**, .38 Special, Double Action, Swing-out Cylinder, Chrome, *Modern*	45.00	65.00	60.00
☐ **Buffalo Scout**, .22LR/.22 WMR Combo, Single Action, Western Style, *Modern*	35.00	55.00	55.00

	V.G.	Exc.	Prior Year Exc. Value
☐ **Buffalo**, .22 L.R.R.F., Single Action, Western Style, *Modern*	30.00	45.00	45.00
☐ **Guardian**, .22 L.R.R.F., Double Action, Swing-out Cylinger, *Modern*	25.00	40.00	40.00
☐ **Guardian**, .22 L.R.R.F., Double Action, Swing-out Cylinder, Chrome, *Modern*	30.00	45.00	45.00
☐ **Guardian**, .32 S & W, Double Action, Swing-out Cylinder, *Modern*	25.00	40.00	40.00
☐ **Guardian**, .32 S & W, Double Action, Swing-out Cylinder, Chrome, *Modern*	30.00	45.00	45.00
☐ **Hombre**, .357 Mag, Single Action, Western Style, Steel Frame, *Modern*	75.00	115.00	110.00
☐ **Hombre**, .44 Mag, Single Action, Western Style, Steel Frame, *Modern*	85.00	135.00	130.00
☐ **Hombre**, .45 L.C., Single Action, Western Style, Steel Frame, *Modern*	75.00	115.00	110.00
☐ **Legend**, .22LR/.22 WMR Combo, Single Action, Western Style, Steel Frame, *Modern*	50.00	70.00	65.00
☐ **Legend**, .22 L.R.R.F., Single Action, Western Style, Steel Frame, *Modern*	30.00	50.00	45.00
☐ **Texas Ranger**, .22LR/.22 WMR Combo, Single Action, Western Style, Steel Frame, *Modern*	30.00	45.00	—
☐ **Titan Tiger**, .38 Spec., Double Action, Blue, *Modern*	50.00	75.00	75.00

HANDGUN, SEMI-AUTOMATIC

	V.G.	Exc.	Prior Year Exc. Value
☐ **Best**, .25 ACP, Hammer, Steel Frame, Blue, *Modern*	65.00	100.00	95.00
☐ **Best**, .32 ACP, Hammer, Steel Frame, Blue, *Modern*	70.00	110.00	105.00
☐ **Guardian**, .25 ACP, Hammer, Blue, *Modern*	25.00	35.00	35.00
☐ **Guardian**, .25 ACP, Hammer, Chrome, *Modern*	25.00	35.00	35.00
☐ **Guardian**, .25 ACP, Hammer, Gold Plated, *Modern*	25.00	40.00	40.00
☐ **Interdynamics KG-9**, 9mm Luger, Clip Fed, *Modern*	225.00	325.00	325.00
☐ **Interdynamics Mini-99**, 9mm Luger, Clip Fed, *Modern*	135.00	200.00	—
☐ **Titan**, .25 ACP, Hammer, Blue, *Modern*	25.00	35.00	35.00
☐ **Titan**, .25 ACP, Hammer, Chrome, *Modern*	25.00	40.00	40.00
☐ **Super Titan II**, .32 ACP, Hammer, Steel Frame, Blue, 13 Shot, *Modern*	85.00	130.00	125.00
☐ **Titan**, .32 ACP, Hammer, Steel Frame, Blue, *Modern*	50.00	80.00	75.00
☐ **Titan**, .32 ACP, Hammer, Steel Frame, Chrome, *Modern*	55.00	85.00	80.00
☐ **Titan**, .32 ACP, Hammer, Steel Frame, Engraved, Chrome, *Modern*	65.00	95.00	90.00
☐ **Titan**, .32 ACP, Hammer, Steel Frame, Engraved, Blue, *Modern*	60.00	90.00	85.00
☐ **Super Titan II**, .380 ACP, Hammer, Steel Frame, Blue, 12 Shot, *Modern*	95.00	140.00	135.00
☐ **Titan**, .380 ACP, Hammer, Steel Frame, Blue, *Modern*	65.00	100.00	95.00
☐ **Titan**, .380 ACP, Hammer, Steel Frame, Chrome, *Modern*	75.00	115.00	110.00

	V.G.	Exc.	Prior Year Exc. Value
☐ **Titan**, .380 ACP, Hammer, Steel Frame, Engraved, Blue, *Modern*	**90.00**	**135.00**	**130.00**
☐ **Titan**, .380 ACP, Hammer, Steel Frame, Engraved, Chrome, *Modern*	**95.00**	**140.00**	**135.00**
☐ **TZ-75**, 9mm Luger, Clip Fed, Double Action, Hammer, Adjustable Sights, Wood Grips, *Modern*	**175.00**	**235.00**	—
RIFLE, FLINTLOCK			
☐ **Kentucky**, .45, Reproduction, *Antique*	**55.00**	**85.00**	**85.00**
☐ **Kentucky**, .45, Engraved, Reproduction, *Antique*	**60.00**	**85.00**	**85.00**
RIFLE, PERCUSSION			
☐ **Berdan**, .45, Reproduction, *Antique*	**50.00**	**80.00**	**80.00**
☐ **Kentucky**, .45, Reproduction, *Antique*	**50.00**	**80.00**	**80.00**
☐ **Kentucky**, .45, Engraved, Reproduction, *Antique*	**55.00**	**80.00**	**80.00**
☐ **Zoave**, .58, Reproduction, *Antique*	**60.00**	**95.00**	**95.00**
COMBINATION WEAPON, OVER-UNDER			
☐ **Combo**, 30/30-20 Ga., *Modern*	**45.00**	**75.00**	**75.00**
SHOTGUN, DOUBLE BARREL, OVER-UNDER			
☐ **OU**, 12 and 20 Ga., Field Grade, Vent Rib, *Modern*	**110.00**	**165.00**	**160.00**
☐ **OU 12 T**, 12 Ga., Trap Grade, Vent Rib, *Modern*	**135.00**	**175.00**	**170.00**
☐ **OU-S**, 12 and 20 Ga., Skeet Grade, Vent Rib, *Modern*	**135.00**	**175.00**	**170.00**
SHOTGUN, DOUBLE BARREL, SIDE-BY-SIDE			
☐ **DB**, Various Gauges, Hammerless, *Modern*	**70.00**	**125.00**	**110.00**
☐ **DB Riot**, Various Gauges, Hammerless, *Modern*	**70.00**	**125.00**	**110.00**
☐ **Brute**, Various Gauges, Short Barrels, Short Stock, *Modern*	**95.00**	**155.00**	**150.00**
SHOTGUN, SINGLESHOT			
☐ **SB 40**, 12 Ga., Hammer, Button Break, *Modern*	**25.00**	**45.00**	**45.00**
☐ **SB 41**, 20 Ga., Hammer, Button Break, *Modern*	**25.00**	**45.00**	**45.00**
☐ **SB 42**, .410 Ga., Hammer, Button Break, *Modern*	**25.00**	**45.00**	**45.00**
☐ **SB Youth**, Various Gauges, Hammer, *Modern*	**25.00**	**35.00**	**35.00**
☐ **SB 12 16 20 .410**, Various Gauges, Hammer, *Modern*	**25.00**	**40.00**	
☐ **S.O.B.**, 12 and 20 Gauges, Short Barrel, Short Stock, *Modern*	**35.00**	**55.00**	

FIEHL & WEEKS FIRE ARMS MFG. CO.

Philadelphia, Pa., c. 1895.

	V.G.	Exc.	Prior Year Exc. Value
HANDGUN, REVOLVER			
☐ **.32 S & W**, 5 Shot, Top Break, Hammerless, Double Action, *Modern*	**55.00**	**100.00**	**95.00**

FIEL

Erquiaga, Muguruzu y Cia., Eibar, Spain, c. 1920.

	V.G.	Exc.	Prior Year Exc. Value
HANDGUN, SEMI-AUTOMATIC			
☐ **Fiel #1**, .25 ACP, Clip Fed, Eibar Style, *Curio*	**95.00**	**135.00**	**125.00**
☐ **Fiel #1**, .32 ACP, Clip Fed, Eibar Style, *Curio*	**100.00**	**145.00**	**140.00**
☐ **Fiel #2**, .25 ACP, Clip Fed, Breech Bolt, *Curio*	**135.00**	**210.00**	**195.00**

FIGTHORN, ANDREW

Reading, Pa. 1779-1790, see Kentucky Rifles.

	V.G.	Exc.	Prior Year Exc. Value

FINNISH LION

Made by Valmet, Jyvaskyla, Finland

RIFLE, BOLT ACTION

	V.G.	Exc.	Prior Year Exc. Value
☐ **Standard**, .22 L.R.R.F., Singleshot, Target Rifle, Target Stock, Target Sights, U.I.T. Rifle, *Modern*	325.00	450.00	440.00
☐ **Match**, .22 L.R.R.F., Singleshot, Target Rifle, Thumbhole Stock, Target Sights, *Modern*	375.00	540.00	525.00
☐ **Champion**, 22 L.R.R.F., Singleshot, Free Rifle, Thumbhole Stock, Target Sights, Heavy Barrel, *Modern*	395.00	625.00	595.00

FIREARMS, CUSTOM MADE

This category covers some of the myriad special firearms that are built to an individual's specifications by a competent gunsmith, and not by the original factory. Most firearms in this class will appeal only to a person who happens to want the same special features, and because of this many of these guns will sell for less than the cost of the conversion.

HANDGUN, REVOLVER

	V.G.	Exc.	Prior Year Exc. Value
☐ **P.P.C. Conversion**, .38 Special, Heavy Barrel, Rib with Target Sights, Target Trigger, Target Grips, *Modern*	185.00	300.00	300.00
☐ **"F.B.I." Conversion**, .38 Special, Cut Trigger Guard, Spurless Hammer, Short Barrel, *Modern*	150.00	240.00	235.00
☐ **Recoil Compensation Devices or Ports**, *Add* **$25.00-$45.00**			

HANDGUN, SEMI-AUTOMATIC

	V.G.	Exc.	Prior Year Exc. Value
☐ **M1911A1**, Double Action Conversion, *Add* **$95.00-$175.00**			
☐ **M1911A1**, I.P.S.C. Conversion, Extended Trigger Guard, Ambidextrous Safety, Special Slide Release, Ported, Target Sights, Extended Grip Safety, *Modern*	325.00	460.00	—
☐ **M1911A1**, Combat Conversion, Extended Trigger Guard, Ambidextrous Safety, Special Slide Release, Ported, Combat Sights, *Modern*	290.00	425.00	400.00

HANDGUN, SINGLESHOT

	V.G.	Exc.	Prior Year Exc. Value
☐ **Silhouette Pistol**, Various Calibers, Bolt Action, Thumbhole Stock, Target Sights, Target Trigger, *Modern*	250.00	400.00	400.00

HANDGUN, PERCUSSION

	V.G.	Exc.	Prior Year Exc. Value
☐ **Target Revolver**, Various Calibers, Tuned, Target Sights, Reproduction, *Antique*	95.00	150.00	145.00

RIFLE, BOLT ACTION

	V.G.	Exc.	Prior Year Exc. Value
☐ **Sporting Rifle**, Various Calibers, Checkered Stock, Recoil Pad, Simple Military Conversion, *Modern*	85.00	145.00	140.00
☐ **Sporting Rifle**, Various Calibers, Fancy Wood, Recoil Pad, Fancy Military Conversion, *Modern*	250.00	400.00	400.00
☐ **Sporting Rifle**, Various Calibers, Plain Stock, Commercial Parts, *Modern*	90.00	165.00	165.00

	V.G.	Exc.	Prior Year Exc. Value
☐ **Sporting Rifle**, Various Calibers, Fancy Stock, High Quality Commercial Parts, Fancy Checkering, Stock Inlays, *Modern*	475.00	975.00	950.00
☐ **Sporting Rifle**, Various Calibers, Fancy Stock, High Quality Commercial Parts, Fancy Checkering, Stock Inlays, Engraved, *Modern*	750.00	1,500.00	1,500.00
☐ **Sporting Rifle**, Various Calibers, Fancy Stock, High Quality Commercial Parts, Fancy Checkering, Stock Inlays, Engraved, Gold Inlays, *Modern*	950.00	2,500.00	2,500.00
☐ **Sporting Rifle**, Various Calibers, Mauser 1871 Action, Checkered Stock, *Antique*	160.00	265.00	250.00
RIFLE, SINGLESHOT			
☐ **Target Rifle**, Centerfire Calibers, Plain, Target Sights, Built on Various Bolt Actions, *Modern*	260.00	390.00	375.00
☐ **Target Rifle**, Centerfire Calibers, Plain, Target Sights, Built on Various Moving Block Actions, *Modern*	185.00	290.00	275.00
☐ **Target Rifle**, Centerfire Calibers, Fancy, Target Sights, Built on Various Moving Block Actions, *Modern*	295.00	425.00	400.00
☐ **Target Rifle**, Rimfire Calibers, Plain, Target Sights, Built on Various Moving Block Actions, *Modern*	170.00	265.00	250.00
SHOTGUN, SLIDE ACTION			
☐ **Combat Conversion**, 12 Ga., Short Barrel, Extended Magazine Tube, Folding Stock, Rifle Sights, *Modern*	145.00	275.00	250.00
☐ **Competition Conversion**, Various Gauges, High Rib, Recoil Reducer in Stock, Fancy Wood, *Modern*	235.00	375.00	350.00
SHOTGUN, DOUBLE BARREL, OVER-UNDER			
☐ **Trap Conversion**, 12 Ga., Recoil Reducer in Stock, Release Triggers, Throated Chambers, Trap Pad, *Add* **$275.00-$400.00**			

FIREARMS CO. LTD.

Made in England for Mandall Shooting Supplies.

	V.G.	Exc.	Prior Year Exc. Value
RIFLE, BOLT ACTION			
☐ **Alpine Standard**, Various Calibers, Checkered Stock, Recoil Pad, Open Rear Sight, *Modern*	175.00	285.00	275.00
☐ **Alpine Custom**, Various Calibers, Checkered Stock, Recoil Pad, Open Rear Sight, *Modern*	220.00	320.00	300.00

FIREARMS INTERNATIONAL

Washington, D.C.

	V.G.	Exc.	Prior Year Exc. Value
HANDGUN, REVOLVER			
☐ **Regent**, .22 L.R.R.F., 8 Shot, Various Barrel Lengths, Blue, *Modern*	40.00	60.00	60.00
☐ **Regent**, .22 L.R.R.F., 7 Shot, Various Barrel Lengths, Blue, *Modern*	45.00	65.00	65.00

	V.G.	Exc.	Prior Year Exc. Value
HANDGUN, SEMI-AUTOMATIC			
☐ **Combo**, .22 L.R.R.F., Unique Model L Pistol with Conversion Kit for Stocked Rifle, *Modern*	85.00	140.00	130.00
☐ **Model D**, .380 ACP, Clip Fed, Adjustable Sights, Blue, *Modern*	95.00	145.00	140.00
☐ **Model D**, .380 ACP, Clip Fed, Adjustable Sights, Chrome *Modern*	110.00	155.00	150.00
☐ **Model D**, .380 ACP, Clip Fed, Adjustable Sights, Matt Blue, *Modern*	100.00	145.00	140.00
SHOTGUN, DOUBLE BARREL, SIDE-BY-SIDE			
☐ **Model 400**, Various Gauges, Single Trigger, Checkered Stock, *Modern*	150.00	215.00	200.00
☐ **Model 400E**, Various Gauges, Single Selective Trigger, Checkered Stock, Selective Ejector, Vent Rib, *Modern*	185.00	265.00	250.00
☐ **Model 400E**, Various Gauges, Single Selective Trigger, Selective Ejector, *Modern* *165.00*	250.00	240.00	

FIREARMS SPECIALTIES

Owosso, Mich., c. 1972.

	V.G.	Exc.	Prior Year Exc. Value
HANDGUN, REVOLVER			
☐ **.45/70 Custom Revolver**, Brass Frame, Single Action, Western Style, *Modern*	365.00	575.00	550.00

FIREBIRD

Made by Femaru for German exporter for U.S. sales.

	V.G.	Exc.	Prior Year Exc. Value
HANDGUN, SEMI-AUTOMATIC			
☐ **Tokagypt Type**, 9mm Luger, Clip Fed, Blue, *Modern*	400.00	600.00	550.00

FITCH & WALDO

New York City, c.1862-67.

	V.G.	Exc.	Prior Year Exc. Value
HANDGUN, REVOLVER			
☐ **Pocket Model, .31, 5 Shot, *Antique***	130.00	250.00	235.00

FLINTLOCK, UNKNOWN MAKER

Also see Miquelet-Lock, Unknown Maker and Snaphaunce, Unknown Maker.

	V.G.	Exc.	Prior Year Exc. Value
HANDGUN, FLINTLOCK			
☐ **.28**, English, Pocket Pistol, Queen Anne Style, Box Lock, Screw Barrel, Plain, *Antique*	270.00	450.00	425.00
☐ **.40**, India Herdsman Pistol, Long Tapered Round Barrel, Silver Furniture, *Antique*	410.00	635.00	625.00
☐ **.45**, French, Mid-1700's, Screw Barrel, Long Cannon Barrel, Silver Furniture, *Antique*	800.00	1,250.00	1,200.00
☐ **.60**, Continental, Early 1700's, Holster Pistol, Half-Octagon Barrel, Engraved, High Quality, *Antique*	1,500.00	2,300.00	2,200.00
☐ **.60**, Oval Bore, Box Lock, Pocket Pistol, Steel Furniture, *Antique*	500.00	795.00	775.00
☐ **.62**, Crantham English, Holster Pistol, Brass Furniture, Plain, *Antique*	300.00	420.00	400.00
☐ **.63**, Spanish, Mid-1600's, Holster Pistol, Silver Inlay, Engraved, *Antique*	2,200.00	3,500.00	3,300.00
☐ **.68**, Tower, Continental, Plain, *Antique*	225.00	325.00	325.00
☐ **.65**, Arabian, Holster Pistol, Flared, Round Barrel, Low Quality, *Antique*	175.00	250.00	250.00
☐ **English Lock**, Mid-1600's, Military, Holster Pistol, Iron Mounts, Plain, *Antique*	2,500.00	4,500.00	4,400.00

	V.G.	Exc.	Prior Year Exc. Value
☐ **English**, Early 1700's, Pocket Pistol, Queen Anne Style, Box Lock, Screw Barrel, All Metal, *Antique*	325.00	550.00	525.00
☐ **English**, Early 1700's, Pocket Pistol, Box Lock, Double Barrel, Screw Barrel, Low Quality, *Antique*	350.00	525.00	525.00
☐ **English**, Mid-1600's, Button Triger, Brass Barrel, Octagon Fish-tail Butt, *Antique*	1,350.00	2,500.00	2,250.00
☐ **French Officer's Type**, c. 1650, Steel Furniture, Rifled, *Antique*	1,250.00	2,300.00	2,250.00
☐ **French Sedan Mid-1600's**, Long Screw Barrel, Rifled, Plain, *Antique*	1,500.00	2,500.00	2,450.00

RIFLE, FLINTLOCK

	V.G.	Exc.	Prior Year Exc. Value
☐ **.64**, Continental, Carbine, Musket, Brass Furniture, *Antique*	320.00	495.00	475.00
☐ **.72**, Continental, 1650, Musket, Brass Furniture, Plain, *Antique*	675.00	975.00	950.00

SHOTGUN, FLINTLOCK

	V.G.	Exc.	Prior Year Exc. Value
☐ **.65**, American Hudson Valley, *Antique*	700.00	1,250.00	1,250.00

F.N.

Fabrique Nationale, Herstal, Belgium from 1889. Also see Browning, Belgian Military.

AUTOMATIC WEAPON, ASSAULT RIFLE

	V.G.	Exc.	Prior Year Exc. Value
☐ **FN-CAL,** .223 Rem., Clip Fed, Commercial, *Class 3*	1150.00	1750.00	1800.00
☐ **FN-FAL,** .308 Win., Clip Fed, Commercial, *Class 3*	900.00	1300.00	1350.00
☐ **FN-FAL,** .308 Win., Clip Fed, Folding Stock, Commercial, *Class 3*	1125.00	1700.00	1750.00
☐ **FN-FAL G-1,** .308 Win., Clip Fed, Heavy Barrel, Bipod, Sniper, with Scope, *Class 3*	1875.00	3300.00	3500.00
☐ **FN-FAL L2A1,** .308 Win., Clip Fed, Heavy Barrel, Bipod, Commercial, *Class 3*	1150.00	1700.00	1800.00
☐ **FN-FAL "Para,"** .308 Win., Clip Fed, Folding Stock, Lightweight, Commercial, *Class 3*	1225.00	1625.00	1700.00

AUTOMATIC WEAPON, LIGHT MACHINE GUN

	V.G.	Exc.	Prior Year Exc. Value
☐ **FN M.A.G. 58,** .308 Win., Belt Fed, Bipod, *Class 3*	2700.00	3600.00	3700.00
☐ **FN M.A.G. 58,** .308 Win., Belt Fed, Tripod, *Class 3*	3675.00	4825.00	5000.00

RIFLE, BOLT ACTION

	V.G.	Exc.	Prior Year Exc. Value
☐ **Model 1925,** .22 L.R.R.F., Singleshot, *Modern*	35.00	50.00	60.00
☐ **Model 1925 Deluxe,** .22 L.R.R.F., Singleshot, Checkered Stock, *Modern*	50.00	75.00	85.00
☐ **Mauser 98 Military Style,** 30/06, Military Finish, Military Stock, Commercial, *Modern*	100.00	210.00	245.00
☐ **Mauser 98 Military Style,** Various Military Calibers, Military Finish, Military Stock, Commercial, *Modern*	85.00	140.00	185.00
☐ **Mauser Deluxe,** Various Calibers, Sporting Rifle, Checkered Stock, *Modern*	220.00	410.00	495.00
☐ **Mauser Deluxe Presentation,** Various Calibers, Sporting Rifle, Fancy Wood, Engraved, *Modern*	510.00	750.00	975.00

Fitch & Waldo Pocket Revolver, .31 Caliber

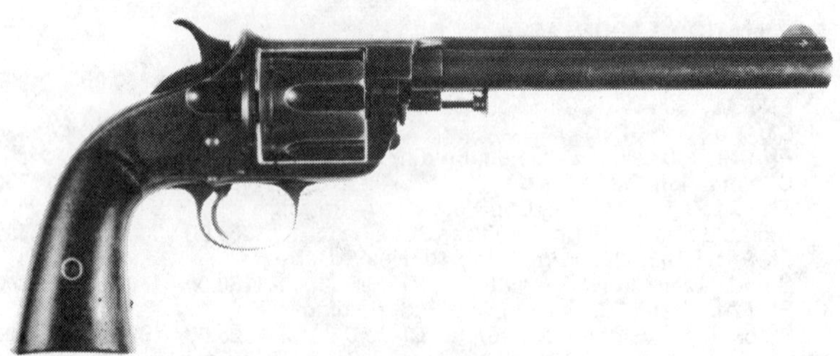

Forehand & Wadsworth Old Army Model, .44 Caliber

	V.G.	Exc.	Prior Year Exc. Value
☐ **Mauser Supreme,** Various Calibers, Sporting Rifle, Checkered Stock, *Modern*	360.00	475.00	550.00
☐ **Mauser Supreme,** Various Calibers, Sporting Rifle, Checkered Stock, Magnum, *Modern*	380.00	525.00	600.00
RIFLE, SEMI-AUTOMATIC			
☐ **FN FAL,** .308 Win., Clip Fed, Commercial, *Modern*	750.00	1100.00	1150.00
☐ **FN LAR Competition,** .308 Win., Clip Fed, Commercial, Flash Hider, *Modern*	770.00	1200.00	1250.00
☐ **FN LAR Paratrooper,** .308 Win., Clip Fed, Commercial, Folding Stock, *Modern*	850.00	1250.00	1300.00
☐ **FN LAR Heavy Barrel,** .308 Win., Clip Fed, Commercial, Synthetic Stock, Bipod, *Modern*	900.00	1425.00	1500.00
☐ **FN LAR Heavy Barrel,** .308 Win., Clip Fed, Commercial, Wood Stock, Bipod, *Modern*	935.00	1550.00	1600.00
☐ **FNC Competition,** .223 Rem., Clip Fed, Commercial, Flash Hider, *Modern*	470.00	625.00	700.00
☐ **FNC Paratrooper,** .223 Rem., Clip Fed, Commercial, Folding Stock, *Modern*	650.00	1000.00	1050.00
☐ **Model 1949,** 30/06, Clip Fed, Military, *Modern*	250.00	375.00	495.00
☐ **Model 1949,** 7mm or 8mm Mauser, Clip Fed, Military, *Modern*	160.00	270.00	375.00
☐ **M-49 Egyptian,** 8mm Mauser, Clip Fed, Military, *Modern*	170.00	285.00	395.00
☐ **SHOTGUN, BOLT ACTION**			
☐ **9mm Shotshell,** *Modern*	80.00	125.00	125.00

FOLGER, WILLIAM H.

Barnsville, Ohio 1830-1854, also See Kentucky Rifles.

FOLK'S GUN WORKS

Bryan, Ohio 1860-1891.

	V.G.	Exc.	Prior Year Exc. Value
RIFLE, SINGLESHOT			
☐ **.32 L.R.R.F.**, Side Lever, Octagon Barrel, *Antique*	240.00	365.00	355.00

FONDERSMITH, JOHN

Strasburg, Pa. 1749-1801. See Kentucky Rifles, U.S. Military.

FORBES, F.F.

Made by Crescent, c. 1900.

	V.G.	Exc.	Prior Year Exc. Value
SHOTGUN, DOUBLE BARREL, SIDE-BY-SIDE			
☐ **Various Gauges**, Outside Hammers, Damascus Barrel, *Modern*	80.00	155.00	150.00
☐ **Various Gauges**, Hammerless, Steel Barrel, *Modern*	115.00	185.00	175.00
☐ **Various Gauges**, Hammerless, Damascus Barrel, *Modern*	80.00	155.00	150.00
☐ **Various Gauges**, Outside Hammers, Steel Barrel, *Modern*	110.00	180.00	175.00
SHOTGUN, SINGLESHOT			
☐ **Various Gauges**, Hammer, Steel Barrel, *Modern*	45.00	75.00	75.00

FOREHAND ARMS CO.

HANDGUN, REVOLVER

	V.G.	Exc.	Prior Year Exc. Value
☐ **.32 S & W**, 5 Shot, Double Action, Solid Frame, 2" Barrel, *Antique*	55.00	95.00	90.00
☐ **.38 S & W**, 5 Shot, Double Action, Solid Frame, 2" Barrel, *Antique*	55.00	95.00	90.00
☐ **Perfection Automatic**, .32 S & W, 5 Shot, Double Action, Top Break, Hammerless, *Antique*	75.00	130.00	120.00
☐ **Perfection Automatic**, .32 S & W, 5 Shot, Double Action, Top Break, *Antique*	65.00	110.00	100.00

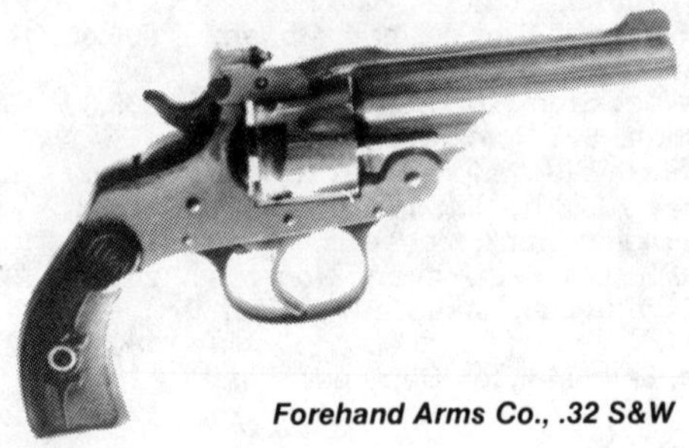

Forehand Arms Co., .32 S&W

FOREHAND & WADSWORTH

Worcester, Mass. Successors and sons-in-law To Ethan Allen 1871-1902. In 1872 the name was changed to Forehand & Wadsworth, in 1890 to Forehand Arms Co.

HANDGUN, REVOLVER

	V.G.	Exc.	Prior Year Exc. Value
☐ **.22 Short R.F.**, Single Action, Spur Trigger, Solid Frame, Side Hammer, *Antique*	100.00	190.00	185.00
☐ **.22 Short R.F.**, 7 Shot, Single Action, Solid Frame, *Antique*	90.00	150.00	145.00
☐ **.30 Short R.F.**, Single Action, Spur Trigger, Solid Frame, Side Hammer, *Antique*	95.00	175.00	170.00
☐ **.32 Short R.F.**, Single Action, Spur Trigger, Solid Frame, Side Hammer, *Antique*	100.00	190.00	185.00
☐ **.44 Short R.F.**, Single Action, Spur Trigger, Solid Frame, Side Hammer, *Antique*	140.00	225.00	215.00
☐ **Army**, .38 Long R.F., 6 Shot, Single Action, Solid Frame, *Antique*	375.00	525.00	495.00
☐ **British Bulldog**, .32 S & W, 7 Shot, Double Action, Solid Frame, *Antique*	55.00	95.00	95.00
☐ **British Bulldog**, .38 S & W, 6 Shot, Double Action, Solid Frame, *Antique*	55.00	95.00	95.00
☐ **British Bulldog**, .44 S & W, 5 Shot, Double Action, Solid Frame, *Antique*	70.00	120.00	120.00
☐ **Bulldog**, .38 Long R.F., 5 Shot, Single Action, Solid Frame, 2" Barrel, *Antique*	85.00	150.00	150.00
☐ **Bulldog**, .44 S & W, 5 Shot, Double Action, Solid Frame, 2" Barrel, *Antique*	70.00	120.00	120.00
☐ **New Navy**, .44 Russian, 6 Shot, Double Action, Solid Frame, 6" Barrel, *Antique*	340.00	525.00	495.00

	V.G.	Exc.	Prior Year Exc. Value
☐ **Old Army,** .44 Russian, 6 Shot, Single Action, Solid Frame, 7" Barrel, *Antique*	160.00	420.00	420.00
☐ **Pocket Model,** .32 S & W Long, 6 Shot, Double Action, Top Break, *Antique*	55.00	95.00	95.00
☐ **Russian Model,** .32 Short R.F., 5 Shot, Single Action, Solid Frame, Spur Trigger, *Antique*	135.00	195.00	185.00
☐ **Swamp Angel,** .41 Short R.F., 5 Shot, Single Action, Solid Frame, Spur Trigger, *Antique*	120.00	200.00	200.00
☐ **Terror,** .32 Short R.F., 5 Shot, Single Action, Solid Frame, Spur Trigger, *Antique*	90.00	165.00	160.00

HANDGUN, SINGLESHOT

	V.G.	Exc.	Prior Year Exc. Value
☐ **.22 Short R.F.,** Spur Trigger, Side-swing Barrel, *Antique*	175.00	260.00	250.00
☐ **.41 Short R.F.,** Spur Trigger, Side-swing Barrel, *Antique*	225.00	365.00	350.00

FOREVER YOURS

Flaig's Lodge, Millvale, Pa.

SHOTGUN, DOUBLE BARREL, OVER-UNDER

	V.G.	Exc.	Prior Year Exc. Value
☐ **Various Gauges**, Automatic Ejector, Checkered Stock, Vent Rib, Double Trigger, *Modern*	420.00	640.00	625.00
☐ **Various Gauges**, Automatic Ejector, Checkered Stock, Vent Rib, Single Trigger, *Modern*	470.00	690.00	675.00

FOULKES, ADAM

Easton & Allentown, Pa. 1773-1794. See Kentucky Rifles and U.S. Military.

FOUR ACE CO.

Brownsville, Texas.

HANDGUN, SINGLESHOT

☐ **Four Ace**, Derringer, Presentation Case *Add* **$10.00-$15.00**

	V.G.	Exc.	Prior Year Exc. Value
☐ **Four Ace Model 200**, .22 Short R.F., Derringer, 4 Shot, Spur Trigger, *Modern*	30.00	45.00	45.00
☐ **Four Ace Model 200**, .22 Short R.F., Derringer, 4 Shot, Spur Trigger, Nickel Plated, Gold Plated, *Modern*	40.00	55.00	55.00
☐ **Four Ace Model 202**, .22 L.R.R.F., Derringer, 4 Shot, Spur Trigger, Nickel Plated, Gold Plated, *Modern*	45.00	60.00	60.00
☐ **Four Ace Model**, 202, .22 L.R.R.F., Derringer, 4 Shot, Spur Trigger, *Modern*	35.00	50.00	50.00
☐ **Four Ace Model 204**, .22 L.R.R.F., Derringer, 4 Shot, Spur Trigger, Stainless Steel, *Modern*	45.00	65.00	65.00
☐ **Little Ace Model 300**, .22 Short R.F., Derringer, Side-swing Barrel, Spur Trigger, *Modern*	25.00	40.00	40.00

FOX, A.H. GUN CO.

Philadelphia, Pa. Formerly Philadelphia Arms Co., now a subsidiary of Savage Arms Co., 1930 to date. Also see Savage Arms Co.

SHOTGUN, DOUBLE BARREL, SIDE-BY-SIDE

☐ **Various Gauges**, Single Selective Trigger *Add* **$175.00-$295.00**

	V.G.	Exc.	Prior Year Exc. Value
☐ **Various Gauges**, For Vent Rib *Add* **$175.00-$295.00**			
☐ **Various Gauges**, Beavertail Forend *Add* **10%-15%**			
☐ **Various Gauges**, For Single Trigger *Add* **$125.00-$200.00**			
☐ **Various Grades**, for 20 Ga. *Add* **50%-75%**			
☐ **A Grade**, Various Gauges, Box Lock, Light Engraving, Checkered Stock, *Modern*	**550.00**	**750.00**	**725.00**
☐ **AE Grade**, Various Gauges, Box Lock, Light Engraving, Checkered Stock, Automatic Ejector, *Modern*	**695.00**	**975.00**	**950.00**
☐ **BE Grade**, Various Gauges, Box Lock, Engraved, Checkered Stock, Automatic Ejector, *Modern*	**890.00**	**1,275.00**	**1,200.00**
☐ **CE Grade**, Various Gauges, Box Lock, Engraved, Fancy Checkering, Automatic Ejector, *Modern*	**1,100.00**	**1,725.00**	**1,650.00**
☐ **DE Grade**, Various Gauges, Box Lock, Fancy Engraving, Fancy Checkering, Fancy Wood, Automatic Ejector, *Modern*	**3,950.00**	**5,775.00**	**5,500.00**
☐ **FE Grade**, Various Gauges, Box Lock, Fancy Engraving, Fancy Checkering, Fancy Wood, Automatic Ejector, *Modern*	**6,500.00**	**9,575.00**	**9,250.00**
☐ **GE Grade**, Various Gauges, Box Lock, Fancy Engraving, Fancy Checkering, Fancy Wood, Automatic Ejector, *Modern*	**9,950.00**	**16,750.00**	**15,750.00**
☐ **HE Grade**, 12 and 20 Gauge, Box Lock, Light Engraving, Checkered Stock, Automatic Ejector, *Modern*	**675.00**	**965.00**	**925.00**
☐ **Skeeter Grade**, 12 and 20 Gauge, Box Lock, Skeet Grade, Beavertail Forend, Vent Rib, Automatic Ejector, *Modern*	**950.00**	**1,475.00**	**1,400.00**
☐ **SP Grade**, Various Gauges, Box Lock, Checkered Stock, *Modern*	**365.00**	**525.00**	**500.00**
☐ **SP Grade**, Various Gauges, Box Lock, Checkered Stock, Automatic Ejector, *Modern*	**395.00**	**575.00**	**550.00**
☐ **SP Grade**, Various Gauges, Box Lock, Skeet Grade, Checkered Stock, *Modern*	**395.00**	**575.00**	**550.00**
☐ **SP Grade**, Various Gauges, Box Lock, Skeet Grade, Automatic Ejector, Checkered Stock, *Modern*	**475.00**	**650.00**	**625.00**
☐ **Sterlingworth**, Various Gauges, Box Lock, Checkered Stock, Hammerless, *Modern*	**345.00**	**500.00**	**475.00**
☐ **Sterlingworth**, Various Gauges, Box Lock, Checkered Stock, Hammerless, Automatic Ejector, *Modern*	**475.00**	**650.00**	**625.00**
☐ **Sterlingworth**, Various Gauges, Box Lock, Skeet Grade, Checkered Stock, *Modern*	**425.00**	**575.00**	**550.00**
☐ **Sterlingworth**, Various Gauges, Box Lock, Skeet Grade, Checkered Stock, Automatic Ejector, *Modern*	**550.00**	**820.00**	**775.00**
☐ **Sterlingworth Deluxe**, Various Gauges, Box Lock, Checkered Stock, Hammerless, Recoil Pad, *Modern*	**445.00**	**600.00**	**575.00**
☐ **Sterlingworth Deluxe**, Various Gauges, Box Lock, Checkered Stock, Hammerless, Recoil Pad, Automatic Ejector, *Modern*	**585.00**	**835.00**	**775.00**

	V.G.	Exc.	Prior Year Exc. Value
☐ **XE Grade**, Various Gauges, Box Lock, Fancy Engraving, Fancy Checkering, Fancy Wood, Automatic Ejector, *Modern*	2,050.00	2,925.00	2,750.00
SHOTGUN, SINGLESHOT			
☐ **JE Grade**, 12 Gauge, Trap Grade, Vent Rib, Automatic Ejector, Engraved, Fancy Checkering, *Modern*	1,295.00	1,725.00	1,675.00
☐ **KE Grade**, 12 Gauge, Trap Grade, Vent Rib, Automatic Ejector, Engraved, Fancy Checkering, *Modern*	1,700.00	2,350.00	2,275.00
☐ **LE Grade**, 12 Gauge, Trap Grade, Vent Rib, Automatic Ejector, Fancy Engraving, Fancy Checkering, *Modern*	2,350.00	3,300.00	3,175.00
☐ **ME Grade**, 12 Gauge, Trap Grade, Vent Rib, Automatic Ejector, Fancy Engraving, Fancy Checkering, *Modern*	4,625.00	6,900.00	6,750.00

FOX

Foxco Products, Inc. Manchester, Conn. Also see Demro, T.A.C.

	V.G.	Exc.	Prior Year Exc. Value
RIFLE, SEMI-AUTOMATIC			
☐ **9mm Luger or .45 ACP**, Clip Fed, *Modern*	165.00	250.00	250.00

FRANCAIS

France, made by Manufacture D'Armes Automatiques Francaise.

	V.G.	Exc.	Prior Year Exc. Value
HANDGUN, SEMI-AUTOMATIC			
☐ **Prima**, .25 ACP, Clip Fed, *Modern*	90.00	145.00	140.00

FRANCHI

Brescia, Italy, now imported by F.I.E.

	V.G.	Exc.	Prior Year Exc. Value
RIFLE, SEMI-AUTOMATIC			
☐ **Centennial**, .22 L.R.R.F., Checkered Stock, Tube Feed, Takedown, *Modern*	150.00	225.00	220.00
☐ **Centennial Deluxe**, .22 L.R.R.F., Checkered Stock, Tube Feed, Takedown, Light Engraving, *Modern*	225.00	335.00	325.00
☐ **Centennial Gallery**, .22 Short R.F., Checkered Stock, Tube Feed, Takedown, *Modern*	140.00	210.00	200.00
SHOTGUN, DOUBLE BARREL, OVER-UNDER			
☐ **Alcione Super**, 12, Vent Rib, Single Selective Trigger, Automatic Ejector, Engraved, *Modern*	325.00	500.00	450.00
☐ **Alcione Super Deluxe**, 12, Vent Rib, Single Selective Trigger, Automatic Ejector, Engraved, *Modern*	550.00	775.00	625.00
☐ **Aristocrat**, 12 Ga., Field Grade, Automatic Ejectors, Single Selective Trigger, Vent Rib, *Modern*	395.00	600.00	575.00
☐ **Aristocrat**, 12 Ga., Imperial Grade, Automatic Ejectors, Single Selective Trigger, Vent Rib, *Modern*	1,300.00	1,850.00	1,750.00
☐ **Aristocrat**, 12 Ga., Monte Carlo Grade, Automatic Ejectors, Single Selective Trigger, Vent Rib, *Modern*	1,850.00	2,675.00	2,600.00

	V.G.	Exc.	Prior Year Exc. Value
☐ **Barrage Skeet**, 12 Ga., Vent Rib, Single Selective Trigger, Automatic Ejector, Recoil Pad, *Modern*	675.00	945.00	900.00
☐ **Barrage Trap**, 12 Ga., Vent Rib, Single Selective Trigger, Automatic Ejector, Recoil Pad, *Modern*	665.00	945.00	900.00
☐ **Dragon Skeet**, 12 Ga., Vent Rib, Single Selective Trigger, Automatic Ejector, Recoil Pad, *Modern*	475.00	650.00	625.00
☐ **Dragon Trap**, 12 Ga., Vent Rib, Single Selective Trigger, Automatic Ejector, Recoil Pad, *Modern*	475.00	650.00	625.00
☐ **Falconet Buckskin**, 12 and 20 Ga., Vent Rib, Single Selective Trigger, Automatic Ejector, *Modern*	325.00	460.00	435.00
☐ **Falconet Ebony**, 12 and 20 Ga., Vent Rib, Single Selective Trigger, Automatic Ejector, *Modern*	300.00	435.00	415.00
☐ **Falconet Peregrine 400**, 12 and 20 Ga., Vent Rib, Single Selective Trigger, Automatic Ejector, *Modern*	315.00	435.00	415.00
☐ **Falconet Peregrine 451**, 12 and 20 Ga., Vent Rib, Single Selective Trigger, Automatic Ejector, *Modern*	355.00	475.00	450.00
☐ **Falconet Pigeon**, 12 Ga. Vent Rib, Single Selective Trigger, Automatic Ejector, Fancy Engraving, Fancy Checkering, *Modern*	985.00	1,400.00	1,350.00
☐ **Falconet Silver**, 12 Ga., Vent Rib, Single Selective Trigger, Automatic Ejector, *Modern*	345.00	490.00	465.00
☐ **Falconet Super**, 12 Ga., Vent Rib, Single Selective Trigger, Automatic Ejector, *Modern*	365.00	515.00	485.00
☐ **Falconet Super Deluxe**, 12 Ga., Vent Rib, Single Selective Trigger, Automatic Ejector, *Modern*	500.00	700.00	625.00
☐ **Model 255**, 12 Ga., Vent Rib, Single Selective Trigger, Automatic Ejector, *Modern*	295.00	435.00	410.00
☐ **Model 2003**, 12 Ga. Trap Grade, Vent Rib, Single Selective Trigger, Automatic Ejector, *Modern*	790.00	1,100.00	1,050.00
☐ **Model 2005/2**, 12 Ga., Trap Grade, Vent Rib, Single Selective Trigger, Automatic Ejector, Extra Shotgun Barrel, *Modern*	995.00	1,800.00	1,750.00
☐ **Model 2005/3**, 12 Ga., Trap Grade, Vent Rib, Single Selective Trigger, Automatic Ejector, Extra Shotgun Barrel, Custom Choke, *Modern*	1,550.00	2,150.00	2,100.00
SHOTGUN, DOUBLE BARREL, SIDE-BY-SIDE			
☐ **Airone**, 12 Ga., Box Lock, Hammerless, Checkered Stock, Automatic Ejector, *Modern*	565.00	775.00	750.00
☐ **Astore**, 12 Ga., Box Lock, Hammerless, Checkered Stock, *Modern*	455.00	600.00	575.00
☐ **Astore S**, 12 Ga., Box Lock, Hammerless, Checkered Stock, Light Engraving, *Modern*	935.00	1,400.00	1,350.00
☐ **Condor**, Various Gauges, Sidelock, Engraved, Checkered Stock, Automatic Ejector, *Modern*	2,400.00	3,300.00	3,200.00
☐ **Imperial**, Various Gauges, Sidelock, Engraved, Checkered Stock, Automatic Ejector, *Modern*	3,600.00	4,625.00	4,500.00
☐ **Imperial Monte Carlo #11**, Various Gauges, Sidelock, Fancy Engraving, Fancy Checkering, Automatic Ejector, *Modern*	7,425.00	9,650.00	9,500.00
☐ **Imperial Monte Carlo Extra**, Various Gauges, Sidelock, Fancy Engraving, Fancy Checkering, Automatic Ejector, *Modern*	8,850.00	12,250.00	11,500.00

	V.G.	Exc.	Prior Year Exc. Value
☐ **Imperial Monte Carlo #5**, Various Gauges, Sidelock, Fancy Engraving, Fancy Checkering, Automatic Ejector, *Modern*	7,500.00	9,950.00	9,750.00
☐ **Imperial S**, Various Gauges, Sidelock, Engraved, Checkered Stock, Automatic Ejector, *Modern*	3,500.00	4,675.00	4,550.00
SHOTGUN, SEMI-AUTOMATIC			
☐ **Dynamic (Heavy)**, 12 Ga., Plain Barrel, *Modern*	170.00	250.00	240.00
☐ **Dynamic (Heavy)**, 12 Ga., Vent Rib, *Modern*	165.00	255.00	250.00
☐ **Dynamic (Heavy)**, 12 Ga., Skeet Grade, Vent Rib, Checkered Stock, *Modern*	190.00	275.00	270.00
☐ **Dynamic (Heavy)**, 12 Ga., Checkered Stock, Slug, Open Rear Sight, *Modern*	195.00	285.00	275.00
☐ **Eldorado**, 12 and 20 Ga., Vent Rib, Engraved, Fancy Checkering, Lightweight, *Modern*	290.00	385.00	375.00
☐ **Hunter**, 12 and 20 Ga., Vent Rib, Engraved, Checkered Stock, Lightweight, *Modern*	230.00	340.00	340.00
☐ **Model 500**, 12 Ga., Vent Rib, Checkered Stock, Engraved, *Modern*	245.00	325.00	325.00
☐ **Model 500**, 12 Ga., Vent Rib, Checkered Stock, *Modern*	195.00	250.00	245.00
☐ **Slug Gun**, 12 and 20 Ga., Open Rear Sight, Sling Swivels, *Modern*	195.00	295.00	275.00
☐ **SPAS 12**, 12 Gauge, Combat Shotgun, Folding Stock, Rifle Sights, Lightweight, *Modern*	295.00	425.00	—
☐ **Standard**, 12 and 20 Ga., Plain Barrel, Lightweight, Checkered Stock, *Modern*	195.00	275.00	260.00
☐ **Standard**, 12 and 20 Ga., Solid Rib, Lightweight, Checkered Stock, *Modern*	190.00	270.00	250.00
☐ **Standard**, 12 and 20 Ga., Vent Rib, Lightweight, Checkered Stock, *Modern*	200.00	295.00	275.00
☐ **Standard Magnum**, 12 and 20 Gauges, Vent Rib, Lightweight, Checkered Stock, *Modern*	230.00	315.00	310.00
☐ **Superange (Heavy)**, 12 and 20 Gauges, Magnum, Plain Barrel, Checkered Stock, *Modern*	180.00	255.00	250.00
☐ **Superange (Heavy)**, 12 and 20 Gauges, Magnum, Vent Rib, Checkered Stock, *Modern*	195.00	290.00	285.00
☐ **Wildfowler (Heavy)**, 12 and 20 Gauges, Magnum, Vent Rib, Checkered Stock, Engraved, *Modern*	250.00	340.00	340.00
SHOTGUN, SINGLESHOT			
☐ **Model 2004**, 12 Ga., Trap Grade, Vent Rib, Automatic Ejector, *Modern*	775.00	1,100.00	1,075.00
☐ **Model 3000/2**, 12 Ga., Trap Grade, Vent Rib, Automatic Ejector, with Choke Tubes, *Modern*	1,335.00	2,050.00	2,000.00

FRANCI, PIERO INZI

Brescia, Italy, c. 1640.

	V.G.	Exc.	Prior Year Exc. Value
HANDGUN, WHEEL-LOCK			
☐ **Octagon-Barrel**, Dagger Handle Butt, *Antique*	2,600.00	3,700.00	3,650.00

FRANCOTTE, AUGUST

Liege, Belgium 1844 to date, also London, England 1877-1893.

	V.G.	Exc.	Prior Year Exc. Value
HANDGUN, REVOLVER			
☐ **Military Style, Various Calibers, Double Action,** *Antique*	85.00	145.00	135.00

	V.G.	Exc.	Prior Year Exc. Value
☐ **Bulldog**, Various Calibers, Double Action, Solid Frame, *Curio*	75.00	125.00	125.00
HANDGUN, SEMI-AUTOMATIC			
☐ **Vest Pocket**, .25 ACP, Clip Fed, *Curio*	215.00	325.00	295.00
HANDGUN, SINGLESHOT			
☐ **Target Pistol**, .22 L.R.R.F., Toggle Breech, *Modern*	245.00	375.00	350.00
RIFLE, DOUBLE BARREL, SIDE-BY-SIDE			
☐ **Luxury Double**, .458 Win., Sidelock, Hammerless, Double Triggers, Fancy Engraving, *Modern*	9,950.00	15,000.00	15,000.00
SHOTGUN, DOUBLE BARREL, SIDE-BY-SIDE			
☐ **A & F #14**, Various Gauges, Box Lock, Automatic Ejector, Checkered Stock, Engraved, Hammerless, *Modern*	2,250.00	2,975.00	2,950.00
☐ **A & F #20**, Various Gauges, Box Lock, Automatic Ejector, Checkered Stock, Engraved, Hammerless, *Modern*	2,700.00	3,475.00	3,450.00
☐ **A & F #25**, Various Gauges, Box Lock, Automatic Ejector, Checkered Stock, Engraved, Hammerless, *Modern*	3,200.00	4,000.00	4,000.00
☐ **A & F #30**, Various Gauges, Box Lock, Automatic Ejector, Checkered Stock, Fancy Engraving, Hammerless, *Modern*	3,600.00	4,500.00	4,450.00
☐ **A & F #45**, Various Gauges, Box Lock, Automatic Ejector, Checkered Stock, Fancy Engraving, Hammerless, *Modern*	4,250.00	5,250.00	5,250.00
☐ **A & F Jubilee**, Various Gauges, Box Lock, Automatic Ejector, Checkered Stock, Light Engraving, Hammerless, *Modern*	2,150.00	3,000.00	3,000.00
☐ **A & F Knockabout**, Various Gauges, Box Lock, Automatic Ejector, Checkered Stock, Hammerless, *Modern*	1,450.00	2,250.00	2,250.00
☐ **Francotte Original**, Various Gauges, Box Lock, Automatic Ejector, Checkered Stock, Hammerless, Engraved, *Modern*	2,150.00	2,900.00	2,900.00
☐ **Francotte Special**, Various Gauges, Box Lock, Automatic Ejector, Checkered Stock, Hammerless, Light Engraving, *Modern*	1,600.00	2,400.00	2,400.00
☐ **Model 10/18E/628**, Various Gauges, Box Lock, Automatic Ejector, Checkered Stock, Hammerless, Light Engraving, *Modern*	2,950.00	3,750.00	3,750.00
☐ **Model 10594**, Various Gauges, Box Lock, Automatic Ejector, Checkered Stock, Hammerless, Engraved, *Modern*	2,300.00	3,100.00	3,100.00
☐ **Model 11/18E**, Various Gauges, Box Lock, Automatic Ejector, Checkered Stock, Hammerless, Engraved, *Modern*	2,300.00	3,100.00	3,100.00
☐ **Model 120.HE/328**, Various Gauges, Sidelock, Automatic Ejector, Checkered Stock, Hammerless, Fancy Engraving, *Modern*	6,750.00	8,500.00	8,500.00
☐ **Model 4996**, Various Gauges, Box Lock, Automatic Ejector, Checkered Stock, Hammerless, Light Engraving, *Modern*	1,650.00	2,475.00	2,450.00

Francotte Bulldog Revolver

Francotte .25 ACP Pistol

	V.G.	Exc.	Prior Year Exc. Value
☐ **Model 6886**, Various Gauges, Box Lock, Automatic Ejector, Checkered Stock, Hammerless, *Modern*	1,450.00	2,300.00	2,300.00
☐ **Model 6930**, Various Gauges, Box Lock, Automatic Ejector, Checkered Stock, Hammerless, Light Engraving, *Modern*	1,600.00	2,400.00	2,400.00
☐ **Model 6982**, Various Gauges, Box Lock, Automatic Ejector, Checkered Stock, Hammerless, Engraved, *Modern*	2,500.00	3,300.00	3,300.00
☐ **Model 8455**, Various Gauges, Box Lock, Automatic Ejector, Checkered Stock, Hammerless, *Modern*	2,600.00	3,500.00	3,450.00
☐ **Model 8457**, Various Gauges, Box Lock, Automatic Ejector, Checkered Stock, Hammerless, Engraved, *Modern*	2,350.00	3,000.00	3,000.00
☐ **Model 9/40.SE**, Various Gauges, Box Lock, Automatic Ejector, Checkered Stock, Hammerless, Fancy Engraving, *Modern*	6,800.00	9,750.00	9,500.00
☐ **Model 9/40E/38321**, Various Gauges, Box Lock, Automatic Ejector, Checkered Stock, Hammerless, Engraved, *Modern*	3,100.00	4,000.00	3,900.00
☐ **Model SOB.E/11082**, Various Gauges, Box Lock, Automatic Ejector, Checkered Stock, Hammerless, Engraved, *Modern*	4,475.00	5,900.00	5,850.00

FRANKLIN, C.W.

Belgium, c. 1900.

SHOTGUN, DOUBLE BARREL, SIDE-BY-SIDE

	V.G.	Exc.	Prior Year Exc. Value
☐ **Various Gauges**, Outside Hammers, Damascus Barrel, *Modern*	80.00	155.00	150.00
☐ **Various Gauges**, Hammerless, Steel Barrel, *Modern*	115.00	185.00	175.00
☐ **Various Gauges**, Hammerless, Damascus Barrel, *Modern*	80.00	155.00	150.00
☐ **Various Gauges**, Outside Hammers, Steel Barrel, *Modern*	110.00	180.00	175.00

SHOTGUN, SINGLESHOT

	V.G.	Exc.	Prior Year Exc. Value
☐ **Various Gauges**, Hammer, Steel Barrel, *Modern*	45.00	75.00	75.00

	V.G.	Exc.	Prior Year Exc. Value

FRANKONIA

Franconia Jagd, arms dealers and manufacturers in West Germany.

RIFLE, SINGLESHOT

	V.G.	Exc.	Prior Year Exc. Value
☐ **Heeren Rifle**, Various Calibers, Fancy Engraving, Fancy wood, Octagon Barrel, *Modern*	1,650.00	2,600.00	2,400.00
☐ **Heeren Rifle**, Various Calibers, Fancy Engraving, Fancy wood, Round Barrel, *Modern*	1,250.00	1,950.00	1,850.00

RIFLE, BOLT ACTION

	V.G.	Exc.	Prior Year Exc. Value
☐ **Favorit**, Various Calibers, Set Triggers, Checkered Stock, *Modern*	175.00	270.00	250.00
☐ **Favorit Deluxe**, Various Calibers, Set Triggers, Checkered Stock, *Modern*	215.00	290.00	270.00
☐ **Favorit Leichtmodell**, Various Calibers, Lightweight, Set Triggers, Checkered Stock, *Modern*	260.00	395.00	370.00
☐ **Safari**, Various Calibers, Target Trigger, Checkered Stock, *Modern*	275.00	410.00	385.00
☐ **Stutzen**, Various Calibers, Carbine, Set Triggers, Full Stock, *Modern*	215.00	290.00	265.00

FRASER (FORMERLY BAUER FIREARMS)

Fraser, Mich.

HANDGUN, SEMI-AUTOMATIC

	V.G.	Exc.	Prior Year Exc. Value
☐ **.25 ACP**, Stainless Steel, Clip Fed, Hammerless, Browning Baby Style, *Modern*	65.00	90.00	—

FRASER, D. & J.

Edinburgh, Scotland 1870-1900.

RIFLE, DOUBLE BARREL, SIDE-BY-SIDE

	V.G.	Exc.	Prior Year Exc. Value
☐ **.360 N.E. #2**, Automatic Ejector, Express Sights, Engraved, Extra Set of Barrels, Cased with Accessories, *Modern*	6,350.00	8,500.00	8,300.00

FRAZIER, JAY

Tyler, Wash., c. 1974.

RIFLE, SINGLESHOT

	V.G.	Exc.	Prior Year Exc. Value
☐ **Creedmore Rifle**, Various Calibers, Single Set Trigger, Vernier Sights, Skeleton Buttplate, Pistol Grip Stock, *Modern*	550.00	775.00	750.00
☐ **Schuetzen Rifle**, Various Calibers, Single Set Trigger, Vernier Sights, Helm Buttplate, Palm Rest, False Muzzle, *Modern*	550.00	775.00	750.00

FRAZIER, CLARK K.

Rawson, Ohio.

RIFLE, PERCUSSION

	V.G.	Exc.	Prior Year Exc. Value
☐ **Matchmate Offhand**, Various Calibers, Under-Hammer, Thumbhole Stock, Heavy Barrel, Reproduction, *Antique*	420.00	640.00	625.00

FREEDOM ARMS

Freedom, Wyo.

	V.G.	Exc.	Prior Year Exc. Value
HANDGUN, REVOLVER			
☐ **FA-S**, .22 L.R.R.F., Stainless Steel, Matt Finish, Spur Trigger, 1" Barrel, Single Action, *Modern*	60.00	85.00	80.00
☐ **FA-L**, .22 L.R.R.F., Stainless Steel, Matt Finish, Spur Trigger, 1¾" Barrel, Single Action, *Modern*	65.00	90.00	85.00
☐ **FA-S**, .22 W.M.R., Stainless Steel, Matt Finish, Spur Trigger, 1" Barrel, Single Action, *Modern*	70.00	105.00	95.00
☐ **FA-L**, .22 W.M.R., Stainless Steel, Matt Finish, Spur Trigger, 1¾" Barrel, Single Action, *Modern*	75.00	110.00	100.00
☐ **FA-BG**, .22 L.R.R.F., Stainless Steel, Spur Trigger, 3" Barrel, Single Action, *Modern*	70.00	110.00	100.00
☐ **FA-BG**, .22 W.M.R., Stainless Steel, Spur Trigger, 3" Barrel, Single Action, *Modern*	75.00	120.00	110.00
☐ **For High Gloss Finish** *Add* **$5.00-$10.00**			

FRENCH MILITARY

	V.G.	Exc.	Prior Year Exc. Value
AUTOMATIC WEAPON, LIGHT MACHINE GUN			
☐ **CSRG 1915 Chauchat,** 8 x 50R Lebel, Clip Fed, Bipod, *Class 3*	675.00	945.00	945.00
AUTOMATIC WEAPON, SUBMACHINE GUN			
☐ **MAS 38,** 7.65 MAS, Clip Fed, Wood Stock, Dewat, *Class 3*	495.00	750.00	750.00
☐ **MAS 38,** 7.65 MAS, Clip Fed, Wood Stock, *Class 3*	935.00	1400.00	1400.00
HANDGUN, FLINTLOCK			
☐ **.69 Charleville 1810,** Cavalry Pistol, Brass Furniture, Plain, *Antique*	575.00	900.00	850.00
☐ **.69 Charleville 1777,** Cavalry Pistol, Brass Frame, Belt Hook, *Antique*	685.00	1075.00	975.00
☐ **.69,** Model 1763, Belt Pistol, Military, *Antique*	1025.00	1650.00	1525.00
HANDGUN, PERCUSSION			
☐ **.69 AN XIII,** Officer's Pistol, Made in France, *Antique*	310.00	490.00	475.00
☐ **.69 AN XIII,** Officer's Pistol, Made in Occupied Country, *Antique*	420.00	600.00	575.00
☐ **.69 Charleville 1810 Cavalry Pistol,** Brass Furniture, Converted from Flintlock, Plain, *Antique*	385.00	530.00	495.00
HANDGUN, REVOLVER			
☐ **Model 1873,** 11mm French Ordnance, Double Action, Solid Frame, *Antique*	175.00	260.00	245.00
☐ **Model 1873 Officer's,** 11mm French Ordnance, Double Action, Solid Frame, *Antique*	185.00	290.00	275.00
☐ **Model 1892,** 8mm Lebel Revolver, Double Action, Solid Frame, *Curio*	110.00	165.00	185.00
☐ **Model 1915,** 8mm Lebel Revolver, Double Action, Solid Frame, Spanish Contract, *Curio*	80.00	125.00	185.00
HANDGUN, SEMI-AUTOMATIC			
☐ **Model 1935-A,** 7.65 MAS, Clip Fed, Blued, *Curio*	60.00	100.00	170.00
☐ **Model 1935-A,** 7.65 MAS, Clip Fed, Black Paint, *Curio*	55.00	100.00	160.00

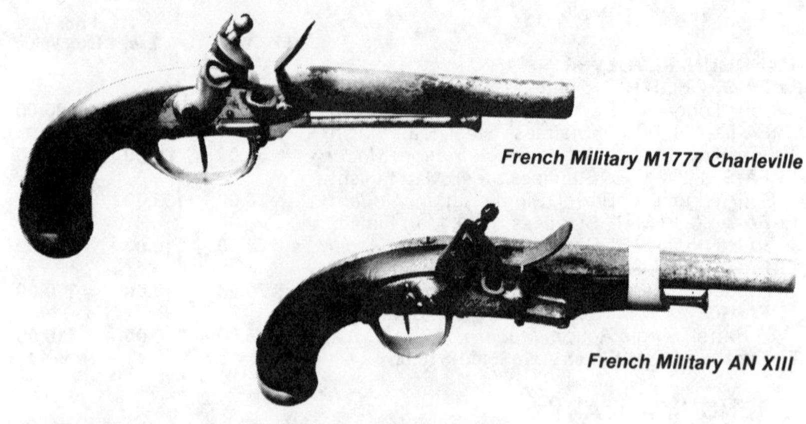

French Military M1777 Charleville

French Military AN XIII

French Military M1935A

French Military M1950

French Military M1873 Revolver

	V.G.	Exc.	Prior Year Exc. Value
☐ **Model 1935-A,** 7.65 MAS, Clip Fed, Nazi Proofed, *Curio*	105.00	170.00	225.00
☐ **Model 1935-S,** 7.65 MAS, M.A.C., Clip Fed, *Curio*	60.00	95.00	160.00
☐ **Model 1935-S,** 7.65 MAS, M.A.C., Clip Fed, Nazi Proofed, *Curio*	90.00	135.00	210.00
☐ **Model 1935-S,** 7.65 MAS, M.A.S., Clip Fed, *Curio*	55.00	95.00	165.00
☐ **Model 1935-S,** 7.65 MAS, M.A.C. M-1, Clip Fed, *Curio*	55.00	95.00	170.00
☐ **Model 1935-S,** 7.65 MAS, M.A.S., Clip Fed, Nazi Proofed, *Curio*	110.00	160.00	215.00
☐ **Model 1935-S,** 7.65 MAS, M.A.T., Clip Fed, *Curio*	90.00	130.00	190.00
☐ **Model 1935-S,** 7.65 MAS, M.A.T., Clip Fed, Nazi Proofed, *Curio*	115.00	165.00	235.00
☐ **Model 1935-S,** 7.65 MAS, SAGEM M-1, Clip Fed, *Curio*	70.00	110.00	170.00
☐ **Model 1935-S,** 7.65 MAS, SAGEM M-1, Clip Fed, Nazi Proofed, *Curio*	100.00	150.00	225.00
☐ **Model 1935-S,** 7.65 MAS, SACM, Clip Fed, *Curio*	60.00	105.00	170.00
☐ **Model 1935-S,** 7.65 MAS, SAGEM M-1, Clip Fed, Nazi Proofed, *Curio*	95.00	145.00	215.00
☐ **Model 1950,** 9mm Luger, M.A.S., Clip Fed, *Modern*	300.00	465.00	465.00
RIFLE, BOLT ACTION			
☐ **6.5 x 53.5 Daudetau,** Carbine, *Curio*	90.00	130.00	200.00
☐ **Model 1874,** 11 x 59R Gras, *Antique*	100.00	170.00	155.00
☐ **Model 1874,** 11 x 59R Gras, Carbine, *Antique*	135.00	200.00	180.00
☐ **Model 1886/93 Lebel,** 8 x 50R Lebel, *Curio*	60.00	100.00	140.00
☐ **Model 1907/15 Remington,** 8 x 50R Lebel, *Curio*	65.00	105.00	150.00
☐ **Model 1916 St. Etienne,** 8 x 50R Lebel, Carbine, *Curio*	75.00	115.00	165.00
☐ **Model 1936 MAS,** 7.5 x 54 MAS, with Bayonet, *Curio*	95.00	145.00	200.00
RIFLE, FLINTLOCK			
☐ **.69,** Model 1763 Charleville 1st. Type, Musket, *Antique*	1000.00	1700.00	1300.00
☐ **.69,** Model 1763/66 Charleville, Musket, *Antique*	850.00	1200.00	975.00
RIFLE, PERCUSSION			
☐ **Model 1840,** Short Rifle, *Antique*	480.00	825.00	735.00

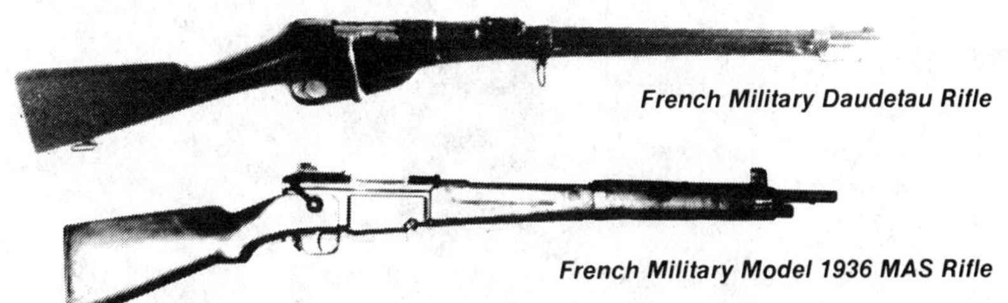

French Military Daudetau Rifle

French Military Model 1936 MAS Rifle

FROMMER

Made by Femaru-Fegyver-Es Gepgyar R.T., (Fegyvergyar) Budapest, Hungary. All see Femaru.

HANDGUN, SEMI-AUTOMATIC

	V.G.	Exc.	Prior Year Exc. Value
☐ **Baby Stop,** .32 ACP, Clip Fed, *Modern*	145.00	205.00	225.00
☐ **Baby Stop,** .380 ACP, Clip Fed, *Modern*	190.00	270.00	280.00
☐ **Liliput,** .22 L.R.R.F., Clip Fed, *Modern*	300.00	400.00	425.00
☐ **Liliput,** .25 ACP, Clip Fed, *Modern*	200.00	270.00	295.00
☐ **Roth-Frommer Model 1901,** 8mm Roth Sauer, Fixed Magazine, Commercial, *Curio*	1150.00	1700.00	1800.00
☐ **Roth-Frommer Model 1901,** 8mm Roth Sauer, Fixed Magazine, Military Test, *Curio*	1450.00	2050.00	2200.00
☐ **Roth-Frommer Model 1906,** 7.65mm Roth Sauer, Clip Fed, Commercial, *Curio*	850.00	1425.00	1500.00
☐ **Roth-Frommer Model 1906,** 7.65mm Roth Sauer, Fixed Magazine, Commercial, *Curio*	725.00	1300.00	1350.00
☐ **Roth-Frommer Model 1910,** .32 ACP, Fixed Magazine, Commercial, *Curio*	800.00	1250.00	1300.00
☐ **Roth-Frommer Model 1910,** .32 ACP, Fixed Magazine, Police, *Curio*	950.00	1475.00	1550.00
☐ **Stop,** .32 ACP, Commercial, Clip Fed, *Modern*	135.00	165.00	180.00
☐ **Stop,** .32 ACP, WW-1 Military, Clip Fed, *Modern*	75.00	135.00	165.00
☐ **Stop,** .32 ACP, M-19 Military, Clip Fed, *Modern*	85.00	145.00	175.00
☐ **Stop,** .32 ACP, Police, Clip Fed, *Modern*	135.00	170.00	185.00
☐ **Stop,** .380 ACP, Military, Clip Fed, *Modern*	150.00	210.00	275.00
☐ **Stop,** .32 ACP, Commercial, Clip Fed, *Modern*	140.00	200.00	220.00

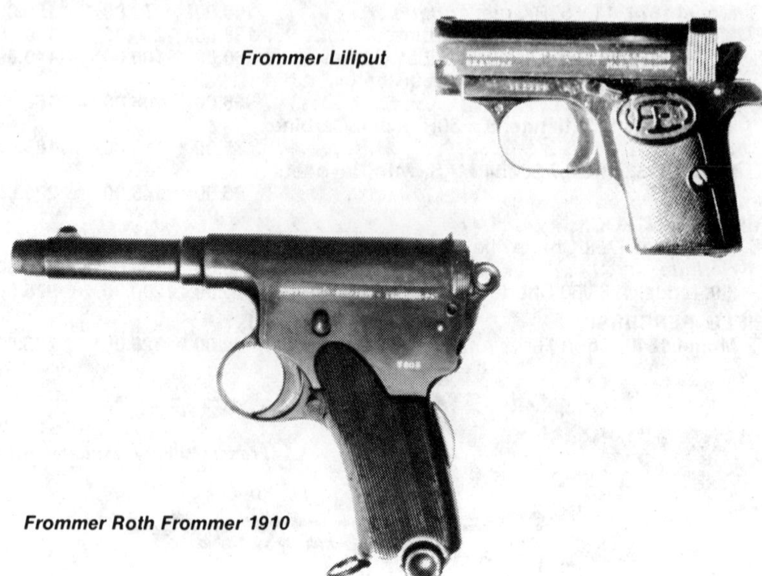

Frommer Liliput

Frommer Roth Frommer 1910

	V.G.	Exc.	Prior Year Exc. Value

FRONTIER
Made by Norwich Falls Pistol Co., c. 1880.

HANDGUN, REVOLVER

	V.G.	Exc.	Prior Year Exc. Value
☐ **.32 Short R.F.**, 5 Shot, Spur Trigger, Solid Frame, Single Action, *Antique*	95.00	170.00	170.00

FRYBERG, ANDREW
Hopkintown, Mass., c. 1905.

HANDGUN, REVOLVER

	V.G.	Exc.	Prior Year Exc. Value
☐ **.32 S & W**, 5 Shot, Top Break, Hammerless, Double Action, *Modern*	55.00	100.00	95.00
☐ **.32 S & W**, 5 Shot, Top Break, Double Action, *Modern*	55.00	100.00	95.00
☐ **.38 S & W**, 5 Shot, Top Break, Double Action, Hammerless, *Modern*	55.00	100.00	95.00
☐ **.38 S & W**, 5 Shot, Top Break, Double Action, *Modern*	55.00	100.00	95.00

FTL
Covina, Calif.

HANDGUN, SEMI-AUTOMATIC

	V.G.	Exc.	Prior Year Exc. Value
☐ **.22 L.R.R.F.**, Clip Fed, Chrome Plated, *Modern*	85.00	135.00	130.00

GALAND, CHARLES FRANCOIS
From 1865 until about 1910 with plants in London, England, Paris, France, and Liege, Belgium.

HANDGUN, REVOLVER

	V.G.	Exc.	Prior Year Exc. Value
☐ **Galand**, Various Calibers, Double Action, Underlever Extraction, *Curio*	175.00	295.00	275.00
☐ **Galand-Perrin**, Various Calibers, Double Action, Underlever Extraction, *Curio*	165.00	285.00	270.00
☐ **Galand & Sommerville**, .38 C.F., Double Action, Underlever Extraction, *Curio*	175.00	295.00	275.00
☐ **Galand & Sommerville**, .450 C.F., Double Action, Underlever Extraction, *Curio*	190.00	325.00	300.00
☐ **Le Novo**, .25 ACP, Double Action, Folding Trigger, *Curio*	80.00	135.00	130.00

SHOTGUN, PERCUSSION

	V.G.	Exc.	Prior Year Exc. Value
☐ **Various Gauges**, Checkered Stock, Double Barrel, Plain, *Antique*	135.00	210.00	200.00

SHOTGUN, DOUBLE BARREL, SIDE-BY-SIDE

	V.G.	Exc.	Prior Year Exc. Value
☐ **Various Gauges**, Checkered Stock, Plain, Hammers, *Curio*	95.00	155.00	150.00

GALEF
Importers in N.Y.C.

HANDGUN, REVOLVER

	V.G.	Exc.	Prior Year Exc. Value
☐ **Stallion**, .22LR/.22 WMR Combo, Western Style, Single Action, *Modern*	65.00	95.00	95.00

HANDGUN, SEMI-AUTOMATIC

	V.G.	Exc.	Prior Year Exc. Value
☐ **Brigadier**, 9mm Luger, Beretta, Clip Fed, *Modern*	180.00	285.00	275.00

	V.G.	Exc.	Prior Year Exc. Value
☐ **Cougar**, .380 ACP, Beretta, Clip Fed, *Modern*	135.00	210.00	200.00
☐ **Jaguar**, .22 L.R.R.F., Beretta, Clip Fed, *Modern*	110.00	185.00	175.00
☐ **Puma**, .32 ACP, Beretta, Clip Fed, *Modern*	110.00	180.00	175.00
☐ **Sable**, .22 L.R.R.F., Beretta, Clip Fed, Adjustable Sights, *Modern*	145.00	215.00	200.00
RIFLE, BOLT ACTION			
☐ **BSA Monarch**, Various Calibers, Checkered Stock, *Modern*	160.00	250.00	245.00
☐ **BSA Monarch**, Various Calibers, Checkered Stock, Magnum Action, *Modern*	185.00	275.00	265.00
☐ **BSA Monarch Varmint**, Various Calibers, Checkered Stock, Heavy Barrel, *Modern*	195.00	290.00	275.00
SHOTGUN, DOUBLE BARREL, OVER-UNDER			
☐ **Golden Snipe**, 12 Ga., Trap Grade, Single Trigger, Automatic Ejector, Engraved, Checkered Stock, *Modern*	375.00	490.00	475.00
☐ **Golden Snipe**, 12 and 20 Gauges, Beretta, Single Trigger, Automatic Ejector, Engraved, Fancy Checkering, *Modern*	310.00	400.00	390.00
☐ **Golden Snipe**, 12 and 20 Gauges, Beretta, Single Selective Trigger, Automatic Ejector, Engraved, Fancy Checkering, *Modern*	360.00	475.00	465.00
☐ **Golden Snipe**, 12 and 20 Gauges, Skeet Grade, Single Trigger, Automatic Ejector, Engraved, Checkered Stock, *Modern*	370.00	490.00	475.00
☐ **Golden Snipe Deluxe**, 12 and 20 Gauges, Beretta, Single Selective Trigger, Automatic Ejector, Fancy Engraving, Fancy Checkering, *Modern*	390.00	525.00	500.00
☐ **Silver Snipe**, 12 Ga., Trap Grade, Single Trigger, Vent Rib, Engraved, Checkered Stock, *Modern*	320.00	435.00	400.00
☐ **Silver Snipe**, 12 and 20 Gauges, Skeet Grade, Single Trigger, Vent Rib, Engraved, Checkered Stock, *Modern*	320.00	430.00	400.00
☐ **Silver Snipe**, 12 and 20 Gauges, Beretta, Single Trigger, Checkered Stock, *Modern*	255.00	340.00	325.00
☐ **Silver Snipe**, 12 and 20 Gauges, Beretta, Single Selective Trigger, Checkered Stock, Light Engraving, *Modern*	290.00	380.00	365.00
☐ **Zoli Golden Snipe**, 12 and 20 Gauges, Vent Rib, Single Trigger, Adjustable Choke, Engraved, Checkered Stock, *Modern*	340.00	460.00	435.00
☐ **Zoli Silver Snipe**, 12 and 20 Gauges, Vent Rib, Single Trigger, Engraved, Checkered Stock, *Modern*	285.00	385.00	370.00
SHOTGUN, DOUBLE BARREL, SIDE-BY-SIDE			
☐ **M213CH**, 10 Ga. 3½", Double Trigger, Checkered Stock, Light Engraving, Recoil Pad, *Modern*	165.00	250.00	235.00
☐ **M213CH**, Various Gauges, Double Trigger, Checkered Stock, Light Engraving, Recoil Pad, *Modern*	135.00	175.00	165.00
☐ **Silver Hawk**, 10 Ga. 3½", Beretta, Double Trigger, Magnum, *Modern*	375.00	490.00	475.00
☐ **Silver Hawk**, 12 and 20 Gauges, Double Trigger, Engraved, Checkered Stock, *Modern*	285.00	375.00	365.00

	V.G.	Exc.	Prior Year Exc. Value
☐ **Silver Hawk**, 12 Ga. Mag. 3", Beretta, Double Trigger, Magnum, *Modern*	285.00	375.00	365.00
☐ **Silver Hawk**, 12 Ga. Mag. 3", Beretta, Single Trigger, Magnum, *Modern*	340.00	435.00	425.00
☐ **Silver Hawk**, Various Gauges, Beretta, Double Trigger, Lightweight, *Modern*	230.00	325.00	315.00
☐ **Silver Hawk**, Various Gauges, Beretta, Double Trigger, Lightweight, *Modern*	285.00	385.00	375.00
☐ **Zabala 213**, 10 Ga. 3½", Double Trigger, *Modern*	140.00	200.00	200.00
☐ **Zabala 213**, 12 and 20 Gauges, Double Trigger, *Modern*	120.00	165.00	160.00
☐ **Zabala 213**, 12 and 20 Gauges, Double Trigger, Vent Rib, *Modern*	125.00	175.00	170.00
☐ **Zabala Police**, 12 and 20 Gauges, Double Trigger, *Modern*	125.00	180.00	175.00
SHOTGUN, SEMI-AUTOMATIC			
☐ **Gold Lark**, 12 Ga., Beretta, Vent Rib, Light Engraving, Checkered Stock, *Modern*	150.00	235.00	225.00
☐ **Ruby Lark**, 12 Ga., Beretta, Vent Rib, Fancy Engraving, Fancy Checkering, *Modern*	240.00	350.00	350.00
☐ **Silver Gyrfalcon**, 12 Ga., Beretta, Checkered Stock, *Modern*	70.00	125.00	120.00
☐ **Silver Lark**, 12 Ga., Beretta, Checkered Stock, *Modern*	95.00	165.00	165.00
SHOTGUN, SINGLESHOT			
☐ **Companion**, Various Gauges, Folding Gun, Checkered Stock, *Modern*	35.00	55.00	55.00
☐ **Companion**, Various Gauges, Folding Gun, Checkered Stock, Vent Rib, *Modern*	45.00	65.00	65.00
☐ **Monte Carlo**, 12 Ga., Trap Grade, Vent Rib, Engraved, Checkered Stock, *Modern*	145.00	210.00	200.00
SHOTGUN, SLIDE ACTION			
☐ **Gold Pigeon**, 12 Ga., Beretta, Vent Rib, Fancy Engraving, Fancy Checkering, *Modern*	225.00	350.00	350.00
☐ **Ruby Pigeon**, 12 Ga., Beretta, Vent Rib, Fancy Engraving, Fancy Checkering, *Modern*	345.00	450.00	450.00
☐ **Silver Pigeon**, 12 Ga., Beretta, Light Engraving, Checkered Stock, *Modern*	95.00	140.00	135.00

GALESI

Industria Armi Galesi, Brescia, Italy since 1910.

HANDGUN, SEMI-AUTOMATIC			
☐ **Model 506**, .22 L.R.R.F., Clip Fed, *Modern*	75.00	125.00	120.00
☐ **Model 6**, .22 Long R.F., Clip Fed, *Modern*	70.00	100.00	95.00
☐ **Model 6**, .25 ACP, Clip Fed, *Modern*	65.00	95.00	90.00
☐ **Model 9**, .22 L.R.R.F., Clip Fed, *Modern*	80.00	130.00	125.00
☐ **Model 9**, .32 ACP, Clip Fed, *Modern*	85.00	140.00	135.00
☐ **Model 9**, .380 ACP, Clip Fed, *Modern*	90.00	155.00	150.00

GALLATIN, ALBERT

See Kentucky Rifles and Pistols.

Galesi Model 9 Pistol

Galesi Revolver

	V.G.	Exc.	Prior Year Exc. Value
GALLUS			
Retoloza Hermanos, Eibar, Spain, c. 1920.			
HANDGUN, SEMI-AUTOMATIC			
☐ **.25 ACP**, Clip Fed, Blue, *Modern*	85.00	130.00	125.00
GAMBA			
Renato Gamba, Brescia, Italy.			
RIFLE, SINGLESHOT			
☐ **Mustang**, Various Calibers, Holland Type Sidelock Action, Set Triggers, Checkered Stock, Engraved, Zeiss Scope, *Modern*	4,000.00	6,250.00	6,250.00
☐ **RIFLE, DOUBLE BARREL, OVER-UNDER**			
☐ **Safari**, Various Calibers, Boxlock, Checkered Stock, Engraved, Double Triggers, *Modern*	3,500.00	5,750.00	5,750.00
SHOTGUN, DOUBLE BARREL, SIDE-BY-SIDE			
☐ **London**, 12 or 20 Ga., Sidelock, Checkered Stock, Engraved, *Modern*	1,800.00	2,500.00	2,450.00
☐ **Oxford**, 12 or 20 Ga., Boxlock, Checkered Stock, Engraved, *Modern*	700.00	1,100.00	1,050.00
GANDER. PETER			
Lancaster, Pa. 1779-1782, see Kentucky Rifles.			
GARATE, ANITUA			
Eibar, Spain, c. 1915.			
HANDGUN, REVOLVER			
☐ **Pistol O.P. #1 Mk.I**, .455 Webley, British Military, *Curio*	160.00	265.00	250.00
HANDGUN, SEMI-AUTOMATIC			
☐ **.32 ACP**, Clip Fed, Long Grip, *Modern*	130.00	195.00	185.00
GARBI			
Armas Garbi, Eibar, Spain.			

	V.G.	Exc.	Prior Year Exc. Value
SHOTGUN, DOUBLE BARREL, SIDE-BY-SIDE			
☐ **Model 51**, Various Gauges, Boxlock, Checkered Stock, Engraved, *Modern*	265.00	390.00	375.00
☐ **Model 60**, Various Gauges, Sidelock, Checkered Stock, Engraved, *Modern*	420.00	565.00	550.00
☐ **Model 60**, Various Gauges, Sidelock, Checkered Stock, Engraved, Automatic Ejectors, *Modern*	585.00	775.00	750.00

GARRISON

Made by Hopkins & Allen, c. 1880-1890.

	V.G.	Exc.	Prior Year Exc. Value
HANDGUN, REVOLVER			
☐ **.22 Short R.F.**, 7 Shot, Spur Trigger, Solid Frame, Single Action, *Antique*	95.00	175.00	170.00

GARRUCHA

Made by Amadeo Rossi, Sao Leopoldo, Brazil.

	V.G.	Exc.	Prior Year Exc. Value
HANDGUN, DOUBLE BARREL, SIDE-BY-SIDE			
☐ **.22 L.R.R.F.**, Double Triggers, Outside Hammers, *Modern*	30.00	55.00	55.00

GASSER

Leopold Gasser, Vienna, Austria.

	V.G.	Exc.	Prior Year Exc. Value
HANDGUN, REVOLVER			
☐ **Montenegrin Gasser**, 11mm Montenegrin, Double Action, Break Top, Ring Extractor, *Antique*	195.00	290.00	275.00
☐ **Rast & Gasser**, 8mm R&G, Double Action, Solid Frame, *Curio*	145.00	235.00	220.00

GASTINE RENETTE

Paris, France since 1812.

	V.G.	Exc.	Prior Year Exc. Value
RIFLE, DOUBLE BARREL, SIDE-BY-SIDE			
☐ **Chapuis Standard**, Various Calibers, Boxlock Action, Engraved, Checkered Stock, Double Trigger, Open Sights, *Modern*	1,200.00	1,750.00	—
☐ **Chapuis de Luxe**, Various Calibers, Boxlock Action With Sideplates, Fancy Engraving, Checkered Stock, Double Trigger, Open Sights, *Modern*	1,500.00	2,100.00	—
☐ **Chapuis President**, Various Calibers, Boxlock Action With Sideplates, Engraved, Gold Inlays, Checkered Stock, Double Trigger, Open Sights, *Modern*	1,800.00	2,350.00	—
☐ **Chapuis**, For Claw Mounts *Add* **$100.00-$150.00**			
☐ **Chapuis**, With 20 Gauge Barrels *Add* **$325.00-$550.00**			
SHOTGUN, DOUBLE BARREL, SIDE-BY-SIDE			
☐ **Model 353**, 12 or 20 Gauge, Sidelock Action, Fancy Engraving, Fancy Wood, Checkered Stock, Double Trigger, *Modern*	4,850.00	7,000.00	—
☐ **Model 202**, 12 or 20 Gauge, Boxlock Action With Sideplates, Fancy Engraving, Fancy Wood, Checkered Stock, Double Trigger, *Modern*	1,750.00	2,450.00	—

	V.G.	Exc.	Prior Year Exc. Value
☐ **Model 98**, 12 or 20 Gauge, Boxlock Action, Engraved, Fancy Wood, Checkered Stock, Double Trigger, *Modern*	1,350.00	1,850.00	—
☐ **Model 105**, 12 or 20 Gauge, Boxlock Action, Engraved, Fancy Wood, Checkered Stock, Double Trigger, *Modern*	1,000.00	1,400.00	—
SHOTGUN, DOUBLE BARREL, OVER-UNDER			
☐ **Bretton Baby Standard**, Lightweight, Double Trigger, Checkered Stock, *Modern*	225.00	350.00	—
☐ **Bretton Baby Elite**, Lightweight, Double Trigger, Checkered Stock, *Modern*	230.00	360.00	—
☐ **Bretton Baby Luxe**, Lightweight, Double Trigger, Checkered Stock, Engraved, Chrome Frame, *Modern*	260.00	385.00	—

GATLING ARMS & AMMUNITION CO.

Birmingham, England, c. 1890.

HANDGUN, REVOLVER

☐ **Dimancea**, .450 C.F., Hammerless, Twist Opening, Double Action, *Antique*	475.00	750.00	725.00

GAULOIS

Tradename used by Mre. Francaise de Armes et Cycles de St. Etienne, France 1897-1910.

HANDGUN, MANUAL REPEATER

☐ **Palm Pistol**, 8mm, Engraved, *Curio*	325.00	525.00	475.00

GAUTEC, PETER

Lancaster, Pa. c. 1780 Kentucky Rifles & Pistols.

GAVAGE

Fab. d'Armes de Guerre de Haute Precision Armand Gavage, Leige, Belgium, c. 1940.

HANDGUN, SEMI-AUTOMATIC

☐ **.32 ACP**, Clip Fed, Blue, *Modern*	165.00	275.00	265.00
☐ **.32 ACP**, Clip Fed, Blue, Nazi-Proofed, *Modern*	240.00	350.00	335.00

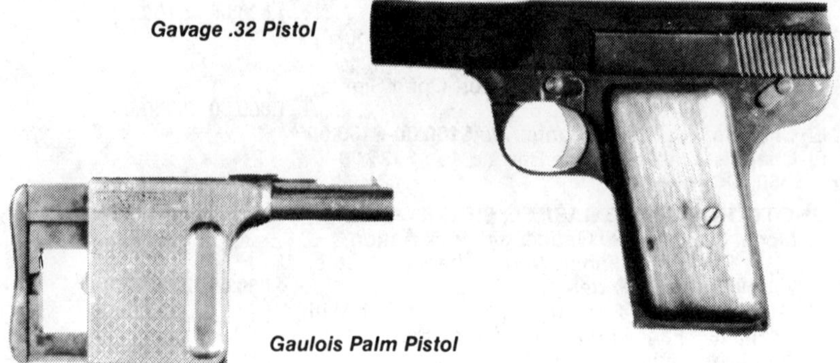

Gavage .32 Pistol

Gaulois Palm Pistol

	V.G.	Exc.	Prior Year Exc. Value

GECADO
Suhl, Germany, by G.C. Dornheim

HANDGUN, SEMI-AUTOMATIC

	V.G.	Exc.	Prior Year Exc. Value
☐ **Model 11**, .25 ACP, Clip Fed, *Modern*	75.00	125.00	125.00

GECO
Tradename used by Gustav Genschow, Hamburg, Germany.

HANDGUN, REVOLVER

	V.G.	Exc.	Prior Year Exc. Value
☐ **Velo Dog**, .25 ACP, Double Action, *Modern*	70.00	110.00	100.00
☐ **Bulldog**, .32 ACP, Double Action, *Modern*	70.00	110.00	110.00

SHOTGUN, DOUBLE BARREL, SIDE-BY-SIDE

	V.G.	Exc.	Prior Year Exc. Value
☐ **12 Gauge**, Checkered Stock, Double Triggers, Plain, *Modern*	95.00	155.00	145.00

GEM
Made by Bacon Arms Co., c. 1880.

HANDGUN, REVOLVER

	V.G.	Exc.	Prior Year Exc. Value
☐ **.22 Short R.F.**, 7 Shot, Spur Trigger, Solid Frame, Single Action, *Antique*	135.00	200.00	200.00

GEM
Made by J. Stevens Arms & Tool, Chicopee Falls, Mass.

HANDGUN, SINGLESHOT

	V.G.	Exc.	Prior Year Exc. Value
☐ **.22 or .30 R.F.**, Side-Swing Barrel, Spur Trigger, *Antique*	110.00	185.00	175.00

GERMAN MILITARY
Also See: Walther, Mauser, Luger.

AUTOMATIC WEAPON, ASSAULT RIFLE

	V.G.	Exc.	Prior Year Exc. Value
☐ **FG 42 (Type 2),** 8mm Mauser, Clip Fed, Wood Stock, *Class 3*	7225.00	8800.00	8750.00
☐ **MP43,** 8mm Mauser, Clip Fed, *Class 3*	530.00	860.00	845.00
☐ **MP44,** 8mm Mauser, Clip Fed, *Class 3*	580.00	910.00	885.00

AUTOMATIC WEAPON, HEAVY MACHINE GUN

	V.G.	Exc.	Prior Year Exc. Value
☐ **MG-08 Sledge Mount,** 8mm Mauser, Belt Fed, *Class 3*	1800.00	2500.00	2400.00
☐ **MG-08/15,** 8mm Mauser, Belt Fed, Bipod, *Class 3,*	825.00	1400.00	1400.00
☐ **MG-42,** 8mm Mauser, Belt Fed, Bipod, *Class 3*	695.00	995.00	995.00

AUTOMATIC WEAPON, LIGHT MACHINE GUN

	V.G.	Exc.	Prior Year Exc. Value
☐ **MG-34,** 8mm Mauser, Belt Fed, High Quality, Bipod, *Class 3*	1800.00	2725.00	2600.00

AUTOMATIC WEAPON, SUBMACHINE GUN

	V.G.	Exc.	Prior Year Exc. Value
☐ **EMP,** 9mm Luger, Clip Fed, *Class 3*	825.00	1400.00	1350.00
☐ **MP 18/1,** 9mm Luger, Drum Magazine, Bergmann, Wood Stock, Military, *Class 3*	1450.00	2475.00	2325.00
☐ **MP 18/1,** 9mm Luger, Drum Magazine, Bergmann, Wood Stock, Military, Dewat, *Class 3*	400.00	600.00	550.00
☐ **MP 18/1 (Modified),** 9mm Luger, Clip Fed, Bergmann, Wood Stock, Military, *Class 3*	895.00	1550.00	1550.00
☐ **MP 3008,** 9mm Luger, Clip Fed, Military, *Class 3*	1700.00	2500.00	2500.00
☐ **MP 35/1,** 9mm Luger, Clip Fed, Bergmann, Wood Stock, Military, *Class 3*	995.00	1700.00	1700.00

	V.G.	Exc.	Prior Year Exc. Value
☐ **MP 38,** 9mm Luger, Clip Fed, Schmeisser, Military, Folding Stock, *Class 3*	1600.00	2400.00	2400.00
☐ **MP 38/40,** 9mm Luger, Clip Fed, Schmeisser, Military, Folding Stock, *Class 3*	1600.00	2550.00	2550.00
☐ **MP 40,** 9mm Luger, Clip Fed, Schmeisser, Military, Folding Stock, *Class 3*	825.00	1250.00	1250.00
☐ **MP 40/1,** 9mm Luger, Clip Fed, Schmeisser, Military, Folding Stock, *Class 3*	730.00	1150.00	1150.00
HANDGUN, FLINTLOCK			
☐ **Model 1830,** .63, Military, *Antique*	430.00	600.00	575.00
HANDGUN, PERCUSSION			
☐ **Model 1860,** .63, Military, *Antique*	265.00	390.00	365.00
HANDGUN, REVOLVER			
☐ **Model 1879 Troopers Model,** 11mm German Service, Solid Frame, Single Action, Safety, 7″ Barrel, 6 Shot, *Antique*	265.00	400.00	375.00
☐ **Model 1883 Officers' Model,** 11mm German Service, Solid Frame, Single Action, Safety, 5″ Barrel, 6 Shot, *Antique*	245.00	350.00	325.00
RIFLE, BOLT ACTION			
☐ **GEW 88 Commission,** 8 x 57 JRS, Clip Fed, *Antique*	55.00	90.00	80.00
☐ **GEW 98 (Average),** 8mm Mauser, Military, *Curio*	100.00	145.00	190.00
☐ **GEW 98 Sniper,** 8mm Mauser, Scope Mounted, Military, *Curio*	520.00	690.00	975.00
☐ **K98K Sniper,** 8mm Mauser, Scope Mounted, Military, *Curio*	330.00	450.00	600.00
☐ **KAR 98 (Average),** 8mm Mauser, Military, Carbine, *Curio*	100.00	160.00	195.00
☐ **KAR 98A (Average),** 8mm Mauser, Military, Carbine, *Curio*	100.00	160.00	195.00
☐ **M-95,** 8mm Mauser, Steyr-Mannlicher, German Military, Nazi-Proofed, *Curio*	85.00	125.00	165.00
☐ **M-95,** 8mm Mauser, Steyr-Mannlicher, German Military, Carbine, Nazi-Proofed, *Curio*	80.00	115.00	155.00
☐ **Model 1871 Mauser,** .43 Mauser, Singleshot, Military, *Antique*	200.00	325.00	295.00
☐ **Model 1871 Mauser,** .43 Mauser, Carbine, Singleshot, Military, *Antique*	300.00	425.00	395.00
☐ **Model 71/84 Mauser,** .43 Mauser, Tube Feed, Military, *Antique*	210.00	350.00	320.00
☐ **Model 45 Mauser,** .22 L.R.R.F., Training Rifle, Military, *Curio*	120.00	170.00	225.00
☐ **Model 1936 Falke KK,** .22 L.R.R.F., Training Rifle, Military, *Curio*	35.00	70.00	100.00
☐ **Model 29/40,** 8mm Mauser, Nazi-Proofed, Military, *Curio*	80.00	120.00	185.00
☐ **Model 33/40,** 8mm Mauser, Nazi-Proofed, Military, *Curio*	100.00	150.00	225.00
☐ **VK-98,** 8mm Mauser, Nazi-Proofed, Military, *Curio*	130.00	190.00	260.00
☐ **VZ-24 BRNO,** 8mm Mauser, Nazi-Proofed, Military, *Curio*	80.00	145.00	175.00
☐ **Needle Gun,** 11mm, Singleshot, Military, *Antique*	220.00	565.00	500.00

	V.G.	Exc.	Prior Year Exc. Value
RIFLE, PERCUSSION			
☐ **M1839,** .69, Musket, Brass Furniture, Military, *Antique*	275.00	430.00	395.00
☐ **M1842,** .75, Musket, Brass Furniture, Military, *Antique*	235.00	350.00	325.00
RIFLE, SEMI-AUTOMATIC			
☐ **G43,** 8mm Mauser, Clip Fed, 10 Shot, Military, *Curio*	190.00	265.00	345.00
☐ **GEW 41,** 8mm Mauser, 10 Shot, Military, *Curio*	280.00	420.00	475.00
☐ **GEW 41 (W),** 8mm Mauser, 10 Shot, Military, *Curio*	265.00	385.00	450.00
☐ **KAR 43 Sniper,** 8mm Mauser, Scope Mounted, Clip Fed, 10 Shot, Military, *Curio*	375.00	650.00	740.00
☐ **VG 2,** 8mm Mauser, Clip Fed, 10 Shot, Military, *Curio*	235.00	315.00	450.00
RIFLE, SINGLESHOT			
☐ **Model 1869 Werder,** 11.5mm, Bavarian, *Antique*	460.00	725.00	675.00

German Military Model 1879 Revolver

German Military Model 1883 Revolver

German Military Model 1871 Rifle

German Military Model 1871/84 Rifle

	V.G.	Exc.	Prior Year Exc. Value

GESSCER, GEORG
Saxony, 1591-1611.

HANDGUN, WHEEL-LOCK

	V.G.	Exc.	Prior Year Exc. Value
☐ **Pair**, Military, Inlays, Pear Pommel, Medium Ornamentation, *Antique*	15,000.00	20,000.00	20.000.00

GEVARM
Gevelot, St. Etienne, France.

RIFLE, SEMI-AUTOMATIC

	V.G.	Exc.	Prior Year Exc. Value
☐ **Model A3**, .22 L.R.R.F., Target Sights, Clip Fed, *Modern*	95.00	160.00	160.00
☐ **Model A6**, .22 L.R.R.F., Open Sights, Clip Fed, *Modern*	75.00	125.00	125.00
☐ **Model A7**, .22 L.R.R.F., Target Sights, Clip Fed, *Modern*	110.00	190.00	185.00
☐ **.32 S & W**, 5 Shot, Double Action, Top Break, *Modern*	50.00	100.00	95.00
☐ **.38 S & W**, 5 Shot, Double Action, Top Break, *Modern*	55.00	100.00	95.00

GIBRALTER
Made by Stevens Arms.

SHOTGUN, SINGLESHOT

	V.G.	Exc.	Prior Year Exc. Value
☐ **Model 116**, Various Gauges, Hammer, Automatic Ejector, Raised Matted Rib, *Modern*	45.00	65.00	65.00

GILL, THOMAS
London, England 1770-1812.

HANDGUN, FLINTLOCK

	V.G.	Exc.	Prior Year Exc. Value
☐ **.68**, Pocket Pistol, Octagon Barrel, Plain, High Quality, *Antique*	665.00	975.00	950.00

GLASER WAFFEN
Zurich, Switzerland.

HANDGUN, SINGLESHOT

	V.G.	Exc.	Prior Year Exc. Value
☐ **Target Pistol**, .22 L.R.R.F., Toggle Breech, Francotte, *Modern*	245.00	375.00	350.00

RIFLE, BOLT ACTION

	V.G.	Exc.	Prior Year Exc. Value
☐ **Custom Rifle**, Various Calibers, Fancy Wood, *Modern*	635.00	1,050.00	1,000.00

RIFLE, SINGLESHOT

	V.G.	Exc.	Prior Year Exc. Value
☐ **Heeren Rifle**, Various Calibers, Engraved, Fancy Wood, *Modern*	1,600.00	2,500.00	2,400.00

	V.G.	Exc.	Prior Year Exc. Value

GLASSBRENNER, DAVID
Lancaster, Pa., c. 1800. See Kentucky Rifles.

GLAZIER, JOHN
Belleville, Ind., c. 1820. See Kentucky Rifles.

GLENFIELD
See Marlin.

GLENN, ROBERT
Edinburgh, Scotland, c. 1860. Made fine copies of Highland Pistols.

HANDGUN, SNAPHAUNCE

	V.G.	Exc.	Prior Year Exc. Value
☐ **Replica Highland**, All Brass, Engraved, Ovoid Pommel, *Antique*	1,900.00	3,000.00	2,850.00

GLISENTI
Soc. Siderugica Glisenti, Turin, Italy, c. 1889-1930.

HANDGUN, REVOLVER

	V.G.	Exc.	Prior Year Exc. Value
☐ **MI889**, 10.4mm Glisenti, Double Action, Folding Trigger, Military, *Curio*	90.00	145.00	135.00
☐ **MI889**, 10.4mm Glisenti, Double Action, Trigger Guard, Military, *Curio*	85.00	135.00	130.00

HANDGUN, SEMI-AUTOMATIC

	V.G.	Exc.	Prior Year Exc. Value
☐ **Brixia**, 9mm Glisenti, Clip Fed, Hard Rubber Grips, *Modern*	275.00	400.00	350.00
☐ **M910 Army**, 9mm Glisenti, Clip Fed, Wood Grips, *Modern*	275.00	425.00	375.00
☐ **M910 Navy**, 9mm Glisenti, Clip Fed, Hard Rubber Grips, *Modern*	250.00	400.00	350.00
☐ **M906**, 7.63 Mauser, Clip Fed, Military, *Modern*	325.00	500.00	425.00

GOLDEN EAGLE
Nikko Arms Co. Ltd., Japan.

RIFLE, BOLT ACTION

	V.G.	Exc.	Prior Year Exc. Value
☐ **Model 7000**, Various Calibers, Grade 1, Checkered Stock, *Modern*	245.00	395.00	375.00
☐ **Model 7000**, Various African Calibers, Grade 1, Checkered Stock, *Modern*	290.00	420.00	400.00
☐ **Model 7000**, Various Calibers, Grade 2, Checkered Stock, *Modern*	290.00	420.00	400.00
☐ **Model 7000**, Various African Calibers, Grade 2, Checkered Stock, *Modern*	340.00	475.00	450.00

SHOTGUN, DOUBLE BARREL, OVER-UNDER

	V.G.	Exc.	Prior Year Exc. Value
☐ **Model 5000**, 12 and 20 Gauges, Field Grade, Vent Rib, Checkered Stock, Light Engraving, Gold Overlay, *Modern*	420.00	595.00	575.00
☐ **Model 5000**, 12 and 20 Gauges, Skeet Grade, Vent Rib, Checkered Stock, Light Engraving, Gold Overlay, *Modern*	490.00	695.00	675.00
☐ **Model 5000**, 12 and 20 Gauges, Trap Grade, Vent Rib, Checkered Stock, Light Engraving, Gold Overlay, *Modern*	440.00	695.00	675.00

	V.G.	Exc.	Prior Year Exc. Value
☐ **Model 5000**, 12 and 20 Gauges, Field Grade 2, Vent Rib, Checkered Stock, Light Engraving, Gold Overlay, *Modern*	525.00	695.00	675.00
☐ **Model 5000**, 12 and 20 Gauges, Skeet Grade 2, Vent Rib, Checkered Stock, Light Engraving, Gold Overlay, *Modern*	595.00	775.00	750.00
☐ **Model 5000**, 12 and 20 Gauges, Trap Grade 2, Vent Rib, Checkered Stock, Light Engraving, Gold Overlay, *Modern*	575.00	730.00	700.00
☐ **Model 5000 Grandee**, 12 and 20 Gauges, Field Grade 3, Vent Rib, Checkered Stock, Fancy Engraving, Gold Overlay, *Modern*	1,685.00	2,550.00	2,500.00
☐ **Model 5000 Grandee**, 12 and 20 Gauges, Skeet Grade 3, Vent Rib, Checkered Stock, Fancy Engraving, Gold Overlay, *Modern*	1,895.00	2,800.00	2,750.00
☐ **Model 5000 Grandee**, 12 Ga., Trap Grade 3, Vent Rib, Checkered Stock, Fancy Engraving, Gold Overlay, *Modern*	1,895.00	2,800.00	2,750.00

GONTER, PETER

Lancaster, Pa. 1770-1778. See Kentucky Rifles.

GOFF, DANIEL

London, England 1779-1810.

HANDGUN, FLINTLOCK

	V.G.	Exc.	Prior Year Exc. Value
☐ **Duelling Pistols**, .50, Cased pair, with Accessories, *Antique*	1,495.00	2,400.00	2,350.00

GOLCHER, JAMES

Philadelphia, Pa. 1820-1833.

GOLCHER, JOHN

Easton, Pa., c. 1775.

GOLCHER, JOSEPH

Philadelphia, Pa., c. 1800.

GOOSE GUN

Made by Stevens Arms.

SHOTGUN, SINGLESHOT

	V.G.	Exc.	Prior Year Exc. Value
☐ **Model 89 Dreadnaught**, Various Gauges, Hammer, *Modern*	45.00	65.00	65.00

GOVERNOR

Made by Bacon Arms Co.

HANDGUN, REVOLVER

	V.G.	Exc.	Prior Year Exc. Value
☐ **.22 Short R.F.**, 7 Shot, Spur Trigger, Solid Frame, Single Action, *Antique*	95.00	165.00	160.00

GOVERNOR

Various makers, c. 1880.

	V.G.	Exc.	Prior Year Exc. Value
HANDGUN, REVOLVER			
☐ **.32 S & W**, 5 Shot, Double Action, Top Break, *Modern*	50.00	95.00	95.00
☐ **.38 S & W**, 5 Shot, Double Action, Top Break, *Modern*	55.00	100.00	95.00

GRAEFF, WM.

Reading, Pa. 1751-1784. See Kentucky Rifles.

GRANT HAMMOND

New Haven, Conn. 1915-1917.

	V.G.	Exc.	Prior Year Exc. Value
HANDGUN, SEMI-AUTOMATIC			
☐ **U.S. Test**, .45 ACP, Clip Fed, Hammer, *Curio*	4,600.00	7,650.00	7,500.00

GRANT, W.L.

	V.G.	Exc.	Prior Year Exc. Value
HANDGUN, REVOLVER			
☐ **.22 Long R.F.**, 6 Shot, Single Action, Solid Frame, Spur Trigger, *Antique*	145.00	230.00	220.00
☐ **.32 Short R.F.**, 6 Shot, Single Action, Solid Frame, Spur Trigger, *Antique*	165.00	250.00	235.00

GRAVE, JOHN

Lancaster, Pa. 1769-1773. See Kentucky Rifles.

GREAT WESTERN

Venice, Calif. 1954-1962. Moved to North Hollywood, Calif. in 1959.

	V.G.	Exc.	Prior Year Exc. Value
HANDGUN, REVOLVER			
☐ **Frontier**, .22 L.R.R.F., Single Action, Western Style, *Modern*	30.00	50.00	50.00
☐ **Frontier**, Various Calibers, Single Action, Western Style, *Modern*	40.00	65.00	65.00
☐ **Deputy**, .22 L.R.R.F., Single Action, Western Style, *Modern*	30.00	50.00	50.00
☐ **Deputy**, .22 L.R.R.F., Single Action, Western Style, *Modern*	30.00	50.00	50.00
☐ **Buntline**, Various Calibers, Single Action, Western Style, *Modern*	50.00	75.00	70.00
HANDGUN, DOUBLE BARREL, OVER-UNDER			
☐ **Double Derringer**, .38 Spec., Remington Copy, *Modern*	30.00	45.00	45.00

GREAT WESTERN GUN WORKS

Pittsburg, Pa. 1860 to about 1923.

	V.G.	Exc.	Prior Year Exc. Value
HANDGUN, REVOLVER			
☐ **.22 Short R.F.**, 7 Shot, Spur Trigger, Solid Frame, Single Action, *Antique*	95.00	165.00	160.00
RIFLE, PERCUSSION			
☐ **No. 5**, Various Calibers, Various Barrel Lengths, Plains Rifle, Octagon Barrel, Brass Fittings, *Antique*	365.00	575.00	550.00

GREEK MILITARY

RIFLE, BOLT ACTION

	V.G.	Exc.	Prior Year Exc. Value
☐ **M 1903 Mannlicher Schoenauer,** 6.5mm M.S., Military, *Curio*	50.00	90.00	130.00
☐ **M 1903 Mannlicher Schoenauer,** 8mm Mauser, Military, *Curio*	55.00	95.00	140.00
☐ **M 1930 Greek,** 8mm Mauser, Military, *Curio*	55.00	100.00	155.00

GREENER, W.W.

Established in 1829 in Northumberland, England as W. Greener, moved to Birmingham, England in 1844; name changed to W.W. Greener in 1860, and to W.W. Greener & Son in 1879.

SHOTGUN, DOUBLE BARREL, SIDE-BY-SIDE

☐ **Various Gauges**, Single Non-Selective Trigger *Add* **$185.00-$280.00**

☐ **Various Gauges**, Single Selective Trigger *Add* **$265.00-$385.00**

	V.G.	Exc.	Prior Year Exc. Value
☐ **Crown DH-55**, Various Gauges, Box Lock, Automatic Ejector, Checkered Stock, Fancy Engraving, *Modern*	1,875.00	2,700.00	2,675.00
☐ **Empire**, 12 Ga. Mag. 3", Box Lock, Hammerless, Light Engraving, Checkered Stock, *Modern*	890.00	1,395.00	1,375.00
☐ **Empire**, 12 Ga. Mag. 3", Box Lock, Hammerless, Light Engraving, Checkered Stock, Automatic Ejector, *Modern*	995.00	1,800.00	1,775.00
☐ **Empire Deluxe**, 12 Ga. Mag. 3", Box Lock, Hammerless, Engraved, Checkered Stock, *Modern*	1,075.00	1,800.00	1,775.00
☐ **Empire Deluxe**, 12 Ga. Mag. 3", Box Lock, Hammerless, Engraved, Checkered Stock, Automatic Ejector, *Modern*	1,250.00	2,000.00	1,975.00
☐ **Far-Killer F35**, 10 Ga. 3½", Box Lock, Hammerless, Engraved, Checkered Stock, *Modern*	1,175.00	1,950.00	1,900.00
☐ **Far-Killer F35**, 10 Ga. 3½", Box Lock, Hammerless, Engraved, Checkered Stock, Automatic Ejector, *Modern*	1,875.00	2,825.00	2,750.00
☐ **Far-Killer F35**, 12 Ga. Mag. 3", Box Lock, Hammerless, Engraved, Checkered Stock, *Modern*	1,635.00	2,300.00	2,275.00
☐ **Far-Killer F35**, 12 Ga. Mag. 3", Box Lock, Hammerless, Engraved, Checkered Stock, Automatic Ejector, *Modern*	1,895.00	2,800.00	2,775.00
☐ **Far-Killer F35**, 8 Ga., Box Lock, Hammerless, Engraved, Checkered Stock, *Modern*	1,425.00	2,300.00	2,275.00
☐ **Far-Killer F35**, 8 Ga., Box Lock, Hammerless, Engraved, Checkered Stock, Automatic Ejector, *Modern*	2,000.00	3,000.00	2,975.00
☐ **Jubilee DH-35**, Various Gauges, Box Lock, Automatic Ejector, Checkered Stock, Engraved, *Modern*	1,225.00	2,000.00	1,975.00
☐ **Royal DH-75**, Various Gauges, Box Lock, Automatic Ejector, Checkered Stock, Fancy Engraving, *Modern*	2,535.00	3,525.00	3,475.00

	V.G.	Exc.	Prior Year Exc. Value
☐ **Sovereign DH-40**, Various Gauges, Box Lock, Automatic Ejector, Checkered Stock, Engraved, *Modern*	1,675.00	2,575.00	2,525.00
SHOTGUN, SINGLESHOT			
☐ **G. P. Martini**, 12 Ga., Checkered Stock, Takedown, *Modern*	170.00	295.00	275.00

GREGORY

Mt. Vernon, Ohio 1837-1842. See Kentucky Rifles.

GREIFELT & CO.

Suhl, Germany from 1885.

	V.G.	Exc.	Prior Year Exc. Value
COMBINATION WEAPON, OVER-UNDER			
☐ **Various Calibers**, Solid Rib, Engraved, Checkered Stock, *Modern*	2,935.00	4,000.00	3,950.00
☐ **Various Calibers**, Solid Rib, Engraved, Checkered Stock, Automatic Ejector, *Modern*	3,875.00	5,025.00	4,950.00
COMBINATION WEAPON, DRILLING			
☐ **Various Calibers**, Fancy Wood, Fancy Checkering, Engraved, *Modern*	3,500.00	4,750.00	4,650.00
☐ **Various Calibers**, Engraved, Checkered Stock, *Modern*	2,600.00	3,700.00	3,600.00
RIFLE, BOLT ACTION			
☐ **Sport**, .22 Hornet, Checkered Stock, Express Sights, *Modern*	525.00	800.00	775.00
SHOTGUN, DOUBLE BARREL, OVER-UNDER			
☐ **Various Gauges**, Single Trigger *Add* **$245.00-$350.00**			
☐ **Various Gauges**, For Vent Rib *Add* **$195.00-$300.00**			
☐ **#1**, .410 Ga., Automatic Ejector, Fancy Engraving, Checkered Stock, Fancy Wood, Solid Rib, *Modern*	4,100.00	5,625.00	5,500.00
☐ **#1**, Various Gauges, Automatic Ejector, Fancy Engraving, Checkered Stock, Fancy Wood, Solid Rib, *Modern*	2,950.00	3,875.00	3,800.00
☐ **#3**, .410 Ga., Automatic Ejector, Engraved, Checkered Stock, Solid Rib, *Modern*	2,975.00	3,900.00	3,850.00
☐ **#3**, Various Gauges, Automatic Ejector, Engraved, Checkered Stock, Solid Rib, *Modern*	1,825.00	2,500.00	2,400.00
☐ **Model 143E**, Various Gauges, Automatic Ejector, Engraved, Checkered Stock, Solid Rib, Double Trigger, *Modern*	1,250.00	2,000.00	1,950.00
☐ **Model 143E**, Various Gauges, Automatic Ejector, Engraved, Checkered Stock, Vent Rib, Single Selective Trigger, *Modern*	1,635.00	2,300.00	2,250.00
SHOTGUN, DOUBLE BARREL, SIDE-BY-SIDE			
☐ **Model 103**, 12 and 16 Gauges, Box Lock, Double Trigger, Checkered Stock, Light Engraving, *Modern*	775.00	1,100.00	1,050.00
☐ **Model 103E**, 12 and 16 Gauges, Box Lock, Double Trigger, Checkered Stock, Light Engraving, Automatic Ejector, *Modern*	995.00	1,400.00	1,375.00

	V.G.	Exc.	Prior Year Exc. Value
☐ **Model 22**, 12 and 16 Gauges, Box Lock, Double Trigger, Checkered Stock, Engraved, *Modern*	685.00	1,050.00	1,000.00
☐ **Model 22E**, 12 and 16 Gauges, Box Lock, Double Trigger, Checkered Stock, Engraved, Automatic Ejector, *Modern*	995.00	1,500.00	1,450.00

GREYHAWK ARMS CORP.

South El Monte, Calif., c. 1975.

RIFLE, SINGLESHOT

	V.G.	Exc.	Prior Year Exc. Value
☐ **Model 74**, Various Calibers, Rolling Block, Octagon Barrel, Open Rear Sight, Reproduction, *Modern*	85.00	125.00	125.00

GRIFFEN & HOWE

N.Y.C. 1923, absorbed by Abercrombie & Fitch 1930.

RIFLE, BOLT ACTION

	V.G.	Exc.	Prior Year Exc. Value
☐ **Mauser 98**, .30/06, Sporterized, Engraved, Fancy Wood, Fancy Checkering, *Modern*	995.00	1,800.00	1,750.00
☐ **Mauser 98**, .30/06, Sporterized, Fancy Engraving, Fancy Wood, Fancy Checkering, Gold Inlays, *Modern*	3,000.00	4,500.00	4,500.00
☐ **Springfield**, .30/06, Sporterized, Engraved, Fancy Wood, Fancy Checkering, *Modern*	975.00	1,775.00	1,750.00
☐ **Springfield**, .30/06, Sporterized, Fancy Engraving, Fancy Wood, Fancy Checkering, *Modern*	1,950.00	3,250.00	3,250.00
☐ **Winchester M70**, .30/06, Sporterized, Engraved, Fancy Wood, Fancy Checkering, *Modern*	1,200.00	1,975.00	1,950.00

GROOM, RICHARD

London, England, c. 1855.

HANDGUN, FLINTLOCK

	V.G.	Exc.	Prior Year Exc. Value
☐ **.68**, East India Company, Calvary Pistol, Military, Tapered Round Barrel, Brass Furniture, *Antique*	995.00	1,850.00	1,800.00

GROSS ARMS CO.

Tiffin, Ohio 1862-1865.

HANDGUN, REVOLVER

	V.G.	Exc.	Prior Year Exc. Value
☐ **.22 Short R.F.**, 7 Shot, Spur Trigger, Tip-Up, *Antique*	365.00	625.00	600.00
☐ **.25 Short R.F.**, 6 Shot, Single Action, Spur Trigger, Tip-Up, *Antique*	370.00	650.00	625.00
☐ **.32 Short R.F.**, 5 Shot, Spur Trigger, Tip-Up, *Antique*	370.00	625.00	600.00

GRUENEL

Gruenig & Elmiger, Malters, Switzerland.

RIFLE, BOLT ACTION

	V.G.	Exc.	Prior Year Exc. Value
☐ **Model K 31**, .308 Win., U.I.T. Target Rifle, Target Sights, Ventilated Forestock, *Modern*	545.00	875.00	850.00

	V.G.	Exc.	Prior Year Exc. Value
☐ **Match 300m**, Various Calibers, Offhand Target Rifle, Target Sights, Ventilated Forestock, Palm Rest, Hook Buttplate, *Modern*	695.00	1,125.00	1,075.00
☐ **U.I.T. Standard**, .308 Win., Target Rifle, Target Sights, Ventilated Forestock, *Modern*	495.00	750.00	725.00

GUARDIAN

Made by Bacon Arms Co., c. 1880.

HANDGUN, REVOLVER

	V.G.	Exc.	Prior Year Exc. Value
☐ **.22 Short R.F.**, 7 Shot, Spur Trigger, Solid Frame, Single Action, *Antique*	95.00	165.00	160.00
☐ **.32 Short R.F.**, 5 Shot, Spur Trigger, Solid Frame, Single Action, *Antique*	95.00	175.00	170.00

GUMPH, CHRISTOPHER

Lancaster, Pa. 1779-1803. See Kentucky Rifles and Pistols.

GUSTAF, CARL

See Husqvarna.

GUSTLOFF WERKE

Suhl, Germany

HANDGUN, SEMI-AUTOMATIC

	V.G.	Exc.	Prior Year Exc. Value
☐ **.32 ACP,** Clip Fed, Hammer, Single Action, *Modern*	1075.00	1800.00	1900.00
☐ **.380 ACP,** Clip Fed, Hammer, Single Action, *Modern*	1950.00	3100.00	3300.00

RIFLE, BOLT ACTION

	V.G.	Exc.	Prior Year Exc. Value
☐ **Mauser M98,** 8mm Mauser, Military, *Curio*	60.00	95.00	155.00
☐ **Model KKW,** .22 L.R.R.F., Pre-WW2, Singleshot, Tangent Sights, Military Style Stock, *Modern*	290.00	410.00	435.00

SHOTGUN, DOUBLE BARREL, SIDE-BY-SIDE

	V.G.	Exc.	Prior Year Exc. Value
☐ **16 Ga.,** Engraved, Color Case Hardened Frame, *Modern*	360.00	490.00	500.00

GYROJET

See M.B. Associates.

Gustloff Werke .32 Pistol

	V.G.	Exc.	Prior Year Exc. Value

HACKETT, EDWIN AND GEORGE
London, England, c. 1870.

SHOTGUN, DOUBLE BARREL, SIDE-BY-SIDE

	V.G.	Exc.	Prior Year Exc. Value
☐ **10 Ga. 2⅞"**, Damascus Barrel, Plain, *Antique*	135.00	200.00	190.00

HADDEN, JAMES
Philadelphia, Pa., c. 1769. See Kentucky Rifles and Pistols.

HAEFFER, JOHN
Lancaster, Pa., c. 1800. See Kentucky Rifles and Pistols.

HAENEL, C.G.
C.G. Haenel Waffen und Fahrradfabrik, Suhl, Germany 1840-1945

HANDGUN, SEMI-AUTOMATIC

	V.G.	Exc.	Prior Year Exc. Value
☐ **Schmiesser Model 1**, .25 ACP, Clip Fed, *Modern*	155.00	245.00	225.00
☐ **Schmiesser Model 2**, .25 ACP, Clip Fed, *Modern*	175.00	290.00	275.00

RIFLE, BOLT ACTION

	V.G.	Exc.	Prior Year Exc. Value
☐ **Model 88**, Various Calibers, Sporting Rifle, Half-Octagon Barrel, Open Rear Sight, *Modern*	200.00	345.00	335.00
☐ **Model 88 Sporter**, Various Calibers, 5 Shot Clip, Half-Octagon Barrel, Open Rear Sight, *Modern*	225.00	385.00	375.00

HAFDASA
Hispano Argentina Fab. de Automoviles, Buenos Aires, Argentina, c. 1935.

HANDGUN, SEMI-AUTOMATIC

	V.G.	Exc.	Prior Year Exc. Value
☐ **.22 L.R.R.F.**, Blowback, *Modern*	225.00	325.00	325.00

HALF-BREED
Made by Hopkins & Allen, c. 1880.

HANDGUN, REVOLVER

	V.G.	Exc.	Prior Year Exc. Value
☐ **.32 Short R.F.**, 5 Shot, Spur Trigger, Solid Frame, Single Action, *Antique*	95.00	170.00	170.00

HAMMERLI
Lenzburg, Switzerland.

HANDGUN, REVOLVER

	V.G.	Exc.	Prior Year Exc. Value
☐ **Virginian**, .357 Magnum, Single Action, Western Style, *Modern*	145.00	200.00	200.00
☐ **Virginian**, .45 Colt, Single Action, Western Style, *Modern*	145.00	225.00	225.00

HANDGUN, SEMI-AUTOMATIC

	V.G.	Exc.	Prior Year Exc. Value
☐ **Model 200 Walther Olympia**, .22 L.R.R.F., Target Pistol, *Modern*	360.00	520.00	500.00
☐ **Model 200 Walther Olympia**, .22 L.R.R.F., Target Pistol, Muzzle Brake, *Modern*	415.00	570.00	550.00
☐ **Model 201 Walther Olympia**, .22 L.R.R.F., Target Pistol, Adjustable Grips, *Modern*	365.00	520.00	500.00
☐ **Model 202 Walther Olympia**, .22 L.R.R.F., Target Pistol, Adjustable Grips, *Modern*	415.00	570.00	550.00

Hafdasa

Haenel Schmeisser Model 1

	V.G.	Exc.	Prior Year Exc. Value
□ **Model 203 Walther Olympia**, .22 L.R.R.F., Target Pistol, Adjustable Grips, *Modern*	470.00	625.00	600.00
□ **Model 203 Walther Olympia**, .22 L.R.R.F., Target Pistol, Adjustable Grips, Muzzle Brake, *Modern*	485.00	695.00	675.00
□ **Model 204 Walther Olympia**, .22 L.R.R.F., Target Pistol, *Modern*	485.00	695.00	675.00
□ **Model 204 Walther Olympia**, .22 L.R.R.F., Target Pistol, Muzzle Brake, *Modern*	570.00	750.00	725.00
□ **Model 205 Walther Olympia**, .22 L.R.R.F., Target Pistol, Fancy Wood, *Modern*	570.00	750.00	725.00
□ **Model 205 Walther Olympia**, .22 L.R.R.F., Target Pistol, Fancy Wood, Muzzle Brake, *Modern*	625.00	800.00	785.00
□ **Model 206**, .22 L.R.R.F., Target Pistol, *Modern*	420.00	595.00	575.00
□ **Model 207**, .22 L.R.R.F., Target Pistol, Adjustable Grips, *Modern*	545.00	675.00	650.00
□ **Model 208**, .22 L.R.R.F., Target Pistol, Clip Fed, Adjustable Grips, *Modern*	545.00	800.00	775.00
□ **Model 208**, .22 L.R.R.F., Target Pistol, Clip Fed, Adjustable Grips, Left-Hand, *Modern*	570.00	810.00	785.00
□ **Model 209**, .22 Short R.F., Target Pistol, 5 Shot Clip, Muzzle Brake, *Modern*	490.00	670.00	650.00
□ **Model 210**, .22 L.R.R.F., Target Pistol, *Modern*	470.00	645.00	625.00
□ **Model 210**, .22 L.R.R.F., Target Pistol, Adjustable Grips, *Modern*	490.00	670.00	650.00
□ **Model 211**, .22 L.R.R.F., Target Pistol, Clip Fed, *Modern*	520.00	775.00	750.00
□ **Model 212 SIG**, .22 L.R.R.F., Target Pistol, Clip Fed, *Modern*	625.00	825.00	790.00
□ **Model 215**, .22 L.R.R.F., Target Pistol, Clip Fed, *Modern*	490.00	690.00	675.00
□ **Model 230-1**, .22 Short R.F., Target Pistol, 5 Shot Clip, *Modern*	520.00	725.00	700.00

	V.G.	Exc.	Prior Year Exc. Value
☐ **Model 230-2**, .22 Short R.F., Target Pistol, 5 Shot Clip, Adjustable Grips, *Modern*	570.00	795.00	770.00
☐ **Model 230-2**, .22 Short R.F., Target Pistol, 5 Shot Clip, Adjustable Grips, Left-Hand, *Modern*	595.00	810.00	785.00
☐ **Model P-240 SIG**, .22 L.R.R.F., Target Pistol, Clip Fed, Conversion Unit Only, *Modern*	390.00	545.00	525.00
☐ **Model P-240 SIG**, .32 S & W Long, Clip Fed, Target Pistol, Cased with Accessories, *Modern*	545.00	795.00	775.00
☐ **Model P-240 SIG**, .38 Special, Clip Fed, Target Pistol, Cased with Accessories, *Modern*	575.00	845.00	825.00
HANDGUN, SINGLESHOT			
☐ **Model 100**, .22 L.R.R.F., Target Pistol, *Modern*	450.00	585.00	575.00
☐ **Model 100 Deluxe**, .22 L.R.R.F., Target Pistol, *Modern*	475.00	665.00	650.00
☐ **Model 101**, .22 L.R.R.F., Target Pistol, *Modern*	475.00	635.00	625.00
☐ **Model 102**, .22 L.R.R.F., Target Pistol, *Modern*	450.00	620.00	600.00
☐ **Model 102 Deluxe**, .22 L.R.R.F., Target Pistol, *Modern*	500.00	685.00	675.00
☐ **Model 103**, .22 L.R.R.F., Target Pistol, Carved, Inlays, *Modern*	500.00	740.00	725.00
☐ **Model 103**, .22 L.R.R.F., Target Pistol, Carved, *Modern*	450.00	665.00	650.00
☐ **Model 104**, .22 L.R.R.F., Target Pistol, Round Barrel, *Modern*	350.00	615.00	600.00
☐ **Model 105**, .22 L.R.R.F., Target Pistol, Octagon Barrel, *Modern*	475.00	665.00	650.00
☐ **Model 106**, .22 L.R.R.F., Target Pistol, Round Barrel, *Modern*	450.00	640.00	625.00
☐ **Model 107**, .22 L.R.R.F., Target Pistol, Octagon Barrel, *Modern*	525.00	735.00	725.00
☐ **Model 107 Deluxe**, .22 L.R.R.F., Target Pistol, Octagon Barrel, Engraved, *Modern*	625.00	950.00	950.00
☐ **Model 110**, .22 L.R.R.F., Target Pistol, *Modern*	425.00	615.00	600.00
☐ **Model 120**, .22 L.R.R.F., Target Pistol, Heavy Barrel, *Modern*	350.00	510.00	500.00
☐ **Model 120**, .22 L.R.R.F., Target Pistol, Heavy Barrel, Adjustable Grips, *Modern*	375.00	535.00	525.00
☐ **Model 120**, .22 L.R.R.F., Target Pistol, Heavy Barrel, Left-Hand, Adjustable Grips, *Modern*	375.00	540.00	535.00
☐ **Model 120-1**, .22 L.R.R.F., Target Pistol, *Modern*	350.00	500.00	500.00
☐ **Model 120-2**, .22 L.R.R.F., Target Pistol, Adjustable Grips, *Modern*	375.00	525.00	525.00
☐ **Model 120-2**, .22 L.R.R.F., Target Pistol, Adjustable Grips, Left-Hand, *Modern*	375.00	540.00	535.00
☐ **Model 150**, .22 L.R.R.F., Target Pistol, *Modern*	650.00	900.00	900.00
☐ **Model 152 Electronic**, .22 L.R.R.F., Target Pistol, *Modern*	550.00	865.00	850.00
RIFLE, BOLT ACTION			
☐ **Model 45**, .22 L.R.R.F., Singleshot, Thumbhole Stock, Target Sights, with Accessories, *Modern*	420.00	585.00	575.00
☐ **Model 54**, .22 L.R.R.F., Singleshot, Thumbhole Stock, Target Sights, with Accessories, *Modern*	420.00	585.00	575.00
☐ **Model 503**, .22 L.R.R.F., Singleshot, Thumbhole Stock, Target Sights, with Accessories, *Modern*	420.00	585.00	575.00

	V.G.	Exc.	Prior Year Exc. Value
☐ **Model 506**, .22 L.R.R.F., Singleshot, Thumbhole Stock, Target Sights, with Accessories, *Modern*	440.00	625.00	600.00
☐ **Olympia 300 Meter**, Various Calibers, Singleshot, Thumbhole Stock, Target Sights, with Accessories, *Modern*	490.00	720.00	700.00
☐ **Tanner**, Various Calibers, Singleshot, Thumbhole Stock, Target Sights, with Accessories, *Modern*	590.00	845.00	825.00
☐ **Sporting Rifle**, Various Calibers, Set Triggers, Fancy Wood, Checkered Stock, Open Sights, *Modern*	395.00	590.00	575.00

HAMPTON, JOHN

Dauphin County, Pa. See Kentucky Rifles and Pistols.

HARD PAN

Made by Hood Firearms, c. 1875.

HANDGUN, REVOLVER

	V.G.	Exc.	Prior Year Exc. Value
☐ **.22 Short R.F.**, 7 Shot, Spur Trigger, Solid Frame, Single Action, *Antique*	95.00	165.00	160.00
☐ **.32 Short R.F.**, 5 Shot, Spur Trigger, Solid Frame, Single Action, *Antique*	95.00	170.00	170.00

HARPERS FERRY ARMS CO.

RIFLE, FLINTLOCK

	V.G.	Exc.	Prior Year Exc. Value
☐ **.72 Lafayette**, Musket, Reproduction, *Antique*	175.00	280.00	275.00

RIFLE, PERCUSSION

	V.G.	Exc.	Prior Year Exc. Value
☐ **.51 Maynard**, Carbine, Breech Loader, Reproduction, *Antique*	140.00	190.00	185.00
☐ **.58**, 1861 Springfield, Rifled, Musket, Reproduction, *Antique*	140.00	190.00	185.00

HARRINGTON & RICHARDSON ARMS CO.

Worcester, Mass. Successors to Wesson & Harrington, 1874 to Date.

AUTOMATIC WEAPON, ASSAULT RIFLE

	V.G.	Exc.	Prior Year Exc. Value
☐ **T-48,** .308 Win., Clip Fed, Military, *Class 3*	2550.00	3600.00	3500.00

AUTOMATIC WEAPON, SUBMACHINE GUN

	V.G.	Exc.	Prior Year Exc. Value
☐ **Riesing M50,** .45 ACP, Commercial, Clip Fed, *Class 3*	290.00	450.00	425.00

HANDGUN, REVOLVER

	V.G.	Exc.	Prior Year Exc. Value
☐ **Abilene Anniversary,** .22 L.R.R.F., Commemorative, *Curio*	67.00	100.00	105.00
☐ **American,** Various Calibers, Double Action, Solid Frame, *Modern*	48.00	85.00	80.00
☐ **Auto Ejecting,** Various Calibers, Top Break, Hammer, Double Action, *Modern*	68.00	120.00	115.00
☐ **Bobby,** Various Calibers, 6 Shot, Top Break, Double Action, *Modern*	63.00	100.00	95.00
☐ **Bulldog,** Various Calibers, Double Action, Solid Frame, *Modern*	47.00	85.00	80.00
☐ **Defender,** .38 S & W, Top Break, 6 Shot, Double Action, Adjustable Sights, *Modern*	70.00	110.00	100.00

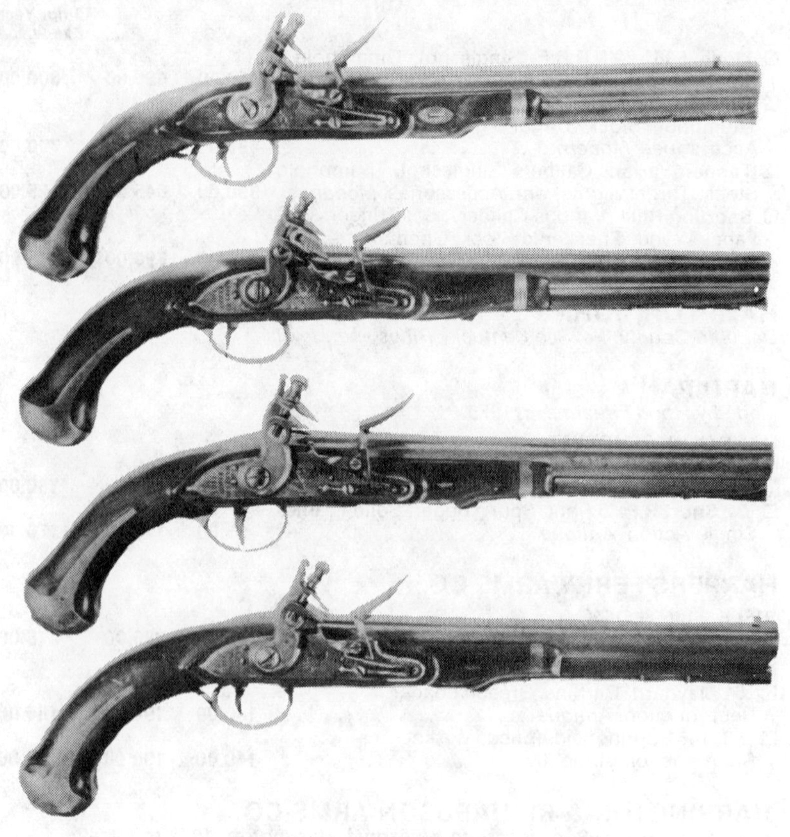

Harper's Ferry M1806 & M1807 Flintlock Pistols

	V.G.	Exc.	Prior Year Exc. Value
☐ **Expert,** .22 L.R.R.F., Top Break, 9 Shot, Double Action, Wood Grips, *Modern*	90.00	140.00	135.00
☐ **Expert,** .22 W.R.F., Top Break, 9 Shot, Double Action, Wood Grips, *Modern*	95.00	150.00	145.00
☐ **Hammerless,** Various Calibers, Double Action, Solid Frame, *Modern*	55.00	100.00	95.00
☐ **Hunter (Early),** .22 L.R.R.F., 7 Shot, Solid Frame, Wood Grips, Double Action, *Modern*	65.00	100.00	95.00
☐ **Hunter (Later),** .22 L.R.R.F., 9 Shot, Solid Frame, Wood Grips, Double Action, *Modern*	60.00	95.00	90.00
☐ **Model 199,** .22 L.R.R.F., Single Action, 9 Shot, Top Break, Adjustable Sights, *Modern*	55.00	95.00	90.00
☐ **Model 4,** Various Calibers, Double Action, Solid Frame, *Modern*	52.00	95.00	90.00
☐ **Model 40,** Various Calibers, Top Break, Hammerless, Double Action, *Modern*	70.00	115.00	110.00
☐ **Model 5,** .32 S & W Double Action, 5 Shot, Solid Frame, *Modern*	45.00	90.00	85.00
☐ **Model 6,** .22 L.R.R.F., Double Action, 7 Shot, Solid Frame, *Modern*	45.00	90.00	85.00
☐ **Model 603,** .22 W.M.R., 9 Shot, Solid Frame, Double Action, Swing-Out Cylinder, Adjustable Sights, *Modern*	67.00	105.00	95.00
☐ **Model 604,** .22 W.M.R., 9 Shot, Solid Frame, Double Action, Swing-Out Cylinder, Adjustable Sights, *Modern*	65.00	100.00	95.00
☐ **Model 622,** .22 L.R.R.F., Solid Frame, 6 Shot, Double Action, *Modern*	40.00	60.00	60.00
☐ **Model 632,** .32 S & W Long, Solid Frame, 6 Shot, Double Action, *Modern*	40.00	60.00	60.00
☐ **Model 633,** .32 S & W Long, Solid Frame, 6 Shot, Chrome, Double Action, *Modern*	42.00	70.00	65.00
☐ **Model 649,** .22LR/.22 W.M.R. Combo, Western Style, 9 Shot, Double Action, Adjustable Sights, *Modern*	45.00	70.00	65.00
☐ **Model 650,** .22LR/.22 W.M.R. Combo, Western Style, 9 Shot, Double Action, Adjustable Sights, *Modern*	50.00	75.00	70.00
☐ **Model 666,** .22LR/.22 W.M.R. Combo, Solid Frame, 9 Shot, Double Action, *Modern*	42.00	70.00	65.00
☐ **Model 676,** .22 LR/.22 W.M.R. Combo, Western Style, 9 Shot, Double Action, Adjustable Sights, *Modern*	60.00	95.00	85.00
☐ **Model 676-12″**, .22LR/.22 W.M.R. Combo, Western Style, 9 Shot, Double Action, Adjustable Sights, *Modern*	60.00	85.00	75.00
☐ **Model 686,** .22LR/.22 W.M.R. Combo, Western Style, 9 Shot, Double Action, Adjustable Sights, *Modern*	65.00	100.00	90.00
☐ **Model 732,** .32 S & W Long, Solid Frame, 6 Shot, Double Action, Swing-Out Cylinder, *Modern*	45.00	65.00	65.00
☐ **Model 733,** .32 S & W Long, Solid Frame, 6 Shot, Double Action, Swing-Out Cylinder, *Modern*	53.00	75.00	70.00
☐ **Model 766,** .22 L.R.R.F., Top Break, 7 Shot, Double Action, Wood Grips, *Modern*	85.00	135.00	125.00

	V.G.	Exc.	Prior Year Exc. Value
☐ **Model 766,** .22 W.R.F., Top Break, 7 Shot, Double Action, Wood Grips, *Modern*	90.00	150.00	140.00
☐ **Model 826,** .22 W.M.R., 6 Shot, Double Action, Adjustable Sights, Swing-Out Cylinder, *Modern*	65.00	100.00	95.00
☐ **Model 829,** .22 L.R.R.F., 9 Shot, Double Action, Adjustable Sights, Swing-Out Cylinder, *Modern*	65.00	100.00	95.00
☐ **Model 832,** .32 S & W, 6 Shot, Double Action, Adjustable Sights, Swing-Out Cylinder, *Modern*	65.00	100.00	95.00
☐ **Model 900,** .22 L.R.R.F., Solid Frame, 9 Shot, Double Action, *Modern*	37.00	55.00	55.00
☐ **Model 901,** .22 L.R.R.F., Solid Frame, 9 Shot, Double Action, *Modern*	37.00	55.00	55.00
☐ **Model 922 (Early),** .22 L.R.R.F., 9 Shot, Solid Frame, Wood Grips, Octagon Barrel, Double Action, *Modern*	65.00	95.00	90.00
☐ **Model 922 (Early),** .22 L.R.R.F., 9 Shot, Solid Frame, Double Action, *Modern*	58.00	90.00	85.00
☐ **Model 922 (Early),** .22 L.R.R.F., 9 Shot, Solid Frame, Pocket Pistol, Double Action, *Modern*	58.00	90.00	85.00
☐ **Model 922 (Late),** .22 L.R.R.F., 9 Shot, Solid Frame, Swing-Out Cylinder, Double Action, *Modern*	37.00	55.00	55.00
☐ **Model 925,** .22 L.R.R.F., 9 Shot, Solid Frame, Double Action, Swing-Out Cylinder, *Modern*	48.00	70.00	70.00
☐ **Model 925,** .38 S & W, Solid Frame, 5 Shot, Adjustable Sights, *Modern*	53.00	80.00	75.00
☐ **Model 926,** .22 L.R.R.F., 5 Shot, Solid Frame, Adjustable Sights, *Modern*	53.00	80.00	75.00
☐ **Model 926,** .38 S & W, Solid Frame, 5 Shot, Adjustable Sights, *Modern*	53.00	80.00	75.00
☐ **Model 929,** .22 L.R.R.F., 9 Shot, Solid Frame, Double Action, Swing-Out Cylinder, *Modern*	42.00	55.00	55.00
☐ **Model 930,** .22 L.R.R.F., 9 Shot, Solid Frame, Double Action, Swing-Out Cylinder, Adjustable Sights, *Modern*	48.00	65.00	65.00
☐ **Model 939,** .22 L.R.R.F., 9 Shot, Solid Frame, Double Action, Swing-Out Cylinder, Adjustable *Modern*	45.00	70.00	70.00
☐ **Model 940,** .22 L.R.R.F., 9 Shot, Solid Frame, Double Action, Swing-Out Cylinder, *Modern*	48.00	70.00	70.00
☐ **Model 949,** .22 L.R.R.F., 9 Shot, Western Style, Double Action, Adjustable Sights, *Modern*	42.00	60.00	60.00
☐ **Model 950,** .22 L.R.R.F., 9 Shot, Western Style, Double Action, Adjustable Sights, *Modern*	42.00	60.00	60.00
☐ **Model 970,** .22, Checkered Grip, *Modern*	50.00	75.00	70.00
☐ **Model 999 (Early),** .22 L.R.R.F., 9 Shot, Top Break, Double Action, Adjustable Sights, *Modern*	58.00	85.00	85.00
☐ **Model 999 (Early),** .22 W.R.F., Top Break, 9 Shot, Double Action, Adjustable Sights, *Modern*	80.00	135.00	130.00
☐ **Model 999 (Late),** .22 L.R.R.F., Top Break, 9 Shot, Double Action, Adjustable Sights, *Modern*	47.00	70.00	70.00
☐ **New Defender,** .22 L.R.R.F., Top Break, 9 Shot, Double Action, Wood Grips, Adjustable Sights, *Modern*	85.00	125.00	120.00
☐ **Premier,** Various Calibers, Top Break, Hammer, Double Action, *Modern*	75.00	130.00	120.00

H & R .32 Pistol

H & R American .44

H & R Auto Ejecting

	V.G.	Exc.	Prior Year Exc. Value
☐ **Special,** .22 L.R.R.F., Top Break, 9 Shot, Double Action, Wood Grips, *Modern*	90.00	135.00	125.00
☐ **Special,** .22 W.R.F., Top Break, 9 Shot, Double Action, Wood Grips, *Modern*	95.00	150.00	140.00
☐ **Target (Early),** .22 L.R.R.F., Top Break, 9 Shot, Double Action, Wood Grips, *Modern*	85.00	125.00	120.00
☐ **Target (Early),** .22 W.R.F., Top Break, 9 Shot, Double Action, Wood Grips, *Modern*	90.00	135.00	125.00
☐ **Target (Hi Speed),** .22 W.R.F., Top Break, 9 Shot, Double Action, Wood Grips, *Modern*	95.00	140.00	135.00
☐ **Target (Hi Speed),** .22 L.R.R.F., Top Break, 9 Shot, Double Action, Wood Grips, *Modern*	85.00	130.00	125.00
☐ **Trapper,** .22 L.R.R.F., 7 Shot, Solid Frame, Wood Grips, Double Action, *Modern*	70.00	100.00	95.00
☐ **Vest Pocket,** Various Calibers, Double Action, Solid Frame, Spurless Hammer, *Modern*	55.00	90.00	85.00
☐ **Young America,** Various Calibers, Double Action, Solid Frame, *Modern*	55.00	90.00	85.00
HANDGUN, SEMI-AUTOMATIC			
☐ **Self-Loading,** .25 ACP, Clip Fed, *Modern*	160.00	300.00	270.00
☐ **Self-Loading,** .32 ACP, Clip Fed, *Modern*	155.00	250.00	235.00

	V.G.	Exc.	Prior Year Exc. Value
HANDGUN, SINGLESHOT			
☐ **U.S.R.A. Target,** .22 L.R.R.F., Top Break, Adjustable Sights, Wood Grips, *Modern*	200.00	375.00	350.00
RIFLE, BOLT ACTION			
☐ **Model 250 Sportster,** .22 L.R.R.F., 5 Shot Clip, Open Rear Sight, *Modern*	37.00	53.00	50.00
☐ **Model 251 Sportster,** .22 L.R.R.F., 5 Shot Clip, Lyman Sights, *Modern*	42.00	65.00	60.00
☐ **Model 265 Reg'lar,** .22 L.R.R.F., Clip Fed, Peep Sights, *Modern*	37.00	58.00	55.00
☐ **Model 300,** Various Calibers, Cheekpiece, Monte Carlo Stock, Checkered Stock, *Modern*	235.00	330.00	315.00
☐ **Model 301,** Various Calibers, Checkered Stock, Mannlicher, *Modern*	260.00	380.00	375.00
☐ **Model 317,** Various Calibers, Checkered Stock, Monte Carlo Stock, *Modern*	225.00	310.00	300.00
☐ **Model 317P,** .223 Rem., Fancy Checkering, Monte Carlo Stock, Fancy Wood, *Modern*	335.00	485.00	475.00
☐ **Model 330,** Various Calibers, Checkered Stock, Monte Carlo Stock, *Modern*	180.00	260.00	250.00
☐ **Model 333,** Various Calibers, Monte Carlo Stock, *Modern*	180.00	260.00	250.00
☐ **Model 340,** Various Calibers, Monte Carlo Stock, Recoil Pad, *Modern*	200.00	280.00	275.00
☐ **Model 365 ACE,** .22 L.R.R.F., Singleshot, Peep Sights, *Modern*	32.00	48.00	45.00
☐ **Model 370,** Various Calibers, Target Stock, Heavy Barrel, *Modern*	205.00	345.00	335.00
☐ **Model 450 Medalist,** .22 L.R.R.F., 5 Shot Clip, No Sights, Target Stock, *Modern*	100.00	140.00	135.00
☐ **Model 451 Medalist,** .22 L.R.R.F., 5 Shot Clip, Lyman Sights, Target Stock, *Modern*	125.00	170.00	160.00
☐ **Model 465 Targeteer,** .22 L.R.R.F., Clip Fed, Peep Sights, *Modern*	60.00	85.00	80.00
☐ **Model 465 Targeteer Jr.,** .22 L.R.R.F., Clip Fed, Peep Sights, *Modern*	60.00	85.00	80.00
☐ **Model 750 Pioneer,** .22 L.R.R.F., Singleshot, Open Rear Sight, *Modern*	32.00	50.00	45.00
☐ **Model 751 Pioneer,** .22 L.R.R.F., Singleshot, Open Rear Sight, Mannlicher, *Modern*	38.00	60.00	55.00
☐ **Model 765 Pioneer,** .22 L.R.R.F., Singleshot, Open Rear Sight, *Modern*	23.00	38.00	35.00
☐ **Model 852 Fieldsman,** .22 L.R.R.F., Tube Feed, Open Rear Sight, *Modern*	43.00	65.00	60.00
☐ **Model 865 Plainsman,** .22 L.R.R.F., 5 Shot Clip, Open Rear Sight, *Modern*	43.00	65.00	60.00
☐ **Model 866 Plainsman,** .22 L.R.R.F., 5 Shot Clip, Open Rear Sight, Mannlicher, *Modern*	43.00	70.00	65.00
☐ **Model 5200 Match,** .22 L.R.R.F., Target Rifle, Single Shot, Heavy Barrel, No Sights, *Modern*	200.00	270.00	270.00
☐ **Model 5200 Sporter,** .22 L.R.R.F., Target Rifle, Clip Fed, Target Sights, Checkered Stock, *Modern*	200.00	270.00	270.00

	V.G.	Exc.	Prior Year Exc. Value
RIFLE, PERCUSSION			
☐ **Huntsman .45,** Top Break, Side Lever, Rifled, Reproduction, *Antique*	58.00	90.00	85.00
☐ **Huntsman .50,** Top Break, Side Lever, Rifled, Reproduction, *Antique*	53.00	80.00	75.00
☐ **Model 175,** .45 or .58 Caliber, Springfield Style, Open Sights, Reproduction, *Antique*	100.00	165.00	155.00
☐ **Model 175 Deluxe,** .45 or .58 Caliber, Springfield Style, Open Sights, Checkered Stock, Reproduction, *Antique*	165.00	260.00	250.00
RIFLE, SEMI-AUTOMATIC			
☐ **Model 150 Leatherneck,** .22 L.R.R.F., 5 Shot Clip, Open Rear Sight, *Modern*	53.00	75.00	70.00
☐ **Model 151 Leatherneck,** .22 L.R.R.F., 5 Shot Clip, Peep Sights, *Modern*	60.00	85.00	80.00
☐ **Model 165 Leatherneck,** .22 L.R.R.F., Clip Fed, Heavy Barrel, Peep Sights, *Modern*	80.00	115.00	110.00
☐ **Model 308,** Various Calibers, Checkered Stock, Monte Carlo Stock, *Modern*	200.00	300.00	285.00
☐ **Model 360,** Various Calibers, Checkered Stock, Monte Carlo Stock, *Modern*	190.00	285.00	275.00
☐ **Model 361,** Various Calibers, Checkered Stock, Monte Carlo Stock, *Modern*	205.00	310.00	300.00
☐ **Model 60 Reising,** .45 ACP, Clip Fed, Carbine, Open Rear Sight, *Modern*	280.00	390.00	375.00
☐ **Model 65 General,** .22 L.R.R.F., Clip Fed, Heavy Barrel, Peep Sights, *Modern*	140.00	235.00	225.00
☐ **Model 700,** .22 W.M.R., Monte Carlo Stock, 5 Shot Clip, *Modern*	90.00	135.00	130.00
☐ **Model 700 Deluxe,** .22 W.M.R., Monte Carlo Stock, 5 Shot Clip, *Modern*	150.00	210.00	220.00
☐ **Model 800 Lynx,** .22 L.R.R.F., Clip Fed, Open Rear Sight, *Modern*	48.00	70.00	65.00
RIFLE, SINGLESHOT			
☐ **1871 Springfield Deluxe,** .45-70 Government, Trap Door Action, Carbine, Light Engraving, *Modern*	175.00	230.00	215.00
☐ **1871 Springfield Officers',** .45-70 Government, Commemorative, Trap Door Action, *Curio*	205.00	330.00	350.00
☐ **1871 Springfield Standard,** .45-70 Government, Trap Door Action, Carbine, *Modern*	130.00	190.00	175.00
☐ **1873 Springfield Officers',** .45-70 Government, Trap Door Action, Light Engraving, Peep Sights, *Modern*	190.00	280.00	265.00
☐ **1873 Springfield Standard,** .45-70 Government, Trap Door Action, Commemorative, *Modern*	160.00	210.00	230.00
☐ **Custer Memorial Enlisted Model,** .45-70 Government, Commemorative, Trap Door Action, Carbine, Fancy Engraving, Fancy Wood, *Curio*	1450.00	2175.00	2500.00
☐ **Custer Memorial Officers' Model,** .45-70 Government, Commemorative, Trap Door Action, Carbine, Fancy Engraving, Fancy Wood, *Curio*	2300.00	3350.00	3700.00
☐ **Little Big Horn Springfield Officers',** .45-70 Government, Commemorative, Trap Door Action, Carbine, *Curio*	185.00	265.00	275.00

Harrington & Richardson, M649, .22 Caliber

Harrington & Richardson M900, .22 Caliber

Harrington & Richardson M929, .22 Caliber

Harrington & Richardson M970, .22 Caliber

	V.G.	Exc.	Prior Year Exc. Value
☐ **Little Big Horn Springfield Standard,** .45-70 Government, Commemorative, Trap Door Action, Carbine, *Curio*	145.00	200.00	220.00
☐ **Model 172 Springfield,** .45-70 Government, Trap Door Action, Carbine, Engraved, Silver Plated, Tang Sights, Checkered Stock, *Modern*	630.00	850.00	825.00
☐ **Model 157,** Various Calibers, Top Break, Side Lever, Automatic Ejector, Open Rear Sight, Mannlicher, *Modern*	47.00	68.00	65.00
☐ **Model 158 Topper,** Various Calibers, Top Break, Side Lever, Automatic Ejector, Open Rear Sight, *Modern*	38.00	60.00	55.00
☐ **Model 158 Topper,** Various Calibers, Top Break, Side Lever, Automatic Ejector, Open Rear Sight, Extra Set of Rifle Barrels, *Modern*	59.00	80.00	75.00
☐ **Model 158 Topper,** Various Calibers, Top Break, Side Lever, Automatic Ejector, Open Rear Sight, Extra Shotgun Barrel, *Modern*	55.00	75.00	70.00
☐ **Model 163,** Various Calibers, Top Break, Side Lever, Automatic Ejector, Open Rear Sight, *Modern*	43.00	63.00	60.00
☐ **Model 755 Sahara,** .22 L.R.R.F., Singleshot, Open Rear Sight, Mannlicher, *Modern*	32.00	48.00	45.00
☐ **Model 760 Sahara,** .22 L.R.R.F., Singleshot, Open Rear Sight, *Modern*	27.00	43.00	40.00
☐ **Shikari,** .44 Magnum, Top Break, Side Lever, Automatic Ejector, *Modern*	48.00	70.00	65.00
☐ **Shikari,** .45-70 Government, Top Break, Side Lever, Automatic Ejector, *Modern*	53.00	80.00	75.00
RIFLE, SLIDE ACTION			
☐ **Model 422,** .22 L.R.R.F., Tube Feed, Open Rear Sight, *Modern*	70.00	100.00	95.00
SHOTGUN, BOLT ACTION			
☐ **Model 348 Gamemaster,** 12 and 16 Gauges, Tube Feed, Takedown, *Modern*	37.00	60.00	55.00
☐ **Model 349 Deluxe,** 12 and 16 Gauges, Tube Feed, Takedown, Adjustable Choke, *Modern*	48.00	70.00	65.00
☐ **Model 351 Huntsman,** 12 and 16 Gauges, Tube Feed, Takedown, Monte Carlo Stock, Adjustable Choke, *Modern*	48.00	70.00	65.00
SHOTGUN, DOUBLE BARREL, OVER-UNDER			
☐ **Model 1212,** 12 Ga., Field Grade, Vent Rib, Single Selective Trigger, *Modern*	250.00	360.00	350.00
☐ **Model 1212 Waterfowl,** 12 Ga. Mag. 3″, Field Grade, Vent Rib, Single Selective Trigger, *Modern*	260.00	380.00	370.00
SHOTGUN, DOUBLE BARREL, SIDE-BY-SIDE			
☐ **Model 404,** Various Gauges, Hammerless, *Modern*	130.00	175.00	170.00
☐ **Model 404C,** Various Gauges, Hammerless, Checkered Stock, *Modern*	130.00	175.00	170.00
SHOTGUN, PERCUSSION			
☐ **Huntsman 12 Ga.,** Top Break, Side Lever, Reproduction, *Antique*	58.00	85.00	80.00

	V.G.	Exc.	Prior Year Exc. Value
SHOTGUN, SEMI-AUTOMATIC			
☐ **Model 403,** .410 Ga., Takedown, *Modern*	130.00	180.00	170.00
SHOTGUN, SINGLESHOT			
☐ **Folding Gun,** Various Gauges, Top Break, Hammer, Automatic Ejector, *Modern*	42.00	65.00	60.00
☐ **Model #1 Harrich,** 12 Ga., Vent Rib, Engraved, Fancy Checkering, *Modern*	1195.00	1600.00	1575.00
☐ **Model 148,** Various Gauges, Top Break, Side Lever, Automatic Ejector, *Modern*	32.00	53.00	50.00
☐ **Model 158,** Various Gauges, Top Break, Side Lever, Automatic Ejector, *Modern*	32.00	53.00	50.00
☐ **Model 159,** Various Gauges, Top Break, Side Lever, Automatic Ejector, *Modern*	40.00	63.00	60.00
☐ **Model 162 Buck,** 12 Ga., Top Break, Side Lever, Automatic Ejector, Peep Sights, *Modern*	37.00	63.00	60.00
☐ **Model 176,** 10 Ga. 3½", Top Break, Side Lever, Automatic Ejector, *Modern*	37.00	63.00	60.00
☐ **Model 188 Deluxe,** Various Gauges, Top Break, Side Lever, Automatic Ejector, *Modern*	28.00	47.00	45.00
☐ **Model 198 Deluxe,** Various Gauges, Top Break, Side Lever, Automatic Ejector, *Modern*	28.00	47.00	45.00
☐ **Model 3,** Various Gauges, Top Break, Hammerless, Automatic Ejector, *Modern*	37.00	62.00	60.00
☐ **Model 459 Youth,** Various Gauges, Top Break, Side Lever, Automatic Ejector, *Modern*	33.00	53.00	50.00
☐ **Model 48,** Various Gauges, Top Break, Hammer, Automatic Ejector, *Modern*	33.00	47.00	45.00
☐ **Model 480 Youth,** Various Gauges, Top Break, Side Lever, Automatic Ejector, *Modern*	33.00	47.00	45.00
☐ **Model 488 Deluxe,** Various Gauges, Top Break, Hammer, Automatic Ejector, *Modern*	38.00	53.00	50.00
☐ **Model 490 Youth,** Various Gauges, Top Break, Side Lever, Automatic Ejector, *Modern*	33.00	47.00	45.00
☐ **Model 5,** Various Gauges, Top Break, Lightweight, Automatic Ejector, *Modern*	48.00	75.00	70.00
☐ **Model 6,** Various Gauges, Top Break, Heavyweight, Automatic Ejector, *Modern*	48.00	80.00	75.00
☐ **Model 7,** Various Gauges, Top Break, Automatic Ejector, *Modern*	37.00	60.00	55.00
☐ **Model 8 Standard,** Various Gauges, Top Break, Automatic Ejector, *Modern*	37.00	60.00	55.00
☐ **Model 9,** Various Gauges, Top Break, Automatic Ejector, *Modern*	37.00	60.00	55.00
☐ **Model 98,** Various Gauges, Top Break, Side Lever, Automatic Ejector, *Modern*	37.00	55.00	50.00
SHOTGUN, SLIDE ACTION			
☐ **Model 400,** Various Gauges, Solid Frame, *Modern*	95.00	155.00	150.00
☐ **Model 401,** Various Gauges, Solid Frame, Adjustable Choke, *Modern*	100.00	160.00	155.00
☐ **Model 402,** .410 Ga., Solid Frame, *Modern*	95.00	155.00	150.00
☐ **Model 440,** Various Gauges, Solid Frame, *Modern*	100.00	160.00	155.00
☐ **Model 400,** Various Gauges, Solid Frame, Vent Rib, *Modern*	115.00	170.00	165.00

HARRIS, HENRY

Payton, Pa. 1779-1783. See Kentucky Rifles.

HARRISON ARMS CO.

Made in Belgium for Sickles & Preston, Davenport, Iowa.

	V.G.	Exc.	Prior Year Exc. Value
SHOTGUN, DOUBLE BARREL, SIDE-BY-SIDE			
☐ **Various Gauges**, Outside Hammers, Damascus Barrel, *Modern*	80.00	155.00	150.00
☐ **Various Gauges**, Hammerless, Steel Barrel, *Modern*	115.00	185.00	175.00
☐ **Various Gauges**, Hammerless, Damascus Barrel, *Modern*	80.00	155.00	150.00
☐ **Various Gauges**, Outside Hammers, Steel Barrel, *Modern*	110.00	180.00	175.00
SHOTGUN, SINGLESHOT			
☐ **Various Gauges**, Hammer, Steel Barrel, *Modern*	45.00	75.00	75.00

HARTFORD ARMS & EQUIPMENT CO.

Hartford, Conn. 1929-1930.

	V.G.	Exc.	Prior Year Exc. Value
HANDGUN, MANUAL REPEATER			
☐ **.22 L.R.R.F.**, Clip Fed, Target Pistol, *Curio*	335.00	475.00	425.00
HANDGUN, SEMI-AUTOMATIC			
☐ **Model 1928**, .22 L.R.R.F., Clip Fed, Target Pistol, *Curio*	300.00	415.00	390.00
HANDGUN, SINGLESHOT			
☐ **.22 L.R.R.F.**, Target Pistol, *Curio*	350.00	500.00	400.00

HARTFORD ARMS CO.

Made by Norwich Falls Pistol Co., c. 1880.

	V.G.	Exc.	Prior Year Exc. Value
HANDGUN, REVOLVER			
☐ **.32 Short R.F.**, 5 Shot, Spur Trigger, Solid Frame, Single Action, *Antique*	95.00	165.00	160.00

HARTFORD ARMS CO.

Made by Crescent for Simmons Hardware Co., St. Louis, Mo.

	V.G.	Exc.	Prior Year Exc. Value
SHOTGUN, DOUBLE BARREL, SIDE-BY-SIDE			
☐ **Various Gauges**, Outside Hammers, Damascus Barrel, *Modern*	80.00	155.00	150.00
☐ **Various Gauges**, Hammerless, Steel Barrel, *Modern*	115.00	185.00	175.00
☐ **Various Gauges**, Hammerless, Damascus Barrel, *Modern*	80.00	155.00	150.00
☐ **Various Gauges**, Outside Hammers, Steel Barrel, *Modern*	110.00	180.00	175.00
SHOTGUN, SINGLESHOT			
☐ **Various Gauges**, Hammer, Steel Barrel, *Modern*	45.00	75.00	75.00

HARVARD

Made by Crescent, c. 1900.

	V.G.	Exc.	Prior Year Exc. Value
SHOTGUN, DOUBLE BARREL, SIDE-BY-SIDE			
☐ **Various Gauges**, Outside Hammers, Damascus Barrel, *Modern*	80.00	155.00	150.00
☐ **Various Gauges**, Hammerless, Steel Barrel, *Modern*	115.00	185.00	175.00
☐ **Various Gauges**, Hammerless, Damascus Barrel, *Modern*	80.00	155.00	150.00
☐ **Various Gauges**, Outside Hammers, Steel Barrel, *Modern*	110.00	180.00	175.00
SHOTGUN, SINGLESHOT			
☐ **Various Gauges**, Hammer, Steel Barrel, *Modern*	45.00	75.00	75.00

HAUCK, WILBUR

West Arlington, Vt., c. 1950.

RIFLE, SINGLESHOT			
☐ **Target Rifle**, Various Calibers, Target Sights, Target Stock, Adjustable Trigger, *Modern*	320.00	485.00	475.00

HAWES FIREARMS

Van Nuys, Calif.

HANDGUN, REVOLVER			
☐ **Montana Marshall**, .22 L.R.R.F./.22 W.M.R. Combo, Western Style, Single Action, Brass Grip Frame, *Modern*	55.00	80.00	80.00
☐ **Montana Marshall**, .22 L.R.R.F., Western Style, Single Action, Brass Grip Frame, *Modern*	45.00	75.00	75.00
☐ **Montana Marshall**, .357 Magnum/9mm Combo, Western Style, Single Action, Brass Grip Frame, *Modern*	125.00	165.00	165.00
☐ **Montana Marshall**, .44 Magnum, Western Style, Single Action, Brass Grip Frame, *Modern*	110.00	145.00	140.00
☐ **Montana Marshall**, .44 Magnum/.44-40 Combo, Western Style, Single Action, Brass Grip Frame, *Modern*	135.00	180.00	175.00
☐ **Montana Marshall**, .45 Colt, Western Style, Single Action, Brass Grip Frame, *Modern*	110.00	150.00	145.00
☐ **Montana Marshall**, .45 Colt/.45 ACP Combo, Western Style, Single Action, Brass Grip Frame, *Modern*	145.00	200.00	190.00
☐ **Silver City Marshall**, .22 L.R.R.F./.22 W.M.R. Combo, Western Style, Single Action, Brass Grip Frame, *Modern*	50.00	90.00	85.00
☐ **Silver City Marshall**, .22 L.R.R.F., Western Style, Single Action, Brass Grip Frame, *Modern*	45.00	75.00	75.00
☐ **Silver City Marshall**, .357 Magnum/9mm Combo, Western Style, Single Action, Brass Grip Frame, *Modern*	125.00	175.00	170.00
☐ **Silver City Marshall**, .44 Magnum, Western Style, Single Action, Brass Grip Frame, *Modern*	120.00	165.00	155.00
☐ **Silver City Marshall**, .44 Magnum/.44-40 Combo, Western Style, Single Action, Brass Grip Frame, *Modern*	135.00	185.00	170.00
☐ **Silver City Marshall**, .45 Colt, Western Style, Single Action, Brass Grip Frame, *Modern*	120.00	160.00	155.00

	V.G.	Exc.	Prior Year Exc. Value
☐ **Silver City Marshall**, .45 Colt/.45 ACP Combo, Western Style, Single Action, Brass Grip Frame, *Modern*	145.00	200.00	195.00
☐ **Texas Marshall**, .22 L.R.R.F./.22 W.M.R. Combo, Western Style, Single Action, Nickel Plated, *Modern*	55.00	90.00	85.00
☐ **Texas Marshall**, .22 L.R.R.F., Western Style, Single Action, Nickel Plated, *Modern*	45.00	75.00	75.00
☐ **Texas Marshall**, .357 Magnum, Western Style, Single Action, Nickel Plated, *Modern*	115.00	155.00	150.00
☐ **Texas Marshall**, .357 Magnum/9mm Combo, Western Style, Single Action, Nickel Plated, *Modern*	130.00	185.00	180.00
☐ **Texas Marshall**, .44 Magnum, Western Style, Single Action, Nickel Plated, *Modern*	125.00	170.00	170.00
☐ **Texas Marshall**, .44 Magnum/.44-40 Combo, Western Style, Single Action, Nickel Plated, *Modern*	145.00	195.00	190.00
☐ **Texas Marshall**, .45 Colt, Western Style, Single Action, Nickel Plated, *Modern*	115.00	155.00	150.00
☐ **Texas Marshall**, .45 Colt/.45 ACP Combo, Western Style, Single Action, Nickel Plated, *Modern*	150.00	200.00	195.00
☐ **Denver Marshall**, .22 L.R.R.F./.22 W.M.R. Combo, Western Style, Single Action, Adjustable Sights, *Modern*	55.00	90.00	85.00
☐ **Denver Marshall**, .22 L.R.R.F., Western Style, Single Action, Brass Grip Frame, Adjustable Sights, *Modern*	45.00	75.00	75.00
☐ **Chief Marshall**, .357 Magnum, Western Style, Single Action, Brass Grip Frame, Adjustable Sights, *Modern*	115.00	150.00	145.00
☐ **Chief Marshall**, .44 Magnum, Western Style, Single Action, Brass Grip Frame, Adjustable Sights, *Modern*	120.00	160.00	155.00
☐ **Chief City Marshall**, .45 Colt, Western Style, Single Action, Brass Grip Frame, Adjustable Sights, *Modern*	110.00	155.00	155.00
HANDGUN, SINGLESHOT			
☐ **Stevens Favorite Copy**, .22 L.R.R.F., Tip-Up, Rosewood Grips, *Modern*	50.00	80.00	75.00
☐ **Stevens Favorite Copy**, .22 L.R.R.F., Tip-Up, Plastic Grips, *Modern*	50.00	80.00	75.00
☐ **Stevens Favorite Copy**, .22 L.R.R.F., Tip-Up, Plastic Grips, Target Sights, *Modern*	50.00	85.00	80.00
HANDGUN, SEMI-AUTOMATIC			
☐ **.25 ACP**, Clip Fed, *Modern*	65.00	100.00	95.00

HAWKIN, J. & S.

Jacob and Samuel Hawkin, St. Louis, Mo. 1822-1862. John Gemmer purchased the business and continued it until 1890.

RIFLE, PERCUSSION

	V.G.	Exc.	Prior Year Exc. Value
☐ **Hawkin Plains Rifle**, Various Calibers, Hawkin Style, *Antique*	3,300.00	6,500.00	6,500.00

	V.G.	Exc.	Prior Year Exc. Value
☐ **Gemmer Plains Rifle**, Various Calibers, Hawkin Style, *Antique*	2,500.00	4,500.00	4,500.00

HAWKINS, HENRY

Schenectady, N.Y. 1769-1775. See Kentucky Rifles.

H & D

Henrion & Dassy, Liege, Belgium, c. 1900.

HANDGUN, SEMI-AUTOMATIC

	V.G.	Exc.	Prior Year Exc. Value
☐ **H & D Patent**, .25 ACP, Clip Fed, *Curio*	375.00	600.00	575.00

H.D.H.

Mre. D'Armes HDH, Liege, Belgium, c. 1910.

HANDGUN, REVOLVER

	V.G.	Exc.	Prior Year Exc. Value
☐ **20 Shot**, Various Calibers, Over-Under Barrels, Two Row Cylinder, Double Action, *Curio*	150.00	250.00	250.00
☐ **10 Shot**, Various Calibers, Double Action, *Curio*	95.00	170.00	165.00
☐ **Ordnance Type**, Various Calibers, Double Action *Curio*	115.00	170.00	165.00
☐ **Constabulary Type**, Various Calibers, Double Action, *Curio*	80.00	135.00	130.00
☐ **Velo-Dog**, Various Calibers, Folding Trigger, Double Action, *Curio*	70.00	110.00	110.00
☐ **Velo-Dog**, Various Calibers, Folding Trigger, Double Action, Hammerless, *Curio*	70.00	110.00	110.00

HECKERT, PHILIP

York, Pa. 1769-1779. See Kentucky Rifles and Pistols.

HECKLER & KOCH

Oberndorf/Neckar, Germany.

AUTOMATIC WEAPON, ASSAULT RIFLE

	V.G.	Exc.	Prior Year Exc. Value
☐ **Model G3**, .308 Win., Clip Fed, *Class 3*	475.00	700.00	700.00
☐ **Model G3A3**, .308 Win., Clip Fed, *Class 3*	575.00	825.00	825.00
☐ **Model G3A4**, .308 Win., Clip Fed, *Class 3*	675.00	900.00	900.00
☐ **Model G3A4**, .308 Win., Clip Fed, with Conversion Kit, *Class 3*	750.00	1,025.00	1,050.00
☐ **Model HK33**, .223 Rem., Clip Fed, *Class 3*	325.00	450.00	450.00

AUTOMATIC WEAPON, SUBMACHINE GUN

	V.G.	Exc.	Prior Year Exc. Value
☐ **Model MP5A2**, 9mm Luger, Clip Fed, *Class 3*	450.00	695.00	675.00
☐ **Model MP5A3**, 9mm Luger, Clip Fed, Folding Stock, *Class 3*	600.00	825.00	825.00

HANDGUN, SEMI-AUTOMATIC

	V.G.	Exc.	Prior Year Exc. Value
☐ **HK-4**, .22 L.R.R.F., Clip Fed, Double Action, *Modern*	210.00	285.00	300.00
☐ **HK-4**, .25 ACP, Clip Fed, Double Action, *Modern*	200.00	280.00	290.00
☐ **HK-4**, .32 ACP, Clip Fed, Double Action, German Police, *Modern*	135.00	170.00	—
☐ **HK-4**, .32 ACP, Clip Fed, Double Action, French Made, *Modern*	145.00	200.00	—

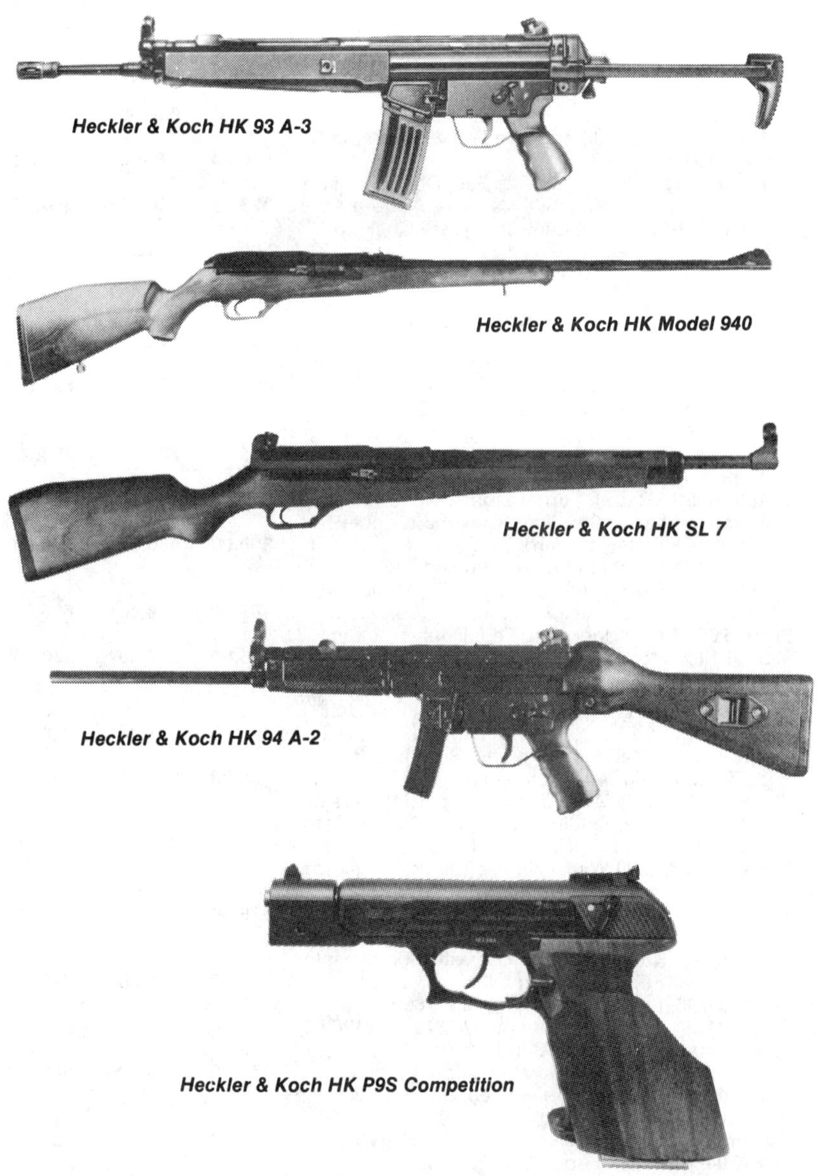

Heckler & Koch HK 93 A-3

Heckler & Koch HK Model 940

Heckler & Koch HK SL 7

Heckler & Koch HK 94 A-2

Heckler & Koch HK P9S Competition

	V.G.	Exc.	Prior Year Exc. Value
☐ **HK-4**, .32 ACP, Clip Fed, Double Action, *Modern*	200.00	285.00	300.00
☐ **HK-4**, .380 ACP, Clip Fed, Double Action, *Modern*	220.00	300.00	325.00
☐ **HK-4**, Various Calibers, Clip Fed, Conversion Kit Only, Each	50.00	70.00	70.00
☐ **HK-4**, Various Calibers, Clip Fed, Double Action, with Conversion Kits All 4 Calibers, *Modern*	325.00	450.00	450.00
☐ **HK P-7 (PSP)**, 9mm Luger, Squeeze Cocking, *Modern*	300.00	425.00	440.00
☐ **HK P-9S**, .45 ACP, Clip Fed, Double Action, *Modern*	320.00	400.00	500.00
☐ **HK P-9S**, .45 ACP, Target Model, Clip Fed, Double Action, *Modern*	380.00	475.00	575.00
☐ **HK P-9S**, .45 ACP, with Extra 8" Barrel, Clip Fed, Double Action, *Modern*	420.00	525.00	625.00
☐ **P-9S Competition Kit**, 9mm Luger, Clip Fed, Double Action, Extra Barrel, Target Sights, Target Grips, *Modern*	535.00	770.00	850.00
☐ **P-9S Target**, 9mm Luger, Clip Fed, Double Action, 5½" Barrel, Target Sights, *Modern*	380.00	475.00	575.00
☐ **P-9S Combat**, 9mm Luger, Clip Fed, Double Action, 4" Barrel, *Modern*	300.00	400.00	500.00
☐ **P-9S Combat**, 9mm Luger, Clip Fed, Double Action, 4" Barrel, with .30 Luger Conversion Kit, *Modern*	465.00	625.00	650.00
☐ **VP-70Z**, 9mm Luger, Clip Fed, Double Action, 18 Shot Clip, *Modern*	225.00	300.00	350.00
RIFLE, SEMI-AUTOMATIC			
☐ **HK 91**, .22 L.R.R.F., Clip Fed, Conversion Unit Only	175.00	225.00	240.00
☐ **HK 91 A-2**, .308 Win., Clip Fed, Sporting Version of Military Rifle, with Compensator, *Modern*	425.00	500.00	525.00
☐ **HK 91 A-3**, .308 Win., Clip Fed, Sporting Version of Military Rifle, Folding Stock with Compensator, *Modern*	450.00	560.00	650.00
☐ **HK 91 A-4**, .308 Win., Clip Fed, Sporting Version of Military Rifle, with Compensator, Polygonal Rifling, *Modern*	475.00	675.00	675.00
☐ **HK 91 A-5**, .308 Win., Clip Fed, Sporting Version of Military Rifle, Folding Stock with Compensator, Polygonal Rifling, *Modern*	575.00	825.00	825.00
☐ **HK 91/93**, Light Bipod, *Add* **$40.00-$60.00**			
☐ **HK 91/93**, For Scope Mount *Add* **$75.00-$120.00**			
☐ **HK 93 A-2**, .223 Rem., Clip Fed, Sporting Version of Military Rifle, with Compensator, *Modern*	375.00	500.00	500.00
☐ **HK 93 A-3**, .223 Rem., Clip Fed, Sporting Version of Military Rifle, Folding Stock, with Compensator, *Modern*	440.00	550.00	625.00
☐ **HK 94 A-2**, 9mm Luger, Clip Fed, Sporting Version of MP5 S.M.G., Standard Stock, *Modern*	410.00	500.00	—
☐ **HK 94 A-3**, 9mm Luger, Clip Fed, Sporting Version of MP5 S.M.G., Folding Stock, *Modern*	445.00	560.00	—
☐ **Model 270**, .22 L.R.R.F., Clip Fed, Checkered Stock, Open Rear Sight, *Modern*	145.00	200.00	250.00

	V.G.	Exc.	Prior Year Exc. Value
☐ **Model 300**, .22 WMR, Clip Fed, Checkered Stock, Open Rear Sight, *Modern*	190.00	275.00	300.00
☐ **Model 630**, .223 Rem., Clip Fed, Checkered Stock, Open Rear Sight, *Modern*	325.00	450.00	450.00
☐ **HK 770**, .308 Win., Sporting Rifle, Checkered Stock, Monte Carlo Stock, *Modern*	325.00	450.00	450.00
☐ **Model 940**, .30/06, Clip Fed, Checkered Stock, Open Rear Sight, *Modern*	385.00	460.00	550.00
☐ **Model SL 6**, .223 Rem., Clip Fed, Military Style Carbine, Open Rear Sight, *Modern*	300.00	400.00	—
☐ **Model SL 7**, .308 Win., Clip Fed, Military Style Carbine, Open Rear Sight, *Modern*	300.00	400.00	—

Hege AP-66 .32

HEGE

Tradename of Hebsacker Gesellschaft and Hege GmbH, established in 1959 in Schwabisch Halle, West Germany. Now in Uberlingen/Bodensee, West Germany. Also see Beeman's.

COMBINATION WEAPON, OVER-UNDER

☐ **President**, Various Calibers, Box Lock, Solid Rib, Double Trigger, Checkered Stock, *Modern*	475.00	695.00	675.00

HANDGUN, PERCUSSION

☐ **Silber Pistol**, .33 Caliber, French Style, Engraved, Gold Inlays, Cased, Reproduction, *Antique*	400.00	600.00	—
☐ **Silber Pistol**, .33 Caliber, British Style, Engraved, Cased, Reproduction, *Antique*	300.00	400.00	—

HANDGUN, SEMI-AUTOMATIC

☐ **AP-63**, .32 ACP, Clip Fed, Double Action, *Modern*	215.00	295.00	295.00
☐ **AP-66**, .32 ACP, Clip Fed, Double Action, *Modern*	150.00	235.00	225.00
☐ **AP-66**, .380 ACP, Clip Fed, Double Action, *Modern*	175.00	250.00	250.00

RIFLE, MATCHLOCK

☐ **Zeughaus Musket**, .63 Caliber, Heavy Swiss Style, Plain, Reproduction, *Antique*	185.00	250.00	—

HEINZELMANN, C.E.

Plochingen, Germany 1921-1928.

HANDGUN, SEMI-AUTOMATIC

☐ **Heim**, .25 ACP, Clip Fed, Blue, *Curio*	390.00	575.00	550.00

	V.G.	Exc.	Prior Year Exc. Value

HELFRICHT
Alfred Krauser Waffenfabrik, Zella Mehlis, Germany 1921-1929.

HANDGUN, SEMI-AUTOMATIC

	V.G.	Exc.	Prior Year Exc. Value
☐ **Model 1**, .25 ACP, Clip Fed, *Curio*	315.00	450.00	425.00
☐ **Model 2**, .25 ACP, Clip Fed, *Curio*	295.00	425.00	400.00
☐ **Model 3**, .25 ACP, Clip Fed, *Curio*	295.00	425.00	400.00
☐ **Model 4**, .25 ACP, Clip Fed, *Curio*	275.00	395.00	375.00

HELVICE
Fab. D'Armes de Guerre de Grand Precision, Eibar Spain.

HANDGUN, SEMI-AUTOMATIC

	V.G.	Exc.	Prior Year Exc. Value
☐ **.25 ACP**, Clip Fed, Modern	85.00	135.00	125.00

HENNCH, PETER
Lancaster, Pa. 1770-1774. See Kentucky Rifles.

HENRY, ALEXANDER
Edinburgh, Scotland 1869-1895.

RIFLE, DOUBLE BARREL, SIDE-BY-SIDE

	V.G.	Exc.	Prior Year Exc. Value
☐ **.500/450 Mag. BPE**, Damascus Barrel, Engraved, Fancy Checkering, Ornate, Cased with Accessories, Hammerless, *Antique*	3,250.00	4,650.00	4,500.00

HENRY GUN CO.
Belgium, c. 1900.

SHOTGUN, DOUBLE BARREL, SIDE-BY-SIDE

	V.G.	Exc.	Prior Year Exc. Value
☐ **Various Gauges**, Outside Hammers, Damascus Barrel, *Modern*	110.00	180.00	175.00
☐ **Various Gauges**, Hammerless, Steel Barrel, *Modern*	135.00	200.00	200.00
☐ **Various Gauges**, Hammerless, Damascus Barrel, *Modern*	110.00	180.00	175.00
☐ **Various Gauges**, Outside Hammers, Steel Barrel, *Modern*	125.00	190.00	190.00

SHOTGUN, SINGLESHOT

	V.G.	Exc.	Prior Year Exc. Value
☐ **Various Gauges**, Hammer, Steel Barrel, *Modern*	55.00	85.00	85.00

HERCULES
Made by Stevens Arms.

SHOTGUN, DOUBLE BARREL, SIDE-BY-SIDE

	V.G.	Exc.	Prior Year Exc. Value
☐ **M 315**, Various Gauges, Hammerless, Steel Barrel, *Modern*	100.00	175.00	170.00
☐ **Model 215**, 12 and 16 Gauges, Outside Hammers, Steel Barrel, *Modern*	100.00	165.00	160.00
☐ **Model 311**, Various Gauges, Hammerless, Steel Barrel, *Modern*	110.00	185.00	175.00
☐ **Model 3151**, Various Gauges, Hammerless, Recoil Pad, Front & Rear Bead Sights, *Modern*	120.00	190.00	185.00
☐ **Model 5151**, Various Gauges, Hammerless, Steel Barrel, *Modern*	100.00	180.00	175.00

	V.G.	Exc.	Prior Year Exc. Value
SHOTGUN, SINGLESHOT			
☐ **Model 94**, Various Gauges, Takedown, Automatic Ejector, Plain Hammer, *Modern*	40.00	65.00	60.00

HERMETIC

Tradename used by Bernadon-Martin, St. Etienne, France, c. 1912.

	V.G.	Exc.	Prior Year Exc. Value
HANDGUN, SEMI-AUTOMATIC			
☐ **B.M.**, .32 ACP, Clip Fed, *Curio*	225.00	320.00	295.00

HERMITAGE

Made by Stevens Arms.

	V.G.	Exc.	Prior Year Exc. Value
SHOTGUN, SINGLESHOT			
☐ **Model 90**, Various Gauges, Takedown, Automatic Ejector, Plain Hammer, *Modern*	45.00	65.00	60.00

HERMITAGE ARMS CO.

Made by Crescent for Grey & Dudley Hdw. Co., Nashville, Tenn.

	V.G.	Exc.	Prior Year Exc. Value
SHOTGUN, DOUBLE BARREL, SIDE-BY-SIDE			
☐ **Various Gauges**, Outside Hammers, Damascus Barrel, *Modern*	80.00	155.00	150.00
☐ **Various Gauges**, Hammerless, Steel Barrel, *Modern*	115.00	185.00	175.00
☐ **Various Gauges**, Hammerless, Damascus Barrel, *Modern*	80.00	155.00	150.00
☐ **Various Gauges**, Outside Hammers, Steel Barrel, *Modern*	110.00	180.00	175.00
SHOTGUN, SINGLESHOT			
☐ **Various Gauges**, Hammer, Steel Barrel, *Modern*	45.00	75.00	75.00

HERMITAGE GUN CO.

Made by Crescent for Grey & Dudley Hdw. Co., Nashville, Tenn.

	V.G.	Exc.	Prior Year Exc. Value
SHOTGUN, DOUBLE BARREL, SIDE-BY-SIDE			
☐ **Various Gauges**, Outside Hammers, Damascus Barrel, *Modern*	80.00	155.00	150.00
☐ **Various Gauges**, Hammerless, Steel Barrel, *Modern*	115.00	185.00	175.00
☐ **Various Gauges**, Hammerless, Damascus Barrel, *Modern*	80.00	155.00	150.00
☐ **Various Gauges**, Outside Hammers, Steel Barrel, *Modern*	110.00	180.00	175.00
SHOTGUN, SINGLESHOT			
☐ **Various Gauges**, Hammer, Steel Barrel, *Modern*	45.00	75.00	75.00

HERO

Made by Rupertus Arms for Tryon Bros. Co., c. 1880.

	V.G.	Exc.	Prior Year Exc. Value
HANDGUN, REVOLVER			
☐ **.22 Short R.F.**, 7 Shot, Spur Trigger, Solid Frame, Single Action, *Antique*	95.00	165.00	160.00
☐ **.32 Short R.F.**, 5 Shot, Spur Trigger, Solid Frame, Single Action, *Antique*	95.00	170.00	170.00
☐ **.38 Short R.F.**, 5 Shot, Spur Trigger, Solid Frame, Single Action, *Antique*	95.00	180.00	180.00

	V.G.	Exc.	Prior Year Exc. Value
☐ **.41 Short R.F.**, 5 Shot, Spur Trigger, Solid Frame, Single Action, *Antique*	120.00	200.00	200.00

HEROLD

Tradename of Franz Jager & Co., Suhl, Germany 1923-1939.

	V.G.	Exc.	Prior Year Exc. Value
Herold Repetierbuchse, .22 Hornet, Set Triggers, Checkered Stock, *Modern*	520.00	765.00	750.00

HERTERS

Distributer & Importer in Waseca, Minn.

	V.G.	Exc.	Prior Year Exc. Value
HANDGUN, REVOLVER			
☐ **Guide**, .22 L.R.R.F., Swing-Out Cylinder, Double Action, *Modern*	30.00	50.00	45.00
☐ **Power-Mag**, .357 Magnum, Western Style, Single Action, *Modern*	50.00	85.00	80.00
☐ **Power-Mag**, .401 Herter Mag., Western Style, Single Action,	50.00	85.00	80.00
☐ **Power-Mag**, .44 Magnum, Western Style, Single Action, *Modern*	65.00	100.00	95.00
☐ **Western**, .22 L.R.R.F., Single Action, Western Style, *Modern*	30.00	50.00	45.00
RIFLE, BOLT ACTION			
☐ **Model J-9 Hunter**, Various Calibers, Plain, Monte Carlo Stock, *Modern*	140.00	200.00	195.00
☐ **Model J-9 Presentation**, Various Calibers, Checkered Stock, Monte Carlo Stock, Sling Swivels, *Modern*	155.00	225.00	220.00
☐ **Model J-9 Supreme**, Various Calibers, Checkered Stock, Monte Carlo Stock, Sling Swivels, *Modern*	155.00	225.00	220.00
☐ **Model U-9 Hunter**, Various Calibers, Plain, Monte Carlo Stock, *Modern*	140.00	190.00	185.00
☐ **Model U-9 Presentation**, Various Calibers, Checkered Stock, Sling Swivels, Monte Carlo Stock, *Modern*	155.00	225.00	220.00
☐ **Model U-9 Supreme**, Various Calibers, Checkered Stock, Sling Swivels, Monte Carlo Stock, *Modern*	150.00	195.00	190.00
SHOTGUN, SINGLESHOT			
☐ **Model 151**, Various Gauges, Hammer, *Modern*	30.00	45.00	40.00
SHOTGUN, SEMI-AUTOMATIC			
☐ **Model SL-18**, 12 Ga. 3", Checkered Stock, *Modern*	185.00	255.00	250.00

HESS, JACOB

Stark Co., Ohio 1842-1860. See Kentucky Rifles.

HESS, SAMUEL

Lancaster, Pa., c. 1771. See Kentucky Rifles.

HEYM

Franz W. Heym, 1934-1945 in Suhl, Germany, now in Munnerstadt, West Germany.

	V.G.	Exc.	Prior Year Exc. Value
COMBINATION WEAPON, DRILLING			
☐ **Model 33**, Various Calibers, Hammerless, Double Triggers, Engraved, Checkered Stock, Express Sights, *Modern*	2,650.00	3,600.00	3,500.00
☐ **Model 37**, Various Calibers, Hammerless, Sidelock, Engraved, Checkered Stock, *Modern*	2,975.00	4,000.00	3,950.00
☐ **Model 37**, Various Calibers, Hammerless, Sidelock, Double Rifle Barrels, Engraved, Checkered Stock, *Modern*	3,800.00	5,500.00	5,400.00
☐ **Model 37 Deluxe**, Various Calibers, Hammerless, Sidelock, Double Rifle Barrels, Engraved, Checkered Stock, *Modern*	4,300.00	5,900.00	5,800.00
COMBINATION WEAPON, OVER-UNDER			
☐ **Model 22S**, Various Calibers, Single Set Trigger, Checkered Stock, Light Engraving, *Modern*	775.00	1,200.00	1,150.00
☐ **Model 55BF (77BF)**, Various Calibers, Boxlock, Double Triggers, Checkered Stock, Engraved, *Modern*	1,750.00	2,550.00	2,500.00
☐ **Model 55BFSS (77BFSS)**, Various Calibers, Sidelock, Double Triggers, Checkered Stock, *Modern*	3,475.00	4,300.00	4,200.00
RIFLE, DOUBLE BARREL, OVER-UNDER			
☐ **Model 55B (77B)**, Various Calibers, Boxlock, Engraved, Checkered Stock, *Modern*	1,875.00	2,750.00	2,700.00
☐ **Model 55BSS (77BSS)**, Various Calibers, Sidelock, Engraved, Checkered Stock, *Modern*	3,350.00	4,350.00	4,300.00
SHOTGUN, DOUBLE BARREL, OVER-UNDER			
☐ **Model 55F (77F)**, Various Gauges, Boxlock, Engraved, Checkered Stock, Double Triggers, *Modern*	1,675.00	2,550.00	2,500.00
☐ **Model 55FSS (77FSS)**, Various Gauges, Sidelock, Engraved, Checkered Stock, Double Triggers, *Modern*	2,650.00	3,575.00	3,500.00
RIFLE, BOLT ACTION			
☐ **Model SR-20**, Various Calibers, Fancy Wood, Double Set Triggers, *Modern*	435.00	600.00	595.00
☐ **Model SR-20**, Various Calibers, Fancy Wood, Double Set Triggers, Left Hand, *Modern*	540.00	725.00	695.00
RIFLE, SINGLESHOT			
☐ **Model HR-30**, Various Calibers, Fancy Wood, Engraved, Single Set Trigger, Ruger Action, Round Barrel, *Modern*	975.00	1,575.00	1,500.00
☐ **Model HR-38**, Various Calibers, Fancy Wood, Engraved, Single Set Trigger, Ruger Action, Octagon Barrel, *Modern*	1,150.00	1,750.00	1,700.00

HIGGINS, J.C.

Trade Name used by Sears-Roebuck.

	V.G.	Exc.	Prior Year Exc. Value
HANDGUN, REVOLVER			
☐ **Model 88**, .22 L.R.R.F., *Modern*	45.00	70.00	65.00
☐ **Model 88 Fisherman**, .22 L.R.R.F., *Modern*	45.00	70.00	65.00
☐ **Ranger**, .22 L.R.R.F., *Modern*	45.00	70.00	65.00

	V.G.	Exc.	Prior Year Exc. Value
HANDGUN, SEMI-AUTOMATIC			
☐ **Model 80**, .22 L.R.R.F., Clip Fed, Hammerless, *Modern*	70.00	105.00	95.00
☐ **Model 85**, .22 L.R.R.F., Clip Fed, Hammer, *Modern*	85.00	125.00	120.00
RIFLE, BOLT ACTION			
☐ **Model 228**, .22 L.R.R.F., Clip Fed, *Modern*	30.00	50.00	45.00
☐ **Model 229**, .22 L.R.R.F., Tube Feed, *Modern*	35.00	55.00	50.00
☐ **Model 245**, .22 L.R.R.F., Singleshot, *Modern*	20.00	40.00	35.00
☐ **Model 51**, Various Calibers, Checkered Stock, *Modern*	160.00	225.00	225.00
☐ **Model 51 Special**, Various Calibers, Checkered Stock, Light Engraving, *Modern*	220.00	300.00	300.00
RIFLE, LEVER ACTION			
☐ **.22 WMR**, *Modern*	55.00	85.00	80.00
☐ **Model 45**, Various Calibers, Tube Feed, Carbine, *Modern*	50.00	80.00	75.00
RIFLE, SEMI-AUTOMATIC			
☐ **Model 25**, .22 L.R.R.F., Clip Fed, *Modern*	30.00	55.00	50.00
☐ **Model 31**, .22 L.R.R.F., Tube Feed, *Modern*	40.00	65.00	65.00
RIFLE, SLIDE ACTION			
☐ **Model 33**, .22 L.R.R.F., Tube Feed, *Modern*	45.00	65.00	55.00
SHOTGUN, BOLT ACTION			
☐ **Model 10**, Various Gauges, Tube Feed, 5 Shot, *Modern*	45.00	65.00	60.00
☐ **Model 11**, Various Gauges, Tube Feed, 3 Shot, *Modern*	40.00	55.00	50.00
SHOTGUN, DOUBLE BARREL, SIDE-BY-SIDE			
☐ **Various Calibers**, Plain, Takedown, Hammerless, *Modern*	110.00	170.00	165.00
SHOTGUN, SEMI-AUTOMATIC			
☐ **Model 66**, 12 Ga., Plain Barrel, *Modern*	95.00	160.00	155.00
☐ **Model 66**, 12 Ga., Plain Barrel, Adjustable Choke, *Modern*	95.00	170.00	165.00
☐ **Model 66**, 12 Ga., Vent Rib, Adjustable Choke, *Modern*	100.00	170.00	170.00
☐ **Model 66 Deluxe**, 12 Ga., *Modern*	100.00	175.00	175.00
SHOTGUN, SINGLESHOT			
☐ **Various Calibers**, Takedown, Adjustable Choke, Plain, Hammer, *Modern*	35.00	55.00	50.00
SHOTGUN, SLIDE ACTION			
☐ **Model 20 Deluxe**, 12 Ga., *Modern*	90.00	145.00	140.00
☐ **Model 20 Deluxe**, 12 Ga., Vent Rib, Adjustable Choke, *Modern*	95.00	155.00	155.00
☐ **Model 20 Special**, 12 Ga., Vent Rib, Adjustable Choke, *Modern*	135.00	190.00	190.00
☐ **Model 20 Standard**, 12 Ga., *Modern*	90.00	135.00	130.00

HIGH STANDARD

High Standard Mfg. Co. 1926 to the present, first in New Haven, Conn., then as High Standard Sporting Firearms in Hamden, Conn., now as High Standard, Inc. in East Hartford, Conn. All High Standard machinery was sold at auction October 5, 1984.

	V.G.	Exc.	Prior Year Exc. Value
HANDGUN, DOUBLE BARREL, OVER-UNDER			
☐ **Derringer,** .22 L.R.R.F., Double Action, 2 Shot, *Modern*	65.00	115.00	110.00
☐ **Derringer,** .22 WMR, Double Action, 2 Shot, *Modern*	70.00	120.00	115.00
☐ **Derringer,** .22 L.R.R.F., Double Action, Top Break, Nickel Plated, Hammerless, Cased, *Modern*	75.00	120.00	120.00
☐ **Derringer,** .22 WMR, Double Action, Top Break, Nickel Plated, Hammerless, Cased, *Modern*	75.00	130.00	125.00
☐ **Derringer,** .22 L.R.R.F., Double Action, Top Break, Electroless Nickel Plated, Hammerless, Walnut Grips, Cased, *Modern*	72.00	120.00	120.00
☐ **Derringer,** .22 WMR, Double Action, Top Break, Electroless Nickel Plated, Hammerless, Walnut Grips, Cased, *Modern*	75.00	130.00	125.00
☐ **Gold Derringer,** .22 WMR, Double Action, 2 Shot, *Modern*	125.00	175.00	170.00
☐ **Presidential Derringer,** .22 WMR, Double Action, Top Break, Gold Plated, Hammerless, Cased, *Modern*	150.00	225.00	220.00
HANDGUN, PERCUSSION			
☐ **.36,** Griswald & Gunnison, Revolver, Commemorative, Cased, Reproduction, *Antique*	150.00	215.00	250.00
☐ **.36 Leech & Rigdon,** Revolver, Commemorative, Cased, Reproduction, *Antique*	150.00	215.00	250.00
☐ **.36 Schneider & Glassick,** Revolver, Commemorative, Cased, Reproduction, *Antique*	210.00	320.00	350.00
HANDGUN, REVOLVER			
☐ **For Nickel Plating,** *Add* **$7.50-$12.50**			
☐ **Camp Gun,** .22 L.R.R.F., Double Action, Swing-Out Cylinder, Adjustable Sights, *Modern*	75.00	100.00	95.00
☐ **Camp Gun,** .22 WMR, Double Action, Swing-Out Cylinder, Adjustable Sights, *Modern*	80.00	115.00	110.00
☐ **Crusader,** Deluxe Pair, .44 Mag. & .45 Colt, Commemorative, Double Action, Swing-Out Cylinder, Gold Inlays, Engraved, *Modern*	1200.00	2600.00	2950.00
☐ **Double-Nine,** .22LR/.22 WMR Combo, Double Action, Western Style, Alloy Frame, *Modern*	60.00	95.00	90.00
☐ **Double-Nine,** .22LR/.22 WMR Combo, Double Action, Western Style, *Modern*	85.00	130.00	125.00
☐ **Double-Nine,** .22 L.R.R.F., Double Action, Western Style, *Modern*	65.00	105.00	100.00
☐ **Double-Nine Deluxe,** .22LR/.22 WMR Combo, Double Action, Western Style, Adjustable Sights, *Modern*	95.00	145.00	140.00
☐ **Durango,** .22 L.R.R.F., Double Action, Western Style, *Modern*	65.00	105.00	100.00
☐ **High Sierra,** .22LR/.22 WMR Combo, Double Action, Western Style, Octagon Barrel, *Modern*	85.00	140.00	135.00
☐ **High Sierra Deluxe,** .22LR/.22 WMR Combo, Double Action, Western Style, Octagon Barrel, Adjustable Sights, *Modern*	100.00	165.00	155.00
☐ **Longhorn,** .22LR/.22 WMR Combo, Double Action, Western Style, Alloy Frame, *Modern*	65.00	100.00	95.00

	V.G.	Exc.	Prior Year Exc. Value
☐ **Longhorn,** .22LR/.22 WMR Combo, Double Action, Western Style, *Modern*	95.00	140.00	135.00
☐ **Longhorn,** .22LR/.22 WMR Combo, Double Action, Adjustable Sights, Western Style, *Modern*	105.00	165.00	155.00
☐ **Natchez,** .22LR/.22 WMR Combo, Double Action, Western Style, Birdshead Grip, Alloy Frame, *Modern*	65.00	100.00	90.00
☐ **Posse,** .22LR/.22 WMR Combo, Double Action, Western Style, Brass Gripframe, *Modern*	80.00	130.00	125.00
☐ **Sentinel,** .22 L.R.R.F., Double Action, Swing-Out Cylinder, *Modern*	50.00	95.00	90.00
☐ **Sentinel Deluxe,** .22 L.R.R.F., Double Action, Swing-Out Cylinder, *Modern*	55.00	95.00	90.00
☐ **Sentinel Imperial,** .22 L.R.R.F., Double Action, Swing-Out Cylinder, *Modern*	55.00	95.00	90.00
☐ **Sentinel Mk III,** .357 Magnum, Double Action, Swing-Out Cylinder, Adjustable Sights, *Modern*	120.00	170.00	165.00
☐ **Sentinel Mk II,** .357 Magnum, Double Action, Swing-Out Cylinder, *Modern*	100.00	150.00	145.00
☐ **Sentinel Mk. I,** .22 L.R.R.F., Double Action, Swing-Out Cylinder, *Modern*	70.00	105.00	100.00
☐ **Sentinel Mk. I,** .22 L.R.R.F., Double Action, Swing-Out Cylinder, Adjustable Sights, *Modern*	80.00	120.00	115.00
☐ **Sentinel Mk. IV,** .22 L.R.R.F., Double Action, Swing-Out Cylinder, Adjustable Sights, *Modern*	115.00	160.00	155.00
☐ **Sentinel Mk. IV,** .22 WMR, Double Action, Swing-Out Cylinder, Adjustable Sights, *Modern*	120.00	165.00	160.00
☐ **Sentinel Mk. IV,** .22 WMR, Double Action, Swing-Out Cylinder, *Modern*	85.00	130.00	125.00
☐ **Sentinel Snub,** .22 L.R.R.F., Double Action, Swing-Out Cylinder, *Modern*	55.00	95.00	90.00
HANDGUN, SEMI-AUTOMATIC			
☐ **For Nickel Plating,** *Add* **$20.00-$35.00**			
☐ **"Benner Olympic,"** .22 L.R.R.F., Supermatic, Military, Engraved, *Curio*	575.00	850.00	900.00
☐ **Citation (Early),** .22 L.R.R.F., Supermatic, Clip Fed, Hammerless, Tapered Barrel, *Modern*	140.00	190.00	185.00
☐ **Citation (Early),** .22 L.R.R.F., Supermatic, Clip Fed, Hammerless, Heavy Barrel, *Modern*	130.00	185.00	175.00
☐ **Citation (Late),** .22 L.R.R.F., Supermatic, Military, Hammerless, Frame-Mounted Rear Sight, Fluted Barrel, *Modern*	160.00	245.00	245.00
☐ **Citation (Late),** .22 L.R.R.F., Supermatic, Military, Hammerless, Frame-Mounted Rear Sight, Heavy Barrel, *Modern*	155.00	225.00	225.00
☐ **Citation (Late),** .22 L.R.R.F., Supermatic, Clip Fed, Hammerless, Frame-Mounted Rear Sight, Heavy Barrel, *Modern*	150.00	225.00	220.00
☐ **Dura-Matic,** .22 L.R.R.F., Clip Fed, Hammerless, *Modern*	85.00	145.00	130.00
☐ **Field King,** .22 L.R.R.F., Clip Fed, Hammerless, Heavy Barrel, *Modern*	105.00	160.00	145.00
☐ **Flight King,** .22 Short R.F., Clip Fed, Hammerless, Lightweight, *Modern*	100.00	150.00	135.00

High Standard Sentinel

High Standard Sharpshooter

High Standard Olympic O.S.U.

High Standard Victor

High Standard Longhorn

High Standard Trophy

High Standard Sport King

	V.G.	Exc.	Prior Year Exc. Value
□ **Flight King,** .22 Short R.F., Clip Fed, Hammerless, Lightweight, Extra Barrel, *Modern*	135.00	195.00	175.00
□ **Flight King,** .22 Short R.F., Clip Fed, Hammerless, *Modern*	105.00	165.00	150.00
□ **Flight King,** .22 Short R.F., Clip Fed, Hammerless, Extra Barrel, *Modern*	135.00	190.00	175.00
□ **H-DM (O.S.S.),** .22 Short R.F., Clip Fed, Silencer, Hammer, *Class 3*	560.00	800.00	775.00
□ **Model A,** .22 L.R.R.F., Clip Fed, Hammerless, *Curio*	175.00	250.00	235.00
□ **Model B,** .22 L.R.R.F., Clip Fed, Hammerless, *Curio*	180.00	265.00	240.00
□ **Model B,** .22 L.R.R.F., Navy, Clip Fed, Hammerless, *Curio*	325.00	525.00	475.00
□ **Model C,** .22 Short R.F., Clip Fed, Hammerless, *Curio*	190.00	275.00	250.00
□ **Model D,** .22 L.R.R.F., Clip Fed, Hammerless, Heavy Barrel, *Curio*	190.00	280.00	250.00
□ **Model E,** .22 L.R.R.F., Clip Fed, Hammerless, Heavy Barrel, Target Grips, *Curio*	230.00	360.00	325.00
□ **Model G-380,** .380 ACP, Clip Fed, Hammer, Takedown, *Curio*	275.00	390.00	350.00
□ **Model G-B,** .22 L.R.R.F., Clip Fed, Hammerless, Takedown, *Curio*	170.00	240.00	215.00
□ **Model G-B,** .22 L.R.R.F., Clip Fed, Hammerless, Takedown, Extra Barrel, *Curio*	185.00	280.00	245.00
□ **Model G-D,** .22 L.R.R.F., Clip Fed, Hammerless, Takedown, *Curio*	185.00	290.00	260.00
□ **Model G-D,** .22 L.R.R.F., Clip Fed, Hammerless, Takedown, Extra Barrel, *Curio*	210.00	315.00	280.00
□ **Model G-E,** .22 L.R.R.F., Clip Fed, Hammerless, Takedown, Extra Barrel, *Curio*	280.00	400.00	350.00
□ **Model G-E,** .22 L.R.R.F., Clip Fed, Hammerless, Takedown, *Curio*	195.00	305.00	285.00
□ **Model G-O,** .22 Short R.F., Clip Fed, Hammerless, Takedown, Extra Barrel, *Curio*	290.00	400.00	375.00
□ **Model G-O,** .22 Short R.F., Clip Fed, Hammerless, Takedown, *Curio*	270.00	350.00	325.00
□ **Model H-A,** .22 L.R.R.F., Clip Fed, Hammer, *Curio*	150.00	250.00	225.00
□ **Model H-B,** .22 L.R.R.F., Clip Fed, Hammer, *Curio*	165.00	250.00	225.00
□ **Model H-D,** .22 L.R.R.F., Clip Fed, Hammer, Heavy Barrel, *Curio*	170.00	265.00	235.00
□ **Model H-D Military,** .22 L.R.R.F., Clip Fed, Hammer, Heavy Barrel, Thumb Safety, *Curio*	200.00	310.00	275.00
□ **Model H-E,** .22 L.R.R.F., Clip Fed, Hammer, Heavy Barrel, Target Grips, *Curio*	215.00	325.00	300.00
□ **Model SB,** .22 L.R.R.F., Clip Fed, Hammerless, Smoothbore, *Class 3*	145.00	210.00	195.00
□ **Olympic,** .22 Short R.F., Clip Fed, Hammerless, *Modern*	180.00	250.00	235.00
□ **Olympic,** .22 Short R.F., Clip Fed, Hammerless, Extra Barrel, *Modern*	200.00	280.00	265.00
□ **Olympic I.S.U.,** .22 Short R.F., Supermatic, Clip Fed, Hammerless, Military, *Modern*	190.00	260.00	240.00

	V.G.	Exc.	Prior Year Exc. Value
☐ **Olympic I.S.U.,** .22 Short R.F., Supermatic, Clip Fed, Hammerless, *Modern*	185.00	245.00	235.00
☐ **Olympic I.S.U.,** .22 Short R.F., Clip Fed, Hammerless, Military, Frame-Mounted Rear Sight, *Modern*	190.00	260.00	250.00
☐ **Olympic I.S.U.,** .22 Short R.F., Clip Fed, Hammerless, Frame-Mounted Rear Sight, *Modern*	195.00	265.00	250.00
☐ **Plinker,** .22 L.R.R.F., Clip Fed, Hammer, *Modern*	100.00	155.00	135.00
☐ **Sharpshooter,** .22 L.R.R.F., Clip Fed, Hammerless, *Modern*	115.00	175.00	160.00
☐ **Sharpshooter (Late),** .22 L.R.R.F., Military Grip, Clip Fed, Hammerless, *Modern*	155.00	230.00	220.00
☐ **Sport King,** .22 L.R.R.F., Clip Fed, Hammerless, Lightweight, *Modern*	95.00	140.00	135.00
☐ **Sport King,** .22 L.R.R.F., Clip Fed, Hammerless, Lightweight, Extra Barrel, *Modern*	120.00	170.00	160.00
☐ **Sport King,** .22 L.R.R.F., Clip Fed, Hammerless, *Modern*	120.00	170.00	160.00
☐ **Sport King,** .22 L.R.R.F., Clip Fed, Hammerless, Extra Barrel, *Modern*	120.00	170.00	160.00
☐ **Sport King (Late),** .22 L.R.R.F., Military Grip,Clip Fed, Hammerless, *Modern*	150.00	195.00	185.00
☐ **Supermatic,** .22 L.R.R.F., Clip Fed, Hammerless, *Modern*	140.00	190.00	180.00
☐ **Supermatic,** .22 L.R.R.F., Clip Fed, Hammerless, Extra Barrel, *Modern*	160.00	235.00	225.00
☐ **Survival Pack,** .22 L.R.R.F., Sharpshooter (Late), Electroless Nickel Plated, Cased with Accessories, *Modern*	170.00	250.00	245.00
☐ **Tournament,** .22 L.R.R.F., Supermatic, Clip Fed, Hammerless, *Modern*	140.00	195.00	185.00
☐ **Tournament,** .22 L.R.R.F., Supermatic, Clip Fed, Hammerless, Military, *Modern*	155.00	215.00	200.00
☐ **Trophy (Early),** .22 L.R.R.F., Supermatic, Clip Fed, Hammerless, *Modern*	165.00	235.00	215.00
☐ **Trophy (Late),** .22 L.R.R.F., Supermatic, Military, Hammerless, Frame-Mounted Rear Sight, Fluted Barrel, *Modern*	175.00	230.00	225.00
☐ **Trophy (Late),** .22 L.R.R.F., Supermatic, Military, Hammerless, Frame-Mounted Rear Sight, Heavy Barrel, *Modern*	180.00	260.00	255.00
☐ **Victor,** .22 L.R.R.F., Heavy Barrel, Military Grip, Solid Rib, Target Sights, *Modern*	205.00	300.00	290.00
☐ **Victor,** .22 L.R.R.F., Heavy Barrel, Military Grip, Vent Rib, Target Sights, *Modern*	230.00	315.00	310.00
☐ **10-X Custom,** .22 L.R.R.F., Heavy Barrel, Military Grip, Target Sights, *Modern*	360.00	470.00	475.00

RIFLE, BOLT ACTION

	V.G.	Exc.	Prior Year Exc. Value
☐ **Hi Power,** Various Calibers, Field Grade, *Modern*	165.00	205.00	200.00
☐ **Hi Power Deluxe,** Various Calibers, Monte Carlo Stock, Checkered Stock, *Modern*	190.00	240.00	235.00

	V.G.	Exc.	Prior Year Exc. Value
RIFLE, SLIDE ACTION			
☐ **.22 L.R.R.F.,** Flight-King, Tube Feed, Monte Carlo Stock, *Modern*	75.00	115.00	110.00
RIFLE, SEMI-AUTOMATIC			
☐ **Sport King,** .22 L.R.R.F., Field Grade, Tube Feed, *Modern*	65.00	100.00	95.00
☐ **Sport King,** .22 L.R.R.F., Field Grade, Carbine, Tube Feed, *Modern*	75.00	110.00	100.00
☐ **Sport King Deluxe,** .22 L.R.R.F., Tube Feed, Monte Carlo Stock, Checkered Stock, *Modern*	75.00	110.00	100.00
☐ **Sport King Special,** .22 L.R.R.F., Tube Feed, Monte Carlo Stock, *Modern*	65.00	95.00	95.00
SHOTGUN, SEMI-AUTOMATIC			
☐ **Trap Grade,** Vent Rib, Recoil Pad, *Modern*	145.00	200.00	195.00
☐ **Skeet Grade,** Vent Rib, Recoil Pad, *Modern*	145.00	200.00	195.00
☐ **12 Ga.,** Supermatic, Field Grade, *Modern*	110.00	165.00	160.00
☐ **20 Ga.,** Mag., Supermatic, Field Grade, *Modern*	115.00	160.00	160.00
☐ **20 Ga.,** Mag., Supermatic, Skeet Grade, Vent Rib, *Modern*	145.00	190.00	190.00
☐ **Deer Gun,** 12 Ga., Supermatic, Open Rear Sight, Recoil Pad, *Modern*	135.00	195.00	190.00
☐ **Deluxe,** Recoil Pad, *Modern*	120.00	165.00	165.00
☐ **Deluxe,** Recoil Pad, Vent Rib, *Modern*	145.00	190.00	185.00
☐ **Deluxe,** 20 Ga. Mag., Supermatic, Recoil Pad, *Modern*	120.00	170.00	165.00
☐ **Deluxe,** 20 Ga. Mag., Supermatic, Recoil Pad, Vent Rib, *Modern*	145.00	195.00	190.00
☐ **Duck Gun,** 12 Ga. Mag. 3″, Supermatic, Recoil Pad, Field Grade, *Modern*	145.00	200.00	195.00
☐ **Duck Gun,** 12 Ga. Mag. 3″, Supermatic, Vent Rib, Recoil Pad, *Modern*	150.00	200.00	195.00
☐ **Model 10,** 12 Ga., Riot Gun, *Modern*	230.00	365.00	350.00
☐ **Special,** 12 Ga., Field Grade, Adjustable Choke, *Modern*	135.00	190.00	185.00
☐ **Special,** 20 Ga. Mag., Supermatic, Field Grade, Adjustable Choke, *Modern*	140.00	190.00	190.00
☐ **Trophy,** Recoil Pad, Vent Rib, Adjustable Choke, *Modern*	165.00	220.00	215.00
☐ **Trophy,** 20 Ga. Mag., Supermatic, Recoil Pad, Vent Rib, Adjustable Choke, *Modern*	170.00	225.00	220.00
SHOTGUN, SLIDE ACTION			
☐ **.410 Ga. 3″,** Flight-King, Field Grade, *Modern*	95.00	145.00	140.00
☐ **.410 Ga. 3″,** Flight-King, Skeet Grade, *Modern*	125.00	170.00	165.00
☐ **12 Ga.,** Flight-King, Trap Grade, Vent Rib, Recoil Pad, *Modern*	125.00	170.00	165.00
☐ **12 Ga.,** Flight-King, Skeet Grade, Vent Rib, Recoil Pad, *Modern*	120.00	160.00	160.00
☐ **12 and 20 Gauges,** Flight-King, Field Grade, *Modern*	90.00	150.00	140.00
☐ **28 Ga.,** Flight-King, Field Grade, *Modern*	100.00	160.00	145.00
☐ **28 Ga.,** Flight-King, Skeet Grade, Vent Rib, *Modern*	120.00	165.00	165.00
☐ **Brush Gun,** 12 Ga., Flight-King, Open Rear Sight, *Modern*	95.00	145.00	145.00

	V.G.	Exc.	Prior Year Exc. Value
☐ **Deluxe,** .410 Ga. 3″ , Flight-King, Vent Rib, *Modern*	100.00	150.00	145.00
☐ **Deluxe,** 12 and 20 Gauges, Flight-King, Recoil Pad, *Modern*	90.00	130.00	130.00
☐ **Deluxe,** 12 and 20 Gauges, Flight-King, Recoil Pad, Vent Rib, *Modern*	100.00	150.00	145.00
☐ **Deluxe,** .28 Ga., Flight-King, Vent Rib, *Modern*	110.00	160.00	155.00
☐ **Deluxe Brush Gun,** 12 Ga., Flight-King, Peep Sights, Sling Swivels, *Modern*	115.00	165.00	160.00
☐ **Riot,** 12 Ga., Flight-King, Plain Barrel, *Modern*	110.00	155.00	150.00
☐ **Riot,** 12 Ga., Flight-King, Open Rear Sight, *Modern*	120.00	170.00	165.00
☐ **Sepcial,** 12 and 20 Gauges, Flight-King, Field Grade, Adjustable Choke, *Modern*	100.00	145.00	140.00
☐ **Trophy,** 12 and 20 Gauges, Flight-King, Recoil Pad, Vent Rib, Adjustable Choke, *Modern*	125.00	175.00	165.00
SHOTGUN, DOUBLE BARREL, OVER-UNDER			
☐ **Shadow Indy,** 12 Ga., Single Selective Trigger, Selective Ejectors, Checkered Stock, Engraved, *Modern*	450.00	585.00	575.00
☐ **Shadow Seven,** 12 Ga., Single Selective Trigger, Selective Ejectors, Checkered Stock, Light Engraving, *Modern*	340.00	495.00	485.00

HIJO

Tradename used by Sloan's of N.Y.C.

HANDGUN, SEMI-AUTOMATIC

	V.G.	Exc.	Prior Year Exc. Value
☐ **Hijo**, .25 ACP, Clip Fed, *Modern*	65.00	100.00	95.00
☐ **Hijo Military**, .22 L.R.R.F., Clip Fed, *Modern*	70.00	110.00	100.00

HILL, S.W.

See Kentucky Rifles and Pistols.

HILLEGAS, J.

Pottsville, Pa. 1810-1830. See Kentucky Rifles.

HILLIARD, D.H. & GEORGE C.

D.H. Hilliard, Cornish, New Hampshire, 1842-1877, taken over by George C. Hilliard and operated 1877-1880.

HANDGUN, PERCUSSION

	V.G.	Exc.	Prior Year Exc. Value
☐ **.34**, Underhammer Target Pistol, *Antique*	220.00	325.00	300.00

HINO-KOMORO

Kumaso Hino and Tomisiro Komoro, Tokyo, Japan, c. 1910.

HANDGUN, SEMI-AUTOMATIC

	V.G.	Exc.	Prior Year Exc. Value
☐ **Blow-Forward**, .32 ACP, Clip Fed, *Curio*	1,525.00	2,700.00	2,500.00

HOCKLEY, JAMES

Chester County, Pa. 1769-1771. See Kentucky Rifles.

HOLDEN, CYRUS B.

Worcester, Mass., c. 1861-1880.

	V.G.	Exc.	Prior Year Exc. Value
SHOTGUN, SINGLESHOT			
☐ **Model 1862**, .44 Henry, Octagon Barrel, *Antique*	300.00	550.00	550.00
☐ **Tip-Up**, .22 R.F., Nickel Plated Frame, Blued Barrel, *Antique*	300.00	450.00	450.00

HOLLAND & HOLLAND

London, England since 1835.

	V.G.	Exc.	Prior Year Exc. Value
RIFLE, BOLT ACTION			
☐ **Best Quality**, Various Calibers, Express Sights, Fancy Checkering, Engraved, *Modern*	1,750.00	2,900.00	2,850.00
☐ **Best Quality**, Various Calibers, Express Sights, Checkered Stock, *Modern*	1,275.00	2,000.00	1,975.00
RIFLE, DOUBLE BARREL, SIDE-BY-SIDE			
☐ **#2**, Various Calibers, Sidelock, Checkered Stock, Engraved, Hammerless, *Modern*	5,600.00	9,000.00	8,775.00
☐ **Deluxe**, Various Calibers, Sidelock, Automatic Ejector, Fancy Engraving, Fancy Checkering, Double Trigger, *Modern*	12,000.00	16,000.00	16,500.00
☐ **Royal**, Various Calibers, Sidelock, Automatic Ejector, Fancy Engraving, Fancy Checkering, Double Trigger, *Modern*	6,700.00	10,000.00	10,500.00
☐ **Special Order**, Various Calibers, Sidelock, Fancy Checkering, Fancy Engraving, Hammerless, *Modern*	11,000.00	16,000.00	16,500.00
SHOTGUN, DOUBLE BARREL, OVER-UNDER			
☐ **Deluxe Royal**, 12 Ga., Sidelock, Automatic Ejector, Fancy Engraving, Fancy Checkering, Double Triggers, *Modern*	12,000.00	16,500.00	17,000.00
☐ **Deluxe Royal**, 12 Ga., Sidelock Automatic Ejector, Fancy Engraving, Fancy Checkering, Single Trigger, *Modern*	14,000.00	19,000.00	20,000.00
☐ **Royal Model (Late)**, 12 Ga., Sidelock, Automatic Ejector, Fancy Engraving, Fancy Checkering, Double Triggers, *Modern*	9,000.00	14,000.00	14,500.00
☐ **Royal Model (Late)**, 12 Ga., Sidelock, Automatic Ejector, Fancy Engraving, Fancy Checkering, Single Trigger, *Modern*	10,000.00	15,000.00	15,000.00
☐ **Royal Model (Old)**, 12 Ga., Sidelock, Automatic Ejector, Fancy Engraving, Fancy Checkering, Double Triggers, *Modern*	8,000.00	11,000.00	11,500.00
☐ **Royal Model (Old)**, 12 Ga., Sidelock, Automatic Ejector, Fancy Engraving, Fancy Checkering, Single Trigger, *Modern*	9,000.00	13,000.00	13,000.00
SHOTGUN, DOUBLE BARREL, SIDE-BY-SIDE			
☐ **Badminton**, Various Gauges, Sidelock, Automatic Ejector, Fancy Engraving, Fancy Checkering, Double Triggers, *Modern*	5,000.00	7,500.00	7,750.00
☐ **Badminton**, Various Gauges, Sidelock, Automatic Ejector, Fancy Engraving, Fancy Checkering, Single Trigger, *Modern*	5,500.00	8,000.00	8,250.00
☐ **Centenary Badminton**, 12 Ga. 2", Sidelock, Automatic Ejector, Fancy Engraving, Fancy Checkering, Double Triggers, *Modern*	5,000.00	7,000.00	7,250.00

	V.G.	Exc.	Prior Year Exc. Value
☐ **Centenary Deluxe**, 12 Ga. 2", Sidelock, Automatic Ejector, Fancy Engraving, Fancy Checkering, Double Triggers, *Modern*	8,750.00	13,000.00	13,500.00
☐ **Centenary Dominion**, 12 Ga. 2", Sidelock, Automatic Ejector, Engraved, Checkered Stock, Double Triggers, *Modern*	2,750.00	4,500.00	4,650.00
☐ **Cententary Royal**, 12 Ga. 2", Sidelock, Automatic Ejector, Fancy Engraving, Fancy Checkering, Double Triggers, *Modern*	8,500.00	11,500.00	11,750.00
☐ **Deluxe**, Various Gauges, Sidelock, Automatic Ejector, Fancy Engraving, Fancy Checkering, Double Triggers, *Modern*	8,750.00	13,000.00	13,250.00
☐ **Deluxe**, Various Gauges, Sidelock, Automatic Ejector, Fancy Engraving, Fancy Checkering, Single Trigger, *Modern*	9,250.00	13,500.00	14,000.00
☐ **Dominion**, Various Gauges, Sidelock, Automatic Ejector, Engraved, Checkered Stock, Double Triggers, *Modern*	2,800.00	4,750.00	4,700.00
☐ **Northwood**, Various Gauges, Boxlock, Automatic Ejector, Checkered Stock, Engraved, *Modern*	1,750.00	2,700.00	2,650.00
☐ **Riviera**, Various Gauges, Extra Shotgun Barrel, Automatic Ejector, Fancy Engraving, Fancy Checkering, Double Triggers, *Modern*	6,000.00	9,500.00	9,750.00
☐ **Royal**, Various Gauges, Sidelock, Automatic Ejector, Fancy Engraving, Fancy Checkering, Double Triggers, *Modern*	8,500.00	12,000.00	12,000.00
☐ **Royal**, Various Gauges, Sidelock, Automatic Ejector, Fancy Engraving, Fancy Checkering, Single Trigger, *Modern*	8,750.00	14,000.00	14,000.00
☐ **Royal Ejector Grade**, 12 Ga. Mag. 3", Single Selective Trigger, Vent Rib, Pistol-Grip Stock, Cased with Accessories, *Modern*	11,000.00	16,000.00	16,500.00
SHOTGUN, SINGLESHOT			
☐ **Standard Super Trap**, 12 Ga., Boxlock, Automatic Ejector, Vent Rib, Fancy Engraving, Checkered Stock, *Modern*	5,500.00	8,500.00	8,250.00
☐ **Deluxe Super Trap**, 12 Ga., Boxlock, Automatic Ejector, Vent Rib, Fancy Engraving, Checkered Stock, *Modern*	6,500.00	9,250.00	9,000.00
☐ **Exhibition Super Trap**, 12 Ga., Boxlock, Automatic Ejector, Vent Rib, Fancy Engraving, Checkered Stock, *Modern*	7,750.00	12,000.00	12,000.00

HOLLIS, CHAS. & SONS

London, England.

SHOTGUN, DOUBLE BARREL, SIDE-BY-SIDE

☐ **12 Ga.**, Hammerless, Engraved, Fancy Checkering, Fancy Wood, *Modern*	2,150.00	2,900.00	2,875.00

HOLLIS, RICHARD

London, England 1800-1850.

HANDGUN, FLINTLOCK

☐ **.68**, Holster Pistol, Round Barrel, Brass Furniture, Plain, *Antique*	500.00	765.00	750.00

	V.G.	Exc.	Prior Year Exc. Value
SHOTGUN, PERCUSSION			
☐ **12 Ga.**, Double Barrels, Double Triggers, Hook Breech, Light Engraving, Checkered Stock, *Antique*	325.00	500.00	

HOLMES, BILL

Fayetteville, Ark.

	V.G.	Exc.	Prior Year Exc. Value
SHOTGUN, SINGLESHOT			
☐ **Supertrap**, 12 Ga., Various Action Types, Checkered Stock, *Modern*	1,100.00	1,750.00	1,750.00

HOOD FIRE ARMS CO.

Norwich, Conn., c. 1875

	V.G.	Exc.	Prior Year Exc. Value
HANDGUN, REVOLVER			
☐ **.32 Short R.F.**, 5 Shot, Spur Trigger, Solid Frame, Single Action, *Antique*	95.00	165.00	160.00

HOPKINS & ALLEN

Norwich, Conn. 1868-1917, taken over by Marlin-Rockwell in 1917. Later purchased by Numrich Arms Corp., West Hurley, N.Y., and now in Hawthorne, N.J.

	V.G.	Exc.	Prior Year Exc. Value
HANDGUN, PERCUSSION			
☐ **"Boot Pistol,"** .36, Under-Hammer, Octagon Barrel, Reproduction, (Numrich), *Antique*	28.00	50.00	45.00
HANDGUN, REVOLVER			
☐ **Model 1876 Army,** .44-40 WCF, Solid Frame, Single Action, 6 Shot, Finger-Rest Trigger Guard, *Antique*	365.00	600.00	575.00
☐ **Safety Police,** .22 L.R.R.F., Top Break, Double Action, Various Barrel Lengths, *Modern*	75.00	125.00	125.00
☐ **Safety Police,** .32 S & W, Top Break, Double Action, Various Barrel Lengths, *Modern*	70.00	125.00	120.00
☐ **Safety Police,** .38 S & W, Top Break, Double Action, Various Barrel Lengths, *Modern*	70.00	125.00	120.00
☐ **XL .30 Long,** .30 Long R.F., Solid Frame, Spur Trigger, Single Action, 5 Shot, *Antique*	110.00	165.00	160.00
☐ **XL 1 Double Action,** .22 Short R.F., Solid Frame, Folding Hammer, *Modern*	75.00	105.00	100.00
☐ **XL 3 Double Action,** .32 S & W, Solid Frame, Folding Hammer, *Modern*	65.00	105.00	100.00
☐ **XL Bulldog,** .32 S & W, Solid Frame, Folding Hammer, *Modern*	65.00	105.00	100.00
☐ **XL Bulldog,** .32 Short R.F., Solid Frame, Folding Hammer, *Modern*	60.00	95.00	90.00
☐ **XL Bulldog,** .38 S & W, Solid Frame, Folding Hammer, *Modern*	65.00	105.00	100.00
☐ **XL CR .22 Short R.F.,** Solid Frame, Spur Trigger, Single Action, 7 Shot, *Antique*	100.00	160.00	155.00
☐ **XL Double Action,** .32 S & W, Solid Frame, Folding Hammer, *Modern*	65.00	105.00	100.00
☐ **XL Double Action,** .38 S & W, Solid Frame, Folding Hammer, *Modern*	65.00	105.00	100.00
☐ **XL Navy,** .38 Short R.F., Solid Frame, Single Action, 6 Shot, *Antique*	330.00	475.00	450.00

	V.G.	Exc.	Prior Year Exc. Value
☐ **XL No. 1,** .22 Short R.F., Solid Frame, Spur Trigger, Single Action, 7 Shot, *Antique*	135.00	185.00	180.00
☐ **XL No. 2,** .30 Short R.F., Solid Frame, Spur Trigger, Single Action, 5 Shot, *Antique*	135.00	190.00	185.00
☐ **XL No. 3,** .32 Short R.F., Solid Frame, Spur Trigger, Single Action, 5 Shot, Safety Cylinder, *Antique*	145.00	200.00	190.00
☐ **XL No. 4,** .38 Short R.F., Solid Frame, Spur Trigger, Single Action, 5 Shot, *Antique*	145.00	200.00	190.00
☐ **XL No. 5,** .38 S & W, Solid Frame, Spur Trigger, Single Action, 5 Shot, *Antique*	230.00	380.00	370.00
☐ **XL No. 5,** .38 Short R.F., Solid Frame, Spur Trigger, Single Action, 5 Shot, Safety Cylinder, Engraved, *Antique*	290.00	350.00	325.00
☐ **XL No. 6,** .41 Short R.F., Solid Frame, Spur Trigger, Single Action, 5 Shot, *Antique*	150.00	230.00	220.00
☐ **XL No. 7,** .41 Short R.F., Solid Frame, Spur Trigger, Single Action, 5 Shot, Swing-Out Cylinder, *Antique*	160.00	275.00	265.00
☐ **XL No. 8 (Army),** .44 R.F., Solid Frame, Single Action, 6 Shot, *Antique*	380.00	560.00	545.00
☐ **XL Police,** .38 Short R.F., Solid Frame, Single Action, 6 Shot, *Antique*	130.00	180.00	175.00
HANDGUN, SINGLESHOT			
☐ **Ladies Garter Pistol,** .22 Short R.F., Tip-Up, Folding Trigger, Single Action, *Antique*	95.00	140.00	135.00
☐ **New Model Target,** .22 L.R.R.F., Top Break, 10″ Barrel, Adjustable Sights, Target Grips, *Modern*	250.00	360.00	345.00
☐ **XL Derringer,** .41 Short R.F., Spur Trigger, Single Action, *Antique*	380.00	600.00	575.00
RIFLE, BOLT ACTION			
☐ **American Military,** .22 L.R.R.F., Singleshot, Takedown, Open Rear Sight, Round Barrel, *Modern*	145.00	200.00	195.00
RIFLE, FLINTLOCK			
☐ **"Kentucky,"** .31, Octagon Barrel, Full-Stocked, Brass Furniture, Reproduction, (Numrich), *Antique*	135.00	185.00	180.00
☐ **"Kentucky,"** .36, Octagon Barrel, Full-Stocked, Brass Furniture, Reproduction, (Numrich), *Antique*	140.00	185.00	180.00
☐ **"Kentucky,"** .45, Octagon Barrel, Full-Stocked, Brass Furniture, Reproduction, (Numrich), *Antique*	150.00	195.00	190.00
☐ **"Minuteman Brush,"** .45, Octagon Barrel, Full-Stocked, Carbine, Reproduction, (Numrich), *Antique*	140.00	195.00	190.00
☐ **"Minuteman Brush,"** .50, Octagon Barrel, Full-Stocked, Carbine, Reproduction, (Numrich), *Antique*	140.00	195.00	190.00
☐ **"Minuteman,"** .31, Octagon Barrel, Full-Stocked, Brass Furniture, Reproduction, (Numrich), *Antique*	135.00	185.00	180.00

	V.G.	Exc.	Prior Year Exc. Value
☐ **"Minuteman,"** .36, Octagon Barrel, Full-Stocked, Brass Furniture, Reproduction, (Numrich), *Antique*	140.00	185.00	180.00
☐ **"Minuteman,"** .45, Octagon Barrel, Full-Stocked, Brass Furniture, Reproduction, (Numrich), *Antique*	150.00	195.00	190.00
☐ **"Minuteman,"** .50, Octagon Barrel, Full-Stocked, Brass Furniture, Reproduction, (Numrich), *Antique*	155.00	195.00	190.00
☐ **"Pennsylvania,"** .31, Octagon Barrel, Half-Stocked, Brass Furniture, Reproduction, (Numrich), *Antique*	130.00	180.00	175.00
☐ **"Pennsylvania,"** .36, Octagon Barrel, Half-Stocked, Brass Furniture, Reproduction, (Numrich), *Antique*	135.00	180.00	175.00
☐ **"Pennsylvania,"** .45, Octagon Barrel, Half-Stocked, Brass Furniture, Reproduction, (Numrich), *Antique*	135.00	190.00	185.00
☐ **"Pennsylvania,"** .50, Octagon Barrel, Half-Stocked, Brass Furniture, Reproduction, (Numrich), *Antique*	140.00	190.00	185.00
RIFLE, PERCUSSION			
☐ **"Buggy Deluxe,"** .36, Under-Hammer, Octagon Barrel, Carbine, Reproduction, (Numrich), *Antique*	75.00	105.00	100.00
☐ **"Buggy Deluxe,"** .45, Under-Hammer, Octagon Barrel, Carbine, Reproduction, (Numrich), *Antique*	80.00	115.00	110.00
☐ **"Deer Stalker,"** .58, Under-Hammer, Octagon Barrel, Reproduction, (Numrich), *Antique*	80.00	105.00	100.00
☐ **"Heritage,"** .36, Under-Hammer, Octagon Barrel, Brass Furniture, Reproduction, (Numrich), *Antique*	75.00	115.00	110.00
☐ **"Heritage,"** .45, Under-Hammer, Octagon Barrel, Brass Furniture, Reproduction, (Numrich), *Antique*	80.00	120.00	115.00
☐ **"Kentucky,"** .31, Full-Stocked, Octagon Barrel, Brass Furniture, Reproduction, (Numrich), *Antique*	135.00	180.00	175.00
☐ **"Kentucky,"** .36, Full-Stocked, Octagon Barrel, Brass Furniture, Reproduction, (Numrich), *Antique*	140.00	180.00	175.00
☐ **"Kentucky,"** .45, Full-Stocked, Octagon Barrel, Brass Furniture, Reproduction, (Numrich), *Antique*	145.00	185.00	180.00
☐ **"Minuteman Brush,"** .45, Full-Stocked, Octagon Barrel, Carbine, Reproduction, (Numrich), *Antique*	135.00	185.00	180.00

Hopkins & Allen Heritage Rifle

	V.G.	Exc.	Prior Year Exc. Value
☐ **"Minuteman Brush,"** .50, Full-Stocked, Octagon Barrel, Carbine, Reproduction, (Numrich), *Antique*	130.00	185.00	180.00
☐ **"Minuteman,"** .31, Full-Stocked, Octagon Barrel, Brass Furniture, Reproduction, (Numrich), *Antique*	125.00	180.00	175.00
☐ **"Minuteman,"** .36, Full-Stocked, Octagon Barrel, Brass Furniture, Reproduction, (Numrich), *Antique*	130.00	180.00	175.00
☐ **"Minuteman,"** .45, Full-Stocked, Octagon Barrel, Brass Furniture, Reproduction, (Numrich), *Antique*	130.00	185.00	180.00
☐ **"Minuteman,"** .50, Full-Stocked, Octagon Barrel, Brass Furniture, Reproduction, (Numrich), *Antique*	135.00	185.00	180.00
☐ **"Offhand Deluxe,"** .36, Under-Hammer, Octagon Barrel, Reproduction, (Numrich), *Antique*	60.00	105.00	100.00
☐ **"Offhand Deluxe,"** .45, Under-Hammer, Octagon Barrel, Reproduction, (Numrich), *Antique*	65.00	105.00	100.00
☐ **"Offhand Deluxe,"** .45, Under-Hammer, Octagon Barrel, Reproduction, (Numrich), *Antique*	65.00	105.00	100.00
☐ **"Pennsylvania,"** .31, Half-Stocked, Octagon Barrel, Brass Furniture, Reproduction, (Numrich), *Antique*	125.00	170.00	165.00
☐ **"Pennsylvania,"** .36, Half-Stocked, Octagon Barrel, Brass Furniture, Reproduction, (Numrich), *Antique*	130.00	170.00	165.00
☐ **"Pennsylvania,"** .45, Half-Stocked, Octagon Barrel, Brass Furniture, Reproduction, (Numrich), *Antique*	130.00	175.00	170.00
☐ **"Pennsylvania,"** .50, Half-Stocked, Octagon Barrel, Brass Furniture, Reproduction, (Numrich), *Antique*	135.00	175.00	170.00
☐ **"Target,"** .45, Under-Hammer, Octagon Barrel, Reproduction, (Numrich), *Antique*	60.00	100.00	95.00
☐ **.45,** Double Barrel, Over-Under, Swivel Breech, Brass Furniture, Reproduction, (Numrich), *Antique*	80.00	125.00	120.00

RIFLE, SINGLESHOT

	V.G.	Exc.	Prior Year Exc. Value
☐ **Model 1888 (XL),** Various Calibers, Falling Block, Takedown, Lever Action, Round Barrel, Open Rear Sight, *Antique*	235.00	375.00	350.00
☐ **Model 1888 Junior,** .22 L.R.R.F., Falling Block, Takedown, Lever Action, Round Barrel, Open Rear Sight, *Antique*	105.00	160.00	155.00
☐ **No. 1922 New Model Junior,** .22 L.R.R.F., Falling Block, Takedown, Lever Action, Octagon Barrel, Open Rear Sight, *Modern*	145.00	235.00	225.00
☐ **No. 1925 New Model Junior,** .25 Short R.F., Falling Block, Takedown, Lever Action, Octagon Barrel, Open Rear Sight, *Modern*	165.00	265.00	250.00
☐ **No. 1932 New Model Junior,** .32 Long R.F., Falling Block, Takedown, Lever Action, Octagon Barrel, Open Rear Sight, *Modern*	155.00	255.00	245.00

	V.G.	Exc.	Prior Year Exc. Value
☐ **No. 1938 New Model Junior,** .38 S & W, Falling Block, Takedown, Lever Action, Octagon Barrel, Open Rear Sight, *Modern*	185.00	275.00	260.00
☐ **No. 2922 New Model Junior,** .22 L.R.R.F., Falling Block, Takedown, Lever Action, Octagon Barrel, Checkered Stock, Open Rear Sight, *Modern*	165.00	260.00	245.00
☐ **No. 2925 New Model Junior,** .25 Short R.F., Falling Block, Takedown, Lever Action, Octagon Barrel, Checkered Stock, Open Rear Sight, *Modern*	180.00	275.00	260.00
☐ **No. 2932 New Model Junior,** .32 Long R.F., Falling Block, Takedown, Lever Action, Octagon Barrel, Checkered Stock, Open Rear Sight, *Modern*	180.00	275.00	260.00
☐ **No. 2938 New Model Junior,** .38 S & W, Falling Block, Takedown, Lever Action, Octagon Barrel, Checkered Stock, Open Rear Sight, *Modern*	220.00	310.00	300.00
☐ **No. 3922 Schuetzen Target,** .22 L.R.R.F., Falling Block, Takedown, Lever Action, Octagon Barrel, Checkered Stock, Swiss Buttplate, *Modern*	440.00	660.00	635.00
☐ **No. 3925 Schuetzen Target,** .25-20 WCF, Falling Block, Takedown, Lever Action, Octagon Barrel, Checkered Stock, Swiss Buttplate, *Modern*	510.00	750.00	725.00
☐ **No. 722,** .22 L.R.R.F., Rolling Block, Takedown, Round Barrel, Open Rear Sight, *Modern*	85.00	135.00	125.00
☐ **No. 822,** .22 L.R.R.F., Rolling Block, Takedown, Lever Action, Round Barrel, Open Rear Sight, *Modern*	100.00	160.00	150.00
☐ **No. 832,** .32 Short R.F., Rolling Block, Takedown, Lever Action, Round Barrel, Open Rear Sight, *Modern*	105.00	170.00	160.00
☐ **No. 922 New Model Junior,** .22 L.R.R.F., Falling Block, Takedown, Lever Action, Round Barrel, Open Rear Sight, *Modern*	115.00	170.00	160.00
☐ **No. 925 New Model Junior,** .25 Short R.F., Falling Block, Takedown, Lever Action, Round Barrel, Open Rear Sight, *Modern*	105.00	170.00	160.00
☐ **No. 932 New Model Junior,** .32 Long R.F., Falling Block, Takedown, Lever Action, Round Barrel, Open Rear Sight, *Modern*	105.00	170.00	160.00
☐ **No. 938 New Model Junior,** .38 S & W, Falling Block, Takedown, Lever Action, Round Barrel, Open Rear Sight, *Modern*	155.00	240.00	220.00
☐ **Noiseless,** .22 L.R.R.F., Falling Block, Takedown, Lever Action, Round Barrel, Silencer, *Class 3*	305.00	450.00	425.00
SHOTGUN, DOUBLE BARREL, SIDE-BY-SIDE			
☐ **No. 100,** 12 and 16 Ga., Double Trigger, Outside Hammers, Checkered Stock, Steel Barrel, *Modern*	100.00	160.00	155.00
☐ **No. 110,** 12 and 16 Ga., Double Trigger, Hammerless, Checkered Stock, Steel Barrel, *Modern*	130.00	175.00	170.00
SHOTGUN, SINGLESHOT			
☐ **New Model,** Various Gauges, Hammer, Top Break, Steel Barrel, *Modern*	45.00	65.00	65.00

	V.G.	Exc.	Prior Year Exc. Value
☐ **New Model**, Various Gauges, Hammer, Top Break, Steel Barrel, Automatic Ejector, Checkered Stock, *Modern*	50.00	85.00	85.00
☐ **New Model**, Various Gauges, Hammer, Top Break, Damascus Barrel, Checkered Stock, *Modern*	45.00	70.00	70.00

HOPKINS, C.W.

Made by Bacon Mfg. Co., Norwich, Conn.

HANDGUN, REVOLVER

	V.G.	Exc.	Prior Year Exc. Value
☐ **.32 Short R.F.**, Single Action, Solid Frame, Swing-Out Cylinder, *Antique*	220.00	335.00	325.00
☐ **.38 Long R.F.**, Single Action, Solid Frame, Swing-Out Cylinder, *Antique*	365.00	625.00	600.00

HOROLT, LORENZ

Nuremberg, Germany, c. 1600.

HANDGUN, WHEEL-LOCK

	V.G.	Exc.	Prior Year Exc. Value
☐ **Long Barreled**, Holster Pistol, Hexagonal Ball Pommel, Light Ornamentation, *Antique*	6,250.00	7,950.00	7,750.00

HOWARD ARMS

Made by Meriden Firearms Co.

HANDGUN, REVOLVER

	V.G.	Exc.	Prior Year Exc. Value
☐ **.32 S & W**, 5 Shot, Double Action, Top Break, *Modern*	55.00	100.00	95.00
☐ **.38 S & W**, 5 Shot, Double Action, Top Break, *Modern*	55.00	100.00	95.00

HOWARD ARMS

Made by Cresent for Fred Bifflar & Co.

SHOTGUN, DOUBLE BARREL, SIDE-BY-SIDE

	V.G.	Exc.	Prior Year Exc. Value
☐ **Various Gauges**, Outside Hammers, Damascus Barrel, *Modern*	95.00	170.00	175.00
☐ **Various Gauges**, Hammerless, Steel Barrel, *Modern*	115.00	185.00	200.00
☐ **Various Gauges**, Hammerless, Damascus Barrel, *Modern*	90.00	165.00	175.00
☐ **Various Gauges**, Outside Hammers, Steel Barrel, *Modern*	115.00	180.00	190.00

SHOTGUN, SINGLESHOT

	V.G.	Exc.	Prior Year Exc. Value
☐ **Various Gauges**, Hammer, Steel Barrel, *Modern*	45.00	75.00	85.00

HOWARD BROTHERS

Detroit, Mich., c. 1868.

RIFLE, SINGLESHOT

	V.G.	Exc.	Prior Year Exc. Value
☐ **.44 Henry R.F., Round Barrel,** *Antique*	325.00	495.00	475.00

HOUILLER, BLANCHAR

Paris, France, c. 1845.

	V.G.	Exc.	Prior Year Exc. Value
HANDGUN, PERCUSSION			
☐ **Pepperbox**, .48, 6 Shot, *Antique*	365.00	490.00	475.00

HUMBERGER, PETER JR.

Ohio 1791-1852. See Kentucky Rifles.

HUMBERGER, PETER SR.

Pa. 1774-1791, then Ohio 1791-1811. See Kentucky Rifles.

HUMMER

Belgium, for Lee Hdw., Kansas.

	V.G.	Exc.	Prior Year Exc. Value
SHOTGUN, DOUBLE BARREL, SIDE-BY-SIDE			
☐ **Various Gauges**, Outside Hammers, Damascus Barrel, *Modern*	90.00	170.00	175.00
☐ **Various Gauges**, Hammerless, Steel Barrel, *Modern*	120.00	190.00	200.00
☐ **Various Gauges**, Outside Hammers, Steel Barrel, *Modern*	115.00	180.00	190.00
SHOTGUN, SINGLESHOT			
☐ **Various Gauges**, Hammer, Steel Barrel, *Modern*	50.00	80.00	85.00

HUNGARIAN MILITARY

	V.G.	Exc.	Prior Year Exc. Value
AUTOMATIC WEAPON, SUBMACHINE GUN			
☐ **43M,** 9mm Mauser Export, Clip Fed, Retarded Blowback, *Class 3*	785.00	1175.00	1150.00
HANDGUN, SEMI-AUTOMATIC			
☐ **19M Frommer Stop,** .380 ACP, Clip Fed, Blue, Military, *Curio*	135.00	200.00	275.00
☐ **29M Femaru,** .380 ACP, Clip Fed, Blue, Military, *Curio*	110.00	160.00	235.00
☐ **37M Femaru,** .380 ACP, Clip Fed, Blue, Military, *Curio*	100.00	145.00	200.00
RIFLE, BOLT ACTION			
☐ **1943M,** 8mm Mauser, Mannlicher, Military, *Curio*	80.00	125.00	180.00
☐ **8mm 1935M,** Mannlicher, Military, *Curio*	50.00	75.00	150.00

Hungarian Military 37M Femaru

HUNTER ARMS
See L.C. Smith.

HUNTING WORLD
N.Y.C.

SHOTGUN, DOUBLE BARREL, SIDE-BY-SIDE

	V.G.	Exc.	Prior Year Exc. Value
☐ **Royal Deluxe Game Gun**, 12 or 20 Gauges, Sidelock, Fancy Wood, Engraved, *Modern*	3,500.00	4,350.00	4,500.00

HUSQVARNA VAPENFABRIK AKITIEBOLAG
Husqvarna, Sweden.

HANDGUN, REVOLVER

	V.G.	Exc.	Prior Year Exc. Value
☐ **Model 1887 Swedish Nagent,** 7.5mm, Double Action, Blue, Military, *Antique*	165.00	250.00	225.00

HANDGUN, SEMI-AUTOMATIC

	V.G.	Exc.	Prior Year Exc. Value
☐ **Model 07,** 9mm Browning Long, Clip Fed, Swedish Military, *Modern*	130.00	190.00	250.00
☐ **Model 07,** 9mm Browning Long, Clip Fed, Belgian Military, *Modern*	135.00	200.00	270.00

Husqvarna M1907 Pistol

Husqvarna M1887 Revolver

RIFLE, BOLT ACTION

	V.G.	Exc.	Prior Year Exc. Value
☐ **Various Calibers**, Sporting Rifle, Checkered Stock, *Modern*	200.00	290.00	285.00
☐ **1000 Super Grade**, Various Calibers, Sporting Rifle, Checkered Stock, Monte Carlo Stock, *Modern*	225.00	325.00	325.00
☐ **1100 Deluxe**, Various Calibers, Sporting Rifle, Checkered Stock, *Modern*	225.00	325.00	325.00
☐ **1622**, .22 L.R.R.F., Clip Fed, Sling Swivels, *Modern*	55.00	80.00	75.00
☐ **1951**, Various Calibers, Sporting Rifle, Checkered Stock, *Modern*	200.00	285.00	275.00
☐ **3000 Crown Grade**, Various Calibers, Sporting Rifle, Checkered Stock, Monte Carlo Stock, *Modern*	275.00	375.00	375.00
☐ **3100 Crown Grade**, Various Calibers, Sporting Rifle, Checkered Stock, *Modern*	275.00	375.00	375.00

	V.G.	Exc.	Prior Year Exc. Value
☐ **4000**, Various Calibers, Sporting Rifle, Checkered Stock, Lightweight, Monte Carlo Stock, *Modern*	275.00	375.00	375.00
☐ **4100**, Various Calibers, Sporting Rifle, Checkered Stock, Lightweight, *Modern*	275.00	375.00	375.00
☐ **456**, Various Calibers, Sporting Rifle, Checkered Stock, Lightweight, Full-Stocked, *Modern*	300.00	400.00	400.00
☐ **6000 Imperial**, Various Calibers, Sporting Rifle, Checkered Stock, Fancy Wood, Express Sights, *Modern*	325.00	450.00	450.00
☐ **7000 Imperial**, Various Calibers, Sporting Rifle, Checkered Stock, Lightweight, Express Sights, *Modern*	325.00	450.00	450.00
☐ **8000 Imperial Grade**, Various Calibers, Sporting Rifle, Checkered Stock, Engraved, Monte Carlo Stock, Fancy Wood, *Modern*	350.00	475.00	475.00
☐ **9000 Crown Grade**, Various Calibers, Sporting Rifle, Checkered Stock, Monte Carlo Stock, *Modern*	275.00	375.00	375.00
☐ **Gustav CG-T**, Various Calibers, Singleshot, Target Stock, Heavy Barrel, *Modern*	200.00	275.00	270.00
☐ **Gustav Grade II**, Various Calibers, Sporting Rifle, Checkered Stock, *Modern*	280.00	400.00	400.00
☐ **Gustav Grade II**, Various Calibers, Sporting Rifle, Checkered Stock, Left-Hand, *Modern*	290.00	420.00	420.00
☐ **Gustav Grade II**, Various Calibers, Sporting Rifle, Checkered Stock, Magnum Action, *Modern*	285.00	420.00	410.00
☐ **Gustav Grade III**, Various Calibers, Sporting Rifle, Checkered Stock, Magnum Action, Left-Hand, *Modern*	285.00	425.00	425.00
☐ **Gustav Grade III**, Various Calibers, Sporting Rifle, Checkered Stock, Magnum Action, Light Engraving, Left-Hand, *Modern*	325.00	475.00	475.00
☐ **Gustav Grade III**, Various Calibers, Sporting Rifle, Checkered Stock, Magnum Action, Light Engraving, *Modern*	325.00	475.00	475.00
☐ **Gustav Grade III**, Various Calibers, Sporting Rifle, Checkered Stock, Light Engraving, *Modern*	325.00	475.00	475.00
☐ **Gustav Grade III**, Various Calibers, Sporting Rifle, Checkered Stock, Light Engraving, Left-Hand, *Modern*	325.00	475.00	475.00
☐ **Gustav Grade V**, Various Calibers, Sporting Rifle, Checkered Stock, Engraved, *Modern*	450.00	670.00	650.00
☐ **Gustav Grade V**, Various Calibers, Sporting Rifle, Checkered Stock, Engraved, Left-Hand, *Modern*	450.00	670.00	650.00
☐ **Gustav Grade V**, Various Calibers, Sporting Rifle, Checkered Stock, Engraved, Magnum Action, *Modern*	450.00	670.00	650.00
☐ **Gustav Grade V**, Various Calibers, Sporting Rifle, Checkered Stock, Engraved, Magnum Action, Left-Hand, *Modern*	450.00	675.00	650.00
☐ **Gustav Swede**, Various Calibers, Sporting Rifle, Checkered Stock, *Modern*	200.00	320.00	300.00
☐ **Gustav Swede Deluxe**, Various Calibers, Sporting Rifle, Checkered Stock, Light Engraving, *Modern*	265.00	345.00	335.00

	V.G.	Exc.	Prior Year Exc. Value
☐ **Gustav V-T**, Various Calibers, Varmint, Target Stock, Heavy Barrel, *Modern*	300.00	425.00	425.00
☐ **P 3000 Presentation**, Various Calibers, Sporting Rifle, Checkered Stock, Engraved, Fancy Wood, *Modern*	460.00	670.00	650.00

HUTZ, BENJAMIN

Lancaster, Pa. c. 1802. See Kentucky Rifles.

HVA

See Husqvarna.

HY HUNTER

Burbank, Calif.

HANDGUN, REVOLVER

	V.G.	Exc.	Prior Year Exc. Value
☐ **Chicago Cub**, .22 Short, 6 Shot, Folding Trigger, *Modern*	20.00	35.00	35.00
☐ **Detective**, .22 L.R.R.F., Double Action, 6 Shot, *Modern*	25.00	45.00	40.00
☐ **Detective**, .22 W.M.R., Double Action, 6 Shot, *Modern*	25.00	45.00	40.00
☐ **Frontier Six Shooter**, .22 L.R.R.F., Single Action, Western Style, *Modern*	40.00	60.00	55.00
☐ **Frontier Six Shooter**, .22 LR/.22 WRF Combo, Single Action, Western Style, *Modern*	40.00	60.00	55.00
☐ **Frontier Six Shooter**, .357 Mag., Single Action, Western Style, *Modern*	65.00	95.00	90.00
☐ **Frontier Six Shooter**, .44 Mag., Single Action, Western Style, *Modern*	90.00	140.00	135.00
☐ **Frontier Six Shooter**, ".45 Mag.", Single Action, Western Style, *Modern*	75.00	125.00	120.00

HANDGUN, SEMI-AUTOMATIC

	V.G.	Exc.	Prior Year Exc. Value
☐ **Maxim**, .25 ACP, Clip Fed, *Modern*	50.00	75.00	70.00
☐ **Militar, .22 L.R.R.F., Double Action, Hammer, Clip Fed, Blue,** *Modern*	55.00	85.00	80.00
☐ **Militar**, .32 ACP, Double Action, Hammer, Clip Fed, Blue, *Modern*	60.00	95.00	95.00
☐ **Militar**, .380 ACP, Double Action, Hammer, Clip Fed, Blue, *Modern*	65.00	100.00	95.00
☐ **Panzer**, .22 L.R.R.F., Clip Fed, Blue, *Modern*	45.00	70.00	65.00
☐ **Stingray**, .25 ACP, Clip Fed, Blue, *Modern*	45.00	65.00	65.00
☐ **Stuka**, .22 Long, Clip Fed, Blue, *Modern*	45.00	70.00	65.00

HANDGUN, DOUBLE BARREL, OVER-UNDER

	V.G.	Exc.	Prior Year Exc. Value
☐ **Automatic Derringer**, .22 L.R.R.F., Blue, *Modern*	30.00	45.00	40.00

HANDGUN, SINGLESHOT

	V.G.	Exc.	Prior Year Exc. Value
☐ **Accurate Ace**, .22 Short, Flobert Type, Chrome Plated, *Modern*	20.00	45.00	40.00
☐ **Favorite**, .22 L.R.R.F., Stevens Copy, *Modern*	40.00	60.00	55.00
☐ **Favorite**, .22 W.M.R., Stevens Copy, *Modern*	45.00	70.00	65.00
☐ **Gold Rush Derringer**, .22 L.R.R.F., Spur Trigger, *Modern*	30.00	45.00	40.00
☐ **Target**, .22 L.R.R.F., Bolt Action, *Modern*	35.00	50.00	45.00
☐ **Target**, .22 W.M.R., Bolt Action, *Modern*	45.00	55.00	50.00

	V.G.	Exc.	Prior Year Exc. Value
RIFLE, BOLT ACTION			
☐ **Maharaja**, Various Calibers, Various Actions, Custom Made, Fancy Engraving, Fancy Wood, Fancy Inlays, Gold Plated, *Modern*	3,875.00	5,750.00	5,500.00

HYPER

Jenks, Okla.

RIFLE, SINGLESHOT			
☐ **Hyper-Single Rifle**, Various Calibers, Fancy Wood, No Sights, Falling Block, Fancy Checkering, *Modern*	750.00	1,000.00	1,000.00
☐ **Hyper-Single Rifle**, Various Calibers, Fancy Wood, No Sights, Falling Block, Fancy Checkering, Stainless Steel Barrel, *Modern*	775.00	1,100.00	1,100.00

HY SCORE ARMS

Brooklyn, N.Y.

HANDGUN, REVOLVER			
☐ **.22 L.R.R.F., Double Action,** *Modern*	20.00	35.00	35.00

IAB

Puccinelli Co., San Anselmo, Calif.

SHOTGUN, DOUBLE BARREL, OVER-UNDER			
☐ **C-300 Combo**, 12 Ga., Vent Rib, Single Selective Trigger, Checkered Stock, with 2 Extra Single Barrels, *Modern*	1,675.00	2,500.00	2,450.00
☐ **C-300 Super Combo**, 12 Ga., Vent Rib, Single Selective Trigger, Checkered Stock, with 2 Extra Single Barrels, *Modern*	2,250.00	3,025.00	2,975.00
SHOTGUN, SINGLESHOT			
☐ **S-300**, 12 Ga., Vent Rib, Checkered Stock, Trap Grade, *Modern*	875.00	1,325.00	1,300.00

I G

Grey, of Dundee, c. 1630.

HANDGUN, SNAPHAUNCE			
☐ **Belt Pistol**, Engraved, Ovoid Pommel, All Metal, *Antique*	15,750.00	22,500.00	20,000.00

IMPERIAL

Maker unknown, c. 1880.

HANDGUN, REVOLVER			
☐ **.22 Short R.F.**, 7 Shot, Spur Trigger, Solid Frame, Single Action, *Antique*	95.00	165.00	160.00
☐ **.32 Short R.F.**, 5 Shot, Spur Trigger, Solid Frame, Single Action, *Antique*	95.00	170.00	170.00

IMPERIAL ARMS

Made by Hopkins & Allen, c. 1880.

	V.G.	Exc.	Prior Year Exc. Value
HANDGUN, REVOLVER			
☐ **.32 Short R.F.**, 5 Shot, Spur Trigger, Solid Frame, Single Action, *Antique*	95.00	165.00	160.00
☐ **.38 Short R.F.**, 5 Shot, Spur Trigger, Solid Frame, Single Action, *Antique*	95.00	170.00	175.00

I.N.A.

Industria Nacional de Armas, Sao Paulo, Brazil.

	V.G.	Exc.	Prior Year Exc. Value
HANDGUN, REVOLVER			
☐ **Tiger**, .22 L.R.R.F., Single Action, Western Style, *Modern*	40.00	65.00	65.00
☐ **Tiger**, .32 S&W Long, Single Action, Western Style, *Modern*	45.00	70.00	70.00

INDIA MILITARY

	V.G.	Exc.	Prior Year Exc. Value
AUTOMATIC WEAPON, HEAVY MACHINE GUN			
☐ **Bira Gun,** .450/.577 Martini-Henry, Drum Magazine, Carriage Mount, Twin Barrels, *Antique*	7250.00	11000.00	10000.00
RIFLE, BOLT ACTION			
☐ **S.M.L.E. No. 1 Mk.III,** .303 British, Clip Fed, Ishapore, *Curio*	50.00	90.00	145.00

INDIAN ARMS

Detroit, Mich., c. 1976.

HANDGUN, SEMI-AUTOMATIC

☐ **.380 ACP**, Clip Fed, Stainless Steel, Vent Rib, Double Action, *Modern* **315.00475.00425.00**

INDIAN SALES

Cheyenne, Wyo.

	V.G.	Exc.	Prior Year Exc. Value
HANDGUN, REVOLVER			
☐ **HS-21,** .22, L.R.R.F., Double Action, Blue, *Modern*	20.00	30.00	30.00
HANDGUN, SEMI-AUTOMATIC			
☐ **Model 4,** .25 ACP, Clip Fed, Blue, *Modern*	60.00	85.00	80.00

INGRAM

Invented by Gordon Ingram. Made by Police Ordnance Co., Los Angeles, Calif. and Military Armament Corp., Georgia.

	V.G.	Exc.	Prior Year Exc. Value
AUTOMATIC WEAPON, SUBMACHINE GUN			
☐ **M-10 M A C,** .45, ACP, Clip Fed, Folding Stock, Commercial, *Class 3*	145.00	195.00	175.00
☐ **M-10 M A C,** .45, ACP, Clip Fed, Folding Stock, Commercial, Silencer, *Class 3*	235.00	325.00	275.00
☐ **M-10 M A C,** 9mm Luger, Clip Fed, Folding Stock, Commercial, *Class 3*	145.00	200.00	175.00
☐ **M-10 M A C,** 9mm Luger, Clip Fed, Folding Stock, Commercial, Silencer, *Class 3*	225.00	315.00	275.00
☐ **M-11 M A C,** .380 ACP, Clip Fed, Folding Stock, Commercial, *Class 3*	320.00	400.00	375.00

	V.G.	Exc.	Prior Year Exc. Value
☐ **M-11 M A C**, .380 ACP, Clip Fed, Folding Stock, Commercial, Silencer, *Class 3*	425.00	540.00	500.00
☐ **M6 Ingram**, .45 ACP, Clip Fed, Commercial, *Class 3*	275.00	375.00	375.00

INGRAM, CHARLES

Glasgow, Scotland, c. 1860.

SHOTGUN, DOUBLE BARREL, SIDE-BY-SIDE

	V.G.	Exc.	Prior Year Exc. Value
☐ **Extra Set of Rifle Barrels**, High Quality, Cased with Accessories, Engraved, Checkered Stock, *Antique*	5,000.00	7,250.00	7,000.00

INHOFF, BENEDICT

Berks County, Pa. 1781-1783. See Kentucky Rifles.

INTERCHANGEABLE

Belgium, Trade Name Schoverlin-Daley & Gales, c. 1880.

SHOTGUN, DOUBLE BARREL, SIDE-BY-SIDE

	V.G.	Exc.	Prior Year Exc. Value
☐ **Various Gauges**, Outside Hammers, Damascus Barrel, *Modern*	95.00	155.00	150.00

INTERDYNAMIC

Miami, Fla., c. 1979. Now made by F.I.E.

HANDGUN, SEMI-AUTOMATIC

	V.G.	Exc.	Prior Year Exc. Value
☐ **KG-9**, 9mm Luger, Clip Fed, SMG Styling, *Modern*	200.00	300.00	325.00
☐ **KG-9**, 9mm Luger, Clip Fed, SMG Styling, Serial Number Higher Than 4089, *Class 3*	165.00	225.00	250.00

INTERNATIONAL

Made by Hood Firearms, c. 1875.

HANDGUN, REVOLVER

	V.G.	Exc.	Prior Year Exc. Value
☐ **.22 Short R.F.**, 7 Shot, Spur Trigger, Solid Frame, Single Action, *Antique*	95.00	165.00	160.00
☐ **.32 Short R.F.**, 5 Shot, Spur Trigger, Solid Frame, Single Action, *Antique*	95.00	170.00	170.00

INTERNATIONAL DISTRIBUTERS

Miami, Florida.

RIFLE, BOLT ACTION

	V.G.	Exc.	Prior Year Exc. Value
☐ **Mauser Type**, Various Calibers, Checkered Stock, Sling Swivels, Recoil Pad, *Modern*	145.00	200.00	200.00

INTERSTATE ARMS CO.

Made by Crescent for Townley Metal & Hdw., Kansas City, Mo.

SHOTGUN, DOUBLE BARREL, SIDE-BY-SIDE

	V.G.	Exc.	Prior Year Exc. Value
☐ **Various Gauges**, Outside Hammers, Damascus Barrel, *Modern*	110.00	180.00	175.00
☐ **Various Gauges**, Hammerless, Steel Barrel, *Modern*	135.00	190.00	200.00

	V.G.	Exc.	Prior Year Exc. Value
☐ **Various Gauges**, Hammerless, Damascus Barrel, *Modern*	100.00	180.00	175.00
☐ **Various Gauges**, Outside Hammers, Steel Barrel, *Modern*	125.00	185.00	190.00
SHOTGUN, SINGLESHOT			
☐ **Various Gauges**, Hammer, Steel Barrel, *Modern*	55.00	80.00	85.00

I P

Probably German, 1580-1600.

RIFLE, WHEEL-LOCK			
☐ **.60**, German Style, Brass Furniture, Light Ornamentation, Horn Inlays, Set Trigger, *Antique*	3,250.00	4,450.00	4,000.00

ISRAELI MILITARY

This list includes both military arms and the commercial arms made by Israeli Military Industries (I.M.I.). Also see Magnum Research, Inc. (M.R.I.).

AUTOMATIC WEAPON, SUBMACHINE GUN			
☐ **UZI**, 9mm Luger, Clip Fed, Silencer, *Class 3*	650.00	800.00	850.00
☐ **UZI**, 9mm Luger, Clip Fed, Folding Stock, *Class 3*	475.00	600.00	650.00
☐ **UZI**, 9mm Luger, Clip Fed, Folding Stock, Commercial Conversion, *Class 3*	300.00	450.00	450.00
HANDGUN, REVOLVER			
☐ **S & W Model 10 Copy**, 9mm Luger, Solid Frame, Swing-Out Cylinder, Double Action, Military, *Modern*	420.00	595.00	575.00
RIFLE, SEMI-AUTOMATIC			
☐ **Galil**, .223 Rem., Clip Fed, Assault Rifle, Folding Stock, *Modern*	600.00	800.00	900.00
☐ **Galil**, .308 Win., Clip Fed, Assault Rifle, Folding Stock, *Modern*	675.00	900.00	1,000.00
☐ **UZI**, 9mm Luger, Clip Fed, Folding Stock, Commercial, *Modern*	300.00	430.00	450.00

ITALGUNS INTERNATIONAL

Cusago, Italy

COMBINATION WEAPON, OVER-UNDER			
☐ **Various Calibers**, Checkered Stock, Double Triggers, *Modern*	220.00	315.00	300.00
HANDGUN, REVOLVER			
☐ **Western Style**, Various Calibers, Single Action, *Modern*	95.00	135.00	125.00
☐ **Western Style**, Various Calibers, Single Action, Automatic Hammer Safety, *Modern*	100.00	140.00	135.00
SHOTGUN, DOUBLE BARREL, OVER-UNDER			
☐ **Model 125**, 12 Gauge, Checkered Stock, Vent Rib, Double Triggers, *Modern*	155.00	210.00	200.00
☐ **Model 150**, 12 or 20 Gauges, Checkered Stock, Vent Rib, Single Trigger, *Modern*	180.00	235.00	225.00

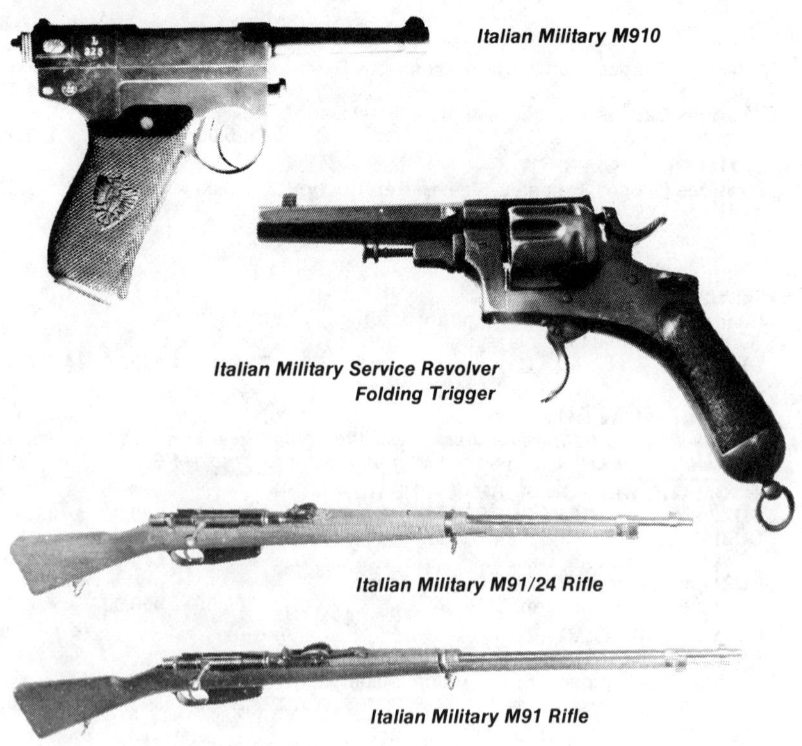

Italian Military M910

Italian Military Service Revolver Folding Trigger

Italian Military M91/24 Rifle

Italian Military M91 Rifle

ITALIAN MILITARY

Also See Beretta.

	V.G.	Exc.	Prior Year Exc. Value
AUTOMATIC WEAPON, ASSAULT RIFLE			
☐ **BM59,** .308 Win., Clip Fed, Bipod, *Class 3*	660.00	910.00	895.00
AUTOMATIC WEAPON, SUBMACHINE GUN			
☐ **MP 38/44,** 9mm Luger, Clip Fed, Military, *Class 3*	675.00	835.00	825.00
☐ **MP 38/49,** 9mm Luger, Clip Fed, Wood Stock, Military, *Class 3*	300.00	400.00	395.00
☐ **MP 38A,** 9mm Luger, Clip Fed, Military, *Class 3*	590.00	775.00	750.00
HANDGUN, REVOLVER			
☐ **Service Revolver,** 10.4mm, Double Action, 6 Shot, Folding Trigger, *Curio*	60.00	110.00	150.00
☐ **Service Revolver,** 10.4mm, Double Action, 6 Shot, Trigger Guard, *Curio*	60.00	110.00	150.00
HANDGUN, SEMI-AUTOMATIC			
☐ **Brixia,** 9mm Glisenti, Clip Fed, Military, *Curio*	190.00	285.00	400.00
☐ **M910 Army,** 9mm Glisenti, Clip Fed, Military, *Curio*	190.00	285.00	400.00
☐ **M 1934 Beretta,** .380 ACP, Clip Fed, Military, *Modern*	80.00	130.00	190.00

	V.G.	Exc.	Prior Year Exc. Value
RIFLE, BOLT ACTION			
☐ **M1891,** 6.5 x 52 Mannlicher-Carcano, Military, *Modern*	40.00	70.00	110.00
☐ **M 38,** 7.35mm Carcano, Military, *Modern*	40.00	70.00	110.00
☐ **M91 T.S.,** 6.5 x 52 Mannlicher-Carcano, Carbine, Folding Bayonet, Military, *Modern*	45.00	75.00	120.00
☐ **M91 T.S. (Late),** 6.5 x 52 Mannlicher-Carcano, Carbine, Folding Bayonet, Military, *Modern*	35.00	55.00	95.00
☐ **M91/24,** 6.5 x 52 Mannlicher-Carcano, Carbine, Military, *Modern*	35.00	55.00	100.00
☐ **M91/24,** 6.5 x 52 Mannlicher-Carcano, Military, *Modern*	35.00	55.00	90.00
☐ **Vetterli M1870/1887,** 10.4 x 47R Italian Vetterli, *Antique*	70.00	110.00	100.00
☐ **Vetterli M1870/87/15,** 6.5 x 52 Mannlicher-Carcano, *Antique*	75.00	120.00	110.00

ITHACA GUN CO.

Ithaca, N.Y. 1873 to Date. Absorbed Lefever Arms Co., Syracuse Arms Co., Union Firearms Co., and Wilkes Barre Gun Co.

	V.G.	Exc.	Prior Year Exc. Value
COMBINATION WEAPON, OVER-UNDER			
☐ **LSA 55 Turkey Gun,** 12 Ga./.222, Open Rear Sight, Monte Carlo Stock, *Modern*	290.00	385.00	380.00
RIFLE, BOLT ACTION			
☐ **BSA CF 2,** Various Calibers, Magnum Action, Monte Carlo Stock, Checkered Stock, *Modern*	200.00	290.00	285.00
☐ **LSA 55,** Various Calibers, Monte Carlo Stock, Cheekpiece, Heavy Barrel, *Modern*	280.00	350.00	350.00
☐ **LSA-55,** Various Calibers, Monte Carlo Stock, Open Rear Sight, *Modern*	220.00	300.00	290.00
☐ **LSA-55 Deluxe,** Various Calibers, Monte Carlo Stock, Cheekpiece, No Sights, Scope Mounts, *Modern*	285.00	355.00	345.00
☐ **LSA-65,** Various Calibers, Monte Carlo Stock, Open Rear Sight, *Modern*	250.00	340.00	320.00
☐ **LSA-65 Deluxe,** Various Calibers, Monte Carlo Stock, Cheekpiece, No Sights, Scope Mounts, *Modern*	270.00	350.00	345.00
RIFLE, LEVER ACTION			
☐ **Model 49,** .22 L.R.R.F., Singleshot, *Modern*	37.00	55.00	50.00
☐ **Model 49,** .22 WMR, Singleshot, *Modern*	43.00	60.00	55.00
☐ **Model 49 Deluxe,** .22 L.R.R.F., Singleshot, Fancy Wood, *Modern*	48.00	65.00	60.00
☐ **Model 49 Presentation,** .22 L.R.R.F., Singleshot, Engraved, Fancy Checkering, *Modern*	125.00	175.00	170.00
☐ **Model 49 R,** .22 L.R.R.F., Tube Feed, *Modern*	53.00	80.00	75.00
☐ **Model 49 St. Louis,** .22 L.R.R.F., Bicentennial, Fancy Wood, Singleshot, *Curio*	105.00	155.00	150.00
☐ **Model 49 Youth,** .22 L.R.R.F., Singleshot, *Modern*	37.00	53.00	50.00
☐ **Model 72,** .22 L.R.R.F., Tube Feed, *Modern*	90.00	125.00	120.00
☐ **Model 72,** .22 WMR, Tube Feed, *Modern*	100.00	145.00	140.00
☐ **Model 72 Deluxe,** .22 L.R.R.F., Tube Feed, Octagon Barrel, *Modern*	120.00	170.00	165.00

	V.G.	Exc.	Prior Year Exc. Value
RIFLE, SEMI-AUTOMATIC			
☐ **X-15 Lightning,** .22 L.R.R.F., Clip Fed, *Modern*	60.00	85.00	80.00
☐ **X5 C Lightning,** .22 L.R.R.F., Clip Fed, *Modern*	65.00	90.00	85.00
☐ **X5 T Lightning,** .22 L.R.R.F., Tube Feed, *Modern*	65.00	90.00	85.00
SHOTGUN, DOUBLE BARREL, OVER-UNDER			
☐ **Model 500,** 12 and 20 Gauges, Field Grade, Selective Ejector, Vent Rib, *Modern*	285.00	400.00	385.00
☐ **Model 500,** 12 Ga. Mag. 3″, Field Grade, Selective Ejector, Vent Rib, *Modern*	295.00	410.00	395.00
☐ **Model 600,** 12 Ga., Trap Grade, Selective Ejector, Vent Rib, *Modern*	390.00	550.00	520.00
☐ **Model 600,** 12 Ga., Trap Grade, Selective Ejector, Vent Rib, Monte Carlo Stock, *Modern*	390.00	550.00	520.00
☐ **Model 600,** 12 and 20 Gauges, Field Grade, Selective Ejector, Vent Rib, *Modern*	375.00	520.00	500.00
☐ **Model 600,** 12 and 20 Gauges, Skeet Grade, Selective Ejector, Vent Rib, *Modern*	385.00	550.00	520.00
☐ **Model 600,** 20 and .410 Gauges, Skeet Grade, Selective Ejector, Vent Rib, *Modern*	400.00	560.00	535.00
☐ **Model 600 Combo Set,** Various Gauges, Skeet Grade, Selective Ejector, Vent Rib, Cased, *Modern*	875.00	1300.00	1250.00
☐ **Model 680 English,** 12 and 20 Gauges, Field Grade, Selective Ejector, Vent Rib, *Modern*	420.00	540.00	525.00
☐ **Model 700,** 12 Ga., Trap Grade, Selective Ejector, Vent Rib, *Modern*	475.00	650.00	625.00
☐ **Model 700,** 12 Ga., Trap Grade, Selective Ejector, Vent Rib, Monte Carlo Stock, *Modern*	475.00	650.00	625.00
☐ **Model 700,** 12 and 20 Gauges, Skeet Grade, Selective Ejector, Vent Rib, *Modern*	475.00	650.00	625.00
☐ **Model 700 Combo Set,** Various Gauges, Skeet Grade, Selective Ejector, Vent Rib, Cased, *Modern*	1025.00	1725.00	1675.00
☐ **Perazzi Light Game Model,** 12 Ga., Automatic Ejector, Vent Rib, Single Trigger, *Modern*	900.00	1400.00	1350.00
☐ **Perazzi Competition 1,** 12 Ga., Trap Grade, Automatic Ejector, Vent Rib, Single Trigger, Cased, *Modern*	900.00	1400.00	1350.00
☐ **Perazzi Competition 1,** 12 Ga., Skeet Grade, Automatic Ejector, Vent Rib, Single Trigger, Cased, *Modern*	900.00	1400.00	1350.00
☐ **Perazzi Mirage,** 12 Ga., Trap Grade, Automatic Ejector, Vent Rib, Cased, *Modern*	1400.00	2000.00	1925.00
☐ **Perazzi Mirage 4-Barrel Set,** Various Gauges, Skeet Grade, Automatic Ejector, Vent Rib, Cased, *Modern*	3500.00	4800.00	4600.00
☐ **Perazzi MT-6,** 12 Ga., Trap Grade, Automatic Ejector, Vent Rib, Cased, *Modern*	1800.00	2600.00	2525.00
☐ **Perazzi MT-6,** 12 Ga., Skeet Grade, Automatic Ejector, Vent Rib, Cased, *Modern*	1850.00	2650.00	2575.00
☐ **Perazzi MX-8,** 12 Ga., Trap Grade, Automatic Ejector, Vent Rib, Cased, *Modern*	1325.00	2050.00	2000.00
☐ **Perazzi MX-8 Combo,** 12 Ga., Trap Grade, Automatic Ejector, Vent Rib, Cased, *Modern*	2075.00	2950.00	2850.00

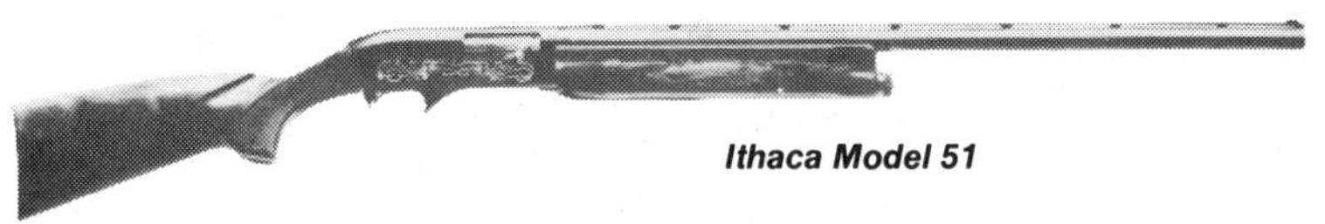

Ithaca Model 51

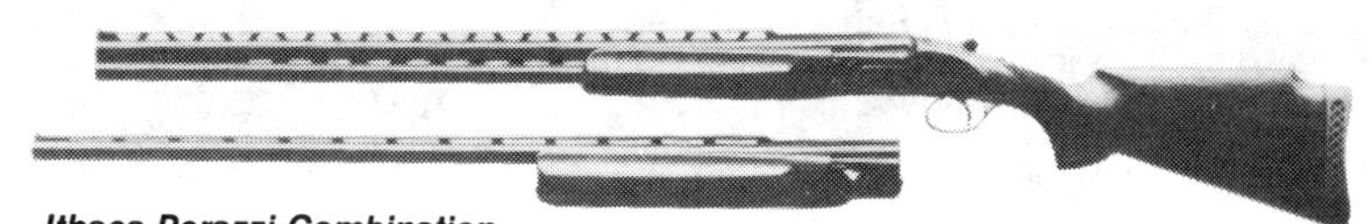

Ithaca Perazzi Combination

	V.G.	Exc.	Prior Year Exc. Value
SHOTGUN, DOUBLE BARREL, SIDE-BY-SIDE			
☐ **Early Model,** Serial Numbers under 425,000, *Deduct* **50%**			
☐ **Outside Hammers,** *Deduct Another* **20%-30%**			
☐ **Various Gauges,** Field Grade, Hammerless, Magnum, Beavertail Forend, *Modern*	625.00	825.00	800.00
☐ **Various Gauges,** Field Grade, Hammerless, Beavertail Forend, Double Trigger, *Modern*	575.00	760.00	735.00
☐ **Various Gauges,** Field Grade, Hammerless, Double Trigger, Checkered Stock, *Modern*	390.00	575.00	550.00
☐ **Various Gauges,** Field Grade, Hammerless, Magnum, Double Trigger, *Modern*	435.00	620.00	600.00
☐ **#1 E Grade,** Various Gauges, Hammerless, Automatic Ejector, Beavertail Forend, Double Trigger, *Modern*	750.00	1050.00	1025.00
☐ **#1 E Grade,** Various Gauges, Hammerless, Automatic Ejector, Magnum, Beavertail Forend, Double Trigger, *Modern*	875.00	1300.00	1250.00
☐ **#1 E Grade,** Various Gauges, Hammerless, Automatic Ejector, Magnum, Double Trigger, *Modern*	775.00	1150.00	1100.00
☐ **#1 E Grade,** Various Gauges, Hammerless, Automatic Ejector, Light Engraving, Checkered Stock, Double Trigger, *Modern*	650.00	900.00	875.00
☐ **#1 Grade,** Various Gauges, Hammerless, Magnum, Double Trigger, Light Engraving, Checkered Stock, *Modern*	580.00	800.00	790.00
☐ **#1 Grade,** Various Gauges, Hammerless, Double Trigger, Checkered Stock, Light Engraving, *Modern*	475.00	690.00	665.00
☐ **#1 Grade,** Various Gauges, Hammerless, Magnum, Beavertail Forend, Double Trigger, *Modern*	670.00	975.00	945.00
☐ **#1 Grade,** Various Gauges, Hammerless, Beavertail Forend, Light Engraving, Checkered Stock, Double Trigger, *Modern*	580.00	810.00	795.00
☐ **#2 E Grade,** Various Gauges, Hammerless, Automatic Ejector, Magnum, Beavertail Forend, Double Trigger, *Modern*	985.00	1400.00	1350.00

	V.G.	Exc.	Prior Year Exc. Value
☐ **#2 E Grade,** Various Gauges, Hammerless, Automatic Ejector, Magnum, Double Trigger, *Modern*	775.00	1150.00	1100.00
☐ **#2 E Grade,** Various Gauges, Hammerless, Automatic Ejector, Beavertail Forend, Double Trigger, *Modern*	825.00	1250.00	1200.00
☐ **#2 E Grade,** Various Gauges, Hammerless, Automatic Ejector, Double Trigger, Engraved, Checkered Stock, *Modern*	725.00	1075.00	1025.00
☐ **#2 Grade,** Various Gauges, Hammerless, Magnum, Beavertail Forend, Double Trigger, *Modern*	750.00	1100.00	1050.00
☐ **#2 Grade,** Various Gauges, Hammerless, Magnum, Beavertail Forend, Double Trigger, *Modern*	750.00	1100.00	1050.00
☐ **#2 Grade,** Various Gauges, Hammerless, Beavertail Forend, Double Trigger, Engraved, Checkered Stock, *Modern*	650.00	875.00	845.00
☐ **#2 Grade,** Various Gauges, Hammerless, Magnum, Double Trigger, Engraved, Checkered Stock, *Modern*	675.00	900.00	865.00
☐ **#2 Grade,** Various Gauges, Hammerless, Double Trigger, Engraved, Checkered Stock, *Modern*	465.00	700.00	675.00
☐ **#3 E Grade,** Various Gauges, Hammerless, Magnum, Beavertail Forend, Automatic Ejector, Double Trigger, *Modern*	1150.00	1650.00	1600.00
☐ **#3 E Grade,** Various Gauges, Hammerless, Magnum, Double Trigger, Engraved, Checkered Stock, *Modern*	975.00	1475.00	1425.00
☐ **#3 E Grade,** Various Gauges, Hammerless, Beavertail Forend, Automatic Ejector, Double Trigger, *Modern*	925.00	1400.00	1350.00
☐ **#3 E Grade,** Various Gauges, Hammerless, Double Trigger, Engraved, Checkered Stock, Automatic Ejector, *Modern*	850.00	1350.00	1300.00
☐ **#3 Grade,** Various Gauges, Hammerless, Magnum, Beavertail Forend, Double Trigger, *Modern*	850.00	1350.00	1300.00
☐ **#3 Grade,** Various Gauges, Hammerless, Magnum, Double Trigger, Engraved, Checkered Stock, *Modern*	775.00	1250.00	1200.00
☐ **#3 Grade,** Various Gauges, Hammerless, Beavertail Forend, Engraved, Checkered Stock, Double Trigger, *Modern*	750.00	1150.00	1100.00
☐ **#3 Grade,** Various Gauges, Hammerless, Double Trigger, Engraved, Checkered Stock, *Modern*	800.00	1200.00	1150.00
☐ **#4 E Grade,** Various Gauges, Hammerless, Automatic Ejector, Vent Rib, Beavertail Forend, *Modern*	2300.00	3250.00	3000.00
☐ **#4 E Grade,** Various Gauges, Hammerless, Automatic Ejector, Vent Rib, Fancy Checkering, Fancy Engraving, *Modern*	2050.00	2750.00	2650.00
☐ **#4 E Grade,** Various Gauges, Hammerless, Automatic Ejector, Beavertail Forend, Fancy Checkering, Fancy Engraving, *Modern*	1750.00	2400.00	2300.00
☐ **#4 E Grade,** Various Gauges, Hammerless, Automatic Ejector, Fancy Checkering, Fancy Engraving, Double Trigger, *Modern*	1400.00	2150.00	2050.00

	V.G.	Exc.	Prior Year Exc. Value
☐ **#5 E Grade,** Various Gauges, Hammerless, Automatic Ejector, Vent Rib, Beavertail Forend, *Modern*	3 250.00	4150.00	4000.00
☐ **#5 E Grade,** Various Gauges, Hammerless, Automatic Ejector, Vent Rib, Fancy Checkering, Fancy Engraving, *Modern*	3100.00	4150.00	4000.00
☐ **#5 E Grade,** Various Gauges, Hammerless, Automatic Ejector, Beavertail Forend, Fancy Checkering, Fancy Engraving, *Modern*	2875.00	3750.00	3600.00
☐ **#5 E Grade,** Various Gauges, Hammerless, Automatic Ejector, Fancy Checkering, Fancy Engraving, Double Trigger, *Modern*	2825.00	3600.00	3500.00
☐ **#7 E Grade,** Various Gauges, Hammerless, Automatic Ejector, Vent Rib, Beavertail Forend, *Modern*	6850.00	8700.00	8700.00
☐ **#7 E Grade,** Various Gauges, Hammerless, Automatic Ejector, Vent Rib, Fancy Checkering, Fancy Engraving, *Modern*	6700.00	8350.00	8350.00
☐ **#7 E Grade,** Various Gauges, Hammerless, Automatic Ejector, Beavertail Forend, Fancy Checkering, Fancy Engraving, *Modern*	6600.00	8100.00	8100.00
☐ **#7 E Grade,** Various Gauges, Hammerless, Automatic Ejector, Fancy Checkering, Fancy Engraving, Double Trigger, *Modern*	6350.00	8000.00	7900.00
☐ **$2000 Grade,** Various Gauges, Hammerless, Automatic Ejector, Single Selective Trigger, Ornate, *Modern*	7500.00	11000.00	11000.00
☐ **$2000 Grade,** Various Gauges, Hammerless, Automatic Ejector, Single Selective Trigger, Vent Rib, Ornate, *Modern*	8200.00	12000.00	12000.00
☐ **$2000 Grade,** Various Gauges, Hammerless, Automatic Ejector, Single Selective Trigger, Beavertail Forend, Ornate, *Modern*	7700.00	11000.00	11000.00
☐ **$2000 Grade,** Various Gauges, Hammerless, Automatic Ejector, Single Selective Trigger, Vent Rib, Beavertail Forend, *Modern*	8250.00	12500.00	12500.00
☐ **Model 100,** 12 and 20 Gauges, Hammerless, Field Grade, *Modern*	210.00	295.00	285.00
☐ **Model 200 E,** 12 and 20 Gauges, Hammerless, Selective Ejector, Field Grade, *Modern*	290.00	385.00	380.00
☐ **Model 200 E,** 12 and 20 Gauges, Hammerless, Selective Ejector, Skeet Grade, *Modern*	310.00	390.00	385.00
☐ **Model 280 English,** 12 and 20 Gauges, Hammerless, Selective Ejector, Field Grade, *Modern*	315.00	440.00	420.00

SHOTGUN, LEVER ACTION

	V.G.	Exc.	Prior Year Exc. Value
☐ **Model 66 Supersingle,** Various Gauges, Singleshot, *Modern*	42.00	58.00	55.00
☐ **Model 66 Buck,** Various Gauges, Singleshot, Open Rear Sight, *Modern*	42.00	65.00	60.00
☐ **Model 66 Youth,** Various Gauges, Singleshot, *Modern*	37.00	58.00	55.00

SHOTGUN, PISTOL

	V.G.	Exc.	Prior Year Exc. Value
☐ **Auto Burglar,** Various Gauges, Double Barrel, Side by Side, Short Shotgun, *Class 3*	435.00	620.00	600.00

	V.G.	Exc.	Prior Year Exc. Value
SHOTGUN, SEMI-AUTOMATIC			
☐ **300 Standard,** 12 and 20 Gauges, *Modern*	150.00	190.00	185.00
☐ **300 Standard,** 12 and 20 Gauges, Vent Rib, *Modern*	155.00	200.00	195.00
☐ **300 XL Standard,** 12 and 20 Gauges, *Modern*	160.00	200.00	195.00
☐ **300 XL Standard,** 12 and 20 Gauges, Vent Rib, *Modern*	175.00	230.00	225.00
☐ **900 Deluxe,** 12 and 20 Gauges, Vent Rib, *Modern*	165.00	980.00	965.00
☐ **900 XL,** 12 Ga., Trap Grade, *Modern*	190.00	260.00	250.00
☐ **900 XL,** 12 Ga., Trap Grade, Monte Carlo Stock, *Modern*	190.00	260.00	250.00
☐ **900 XL,** 12 and 20 Gauges, Skeet Grade, *Modern*	185.00	245.00	240.00
☐ **900 XL Deluxe,** 12 and 20 Gauges, Vent Rib, *Modern*	185.00	230.00	225.00
☐ **900 XL Slug,** 12 and 20 Gauges, Open Rear Sight, *Modern*	175.00	230.00	225.00
☐ **Mag 10 Deluxe,** 10 Ga. 3½", Takedown, Vent Rib, Fancy Wood, Checkered Stock, *Modern*	415.00	510.00	495.00
☐ **Mag 10 Standard,** 10 Ga. 3½", Takedown, Vent Rib, Recoil Pad, Checkered Stock, Sling Swivels, *Modern*	310.00	405.00	400.00
☐ **Mag 10 Standard,** 10 Ga. 3½", Takedown, Recoil Pad, Checkered Stock, Sling Swivels, *Modern*	270.00	360.00	350.00
☐ **Mag 10 Supreme,** 10 Ga. 3½", Takedown, Vent Rib, Fancy Wood, Engraved, Checkered Stock, *Modern*	525.00	630.00	625.00
☐ **Model 51,** 12 and 20 Gauges, Takedown, Vent Rib, Recoil Pad, Magnum, *Modern*	200.00	270.00	265.00
☐ **Model 51 Deerslayer,** 12 Ga., Takedown, Open Rear Sight, Sling Swivels, *Modern*	195.00	260.00	255.00
☐ **Model 51 Deluxe,** 12 Ga., Trap Grade, Takedown, Checkered Stock, Fancy Wood, Recoil Pad, *Modern*	275.00	330.00	325.00
☐ **Model 51 Deluxe,** 12 Ga., Trap Grade, Monte Carlo Stock, Fancy Wood, Recoil Pad, *Modern*	285.00	345.00	340.00
☐ **Model 51 Deluxe,** 12 and 20 Gauges, Skeet Grade, Takedown, Checkered Stock, Fancy Wood, Recoil Pad, *Modern*	225.00	295.00	290.00
☐ **Model 51 Standard,** 12 and 20 Gauges, Takedown, Checkered Stock, *Modern*	175.00	230.00	225.00
☐ **Model 51 Standard,** 12 and 20 Gauges, Takedown, Vent Rib, Checkered Stock, *Modern*	195.00	255.00	250.00
SHOTGUN, SINGLESHOT			
☐ **$5000 Grade,** 12 Ga., Trap Grade, Automatic Ejector, Ornate, *Modern*	4150.00	5050.00	5000.00
☐ **4 E Grade,** 12 Gauge, Trap Grade, Automatic Ejector, Engraved, Fancy Checkering, *Modern*	2250.00	3025.00	3000.00
☐ **5 E Grade,** 12 Gauge, Trap Grade, Automatic Ejector, Fancy Engraving, Fancy Checkering, *Modern*	3075.00	3950.00	3900.00
☐ **7 E Grade,** 12 Gauge, Trap Grade, Automatic Ejector, Fancy Engraving, Fancy Checkering, *Modern*	3375.00	4300.00	4250.00

	V.G.	Exc.	Prior Year Exc. Value
☐ **Century 12 Ga.,** Trap Grade, Automatic Ejector, Engraved, Checkered Stock, *Modern*	335.00	450.00	445.00
☐ **Century II,** 12 Ga., Trap Grade, Automatic Ejector, Engraved, Checkered Stock, *Modern*	355.00	485.00	475.00
☐ **Perazzi Competition 1,** 12 Ga., Trap Grade, Automatic Ejector, Vent Rib, Cased, *Modern*	1050.00	1500.00	1475.00
☐ **Victory Grade,** 12 Ga., Automatic Ejector, Checkered Stock, Vent Rib, Trap Grade, *Modern*	775.00	1200.00	1150.00

SHOTGUN, SLIDE ACTION

	V.G.	Exc.	Prior Year Exc. Value
☐ **Model 37,** for Extra Barrel, *Add* **$50.00-$75.00**			
☐ **Model 37,** Extra Vent Rib Barrel, *Add* **$60.00-$85.00**			
☐ **Model 37,** 12 Ga., Takedown, Bicentennial, Engraved, Fancy Wood, Checkered Stock, *Modern*	465.00	580.00	565.00
☐ **Model 37,** Various Gauges, Takedown, Plain, *Modern*	100.00	145.00	140.00
☐ **Model 37 Deerslayer,** Various Gauges, Takedown, Checkered Stock, Recoil Pad, Open Rear Sight, *Modern*	145.00	195.00	185.00
☐ **Model 37 Deerslayer,** Various Gauges, Takedown, Fancy Wood, Checkered Stock, Recoil Pad, Open Rear Sight, *Modern*	155.00	225.00	220.00
☐ **Model 37 DSPS,** 12 Ga., Takedown, Checkered Stock, 8 Shot, Open Rear Sight, *Modern*	155.00	225.00	220.00
☐ **Model 37 DSPS,** 12 Ga., Takedown, Checkered Stock, 5 Shot, Open Rear Sight, *Modern*	150.00	210.00	200.00
☐ **Model 37 M & P,** 12 Ga., Takedown, Parkerized, 5 Shot, *Modern*	140.00	200.00	195.00
☐ **Model 37 M & P,** Bayonet & Adapter, *Add* **$25.00-$45.00**			
☐ **Model 37-V Standard,** Various Gauges, Takedown, Checkered Stock, Vent Rib, *Modern*	150.00	200.00	195.00
☐ **Model 37 Standard,** Various Gauges, Takedown, Checkered Stock, *Modern*	130.00	175.00	170.00
☐ **Model 37 Supreme,** Various Gauges, Takedown, Trap Grade, Fancy Wood, Checkered Stock, *Modern*	265.00	380.00	365.00
☐ **Model 37 Supreme,** Various Gauges, Takedown, Skeet Grade, Fancy Wood, Checkered Stock, *Modern*	265.00	380.00	365.00
☐ **Model 37-$1000 Grade,** Various Gauges, Takedown, Fancy Wood, Fancy Checkering, Fancy Engraving, Gold Inlays, *Modern*	2750.00	4000.00	3900.00
☐ **Model 37-$3000 Grade,** Various Gauges, Takedown, Fancy Wood, Fancy Checkering, Fancy Engraving, Gold Inlays, *Modern*	3100.00	4000.00	3900.00
☐ **Model 37-D,** Various Gauges, Takedown, Checkered Stock, Beavertail Forend, *Modern*	125.00	165.00	160.00
☐ **Model 37-Deluxe,** Various Gauges, Takedown, Checkered Stock, Recoil Pad, *Modern*	140.00	175.00	170.00
☐ **Model 37-Deluxe,** Various Gauges, Takedown, Checkered Stock, Recoil Pad, Vent Rib, *Modern*	165.00	215.00	210.00

	V.G.	Exc.	Prior Year Exc. Value
☐ **Model 37-R,** Various Gauges, Takedown, Solid Rib, Checkered Stock, *Modern*	130.00	170.00	165.00
☐ **Model 37-R,** Various Gauges, Takedown, Solid Rib, Plain, *Modern*	125.00	165.00	160.00
☐ **Model 37-R Deluxe,** Various Gauges, Takedown, Solid Rib, Fancy Wood, Checkered Stock, *Modern*	165.00	215.00	210.00
☐ **Model 37-S,** Various Gauges, Takedown, Skeet Grade, Checkered Stock, Fancy Wood, *Modern*	230.00	325.00	320.00
☐ **Model 37-T,** Various Gauges, Takedown, Trap Grade, Checkered Stock, Fancy Wood, *Modern*	230.00	325.00	320.00

IVER JOHNSON

Started as Johnson & Bye 1871 in Worcester, Mass. In 1883 became Iver Johnson's Arms & Cycle Works. 1891 to 1982 at Fitchburg, Mass., now located in Jacksonville, Ark.

HANDGUN, PERCUSSION

	V.G.	Exc.	Prior Year Exc. Value
☐ **Prince,** .30, Singleshot, Spur Trigger, Various Barrel Lengths, Screw Barrel, *Antique*	255.00	330.00	325.00
☐ **Uncle Sam 1871,** .30, Singleshot, Spur Trigger, Various Barrel Lengths, *Antique*	230.00	300.00	295.00
☐ **.36 1861 Navy,** Revolver, Reproduction, *Antique*	53.00	80.00	75.00
☐ **.36 New Model Navy,** Revolver, Reproduction, *Antique*	42.00	68.00	65.00
☐ **.36 Pocket Model,** Revolver, Reproduction, *Antique*	53.00	80.00	75.00
☐ **.36 Remington Army,** Revolver, Reproduction, *Antique*	53.00	80.00	75.00
☐ **.44 1860 Army,** Revolver, Reproduction, *Antique*	53.00	80.00	75.00
☐ **.44 Confederate Army,** Revolver, Reproduction, *Antique*	37.00	60.00	55.00
☐ **.44 Remington Army,** Revolver, Reproduction, *Antique*	53.00	80.00	75.00
☐ **.44 Remington Target,** Revolver, Reproduction, *Antique*	65.00	100.00	95.00

HANDGUN, REVOLVER

	V.G.	Exc.	Prior Year Exc. Value
☐ **.22 Supershot,** .22 L.R.R.F., 7 Shot, Blue, Wood Grips, Top Break, Double Action, *Modern*	58.00	95.00	90.00
☐ **Armsworth M855,** .22 L.R.R.F., 8 Shot, Single Action, Top Break, Adjustable Sights, Wood Grips, *Modern*	70.00	120.00	110.00
☐ **Cadet,** .22 WMR, 8 Shot, Solid Frame, Double Action, Plastic Stock, Blue, *Modern*	48.00	75.00	70.00
☐ **Cadet,** .32 S & W Long, 5 Shot, Solid Frame Double Action, Plastic Stock, Nickel Plated, *Modern*	42.00	70.00	65.00
☐ **Cadet,** .32 S & W, 5 Shot, Solid Frame, Double Action, Plastic Stock, Blue, *Modern*	37.00	65.00	60.00
☐ **Cadet,** .38 Special, 5 Shot, Solid Frame, Double Action, Plastic Stock, Blue, *Modern*	42.00	70.00	65.00
☐ **Cadet,** .38 Special, 5 Shot, Solid Frame, Double Action, Plastic Stock, Nickel Plated, *Modern*	48.00	75.00	70.00

	V.G.	Exc.	Prior Year Exc. Value
☐ **Cattleman,** .357 Magnum, Single Action, Western Style, Color Case Hardened Frame, Various Barrel Lengths, *Modern*	105.00	150.00	145.00
☐ **Cattleman,** .44 Magnum, Single Action, Western Style, Color Case Hardened Frame, Various Barrel Lengths, *Modern*	135.00	175.00	170.00
☐ **Cattleman,** .45 Colt, Single Action, Western Style, Color Case Hardened Frame, Various Barrel Lengths, *Modern*	110.00	155.00	150.00
☐ **Cattleman Buckhorn,** .357 Magnum, Single Action, Western Style, Color Case Hardened Frame, Adjustable Sights, Various Barrel Lengths, *Modern*	105.00	150.00	145.00
☐ **Cattleman Buckhorn,** .357 Magnum, Single Action, Western Style, Color Case Hardened Frame, Adjustable Sights, 12" Barrel, *Modern*	140.00	195.00	185.00
☐ **Cattleman Buckhorn,** .44 Magnum, Single Action, Western Style, Color Case Hardened Frame, Adjustable Sights, Various Barrel Lengths, *Modern*	145.00	195.00	185.00
☐ **Cattleman Buckhorn,** .44 Magnum, Single Action, Western Style, Color Case Hardened Frame, *Modern*	130.00	175.00	170.00
☐ **Cattleman Buckhorn,** .45 Colt, Single Action, Western Style, Color Case Hardened Frame, Adjustable Sights, Various Barrel Lengths, *Modern*	115.00	170.00	165.00
☐ **Cattleman Buckhorn,** .45 Colt, Single Action, Western Style, Color Case Hardened Frame, Adjustable Sights, 12" Barrel, *Modern*	145.00	200.00	190.00
☐ **Cattleman Buntline,** .357 Magnum, Single Action, Western Style, with Detachable Shoulder Stock, Adjustable Sights, 18" Barrel, *Modern*	225.00	315.00	295.00
☐ **Cattleman Buntline,** .44 Magnum, Single Action, Western Style, with Detachable Shoulder Stock, Adjustable Sights, 18" Barrel, *Modern*	235.00	320.00	310.00
☐ **Cattleman Buntline,** .45 Colt, Single Action, Western Style, with Detachable Shoulder Stock, Adjustable Sights, 18" Barrel, *Modern*	220.00	310.00	300.00
☐ **Cattleman Trailblazer,** .22LR/.22 WMR Combo, Single Action, Western Style, Color Case Hardened Frame, Adjustable Sights, *Modern*	100.00	145.00	140.00
☐ **Champion Target,** .22 L.R.R.F., 8 Shot, Single Action, Top Break, Adjustable Sights, Wood Grips, *Modern*	80.00	130.00	125.00
☐ **Model 1900,** .22 L.R.R.F., 7 Shot, Blue, Double Action, Solid Frame, *Modern*	58.00	100.00	95.00
☐ **Model 1900,** .22 L.R.R.F., 7 Shot, Nickel Plated, Double Action, Solid Frame, *Modern*	55.00	100.00	95.00
☐ **Model 1900,** .32 S & W Long, 6 Shot, Blue, Double Action, Solid Frame, *Modern*	58.00	100.00	95.00
☐ **Model 1900,** .32 S & W Long, 6 Shot, Nickel Plated, Double Action, Solid Frame, *Modern*	58.00	100.00	95.00
☐ **Model 1900,** .32 Short R.F., 6 Shot, Blue, Double Action, Solid Frame, *Modern*	58.00	100.00	95.00

	V.G.	Exc.	Prior Year Exc. Value
☐ **Model 1900,** .32 Short R.F., 6 Shot, Nickel Plated, Double Action, Solid Frame, *Modern*	63.00	105.00	100.00
☐ **Model 1900,** .38 S & W, 5 Shot, Blue, Double Action, Solid Frame, *Modern*	63.00	105.00	100.00
☐ **Model 1900,** .38 S & W, 5 Shot, Nickel Plated, Double Action, Solid Frame, *Modern*	68.00	120.00	115.00
☐ **Model 1900 Target,** .22 L.R.R.F., 7 Shot, Blue, Wood Grips, Solid Frame, Double Action, *Modern*	75.00	130.00	125.00
☐ **Model 50A Sidewinder,** .22 L.R.R.F., 8 Shot, Solid Frame, Double Action, Plastic Stock, Western Style, *Modern*	47.00	70.00	65.00
☐ **Model 50A Sidewinder,** .22 L.R.R.F., 8 Shot, Solid Frame, Double Action, Wood Grips, Western Style, *Modern*	53.00	75.00	70.00
☐ **Model 55,** .22 L.R.R.F., 8 Shot, Solid Frame, Double Action, Wood Grips, Blue, *Modern*	42.00	70.00	65.00
☐ **Model 55-S Cadet,** .32 S & W, 5 Shot, Solid Frame, Double Action, Plastic Stock, Blue, *Modern*	42.00	70.00	65.00
☐ **Model 55-S Cadet,** .38 S & W, 5 Shot, Solid Frame, Double Action, Plastic Stock, Blue, *Modern*	42.00	70.00	65.00
☐ **Model 55-SA Cadet,** .22 L.R.R.F., 8 Shot, Solid Frame, Double Action, Plastic, Blue, *Modern*	42.00	70.00	65.00
☐ **Model 55-SA Cadet,** .32 S & W, 5 Shot, Solid Frame, Double Action, Plastic Stock, Blue, *Modern*	42.00	70.00	65.00
☐ **Model 55-SA Cadet,** .38 S & W, 5 Shot, Solid Frame, Double Action, Plastic Stock, Blue, *Modern*	48.00	75.00	70.00
☐ **Model 55A,** .22 L.R.R.F., 8 Shot, Solid Frame, Double Action, Wood Grips, Blue, *Modern*	43.00	70.00	65.00
☐ **Model 55A,** .22 L.R.R.F., 8 Shot, Solid Frame, Double Action, Wood Grips, Blue, *Modern*	43.00	70.00	65.00
☐ **Model 55A,** .22 L.R.R.F., 8 Shot, Solid Frame, Double Action, Plastic Stock, Blue, *Modern*	43.00	70.00	65.00
☐ **Model 55S,** .22 L.R.R.F., 8 Shot, Solid Frame, Double Action, Plastic Stock, Blue, *Modern*	43.00	70.00	65.00
☐ **Model 57 Target,** .22 L.R.R.F., 8 Shot, Solid Frame, Double Action, Plastic Stock, Adjustable Sights, *Modern*	48.00	75.00	70.00
☐ **Model 57 Target,** .22 L.R.R.F., 8 Shot, Solid Frame, Double Action, Wood Grips, Adjustable Sights, *Modern*	48.00	75.00	70.00
☐ **Model 57-A Target,** .22 L.R.R.F., 8 Shot, Solid Frame, Double Action, Plastic Stock, Adjustable Sights, *Modern*	53.00	80.00	75.00
☐ **Model 57-A Target,** .22 L.R.R.F., 8 Shot, Solid Frame, Double Action, Wood Grips, Adjustable Sights, *Modern*	53.00	80.00	75.00
☐ **Model 66 Trailsman,** .22 L.R.R.F., 8 Shot, Top Break, Double Action, Wood Grips, Adjustable Sights, *Modern*	53.00	80.00	75.00

	V.G.	Exc.	Prior Year Exc. Value
☐ **Model 67 Viking,** .22 L.R.R.F., 8 Shot, Top Break, Double Action, Plastic Stock, Adjustable Sights, *Modern*	55.00	75.00	75.00
☐ **Model 76S Viking,** .22 L.R.R.F., 8 Shot, Top Break, Double Action, Plastic Stock, Adjustable Sights, *Modern*	50.00	70.00	70.00
☐ **Model 67S Viking,** .32 S & W, 5 Shot, Top Break, Double Action, Plastic Stock, Adjustable Sights, *Modern*	55.00	75.00	75.00
☐ **Model 67S Viking,** .38 S & W, 5 Shot, Top Break, Double Action, Plastic Stock, Adjustable Sights, *Modern*	48.00	65.00	60.00
☐ **Petite,** .22 Short, Nickel Plated, Folding Trigger, 5 Shot, "Baby" Style, *Antique*	210.00	330.00	300.00
☐ **Safety,** .22 L.R.R.F., 7 Shot, Top Break, Double Action, Hammer, Blue, *Modern*	70.00	105.00	100.00
☐ **Safety,** .22 L.R.R.F., 7 Shot, Top Break, Double Action, Hammer, Nickel Plated, *Modern*	80.00	130.00	120.00
☐ **Safety,** .22 L.R.R.F., 7 Shot, Top Break, Double Action, Hammerless, Blue, *Modern*	80.00	130.00	120.00
☐ **Safety,** .22 L.R.R.F., 7 Shot, Top Break, Double Action, Hammerless, Nickel Plated, *Modern*	80.00	135.00	125.00
☐ **Safety,** .32 S & W, 5 Shot, Top Break, Double Action, Hammer, Nickel Plated, *Modern*	75.00	130.00	120.00
☐ **Safety,** .32 S & W, 5 Shot, Top Break, Double Action, Hammer, Blue, *Modern*	65.00	105.00	100.00
☐ **Safety,** .32 S & W, 5 Shot, Top Break, Double Action, Hammerless, Blue, *Modern*	80.00	130.00	120.00
☐ **Safety,** .32 S & W, 5 Shot, Top Break, Double Action, Hammerless, Nickel Plated, *Modern*	80.00	135.00	125.00
☐ **Safety,** .32 S & W Long, 6 Shot, Top Break, Double Action, Hammer, Blue, *Modern*	70.00	105.00	100.00
☐ **Safety,** .32 S & W Long, 6 Shot, Top Break, Double Action, Hammer, Nickel Plated, *Modern*	80.00	120.00	115.00
☐ **Safety,** .32 S & W Long, 6 Shot, Top Break, Double Action, Hammerless, Blue, *Modern*	75.00	115.00	110.00
☐ **Safety,** .38 S & W, 5 Shot, Top Break, Double Action, Hammerless, Nickel Plated, *Modern*	80.00	130.00	125.00
☐ **Sealed 8 Protector,** .22 L.R.R.F., 8 Shot, Blue, Wood Grips, Top Break, Double Action, *Modern*	80.00	125.00	120.00
☐ **Sealed 8 Supershot,** .22 L.R.R.F., Adjustable Sights, Blue, Wood Grips, Top Break, Double Action, *Modern*	85.00	130.00	125.00
☐ **Sealed 8 Target,** .22 L.R.R.F., 8 Shot, Blue, Wood Grips, Solid Frame, Double Action, *Modern*	75.00	115.00	110.00
☐ **Sidewinder,** .22LR/.22WMR Combo, Western Style, 4″ Barrel, Adjustable Sights, *Modern*	70.00	95.00	90.00
☐ **Sidewinder,** .22LR/.22 WMR Combo, Western Style, 6″ Barrel, Adjustable Sights, *Modern*	70.00	95.00	90.00
☐ **Supershot 9,** .22 L.R.R.F., 9 Shot, Adjustable Sights, Blue, Wood Grips, Top Break, *Modern*	80.00	120.00	115.00
☐ **Supershot M 844,** .22 L.R.R.F., 8 Shot, Double Action, Top Break, Adjustable Sights, Wood Grips, *Modern*	70.00	95.00	90.00

	V.G.	Exc.	Prior Year Exc. Value
☐ **Swing Out,** .22 L.R.R.F., Swing-Out Cylinder, Various Barrel Lengths, Double Action, Wood Grips, Blue, *Modern*	68.00	95.00	90.00
☐ **Swing Out,** .22 L.R.R.F., Swing-Out Cylinder, 4″ Barrel, Double Action, Wood Grips, Blue, *Modern*	72.00	100.00	95.00
☐ **Swing Out,** .22 L.R.R.F., Swing-Out Cylinder, 4″ Barrel, Double Action, Adjustable Sights, Blue, *Modern*	95.00	135.00	130.00
☐ **Swing Out,** .22 L.R.R.F., Swing-Out Cylinder, 6″ Barrel, Double Action, Adjustable Sights, Blue, *Modern*	80.00	115.00	110.00
☐ **Swing Out,** .22 WMR, Swing-Out Cylinder, Various Barrel Lengths, Double Action, Wood Grips, Blue,*M odern*	67.00	95.00	90.00
☐ **Swing Out,** .22 WMR, Swing-Out Cylinder, 4″ Barrel, Double Action, Wood Grips, Blue, *Modern*	67.00	100.00	95.00
☐ **Swing Out,** .22 WMR, Swing-Out Cylinder, 4″ Barrel, Double Action, Adjustable Sights, Blue, *Modern*	95.00	135.00	130.00
☐ **Swing Out,** .22 WMR, Swing-Out Cylinder, 6″ Barrel, Double Action, Adjustable Sights, Blue, *Modern*	72.00	115.00	110.00
☐ **Swing Out,** .32 S & W Long, Swing-Out Cylinder, Various Barrel Lengths, Double Action, Wood Grips, Blue, *Modern*	67.00	90.00	85.00
☐ **Swing Out,** .32 S & W Long, Swing-Out Cylinder, Various Barrel Lengths, Double Action, Wood Grips, Nickel Plated, *Modern*	67.00	100.00	95.00
☐ **Swing Out,** .32 S & W Long, Swing-Out Cylinder, 4″ Barrel, Double Action, Wood Grips, Blue, *Modern*	67.00	100.00	95.00
☐ **Swing Out,** .32 S & W Long, Swing-Out Cylinder, 4″ Barrel, Double Action, Adjustable Sights, Blue, *Modern*	95.00	135.00	130.00
☐ **Swing Out,** .32 S & W Long, Swing-Out Cylinder, 6″ Barrel, Double Action, Adjustable Sights, Blue, *Modern*	80.00	115.00	110.00
☐ **Swing Out,** .38 Special, Swing-Out Cylinder, Various Barrel Lengths, Double Action, Wood Grips, Blue, *Modern*	67.00	100.00	95.00
☐ **Swing Out,** .38 Special, Swing-Out Cylinder, Various Barrel Lengths, Double Action, Wood Grips, Nickel Plated, *Modern*	67.00	105.00	100.00
☐ **Swing Out,** .38 Special, Swing-Out Cylinder, 4″ Barrel, Double Action, Wood Grips, Blue, *Modern*	67.00	105.00	100.00
☐ **Swing Out,** .38 Special, Swing-Out Cylinder, 4″ Barrel, Double Action, Adjustable Sights, Blue, *Modern*	95.00	140.00	135.00
☐ **Swing Out,** .38 Special, Swing-Out Cylinder, 6″ Barrel, Double Action, Adjustable Sights, Blue, *Modern*	80.00	120.00	115.00
☐ **Swing Out Model 1879,** .38 S & W, 5 Shot, Swing Right, Forward Hinge, Solid Frame, *Antique*	200.00	275.00	265.00

	V.G.	Exc.	Prior Year Exc. Value
☐ **Target 9,** .22 L.R.R.F., 9 Shot, Blue, Solid Frame, Wood Grips, Double Action, *Modern*	67.00	100.00	95.00
☐ **Trigger-Cocking,** .22 L.R.R.F., 8 Shot, Single Action, Top Break, Adjustable Sights, Wood Grips, *Modern*	80.00	125.00	120.00
HANDGUN, SEMI-AUTOMATIC			
☐ **Model TP-22,** .22 L.R.R.F., Double Action, Hammer, Clip Fed, Blue, *Modern*	80.00	110.00	110.00
☐ **Model TP-25,** .25 ACP, Double Action, Hammer, Clip Fed, Blue, *Modern*	75.00	110.00	110.00
☐ **PP30 Enforcer,** .30 M1 Carbine, Clip Fed, Blue, *Modern*	125.00	195.00	195.00
☐ **PP30S Enforcer,** .30 M1 Carbine, Clip Fed, Stainless, *Modern*	145.00	230.00	225.00
☐ **Trailsman,** .22 L.R.R.F., Clip Fed, Blue, *Modern*	95.00	120.00	120.00
☐ **X-300 Pony,** .380 ACP, Hammer, Clip Fed, Blue, *Modern*	115.00	155.00	150.00
☐ **X-300 Pony,** .380 ACP, Hammer, Clip Fed, Nickel Plated, *Modern*	120.00	165.00	160.00
☐ **X-300 Pony,** .380 ACP, Hammer, Clip Fed, Matt Blue, *Modern*	115.00	155.00	150.00
HANDGUN, SINGLESHOT			
☐ **Eclipse 1872,** .22 R.F., Spur Trigger, Side-Swing Barrel, Hammer, *Antique*	170.00	230.00	225.00
RIFLE, BOLT ACTION			
☐ **Model 2X,** .22 L.R.R.F., Singleshot, Takedown, *Modern*	33.00	60.00	55.00
☐ **Model X,** .22 L.R.R.F., Singleshot, Takedown, *Modern*	33.00	60.00	55.00
RIFLE, SEMI-AUTOMATIC			
☐ **PM30P,** .30 Carbine, Clip Fed, Telescoping Stock, Carbine, *Modern*	135.00	190.00	190.00
☐ **PM30G,** .30 Carbine, Clip Fed, Military Style, Carbine, *Modern*	125.00	165.00	165.00
☐ **PM5.7 Spitfire,** 5.7 Spitfire, Clip Fed, Military Style, *Modern*	120.00	165.00	160.00
☐ **PM30PS Paratrooper,** .30 M1 Carbine, Clip Fed, Stainless, *Modern*	160.00	230.00	225.00
☐ **PM5.7S Spitfire,** 5.7 Spitfire, Clip Fed, Military Style, *Modern*	160.00	205.00	205.00
☐ **PP30GS Standard,** .30 M1 Carbine, Clip Fed, Stainless, *Modern*	145.00	205.00	205.00
☐ **SC30S,** .30 Carbine, Clip Fed, Plastic Stock, Carbine, *Modern*	130.00	175.00	175.00
☐ **SC30F,** .30 Carbine, Clip Fed, Folding Stock, Carbine, *Modern*	155.00	200.00	200.00
☐ **SC5.7S,** 5.7 Spitfire, Clip Fed, Plastic Stock, *Modern*	135.00	170.00	170.00
☐ **SC5.7S,** 5.7 Spitfire, Clip Fed, Folding Stock, Carbine, *Modern*	155.00	200.00	200.00
☐ **SC30S,** .30 Carbine, Clip Fed, Plastic Stock, Carbine, Stainless, *Modern*	160.00	210.00	210.00
☐ **SC30F,** .30 Carbine, Clip Fed, Folding Stock, Carbine, Stainless, *Modern*	185.00	240.00	240.00
☐ **SC5.7S,** 5.7 Spitfire, Clip Fed, Plastic Stock, Stainless, *Modern*	155.00	210.00	210.00

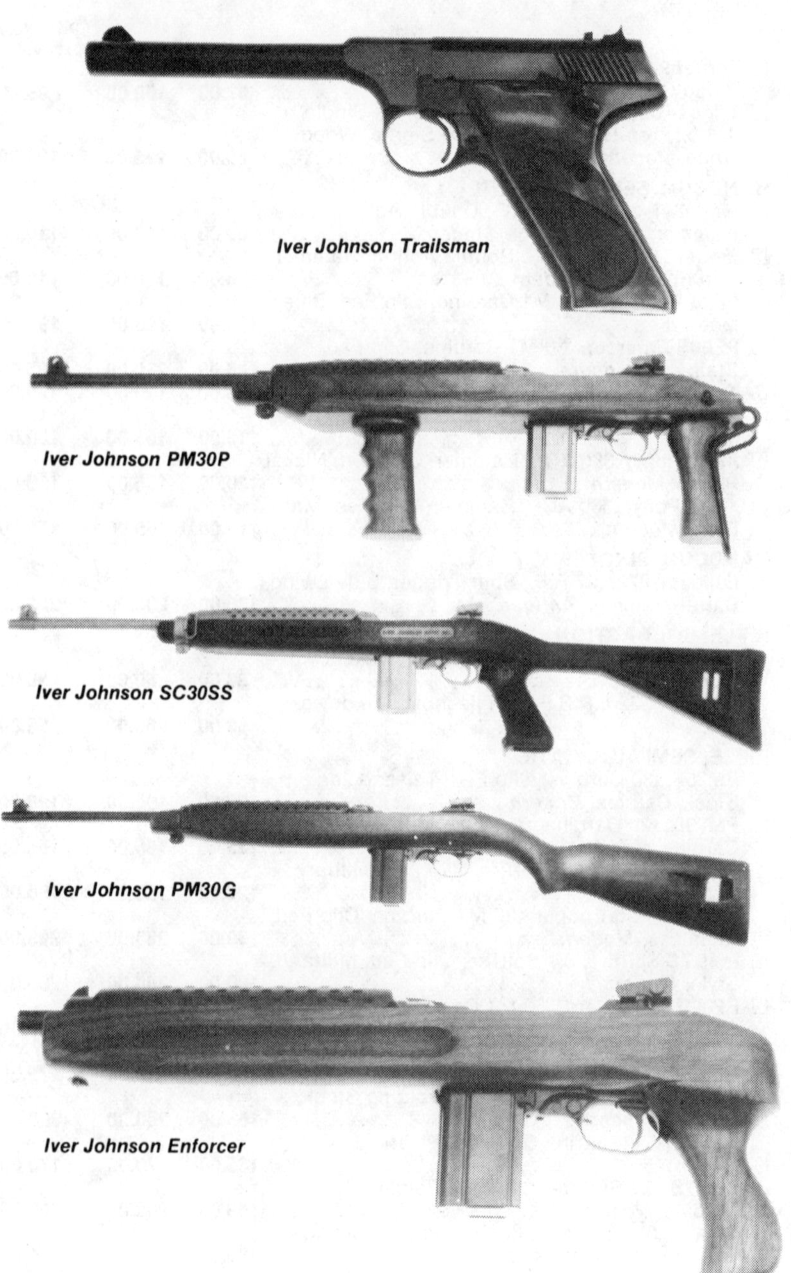

Iver Johnson Trailsman

Iver Johnson PM30P

Iver Johnson SC30SS

Iver Johnson PM30G

Iver Johnson Enforcer

	V.G.	Exc.	Prior Year Exc. Value
☐ **SC5.7S,** 5.7 Spitfire, Clip Fed, Folding Stock, Carbine, Stainless, *Modern*	175.00	235.00	235.00
SHOTGUN, DOUBLE BARREL, OVER-UNDER			
☐ **Silver Shadow,** 12 Gauge, Single Trigger, Checkered Stock, *Modern*	200.00	300.00	275.00
☐ **Silver Shadow,** 12 Gauge, Double Trigger, Checkered Stock, *Modern*	190.00	275.00	250.00
☐ **Silver Shadow,** 12 Gauge, Double Trigger, Checkered Stock, Light Engraving, Vent Rib, *Modern*	175.00	260.00	245.00
☐ **Silver Shadow,** 12 Gauge, Single Trigger, Checkered Stock, Light Engraving, Vent Rib, *Modern*	195.00	290.00	265.00
SHOTGUN, DOUBLE BARREL, SIDE-BY-SIDE			
☐ **Hercules,** Various Gauges, Double Trigger, Checkered Stock, Hammerless, *Modern*	195.00	300.00	275.00
☐ **Hercules,** Various Gauges, Double Trigger, Automatic Ejector, Hammerless, Checkered Stock, *Modern*	230.00	360.00	340.00
☐ **Hercules,** Various Gauges, Single Trigger, Hammerless, Checkered Stock, *Modern*	275.00	395.00	375.00
☐ **Hercules,** Various Gauges, Single Trigger, Automatic Ejector, Hammerless, Checkered Stock, *Modern*	310.00	440.00	415.00
☐ **Hercules,** Various Gauges, Single Selective Trigger, Hammerless, Checkered Stock, *Modern*	325.00	470.00	435.00
☐ **Hercules,** Various Gauges, Single Selective Trigger, Automatic Ejector, Hammerless, Checkered Stock, *Modern*	365.00	510.00	465.00
☐ **Knox-All,** Various Gauges, Double Trigger, Hammer, Checkered Stock, *Modern*	185.00	285.00	265.00
☐ **Skeeter,** Various Gauges, Double Trigger, Hammerles, *Modern*	290.00	435.00	415.00
☐ **Skeeter,** Various Gauges, Skeet Grade, Double Trigger, Automatic Ejector, Hammerless, *Modern*	360.00	540.00	495.00
☐ **Skeeter,** Various Gauges, Skeet Grade, Single Trigger, Hammerless, *Modern*	330.00	515.00	470.00
☐ **Skeeter,** Various Gauges, Skeet Grade, Single Trigger, Automatic Ejector, Hammerless, *Modern*	395.00	550.00	500.00
☐ **Skeeter,** Various Gauges, Skeet Grade, Single Selective Trigger, Hammerless, *Modern*	405.00	565.00	525.00
☐ **Skeeter,** Various Gauges, Skeet Grade, Single Selective Trigger, Automatic Ejector, Hammerless, *Modern*	395.00	530.00	495.00
☐ **Super,** 12 Gauge, Trap Grade, Double Trigger, Hammerless, *Modern*	450.00	575.00	550.00
☐ **Super,** 12 Gauge, Trap Grade, Single Trigger, Hammerless, *Modern*	520.00	650.00	620.00
☐ **Super,** 12 Gauge, Trap Grade, Single Selective Trigger, Hammerless, *Modern*	600.00	775.00	725.00

	V.G.	Exc.	Prior Year Exc. Value
SHOTGUN, SINGLESHOT			
☐ **Side Snap,** 12 Gauge, Steel Barrel, Hammer, *Antique*	55.00	80.00	75.00
☐ **Side Snap,** 12 Gauge, Damascus Barrel, Hammer, *Antique*	48.00	70.00	65.00
☐ **Top Snap,** 12 Gauge, Steel Barrel, Hammer, *Antique*	60.00	90.00	80.00
☐ **12 Gauge,** Trap Grade, Vent Rib, Checkered Stock, *Modern*	85.00	150.00	135.00
☐ **Champion,** Various Gauges, Automatic Ejector, *Modern*	50.00	70.00	65.00
☐ **Mat Rib Grade,** Various Gauges, Raised Matted Rib, Automatic Ejector, Checkered Stock, *Modern*	55.00	90.00	85.00

IZARRA

Made by Bonifacio Echeverra, Eibar, Spain, c. 1918.

	V.G.	Exc.	Prior Year Exc. Value
HANDGUN, SEMI-AUTOMATIC			
☐ **.32 ACP**, Clip Fed, Long Grip, *Modern*	135.00	175.00	165.00

J & R

Burbank, Calif.

	V.G.	Exc.	Prior Year Exc. Value
RIFLE, SEMI-AUTOMATIC			
☐ **Model 68**, 9mm Luger, Clip Fed, Flash Hider, Takedown, *Modern*	125.00	175.00	175.00

JACKRABBIT

Continental Arms Corp., N.Y.C., c. 1960.

	V.G.	Exc.	Prior Year Exc. Value
RIFLE, SINGLESHOT			
☐ **Handy Gun**, .44 Magnum, Detachable Shoulder Stock, *Modern*	50.00	80.00	75.00
SHOTGUN, SINGLESHOT			
☐ **Handy Gun**, .410 3", Detachable Shoulder Stock, *Modern*	45.00	75.00	70.00

JACKSON ARMS CO.

Made by Crescent for C.M. McClung & Co., Knoxville, Tenn.

	V.G.	Exc.	Prior Year Exc. Value
SHOTGUN, DOUBLE BARREL, SIDE-BY-SIDE			
☐ **Various Gauges**, Outside Hammers, Damascus Barrel, *Modern*	100.00	170.00	175.00
☐ **Various Gauges**, Hammerless, Steel Barrel, *Modern*	135.00	200.00	200.00
☐ **Various Gauges**, Hammerless, Damascus Barrel, *Modern*	100.00	175.00	175.00
☐ **Various Gauges**, Outside Hammers, Steel Barrel, *Modern*	125.00	195.00	190.00
SHOTGUN, SINGLESHOT			
☐ **Various Gauges**, Hammer, Steel Barrel, *Modern*	55.00	80.00	85.00

JACKSON HOLE RIFLE CO.

Jackson Hole, Wyo., c. 1970.

	V.G.	Exc.	Prior Year Exc. Value
RIFLE, BOLT ACTION			
☐ **Sportsman**, Various Calibers, with 3 Interchangable Barrels, Checkered Stock, *Modern*	450.00	600.00	575.00
☐ **Custom**, Various Calibers, with 3 Interchangable Barrels, Fancy Checkering, Fancy Wood, *Modern*	600.00	865.00	845.00
☐ **Presentation**, Various Calibers, with 3 Interchangable Barrels, Fancy Checkering, Fancy Wood, Engraved, *Modern*	750.00	1,100.00	1,050.00

JAGA

Frantisek Dusek. Opocno, Czechoslovakia, c. 1930.

HANDGUN, SEMI-AUTOMATIC	V.G.	Exc.	Prior Year Exc. Value
☐ **.25 ACP**, Clip Fed, Blue, *Modern*	85.00	135.00	125.00

JAGER

Suhl, Germany.

HANDGUN, SEMI-AUTOMATIC	V.G.	Exc.	Prior Year Exc. Value
☐ **.32 ACP**, Clip Fed, Military, *Modern*	275.00	450.00	425.00
☐ **.32 ACP**, Clip Fed, Commercial, *Modern*	220.00	365.00	400.00

JAGER

HANDGUN, REVOLVER	V.G.	Exc.	Prior Year Exc. Value
☐ **Jager**, .22LR/.22 WMR Combo, Single Action, Western Style, Adjustable Sights, *Modern*	70.00	100.00	95.00
☐ **Jager**, .22LR/.22 WMR Combo, Single Action, Western Style, *Modern*	65.00	95.00	90.00
☐ **Jager Centerfire**, Various Calibers, Single Action, Western Style, Adjustable Sights, *Modern*	85.00	125.00	125.00
☐ **Jager Centerfire**, Various Calibers, Single Action, Western Style, *Modern*	75.00	115.00	115.00

JAGER, F. & CO.

See Herold.

JANSSEN FRERES

Liege, Belgium, c. 1925

SHOTGUN, DOUBLE BARREL, SIDE-BY-SIDE	V.G.	Exc.	Prior Year Exc. Value
☐ **Various Gauges**, Hammerless, Steel Barrel, *Modern*	115.00	180.00	170.00

JAPANESE MILITARY

AUTOMATIC WEAPON, LIGHT MACHINE GUN	V.G.	Exc.	Prior Year Exc. Value
☐ **Type 92 (Lewis)**, 7.7mm Jap, Drum Magazine, Bipod, Military, *Class 3*	750.00	1,000.00	975.00
☐ **Type 96**, 6.5 x 50 Arisaka, Clip Fed, Bipod, Military, *Class 3*	700.00	950.00	925.00
☐ **Type 96**, 6.5 x 50 Arisaka, Clip Fed, Bipod, Military, Scope Mounted, *Class 3*	900.00	1,350.00	1,300.00
☐ **Type 99**, 7.7mm Jap, Clip Fed, Bipod, Scope Mounted, Military, *Class 3*	1,250.00	1,750.00	1,650.00

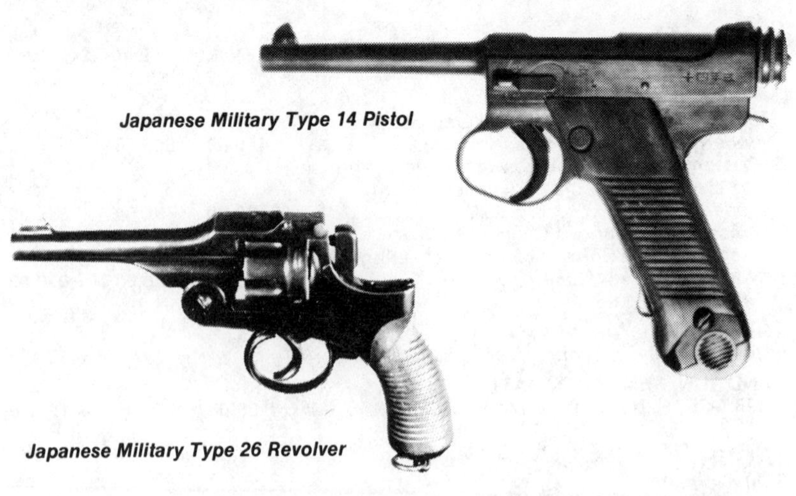

Japanese Military Type 14 Pistol

Japanese Military Type 26 Revolver

Japanese Military Type 99 Rifle

	V.G.	Exc.	Prior Year Exc. Value
☐ **Type 99**, 7.7mm Jap, Clip Fed, Bipod, Military, *Class 3*	700.00	975.00	950.00
AUTOMATIC WEAPON, SUBMACHINE GUN			
☐ **Type 100**, 8mm Nambu, Clip Fed, Wood Stock, *Class 3*	895.00	1,450.00	1,400.00
HANDGUN, REVOLVER			
☐ **Model 26**, 9mm, Military, *Curio*	150.00	225.00	195.00
HANDGUN, SEMI-AUTOMATIC			
☐ **Baby Nambu**, 7mm Nambu, Clip Fed, Military, *Curio*	975.00	1,725.00	1,650.00
☐ **Baby Nambu**, 7mm Nambu, Presentation, Military, Clip Fed, Military, *Curio*	1,400.00	2,100.00	2,000.00
☐ **Type 14 Nambu**, 8mm Nambu, Clip Fed, Small Trigger Guard, Military, *Curio*	275.00	450.00	400.00
☐ **Type 14 Nambu**, 8mm Nambu, Clip Fed, Large Trigger Guard, Military, *Curio*	225.00	350.00	350.00
☐ **Type 1902 "Grandpa"**, 8mm Nambu, Tokyo Arsenal, Clip Fed, Military, *Curio*	700.00	1,100.00	995.00
☐ **Type 1904 "Papa"**, 8mm Nambu, TGE Navy, Clip Fed, Military, *Curio*	575.00	800.00	775.00
☐ **Type 1904 "Papa"**, 8mm Nambu, TGE Commercial, Clip Fed, *Curio*	650.00	875.00	850.00

	V.G.	Exc.	Prior Year Exc. Value
☐ **Type 1904 "Papa",** 8mm Nambu, TGE Commercial, Slotted for Shoulder Stock, Clip Fed, *Curio*	875.00	1150.00	1600.00
☐ **Type 1904 "Papa",** 8mm Nambu, Tokyo Arsenal, Clip Fed, Military, *Curio*	350.00	510.00	700.00
☐ **Type 1904 "Papa",** 8mm Nambu, Thailand, Clip Fed, Military, *Curio*	1000.00	1500.00	2100.00
☐ **Type 94,** 8mm Nambu, Clip Fed, Military, *Curio*	130.00	190.00	295.00

RIFLE, BOLT ACTION

The following World War I and World War II rifles were made by a few national armories: Nagoya, Tokyo, Kokura, Jinsen, and Inchon (located in occupied Korea) and the private plant of Chuo Kogyo Kabushiki.

In dealing with Japanese weapons, remember that when it says "Type 38 or Type 99" this is not the year of manufacture in the Roman calendar system but a Japanese calendar denoting the reign of their emperor. For example, Type 38 would mean it was adopted in 1905 and Type 99 would have been adopted in 1939.

	V.G.	Exc.	Prior Year Exc. Value
☐ **Model 38 (1905),** 6.5 x 50 Arisaka, Military, *Curio*	50.00	90.00	140.00
☐ **Model 38 (1905),** 6.5 x 50 Arisaka, Military, Carbine, *Curio*	50.00	90.00	140.00
☐ **Model 44 (1911),** 6.5 x 50 Arisaka, Military, Carbine, *Curio*	50.00	90.00	140.00
☐ **Model 99 (1939),** 7.7 x 58 Arisaka, Military, Open Rear Sight, *Curio*	50.00	90.00	145.00
☐ **Type 30 (1897),** 6.5 Arisaka, Bolt Action, 31-Inch Barrel, Often Referred To As The "Hook Safety Rifle," *Curio*	40.00	85.00	125.00
☐ **Type 38 Carbine,** 6.5 Cal., Arisaka, 19-Inch Barrel, Modified For Paratroop Use By The Edition Of A Hinge To The Wrist Of The Stock For Folding, Somewhat Rare, *Curio*	60.00	95.00	150.00
☐ **Type 38,** 6.5 x 50 Arisaka, Late Model, Military, *Curio*	50.00	75.00	135.00
☐ **Type 44,** 6.5 x 50 Arisaka, Folding Bayonet, Military, *Curio*	90.00	135.00	200.00
☐ **Type 97 Sniper Rifle,** Arisaka, 31-Inch Barrel, Specially Selected For Extreme Accuracy And Then Fitted With Telescopic Sight, *Curio*	90.00	135.00	200.00
☐ **Type 99,** 7.7 x 58 Arisaka, Aircraft Sights Dust Cover, Military, *Curio*	55.00	100.00	160.00
☐ **Type 99,** 7.7 Cal., Arisaka, 31-Inch Barrel, Five Shot Mauser Type Magazine, Bolt Action, Long Barrel Infantry Model, Becoming Scarce, *Curio*	35.00	60.00	100.00
☐ **Type 99, Type 2 Take Down Rifle,** 7.7 Cal., Arisaka, 25-Inch Barrel, A Standard Type 99 Rifle Modified To Break In Half For Compact Paratroop Use, Very Rare, *Curio*	120.00	150.00	200.00
☐ **Japanese "Siamese Mauser",** 8 x 52R Cal., Made By Japan For The Government Of Siam In The Early 1920s. A Modified 98 Mauser, Bolt Action, 30-Inch Barrel, *Curio*	30.00	50.00	75.00

	V.G.	Exc.	Prior Year Exc. Value
JENNINGS FIREARMS, INC.			
Chino, Calif., current.			
HANDGUN, SEMI-AUTOMATIC			
☐ **Model J-22**, .22 L.R.R.F., Clip Fed, Black Teflon Plate, *Modern*	35.00	50.00	65.00
☐ **Model J-22**, .22 L.R.R.F., Clip Fed, Satin Nickel Plate, *Modern*	35.00	50.00	65.00
JEWEL			
Made by Hood Firearms Co., c. 1876.			
HANDGUN, REVOLVER			
☐ **#1**, .22 Short R.F., 7 Shot, Spur Trigger, Solid Frame, Single Action, *Antique*	90.00	165.00	160.00
JIEFFCO			
Mre. Liegoise d'Armes a Feu Robar et Cie, Liege, Belgium, c. 1912-1914.			
HANDGUN, SEMI-AUTOMATIC			
☐ **.25 ACP**, Clip Fed, Blue, *Curio*	195.00	290.00	275.00
☐ **.32 ACP**, Clip Fed, Blue, *Curio*	185.00	275.00	260.00
JIEFFCO			
Tradename used by Davis-Warner on pistols made by Robar et Cie., c. 1920.			
HANDGUN, SEMI-AUTOMATIC			
☐ **New Model Melior**, .25 ACP, Clip Fed, *Curio*	120.00	170.00	155.00
J.G.L.			
Jos. G. Landmann, Holstein, W. Germany, c. 1968.			
RIFLE, SEMI-AUTOMATIC			
☐ **JGL-68 Model 1**, .22 L.R.R.F., Clip Fed, Carbine Style, *Modern*	55.00	75.00	70.00
☐ **JGL-68 Model 2**, .22 L.R.R.F., Clip Fed, Vertical Grip & Foregrip, *Modern*	65.00	85.00	80.00
☐ **JGL-68 Model 3**, .22 L.R.R.F., Clip Fed, Vertical Grip, *Modern*	55.00	80.00	75.00
JOFFRE			
Spain, Unknown Maker, c. 1900.			
HANDGUN, SEMI-AUTOMATIC			
☐ **M1916**, .32 ACP, Clip Fed, *Modern*	85.00	130.00	125.00

JOHNSON AUTOMATICS

Providence, R.I. Also see U.S. Military.

	V.G.	Exc.	Prior Year Exc. Value
RIFLE, BOLT ACTION			
☐ **Diamond Cherry Featherweight**, Various Calibers, Engraved, Carved Cherry Stock, Muzzle Brake, *Modern*	785.00	1,200.00	1,100.00
☐ **Honey Featherweight**, Various Calibers, Engraved, Carved Stock, Muzzle Brake, Gold and Silver Inlays, *Modern*	1,300.00	2,075.00	2,000.00
☐ **Laminar Sporter**, Various Calibers, Laminated Stock, *Modern*	475.00	725.00	700.00
RIFLE, SEMI-AUTOMATIC			
☐ **Model 1941**, .30-06 Springfield, Military, *Curio*	485.00	700.00	650.00
☐ **Model 1941**, 7mm Mauser, Military, *Modern*	575.00	800.00	750.00

JO-LO-AR

Hijos de Arrizabalaga, Eibar, Spain, c. 1920.

	V.G.	Exc.	Prior Year Exc. Value
HANDGUN, SEMI-AUTOMATIC			
☐ **.380 ACP**, Tip-up, Clip Fed, Hammer, Spur Trigger, Military, *Modern*	170.00	250.00	240.00
☐ **9mm Bergmann**, Tip-up, Clip Fed, Hammer, Spur Trigger, Military, *Modern*	135.00	200.00	200.00

JONES, CHARLES

Lancaster, Pa. 1780. See Kentucky Rifles.

JONES, J.N. & CO.

London, England, c. 1760.

	V.G.	Exc.	Prior Year Exc. Value
HANDGUN, FLINTLOCK			
☐ **.60**, George III, Navy Pistol, Brass Barrel, Brass Furniture, Military, *Antique*	625.00	1,000.00	950.00
HANDGUN, PERCUSSION			
☐ **.58**, Holster Pistol, Converted from Flintlock, Brass Furniture, Plain, *Antique*	485.00	715.00	650.00

JUPITER

Fabrique d'Armes de Guerre de Grand Precision, Eibar, Spain.

	V.G.	Exc.	Prior Year Exc. Value
HANDGUN, SEMI-AUTOMATIC			
☐ **.32 ACP**. Clip Fed, Blue, *Curio*	90.00	140.00	135.00

KABA SPEZIAL

Made by August Menz, Suhl, Germany, for Karl Bauer & Co., Berlin, Germany, c. 1925.

	V.G.	Exc.	Prior Year Exc. Value
HANDGUN, SEMI-AUTOMATIC			
☐ **Liliput**, .25 ACP, Clip Fed, Blue, *Modern*	175.00	240.00	225.00
☐ **Liliput**, .32 ACP, Clip Fed, Blue, *Modern*	190.00	265.00	250.00

KABA SPEZIAL

Made by Francisco Arizmendi, Eibar, Spain.

	V.G.	Exc.	Prior Year Exc. Value
HANDGUN, SEMI-AUTOMATIC			
☐ **.25 ACP, Clip Fed, Blue,** *Modern*	125.00	165.00	155.00

KART

	V.G.	Exc.	Prior Year Exc. Value
HANDGUN, SEMI-AUTOMATIC			
☐ **Target**, .22 L.R.R.F., Clip Fed, M1911 Frame, 6" Barrel, *Modern*	440.00	625.00	600.00
☐ **For Colt Government Target**, .22 L.R.R.F., Conversion Unit Only	145.00	190.00	185.00

KASSNAR IMPORTS

Harrisburg, Pa.

	V.G.	Exc.	Prior Year Exc. Value
RIFLE, BOLT ACTION			
☐ **Model M-14S**, .22 L.R.R.F., Clip Fed, Checkered Stock, *Modern*	45.00	65.00	60.00
☐ **Model M-15S**, .22 WMR, Clip Fed, Checkered Stock, *Modern*	50.00	80.00	75.00
☐ **Model M-1400**, .22 L.R.R.F., Clip Fed, Checkered Stock, *Modern*	50.00	70.00	70.00
☐ **Model M-1500**, .22 WMR, Clip Fed, Checkered Stock, *Modern*	55.00	85.00	85.00
☐ **Parker Hale Midland**, Various Calibers, Checkered Stock, Open Sights, *Modern*	160.00	220.00	195.00
☐ **Parker Hale Super**, Various Calibers, Checkered Stock, Open Sights, Monte Carlo Stock, *Modern*	195.00	285.00	275.00
☐ **Parker Hale Varmint**, Various Calibers, Checkered Stock, Open Sights, Varmint Stock, *Modern*	195.00	285.00	275.00
RIFLE, SEMI-AUTOMATIC			
☐ **Model M-16**, .22 L.R.R.F., Clip Fed, Military Style, *Modern*	55.00	80.00	75.00
☐ **Model M-20S**, .22 L.R.R.F., *Modern*	40.00	65.00	60.00
SHOTGUN, DOUBLE BARREL, OVER-UNDER			
☐ **Fias SK-1**, 12 and 20 Gauges, Double Trigger, Checkered Stock, *Modern*	240.00	335.00	320.00
☐ **Fias SK-3**, 12 and 20 Gauges, Single Selective Trigger, Checkered Stock, *Modern*	265.00	375.00	360.00
☐ **Fias SK-4**, 12 and 20 Gauges, Single Selective Trigger, Checkered Stock, Automatic Ejector, *Modern*	325.00	435.00	400.00

	V.G.	Exc.	Prior Year Exc. Value
☐ **Fias SK-4D**, 12 and 20 Gauges, Single Selective Trigger, Fancy Checkering, Fancy Wood, Engraved, Automatic Ejector, *Modern*	340.00	455.00	425.00
☐ **Fias SK-4T**, 12 Ga., Trap Grade, Single Selective Trigger, Automatic Ejector, Checkered Stock, Wide Vent Rib, *Modern*	340.00	455.00	425.00
SHOTGUN, DOUBLE BARREL, SIDE-BY-SIDE			
☐ **Zabala**, Various Gauges, Checkered Stock, Double Triggers, *Modern*	180.00	260.00	245.00
SHOTGUN, SINGLESHOT			
☐ **Taiyojuki**, Various Gauges, Top Break, Plain, *Modern*	30.00	45.00	40.00

KEFFER, JACOB

Lancaster, Pa., c. 1802. See Kentucky Rifles and Pistols.

KEIM, JOHN

Reading, Pa. 1820-1839. See Kentucky Rifles and Pistols.

KENTUCKY RIFLES AND PISTOLS

The uniquely American "Kentucky" (or, as some prefer, "Pennsylvania") expressed in wood & metal the attitude of strength and independence that fostered our young nation. For the most part Kentuckys are custom guns, and, aside from general style similarities, virtually all are different, even those by the same maker. To add to the problem of price generalization, gunsmiths purchased parts from various makers and there may be three different names on a single gun or none at all. The main considerations in determining value are: 1. Type of ignition; 2. Quality of workmanship; 3. Decoration; 4. Orginality; 5. Condition. Except for orginality this list also applies to contemporary makers.

	V.G.	Exc.	Prior Year Exc. Value
RIFLES, FLINTLOCK			
☐ **Moderate Quality**, Plain, *Antique*	675.00	1,300.00	1,200.00
☐ **Moderate Quality**, Medium Decoration, *Antique*	2,000.00	4,400.00	4,200.00
☐ **High Quality**, Fancy Decoration, *Antique*	3,500.00	6,300.00	6,000.00
☐ **Over-Under**, Swivel-Breech, Plain, *Antique*	875.00	1,700.00	1,600.00
☐ **Over-Under**, Swivel-Breech, Medium Quality, *Antique*	3,500.00	5,750.00	5,600.00
☐ **Over-Under**, Swivel-Breech, High Quality, *Antique*	4,600.00	8,650.00	8,500.00
☐ **Deduct 30%-40%**, if Converted from Percussion			
RIFLES, PERCUSSION			
☐ **Moderate Quality**, Plain, *Antique*	635.00	1,300.00	1,200.00
☐ **Moderate Quality**, Medium Decoration, *Antique*	875.00	1,800.00	1,750.00
☐ **High Quality**, Fancy Decoration, *Antique*	3,150.00	5,650.00	5,500.00
☐ **Over-Under**, Medium Quality, Swivel Breech, Plain, *Antique*	585.00	1,200.00	1,100.00
☐ **Over-Under**, Medium Quality, Swivel-Breech, *Antique*	1,375.00	2,650.00	2,500.00
☐ **Over-Under**, High Quality, Swivel-Breech, *Antique*	2,500.00	4,200.00	4,000.00
☐ **Add 20%**, if converted from Flintlock to Percussion			
PISTOLS, FLINTLOCK			
☐ **Moderate Quality**, Medium Decoration, *Antique*	1,825.00	3,400.00	3,250.00

	V.G.	Exc.	Prior Year Exc. Value
☐ **High Quality**, Fancy Decoration, *Antique*	3,600.00	6,875.00	6,750.00

PISTOLS, PERCUSSION (ORIGINAL)

☐ **Moderate Quality**, Medium Decoration, *Antique*	1,675.00	2,500.00	2,400.00
☐ **High Quality**, Fancy Decoration, *Antique*	2,800.00	3,875.00	3,750.00

PISTOLS, PERCUSSION (CONVERTED FROM FLINTLOCK)

☐ **Moderate Quality**, Medium Decoration, *Antique*	875.00	1,500.00	1,450.00
☐ **High Quality**, Fancy Decoration, *Antique*	1,675.00	2,500.00	2,400.00

Arms with signatures are more desirable than those without markings. No name-deduct **10%-15%**. *If of recent vintage, and handmade, use this chart and deduct* **50%**.

KETLAND & CO.

Birmingham & London, England 1760-1831. Also See Kentucky Rifles.

HANDGUN, FLINTLOCK

☐ **.58**, Holster Pistol, Plain, Tapered Round Barrel, Brass Furniture, *Antique*	625.00	995.00	975.00
☐ **.62**, Belt Pistol, Brass Barrel, Brass Furniture, Light Ornamentation, *Antique*	645.00	1,045.00	995.00

KETLAND, T.

Birmingham, England 1750-1829.

HANDGUN, FLINTLOCK

☐ **.69**, Pair, Belt Pistol, Brass Furniture, Plain, *Antique*	1,500.00	2,400.00	2,250.00

RIFLE, FLINTLOCK

☐ **.65**, Officers Model Brown Bess, Musket, Military, *Antique*	2,325.00	3,400.00	3,250.00
☐ **.73**, 2nd. Model Brown Bess, Musket, Military, *Antique*	1,200.00	2,250.00	2,150.00

KETLAND, WILLIAM & CO.

HANDGUN, FLINTLOCK

☐ **.63**, Holster Pistol, Round Barrel, Plain, *Antique*	565.00	895.00	850.00

KETTNER, ED

Suhl, Thuringia, Germany 1922-1939.

COMBINATION WEAPON, DRILLING

☐ **12x12 x 10.75x65R Collath**, Engraved, Checkered Stock, Sling Swivels, *Modern*	875.00	1,550.00	1,450.00

KIMBALL, J.M. ARMS CO.

Detroit, Mich., c. 1955.

HANDGUN, SEMI-AUTOMATIC

☐ **Standard Model**, .30 Carbine, Clip Fed, Blue, *Modern*	475.00	750.00	700.00
☐ **Standard Model**, .30 Carbine, Clip Fed, Blue, Grooved Chamber, *Modern*	525.00	850.00	800.00
☐ **Standard Model**, .22 Hornet, Clip Fed, Blue, *Modern*	1,100.00	1,650.00	1,650.00

	V.G.	Exc.	Prior Year Exc. Value
☐ **Standard Model**, .38 Special, Clip Fed, Blue, *Modern*	800.00	1,200.00	1,200.00
☐ **Target Model**, .30 Carbine, Clip Fed, Blue, Adjustable Sights, *Modern*	525.00	850.00	800.00
☐ **Combat Model**, .30 Carbine, Clip Fed, Blue, Short Barrel, *Modern*	475.00	725.00	700.00

KIMBER

Clackamas, Ore.

RIFLE, BOLT ACTION

	V.G.	Exc.	Prior Year Exc. Value
☐ **Model 82 Cascade**, .22 L.R.R.F., Checkered Stock, Clip Fed, No Sights, Monte Carlo Stock, *Modern*	245.00	335.00	325.00
☐ **Model 82 Cascade**, .22 W.M.R., Checkered Stock, Clip Fed, No Sights, Monte Carlo Stock, *Modern*	265.00	350.00	340.00
☐ **Model 82 Classic**, .22 L.R.R.F., Checkered Stock, Clip Fed, No Sights, *Modern*	240.00	320.00	315.00
☐ **Model 82 Classic**, .22 W.M.R., Checkered Stock, Clip Fed, No Sights, *Modern*	255.00	330.00	325.00

KIMEL INDUSTRIES

Matthews, N.C.

HANDGUN, DOUBLE BARREL, OVER-UNDER

	V.G.	Exc.	Prior Year Exc. Value
☐ **Twist**, .22 Short R.F., Swivel Breech, Derringer, Spur Trigger, *Modern*	20.00	35.00	35.00

KING NITRO

Made by Stevens Arms.

RIFLE, BOLT ACTION

	V.G.	Exc.	Prior Year Exc. Value
☐ **Model 53**, .22 L.R.R.F., Singleshot, Takedown, *Modern*	35.00	50.00	45.00

SHOTGUN, DOUBLE BARREL, SIDE-BY-SIDE

	V.G.	Exc.	Prior Year Exc. Value
☐ **M 315 Various Gauges**, Hammerless, Steel Barrel, *Modern*	110.00	175.00	165.00

KINGLAND SPECIAL

Made by Crescent for Geller, Wards & Hasner St. Louis, Mo.

SHOTGUN, DOUBLE BARREL, SIDE-BY-SIDE

	V.G.	Exc.	Prior Year Exc. Value
☐ **Various Gauges**, Outside Hammers, Damascus Barrel, *Modern*	100.00	170.00	175.00
☐ **Various Gauges**, Hammerless, Steel Barrel, *Modern*	135.00	190.00	200.00
☐ **Various Gauges**, Hammerless, Damascus Barrel, *Modern*	100.00	170.00	175.00
☐ **Various Gauges**, Outside Hammers, Steel Barrel, *Modern*	125.00	185.00	190.00

SHOTGUN, SINGLESHOT

	V.G.	Exc.	Prior Year Exc. Value
☐ **Various Gauges**, Hammer, Steel Barrel, *Modern*	55.00	85.00	85.00

KINGLAND 10-STAR

Made by Crescent for Geller, Wards & Hasner St. Louis, Mo. See Kingsland Special

	V.G.	Exc.	Prior Year Exc. Value
KIRIKKALE			
Makina ve Kimya Endustrisi Kurumu Kirrikale, Ankara, Turkey.			
HANDGUN, SEMI-AUTOMATIC			
☐ **MKE**, .380 ACP, Clip Fed, Double Action, *Modern*	140.00	200.00	185.00
KITTEMAUG			
Maker Unknown, c. 1880.			
HANDGUN, REVOLVER			
☐ **.32 Short R.F.**, 5 Shot, Spur Trigger, Solid Frame, Single Action, *Antique*	95.00	165.00	160.00
KLEINGUENTHER'S			
Seguin, Texas.			
HANDGUN, REVOLVER			
☐ **Reck R-18**, .357 Magnum, Adjustable Sights, Western Style, Single Action, *Modern*	65.00	110.00	100.00
RIFLE, BOLT ACTION			
☐ **K-10**, .22 L.R.R.F., Single Shot, Tangent Sights, *Modern*	35.00	50.00	45.00
☐ **K-12**, .22 L.R.R.F., Clip Fed, Checkered Stock, *Modern*	50.00	75.00	70.00
☐ **K-13**, .22 W.M.R., Clip Fed, Checkered Stock, *Modern*	80.00	120.00	110.00
☐ **K-14 Insta-fire**, Various Calibers, Checkered Stock, No Sights, Recoil Pad, *Modern*	310.00	420.00	395.00
☐ **K-15 Insta-fire**, Various Calibers, Checkered Stock, No Sights, Recoil Pad, *Modern*	370.00	595.00	575.00
☐ **K-15**, .22 L.R.R.F., Clip Fed, Checkered Stock, *Modern*	60.00	110.00	100.00
☐ **V2130**, Various Calibers, Checkered Stock, Recoil Pad, *Modern*	155.00	220.00	200.00
RIFLE, DOUBLE BARREL, OVER-UNDER			
☐ **Model 222**, .22 WMR, Plain, *Modern*	85.00	130.00	120.00
SHOTGUN, DOUBLE BARREL, OVER-UNDER			
☐ **Condor**, 12 Gauge, Skeet Grade, Single Selective Trigger, Automatic Ejector, Wide Vent Rib, *Modern*	345.00	450.00	435.00
☐ **Condor**, 12 Gauge, Single Selective Trigger, Automatic Ejector, Vent Rib, *Modern*	320.00	425.00	400.00
SHOTGUN, DOUBLE BARREL, SIDE-BY-SIDE			
☐ **Brescia**, 12 Gauge, Hammerless, Light Engraving, Double Trigger, *Modern*	175.00	240.00	225.00
SHOTGUN, SEMI-AUTOMATIC			
☐ **12 Ga.**, Checkered Stock, Vent Rib, Engraved, Right Hand, *Modern*	145.00	195.00	185.00
☐ **12 Ga.**, Checkered Stock, Vent Rib, Engraved, Left Hand, *Modern*	160.00	220.00	200.00

KLETT, SIMON

Probably Leipzig, c. 1620.

	V.G.	Exc.	Prior Year Exc. Value
RIFLE, WHEEL-LOCK			
☐ **.54**, Rifled, Octagon Barrel, Brass Furniture, Medium Ornamentation, Engraved, High Quality, *Antique*	6,200.00	9,750.00	9,500.00

KNICKERBOCKER

Made by Crescent for H & D Folsom, c. 1900.

	V.G.	Exc.	Prior Year Exc. Value
SHOTGUN, DOUBLE BARREL, SIDE-BY-SIDE			
☐ **Various Gauges**, Hammerless, *Modern*	135.00	190.00	200.00
☐ **Various Gauges**, Outside Hammers, *Modern*	125.00	185.00	190.00

KNICKERBOCKER

Made by Stevens Arms.

	V.G.	Exc.	Prior Year Exc. Value
SHOTGUN, DOUBLE BARREL, SIDE-BY-SIDE			
☐ **Model 311**, Various Gauges, Hammerless, Steel Barrel, *Modern*	115.00	180.00	165.00

KNOCKABOUT

Made by Stevens Arms.

	V.G.	Exc.	Prior Year Exc. Value
SHOTGUN, DOUBLE BARREL, SIDE-BY-SIDE			
☐ **Model 311**, Various Guages, Hammerless, Steel Barrel, *Modern*	115.00	180.00	165.00

KNOXALL

Made by Crescent, c. 1900.

	V.G.	Exc.	Prior Year Exc. Value
SHOTGUN, DOUBLE BARREL, SIDE-BY-SIDE			
☐ **Various Gauges**, Hammerless, Steel Barrel, *Modern*	135.00	190.00	200.00
☐ **Various Gauges**, Outside Hammers, Steel Barrel, *Modern*	125.00	185.00	190.00

KODIAK MFG. CO.

North Haven, Conn., c. 1965.

	V.G.	Exc.	Prior Year Exc. Value
RIFLE, BOLT ACTION			
☐ **Model 98 Brush Carbine**, Various Calibers, Checkered Stock, *Modern*	95.00	155.00	145.00
☐ **Model 99 Deluxe Brush Carbine**, Various Calibers, Checkered Stock, *Modern*	110.00	165.00	155.00
☐ **Model 100 Deluxe Rifle**, Various Calibers, Checkered Stock, *Modern*	115.00	175.00	160.00
☐ **Model 100M Deluxe Rifle**, Various Magnum Calibers, Checkered Stock, *Modern*	135.00	185.00	175.00
☐ **Model 101 Ultra**, Various Calibers, Monte Carlo Stock, *Modern*	140.00	185.00	175.00
☐ **Model 101M Ultra**, Various Magnum Calibers, Monte Carlo Stock, *Modern*	155.00	200.00	190.00
☐ **Model 102 Ultra Varmint**, Various Calibers, Heavy Barrel, *Modern*	155.00	200.00	190.00
RIFLE, SEMI-AUTOMATIC			
☐ **Model 260 Autoloader**, .22 L.R.R.F., Tube Feed, Open Sights, 22" Barrel, *Modern*	65.00	90.00	85.00

	V.G.	Exc.	Prior Year Exc. Value
☐ **Model 260 Magnum**, .22 W.M.R., Tube Feed, Open Sights, 22" Barrel, *Modern*	85.00	130.00	125.00
☐ **Model 260 Autoloader Carbine**, .22 L.R.R.F., Tube Feed, Open Sights, 20" Barrel, *Modern*	75.00	95.00	90.00
☐ **Model 260 Magnum Carbine**, .22 W.M.R., Tube Feed, Open Sights, 20" Barrel, *Modern*	95.00	140.00	135.00

KOHOUT & SPOL

Kdyne, Czechoslovakia.

HANDGUN, SEMI-AUTOMATIC

	V.G.	Exc.	Prior Year Exc. Value
☐ **Mars**, .25 ACP, Clip Fed, *Modern*	110.00	170.00	155.00
☐ **Mars**, .32 ACP, Clip Fed, *Modern*	130.00	180.00	165.00

KOMMER, THEODOR

Zella Mehlis, Germany, c. 1920.

HANDGUN, SEMI-AUTOMATIC

	V.G.	Exc.	Prior Year Exc. Value
☐ **Model I**, .25 ACP, Clip Fed, *Modern*	245.00	400.00	385.00
☐ **Model II**, .25 ACP, Clip Fed, *Modern*	185.00	275.00	265.00
☐ **Model III**, .25 ACP, Clip Fed, *Modern*	260.00	390.00	375.00
☐ **Model IV**, .32 ACP, Clip Fed, *Modern*	295.00	410.00	390.00

Kommer Model 1

Kommer Model 2

Kommer Model 4

KORTH

Wilhelm Korth Waffenfabrik, Ratzburg, West Germany.

HANDGUN, REVOLVER

	V.G.	Exc.	Prior Year Exc. Value
☐ **Target**, .22 L.R.R.F., 6 Shot, *Modern*	400.00	600.00	600.00
☐ **Target**, .22 L.R.R.F., 6 Shot, *Modern*	400.00	600.00	600.00

KRAFT, JACOB

Lancaster, Pa. 1771-1782. See Kentucky Rifles and Pistols.

KRICO

Stuttgart, West Germany. Also see Beeman's.

RIFLE, BOLT ACTION

	V.G.	Exc.	Prior Year Exc. Value
☐ **.222 Rem. Rifle**, Checkered Stock, Double Set Triggers, *Modern*	325.00	475.00	450.00
☐ **.222 Rem. Carbine**, Checkered Stock, Double Set, Triggers, *Modern*	350.00	500.00	475.00
☐ **Model DJV**, .22 Various Calibers, Checkered Target Stock, Double Set Triggers, *Modern*	325.00	450.00	425.00
☐ **Special Varmint**, .222 Rem., Checkered Stock, Heavy Barrel, Double Set Triggers, *Modern*	325.00	475.00	450.00
☐ **Krico Model 302**, .22 L.R.R.F., Clip Fed, Checkered Stock, Open Sights, *Modern*	225.00	300.00	—
☐ **Krico Model 304**, .22 L.R.R.F., Clip Fed, Checkered Stock, Mannlicher Stock, Set Triggers, Open Sights, *Modern*	275.00	375.00	—
☐ **Model 311**, .22 L.R.R.F., Checkered Stock, Double Set Trigger, *Modern*	185.00	265.00	250.00
☐ **Krico Model 340**, .22 L.R.R.F., Metallic Silhouette Match Rifle, Clip Fed, Checkered Stock, Target Stock, *Modern*	325.00	430.00	—
☐ **Krico Model 340**, .22 L.R.R.F., Mini-Sniper Match Rifle, Clip Fed, Checkered Stock, Target Stock, *Modern*	350.00	475.00	—
☐ **Model 351**, .22 WMR, Checkered Stock, Double Set Triggers, *Modern*	220.00	290.00	275.00
☐ **Model 354**, .22 WMR, Checkered Stock, Double Set Triggers, *Modern*	250.00	345.00	325.00
☐ **Krico Model 400**, .22 Hornet, Clip Fed, Checkered Stock, Open Sights, *Modern*	325.00	425.00	—
☐ **Krico Model 420**, .22 Hornet, Clip Fed, Checkered Stock, Set Triggers, Mannlicher Stock, Open Sights, Sling Swivels, *Modern*	350.00	465.00	—
☐ **Krico Model 600**, Various Calibers, Clip Fed, Checkered Stock, Open Sights, Sling Swivels, Recoil Pad, *Modern*	450.00	635.00	—
☐ **Model 600 Export**, Various Calibers, Checkered Stock, Double Set Triggers, *Modern*	225.00	310.00	275.00
☐ **Model 600 Luxus**, Various Calibers, Checkered Stock, Double Set Triggers, *Modern*	255.00	360.00	325.00
☐ **Krico Model 620**, Various Calibers, Clip Fed, Checkered Stock, Set Triggers, Mannlicher Stock, Open Sights, Sling Swivels, *Modern*	465.00	650.00	—
☐ **Model 620 Luxus**, Various Calibers, Checkered Stock, Double Set Triggers, *Modern*	315.00	450.00	375.00

	V.G.	Exc.	Prior Year Exc. Value
☐ **Krico Model 640**, Various Calibers, Deluxe Varmint Rifle, Clip Fed, Checkered Stock, Target Stock, *Modern*	450.00	630.00	—
☐ **Krico Model 650**, Various Calibers, Sniper/Match Rifle, Clip Fed, Checkered Stock, Target Stock, *Modern*	575.00	800.00	—
☐ **Krico Model 700**, Various Calibers, Clip Fed, Checkered Stock, Open Sights, Sling Swivels, Recoil Pad, *Modern*	450.00	635.00	—
☐ **Model 700 Export**, Various Calibers, Checkered Stock, Double Set Triggers, *Modern*	290.00	400.00	295.00
☐ **Model 700 Luxus**, Various Calibers, Checkered Stock, Double Set Triggers, *Modern*	325.00	450.00	345.00
☐ **Krico Model 720**, Various Calibers, Clip Fed, Checkered Stock, Set Triggers, Mannlicher Stock, Open Sights, Sling Swivels, *Modern*	465.00	650.00	—
☐ **Model 720 Luxus**, Various Calibers, Checkered Stock, Double Set Triggers, *Modern*	345.00	475.00	385.00

KRIEGHOFF GUN CO.

Suhl, Germany 1929-1945, and from 1945 to date in Ulm, West Germany. Also see Shotguns of Ulm.

COMBINATION WEAPON, OVER-UNDER

	V.G.	Exc.	Prior Year Exc. Value
☐ **Teck**, Various Calibers, Hammerless, Engraved, Fancy Checkering, *Modern*	1,850.00	2,650.00	2,500.00
☐ **Teck Dural**, Various Calibers, Hammerless, Engraved, Fancy Checkering, Lightweight, *Modern*	1,900.00	2,750.00	2,600.00
☐ **Ulm**, Various Calibers, Hammerless, Engraved, Fancy Checkering, Sidelock, *Modern*	3,450.00	4,300.00	4,150.00
☐ **Ulm Dural**, Various Calibers, Hammerless, Engraved, Fancy Checkering, Sidelock, *Modern*	3,450.00	4,300.00	4,150.00
☐ **Ulm Primus**, Various Calibers, Hammerless, Engraved, Fancy Checkering, Sidelock, *Modern*	3,500.00	4,650.00	4,450.00
☐ **Ulm Primus**, Various Calibers, Hammerless, Engraved, Fancy Checkering, Sidelock, Lightweight, *Modern*	4,350.00	5,750.00	5,500.00

COMBINATION WEAPON, DRILLING

	V.G.	Exc.	Prior Year Exc. Value
☐ **Neptun**, Various Calibers, Hammerless, Engraved, Fancy Checkering, Sidelock, *Modern*	3,400.00	4,475.00	4,350.00
☐ **Neptun Dural**, Various Calibers, Hammerless, Engraved, Fancy Checkering, Sidelock, *Modern*	3,500.00	4,500.00	4,350.00
☐ **Neptun Primus**, Various Calibers, Hammerless, Fancy Checkering, Fancy Engraving, Sidelock, *Modern*	4,250.00	5,500.00	5,250.00
☐ **Neptun Primus**, Various Calibers, Hammerless, Fancy Checkering, Fancy Engraving, Sidelock, Lightweight, *Modern*	4,250.00	5,500.00	5,250.00
☐ **Neptun Primus M**, Various Calibers, Hammerless, Fancy Engraving, Fancy Checkering, Sidelock, *Modern*	9,950.00	15,000.00	14,750.00
☐ **Trumpf**, Various Calibers, Hammerless, Engraved, Fancy Checkering, *Modern*	2,350.00	3,100.00	2,950.00

	V.G.	Exc.	Prior Year Exc. Value
☐ **Trumpf Dural**, Various Calibers, Hammerless, Engraved, Fancy Checkering, Lightweight, *Modern*	2,350.00	3,100.00	2,950.00
RIFLE, DOUBLE BARREL, OVER-UNDER			
☐ **Teck**, Various Calibers, Hammerless, Engraved, Fancy Checkering, Magnum, *Modern*	2,650.00	3,500.00	3,300.00
☐ **Teck**, Various Calibers, Hammerless, Engraved, Fancy Checkering, *Modern*	2,100.00	2,700.00	2,550.00
☐ **Ulm**, Various Calibers, Hammerless, Engraved, Fancy Checkering, Magnum, Sidelock, *Modern*	3,850.00	4,700.00	4,500.00
☐ **Ulm**, Various Calibers, Hammerless, Engraved, Fancy Checkering, Sidelock, *Modern*	3,450.00	4,300.00	4,150.00
☐ **Ulm Primus**, Various Calibers, Hammerless, Engraved, Fancy Checkering, Magnum, Sidelock, *Modern*	4,275.00	5,300.00	5,150.00
☐ **Ulm Primus**, Various Calibers, Hammerless, Engraved, Fancy Checkering, Sidelock, *Modern*	3,800.00	4,975.00	4,850.00
SHOTGUN, DOUBLE BARREL, OVER-UNDER			
☐ **Extra Barrel**, *Add* **$625.00-$800.00**			
☐ **Crown**, 12 Gauge, Trap Grade, *Modern*	7,650.00	10,100.00	9,950.00
☐ **Crown Combo**, Various Gauges, Skeet Grade, Four Barrel Set, *Modern*	14,000.00	17,950.00	17,500.00
☐ **Exhibition**, 12 Gauge, Trap Grade, *Modern*	19,850.00	26,250.00	25,500.00
☐ **Exhibition Combo**, Various Gauges, Skeet Grade, Four Barrel Set, *Modern*	25,500.00	30,500.00	29,500.00
☐ **Monte Carlo**, 12 Gauge, Trap Grade, *Modern*	6,950.00	9,750.00	9,000.00
☐ **Monte Carlo Combo**, Various Gauges, Skeet Grade, Four Barrel Set, *Modern*	9,750.00	14,500.00	14,000.00
☐ **Munchen Combo**, Various Gauges, Skeet Grade, Four Barrel Set, *Modern*	5,750.00	7300.00	7,000.00
☐ **San Remo**, 12 Gauge, Trap Grade, *Modern*	3,450.00	4,400.00	4,250.00
☐ **San Remo Combo**, Various Gauges, Skeet Grade, Four Barrel Set, *Modern*	6,650.00	7,900.00	7,750.00
☐ **Standard**, 12 Gauge, Trap Grade, *Modern*	1,500.00	2,050.00	1,950.00
☐ **Standard**, 12 Gauge, Field Grade, *Modern*	1,750.00	2,350.00	2,250.00
☐ **Standard**, Various Gauges, Skeet Grade, *Modern*	1,750.00	2,350.00	2,250.00
☐ **Standard Combo**, 12 Gauge, Trap Grade, Two Barrel Set, *Modern*	2,300.00	2,975.00	2,850.00
☐ **Standard Combo**, Various Gauges, Skeet Grade, Four Barrel Set, *Modern*	4,300.00	5,650.00	5,500.00
☐ **Super Crown**, 12 Gauge, Trap Grade, *Modern*	9,950.00	14,000.00	13,500.00
☐ **Super Crown Combo**, Various Gauges, Skeet Grade, Four Barrel Set, *Modern*	14,500.00	20,000.00	19,500.00
☐ **Teck**, Various Gauges, Hammerless, Engraved, Fancy Checkering, *Modern*	1,850.00	2,500.00	2,400.00
☐ **Teck**, Various Gauges, Hammerless, Engraved, Fancy Checkering, Single Trigger, *Modern*	1,900.00	2,625.00	2,500.00
☐ **Teck Dural**, Various Gauges, Hammerless, Engraved, Fancy Checkering, Lightweight, *Modern*	1,800.00	2,550.00	2,450.00
☐ **Ulm**, Various Gauges, Hammerless, Engraved, Fancy Checkering, Sidelock, *Modern*	2,850.00	3,550.00	3,400.00
☐ **Ulm**, Various Gauges, Hammerless, Engraved, Fancy Checkering, Sidelock, Lightweight, *Modern*	2,800.00	3,475.00	3,350.00

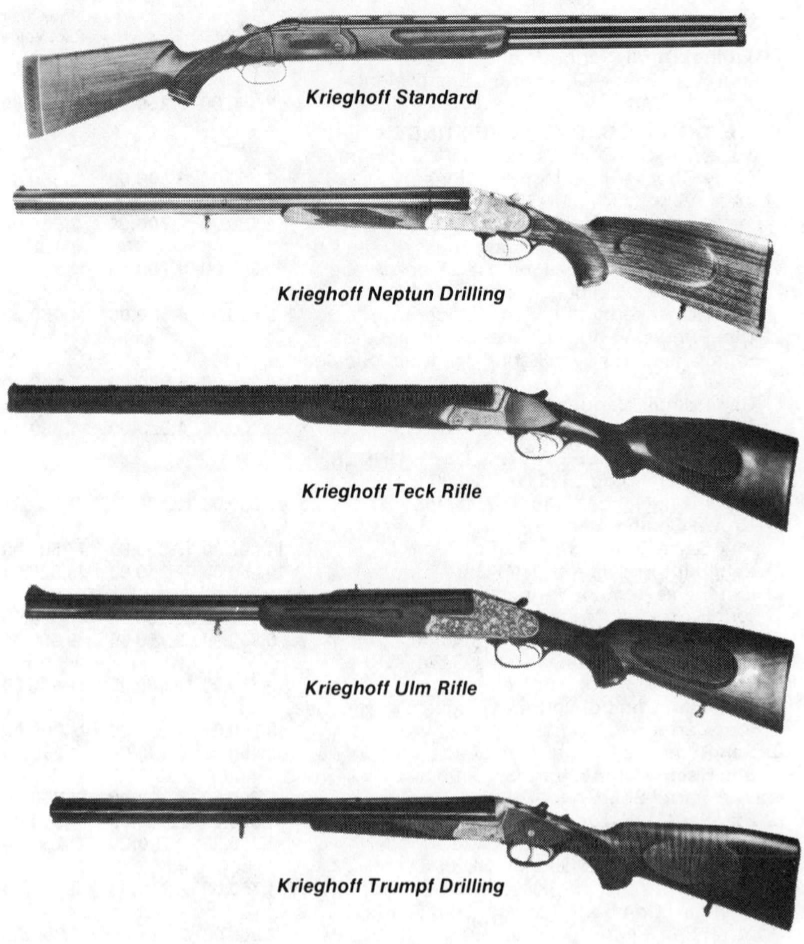

Krieghoff Standard

Krieghoff Neptun Drilling

Krieghoff Teck Rifle

Krieghoff Ulm Rifle

Krieghoff Trumpf Drilling

	V.G.	Exc.	Prior Year Exc. Value
☐ **Ulm-Primus**, Various Gauges, Hammerless, Engraved, Fancy Checkering, Sidelock, *Modern*	3,650.00	4,500.00	4,350.00
☐ **Ulm-Primus**, Various Gauges, Hammerless, Engraved, Fancy Checkering, Sidelock, Lightweight, *Modern*	3,650.00	4,600.00	4,450.00
☐ **Vandalia Rib**, 12 Gauge, Trap Grade, *Modern*	1,900.00	2,550.00	2,450.00
☐ **Vandalia Rib Combo**, Various Gauges, Skeet Grade, Four Barrel Set, *Modern*	3,400.00	4,200.00	4,000.00

KRUSCHITZ
Vienna, Austria.

RIFLE, BOLT ACTION

	V.G.	Exc.	Prior Year Exc. Value
☐ **Mauser 98**, .30/06, Checkered Stock, Double Set Triggers, *Modern*	215.00	295.00	280.00

KROYDEN
Tradename used by Savage Arms Corp.

RIFLE, SEMI-AUTOMATIC

	V.G.	Exc.	Prior Year Exc. Value
☐ **.22 L.R.R.F.**, Tube Feed, Plain Stock, *Modern*	40.00	60.00	55.00

KYNOCH GUN FACTORY
Birmingham, England.

HANDGUN, REVOLVER

	V.G.	Exc.	Prior Year Exc. Value
☐ **Schlund**, .476 Eley, Hammerless, Top Break, Double Trigger Cocking, *Antique*	475.00	735.00	700.00

Kynoch Schlund Revolver

LAHTI
Developed and made by Valtion Kivaarithedas, Jyvaskyla, Finland. Also made by Husqvarna in Sweden.

HANDGUN, SEMI-AUTOMATIC

	V.G.	Exc.	Prior Year Exc. Value
☐ **L-35 Finnish,** 9mm Luger, Clip Fed, Military, *Curio*	400.00	620.00	875.00
☐ **M 40 Swedish,** 9mm Luger, Clip Fed, Military, *Modern*	120.00	190.00	290.00

LAKESIDE
Made by Crescent for Montgomery Ward & Co., c. 1900.

SHOTGUN, DOUBLE BARREL, SIDE-BY-SIDE

	V.G.	Exc.	Prior Year Exc. Value
☐ **Various Gauges**, Outside Hammers, Damascus Barrel, *Modern*	100.00	170.00	175.00
☐ **Various Gauges**, Hammerless, Steel Barrel, *Modern*	135.00	190.00	200.00
☐ **Various Gauges**, Hammerless, Damascus Barrel, *Modern*	100.00	170.00	175.00

	V.G.	Exc.	Prior Year Exc. Value
☐ **Various Gauges**, Outside Hammers, Steel Barrel, *Modern*	125.00	185.00	190.00
SHOTGUN, SINGLESHOT			
☐ **Various Gauges**, Hammer, Steel Barrel, *Modern*	55.00	85.00	85.00

LAMES

Chiavari, Italy.

	V.G.	Exc.	Prior Year Exc. Value
SHOTGUN, DOUBLE BARREL, OVER-UNDER			
☐ **12 Gauge Mag. 3"**, Field Grade, Automatic Ejector, Single Selective Trigger, Vent Rib, Checkered Stock, *Modern*	275.00	365.00	350.00
☐ **12 Gauge Mag. 3"**, Skeet Grade, Automatic Ejector, Single Selective Trigger, Vent Rib, Checkered Stock, *Modern*	325.00	420.00	400.00
☐ **12 Gauge Mag. 3"**, Trap Grade, Automatic Ejector, Single Selective Trigger, Vent Rib, Checkered Stock, *Modern*	325.00	420.00	400.00
☐ **12 Gauge Mag. 3"**, Trap Grade, Automatic Ejector, Single Selective Trigger, Vent Rib, Monte Carlo Stock, *Modern*	375.00	475.00	450.00
☐ **California**, 12 Gauge Mag. 3", Trap Grade, Automatic Ejector, Single Selective Trigger, Vent Rib, Checkered Stock, *Modern*	490.00	635.00	600.00

LANBER

Lanber Armas, S.A., Vizcaya, Spain.

	V.G.	Exc.	Prior Year Exc. Value
SHOTGUN, DOUBLE BARREL, OVER-UNDER			
☐ **Model 844 ST**, 12 Gauge, Double Triggers, Checkered Stock, Light Engraving, *Modern*	220.00	320.00	—
☐ **Model 844 MST**, 12 Gauge 3", Double Triggers, Checkered Stock, Light Engraving, *Modern*	225.00	330.00	—
☐ **Model 844 EST**, 12 Gauge, Automatic Ejectors, Double Triggers, Checkered Stock, Light Engraving, *Modern*	280.00	390.00	—
☐ **Model 844 EST CHR**, 12 Gauge, Automatic Ejectors, Double Triggers, Checkered Stock, Light Engraving, *Modern*	270.00	375.00	—
☐ **Model 2004 LCH**, 12 Gauge, Automatic Ejector, Single Trigger, Checkered Stock, Light Engraving, Lanber Choke, *Modern*	345.00	450.00	—
☐ **Model 2008 LCH**, 12 Gauge, Automatic Ejector, Single Trigger, Checkered Stock, Light Engraving, Lanber Choke, *Modern*	465.00	600.00	—
☐ **Model 2009 LCH**, 12 Gauge, Trap Grade, Automatic Ejector, Single Trigger, Checkered Stock, Light Engraving, Lanber Choke, *Modern*	465.00	600.00	—

LANCASTER, CHARLES

London, England 1889-1936.

	V.G.	Exc.	Prior Year Exc. Value
RIFLE, BOLT ACTION			
☐ **Various Calibers**, Sporting Rifle, Checkered Stock, *Modern*	575.00	895.00	875.00

LANCELOT

	V.G.	Exc.	Prior Year Exc. Value
HANDGUN, SEMI-AUTOMATIC			
☐ **.25 ACP**, Clip Fed, Blue, *Modern*	140.00	195.00	185.00

LANE & READ

Boston, Mass. 1826-1835.

	V.G.	Exc.	Prior Year Exc. Value
SHOTGUN, PERCUSSION			
☐ **28 Gauge**, Double Barrel, Side by Side, Light Engraving, Checkered Stock, *Antique*	340.00	465.00	445.00

LANG, JOSEPH

London, England, established in 1821.

	V.G.	Exc.	Prior Year Exc. Value
HANDGUN, PERCUSSION			
☐ **Pair**, Double Barrel, Over-Under, Officer's Belt Pistol, Light Engraving, Cased With Accessories, *Antique*	3,600.00	4,600.00	4,650.00
SHOTGUN, SINGLESHOT			
☐ **12 Gauge**, Plain, Trap Grade, *Modern*	950.00	1,400.00	1,450.00

LANGENHAN

Friedrich Langenhan Gewehr u. Fahrradfabrik, Zella Mehlis, Germany.

	V.G.	Exc.	Prior Year Exc. Value
HANDGUN, SEMI-AUTOMATIC			
☐ **Model I**, .32 ACP, Clip Fed, Military, *Modern*	160.00	235.00	225.00
☐ **Model II**, .25 ACP, Clip Fed, *Modern*	175.00	275.00	275.00
☐ **Model III**, .25 ACP, Clip Fed, *Modern*	200.00	300.00	300.00

Langenhan Model I

Langenhan Model III

LA SALLE

Tradename used by Manufrance.

	V.G.	Exc.	Prior Year Exc. Value
SHOTGUN, SLIDE ACTION			
☐ **12 Gauge Mag. 3″**, Field Grade, Plain, *Modern*	85.00	140.00	135.00
☐ **12 Gauge Mag. 3″**, Checkered Stock, Fancy Wood, *Modern*	100.00	150.00	145.00
☐ **20 Gauge Mag.**, Field Grade, Plain, *Modern*	85.00	135.00	130.00
SHOTGUN, SEMI-AUTOMATIC			
☐ **Custom**, 12 Ga., Checkered Stock, *Modern*	125.00	175.00	175.00

LAURONA

Spain.

	V.G.	Exc.	Prior Year Exc. Value
SHOTGUN, DOUBLE BARREL, OVER-UNDER			
☐ **Model 67-G**, 12 Gauge 3″, Checkered Stock, Vent Rib, Double Triggers, *Modern*	165.00	225.00	220.00

LE BARON

	V.G.	Exc.	Prior Year Exc. Value
RIFLE, FLINTLOCK			
☐ **.69 Presentation**, Silver Furniture, Fancy Wood, Fancy Checkering, Fancy Engraving, *Antique*	3,250.00	4,300.00	4,250.00

LE BASQUE

	V.G.	Exc.	Prior Year Exc. Value
HANDGUN, SEMI-AUTOMATIC			
☐ **.32 ACP**, Clip Fed, Blue, *Modern*	140.00	200.00	195.00

Le Francaise Military

Le Francaise Policeman

	V.G.	Exc.	Prior Year Exc. Value

LE FRANCAISE

Mre. Francaise de Armes et Cycles de St. Etienne, St. Etienne, France.

HANDGUN, SEMI-AUTOMATIC

	V.G.	Exc.	Prior Year Exc. Value
☐ **Champion**, .25 ACP, Clip Fed, Long Grip, *Modern*	195.00	285.00	215.00
☐ **Le Francais**, .32 ACP, Clip Fed, *Modern*	285.00	420.00	400.00
☐ **Military Model**, 9mm French Long, Clip Fed, *Modern*	575.00	875.00	875.00
☐ **Pocket Model**, .25 ACP, Clip Fed, *Modern*	140.00	210.00	200.00
☐ **Policeman**, .25 ACP, Clip Fed, *Modern*	200.00	285.00	295.00
☐ **Staff Officer's**, .25 ACP, Clip Fed, *Modern*	235.00	350.00	325.00

LE MARTINY

HANDGUN, SEMI-AUTOMATIC

	V.G.	Exc.	Prior Year Exc. Value
☐ **.25 ACP**, Clip Fed, Blue, *Modern*	95.00	140.00	135.00

LE MONOBLOC

Jules Jacquemart, Liege, Belgium, c. 1910.

HANDGUN, SEMI-AUTOMATIC

	V.G.	Exc.	Prior Year Exc. Value
☐ **.25 ACP**, Clip Fed, *Modern*	275.00	385.00	375.00

LE SANS PARIEL

Mre. d'Armes des Pyrenees.

HANDGUN, SEMI-AUTOMATIC

	V.G.	Exc.	Prior Year Exc. Value
☐ **.25 ACP**, Clip Fed, Blue, *Modern*	95.00	140.00	135.00

LE TOUTACIER

Mre. d'Armes des Pyrenees.

HANDGUN, SEMI-AUTOMATIC

	V.G.	Exc.	Prior Year Exc. Value
☐ **.25 ACP**, Clip Fed, Blue, *Modern*	90.00	135.00	135.00

LEADER

Possibly Hopkins & Allen, c. 1880.

HANDGUN, REVOLVER

	V.G.	Exc.	Prior Year Exc. Value
☐ **.22 Short R.F.**, 7 Shot, Spur Trigger, Solid Frame, Single Action, *Antique*	90.00	165.00	160.00
☐ **.32 Short R.F.**, 5 Shot, Spur Trigger, Solid Frame, Single Action, *Antique*	95.00	170.00	170.00

LEADER GUN CO.

Made by Crescent for Charles Willian Stores Inc., c. 1900.

SHOTGUN, DOUBLE BARREL, SIDE-BY-SIDE

	V.G.	Exc.	Prior Year Exc. Value
☐ **Various Gauges**, Outside Hammers, Damascus Barrel, *Modern*	100.00	170.00	175.00
☐ **Various Gauges**, Hammerless, Steel Barrel, *Modern*	135.00	190.00	200.00
☐ **Various Gauges**, Hammerless, Damascus Barrel, *Modern*	100.00	170.00	175.00
☐ **Various Gauges**, Outside Hammers, Steel Barrel, *Modern*	125.00	185.00	190.00

SHOTGUN, SINGLESHOT

	V.G.	Exc.	Prior Year Exc. Value
☐ **Various Gauges**, Hammer, Steel Barrel, *Modern*	55.00	85.00	85.00

LEATHER, JACOB

York, Pa. 1779-1802. See U.S. Military, Kentucky Rifles.

LEE ARMS CO.

Wilkes-Barre, Pa. c. 1870. Also See Red Jacket

HANDGUN, REVOLVER

	V.G.	Exc.	Prior Year Exc. Value
☐ **.22 Short R.F.**, 7 Shot, Spur Trigger, Solid Frame, Single Action, *Antique*	95.00	165.00	160.00
☐ **.32 Short R.F.**, Spur Trigger, Nickel Plated, *Antique*	85.00	145.00	140.00
☐ **.32 Short R.F.**, 5 Shot, Spur Trigger, Solid Frame, Single Action, *Antique*	90.00	165.00	160.00

LEBEAU-COURALLY

Lebeau-Courally Continental Firearms, Liege, Belgium since 1865.

RIFLE, DOUBLE BARREL, SIDE-BY-SIDE

	V.G.	Exc.	Prior Year Exc. Value
☐ **Ardennes**, Various Calibers, Fancy Engraving, Double Triggers, Checkered Stock, Automatic Ejector, Boxlock, Fancy Wood, *Modern*	2,250.00	2,975.00	—
☐ **St. Hubert**, Varoius Calibers, Fancy Engraving, Double Triggers, Checkered Stock, Automatic Ejector, Sidelocks, Fancy Wood, *Modern*	5,200.00	6,750.00	—

SHOTGUN, DOUBLE BARREL, SIDE-BY-SIDE

	V.G.	Exc.	Prior Year Exc. Value
☐ **Grand Russe**, 12 Gauge, Fancy Engraving, Double Triggers, Checkered Stock, Automatic Ejector, Boxlock, Fancy Wood, *Modern*	2,250.00	3,100.00	—
☐ **Sologne**, 12 Gauge, Medium Engraving, Double Triggers, Checkered Stock, Automatic Ejector, Boxlock with Sideplates, Fancy Wood, *Modern*	2,250.00	3,100.00	—
☐ **Imperial**, 12 Gauge, Fancy Engraving, Double Triggers, Checkered Stock, Automatic Ejector, Self-Opening, Sidelocks, Fancy Wood, *Modern*	7,500.00	9,950.00	—
☐ **Prince Koudacheff**, 12 Gauge, Fancy Engraving, Double Triggers, Checkered Stock, Automatic Ejector, Sidelocks, Fancy Wood, *Modern*	5,300.00	6,750.00	—
☐ **Royal Gordon**, 12 Gauge, Fancy Engraving, Double Triggers, Checkered Stock, Automatic Ejector, Detachable Sidelocks, Fancy Wood, *Modern*	5,500.00	6,950.00	—
☐ **Weisbaden**, 12 Gauge, Fancy Engraving, Double Triggers, Checkered Stock, Automatic Ejector, Sidelocks, Fancy Wood, *Modern*	5,500.00	6,950.00	—
☐ **Washington**, 12 Gauge, Fancy Engraving, Double Triggers, Checkered Stock, Automatic Ejector, Detachable Sidelocks, Fancy Wood, *Modern*	5,950.00	7,250.00	—

LEE SPECIAL

Made by Crescent for Lee Hardware, Salina, Kans. c. 1900.

SHOTGUN, DOUBLE BARREL, SIDE-BY-SIDE

	V.G.	Exc.	Prior Year Exc. Value
☐ **Various Gauges**, Outside Hammers, Damascus Barrel, *Modern*	100.00	170.00	175.00
☐ **Various Gauges**, Hammerless, Steel Barrel, *Modern*	135.00	190.00	200.00

	V.G.	Exc.	Prior Year Exc. Value
☐ **Various Gauges**, Hammerless, Damascus Barrel, *Modern*	100.00	170.00	175.00
☐ **Various Gauges**, Outside Hammers, Steel Barrel, *Modern*	125.00	185.00	190.00

SHOTGUN, SINGLESHOT

☐ **Various Gauges**, Hammer, Steel Barrel, *Modern*	55.00	85.00	85.00

LEE'S MUNNER SPECIAL

Made by Crescent for Lee Hardware, Salina, Kans.

SHOTGUN, DOUBLE BARREL, SIDE-BY-SIDE

☐ **Various Gauges**, Outside Hammers, Damascus Barrel, *Modern*	100.00	170.00	175.00
☐ **Various Gauges**, Hammerless, Steel Barrel, *Modern*	135.00	190.00	200.00
☐ **Various Gauges**, Hammerless, Damascus Barrel, *Modern*	100.00	170.00	175.00
☐ **Various Gauges**, Outside Hammers, Steel Barrel, *Modern*	125.00	185.00	190.00

SHOTGUN, SINGLESHOT

☐ **Various Gauges**, Hammer, Steel Barrel, *Modern*	55.00	85.00	85.00

LEFAUCHEUX

Paris, France.

HANDGUN, REVOLVER

☐ **9mm Pinfire**, Double Action, Folding Trigger, Belgian, *Antique*	110.00	175.00	160.00
☐ **9mm Pinfire**, Double Action, Paris, *Antique*	190.00	295.00	275.00
☐ **12mm Pinfire**, Model 1863, Double Action, Finger Rest Trigger Guard, *Antique*	220.00	325.00	300.00

SHOTGUN, DOUBLE BARREL, SIDE-BY-SIDE

☐ **Various Pinfire Gauges**, Double Triggers, Hammers, *Antique*	85.00	145.00	125.00

LEFEVER SONS & CO.

Syracuse, N.Y. Nichols & Lefever, 1876-1878; D.M. Lefever, 1879-1889; Lefever Arms Co. 1889-1899; Lefever, Sons & Co. 1899-1926. Purchased by Ithaca Gun Co. 1926.

SHOTGUN, DOUBLE BARREL, SIDE-BY-SIDE

☐ **#1000 Grade**, Various Gauges, Sidelock, Hammerless, Fancy Checkering, Fancy Engraving, Monte Carlo Stock, *Modern*	8,100.00	10,450.00	9,950.00
☐ **4AA**, Various Gauges, Box Lock, Hammerless, Automatic Ejector, Fancy Checkering, Fancy Engraving, Monte Carlo Stock, *Modern*	3,500.00	4,300.00	4,150.00
☐ **5BE**, Various Guages, Box Lock, Hammerless, Fancy Checkering, Automatic Ejector, Fancy Engraving, *Modern*	2,450.00	3,300.00	3,150.00
☐ **6CE**, Various Gauges, Box Lock, Hammerless, Fancy Checkering, Automatic Ejector, Fancy Engraving, *Modern*	1,800.00	2,500.00	2,400.00
☐ **7DE**, Various Guages, Box Lock, Hammerless, Fancy Checkering, Automatic Ejector, Fancy Engraving, *Modern*	1,550.00	2,250.00	2,150.00

	V.G.	Exc.	Prior Year Exc. Value
☐ **8EE**, Various Gauges, Box Lock, Hammerless, Checkered Stock, Automatic Ejector, Engraved, *Modern*	995.00	1,650.00	1,600.00
☐ **9FE**, Various Gauges, Box Lock, Hammerless, Checkered Stock, Automatic Ejector, Engraved, *Modern*	875.00	1,325.00	1,250.00
☐ **A**, Various Gauges, Sidelock, Hammerless, Fancy Checkering, Fancy Engraving, Monte Carlo Stock, *Modern*	2,650.00	3,575.00	3,450.00
☐ **AA**, Various Gauges, Sidelock, Hammerless, Fancy Checkering, Fancy Engraving, Monte Carlo Stock, *Modern*	3,500.00	4,250.00	4,100.00
☐ **B**, Various Gauges, Sidelock, Hammerless, Fancy Checkering, Fancy Engraving, Monte Carlo Stock, *Modern*	2,225.00	2,825.00	2,750.00
☐ **BE**, Various Gauges, Sidelock, Hammerless, Fancy Checkering, Fancy Engraving, Monte Carlo Stock, Automatic Ejector, *Modern*	2,500.00	3,100.00	2,950.00
☐ **C**, Various Gauges, Sidelock, Hammerless, Fancy Checkering, Fancy Engraving, Monte Carlo Stock, *Modern*	1,750.00	2,325.00	2,250.00
☐ **CE**, Various Gauges, Sidelock, Hammerless, Fancy Checkering, Fancy Engraving, Monte Carlo Stock, Automatic Ejector, *Modern*	1,800.00	2,450.00	2,350.00
☐ **D**, Various Gauges, Sidelock, Hammerless, Fancy Checkering, Engraved, Monte Carlo Stock, *Modern*	1,450.00	1,975.00	1,900.00
☐ **DE**, Various Gauges, Sidelock, Hammerless, Fancy Checkering, Engraved, Monte Carlo Stock, Automatic Ejector, *Modern*	1,550.00	2,250.00	2,150.00
☐ **D S**, Various Gauges, Sidelock, Hammerless, Checkered Stock, *Modern*	450.00	600.00	575.00
☐ **D SE**, Various Gauges, Sidelock, Hammerless, Checkered Stock, Automatic Ejector, *Modern*	550.00	795.00	750.00
☐ **E**, Various Gauges, Sidelock, Hammerless, Fancy Checkering, Engraved, *Modern*	995.00	1,550.00	1,500.00
☐ **EE**, Various Gauges, Sidelock, Hammerless, Fancy Checkering, Engraved, *Modern*	1,295.00	1,900.00	1,800.00
☐ **Excelsior**, Various Gauges, Box Lock, Hammerless, Checkered Stock, Automatic Ejector, Light Engraving, *Modern*	770.00	995.00	975.00
☐ **F**, Various Gauges, Sidelock, Hammerless, Checkered Stock, Engraved, *Modern*	950.00	1,400.00	1,350.00
☐ **FE**, Various Gauges, Sidelock, Hammerless, Checkered Stock, Engraved, Automatic Ejector, *Modern*	995.00	1,500.00	1,450.00
☐ **G**, Various Gauges, Sidelock, Hammerless, Checkered Stock, Light Engraving, *Modern*	650.00	895.00	850.00
☐ **GE**, Various Gauges, Sidelock, Hammerless, Checkered Stock, Light Engraving, Automatic Ejector, *Modern*	750.00	1,025.00	975.00
☐ **H**, Various Gauges, Sidelock, Hammerless, Checkered Stock, Light Engraving, *Modern*	550.00	725.00	675.00
☐ **HE**, Various Gauges, Sidelock, Hammerless, Checkered Stock, Light Engraving, Automatic Ejector, *Modern*	575.00	865.00	825.00

	V.G.	Exc.	Prior Year Exc. Value
☐ **Nitro Special**, Various Gauges, Box Lock, Double Trigger, Checkered Stock, *Modern*	295.00	425.00	400.00
☐ **Nitro Special**, Various Gauges, Box Lock, Single Trigger, Checkered Stock, *Modern*	370.00	500.00	475.00
☐ **Optimus**, Various Gauges, Sidelock, Hammerless, Fancy Checkering, Fancy Engraving, Monte Carlo Stock, *Modern*	5,200.00	7,350.00	7,000.00
☐ **Uncle Dan**, Various Gauges, Box Lock, Hammerless, Automatic Ejector, Fancy Checkering, Fancy Engraving, Monte Carlo Stock, *Modern*	5,200.00	7,350.00	7,000.00

SHOTGUN, SINGLESHOT

	V.G.	Exc.	Prior Year Exc. Value
☐ **12 Gauge**, Trap Grade, Hammerless, Vent Rib, Checkered Stock, Automatic Ejector, *Modern*	225.00	325.00	300.00
☐ **D.M. Lefever**, 12 Gauge, Trap Grade, Hammerless, Vent Rib, Checkered Stock, Automatic Ejector, *Modern*	425.00	650.00	630.00
☐ **Long Range**, Various Gauges, Field Grade, Hammerless, Checkered Stock, *Modern*	110.00	160.00	140.00

LEFEVRE, PHILIP

Beaver Valley, Pa. 1731-1756. See Kentucky Rifles.

LEFEVRE, SAMUEL

Strasbourg, Pa. 1770-1771. See Kentucky Rifles and Pistols.

LEIGH, HENRY

Belgium, c. 1890.

SHOTGUN, DOUBLE BARREL, SIDE-BY-SIDE

	V.G.	Exc.	Prior Year Exc. Value
☐ **Various Gauges**, Outside Hammers, Damascus Barrel, *Modern*	90.00	155.00	150.00

LEITNER, ADAM

York Co, Pa. See Kentucky Rifles and Pistols.

LENNARD

Lancaster, Pa. 1770-1772. See Kentucky Rifles and Pistols.

LEONHARDT

H.M. Gering & Co., Arnstadt, Germany, c. 1917.

HANDGUN, SEMI-AUTOMATIC

	V.G.	Exc.	Prior Year Exc. Value
☐ **Army**, .32 ACP, Clip Fed, *Modern*	135.00	200.00	175.00
☐ **Gering**, .32 ACP, Clip Fed, *Modern*	145.00	210.00	190.00

LEPAGE

Made by Manufacture D'Armes Le Page, Liege, Belgium.

HANDGUN, SEMI-AUTOMATIC

	V.G.	Exc.	Prior Year Exc. Value
☐ **.25 ACP**, Clip Fed, *Modern*	175.00	250.00	245.00
☐ **.32 ACP**, Clip Fed, *Modern*	280.00	390.00	375.00
☐ **.380 ACP**, Clip Fed, Adjustable Sights, *Modern*	300.00	440.00	425.00
☐ **9mm Browning Long**, Clip Fed, Adjustable Sights, *Modern*	440.00	600.00	575.00

Leonhardt Gering

LePage

Lepco

	V.G.	Exc.	Prior Year Exc. Value
☐ **9mm Browning Long**, Clip Fed, Adjustable Sights, Detachable Shoulder Stock, *Class 3*	675.00	900.00	875.00

LEPCO

HANDGUN, SEMI-AUTOMATIC

	V.G.	Exc.	Prior Year Exc. Value
☐ **.25 ACP**, Clip Fed, Blue, *Modern*	85.00	130.00	125.00

L.E.S.

Skokie, Ill.

HANDGUN, SEMI-AUTOMATIC

	V.G.	Exc.	Prior Year Exc. Value
☐ **P-18**, 9mm Luger, Matte Stainless Steel, Clip Fed, Hammer, Double Action, *Modern*	185.00	245.00	245.00
☐ **P-18 Deluxe**, 9mm Luger, Polished Stainless Steel, Clip Fed, Hammer, Double Action, *Modern*	225.00	300.00	300.00
☐ **P-18**, 9mm Luger, Matte Stainless Steel, Clip Fed, Hammer, Single Action, *Modern*	160.00	220.00	220.00
☐ **P-18 Deluxe**, 9mm Luger, Polished Stainless Steel, Clip Fed, Hammer, Single Action, *Modern*	200.00	275.00	275.00

LESCHER

Philadelphia, Pa., c. 1730. See Kentucky Rifles and Pistols.

LESCONNE, A.

Maybe French, c. 1650.

	V.G.	Exc.	Prior Year Exc. Value
HANDGUN, FLINTLOCK			
☐ **Pair**, Engraved, Silver Inlay, Long Screw Barrel, Rifled, Belt Hook, *Antique*	7,500.00	10,000.00	10,000.00

LIBERTY
Made by Hood Firearms, 1880-1900.

HANDGUN, REVOLVER	V.G.	Exc.	Prior Year Exc. Value
☐ **.22 Short R.F.**, 7 Shot, Spur Trigger, Solid Frame, Single Action, *Antique*	90.00	165.00	160.00
☐ **.32 Short R.F.**, 5 Shot, Spur Trigger, Solid Frame, Single Action, *Antique*	95.00	170.00	170.00

LIBERTY
Montrose, Calif.

HANDGUN, REVOLVER	V.G.	Exc.	Prior Year Exc. Value
☐ **Mustang**, .22LR/.22 WMR Combo, Single Action, Western Style, Adjustable Sights, *Modern*	30.00	45.00	45.00
☐ **Mustang**, .22 L.R.R.F., Single Action, Western Style, Adjustable Sights, *Modern*	25.00	40.00	40.00

Liberty M1924 **Liberty Long Grip**

LIBERTY
Retolaza Hermanos, Eibar, Spain, c. 1920.

HANDGUN, SEMI-AUTOMATIC	V.G.	Exc.	Prior Year Exc. Value
☐ **M1924**, .32 ACP, Clip Fed, *Modern*	100.00	145.00	130.00
☐ **Model 1914**, .32 ACP, Clip Fed, Blue, *Modern*	110.00	160.00	150.00
☐ **.25 ACP**, Clip Fed, Blue, Long Grip, *Modern*	120.00	175.00	145.00

LIBERTY CHIEF
Miroku Firearms, Kochi, Japan.

HANDGUN, REVOLVER	V.G.	Exc.	Prior Year Exc. Value
☐ **Model 6**, .38 Spec., Double Action, Blue, *Modern*	80.00	130.00	125.00

LIBIA
Made by Beistegui Hermanos, c. 1920.

	V.G.	Exc.	Prior Year Exc. Value
HANDGUN, SEMI-AUTOMATIC			
☐ **.25 ACP**, Clip Fed, Blue, *Modern*	140.00	195.00	185.00
☐ **.32 ACP**, Clip Fed, Blue, *Modern*	165.00	225.00	215.00

LIEGEOISE D'ARMES A FEU

Robar et Cie., Liege, Belgium, c. 1920.

	V.G.	Exc.	Prior Year Exc. Value
HANDGUN, SEMI-AUTOMATIC			
☐ **Spanish Copy**, .25 ACP, Blue, Clip Fed, *Curio*	90.00	130.00	125.00
☐ **Spanish Copy**, .32 ACP, Blue, Clip Fed, *Curio*	90.00	140.00	135.00
☐ **New Model Melior**, .25 ACP, Clip Fed, Blue, *Curio*	135.00	175.00	170.00

LIGHTNING

Echave y Arizmendi, Eibar, Spain, c. 1920.

	V.G.	Exc.	Prior Year Exc. Value
HANDGUN, SEMI-AUTOMATIC			
☐ **.25 ACP**, Clip Fed, Blue, *Modern*	90.00	135.00	125.00

LIGNITZ, I.H.

Continental, c. 1650.

	V.G.	Exc.	Prior Year Exc. Value
HANDGUN, WHEEL-LOCK			
☐ **Brass Barrel**, Holster Pistol, Medium Ornamentation, *Antique*	5,300.00	7,000.00	6,750.00

LIGNOSE

Successors to Theodor Bergmann, Suhl, Germany, c. 1925.

	V.G.	Exc.	Prior Year Exc. Value
HANDGUN, SEMI-AUTOMATIC			
☐ **For Original Wood Grips** *Add* **10%-15%**			
☐ **Model 2**, .25 ACP, Clip Fed, *Modern*	200.00	295.00	285.00
☐ **Model 2A**, .25 ACP, Clip Fed, Einhand, Steel Cocking Piece, *Modern*	185.00	265.00	260.00
☐ **Model 2A**, .25 ACP, Clip Fed, Einhand, Brass Cocking Piece, *Modern*	195.00	280.00	270.00
☐ **Model 3**, .25 ACP, Clip Fed, Long Grip, *Modern*	240.00	335.00	325.00
☐ **Model 3A**, .25 ACP, Clip Fed, Long Grip, Einhand, Steel Cocking Piece, *Modern*	190.00	285.00	280.00
☐ **Model 3A**, .25 ACP, Clip Fed, Long Grip, Einhand, Brass Cocking Piece, *Modern*	200.00	300.00	290.00

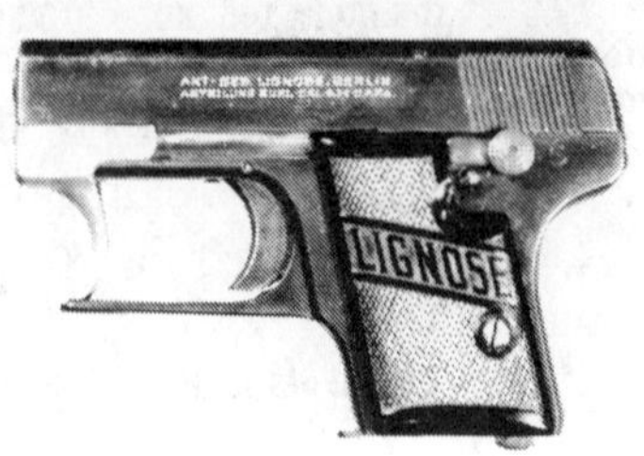

Lignose 3A

	V.G.	Exc.	Prior Year Exc. Value

LILIPUT
August Menz, Suhl, Germany, c. 1920.

HANDGUN, SEMI-AUTOMATIC

	V.G.	Exc.	Prior Year Exc. Value
☐ **4.25mm Liliput**, Clip Fed, Blue, *Curio*	395.00	575.00	545.00
☐ **25 ACP**, Clip Fed, Blue, *Modern*	195.00	285.00	265.00

LION
Made by Johnson Bye & Co., c. 1870-1880. Sold by J.P. Lovell, Boston, Mass.

HANDGUN, REVOLVER

	V.G.	Exc.	Prior Year Exc. Value
☐ **#1**, .22 Short R.F., 7 Shot, Spur Trigger, Solid Frame, Single Action, *Antique*	90.00	165.00	160.00
☐ **#2**, .32 Short R.F., 5 Shot, Spur Trigger, Solid Frame, Single Action, *Antique*	95.00	170.00	170.00
☐ **#3**, .38 Short R.F., 5 Shot, Spur Trigger, Solid Frame, Single Action, *Antique*	95.00	175.00	175.00
☐ **#4**, .41 Short R.F., 5 Shot, Spur Trigger, Solid Frame, Single Action, *Antique*	110.00	185.00	185.00

LITTLE GIANT
Made by Bacon Arms Co., c. 1880.

HANDGUN, REVOLVER

	V.G.	Exc.	Prior Year Exc. Value
☐ **.22 Short R.F.**, 7 Shot, Spur Trigger, Solid Frame, Single Action, *Antique*	95.00	165.00	160.00

LITTLE GIANT
Made by Bacon Arms Co., c. 1880.

HANDGUN, REVOLVER

	V.G.	Exc.	Prior Year Exc. Value
☐ **.22 Short R.F.**, 7 Shot, Spur Trigger, Solid Frame, Single Action, *Antique*	95.00	165.00	160.00

LITTLE JOHN
Made by Hood Firearms., c. 1876.

HANDGUN, REVOLVER

	V.G.	Exc.	Prior Year Exc. Value
☐ **.22 Short R.F.**, 7 Shot, Spur Trigger, Solid Frame, Single Action, *Antique*	95.00	165.00	160.00

LITTLE JOKER
Made by John M. Marlin, New Haven, Conn. 1873-1875.

HANDGUN, REVOLVER

	V.G.	Exc.	Prior Year Exc. Value
☐ **.22 Short R.F.**, 7 Shot, Spur Trigger, Solid Frame, Single Action, *Antique*	115.00	195.00	175.00

LITTLE PET
Made by Stevens Arms.

SHOTGUN, SINGLESHOT

	V.G.	Exc.	Prior Year Exc. Value
☐ **Model 958**, .410 Gauge, Automatic Ejector, Hammer, *Modern*	40.00	60.00	55.00
☐ **Model 958**, 32 Gauge, Automatic Ejector, Hammer, *Modern*	50.00	70.00	65.00

	V.G.	Exc.	Prior Year Exc. Value

LITTLE TOM

Alois Tomiska, Pilsen, Czechoslovakia 1909-1918.

HANDGUN, SEMI-AUTOMATIC

	V.G.	Exc.	Prior Year Exc. Value
☐ **.25 ACP**, Clip Fed, Blue, Hammer, *Curio*	**300.00**	**420.00**	**395.00**
☐ **.32 ACP**, Clip Fed, Blue, Hammer, *Curio*	**365.00**	**485.00**	**465.00**

LITTLE TOM

Wiener Waffenfabrik, Vienna, Austria 1918-1925.

HANDGUN, SEMI-AUTOMATIC

	V.G.	Exc.	Prior Year Exc. Value
☐ **.25 ACP**, Clip Fed, Blue, Hammer, *Curio*	**275.00**	**365.00**	**350.00**

LJUTIC INDUSTRIES, INC.

Yakima, Wash.

SHOTGUN, DOUBLE BARREL, OVER-UNDER

	V.G.	Exc.	Prior Year Exc. Value
☐ **Bi Gun**, 12 Gauge, High Rib, Live Pigeon, Checkered Stock, Choke Tubes, *Modern*	**3,300.00**	**4,300.00**	**4,250.00**
☐ **Bi Gun**, 12 Gauge, Vent Rib, Trap Grade, Checkered Stock, *Modern*	**3,250.00**	**4,100.00**	**4,000.00**
☐ **Bi Gun Set**, Various Calibers, Vent Rib, Skeet Grade, Checkered Stock, With 4 Sets of Barrels, *Modern*	**6,500.00**	**8,900.00**	**8,750.00**

SHOTGUN, SEMI-AUTOMATIC

	V.G.	Exc.	Prior Year Exc. Value
☐ **Bi Matic**, 12 Gauge, Vent Rib, Trap Grade, Checkered Stock, *Modern*	**1,500.00**	**2,100.00**	**2,000.00**

SHOTGUN, SINGLESHOT

	V.G.	Exc.	Prior Year Exc. Value
☐ **Dyn-A-Trap**, 12 Gauge, Trap Grade, Checkered Stock, Vent Rib, *Modern*	**775.00**	**1,200.00**	**1,150.00**
☐ **Dyn-A-Trap**, 12 Gauge, Release Trigger *Add* **$95.00-$150.00**			
☐ **Dyn-A-Trap**, 12 Gauge, for Custom Stock *Add* **$115.00-$170.00**			
☐ **Mono-Gun**, 12 Gauge, Trap Grade, Checkered Stock, Vent Rib, *Modern*	**1,750.00**	**2,600.00**	**2,500.00**
☐ **Mono-Gun**, 12 Gauge, Trap Grade, Checkered Stock, Olympic Rib, *Modern*	**2,400.00**	**3,100.00**	**3,000.00**
☐ **Mono-Gun**, 12 Gauge, For Extra Barrel *Add* **$350.00-$565.00**			
☐ **Mono-Gun**, 12 Gauge, Release Trigger *Add* **$150.00-$220.00**			
☐ **Mono-Gun**, 12 Gauge, Trap Grade, Checkered Stock, Vent Rib, Adjustable Pattern, *Modern*	**2,400.00**	**3,100.00**	**3,000.00**
☐ **X-73**, 12 Gauge, Trap Grade, Checkered Stock, Vent Rib, *Modern*	**775.00**	**1,200.00**	**1,150.00**
☐ **X-73**, 12 Gauge, For Extra Barrel *Add* **$300.00-$435.00**			
☐ **X-73**, 12 Gauge, Release Trigger *Add* **$150.00-$220.00**			

LLAMA

Gabilondo y Cia., Elgoibar, Spain from 1930 to date. Imported by Stoeger Arms.

HANDGUN, REVOLVER

☐ **Chrome Plate** *Add* **20%-30%**
☐ **Engraving** *Add* **25%-35%**

	V.G.	Exc.	Prior Year Exc. Value
☐ **Gold Damascening** *Add* **300%-400%**			
☐ **Commanche I**, .22 L.R.R.F., Swing-Out Cylinder, Double Action, Blue, *Modern*	125.00	175.00	175.00
☐ **Commanche II**, .38 Special, Swing-Out Cylinder, Double Action, Blue, *Modern*	125.00	175.00	175.00
☐ **Commanche III**, .357 Magnum, Swing-Out Cylinder, Double Action, Blue, *Modern*	140.00	200.00	200.00
☐ **Martial**, .22 L.R.R.F., Swing-Out Cylinder, Double Action, Blue, *Modern*	95.00	145.00	145.00
☐ **Martial**, .22 WMR, Swing-Out Cylinder, Double Action, Blue, *Modern*	115.00	160.00	160.00
☐ **Martial**, .38 Special, Swing-Out Cylinder, Double Action, Blue, *Modern*	100.00	145.00	145.00
☐ **Super Commanche**, .357 Magnum, Swing-Out Cylinder, Double Action, Blue, *Modern*	160.00	220.00	220.00
☐ **Super Commanche**, .44 Magnum, Swing-Out Cylinder, Double Action, Blue, *Modern*	240.00	325.00	325.00

HANDGUN, SEMI-AUTOMATIC

	V.G.	Exc.	Prior Year Exc. Value
☐ **Chrome Plate** *Add* **20%-30%**			
☐ **Engraving** *Add* **25%-35%**			
☐ **Gold Damascening** *Add* **300%-400%**			
☐ **Model I**, .32 ACP, Clip Fed, Blue, *Modern*	120.00	165.00	160.00
☐ **Model II**, .380 ACP, Clip Fed, Blue, *Modern*	120.00	185.00	175.00
☐ **Model III**, .380 ACP, Clip Fed, Blue, *Modern*	125.00	175.00	170.00
☐ **Model IIIA**, .380 ACP, Clip Fed, Grip Safety, Blue, *Modern*	145.00	190.00	190.00
☐ **Model IV**, 9mm Bergmann, Clip Fed, Blue, *Modern*	120.00	170.00	165.00
☐ **Model IX**, .45 ACP, Clip Fed, Blue, *Modern*	140.00	190.00	190.00
☐ **Model IXA**, .45 ACP, Clip Fed, Blue, *Modern*	150.00	225.00	220.00
☐ **Model V**, .38 ACP, Clip Fed, Blue, *Modern*	140.00	190.00	185.00
☐ **Model VII**, .38 ACP, Clip Fed, Blue, *Modern*	145.00	190.00	190.00
☐ **Model VIII**, .38 ACP, Grip Safety, Blue, *Modern*	160.00	225.00	225.00
☐ **Model X**, .32 ACP, Clip Fed, Blue, *Modern*	120.00	165.00	165.00
☐ **Model XA**, .32 ACP, Clip Fed, Grip Safety, Blue, *Modern*	135.00	190.00	185.00
☐ **Model XI**, 9mm Luger, Clip Fed, Blue, *Modern*	150.00	225.00	225.00
☐ **Model XV**, .22 L.R.R.F., Clip Fed, Grip Safety, Blue, *Modern*	130.00	185.00	180.00
☐ **Omni**, 9mm Luger or .45 ACP, Clip Fed, Double Action, Blue, Military, *Antique*	165.00	250.00	225.00

LOBINGER, JOHANN

Vienna, Austria, c. 1780.

RIFLE, FLINTLOCK

	V.G.	Exc.	Prior Year Exc. Value
☐ **Yaeger**, Smoothbore, Half-Octagon Barrel, Silver Furniture, Carved, *Antique*	2,650.00	3,700.00	3,500.00

LONGINES

Cooperative Orbea, Eibar, Spain, c. 1920.

HANDGUN, SEMI-AUTOMATIC

	V.G.	Exc.	Prior Year Exc. Value
☐ **.32 ACP**, Clip Fed, *Modern*	145.00	200.00	185.00

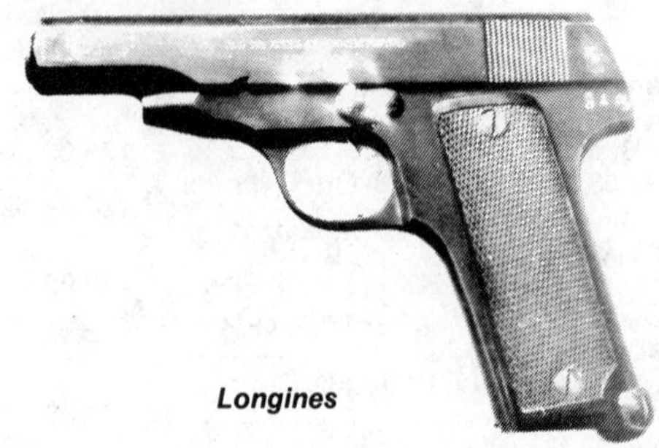

Longines

	V.G.	Exc.	Prior Year Exc. Value
LONG RANGE WONDER			
Tradename used by Sears, Roebuck & Co.			
SHOTGUN, SINGLESHOT			
☐ **12 Ga.**, Hammer, Break-Open, *Modern*	40.00	60.00	55.00
LONG TOM			
Made by Stevens Arms.			
SHOTGUN, SINGLESHOT			
☐ **Model 90**, Various Gauges, Takedown, Automatic Ejector, Plain, Hammer, *Modern*	40.00	60.00	55.00
☐ **Model 95**, 12 and 16 Gauges, Hammer, Automatic Ejector, *Modern*	40.00	60.00	55.00
LOOKING GLASS			
Domingo Acha and Acha Hermanos, Ermua, Spain, c. 1920.			
HANDGUN, SEMI-AUTOMATIC			
☐ **.25 ACP**, Clip Fed, Hammer, *Modern*	110.00	150.00	145.00
☐ **.25 ACP**, Clip Fed, Hammerless, *Modern*	90.00	130.00	125.00
☐ **.32 ACP**, Clip Fed, Long Grip, Hammerless, *Modern*	95.00	140.00	135.00
☐ **.32 ACP**, Clip Fed, Long Grip, Hammer, *Modern*	115.00	160.00	150.00
LORD, J.			
Orwigsburg, Pa. 1842-55. See Kentucky Rifles.			
LOWELL ARMS CO.			
Lowell, Mass. 1864-68.			
HANDGUN, REVOLVER			
☐ **.22 Short R.F.**, 7 Shot, Spur Trigger, Tip-up, *Antique*	230.00	345.00	325.00
.32 Long R.F., 6 Shot, Spur Trigger, Tip-up, Single Action, *Antique*	175.00	265.00	250.00
.38 Long R.F., 6 Shot, Spur Trigger, Tip-up, Single Action, *Antique*	265.00	390.00	375.00

	V.G.	Exc.	Prior Year Exc. Value
RIFLE, SINGLESHOT			
☐ **.38 Long R.F.,** *Antique*	235.00	365.00	350.00

LOWER, J.P.

Philadelphia, Pa., c. 1875.

	V.G.	Exc.	Prior Year Exc. Value
HANDGUN, REVOLVER			
☐ **.22 Long R.F.**, 7 Shot, Single Action, Solid Frame, Spur Trigger, *Antique*	115.00	185.00	180.00
☐ **.32 Long R.F.**, 7 Shot, Single Action, Solid Frame, Spur Trigger, *Antique*	125.00	200.00	190.00

LUGER

Made by various companies for commercial and military use from 1900-45. Also see Mauser Parabellum.

	V.G.	Exc.	Prior Year Exc. Value
HANDGUN, SEMI-AUTOMATIC			
☐ **1900 Commercial,** .30 Luger, *Curio*	700.00	1600.00	2500.00
☐ **1900 Eagle,** .30 Luger, *Curio*	650.00	1400.00	2000.00
☐ **1900 Swiss Commercial,** .30 Luger, *Curio*	700.00	1600.00	2500.00
☐ **1900 Swiss Military,** .30 Luger, *Curio*	750.00	1500.00	2200.00
☐ **1900 Swiss Military,** .30 Luger, Wide Trigger, *Curio*	875.00	1850.00	2700.00
☐ **1902,** .30 Luger and 9mm Luger, Carbine, Blue, *Curio*	1900.00	4000.00	5750.00
☐ **1902,** 9mm Luger, Cartridge Counter, *Curio*	2800.00	5300.00	7500.00
☐ **1902 Commercial,** 9mm Luger, *Curio*	2200.00	4300.00	5800.00
☐ **1902 Eagle,** 9mm Luger, *Curio*	1800.00	3500.00	4500.00
☐ **1902 Prototype,** .30 Luger and 9mm Luger, *Curio*	5100.00	9950.00	14750.00
☐ **1902 Test,** .30 Luger, and 9mm Luger, *Curio*	1350.00	3000.00	4500.00
☐ **1902-3 Presentation,** .30 Luger, Carbine, *Curio*	17000.00	28000.00	34000.00
☐ **1903 Commercial,** .30 Luger, *Curio*	3200.00	5800.00	7500.00
☐ **1904 Navy,** 9mm Luger, *Curio*	3400.00	6700.00	11000.00
☐ **1906 Brazilian,** .30 Luger, *Curio*	590.00	1125.00	1800.00
☐ **1906 Bulgarian,** 9mm Luger, *Curio*	1900.00	3750.00	6000.00
☐ **1906 Bulgarian,** .30 Luger, *Curio*	2300.00	3875.00	6150.00
☐ **1906 Commercial,** .30 Luger, *Curio*	600.00	1175.00	1850.00
☐ **1906 Commercial,** 9mm Luger, *Curio*	820.00	1800.00	2500.00
☐ **1906 Dutch,** 9mm Luger, *Curio*	600.00	1175.00	1800.00
☐ **1906 Eagle,** .30 Luger, *Curio*	675.00	1400.00	2000.00
☐ **1906 Eagle,** 9mm Luger, *Curio*	850.00	1500.00	2250.00
☐ **1906 French,** .30 Luger, *Curio*	3200.00	6700.00	8000.00
☐ **1906 Navy Commercial,** 9mm Luger, *Curio*	2250.00	3675.00	5000.00
☐ **1906 Navy Military,** 9mm Luger, *Curio*	700.00	1700.00	2550.00
☐ **1906 Portuguese Army,** .30 Luger, *Curio*	650.00	1100.00	1475.00
☐ **1906 Portuguese Navy Crown,** .30 Luger and 9mm Luger, *Curio*	3800.00	8500.00	12750.00
☐ **1906 Portuguese Navy,** RP, .30 Luger, *Curio*	2000.00	3350.00	5150.00
☐ **1906 Russian,** 9mm Luger, *Curio*	3175.00	6750.00	10500.00
☐ **1906 Swiss Commercial,** .30 Luger, *Curio*	900.00	2000.00	3750.00
☐ **1906 Swiss Military,** .30 Luger, *Curio*	550.00	975.00	1700.00
☐ **1906 Swiss Police,** .30 Luger, *Curio*	650.00	1400.00	2000.00
☐ **1908 Bolivian,** 9mm Luger, *Curio*	3800.00	6000.00	9350.00
☐ **1908 Bulgarian,** 9mm Luger, *Curio*	650.00	1450.00	2300.00

Luger 1906 Commercial

Luger 1940 42 with Snail Drum

Luger 1902 Commercial

Luger 1906 Navy

Luger VOPO

	V.G.	Exc.	Prior Year Exc. Value
☐ **1908 DWM Commercial,** 9mm Luger, *Curio*	420.00	810.00	1200.00
☐ **1908 Military,** 9mm Luger, *Curio*	385.00	650.00	1000.00
☐ **1908 Navy Commercial,** .30 Luger, *Curio*	1075.00	2500.00	4200.00
☐ **1908 Navy Military,** 9mm Luger, *Curio*	650.00	1380.00	2200.00
☐ **1913 Commercial,** 9mm Luger, *Curio*	475.00	1100.00	1775.00
☐ **1914 Commercial,** 9mm Luger, *Curio*	475.00	1100.00	1800.00
☐ **1914 Artillery,** 9mm Luger, *Curio*	475.00	1100.00	1800.00
☐ **1914 Military,** 9mm Luger, *Curio*	350.00	550.00	975.00
☐ **1914 Navy,** 9mm Luger, *Curio*	590.00	1075.00	1675.00
☐ **1918 Spandau,** 9mm Luger, *Curio*	2200.00	4300.00	6750.00
☐ **1920 Abercrombie & Fitch,** .30 Luger and 9mm Luger, *Curio*	2100.00	4000.00	6000.00
☐ **1920 Artillery,** 9mm Luger, *Curio*	360.00	800.00	1600.00
☐ **1920 Commercial,** .30 Luger and 9mm Luger, *Curio*	275.00	550.00	925.00
☐ **1920 Navy,** 9mm Luger, *Curio*	650.00	1300.00	2350.00
☐ **1920 Simson,** 9mm Luger, *Curio*	300.00	625.00	1100.00
☐ **1920 Swiss Commercial,** .30 Luger and 9mm Luger, *Curio*	625.00	950.00	1700.00
☐ **1920 Swiss Rework,** .30 Luger and 9mm Luger, *Curio*	650.00	1175.00	1900.00
☐ **1920-22,** .30 Luger and 9mm Luger, *Curio*	275.00	500.00	900.00
☐ **1921 Krieghoff,** .30 Luger, *Curio*	485.00	900.00	1800.00
☐ **1923 Arabian,** .30 Luger, *Curio*	300.00	575.00	1150.00
☐ **1923 Commercial,** .30 Luger and 9mm Luger, *Curio*	275.00	550.00	1050.00
☐ **1923 Commercial Krieghoff,** 9mm Luger, *Curio*	390.00	800.00	1400.00
☐ **1923 Commercial "Safe-Loaded",** .30 Luger and 9mm Luger, *Curio*	395.00	810.00	1900.00
☐ **1923 Dutch,** 9mm Luger, *Curio*	380.00	770.00	1300.00
☐ **1923 Russian,** .30 Luger, *Curio*	875.00	1900.00	3000.00
☐ **1923 Simson Commercial,** 9mm Luger, *Curio*	380.00	1100.00	2200.00
☐ **1923 Simson Military,** 9mm Luger, *Curio*	550.00	1300.00	2400.00
☐ **1923 Stoeger,** .30 Luger and 9mm Luger, *Curio*	1850.00	3275.00	5400.00
☐ **1924 Bern,** .30 Luger, *Curio*	700.00	1475.00	2500.00
☐ **1924-7 Simson,** 9mm Luger, *Curio*	600.00	1300.00	2300.00
☐ **1929 Bern,** .30 Luger and 9mm Luger, *Curio*	675.00	1550.00	3500.00
☐ **1929-33 Riff,** 9mm Luger, *Curio*	290.00	670.00	995.00
☐ **1929-33 Sneak,** 9mm Luger, *Curio*	320.00	775.00	1200.00
☐ **1930-33 Death Head,** 9mm Luger, *Curio*	410.00	950.00	1450.00
☐ **1933 Finnish Army,** 9mm Luger, *Curio*	450.00	1175.00	2000.00
☐ **1933 K.I.,** 9mm Luger, *Curio*	500.00	1150.00	1700.00
☐ **1933 Stoeger,** .30 Luger and 9mm Luger, *Curio*	2275.00	3900.00	5900.00
☐ **1933-35 Dutch,** 9mm Luger, *Curio*	810.00	1450.00	2300.00
☐ **1933-35 Mauser Commercial,** 9mm Luger, *Curio*	670.00	1175.00	2250.00
☐ **1934 P Commercial, Krieghoff,** .30 Luger and 9mm Luger, *Curio*	950.00	1750.00	3400.00
☐ **1934 P Commercial, Krieghoff,** 9mm Luger, *Curio*	900.00	1600.00	3000.00
☐ **1934 Sideframe, Krieghoff,** 6″ Barrel, 9mm Luger, *Curio*	2800.00	5300.00	7450.00
☐ **1934 Sideframe,** 9mm Luger, Krieghoff, 6″ Barrel, *Curio*	2600.00	4500.00	5900.00
☐ **1934 Simson,** 9mm Luger, *Curio*	630.00	1150.00	1950.00
☐ **1935 Portuguese,** .30 Luger, *Curio*	420.00	850.00	1325.00

	V.G.	Exc.	Prior Year Exc. Value
☐ **1936 Persian,** 9mm Luger, *Curio*	2300.00	4900.00	8000.00
☐ **1936-37,** 9mm Luger, Krieghoff, *Curio*	630.00	1400.00	2700.00
☐ **1936-39,** .30 Luger and 9mm Luger, 4″ Barrel, *Curio*	295.00	600.00	1100.00
☐ **1936-40 Dutch Banner,** 9mm Luger, *Curio*	470.00	950.00	1750.00
☐ **1936-9 S/42,** 9mm Luger, *Curio*	270.00	575.00	900.00
☐ **1937-39 Banner Commercial,** .30 Luger, 4″ Barrel, *Curio*	950.00	1450.00	2750.00
☐ **1938,** 9mm Luger, Krieghoff, *Curio*	1675.00	3100.00	4250.00
☐ **1939-40 42,** 9mm Luger, *Curio*	230.00	410.00	750.00
☐ **1940,** 9mm Luger, Krieghoff, *Curio*	640.00	1350.00	2200.00
☐ **1940 42/42 byf,** 9mm Luger, *Curio*	385.00	1175.00	2000.00
☐ **1940 Mauser Banner,** .30 Luger and 9mm Luger, *Curio*	450.00	910.00	1600.00
☐ **1940-1 S/42,** 9mm Luger, *Curio*	420.00	590.00	1050.00
☐ **1941-2 byf,** 9mm Luger, *Curio*	280.00	500.00	725.00
☐ **1941-4,** 9mm Luger, Krieghoff, *Curio*	1200.00	1950.00	3000.00
☐ **1945,** 9mm Luger, Krieghoff, *Curio*	2100.00	3500.00	4700.00
☐ **36,** 9mm Luger, Krieghoff, *Curio*	630.00	1200.00	2200.00
☐ **41 & 42 Banner,** 9mm Luger, *Curio*	410.00	635.00	1200.00
☐ **42/41,** 9mm Luger, *Curio*	480.00	650.00	1200.00
☐ **Artillery, Stock Only,** *Curio*	170.00	320.00	475.00
☐ **Austrian Banner,** 9mm Luger, *Curio*	420.00	700.00	1300.00
☐ **Banner Commercial,** .30 Luger, 4″ Barrel, *Curio*	1000.00	1675.00	2425.00
☐ **Bulgarian,** .30 Luger, *Curio*	3200.00	5400.00	7500.00
☐ **Cutaway,** 9mm Luger, *Curio*	1300.00	2700.00	4100.00
☐ **Double Date,** 9mm Luger, *Curio*	310.00	670.00	950.00
☐ **Engraved, Original,** 9mm Luger, *Curio*	2800.00	5175.00	7000.00
☐ **Finnish Prison,** .30 Luger and 9mm Luger, *Curio*	2300.00	4500.00	6000.00
☐ **G-S/42,** 9mm Luger, *Curio*	490.00	875.00	1625.00
☐ **G-S/42,** DWM, 9mm Luger, *Curio*	550.00	950.00	1900.00
☐ **G.L. Baby,** 9mm Luger, *Curio*	18000.00	30000.00	35000.00
☐ **Ideal,** Holster Stock, *Curio*	275.00	460.00	675.00
☐ **K U,** 9mm Luger, *Curio*	525.00	900.00	1650.00
☐ **K-S/42,** 9mm Luger, *Curio*	600.00	1075.00	1850.00
☐ **K-S/42 Navy,** 9mm Luger, *Curio*	950.00	1775.00	3000.00
☐ **Mauser Banner Commercial,** 9mm Luger, *Curio*	530.00	925.00	1650.00
☐ **Navy, Stock Only,** *Curio*	210.00	550.00	900.00
☐ **Post War,** 9mm Luger, Krieghoff, *Curio*	625.00	1575.00	2600.00
☐ **S/42 Navy,** 9mm Luger, *Curio*	450.00	1000.00	1800.00
☐ **Snail Drum,** Magazine, *Curio*	150.00	310.00	465.00
☐ **Stoeger (New) STLR,** .22 L.R.R.F., Clip Fed, Alloy Frame, *Modern*	45.00	85.00	120.00
☐ **Stoeger (New) STLR,** .22 L.R.R.F., Clip Fed, Alloy Frame, Checkered Wood Grips, Early, *Modern*	50.00	95.00	135.00
☐ **Stoeger (New) STLR,** .22 L.R.R.F., Clip Fed, Steel Frame, *Modern*	52.00	98.00	140.00
☐ **Stoeger (New) TLR,** .22 L.R.R.F., Clip Fed, Adjustable Sights, *Modern*	50.00	95.00	135.00
☐ **Turkish,** 9mm Luger, *Curio*	5600.00	13000.00	15000.00
☐ **U.S. Test Eagle,** .30 Luger, *Curio*	1200.00	2600.00	3400.00
☐ **Vickers Commercial,** 9mm Luger, *Curio*	1150.00	2600.00	3400.00
☐ **Vickers Military,** 9mm Luger, *Curio*	680.00	1400.00	2300.00
☐ **VOPO,** 9mm Luger, Clip Fed, *Modern*	310.00	500.00	675.00

	V.G.	Exc.	Prior Year Exc. Value

LUR-PANZER
Echave y Arizmendi, Eibar, Spain.

HANDGUN, SEMI-AUTOMATIC

	V.G.	Exc.	Prior Year Exc. Value
☐ **Luger Type**, .22 L.R.R.F., Toggle Action, Clip Fed, *Modern*	95.00	155.00	145.00

LYMAN GUN SIGHT CORP.
Middlefield, Conn.

HANDGUN, PERCUSSION

	V.G.	Exc.	Prior Year Exc. Value
☐ **.36 1851 Navy**, Color Case Hardened Frame, Engraved Cylinder, Reproduction, *Antique*	65.00	95.00	95.00
☐ **.36 New Model Navy**, Brass Trigger Guard, Solid Frame, Reproduction, *Antique*	55.00	85.00	85.00
☐ **.44 1860 Army**, Color Case Hardened Frame, Engraved Cylinder, Reproduction, *Antique*	70.00	95.00	95.00
☐ **.44 New Model Army**, Brass Trigger Guard, Solid Frame, Reproduction, *Antique*	70.00	95.00	95.00

RIFLE, FLINTLOCK

	V.G.	Exc.	Prior Year Exc. Value
☐ **Plains Rifle**, Various Calibers, Brass Furniture, Set Trigger, Reproduction, *Antique*	150.00	210.00	215.00

RIFLE, PERCUSSION

	V.G.	Exc.	Prior Year Exc. Value
☐ **Plains Rifle**, Various Calibers, Brass Furniture, Set Trigger, Reproduction, *Antique*	120.00	170.00	175.00
☐ **Trade Rifle**, Various Calibers, Brass Furniture, Set Trigger, Reproduction, *Antique*	100.00	150.00	150.00

RIFLE, SINGLESHOT

	V.G.	Exc.	Prior Year Exc. Value
☐ **Centennial**, 45/70 Government, Ruger #1, Commemorative, Cased with Accessories, *Modern*	900.00	1,425.00	1,400.00

MAADI

RIFLE, SEMI-AUTOMATIC

	V.G.	Exc.	Prior Year Exc. Value
☐ **Paratrooper AKM**, 7.62 x 39mm, Clip Fed, Assault Rifle, *Modern*	650.00	1,025.00	975.00
☐ **Standard AKM**, 7.62 x 39mm, Clip Fed, Assault Rifle, *Modern*	600.00	900.00	875.00

MAB
Mre. d'Armes Automatiques Bayonne, Bayonne, France since 1921.

HANDGUN, SEMI-AUTOMATIC

☐ **Nazi Proofs** *Add* **20%-30%**
☐ **Nazi Navy Proofs** *Add* **40%-50%**
☐ **W.A.C Markings**, *Deduct* **5%-10%**

	V.G.	Exc.	Prior Year Exc. Value
☐ **Modele A**, .25 ACP, Clip Fed, *Modern*	95.00	145.00	135.00
☐ **Modele B**, .25 ACP, Clip Fed, *Modern*	145.00	220.00	200.00
☐ **Modele C**, .32 ACP, Clip Fed, *Modern*	125.00	175.00	165.00
☐ **Modele C**, .380 ACP, Clip Fed, *Modern*	150.00	210.00	195.00
☐ **Modele C/D**, .32 ACP, Clip Fed, *Modern*	115.00	155.00	145.00
☐ **Modele C/D**, .380 ACP, Clip Fed, *Modern*	125.00	180.00	165.00
☐ **Modele D**, .32 ACP, Clip Fed, *Modern*	100.00	150.00	140.00
☐ **Modele D**, .32 ACP, Clip Fed, French Military, *Modern*	150.00	225.00	200.00

	V.G.	Exc.	Prior Year Exc. Value
☐ **Modele D**, .380 ACP, Clip Fed, *Modern*	115.00	160.00	150.00
☐ **Modele E**, .25 ACP, Clip Fed, Long Grip, *Modern*	135.00	200.00	190.00
☐ **Modele F**, .22 L.R.R.F., Clip Fed, Hammer, 3" Barrel, *Modern*	120.00	185.00	180.00
☐ **Modele F**, .22 L.R.R.F., Clip Fed, Hammer, 5" Barrel, *Modern*	125.00	190.00	185.00
☐ **Modele F**, .22 L.R.R.F., Clip Fed, Hammer, 3" Barrel, *Modern*	140.00	200.00	190.00
☐ **Modele G**, .22 L.R.R.F., Clip Fed, *Modern*	95.00	140.00	135.00
☐ **Modele GZ**, .22 L.R.R.F., Clip Fed, Blue, *Modern*	120.00	155.00	150.00
☐ **Modele GZ**, .22 L.R.R.F., Clip Fed, Green, *Modern*	125.00	165.00	160.00
☐ **Modele GZ**, .25 ACP, Clip Fed, *Modern*	135.00	175.00	170.00
☐ **Modele Le Chasseur**, .22 L.R.R.F., Clip Fed, Hammer, Target Grips, *Modern*	145.00	200.00	190.00
☐ **Modele PA-15**, 9mm Luger, Clip Fed, Hammer, *Modern*	230.00	325.00	300.00
☐ **Modele R Para**, 9mm Luger, Clip Fed, Hammer, *Curio*	230.00	325.00	300.00
☐ **Modele R Court**, .32 ACP, Clip Fed, Hammer, *Modern*	170.00	260.00	240.00
☐ **Modele R Longue**, 7.65 MAS, Clip Fed, Hammer, *Modern*	170.00	245.00	220.00

MAB Modele A

MAB Modele D

MAB Modele F

	V.G.	Exc.	Prior Year Exc. Value

M.A.C. (Military Armament Corp)

Also see Ingram. See Ruger and Remington for Silenced Adaptations.

AUTOMATIC WEAPON, ASSAULT RIFLE

	V.G.	Exc.	Prior Year Exc. Value
☐ **M16-M.A.C.**,.22 L.R.R.F., Clip Fed, Conversion Unit Only, *Class 3*	95.00	135.00	125.00

AUTOMATIC WEAPON, SUBMACHINE GUN

	V.G.	Exc.	Prior Year Exc. Value
☐ **M-10 M A C**, .45 ACP, Clip Fed, Folding Stock, Commercial, *Class 3*	155.00	215.00	195.00
☐ **M-10 M A C**, .45 ACP, Clip Fed, Folding Stock, Commercial, Silencer, *Class 3*	235.00	325.00	300.00
☐ **M-10 M A C**, 9mm Luger, Clip Fed, Folding Stock, Commercial, *Class 3*	160.00	220.00	200.00
☐ **M-10 M A C**, 9 mm Luger, Clip Fed, Folding Stock, Commercial, Silencer, *Class 3*	235.00	320.00	300.00
☐ **M-11 M A C**, .380 ACP, Clip Fed, Folding Stock, Commercial, *Class 3*	340.00	425.00	400.00
☐ **M-11 M A C**, .380 ACP, Clip Fed, Folding Stock, Commercial, Silencer, *Class 3*	435.00	550.00	535.00

HANDGUN, SEMI-AUTOMATIC

	V.G.	Exc.	Prior Year Exc. Value
☐ **Model 200 S.A.P.**, 9mm Luger, Clip Fed, *Modern*	195.00	285.00	275.00

RIFLE, BOLT ACTION

	V.G.	Exc.	Prior Year Exc. Value
☐ **Model 40-XB Sniper (MAC)**, .308 Win., Heavy Barrel, Scope Mounted, Silencer, *Class 3*	570.00	775.00	750.00

MACLOED

Doune, Scotland 1711-1750.

HANDGUN, FLINTLOCK

	V.G.	Exc.	Prior Year Exc. Value
☐ **.54**, All Steel, Engraved, Ram's Horn Butt, *Antique*	2,950.00	3,400.00	3,250.00

MAICHE, A.

France.

HANDGUN, FLINTLOCK

	V.G.	Exc.	Prior Year Exc. Value
☐ **.56**, Brass Mountings, Holster Pistol, *Antique*	385.00	575.00	550.00

MALTBY-CURTIS

Agent for Norwich Pistol Co. 1875-1881.

HANDGUN, REVOLVER

	V.G.	Exc.	Prior Year Exc. Value
☐ **.22 Short R.F.**, 7 Shot, Spur Trigger, Solid Frame, Single Action, *Antique*	95.00	165.00	160.00
☐ **.32 Short R.F.**, 5 Shot, Spur Trigger, Solid Frame, Single Action, *Antique*	95.00	170.00	170.00

MALTBY-HENLEY & CO.

N.Y.C. 1878-1889. Made by Columbia Armory, Tenn.

HANDGUN, REVOLVER

	V.G.	Exc.	Prior Year Exc. Value
☐ **.22 L.R.R.F.**, 7 Shot, Double Action, Hammerless, Top Break, *Curio*	55.00	95.00	95.00
☐ **.32 S & W**, 5 Shot, Top Break, Hammerless, Double Action, *Curio*	60.00	100.00	95.00

	V.G.	Exc.	Prior Year Exc. Value
☐ **.38 S & W**, 5 Shot, Top Break, Hammerless, Double Action, *Curio*	65.00	105.00	95.00

MAMBA

Made by Relay Products in Johannesburg, South Africa, and Navy Arms in the U.S.

HANDGUN, SEMI-AUTOMATIC

	V.G.	Exc.	Prior Year Exc. Value
☐ **Relay Mamba**, 9mm Luger, Stainless, Double Action, *Modern*	335.00	465.00	450.00
☐ **Rhodesian Mamba**, 9mm Luger, Stainless, Double Action, *Modern*	1,350.00	2,000.00	2,000.00
☐ **Navy Mamba**, 9mm Luger, Stainless, Double Action, *Modern*	230.00	320.00	300.00

MANHATTAN FIREARMS MFG. CO.

N.Y.C. & Newark, N.J. 1849-1864.

HANDGUN, PERCUSSION

	V.G.	Exc.	Prior Year Exc. Value
☐ **Hero,** Singleshot, Derringer, *Antique*	140.00	210.00	195.00
☐ **Bar Hammer,** Double Action, Screw Barrel, Singleshot, *Antique*	145.00	235.00	225.00
☐ **Pepperbox,** .28, 3 Shot, Double Action, *Antique*	265.00	495.00	475.00
☐ **Pepperbox,** .28, 6 Shot, Double Action, *Antique*	195.00	345.00	325.00
☐ **Revolver,** .36, Navy Model, Single Action, *Antique*	340.00	550.00	525.00
☐ **Revolver,** .36, Pocket Model, Single Action, *Antique*	195.00	345.00	335.00
☐ **Revolver, M2,** .22 Cal. Cartridge, *Antique*	100.00	200.00	190.00

MANHURIN

Mre. de Machines du Haut-Rhin, Mulhouse-Bourtzwiller, France. Also see Walther.

HANDGUN, REVOLVER

	V.G.	Exc.	Prior Year Exc. Value
☐ **Model 73**, .357 Magnum, Police Model, Double Action, Swing-Out Cylinder, *Modern*	375.00	500.00	500.00
☐ **Model 73**, .357 Magnum, Target Model, Double Action, Swing-Out Cylinder, *Modern*	450.00	600.00	600.00

MANN

Fritz Mann Werkzeugfabrik, Suhl, Germany 1919-1924.

HANDGUN, SEMI-AUTOMATIC

	V.G.	Exc.	Prior Year Exc. Value
☐ **Model Wt**, .25 ACP, Clip Fed, *Modern*	175.00	260.00	245.00
☐ **Pocket**, .32 ACP, Clip Fed, *Modern*	215.00	300.00	285.00
☐ **Pocket**, .380 ACP, Clip Fed, *Modern*	245.00	340.00	325.00

MANN, MICHEL

Uhlenberg, Germany, c. 1630.

HANDGUN, WHEEL-LOCK

	V.G.	Exc.	Prior Year Exc. Value
☐ **Miniature**, All Metal, Gold Damascened, Ball Pommel, *Antique*	2,200.00	3,650.00	3,500.00

MANNLICHER-SCHOENAUER

Steyr-Daimler-Puch, Steyr, Austria.

Manhatten Second Model, .22 Caliber

Manhatten Bar Hammer, .31 Caliber

Mann Pocket

	V.G.	Exc.	Prior Year Exc. Value
RIFLE, DOUBLE BARREL, OVER-UNDER			
☐ **Safari 72**, .375 H & H Mag., Checkered Stock, Engraved, Double Trigger, *Modern*	2,475.00	3,450.00	3,400.00
☐ **Safari 77**, Various Calibers, Checkered Stock, Engraved, Double Trigger, Automatic Ejector, *Modern*	3,500.00	4,500.00	4,400.00
RIFLE, BOLT ACTION			
☐ **Alpine**, Various Caliber, Sporting Rifle, Full-Stocked, *Modern*	360.00	475.00	465.00
☐ **Custom M-S**, Various Calibers, Sporting Rifle, Scope Mounted, Carbine, *Modern*	390.00	690.00	675.00
☐ **Custom M-S**, Various Calibers, Sporting Rifle, Scope Mounted, *Modern*	390.00	690.00	675.00
☐ **High Velocity**, Various Calibers, Sporting Rifle, Set Trigger, *Modern*	540.00	825.00	800.00
☐ **High Velocity**, Various Calibers, Sporting Rifle, Takedown, Set Trigger, *Modern*	570.00	875.00	850.00
☐ **M-72 LM**, Various Calibers, Sporting Rifle, Full-Stocked, *Modern*	425.00	750.00	725.00
☐ **M-72 S**, Various Calibers, Sporting Rifle, *Modern*	520.00	835.00	800.00
☐ **M-72 T**, Various Calibers, Sporting Rifle, *Modern*	570.00	875.00	850.00
☐ **Magnum M-S**, Various Calibers, Sporting Rifle, Monte Carlo Stock, Set Trigger, *Modern*	570.00	875.00	850.00
☐ **MCA**, Various Calibers, Sporting Rifle, Carbine, Monte Carlo Stock, *Modern*	635.00	940.00	900.00
☐ **MCA**, Various Calibers, Sporting Rifle, Monte Carlo Stock, *Modern*	630.00	935.00	900.00
☐ **Model 1903**, Various Calibers, Sporting Rifle, Carbine, Set Trigger, Full-Stocked, *Modern*	570.00	830.00	800.00
☐ **Model 1905**, 9 x 56 M.S., Sporting Rifle, Carbine, Set Trigger, Full-Stocked, *Modern*	490.00	750.00	725.00
☐ **Model 1908**, Various Calibers, Sporting Rifle, Carbine, Set Trigger, Full-Stocked, *Modern*	440.00	725.00	700.00
☐ **Model 1910**, 9.5 x 57 M.S., Sporting Rifle, Carbine, Set Trigger, Full-Stocked, *Modern*	470.00	750.00	725.00
☐ **Model 1924**, .30-06 Springfield, Sporting Rifle, Carbine, Set Trigger, Full-Stocked, *Modern*	630.00	975.00	950.00
☐ **Model 1950**, 6.5 x 54 M.S., Sporting Rifle, Carbine, Set Trigger, Full-Stocked, *Modern*	425.00	700.00	675.00

	V.G.	Exc.	Prior Year Exc. Value
☐ **Model 1950**, Various Calibers, Sporting Rifle, Set Trigger, *Modern*	465.00	775.00	750.00
☐ **Model 1950**, Various Calibers, Sporting Rifle, Carbine, Set Trigger, Full-Stocked, *Modern*	495.00	800.00	750.00
☐ **Model 1952**, 6.5 x 54 M.S., Sporting Rifle, Carbine, Set Trigger, Full-Stocked, *Modern*	440.00	750.00	725.00
☐ **Model 1952**, Various Calibers, Sporting Rifle, Carbine, Set Trigger, Full-Stocked, *Modern*	470.00	775.00	750.00
☐ **Model 1952**, Various Calibers, Sporting Rifle, Set Trigger, *Modern*	470.00	775.00	750.00
☐ **Model 1956**, Various Calibers, Sporting Rifle, Carbine, Set Trigger, Full-Stocked, *Modern*	470.00	775.00	750.00
☐ **Model 1956**, Various Calibers, Sporting Rifle, Set Trigger, *Modern*	470.00	775.00	750.00
☐ **Premier**, Various Calibers, Sporting Rifle, Magnum Action, Fancy Checkering, Engraved, *Modern*	775.00	1,250.00	1,200.00
☐ **Premier**, Various Calibers, Sporting Rifle, Fancy Checkering, Engraved, *Modern*	465.00	625.00	600.00
☐ **Model SSG**, .308 Win., Synthetic Target Stock, Set Triggers, *Modern*	375.00	495.00	475.00
☐ **Model SSG Match**, .308 Win., Synthetic Target Stock, Set Triggers, Walther Peep Sights, *Modern*	470.00	625.00	600.00
☐ **Model ML 79**, Various Calibers, Checkered Stock, Set Trigger, *Modern*	495.00	735.00	700.00
☐ **Model L Varmint**, Various Calibers, Checkered Stock, Set Trigger, *Modern*	370.00	495.00	475.00
☐ **Model M**, Various Calibers, Checkered Stock, Set Trigger, *Modern*	390.00	575.00	550.00
☐ **Model M Professional**, Various Calibers, Checkered Stock, Set Trigger, *Modern*	265.00	395.00	375.00
☐ **Model S/T Magnum**, Various Calibers, Checkered Stock, Set Trigger, *Modern*	445.00	650.00	625.00
☐ **Model S**, Various Calibers, Checkered Stock, Set Trigger, *Modern*	440.00	650.00	625.00
RIFLE, DOUBLE BARREL, SIDE-BY-SIDE			
☐ **Mustang**, Various Calibers, Standard, Checkered Stock, Sidelock, *Modern*	3,950.00	5,850.00	5,750.00
☐ **Mustang**, Various Calibers, Standard, Checkered Stock, Sidelock, Engraved, *Modern*	4,500.00	6,000.00	6,000.00
SHOTGUN, DOUBLE BARREL, OVER-UNDER			
☐ **Edinbourgh**, 12 Ga., Checkered Stock, Vent Rib, *Modern*	975.00	1,475.00	1,400.00
SHOTGUN, DOUBLE BARREL, SIDE-BY-SIDE			
☐ **Ambassador English**, 12 and 20 Gauges, Checkered Stock, Sidelock, Automatic Ejectors, Engraved, *Modern*	5,350.00	7,350.00	7,250.00
☐ **Ambassador Extra**, 12 and 20 Gauges, Checkered Stock, Sidelock, Automatic Ejectors, Engraved, *Modern*	5,200.00	7,150.00	7,000.00
☐ **Ambassador Golden Black**, 12 and 20 Gauges, Checkered Stock, Sidelock, Automatic Ejectors, Engraved, Gold Inlays, *Modern*	6,700.00	9,250.00	9,000.00

	V.G.	Exc.	Prior Year Exc. Value
☐ **Ambassador Executive**, 12 and 20 Gauges, Checkered Stock, Sidelock, Automatic Ejectors, Fancy Engraving, *Modern*	11,000.00	15,000.00	15,000.00
☐ **Oxford Field**, 12 and 20 Gauges, Checkered Stock, Automatic Ejectors, Engraved, *Modern*	825.00	1,250.00	1,200.00
☐ **London**, 12 and 20 Gauges, Checkered Stock, Sidelock, Automatic Ejectors, Engraved, Cased, *Modern*	1,850.00	2,450.00	2,400.00

MANTON, J. & CO.

Belgium, c. 1900.

SHOTGUN, DOUBLE BARREL, SIDE-BY-SIDE

	V.G.	Exc.	Prior Year Exc. Value
☐ **Various Gauges**, Outside Hammers, Damascus Barrel, *Modern*	100.00	170.00	175.00
☐ **Various Gauges**, Hammerless, Steel Barrel, *Modern*	135.00	190.00	200.00
☐ **Various Gauges**, Hammerless, Damascus Barrel, *Modern*	100.00	170.00	175.00
☐ **Various Gauges**, Outside Hammers, Steel Barrel, *Modern*	125.00	185.00	190.00

SHOTGUN, SINGLESHOT

	V.G.	Exc.	Prior Year Exc. Value
☐ **Various Gauges**, Hammer, Steel Barrel, *Modern*	55.00	85.00	85.00

MANTON, JOSEPH

London, England 1795-1835.

HANDGUN, FLINTLOCK

	V.G.	Exc.	Prior Year Exc. Value
☐ **Pair**, Octagon Barrel, Duelling Pistols, Gold Inlays, Light Engraving, Cased with Accessories, *Antique*	3,550.00	4,625.00	4,500.00

HANDGUN, PERCUSSION

	V.G.	Exc.	Prior Year Exc. Value
☐ **.55**, Pair, Duelling Pistols, Octagon Barrel, Light Ornamentation, Cased with Accessories, *Antique*	3,750.00	4,800.00	4,750.00

SHOTGUN, PERCUSSION

	V.G.	Exc.	Prior Year Exc. Value
☐ **12 Ga. Double Barrel**, Side by Side, Damascus Barrels, Light Engraving, Gold Inlays, *Antique*	445.00	630.00	600.00

MANUFRANCE

Manufacture Francaise de Armes et Cycles de St. Etienne, St. Etienne, France. Also see Le Francaise.

HANDGUN, SEMI-AUTOMATIC

	V.G.	Exc.	Prior Year Exc. Value
☐ **Model 1911 Astra-Manufrance**, .32 ACP, CLip Fed, Blue, *Curio*	95.00	165.00	155.00

RIFLE, SEMI-AUTOMATIC

	V.G.	Exc.	Prior Year Exc. Value
☐ **Reina**, .22 L.R.R.F., Carbine, Clip Fed, *Modern*	90.00	145.00	145.00
☐ **Sniper**, .22 W.M.R., Carbine, Clip Fed, *Modern*	135.00	190.00	185.00

RIFLE, BOLT ACTION

	V.G.	Exc.	Prior Year Exc. Value
☐ **Mauser K98 Sporter**, .270 Win., Sporterized, Plain, *Modern*	85.00	135.00	130.00
☐ **Mauser K98 Sporter**, .270 Win., Sporterized, Checkered Stock, *Modern*	95.00	145.00	140.00
☐ **Club**, .22 L.R.R.F., Singleshot, Carbine, *Modern*	60.00	90.00	85.00

	V.G.	Exc.	Prior Year Exc. Value
☐ **Club**, .22 L.R.R.F., Singleshot, Carbine, Checkered Stock, *Modern*	65.00	100.00	95.00
☐ **Buffalo Match**, .22 L.R.R.F., Target Rifle, *Modern*	110.00	160.00	150.00
☐ **Rival**, 375 H & H Mag., Checkered Stock, *Modern*	180.00	285.00	275.00
SHOTGUN, DOUBLE BARREL, OVER-UNDER			
☐ **Falcor Field**, 12 Ga., Vent Rib, Automatic Ejector, Single Selective Trigger, Checkered Stock, *Modern*	450.00	600.00	600.00
☐ **Falcor Trap**, 12 Ga., Vent Rib, Automatic Ejector, Single Selective Trigger, Checkered Stock, *Modern*	500.00	650.00	650.00
☐ **Falcor Sport**, 12 Ga., Vent Rib, Automatic Ejector, Single Selective Trigger, Checkered Stock, Extra Barrels, *Modern*	600.00	750.00	750.00
SHOTGUN, DOUBLE BARREL, SIDE-BY-SIDE			
☐ **Ideal DeLuxe**, 12 Ga. 3", Fancy Engraving, Checkered Stock, Double Triggers, *Modern*	1,250.00	1,750.00	1,750.00
☐ **Ideal Prestige**, 12 Ga. 3", Fancy Engraving, Checkered Stock, Double Triggers, *Modern*	1,750.00	2,500.00	2,500.00
☐ **Robust**, 12 Ga. 3", Checkered Stock, Double Triggers, *Modern*	250.00	365.00	350.00
☐ **Robust Luxe**, 12 Ga. 3", Engraved, Automatic Ejectors, Checkered Stock, Double Triggers, *Modern*	400.00	600.00	600.00
SHOTGUN, SEMI-AUTOMATIC			
☐ **Perfex Special**, 12 Ga. Mag. 3", Open Sights, Short Barrel, Checkered Stock, *Modern*	250.00	365.00	350.00
☐ **Perfex**, 12 Ga. Mag. 3", Checkered Stock, *Modern*	225.00	335.00	325.00
SHOTGUN, SINGLESHOT			
☐ **Simplex**, 12 Gauge, Sling Swivels, *Modern*	80.00	125.00	120.00
SHOTGUN, SLIDE ACTION			
☐ **Rapid**, 12 or 16 Gauges, Plain, *Modern*	125.00	170.00	165.00

MARK X

Made in Zestavia, Yugoslavia. Imported by Interarms.

	V.G.	Exc.	Prior Year Exc. Value
RIFLE, BOLT ACTION			
☐ **Alaskan**, Various Calibers, Magnum, Open Rear Sight, Checkered Stock, Sling Swivels, *Modern*	195.00	285.00	275.00
☐ **Cavalier**, Various Calibers, Cheekpiece, Checkered Stock, Open Rear Sight, Sling Swivels, *Modern*	180.00	265.00	260.00
☐ **Mannlicher**, Various Calibers, Carbine, Full-Stocked, Checkered Stock, Open Rear Sight, Sling Swivels, *Modern*	195.00	285.00	275.00
☐ **Marquis**, Various Calibers, Carbine, Mauser Action, *Modern*	430.00	460.00	
☐ **Standard**, Various Calibers, Checkered Stock, Open Rear Sight, Sling Swivels, *Modern*	160.00	235.00	225.00
☐ **Viscount**, Various Calibers, Plain, Open Rear Sight, Checkered Stock, Sling Swivels, *Modern*	130.00	180.00	175.00

MARKWELL ARMS CO.

Chicago, Ill.

	V.G.	Exc.	Prior Year Exc. Value
HANDGUN, PERCUSSION			
☐ **.41 Derringer**, Singleshot, Brass Furniture, Reproduction, *Antique*	20.00	30.00	30.00
☐ **.44 C S A 1860**, Revolver, 6 Shot, Brass Frame, Reproduction, *Antique*	40.00	65.00	60.00
☐ **.44 New Army**, Revolver, 6 Shot, Brass Trigger Guard, Reproduction, *Antique*	40.00	65.00	65.00
☐ **.45 Colonial**, Singleshot, Brass Furniture, Reproduction, *Antique*	20.00	35.00	35.00
☐ **.45 Kentucky**, Singleshot, Brass Furniture, Reproduction, *Antique*	30.00	45.00	45.00
☐ **.45 Loyalist**, Singleshot, Brass Furniture, Set Trigger, Adjustable Sights, Reproduction, *Antique*	45.00	65.00	65.00
RIFLE, PERCUSSION			
☐ **.45 Hawken**, Brass Furniture, Reproduction, *Antique*	60.00	90.00	90.00
☐ **.45 Kentucky**, Brass Furniture, Reproduction, *Antique*	50.00	75.00	75.00
☐ **.45 Super Kentucky**, Brass Furniture, Set Trigger, Reproduction, *Antique*	70.00	110.00	110.00

MARLIN FIREARMS CO.

New Haven, Conn. J.M. Marlin from 1870-1881. Marlin Firearms from 1881-1915. Marlin-Rockwell Corp. 1915-1926. From 1926 to Date as Marlin Firearms Co. Also See Ballard.

	V.G.	Exc.	Prior Year Exc. Value
AUTOMATIC WEAPON, HEAVY MACHINE GUN			
☐ **M1906 Marlin,** .30-06 Springfield, Belt Fed, Tripod, Potato Digger, Military, *Class 3*	1675.00	2500.00	2450.00
☐ **M1906 Marlin,** .303 British, Belt Fed, Tripod, Potato Digger, Military, *Class 3*	1600.00	2450.00	2400.00
☐ **M1906 Marlin,** .308 Win., Belt Fed, Tripod, Potato Digger, Military, *Class 3*	1500.00	2275.00	2200.00
☐ **M1917 Marlin,** .30-06 Springfield, Belt Fed, Tripod, Potato Digger, Military, *Class 3*	1725.00	2350.00	2300.00
HANDGUN, REVOLVER			
☐ **Standard 1875,** .30 R.F., Tip Up, Spur Trigger, *Antique*	120.00	190.00	185.00
☐ **XX Standard 1873,** .22 R.F., Tip Up, Spur Trigger, *Antique*	120.00	200.00	190.00
☐ **XX Standard 1873,** .22 R.F., Tip Up, Spur Trigger, Octagon Barrel, *Antique*	130.00	210.00	200.00
☐ **XXX Standard 1872,** .30 R.F., Tip Up, Spur Trigger, *Antique*	120.00	190.00	185.00
☐ **XXX Standard 1872,** .30 R.F., Tip Up, Spur Trigger, Octagon Barrel, *Antique*	135.00	230.00	215.00
☐ **Model 1887,** .32 and .38, Double Action, Top Break, *Antique*	115.00	195.00	180.00
RIFLE, BOLT ACTION			
☐ **Glenfield M10,** .22 L.R.R.F., Singleshot, *Modern*	28.00	42.00	40.00
☐ **Glenfield M20,** .22 L.R.R.F., Clip Fed, *Modern*	37.00	55.00	50.00

	V.G.	Exc.	Prior Year Exc. Value
☐ **Model 100,** .22 L.R.R.F., Singleshot, Open Rear Sight, Takedown, *Modern*	32.00	43.00	40.00
☐ **Model 100-S,** .22 L.R.R.F., Singleshot, Peep Sights, Takedown, *Modern*	53.00	75.00	70.00
☐ **Model 100-SB,** .22 L.R.R.F., Singleshot, Smoothbore, Takedown, *Modern*	32.00	43.00	40.00
☐ **Model 101,** .22 L.R.R.F., Singleshot, Open Rear Sight, Takedown, Beavertail Forend, *Modern*	32.00	50.00	45.00
☐ **Model 101-DL,** .22 L.R.R.F., Singleshot, Takedown, Peep Sights, Beavertail Forend, *Modern*	38.00	50.00	45.00
☐ **Model 122,** .22 L.R.R.F., Singleshot, Open Rear Sight, Monte Carlo Stock, *Modern*	32.00	50.00	45.00
☐ **Model 322 (Sako),** .222 Rem., Clip Fed, Peep Sights, Checkered Stock, *Modern*	180.00	290.00	280.00
☐ **Model 455 (FN),** Various Calibers, Peep Sights, Monte Carlo Stock, Checkered Stock, *Modern*	180.00	295.00	285.00
☐ **Model 65,** .22 L.R.R.F., Singleshot, Open Rear Sight, *Modern*	32.00	50.00	45.00
☐ **Model 65E,** .22 L.R.R.F., Singleshot, Peep Sights, *Modern*	32.00	50.00	45.00
☐ **Model 780,** .22 L.R.R.F., Clip Fed, Open Rear Sight, *Modern*	43.00	70.00	65.00
☐ **Model 781,** .22 L.R.R.F., Tube Feed, Open Rear Sight, *Modern*	48.00	75.00	70.00
☐ **Model 782,** .22 WMR, Clip Fed, Open Rear Sight, *Modern*	53.00	80.00	75.00
☐ **Model 783,** .22 WMR, Tube Feed, Open Rear Sight, *Modern*	53.00	80.00	75.00
☐ **Model 80,** .22 L.R.R.F., Clip Fed, Open Rear Sight, Takedown, *Modern*	42.00	60.00	55.00
☐ **Model 80 DL,** .22 L.R.R.F., Clip Fed, Beavertail Forend, Takedown, Peep Sights, *Modern*	42.00	70.00	65.00
☐ **Model 80C,** .22 L.R.R.F., Clip Fed, Beavertail Forend, Takedown, Open Rear Sight, *Modern*	48.00	65.00	60.00
☐ **Model 80E,** .22 L.R.R.F., Clip Fed, Peep Sights, Takedown, *Modern*	42.00	60.00	55.00
☐ **Model 81,** .22 L.R.R.F., Tube Feed, Takedown, Open Rear Sight, *Modern*	53.00	70.00	65.00
☐ **Model 81C,** .22 L.R.R.F., Tube Feed, Takedown, Open Rear Sight, Beavertail Forend, *Modern*	48.00	70.00	65.00
☐ **Model 81DL,** .22 L.R.R.F., Tube Feed, Takedown, Peep Sights, Beavertail Forend, *Modern*	43.00	65.00	60.00
☐ **Model 81E,** .22 L.R.R.F., Tube Feed, Takedown, Peep Sights, *Modern*	43.00	65.00	60.00
☐ **Model 81G,** .22 L.R.R.F., Tube Feed, Takedown, Open Rear Sight, Beavertail Forend, *Modern*	43.00	65.00	60.00
☐ **Model 980,** .22 WMR, Clip Fed, Monte Carlo Stock, Open Rear Sight, *Modern*	60.00	80.00	75.00

RIFLE, LEVER ACTION

	V.G.	Exc.	Prior Year Exc. Value
☐ **Centennial Set 336-39,** Fancy Checkering, Fancy Wood, Engraved, Brass Furniture, *Modern*	725.00	1200.00	1150.00
☐ **Glenfield M 30 A,** .30-30 Win., Tube Feed, *Modern*	105.00	145.00	140.00

Marlin Cased Centennial Pair

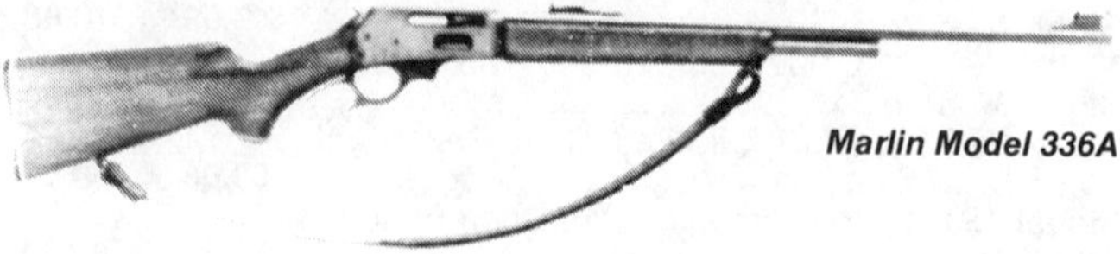

Marlin Model 336A

Marlin Model 783

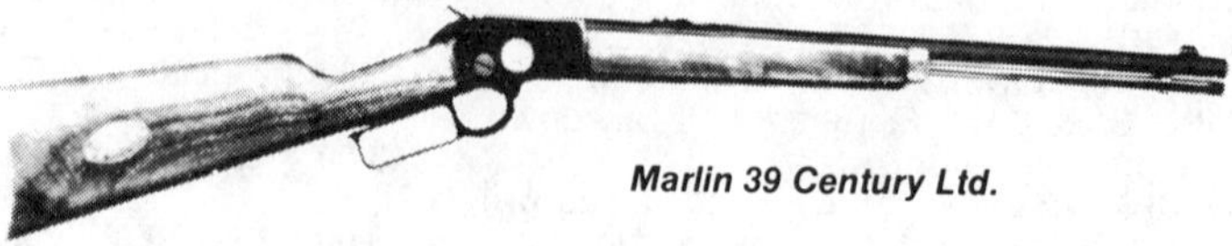

Marlin 39 Century Ltd.

Marlin Model 99M1

	V.G.	Exc.	Prior Year Exc. Value
☐ **M1894 (Late),** .357 Magnum, Tube Feed, Open Rear Sight, *Modern*	145.00	195.00	180.00
☐ **M1894 (Late),** .41 Magnum, Tube Feed, Open Rear Sight, *Modern*	130.00	180.00	165.00
☐ **M1894 (Late),** .44 Magnum, Tube Feed, Open Rear Sight, *Modern*	130.00	180.00	165.00
☐ **M1895 (Late),** .45-70 Government, Tube Feed, Open Rear Sight, *Modern*	150.00	190.00	185.00
☐ **Model 1881 Standard,** Various Calibers, Tube Feed, Open Rear Sight, *Antique*	450.00	715.00	695.00
☐ **Model 1888,** Various Calibers, Tube Feed, Open Rear Sight, *Antique*	550.00	875.00	850.00
☐ **Model 1889 Standard,** Various Calibers, Tube Feed, Open Rear Sight, *Antique*	300.00	515.00	495.00
☐ **Model 1891,** .22 L.R.R.F., Tube Feed, Open Rear Sight, *Antique*	300.00	410.00	395.00
☐ **Model 1892,** Various Calibers, Tube Feed, Open Rear Sight, *Antique*	275.00	400.00	375.00
☐ **Model 1892 Over #177382,** Various Calibers, Tube Feed, *Modern*	250.00	350.00	325.00
☐ **Model 1893,** Various Calibers, Tube Feed, Solid Frame, Octagon Barrel, *Antique*	335.00	475.00	450.00
☐ **Model 1893,** Various Calibers, Tube Feed, Solid Frame, Round Barrel, *Antique*	275.00	410.00	395.00
☐ **Model 1893,** Various Calibers, Tube Feed, Solid Frame, Round Barrel, Carbine, *Antique*	440.00	575.00	550.00
☐ **Model 1893,** Various Calibers, Tube Feed, Takedown, Octagon Barrel, *Antique*	465.00	600.00	575.00
☐ **Model 1893,** Various Calibers, Tube Feed, Takedown, Round Barrel, *Antique*	360.00	500.00	475.00
☐ **Model 1893,** Various Calibers, Tube Feed, Sporting Carbine, 5 Shot, *Antique*	490.00	670.00	635.00
☐ **Model 1893,** Various Calibers, Tube Feed, Sporting Carbine, Takedown, 5 Shot, *Antique*	550.00	700.00	675.00
☐ **Model 1893,** Various Calibers, Tube Feed, Full-Stocked, with Bayonet, *Antique*	1850.00	2850.00	2800.00
☐ **Model 1893 over #177304,** Various Calibers, Tube Feed, Solid Frame, Octagon Barrel, *Modern*	340.00	470.00	450.00
☐ **Model 1893 over #177304,** Various Calibers, Tube Feed, Solid Frame, Round Barrel, *Modern*	280.00	400.00	375.00
☐ **Model 1893 over #177304,** Various Calibers, Tube Feed, Solid Frame, Round Barrel, Carbine, *Modern*	410.00	515.00	495.00
☐ **Model 1893 over #177304,** Various Calibers, Tube Feed, Takedown, Octagon Barrel, *Modern*	380.00	500.00	475.00
☐ **Model 1893 over #177304,** Various Calibers, Tube Feed, Takedown, Round Barrel, *Modern*	300.00	400.00	375.00
☐ **Model 1893 over #177304,** Various Calibers, Tube Feed, Sporting Carbine, 5 Shot, *Modern*	410.00	500.00	475.00
☐ **Model 1893 over #177304,** Various Calibers, Tube Feed, Sporting Carbine, Takedown, 5 Shot, *Modern*	485.00	675.00	640.00
☐ **Model 1893 over #177304,** Various Calibers, Tube Feed, Full-Stocked, with Bayonet, *Modern*	1700.00	2950.00	2875.00
☐ **Model 1894,** Various Calibers, Tube Feed, Takedown, Octagon Barrel, *Antique*	485.00	625.00	600.00

	V.G.	Exc.	Prior Year Exc. Value
☐ **Model 1894,** Various Calibers, Tube Feed, Takedown, Round Barrel, *Antique*	435.00	575.00	550.00
☐ **Model 1894,** Various Calibers, Tube Feed, Solid Frame, Octagon Barrel, *Antique*	360.00	500.00	475.00
☐ **Model 1894,** Various Calibers, Tube Feed, Solid Frame, Round Barrel, *Antique*	300.00	410.00	395.00
☐ **Model 1894 over #175431,** Various Calibers, Tube Feed, Takedown, Octagon Barrel, *Modern*	490.00	625.00	600.00
☐ **Model 1894 over #175431,** Various Calibers, Tube Feed, Takedown, Round Barrel, *Modern*	340.00	475.00	450.00
☐ **Model 1894 over #175431,** Various Calibers, Tube Feed, Solid Frame, Octagon Barrel, *Modern*	335.00	475.00	450.00
☐ **Model 1894 over #175431,** Various Calibers, Tube Feed, Solid Frame, Round Barrel, *Modern*	280.00	400.00	375.00
☐ **Model 1895,** Various Calibers, Tube Feed, Solid Frame, Round Barrel, *Antique*	545.00	825.00	800.00
☐ **Model 1895,** Various Calibers, Tube Feed, Solid Frame, Octagon Barrel, *Antique*	510.00	775.00	750.00
☐ **Model 1895,** Various Calibers, Tube Feed, Takedown, Octagon Barrel, *Antique*	550.00	900.00	885.00
☐ **Model 1895,** Various Calibers, Tube Feed, Takedown, Round Barrel, *Antique*	550.00	900.00	885.00
☐ **Model 1895 over #167531,** Various Calibers, Tube Feed, Solid Frame, Round Barrel, *Modern*	410.00	700.00	675.00
☐ **Model 1895 over #167531,** Various Calibers, Tube Feed, Solid Frame, Octagon Barrel, *Modern*	460.00	750.00	725.00
☐ **Model 1895 over #167531,** Various Calibers, Tube Feed, Takedown, Octagon Barrel, *Modern*	490.00	825.00	800.00
☐ **Model 1895 over #167531,** Various Calibers, Tube Feed, Takedown, Round Barrel, *Modern*	460.00	800.00	775.00
☐ **Model 1897,** .22 L.R.R.F., Tube Feed, Takedown, *Antique*	275.00	400.00	375.00
☐ **Model 1897 over #177197,** .22 L.R.R.F., Tube Feed, Takedown, *Modern*	250.00	375.00	350.00
☐ **Model 336,** .219 Zipper, Tube Feed, Sporting Carbine, Open Rear Sight, 5 Shot, *Modern*	225.00	350.00	325.00
☐ **Model 336,** Various Calibers, Tube Feed, Sporting Carbine, Open Rear Sight, 5 Shot, *Modern*	120.00	165.00	155.00
☐ **Model 336 Marauder,** Various Calibers, Tube Feed, Carbine, Open Rear Sight, Straight Grip, *Modern*	175.00	275.00	265.00
☐ **Model 336 Zane Grey,** .30-30 Win., Tube Feed, Octagon Barrel, Open Rear Sight, *Modern*	165.00	230.00	225.00
☐ **Model 336A,** Various Calibers, Tube Feed, Sporting Rifle, Open Rear Sight, 5 Shot, *Modern*	120.00	165.00	160.00
☐ **Model 336A-DL,** Various Calibers, Tube Feed, Sporting Rifle, Open Rear Sight, 5 Shot, Checkered Stock, *Modern*	130.00	170.00	165.00
☐ **Model 336C,** Various Calibers, Tube Feed, Carbine, Open Rear Sight, *Modern*	115.00	165.00	160.00
☐ **Model 336T,** .44 Magnum, Tube Feed, Carbine, Open Rear Sight, Straight Grip, *Modern*	135.00	180.00	175.00

	V.G.	Exc.	Prior Year Exc. Value
☐ **Model 336T,** Various Calibers, Tube Feed, Carbine, Open Rear Sight, Straight Grip, *Modern*	115.00	165.00	155.00
☐ **Model 36,** Various Calibers, Tube Feed, Beavertail Forend, Open Rear Sight, Carbine, *Modern*	160.00	230.00	215.00
☐ **Model 36,** Various Calibers, Tube Feed, Beavertail Forend, Open Rear Sight, Sporting Carbine, 5 Shot, *Modern*	160.00	235.00	220.00
☐ **Model 36A,** Various Calibers, Tube Feed, Beavertail Forend, Open Rear Sight, 5 Shot, *Modern*	160.00	235.00	220.00
☐ **Model 36DL,** Various Calibers, Tube Feed, Fancy Checkering, Open Rear Sight, 5 Shot, *Modern*	185.00	285.00	270.00
☐ **Model 39,** .22 L.R.R.F., Takedown, Tube Feed, Hammer, Octagon Barrel, *Modern*	180.00	285.00	270.00
☐ **Model 39 Article II,** .22 L.R.R.F., Takedown, Tube Feed, Hammer, Octagon Barrel, *Modern*	150.00	230.00	220.00
☐ **Model 39 Article II,** .22 L.R.R.F., Takedown, Tube Feed, Hammer, Octagon Barrel, Carbine, *Modern*	150.00	235.00	225.00
☐ **Model 39 Century,** .22 L.R.R.F., Takedown, Tube Feed, Hammer, Octagon Barrel, *Modern*	150.00	230.00	220.00
☐ **Model 39 M,** .22 L.R.R.F., Takedown, Tube Feed, Hammer, Round Barrel, Carbine, *Modern*	100.00	140.00	135.00
☐ **Model 39A,** .22 L.R.R.F., Takedown, Tube Feed, Hammer, Round Barrel, *Modern*	95.00	145.00	140.00
☐ **Model 39A Mountie,** .22 L.R.R.F., Takedown, Tube Feed, Hammer, Round Barrel, *Modern*	105.00	150.00	145.00
☐ **Model 444,** .444 Marlin, Tube Feed, Monte Carlo Stock, Open Rear Sight, Straight Grip, *Modern*	140.00	190.00	180.00
☐ **Model 56,** .22 L.R.R.F., Clip Fed, Open Rear Sight, Monte Carlo Stock, *Modern*	63.00	100.00	90.00
☐ **Model 57,** .22 L.R.R.F., Tube Feed, Open Rear Sight, Monte Carlo Stock, *Modern*	63.00	100.00	90.00
☐ **Model 57M,** .22 WMR, Tube Feed, Open Rear Sight, Monte Carlo Stock, *Modern*	75.00	105.00	100.00
☐ **Model 62,** Various Calibers, Clip Fed, Open Rear Sight, Monte Carlo Stock, *Modern*	100.00	155.00	145.00
RIFLE, SEMI-AUTOMATIC			
☐ **Glenfield M40,** .22 L.R.R.F., Tube Feed, *Modern*	48.00	65.00	60.00
☐ **Glenfield M60,** .22 L.R.R.F., Tube Feed, *Modern*	37.00	53.00	50.00
☐ **Model 49 DL,** .22 L.R.R.F., Tube Feed, Open Rear Sight, *Modern*	43.00	65.00	60.00
☐ **Model 50,** .22 L.R.R.F., Clip Fed, Open Rear Sight, Takedown, *Modern*	43.00	65.00	60.00
☐ **Model 50E,** .22 L.R.R.F., Clip Fed, Peep Sights, Takedown, *Modern*	43.00	65.00	60.00
☐ **Model 88C,** .22 L.R.R.F., Tube Feed, Takedown, Open Rear Sight, *Modern*	48.00	65.00	60.00
☐ **Model 88DL,** .22 L.R.R.F., Tube Feed, Takedown, Peep Sights, *Modern*	48.00	70.00	65.00
☐ **Model 89 DL,** .22 L.R.R.F., Clip Fed, Takedown, Peep Sights, *Modern*	48.00	70.00	65.00

	V.G.	Exc.	Prior Year Exc. Value
☐ **Model 89C,** .22 L.R.R.F., Clip Fed, Takedown, Open Rear Sight, *Modern*	48.00	70.00	65.00
☐ **Model 98,** .22 L.R.R.F., Tube Feed, Solid Frame, Open Rear Sight, Monte Carlo Stock, *Modern*	48.00	70.00	65.00
☐ **Model 989,** .22 L.R.R.F., Clip Fed, Open Rear Sight, Monte Carlo Stock, *Modern*	48.00	63.00	60.00
☐ **Model 989 G,** .22 L.R.R.F., Clip Fed, Open Rear Sight, Monte Carlo Stock, *Modern*	48.00	68.00	65.00
☐ **Model 990,** .22 L.R.R.F., Tube Feed, Open Rear Sight, Monte Carlo Stock, *Modern*	48.00	68.00	65.00
☐ **Model 995,** .22 L.R.R.F., Clip Fed, Open Rear Sight, *Modern*	48.00	63.00	60.00
☐ **Model 99,** .22 L.R.R.F., Tube Feed, Open Rear Sight, *Modern*	43.00	63.00	60.00
☐ **Model 99 M-1,** .22 L.R.R.F., Tube Feed, Open Rear Sight, Monte Carlo Stock, *Modern*	48.00	63.00	60.00
☐ **Model 99 M-2,** .22 L.R.R.F., Clip Fed, Open Rear Sight, *Modern*	43.00	58.00	55.00
☐ **Model 99C,** .22 L.R.R.F., Tube Feed, Open Rear Sight, Monte Carlo Stock, *Modern*	48.00	58.00	55.00
☐ **Model 99DL,** .22 L.R.R.F., Tube Feed, Open Rear Sight, Monte Carlo Stock, *Modern*	48.00	58.00	55.00
☐ **Model A-1,** .22 L.R.R.F., Clip Fed, Takedown, Open Rear Sight, *Modern*	43.00	58.00	55.00
☐ **Model A-1E,** .22 L.R.R.F., Clip Fed, Takedown, Peep Sights, *Modern*	43.00	58.00	55.00
RIFLE, SLIDE ACTION			
☐ **Model 18,** .22 L.R.R.F., Solid Frame, Tube Feed, Hammer, *Modern*	155.00	250.00	240.00
☐ **Model 20,** .22 L.R.R.F., Takedown, Tube Feed, Hammer, Octagon Barrel, *Modern*	160.00	225.00	220.00
☐ **Model 25,** .22 Short R.F., Takedown, Tube Feed, Hammer, *Modern*	180.00	300.00	290.00
☐ **Model 27,** Various Calibers, Takedown, Tube Feed, Hammer, Octagon Barrel, *Modern*	180.00	275.00	265.00
☐ **Model 27-S,** Various Calibers, Takedown, Tube Feed, Hammer, Round Barrel, *Modern*	180.00	270.00	260.00
☐ **Model 29,** .22 L.R.R.F., Takedown, Tube Feed, Hammer, Round Barrel, *Modern*	160.00	245.00	235.00
☐ **Model 32,** .22 L.R.R.F., Takedown, Tube Feed, Hammerless, Octagon Barrel, *Modern*	160.00	240.00	235.00
☐ **Model 38,** .22 L.R.R.F., Takedown, Tube Feed, Hammerless, Octagon Barrel, *Modern*	160.00	235.00	230.00
SHOTGUN, LEVER ACTION			
☐ **Four-Tenner,** .410 Ga., Tube Feed, *Modern*	390.00	565.00	550.00
SHOTGUN, SLIDE ACTION			
☐ **Model 1898 Field,** 12 Ga., Hammer, Tube Feed, *Modern*	160.00	340.00	325.00
☐ **Model 1898 B,** 12 Ga., Hammer, Tube Feed, Checkered Stock, *Modern*	190.00	390.00	375.00
☐ **Model 1898 C,** 12 Ga., Hammer, Tube Feed, Checkered Stock, Fancy Wood, Light Engraving, *Modern*	490.00	750.00	725.00

Marlin Model 49DL

Marlin Model 989M2

Marlin Model 39A

Marlin Model 55 Slug Gun

Marlin Model 1891

Marlin Model 780

	V.G.	Exc.	Prior Year Exc. Value
☐ **Model 1898 D,** 12 Ga., Hammer, Tube Feed, Checkered Stock, Fancy Wood, Engraved, *Modern*	890.00	1525.00	1500.00
☐ **Model 19 Field,** 12 Ga., Hammer, Tube Feed, *Modern*	140.00	275.00	260.00
☐ **Model 19 B,** 12 Ga., Hammer, Tube Feed, Checkered Stock, *Modern*	190.00	400.00	375.00
☐ **Model 19 C,** 12 Ga., Hammer, Tube Feed, Checkered Stock, Fancy Wood, Light Engraving, *Modern*	390.00	550.00	535.00
☐ **Model 19 D,** 12 Ga., Hammer, Tube Feed, Checkered Stock, Fancy Wood, Engraved, *Modern*	785.00	1200.00	1150.00
☐ **Model 21 Field,** 12 Ga., Hammer, Tube Feed, *Modern*	135.00	270.00	260.00
☐ **Model 21 B,** 12 Ga., Hammer, Tube Feed, Checkered Stock, *Modern*	190.00	385.00	365.00
☐ **Model 21 C,** 12 Ga., Hammer, Tube Feed, Checkered Stock, Fancy Wood, Light Engraving, *Modern*	375.00	540.00	525.00
☐ **Model 21 D,** 12 Ga., Hammer, Tube Feed, Checkered Stock, Fancy Wood, Engraved, *Modern*	775.00	1175.00	1125.00
☐ **Model 24 Field,** 12 Ga., Hammer, Tube Feed, *Modern*	155.00	290.00	285.00
☐ **Model 24 B,** 12 Ga., Hammer, Tube Feed, Checkered Stock, *Modern*	240.00	400.00	390.00
☐ **Model 24 C,** 12 Ga., Hammer, Tube Feed, Checkered Stock, Fancy Wood, Light Engraving, *Modern*	375.00	550.00	525.00
☐ **Model 24 D,** 12 Ga., Hammer, Tube Feed, Checkered Stock, Fancy Wood, Engraved, *Modern*	775.00	1250.00	1225.00
☐ **Model 16 Field,** 12 Ga., Hammer, Tube Feed, *Modern*	155.00	295.00	285.00
☐ **Model 16 B,** 12 Ga., Hammer, Tube Feed, Checkered Stock, *Modern*	240.00	400.00	385.00
☐ **Model 16 C,** 12 Ga., Hammer, Tube Feed, Checkered Stock, Fancy Wood, Light Engraving, *Modern*	375.00	560.00	530.00
☐ **Model 16 D,** 12 Ga., Hammer, Tube Feed, Checkered Stock, Fancy Wood, Engraved, *Modern*	775.00	1250.00	1225.00
☐ **Model 30 Field,** 12 Ga., Hammer, Tube Feed, *Modern*	155.00	290.00	285.00
☐ **Model 30 B,** 12 Ga., Hammer, Tube Feed, Checkered Stock, *Modern*	240.00	395.00	385.00
☐ **Model 30 C,** 12 Ga., Hammer, Tube Feed, Checkered Stock, Fancy Wood, Light Engraving, *Modern*	375.00	550.00	525.00

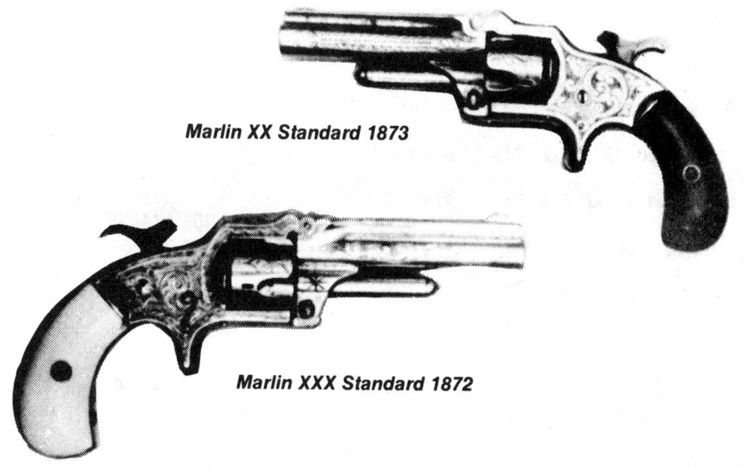

Marlin XX Standard 1873

Marlin XXX Standard 1872

	V.G.	Exc.	Prior Year Exc. Value
☐ **Model 30 D,** 12 Ga., Hammer, Tube Feed, Checkered Stock, Fancy Wood, Engraved, *Modern*	775.00	1270.00	1235.00
☐ **Model 28 Field,** 12 Ga., Hammerless, Tube Feed, *Modern*	180.00	340.00	320.00
☐ **Model 28 B,** 12 Ga., Hammerless, Tube Feed, Checkered Stock, *Modern*	300.00	500.00	475.00
☐ **Model 28 C,** 12 Ga., Hammerless, Tube Feed, Checkered Stock, Fancy Wood, Light Engraving, *Modern*	450.00	675.00	650.00
☐ **Model 28 D,** 12 Ga., Hammerless, Tube Feed, Checkered Stock, Fancy Wood, Engraved, *Modern*	850.00	1450.00	1400.00
☐ **Model 28 Trap,** 12 Ga., Hammerless, Tube Feed, *Modern*	340.00	490.00	470.00
☐ **Model 31 Field,** 12 Ga., Hammerless, Tube Feed, *Modern*	180.00	360.00	345.00
☐ **Model 31 B,** 12 Ga., Hammerless, Tube Feed, Checkered Stock, *Modern*	290.00	490.00	470.00
☐ **Model 31 C,** 12 Ga., Hammerless, Tube Feed, Checkered Stock, Fancy Wood, Light Engraving, *Modern*	450.00	675.00	650.00
☐ **Model 31 D,** 12 Ga., Hammerless, Tube Feed, Checkered Stock, Fancy Wood, Engraved, *Modern*	850.00	1450.00	1400.00
☐ **Model 17 Field,** 12 Ga., Hammer, Tube Feed, *Modern*	180.00	350.00	325.00
☐ **Model 26 Field,** 12 Ga., Hammer, Tube Feed, *Modern*	175.00	300.00	290.00
☐ **Model 44 Field,** 12 Ga., Hammerless, Tube Feed, *Modern*	200.00	340.00	320.00
☐ **Model 63 Field,** 12 Ga., Hammerless, Tube Feed, *Modern*	165.00	285.00	265.00
☐ **Premier Mark I,** 12 Ga., Hammerless, Tube Feed, *Modern*	115.00	165.00	155.00

	V.G.	Exc.	Prior Year Exc. Value
☐ **Premier Mark II,** 12 Ga., Hammerless, Tube Feed, *Modern*	135.00	185.00	180.00
☐ **Premier Mark IV,** 12 Ga., Hammerless, Tube Feed, Vent Rib, *Modern*	195.00	290.00	275.00
☐ **Model 120,** 12 Ga. 3″, Hammerless, Tube Feed, *Modern*	135.00	165.00	160.00
☐ **Glenfield Model 778,** 12 Ga., Hammerless, Tube Feed, *Modern*	95.00	145.00	140.00
SHOTGUN, DOUBLE BARREL, OVER-UNDER			
☐ **Model 90,** 12 and 16 Gauges, Checkered Stock, Double Triggers, *Modern*	250.00	375.00	370.00
☐ **Model 90,** 20 and .410 Gauges, Checkered Stock, Double Triggers, *Modern*	300.00	450.00	425.00
☐ **Model 90,** 12 and 16 Gauges, Checkered Stock, Single Triggers, *Modern*	300.00	435.00	420.00
☐ **Model 90,** 20 and 16 Gauges, Checkered Stock, Single Triggers, *Modern*	385.00	510.00	490.00
SHOTGUN, BOLT ACTION			
☐ **Model 55,** Various Gauges, Clip Fed, *Modern*	53.00	68.00	65.00
☐ **Model 55,** Various Gauges, Clip Fed, Adjustable Choke, *Modern*	58.00	80.00	75.00
☐ **Model 55 Goose Gun,** 12 Ga. 3″, Clip Fed, *Modern*	58.00	80.00	75.00
☐ **Model 55,** 12 Ga. 3″, Clip Fed, Adjustable Choke, *Modern*	58.00	80.00	75.00
☐ **Model 55S,** 12 Ga. 3″, Clip Fed, *Modern*	58.00	80.00	75.00
☐ **Model Super Goose,** 10 Ga. 3½″, Clip Fed, *Modern*	95.00	150.00	140.00
☐ **Glenfield 50,** 12 Ga. 3″, Clip Fed, *Modern*	53.00	75.00	70.00

MAROCCINI

Fabricca Fucili da Caccia di Luciano Maroccini, Gardone Val Trompia, Italy.

	V.G.	Exc.	Prior Year Exc. Value
SHOTGUN, DOUBLE BARREL, OVER-UNDER			
☐ **Mistral**, Various Gauges, Checkered Stock, Sling Swivels, Double Triggers, Boxlock, *Modern*	125.00	165.00	—
☐ **Mistral Trap**, Various Gauges, Checkered Stock, Single Trigger, Boxlock, Automatic Ejectors, *Modern*	150.00	200.00	—
☐ **Commander**, 12 Gauge Magnum, Police Style, Detachable Buttstock, Double Triggers, Boxlock, *Modern*	140.00	180.00	—
SHOTGUN, DOUBLE BARREL, SIDE-BY-SIDE			
☐ **Mondial**, 12 Gauge, Checkered Stock, Sling Swivels, Double Triggers, Boxlock, *Modern*	145.00	195.00	—

MARQUIS OF LORNE

Made by Hood Arms Co. Norwich, Conn., c. 1880.

	V.G.	Exc.	Prior Year Exc. Value
HANDGUN, REVOLVER			
☐ **.22 Short R.F.**, 7 Shot, Spur Trigger, Solid Frame, Single Action, *Antique*	95.00	165.00	160.00
☐ **.32 Short R.F.**, 5 Shot, Spur Trigger, Solid Frame, Single Action, *Antique*	95.00	170.00	170.00

	V.G.	Exc.	Prior Year Exc. Value

MARS
Unknown maker, Spain, c. 1920.

HANDGUN, SEMI-AUTOMATIC

	V.G.	Exc.	Prior Year Exc. Value
☐ **Automat Pistole Mars**, .25 ACP, Clip Fed, *Modern*	140.00	195.00	190.00

MARS
Kohout & Spolecnost, Kydne, Czechoslovakia, c. 1925.

HANDGUN, SEMI-AUTOMATIC

	V.G.	Exc.	Prior Year Exc. Value
☐ **Mars**, .25 ACP, Clip Fed, Blue, *Modern*	165.00	245.00	235.00
☐ **Mars**, .32 ACP, Clip Fed, Blue, *Modern*	185.00	275.00	265.00

MARS AUTOMATIC PISTOL SYNDICATE
Distributers of the Gabbet-Fairfax pistol made by Webley & Scott, Birmingham, England, c. 1902.

HANDGUN, SEMI-AUTOMATIC

	V.G.	Exc.	Prior Year Exc. Value
☐ **9mm**, Clip Fed, Blue, Hammer, *Curio*	2,575.00	3,650.00	3,500.00
☐ **.45 Long**, Clip Fed, Blue, Hammer, *Curio*	3,600.00	4,700.00	4,500.00

MARSHWOOD
Made by Stevens Arms.

SHOTGUN, DOUBLE BARREL, SIDE-BY-SIDE

	V.G.	Exc.	Prior Year Exc. Value
☐ **M 315**, Various Gauges, Hammerless, Steel Barrel, *Modern*	110.00	165.00	160.00

MARSTON, STANHOPE
N.Y.C., c. 1850.

HANDGUN, PERCUSSION

	V.G.	Exc.	Prior Year Exc. Value
☐ **Swivel Breech**, .31, Two Barrels, Ring Trigger, Bar Hammer, *Antique*	435.00	695.00	675.00

MARSTON, WILLIAM W.
N.Y.C. 1850-1863

HANDGUN, PERCUSSION

	V.G.	Exc.	Prior Year Exc. Value
☐ **Pepperbox**, .31, Double Action, 6 Shot, Bar Hammer, *Antique*	235.00	400.00	385.00
☐ **Single Shot**, .36, Bar Hammer, Double Action, Screw Barrel, *Antique*	160.00	235.00	220.00
☐ **Single Shot**, .36, Bar Hammer, Single Action, Screw Barrel, *Antique*	175.00	245.00	235.00
☐ **Breech Loader**, .36, Half Octagon Barrel, Engraved, *Antique*	750.00	1,325.00	1,275.00

MARTE
Erquiaga, Muguruzu y Cia., Eibar, Spain, c. 1920.

HANDGUN, SEMI-AUTOMATIC

	V.G.	Exc.	Prior Year Exc. Value
☐ **.25 ACP**, Clip Fed, Blue, *Curio*	90.00	135.00	125.00

MARTIAN
Martin A Bascaran, Eibar, Spain 1916-1927.

Martian

	V.G.	Exc.	Prior Year Exc. Value
HANDGUN, SEMI-AUTOMATIC			
☐ **.25 ACP**, Clip Fed, Trigger Guard Takedown, *Curio*	175.00	235.00	225.00
☐ **.32 ACP**, Clip Fed, Trigger Guard Takedown, *Curio*	180.00	270.00	260.00
☐ **.25 ACP**, Clip Fed, Eibar Type, *Modern*	95.00	135.00	125.00
☐ **.32 ACP**, Clip Fed, Eibar Type, *Modern*	110.00	165.00	155.00

MARTIAN COMMERCIAL

Martin A Bascaran, Eibar, Spain 1919-1927.

	V.G.	Exc.	Prior Year Exc. Value
HANDGUN, SEMI-AUTOMATIC			
☐ **.25 ACP**, Clip Fed, Eibar Type, *Modern*	90.00	135.00	125.00
☐ **.25 ACP**, Clip Fed, Eibar Type, *Modern*	110.00	160.00	150.00

MARTIN, ALEXANDER

Glasgow & Aberdeen, Scotland 1922-1928.

	V.G.	Exc.	Prior Year Exc. Value
RIFLE, BOLT ACTION			
☐ **.303 British**, Sporting Rifle, Express Sights, Engraved, Fancy Wood, Cased, *Modern*	775.00	1,300.00	1,200.00

MASSACHUSETTS ARMS

Made by Stevens Arms.

	V.G.	Exc.	Prior Year Exc. Value
SHOTGUN, DOUBLE BARREL, SIDE-BY-SIDE			
☐ **Model 311**, Various Gauges, Hammerless, Steel Barrel, *Modern*	110.00	175.00	165.00
SHOTGUN, SINGLESHOT			
☐ **Model 90**, Various Gauges, Takedown, Automatic Ejector, Plain, Hammer, *Modern*	45.00	65.00	60.00
☐ **Model 94**, Various Gauges, Takedown, Automatic Ejector, Plain, Hammer, *Modern*	45.00	65.00	60.00

MASSACHUSETTS ARMS CO.

Chicopee Falls, Mass. 1850-1866. Also see Adams.

	V.G.	Exc.	Prior Year Exc. Value
HANDGUN, PERCUSSION			
☐ **Maynard Pocket Revolver**, .28, 6 Shot, *Antique*	265.00	375.00	350.00
☐ **Maynard Belt Revolver**, .31, 6 Shot, *Antique*	390.00	525.00	500.00

	V.G.	Exc.	Prior Year Exc. Value
☐ **Wesson & Leavitt Belt Revolver**, .31, 6 Shot, *Antique*	330.00	500.00	475.00
☐ **Wesson & Leavitt Dragoon Revolver**, .40, 6 Shot, *Antique*	725.00	1,250.00	1,200.00

MATCHLOCK ARMS, UNKNOWN MAKER

RIFLE, MATCHLOCK

	V.G.	Exc.	Prior Year Exc. Value
☐ **.45**, India Mid-1600's, 4 Shot, Revolving Cylinder, Light Ornamentation, Brass Furniture, *Antique*	1,000.00	1,700.00	1,700.00
☐ **.57**, Japanese Full Stock Musket, Octagon Barrel, Silver Inlay, Brass Furniture, *Antique*	500.00	750.00	750.00

MATADOR

Made in Spain for Firearms International, Washington, D.C.

SHOTGUN, DOUBLE BARREL, SIDE-BY-SIDE

	V.G.	Exc.	Prior Year Exc. Value
☐ **Matador II**, 12 or 20 Gauges, Checkered Stock, Single Trigger, Selective Ejectors, *Modern*	155.00	235.00	225.00

MAUSER

Germany Gebruder Mauser et Cie from 1864-1890. From 1890 to date is known as Mauser Werke. Also See German Military, Luger.

AUTOMATIC WEAPON, MACHINE-PISTOL

	V.G.	Exc.	Prior Year Exc. Value
☐ **M1912,** 7.63 Mauser, with Detachable Shoulder Stock, *Class 3*	775.00	1400.00	1400.00
☐ **M1930,** 7.63 Mauser, with Detachable Shoulder Stock, *Class 3*	3350.00	4200.00	4200.00
☐ **MP1932,** 7.63 Mauser, with Detachable Shoulder Stock, *Class 3*	3350.00	4200.00	4200.00

HANDGUN, REVOLVER

	V.G.	Exc.	Prior Year Exc. Value
☐ **Colt Type,** .38 Spec., Double Action, 6 Shot, 2″ Barrel, *Modern*	110.00	170.00	225.00
☐ **M 78 Zig Zag,** Tip-Up, Fancy Engraving, *Antique*	3400.00	4900.00	4900.00
☐ **M 78 Zig Zag,** 9mm Mauser, Tip-Up, *Antique*	1400.00	2700.00	2700.00
☐ **M 78 Zig Zag,** 10.6mm, Tip-Up, *Antique*	2550.00	3550.00	3550.00
☐ **M 78 Zig Zag,** 7.6mm, Tip-Up, *Antique*	2050.00	2900.00	2900.00

HANDGUN, SEMI-AUTOMATIC

	V.G.	Exc.	Prior Year Exc. Value
☐ **Chinese Shansei,** .45 ACP, With Shoulder Stock, *Curio*	3600.00	4800.00	5100.00
☐ **HSC,** .32 ACP, Pre-War, Prototype, Commercial, *Modern*	520.00	900.00	1200.00
☐ **HSC,** .32 ACP, Post-War, Prototype, Commercial, *Modern*	325.00	490.00	600.00
☐ **HSC,** .32 ACP, Pre-War, Nazi-Proofed, Commercial, *Modern*	180.00	260.00	345.00
☐ **HSC,** .32 ACP, Post-War, Blue, *Modern*	135.00	200.00	275.00
☐ **HSC,** .32 ACP, Nickel Plated, Post-War, *Modern*	150.00	215.00	300.00
☐ **HSC,** .380 ACP, Blue, Post-War, *Modern*	145.00	210.00	290.00
☐ **HSC,** .380 ACP, Nickel Plated, Post-War, *Modern*	155.00	225.00	315.00
☐ **HSC 1 of 5,000,** .380 ACP, Blue, Post-War, Cased, *Modern*	150.00	205.00	280.00

Mauser M 78 Zig Zag

Mauser M1910

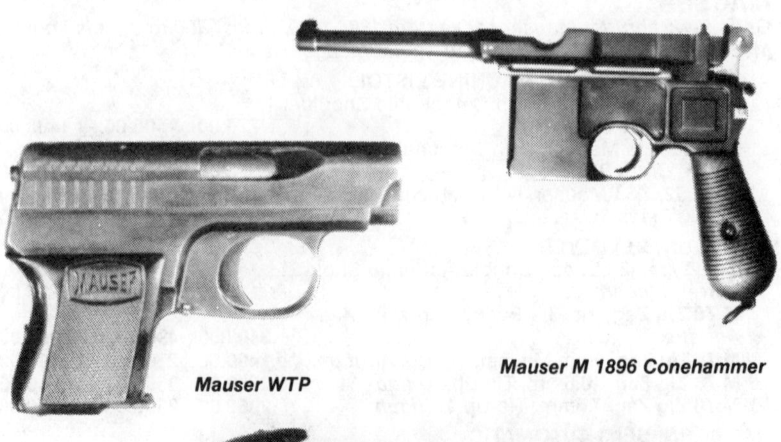

Mauser M 1896 Conehammer

Mauser WTP

Mauser M 1896 WW I with Holster Stock

	V.G.	Exc.	Prior Year Exc. Value
☐ **HSC French,** .32 ACP, Nazi-Proofed, *Curio*	175.00	240.00	345.00
☐ **HSC Navy,** .32 ACP, Nazi-Proofed, *Curio*	320.00	450.00	515.00
☐ **HSC NSDAP SA,** .32 ACP, Nazi-Proofed, *Curio*	330.00	490.00	580.00
☐ **HSC Police,** .32 ACP, Nazi-Proofed, *Curio*	235.00	310.00	380.00
☐ **HSC Swiss,** .32 ACP, Nazi-Proofed, *Curio*	500.00	700.00	875.00
☐ **M 1896,** 7.63 Mauser, 10 Shot, Conehammer, *Curio*	1000.00	1800.00	2050.00
☐ **M 1896,** 7.63 Mauser, 10 Shot, with Loading Lever, *Curio*	710.00	1400.00	1750.00
☐ **M 1896,** 7.63 Mauser, Conehammer, with Shoulder Stock, *Curio*	1230.00	2100.00	2600.00
☐ **M 1896,** 7.63 Mauser, with Loading Lever, with Shoulder Stock, *Curio*	900.00	1750.00	2100.00
☐ **M 1896,** 7.63 Mauser, with Loading Lever, Transitional, *Curio*	995.00	1600.00	1600.00
☐ **M 1896,** 7.63 Mauser, Slabside, *Curio*	850.00	1300.00	1300.00
☐ **M 1896 (Early),** 7.63 Mauser, Small Ring, *Curio*	850.00	1325.00	1325.00
☐ **M 1896 Italian,** 7.63 Mauser, Slabside, *Curio*	1350.00	1925.00	1925.00
☐ **M 1896 Shallow Mill,** 7.63 Mauser, with Loading Lever, *Curio*	675.00	1150.00	1700.00
☐ **M 1896 Turkish,** 7.63 Mauser, Conehammer, *Curio*	1750.00	2600.00	2600.00
☐ **M 1912,** .45 ACP, Clip Fed, *Curio*	4350.00	5650.00	5650.00
☐ **M 1921,** .45 ACP, Clip Fed, *Curio*	2350.00	3350.00	3350.00
☐ **M 1921,** 9mm Luger, Clip Fed, *Curio*	3500.00	4650.00	4650.00
☐ **M 1895,** 7.65 Borchardt, *Antique*	2375.00	3550.00	3550.00
☐ **M 1896,** 6-Shot Model *Add* **75%-100%**			
☐ **M 1896,** 20-Shot Model *Add* **50%-80%**			
☐ **M 1896,** 40-Shot Model *Add* **100%**			
☐ **M 1896,** Factory Engraving *Add* **300%**			
☐ **M 1896,** Original Holster Stock *Add* **20%-35%**			
☐ **M 1896,** 7.63 Mauser, Pre-War, Commercial, *Curio*	750.00	1175.00	1175.00
☐ **M 1896 1920 Police,** 7.63 Mauser, *Curio*	635.00	1075.00	1075.00
☐ **M 1896 Banner,** 7.63 Mauser, *Curio*	935.00	1500.00	1500.00
☐ **M 1896 Bolo,** 7.63 Mauser, Post-War, *Curio*	945.00	1525.00	1525.00
☐ **M 1896 French Police,** 7.63 Mauser, *Curio*	1425.00	2100.00	2100.00
☐ **M 1896 Persian,** 7.63 Mauser, *Curio*	1575.00	2450.00	2450.00
☐ **M 1896 WW I,** 7.63 Mauser, Commercial, *Curio*	510.00	720.00	1100.00
☐ **M 1896 WW I,** 7.63 Mauser, Military, *Curio*	510.00	720.00	1100.00
☐ **M 1896 WW I,** 9mm Luger, Military, *Curio*	530.00	790.00	1200.00
☐ **M 1906/08,** 7.63 Mauser, Clip Fed, *Curio*	2600.00	3650.00	3650.00
☐ **M 1910,** .25 ACP, Clip Fed, *Curio*	140.00	230.00	320.00
☐ **M 1910/14,** .25 ACP, Clip Fed, *Curio*	150.00	240.00	340.00
☐ **M 1910/34,** .25 ACP, Clip Fed, *Modern*	250.00	370.00	485.00
☐ **M 1912,** 9mm Luger, Clip Fed, *Curio*	2000.00	2750.00	3125.00
☐ **M 1914 Presentation Humpback,** 4mm, Clip Fed, Fancy Grips, *Curio*	6150.00	9200.00	9200.00
☐ **M 1914 Humpback,** .32 ACP, Long Barrel, Clip Fed, *Curio*	1500.00	2500.00	2500.00
☐ **M 1914 Transition Humpback,** .32 ACP, Clip Fed, *Curio*	1250.00	2000.00	2000.00
☐ **M 1914 Late Humpback,** .32 ACP, Clip Fed, *Curio*	1000.00	1800.00	1800.00
☐ **M 1914 Early,** .32 ACP, Clip Fed, *Curio*	180.00	310.00	425.00

	V.G.	Exc.	Prior Year Exc. Value
☐ **M 1914 War Commercial,** .32 ACP, Clip Fed, *Curio*	230.00	325.00	440.00
☐ **M 1914 Post-War,** .32 ACP, Clip Fed, *Modern*	210.00	310.00	325.00
☐ **M 1914 Army,** .32 ACP, Clip Fed, *Curio*	125.00	180.00	295.00
☐ **M 1914 Navy,** .32 ACP, Clip Fed, *Curio*	300.00	375.00	550.00
☐ **M 1914/34,** .32 ACP, Clip Fed, *Modern*	150.00	240.00	320.00
☐ **M 1930,** 7.63 Mauser, Commercial, *Curio*	550.00	750.00	1300.00
☐ **M 1930,** 9mm Luger, Commercial, *Curio*	500.00	700.00	1200.00
☐ **M 1934,** .32 ACP, Clip Fed, *Modern*	140.00	230.00	320.00
☐ **M 1934 Navy,** .32 ACP, Clip Fed, *Curio*	190.00	300.00	465.00
☐ **M 1934 Police,** .32 ACP, Clip Fed, *Curio*	180.00	290.00	450.00
☐ **Model Nickl HSV,** 9mm Luger, Clip Fed, *Modern*	3550.00	4600.00	4600.00
☐ **Parabellum 75th. Anniversary,** 9mm Luger, 12″ Barrel, Grip Safety, Forestock, Detachable Buttstock, *Class 3*	3000.00	4000.00	4000.00
☐ **Parabellum PO 8,** .30 Luger, 6″ Barrel, Grip Safety, *Modern*	435.00	545.00	545.00
☐ **Parabellum Model 1902 Cartridge Counter,** 9mm Luger, 4″ Barrel, Grip Safety, *Modern*	1700.00	2450.00	2450.00
☐ **Parabellum PO 8,** .30 Luger, 4″ Barrel, Grip Safety, *Modern*	460.00	565.00	565.00
☐ **Parabellum PO 8,** 9mm Luger, Various Barrel Lengths, Grip Safety, *Modern*	435.00	520.00	520.00
☐ **Parabellum Swiss,** .30 Luger, 6″ Barrel, Grip Safety, *Modern*	360.00	475.00	475.00
☐ **Parabellum Swiss,** 9mm Luger, 4″ Barrel, Grip Safety, *Modern*	360.00	475.00	475.00
☐ **Parabellum Bulgarian,** .30 Luger, Grip Safety, Commemorative, *Modern*	1000.00	1800.00	1800.00
☐ **Parabellum Russian,** .30 Luger, Grip Safety, Commemorative, *Modern*	1000.00	1800.00	1800.00
☐ **Parabellum Kriegsmarine,** 9mm Luger, Grip Safety, Commemorative, *Modern*	2000.00	3000.00	3000.00
☐ **Parabellum Sport,** .30 or 9mm Luger, Heavy Barrel, Target Sights, *Modern*	800.00	1400.00	1400.00
☐ **W T P,** .25 ACP, Clip Fed, *Modern*	275.00	400.00	400.00
☐ **W T P - T 6.35,** .25 ACP, Clip Fed, *Modern*	375.00	550.00	550.00
☐ **W T P 2,** .25 ACP, Clip Fed, *Modern*	325.00	425.00	425.00

Mauser M 1914

	V.G.	Exc.	Prior Year Exc. Value
RIFLE, BOLT ACTION			
☐ **Various Calibers,** Sporting Rifle, Set Trigger, Pre-WWI, Short Action, *Modern*	450.00	620.00	620.00
☐ **Various Calibers,** Sporting Rifle, Set Trigger, Pre-WWI, Carbine, Full-Stocked, *Modern*	450.00	620.00	620.00
☐ **Various Calibers,** Sporting Rifle, Pre-WWI, Military, Commercial, *Modern*	285.00	410.00	525.00
☐ **Model 10 Varminter,** .22-250, Post-War, Heavy Barrel, Monte Carlo Stock, Checkered Stock, *Modern*	250.00	390.00	390.00
☐ **Model 2000,** Various Calibers, Post-War, Monte Carlo Stock, Checkered Stock, *Modern*	250.00	370.00	370.00
☐ **Model 3000,** Various Calibers, Post-War, Monte Carlo Stock, *Modern*	300.00	420.00	420.00
☐ **Model 3000,** Various Calibers, Post-War, Left-Hand, Monte Carlo Stock, Checkered Stock, *Modern*	300.00	430.00	430.00
☐ **Model 3000,** Various Calibers, Post-War, Magnum Action, Monte Carlo Stock, Checkered Stock, *Modern*	300.00	430.00	430.00
☐ **Model 3000,** Various Calibers, Post-War, Left-Hand, Magnum Action, Monte Carlo Stock, Checkered Stock, *Modern*	315.00	445.00	445.00
☐ **Model 4000,** Various Calibers, Varmint, Fancy Checkering, Flared, *Modern*	320.00	440.00	440.00
☐ **Model 660,** Various Calibers, Post-War, Takedown, Monte Carlo Stock, Checkered Stock, *Modern*	675.00	850.00	850.00
☐ **Model 660 Safari,** Various Calibers, Post-War, Takedown, Monte Carlo Stock, Checkered Stock, Magnum, *Modern*	750.00	975.00	975.00
☐ **Model 98,** Various Calibers, Sporting Rifle, Full-Stocked, Pre-WW2, Military, Commercial, *Modern*	300.00	420.00	545.00
☐ **Model A,** Various Calibers, Sporting Rifle, Pre-WW2, Short Action, *Modern*	470.00	630.00	775.00
☐ **Model A,** Various Calibers, Sporting Rifle, Pre-WW2, Magnum Action, *Modern*	480.00	645.00	800.00
☐ **Model A British,** Various Calibers, Sporting Rifle, Express Sights, Pre-WW2, *Modern*	310.00	435.00	675.00
☐ **Model A British,** Various Calibers, Sporting Rifle, Peep Sights, Pre-WW2, Octagon Barrel, Set Trigger, *Modern*	470.00	670.00	825.00
☐ **Model B,** Various Calibers, Sporting Rifle, Pre-WW2, Set Trigger, Express Sights, *Modern*	340.00	480.00	650.00
☐ **Model B,** Various Calibers, Sporting Rifle, Pre-WW2, Octagon Barrel, Set Trigger, *Modern*	360.00	545.00	750.00
☐ **Model DSM 34,** .22 L.R.R.F., Pre-WW2, Singleshot, Tangent Sights, Military Style Stock, *Modern*	190.00	310.00	475.00
☐ **Model EL 320,** .22 L.R.R.F., Pre-WW2, Singleshot, Sporting Rifle, Adjustable Sights, *Modern*	145.00	230.00	345.00
☐ **Model EN 310,** .22 L.R.R.F., Pre-WW2, Singleshot, Open Rear Sight, *Modern*	120.00	195.00	280.00
☐ **Model ES 340,** .22 L.R.R.F., Pre-WW2, Singleshot, Tangent Sights, Sporting Rifle, *Modern*	125.00	205.00	300.00

	V.G.	Exc.	Prior Year Exc. Value
☐ **Model ES 340B,** .22 L.R.R.F., Pre-WW2, Singleshot, Tangent Sights, Sporting Rifle, *Modern*	160.00	250.00	310.00
☐ **Model ES 350,** .22 L.R.R.F., Pre-WW2, Singleshot, Target Sights, Target Stock, *Modern*	250.00	370.00	490.00
☐ **Model ES 350B,** .22 L.R.R.F., Pre-WW2, Singleshot, Target Sights, Target Stock, *Modern*	225.00	340.00	435.00
☐ **Model K,** Various Calibers, Sporting Rifle, Pre-WW2, Short Action, *Modern*	325.00	480.00	590.00
☐ **Model KKW,** .22 L.R.R.F., Pre-WW2, Singleshot, Tangent Sights, Military Style Stock, *Modern*	240.00	375.00	470.00
☐ **Model M,** Various Calibers, Sporting Rifle, Full-Stocked, Set Trigger, Express Sights, Carbine, *Modern*	535.00	690.00	690.00
☐ **Model M,** Various Calibers, Sporting Rifle, Pre-WW2, Full-Stocked, Tangent Sights, Carbine, *Modern*	320.00	480.00	590.00
☐ **Model MM 410,** .22 L.R.R.F., Pre-WW2, 5 Shot Clip, Tangent Sights, Sporting Rifle, *Modern*	190.00	285.00	350.00
☐ **Model MM 410B,** .22 L.R.R.F., Pre-WW2, 5 Shot Clip, Tangent Sights, Sporting Rifle, *Modern*	250.00	370.00	490.00
☐ **Model MS 350B,** .22 L.R.R.F., Pre-WW2, 5 Shot Clip, Target Sights, Target Stock, *Modern*	300.00	435.00	540.00
☐ **Model MS 420,** .22 L.R.R.F., Pre-WW2, 5 Shot Clip, Tangent Sights, Sporting Rifle, *Modern*	180.00	270.00	365.00
☐ **Model MS 420B,** .22 L.R.R.F., Pre-WW2, 5 Shot Clip, Tangent Sights, Target Stock, *Modern*	280.00	390.00	485.00
☐ **Model S,** Various Calibers, Sporting Rifle, Pre-WW2, Full-Stocked, Set Trigger, Carbine, *Modern*	335.00	465.00	590.00
☐ **Standard,** Various Calibers, Sporting Rifle, Set Trigger, Pre-WW1, *Modern*	360.00	495.00	670.00
RIFLE, DOUBLE BARREL, OVER-UNDER			
☐ **Model Aristocrat,** .375 H & H Magnum, Fancy Checkering, Engraved, Open Rear Sight, Cheekpiece, Double Trigger, *Modern*	1300.00	2000.00	2000.00
☐ **Model Aristocrat,** Various Calibers, Fancy Checkering, Engraved, Open Rear Sight, Checkpiece, Double Trigger, *Modern*	1050.00	1500.00	1500.00
RIFLE, SEMI-AUTOMATIC			
☐ **M1896,** 7.63 Mauser, Carbine, *Curio*	3175.00	4500.00	5200.00
SHOTGUN, BOLT ACTION			
☐ **16 Gauge,** *Modern*	85.00	135.00	135.00
SHOTGUN, DOUBLE BARREL, OVER-UNDER			
☐ **Model 610,** 12 Gauge, Trap Grade, Vent Rib, Checkered Stock, *Modern*	620.00	890.00	890.00
☐ **Model 610,** 12 Gauge, Skeet Grade, with Conversion Kit, Vent Rib, Checkered Stock, *Modern*	1150.00	1550.00	1550.00
☐ **Model 620,** 12 Gauge, Automatic Ejector, Single Selective Trigger, Vent Rib, Fancy Wood, *Modern*	670.00	950.00	950.00

	V.G.	Exc.	Prior Year Exc. Value
☐ **Model 620**, 12 Gauge, Automatic Ejector, Single Trigger, Vent Rib, Fancy Wood, *Modern*	640.00	900.00	875.00
☐ **Model 620**, 12 Gauge, Automatic Ejector, Double Trigger, Vent Rib, Fancy Wood, *Modern*	585.00	850.00	825.00
☐ **Model 71E**, 12 Gauge, Field Grade, Double Trigger, Checkered Stock, *Modern*	285.00	370.00	350.00
☐ **Model 72E**, 12 Gauge, Trap Grade, Checkered Stock, Light Engraving, *Modern*	365.00	495.00	475.00
☐ **Model 72E**, 12 Gauge, Skeet Grade, Checkered Stock, Light Engraving, *Modern*	360.00	490.00	475.00
SHOTGUN, DOUBLE BARREL, SIDE-BY-SIDE			
☐ **Model 496**, 12 Gauge, Trap Grade, Vent Rib, Single Trigger, Checkered Stock, Box Lock, *Modern*	385.00	525.00	500.00
☐ **Model 545**, 12 and 20 Gauges, Single Trigger, Recoil Pad, Checkered Stock, Box Lock, *Modern*	355.00	465.00	450.00
☐ **Model 580**, 12 Gauge, Engraved, Fancy Checkering, Fancy Wood, *Modern*	640.00	900.00	875.00
SHOTGUN, SINGLESHOT			
☐ **Model 496**, 12 Gauge, Trap Grade, Engraved, Checkered Stock, *Modern*	360.00	490.00	475.00
☐ **Model 496 Competition**, 12 Gauge, Trap Grade, Engraved, Fancy Wood, Fancy Checkering, *Modern*	490.00	675.00	650.00

MAYESCH

Lancaster, Pa. 1760-1770. See Kentucky Rifles and Pistols.

MAYER & SOEHNE

Arnsberg, W. Germany.

HANDGUN, REVOLVER

☐ **Target**, .22 L.R.R.F., Break Top, 5 Shot, Target Sights, Double Action, *Modern*	75.00	120.00	115.00

MAYOR, FRANCOIS

Lausanne, Switzerland.

HANDGUN, SEMI-AUTOMATIC

☐ **Rochat**, .25 ACP, Clip Fed, *Modern*	465.00	625.00	600.00

M.B. ASSOCIATES

San Ramon, Calif.

HANDGUN, ROCKET PISTOL

☐ **Gyrojet**, For Nickel Plating, *Add* **10%-15%**

☐ **Gyrojet**, For U.S. Property Stamping *Add* **75%-100%**

☐ **Gyrojet Mark I Model A**, Clip Fed, *Modern*	700.00	900.00	875.00
☐ **Gyrojet Mark I Model A Exp.**, Clip Fed, *Modern*	925.00	1,475.00	1,400.00
☐ **Gyrojet Mark II Model B**, Clip Fed, *Modern*	525.00	750.00	700.00
☐ **Gyrojet Mark II Model B Exp.**, Clip Fed, *Modern*	775.00	1,265.00	1,200.00
☐ **Gyrojet Mark II Model B Snub**, Clip Fed, *Modern*	575.00	825.00	775.00
☐ **Gyrojet Mark II Model C**, Clip Fed, *Modern*	425.00	590.00	550.00
☐ **Gyrojet Mark II B**, Clip Fed, Presentation, Cased with Accessories, *Modern*	950.00	1,500.00	1,450.00

	V.G.	Exc.	Prior Year Exc. Value

MCCOY, ALEXANDER
Philadelphia, Pa. 1779. See Kentucky Rifles.

MCCOY, KESTER
Lancaster County, Pa. See Kentucky Rifles and Pistols.

MCCULLOUGH, GEORGE
Lancaster, Pa. 1770-1773. See Kentucky Rifles.

MEIER, ADOLPHUS
St. Louis, Mo. 1845-1850.

RIFLE, PERCUSSION

	V.G.	Exc.	Prior Year Exc. Value
☐ **.58 Plains Type**, Double Barrel, Side by Side, Half-Octagon Barrel, Rifled, Plain, *Antique*	1,250.00	1,900.00	1,850.00

MELIOR
Liege, Belgium. Made by Robar et Cie. 1900-1959.

HANDGUN, SEMI-AUTOMATIC

	V.G.	Exc.	Prior Year Exc. Value
☐ **New Model Pocket**, .22 L.R.R.F., Clip Fed, *Modern*	135.00	195.00	185.00
☐ **New Model Pocket**, .32 ACP, Clip Fed, *Modern*	120.00	170.00	160.00
☐ **New Model Pocket**, .380 ACP, Clip Fed, *Modern*	125.00	190.00	175.00
☐ **New Model Vest Pocket**, .22 Long R.F., Clip Fed, *Modern*	115.00	170.00	160.00
☐ **New Model Vest Pocket**, .25 ACP, Clip Fed, *Modern*	115.00	170.00	160.00
☐ **Old Model Pocket**, .32 ACP, Clip Fed, *Modern*	125.00	180.00	165.00
☐ **Old Model Vest Pocket**, .25 ACP, Clip Fed, *Modern*	120.00	180.00	165.00
☐ **Target**, .22 L.R.R.F., Clip Fed, Long Barrel, *Modern*	160.00	240.00	225.00

MENDOZA
Mexico City, Mexico.

HANDGUN, SINGLESHOT

	V.G.	Exc.	Prior Year Exc. Value
☐ **K-62**, .22 L.R.R.F., *Modern*	65.00	120.00	115.00

RIFLE, BOLT ACTION

	V.G.	Exc.	Prior Year Exc. Value
☐ **Modelo Conejo**, .22 L.R.R.F., 2 Shot, *Modern*	95.00	165.00	160.00

MENTA
Made by August Menz, Suhl, Germany, c. 1916.

	V.G.	Exc.	Prior Year Exc. Value
☐ **.25 ACP**, Clip Fed, *Modern*	350.00	450.00	450.00
☐ **.32 ACP**, Clip Fed, Military, *Modern*	145.00	240.00	220.00
☐ **.32 ACP**, Clip Fed, Commercial, *Modern*	145.00	215.00	215.00

MENZ, AUGUST
Suhl, Germany. 1912-1924

HANDGUN, SEMI—AUTOMATIC

	V.G.	Exc.	Prior Year Exc. Value
☐ **Lilliput**, .25 ACP, Clip Fed. *Curio*	195.00	275.00	240.00

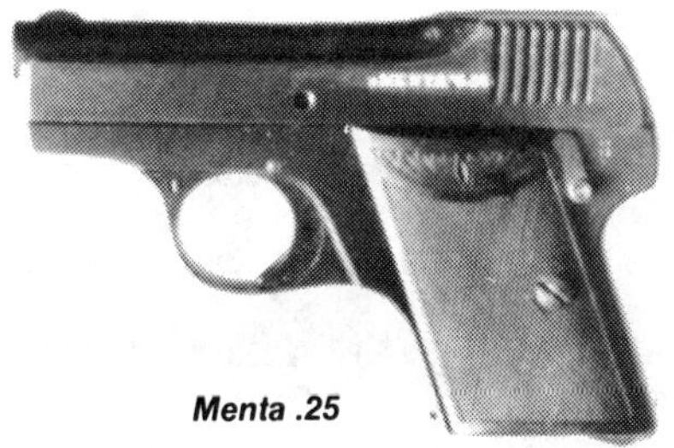

Menta .25

Menta .32

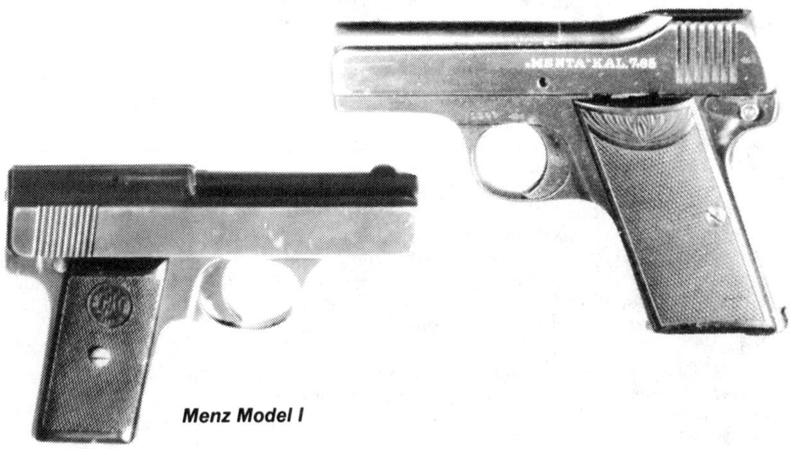

Menz Model I

	V.G.	Exc.	Prior Year Exc. Value
☐ **Model I**, .32 ACP, Clip Fed, *Curio*	195.00	295.00	265.00
☐ **Model II**, .32 ACP, Clip Fed, *Curio*	225.00	345.00	325.00
☐ **Model III**, .32 ACP, Clip Fed, Hammer, *Curio*	230.00	355.00	325.00
☐ **P & B Special**, .32 ACP, Clip Fed, Hammer, Double Action, *Curio*	425.00	550.00	475.00
☐ **P & B Special**, .380 ACP, Clip Fed, Hammer, Double Action, *Curio*	575.00	800.00	650.00

MERCURY

Made by Robar et Cie., Liege, Belgium for Tradewinds.

HANDGUN, SEMI-AUTOMATIC

☐ **M 622 VP**, .22 L.R.R.F., Clip Fed, *Modern*	100.00	155.00	140.00

SHOTGUN, DOUBLE BARREL, SIDE-BY-SIDE

☐ **Mercury**, 10 Gauge 3″, Hammerless, Magnum, Checkered Stock, Double Trigger, *Modern*	170.00	265.00	250.00
Mercury, 12 and 20 Gauges, Hammerless, Magnum, Checkered Stock, Double Trigger, *Modern*	160.00	220.00	200.00

MERIDEN FIRE ARMS CO.

Meriden, Conn. 1907-1909.

	V.G.	Exc.	Prior Year Exc. Value
HANDGUN, REVOLVER			
☐ **.38 S & W**, 5 Shot, Top Break, Hammerless, Double Action, *Modern*	**65.00**	**100.00**	**95.00**
RIFLE, SINGLESHOT			
☐ **Model 10**, .22 L.R.R.F., *Modern*	**50.00**	**70.00**	**65.00**
RIFLE, SLIDE ACTION			
☐ **Model 15**, .22 L.R.R.F., Tube Feed, *Modern*	**145.00**	**220.00**	**225.00**

MERKEL

Gebruder Merkel, Suhl, Germany from 1920. After WW II, VEB Fahrzeug u. Jagdwaffenwerk Ernst Thalmann, Suhl, East Germany.

COMBINATION WEAPON, OVER-UNDER			
☐ **Model 210**, Various Calibers, Pre-WW2, Engraved, Checkered Stock, *Modern*	**900.00**	**1,300.00**	**1,250.00**
☐ **Model 210E**, Various Calibers, Engraved, Checkered Stock, Automatic Ejector, *Modern*	**1,000.00**	**1,450.00**	**1,400.00**
☐ **Model 211**, Various Calibers, Pre-WW2, Engraved, Checkered Stock, *Modern*	**1,250.00**	**1,700.00**	**1,650.00**
☐ **Model 211E**, Various Calibers, Engraved, Checkered Stock, Automatic Ejector, *Modern*	**1,350.00**	**1,800.00**	**1,750.00**
☐ **Model 212**, Various Calibers, Pre-WW2, Fancy Engraving, Fancy Checkering, *Modern*	**1,400.00**	**1,800.00**	**1,750.00**
☐ **Model 212E**, Various Calibers, Pre-WW2, Fancy Engraving, Fancy Checkering, Automatic Ejector, *Modern*	**1,700.00**	**2,400.00**	**2,350.00**
☐ **Model 213E**, Various Calibers, Sidelock, Fancy Checkering, Fancy Engraving, Automatic Ejector, *Modern*	**2,350.00**	**3,000.00**	**3,000.00**
☐ **Model 214E**, Various Calibers, Pre-WW2, Sidelock, Fancy Checkering, Fancy Engraving, Automatic Ejector, *Modern*	**2,350.00**	**3,000.00**	**3,000.00**
☐ **Model 310**, Various Calibers, Pre-WW2, Engraved, Checkered Stock, *Modern*	**1,300.00**	**1,850.00**	**1,800.00**
☐ **Model 310E**, Various Calibers, Pre-WW2, Engraved, Checkered Stock, Automatic Ejector, *Modern*	**1,700.00**	**2,400.00**	**2,350.00**
☐ **Model 311**, Various Calibers, Pre-WW2, Fancy Engraving, Fancy Checkering, *Modern*	**1,500.00**	**2,175.00**	**2,100.00**
☐ **Model 311E**, Various Calibers, Pre-WW2, Fancy Engraving, Fancy Checkering, Automatic Ejector, *Modern*	**1,700.00**	**2,465.00**	**2,400.00**
☐ **Model 312**, Various Calibers, Pre-WW2, Fancy Engraving, Fancy Checkering, Automatic Ejector, *Modern*	**2,000.00**	**2,800.00**	**2,750.00**
☐ **Model 313**, Various Calibers, Sidelock, Fancy Checkering, Fancy Engraving, Automatic Ejector, *Modern*	**4,000.00**	**5,500.00**	**5,400.00**
☐ **Model 314**, Various Calibers, Sidelock, Fancy Checkering, Fancy Engraving, Automatic Ejector, *Modern*	**5,750.00**	**7,375.00**	**7,250.00**
☐ **Model 410**, Various Calibers, Pre-WW2, Engraved, Checkered Stock, *Modern*	**850.00**	**1,300.00**	**1,250.00**

	V.G.	Exc.	Prior Year Exc. Value
☐ **Model 410E**, Various Calibers, Pre-WW2, Engraved, Checkered Stock, Automatic Ejector, *Modern*	900.00	1,400.00	1,350.00
☐ **Model 411**, Various Calibers, Pre-WW2, Engraved, Checkered Stock, *Modern*	1,000.00	1,550.00	1,500.00
☐ **Model 411E**, Various Calibers, Pre-WW2, Engraved, Checkered Stock, Automatic Ejector, *Modern*	1,200.00	1,700.00	1,650.00
COMBINATION WEAPON, DRILLING			
☐ **Model 142**, Various Calibers, Pre-WW2, Double Trigger, Engraved, Checkered Stock, *Modern*	3,000.00	3,800.00	3,750.00
☐ **Model 144**, Various Calibers, Pre-WW2, Double Trigger, Engraved, Checkered Stock, *Modern*	3,100.00	3,875.00	3,800.00
☐ **Model 145**, Various Calibers, Pre-WW2, Double Trigger, Engraved, Checkered Stock, *Modern*	2,800.00	3,650.00	3,550.00
RIFLE, DOUBLE BARREL, OVER-UNDER			
☐ **Model 220**, Various Calibers, Pre-WW2, Checkered Stock, Engraved, *Modern*	875.00	1,300.00	1,250.00
☐ **Model 220E**, Various Calibers, Engraved, Checkered Stock, Automatic Ejector, *Modern*	975.00	1,400.00	1,350.00
☐ **Model 221**, Various Calibers, Pre-WW2, Checkered Stock, Engraved, *Modern*	975.00	1,350.00	1,300.00
☐ **Model 221E**, Various Calibers, Engraved, Checkered Stock, Automatic Ejector, *Modern*	1,350.00	1,925.00	1,850.00
☐ **Model 320**, Various Calibers, Pre-WW2, Checkered Stock, Engraved, *Modern*	1,350.00	1,925.00	1,850.00
☐ **Model 320E**, Various Calibers, Pre-WW2, Checkered Stock, Engraved, Automatic Ejector, *Modern*	1,750.00	2,500.00	2,400.00
☐ **Model 321**, Various Calibers, Pre-WW2, Fancy Engraving, Fancy Checkering, *Modern*	1,650.00	2,300.00	2,250.00
☐ **Model 321E**, Various Calibers, Pre-WW2, Fancy Engraving, Fancy Checkering, Automatic Ejector, *Modern*	1,900.00	2,600.00	2,500.00
☐ **Model 322**, Various Calibers, Pre-WW2, Fancy Engraving, Fancy Checkering, Automatic Ejector, *Modern*	2,000.00	2,775.00	2,800.00
☐ **Model 323**, Various Calibers, Sidelock, Fancy Checkering, Fancy Engraving, Automatic Ejector, *Modern*	4,400.00	5,800.00	5,750.00
☐ **Model 324**, Various Calibers, Sidelock, Fancy Checkering, Fancy Engraving, Automatic Ejector, *Modern*	6,000.00	7,500.00	7,500.00
SHOTGUN, DOUBLE BARREL, OVER-UNDER			
☐ **Model 100**, Various Gauges, Pre-WW2, Plain Barrel, Checkered Stock, *Modern*	575.00	750.00	725.00
☐ **Model 100**, Various Gauges, Pre-WW2, Raised Matted Rib, Checkered Stock, *Modern*	625.00	800.00	775.00
☐ **Model 101**, Various Gauges, Pre-WW2, Raised Matted Rib, Checkered Stock, Light Engraving, *Modern*	650.00	875.00	850.00
☐ **Model 101E**, Various Gauges, Pre-WW2, Raised Matted Rib, Checkered Stock, Light Engraving, Automatic Ejector, *Modern*	700.00	975.00	950.00

	V.G.	Exc.	Prior Year Exc. Value
☐ **Model 200**, Various Gauges, Pre-WW2, Raised Matted Rib, Checkered Stock, Light Engraving, *Modern*	900.00	1,300.00	1,250.00
☐ **Model 200E**, Various Gauges, Pre-WW2, Raised Matted Rib, Checkered Stock, Light Engraving, Automatic Ejector, *Modern*	1,100.00	1,700.00	1,650.00
☐ **Model 201**, Various Gauges, Pre-WW2, Raised Matted Rib, Checkered Stock, Engraved, *Modern*	1,000.00	1,600.00	1,550.00
☐ **Model 201E**, Various Gauges, Pre-WW2, Raised Matted Rib, Checkered Stock, Engraved, Automatic Ejector, *Modern*	1,250.00	1,875.00	1,800.00
☐ **Model 202**, Various Gauges, Pre-WW2, Raised Matted Rib, Fancy Checkering, Fancy Engraving, *Modern*	1,300.00	1,900.00	1,850.00
☐ **Model 202E**, Various Gauges, Pre-WW2, Raised Matted Rib, Fancy Checkering, Fancy Engraving, Automatic Ejector, *Modern*	1,750.00	2,500.00	2,400.00
☐ **Model 203E**, Various Gauges, Sidelock, Fancy Checkering, Fancy Engraving, Automatic Ejector, *Modern*	2,350.00	3,300.00	3,200.00
☐ **Model 203E**, Various Gauges, Sidelock, Single Selective Trigger, Automatic Ejector, Fancy Checkering, Fancy Engraving, *Modern*	3,450.00	4,700.00	4,650.00
☐ **Model 204E**, Various Gauges, Pre-WW2, Sidelock, Fancy Checkering, Fancy Engraving, Automatic Ejector, *Modern*	2,600.00	3,500.00	3,500.00
☐ **Model 300**, Various Gauges, Pre-WW2, Raised Matted Rib, Checkered Stock, Engraved, *Modern*	1,450.00	1,950.00	1,900.00
☐ **Model 300E**, Various Gauges, Pre-WW2, Raised Matted Rib, Checkered Stock, Engraved, Automatic Ejector, *Modern*	1,750.00	2,500.00	2,400.00
☐ **Model 301**, Various Gauges, Pre-WW2, Raised Matted Rib, Fancy Checkering, Engraved, *Modern*	1,600.00	2,400.00	2,300.00
☐ **Model 301E**, Various Gauges, Pre-WW2, Raised Matted Rib, Fancy Checkering, Engraved, Automatic Ejector, *Modern*	1,950.00	2,600.00	2,550.00
☐ **Model 302**, Various Gauges, Pre-WW2, Raised Matted Rib, Fancy Checkering, Fancy Engraving, Automatic Ejector, *Modern*	2,350.00	3,150.00	3,100.00
☐ **Model 303E**, Various Gauges, Sidelock, Single Selective Trigger, Automatic Ejector, Fancy Engraving, Fancy Checkering, *Modern*	4,250.00	5,700.00	5,600.00
☐ **Model 304E**, Various Gauges, Sidelock, Single Selective Trigger, Automatic Ejector, Fancy Engraving, Fancy Checkering, *Modern*	6,000.00	7,500.00	7,500.00
☐ **Model 400**, Various Gauges, Pre-WW2, Raised Matted Rib, Checkered Stock, Engraved, *Modern*	775.00	1,100.00	1,050.00
☐ **Model 400E**, Various Gauges, Pre-WW2, Raised Matted Rib, Checkered Stock, Engraved, Automatic Ejector, *Modern*	850.00	1,350.00	1,300.00
☐ **Model 401**, Various Gauges, Pre-WW2, Raised Matted Rib, Checkered Stock, Fancy Engraving, *Modern*	975.00	1,450.00	1,425.00

	V.G.	Exc.	Prior Year Exc. Value
☐ **Model 401E**, Various Gauges, Pre WW-2, Raised Matted Rib, Checkered Stock, Fancy Engraving, Automatic Ejector, *Modern*	1,100.00	1,650.00	1,600.00
SHOTGUN, DOUBLE BARREL, SIDE-BY-SIDE			
☐ **Model 127**, Various Gauges, Pre-WW2, Sidelock, Fancy Engraving, Fancy Checkering, Automatic Ejector, *Modern*	5,500.00	7,200.00	7,000.00
☐ **Model 130**, Various Gauges, Pre-WW2, Fancy Engraving, Fancy Checkering, Automatic Ejector, *Modern*	2,900.00	3,800.00	3,700.00
☐ **Model 147E**, Various Gauges, Fancy Checkering, Fancy Engraving, *Modern*	850.00	1,150.00	1,100.00
☐ **Model 147E**, Various Gauges, Fancy Checkering, Fancy Engraving, Single Selective Trigger, *Modern*	950.00	1,350.00	1,300.00
☐ **Model 147S**, Various Gauges, Fancy Checkering, Fancy Engraving, Sidelock, *Modern*	1,850.00	2,550.00	2,500.00
☐ **Model 147S**, Various Gauges, Fancy Checkering, Fancy Engraving, Sidelock, Single Selective Trigger, *Modern*	1,950.00	2,875.00	2,800.00
☐ **Model 47E**, Various Gauges, Checkered Stock, Engraved, *Modern*	650.00	875.00	850.00
☐ **Model 47E**, Various Gauges, Single Selective Trigger, Checkered Stock, Engraved, *Modern*	700.00	1,025.00	975.00
☐ **Model 47S**, Various Gauges, Sidelock, Checkered Stock, Engraved, *Modern*	1,250.00	1,850.00	1,800.00
☐ **Model 47S**, Various Gauges, Sidelock, Single Selective Trigger, Checkered Stock, Engraved, *Modern*	1,400.00	2,100.00	2,000.00

MERRILL CO.

Formerly in Rockwell City, Iowa, now in Fullerton, Calif.

HANDGUN, SINGLESHOT

☐ **Sportsman**, For Extra Barrel *Add* **$75.00-$110.00**

☐ **Sportsman**, For Extra 14" Barrel and Dies *Add* **$125.00-$185.00**

☐ **Sportsman**, Wrist Attachment *Add* **$15.00-$25.00**

	V.G.	Exc.	Prior Year Exc. Value
☐ **Sportsman**, Various Calibers, Target Pistol, Top Break, Adjustable Sights, Vent Rib, *Modern*	175.00	270.00	265.00

MERRIMAC ARMS & MFG. CO.

Newburyport, Mass. Absorbed by Brown Mfg. Co. Worcester, Mass. 1861-1866. Also see Ballard.

	V.G.	Exc.	Prior Year Exc. Value
HANDGUN, SINGLESHOT			
☐ **Southerner**, .41 Short R.F., Derringer, Iron Frame, Light Engraving, *Antique*	340.00	450.00	425.00
RIFLE, DOUBLE BARREL, SIDE-BY-SIDE			
☐ **Various Calibers**, Octagon Barrel, *Antique*	785.00	1,100.00	1,000.00
SHOTGUN, SINGLESHOT			
☐ **20 Gauge**, Falling Block, *Antique*	195.00	285.00	275.00

MERWIN & BRAY

Worcester, Mass. 1864-1868. Became Merwin & Simpkins in 1868 and also Merwin-Taylor & Simpkins the same year, also within the same year became Merwin, Hulbert & Co. Also see Ballard, Merwin, Hulbert & Co.

	V.G.	Exc.	Prior Year Exc. Value
HANDGUN, REVOLVER			
☐ **.22 Short R.F.**, 7 Shot, Single Action, Solid Frame, Spur Trigger, *Antique*	**120.00**	**185.00**	**165.00**
☐ **.28 Cup Primed Cartridge**, 6 Shot, Single Action, Spur Trigger, Solid Frame, *Antique*	**120.00**	**190.00**	**175.00**
☐ **.30 Cup Primed Cartridge**, 6 Shot, Single Action, Spur Trigger, Solid Frame, *Antique*	**125.00**	**200.00**	**185.00**
☐ **.31 R.F.**, 6 Shot, Single Action, Solid Frame, Spur Trigger, *Antique*	**110.00**	**170.00**	**160.00**
☐ **.32 Short R.F.**, 6 Shot, Single Action, Solid Frame, Spur Trigger, *Antique*	**120.00**	**180.00**	**170.00**
☐ **.42 Cup Primed Cartridge**, 6 Shot, Single Action, Spur Trigger, Solid Frame, *Antique*	**160.00**	**240.00**	**225.00**
☐ **.42 Cup Primed Cartridge**, 6 Shot, Single Action, Spur Trigger, Solid Frame, 6" Barrel, *Antique*	**280.00**	**400.00**	**375.00**
☐ **"Navy"**, .32 Short R.F., 6 Shot, Single Action, Solid Frame, Finger-Rest Trigger Guard, *Antique*	**300.00**	**450.00**	**425.00**
☐ **"Navy"**, .38 Short R.F., 6 Shot, Single Action, Solid Frame, Finger-Rest Trigger Guard, *Antique*	**375.00**	**500.00**	**475.00**
☐ **"Original"**, .28 Cup Primed Cartridge, 6 Shot, Single Action, Spur Trigger, Tip-Up, *Antique*	**495.00**	**665.00**	**625.00**
☐ **"Original"**, .30 Cup Primed Cartridge, 6 Shot, Single Action, Spur Trigger, Tip-Up, *Antique*	**540.00**	**700.00**	**675.00**
☐ **"Original"**, .42 Cup Primed Cartridge, 6 Shot, Single Action, Spur Trigger, Tip-Up, *Antique*	**595.00**	**765.00**	**725.00**
☐ **"Original"**, Various Cup-Primed Calibers, Extra Cylinder, Percussion, *Add* **$95.00-$160.00**			
☐ **Reynolds**, .25 Short R.F., 5 Shot, Single Action, Spur Trigger, 3" Barrel, *Antique*	**120.00**	**185.00**	**175.00**
HANDGUN, SINGLESHOT			
☐ **.32 Short R.F.**, Side-Swing Barrel, Brass Frame, 3" Barrel, Spur Trigger, *Antique*	**115.00**	**180.00**	**165.00**

MERWIN, HULBERT & CO.

Successors to Merwin & Bray, et al. in 1868, and became Hulbert Bros. in 1892. Out of business in 1896.

	V.G.	Exc.	Prior Year Exc. Value
HANDGUN, REVOLVER			
☐ **Army Model**, Extra Barrel, *Add* **$145.00-$200.00**			
☐ **Army Model**, "Safety Hammer", *Add* **$40.00-$65.00**			
☐ **Army Model**, .44-40 WCF, Belt Pistol, 7" Barrel, Double Action, Round Butt, 6 Shot, *Antique*	**390.00**	**595.00**	**550.00**
☐ **Army Model**, .44-40 WCF, Belt Pistol, 7" Barrel, Single Action, Square-Butt, 6 Shot, *Antique*	**470.00**	**675.00**	**625.00**
☐ **Army Model**, .44-40 WCF, Pocket Pistol, 3½" Barrel, Double Action, Round Butt, 6 Shot, *Antique*	**380.00**	**545.00**	**500.00**

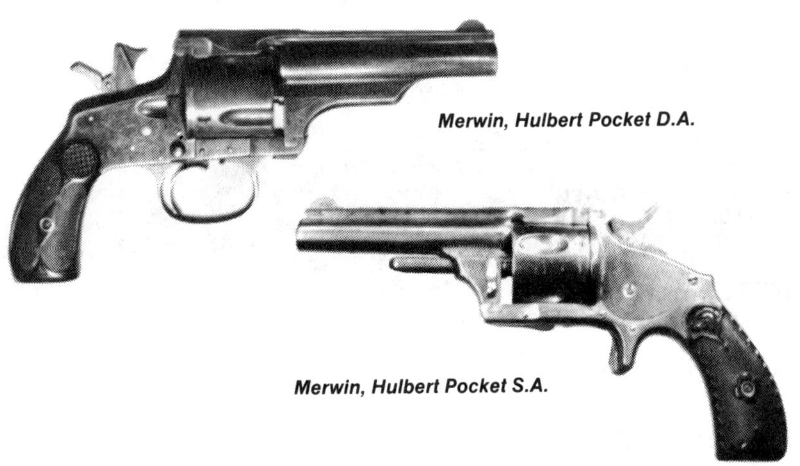
Merwin, Hulbert Pocket D.A.

Merwin, Hulbert Pocket S.A.

	V.G.	Exc.	Prior Year Exc. Value
☐ **Army Model**, .44-40 WCF, Pocket Pistol, 3½" Barrel, Single Action, Square-Butt, 6 Shot, *Antique*	390.00	565.00	525.00
☐ **Pocket Model**, .32 S & W, 5 Shot, Double Action, *Antique*	160.00	275.00	265.00
☐ **Target Model**, .32 S & W, 7 Shot, Double Action, *Antique*	195.00	325.00	300.00

MERVEILLEUX
Rouchouse, Paris, France.

HANDGUN, MANUAL REPEATER

☐ **Palm Pistol**, 6mm, Engraved, Nickel Plated, *Curio*	350.00	500.00	475.00

MESSERSMITH, JACOB
Lancaster, Pa. 1779-1782. See Kentucky Rifles & Pistols.

METEOR
Made by Stevens Arms.

RIFLE, BOLT ACTION

☐ **Model 52**, .22 L.R.R.F., Singleshot, Takedown, *Modern*	35.00	50.00	45.00

METROPOLITAN
Made by Crescent for Siegel Cooper Co., N.Y.C., c. 1900.

SHOTGUN, DOUBLE BARREL, SIDE-BY-SIDE

☐ **Various Gauges,** Outside Hammers, Damascus Barrel, *Modern*	100.00	170.00	175.00
☐ **Various Gauges,** Hammerless, Steel Barrel, *Modern*	135.00	190.00	200.00
☐ **Various Gauges,** Hammerless, Damascus Barrel, *Modern*	100.00	170.00	175.00

	V.G.	Exc.	Prior Year Exc. Value
SHOTGUN, SINGLESHOT			
☐ **Various Gauges**, Hammer, Steel Barrel, *Modern*	55.00	85.00	85.00

METROPOLITAN POLICE

Made by Norwich Falls Pistol Co. Norwich, Conn., c. 1885.

HANDGUN, REVOLVER

☐ **.32 Short R.F.**, 5 Shot, Spur Trigger, Solid Frame, Single Action, *Antique*	95.00	165.00	160.00

METZGER, J.

Lancaster, Pa., c. 1728. See Kentucky Rifles.

MEUHIRTER, S.

See Kentucky Rifles.

MEXICAN MILITARY

HANDGUN, SEMI-AUTOMATIC			
☐ **Obregon**, .45 ACP, Clip Fed, Military, *Modern*	250.00	375.00	350.00
RIFLE, BOLT ACTION			
☐ **M1902 Mauser**, 7mm, Military, *Modern*	125.00	180.00	175.00
☐ **M1936 Mauser**, 7mm, Military, *Modern*	145.00	195.00	195.00
RIFLE, SEMI-AUTOMATIC			
☐ **M1908 Mondragon**, 7mm, Clip Fed, S.I.G., *Curio*	495.00	800.00	775.00

MIDLAND

Imported from England by Jana International, c. 1973.

RIFLE, BOLT ACTION

☐ **Midland**, Various Calibers, Checkered Stock, Open Sights, *Modern*	175.00	265.00	250.00

MIIDA

Tradename of Marubeni America Corp. on Japanese shotguns.

SHOTGUN, DOUBLE BARREL, OVER-UNDER

☐ **Model 2100**, 12 Gauge, Skeet Grade, Checkered Stock, Engraved, Single Selective Trigger, Vent Rib, *Modern*	385.00	495.00	495.00
☐ **Model 2200 S**, 12 Gauge, Skeet Grade, Checkered Stock, Engraved, Single Selective Trigger, wide Vent Rib, *Modern*	445.00	585.00	575.00
☐ **Model 2200 T**, 12 Gauge, Trap Grade, Checkered Stock, Engraved, Single Selective Trigger, Wide Vent Rib, *Modern*	485.00	650.00	635.00
☐ **Model 2300 S**, 12 Gauge, Skeet Grade, Fancy Wood, Engraved, Single Selective Trigger, Vent Rib, *Modern*	485.00	650.00	635.00
☐ **Model 2300 T**, 12 Gauge, Trap Grade, Fancy Wood, Engraved, Single Selective Trigger, Vent Rib, *Modern*	520.00	700.00	685.00

	V.G.	Exc.	Prior Year Exc. Value
☐ **Model 612**, 12 Gauge, Field Grade, Checkered Stock, Light Engraving, Single Selective Trigger, Vent Rib, *Modern*	390.00	500.00	485.00
☐ **Model Grandee**, 12 Gauge, Fancy Engraving, Fancy Wood, Gold Inlays, Single Selective Trigger, Vent Rib, *Modern*	950.00	1,450.00	1,400.00

MIKROS

Tradename of Manufacture D'Armes Des Pyrenees, Heydaye, France, 1934-1939, 1958 to date.

HANDGUN, SEMI-AUTOMATIC

☐ **.25 ACP**, Clip Fed, Magazine Disconnect, *Modern*	125.00	170.00	165.00
☐ **.32 ACP**, Clip Fed, Magazine Disconncet, *Modern*	125.00	170.00	165.00
☐ **KE**, .22 Short R.F., Clip Fed, Hammer, Magazine Disconnect, 2" Barrel, *Modern*	90.00	140.00	135.00
☐ **KE**, .22 Short R.F., Clip Fed, Hammer, Magazine Disconnect, 4" Barrel, *Modern*	95.00	145.00	140.00
☐ **KE**, .22 Short R.F., Clip Fed, Hammer, Magazine Disconnect, 2" Barrel, Lightweight, *Modern*	85.00	130.00	125.00
☐ **KE**, .22 Short R.F., Clip Fed, Hammer, Magazine Disconnect, 4" Barrel, Lightweight, *Modern*	80.00	125.00	120.00
☐ **KN**, .25 ACP, Clip Fed, Hammer, Magazine Disconnect, 2" Barrel, *Modern*	85.00	125.00	120.00
☐ **KN**, .25 ACP, Clip Fed, Hammer, Magazine Disconnect, 2" Barrel, Lightweight, *Modern*	85.00	130.00	125.00

MILITARY

Retolaza Hermanos, Eibar, Spain, c. 1915.

HANDGUN, SEMI-AUTOMATIC

☐ **Model 1914**, .32 ACP, Clip Fed, *Modern*	95.00	145.00	135.00

MILLER, MATHIAS

Easton, Pa. 1771-1788. See Kentucky Rifles.

MILLS, BENJAMIN

Charlottesville, N.C. 1784-1790, 1790-1814 at Harrodsburg, Ky. See Kentucky Rifles, U.S. Military.

MINNEAPOLIS FIREARMS CO.

Minneapolis, Minn., c. 1883.

HANDGUN, PALM PISTOL

☐ **The Protector**, .32 Extra Short R.F., Nickel Plated, *Antique*	375.00	600.00	550.00

MIQUELET-LOCK, UNKNOWN MAKER

HANDGUN, MIQUELET-LOCK

☐ **.52 Arabian**, Holster Pistol, Tapered Round Barrel, Low Quality, *Antique*	245.00	350.00	325.00
☐ **.55**, Russian Cossack Type, Tapered Round Barrel, Steel Furniture, Silver Furniture, *Antique*	575.00	825.00	800.00

	V.G.	Exc.	Prior Year Exc. Value
☐ **Central Italian 1700's**, Holster Pistol, Brass Furniture, Brass Overlay Stock, Medium Quality, *Antique*	1,600.00	2,400.00	2,350.00
☐ **Pair Late 1700's**, Pocket Pistol, Medium Quality, Brass Furniture, Light Ornamentation, *Antique*	1,000.00	1,650.00	1,600.00
☐ **Pair Spanish Late 1600's**, Belt Hook, Brass Overlay Stock, High Quality, *Antique*	14,000.00	20,000.00	20,000.00
☐ **Pair Cominazzo Early 1700's**, Steel Inlay, Medium Quality, Holster Pistol, *Antique*	2,300.00	3,500.00	3,500.00
☐ **Ripoll Type Late 1600's**, Blunderbuss, Brass Inlay, *Antique*	3,500.00	4,350.00	4,250.00
☐ **Ripoll Type Late 1600's**, Blunderbuss, Silver Inlay, *Antique*	5,500.00	7,250.00	7,000.00
RIFLE, MIQUELET-LOCK			
☐ **Mid-Eastern**, Gold Inlays, Cannon Barrel, Front & Rear Bead Sights, Silver Overlay Stock, Silver Furniture, *Antique*	2,500.00	3,600.00	3,350.00
☐ **Mid-Eastern 1700's**, Damascus Barrel, Gold Inlays, Many Semi-Precious Gem Inlays, Silver Furniture, Ornate, *Antique*	4,200.00	7,000.00	6,500.00

MIROKU

Tokyo, Japan.

	V.G.	Exc.	Prior Year Exc. Value
HANDGUN, REVOLVER			
☐ **Model 6**, .38 Spec., Double Action, Swing-Out Cylinder, *Modern*	90.00	130.00	125.00
RIFLE, LEVER ACTION			
☐ **Center Fire**, Various Calibers, Checkered Stock, Clip Fed, *Modern*	150.00	235.00	220.00
☐ **.22 L.R.R.F.**, Tube Feed, Plain, *Modern*	150.00	240.00	225.00
RIFLE, SEMI-AUTOMATIC			
☐ **.22 L.R.R.F.**, Takedown, Tube Feed Through Butt, *Modern*	120.00	180.00	165.00

Miroku .22 Auto

Miroku Model 3800

Miroku .22 Lever Action

	V.G.	Exc.	Prior Year Exc. Value
RIFLE, SINGLESHOT			
☐ **Model 78**, Various Calibers, Checkered Stock, Falling Block, *Modern*	220.00	325.00	300.00
SHOTGUN, DOUBLE BARREL, OVER-UNDER			
☐ **Model 3800**, 12 Ga., Checkered Stock, Vent Rib, *Modern*	320.00	450.00	425.00
☐ **Model H.S.W. DeLuxe**, 12 Ga., Checkered Stock, Vent Rib, Engraved, *Modern*	660.00	925.00	900.00

MISSISSIPPI VALLEY ARMS CO.

Made by Crescent for Shapleigh Hardware, St. Louis, Mo.

	V.G.	Exc.	Prior Year Exc. Value
SHOTGUN, DOUBLE BARREL, SIDE-BY-SIDE			
☐ **Various Gauges**, Outside Hammers, Damascus Barrel, *Modern*	100.00	170.00	175.00
☐ **Various Gauges**, Hammerless, Steel Barrel, *Modern*	135.00	190.00	200.00
☐ **Various Gauges**, Hammerless, Damascus Barrel, *Modern*	100.00	170.00	175.00
☐ **Various Gauges**, Outside Hammers, Steel Barrel, *Modern*	125.00	185.00	190.00
SHOTGUN, SINGLESHOT			
☐ **Various Gauges**, Hammer, Steel Barrel, *Modern*	55.00	85.00	85.00

MITCHELL ARMS

	V.G.	Exc.	Prior Year Exc. Value
HANDGUN, DOUBLE BARREL, OVER-UNDER			
☐ **Derringer**, .357 Magnum, Spur Trigger, *Modern*	65.00	100.00	95.00
HANDGUN, REVOLVER			
☐ **Army Target**, Various Calibers, Single Action, Western Style, *Modern*	100.00	150.00	150.00

MITRAILLEUSE

Mre. de Armes et Cycles de St. Etienne, St. Etienne, France, c. 1893-1897.

	V.G.	Exc.	Prior Year Exc. Value
HANDGUN, PALM PISTOL			
☐ **Mitrailleuse**, 8mm, Engraved, Nickel Plated, *Antique*	375.00	525.00	475.00

MOHAWK

Made by Crescent for Blish, Mize & Stillman, c. 1900.

	V.G.	Exc.	Prior Year Exc. Value
SHOTGUN, DOUBLE BARREL, SIDE-BY-SIDE			
☐ **Various Gauges**, Outside Hammers, Damascus Barrel, *Modern*	100.00	170.00	175.00
☐ **Various Gauges**, Hammerless, Steel Barrel, *Modern*	135.00	190.00	200.00
☐ **Various Gauges**, Hammerless, Damascus Barrel, *Modern*	100.00	170.00	175.00
☐ **Various Gauges**, Outside Hammers, Steel Barrel, *Modern*	125.00	185.00	190.00
SHOTGUN, SINGLESHOT			
☐ **Various Gauges**, Hammer, Steel Barrel, *Modern*	55.00	85.00	85.00

MOLL, DAVID

Hellerstown, Pa. 1814-1833. See Kentucky Rifles.

	V.G.	Exc.	Prior Year Exc. Value

MOLL, JOHN
Hellerstown, Pa. 1770-1794. See Kentucky Rifles.

MOLL, JOHN III
Hellerstown, Pa. 1824-1863. See Kentucky Rifles.

MOLL, JOHN, JR.
Hellerstown, Pa. 1794-1824. See Kentucky Rifles.

MOLL, PETER
Hellerstown, Pa. 1804-1833 with Brother John Moll Jr. Made Some of the Finest Kentucky Rifles in Pa. See Kentucky Rifles.

MONARCH
Maker Unknown c. 1880

HANDGUN, REVOLVER

	V.G.	Exc.	Prior Year Exc. Value
☐ **.32 Short R.F.**, 5 Shot, Spur Trigger, Solid Frame, Single Action, *Antique*	95.00	165.00	160.00

MONARCH
Made by Hopkins & Allen, c. 1880.

HANDGUN, REVOLVER

	V.G.	Exc.	Prior Year Exc. Value
☐ **#1**, .22 Short R.F., 7 Shot, Spur Trigger, Solid Frame, Single Action, *Antique*	95.00	165.00	160.00
☐ **#2**, .32 Short R.F., 5 Shot, Spur Trigger, Solid Frame, Single Action, *Antique*	95.00	170.00	170.00
☐ **#3**, .38 Short R.F., 5 Shot, Spur Trigger, Solid Frame, Single Action, *Antique*	95.00	175.00	175.00
☐ **#4**, .41 Short R.F., 5 Shot, Spur Trigger, Solid Frame, Single Action, *Antique*	110.00	190.00	190.00

MONDIAL
Gaspar Arrizaga, Eibar, Spain.

HANDGUN, SEMI-AUTOMATIC

	V.G.	Exc.	Prior Year Exc. Value
☐ **Model 1**, .25 ACP, Clip Fed, Grip Safety, Magazine Disconnect, *Modern*	165.00	250.00	235.00
☐ **Model 2**, .25 ACP, Clip Fed, Blue, *Modern*	140.00	190.00	175.00

MONITOR
Made by Stevens Arms.

SHOTGUN, DOUBLE BARREL, SIDE-BY-SIDE

	V.G.	Exc.	Prior Year Exc. Value
☐ **Model 311**, Various Gauges, Hammerless, Steel Barrel, *Modern*	115.00	180.00	165.00

SHOTGUN, SINGLESHOT

	V.G.	Exc.	Prior Year Exc. Value
☐ **Model 90**, Various Gauges, Takedown, Automatic Ejector, Plain, Hammer, *Modern*	45.00	65.00	60.00

MOORE PATENT FIRE ARMS CO.
Brooklyn, N.Y. 1863-1883.

HANDGUN, SINGLESHOT

	V.G.	Exc.	Prior Year Exc. Value
☐ **.41 Short R.F.**, Derringer, Brass Frame, *Antique*	340.00	450.00	425.00

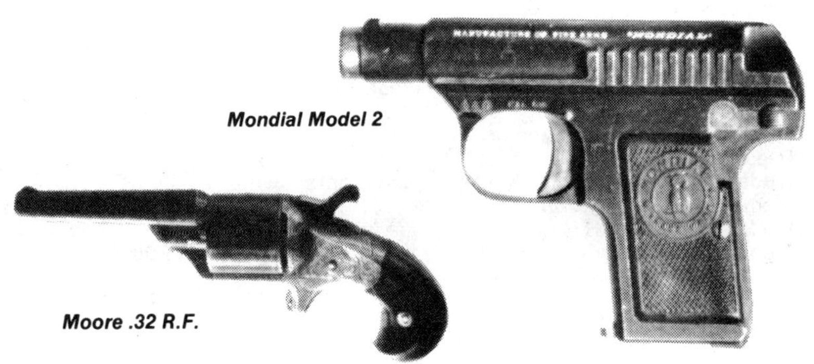

Mondial Model 2

Moore .32 R.F.

	V.G.	Exc.	Prior Year Exc. Value
HANDGUN, REVOLVER			
☐ **.32 T.F.**, Spur Trigger, Single Action, Brass Frame, No Extractor, *Antique*	185.00	290.00	275.00
☐ **.32 T.F.**, Spur Trigger, Single Action, Brass Frame, *Antique*	160.00	275.00	250.00
☐ **Williamson's Patent**, .32 T.F., Brass Frame, Hook Extractor, *Antique*	175.00	250.00	240.00

MORRONE

Rhode Island Arms Co., Hope Valley, R.I., c. 1951.

	V.G.	Exc.	Prior Year Exc. Value
SHOTGUN, DOUBLE BARREL, OVER-UNDER			
☐ **Model 46**, 12 Ga., Single Trigger, Plain Barrels, Checkered Stock, *Modern*	425.00	650.00	650.00
☐ **Model 46**, 20 Ga., Single Trigger, Vent Rib, Checkered Stock, *Modern*	675.00	950.00	950.00

MORTIMER, H.W. & SON

London, England 1800-1802.

	V.G.	Exc.	Prior Year Exc. Value
HANDGUN, FLINTLOCK			
☐ **.45**, 4 Barrel Duckfoot, Pocket Pistol, Steel Barrel and Frame, Plain, *Antique*	3,500.00	4,400.00	4,250.00

MOSSBERG, O.F. & SONS

New Haven, Conn. 1919 to date. Fitchburg & Chicopee Falls, Mass. 1892-1919 as Oscar F. Mossberg.

	V.G.	Exc.	Prior Year Exc. Value
HANDGUN, MANUAL REPEATER			
☐ **Brownie,** .22 L.R.R.F., Top Break, Double Action, Rotating Firing Pin, 4 Barrels, 4 Shot, *Modern*	160.00	245.00	235.00
HANDGUN, REVOLVER			
☐ **Abilene,** .357 Mag., Single Action, Western Style, Adjustable Sights, Various Barrel Lengths, *Modern*	150.00	220.00	210.00
☐ **Abilene,** .44 Mag., Single Action, Western Style, Adjustable Sights, Various Barrel Lengths, *Modern*	165.00	230.00	225.00
☐ **Abilene Silhouette,** .357 Mag., Single Action, Western Style, Adjustable Sights, 10″ Barrel, *Modern*	180.00	260.00	250.00

RIFLE, BOLT ACTION

	V.G.	Exc.	Prior Year Exc. Value
☐ **Model 10,** .22 L.R.R.F., Singleshot, Takedown, *Modern*	48.00	63.00	60.00
☐ **Model 14,** .22 L.R.R.F., Singleshot, Takedown, Peep Sights, *Modern*	53.00	68.00	65.00
☐ **Model 14OB,** .22 L.R.R.F., Clip Fed, Peep Sights, Monte Carlo Stock, *Modern*	53.00	80.00	75.00
☐ **Model 14OK,** .22 L.R.R.F., Clip Fed, Open Rear Sight, Monte Carlo Stock, *Modern*	48.00	75.00	70.00
☐ **Model 142A,** .22 L.R.R.F., Clip Fed, Peep Sights, *Modern*	58.00	85.00	80.00
☐ **Model 142A,** .22 L.R.R.F., Clip Fed, Carbine, Monte Carlo Stock, Peep Sights, *Modern*	53.00	85.00	80.00
☐ **Model 142K,** .22 L.R.R.F., Clip Fed, Open Rear Sight, *Modern*	58.00	85.00	80.00
☐ **Model 142K,** .22 L.R.R.F., Clip Fed, Carbine, Monte Carlo Stock, *Modern*	47.00	68.00	65.00
☐ **Model 144,** .22 L.R.R.F., Clip Fed, Heavy Barrel, Target Stock, Target Sights, *Modern*	85.00	125.00	120.00
☐ **Model 144LS,** .22 L.R.R.F., Clip Fed, Heavy Barrel, Lyman Sights, Target Stock, *Modern*	90.00	135.00	125.00
☐ **Model 146B,** .22 L.R.R.F., Takedown, Tube Feed, Monte Carlo Stock, Peep Sights, *Modern*	58.00	85.00	80.00
☐ **Model 20,** .22 L.R.R.F., Singleshot, Takedown, *Modern*	53.00	68.00	65.00
☐ **Model 25,** .22 L.R.R.F., Singleshot, Takedown, Peep Sights, *Modern*	53.00	68.00	65.00
☐ **Model 25A,** .22 L.R.R.F., Singleshot, Takedown, Peep Sights, *Modern*	53.00	75.00	70.00
☐ **Model 26B,** .22 L.R.R.F., Singleshot, Takedown, Peep Sights, *Modern*	42.00	63.00	60.00
☐ **Model 26C,** .22 L.R.R.F., Singleshot, Takedown, Open Rear Sight, *Modern*	42.00	60.00	55.00
☐ **Model 30,** .22 L.R.R.F., Singleshot, Takedown, Peep Sights, *Modern*	48.00	68.00	65.00
☐ **Model 32OB,** .22 L.R.R.F., Singleshot, Peep Sights, *Modern*	53.00	75.00	70.00
☐ **Model 320K,** .22 L.R.R.F., Singleshot, Open Rear Sight, Monte Carlo Stock, *Modern*	42.00	60.00	55.00
☐ **Model 321K,** .22 L.R.R.F., Singleshot, Open Rear Sight, *Modern*	33.00	53.00	50.00
☐ **Model 340B,** .22 L.R.R.F., Clip Fed, Peep Sights, *Modern*	58.00	80.00	75.00
☐ **Model 340K,** .22 L.R.R.F., Clip Fed, Open Rear Sight, *Modern*	47.00	68.00	65.00
☐ **Model 340M,** .22 L.R.R.F., Clip Fed, Full-Stocked, Carbine, *Modern*	63.00	90.00	85.00
☐ **Model 341,** .22 L.R.R.F., Clip Fed, Open Rear Sight, *Modern*	52.00	75.00	70.00
☐ **Model 342K,** .22 L.R.R.F., Clip Fed, Open Rear Sight, *Modern*	48.00	68.00	65.00
☐ **Model 346B,** .22 L.R.R.F., Tube Feed, Peep Sights, Monte Carlo Stock, *Modern*	58.00	85.00	80.00
☐ **Model 346K,** .22 L.R.R.F., Tube Feed, Monte Carlo Stock, Open Rear Sight, *Modern*	53.00	75.00	70.00

	V.G.	Exc.	Prior Year Exc. Value
☐ **Model 352K,** .22 L.R.R.F., Clip Fed, Monte Carlo Stock, Open Rear Sight, Carbine, *Modern*	58.00	85.00	80.00
☐ **Model 450,** .22 L.R.R.F., Tube Feed, Monte Carlo Stock, Checkered Stock, Open Rear Sight, *Modern*	58.00	90.00	85.00
☐ **Model 432,** .22 L.R.R.F., Tube Feed, Western Style, Carbine, *Modern*	58.00	85.00	80.00
☐ **Model 50,** .22 L.R.R.F., Takedown, Tube Feed, Open Rear Sight, *Modern*	58.00	85.00	80.00
☐ **Model 51,** .22 L.R.R.F., Takedown, Tube Feed, Peep Sight, *Modern*	63.00	90.00	85.00
☐ **Model 51M,** .22 L.R.R.F., Takedown, Tube Feed, Peep Sight, Full-Stocked, *Modern*	63.00	90.00	85.00
RIFLE, SINGLESHOT			
☐ **Model L,** .22 L.R.R.F., Lever Action, Falling Block, Takedown, *Modern*	165.00	225.00	220.00
RIFLE, SLIDE ACTION			
☐ **Model K,** .22 L.R.R.F., Takedown, Tube Feed, Hammerless, *Modern*	58.00	90.00	85.00
☐ **Model M,** .22 L.R.R.F., Takedown, Tube Feed, Hammerless, Octagon Barrel, *Modern*	80.00	120.00	110.00
RIFLE, LEVER ACTION			
☐ **Model 400,** .22 L.R.R.F., Tube Feed, Open Rear Sight, *Modern*	58.00	85.00	80.00
☐ **Model 402,** .22 L.R.R.F., Tube Feed, Open Rear Sight, Monte Carlo Stock, *Modern*	65.00	90.00	85.00
☐ **Model 472C,** Various Calibers, Straight Grip, Tube Feed, Open Rear Sight, Carbine, *Modern*	95.00	140.00	135.00
☐ **Model 472P,** Various Calibers, Pistol-Grip Stock, Tube Feed, Open Rear Sight, Carbine, *Modern*	90.00	135.00	130.00
☐ **RM-7,** Various Calibers, Open Sights, *Modern*	145.00	190.00	185.00
RIFLE, SEMI-AUTOMATIC			
☐ **Model 151K,** .22 L.R.R.F., Takedown, Tube Feed, Open Rear Sight, *Modern*	63.00	90.00	85.00
☐ **Model 151M,** .22 L.R.R.F., Takedown, Tube Feed, Peep Sights, Full-Stocked, *Modern*	70.00	90.00	85.00
☐ **Model 152,** .22 L.R.R.F., Clip Fed, Monte Carlo Stock, Peep Sights, Carbine, *Modern*	63.00	90.00	85.00
☐ **Model 152K,** .22 L.R.R.F., Clip Fed, Monte Carlo Stock, Open Rear Sight, Carbine, *Modern*	58.00	95.00	90.00
☐ **Model 350K,** .22 L.R.R.F., Clip Fed, Monte Carlo Stock, Open Rear Sight, *Modern*	53.00	90.00	80.00
☐ **Model 351C,** .22 L.R.R.F., Tube Feed, Monte Carlo Stock, Open Rear Sight, Carbine, *Modern*	58.00	90.00	80.00
☐ **Model 351K,** .22 L.R.R.F., Tube Feed, Monte Carlo Stock, Open Rear Sight, *Modern*	53.00	80.00	75.00

	V.G.	Exc.	Prior Year Exc. Value
☐ **Model 35,** .22 L.R.R.F., Singleshot, Target Stock, Target Sights, *Modern*	85.00	130.00	125.00
☐ **Model 35A,** .22 L.R.R.F., Singleshot, Target Stock, Target Sights, *Modern*	73.00	125.00	120.00
☐ **Model 35A-LS,** .22 L.R.R.F., Singleshot, Target Stock, Lyman Sights, *Modern*	85.00	130.00	125.00
☐ **Model 35B,** .22 L.R.R.F., Singleshot, Target Sights, Heavy Barrel, Target Stock, *Modern*	85.00	125.00	120.00
☐ **Model 40,** .22 L.R.R.F., Takedown, Tube Feed, Open Rear Sight, *Modern*	52.00	73.00	70.00
☐ **Model 42,** .22 L.R.R.F., Takedown, Clip Fed, Open Rear Sight, *Modern*	52.00	73.00	70.00
☐ **Model 42A,** .22 L.R.R.F., Takedown, Clip Fed, Peep Sights, *Modern*	52.00	73.00	70.00
☐ **Model 42B,** .22 L.R.R.F., Takedown, 5 Shot Clip, Peep Sights, *Modern*	52.00	73.00	70.00
☐ **Model 42C,** .22 L.R.R.F., Takedown, 5 Shot Clip, Open Rear Sight, *Modern*	47.00	73.00	70.00
☐ **Model 42M,** .22 L.R.R.F., Takedown, Clip Fed, Full-Stocked, Peep Sights, *Modern*	58.00	85.00	80.00
☐ **Model 42MB (British),** .22 L.R.R.F., Takedown, Clip Fed, Full-Stocked, Peep Sights, *Modern*	80.00	110.00	105.00
☐ **Model 43,** .22 L.R.R.F., Clip Fed, Heavy Barrel, Target Sights, Target Stock, *Modern*	80.00	115.00	110.00
☐ **Model 44,** .22 L.R.R.F., Takedown, Tube Feed, Open Rear Sight, *Modern*	58.00	80.00	75.00
☐ **Model 44 US,** .22 L.R.R.F., Clip Fed, Target Sights, Target Stock, Heavy Barrel, *Modern*	95.00	145.00	140.00
☐ **Model 448,** .22 L.R.R.F., Target Stock, Clip Fed, Target Sights, *Modern*	85.00	130.00	125.00
☐ **Model 45,** .22 L.R.R.F., Takedown, Tube Feed, Peep Sights, *Modern*	53.00	75.00	70.00
☐ **Model 45A,** .22 L.R.R.F., Takedown, Tube Feed, Peep Sights, *Modern*	58.00	75.00	70.00
☐ **Model 45AC,** .22 L.R.R.F., Takedown, Tube Feed, Open Rear Sight, *Modern*	58.00	75.00	70.00
☐ **Model 45B,** .22 L.R.R.F., Takedown, Tube Feed, Ope Rear Sight, *Modern*	58.00	80.00	75.00
☐ **Model 45B,** .22 L.R.R.F., Takedown, Tube Feed, Open Rear Sight, *Modern*	65.00	85.00	80.00
☐ **Model 45C,** .22 L.R.R.F., Takedown, Tube Feed, no Sights, *Modern*	58.00	80.00	75.00
☐ **Model 46,** .22 L.R.R.F., Takedown, Tube Feed, Peep Sights, *Modern*	70.00	95.00	90.00
☐ **Model 46A-LS,** .22 L.R.R.F., Takedown, Tube Feed, Lyman Sights, *Modern*	70.00	110.00	105.00
☐ **Model 46AC,** .22 L.R.R.F., Takedown, Tube Feed, Open Rear Sight, *Modern*	58.00	80.00	75.00
☐ **Model 46B,** .22 L.R.R.F., Takedown, Tube Feed, Peep Sights, *Modern*	58.00	80.00	75.00
☐ **Model 46M,** .22 L.R.R.F., Takedown, Tube Feed, Full-Stocked, Peep Sights, *Modern*	63.00	105.00	100.00
☐ **Model 46T,** .22 L.R.R.F., Takedown, Tube Feed, Heavy Barrel, Target Stock, Peep Sights, *Modern*	70.00	105.00	100.00

Mossberg Abilene, .357 Magnum

Mossberg Abilene, .44 Magnum

Mossberg 395 K, 12 Gauge

	V.G.	Exc.	Prior Year Exc. Value
☐ **Model 83D,** .410 Ga., Takedown, 3 Shot, *Modern*	48.00	68.00	65.00
☐ **Model 85D,** .20 Ga. Takedown, 3 Shot, Adjustable Choke, *Modern*	48.00	68.00	65.00

SHOTGUN, BOLT ACTION

	V.G.	Exc.	Prior Year Exc. Value
☐ **Model 173,** .410 Ga. Takedown, Singleshot, *Modern*	42.00	65.00	60.00
☐ **Model 173Y,** .410 Ga., Clip Fed, Singleshot, *Modern*	42.00	65.00	60.00
☐ **Model 183D,** .410 Ga., Takedown, 3 Shot, *Modern*	48.00	70.00	65.00
☐ **Model 183K,** .410 Ga., Takedown, Adjustable Choke, Clip Fed, *Modern*	48.00	70.00	65.00
☐ **Model 183T,** .410 Ga., Clip Fed, *Modern*	48.00	75.00	70.00
☐ **Model 185D,** 20 Ga., Takedown, 3 Shot, *Modern*	48.00	70.00	65.00
☐ **Model 185K,** 20 Ga., Takedown, 3 Shot, Adjustable Choke, *Modern*	48.00	70.00	65.00
☐ **Model 19OD,** 16 Ga., Takedown, Clip Fed, *Modern*	48.00	70.00	65.00
☐ **Model 19OK,** 16 Ga., Takedown, Adjustable Choke, Clip Fed, *Modern*	49.00	70.00	65.00
☐ **Model 195D,** 12 Ga., Takedown, Clip Fed, *Modern*	53.00	75.00	70.00
☐ **Model 195K,** 12 Ga., Takedown, Adjustable Choke, Clip Fed, *Modern*	53.00	75.00	70.00
☐ **Model 385K,** 20 Ga., Clip Fed, Adjustable Choke, *Modern*	58.00	80.00	75.00
☐ **Model 385T,** 20 Ga., Clip Fed, *Modern*	53.00	75.00	70.00
☐ **Model 39OK,** 16 Ga., Clip Fed, Adjustable Choke, *Modern*	58.00	80.00	75.00
☐ **Model 39OT,** 16 Ga., Clip Fed, *Modern*	53.00	75.00	70.00
☐ **Model 395K,** 12 Ga. Mag. 3″, Clip Fed, Adjustable Choke, *Modern*	58.00	80.00	75.00
☐ **Model 395S,** 12 Ga. Mag. 3″, Clip Fed, Open Rear Sight, *Modern*	53.00	80.00	75.00
☐ **Model 395T,** 12 Ga., Clip Fed, *Modern*	53.00	75.00	70.00
☐ **Model 73,** .410 Ga., Takedown, Singleshot, *Modern*	42.00	60.00	55.00
☐ **Model 64OK,** .22 WMR, 5 Shot Clip, Monte Carlo Stock, Open Rear Sight, *Modern*	68.00	90.00	85.00
☐ **Model 800,** Various Calibers, Open Rear Sight, Monte Carlo Stock, *Modern*	140.00	190.00	185.00
☐ **Model 800D,** Various Calibers, Monte Carlo Stock, Cheekpiece, Checkered Stock, Open Rear Sight, *Modern*	160.00	200.00	195.00
☐ **Model 800M,** Various Calibers, Open Rear Sight, Full-Stocked, *Modern*	155.00	200.00	195.00
☐ **Model 800SM,** Various Calibers, Scope Mounted, Monte Carlo Stock, *Modern*	170.00	230.00	225.00
☐ **Model 800V,** Various Calibers, no Sights, Monte Carlo Stock, Heavy Barrel, *Modern*	160.00	200.00	195.00
☐ **Model 810,** Various Calibers, Magnum Action, Open Rear Sight, Monte Carlo Stock, *Modern*	165.00	205.00	200.00
☐ **Model 810,** Various Calibers, Open Rear Sight, Long Action, Monte Carlo Stock, *Modern*	160.00	205.00	200.00
☐ **Model B,** .22 L.R.R.F., Singleshot, Takedown, *Modern*	32.00	52.00	50.00

	V.G.	Exc.	Prior Year Exc. Value
☐ **Model L42A,** .22 L.R.R.F., Takedown, Clip Fed, Peep Sights, Left-Hand, *Modern*	58.00	90.00	85.00
☐ **Model L43,** .22 L.R.R.F., Clip Fed, Heavy Barrel, Target Sights, Target Stock, Left-Hand, *Modern*	95.00	135.00	130.00
☐ **Model L45A,** .22 L.R.R.F., Takedown, Tube Feed, Peep Sights, *Modern*	65.00	90.00	85.00
☐ **Model L46A-LS,** .22 L.R.R.F., Takedown, Tube Feed, Lyman Sights, Left-Hand, *Modern*	75.00	125.00	120.00
☐ **Model R,** .22 L.R.R.F., Takedown, Tube Feed, Open Rear Sight, *Modern*	42.00	63.00	60.00
SHOTGUN, SLIDE ACTION			
☐ **Cruiser,** 12 Ga., One-Hand Grip, Nickel Plated, *Modern*	145.00	200.00	195.00
☐ **Model 200D,** 12 Ga., Clip Fed, Adjustable Choke, *Modern*	58.00	95.00	90.00
☐ **Model 200K,** 12 Ga., Clip Fed, Adjustable Choke, *Modern*	63.00	100.00	95.00
☐ **Model 500 Super,** Checkered Stock, Vent Rib, *Modern*	130.00	185.00	180.00
☐ **Model 500A,** 12 Ga. Mag. 3″, Field Grade, *Modern*	115.00	160.00	155.00
☐ **Model 500AA,** 12 Ga. Mag. 3″, Trap Grade, *Modern*	145.00	195.00	190.00
☐ **Model 500AK,** Field Grade, Adjustable Choke, *Modern*	120.00	165.00	160.00
☐ **Model 500AKR,** Field Grade, Adjustable Choke, Vent Rib, *Modern*	130.00	175.00	170.00
☐ **Model 500AM,** Field Grade, Magnum, *Modern*	115.00	155.00	150.00
☐ **Model 500AMR,** Field Grade, Magnum, Vent Rib, *Modern*	125.00	165.00	160.00
☐ **Model 500AR,** Field Grade, Vent Rib, *Modern*	125.00	160.00	155.00
☐ **Model 500AS,** Field Grade, Open Rear Sight, *Modern*	130.00	170.00	165.00
☐ **Model 500ATR,** Trap Grade, Vent Rib, *Modern*	135.00	190.00	185.00
☐ **Model 500AHTD,** Trap Grade, High Vent Rib, with Choke Tubes, *Modern*	235.00	315.00	300.00
☐ **Model 500B,** 16 Ga., Field Grade, *Modern*	105.00	160.00	150.00
☐ **Model 500BK,** 16 Ga., Adjustable Choke, *Modern*	105.00	150.00	145.00
☐ **Model 500BS,** 16 Ga., Open Rear Sight, *Modern*	115.00	155.00	150.00
☐ **Model 500C,** 20 Ga., Field Grade, *Modern*	105.00	155.00	150.00
☐ **Model 500CK,** 20 Ga., Field Grade, Adjustable Choke, *Modern*	115.00	160.00	155.00
☐ **Model 500CKR,** 20 Ga., Field Grade, Vent Rib, Adjustable Choke, *Modern*	115.00	165.00	160.00
☐ **Model 500CR,** 20 Ga., Field Grade, Vent Rib, *Modern*	115.00	160.00	155.00
☐ **Model 500CS,** 20 Ga., Field Grade, Open Rear Sight, *Modern*	115.00	160.00	155.00
☐ **Model 500E,** .410 Ga., Field Grade, *Modern*	105.00	150.00	145.00
☐ **Model 500EK,** .410 Ga., Field Grade, Adjustable Choke, *Modern*	115.00	155.00	150.00
☐ **Model 500EKR,** .410 Ga., Field Grade, Vent Rib, Adjustable Choke, *Modern*	120.00	175.00	165.00
☐ **Model 500ER,** .410 Ga., Field Grade, Vent Rib, *Modern*	115.00	165.00	155.00

MOSTER, GEO.

Lancaster, Pa. 1771-1779. See Kentucky Rifles and Pistols.

M.R.I. Eagle

M.R.I.

Magnum Research, Inc., Minneapolis, Minn. Also see Israeli Military.

	V.G.	Exc.	Prior Year Exc. Value
HANDGUN, SEMI-AUTOMATIC			
☐ **Eagle**, .357 Magnum, Clip Fed, Interchangeable Barrels, Gas Operated, Blue, *Modern*	385.00	495.00	—

M.S.

Modesto Santos, Eibar, Spain, c. 1920.

	V.G.	Exc.	Prior Year Exc. Value
HANDGUN, SEMI-AUTOMATIC			
☐ **Model 1920**, .25 ACP, Clip Fed, Blue, *Curio*	90.00	135.00	130.00
☐ **Action**, .32 ACP, Clip Fed, Blue, *Curio*	105.00	145.00	135.00

MT. VERNON ARMS

Belgium, c. 1900.

	V.G.	Exc.	Prior Year Exc. Value
SHOTGUN, DOUBLE BARREL, SIDE-BY-SIDE			
☐ **Various Gauges**, Outside Hammers, Damascus Barrel, *Modern*	100.00	170.00	175.00
☐ **Various Gauges**, Hammerless, Steel Barrel, *Modern*	135.00	190.00	200.00
☐ **Various Gauges**, Hammerless, Damascus Barrel, *Modern*	100.00	170.00	175.00
☐ **Various Gauges**, Outside Hammers, Steel Barrel, *Modern*	125.00	185.00	190.00
SHOTGUN, SINGLESHOT			
☐ **Various Gauges**, Hammer, Steel Barrel, *Modern*	55.00	85.00	85.00

MOUNTAIN EAGLE

Made by Hopkins & Allen, c. 1880.

	V.G.	Exc.	Prior Year Exc. Value
HANDGUN, REVOLVER			
☐ **.32 Short R.F.**, 5 Shot, Spur Trigger, Solid Frame, Single Action, *Antique*	95.00	165.00	160.00

	V.G.	Exc.	Prior Year Exc. Value

MUGICA

Jose Mugica, Eibar, Spain, tradename on Llama pistols. See Llama for equivilent models.

MUSGRAVE

South Africa.

RIFLE, BOLT ACTION

	V.G.	Exc.	Prior Year Exc. Value
☐ **Mk. III**, Various Calibers, Checkered Stock, *Modern*	170.00	240.00	225.00
☐ **Valiant NR6**, Various Calibers, Checkered Stock, *Modern*	165.00	215.00	200.00
☐ **Premier NR5**, Various Calibers, Checkered Stock, *Modern*	225.00	285.00	275.00

MUSKETEER

Tradename used by Firearms International, Washington, D.C., c. 1968.

RIFLE, BOLT ACTION

	V.G.	Exc.	Prior Year Exc. Value
☐ **Carbine**, Various Calibers, Monte Carlo Stock, Checkered Stock, Sling Swivels, *Modern*	165.00	230.00	225.00
☐ **Deluxe**, Various Calibers, Monte Carlo Stock, Checkered Stock, Sling Swivels, *Modern*	190.00	260.00	250.00
☐ **Sporter**, Various Calibers, Monte Carlo Stock, Checkered Stock, Sling Swivels, *Modern*	175.00	240.00	235.00
☐ **Mannlicher**, Various Calibers, Full Stock, *Modern*	160.00	245.00	240.00

MUTTI, GEROLIMO

Brescia, c. 1680.

HANDGUN, SNAPHAUNCE

	V.G.	Exc.	Prior Year Exc. Value
☐ **Pair**, Belt Pistol, Brass Mounts, Engraved, Ornate, *Antique*	8,650.00	15,450.00	15,000.00

MUTTI, GIESU

Brescia, c. 1790.

HANDGUN, SNAPHAUNCE

	V.G.	Exc.	Prior Year Exc. Value
☐ **Pair**, Engraved, Belt Hook, Medium Ornamentation, *Antique*	6,750.00	10,000.00	9,750.00

NAPOLEON

Made by Thomas Ryan, Jr., Pistol Mfg. Co., c. 1870-1876.

HANDGUN, REVOLVER

	V.G.	Exc.	Prior Year Exc. Value
☐ **.22 Short R.F.**, 7 Shot, Spur Trigger, Solid Frame, Single Action, *Antique*	95.00	165.00	160.00
☐ **.32 Short R.F.**, 5 Shot, Spur Trigger, Solid Frame, Single Action, *Antique*	95.00	170.00	170.00

NATIONAL

Made by Norwich Falls Pistol Co., c. 1880.

HANDGUN, REVOLVER

	V.G.	Exc.	Prior Year Exc. Value
☐ **.32 Short R.F.**, 5 Shot, Spur Trigger, Solid Frame, Single Action, *Antique*	95.00	165.00	160.00

	V.G.	Exc.	Prior Year Exc. Value
☐ **.38 Short R.F.**, 5 Shot, Spur Trigger, Solid Frame, Single Action, *Antique*	95.00	175.00	170.00

HANDGUN, SINGLESHOT

☐ **.41 Short R.F.**, Derringer, all Metal, Light Engraving, *Antique*	190.00	265.00	250.00

NATIONAL ARMS CO.

Made by Crescent, c. 1900.

SHOTGUN, DOUBLE BARREL, SIDE-BY-SIDE

☐ **Various Gauges**, Outside Hammers, Damascus Barrel, *Modern*	100.00	170.00	175.00
☐ **Various Gauges**, Hammerless, Steel Barrel, *Modern*	135.00	190.00	200.00
☐ **Various Gauges**, Hammerless, Damascus Barrel, *Modern*	100.00	170.00	175.00
☐ **Various Gauges**, Outside Hammers, Steel Barrel, *Modern*	125.00	185.00	190.00

SHOTGUN, SINGLESHOT

☐ **Various Gauges**, Hammer, Steel Barrel, *Modern*	55.00	85.00	85.00

NATIONAL ORDNANCE

South El Monte, Calif.

RIFLE, BOLT ACTION

☐ **1903A3**, .30-06 Springfield, Reweld, Military, *Modern*	90.00	135.00	125.00

RIFLE, SEMI-AUTOMATIC

☐ **Garand**, .30-06 Springfield, Reweld, Military, *Modern*	290.00	445.00	425.00
☐ **M-1 Carbine**, .30 Carbine, Clip Fed, Reweld, *Modern*	115.00	150.00	155.00
☐ **M-1 Carbine**, .30 Carbine, Clip Fed, Folding Stock, Reweld, *Modern*	125.00	160.00	165.00
☐ **Tanker Garand**, .308 Win., Reweld, Military, *Modern*	290.00	440.00	425.00

NAVY ARMS

Ridgefield, N.J.

- ☐ **Presentation Case Only,** *Add* **$15.00-$25.00**
- ☐ **A Engraving Pistol,** *Add* **$75.00-$115.00**
- ☐ **B Engraving Pistol,** *Add* **$95.00-$140.00**
- ☐ **C Engraving Pistol,** *Add* **$195.00-$265.00**
- ☐ **A Engraving Rifle,** *Add* **$95.00-$145.00**
- ☐ **B Engraving Rifle,** *Add* **$155.00-$215.00**
- ☐ **C Engraving Rifle,** *Add* **$365.00-$495.00**
- ☐ **Tiffany Grips Only,** *Add* **$95.00-$155.00**
- ☐ **Silver Plating,** *Add* **$65.00-$95.00**

HANDGUN, FLINTLOCK

☐ **.44 "Kentucky"**, Belt Pistol, Reproduction, Brass Furniture, *Antique*	67.00	95.00	90.00
☐ **.44 "Kentucky"**, Belt Pistol, Reproduction, Brass Furniture, Brass Barrel, *Antique*	67.00	95.00	90.00

	V.G.	Exc.	Prior Year Exc. Value
☐ **.577 Scotch Black Watch,** Military, Reproduction, Belt Pistol, all Metal, *Antique*	67.00	100.00	95.00
☐ **.69 M1763 Charleville,** Military, Reproduction, Belt Pistol, *Antique*	175.00	245.00	235.00
☐ **.69 M1763 Charleville,** Military, Reproduction, Belt Pistol, *Antique*	67.00	100.00	95.00
☐ **.69 M1777 Charleville,** Military, Reproduction, Belt Pistol, *Antique*	67.00	100.00	95.00
☐ **.69 Tower,** Military, Reproduction, Belt Pistol, *Antique*	32.00	48.00	45.00
HANDGUN, PERCUSSION			
☐ **.36 M1851 New Navy,** Revolver, Reproduction, Brass Grip Frame, *Antique*	67.00	95.00	90.00
☐ **.36 M1851 New Navy,** Revolver, Reproduction, Silver-Plated Grip Frame, *Antique*	67.00	95.00	90.00
☐ **.36 M1853,** Revolver, Reproduction, Pocket Pistol, 4½" Barrel, *Antique*	67.00	95.00	90.00
☐ **.36 M1853,** Revolver, Reproduction, Pocket Pistol, 5½" Barrel, *Antique*	67.00	95.00	90.00
☐ **.36 M1853,** Revolver, Reproduction, Pocket Pistol, 6½" Barrel, *Antique*	67.00	95.00	90.00
☐ **.36 M1860 Reb,** Revolver, Reproduction, Brass Frame, *Antique*	42.00	63.00	60.00
☐ **.36 M1860 Sheriff,** Revolver, Reproduction, Brass Frame, *Antique*	42.00	63.00	60.00
☐ **.36 M1861,** Revolver, Reproduction, Sheriff's Model, with Short Barrel, *Antique*	63.00	95.00	90.00
☐ **.36 M1861 Navy,** Revolver, Reproduction, Fluted Cylinder, *Antique*	63.00	95.00	90.00
☐ **.36 M1861 Navy,** Revolver, Reproduction, Engraved Cylinder, *Antique*	58.00	90.00	85.00
☐ **.36 M1862 Police,** Revolver, Reproduction, 5 Shot, Brass Grip Frame, Cased with Accessories, *Antique*	95.00	135.00	130.00
☐ **.36 M1862 Police,** Revolver, Reproduction, 5 Shot, Brass Grip Frame, 4½" Barrel, *Antique*	63.00	90.00	85.00
☐ **.36 M1862 Police,** Revolver, Reproduction, 5 Shot, Brass Grip Frame, 5½" Barrel, *Antique*	63.00	90.00	85.00
☐ **.36 M1862 Police,** Revolver, Reproduction, 5 Shot, Brass Grip Frame, 6½" Barrel, *Antique*	63.00	90.00	85.00
☐ **.36 M1862 Police,** Revolver, Reproduction, Fancy Engraving, Silver Plated, Gold Plated, *Antique*	375.00	490.00	470.00
☐ **.36 M1863,** Revolver, Reproduction, Sheriff's Model, with Short Barrel, *Antique*	67.00	95.00	90.00
☐ **.36 Remington,** Revolver, Reproduction, Target Pistol, Adjustable Sights, *Antique*	80.00	115.00	120.00
☐ **.36 Spiller & Burr,** Revolver, Reproduction, Solid Frame, *Antique*	53.00	75.00	70.00
☐ **.44 "Kentucky",** Belt Pistol, Reproduction, Brass Furniture, *Antique*	65.00	90.00	85.00
☐ **.44 "Kentucky",** Belt Pistol, Reproduction, Brass Furniture, Brass Barrel, *Antique*	75.00	105.00	100.00

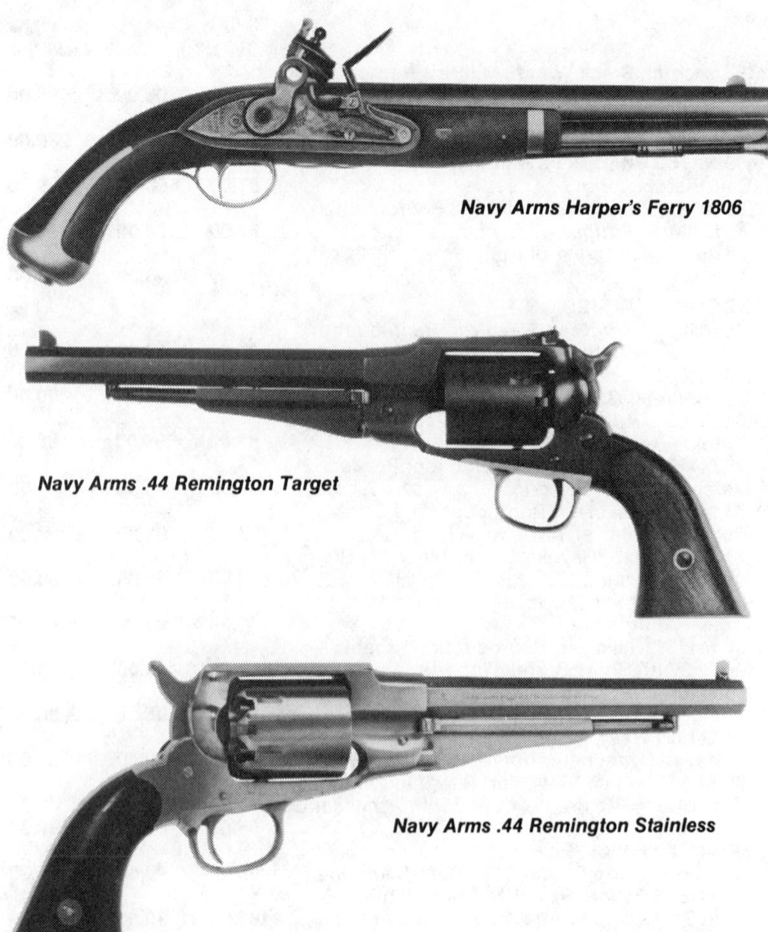
Navy Arms Harper's Ferry 1806

Navy Arms .44 Remington Target

Navy Arms .44 Remington Stainless

	V.G.	Exc.	Prior Year Exc. Value
☐ **.44 First Model Dragoon,** Revolver, Reproduction, Brass Grip Frame, *Antique*	75.00	115.00	110.00
☐ **.44 M1847 Walker,** Revolver, Reproduction, Brass Grip Frame, *Antique*	85.00	125.00	120.00
☐ **.44 M1847 Walker,** Revolver, Reproduction, Brass Grip Frame, Engraved, Gold Inlays, *Antique*	185.00	255.00	240.00
☐ **.44 M1860,** Revolver, Reproduction, Sheriff's Model, with Short Barrel, *Antique*	68.00	95.00	90.00
☐ **.44 M1860 Army,** Revolver, Reproduction, Fluted Cylinder, *Antique*	68.00	95.00	90.00
☐ **.44 M1860 Army,** Revolver, Reproduction, Engraved Cylinder, *Antique*	68.00	95.00	90.00
☐ **.44 M1860 Reb,** Revolver, Reproduction, Brass Frame, *Antique*	43.00	65.00	60.00

	V.G.	Exc.	Prior Year Exc. Value
☐ **.44 M1860 Reb,** Revolver, Reproduction, Shoulder Stock Only	32.00	48.00	45.00
☐ **.44 M1860 Sheriff,** Revolver, Reproduction, Brass Frame, *Antique*	43.00	63.00	60.00
☐ **.44 Remington,** Revolver, Reproduction, Target Pistol, Adjustable Sights, *Antique*	80.00	125.00	120.00
☐ **.44 Remington,** Revolver, Reproduction, Solid Frame, *Antique*	67.00	95.00	90.00
☐ **.44 Remington,** Revolver, Reproduction, Stainless Steel, *Antique*	100.00	145.00	140.00
☐ **.44 Remington Army,** Revolver, Reproduction, Nickel Plated, *Antique*	85.00	125.00	120.00
☐ **.44 Second Model,** Dragoon, Revolver, Reproduction, Brass Grip Frame, *Antique*	78.00	115.00	110.00
☐ **.44 Third Model Dragoon,** Revolver, Reproduction, Buntline, with Detachable Shoulder Stock, *Antique*	135.00	180.00	175.00
☐ **.44 Third Model Dragoon,** Revolver, Reproduction, Brass Grip Frame, *Antique*	85.00	125.00	120.00
☐ **.44 Third Model Dragoon,** Revolver, Reproduction, Brass Grip Frame, with Detachable Shoulder Stock, *Antique*	130.00	170.00	165.00
☐ **.58 M1806,** Harper's Ferry, Reproduction, Brass Furniture, Military, Belt Pistol, *Antique*	65.00	90.00	85.00
☐ **.58 M1855,** Harper's Ferry, Reproduction, Holster Pistol, Military, with Detachable Shoulder Stock, *Antique*	90.00	130.00	125.00
☐ **.58 M1855,** Harper's Ferry, Shoulder Stock Only	27.00	43.00	40.00
HANDGUN, REVOLVER			
☐ **Frontier,** Various Calibers, Color Case Hardened Frame, Single Action, Western Style, *Modern*	115.00	155.00	150.00
☐ **Frontier Target,** .357 Magnum, Color Case Hardened Frame, Single Action, Western Style, Adjustable Sights, with Detachable Shoulder Stock, *Modern*	150.00	210.00	200.00
☐ **Frontier Target,** .45 Colt, Color Case Hardened Frame, Single Action, Western Style, Adjustable Sights, with Detachable Shoulder Stock, *Modern*	155.00	200.00	195.00
☐ **Frontier Target,** Various Calibers, Color Case Hardened Frame, Single Action, Western Style, Adjustable Sights, *Modern*	115.00	155.00	150.00
☐ **M1875 Remington,** .357 Magnum, Color Case Hardened Frame, Western Style, Single Action, *Modern*	120.00	160.00	155.00
☐ **M1875 Remington,** .357 Magnum, Nickel Plated, Western Style, Single Action, *Modern*	135.00	185.00	180.00
☐ **M1875 Remington,** .44-40 WCF, Color Case Hardened Frame, Western Style, Single Action, *Modern*	115.00	160.00	155.00
☐ **M1875 Remington,** .44-40 WCF, Nickel Plated, Western Style, Single Action, *Modern*	135.00	165.00	160.00
☐ **M1875 Remington,** .45 Colt, Color Case Hardened Frame, Western Style, Single Action, *Modern*	125.00	165.00	160.00

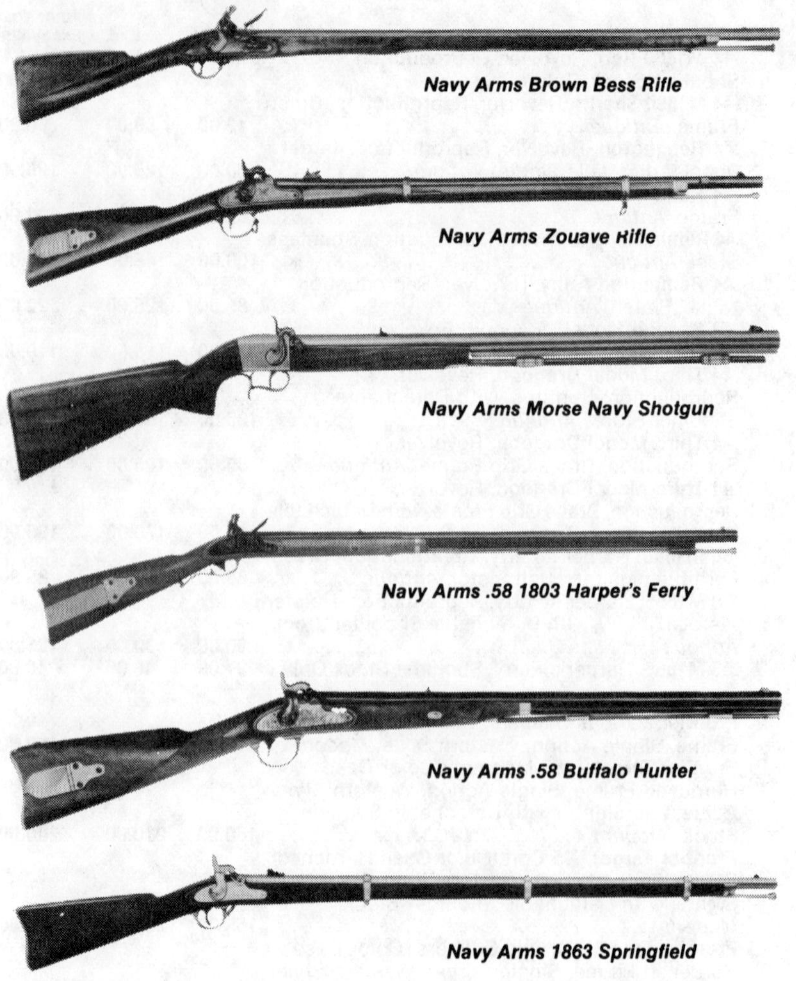

Navy Arms Brown Bess Rifle

Navy Arms Zouave Rifle

Navy Arms Morse Navy Shotgun

Navy Arms .58 1803 Harper's Ferry

Navy Arms .58 Buffalo Hunter

Navy Arms 1863 Springfield

	V.G.	Exc.	Prior Year Exc. Value
☐ **M1875 Remington,** .45 Colt, Stainless Steel, Western Style, Single Action, *Modern*	140.00	180.00	175.00
☐ **M1875 Remington,** .45 Colt, Nickel Plated, Western Style, Single Action, *Modern*	140.00	185.00	180.00
HANDGUN, SINGLESHOT			
☐ **Rolling Block,** .22 Hornet, Half-Octagon Barrel, Color Case Hardened Frame, Adjustable Sights, *Modern*	90.00	135.00	130.00
☐ **Rolling Block,** .22 L.R.R.F., Half-Octagon Barrel, Color Case Hardened Frame, Adjustable Sights, *Modern*	75.00	105.00	100.00
☐ **Rolling Block,** .357 Magnum, Half-Octagon Barrel, Color Case Hardened Frame, Adjustable Sights, *Modern*	90.00	130.00	125.00
RIFLE, BOLT ACTION			
☐ **Mauser '98,** .45-70 Government, Checkered Stock, *Modern*	100.00	145.00	140.00
☐ **Mauser '98,** .45-70 Government, Carbine, Checkered Stock, *Modern*	100.00	145.00	140.00
RIFLE, FLINTLOCK			
☐ **.45 "Kentucky",** Long Rifle, Reproduction, Brass Furniture, *Antique*	125.00	170.00	165.00
☐ **.45 "Kentucky",** Carbine, Reproduction, Brass Furniture, *Antique*	125.00	170.00	165.00
☐ **.58 M1803,** Harper's Ferry, Reproduction, Brass Furniture, Military, *Antique*	130.00	180.00	175.00
☐ **.69 M1795 Springfield,** Modern, Reproduction, Musket, *Antique*	175.00	240.00	235.00
☐ **.69 M1809 Springfield,** Modern, Reproduction, Musket, *Antique*	175.00	240.00	235.00
☐ **.75 Brown Bess,** Modern, Reproduction, Musket, *Antique*	200.00	275.00	250.00
☐ **.75 Brown Bess,** Modern, Reproduction, Carbine, *Antique*	200.00	275.00	250.00
☐ **.75 Brown Bess (Jap),** Modern, Reproduction, Musket, *Antique*	155.00	200.00	190.00
RIFLE, LEVER ACTION			
☐ **M1873 1 of 1000,** .44-40 WCF, Blue Tube, Octagon Barrel, Steel Buttplate, Engraved, *Modern*	515.00	725.00	700.00
☐ **M1873-"101",** .22 L.R.R.F., Color Case Hardened Frame, Tube Feed, Round Barrel, Steel Buttplate, Carbine, *Modern*	150.00	210.00	200.00
☐ **M1873-"101",** .44-40 WCF, Color Case Hardened Frame, Tube Feed, Octagon Barrel, Steel Buttplate, *Modern*	170.00	235.00	225.00
☐ **M1873-"101",** .44-40 WCF, Color Case Hardened Frame, Tube Feed, Round Barrel, Steel Buttplate, Carbine, *Modern*	150.00	210.00	200.00
☐ **M1873-"101",** Trapper, .22 L.R.R.F., Color Case Hardened Frame, Tube Feed, Round Barrel, Steel Buttplate, *Modern*	150.00	210.00	200.00

	V.G.	Exc.	Prior Year Exc. Value
☐ **M1873-"101",** Trapper, .44-40 WCF, Color Case Hardened Frame, Tube Feed, Round Barrel, Steel Buttplate, *Modern*	150.00	210.00	200.00
☐ **Yellowboy,** .22 L.R.R.F., Brass Frame, Tube Feed, Round Barrel, Brass Buttplate, Saddle-Ring Carbine, *Modern*	145.00	200.00	190.00
☐ **Yellowboy,** .38 Special, Brass Frame, Tube Feed, Octagon Barrel, Brass Buttplate, *Modern*	150.00	210.00	200.00
☐ **Yellowboy,** .38 Special, Brass Frame, Tube Feed, Round Barrel, Brass Buttplate, Saddle-Ring Carbine, *Modern*	145.00	200.00	190.00
☐ **Yellowboy,** .44-40 WCF, Brass Frame, Tube Feed, Octagon Barrel, Brass Buttplate, *Modern*	150.00	210.00	200.00
☐ **Yellowboy,** .44-40 WCF, Brass Frame, Tube Feed, Round Barrel, Brass Buttplate, Saddle-Ring Carbine, *Modern*	145.00	200.00	190.00
☐ **Yellowboy Trapper,** .22 L.R.R.F., Brass Frame, Tube Feed, Round Barrel, Brass Buttplate, *Modern*	145.00	200.00	190.00
☐ **Yellowboy Trapper,** .38 Special, Brass Frame, Tube Feed, Round Barrel, Brass Buttplate, *Modern*	145.00	200.00	190.00
☐ **Yellowboy Trapper,** .44-40 WCF, Brass Frame, Tube Feed, Round Barrel, Brass Buttplate, *Modern*	145.00	200.00	190.00
RIFLE, PERCUSSION			
☐ **.44 Remington,** Revolver, Reproduction, Carbine, Brass Furniture, *Antique*	110.00	145.00	140.00
☐ **.45 "Kentucky",** Long Rifle, Reproduction, Brass Furniture, *Antique*	115.00	160.00	155.00
☐ **.45 "Kentucky",** Carbine, Reproduction, Brass Furniture, *Antique*	115.00	155.00	150.00
☐ **.45 "Kentucky",** Carbine, Reproduction, Brass Furniture, *Antique*	115.00	160.00	155.00
☐ **.45 Hawken Hurricane,** Octagon Barrel, Brass Furniture, Reproduction, *Antique*	135.00	175.00	170.00
☐ **.45 Morse,** Octagon Barrel, Brass Frame, Reproduction, *Antique*	85.00	120.00	115.00
☐ **.50 Hawken Hurricane,** Octagon Barrel, Brass Furniture, Reproduction, *Antique*	140.00	180.00	175.00
☐ **.50 Morse,** Octagon Barrel, Brass Frame, Reproduction, *Antique*	85.00	125.00	120.00
☐ **.54 Gallagher,** Carbine, Reproduction, Military, Steel Furniture, *Antique*	145.00	195.00	190.00
☐ **.577 M1853 3-Band,** Military, Reproduction, Musket, (Parker-Hale) *Antique*	190.00	250.00	245.00
☐ **.577 M1858 2-Band,** Military, Reproduction, Rifled, (Parker-Hale) *Antique*	140.00	190.00	185.00
☐ **.577 M1861,** Military, Reproduction, Musketoon, (Parker-Hale) *Antique*	140.00	190.00	185.00
☐ **.58 J.P. Murray Artillery Carbine,** Reproduction, Brass Furniture, Military, *Antique*	100.00	145.00	140.00
☐ **.58 Buffalo Hunter,** Round Barrel, Brass Furniture, Reproduction, *Antique*	115.00	160.00	155.00

	V.G.	Exc.	Prior Year Exc. Value
☐ **.58 Hawken Hunter,** Octagon Barrel, Brass Furniture, Reproduction, *Antique*	**135.00**	**180.00**	**175.00**
☐ **.58 M1841 Mississippi Rifle,** Reproduction, Brass Furniture, Military, *Antique*	**110.00**	**155.00**	**150.00**
☐ **.58 M1863 Springfield,** Military, Reproduction, Rifled, Musket, *Antique*	**130.00**	**175.00**	**170.00**
☐ **.58 M1864 Springfield,** Military, Reproduction, Rifled, Musket, *Antique*	**145.00**	**180.00**	**175.00**
☐ **.58 Morse,** Octagon Barrel, Brass Frame, Reproduction, *Antique*	**90.00**	**130.00**	**125.00**
☐ **.58 Zouave,** Military, Reproduction, *Antique*	**105.00**	**150.00**	**145.00**
☐ **.58 Zouave 1864,** Military, Reproduction, Carbine, Brass Furniture, *Antique*	**105.00**	**150.00**	**145.00**
RIFLE, REVOLVER			
☐ **M1875 Remington,** .357 Magnum, Color Case Hardened Frame, Carbine, Single Action, Brass Furniture, *Modern*	**150.00**	**190.00**	**185.00**
☐ **M1875 Remington,** .44-40 WCF, Color Case Hardened Frame, Carbine, Single Action, Brass Furniture, *Modern*	**150.00**	**190.00**	**185.00**
☐ **M1875 Remington,** .45 Colt, Color Case Hardened Frame, Carbine, Single Action, Brass Furniture, *Modern*	**150.00**	**190.00**	**185.00**
RIFLE, SEMI-AUTOMATIC			
☐ **AP-74,** .22 L.R.R.F., Clip Fed, Plastic Stock, *Modern*	**63.00**	**95.00**	**90.00**
☐ **AP-74,** .22 L.R.R.F., Clip Fed, Wood Stock, *Modern*	**75.00**	**105.00**	**100.00**
☐ **AP-74,** .32 ACP, Clip Fed, Plastic Stock, *Modern*	**75.00**	**105.00**	**100.00**
☐ **AP-74 Commando,** .22 L.R.R.F., Clip Fed, Wood Stock, *Modern*	**75.00**	**105.00**	**100.00**
RIFLE, SINGLESHOT			
☐ **Buffalo,** .45-70 Government, Rolling Block, Color Case Hardened Frame, Octagon Barrel, Open Rear Sight, Various Barrel Lengths, *Modern*	**130.00**	**160.00**	**155.00**
☐ **Buffalo,** .45-70 Government, Rolling Block, Color Case Hardened Frame, Half-Octagon Barrel, Open Rear Sight, Various Barrel Lengths, *Modern*	**120.00**	**155.00**	**150.00**
☐ **Buffalo,** .50 U.S. Carbine, Rolling Block, Color Case Hardened Frame, Octagon Barrel, Open Rear Sight, Various Barrel Lengths, *Modern*	**115.00**	**150.00**	**145.00**
☐ **Buffalo,** .50 U.S. Carbine, Rolling Block, Color Case Hardened Frame, Half-Octagon Barrel, Open Rear Sight, Various Barrel Lengths, *Modern*	**110.00**	**145.00**	**140.00**
☐ **Creedmore,** .45-70 Government, Rolling Block, Color Case Hardened Frame, Octagon Barrel, Vernier Sights, 30″ Barrel, *Modern*	**150.00**	**220.00**	**210.00**
☐ **Creedmore,** .45-70 Government, Rolling Block, Color Case Hardened Frame, Half-Octagon Barrel, Vernier Sights, 30″ Barrel, *Modern*	**150.00**	**205.00**	**195.00**
☐ **Creedmore,** .50 U.S. Carbine, Rolling Block, Color Case Hardened Frame, Octagon Barrel, Vernier Sights, 30″ Barrel, *Modern*	**150.00**	**200.00**	**190.00**

	V.G.	Exc.	Prior Year Exc. Value
☐ **Creedmore,** .50 U.S. Carbine, Rolling Block, Color Case Hardened Frame, Half-Octagon Barrel, Vernier Sights, 30″ Barrel, *Modern*	150.00	195.00	190.00
☐ **Creedmore,** .50-140 Sharps, Rolling Block, Color Case Hardened Frame, Octagon Barrel, Vernier Sights, 30″ Barrel, *Modern*	150.00	200.00	195.00
☐ **Martini,** .45-70 Government, Color Case Hardened Frame, Half-Octagon Barrel, Open Rear Sight, Checkered Stock, *Modern*	185.00	250.00	240.00
☐ **Martini,** .45-70 Government, Color Case Hardened Frame, Octagon Barrel, Open Rear Sight, Checkered Stock, *Modern*	180.00	240.00	235.00
☐ **Rolling Block,** .22 Hornet, Carbine, Color Case Hardened Frame, Adjustable Sights, *Modern*	115.00	150.00	145.00
☐ **Rolling Block,** .22 L.R.R.F., Carbine, Color Case Hardened Frame, Adjustable Sights, *Modern*	100.00	145.00	135.00
☐ **Rolling Block,** .357 Magnum, Carbine, Color Case Hardened Frame, Adjustable Sights, *Modern*	105.00	145.00	140.00
SHOTGUN, PERCUSSION			
☐ **Magnum Deluxe,** 12 Ga., Double Barrel, Side by Side, Reproduction, Outside Hammers, Checkered Stock, *Antique*	155.00	195.00	190.00
☐ **Morse/Navy,** 12 Ga., Singleshot, Reproduction, Brass Frame, *Antique*	90.00	135.00	130.00
☐ **Upland Deluxe,** .12 Ga., Double Barrel, Side by Side, Reproduction, Outside Hammers, Checkered Stock, *Antique*	90.00	135.00	130.00
☐ **Zouave,** 12 Ga., Brass Furniture, Reproduction, *Antique*	95.00	140.00	135.00

NEIHARD, PETER

Northhampton, Pa. 1785-1787. See Kentucky Rifles.

NERO

Made by J. Rupertus Arms Co., c. 1880. Sold by E. Tryon Co.

HANDGUN, REVOLVER			
☐ **.22 Short R.F., 7 Shot, Spur Trigger, Solid Frame, Single Action,** *Antique*	95.00	170.00	160.00
☐ **.32 Short R.F., 5 Shot, Spur Trigger, Solid Frame, Single Action,** *Antique*	95.00	175.00	170.00

NERO

Made by Hopkins & Allen., c. 1880. Sold by C.L. Riker.

HANDGUN, REVOLVER			
☐ **.22 Short R.F., 7 Shot, Spur Trigger, Solid Frame, Single Action,** *Antique*	95.00	165.00	160.00
☐ **.32 Short R.F., 5 Shot, Spur Trigger, Solid Frame, Single Action,** *Antique*	95.00	170.00	170.00

NEW CHIEFTAIN

Made by Stevens Arms.

	V.G.	Exc.	Prior Year Exc. Value
SHOTGUN, SINGLESHOT			
☐ **Model 94**, Various Gauges, Takedown, Automatic Ejector, Plain, Hammer, *Modern*	40.00	65.00	60.00

NEW NAMBU

Shin Chuo Kogyo, Tokyo, Japan, c. 1960.

	V.G.	Exc.	Prior Year Exc. Value
HANDGUN, REVOLVER			
☐ **Model 58**, .38 Spec., Swing-Out Cylinder, Double Action, *Modern*	70.00	120.00	115.00
HANDGUN, SEMI-AUTOMATIC			
☐ **Model 57A**, 9mm Luger, Clip Fed, Blue, *Modern*	145.00	210.00	195.00
☐ **Model 57B**, .32 ACP, Clip Fed, Blue, *Modern*	135.00	185.00	175.00

NEW RIVAL

Made by Crescent for Van Camp Hardwore & Iron Co., Indianapolis, Ind.

	V.G.	Exc.	Prior Year Exc. Value
SHOTGUN, DOUBLE BARREL, SIDE-BY-SIDE			
☐ **Various Gauges**, Outside Hammers, Damascus Barrel, *Modern*	100.00	170.00	175.00
☐ **Various Gauges**, Hammerless, Steel Barrel, *Modern*	135.00	190.00	200.00
☐ **Various Gauges**, Hammerless, Damascus Barrel, *Modern*	100.00	170.00	175.00
☐ **Various Gauges**, Outside Hammers, Steel Barrel, *Modern*	125.00	185.00	190.00
SHOTGUN, SINGLESHOT			
☐ **Various Gauges**, Hammer, Steel Barrel, *Modern*	55.00	85.00	85.00

NEW YORK ARMS CO.

Made by Crescent for Garnet Carter Co. Tenn., c. 1900.

	V.G.	Exc.	Prior Year Exc. Value
SHOTGUN, DOUBLE BARREL, SIDE-BY-SIDE			
☐ **Various Gauges**, Outside Hammers, Damascus Barrel, *Modern*	100.00	170.00	175.00
☐ **Various Gauges**, Hammerless, Steel Barrel, *Modern*	135.00	190.00	200.00
☐ **Various Gauges**, Hammerless, Damascus Barrel, *Modern*	100.00	170.00	175.00
☐ **Various Gauges**, Outside Hammers, Steel Barrel, *Modern*	125.00	185.00	190.00
SHOTGUN, SINGLESHOT			
☐ **Various Gauges**, Hammer, Steel Barrel, *Modern*	55.00	85.00	85.00

NEW YORK PISTOL CO.

N.Y.C., c. 1870.

	V.G.	Exc.	Prior Year Exc. Value
HANDGUN, REVOLVER			
☐ **.22 Short R.F.**, 7 Shot, Spur Trigger, Solid Frame, Single Action, *Antique*	95.00	165.00	160.00
☐ **.32 Short R.F.**, 5 Shot, Spur Trigger, Solid Frame, Single Action, *Antique*	95.00	170.00	165.00

NEWCOMER, JOHN

Lancaster, Pa. 1770-1772. See Kentucky Rifles.

	V.G.	Exc.	Prior Year Exc. Value

NEWHARDT, JACOB
Allentown, Pa. 1770-1777. See Kentucky Rifles.

NEWPORT
Made by Stevens Arms.

SHOTGUN, DOUBLE BARREL, SIDE-BY-SIDE

	V.G.	Exc.	Prior Year Exc. Value
☐ **Model 311**, Various Gauges, Hammerless, Steel Barrel, *Modern*	110.00	180.00	165.00

NEWTON ARMS CO.
Buffalo, N.Y. 1914-1918, reorganized 1918-1930 as Newton Rifle Corp.

RIFLE, BOLT ACTION

	V.G.	Exc.	Prior Year Exc. Value
☐ **1st Type**, Various Calibers, Sporting Rifle, Set Trigger, Checkered Stock, Open Rear Sight, *Modern*	445.00	595.00	575.00
☐ **2nd Type**, Various Calibers, Sporting Rifle, Set Trigger, Checkered Stock, Open Rear Sight, *Modern*	465.00	650.00	625.00
☐ **Newton-Mauser**, Various Calibers, Sporting Rifle, Set Trigger, Checkered Stock, Open Rear Sight, *Modern*	345.00	500.00	475.00

NICHOLS, JOHN
Oxford, England 1730-1775.

HANDGUN, FLINTLOCK

	V.G.	Exc.	Prior Year Exc. Value
☐ **Holster Pistol**, Engraved, Brass Furniture, High Quality, *Antique*	2,550.00	3,500.00	3,450.00

NIKKO SPORTING FIREARMS
Japan Imported by Kanematsu-Gosho U.S.A. Inc., Arlington Heights, Ill.

RIFLE, BOLT ACTION

	V.G.	Exc.	Prior Year Exc. Value
☐ **Model 7000**, Various Calibers, Grade 1, Checkered Stock, *Modern*	200.00	300.00	300.00
☐ **Model 7000**, Various African Calibers, Grade 1, Checkered Stock, *Modern*	225.00	350.00	350.00

SHOTGUN, DOUBLE BARREL, OVER-UNDER

	V.G.	Exc.	Prior Year Exc. Value
☐ **Model 5000**, 12 and 20 Gauges, Field Grade, Vent Rib, Checkered Stock, Light Engraving, Gold Overlay, *Modern*	325.00	465.00	450.00
☐ **Model 5000**, 12 and 20 Gauges, Skeet Grade, Vent Rib, Checkered Stock, Light Engraving, Gold Overlay, *Modern*	400.00	560.00	550.00
☐ **Model 5000**, 12 and 20 Gauges, Trap Grade, Vent Rib, Checkered Stock, Light Engraving, Gold Overlay, *Modern*	400.00	560.00	550.00

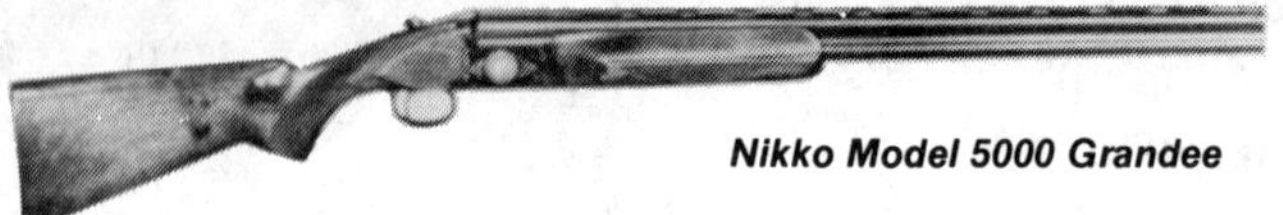

Nikko Model 5000 Grandee

	V.G.	Exc.	Prior Year Exc. Value
☐ **Model 5000**, 12 and 20 Gauges, Field Grade 2, Vent Rib, Checkered Stock, Light Engraving, Gold Overlay, *Modern*	425.00	560.00	550.00
☐ **Model 5000**, 12 and 20 Gauges, Skeet Grade 2, Vent Rib, Checkered Stock, Light Engraving, Gold Overlay, *Modern*	475.00	600.00	600.00
☐ **Model 5000**, 12 and 20 Gauges, Trap Grade 2, Vent Rib, Checkered Stock, Light Engraving, Gold Overlay, *Modern*	475.00	600.00	600.00
☐ **Model 5000 Grandee**, 12 and 20 Gauges, Field Grade 3, Vent Rib, Checkered Stock, Fancy Engraving, Gold Overlay, *Modern*	1,250.00	2,000.00	2,000.00
☐ **Model 5000 Grandee**, 12 and 20 Gauges, Skeet Grade 3, Vent Rib, Checkered Stock, Fancy Engraving, Gold Overlay, *Modern*	1,250.00	2,000.00	2,000.00
☐ **Model 5000 Grandee**, 12 Ga., Trap Grade 3, Vent Rib, Checkered Stock, Fancy Engraving, Gold Overlay, *Modern*	1,250.00	2,000.00	2,000.00

NITRO PROOF

Made by Stevens Arms.

SHOTGUN, SINGLESHOT

	V.G.	Exc.	Prior Year Exc. Value
☐ **Model 115**, Various Gauges, Hammer, Automatic Ejector, *Modern*	45.00	65.00	60.00

NIVA

Kohout & Spolecnost, Kydne, Czechoslovakia.

HANDGUN, SEMI-AUTOMATIC

	V.G.	Exc.	Prior Year Exc. Value
☐ **Niva**, .25 ACP, Clip Fed, Blue, *Modern*	135.00	200.00	185.00

NOBLE

Haydenville, Mass.1950-1971.

RIFLE, BOLT ACTION

	V.G.	Exc.	Prior Year Exc. Value
☐ **98 Mauser**, .30-06 Springfield, Monte Carlo Stock, Open Rear Sight, *Modern*	95.00	145.00	135.00
☐ **Model 10**, .22 L.R.R.F., Singleshot, *Modern*	25.00	45.00	40.00
☐ **Model 20**, .22 L.R.R.F., Singleshot, *Modern*	25.00	45.00	40.00
☐ **Model 222**, .22 L.R.R.F., Singleshot, *Modern*	45.00	55.00	50.00

RIFLE, LEVER ACTION

	V.G.	Exc.	Prior Year Exc. Value
☐ **Model 275**, .22 L.R.R.F., Tube Fed, *Modern*	50.00	80.00	75.00

RIFLE, SEMI-AUTOMATIC

	V.G.	Exc.	Prior Year Exc. Value
☐ **Model 285**, .22 L.R.R.F., Tube Fed, *Modern*	55.00	85.00	80.00

RIFLE, SLIDE ACTION

	V.G.	Exc.	Prior Year Exc. Value
☐ **Model 235**, .22 L.R.R.F., Wood Stock, *Modern*	55.00	85.00	80.00
☐ **Model 33**, .22 L.R.R.F., Plastic Stock, *Modern*	50.00	80.00	75.00
☐ **Model 33A**, .22 L.R.R.F., Wood Stock, *Modern*	55.00	85.00	80.00

SHOTGUN, DOUBLE BARREL, SIDE-BY-SIDE

	V.G.	Exc.	Prior Year Exc. Value
☐ **Model 420**, Various Gauges, Hammerless, Checkered Stock, Recoil Pad, *Modern*	130.00	175.00	165.00
☐ **Model 420EK**, Various Gauges, Hammerless, Checkered Stock, Recoil Pad, Fancy Wood, *Modern*	145.00	200.00	200.00

	V.G.	Exc.	Prior Year Exc. Value
☐ **Model 450E**, Various Gauges, Hammerless, Checkered Stock, Recoil Pad, *Modern*	180.00	290.00	285.00
SHOTGUN, SEMI-AUTOMATIC			
☐ **Model 80**, .410 Ga., *Modern*	115.00	155.00	150.00
SHOTGUN, SLIDE ACTION			
☐ **Model 160 Deergun**, 12 and 20 Gauges, Peep Sights, *Modern*	95.00	150.00	145.00
☐ **Model 166L Deergun**, 12 and 16 Gauges, Peep Sights, *Modern*	95.00	150.00	145.00
☐ **Model 166LP Deergun**, 12 and 16 Gauges, Peep Sights, *Modern*	95.00	150.00	150.00
☐ **Model 200**, 20 Ga., Vent Rib, Adjustable Choke, *Modern*	95.00	145.00	140.00
☐ **Model 200**, 20 Ga., Adjustable Choke, *Modern*	90.00	145.00	140.00
☐ **Model 200**, 20 Ga., *Modern*	90.00	140.00	135.00
☐ **Model 200**, 20 Ga., Trap Grade, *Modern*	95.00	150.00	150.00
☐ **Model 300**, 12 Ga., Vent Rib, Adjustable Choke, *Modern*	110.00	160.00	160.00
☐ **Model 300**, 12 Ga., Adjustable Choke, *Modern*	95.00	145.00	145.00
☐ **Model 300**, 12 Ga., *Modern*	95.00	145.00	140.00
☐ **Model 300**, 12 Ga., Trap Grade, *Modern*	115.00	165.00	160.00
☐ **Model 390**, 12 Ga., Peep Sights, *Modern*	90.00	145.00	140.00
☐ **Model 40**, 12 Ga., Hammerless, Solid Frame, Adjustable Choke, *Modern*	85.00	135.00	130.00
☐ **Model 400**, .410 Ga., Skeet Grade, *Modern*	90.00	140.00	135.00
☐ **Model 400**, .410 Ga., Adjustable Choke, *Modern*	90.00	140.00	135.00
☐ **Model 400**, .410 Ga., Skeet Grade, Adjustable Choke, *Modern*	95.00	155.00	150.00
☐ **Model 400**, .410 Ga., *Modern*	85.00	140.00	135.00
☐ **Model 50**, 12 Ga., Hammerless, Solid Frame, *Modern*	70.00	125.00	110.00
☐ **Model 60**, 12 and 16 Gauges, Hammerless, Solid Frame, Adjustable Choke, *Modern*	85.00	130.00	125.00
☐ **Model 602**, 20 Ga., *Modern*	90.00	140.00	135.00
☐ **Model 602CLP**, 20 Ga., Adjustable Choke, *Modern*	95.00	145.00	145.00
☐ **Model 602RCLP**, 20 Ga., Adjustable Choke, Vent Rib, *Modern*	115.00	155.00	155.00
☐ **Model 602 RLP**, 20 Ga., Vent Rib, *Modern*	90.00	140.00	140.00
☐ **Model 60ACP**, 12 and 16 Gauges, Hammerless, Solid Frame, Adjustable Choke, Vent Rib, *Modern*	80.00	130.00	125.00
☐ **Model 60AF**, 12 and 16 Gauges, Hammerless, Solid Frame, Vent Rib, Adjustable Choke, *Modern*	85.00	135.00	130.00
☐ **Model 60 RCLP**, 12 and 16 Gauges, Hammerless, Solid Frame, Vent Rib, Adjustable Choke, Checkered Stock, *Modern*	85.00	140.00	135.00
☐ **Model 65**, 12 and 16 Gauges, Hammerless, Solid Frame, *Modern*	70.00	125.00	115.00
☐ **Model 662CR**, 20 Ga., Vent Rib, *Modern*	100.00	150.00	150.00
☐ **Model 66CLP**, 12 and 16 Gauges, Adjustable Choke, *Modern*	110.00	155.00	155.00

	V.G.	Exc.	Prior Year Exc. Value
☐ **Model 66RCLP**, 12 and 16 Gauges, Hammerless, Solid Frame, Adjustable Choke, Vent Rib, *Modern*	110.00	155.00	155.00
☐ **Model 66RLP**, 12 and 16 Gauges, Hammerless, Solid Frame, Vent Rib, *Modern*	110.00	150.00	150.00
☐ **Model 66XLP**, 12 and 16 Gauges, Hammerless, Solid Frame, *Modern*	90.00	140.00	135.00
☐ **Model 70**, .410 Ga., *Modern*	70.00	110.00	100.00
☐ **Model 70CLP**, .410 Ga., Hammerless, Solid Frame, Adjustable Choke, *Modern*	90.00	140.00	135.00
☐ **Model 70RL**, .410 Ga., *Modern*	85.00	130.00	125.00
☐ **Model 70X**, .410 Ga., *Modern*	80.00	125.00	120.00
☐ **Model 70XL**, .410 Ga., *Modern*	80.00	130.00	125.00
☐ **Model 757**, 20 Ga., Adjustable Choke, Lightweight, *Modern*	115.00	160.00	160.00

NOCK, HENRY

London & Birmingham, England 1760-1810.

RIFLE, FLINTLOCK

	V.G.	Exc.	Prior Year Exc. Value
☐ **.65**, Ellett Carbine, Musket, Military, *Antique*	995.00	1,700.00	1,650.00

SHOTGUN, PERCUSSION

	V.G.	Exc.	Prior Year Exc. Value
☐ **Fowler**, Converted from Flintlock, Patent Breech, *Antique*	465.00	725.00	700.00

NONPAREIL

Made by Norwich Falls Pistols Co., c. 1880.

HANDGUN, REVOLVER

	V.G.	Exc.	Prior Year Exc. Value
☐ **.32 Short R.F.**, 5 Shot, Spur Trigger, Solid Frame, Single Action, *Antique*	95.00	165.00	160.00

NORTH AMERICAN ARMS CO.

Freedom, Wyo.

HANDGUN, REVOLVER

	V.G.	Exc.	Prior Year Exc. Value
☐ **.454 Casull Magnum**, Single Action, Western Style, Stainless Steel, 5 Shot, *Modern*	345.00	450.00	450.00
☐ **Mini**, .22 Short, 5 Shot, Single Action, Spur Trigger, 1" Barrel, Derringer, *Modern*	65.00	85.00	85.00
☐ **Mini**, .22 L.R.R.F., 5 Shot, Single Action, Spur Trigger, 1" Barrel, Derringer, *Modern*	65.00	85.00	85.00
☐ **Mini**, .22 L.R.R.F., 5 Shot, Single Action, Spur Trigger, 1½" Barrel, Derringer, *Modern*	65.00	90.00	90.00
☐ **Mini**, .22 W.M.R., 5 Shot, Single Action, Spur Trigger, 1" Barrel, Derringer, *Modern*	70.00	100.00	100.00

NORTH VIETNAM MILITARY

AUTOMATIC WEAPON, SUBMACHINE GUN

	V.G.	Exc.	Prior Year Exc. Value
☐ **K50M**, 7.62mm Tokarev, Clip Fed, Folding Stock, *Class 3*	1,450.00	1,850.00	1,750.00

NORTHWESTERNER

Made by Stevens Arms.

	V.G.	Exc.	Prior Year Exc. Value
RIFLE, BOLT ACTION			
☐ **Model 52**, .22 L.R.R.F., Single Action, Takedown, *Modern*	35.00	50.00	45.00
SHOTGUN, SINGLESHOT			
☐ **Model 94**, Various Gauges, Takedown, Automatic Ejector, Plain, Hammer, *Modern*	40.00	60.00	55.00

NORTON

See Budischowsky and American Arms & Ammunition Co.

NORWEGIAN MILITARY

	V.G.	Exc.	Prior Year Exc. Value
HANDGUN, SEMI-AUTOMATIC			
☐ **Mauser Model 1914,** .32 ACP, Blue, Clip Fed, *Modern*	380.00	550.00	800.00
☐ **Model 1914,** .45 ACP, Military, Clip Fed, *Modern*	210.00	340.00	450.00
☐ **Model 1914,** .45 ACP, Military, Clip Fed, Nazi-Proofed, *Modern*	330.00	480.00	600.00
RIFLE, BOLT ACTION			
☐ **Model 1894 Krag,** 6.5 x 55mm, Military, Curio	110.00	155.00	200.00
☐ **Model 1925 Krag Sniper,** 6.5 x 55mm, Military, *Curio*	115.00	165.00	235.00

NORWICH ARMS CO.

Probably made by Norwich Falls Pistols Co.

	V.G.	Exc.	Prior Year Exc. Value
HANDGUN, REVOLVER			
☐ **.22 Short R.F.**, 7 Shot, Spur Trigger, Solid Frame, Single Action, *Antique*	95.00	165.00	160.00
☐ **.32 Short R.F.**, 5 Shot, Spur Trigger, Solid Frame, Single Action, *Antique*	95.00	170.00	170.00

NORWICH ARMS CO.

Made by Crescent, c. 1900.

	V.G.	Exc.	Prior Year Exc. Value
SHOTGUN, DOUBLE BARREL, SIDE-BY-SIDE			
☐ **Various Gauges**, Outside Hammers, Damascus Barrel, *Modern*	100.00	170.00	175.00
☐ **Various Gauges**, Hammerless, Steel Barrel, *Modern*	135.00	190.00	200.00
☐ **Various Gauges**, Hammerless, Damascus Barrel, *Modern*	100.00	170.00	175.00
☐ **Various Gauges**, Outside Hammers, Steel Barrel, *Modern*	125.00	185.00	190.00
SHOTGUN, SINGLESHOT			
☐ **Various Gauges**, Hammer, Steel Barrel, *Modern*	55.00	85.00	85.00

NOT-NAC MFG. CO.

Made by Crescent for Belknap Hardware Co., Louisville, Ky.

	V.G.	Exc.	Prior Year Exc. Value
SHOTGUN, DOUBLE BARREL, SIDE-BY-SIDE			
☐ **Various Gauges**, Outside Hammers, Damascus Barrel, *Modern*	100.00	170.00	175.00
☐ **Various Gauges**, Hammerless, Steel Barrel, *Modern*	135.00	190.00	200.00

	V.G.	Exc.	Prior Year Exc. Value
☐ **Various Gauges**, Hammerless, Damascus Barrel, *Modern*	100.00	170.00	175.00
☐ **Various Gauges**, Outside Hammers, Steel Barrel, *Modern*	125.00	185.00	190.00

SHOTGUN, SINGLESHOT

☐ **Various Gauges**, Hammer, Steel Barrel, *Modern*	55.00	85.00	85.00

NOVA

La France Specialties, San Diego, Calif.

HANDGUN, SEMI-AUTOMATIC

☐ **Nova**, 9mm Luger, Clip Fed, "Electrofilm" Finish, Reduced M1911 Style, *Modern*	375.00	495.00	—

NOYS, R.

Wiltshire, England 1800-1830.

HANDGUN, FLINTLOCK

☐ **Pocket Pistol**, Screw Barrel, Box Lock, Steel Barrel and Frame, Plain, *Antique*	490.00	657.00	650.00

NUMRICH ARMS CO.

West Hurley, N.Y. Also see Auto Ordnance, Thompson, Hopkins & Allen.

HANDGUN, SEMI-AUTOMATIC

☐ **M1911A1**, .45 ACP, Clip Fed, Blue, Military Style, *Modern*	175.00	250.00	245.00
☐ **Model 27A5**, .45 ACP, Clip Fed, Finned Barrel, Adjustable Sights, with Compensator, (Numrich), *Modern*	250.00	350.00	350.00

RIFLE, SEMI-AUTOMATIC

☐ **Model 27A1**, .45 ACP, Clip Fed, without Compensator, *Modern*	250.00	350.00	350.00
☐ **Model 27A1**, .45 ACP, Clip Fed, without Compensator, Cased with Accessories, *Modern*	400.00	475.00	475.00
☐ **Model 27A1 Deluxe**, .45 ACP, Clip Fed, Finned Barrel, Adjustable Sights, with Compensator, *Modern*	265.00	370.00	370.00
☐ **Model 27A3**, .22 L.R.R.F., Clip Fed, Finned Barrel, Adjustable Sights, with Compensator, *Modern*	225.00	350.00	350.00

NUNNEMACHER, ABRAHAM

York, Pa. 1779-1783. See Kentucky Rifles.

OAK LEAF

Made by Stevens Arms.

SHOTGUN, SINGLESHOT

☐ **Model 90**, Various Gauges, Takedown, Automatic Ejector, Plain, Hammer, *Modern*	40.00	60.00	55.00

OCCIDENTAL

Belgium, c. 1880.

SHOTGUN, DOUBLE BARREL, SIDE-BY-SIDE

☐ **Various Gauges**, Outside Hammers, Damascus Barrel, *Modern*	90.00	155.00	150.00

	V.G.	Exc.	Prior Year Exc. Value

OLD TIMER
Made by Stevens Arms.

SHOTGUN, SINGLESHOT

	V.G.	Exc.	Prior Year Exc. Value
☐ **Model 94**, Various Gauges, Takedown, Automatic Ejector, Plain, Hammer, *Modern*	40.00	60.00	55.00

OLYMPIC
Made by Stevens Arms.

SHOTGUN, DOUBLE BARREL, SIDE-BY-SIDE

	V.G.	Exc.	Prior Year Exc. Value
☐ **M 315**, Various Gauges, Hammerless, Steel Barrel, *Modern*	115.00	180.00	165.00
☐ **Model 311**, Various Gauges, Hammerless, Steel Barrel, *Modern*	115.00	180.00	165.00

SHOTGUN, SINGLESHOT

	V.G.	Exc.	Prior Year Exc. Value
☐ **Model 94**, Various Gauges, Takedown, Automatic Ejector, Plain, Hammer, *Modern*	40.00	60.00	55.00

O.M.
Ojanguren y Marcaido, Eibar, Spain, c. 1920.

HANDGUN, REVOLVER

	V.G.	Exc.	Prior Year Exc. Value
☐ **S & W Type**, Various Calibers, Double Action, Swing-Out Cylinder, Blue, *Curio*	70.00	100.00	100.00

OMEGA
Armero Especialistas Reunidas, Eibar, Spain, c. 1925.

HANDGUN, SEMI-AUTOMATIC

	V.G.	Exc.	Prior Year Exc. Value
☐ **.25 ACP**, Clip Fed, *Modern*	80.00	125.00	115.00
☐ **.32 ACP**, Clip Fed, Grip Safety, *Modern*	90.00	140.00	130.00

OMEGA
Torrance, Calif. Made by Hi-Shear Corp. Current.

RIFLE, BOLT ACTION

	V.G.	Exc.	Prior Year Exc. Value
☐ **Omega III**, Various Calibers, no Sights, Fancy Wood, Adjustable Trigger, *Modern*	290.00	420.00	400.00

ORBEA HERMANOS
Orbea Hermanos and Orbea y Cia., Eibar, Spain, c. 1860-1935.

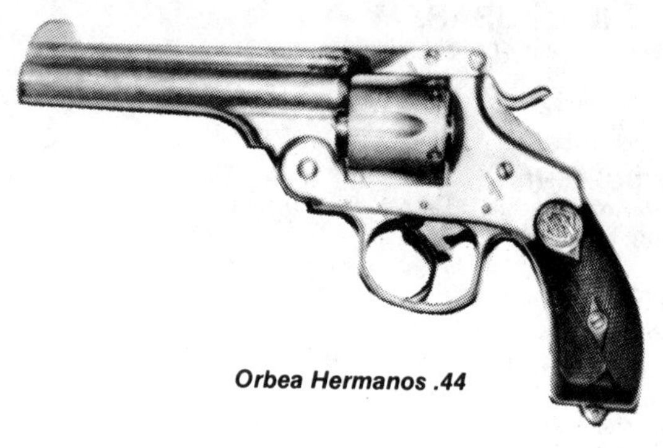

Orbea Hermanos .44

	V.G.	Exc.	Prior Year Exc. Value
HANDGUN, REVOLVER			
☐ **S & W Type**, .44 Russian, Double Action, Top-Break, *Antique*	85.00	130.00	125.00

OREA

Orechowsky, Graz, Austria, c. 1930.

	V.G.	Exc.	Prior Year Exc. Value
RIFLE, SINGLESHOT			
☐ **Heeren Rifle**, Various Calibers, Checkered Stock, Engraved, Fancy Wood, *Modern*	950.00	1,650.00	1,500.00

Ortgies D Pocket

Ortgies H O Vest Pocket

ORTGIES

Germany, 1918-1921, 1921 Taken over by Deutsche-Werke, Erfurt, Germany.

	V.G.	Exc.	Prior Year Exc. Value
HANDGUN, SEMI-AUTOMATIC			
☐ **D Pocket**, .380 ACP, Clip Fed, *Modern*	145.00	195.00	175.00
☐ **H O Pocket**, .380 ACP, Clip Fed, *Modern*	135.00	185.00	165.00
☐ **D Pocket**, .32 ACP, Clip Fed, *Modern*	110.00	170.00	150.00
☐ **D Vest Pocket**, .25 ACP, Clip Fed, *Modern*	140.00	190.00	170.00
☐ **H O Vest Pocket**, .25 ACP, Clip Fed, *Modern*	130.00	180.00	160.00

OSGOOD GUN WORKS

Norwich, Conn., c. 1880.

	V.G.	Exc.	Prior Year Exc. Value
HANDGUN, REVOLVER			
☐ **Duplex**, .22/.32 R.F., 8 Shot .22, Singleshot .32, Two Barrels, Spur Trigger, *Antique*	195.00	350.00	325.00

OUR JAKE

	V.G.	Exc.	Prior Year Exc. Value
HANDGUN, REVOLVER			
☐ **.32 R.F.**, Spur Trigger, Solid Frame, Hammer, *Antique*	90.00	145.00	140.00

OWA

Oesterreichische Werke Anstalt, Vienna, Austria, c. 1920-1925.

	V.G.	Exc.	Prior Year Exc. Value
HANDGUN, SEMI-AUTOMATIC			
☐ **Model 1921 Standard**, .25 ACP, Clip Fed, *Modern*	135.00	175.00	165.00

	V.G.	Exc.	Prior Year Exc. Value
OXFORD ARMS			
Made by Stevens Arms.			
SHOTGUN, DOUBLE BARREL, SIDE-BY-SIDE			
☐ **Model 311**, Various Gauges, Hammerless, Steel Barrel, *Modern*	115.00	180.00	165.00
OXFORD ARMS CO.			
Made by Crescent for Belknap Hdw. Co., Louisville, Ky.			
SHOTGUN, DOUBLE BARREL, SIDE-BY-SIDE			
☐ **Various Gauges**, Outside Hammers, Damascus Barrel, *Modern*	100.00	170.00	175.00
☐ **Various Gauges**, Hammerless, Steel Barrel, *Modern*	135.00	190.00	200.00
☐ **Various Gauges**, Hammerless, Damascus Barrel, *Modern*	100.00	170.00	175.00
☐ **Various Gauges**, Outside Hammers, Steel Barrel, *Modern*	125.00	185.00	190.00
SHOTGUN, SINGLESHOT			
☐ **Various Gauges**, Hammer, Steel Barrel, *Modern*	55.00	85.00	85.00

P.A.F. Junior

	V.G.	Exc.	Prior Year Exc. Value
P.A.F.			
Pretoria Arms Factory, Pretoria, South Africa, c. 1955.			
HANDGUN, SEMI-AUTOMATIC			
☐ **Junior**, For Cocking Indicator *Add* **10%-15%**			
☐ **Junior**, .25 ACP, High Slide, Clip Fed, Blue, *Curio*	115.00	145.00	145.00
☐ **Junior**, .25 ACP, Sight Rib, Clip Fed, Blue, *Curio*	125.00	170.00	165.00
☐ **Junior**, .25 ACP, Low Slide, Clip Fed, Blue, *Curio*	110.00	150.00	150.00
PAGE, T.			
Norwich, England, 1766-1776.			
HANDGUN, FLINTLOCK			
☐ **.60**, Queen Anne Style, Pocket Pistol, Screw Barrel, Box Lock, Brass Furniture, Engraved, *Antique*	975.00	1,550.00	1,450.00

PAGE-LEWIS ARMS CO.

See Stevens, J. Arms & Tool Co. for similar listings.

	V.G.	Exc.	Prior Year Exc. Value

PALMER, THOMAS

Philadelphia, Pa. 1772-1776. See Kentucky Rifles and U.S. Military.

PALMETTO

Made by Stevens Arms.

SHOTGUN, SINGLESHOT

	V.G.	Exc.	Prior Year Exc. Value
☐ **Model 90**, Various Gauges, Takedown, Automatic Ejector, Plain, Hammer, *Modern*	35.00	55.00	55.00
☐ **Model 94**, Various Gauges, Takedown, Automatic Ejector, Plain, Hammer, *Modern*	40.00	60.00	55.00

PANNABECKER, JEFFERSON

Lancaster, Pa. 1790-1810. See Kentucky Rifles.

PANNABECKER, JESSE

Lancaster, Pa. 1833-1860. See Kentucky Rifles.

PANTAX

Tradename used by E. Woerther, Buenos Aires, Argentina.

HANDGUN, SEMI-AUTOMATIC

	V.G.	Exc.	Prior Year Exc. Value
☐ **.22 R.F.**, Clip Fed, Blue, *Modern*	85.00	130.00	125.00

PANZER

G.M.F. Corp., Watertown, Ct.

HANDGUN, DOUBLE BARREL, OVER-UNDER

	V.G.	Exc.	Prior Year Exc. Value
☐ **Panzer**, .22 L.R.R.F., Twist Barrel, Spur Trigger, *Modern*	25.00	40.00	35.00

PARAGON

Made by Stevens Arms.

SHOTGUN, DOUBLE BARREL, SIDE-BY-SIDE

	V.G.	Exc.	Prior Year Exc. Value
☐ **Model 311**, Various Gauges, Hammerless, Steel Barrel, *Modern*	115.00	180.00	165.00

PARAGON

Possibly made by Hopkins & Allen, c. 1880.

HANDGUN, REVOLVER

	V.G.	Exc.	Prior Year Exc. Value
☐ **.32 Short R.F.**, 5 Shot, Spur Trigger, Solid Frame, Single Action, *Antique*	95.00	165.00	160.00

	V.G.	Exc.	Prior Year Exc. Value

PARAMOUNT

Retolaza Hermanos, Eibar, Spain, c. 1920

HANDGUN, SEMI-AUTOMATIC

	V.G.	Exc.	Prior Year Exc. Value
☐ **.32 ACP**, Clip Fed, *Modern*	85.00	130.00	120.00
☐ **M 1914**, .32 ACP, Clip Fed, Long Grip, *Modern*	90.00	135.00	125.00
☐ **Vest Pocket**, .25 ACP, Clip Fed, *Modern*	80.00	125.00	115.00

PARKER BROTHERS

Meriden, Conn. 1868-1934. In 1934 Parker Bros. was taken over by Remington Arms Co.

SHOTGUN, DOUBLE BARREL, SIDE-BY-SIDE

☐ **For Upgrades**, *Deduct* **25%-30%**
☐ **For Plain Extractor**, *Deduct* **30%-45%**
☐ **For Damascus Barrel**,*.Deduct* **60%-75%**
☐ **Single Selective Trigger**, *Add* **$200.00-$325.00**
☐ **Beavertail Forend**, for BHE through A-1, *Add* **$250.00-$350.00**
☐ **Beavertail Forend**, VHE through CHE, *Add* **$200.00-$300.00**
☐ **Extra Barrel**, *Add* **30%-40%**
☐ **Vent Rib**, *Add* **$275.00-$350.00**
☐ **Trap Grade**, *Add* **15%-25%**
☐ **Skeet Grade**, *Add* **15%-25%**
☐ **Outside Hammers with Steel Barrels**, *Deduct* **20%-30%**

	V.G.	Exc.	Prior Year Exc. Value
☐ **A-1 Special**, 12 Ga., Hammerless, Double Trigger, Automatic Ejector, *Modern*	15,000.00	25,000.00	25,000.00
☐ **A-1 Special**, 16 Ga., Hammerless, Double Trigger, Automatic Ejector, *Modern*	12,000.00	18,250.00	18,000.00
☐ **A-1 Special**, 20 Ga., Hammerless, Double Trigger, Automatic Ejector, *Modern*	20,000.00	30,000.00	30,000.00
☐ **A-1 Special**, 28 Ga., Hammerless, Double Trigger, Automatic Ejector, *Modern*	40,000.00	55,000.00	55,000.00
☐ **A-1 Upgrade**, .410 Ga., Hammerless, Double Trigger, Automatic Ejector, *Modern*	8,000.00	15,000.00	15,000.00
☐ **A-1 Upgrade**, 12 and 16 Gauges, Hammerless, Double Trigger, Automatic Ejector, *Modern*	6,500.00	10,000.00	10,000.00
☐ **A-1 Upgrade**, 20 Ga., Hammerless, Double Trigger, Automatic Ejector, *Modern*	6,000.00	9,250.00	9,000.00
☐ **A-1 Upgrade**, 28 Ga., Hammerless, Double Trigger, Automatic Ejector, *Modern*	9,000.00	15,000.00	15,000.00
☐ **AAHE**, 10 Ga., Hammerless, Double Trigger, Automatic Ejector, *Modern*	23,000.00	28,500.00	28,000.00
☐ **AAHE**, 12 Ga., Hammerless, Double Trigger, Automatic Ejector, *Modern*	9,000.00	15,000.00	15,000.00
☐ **AAHE**, 16 Ga., Hammerless, Double Trigger, Automatic Ejector, *Modern*	8,000.00	15,000.00	15,000.00
☐ **AAHE**, 20 Ga., Hammerless, Double Trigger, Automatic Ejector, *Modern*	12,000.00	18,500.00	18,000.00
☐ **AAHE**, 28 Ga., Hammerless, Double Trigger, Automatic Ejector, *Modern*	24,000.00	30,000.00	30,000.00
☐ **AHE**, .410 Ga., Hammerless, Double Trigger, Automatic Ejector, *Modern*	15,000.00	20,500.00	20,000.00
☐ **AHE**, 10 Ga., Hammerless, Double Trigger, Automatic Ejector, *Modern*	15,000.00	20,000.00	20,000.00

	V.G.	Exc.	Prior Year Exc. Value
☐ **AHE**, 12 Ga., Hammerless, Double Trigger, Automatic Ejector, *Modern*	8,000.00	13,000.00	13,000.00
☐ **AHE**, 16 Ga., Hammerless, Double Trigger, Automatic Ejector, *Modern*	8,000.00	12,000.00	12,000.00
☐ **AHE**, 20 Ga., Hammerless, Double Trigger, Automatic Ejector, *Modern*	9,500.00	17,500.00	17,000.00
☐ **AHE**, 28 Ga., Hammerless, Double Trigger, Automatic Ejector, *Modern*	14,000.00	21,450.00	21,000.00
☐ **BHE**, .410 Ga., Hammerless, Double Trigger, Automatic Ejector, *Modern*	13,000.00	19,500.00	19,000.00
☐ **BHE**, 10 Ga., Hammerless, Double Trigger, Automatic Ejector, *Modern*	12,000.00	18,000.00	18,000.00
☐ **BHE**, 12 Ga., Hammerless, Double Trigger, Automatic Ejector, *Modern*	7,500.00	11,000.00	11,000.00
☐ **BHE**, 16 Ga., Hammerless, Double Trigger, Automatic Ejector, *Modern*	7,000.00	10,000.00	10,000.00
☐ **BHE**, 20 Ga., Hammerless, Double Trigger, Automatic Ejector, *Modern*	9,000.00	15,000.00	15,000.00
☐ **BHE**, 28 Ga., Hammerless, Double Trigger, Automatic Ejector, *Modern*	15,000.00	22,500.00	22,000.00
☐ **CHE**, .410 Ga., Hammerless, Double Trigger, Automatic Ejector, *Modern*	8,000.00	13,500.00	13,000.00
☐ **CHE**, 10 Ga., Hammerless, Double Trigger, Automatic Ejector, *Modern*	8,000.00	13,000.00	13,000.00
☐ **CHE**, 12 Ga., Hammerless, Double Trigger, Automatic Ejector, *Modern*	6,000.00	9,250.00	9,000.00
☐ **CHE**, 16 Ga., Hammerless, Double Trigger, Automatic Ejector, *Modern*	5,500.00	8,500.00	8,250.00
☐ **CHE**, 20 Ga., Hammerless, Double Trigger, Automatic Ejector, *Modern*	8,000.00	11,250.00	11,000.00
☐ **CHE**, 28 Ga., Hammerless, Double Trigger, Automatic Ejector, *Modern*	9,500.00	14,500.00	14,000.00
☐ **DHE**, .410 Ga., Hammerless, Double Trigger, Automatic Ejector, *Modern*	6,500.00	10,000.00	9,750.00
☐ **DHE**, 10 Ga., Hammerless, Double Trigger, Automatic Ejector, *Modern*	5,500.00	9,250.00	9,000.00
☐ **DHE**, 12 Ga., Hammerless, Double Trigger, Automatic Ejector, *Modern*	5,000.00	8,750.00	8,500.00
☐ **DHE**, 16 Ga., Hammerless, Double Trigger, Automatic Ejector, *Modern*	4,500.00	8,000.00	8,000.00
☐ **DHE**, 20 Ga., Hammerless, Double Trigger, Automatic Ejector, *Modern*	7,000.00	10,500.00	10,000.00
☐ **DHE**, 28 Ga., Hammerless, Double Trigger, Automatic Ejector, *Modern*	9,000.00	14,500.00	14,000.00
☐ **Early Model**, Various Gauges, Outside Hammers, Damascus Barrel, Under-Lever, *Antique*	675.00	1,200.00	1,100.00
☐ **GHE**, .410 Ga., Hammerless, Double Trigger, Automatic Ejector, *Modern*	4,500.00	8,500.00	8,000.00
☐ **GHE**, 10 Ga. 3½", Hammerless, Double Trigger, Automatic Ejector, *Modern*	4,250.00	8,000.00	8,000.00
☐ **GHE**, 12 Ga., Hammerless, Double Trigger, Automatic Ejector, *Modern*	2,800.00	4,500.00	4,000.00
☐ **GHE**, 16 Ga., Hammerless, Double Trigger, Automatic Ejector, *Modern*	2,800.00	4,000.00	4,000.00
☐ **GHE**, 20 Ga., Hammerless, Double Trigger, Automatic Ejector, *Modern*	4,000.00	9,500.00	9,000.00

	V.G.	Exc.	Prior Year Exc. Value
☐ **GHE**, 28 Ga., Hammerless, Double Trigger, Automatic Ejector, *Modern*	6,000.00	9,500.00	9,000.00
☐ **Invincible**, 12 Ga., Hammerless, Double Trigger, Automatic Ejector, *Modern*		120,000.00+	
☐ **Invincible**, 16 Ga., Hammerless, Double Trigger, Automatic Ejector, *Modern*		65,000.00+	
☐ **Trojan**, 12 and 16 Gauges, Hammerless, Double Trigger, *Modern*	625.00	995.00	950.00
☐ **Trojan**, 20 Ga., Hammerless, Double Trigger, *Modern*	925.00	1,550.00	1,500.00
☐ **Trojan**, 24 Ga., Hammerless, Double Trigger, *Modern*		20,000.00+	
☐ **VHE**, .410 Ga., Hammerless, Double Trigger, Automatic Ejector, *Modern*	4,500.00	8,250.00	8,000.00
☐ **VHE**, 10 Ga. 3½", Hammerless, Double Trigger, Automatic Ejector, *Modern*	3,500.00	7,000.00	7,000.00
☐ **VHE**, 12 Ga., Hammerless, Double Trigger, Automatic Ejector, *Modern*	1,500.00	2,350.00	2,300.00
☐ **VHE**, 16 Ga., Hammerless, Double Trigger, Automatic Ejector, *Modern*	1,500.00	2,250.00	2,200.00
☐ **VHE**, 20 Ga., Hammerless, Double Trigger, Automatic Ejector, *Modern*	4,000.00	8,250.00	8,000.00
☐ **VHE**, 28 Ga., Hammerless, Double Trigger, Automatic Ejector, *Modern*	4,500.00	8,750.00	8,500.00
SHOTGUN, SINGLESHOT			
☐ **S.A.**, 12 Ga., Hammerless, Vent Rib, Automatic Ejector, *Modern*	5,000.00	7,750.00	7,500.00
☐ **S.A.-1 Special**, 12 Ga., Hammerless, Vent Rib, Automatic Ejector, *Modern*	8,000.00	12,500.00	12,000.00
☐ **S.A.A.**, 12 Ga., Hammerless, Vent Rib, Automatic Ejector, *Modern*	6,000.00	9,250.00	9,000.00
☐ **S.B.**, 12 Ga., Hammerless, Vent Rib, Automatic Ejector, *Modern*	4,500.00	6,750.00	6,500.00
☐ **S.C.**, 12 Ga., Hammerless, Vent Rib, Automatic Ejector, *Modern*	3,500.00	5,750.00	5,500.00

PARKER BROTHERS

Imported from Italy by Jana International.

	V.G.	Exc.	Prior Year Exc. Value
SHOTGUN, DOUBLE BARREL, OVER-UNDER			
☐ **Field Model**, 12 Ga. 3", Single Selective Trigger, Automatic Ejectors, Checkered Stock, Engraved, Vent Rib, *Modern*	220.00	325.00	300.00
☐ **Field Model**, 12 Ga., Single Selective Trigger, Automatic Ejectors, Checkered Stock, Engraved, Vent Rib, *Modern*	200.00	300.00	280.00
☐ **Skeet Model**, 12 Ga., Single Selective Trigger, Automatic Ejectors, Checkered Stock, Engraved, Vent Rib, *Modern*	240.00	345.00	325.00
☐ **Monte Carlo Trap Model**, 12 Ga., Single Selective Trigger, Automatic Ejectors, Checkered Stock, Engraved, Vent Rib, *Modern*	265.00	375.00	350.00
☐ **California Trap Model**, 12 Ga., Single Selective Trigger, Automatic Ejectors, Checkered Stock, Engraved, Double Vent Ribs, *Modern*	365.00	525.00	500.00

	V.G.	Exc.	Prior Year Exc. Value

PARKER-HALE
Birmingham, England.

HANDGUN, REVOLVER

	V.G.	Exc.	Prior Year Exc. Value
☐ **S & W Victory**, .22 L.R.R.F., Conversion, Adjustable Sights, *Modern*	85.00	130.00	125.00

RIFLE, BOLT ACTION

	V.G.	Exc.	Prior Year Exc. Value
☐ **Model 1200**, Various Calibers, Checkered Stock, Open Rear Sight, Monte Carlo Stock, *Modern*	160.00	210.00	195.00
☐ **Model 1200M**, Various Calibers, Magnum, Checkered Stock, Open Rear Sight, Monte Carlo Stock, *Modern*	165.00	225.00	220.00
☐ **Model 1200V**, Various Calibers, Heavy Barrel, Checkered Stock, no Sights, Monte Carlo Stock, *Modern*	165.00	225.00	220.00

RIFLE, PERCUSSION

	V.G.	Exc.	Prior Year Exc. Value
☐ **.54 Gallagher**, Breech Loader, Carbine, Brass Furniture, Reproduction, *Antique*	125.00	175.00	170.00
☐ **.58 M1853 Enfield**, Musket, Rifled, 2 Bands, Brass Furniture, Reproduction, *Antique*	140.00	190.00	185.00
☐ **.58 M1858 Enfield Rifle**, Rifled, Brass Furniture, Reproduction, *Antique*	130.00	190.00	190.00
☐ **.58 M1861 Enfield**, Musketoon, Rifled, 2 Bands, Brass Furniture, Reproduction, *Antique*	120.00	170.00	170.00
☐ **.451**, Whitworth Military Target Rifle, 3 Bands, Target Sights, Checkered Stock, Reproduction, *Antique*	250.00	350.00	350.00

SHOTGUN, SEMI-AUTOMATIC

	V.G.	Exc.	Prior Year Exc. Value
☐ **Model 900**, 12 Ga., Checkered Stock, Vent Rib, *Modern*	140.00	200.00	200.00
☐ **Model 900**, 12 Ga. 3", Checkered Stock, Vent Rib, *Modern*	150.00	220.00	220.00

PARKER SAFETY HAMMERLESS
Made by Columbia Armory, Tenn., c. 1890.

HANDGUN, REVOLVER

	V.G.	Exc.	Prior Year Exc. Value
☐ **.32 S & W**, 5 Shot, Top Break, Hammerless, Double Action, *Modern*	60.00	100.00	95.00

PARKER, WILLIAM
London, England 1790-1840.

SHOTGUN, FLINTLOCK

	V.G.	Exc.	Prior Year Exc. Value
☐ **16 Ga.**, Double Barrel, Side by Side, Engraved, High Quality, *Antique*	2,550.00	4,000.00	3,950.00

SHOTGUN, PERCUSSION

	V.G.	Exc.	Prior Year Exc. Value
☐ **14 Ga.**, Single Barrel, Smoothbore, High Quality, Cased with Accessories, *Antique*	895.00	1,500.00	1,450.00

PARKHILL, ANDREW
Phila., Pa. 1778-1785. See Kentucky Rifles and Pistols.

PAROLE
Made by Hopkins & Allen, c. 1880.

	V.G.	Exc.	Prior Year Exc. Value
HANDGUN, REVOLVER			
☐ **.22 Short R.F.**, 7 Shot, Spur Trigger, Solid Frame, Single Action, *Antique*	95.00	165.00	160.00

PARR, J.

Liverpool, England, c. 1810.

RIFLE, FLINTLOCK			
☐ **.75**, 3rd Model Brown Bess, Musket, Military, *Antique*	845.00	1,500.00	1,450.00

PARSONS, HIRAM

Baltimore, Md., c. 1819. See Kentucky Rifles.

PATRIOT

Made by Norwich Falls Pistol Co., c. 1880.

HANDGUN, REVOLVER			
☐ **.32 Short R.F.**, 5 Shot, Spur Trigger, Solid Frame, Single Action, *Antique*	95.00	165.00	160.00

PECK, ABIJAH

Hartford, Conn. See U. S. Military.

PEERLESS

Made by Stevens.

RIFLE, BOLT ACTION			
☐ **Model 056 Buckhorn**, .22 L.R.R.F., 5 Shot Clip, Peep Sights, *Modern*	50.00	70.00	65.00
☐ **Model 066 Buckhorn**, .22 L.R.R.F., Tube Feed, Peep Sights, *Modern*	50.00	70.00	65.00
☐ **Model 53**, .22 L.R.R.F., Singleshot, Takedown, *Modern*	35.00	50.00	45.00

PEERLESS

Made by Crescent H. & D. Folsom, c. 1900.

SHOTGUN, DOUBLE BARREL, SIDE-BY-SIDE			
☐ **Various Gauges**, Outside Hammers, Damascus Barrel, *Modern*	100.00	170.00	175.00
☐ **Various Gauges**, Hammerless, Steel Barrel, *Modern*	135.00	190.00	200.00
☐ **Various Gauges**, Hammerless, Damascus Barrel, *Modern*	100.00	170.00	175.00
☐ **Various Gauges**, Outside Hammers, Steel Barrel, *Modern*	125.00	185.00	190.00
SHOTGUN, SINGLESHOT			
☐ **Various Gauges**, Hammer, Steel Barrel, *Modern*	55.00	85.00	85.00

PENCE, JACOB

Lancaster, Pa. 1771. See Kentucky Rifles and Pistols.

PENETRATOR

Made by Norwich Falls Pistol Co., c. 1880.

	V.G.	Exc.	Prior Year Exc. Value
HANDGUN, REVOLVER			
☐ **.32 Short R.F.**, 5 Shot, Spur Trigger, Solid Frame, Single Action, *Modern*	95.00	165.00	160.00

PENNYPACKER, DANIEL
Berks County, Pa. 1773-1808. See Kentucky Rifles and Pistols.

PENNYPACKER, WM.
Berks County, Pa. 1808-1858. See Kentucky Rifles and Pistols.

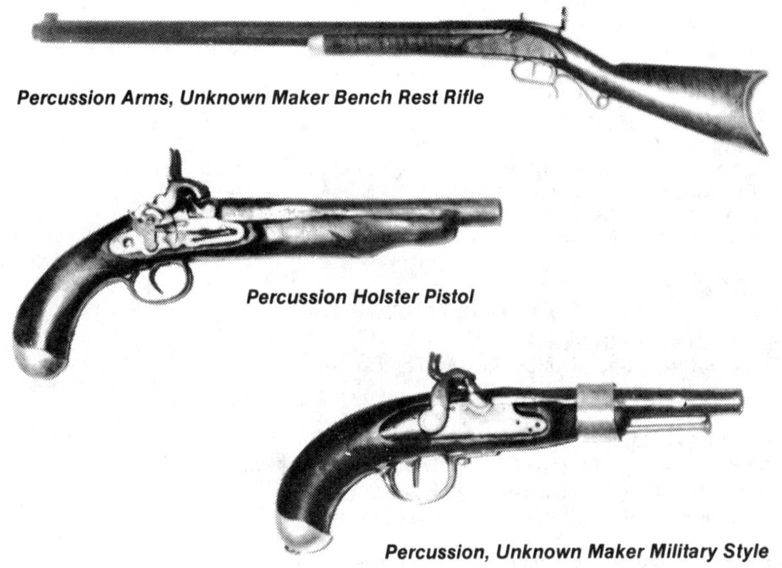

Percussion Arms, Unknown Maker Bench Rest Rifle

Percussion Holster Pistol

Percussion, Unknown Maker Military Style

PERCUSSION ARMS, UNKNOWN MAKER

	V.G.	Exc.	Prior Year Exc. Value
HANDGUN, PERCUSSION			
☐ **.40 English**, 6 Shot, Pepperbox, Pocket Pistol, Light Engraving, German Silver Frame, Steel Barrel, *Antique*	265.00	395.00	375.00
☐ **.45**, Pair French, Target Pistol, Octagon Barrel, Single Set Trigger, Brass Furniture, Cased with Accessories, *Antique*	2,000.00	2,500.00	2,500.00
☐ **.70**, French Sotiau, Belt Pistol, Steel Furniture, Rifled, Octagon Barrel, *Antique*	400.00	575.00	550.00
☐ **Boot Pistol**, Bar Hammer, Screw Barrel, *Antique*	95.00	150.00	150.00
☐ **Boot Pistol**, Boxlock, Screw Barrel, *Antique*	95.00	165.00	150.00
☐ **Boot Pistol**, Sidelock, Derringer Style, *Antique*	120.00	190.00	180.00
☐ **Pair**, Duelling Pistols, Octagon Barrel, Single Set Trigger, German Silver Furniture, Medium Quality, Cased with Accessories, *Antique*	1,400.00	2,000.00	2,000.00

	V.G.	Exc.	Prior Year Exc. Value
HANDGUN, REVOLVER			
☐ **.36**, Navy Colt Type, Belgian Make, Medium Quality, *Antique*	110.00	185.00	175.00
☐ **.45**, Adams Type, Double Action, Octagon Barrel, Plain, Cased with Accessories, *Antique*	600.00	900.00	900.00
RIFLE, PERCUSSION			
☐ **American Indian Trade Gun**, Belgian, Converted from Flintlock, Brass Furniture, *Antique*	500.00	900.00	900.00
☐ **Benchrest**, Various Calibers, Heavy Barrel, Set Triggers, Target Sights, Light Decoration, *Antique*	400.00	765.00	750.00
☐ **Benchrest**, Various Calibers, Heavy Barrel, Set Triggers, Target Sights, Medium Decoration, *Antique*	500.00	950.00	950.00
☐ **German**, Schutzen Rifle, Rifled, Ivory Inlays, Gold Inlays, Ornate, *Antique*	4,000.00	5,550.00	5,500.00
SHOTGUN, PERCUSSION			
☐ **English**, 12 Ga., Double Barrel, Side by Side, Light Ornamentation, Medium Quality, *Antique*	300.00	465.00	450.00
☐ **English**, 12 Ga., Double Barrel, Side by Side, Light Ornamentation, High Quality, Cased with Accessories, *Antique*	500.00	850.00	800.00

PERFECT

Made by Foehl & Weeks. Phila, Pa., c. 1890.

	V.G.	Exc.	Prior Year Exc. Value
HANDGUN, REVOLVER			
☐ **.38 S & W**, 5 Shot, Double Action, Top Break, *Modern*	55.00	100.00	95.00

PERFECTION

Made by Crescent for H. & G. Lipscomb & Co., Nashville, Tenn.

	V.G.	Exc.	Prior Year Exc. Value
SHOTGUN, DOUBLE BARREL, SIDE-BY-SIDE			
☐ **Various Gauges**, Outside Hammers, Damascus Barrel, *Modern*	100.00	170.00	175.00
☐ **Various Gauges**, Hammerless, Steel Barrel, *Modern*	135.00	190.00	200.00
☐ **Various Gauges**, Hammerless, Damascus Barrel, *Modern*	100.00	170.00	175.00
☐ **Various Gauges**, Outside Hammers, Steel Barrel, *Modern*	125.00	185.00	190.00
SHOTGUN, SINGLESHOT			
☐ **Various Gauges**, Hammer, Steel Barrel, *Modern*	55.00	85.00	85.00

PERFECTION AUTOMATIC REVOLVER

Made by Forehand Arms Co.

	V.G.	Exc.	Prior Year Exc. Value
HANDGUN, REVOLVER			
☐ **.32 S & W**, 5 Shot, Double Action, Top Break, *Antique*	55.00	90.00	85.00
☐ **.32 S & W**, 5 Shot, Double Action, Top Break, Hammerless, *Antique*	65.00	100.00	95.00

	V.G.	Exc.	Prior Year Exc. Value

PERLA
Frantisek Dusek, Opocno, Czechoslovakia, c. 1935.

HANDGUN, SEMI-AUTOMATIC

	V.G.	Exc.	Prior Year Exc. Value
☐ **.25 ACP**, Clip Fed, Blue, *Modern*	145.00	220.00	195.00

PETTIBONE, DANIEL
Philadelphia, Pa. 1799-1814.

PHILLIPINE MILITARY

SHOTGUN, SINGLESHOT

	V.G.	Exc.	Prior Year Exc. Value
☐ **WW 2 Guerrilla Weapon,** 12 Ga., *Modern*	30.00	65.00	100.00

PHOENIX
Spain, Tomas de Urizar y Cia., c. 1920.

HANDGUN, SEMI-AUTOMATIC

	V.G.	Exc.	Prior Year Exc. Value
☐ **Vest Pocket**, .25 ACP, Clip Fed, *Modern*	90.00	135.00	125.00

PHOENIX ARMS CO.
Lowell Arms Co., Lowell, Mass., c. 1920.

HANDGUN, SEMI-AUTOMATIC

	V.G.	Exc.	Prior Year Exc. Value
☐ **Vest Pocket**, .25 ACP, Clip Fed, *Curio*	285.00	425.00	395.00

PIC
Made in West Germany for Precise Imports Corp., Suffern, N.Y.

HANDGUN, SEMI-AUTOMATIC

	V.G.	Exc.	Prior Year Exc. Value
☐ **Vest Pocket**, .25 ACP, Clip Fed, *Modern*	55.00	80.00	75.00
☐ **Vest Pocket**, .22 Short R.F., Clip Fed, *Modern*	55.00	80.00	75.00

HANDGUN, REVOLVER

	V.G.	Exc.	Prior Year Exc. Value
☐ **.22 L.R.R.F.**, Double Action, Blue, *Modern*	20.00	35.00	35.00

PICKFATT, HUMPHREY
London, England 1714-1730.

HANDGUN, FLINTLOCK

	V.G.	Exc.	Prior Year Exc. Value
☐ **Pair**, Queen Anne Style, Box Lock, Pocket Pistol, Silver Furniture, *Antique*	2,000.00	2,850.00	2,750.00
☐ **Pair**, Holster Pistol, Engraved, Brass Furniture, High Quality, *Antique*	4,500.00	8,500.00	8,250.00

PIEDMONT
Made by Crescent for Piedmont Hdw. Danville, Pa.

SHOTGUN, DOUBLE BARREL, SIDE-BY-SIDE

	V.G.	Exc.	Prior Year Exc. Value
☐ **Various Gauges**, Outside Hammers, Damascus Barrel, *Modern*	100.00	170.00	175.00
☐ **Various Gauges**, Hammerless, Steel Barrel, *Modern*	135.00	190.00	200.00
☐ **Various Gauges**, Hammerless, Damascus Barrel, *Modern*	100.00	170.00	175.00
☐ **Various Gauges**, Outside Hammers, Steel Barrel, *Modern*	125.00	185.00	190.00

Phoenix Arms Co. .25

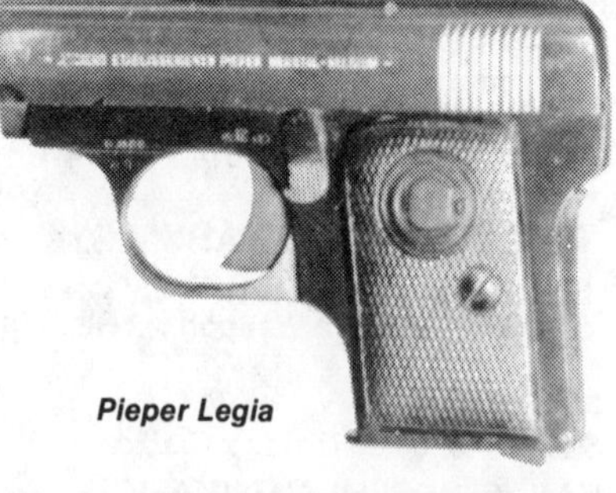

Pieper Legia

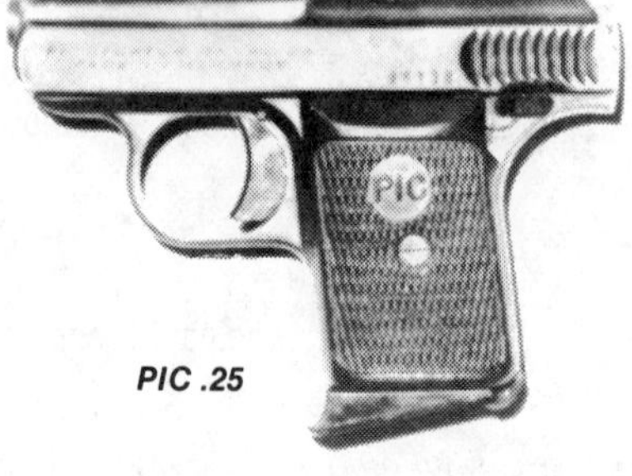

PIC .25

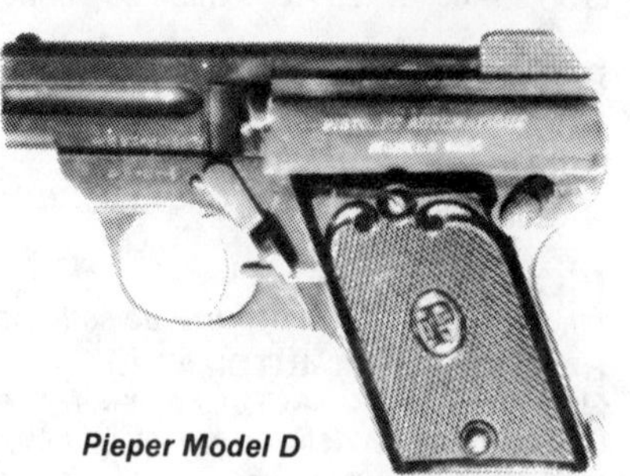

Pieper Model D

	V.G.	Exc.	Prior Year Exc. Value
SHOTGUN, SINGLESHOT			
☐ **Various Gauges**, Hammer, Steel Barrel, *Modern*	55.00	85.00	85.00

PIEPER

Henri Pieper, Herstal, Belgium 1884. Became Nicolas Pieper in 1898, and in 1905 became Anciens Etablissments Pieper.

	V.G.	Exc.	Prior Year Exc. Value
COMBINATION WEAPON, SIDE-BY-SIDE			
☐ **Various Calibers**, Hammer, Open Rear Sight, Checkered Stock, Plain, *Modern*	275.00	395.00	375.00
HANDGUN, SEMI-AUTOMATIC			
☐ **Bayard Model 1908 Pocket**, .25 ACP, Blue, Clip Fed, *Modern*	135.00	190.00	175.00
☐ **Bayard Model 1908 Pocket**, .380 ACP, Blue, Clip Fed, *Modern*	115.00	165.00	155.00
☐ **Bayard Model 1923 Pocket**, .25 ACP, Blue, Clip Fed, *Modern*	120.00	170.00	160.00
☐ **Bayard Model 1923 Pocket**, .32 ACP, Blue, Clip Fed, *Modern*	135.00	210.00	195.00
☐ **Bayard Model 1930 Pocket**, .25 ACP, Blue, Clip Fed, *Modern*	140.00	210.00	195.00

	V.G.	Exc.	Prior Year Exc. Value
☐ **Model A (Army)**, .32 ACP, Clip Fed, 7 Shot, *Modern*	100.00	150.00	140.00
☐ **Model B**, .32 ACP, Clip Fed, 6 Shot, *Modern*	85.00	125.00	120.00
☐ **Model C**, .25 ACP, Clip Fed, Long Grip, *Modern*	125.00	170.00	155.00
☐ **Model C**, .25 ACP, Clip Fed, *Modern*	100.00	140.00	135.00
☐ **Model D (1920)**, .25 ACP, Clip Fed, Tip-Up, *Modern*	120.00	165.00	140.00
☐ **Model Legia**, .25 ACP, Clip Fed, *Modern*	90.00	130.00	120.00
☐ **Model Legia**, .25 ACP, Clip Fed, Long Grip, *Modern*	100.00	145.00	135.00
☐ **Model N**, .32 ACP, Clip Fed, Tip-Up, 7 Shot, *Modern*	100.00	145.00	135.00
☐ **Model O**, .32 ACP, Clip Fed, Tip-Up, 6 Shot, *Modern*	90.00	130.00	120.00
☐ **Model P**, .25 ACP, Clip Fed, Tip-Up, *Modern*	125.00	170.00	160.00
RIFLE, BOLT ACTION			
☐ **Singleshot**, .22 L.R.R.F., Plain, *Curio*	40.00	60.00	55.00
RIFLE, SEMI-AUTOMATIC			
☐ **Pieper/Bayard Carbine**, .22 Short, Checkered Stock, Pistol Grip, *Curio*	50.00	80.00	75.00
☐ **Pieper/Bayard Carbine**, .22 Long, Checkered Stock, Pistol Grip, *Curio*	60.00	95.00	90.00
☐ **Pieper Carbine**, .22 L.R.R.F., Checkered Stock, English Grip, *Curio*	60.00	95.00	90.00
☐ **Pieper Musket**, .22 L.R.R.F., Military Style Stock, *Curio*	65.00	100.00	95.00
☐ **Pieper Musket**, .22 L.R.R.F., Military Style Stock, with Bayonet, *Curio*	85.00	125.00	120.00
SHOTGUN, DOUBLE BARREL, SIDE-BY-SIDE			
☐ **Bayard**, Various Gauges, Hammerless, Boxlock, Light Engraving, Checkered Stock, *Modern*	115.00	185.00	175.00
☐ **Hammer Gun**, Various Gauges, Plain, Steel Barrels, *Modern*	95.00	150.00	135.00
☐ **Hammer Gun**, Various Gauges, Plain, Damascus Barrels, *Modern*	75.00	140.00	125.00
☐ **Hammer Gun**, Various Gauges, Light Engraving, Steel Barrels, *Modern*	115.00	175.00	165.00

PIEPER, ABRAHAM

Lancaster, Pa. 1801-1803. See Kentucky Rifles and Pistols.

PIEPER, HENRI

Also see Pieper

	V.G.	Exc.	Prior Year Exc. Value
COMBINATION WEAPON, SIDE-BY-SIDE			
☐ **Various Calibers**, Double Trigger, Outside Hammers, Side Lever, *Antique*	275.00	395.00	375.00

PINAFORE

Made by Norwich Falls Pistol Co., c. 1880.

	V.G.	Exc.	Prior Year Exc. Value
HANDGUN, REVOLVER			
☐ **.22 Short R.F.**, 7 Shot, Spur Trigger, Solid Frame, Single Action, *Antique*	95.00	165.00	160.00

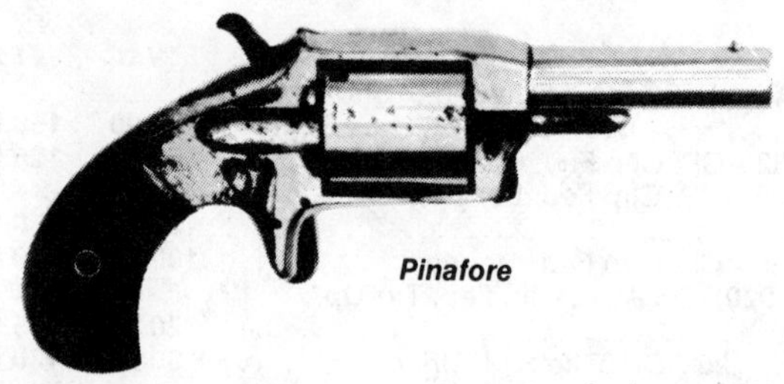

Pinafore

	V.G.	Exc.	Prior Year Exc. Value
PINKERTON			
Gaspar Arizaga, Eibar, Spain, c. 1930.			
HANDGUN, SEMI-AUTOMATIC			
☐ **Browning Type**, .25 ACP, Clip Fed, Blue, *Modern*	95.00	135.00	125.00
☐ **Mondial Type**, .25 ACP, Clip Fed, Blue, *Modern*	135.00	180.00	175.00
PIONEER			
Made by Stevens Arms.			
RIFLE, SEMI-AUTOMATIC			
☐ **Model 87**, .22 L.R.R.F., Tube Feed, Open Rear Sight, *Modern*	55.00	75.00	70.00
PIONEER			
Maker unknown, c. 1880.			
HANDGUN, REVOLVER			
☐ **.38 Short R.F.**, 5 Shot, Spur Trigger, Solid Frame, Single Action, *Antique*	95.00	170.00	170.00
PIONEER ARMS CO.			
Made by Crescent for Kruse Hardware Co. Cincinnati, Ohio.			
SHOTGUN, DOUBLE BARREL, SIDE-BY-SIDE			
☐ **Various Gauges**, Outside Hammers, Damascus Barrel, *Modern*	100.00	170.00	175.00
☐ **Various Gauges**, Hammerless, Steel Barrel, *Modern*	135.00	190.00	200.00
☐ **Various Gauges**, Hammerless, Damascus Barrel, *Modern*	100.00	170.00	175.00
☐ **Various Gauges**, Outside Hammers, Steel Barrel, *Modern*	125.00	185.00	190.00
SHOTGUN, SINGLESHOT			
☐ **Various Gauges**, Hammer, Steel Barrel, *Modern*	55.00	85.00	85.00
PIOTTI			
Brescia, Italy. Currently Imported by Ventura Imports.			
SHOTGUN, DOUBLE BARREL, SIDE-BY-SIDE			
☐ **Gardone**, 12 and 20 Gauges, Sidelock, Automatic Ejector, Double Trigger, Fancy Checkering, Fancy Engraving, *Modern*	1,250.00	1,775.00	1,750.00
☐ **Val Trompia Crown**, 12 and 20 Gauges, Sidelock, Automatic Ejector, Single Selective Trigger, Fancy Checkering, Fancy Engraving, *Modern*	2,600.00	3,850.00	3,750.00

PJK
Bradbury, Calif.

RIFLE, SEMI-AUTOMATIC

	V.G.	Exc.	Prior Year Exc. Value
☐ **M-68**, 9mm Luger, Clip Fed, Carbine, Flash Hider, *Modern*	130.00	185.00	175.00

PLAINFIELD MACHINE CO.
Dunellen, N.J., Also see Iver Johnson.

	V.G.	Exc.	Prior Year Exc. Value
AUTOMATIC WEAPON, SUBMACHINE GUN			
☐ **M-2**, .30 Carbine, Carbine, Commercial, *Class 3*	150.00	195.00	195.00
HANDGUN, SEMI-AUTOMATIC			
☐ **Super Enforcer**, .30 Carbine, Clip Fed, *Modern*	135.00	175.00	165.00
RIFLE, SEMI-AUTOMATIC			
☐ **M-1**, .30 Carbine, Carbine, *Modern*	130.00	175.00	165.00
☐ **M-1**, .30 Carbine, Carbine, Sporting Rifle, *Modern*	125.00	170.00	160.00
☐ **M-1**, 5.7mm Carbine, Carbine, *Modern*	120.00	165.00	155.00
☐ **M-1 Deluxe**, .30 Carbine, Carbine, Sporting Rifle, Monte Carlo Stock, Checkered Stock, *Modern*	145.00	190.00	180.00
☐ **M-1 Paratrooper**, .30 Carbine, Carbine, Folding Stock, *Modern*	145.00	190.00	180.00
☐ **M-1 Presentation**, .30 Carbine, Carbine, Sporting Rifle, Monte Carlo Stock, Fancy Wood, *Modern*	145.00	195.00	185.00

PLAINFIELD ORDNANCE CO.
Middlesex, N.J.

HANDGUN, SEMI-AUTOMATIC

	V.G.	Exc.	Prior Year Exc. Value
☐ **Model 71**, .22 L.R.R.F., Clip Fed, Stainless Steel, *Modern*	75.00	105.00	95.00
☐ **Model 71**, .22 L.R.R.F. and .25 ACP, Clip Fed, Stainless Steel, with Conversion Kit, *Modern*	85.00	125.00	120.00
☐ **Model 71**, .25 ACP, Clip Fed, Stainless Steel, *Modern*	75.00	115.00	110.00
☐ **Model 72**, .22 L.R.R.F., Clip Fed, Lightweight, *Modern*	75.00	115.00	110.00
☐ **Model 72**, .22 L.R.R.F. and .25 ACP, Clip Fed, Lightweight, with Conversion Kit, *Modern*	95.00	140.00	130.00
☐ **Model 72**, .25 ACP, Clip Fed, Lightweight, *Modern*	65.00	105.00	95.00

PLANT'S MFG. CO.
New Haven, Conn. 1860-1866.

HANDGUN, REVOLVER

	V.G.	Exc.	Prior Year Exc. Value
☐ **.28 Cup Primed Cartridge**, 6 Shot, Single Action, Spur Trigger, Solid Frame, *Antique*	140.00	225.00	195.00
☐ **.30 Cup Primed Cartridge**, 6 Shot, Single Action, Spur Trigger, Solid Frame, *Antique*	145.00	230.00	210.00
☐ **.31 R.F.**, 6 Shot, Single Action, Solid Frame, Spur Trigger, *Antique*	135.00	200.00	180.00
☐ **.32 Short R.F.**, 6 Shot, Single Action, Solid Frame, Spur Trigger, *Antique*	135.00	200.00	180.00
☐ **.42 Cup Primed Cartridge**, 6 Shot, Single Action, Spur Trigger, Solid Frame, *Antique*	170.00	265.00	240.00

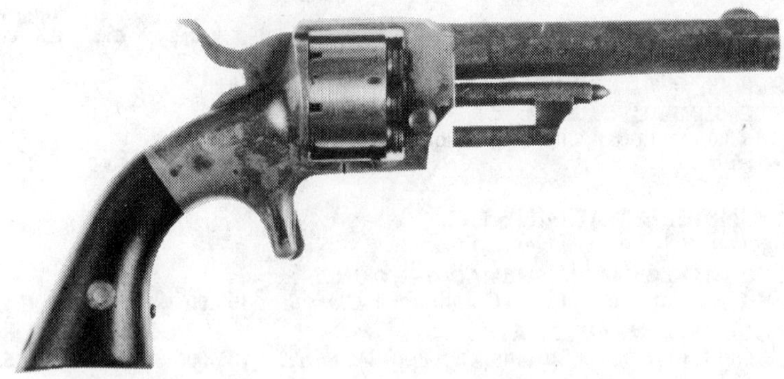

Lucius W. Pond Seven Shot Cartridge Revolver, .22 Caliber

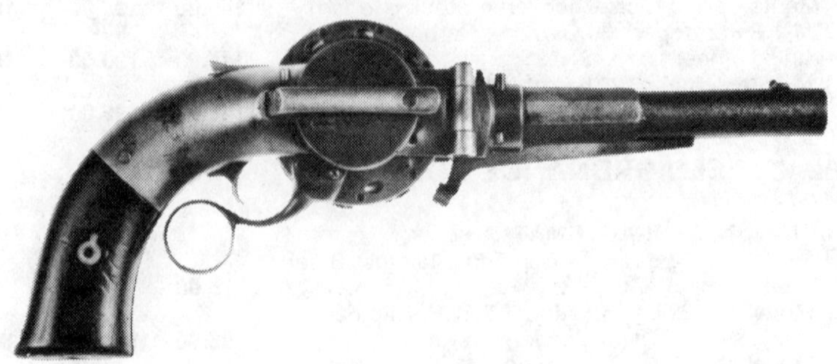

Patrick W. Porter Patent Turret Pistol, .41 Caliber

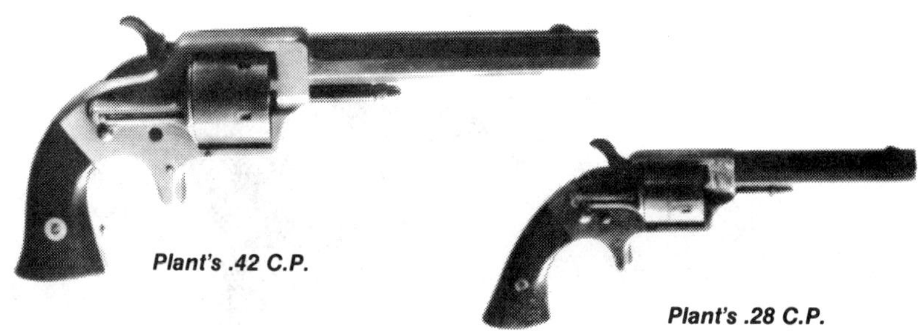
Plant's .42 C.P.

Plant's .28 C.P.

	V.G.	Exc.	Prior Year Exc. Value
☐ **.42 Cup Primed Cartridge**, 6 Shot, Single Action, Spur Trigger, Solid Frame, 6" Barrel, *Antique*	275.00	425.00	395.00
☐ **"Original"**, .28 Cup Primed Cartridge, 6 Shot, Single Action, Spur Trigger, Tip-Up, *Antique*	495.00	675.00	650.00
☐ **"Original"**, .30 Cup Primed Cartridge, 6 Shot, Single Action, Spur Trigger, Tip-Up, *Antique*	520.00	695.00	675.00
☐ **"Original"**, .42 Cup Primed Cartridge, 6 Shot, Single Action, Spur Trigger, Tip-Up, *Antique*	575.00	735.00	695.00
☐ **"Original"**, Various Cup-Primed Calibers, Extra Cylinder, Percussion, *Add* **$110.00-$185.00**			
☐ **Reynolds**, .25 Short R.F., 5 Shot, Single Action, Spur Trigger, 3" Barrel, *Antique*	130.00	190.00	180.00

PLUS ULTRA

Gabilondo y Cia., Eibar, Spain, c. 1930.

HANDGUN, SEMI-AUTOMATIC

☐ **.32 ACP**, Extra Long Grip, Military, *Modern*	375.00	550.00	550.00

POND, LUCIUS

Worcester, Mass., c. 1863-72

HANDGUN, REVOLVER

☐ **Front Loader,** .22, 7 Shot, 3½" bbl., *Antique*	160.00	300.00	290.00

PORTER, PATRICK W.

New York City, c. 1851-54

HANDGUN, PERCUSSION

☐ **Patent Turret Pistol,** .41, 9 Shot, *Antique*	3725.00	7850.00	7325.00

PORTUGUESE MILITARY

RIFLE, BOLT ACTION

☐ **Kropatchek M1886,** 8mm, Tube Feed, *Antique*	70.00	120.00	110.00
☐ **Mauser-Vergueiro,** 6.5mm, Rifle, *Curio*	60.00	100.00	130.00

POUS, EUDAL

Spain, c. 1790.

HANDGUN, MIQUELET-LOCK

☐ **Pair**, Holster Pistol, Low Quality, Light Brass Furniture, *Antique*	1,550.00	2,850.00	2,750.00

PRAGA

Zbrojovka Praga, Prague, Czechoslovakia 1918-1926.

Praga Praha

	V.G.	Exc.	Prior Year Exc. Value
HANDGUN, SEMI-AUTOMATIC			
☐ **Praga**, .25 ACP, Clip Fed, Folding Trigger, *Curio*	145.00	195.00	180.00
☐ **Praha**, .32 ACP, Clip Fed, *Curio*	195.00	265.00	250.00

PRAIRIE KING

Made by Norwich Falls Pistol Co., c. 1880.

	V.G.	Exc.	Prior Year Exc. Value
HANDGUN, REVOLVER			
☐ **.22 Short R.F.**, 7 Shot, Spur Trigger, Solid Frame, Single Action, *Antique*	85.00	145.00	130.00

PREMIER

Tomas de Urizar y Cia., Eibar, Spain, c. 1920.

	V.G.	Exc.	Prior Year Exc. Value
HANDGUN, SEMI-AUTOMATIC			
☐ **.25 ACP**, Clip Fed, Blue, *Modern*	85.00	125.00	120.00

PREMIER

Brooklyn, N.Y.

	V.G.	Exc.	Prior Year Exc. Value
SHOTGUN, DOUBLE BARREL, SIDE-BY-SIDE			
☐ **Ambassador**, Various Calibers, Checkered Stock, Hammerless, Double Trigger, *Modern*	165.00	225.00	220.00
☐ **Brush King**, 12 and 20 Gauges, Checkered Stock, Hammerless, Double Trigger, *Modern*	130.00	175.00	165.00
☐ **Continental**, Various Calibers, Checkered Stock, Outside Hammers, Double Trigger, *Modern*	135.00	190.00	185.00
☐ **Magnum**, 10 Ga. 3½", Checkered Stock, Hammerless, Double Trigger, *Modern*	150.00	210.00	200.00
☐ **Monarch**, Various Calibers, Hammerless, Double Trigger, Checkered Stock, Engraved, Adjustable Choke, *Modern*	250.00	365.00	350.00
☐ **Presentation**, Various Calibers, Adjustable Choke, Double Trigger, Fancy Engraving, Fancy Checkering, Extra Shotgun Barrel, *Modern*	650.00	900.00	900.00
☐ **Regent**, Various Calibers, Checkered Stock, Hammerless, Double Trigger, *Modern*	120.00	165.00	155.00

	V.G.	Exc.	Prior Year Exc. Value
☐ **Regent**, Various Calibers, Checkered Stock, Hammerless, Double Trigger, Extra Shotgun Barrel, *Modern*	210.00	315.00	300.00

PREMIER

Made by Stevens Arms.

RIFLE, BOLT ACTION

	V.G.	Exc.	Prior Year Exc. Value
☐ **Model 52**, .22 L.R.R.F., Singleshot, Takedown, *Modern*	30.00	45.00	40.00
☐ **Model 53**, .22 L.R.R.F., Singleshot, Takedown, *Modern*	35.00	50.00	45.00
☐ **Model 66 Buckhorn**, .22 L.R.R.F., Tube Feed, Open Rear Sight, *Modern*	35.00	60.00	55.00

RIFLE, SLIDE ACTION

	V.G.	Exc.	Prior Year Exc. Value
☐ **Model 75**, .22 L.R.R.F., Tube Feed, Hammerless, *Modern*	90.00	165.00	160.00

PREMIER

Made by Thomas E. Ryan, Norwich, Conn., c. 1870-1876.

HANDGUN, REVOLVER

	V.G.	Exc.	Prior Year Exc. Value
☐ **.22 Short R.F.**, 7 Shot, Spur Trigger, Solid Frame, Single Action, *Antique*	95.00	165.00	160.00
☐ **.38 Long R.F.**, 6 Shot, Spur Trigger, Solid Frame, Single Action, *Antique*	95.00	165.00	160.00

PREMIER TRAIL BLAZER

Made by Stevens Arms.

RIFLE, SLIDE ACTION

	V.G.	Exc.	Prior Year Exc. Value
☐ **Model 75**, .22 L.R.R.F., Tube Feed, Hammerless, *Modern*	90.00	165.00	160.00

PRESCOTT, E.A.

Worcester, Mass. 1860-1874.

HANDGUN, REVOLVER

	V.G.	Exc.	Prior Year Exc. Value
☐ **.22 Short R.F.**, 7 Shot, Spur Trigger, Solid Frame, Single Action, *Antique*	95.00	160.00	150.00
☐ **.30 R.F.**, 6 Shot, Spur Trigger, Solid Frame, Single Action, *Antique*	95.00	165.00	155.00
☐ **.32 Short R.F.**, 6 Shot, Spur Trigger, Solid Frame, Single Action, *Antique*	95.00	165.00	155.00
☐ **"Navy" .32 Short R.F.**, 6 Shot, Single Action, Solid Frame, Finger-Rest Trigger Guard, *Antique*	225.00	325.00	300.00
☐ **"Navy" .38 Short R.F.**, 6 Shot, Single Action, Solid Frame, Finger-Rest Trigger Guard, *Antique*	260.00	350.00	325.00

PRICE, J.W.

Made by Stevens Arms.

SHOTGUN, SINGLESHOT

	V.G.	Exc.	Prior Year Exc. Value
☐ **Model 90**, Various Gauges, Takedown, Automatic Ejector, Plain, Hammer, *Modern*	40.00	60.00	55.00

Prima

Princeps

PRIMA

Mre. d'Armes des Pyrenees, Hendaye, France.

HANDGUN, SEMI-AUTOMATIC

	V.G.	Exc.	Prior Year Exc. Value
☐ **.25 ACP**, Clip Fed, *Modern*	95.00	140.00	135.00

PRINCEPS

Tomas de Urizar, Eibar, Spain, c. 1920.

HANDGUN, SEMI-AUTOMATIC

	V.G.	Exc.	Prior Year Exc. Value
☐ **.32 ACP**, Clip Fed, *Modern*	90.00	135.00	130.00

PRINCESS

Unknown maker, c. 1880.

HANDGUN, REVOLVER

	V.G.	Exc.	Prior Year Exc. Value
☐ **.22 Short R.F.**, 7 Shot, Spur Trigger, Solid Frame, Single Action, *Antique*	95.00	165.00	160.00

PROTECTOR

Made by Norwich Falls Pistol Co., c. 1880.

HANDGUN, REVOLVER

	V.G.	Exc.	Prior Year Exc. Value
☐ **.32 Short R.F.**, 5 Shot, Spur Trigger, Solid Frame, Single Action, *Antique*	95.00	170.00	170.00

PROTECTOR ARMS CO.

Spain, c. 1900.

HANDGUN, SEMI-AUTOMATIC

	V.G.	Exc.	Prior Year Exc. Value
☐ **M 1918**, .25 ACP, Clip Fed, *Modern*	85.00	130.00	125.00

PURDEY, JAMES

RIFLE, DOUBLE BARREL, SIDE-BY-SIDE

	V.G.	Exc.	Prior Year Exc. Value
☐ **.500 #2 Express**, Damascus Barrel, Outside Hammers, Under-Lever, Engraved, Ornate, *Antique*	2,550.00	3,600.00	3,500.00

RIFLE, PERCUSSION

	V.G.	Exc.	Prior Year Exc. Value
☐ **.52**, Double Barrel, Side by Side, Damascus Barrel, Engraved, Fancy Wood, Gold Inlays, Cased with Accessories, *Antique*	5,000.00	6,000.00	6,000.00

PURDEY, JAS. & SONS

London, England, 1816 to Date.

	V.G.	Exc.	Prior Year Exc. Value
RIFLE, DOUBLE BARREL, SIDE-BY-SIDE			
☐ **Various Calibers**, Sidelock, Fancy Engraving, Fancy Checkering, Fancy Wood, *Modern*	8,000.00	14,500.00	14,500.00
RIFLE, BOLT ACTION			
☐ **Sporting Rifle**, Various Calibers, Fancy Wood, Checkered Stock, Express Sights, *Modern*	1,450.00	2,300.00	2,250.00
SHOTGUN, DOUBLE BARREL, OVER-UNDER			
☐ **12 Ga.**, Vent Rib, Single Selective Trigger, Pistol-Grip Stock, *Modern*	9,000.00	16,250.00	16,000.00
☐ **Various Gauges**, Extra Barrels Only **$3000.00-$5000.00**			
☐ **Purdy**, Various Gauges, Sidelock, Automatic Ejector, Double Trigger, Fancy Engraving, Fancy Checkering, *Modern*	7,500.00	12,500.00	12,000.00
☐ **Purdy**, Various Gauges, Sidelock, Automatic Ejector, Single Trigger, Fancy Engraving, Fancy Checkering, *Modern*	9,500.00	14,500.00	14,000.00
☐ **Woodward**, Various Gauges, Sidelock, Automatic Ejector, Double Trigger, Fancy Engraving, Fancy Checkering, *Modern*	7,500.00	10,500.00	10,000.00
☐ **Woodward**, Various Gauges, Sidelock, Automatic Ejector, Single Trigger, Fancy Engraving, Fancy Checkering, *Modern*	11,500.00	17,500.00	17,000.00
SHOTGUN, DOUBLE BARREL, SIDE-BY-SIDE			
☐ **12 Ga.**, Extra Barrel, Vent Rib, Single Selective Trigger, Engraved, Cased with Accessories, *Modern*	12,500.00	18,500.00	18,000.00
☐ **12 Ga.**, Extra Barrels, 10 Ga., Pistol-Grip Stock, Cased with Accessories, *Modern*	12,500.00	18,500.00	18,000.00
☐ **Various Gauges**, Extra Barrels Only $2,600.00-$3,750.00			
☐ **Featherweight**, Various Gauges, Sidelock, Automatic Ejector, Double Trigger, Fancy Engraving, Fancy Checkering, *Modern*	8,500.00	12,500.00	12,000.00
☐ **Featherweight**, Various Gauges, Sidelock, Automatic Ejector, Single Trigger, Fancy Engraving, Fancy Checkering, *Modern*	9,000.00	15,500.00	15,000.00
☐ **Game Gun**, Various Gauges, Sidelock, Automatic Ejector, Double Trigger, Fancy Engraving, Fancy Checkering, *Modern*	8,000.00	13,500.00	13,000.00
☐ **Game Gun**, Various Gauges, Sidelock, Automatic Ejector, Single Trigger, Fancy Engraving, Fancy Checkering, *Modern*	9,000.00	15,500.00	15,000.00
☐ **Pigeon Gun**, 12 Ga., Single Selective Trigger, Vent Rib, Cased Straight Grip, *Modern*	9,000.00	15,500.00	15,000.00
☐ **Pigeon Gun**, Various Gauges, Sidelock, Automatic Ejector, Double Trigger, Fancy Engraving, Fancy Checkering, *Modern*	7,500.00	12,500.00	12,000.00
☐ **Pigeon Gun**, Various Gauges, Sidelock, Automatic Ejector, Single Trigger, Fancy Engraving, Fancy Checkering, *Modern*	8,000.00	13,500.00	13,000.00

	V.G.	Exc.	Prior Year Exc. Value
☐ **Two-Inch**, 12 Ga. 2", Sidelock, Automatic Ejector, Double Trigger, Fancy Engraving, Fancy Checkering, *Modern*	7,000.00	10,500.00	10,000.00
☐ **Two-Inch**, 12 Ga. 2", Sidelock, Automatic Ejector, Single Trigger, Fancy Engraving, Fancy Checkering, *Modern*	8,500.00	12,750.00	12,500.00
SHOTGUN, SINGLESHOT			
☐ **12 Ga.**, Vent Rib, Plain, Trap Grade, *Modern*	6,500.00	10,000.00	9,500.00

PZK

Kohout & Spolecnost, Kydne, Czechoslovakia.

	V.G.	Exc.	Prior Year Exc. Value
HANDGUN, SEMI-AUTOMATIC			
☐ **PZK**, .25 ACP, Clip Fed, *Modern*	145.00	190.00	175.00

QUACKENBUSH

Herkimer, N.Y., c. 1880.

	V.G.	Exc.	Prior Year Exc. Value
RIFLE, SINGLESHOT			
☐ **.22 R.F.**, Side Swing Breech, Nickel Plated, Takedown, *Modern*	115.00	165.00	150.00

QUAIL

Made by Crescent, c. 1900.

	V.G.	Exc.	Prior Year Exc. Value
SHOTGUN, DOUBLE BARREL, SIDE-BY-SIDE			
☐ **Various Gauges**, Outside Hammers, Damascus Barrel, *Modern*	100.00	170.00	175.00
☐ **Various Gauges**, Hammerless, Steel Barrel, *Modern*	135.00	190.00	200.00
☐ **Various Gauges**, Hammerless, Damascus Barrel, *Modern*	100.00	170.00	175.00
☐ **Various Gauges**, Outside Hammers, Steel Barrel, *Modern*	125.00	185.00	190.00
SHOTGUN, SINGLESHOT			
☐ **Various Gauges**, Hammer, Steel Barrel, *Modern*	55.00	85.00	85.00

QUAIL'S FARGO

Tradename used by Dakin Gun Co. and Simmons Specialties.

	V.G.	Exc.	Prior Year Exc. Value
SHOTGUN, DOUBLE BARREL, SIDE-BY-SIDE			
☐ **12 Ga.**, Checkered Stock, Plain, *Modern*	130.00	175.00	165.00

QUEEN CITY

Made by Crescent for Elmira Arms Co., c. 1900.

	V.G.	Exc.	Prior Year Exc. Value
SHOTGUN, DOUBLE BARREL, SIDE-BY-SIDE			
☐ **Various Gauges**, Outside Hammers, Damascus Barrel, *Modern*	100.00	170.00	175.00
☐ **Various Gauges**, Hammerless, Steel Barrel, *Modern*	135.00	190.00	200.00
☐ **Various Gauges**, Hammerless, Damascus Barrel, *Modern*	100.00	170.00	175.00
☐ **Various Gauges**, Outside Hammers, Steel Barrel, *Modern*	125.00	185.00	190.00
SHOTGUN, SINGLESHOT			
☐ **Various Gauges**, Hammer, Steel Barrel, *Modern*	55.00	85.00	85.00

	V.G.	Exc.	Prior Year Exc. Value

RADIUM
Gabilondo y Urresti, Guernica, Spain, c. 1910

HANDGUN, SEMI-AUTOMATIC

	V.G.	Exc.	Prior Year Exc. Value
☐ **.25 ACP**, Fixed Magazine, Side Loading, Blue, *Curio*	185.00	285.00	275.00

RADOM
Fabryka Broni w Radomu, Radom, Poland, c. 1930 through WWII.

HANDGUN, REVOLVER

	V.G.	Exc.	Prior Year Exc. Value
☐ **Ng 30**, 7.62mm Nagant, Gas Seal, Double Action, *Curio*	145.00	215.00	185.00

HANDGUN, SEMI-AUTOMATIC

	V.G.	Exc.	Prior Year Exc. Value
☐ **VIS 1935**, 9mm Luger, Clip Fed, Military, Nazi-Proofed, Early Type, *Modern*	195.00	285.00	225.00
☐ **VIS 1935**, 9mm Luger, Clip Fed, Military, Nazi-Proofed, Late Type, *Modern*	165.00	240.00	225.00
☐ **VIS 1935 Navy**, 9mm Luger, Clip Fed, Military, Nazi-Proofed, *Modern*	550.00	700.00	225.00
☐ **VIS 1935 Polish**, 9mm Luger, Clip Fed, Military, *Modern*	465.00	650.00	225.00

Radom, Polish ***Radom, Early Nazi*** ***Radom, Late Nazi***

RANGER
Made by E.L. Dickinson, Springfield, Mass.

HANDGUN, REVOLVER

	V.G.	Exc.	Prior Year Exc. Value
☐ **#2**, .32 Short R.F., 5 Shot, Spur Trigger, Solid Frame, Single Action, *Antique*	90.00	155.00	150.00

RANGER
Made by Stevens Arms.

	V.G.	Exc.	Prior Year Exc. Value
RIFLE, SLIDE ACTION			
☐ **Model 70**, .22 L.R.R.F., Solid Frame, Hammer, *Modern*	95.00	160.00	150.00
☐ **Model 75**, .22 L.R.R.F., Tube Feed, Hammerless, *Modern*	115.00	175.00	170.00
SHOTGUN, DOUBLE BARREL, SIDE-BY-SIDE			
☐ **Model 315**, Various Gauges, Steel Barrels, Hammerless, *Modern*	115.00	170.00	165.00
☐ **Model 215**, 12 and 16 Gauges, Steel Barrels, Outside Hammers, *Modern*	115.00	170.00	165.00
SHOTGUN, SINGLESHOT			
☐ **Model 89 Dreadnaught**, Varoius Gauges, Hammer, *Modern*	40.00	60.00	60.00

RANGER

Made by Hopkins & Allen, c. 1880.

	V.G.	Exc.	Prior Year Exc. Value
HANDGUN, REVOLVER			
☐ **.22 Short R.F.**, 7 Shot, Spur Trigger, Solid Frame, Single Action, *Antique*	90.00	155.00	150.00
☐ **.32 Short R.F.**, 6 Shot, Spur Trigger, Solid Frame, Single Action, *Antique*	95.00	165.00	160.00

RANGER ARMS, INC.

Gainesville, Tex., c. 1972.

	V.G.	Exc.	Prior Year Exc. Value
RIFLE, BOLT ACTION			
☐ **Bench Rest/Varminter**, Various Calibers, Singleshot, Target Rifle, Thumbhole Stock, Heavy Barrel, Recoil Pad, *Modern*	325.00	465.00	450.00
☐ **Governor Grade**, Various Calibers, Sporting Rifle, Fancy Checkering, Fancy Wood, Recoil Pad, Sling Swivels, *Modern*	300.00	420.00	400.00
☐ **Governor Grade Magnum**, Various Calibers, Sporting Rifle, Fancy Checkering, Fancy Wood, Recoil Pad, Sling Swivels, *Modern*	325.00	470.00	450.00
☐ **Senator Grade**, Various Calibers, Sporting Rifle, Fancy Checkering, Recoil Pad, Sling Swivels, *Modern*	250.00	365.00	350.00
☐ **Senator Grade Magnum**, Various Calibers, Sporting Rifle, Fancy Checkering, Recoil Pad, Sling Swivels, *Modern*	260.00	370.00	360.00
☐ **Statesman Grade**, Various Calibers, Sporting Rifle, Checkered Stock, Recoil Pad, Sling Swivels, *Modern*	175.00	260.00	250.00
☐ **Statesman Grade Magnum**, Various Calibers, Sporting Rifle, Checkered Stock, Recoil Pad, Sling Swivels, *Modern*	185.00	285.00	275.00

RANDALL

Randall Firearms Mfg. Corp., Sun Valley, Calif.

	V.G.	Exc.	Prior Year Exc. Value
HANDGUN, SEMI-AUTOMATIC			
☐ **Compact Model**, Various Calibers, Stainless Steel, M1911A1 Style, Herritt Grips, Adjustable Sights, *Modern*	225.00	300.00	—

	V.G.	Exc.	Prior Year Exc. Value
☐ **Service Model**, Various Calibers, Stainless Steel, M1911A1 Style, Herritt Grips, Adjustable Sights, *Modern*	275.00	350.00	—
☐ **Target Model**, Various Calibers, Stainless Steel, M1911A1 Style, Herritt Grips, Adjustable Sights with Rib, *Modern*	300.00	375.00	—

RASCH

Brunswick, Germany 1790-1810.

RIFLE, FLINTLOCK

	V.G.	Exc.	Prior Year Exc. Value
☐ **Yaeger**, Octagon Barrel, Brass Furniture, Engraved, Carved, Target Sights, *Antique*	2,600.00	3,500.00	3,450.00

RATHFONG, GEORGE

Lancaster, Pa. 1774-1809. See U.S. Military, Kentucky Rifles.

RATHFONG, JACOB

Lancaster, Pa. 1810-1839. See Kentucky Rifles and Pistols.

RAVEN

Raven Arms, Industry, Calif.

HANDGUN, SEMI-AUTOMATIC

	V.G.	Exc.	Prior Year Exc. Value
☐ **P-25**, .25 ACP, Clip Fed, Blue, *Modern*	30.00	40.00	40.00
☐ **P-25**, .25 ACP, Clip Fed, Nickel, *Modern*	30.00	40.00	40.00
☐ **P-25**, .25 ACP, Clip Fed, Chrome, *Modern*	30.00	40.00	40.00
☐ **MP-25**, .25 ACP, Clip Fed, Teflon, *Modern*	35.00	50.00	—
☐ **MP-25**, .25 ACP, Clip Fed, Nickel, *Modern*	35.00	50.00	—
☐ **MP-25**, .25 ACP, Clip Fed, Chrome, *Modern*	35.00	50.00	—

Raven MP-25

REASOR, DAVID

Lancaster, Pa. 1749-1780. See Kentucky Rifles and Pistols.

RECK

Reck Sportwaffenfabrik, Arnsberg, West Germany.

HANDGUN, REVOLVER

	V.G.	Exc.	Prior Year Exc. Value
☐ **.22 L.R.R.F.**, Double Action, Blue, *Modern*	20.00	30.00	30.00

HANDGUN, SEMI-AUTOMATIC

	V.G.	Exc.	Prior Year Exc. Value
☐ **P-8**, .25 ACP, Clip Fed, Blue, *Modern*	40.00	65.00	60.00

	V.G.	Exc.	Prior Year Exc. Value

RED CLOUD

HANDGUN, REVOLVER

	V.G.	Exc.	Prior Year Exc. Value
☐ **.32 Long R.F.**, 5 Shot, Single Action, Solid Frame, Spur Trigger, *Antique*	95.00	165.00	160.00

RED JACKET

Made by Lee Arms, Wilkes-Barre, Pa., c. 1870.

HANDGUN, REVOLVER

	V.G.	Exc.	Prior Year Exc. Value
☐ **.22 Long R.F.**, 7 Shot, Single Action, Solid Frame, Spur Trigger, *Antique*	95.00	165.00	160.00
☐ **.32 Short R.F.**, 5 Shot, Single Action, Solid Frame, Spur Trigger, *Antique*	95.00	170.00	165.00

RED MOUNTAIN ARSENAL

Parowen, Utah

AUTOMATIC WEAPON, SUBMACHINE GUN

	V.G.	Exc.	Prior Year Exc. Value
☐ **Model 80C**, 9mm Luger and .45 ACP Combo, Clip Fed, With Conversion Kit, *Class 3*	260.00	350.00	350.00

REED, JAMES

Lancaster, Pa. 1778-1780. See Kentucky Rifles.

REFORM

August Schueler, Suhl, Germany, c. 1910.

HANDGUN, MANUAL REPEATER

	V.G.	Exc.	Prior Year Exc. Value
☐ **6mm R.F.**, 1 Barrel, Spur Trigger, Hammer, *Curio*	265.00	350.00	175.00
☐ **.25 ACP**, 4 Barrels, Spur Trigger, Hammer, *Curio*	225.00	325.00	140.00
☐ **.25 ACP & 6mm R.F.**, 2 Sets of Barrels, Spur Trigger, Hammer, *Curio*	325.00	425.00	300.00

REFORM

Spain, unknown maker, c. 1920.

HANDGUN, SEMI-AUTOMATIC

	V.G.	Exc.	Prior Year Exc. Value
☐ **.25 ACP**, Clip Fed, Blue, *Curio*	80.00	125.00	120.00

REGENT

Gregorio Bolumburu, Eibar, Spain, c. 1925.

HANDGUN, SEMI-AUTOMATIC

	V.G.	Exc.	Prior Year Exc. Value
☐ **.25 ACP**, Clip Fed, Blue, *Modern*	85.00	130.00	125.00

REGENT

Karl Burgsmuller, Kreiensen, West Germany.

HANDGUN, REVOLVER

	V.G.	Exc.	Prior Year Exc. Value
☐ **.22 L.R.R.F.**, Double Action, Blue *Modern*	25.00	40.00	40.00

REGINA

Gregorio Bolumburu, Eibar, Spain, c. 1920.

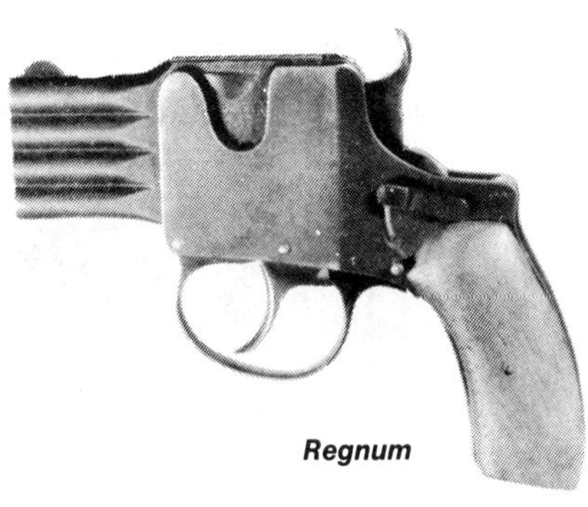

Regnum

Regina Vest Pocket

	V.G.	Exc.	Prior Year Exc. Value
HANDGUN, SEMI-AUTOMATIC			
☐ **Pocket**, .32 ACP, Clip Fed, Blue, *Modern*	85.00	135.00	125.00
☐ **Vest Pocket**, .25 ACP, Clip Fed, Blue, *Modern*	75.00	120.00	110.00

REGNUM

Tradename used by August Menz, Suhl, Germany.

	V.G.	Exc.	Prior Year Exc. Value
HANDGUN, MANUAL REPEATER			
☐ **.25 ACP**, 4 Barrels, Spur Trigger, Hammer, *Modern*	145.00	225.00	145.00

REID PATENT REVOLVERS

Made by W. Irving for James Reid, N.Y. 1862-1884.

	V.G.	Exc.	Prior Year Exc. Value
HANDGUN, REVOLVER			
☐ **.22 Short R.F.**, 7 Shot, Spur Trigger, Solid Frame, Single Action, *Antique*	150.00	275.00	265.00
☐ **.32 Short R.F.**, 7 Shot, Spur Trigger, Solid Frame, Single Action, *Antique*	195.00	355.00	340.00
☐ **.41 Short R.F.**, 5 Shot, Spur Trigger, Solid Frame, Single Action, *Antique*	395.00	575.00	550.00
☐ **My Friend**, .22 R.F., Knuckleduster, 7 Shot, *Antique*	240.00	400.00	375.00
☐ **My Friend**, .32 R.F., Knuckleduster, 7 Shot, *Antique*	300.00	475.00	450.00

REIMS

Azanza y Arrizabalaga, Eibar, Spain, c. 1914.

	V.G.	Exc.	Prior Year Exc. Value
HANDGUN, SEMI-AUTOMATIC			
☐ **1914 Model**, .25 ACP, Clip Fed, *Modern*	85.00	125.00	120.00
☐ **1914 Model**, .32 ACP, Clip Fed, *Modern*	95.00	140.00	135.00

REINA

Mre. d'Armes des Pyrenees, Hendaye, France, c. 1930.

	V.G.	Exc.	Prior Year Exc. Value
HANDGUN, SEMI-AUTOMATIC			
☐ **.32 ACP**, Clip Fed, Blue, *Modern*	95.00	145.00	135.00

REISING

Hartford, Conn. 1916-1924.

	V.G.	Exc.	Prior Year Exc. Value
AUTOMATIC WEAPON, SUBMACHINE GUN			
☐ **M50 Reising**, .45 ACP, Clip Fed, Wood Stock, Military, Cased with Accessories, *Class 3*	265.00	375.00	350.00
☐ **M50 Reising**, .45 ACP, Clip Fed, Wood Stock, Military, *Class 3*	185.00	295.00	275.00
☐ **M55 Reising**, .45 ACP, Clip Fed, Folding Stock, Military, *Class 3*	295.00	400.00	375.00
HANDGUN, SEMI-AUTOMATIC			
☐ **Target (Hartford)**, .22 L.R.R.F., Clip Fed, Hammer, *Modern*	250.00	350.00	325.00
☐ **Target (N.Y.)**, .22 L.R.R.F., Clip Fed, Hammer, *Modern*	355.00	495.00	475.00

REMINGTON ARMS CO.

Eliphalet Remington, Herkimer County, N.Y. 1816-1831. Ilion, N.Y. 1831 to Date. 1856- E. Remington & Sons; 1888- Remington Arms Co.; 1910- Remington Arms U.M.C. Co.; 1925 to Date Remington Arms Co., Ilion, N.Y.

	V.G.	Exc.	Prior Year Exc. Value
HANDGUN, DOUBLE BARREL, OVER-UNDER			
☐ **Elliot Derringer,** 1st. Model, .41 Short R.F., Spur Trigger, Tip-Up, no Extractor, Markings on Sides of Barrel, E. Remington & Sons, *Antique*	430.00	700.00	675.00
☐ **Elliot Derringer,** 2nd. Model, .41 Short R.F., Spur Trigger, Tip-Up, with Extractor, Markings on Sides of Barrel, E. Remington & Sons, *Antique*	360.00	650.00	625.00
☐ **Elliot Derringer,** 3rd. Model, .41 Short R.F., Spur Trigger, Tip-Up, with Extractor, Markings on Top of Barrel, E. Remington & Sons, *Antique*	270.00	450.00	420.00
☐ **Elliot Derringer,** 4th Model, .41 Short R.F., Spur Trigger, Tip-Up, with Extractor, Markings on Top of Barrel, Remington Arms Co., *Curio*	250.00	400.00	375.00
☐ **Elliot Derringer,** 5th Model, .41 Short R.F., Spur Trigger, Tip-Up, with Extractor, Markings on Top of Barrel, *Modern*	220.00	370.00	360.00
☐ **Elliot Derringer,** 6th Model, .41 Short R.F., Spur Trigger, Tip-Up, with Extractor, Remington Arms Co. #'s L75925-L99941, *Modern*	190.00	315.00	315.00
HANDGUN, MANUAL REPEATER			
☐ **Elliot Derringer,** .22 Short R.F., 5 Shot, Double Action, Ring Trigger, Rotating Firing Block, *Antique*	335.00	475.00	450.00
☐ **Elliot Derringer,** .32 Short R.F., 4 Shot, Double Action, Ring Trigger, Rotating Firing Block, *Antique*	315.00	450.00	425.00
☐ **Rider Magazine Pistol,** .32 Extra Short R.F., Tube Feed, Spur Trigger, 5 Shot, *Antique*	400.00	585.00	545.00
HANDGUN, PERCUSSION			
☐ **.31, Beals #1,** Revolver, Pocket Pistol, 5 Shot, Octagon Barrel, 3″ Barrel, *Antique*	325.00	475.00	450.00
☐ **.31, Beals #2,** Revolver, Pocket Pistol, 5 Shot, Octagon Barrel, 3″ Barrel, Spur Trigger, *Antique*	1200.00	1925.00	1850.00
☐ **.31, Beals #3,** Revolver, Octagon Barrel, 4″ Barrel, Spur Trigger, with Loading Lever, *Antique*	675.00	1200.00	1150.00

	V.G.	Exc.	Prior Year Exc. Value
☐ **.31, New Model Pocket,** Revolver, Safety Notches on Cylinder, Spur Trigger, 5 Shot, Octagon Barrel, *Antique*	340.00	575.00	550.00
☐ **.31, Rider Pocket,** Revolver, Double Action, 5 Shot, Octagon Barrel, 3″ Barrel, *Antique*	270.00	495.00	475.00
☐ **.36, Beals Navy,** Revolver, Single Action, Octagon Barrel, 7½″ Barrel, *Antique*	435.00	700.00	675.00
☐ **.36, Belt Model,** Revolver, Safety Notches on Cylinder, Single Action, Octagon Barrel, 6½″ Barrel, *Antique*	380.00	620.00	595.00
☐ **.36, Belt Model,** Revolver, Safety Notches on Cylinder, Double Action, Octagon Barrel, 6½″ Barrel, *Antique*	535.00	960.00	935.00
☐ **.36, Model 1861 Navy,** Revolver, Channeled Loading Lever, Single Action, Octagon Barrel, 7½″ Barrel, *Antique*	440.00	700.00	675.00
☐ **.36, New Model Navy,** Revolver, Safety Notches on Cylinder, Single Action, Octagon Barrel, 7½″ Barrel, *Antique*	480.00	760.00	730.00
☐ **.36, Police Model,** Revolver, Single Action, Octagon Barrel, Various Barrel Lengths, 5 Shot, *Antique*	375.00	575.00	550.00
☐ **.44, Beals Army,** Revolver, Single Action, Octagon Barrel, 8″ Barrel, *Antique*	600.00	975.00	935.00
☐ **.44, Model 1861 Army,** Revolver, Channeled Loading Lever, Single Action, Octagon Barrel, 8″ Barrel, *Antique*	475.00	700.00	675.00
☐ **.44, New Model Army,** Revolver, Safety Notches on Cylinder, Single Action, Octagon Barrel, 7½″ Barrel, *Antique*	430.00	675.00	650.00
HANDGUN, REVOLVER			
☐ **Iroquois,** .22 L.R.R.F., 7 Shot, Solid Frame, Spur Trigger, Single Action, Fluted Cylinder, *Antique*	225.00	350.00	320.00
☐ **Iroquois,** .22 L.R.R.F., 7 Shot, Solid Frame, Spur Trigger, Single Action, Unfluted Cylinder, *Antique*	310.00	450.00	420.00
☐ **Model 1875,** .44-40 WCF, Single Action, Western Style, Solid Frame, *Antique*	700.00	1150.00	1075.00
☐ **Model 1875,** .45 Colt, Single Action, Western Style, Solid Frame, *Antique*	650.00	1100.00	1000.00
☐ **Model 1890,** .44-40 WCF, Single Action, Western Style, Solid Frame, *Antique*	950.00	1750.00	1700.00
☐ **Smoot #1,** .30 Short R.F., 5 Shot, Solid Frame, Spur Trigger, Single Action, *Antique*	170.00	255.00	245.00
☐ **Smoot #2,** .32 Short R.F., 5 Shot, Solid Frame, Spur Trigger, Single Action, *Antique*	150.00	235.00	220.00
☐ **Smoot #3,** .38 Long R.F., 5 Shot, Solid Frame, Spur Trigger, Single Action, Birdhead Grip, *Antique*	200.00	325.00	300.00
☐ **Smoot #3,** .38 Long R.F., 5 Shot, Solid Frame, Spur Trigger, Single Action, Saw Handle Grip, *Antique*	210.00	350.00	335.00
☐ **Smoot #4,** .38 S & W, 5 Shot, Solid Frame, Spur Trigger, Single Action, no Ejector Housing, *Antique*	150.00	235.00	220.00

	V.G.	Exc.	Prior Year Exc. Value
☐ **Smoot #4,** .41 Short R.F., 5 Shot, Solid Frame, Spur Trigger, Single Action, no Ejector Housing, *Antique*	145.00	210.00	195.00
☐ **Zig-Zag Derringer,** .22 Short R.F., Pepperbox, Double Action, 6 Shot, Ring Trigger, *Antique*	800.00	1450.00	1400.00
HANDGUN, SEMI-AUTOMATIC			
☐ **Model 51,** .32 ACP, Early, Clip Fed, Grip Safety, *Modern*	220.00	350.00	325.00
☐ **Model 51,** .380 ACP, Early, Clip Fed, Grip Safety, *Modern*	280.00	430.00	400.00
☐ **Model 51,** .32 ACP, Late, Clip Fed, Grip Safety, *Modern*	210.00	315.00	300.00
☐ **Model 51,** .380 ACP, Late, Clip Fed, Grip Safety, *Modern*	240.00	365.00	350.00
HANDGUN, SINGLESHOT			
☐ **#1 Vest Pocket,** .22 Short R.F., Iron Frame, no Breech Bolt, Spur Trigger, *Antique*	250.00	400.00	375.00
☐ **#2 Vest Pocket,** .30 Short R.F., Iron Frame, "Split Breech" Model, Spur Trigger, *Antique*	350.00	515.00	495.00
☐ **#2 Vest Pocket,** .41 Short R.F., Iron Frame, "Split Breech" Model, Spur Trigger, *Antique*	315.00	465.00	450.00
☐ **Elliot Derringer,** .41 Short R.F., Iron Frame, Birdhead Grip, no Breech Bolt, *Antique*	420.00	600.00	575.00
☐ **Mark III,** 10 Gauge, Signal Pistol, 9″ Barrel, Spur Trigger, Brass Frame, *Curio*	100.00	155.00	150.00
☐ **Model 1865 Navy,** .50 Rem. Navy R.F., Rolling Block, Spur Trigger, 8½″ Barrel, *Antique*	900.00	1400.00	1350.00
☐ **Model 1867 Navy,** .50 Rem. Rolling Block, 7″ Barrel, *Antique*	500.00	750.00	725.00
☐ **Model 1871 Army,** .50 Rem., Rolling Block, 8″ Barrel, *Antique*	380.00	550.00	525.00
☐ **Model 1891 Target,** Rolling Block, 12″ Barrel, *Add* **15%-20%**			
☐ **Model 1891 Target,** Rolling Block, 10″ Barrel, *Add* **15%-20%**			
☐ **Model 1891 Target,** .22 L.R.R.F., Rolling Block, 8″ Barrel, Half-Octagon Barrel, Plain Barrel, *Antique*	750.00	1200.00	1150.00
☐ **Model 1891 Target,** .25 Short R.F., Rolling Block, 8″ Barrel, Half-Octagon Barrel, Plain Barrel, *Antique*	510.00	715.00	695.00
☐ **Model 1891 Target,** .32 Long R.F., Rolling Block, 8″ Barrel, Half-Octagon Barrel, Plain Barrel, *Antique*	585.00	870.00	835.00
☐ **Model 1891 Target,** .32 S & W, Rolling Block, 8″ Barrel, Half-Octagon Barrel, Plain Barrel, *Antique*	710.00	1100.00	1050.00
☐ **Model 1891 Target,** .32-20 WCF, Rolling Block, 8″ Barrel, Half-Octagon Barrel, Plain Barrel, *Antique*	800.00	1300.00	1250.00
☐ **Model 1901 Target,** .22 L.R.R.F., Rolling Block, 10″ Barrel, Checkered Stock, Half-Octagon Barrel, *Modern*	690.00	1050.00	1000.00

	V.G.	Exc.	Prior Year Exc. Value
☐ **Model 1901 Target,** .44 Russian, Rolling Block, 10″ Barrel, Checkered Stock, Half-Octagon Barrel, *Modern*	675.00	1225.00	1225.00
☐ **XP-100,** .221 Rem. Fireball, Bolt Action, Target Nylon Stock, 10½″ Barrel, Vent Rib, Open Sights, Cased, *Modern*	165.00	225.00	225.00
☐ **XP-100 Silhouette,** 7mm BR Rem., Bolt Action, Target Nylon Stock, 15″ Barrel, Vent Rib, Open Sights, Cased, *Modern*	180.00	245.00	245.00
RIFLE, BOLT ACTION			
☐ **Enfield 1914,** .303 British, Full-Stocked, Military, *Curio*	160.00	215.00	200.00
☐ **International (1961),** Various Calibers, Singleshot, Target Stock, no Sights, with Accessories, *Modern*	285.00	410.00	390.00
☐ **Model 1907/15 French,** 8 x 50R Lebel, Military, *Curio*	125.00	170.00	165.00
☐ **Model 1907/15 French,** 8 x 50R Lebel, Carbine, Military, *Curio*	95.00	155.00	155.00
☐ **Model 1917 U.S.,** .30-06 Springfield, Full-Stocked, Military, *Curio*	170.00	250.00	235.00
☐ **Model 30A,** Various Calibers, Sporting Rifle, Plain, Open Rear Sight, *Modern*	180.00	265.00	245.00
☐ **Model 30F Premier,** Various Calibers, Sporting Rifle, Fancy Checkering, Fancy Engraving, Fancy Wood, *Modern*	525.00	675.00	650.00
☐ **Model 30R,** Various Calibers, Sporting Rifle, Plain, Carbine, Open Rear Sight, *Modern*	180.00	250.00	230.00
☐ **Model 30S,** Various Calibers, Sporting Rifle, Checkered Stock, Peep Sights, *Modern*	240.00	345.00	330.00
☐ **Model 33A,** .22 L.R.R.F., Plain, Singleshot, Open Rear Sight, *Modern*	43.00	65.00	60.00
☐ **Model 33A,** .22 L.R.R.F., Plain, Singleshot, Peep Sights, *Modern*	43.00	65.00	60.00
☐ **Model 33NRA,** .22 L.R.R.F., Plain, Singleshot, Peep Sights, Sling Swivels, *Modern*	50.00	75.00	70.00
☐ **Model 341A,** .22 L.R.R.F., Tube Feed, Takedown, Open Rear Sight, *Modern*	60.00	95.00	90.00
☐ **Model 341P,** .22 L.R.R.F., Tube Feed, Takedown, Peep Sights, *Modern*	70.00	110.00	100.00
☐ **Model 341SB,** .22 L.R.R.F., Tube Feed, Takedown, Smoothbore, *Modern*	60.00	85.00	75.00
☐ **Model 34A,** .22 L.R.R.F., Tube Feed, Takedown, Open Rear Sight, *Modern*	65.00	95.00	90.00
☐ **Model 34A,** .22 L.R.R.F., Tube Feed, Takedown, Lyman Sights, *Modern*	65.00	95.00	90.00
☐ **Model 34NRA,** .22 L.R.R.F., Tube Feed, Takedown, Lyman Sights, Target, *Modern*	75.00	110.00	105.00
☐ **Model 37A,** .22 L.R.R.F., 5 Shot Clip, Target Stock, Target Sights, Target Barrel, *Modern*	250.00	350.00	325.00
☐ **Model 37A,** .22 L.R.R.F., 5 Shot Clip, Target Stock, Target Sights, Target Barrel, Fancy Wood, *Modern*	275.00	365.00	345.00
☐ **Model 37AX,** .22 L.R.R.F., 5 Shot Clip, Target Stock, no Sights, Target Barrels, *Modern*	210.00	265.00	255.00

	V.G.	Exc.	Prior Year Exc. Value
☐ **Model 40-XB CF-H2,** Various Calibers, Stainless Steel Barrel, Heavy Barrel, Target Stock, no Sights, *Modern*	275.00	450.00	450.00
☐ **Model 40-XB CF-S2,** Various Calibers, Stainless Steel Barrel, Target Stock, no Sights, *Modern*	300.00	475.00	475.00
☐ **Model 40-XB RF-H2,** .22 L.R.R.F., Heavy Barrel, Target Stock, no Sights, *Modern*	195.00	285.00	275.00
☐ **Model 40-XB RF-S2,** .22 L.R.R.F., Target Stock, no Sights, *Modern*	205.00	290.00	285.00
☐ **Model 40-XB-BR, For 2 oz. Trigger,** *Add* **$40.00-$65.00**			
☐ **Model 40-XB-BR,** Various Calibers, Stainless Steel Barrel, Heavy Barrel, Target Stock, no Sights, *Modern*	410.00	550.00	520.00
☐ **Model 40-XB-CF, For Repeater,** *Add* **$25.00**			
☐ **Model 40X-CFH2,** Various Calibers, Singleshot, Target Stock, no Sights, Heavy Barrel, *Modern*	200.00	295.00	275.00
☐ **Model 40X-CFS2,** Various Calibers, Singleshot, Target Stock, no Sights, *Modern*	185.00	265.00	250.00
☐ **Model 40X-H1,** .22 L.R.R.F., Singleshot, Target Stock, Target Sights, Heavy Barrel, *Modern*	180.00	245.00	230.00
☐ **Model 40X-H2,** .22 L.R.R.F., Singleshot, Target Stock, no Sights, Heavy Barrel, *Modern*	155.00	220.00	210.00
☐ **Model 40X-S1,** .22 L.R.R.F., Singleshot, Target Stock, Target Sights, *Modern*	175.00	225.00	210.00
☐ **Model 40X-S2,** .22 L.R.R.F., Singleshot, Target Stock, no Sights, *Modern*	155.00	205.00	190.00
☐ **Model 40XB Sporter,** .22 L.R.R.F., *Modern*	350.00	450.00	435.00
☐ **Model 40XC National Match,** .308 Winchester, Target Stock, Target Sights, *Modern*	420.00	565.00	545.00
☐ **Model 40XR Position,** .22 L.R.R.F., Target Stock, no Sights, *Modern*	275.00	375.00	350.00
☐ **Model 41A,** .22 L.R.R.F., Takedown, Singleshot, Plain, Open Rear Sight, *Modern*	43.00	65.00	60.00
☐ **Model 41AS,** .22 WRF, Takedown, Singleshot, Plain, Open Rear Sight, *Modern*	43.00	70.00	65.00
☐ **Model 41P,** .22 L.R.R.F., Takedown, Singleshot, Plain, Target Sights, *Modern*	43.00	70.00	65.00
☐ **Model 41SB,** .22 L.R.R.F., Takedown, Singleshot, Plain, Smoothbore, *Modern*	43.00	65.00	60.00
☐ **Model 510A,** .22 L.R.R.F., Singleshot, Open Rear Sight, Plain, Takedown, *Modern*	43.00	70.00	65.00
☐ **Model 510C,** .22 L.R.R.F., Singleshot, Carbine, Plain, Takedown, *Modern*	43.00	70.00	65.00
☐ **Model 510P,** .22 L.R.R.F., Singleshot, Peep Sights, Plain, Takedown, *Modern*	43.00	70.00	65.00
☐ **Model 510SB,** .22 L.R.R.F., Singleshot, Smoothbore, Plain, Takedown, *Modern*	35.00	55.00	55.00
☐ **Model 510X,** .22 L.R.R.F., Singleshot, Plain, *Modern*	32.00	48.00	45.00
☐ **Model 510X,** .22 L.R.R.F., Singleshot, Plain, Smoothbore, *Modern*	32.00	48.00	45.00
☐ **Model 511A,** .22 L.R.R.F., Clip Fed, Open Rear Sight, Plain, Takedown, *Modern*	45.00	65.00	65.00
☐ **Model 511P,** .22 L.R.R.F., Clip Fed, Peep Sights, Plain, Takedown, *Modern*	45.00	70.00	70.00

Remington Smoot #1

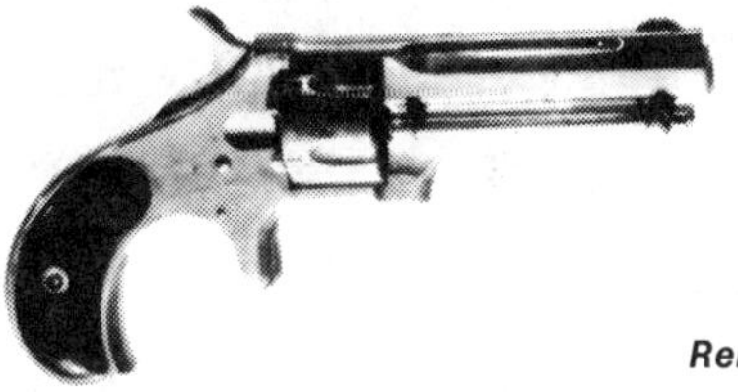

Remington .44 Model 1861 Army

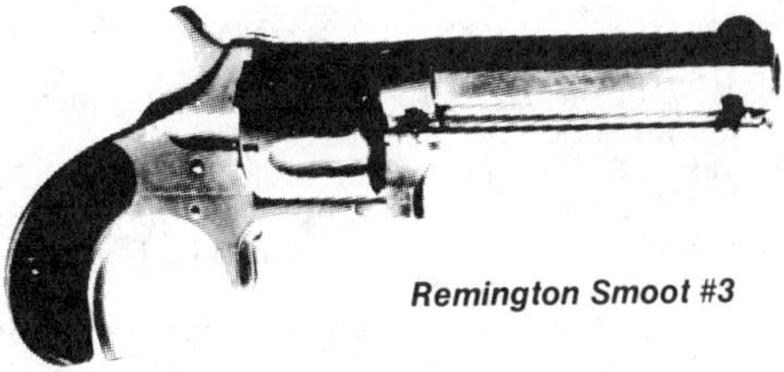

Remington Model 51

Remington Smoot #3

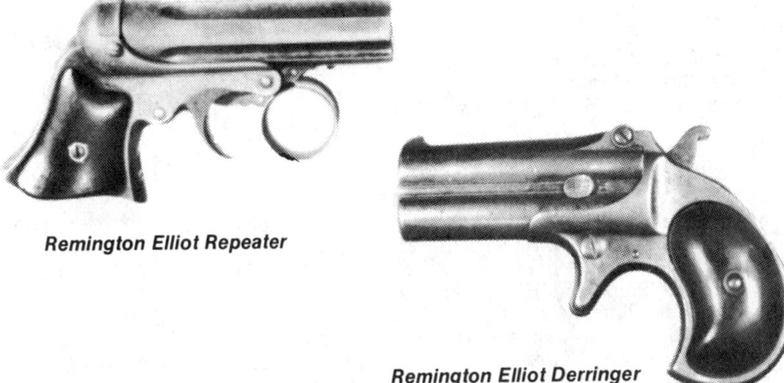

Remington Elliot Repeater

Remington Elliot Derringer

	V.G.	Exc.	Prior Year Exc. Value
☐ **Model 511SB,** .22 L.R.R.F., Clip Fed, Smoothbore, Plain, Takedown, *Modern*	43.00	70.00	65.00
☐ **Model 511X,** .22 L.R.R.F., Clip Fed, Plain, *Modern*	43.00	70.00	65.00
☐ **Model 512A,** .22 L.R.R.F., Tube Feed, Plain, Open Rear Sight, *Modern*	48.00	70.00	65.00
☐ **Model 512P,** .22 L.R.R.F., Tube Feed, Plain, Peep Sights, *Modern*	48.00	75.00	70.00
☐ **Model 512SB,** .22 L.R.R.F., Tube Feed, Plain, Smoothbore, *Modern*	48.00	75.00	70.00
☐ **Model 512X,** .22 L.R.R.F., Tube Feed, Plain, *Modern*	42.00	75.00	65.00
☐ **Model 513SA,** .22 L.R.R.F., Clip Fed, Sporting Rifle, Open Rear Sight, Takedown, Checkered Stock, *Modern*	80.00	135.00	130.00
☐ **Model 513SP,** .22 L.R.R.F., Clip Fed, Sporting Rifle, Peep Sights, Takedown, Checkered Stock, *Modern*	80.00	140.00	130.00
☐ **Model 513TR,** .22 L.R.R.F., Clip Fed, Target Stock, Target Sights, Takedown, *Modern*	100.00	150.00	145.00
☐ **Model 513TX,** .22 L.R.R.F., Clip Fed, Target Stock, no Sights, Takedown, *Modern*	80.00	130.00	125.00
☐ **Model 514,** .22 L.R.R.F., Singleshot, Plain, Open Rear Sight, *Modern*	33.00	48.00	45.00
☐ **Model 514BR (Youth),** .22 L.R.R.F., Singleshot, Plain, Open Rear Sight, *Modern*	33.00	48.00	45.00
☐ **Model 514P,** .22 L.R.R.F., Singleshot, Plain, Peep Sights, *Modern*	33.00	55.00	50.00
☐ **Model 521TL,** .22 L.R.R.F., Takedown, Clip Fed, Target Stock, Lyman Sights, *Modern*	65.00	100.00	95.00
☐ **Model 540XR Position,** .22 L.R.R.F., Target Stock, no Sights, *Modern*	160.00	245.00	235.00
☐ **Model 540XRJR Position,** .22 L.R.R.F., Target Stock, no Sights, *Modern*	145.00	225.00	210.00
☐ **Model 541-S,** .22 L.R.R.F., Clip Fed, Checkered Stock, Fancy Wood, *Modern*	145.00	210.00	195.00
☐ **Model 580,** .22 L.R.R.F., Singleshot, Plain, *Modern*	43.00	65.00	60.00
☐ **Model 580 BR (Youth),** .22 L.R.R.F., Singleshot, Plain, *Modern*	37.00	60.00	55.00
☐ **Model 580 SB,** .22 L.R.R.F., Singleshot, Plain, Smoothbore, *Modern*	42.00	65.00	60.00
☐ **Model 581,** .22 L.R.R.F., Clip Fed, Plain, *Modern*	63.00	90.00	85.00
☐ **Model 581,** .22 L.R.R.F., Clip Fed, Plain, Left-Hand, *Modern*	63.00	95.00	90.00
☐ **Model 582,** .22 L.R.R.F., Tube Feed, Plain, *Modern*	68.00	105.00	100.00
☐ **Model 591,** 5mm Rem. RFM, Clip Fed, Monte Carlo Stock, Plain, *Modern*	95.00	145.00	140.00
☐ **Model 592,** 5mm Rem. RFM, Tube Feed, Monte Carlo Stock, Plain, *Modern*	95.00	145.00	140.00
☐ **Model 600,** Various Calibers, Vent Rib, Carbine, Checkered Stock, *Modern*	155.00	220.00	210.00
☐ **Model 600,** Various Calibers, Vent Rib, Carbine, Magnum, Recoil Pad, Checkered Stock, *Modern*	180.00	265.00	250.00

	V.G.	Exc.	Prior Year Exc. Value
☐ **Model 600 Montana Centennial,** Trap Grade, Carbine, Checkered Stock, Commemorative, *Curio*	205.00	295.00	285.00
☐ **Model 660,** Various Calibers, Carbine, Checkered Stock, *Modern*	155.00	215.00	210.00
☐ **Model 660,** Various Calibers, Carbine, Magnum, Recoil Pad, Checkered Stock, *Modern*	190.00	270.00	260.00
☐ **Model 700 Safari,** Various Calibers, Magnum, Checkered Stock, Fancy Wood, *Modern*	350.00	475.00	465.00
☐ **Model 700ADL,** Various Calibers, Checkered Stock, *Modern*	165.00	230.00	225.00
☐ **Model 700ADL,** Various Calibers, Magnum, Checkered Stock, *Modern*	190.00	250.00	240.00
☐ **Model 700BDL,** Various Calibers, Checkered Stock, Fancy Wood, *Modern*	200.00	285.00	275.00
☐ **Model 700BDL,** Various Calibers, Magnum, Checkered Stock, Fancy Wood, *Modern*	205.00	295.00	285.00
☐ **Model 700BDL,** Various Calibers, Heavy Barrel, Varmint, Checkered Stock, Fancy Wood, *Modern*	230.00	325.00	315.00
☐ **Model 700BDL,** Various Calibers, Checkered Stock, Fancy Wood, Magnum, Left-Hand, *Modern*	230.00	325.00	315.00
☐ **Model 700BDL,** Various Calibers, Checkered Stock, Fancy Wood, Left-Hand, *Modern*	215.00	310.00	300.00
☐ **Model 700C Custom,** Various Calibers, Checkered Stock, Fancy Wood, *Modern*	365.00	510.00	490.00
☐ **Model 700D Peerless,** Various Calibers, Fancy Checkering, Fancy Wood, Engraved, *Modern*	600.00	800.00	770.00
☐ **Model 700F Premier,** Various Calibers, Fancy Checkering, Fancy Wood, Fancy Engraving, *Modern*	1050.00	1550.00	1500.00
☐ **Model 720A,** Various Calibers, Sporting Rifle, Open Rear Sight, *Modern*	170.00	225.00	220.00
☐ **Model 720A,** Various Calibers, Sporting Rifle, Target Sights, *Modern*	195.00	270.00	255.00
☐ **Model 720R,** Various Calibers, Sporting Rifle, Open Rear Sight, Carbine, *Modern*	175.00	250.00	245.00
☐ **Model 720R,** Various Calibers, Sporting Rifle, Target Sights, Carbine, *Modern*	200.00	270.00	260.00
☐ **Model 720S,** Various Calibers, Sporting Rifle, Target Sights, *Modern*	195.00	270.00	260.00
☐ **Model 721,** For .300 H & H Magnum, *Add* **$20.00-$35.00**			
☐ **Model 721 Peerless,** Various Calibers, Long Action, Sporting Rifle, Fancy Wood, Engraved, Fancy Checkering, *Modern*	525.00	715.00	690.00
☐ **Model 721 Premier,** Various Calibers, Long Action, Sporting Rifle, Fancy Wood, Fancy Engraving, Fancy Checkering, *Modern*	850.00	1300.00	1275.00
☐ **Model 721 Special,** Various Calibers, Long Action, Sporting Rifle, Checkered Stock, Fancy Wood, *Modern*	145.00	200.00	190.00
☐ **Model 721A,** Various Calibers, Long Action, Sporting Rifle, Plain, *Modern*	130.00	175.00	170.00

	V.G.	Exc.	Prior Year Exc. Value
☐ **Model 721ADL,** Various Calibers, Long Action, Sporting Rifle, Checkered Stock, *Modern*	145.00	195.00	185.00
☐ **Model 721BDL,** Various Calibers, Long Action, Sporting Rifle, Monte Carlo Stock, Checkered Stock, Fancy Wood, *Modern*	150.00	195.00	190.00
☐ **Model 722,** For .222 Rem. *Add* **$25.00-$35.00**			
☐ **Model 722A,** Various Calibers, Short Action, Sporting Rifle, Plain, *Modern*	125.00	165.00	160.00
☐ **Model 722ADL,** Various Calibers, Short Action, Sporting Rifle, Checkered Stock, *Modern*	145.00	185.00	180.00
☐ **Model 722BDL,** Various Calibers, Short Action, Sporting Rifle, Checkered Stock, Fancy Wood, *Modern*	160.00	225.00	210.00
☐ **Model 722D Peerless,** Various Calibers, Short Action, Sporting Rifle, Fancy Wood, Fancy Checkering, Engraved, *Modern*	510.00	700.00	675.00
☐ **Model 722F Premier,** Various Calibers, Short Action, Sporting Rifle, Fancy Wood, Fancy Engraving, Fancy Checkering, *Modern*	775.00	1025.00	995.00
☐ **Model 725ADL,** Various Calibers, Long Action, Sporting Rifle, Checkered Stock, Fancy Wood, *Modern*	185.00	260.00	250.00
☐ **Model 725ADL,** Various Calibers, Long Action, Magnum, Sporting Rifle, Checkered Stock, Fancy Wood, *Modern*	365.00	490.00	475.00
☐ **Model 725D Peerless,** Various Calibers, Long Action, Sporting Rifle, Engraved, Fancy Checkering, Fancy Wood, *Modern*	550.00	710.00	690.00
☐ **Model 725F Premier,** Various Calibers, Long Action, Sporting Rifle, Fancy Engraving, Fancy Checkering, Fancy Wood, *Modern*	935.00	1350.00	1300.00
☐ **Model 788,** Various Calibers, Clip Fed, Plain, *Modern*	145.00	185.00	175.00
☐ **Model 788,** Various Calibers, Clip Fed, Left-Hand, Plain, *Modern*	155.00	195.00	185.00
☐ **Nylon 10,** .22 L.R.R.F., Singleshot, Plastic Stock, *Modern*	43.00	58.00	55.00
☐ **Nylon 10-SB,** .22 L.R.R.F., Singleshot, Plastic Stock, Smoothbore, *Modern*	37.00	53.00	50.00
☐ **Nylon 12,** .22 L.R.R.F., Tube Feed, Plastic, *Modern*	58.00	85.00	80.00

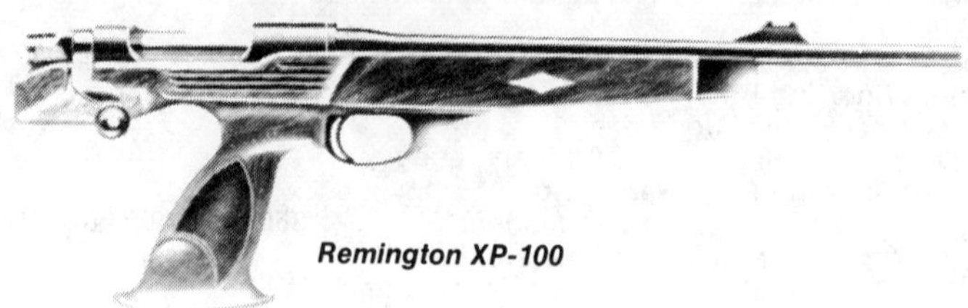

Remington XP-100

	V.G.	Exc.	Prior Year Exc. Value
RIFLE, LEVER ACTION			
☐ **Nylon 76,** .22 L.R.R.F., Tube Feed, Plastic Stock, *Modern*	70.00	105.00	100.00
RIFLE, SEMI-AUTOMATIC			
☐ **Model Four,** Various Calibers, Clip Fed, Sporting Rifle, Open Rear Sight, Checkered Stock, Fancy Wood, *Modern*	230.00	325.00	310.00
☐ **Model 10C Mohawk,** .22 L.R.R.F., Clip Fed, Plastic Stock, *Modern*	48.00	75.00	70.00
☐ **Model 16,** .22 Rem. Automatic R.F., Takedown, Tube Feed, *Modern*	150.00	205.00	200.00
☐ **Model 16D,** .22 Rem. Automatic R.F., Takedown, Tube Feed, Checkered Stock, Engraved, *Modern*	310.00	400.00	390.00
☐ **Model 16F,** .22 Rem. Automatic R.F., Takedown, Tube Feed, Fancy Checkering, Fancy Engraving, *Modern*	675.00	800.00	795.00
☐ **Model 241A,** .22 L.R.R.F., Tube Feed, Takedown, Open Rear Sight, *Modern*	180.00	255.00	250.00
☐ **Model 241A,** .22 Short R.F., Tube Feed, Takedown, Open Rear Sight, *Modern*	170.00	230.00	225.00
☐ **Model 241D,** .22 L.R.R.F., Takedown, Tube Feed, Fancy Checkering, Engraved, *Modern*	305.00	400.00	385.00
☐ **Model 241F,** .22 L.R.R.F., Takedown, Tube Feed, Fancy Checkering, Fancy Engraving, *Modern*	670.00	810.00	790.00
☐ **Model 24A,** .22 L.R.R.F., Takedown, Plain, *Modern*	125.00	170.00	165.00
☐ **Model 24A,** .22 Short R.F., Takedown, Plain, *Modern*	100.00	150.00	145.00
☐ **Model 24C,** .22 L.R.R.F., Takedown, Checkered Stock, *Modern*	130.00	175.00	170.00
☐ **Model 24D Peerless,** .22 L.R.R.F., Takedown, Fancy Checkering, Engraved, *Modern*	360.00	480.00	465.00
☐ **Model 24F Premier,** .22 L.R.R.F., Takedown, Fancy Checkering, Fancy Engraving, *Modern*	750.00	910.00	890.00
☐ **Model 550-2G,** .22 Short R.F., Takedown, Open Rear Sight, Plain, *Modern*	60.00	95.00	90.00
☐ **Model 550A,** .22 L.R.R.F., Takedown, Open Rear Sight, Plain, *Modern*	60.00	90.00	85.00
☐ **Model 550P,** .22 L.R.R.F., Takedown, Peep Sights, Plain, *Modern*	70.00	100.00	95.00
☐ **Model 552A,** .22 L.R.R.F., Tube Feed, Plain, *Modern*	70.00	100.00	95.00
☐ **Model 552BDL,** .22 L.R.R.F., Tube Feed, Checkered Stock, *Modern*	80.00	120.00	115.00
☐ **Model 552C,** .22 L.R.R.F., Tube Feed, Carbine, Plain, *Modern*	70.00	100.00	95.00
☐ **Model 552GS,** .22 Short R.F., Tube Feed, Plain, *Modern*	75.00	115.00	110.00
☐ **Model 740A,** Various Calibers, Clip Fed, Sporting Rifle, Open Rear Sight, Plain, *Modern*	160.00	235.00	225.00
☐ **Model 740ADL,** Various Calibers, Clip Fed, Sporting Rifle, Open Rear Sight, Checkered Stock, *Modern*	165.00	240.00	230.00

	V.G.	Exc.	Prior Year Exc. Value
☐ **Model 740BDL,** Various Calibers, Clip Fed, Sporting Rifle, Open Rear Sight, Checkered Stock, Fancy Wood, *Modern*	185.00	260.00	250.00
☐ **Model 740D Peerless,** Various Calibers, Clip Fed, Sporting Rifle, Open Rear Sight, Fancy Checkering, Engraved, *Modern*	675.00	910.00	885.00
☐ **Model 740F Premier,** Various Calibers, Clip Fed, Sporting Rifle, Open Rear Sight, Fancy Checkering, Fancy Engraving, *Modern*	1025.00	1500.00	1450.00
☐ **Model 7400,** Various Calibers, Clip Fed, Sporting Rifle, Open Rear Sight, Checkered Stock, *Modern*	205.00	280.00	275.00
☐ **Model 742,** .30-06 Springfield, Bicentennial, Clip Fed, *Modern*	205.00	305.00	295.00
☐ **Model 742,** Various Calibers, Clip Fed, Sporting Rifle, Open Rear Sight, Checkered Stock, *Modern*	190.00	275.00	265.00
☐ **Model 742 Canadian Centennial,** Clip Fed, Sporting Rifle, Open Rear Sight, Checkered Stock, Commemorative, *Curio*	205.00	305.00	300.00
☐ **Model 742ADL,** Various Calibers, Clip Fed, Sporting Rifle, Open Rear Sight, Checkered Stock, *Modern*	180.00	250.00	245.00
☐ **Model 742BDL,** Various Calibers, Clip Fed, Sporting Rifle, Open Rear Sight, Checkered Stock, Fancy Wood, *Modern*	190.00	295.00	285.00
☐ **Model 742C,** Various Calibers, Clip Fed, Sporting Rifle, Open Rear Sight, Carbine, Checkered Stock, *Modern*	185.00	275.00	270.00
☐ **Model 742CDL,** Various Calibers, Clip Fed, Sporting Rifle, Open Rear Sight, Carbine, Fancy Wood, *Modern*	195.00	290.00	285.00
☐ **Model 742D Peerless,** Various Calibers, Clip Fed, Sporting Rifle, Open Rear Sight, Fancy Checkering, Engraved, *Modern*	675.00	910.00	890.00
☐ **Model 742F Premier,** Various Calibers, Clip Fed, Sporting Rifle, Open Rear Sights, Fancy Checkering, Engraved, *Modern*	1325.00	1800.00	1745.00
☐ **Model 81A,** Various Calibers, Plain, Takedown, *Modern*	205.00	305.00	300.00
☐ **Model 81D Peerless,** Various Calibers, Takedown, Fancy Checkering, Engraved, *Modern*	535.00	680.00	665.00
☐ **Model 81F Premier,** Various Calibers, Takedown, Fancy Checkering, Fancy Engraving, Fancy Wood, *Modern*	920.00	1300.00	1275.00
☐ **Model 8A Standard,** Various Calibers, Plain, *Modern*	200.00	280.00	275.00
☐ **Model 8C Special,** Various Calibers, Checkered Stock, *Modern*	230.00	350.00	335.00
☐ **Model 8D Peerless,** Various Calibers, Fancy Checkering, Light Engraving, *Modern*	470.00	650.00	625.00
☐ **Model 8E Expert,** Various Calibers, Fancy Checkering, Engraved, *Modern*	630.00	900.00	875.00

	V.G.	Exc.	Prior Year Exc. Value
☐ **Model 8F Premier,** Various Calibers, Fancy Checkering, Fancy Engraving, Fancy Wood, *Modern*	875.00	1225.00	1200.00
☐ **Nylon 11,** .22 L.R.R.F., Clip Fed, Plastic Stock, *Modern*	45.00	70.00	65.00
☐ **Nylon 66,** .22 L.R.R.F., Tube Feed, Plastic Stock, *Modern*	55.00	85.00	80.00
☐ **Nylon 66,** .22 L.R.R.F., Tube Feed, Bicentennial, Plastic Stock, *Modern*	60.00	95.00	90.00
☐ **Nylon 66 GS,** .22 Short R.F., Tube Feed, Plastic Stock, *Modern*	60.00	90.00	85.00
☐ **Model 77,** .22 L.R.R.F., Clip Fed, Plastic Stock, *Modern*	55.00	85.00	80.00
RIFLE, SINGLESHOT			
☐ **Beals,** .32 R.F., Sliding Barrel, Plain, *Antique*	290.00	400.00	375.00
☐ **Hepburn #3,** Various Calibers, Sporting Rifle, Checkered Stock, Hammer, *Curio*	370.00	600.00	575.00
☐ **Model 1,** Various Calibers, Rolling Block, Sporting Rifle, Adjustable Sights, Plain Stock, *Curio*	225.00	375.00	350.00
☐ **Model 1,** Various Calibers, Rolling Block, Target, Adjustable Sights, Checkered Stock, *Curio*	520.00	670.00	650.00
☐ **Model 4,** .22 L.R.R.F., Rolling Block, Takedown, *Modern*	130.00	180.00	175.00
☐ **Model 4S Boy Scout,** .22 L.R.R.F., Rolling Block, Full-Stocked, *Curio*	235.00	405.00	400.00
☐ **Model 4S Boy Scout,** .22 L.R.R.F., Rolling Block, Full-Stocked, with Bayonet, *Curio*	375.00	535.00	525.00
☐ **Model 5,** Various Calibers, Rolling Block, Sporting Rifle, Adjustable Sights, Plain Stock, *Curio*	290.00	460.00	440.00
☐ **Model 6,** .22 L.R.R.F., Rolling Block, Takedown, *Modern*	90.00	150.00	145.00
☐ **Model 6,** .32 Long Rifle, Rolling Block, Takedown, *Modern*	85.00	140.00	135.00
☐ **Model 7,** Various Rimfires, Rolling Block, Target, Adjustable Sights, Checkered Stock, *Curio*	625.00	975.00	950.00
☐ **Model 7,** Various Rimfires, Rolling Block, Target, Swiss Buttplate, Checkered Stock, Adjustable Sights, *Curio*	765.00	1300.00	1275.00
☐ **Model 7,** Various Rimfires, Rolling Block, Target, Swiss Buttplate, Checkered Stock, Peep Sights, *Curio*	775.00	1390.00	1375.00
☐ **1867 Navy,** .50/70 C.F., Military, Carbine, *Antique*	450.00	650.00	625.00
☐ **1867 Cadet Navy,** .50/45 C.F., Military, *Antique*	545.00	750.00	725.00
☐ **Split Breech,** .46 R.F., Military, Carbine, *Antique*	415.00	600.00	575.00
☐ **Split Breech,** .50 R.F., Military, Carbine, *Antique*	530.00	800.00	775.00
RIFLE, SLIDE ACTION			
☐ **Model Six,** Various Calibers, Clip Fed, Sporting Rifle, Open Rear Sight, Monte Carlo Stock, Checkered Stock, *Modern*	200.00	290.00	280.00

	V.G.	Exc.	Prior Year Exc. Value
☐ **Model 12A Standard,** .22 L.R.R.F., Plain Round Barrel, Tube Feed, *Modern*	125.00	170.00	165.00
☐ **Model 12B Gallery,** .22 Short R.F., Plain, Round Barrel, Tube Feed, *Modern*	115.00	160.00	155.00
☐ **Model 12C,** .22 L.R.R.F., Plain, Octagon Barrel, Tube Feed, Target, *Modern*	130.00	210.00	200.00
☐ **Model 12C-NRA,** .22 L.R.R.F., Plain, Octagon Barrel, Tube Feed, Peep Sights, *Modern*	180.00	260.00	255.00
☐ **Model 12CS Special,** .22 WRF., Plain, Octagon Barrel, Tube Feed, *Modern*	140.00	245.00	220.00
☐ **Model 12D Peerless,** .22 L.R.R.F., Checkered Stock, Octagon Barrel, Tube Feed, Light Engraving, *Modern*	335.00	440.00	435.00
☐ **Model 12E Expert,** .22 L.R.R.F., Fancy Checkering, Octagon Barrel, Tube Feed, Engraved, *Modern*	465.00	650.00	625.00
☐ **Model 12F Premier,** .22 L.R.R.F., Fancy Checkering, Octagon Barrel, Tube Feed, Fancy Engraving, Fancy Wood, *Modern*	725.00	900.00	875.00
☐ **Model 121A,** .22 L.R.R.F., Takedown, Tube Feed, Plain, *Modern*	155.00	230.00	225.00
☐ **Model 121A,** .22 Short R.F., Takedown, Tube Feed, Plain, *Modern*	130.00	190.00	185.00
☐ **Model 121D Peerless,** .22 L.R.R.F., Takedown, Tube Feed, Fancy Checkering, Engraved, *Modern*	465.00	615.00	600.00
☐ **Model 121F Premier,** .22 L.R.R.F., Takedown, Tube Feed, Fancy Checkering, Fancy Engraving, *Modern*	775.00	925.00	900.00
☐ **Model 121S,** .22 WRF, Takedown, Tube Feed, Plain, *Modern*	140.00	200.00	195.00
☐ **Model 121SB,** .22 L.R.R.F., Takedown, Tube Feed, Plain, Smoothbore, *Modern*	145.00	185.00	180.00
☐ **Model 14½ A,** Various Calibers, Tube Feed, Short Action, Plain, *Modern*	180.00	280.00	265.00
☐ **Model 14½ R,** Various Calibers, Tube Feed, Short Action, Carbine, Plain Barrel, *Modern*	240.00	330.00	320.00
☐ **Model 141A,** Various Calibers, Takedown, Tube Feed, Plain, *Modern*	180.00	270.00	260.00
☐ **Model 141D Peerless,** Various Calibers, Takedown, Tube Feed, Fancy Checkering, Engraved, *Modern*	465.00	630.00	615.00
☐ **Model 141F Premier,** Various Calibers, Takedown, Tube Feed, Fancy Checkering, Fancy Engraving, *Modern*	875.00	1100.00	1050.00
☐ **Model 141R,** Various Calibers, Takedown, Tube Feed, Plain, Carbine, *Modern*	180.00	255.00	250.00
☐ **Model 14A,** Various Calibers, Tube Feed, Plain, *Modern*	155.00	230.00	225.00
☐ **Model 14C Special,** Various Calibers, Tube Feed, Checkered Stock, *Modern*	185.00	270.00	260.00
☐ **Model 14D Peerless,** Various Calibers, Tube Feed, Fancy Checkering, Engraved, *Modern*	440.00	580.00	565.00
☐ **Model 14F Premier,** Various Calibers, Tube Feed, Fancy Checkering, Fancy Wood, Fancy Engraving, *Modern*	775.00	1050.00	1025.00

	V.G.	Exc.	Prior Year Exc. Value
☐ **Model 14R,** Various Calibers, Tube Feed, Carbine, Plain, *Modern*	195.00	300.00	285.00
☐ **Model 25A,** Various Calibers, Takedown, Plain, *Modern*	155.00	240.00	230.00
☐ **Model 25D Peerless,** Various Calibers, Takedown, Checkered Stock, Engraved, *Modern*	465.00	645.00	620.00
☐ **Model 25F Premier,** Various Calibers, Takedown, Fancy Checkering, Fancy Engraving, *Modern*	830.00	1100.00	1075.00
☐ **Model 25R,** Various Calibers, Takedown, Plain, Carbine, *Modern*	180.00	265.00	260.00
☐ **Model 572,** .22 L.R.R.F., Tube Feed, Open Rear Sight, Lightweight, Fancy Checkering, Chrome, *Modern*	65.00	115.00	110.00
☐ **Model 572A,** .22 L.R.R.F., Tube Feed, Open Rear Sight, Plain, *Modern*	80.00	120.00	115.00
☐ **Model 572BDL,** .22 L.R.R.F., Tube Feed, Open Rear Sight, Checkered Stock, *Modern*	90.00	135.00	130.00
☐ **Model 572SB,** .22 L.R.R.F., Tube Feed, Plain, Smoothbore, *Modern*	75.00	120.00	115.00
☐ **Model 760,** .30-06 Springfield, Bicentennial, Clip Fed, *Modern*	180.00	260.00	250.00
☐ **Model 760A,** Various Calibers, Clip Fed, Sporting Rifle, Open Rear Sight, Plain, *Modern*	155.00	220.00	210.00
☐ **Model 760ADL,** Various Calibers, Clip Fed, Sporting Rifle, Open Rear Sight, Monte Carlo Stock, Checkered Stock, *Modern*	180.00	255.00	245.00
☐ **Model 760BDL,** Various Calibers, Clip Fed, Sporting Rifle, Open Rear Sight, Monte Carlo Stock, Checkered Stock, *Modern*	205.00	280.00	270.00
☐ **Model 760C,** Various Calibers, Clip Fed, Sporting Rifle, Open Rear Sight, Carbine, Plain, *Modern*	175.00	245.00	235.00
☐ **Model 760CDL,** Various Calibers, Clip Fed, Sporting Rifle, Open Rear Sight, Carbine, Checkered Stock, *Modern*	200.00	285.00	275.00
☐ **Model 760D Peerless,** Various Calibers, Clip Fed, Sporting Rifle, Open Rear Sight, Fancy Checkering, Engraved, *Modern*	610.00	875.00	865.00
☐ **Model 760F Premier,** Various Calibers, Clip Fed, Sporting Rifle, Open Rear Sight, Fancy Checkering, Fancy Engraving, *Modern*	1275.00	1800.00	1750.00
☐ **Model 7600,** Various Calibers, Clip Fed, Sporting Rifle, Open Rear Sight, Monte Carlo Stock, Checkered Stock, *Modern*	180.00	260.00	245.00

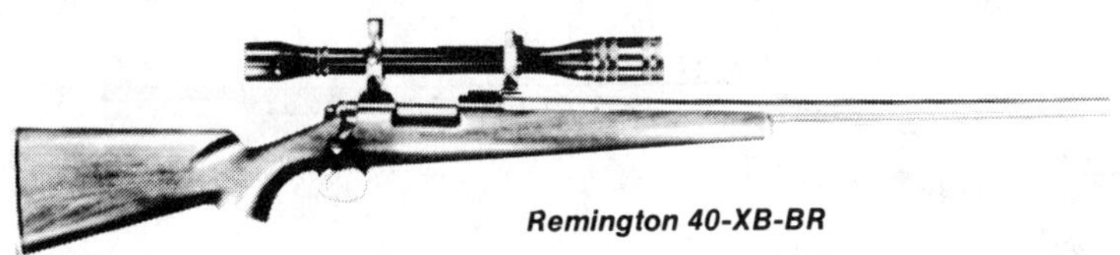

Remington 40-XB-BR

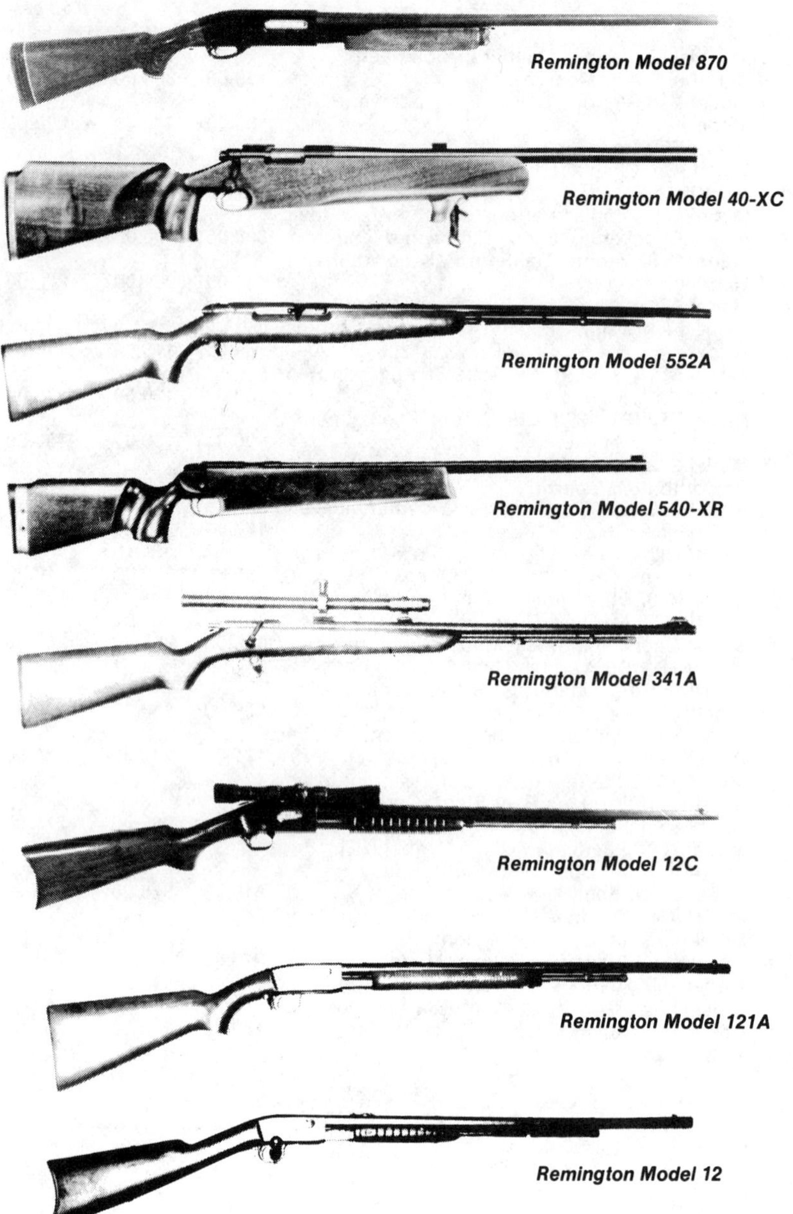

Remington Model 870

Remington Model 40-XC

Remington Model 552A

Remington Model 540-XR

Remington Model 341A

Remington Model 12C

Remington Model 121A

Remington Model 12

	V.G.	Exc.	Prior Year Exc. Value
SHOTGUN, DOUBLE BARREL, OVER-UNDER			
☐ **Model 32,** Raised Solid Rib, *Add* **$55.00-$80.00**			
☐ **Model 32,** for Vent Rib, *Add* **$95.00-$135.00**			
☐ **Model 32,** 12 Ga., Skeet Grade, Engraved, Fancy Checkering, *Modern*	900.00	1250.00	1200.00
☐ **Model 32A,** 12 Ga., Double Trigger, Automatic Ejector, Plain Barrel, Engraved, Checkered Stock, *Modern*	465.00	650.00	625.00
☐ **Model 32A,** 12 Ga., Single Selective Trigger, Automatic Ejector, Plain Barrel, Engraved, Checkered Stock, *Modern*	690.00	1025.00	1000.00
☐ **Model 32D,** 12 Ga., Fancy Checkering, Fancy Wood, Fancy Engraving, *Modern*	1600.00	2350.00	2300.00
☐ **Model 32E,** 12 Ga., Fancy Checkering, Fancy Wood, Fancy Engraving, *Modern*	2175.00	3000.00	2900.00
☐ **Model 32F,** 12 Ga., Fancy Checkering, Fancy Wood, Fancy Engraving, *Modern*	3075.00	4350.00	4300.00
☐ **Model 32TC,** 12 Ga., Trap Grade, Single Selective Trigger, Engraved, Fancy Checkering, *Modern*	1225.00	1750.00	1700.00
☐ **Model 3200,** 12 Ga., Field Grade, Automatic Ejector, Single Selective Trigger, Vent Rib, Checkered Stock, *Modern*	710.00	925.00	900.00
☐ **Model 3200,** 12 Ga., Skeet Grade, Automatic Ejector, Single Selective Trigger, Vent Rib, Checkered Stock, *Modern*	740.00	1150.00	1100.00
☐ **Model 3200,** 12 Ga., Trap Grade, Automatic Ejector, Single Selective Trigger, Vent Rib, Checkered Stock, *Modern*	740.00	1150.00	1100.00
☐ **Model 3200,** 12 Ga. Mag. 3″, Field Grade, Automatic Ejector, Single Selective Trigger, Vent Rib, Checkered Stock, *Modern*	710.00	1000.00	975.00
☐ **Model 3200 Competition,** 12 Ga., Skeet Grade, Automatic Ejector, Single Selective Trigger, Vent Rib, Engraved, *Modern*	900.00	1300.00	1250.00
☐ **Model 3200 Competition,** 12 Ga., Skeet Grade, Automatic Ejector, Single Selective Trigger, Vent Rib, Engraved, Extra Barrels, *Modern*	2875.00	4175.00	4050.00
☐ **Model 3200 Competition,** 12 Ga., Trap Grade, Automatic Ejector, Single Selective Trigger, Vent Rib, Engraved, *Modern*	900.00	1300.00	1250.00
SHOTGUN, DOUBLE BARREL, SIDE-BY-SIDE			
☐ **Model 1882,** Various Gauges, Hammer, Damascus Barrel, Checkered Stock, Double Trigger, *Antique*	280.00	440.00	425.00
☐ **Model 1883,** Various Gauges, Hammer, Damascus Barrel, Checkered Stock, Double Trigger, *Antique*	280.00	440.00	425.00
☐ **Model 1883,** Various Gauges, Hammer, Steel Barrel, Checkered Stock, Double Trigger, *Antique*	310.00	475.00	450.00
☐ **Model 1894 A E,** Various Gauges, Hammerless, Damascus Barrel, Automatic Ejector, Checkered Stock, Double Trigger, *Curio*	215.00	350.00	325.00

	V.G.	Exc.	Prior Year Exc. Value
☐ **Model 1894 A E O,** Various Gauges, Hammerless, Steel Barrel, Automatic Ejector, Checkered Stock, Double Trigger, *Curio*	430.00	575.00	540.00
☐ **Model 1894 A O,** Various Gauges, Hammerless, Steel Barrel, Plain, Checkered Stock, Double Trigger, *Curio*	375.00	510.00	485.00
☐ **Model 1894 B,** Various Gauges, Hammerless, Damascus Barrel, Light Engraving, Checkered Stock, Double Trigger, *Curio*	190.00	275.00	250.00
☐ **Model 1894 B E,** Various Gauges, Hammerless, Damascus Barrel, Automatic Ejector, Light Engraving, Checkered Stock, *Curio*	300.00	425.00	400.00
☐ **Model 1894 B E O,** Various Gauges, Hammerless, Steel Barrel, Automatic Ejector, Light Engraving, Checkered Stock, *Curio*	535.00	775.00	745.00
☐ **Model 1894 B O,** Various Gauges, Hammerless, Steel Barrel, Light Engraving, Checkered Stock, Double Trigger, *Curio*	420.00	550.00	525.00
☐ **Model 1894 C,** Various Gauges, Hammerless, Damascus Barrel, Engraved, Checkered Stock, Double Trigger, *Curio*	315.00	450.00	425.00
☐ **Model 1894 C E,** Various Gauges, Hammerless, Damascus Barrel, Automatic Ejector, Engraved, Checkered Stock, *Curio*	395.00	525.00	500.00
☐ **Model 1894 C E O,** Various Gauges, Hammerless, Steel Barrel, Automatic Ejector, Engraved, Checkered Stock, *Curio*	735.00	1075.00	1000.00
☐ **Model 1894 C O,** Various Gauges, Hammerless, Steel Barrel, Engraved, Checkered Stock, Double Trigger, *Curio*	590.00	800.00	775.00
☐ **Model 1894 D,** Various Gauges, Hammerless, Damascus Barrel, Fancy Engraving, Fancy Checkering, Fancy Wood, *Curio*	500.00	700.00	675.00
☐ **Model 1894 D E,** Various Gauges, Hammerless, Damascus Barrel, Automatic Ejector, Fancy Engraving, Fancy Checkering, *Curio*	595.00	800.00	775.00
☐ **Model 1894 D E O,** Various Gauges, Hammerless, Steel Barrel, Automatic Ejector, Fancy Engraving, Fancy Checkering, *Curio*	925.00	1500.00	1450.00
☐ **Model 1894 D O,** Various Gauges, Hammerless, Steel Barrel, Fancy Engraving, Fancy Checkering, Fancy Wood, *Curio*	735.00	1350.00	1300.00
☐ **Model 1894 E,** Various Gauges, Hammerless, Damascus Barrel, Fancy Engraving, Fancy Checkering, Fancy Wood, *Curio*	750.00	1025.00	985.00
☐ **Model 1894 E E,** Various Gauges, Hammerless, Damascus Barrel, Automatic Ejector, Fancy Engraving, Fancy Checkering, *Curio*	825.00	1200.00	1150.00
☐ **Model 1894 E E O,** Various Gauges, Hammerless, Steel Barrel, Automatic Ejector, Fancy Engraving, Fancy Checkering, *Curio*	1900.00	2700.00	2600.00
☐ **Model 1894 E O,** Various Gauges, Hammerless, Steel Barrel, Fancy Engraving, Fancy Checkering, Fancy Wood, *Curio*	1775.00	2500.00	2400.00

	V.G.	Exc.	Prior Year Exc. Value
☐ **Model 1894 Special,** Various Gauges, Hammerless, Steel Barrel, Automatic Ejector, Fancy Engraving, Fancy Checkering, *Curio*	4200.00	6650.00	6650.00
☐ **Model 1894-A,** Various Gauges, Hammerless, Damascus Barrel, Plain, Checkered Stock, Double Trigger, *Curio*	120.00	195.00	185.00
☐ **Model 1900 K,** 12 and 16 Gauges, Hammerless, Steel Barrel, Plain, Checkered Stock, *Curio*	200.00	350.00	325.00
☐ **Model 1900 K D,** 12 and 16 Gauges, Hammerless, Damascus Barrel, Plain, Checkered Stock, *Curio*	125.00	235.00	220.00
☐ **Model 1900 K E D,** 12 and 16 Gauges, Hammerless, Damascus Barrel, Automatic Ejector, Palm Rest, Checkered Stock, *Curio*	175.00	280.00	265.00
☐ **Model 1900 KE,** 12 and 16 Gauges, Hammerless, Steel Barrel, Automatic Ejector, Plain, Checkered Stock, *Curio*	280.00	410.00	390.00
☐ **Model Parker 920,** 12 Ga., Double Trigger, Checkered Stock, *Modern*	600.00	950.00	950.00
SHOTGUN, SEMI-AUTOMATIC			
☐ **Autoloading,** 12 Ga., for Solid Rib, *Add* **$25.00-$35.00**			
☐ **Autoloading-0,** 12 Ga., Takedown, Riot Gun, Plain, *Modern*	135.00	185.00	180.00
☐ **Autoloading-1,** 12 Ga., Takedown, Plain, *Modern*	140.00	190.00	185.00
☐ **Autoloading-2,** 12 Ga., Takedown, Checkered Stock, *Modern*	180.00	250.00	235.00
☐ **Autoloading-4,** 12 Ga., Takedown, Fancy Checkering, Fancy Wood, Engraved, *Modern*	465.00	625.00	600.00
☐ **Autoloading-6,** 12 Ga., Takedown, Fancy Checkering, Fancy Wood, Fancy Engraving, *Modern*	770.00	1025.00	1000.00
☐ **Model 11,** for Vent Rib, *Add* **$35.00-$45.00**			
☐ **Model 11,** Raised Solid Rib, *Add* **$20.00-$30.00**			
☐ **Model 11 Sportsman,** Various Gauges, Skeet Grade, Vent Rib, Light Engraving, Checkered Stock, *Modern*	230.00	350.00	325.00
☐ **Model 11-48 D Tournament,** Various Gauges, Vent Rib, Fancy Wood, Fancy Engraving, Fancy Checkering, *Modern*	450.00	575.00	550.00
☐ **Model 11-48 Duck,** Various Gauges, Vent Rib, Checkered Stock, *Modern*	140.00	205.00	195.00
☐ **Model 11-48 R,** 12 Ga., Riot Gun, Plain Barrel, *Modern*	105.00	150.00	145.00
☐ **Model 11-48 RSS,** 12 Ga., Open Rear Sight, Slug, Checkered Stock, *Modern*	150.00	205.00	200.00
☐ **Model 11-48 SA,** Various Gauges, Skeet Grade, Vent Rib, Checkered Stock, *Modern*	150.00	225.00	220.00
☐ **Model 11-48A,** Various Gauges, Plain Barrel, *Modern*	120.00	175.00	170.00
☐ **Model 11-48B,** Various Gauges, Vent Rib, Checkered Stock, Fancy Wood, *Modern*	130.00	190.00	185.00

	V.G.	Exc.	Prior Year Exc. Value
☐ **Model 11-48F Premier,** Various Gauges, Vent Rib, Fancy Wood, Fancy Engraving, Fancy Checkering, *Modern*	875.00	1200.00	1150.00
☐ **Model 1100,** for Left Hand, *Add* **$25.00-$35.00**			
☐ **Model 1100,** 12 Ga. Lightweight, *Add* **$15.00-$25.00**			
☐ **Model 1100,** for .28 Ga. or .410 Ga., *Add* **$15.00-$25.00**			
☐ **Model 1100,** 12 Ga., Bicentennial, Skeet Grade, Vent Rib, Checkered Stock, *Modern*	250.00	375.00	350.00
☐ **Model 1100,** Various Gauges, Plain Barrel, Checkered Stock, *Modern*	230.00	325.00	300.00
☐ **Model 1100,** Various Gauges, Vent Rib, Checkered Stock, *Modern*	250.00	360.00	335.00
☐ **Model 1100,** Various Gauges, Plain Barrel, Magnum, Checkered Stock, *Modern*	230.00	310.00	295.00
☐ **Model 1100,** Various Gauges, Vent Rib, Magnum, Checkered Stock, *Modern*	250.00	360.00	345.00
☐ **Model 1100,** Various Gauges, Skeet Grade, Vent Rib, Checkered Stock, *Modern*	255.00	355.00	340.00
☐ **Model 1100 Cutts,** Various Gauges, Skeet Grade, Vent Rib, Checkered Stock, *Modern*	285.00	370.00	355.00
☐ **Model 1100 D Tournament,** Various Gauges, Vent Rib, Fancy Checkering, Fancy Wood, Fancy Engraving, *Modern*	650.00	1050.00	995.00
☐ **Model 1100 Deer Gun,** Various Gauges, Open Rear Sight, Checkered Stock, *Modern*	270.00	375.00	350.00
☐ **Model 1100 F Premier,** Various Gauges, Vent Rib, Fancy Checkering, Fancy Wood, Fancy Engraving, *Modern*	1500.00	2100.00	1950.00
☐ **Model 1100 TA,** 12 Ga., Bicentennial, Trap Grade, Vent Rib, Checkered Stock, *Modern*	300.00	410.00	390.00
☐ **Model 1100 TA,** 12 Ga., Bicentennial, Trap Grade, Vent Rib, Monte Carlo Stock, Checkered Stock, *Modern*	335.00	425.00	410.00
☐ **Model 1100 TA,** 12 Ga., Trap Grade, Vent Rib, Checkered Stock, *Modern*	280.00	400.00	390.00
☐ **Model 1100 TA,** 12 Ga., Trap Grade, Vent Rib, Checkered Stock, Monte Carlo Stock, *Modern*	335.00	435.00	425.00
☐ **Model 11A,** 12 Ga., Plain Barrel, *Modern*	130.00	195.00	190.00
☐ **Model 11A Sportsman,** Various Gauges, Plain Barrel, Light Engraving, *Modern*	135.00	195.00	190.00
☐ **Model 11A,** 12 Gauge, Plain Barrel, Fancy Wood, Checkered Stock, *Modern*	160.00	230.00	225.00
☐ **Model 11A Sportsman,** 12 Gauge, Plain Barrel, Fancy Wood, Light Engraving, Checkered Stock, *Modern*	170.00	265.00	250.00
☐ **Model 11C,** 12 Ga., Plain Barrel, Trap Grade, Fancy Checkering, Fancy Wood, *Modern*	215.00	350.00	325.00
☐ **Model 11D,** 12 Ga., Plain Barrel, Fancy Checkering, Fancy Wood, Fancy Engraving, *Modern*	450.00	600.00	575.00
☐ **Model 11D Sportsman,** Various Gauges, Plain Barrel, Engraved, Fancy Checkering, *Modern*	460.00	615.00	590.00

	V.G.	Exc.	Prior Year Exc. Value
☐ **Model 11E,** 12 Ga., Plain Barrel, Fancy Checkering, Fancy Wood, Fancy Engraving, *Modern*	620.00	750.00	735.00
☐ **Model 11E Sportsman,** Various Gauges, Plain Barrel, Fancy Checkering, Fancy Wood, Fancy Engraving, *Modern*	620.00	775.00	750.00
☐ **Model 11F,** 12 Ga., Plain Barrel, Fancy Checkering, Fancy Wood, Fancy Engraving, *Modern*	750.00	1050.00	1000.00
☐ **Model 11F Sportsman,** Various Gauges, Plain Barrel, Fancy Checkering, Fancy Wood, Fancy Engraving, *Modern*	735.00	1030.00	995.00
☐ **Model 11R,** 12 Ga., Riot Gun, Military, *Modern*	125.00	170.00	165.00
☐ **Model 11R,** 12 Ga., Riot Gun, Commercial, *Modern*	120.00	165.00	160.00
☐ **Model 48-D Sportsman,** Various Gauges, Vent Rib, Fancy Checkering, Fancy Wood, Fancy Engraving, *Modern*	480.00	640.00	625.00
☐ **Model 48-F Sportsman,** Various Gauges, Vent Rib, Fancy Checkering, Fancy Wood, Fancy Engraving, *Modern*	870.00	1200.00	1150.00
☐ **Model 48-SA Sportsman,** Various Gauges, Skeet Grade, Vent Rib, Checkered Stock, *Modern*	155.00	210.00	200.00
☐ **Model 48A Sportsman,** Various Gauges, Plain Barrel, *Modern*	115.00	165.00	160.00
☐ **Model 48B Sportsman,** Various Gauges, Vent Rib, Checkered Stock, *Modern*	130.00	185.00	180.00
☐ **Model 58 ADL,** 12 and 20 Gauges, Vent Rib, Recoil Pad, Checkered Stock, Magnum, *Modern*	170.00	230.00	220.00
☐ **Model 58 ADL,** Various Gauges, Plain Barrel, Checkered Stock, *Modern*	145.00	190.00	185.00
☐ **Model 58 ADL,** Various Gauges, Vent Rib, Checkered Stock, *Modern*	165.00	230.00	225.00
☐ **Model 58 ADX,** Various Gauges, Vent Rib, Checkered Stock, Fancy Wood, *Modern*	165.00	225.00	220.00
☐ **Model 58 BDL,** Various Gauges, Plain Barrel, Checkered Stock, Fancy Wood, *Modern*	165.00	225.00	220.00
☐ **Model 58 BDL,** Various Gauges, Vent Rib, Checkered Stock, Fancy Wood, *Modern*	165.00	230.00	225.00
☐ **Model 58 D Tournament,** Various Gauges, Vent Rib, Fancy Checkering, Fancy Wood, Fancy Engraving, *Modern*	485.00	675.00	650.00
☐ **Model 58 F Premier,** Various Gauges, Vent Rib, Fancy Checkering, Fancy Wood, Fancy Engraving, *Modern*	1050.00	1350.00	1300.00
☐ **Model 58 RSS,** 12 Ga. Slug, Open Rear Sight, Checkered Stock, *Modern*	160.00	215.00	210.00
☐ **Model 58 SA,** Various Gauges, Skeet Grade, Vent Rib, Checkered Stock, *Modern*	190.00	270.00	255.00
☐ **Model 58 TB,** 12 Ga., Trap Grade, Vent Rib, Checkered Stock, *Modern*	190.00	270.00	255.00
☐ **Model 878 A,** 12 Ga., Plain Barrel, *Modern*	115.00	160.00	155.00
☐ **Model 878 A,** 12 Ga., Vent Rib, *Modern*	125.00	170.00	165.00
☐ **Model 878 ADL,** 12 Ga., Plain Barrel, Checkered Stock, *Modern*	125.00	170.00	165.00

	V.G.	Exc.	Prior Year Exc. Value
☐ **Model 878 ADL,** 12 Ga., Vent Rib, Checkered Stock, *Modern*	140.00	190.00	180.00
☐ **Model 878 D,** 12 Ga., Vent Rib, Fancy Checkering, Fancy Wood, Fancy Engraving, *Modern*	485.00	580.00	565.00
☐ **Model 878 F,** 12 Ga., Vent Rib, Fancy Checkering, Fancy Wood, Fancy Engraving, *Modern*	800.00	1050.00	1000.00
☐ **Model 878 SA,** 12 Ga., Skeet Grade, Vent Rib, Checkered Stock, *Modern*	160.00	220.00	215.00
SHOTGUN, SINGLESHOT			
☐ **Model 3 (M1893),** 12 Ga., 24 Ga., 28 Ga., *Add* **$35.00**			
☐ **Model 3 (M1893),** Various Gauges, Takedown, Plain, *Curio*	100.00	135.00	130.00
☐ **Model 9 (M1902),** Various Gauges, Automatic Ejector, Plain, *Curio*	95.00	130.00	125.00
☐ **Model Parker 930,** 12 Ga., Trap Grade, Vent Rib, Automatic Ejector, Fancy Checkering, *Modern*	1075.00	1650.00	1600.00
☐ **Model Parker 930,** 12 Ga., Trap Grade, Vent Rib, Automatic Ejector, Fancy Checkering, Fancy Engraving, *Modern*	1900.00	2800.00	2750.00
SHOTGUN, SLIDE ACTION			
☐ **Model 10A,** 12 Ga., Takedown, Plain, *Modern*	150.00	200.00	195.00
☐ **Model 108,** 12 Ga., Takedown, Checkered Stock, Fancy Wood, *Modern*	180.00	245.00	235.00
☐ **Model 10C,** 12 Ga., Takedown, Fancy Wood, Checkered Stock, *Modern*	190.00	280.00	265.00
☐ **Model 10D,** 12 Ga., Takedown, Fancy Checkering, Fancy Wood, Engraved, *Modern*	460.00	615.00	595.00
☐ **Model 10E,** 12 Ga., Takedown, Fancy Checkering, Fancy Wood, Fancy Engraving, *Modern*	615.00	800.00	775.00
☐ **Model 10F,** 12 Ga., Takedown, Fancy Checkering, Fancy Engraving, Fancy Wood, *Modern*	750.00	1050.00	995.00
☐ **Model 10R,** 12 Ga., Takedown, Riot Gun, Plain, *Modern*	115.00	170.00	160.00
☐ **Model 10S,** 12 Ga., Takedown, Trap Grade, Checkered Stock, *Modern*	175.00	245.00	235.00
☐ **Model 17,** 20 Ga., for Solid Rib, *Add* **$25.00-$40.00**			
☐ **Model 17A,** 20 Ga., Takedown, Plain, *Modern*	170.00	230.00	220.00
☐ **Model 17B,** 20 Ga., Takedown, Checkered Stock, *Modern*	195.00	270.00	260.00
☐ **Model 17C,** 20 Ga., Takedown, Fancy Wood, Checkered Stock, *Modern*	250.00	345.00	335.00
☐ **Model 17D,** 20 Ga., Takedown, Fancy Wood, Fancy Checkering, Engraved, *Modern*	430.00	595.00	575.00
☐ **Model 17E,** 20 Ga., Takedown, Fancy Wood, Fancy Checkering, Fancy Engraving, *Modern*	590.00	825.00	800.00
☐ **Model 17F,** 20 Ga., Takedown, Fancy Wood, Fancy Checkering, Fancy Engraving, *Modern*	830.00	1050.00	1000.00
☐ **Model 17R,** 20 Ga., Takedown, Riot Gun, Plain, *Modern*	140.00	205.00	200.00

	V.G.	Exc.	Prior Year Exc. Value
☐ **Model 1908-0,** 12 Ga., Takedown, Riot Gun, Plain, *Modern*	140.00	205.00	200.00
☐ **Model 1908-1,** 12 Ga., Takedown, Plain, *Modern*	145.00	205.00	200.00
☐ **Model 1908-3,** 12 Ga., Takedown, Checkered Stock, Fancy Wood, *Modern*	175.00	250.00	240.00
☐ **Model 1908-4,** 12 Ga., Takedown, Fancy Checkering, Fancy Wood, Engraved, *Modern*	450.00	575.00	550.00
☐ **Model 1908-6,** 12 Ga., Takedown, Fancy Checkering, Fancy Wood, Fancy Engraving, *Modern*	695.00	1050.00	1000.00
☐ **Model 29,** for Solid Rib, *Add* **$25.00-$35.00**			
☐ **Model 29,** for Vent Rib, *Add* **$35.00-$55.00**			
☐ **Model 29A Sportsman,** 12 Ga., Plain Barrel, Takedown, *Modern*	155.00	235.00	230.00
☐ **Model 29B,** 12 Ga., Checkered Stock, Takedown, *Modern*	165.00	240.00	235.00
☐ **Model 29C,** 12 Ga., Trap Grade, Takedown, *Modern*	190.00	280.00	275.00
☐ **Model 29R,** 12 Ga., Riot Gun, Plain Barrel, *Modern*	120.00	175.00	170.00
☐ **Model 29S,** 12 Ga., Trap Grade, Plain Barrel, Checkered Stock, *Modern*	175.00	240.00	235.00
☐ **Model 29TA,** 12 Ga., Trap Grade, Vent Rib, Checkered Stock, *Modern*	185.00	300.00	285.00
☐ **Model 29TC,** 12 Ga., Trap Grade, Vent Rib, Checkered Stock, Fancy Wood, *Modern*	240.00	350.00	335.00
☐ **Model 29TD,** 12 Ga., Trap Grade, Vent Rib, Fancy Checkering, Fancy Wood, Engraved, *Modern*	390.00	570.00	545.00
☐ **Model 29TE,** 12 Ga., Trap Grade, Vent Rib, Fancy Checkering, Fancy Wood, Fancy Engraving, *Modern*	590.00	750.00	725.00
☐ **Model 29TF,** 12 Ga., Trap Grade, Vent Rib, Fancy Checkering, Fancy Wood, Fancy Engraving, *Modern*	750.00	1025.00	975.00
☐ **Model 31,** for Vent Rib, *Add* **$45.00-$60.00**			
☐ **Model 31,** for Solid Rib, *Add* **$15.00-$30.00**			
☐ **Model 31,** Various Gauges, Skeet Grade, Vent Rib, Checkered Stock, Fancy Wood, *Modern*	350.00	480.00	465.00
☐ **Model 31A,** Various Gauges, Plain Barrel, *Modern*	145.00	200.00	195.00
☐ **Model 31B,** Various Gauges, Plain Barrel, Checkered Stock, Fancy Wood, *Modern*	225.00	350.00	335.00
☐ **Model 31D Tournament,** Various Gauges, Plain Barrel, Checkered Stock, Fancy Wood, Engraved, *Modern*	550.00	725.00	700.00
☐ **Model 31E Expert,** Various Gauges, Plain Barrel, Fancy Checkering, Fancy Wood, Fancy Engraving, *Modern*	650.00	875.00	850.00
☐ **Model 31F Premier,** Various Gauges, Plain Barrel, Fancy Checkering, Fancy Wood, Fancy Engraving, *Modern*	900.00	1375.00	1350.00
☐ **Model 31H Hunter,** Various Gauges, Checkered Stock, Fancy Wood, Plain Barrel, *Modern*	275.00	370.00	350.00
☐ **Model 31R,** 12 Ga., Plain Barrel, Riot Gun, *Modern*	150.00	215.00	200.00

	V.G.	Exc.	Prior Year Exc. Value
☐ **Model 31S,** 12 Ga., Raised Matted Rib, Checkered Stock, Fancy Wood, *Modern*	305.00	465.00	450.00
☐ **Model 31TC,** 12 Ga., Trap Grade, Vent Rib, Recoil Pad, *Modern*	330.00	480.00	465.00
☐ **Model 870,** For Lightweight 20, *Add* **$20.00-$25.00**			
☐ **Model 870,** for .28 Ga. or .410 Ga., *Add* **$20.00-$25.00**			
☐ **Model 870,** for Left-Hand, *Add* **$10.00-$15.00**			
☐ **Model 870,** Various Gauges, Plain Barrel, Checkered Stock, *Modern*	180.00	230.00	225.00
☐ **Model 870,** Various Gauges, Vent Rib, Checkered Stock, *Modern*	200.00	260.00	250.00
☐ **Model 870,** Various Gauges, Plain Barrel, Magnum, Checkered Stock, *Modern*	195.00	245.00	235.00
☐ **Model 870,** Various Gauges, Vent Rib, Magnum, Checkered Stock, *Modern*	225.00	280.00	270.00
☐ **Model 870 All American,** 12 Ga., Trap Grade, Vent Rib, Fancy Checkering, Engraved, *Modern*	490.00	615.00	600.00
☐ **Model 870 Brushmaster,** 12 and 20 Gauges, Open Rear Sight, Recoil Pad, Checkered Stock, *Modern*	185.00	255.00	245.00
☐ **Model 870 Competition,** 12 Ga., Trap Grade, Vent Rib, Checkered Stock, Singleshot, *Modern*	260.00	360.00	345.00
☐ **Model 870 D Tournament,** Various Gauges, Vent Rib, Fancy Checkering, Fancy Wood, Fancy Engraving, *Modern*	650.00	935.00	900.00
☐ **Model 870 Deergun,** 12 Ga., Open Rear Sight, Checkered Stock, *Modern*	180.00	260.00	245.00
☐ **Model 870 F Premier,** Various Gauges, Vent Rib, Fancy Checkering, Fancy Wood, Fancy Engraving, *Modern*	1500.00	2100.00	2000.00
☐ **Model 870 Police,** 12 Ga., Open Rear Sight, *Modern*	180.00	235.00	230.00
☐ **Model 870 Police,** 12 Ga., Plain Barrel, *Modern*	165.00	225.00	220.00
☐ **Model 870 SA,** 12 Ga., Bicentennial, Skeet Grade, Vent Rib, Checkered Stock, *Modern*	200.00	285.00	275.00
☐ **Model 870SA,** Various Gauges, Skeet Grade, Vent Rib, Checkered Stock, *Modern*	205.00	285.00	275.00
☐ **Model 870SA Cutts,** Various Gauges, Skeet Grade, Vent Rib, Checkered Stock, *Modern*	200.00	280.00	270.00
☐ **Model 870SC,** Various Gauges, Skeet Grade, Vent Rib, Checkered Stock, *Modern*	205.00	285.00	275.00
☐ **Model 870TB,** 12 Ga., Trap Grade, Vent Rib, Checkered Stock, *Modern*	200.00	270.00	260.00
☐ **Model 870TB,** 12 Ga., Trap Grade, Vent Rib, Checkered Stock, Monte Carlo Stock, *Modern*	200.00	280.00	270.00
☐ **Model 870TB,** 12 Ga., Bicentennial, Trap Grade, Vent Rib, Checkered Stock, *Modern*	200.00	280.00	270.00
☐ **Model 870TB,** 12 Ga., Bicentennial, Trap Grade, Vent Rib, Checkered Stock, Monte Carlo Stock, *Modern*	200.00	280.00	270.00
☐ **Model 870TC,** 12 Ga., Trap Grade, Vent Rib, Checkered Stock, *Modern*	260.00	350.00	335.00
☐ **Model 870TC,** 12 Ga., Trap Grade, Vent Rib, Checkered Stock, Monte Carlo Stock, *Modern*	265.00	360.00	345.00

	V.G.	Exc.	Prior Year Exc. Value
SILENCED WEAPON RIFLE			
☐ **Rem. 40XB Sniper,** .308 Win., Heavy Barrel, Scope Mounted, Silencer, *Class 3*	600.00	875.00	850.00

REPUBLIC

Spain, unknown maker.

	V.G.	Exc.	Prior Year Exc. Value
HANDGUN, SEMI-AUTOMATIC			
☐ **.32 ACP**, Clip Fed, Long Grip, *Modern*	110.00	150.00	140.00

RETRIEVER

Made by Thomas Ryan, Norwich, Conn. 1870-1876.

	V.G.	Exc.	Prior Year Exc. Value
HANDGUN, REVOLVER			
☐ **.32 Short R.F.**, 5 Shot, Spur Trigger, Solid Frame, Single Action, *Antique*	95.00	165.00	160.00

REVELATION

Trade name used by Western Auto.

	V.G.	Exc.	Prior Year Exc. Value
RIFLE, BOLT ACTION			
☐ **Model 107**, .22 WMR, Clip Fed, *Modern*	45.00	70.00	65.00
☐ **Model 210B**, 7mm Rem. Mag., Checkered Stock, Monte Carlo Stock, *Modern*	140.00	185.00	175.00
☐ **Model 220A**, .308 Win., Checkered Stock, Monte Carlo Stock, *Modern*	125.00	170.00	165.00
☐ **Model 220AD**, .308 Win., Checkered Stock, Monte Carlo Stock, Fancy Wood, *Modern*	150.00	195.00	195.00
☐ **Model 220B**, .243 Win., Checkered Stock, Monte Carlo Stock, *Modern*	125.00	165.00	160.00
☐ **Model 220BD**, .243 Win., Checkered Stock, Monte Carlo Stock, Fancy Wood, *Modern*	150.00	195.00	195.00
☐ **Model 220C**, .22-250, Checkered Stock, Monte Carlo Stock, *Modern*	125.00	165.00	160.00
☐ **Model 220CD**, .22-250, Checkered Stock, Monte Carlo Stock, Fancy Wood, *Modern*	150.00	195.00	195.00
RIFLE, LEVER ACTION			
☐ **Model 117**, .22 L.R.R.F., Tube Feed, *Modern*	50.00	70.00	65.00
RIFLE, SEMI-AUTOMATIC			
☐ **Model 125**, .22 L.R.R.F., Clip Fed, *Modern*	40.00	60.00	55.00
RIFLE, SINGLESHOT			
☐ **Model 100**, .22 L.R.R.F., *Modern*	20.00	35.00	35.00
SHOTGUN, BOLT ACTION			
☐ **Model 312B**, 12 Ga., Clip Fed, *Modern*	35.00	55.00	50.00
☐ **Model 312BK**, 12 Ga., Clip Fed, Adjustable Choke, *Modern*	45.00	65.00	60.00
☐ **Model 316B**, 16 Ga., Clip Fed, *Modern*	35.00	50.00	45.00
☐ **Model 316BK**, 16 Ga., Clip Fed, Adjustable Choke, *Modern*	35.00	55.00	50.00
☐ **Model 325B**, 20 Ga., Clip Fed, *Modern*	40.00	55.00	50.00
☐ **Model 325BK**, 20 Ga., Clip Fed, Adjustable Choke, *Modern*	45.00	55.00	55.00
☐ **Model 330**, .410 Ga., Clip Fed, *Modern*	35.00	50.00	45.00

	V.G.	Exc.	Prior Year Exc. Value
SHOTGUN, SLIDE ACTION			
☐ **Model 310**, Various Gauges, Plain Barrel, Takedown, *Modern*	85.00	135.00	130.00
☐ **Model 31OR**, Various Gauges, Vent Rib, Takedown, *Modern*	90.00	140.00	135.00

REV-O-NOC

Made by Crescent for Hibbard-Spencer-Bartlett Co., Chicago.

	V.G.	Exc.	Prior Year Exc. Value
SHOTGUN, DOUBLE BARREL, SIDE-BY-SIDE			
☐ **Various Gauges**, Outside Hammers, Damascus Barrel, *Modern*	100.00	170.00	175.00
☐ **Various Gauges**, Hammerless, Steel Barrel, *Modern*	135.00	190.00	200.00
☐ **Various Gauges**, Hammerless, Damascus Barrel, *Modern*	100.00	170.00	175.00
☐ **Various Gauges**, Outside Hammers, Steel Barrel, *Modern*	125.00	185.00	190.00
SHOTGUN, SINGLESHOT			
☐ **Various Gauges**, Hammer, Steel Barrel, *Modern*	55.00	85.00	85.00

REYNOLDS, PLANT & HOTCHKISS

Also see Plant's Mfg. Co.

	V.G.	Exc.	Prior Year Exc. Value
HANDGUN, REVOLVER			
☐ **.25 Short R.F.**, 5 Shot, Single Action, Spur Trigger, 3" Barrel, *Antique*	135.00	190.00	175.00

R.G. INDUSTRIES

R.G. tradename belongs to Rohm GmbH, Sontheim/Brenz, W. Germany, and after 1968 also made in Miami, Fla. for American consumption.

	V.G.	Exc.	Prior Year Exc. Value
HANDGUN, DOUBLE BARREL, OVER-UNDER			
☐ **RG-16**, .22 WMR, 2 Shot, Derringer, *Modern*	25.00	35.00	35.00
☐ **RG-17**, .38 Special, 2 Shot, Derringer, *Modern*	25.00	35.00	35.00
HANDGUN, REVOLVER			
☐ **Partner RG-40P**, .38 Special, 6 Shot, Double Action, Swing-Out Cylinder, *Modern*	40.00	65.00	60.00
☐ **RG-14**, .22 L.R.R.F., 6 Shot, Double Action, *Modern*	25.00	35.00	30.00
☐ **RG-23**, .22 L.R.R.F., 6 Shot, Double Action, *Modern*	30.00	45.00	40.00
☐ **RG-30**, .22LR/.22 WMR Combo, 6 Shot, Double Action, Swing-Out Cylinder, *Modern*	35.00	50.00	50.00
☐ **RG-30**, .22 L.R.R.F., 6 Shot, Double Action, Swing-Out Cylinder, *Modern*	25.00	35.00	35.00
☐ **RG-30**, .22 WMR, 6 Shot, Double Action, Swing-Out Cylinder, *Modern*	25.00	40.00	40.00
☐ **RG-30**, .32 S & W Long, 6 Shot, Double Action, Swing-Out Cylinder, *Modern*	25.00	40.00	40.00
☐ **RG-31**, .32 S & W Long, 6 Shot, Double Action, *Modern*	30.00	45.00	40.00
☐ **RG-31**, .38 Special, 5 Shot, Double Action, *Modern*	30.00	45.00	40.00
☐ **RG-38S**, .38 Special, 6 Shot, Double Action, Blue, *Modern*	40.00	60.00	55.00

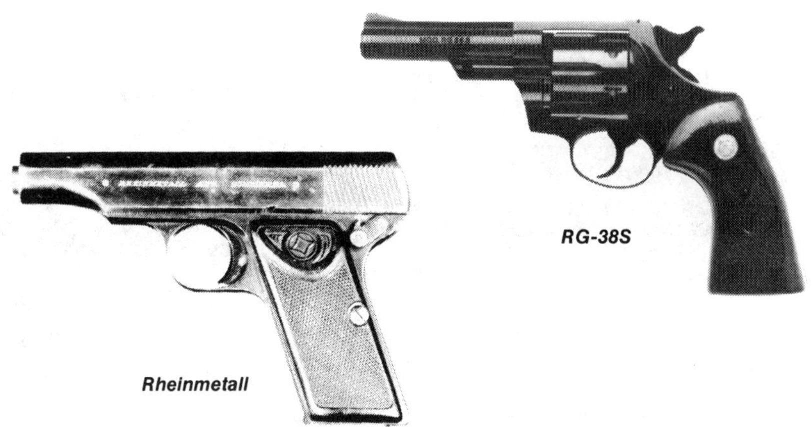
RG-38S

Rheinmetall

	V.G.	Exc.	Prior Year Exc. Value
☐ **RG-38S**, .38 Special, 6 Shot, Double Action, Nickel Plated, *Modern*	40.00	60.00	55.00
☐ **RG-40**, .38 Special, 6 Shot, Double Action, Swing-Out Cylinder, *Modern*	40.00	60.00	55.00
☐ **RG-57**, .357 Magnum, 6 Shot, Double Action, Swing-Out Cylinder, *Modern*	50.00	80.00	80.00
☐ **RG-57**, .44 Magnum, 6 Shot, Double Action, Swing-Out Cylinder, *Modern*	65.00	100.00	100.00
☐ **RG-63**, .22 L.R.R.F., 6 Shot, Double Action, Western Style, *Modern*	25.00	35.00	35.00
☐ **RG-66**, .22LR/.22 WMR Combo, 6 Shot, Single Action, Western Style, *Modern*	25.00	40.00	40.00
☐ **RG-66T**, .22LR/.22 WMR Combo, 6 Shot, Single Action, Western Style, Adjustable Sights, *Modern*	30.00	45.00	45.00
☐ **RG-74**, .22 L.R.R.F., 6 Shot, Double Action, Swing-Out Cylinder, *Modern*	40.00	55.00	50.00
☐ **RG-88**, .357 Magnum, 6 Shot, Double Action, Swing-Out Cylinder, *Modern*	60.00	85.00	85.00
HANDGUN, SEMI-AUTOMATIC			
☐ **RG-25**, .25 ACP, *Modern*	30.00	45.00	45.00
☐ **RG-26**, .25 ACP, *Modern*	30.00	45.00	45.00

RHEINMETALL

Rheinsche Metallwaren u. Maschinenfabrik, Sommerda, Germany 1922-1927.

HANDGUN, SEMI-AUTOMATIC

	V.G.	Exc.	Prior Year Exc. Value
☐ **.32 ACP**, Clip Fed, Blue, *Curio*	215.00	350.00	300.00

RICHARDS, JOHN

London & Birmingham, England 1745-1810.

	V.G.	Exc.	Prior Year Exc. Value
SHOTGUN, FLINTLOCK			
☐ **Blunderbuss**, Half-Octagon, Cannon, Steel Barrel, Folding Bayonet, *Antique*	675.00	975.00	950.00

RICHARDS, W.

Belgium, c. 1900

	V.G.	Exc.	Prior Year Exc. Value
SHOTGUN, DOUBLE BARREL, SIDE-BY-SIDE			
☐ **Various Gauges**, Outside Hammers, Damascus Barrel, *Modern*	100.00	170.00	175.00
☐ **Various Gauges**, Hammerless, Steel Barrel, *Modern*	135.00	190.00	200.00
☐ **Various Gauges**, Hammerless, Damascus Barrel, *Modern*	100.00	170.00	175.00
☐ **Various Gauges**, Outside Hammers, Steel Barrel, *Modern*	125.00	185.00	190.00
SHOTGUN, SINGLESHOT			
☐ **Various Gauges**, Hammer, Steel Barrel, *Modern*	55.00	85.00	85.00

RICHARDSON INDUSTRIES

New Haven, Conn.

	V.G.	Exc.	Prior Year Exc. Value
SHOTGUN, SINGLESHOT			
☐ **Model R-5**, 12 Ga., 24" Barrel, *Modern*	20.00	35.00	35.00

RICHLAND ARMS CO.

Bussfield, Mich.

	V.G.	Exc.	Prior Year Exc. Value
SHOTGUN, DOUBLE BARREL, OVER-UNDER			
☐ **Model 808**, 12 Ga., Single Trigger, Checkered Stock, Vent Rib, *Modern*	225.00	350.00	325.00
☐ **Model 810**, 10 Ga. 3½", Double Trigger, Checkered Stock, Vent Rib, *Modern*	340.00	450.00	425.00
☐ **Model 828**, 28 Ga., Single Trigger, Checkered Stock, *Modern*	235.00	320.00	290.00
☐ **Model 844**, 12 Ga., Single Trigger, Checkered Stock, *Modern*	170.00	240.00	220.00
SHOTGUN, DOUBLE BARREL, SIDE-BY-SIDE			
☐ **Model 200**, Various Gauges, Double Trigger, Checkered Stock, *Modern*	185.00	250.00	240.00
☐ **Model 202**, Various Gauges, Double Trigger, Extra Shotgun Barrel, *Modern*	260.00	335.00	325.00
☐ **Model 707 Deluxe**, 12 and 20 Gauges, Double Trigger, *Modern*	200.00	290.00	275.00
☐ **Model 707 Deluxe**, 12 and 20 Gauges, Double Trigger, Checkered Stock, Extra Shotgun Barrel, *Modern*	260.00	370.00	350.00
☐ **Model 711**, 10 Ga. 3½", Double Trigger, *Modern*	195.00	275.00	265.00
☐ **Model 711**, 12 Ga. Mag. 3", Double Trigger, *Modern*	185.00	235.00	225.00
RIFLE, PERCUSSION			
☐ **Wesson Rifle**, .50, Set Triggers, Target Sights, Reproduction, *Antique*	140.00	200.00	200.00

RICHTER, CHARLES

Made by Crescent for New York Sporting Goods Co. c. 1900.

	V.G.	Exc.	Prior Year Exc. Value
SHOTGUN, DOUBLE BARREL, SIDE-BY-SIDE			
☐ **Various Gauges**, Outside Hammers, Damascus Barrel, *Modern*	100.00	170.00	175.00
☐ **Various Gauges**, Hammerless, Steel Barrel, *Modern*	135.00	190.00	200.00
☐ **Various Gauges**, Hammerless, Damascus Barrel, *Modern*	100.00	170.00	175.00
☐ **Various Gauges**, Outside Hammers, Steel Barrel, *Modern*	125.00	185.00	190.00
SHOTGUN, SINGLESHOT			
☐ **Various Gauges**, Hammer, Steel Barrel, *Modern*	55.00	85.00	85.00

RICKARD ARMS

Made by Crescent for J.A. Rickard Co. Schenectady, N.Y.

	V.G.	Exc.	Prior Year Exc. Value
SHOTGUN, DOUBLE BARREL, SIDE-BY-SIDE			
☐ **Various Gauges**, Outside Hammers, Damascus Barrel, *Modern*	100.00	170.00	175.00
☐ **Various Gauges**, Hammerless, Steel Barrel, *Modern*	135.00	190.00	200.00
☐ **Various Gauges**, Hammerless, Damascus Barrel, *Modern*	100.00	170.00	175.00
☐ **Various Gauges**, Outside Hammers, Steel Barrel, *Modern*	125.00	185.00	190.00
SHOTGUN, SINGLESHOT			
☐ **Various Gauges**, Hammer, Steel Barrel, *Modern*	55.00	85.00	85.00

RIGARMI

Industria Galesi, Brescia, Italy.

	V.G.	Exc.	Prior Year Exc. Value
HANDGUN, SEMI-AUTOMATIC			
☐ **Militar**, .22 L.R.R.F., Clip Fed, Hammer, Double Action, *Modern*	120.00	160.00	155.00
☐ **Pocket**, .32 ACP, Clip Fed, Hammer, Double Action, *Modern*	110.00	155.00	145.00
☐ **RG-217**, .22 Long R.F., Clip Fed, *Modern*	65.00	100.00	95.00
☐ **RG-218**, .22 L.R.R.F., Clip Fed, *Modern*	80.00	125.00	120.00
☐ **RG-219**, .25 ACP, Clip Fed, *Modern*	65.00	100.00	95.00

RIGBY, JOHN & CO.

Dublin, Ireland & London, England from 1867.

	V.G.	Exc.	Prior Year Exc. Value
RIFLE, BOLT ACTION			
☐ **.275 Rigby**, Sporting Rifle, Express Sights, Checkered Stock, *Modern*	1,450.00	2,350.00	2,250.00
☐ **.275 Rigby**, Sporting Rifle, Lightweight, Express Sights, Checkered Stock, *Modern*	1,435.00	2,300.00	2,250.00
☐ **.350 Rigby**, Sporting Rifle, Express Sights, Checkered Stock, *Modern*	1,450.00	2,350.00	2,250.00
☐ **Big Game**, .416 Rigby, Sporting Rifle, Express Sights, Checkered Stock, *Modern*	1,450.00	2,350.00	2,250.00

	V.G.	Exc.	Prior Year Exc. Value
RIFLE, DOUBLE BARREL, SIDE-BY-SIDE			
☐ **Best Grade**, Various Calibers, Sidelock, Double Trigger, Express Sights, Fancy Engraving, Fancy Checkering, *Modern*	7,500.00	13,250.00	13,000.00
☐ **Second Grade**, Various Calibers, Box Lock, Double Trigger, Express Sights, Fancy Engraving, Fancy Checkering, *Modern*	5,500.00	8,750.00	8,500.00
☐ **Third Grade**, Various Calibers, Box Lock, Double Trigger, Express Sights, Engraved, Checkered Stock, *Modern*	4,000.00	5,650.00	5,500.00
SHOTGUN, DOUBLE BARREL, SIDE-BY-SIDE			
☐ **Chatsworth**, Various Gauges, Box Lock, Automatic Ejector, Double Trigger, Fancy Engraving, Fancy Checkering, *Modern*	1,750.00	2,575.00	2,500.00
☐ **Regal**, Various Gauges, Sidelock, Automatic Ejector, Double Trigger, Fancy Engraving, Fancy Checkering, *Modern*	5,750.00	9,250.00	9,000.00
☐ **Sackville**, Various Gauges, Box Lock, Automatic Ejector, Double Trigger, Fancy Engraving, Fancy Checkering, *Modern*	2,100.00	3,150.00	3,000.00
☐ **Sandringham**, Various Gauges, Sidelock, Automatic Ejector, Double Trigger, Fancy Engraving, Fancy Checkering, *Modern*	4,200.00	6,700.00	6,500.00

RINO GALESI

Industria Galesi, Brescia, Italy.

	V.G.	Exc.	Prior Year Exc. Value
HANDGUN, SEMI-AUTOMATIC			
☐ **Model 9**, .25 ACP, Clip Fed, Blue, *Modern*	85.00	120.00	110.00

RIOT

Made by Stevens Arms.

	V.G.	Exc.	Prior Year Exc. Value
SHOTGUN, PUMP			
☐ **Model 520**, 12 Ga., Takedown, *Modern*	105.00	145.00	140.00
☐ **Model 620**, Various Gauges, Takedown, *Modern*	115.00	160.00	150.00

RIPOLI

	V.G.	Exc.	Prior Year Exc. Value
HANDGUN, MIQUELOT-LOCK			
☐ **Ball Butt**, Brass Inlay, Light Ornamentation, *Antique*	1,575.00	2,550.00	2,400.00
☐ **Pair**, Fluted Barrel, Pocket Pistol, Engraved, Silver Furniture, *Antique*	5,250.00	7,300.00	7,000.00

RITTER, JACOB

Phila., Pa. 1775-1783. See Kentucky Rifles and Pistols.

RIVERSIDE ARMS CO.

Made by Stevens Arms & Tool Co.

	V.G.	Exc.	Prior Year Exc. Value
SHOTGUN, DOUBLE BARREL, SIDE-BY-SIDE			
☐ **Model 215**, 12 and 16 Gauges, Outside Hammers, Steel Barrel, *Modern*	115.00	175.00	165.00

	V.G.	Exc.	Prior Year Exc. Value

ROB ROY

Made by Hood Firearms Norwich, Conn., c. 1880.

HANDGUN, REVOLVER

	V.G.	Exc.	Prior Year Exc. Value
☐ **.22 Short R.F.**, 7 Shot, Spur Trigger, Solid Frame, Single Action, *Antique*	95.00	165.00	160.00

ROBBINS & LAWRENCE

Robbins, Kendall & Lawrence, Windsor, Vt. 1844-1857. Became Robbins & Lawrence about 1846. Also see Sharps, U.S. Military.

HANDGUN, PERCUSSION

	V.G.	Exc.	Prior Year Exc. Value
☐ **Pepperbox**, Various Calibers, Ring Trigger, *Antique*	390.00	575.00	550.00

ROBIN HOOD

Made by Hood Firearms Norwich, Conn., c. 1875.

HANDGUN, REVOLVER

	V.G.	Exc.	Prior Year Exc. Value
☐ **.22 Short R.F.**, 7 Shot, Spur Trigger, Solid Frame, Single Action, *Antique*	95.00	165.00	160.00
☐ **.32 Short R.F.**, 5 Shot, Spur Trigger, Solid Frame, Single Action, *Antique*	95.00	170.00	170.00

ROESSER, PETER

Lancaster, Pa. 1741-1782. See Kentucky Rifles and Pistols.

ROGERS & SPENCER

Willowvale, N.Y., c. 1862.

HANDGUN, PERCUSSION

	V.G.	Exc.	Prior Year Exc. Value
☐ **.44 Army**, Single Action, *Antique*	550.00	825.00	775.00

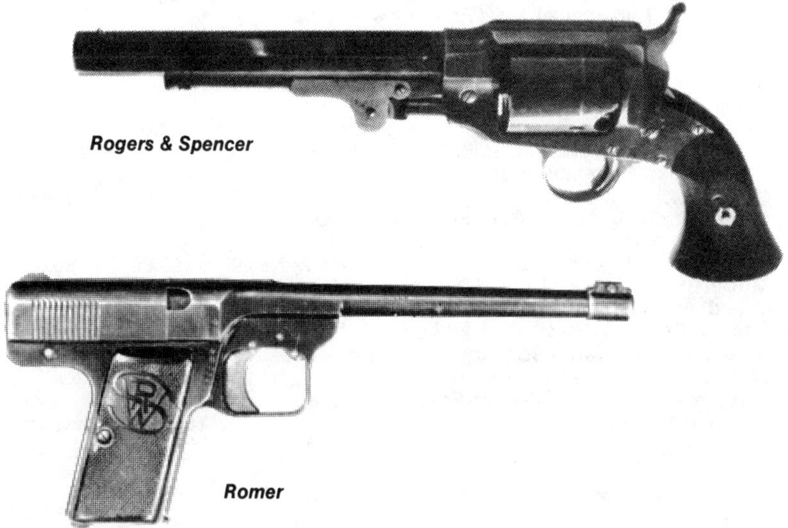

Rogers & Spencer

Romer

	V.G.	Exc.	Prior Year Exc. Value
ROLAND			
Francisco Arizmendi, Eibar, Spain, c. 1922.			
HANDGUN, SEMI-AUTOMATIC			
□ **.25 ACP**, Clip Fed, Blue, *Curio*	85.00	125.00	120.00
□ **.32 ACP**, Clip Fed, Blue, *Curio*	95.00	135.00	130.00
ROME REVOLVER AND NOVELTY WORKS			
Rome, N.Y., c. 1880.			
HANDGUN, REVOLVER			
□ **.32 Short R.F.**, 5 Shot, Spur Trigger, Solid Frame, Single Action, *Antique*	90.00	165.00	160.00
ROMER			
Romerwerke AG, Suhl, Germany, c. 1925.			
HANDGUN, SEMI-AUTOMATIC			
□ **.22 L.R.R.F.**, Clip Fed, 2½" and 6½" Barrels, Blue, *Curio*	640.00	995.00	950.00
□ **.22 L.R.R.F.**, Clip Fed, One Barrel, Blue, *Curio*	545.00	850.00	825.00
ROOP, JOHN			
Allentown, Pa., c. 1775. See Kentucky Rifles.			
ROSSI			
Amadeo Rossi S.A., Sao Leopoldo, Brazil. Also see Garrucha.			
HANDGUN, REVOLVER			
□ **Model 31,** .38 Special, Solid Frame, Swing-Out Cylinder, 5 Shot, 4" Barrel, *Modern*	75.00	110.00	95.00
□ **Model 51,** .22 L.R.R.F., Solid Frame, Swing-Out Cylinder, Adjustable Sights, 5 Shot, 6" Barrel, *Modern*	70.00	100.00	85.00
□ **Model 68/2,** .38 Special, Solid Frame, Swing-Out Cylinder, Adjustable Sights, 5 Shot, 2" Barrel, *Modern*	140.00	160.00	—
□ **Model 68,** .38 Special, Solid Frame, Swing-Out Cylinder, Adjustable Sights, 5 Shot, 3" Barrel, *Modern*	75.00	110.00	95.00
□ **Model 69,** .32 S & W Long, Solid Frame, Swing-Out Cylinder, Adjustable Sights, 5 Shot, 3" Barrel, *Modern*	65.00	95.00	80.00
□ **Model 70,** .22 Short R.F., Solid Frame, Swing-Out Cylinder, Adjustable Sights, 5 Shot, 3" Barrel, *Modern*	65.00	95.00	80.00
□ **Model 88,** .38 Special, Solid Frame, Swing-Out Cylinder, Adjustable Sights, Stainless Steel, 5 Shot, 3" Barrel, *Modern*	95.00	140.00	—
□ **Model 89, The Stainless Lady,** .38 Special, Stainless, 3" Barrel, *Modern*	160.00	180.00	—
□ **Model 94,** .38 Special, Medium Frame, Shrouded Ejector Rod, *Modern*		**To Be Announced**	

Rossi Gallery Rifle

Rossi Mark X, Marquis, Deluxe

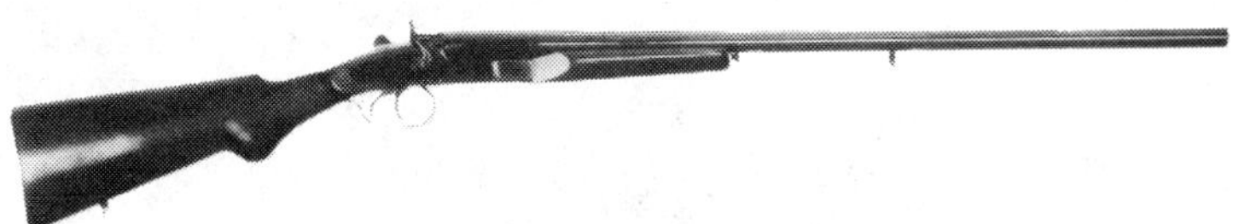

Rossi Overland Shotgun

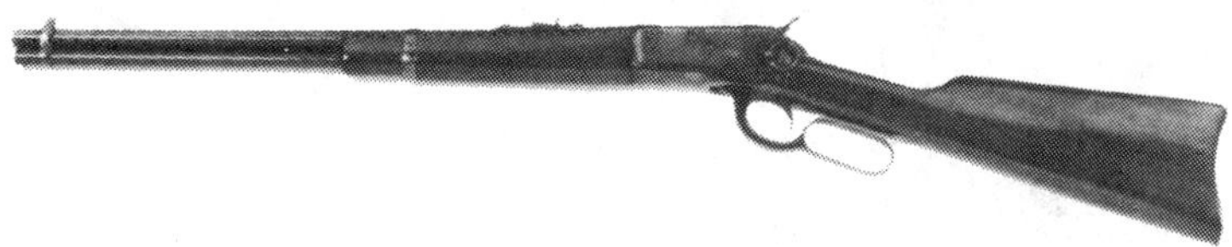

Rossi Saddle Ring Carbine Rifle

	V.G.	Exc.	Prior Year Exc. Value
HANDGUN, SINGLESHOT			
☐ **.22 Short R.F.**, Derringer, *Modern*	35.00	55.00	50.00
RIFLE, SLIDE ACTION			
☐ **Saddle Ring**, .357 Mag., Tube Feed, Hammer, Carbine, *Modern*	120.00	165.00	160.00
☐ **Saddle Ring**, .357 Mag., Tube Feed, Hammer, Carbine, Engraved, *Modern*	160.00	215.00	210.00
☐ **Gallery**, .22 L.R.R.F., Tube Feed, Takedown, Hammer, *Modern*	75.00	125.00	95.00

Rossi Model 68/2

Rossi M94

	V.G.	Exc.	Prior Year Exc. Value
☐ **Gallery,** .22 L.R.R.F., Tube Feed, Takedown, Hammer, Carbine, *Modern*	75.00	125.00	95.00
RIFLE, SLIDE ACTION			
☐ **Mark X Marquis Deluxe**	345.00	369.95	—
SHOTGUN, DOUBLE BARREL, SIDE-BY-SIDE			
☐ **12 Ga. Mag. 3"**, Checkered Stock, Hammerless, Double Trigger, *Modern*	135.00	195.00	180.00
☐ **12 Ga. Mag. 3"**, Hammerless, Double Trigger, *Modern*	130.00	185.00	175.00
☐ **Overland**, 12 and 20 Gauges, Checkered Stock, Outside Hammers, Double Trigger, *Modern*	135.00	180.00	165.00
☐ **Overland**, 12 and 20 Gauges, Outside Hammers, Double Trigger, *Modern*	135.00	180.00	165.00
☐ **Overland II,** Various Gauges, Checkered Stock, Outside Hammers, Double Trigger, *Modern*	150.00	200.00	195.00
☐ **Squire Model 14,** Various Gauges, Hammerless, Double Trigger, *Modern*	135.00	185.00	175.00

	V.G.	Exc.	Prior Year Exc. Value

ROSS RIFLE CO.

Quebec, Canada. Also see Canadian Military.

RIFLE, BOLT ACTION

	V.G.	Exc.	Prior Year Exc. Value
☐ **Canadian Issue**, .303 British, Military, *Modern*	165.00	225.00	220.00
☐ **Model 1903 MK I**, .303 British, Sporting Rifle, Open Rear Sight, *Modern*	275.00	365.00	350.00
☐ **Model 1905 MK II**, Various Calibers, Sporting Rifle, Open Rear Sight, *Modern*	225.00	335.00	325.00
☐ **Model 1910 MK III**, Various Calibers, Sporting Rifle, Open Rear Sight, Checkered Stock, *Modern*	195.00	320.00	295.00

ROTTWEIL

Germany, Imported by Eastern Sports Milford, N.H.

RIFLE, DOUBLE BARREL, OVER-UNDER

	V.G.	Exc.	Prior Year Exc. Value
☐ **Standard Grade**, Various Calibers, Engraved, Fancy Checkering, Open Rear Sight, *Modern*	1,550.00	2,300.00	2,200.00

SHOTGUN, DOUBLE BARREL, OVER-UNDER

	V.G.	Exc.	Prior Year Exc. Value
☐ **Montreal**, 12 Ga., Trap Grade, Vent Rib, Single Selective Trigger, Checkered Stock, *Modern*	1,350.00	1,850.00	1,800.00
☐ **Olympia**, 12 Ga., Skeet Grade, Single Selective Trigger, Automatic Ejector, Vent Rib, Engraved, *Modern*	1,450.00	2,150.00	2,100.00
☐ **Olympia**, 12 Ga., Trap Grade, Single Selective Trigger, Automatic Ejector, Vent Rib, Engraved, *Modern*	1,450.00	2,150.00	2,100.00
☐ **Olympia 72**, 12 Ga., Skeet Grade, Trap Grade, Single Selective Trigger, Checkered Stock, *Modern*	1,250.00	1,850.00	1,800.00
☐ **Supreme**, 12 Ga., Vent Rib, Single Selective Trigger, Checkered Stock, *Modern*	1,150.00	1,750.00	1,700.00
☐ **Supreme**, 12 Ga., Field Grade, Single Selective Trigger, Automatic Ejector, Vent Rib, Engraved, *Modern*	1,450.00	2,150.00	2,100.00
☐ **American**, 12 Ga., Trap Grade, Single Selective Trigger, Automatic Ejector, Vent Rib, Engraved, *Modern*	1,450.00	2,150.00	2,100.00

ROVIRO, ANTONIO

Iqualada, Spain, c. 1790.

HANDGUN, MIQUELET-LOCK

	V.G.	Exc.	Prior Year Exc. Value
☐ **Pair**, Belt Pistol, Belt Hook, Engraved, Light Ornamentation, *Antique*	3,600.00	5,250.00	5,000.00

ROYAL

Possibly Hopkins & Allen, c. 1880.

HANDGUN, REVOLVER

	V.G.	Exc.	Prior Year Exc. Value
☐ **.22 Short R.F.**, 7 Shot, Spur Trigger, Solid Frame, Single Action, *Antique*	90.00	165.00	160.00
☐ **.32 Short R.F.**, 5 Shot, Spur Trigger, Solid Frame, Single Action, *Antique*	95.00	175.00	170.00

ROYAL

M. Zulaika y Cia., Eibar, Spain.

HANDGUN, SEMI-AUTOMATIC

	V.G.	Exc.	Prior Year Exc. Value
☐ **Mauser M1896 Type**, 7.63mm, Blue, *Modern*	265.00	395.00	375.00
☐ **Novelty**, .25 ACP, Clip Fed, Blue, *Curio*	165.00	210.00	195.00
☐ **Novelty**, .32 ACP, Clip Fed, Blue, *Curio*	175.00	225.00	215.00
☐ **.32 ACP**, Clip Fed, Long Grip, *Modern*	130.00	185.00	170.00
☐ **12 Shot**, .32 ACP, Clip Fed, Long Grip, *Modern*	170.00	255.00	235.00

Royal 12 Shot

Royal Novelty .32

Ruby .45

RUBY

Gabilondo y Cia., Vitoria, Spain.

HANDGUN, REVOLVER

☐ **Ruby Extra** For Engraving *Add* **$40.00-$60.00**

☐ **Ruby Extra** For Chrome Plating *Add* **$20.00-$35.00**

	V.G.	Exc.	Prior Year Exc. Value
☐ **Ruby Extra Model 14**, .22 L.R.R.F., Double Action, Blue, Swing-Out Cylinder, *Modern*	50.00	80.00	70.00
☐ **Ruby Extra Model 14**, .32 S & W Long, Double Action, Blue, Swing-Out Cylinder, *Modern*	50.00	80.00	70.00
☐ **Ruby Extra Model 12**, .38 Spec., Double Action, Blue, Swing-Out Cylinder, *Modern*	60.00	85.00	80.00

HANDGUN, SEMI-AUTOMATIC

	V.G.	Exc.	Prior Year Exc. Value
☐ **.32 ACP**, Clip Fed, Blue, *Curio*	125.00	165.00	150.00

RUGER

Sturm, Ruger & Co., Southport, Conn.

☐ **For Bicentennial Stamping,** *Add* **5%-10%**

	V.G.	Exc.	Prior Year Exc. Value
AUTOMATIC WEAPON, SUBMACHINE GUN			
☐ **AC-556,** .223 Rem., Clip Fed, Wood Stock, with Compensator, *Class 3*	210.00	290.00	285.00
☐ **AC-556F,** .223 Rem., Clip Fed, Folding Stock, With Compensator, *Class 3*	230.00	345.00	335.00
☐ **K AC-556,** .223 Rem., Clip Fed, Stainless, Wood Stock, with Compensator, *Class 3*	305.00	390.00	375.00
☐ **K AC-556F,** .223 Rem., Clip Fed, Stainless, Folding Stock, with Compensator, *Class 3*	315.00	415.00	400.00
HANDGUN, REVOLVER			
☐ **Brass Gripframe,** *Add* **$20.00-$30.00**			
☐ **.22 L.R.R.F,** Western Style, Single Action, Blue, Lightweight, Early Model, *Modern*	255.00	350.00	335.00
☐ **BP-7 Old Army Cap and Ball Revolver,** .44 Black Powder, Blue, Walnut Grip, Reproduction, *Antique*	216.00	235.00	230.00
☐ **KBP-7 Old Army Cap and Ball Revolver,** .44 Black Powder, Stainless, Walnut Grip, Reproduction, *Antique*	285.00	300.00	300.00
☐ **KRH-35 Redhawk Double Action Revolver,** .357 Magnum, Stainless, 7½" Barrel, *Modern*	381.00	395.00	395.00
☐ **KRH-355 Redhawk Double Action Revolver,** .357 Magnum, Stainless, 5½" Barrel, *Modern*	381.00	395.00	395.00
☐ **KRH-41 Redhawk Double Action Revolver,** .41 Magnum, Stainless, 7½" Barrel, *Modern*	381.00	395.00	395.00
☐ **KRH-415 Redhawk Double Action Revolver,** .41 Magnum, Stainless, 5½" Barrel, *Modern*	381.00	395.00	395.00
☐ **"Magna-port IV",** .44 Magnum, Western Style, Single Action, Commemorative, *Modern*	900.00	1350.00	1450.00
☐ **"Magna-port V",** .44 Magnum, Western Style, Single Action, Commemorative, *Modern*	935.00	1650.00	1750.00
☐ **Bearcat,** .22 L.R.R.F., Western Style, Single Action, Blue, Brass Gripframe, *Modern*	165.00	240.00	235.00
☐ **Bearcat,** .22 L.R.R.F., Western Style, Single Action, Blue, Aluminum Gripframe, Early Model, *Modern*	190.00	290.00	280.00
☐ **Blackhawk,** .30 Carbine, Western Style, Single Action, Blue, New Model, *Modern*	145.00	175.00	170.00
☐ **Blackhawk,** .30 Carbine, Western Style, Single Action, Blue, *Modern*	160.00	225.00	220.00
☐ **Blackhawk,** .357 Magnum, Western Style, Single Action, Blue, New Model, *Modern*	140.00	170.00	165.00
☐ **Blackhawk,** .357 Magnum, Western Style, Single Action, Blue, *Modern*	160.00	225.00	220.00
☐ **Blackhawk,** .357 Magnum, Western Style, Single Action, Blue, Flat-Top Frame, Early Model, *Modern*	335.00	450.00	435.00
☐ **Blackhawk,** .357 Magnum, Western Style, Single Action, Blue, 10" Barrel, *Modern*	495.00	700.00	675.00

	V.G.	Exc.	Prior Year Exc. Value
☐ **Blackhawk,** .357 Maximum, Western Style, Single Action, Blue, New Model, *Modern*	175.00	250.00	250.00
☐ **Blackhawk,** .357 Magnum, Western Style, Single Action, Stainless Steel, New Model, *Modern*	150.00	195.00	190.00
☐ **Blackhawk,** .357 Magnum/9mm Combo, Western Style, Single Action, Blue, New Model, *Modern*	160.00	215.00	210.00
☐ **Blackhawk,** .357 Magnum/9mm Combo, Western Style, Single Action, Blue, *Modern*	175.00	240.00	235.00
☐ **Blackhawk,** .41 Magnum, Western Style, Single Action, Blue, New Model, *Modern*	135.00	185.00	180.00
☐ **Blackhawk,** .41 Magnum, Western Style, Single Action, Blue, *Modern*	165.00	215.00	210.00
☐ **Blackhawk,** .45 Colt, Western Style, Single Action, Blue, *Modern*	170.00	235.00	220.00
☐ **Blackhawk,** .45 Colt, Western Style, Single Action, Blue, New Model, *Modern*	145.00	190.00	180.00
☐ **Blackhawk,** .45 Colt/.45 ACP Combo, Western Style, Single Action, New Model, Blue, *Modern*	165.00	220.00	210.00
☐ **Blackhawk,** .45 Colt/.45 ACP Combo, Western Style, Single Action, Blue, *Modern*	195.00	265.00	255.00
☐ **Security-Six,** .357 Magnum, Double Action, Swing-Out Cylinder, Stainless Steel, Adjustable Sights, *Modern*	140.00	200.00	215.00
☐ **Security-Six,** .357 Magnum, Double Action, Swing-Out Cylinder, Blue, Adjustable Sights, *Modern*	145.00	185.00	180.00
☐ **Service-Six,** .357 Magnum, Double Action, Swing-Out Cylinder, Blue, *Modern*	125.00	165.00	160.00
☐ **Service-Six,** .357 Magnum, Double Action, Swing-Out Cylinder, Stainless Steel, *Modern*	140.00	190.00	185.00
☐ **Service-Six,** 9mm Luger, Double Action, Swing-Out Cylinder, Blue, *Modern*	130.00	160.00	155.00
☐ **Service-Six,** 9mm Luger, Double Action, Swing-Out Cylinder, Stainless Steel, *Modern*	140.00	190.00	185.00
☐ **Service-Six,** .38 Special, Double Action, Swing-Out Cylinder, Blue, *Modern*	130.00	160.00	155.00
☐ **Service-Six,** .38 Special, Double Action, Swing-Out Cylinder, Stainless Steel, *Modern*	145.00	185.00	180.00
☐ **Single-Six,** .22 L.R.R.F., Western Style, Single Action, Blue, Engraved, Cased, *Modern*	620.00	850.00	825.00
☐ **Single-Six,** .22 L.R.R.F., Western Style, Single Action, Blue, Flat Loading Gate, Early Model, *Modern*	230.00	310.00	300.00
☐ **Single-Six Colorado Centennial,** .22 L.R.R.F., Commemorative, Cased, *Curio*	160.00	250.00	295.00
☐ **Speed-Six,** .357 Magnum, Double Action, Swing-Out Cylinder, Blue, *Modern*	100.00	135.00	130.00
☐ **Speed-Six,** .357 Magnum, Double Action, Swing-Out Cylinder, Stainless Steel, *Modern*	140.00	185.00	180.00
☐ **Speed-Six,** .38 Special, Double Action, Swing-Out Cylinder, Blue, *Modern*	120.00	150.00	145.00
☐ **Speed-Six,** .38 Special, Double Action, Swing-Out Cylinder, Stainless Steel, *Modern*	140.00	185.00	180.00
☐ **Speed-Six,** 9mm Luger, Double Action, Swing-Out Cylinder, Blue, *Modern*	120.00	150.00	145.00

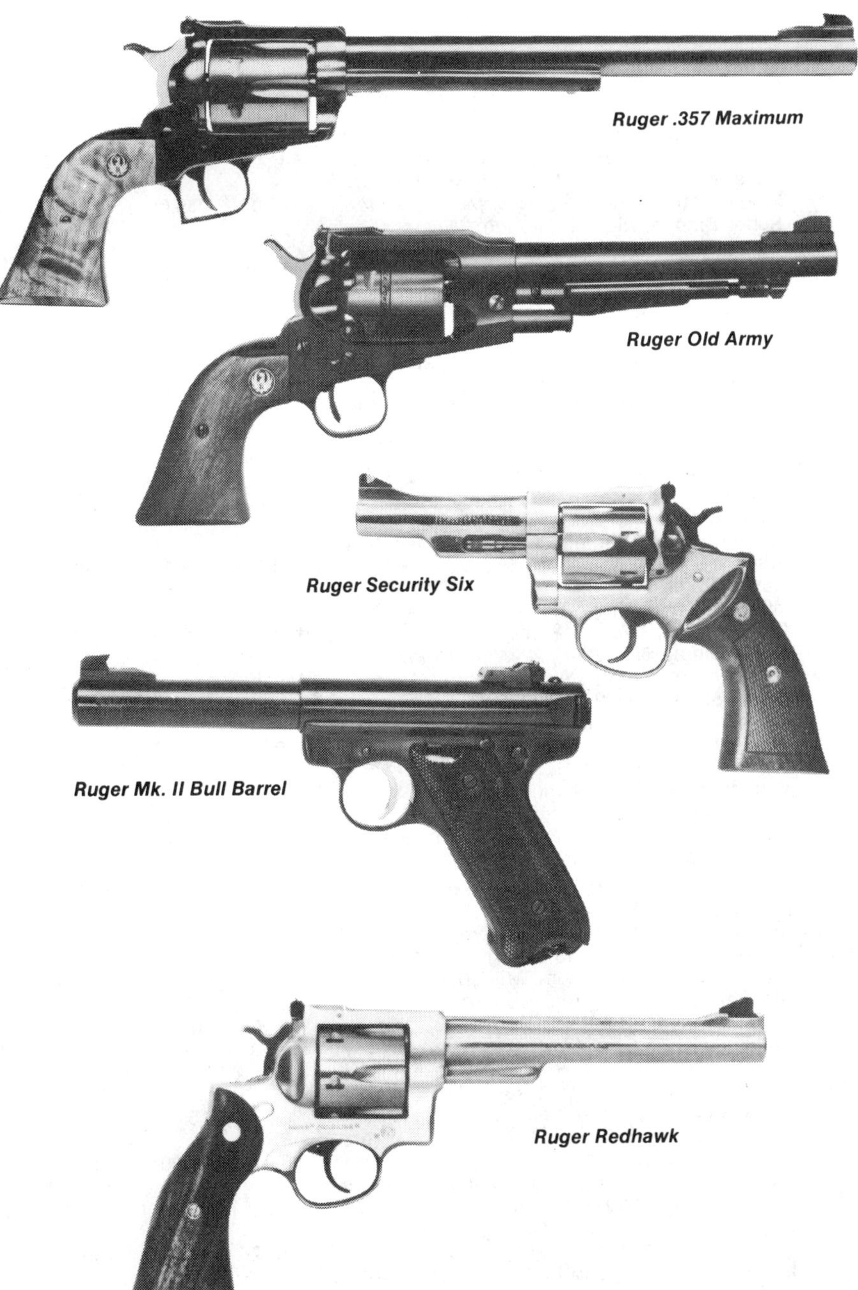

Ruger .357 Maximum

Ruger Old Army

Ruger Security Six

Ruger Mk. II Bull Barrel

Ruger Redhawk

☐ **Super Blackhawk,** .44 Magnum, Western Style, Single Action, Blue, New Model, 10½″ Barrel, *Modern*	145.00	195.00	190.00
☐ **Super Blackhawk,** .44 Magnum, Western Style, Single Action, Blue, New Model, *Modern*	145.00	190.00	185.00
☐ **Super Blackhawk,** .44 Magnum, Western Style, Single Action, Stainless, New Model, *Modern*	170.00	235.00	230.00
☐ **Super Blackhawk,** .44 Magnum, Western Style, Single Action, Stainless, New Model, 10½″ Bull Barrel, *Modern*	170.00	230.00	225.00
☐ **Super Blackhawk,** .44 Magnum, Western Style, Single Action, Stainless, 10½″ Barrel, New Model, *Modern*	170.00	230.00	225.00
☐ **Super Blackhawk,** .44 Magnum, Western Style, Single Action, Blue, *Modern*	195.00	300.00	275.00
☐ **Super Blackhawk,** .44 Magnum, Western Style, Single Action, Blue, Flat-Top Frame, Early Model, *Modern*	510.00	715.00	685.00
☐ **Super Blackhawk,** .44 Magnum, Western Style, Single Action, Blue, 10″ Barrel, *Modern*	550.00	745.00	700.00
☐ **Super Single Six,** .22LR/.22 WMR Combo, Western Style, Single Action, Blue, New Model, *Modern*	100.00	145.00	140.00
☐ **Super Single Six,** .22LR/.22 WMR Combo, Western Style, Single Action, Blue, New Model, 9½″ Barrel, *Modern*	100.00	145.00	140.00
☐ **Super Single Six,** .22LR/.22 WMR Combo, Western Style, Single Action, Blue, *Modern*	140.00	185.00	175.00
☐ **Super Single Six,** .22LR/.22 WMR Combo, Western Style, Single Action, Blue, 9½″ Barrel, *Modern*	150.00	195.00	185.00
☐ **Super Single Six,** .22LR/.22 WMR Combo, Western Style, Single Action, Stainless Steel, New Model, *Modern*	140.00	170.00	165.00
☐ **Redhawk,** .44 Magnum, Double Action, Stainless, Interchangeable Sights, Swing-Out Cylinder, *Modern*	185.00	280.00	275.00
HANDGUN, SEMI-AUTOMATIC			
☐ **Bisley Single Six,** .22 L.R., *Modern*	235.00	258.00	—
☐ **Bisley Single Six,** .32 H&R Magnum, *Modern*	235.00	258.00	—
☐ **Blackhawk,** .357 Magnum, *Modern*	285.00	307.00	—
☐ **Blackhawk,** .41 Magnum, *Modern*	285.00	307.00	—
☐ **Blackhawk,** .44 Magnum, *Modern*	285.00	307.00	—
☐ **Blackhawk,** .45 Colt, *Modern*	285.00	307.00	—
☐ **Bullseye MK I,** .22 L.R.R.F., Clip Fed, Adjustable Sights, Target Pistol, Mag-Na-Port Commemorative, *Modern*	225.00	375.00	375.00
☐ **MK I,** .22 L.R.R.F., Clip Fed, Adjustable Sights, Target Pistol, *Modern*	95.00	150.00	145.00
☐ **MK I,** .22 L.R.R.F., Clip Fed, Adjustable Sights, Target Pistol, Wood Grips, *Modern*	110.00	160.00	155.00
☐ **MK II,** .22 L.R.R.F., Clip Fed, Adjustable Sights, Target Pistol, *Modern*	95.00	145.00	140.00
☐ **MK II,** .22 L.R.R.F., Clip Fed, Adjustable Sights, Stainless, *Modern*	230.00	255.00	270.00
☐ **MK II,** .22 L.R.R.F., Clip Fed, Adjustable Sights, Target Pistol, Bull Barrel, *Modern*	100.00	145.00	140.00

	V.G.	Exc.	Prior Year Exc. Value
☐ **MK II,** .22 L.R.R.F., Clip Fed, Adjustable Sights, Target Pistol, Bull Barrel, Stainless, *Modern*	230.00	255.00	270.00
☐ **MK II Standard,** .22 L.R.R.F., Clip Fed, Fixed Sights, Stainless, *Modern*	200.00	225.00	240.00
☐ **Signature RST-4,** .22 L.R.R.F., Clip Fed, Commemorative, Stainless, *Modern*	375.00	490.00	485.00
☐ **Standard,** .22 L.R.R.F., Clip Fed, *Modern*	95.00	135.00	130.00
☐ **Standard MK II,** .22 L.R.R.F., Clip Fed, *Modern*	90.00	130.00	125.00
☐ **Standard (Under #25600),** .22 L.R.R.F., Clip Fed, Early Model, Blue, *Modern*	195.00	300.00	275.00
HANDGUN, SINGLESHOT			
☐ **Hawkeye,** .256 Win. Mag., Western Style, Single Action, Blue, *Modern*	460.00	650.00	635.00
HANDGUN, PERCUSSION			
☐ **Old Army,** .44, Single Action, Blue, Adjustable Sights, Reproduction, *Antique*	125.00	160.00	155.00
☐ **Old Army,** .44, Single Action, Stainless, Adjustable Sights, Reproduction, *Antique*	140.00	210.00	190.00
RIFLE, BOLT ACTION			
☐ **M-77,** for .338 Win. Mag., *Add* **$10.00-$15.00**			
☐ **M-77,** for .458 Win. Mag., *Add* **$40.00-$50.00**			
☐ **M-77R,** Various Calibers, Checkered Stock, Scope Mounts, no Sights, *Modern*	185.00	270.00	260.00
☐ **M-77RL,** Various Calibers, Checkered Stock, Scope Mounts, Ultra Light, no Sights, *Modern*	225.00	315.00	300.00
☐ **M-77RS,** Various Calibers, Checkered Stock, Open Rear Sight, Scope Mounts, *Modern*	195.00	290.00	275.00
☐ **M-77RS Tropical,** .458 Win. Mag., Checkered Stock, Open Rear Sight, Scope Mounts, *Modern*	250.00	340.00	330.00
☐ **M-77RSI,** Various Calibers, Checkered Stock, Open Rear Sight, Mannlicher Stock, Scope Mounts, *Modern*	225.00	345.00	335.00
☐ **M-77ST,** Various Calibers, Checkered Stock, Open Rear, Sight, *Modern*	185.00	270.00	260.00
☐ **M-77V,** Various Calibers, Heavy Barrel, Varmint, no Sights, Scope Mounts, Checkered Stock, *Modern*	185.00	270.00	260.00
☐ **M-77/22S,** .22 Caliber Rimfire, Detachable Ten Shot Magazine, Blue, *Modern*	290.00	300.00	300.00
☐ **M-77/22R,** .22 Caliber Rimfire, Detachable Ten Shot Magazine, Blue, *Modern*	290.00	300.00	300.00
RIFLE, SEMI-AUTOMATIC			
☐ **10/22,** .22 L.R.R.F., Clip Fed, Plain, *Modern*	68.00	95.00	90.00
☐ **10/22 Canadian Centennial,** .22 L.R.R.F., Commemorative, *Curio*	60.00	110.00	125.00
☐ **10/22 International,** .22 L.R.R.F., Clip Fed, Full-Stocked, *Modern*	100.00	150.00	145.00
☐ **10/22 Sporter I,** .22 L.R.R.F., Clip Fed, Monte Carlo Stock, *Modern*	75.00	115.00	110.00
☐ **10/22 Sporter II,** .22 L.R.R.F., Clip Fed, Checkered Stock, *Modern*	80.00	120.00	115.00
☐ **10/22 Deluxe,** .22 L.R.R.F., Clip Fed, Checkered Stock, *Modern*	80.00	120.00	115.00
☐ **Mini-14,** .223 Rem., Clip Fed, Carbine, *Modern*	165.00	230.00	225.00
☐ **Mini-14,** .223 Rem., Clip Fed, Carbine, Stainless, *Modern*	190.00	270.00	260.00

	V.G.	Exc.	Prior Year Exc. Value
☐ **Mini-14/20 GB,** .223 Rem., Clip Fed, Carbine, with Flash Hider and Bayonet Stud, *Modern*	165.00	230.00	225.00
☐ **Mini-14/20 GB-F,** .223 Rem., Clip Fed, Carbine, Stainless, with Flash Hider and Bayonet Stud, *Modern*	185.00	265.00	260.00
☐ **K Mini-14/20 GB,** .223 Rem., Clip Fed, Carbine, with Flash Hider and Bayonet Stud, Folding Stock, *Modern*	220.00	295.00	290.00
☐ **K Mini-14/20 GB-F,** .223 Rem., Clip Fed, Carbine, Stainless, with Flash Hider and Bayonet Stud, Folding Stock, *Modern*	245.00	325.00	320.00
☐ **Model 44 Deluxe,** .44 Magnum, Tube Feed, Plain, Peep Sights, Sling Swivels, *Modern*	170.00	235.00	230.00

Ruger Mark II Target Model Pistol

Ruger .22 Rimfire Bolt-Action Rifle

Ruger Mark II Standard Model, .22 Caliber Long Rifle

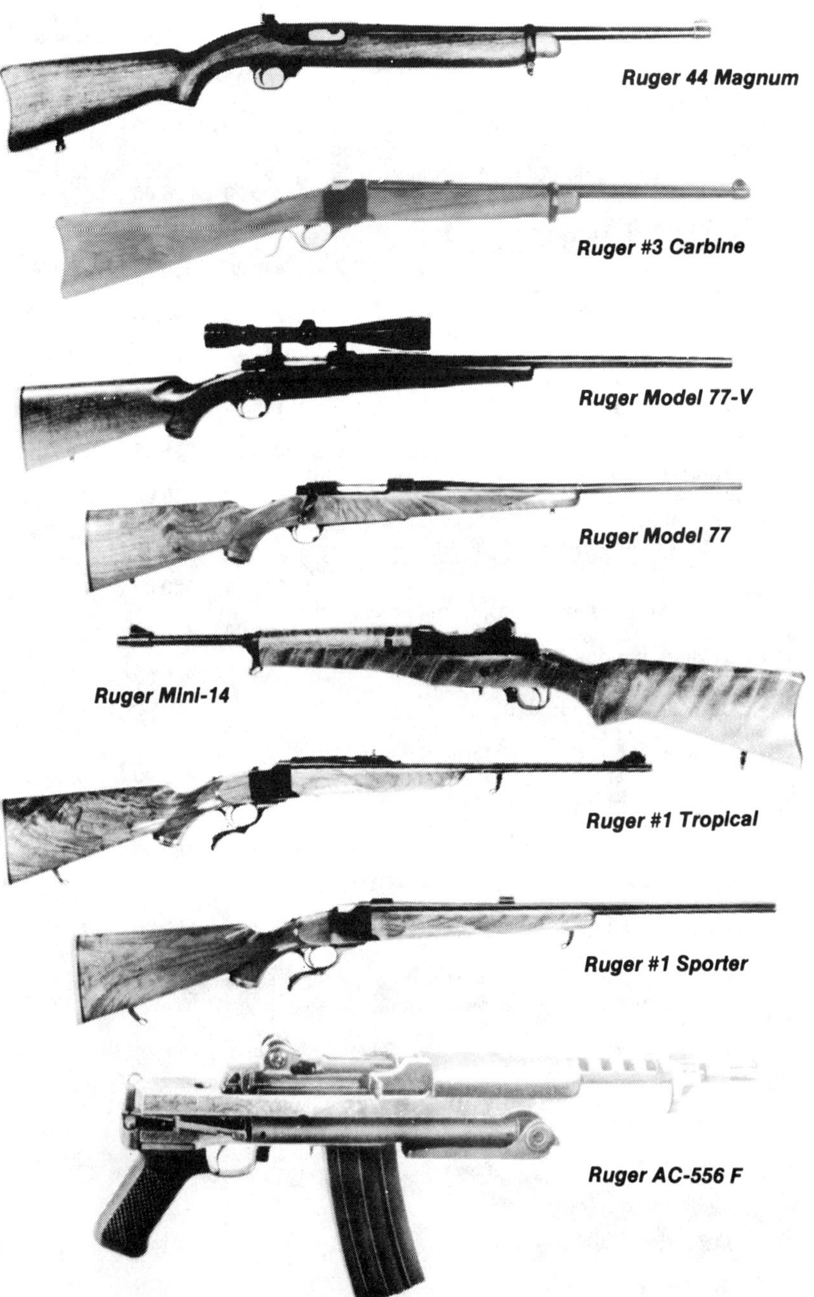

Ruger 44 Magnum

Ruger #3 Carbine

Ruger Model 77-V

Ruger Model 77

Ruger Mini-14

Ruger #1 Tropical

Ruger #1 Sporter

Ruger AC-556 F

	V.G.	Exc.	Prior Year Exc. Value
☐ **Model 44 International,** .44 Magnum, Tube Feed, Full-Stocked, *Modern*	185.00	245.00	240.00
☐ **Model 44 Sporter,** .44 Magnum, Tube Feed, Monte Carlo Stock, *Modern*	185.00	245.00	240.00
☐ **Model 44 Standard,** .44 Magnum, Tube Feed, Plain, Open Rear Sight, *Modern*	165.00	220.00	220.00
☐ **XGI,** .308, *Modern*	390.00	425.00	—

RIFLE, SINGLESHOT

	V.G.	Exc.	Prior Year Exc. Value
☐ **#1 Canadian Centennial Deluxe,** Commemorative, *Curio*	430.00	650.00	800.00
☐ **#1 Light Sporter,** Various Calibers, Open Rear Sight, Checkered Stock, *Modern*	200.00	295.00	280.00
☐ **#1 Medium Sporter,** Various Calibers, Open Rear Sight, Checkered Stock, *Modern*	195.00	295.00	280.00
☐ **#1 Standard Sporter,** Various Calibers, no Sights, Scope Mounts, Checkered Stock, *Modern*	195.00	285.00	275.00
☐ **#1 International,** Various Calibers, Open Rear Sight, Checkered Mannlicher Stock, *Modern*	215.00	305.00	290.00
☐ **#1 Tropical,** Various Calibers, Open Rear Sight, Checkered Stock, *Modern*	200.00	300.00	285.00
☐ **#1 Varminter,** Various Calibers, Heavy Barrel, no Sights, Checkered Stock, *Modern*	200.00	300.00	285.00
☐ **#2 Canadian Centennial Set,** Commemorative, *Curio*	315.00	420.00	500.00
☐ **#3 Canadian Centennial Set,** Commemorative, *Curio*	230.00	310.00	375.00
☐ **#3 Carbine,** Various Calibers, Open Rear Sight, *Modern*	150.00	200.00	195.00

SILENCED WEAPON, PISTOL

	V.G.	Exc.	Prior Year Exc. Value
☐ **MK I (MAC),** .22 L.R.R.F., Semi-Automatic, Adjustable Sights, Clip Fed, Target Pistol, Cased, *Class 3*	420.00	650.00	625.00

SILENCED WEAPON, RIFLE

	V.G.	Exc.	Prior Year Exc. Value
☐ **10/22 (MAC),** .22 L.R.R.F., Semi-Automatic, Clip Fed, Military, *Class 3*	650.00	850.00	825.00

SHOTGUN, DOUBLE BARREL, OVER-UNDER

	V.G.	Exc.	Prior Year Exc. Value
☐ **Red Label,** 12 or 20 Gauges, Checkered Stock, Single Trigger, *Modern*	500.00	650.00	625.00

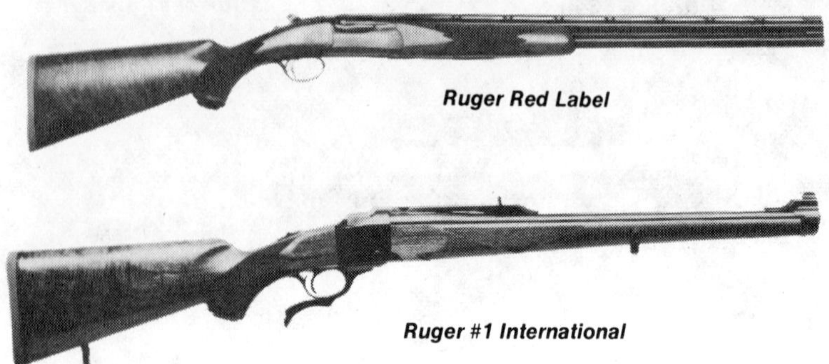

Ruger Red Label

Ruger #1 International

	V.G.	Exc.	Prior Year Exc. Value

RUMMEL
Made by Crescent for A.J. Rummel Arms Co., Toledo, Ohio.

SHOTGUN, DOUBLE BARREL, SIDE-BY-SIDE

	V.G.	Exc.	Prior Year Exc. Value
☐ **Various Gauges**, Outside Hammers, Damascus Barrel, *Modern*	**100.00**	**170.00**	**175.00**
☐ **Various Gauges**, Hammerless, Steel Barrel, *Modern*	**135.00**	**190.00**	**200.00**
☐ **Various Gauges**, Hammerless, Damascus Barrel, *Modern*	**100.00**	**170.00**	**175.00**
☐ **Various Gauges**, Outside Hammers, Steel Barrel, *Modern*	**125.00**	**185.00**	**190.00**

SHOTGUN, SINGLESHOT

	V.G.	Exc.	Prior Year Exc. Value
☐ **Various Gauges**, Hammer, Steel Barrel, *Modern*	**55.00**	**85.00**	**85.00**

RUPERTUS, JACOB
Philadelphia, Pa. 1858-1899.

HANDGUN, DOUBLE BARREL, SIDE-BY-SIDE

	V.G.	Exc.	Prior Year Exc. Value
☐ **.22 Short R.F.,** Derringer, Side-Swing Barrel, Iron Frame, Spur Trigger, *Antique*	**295.00**	**425.00**	**400.00**

HANDGUN, REVOLVER

	V.G.	Exc.	Prior Year Exc. Value
☐ **.22 Short R.F.,** Pepperbox, 8 Shot, Iron Frame, Spur Trigger, *Antique*	**265.00**	**395.00**	**375.00**
☐ **.22 Short R.F.,** 7 Shot, Spur Trigger, Solid Frame, Single Action, *Antique*	**125.00**	**170.00**	**165.00**
☐ **.32 Short R.F.,** 5 Shot, Spur Trigger, Solid Frame, Single Action, *Antique*	**135.00**	**190.00**	**180.00**
☐ **.36 Patent Navy,** Percussion, 6 Shot, *Antique*	**2250.00**	**4650.00**	**4175.00**
☐ **.38 Short R.F.,** 5 Shot, Spur Trigger, Solid Frame, Single Action, *Antique*	**130.00**	**195.00**	**190.00**
☐ **.41 Short R.F.,** 5 Shot, Spur Trigger, Solid Frame, Single Action, *Antique*	**155.00**	**220.00**	**210.00**

HANDGUN, SINGLESHOT

	V.G.	Exc.	Prior Year Exc. Value
☐ **.22 Short R.F.,** Derringer, Side-Swing Barrel, Iron Frame, Spur Trigger, *Antique*	**155.00**	**230.00**	**230.00**
☐ **.32 Short R.F.,** Derringer, Side-Swing Barrel, Iron Frame, Spur Trigger, *Antique*	**145.00**	**190.00**	**185.00**
☐ **.38 Short R.F.,** Derringer, Side-Swing Barrel, Iron Frame, Spur Trigger, *Antique*	**150.00**	**195.00**	**190.00**

RUPP, HERMAN
Pa. 1784. See Kentucky Rifles.

RUPP, JOHN
Allentown, Pa. See U.S. Military, Kentucky Rifles and Pistols.

RUPPERT, WILLIAM
Lancaster, Pa., c. 1776. See U.S. Military, Kentucky Rifles and Pistols.

RUSH, JOHN
Philadelphia, Pa. 1740-1750. See Kentucky Rifles and Pistols.

RUSSIAN MILITARY

AUTOMATIC WEAPON, ASSAULT RIFLE

	V.G.	Exc.	Prior Year Exc. Value
☐ **AVS 36 Simonava,** 7.62 x 39 Russian, Clip Fed, Wood Stock, *Class 3*	**750.00**	**1035.00**	**1035.00**

Russian Military M1890 Communist

Russian Military Tokarev

Russian Military Handgun Percussion

	V.G.	Exc.	Prior Year Exc. Value
AUTOMATIC WEAPON, HEAVY MACHINE GUN			
☐ **Goryunov SG-43,** 7.62 x 39 Russian, Belt Fed, Heavy Barrel, *Class 3*	1375.00	1960.00	1960.00
AUTOMATIC WEAPON, LIGHT MACHINE GUN			
☐ **Degtyarov DP,** 7.62 x 54R Russian, Drum Magazine, Bipod, *Class 3*	1000.00	1725.00	1725.00
AUTOMATIC WEAPON, SUBMACHINE GUN			
☐ **PPS-43,** 7.62mm Tokarev, Clip Fed, Folding Stock, *Class 3*	745.00	1000.00	995.00
☐ **PPSH-41,** 7.62mm Tokarev, Clip Fed, Wood Stock, *Class 3*	550.00	800.00	800.00
HANDGUN, FREE PISTOL			
☐ **MC,** .22 L.R.R.F., Clip Fed, *Modern*	125.00	200.00	250.00
☐ **MCU,** .22 Short, Clip Fed, *Modern*	150.00	260.00	295.00
☐ **Vostok M-T0Z-35,** .22 L.R.R.F., *Modern*	380.00	550.00	700.00
☐ **Vostok M-T0Z-35,** .22 L.R.R.F., Cased with Accessories, *Modern*	620.00	850.00	935.00
HANDGUN, REVOLVER			
☐ **M1890,** 7.62mm Nagent, Gas-Seal Cylinder, Imperial, *Curio*	115.00	170.00	235.00
☐ **M1890,** 7.62mm Nagent, Gas-Seal Cylinder, Police, *Curio*	160.00	230.00	325.00

Russian Military Makarov

	V.G.	Exc.	Prior Year Exc. Value
☐ **M1890,** 7.62mm Nagent, Gas-Seal Cylinder, Communist, *Curio*	100.00	140.00	185.00
HANDGUN, SEMI-AUTOMATIC			
☐ **Makarov,** 9mm Makarov, Clip Fed, Double Action, *Modern*	475.00	750.00	875.00
☐ **Tokarev TT-30,** 7.62mm Tokarev, Clip Fed, *Modern*	290.00	430.00	475.00
☐ **Tokarev TT-33 Early,** 7.62mm Tokarev, Clip Fed, *Modern*	170.00	260.00	290.00

Czarist and Communist plants include: Tula, Izshevsky, and many others. Foreign manufacturers for Czarist Russia include: S.I.G. Neuhasen, Switzerland; St. Etienne, France, and Remington Arms U.S.A. Foreign manufacturers for Moisin-Nagant only. Tokarev and SKS Communist Russia produced.

NOTE: Russian ammo either 7.62 x 54R or 7.62 x 39M43 will not interchange with American 7.62 N.A.T.O. ammunition.

	V.G.	Exc.	Prior Year Exc. Value
RIFLE, BOLT ACTION			
☐ **KK M, CM 2,** .22 L.R.R.F., Match Rifle, Target Sights, *Modern*	250.00	360.00	345.00
☐ **1891 Moisin-Nagant,** 7.62 Cal., 31-Inch Barrel, Bolt Action. (The rear sight of these early rifles are graduated not in meters but in arshins. An arshin is equivalent to .78 yards. After the revolution, Russia adopted the metric system and the sights for the Model 1891/30 and later rifles and carbines are graduated in meters.)	60.00	90.00	100.00
☐ **1891/38 Carbine,** 7.62.54 Cal., 20-Inch Barrel, Hooded Front Sight, Rear Sight Graduated From 100 - 1000 Meters, No Bayonet Mounting	60.00	100.00	125.00
☐ **1891 Remington,** Same As Russian Nagant, Except Made in U.S.A., By Remington For Export To Czarist Russia. (Few were ever delivered. Much higher quality than Russian produced models)	60.00	115.00	150.00

	V.G.	Exc.	Prior Year Exc. Value
☐ **1891/30 Sniper Rifle,** Especially Selected For Accuracy, Bolt Handle Turned Down and Fitted with Either 4xP. E. or 3.5xP. U. Telescopic Sight, (Still in use in Russia.) *Very Rare*	125.00	220.00	250.00
☐ **M1910,** 7.62 x 54R Russian, Military, Carbine, *Modern*	70.00	115.00	135.00
☐ **1938 Russian Tokarev,** Semi-Automatic Gas Operated Rifle, Two Piece Stock, 10 Shot Magazine, Fitted with Muzzlebreak, Cleaning Rod On Right Side Of Stock, First of Tokarev Series	125.00	220.00	250.00
☐ **1940 Tokarev Model,** 24-Inch Barrel, Semi-Automatic Gas Operated Rifle, (Similar to Model 1938 but much more rugged, was very successful action similar to that of Belgian FN Rifle.)	90.00	140.00	200.00
☐ **Russian SKS,** 7.62.39M43 Cal., 20-Inch Barrel, (A Russian attempt to develop a gas operated carbine) 10 Shot Magazine, Folding Bayonet, Very Well Made	115.00	175.00	250.00

RWS

Rheinische-Westfalische Sprengstoff, since 1931. Now Dynamit Nobel AG, Troisdorf-Oberlar, West Germany.

RIFLE, BOLT ACTION

	V.G.	Exc.	Prior Year Exc. Value
☐ **Repeater**, Various Calibers, Checkered Stock, Set Triggers, Open Sights, *Modern*	245.00	335.00	325.00

RYAN, THOMAS

Norwich, Conn., c. 1870.

HANDGUN, REVOLVER

	V.G.	Exc.	Prior Year Exc. Value
☐ **.22 Short R.F.**, 7 Shot, Spur Trigger, Solid Frame, Single Action, *Antique*	95.00	165.00	160.00
☐ **.32 Short R.F.**, 5 Shot, Spur Trigger, Solid Frame, Single Action, *Antique*	95.00	170.00	170.00

SABLE

Belgium, unknown maker.

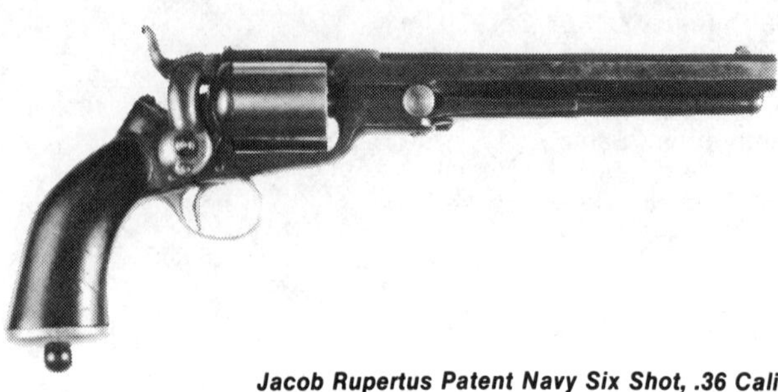

Jacob Rupertus Patent Navy Six Shot, .36 Caliber

	V.G.	Exc.	Prior Year Exc. Value
HANDGUN, REVOLVER			
☐ **Baby Hammerless**, .22 Short R.F., Folding Trigger, *Modern*	70.00	100.00	

SAKO

O.Y. Sako AB, Riihmaki, Finland.

	V.G.	Exc.	Prior Year Exc. Value
RIFLE, BOLT ACTION			
☐ **Deluxe (Garcia)**, Various Calibers, Sporting Rifle, Monte Carlo Stock, Fancy Checkering, Long Action, *Modern*	325.00	435.00	425.00
☐ **Deluxe (Garcia)**, Various Calibers, Sporting Rifle, Monte Carlo Stock, Fancy Checkering, Medium Action, *Modern*	335.00	435.00	425.00
☐ **Deluxe (Garcia)**, Various Calibers, Sporting Rifle, Monte Carlo Stock, Fancy Checkering, Short Action, *Modern*	335.00	435.00	425.00
☐ **Finnbear**, Various Calibers, Sporting Rifle, Monte Carlo Stock, Checkered Stock, Long Action, *Modern*	335.00	435.00	425.00
☐ **Finnbear Carbine**, Various Calibers, Sporting Rifle, Monte Carlo Stock, Checkered Stock, Long Action, Full-Stocked, *Modern*	350.00	465.00	450.00
☐ **Forester**, Various Calibers, Sporting Rifle, Monte Carlo Stock, Checkered Stock, Medium Action, *Modern*	315.00	420.00	400.00
☐ **Forester**, Various Calibers, Sporting Rifle, Monte Carlo Stock, Checkered Stock, Medium Action, Heavy Barrel, *Modern*	315.00	420.00	400.00
☐ **Forester Carbine**, Various Calibers, Sporting Rifle, Monte Carlo Stock, Checkered Stock, Medium Action, Full-Stocked, *Modern*	345.00	475.00	450.00
☐ **Hi-Power Mauser (FN)**, Various Calibers, Sporting Rifle, Monte Carlo Stock, Checkered Stock, *Modern*	290.00	395.00	375.00
☐ **Magnum Mauser (FN)**, Various Calibers, Sporting Rifle, Monte Carlo Stock, Checkered Stock, *Modern*	320.00	435.00	420.00
☐ **Model 74 (Garcia)**, Various Calibers, Sporting Rifle, Monte Carlo Stock, Checkered Stock, Long Action, *Modern*	270.00	375.00	350.00
☐ **Model 74 (Garcia)**, Various Calibers, Sporting Rifle, Monte Carlo Stock, Checkered Stock, Medium Action, *Modern*	270.00	375.00	350.00
☐ **Model 74 (Garcia)**, Various Calibers, Sporting Rifle, Monte Carlo Stock, Checkered Stock, Short Action, *Modern*	270.00	375.00	350.00
☐ **Model 74 (Garcia)**, Various Calibers, Sporting Rifle, Monte Carlo Stock, Checkered Stock, Heavy Barrel, Medium Action, *Modern*	290.00	390.00	365.00
☐ **Model 74 (Garcia)**, Various Calibers, Sporting Rifle, Monte Carlo Stock, Checkered Stock, Heavy Barrel, Short Action, *Modern*	285.00	390.00	365.00
☐ **Model 78 (Stoeger)**, .22 L.R.R.F., Sporting Rifle, Monte Carlo Stock, Checkered Stock, *Modern*	185.00	260.00	250.00
☐ **Model 78 (Stoeger)**, .22 Hornet, Sporting Rifle, Monte Carlo Stock, Checkered Stock, *Modern*	230.00	320.00	300.00

	V.G.	Exc.	Prior Year Exc. Value
☐ **Model 78 (Stoeger)**, .22 W.M.R., Sporting Rifle, Monte Carlo Stock, Checkered Stock, *Modern*	215.00	290.00	280.00
☐ **Model 78 (Stoeger)**, .22 L.R.R.F., Sporting Rifle, Monte Carlo Stock, Checkered Stock, Heavy Barrel, *Modern*	210.00	295.00	285.00
☐ **Vixen**, Various Calibers, Sporting Rifle, Monte Carlo Stock, Checkered Stock, Short Action, *Modern*	250.00	350.00	335.00
☐ **Vixen**, Various Calibers, Sporting Rifle, Monte Carlo Stock, Checkered Stock, Short Action, Heavy Barrel, *Modern*	260.00	375.00	360.00
☐ **Vixen Carbine**, Various Calibers, Sporting Rifle, Monte Carlo Stock, Checkered Stock, Short Action, Full-Stocked, *Modern*	290.00	395.00	380.00

RIFLE, LEVER ACTION

	V.G.	Exc.	Prior Year Exc. Value
☐ **Finnwolf**, Various Calibers, Sporting Rifle, Monte Carlo Stock, Checkered Stock, *Modern*	260.00	395.00	375.00

ST. LOUIS ARMS CO.

Belgium for Shapleigh Hardware Co., c. 1900.

SHOTGUN, DOUBLE BARREL, SIDE-BY-SIDE

	V.G.	Exc.	Prior Year Exc. Value
☐ **Various Gauges**, Outside Hammers, Damascus Barrel, *Modern*	100.00	170.00	175.00
☐ **Various Gauges**, Hammerless, Steel Barrel, *Modern*	135.00	190.00	200.00
☐ **Various Gauges**, Hammerless, Damascus Barrel, *Modern*	100.00	170.00	175.00
☐ **Various Gauges**, Outside Hammers, Steel Barrel, *Modern*	125.00	185.00	190.00

SHOTGUN, SINGLESHOT

	V.G.	Exc.	Prior Year Exc. Value
☐ **Various Gauges**, Hammer, Steel Barrel, *Modern*	55.00	85.00	85.00

SAMPLES, BETHUEL

Urbana, Ohio. See Kentucky Rifles and Pistols.

SANDERSON

Portage, Wisc.

SHOTGUN, DOUBLE BARREL, SIDE-BY-SIDE

	V.G.	Exc.	Prior Year Exc. Value
☐ **M200-S 1**, Various Gauges, Checkered Stock, Automatic Ejectors, Engraved, *Modern*	300.00	400.00	400.00
☐ **Neumann**, Various Gauges, Checkered Stock, Automatic Ejectors, Engraved, *Modern*	175.00	250.00	250.00
☐ **Neumann**, 10 Gauge Mag., Checkered Stock, Automatic Ejectors, Engraved, *Modern*	300.00	400.00	400.00

SARASQUETA, FELIX

Eibar, Spain, imported by Sarasqueta of N.A., Coral Gables, Fla.

SHOTGUN, DOUBLE BARREL, OVER-UNDER

	V.G.	Exc.	Prior Year Exc. Value
☐ **Model 500**, 12 Gauge, Checkered Stock, Boxlock, Light Engraving, Double Triggers, *Modern*	170.00	240.00	—
☐ **Model 510**, 20 Gauge, Checkered Stock, Boxlock with Sideplates, Light Engraving, Double Triggers, *Modern*	150.00	220.00	—

	V.G.	Exc.	Prior Year Exc. Value
SHOTGUN, DOUBLE BARREL, SIDE-BY-SIDE			
☐ **Model 340**, 12 Gauge, Checkered Stock, Sidelock, Light Engraving, Double Triggers, *Modern*	280.00	375.00	—
☐ **Model 210**, 12 Gauge, Checkered Stock, Boxlock, Double Triggers, *Modern*	135.00	180.00	—

SARASQUETA, VICTOR

Victor Sarasqueta, Eibar, Spain from 1934.

	V.G.	Exc.	Prior Year Exc. Value
RIFLE, DOUBLE BARREL, SIDE-BY-SIDE			
☐ **Various Calibers**, Sidelock, Automatic Ejector, Fancy Engraving, Fancy Checkering, *Modern*	1,750.00	2,500.00	2,500.00
SHOTGUN, DOUBLE BARREL, SIDE-BY-SIDE			
☐ **#10**, Various Gauges, Sidelock, Fancy Checkering, Fancy Engraving, *Modern*	675.00	975.00	975.00
☐ **#11**, Various Gauges, Sidelock, Fancy Checkering, Fancy Engraving, *Modern*	900.00	1,225.00	1,200.00
☐ **#12**, Various Gauges, Sidelock, Fancy Checkering, Fancy Engraving, *Modern*	1,200.00	1,450.00	1,450.00
☐ **#2**, Various Gauges, Double Trigger, Checkered Stock, Light Engraving, *Modern*	135.00	195.00	190.00
☐ **#3**, Various Gauges, Double Trigger, Checkered Stock, Light Engraving, *Modern*	190.00	295.00	295.00
☐ **#4**, Various Gauges, Sidelock, Checkered Stock, Light Engraving, *Modern*	240.00	350.00	345.00
☐ **#4E**, Various Gauges, Sidelock, Checkered Stock, Light Engraving, *Modern*	275.00	400.00	400.00
☐ **#5**, Various Gauges, Sidelock, Checkered Stock, Light Engraving, *Modern*	250.00	350.00	350.00
☐ **#5E**, Various Gauges, Sidelock, Checkered Stock, Light Engraving, *Modern*	300.00	440.00	435.00
☐ **#6**, Various Gauges, Sidelock, Fancy Checkering, Engraved, *Modern*	280.00	385.00	375.00
☐ **#6E**, Various Gauges, Sidelock, Fancy Checkering, Engraved, *Modern*	375.00	500.00	495.00
☐ **#7**, Various Gauges, Sidelock, Fancy Checkering, Engraved, *Modern*	375.00	500.00	495.00
☐ **#7E**, Various Gauges, Sidelock, Fancy Checkering, Engraved, *Modern*	450.00	595.00	585.00
☐ **#8**, Various Gauges, Sidelock, Fancy Checkering, Fancy Engraving, *Modern*	565.00	700.00	690.00
☐ **#9**, Various Gauges, Sidelock, Fancy Checkering, Fancy Engraving, *Modern*	675.00	825.00	820.00
☐ **Super Deluxe**, Various Gauges, Sidelock, Fancy Checkering, Fancy Engraving, *Modern*	1,800.00	2,450.00	2,400.00

SATA

Sabotti & Tanfoglio Fabbrica d'Armi, Gardone Val Trompia, Italy.

	V.G.	Exc.	Prior Year Exc. Value
HANDGUN, SEMI-AUTOMATIC			
☐ **.22 Short**, Clip Fed, Blue, *Modern*	90.00	155.00	145.00
☐ **.25 ACP**, Clip Fed, Blue, *Modern*	95.00	160.00	150.00

SAUER, J.P. & SOHN

1855 to date, first in Suhl, now in Eckernforde, West Germany. Also see Hawes.

	V.G.	Exc.	Prior Year Exc. Value
COMBINATION WEAPON, OVER-UNDER			
☐ **BBF**, Various Calibers, Double Trigger, Set Trigger Engraved, Checkered Stock, *Modern*	900.00	1,475.00	1,450.00
☐ **BBF Deluxe**, Various Calibers, Double Trigger, Set Trigger, Fancy Engraving, Fancy Checkering, *Modern*	1,150.00	1,735.00	1,700.00
COMBINATION WEAPON, DRILLING			
☐ **Model 3000E**, Various Calibers, Double Trigger, Engraved, Checkered Stock, *Modern*	1,300.00	1,785.00	1,750.00
☐ **Model 3000E Deluxe**, Various Calibers, Double Trigger, Fancy Engraving, Fancy Checkering, *Modern*	1,450.00	2,200.00	2,100.00
HANDGUN, MANUAL REPEATER			
☐ **Bar Pistole**, 7mm, Double Barrel, 4 Shot, Folding Trigger, *Curio*	275.00	375.00	350.00
HANDGUN, SEMI-AUTOMATIC			
☐ **Behorden**, .32 ACP, Clip Fed, *Modern*	190.00	295.00	275.00
☐ **Behorden**, .32 ACP, Clip Fed, Lightweight, *Modern*	345.00	450.00	425.00
☐ **Behorden 4mm**, .32 ACP, Clip Fed, Extra Barrel, *Modern*	595.00	850.00	800.00
☐ **Behorden Dutch Navy**, .32 ACP, Clip Fed, Military, *Modern*	325.00	425.00	400.00
☐ **Model 1913**, .25 ACP, Clip Fed, *Modern*	165.00	245.00	245.00
☐ **Model 1913**, .32 ACP, Clip Fed, *Modern*	175.00	250.00	250.00
☐ **Model 28**, .25 ACP, Clip Fed, *Modern*	190.00	275.00	275.00
☐ **Model H 38**, .25 ACP, Double Action, Clip Fed, Hammer, *Modern*	385.00	495.00	400.00
☐ **Model H 38**, .32 ACP, Double Action, Clip Fed, Hammer, Commercial, *Modern*	250.00	350.00	325.00
☐ **Model H 38**, .32 ACP, Double Action, Clip Fed, Hammer, Nazi-Proofed, Military, *Modern*	225.00	325.00	280.00
☐ **Model H 38**, .32 ACP, Double Action, Clip Fed, Hammer, Nazi-Proofed, No Safety, Military, *Modern*	200.00	300.00	250.00
☐ **Model H 38**, .32 ACP, Double Action, Clip Fed, Hammer, Lightweight, *Modern*	500.00	675.00	600.00
☐ **Model H 38 Police**, .32 ACP, Double Action, Clip Fed, Hammer, Nazi-Proofed, *Curio*	375.00	500.00	500.00
☐ **W.T.M. 1922**, .25 ACP, Clip Fed, *Modern*	185.00	265.00	250.00
☐ **W.T.M. 1928**, .25 ACP, Clip Fed, *Modern*	200.00	290.00	275.00
☐ **W.T.M. 1928/2**, .25 ACP, Clip Fed, *Modern*	170.00	245.00	235.00
☐ **Roth-Sauer**, 8mm, Clip Fed, *Curio*	600.00	900.00	900.00
RIFLE, BOLT ACTION			
☐ **Mauser Custom**, Various Calibers, Set Trigger, Checkered Stock, Octagon Barrel, *Modern*	335.00	500.00	500.00
SHOTGUN, DOUBLE BARREL, OVER-UNDER			
☐ **Model 66 GR I**, 12 Ga., Single Selective Trigger, Selective Ejector, Hammerless, Sidelock, Engraved, *Modern*	965.00	1,375.00	1,350.00
☐ **Model 66 GR I**, 12 Ga., Skeet Grade, Selective Ejector, Hammerless, Sidelock, Engraved, *Modern*	800.00	1,200.00	1,200.00

Sauer Model H 38

Sauer Bar Pistole

Sauer Roth-Sauer

Sauer Model 1913 .25

	V.G.	Exc.	Prior Year Exc. Value
☐ **Model 66 GR II**, 12 Ga., Single Selective Trigger, Selective Ejector, Hammerless, Sidelock, Fancy Engraving, *Modern*	1,000.00	1,625.00	1,600.00
☐ **Model 66 GR II**, 12 Ga., Skeet Grade, Selective Ejector, Hammerless, Sidelock, Fancy Engraving, *Modern*	925.00	1,250.00	1,250.00
☐ **Model 66 GR II**, 12 Ga., Trap Grade, Selective Ejector, Hammerless, Sidelock, Fancy Engraving, *Modern*	950.00	1,300.00	1,300.00
☐ **Model 66 GR III**, 12 Ga., Single Selective Trigger, Selective Ejector, Hammerless, Sidelock, Fancy Engraving, *Modern*	1,650.00	2,350.00	2,350.00
☐ **Model 66 GR III**, 12 Ga., Skeet Grade, Selective Ejector, Hammerless, Sidelock, Fancy Engraving, *Modern*	1,150.00	1,825.00	1,800.00
☐ **Model 66 GR III**, 12 Ga., Trap Grade, Selective Ejector, Hammerless, Sidelock, Fancy Engraving, *Modern*	1,150.00	1,825.00	1,800.00

	V.G.	Exc.	Prior Year Exc. Value
SHOTGUN, DOUBLE BARREL, SIDE-BY-SIDE			
☐ **.410 Gauge**, Double Trigger, Light Engraving, *Modern*	425.00	620.00	600.00
☐ **Artemis I**, 12 Ga., Single Selective Trigger, Engraved, Checkered Stock, *Modern*	2,450.00	3,500.00	3,500.00
☐ **Artemis II**, 12 Ga., Single Selective Trigger, Fancy Engraving, Fancy Checkering, *Modern*	3,000.00	4,000.00	4,000.00
☐ **Royal**, 12 and 20 Gauges, Single Selective Trigger, Engraved, Checkered Stock, *Modern*	500.00	865.00	850.00
☐ **Model Kim**, Various Gauges, Double Triggers, Checkered Stock, Light Engraving, *Modern*	180.00	285.00	275.00
☐ **Model VIII**, Various Gauges, Double Triggers, Checkered Stock, Light Engraving, *Modern*	175.00	285.00	275.00
☐ **Model VIII DES**, Various Gauges, Single Selective Trigger, Selective Ejectors, Checkered Stock, Light Engraving, *Modern*	175.00	285.00	275.00
☐ **Model VIII DES-01**, Various Gauges, Single Selective Trigger, Selective Ejectors, Checkered Stock, Engraved, *Modern*	250.00	365.00	350.00
☐ **Model VIII DES-07**, Various Gauges, Single Selective Trigger, Selective Ejectors, Checkered Stock, Fancy Engraving, *Modern*	350.00	485.00	475.00
☐ **Model VIII DES-05**, Various Gauges, Single Selective Trigger, Selective Ejectors, Checkered Stock, Fancy Engraving, Sideplates, *Modern*	550.00	795.00	775.00

SAVAGE ARMS CO.

Utica, N.Y. 1893-1899, renamed Savage Arms Co. 1899. J. Stevens Arms Co. Springfield Arms Co. and A.H. Fox are all part of Savage. Also See U.S. Military.

	V.G.	Exc.	Prior Year Exc. Value
AUTOMATIC WEAPON, HEAVY MACHINE GUN			
☐ **M2 Browning,** .50 BMG, Belt Fed, Tripod, *Class 3*	3525.00	4450.00	4400.00
AUTOMATIC WEAPON, SUBMACHINE GUN			
☐ **Thompson M1928A1,** .45 ACP, Clip Fed, with Compensator, Lyman Sights, *Class 3*	1225.00	1700.00	1675.00
COMBINATION WEAPON, OVER-UNDER			
☐ **Model 24,** Various Calibers, Hammer, *Modern*	85.00	130.00	110.00
☐ **Model 24-C,** .22/20 Ga., Hammer, *Modern*	95.00	135.00	125.00
☐ **Model 24-D,** Various Calibers, Hammer, *Modern*	95.00	150.00	135.00
☐ **Model 24-V,** Various Calibers, Checkered Stock, Hammer, *Modern*	115.00	185.00	160.00
☐ **Model 2400,** Various Calibers, Checkered Stock, Hammer, *Modern*	380.00	485.00	475.00
HANDGUN, SEMI-AUTOMATIC			
☐ **Model 1907,** Factory Nickel, *Add* **$35.00-$50.00**			
☐ **Model 1907,** Grade A Engraving (Light), *Add* **$75.00-$100.00**			
☐ **Model 1907,** Grade C Engraving (Fancy), *Add* **$225.00-$325.00**			
☐ **Model 1907 (1908),** .32 ACP, Clip Fed, Burr Cocking Piece, (under #10,899), *Curio*	185.00	255.00	250.00
☐ **Model 1907 (1909),** .32 ACP, Clip Fed, Burr Cocking Piece, (#'s-10,900-70,499), *Curio*	155.00	195.00	190.00
☐ **Model 1907 (1912),** .32 ACP, Clip Fed, Burr Cocking Piece, (Higher # than 70500), *Curio*	140.00	180.00	175.00

	V.G.	Exc.	Prior Year Exc. Value
☐ **Model 1907 (1913),** .380 ACP, Clip Fed, Burr Cocking Piece, *Curio*	**185.00**	**255.00**	**250.00**
☐ **Model 1907 (1914),** .32 ACP, Spur Cocking Piece, *Curio*	**140.00**	**175.00**	**170.00**
☐ **Model 1907 (1914),** .380 ACP, Spur Cocking Piece, *Curio*	**150.00**	**205.00**	**200.00**
☐ **Model 1907 (1918),** .32 ACP, Clip Fed, no Cartridge Indicator, Burr Cocking Piece, (After # 175,000), *Curio*	**125.00**	**165.00**	**160.00**
☐ **Model 1907 (1918),** .32 ACP, Clip Fed, Spur Cocking Piece, (After # 195000), *Curio*	**145.00**	**185.00**	**180.00**
☐ **Model 1907 (1918),** .308 ACP, Clip Fed, Burr Cocking Piece, (After # 10000B), *Curio*	**210.00**	**280.00**	**275.00**
☐ **Model 1907 Military,** .32 ACP, Clip Fed, Burr Cocking Piece, *Curio*	**120.00**	**155.00**	**150.00**
☐ **Model 1907 Military,** .32 ACP, Clip Fed, Burr Cocking Piece, (Portuguese Contract), *Curio*	**270.00**	**360.00**	**350.00**
☐ **Model 1915,** .32 ACP, Clip Fed, Hammerless, Grip Safety, *Curio*	**180.00**	**245.00**	**240.00**
☐ **Model 1915,** .380 ACP, Clip Fed, Hammerless, Grip Safety, *Curio*	**255.00**	**330.00**	**325.00**
☐ **Model 1917,** .32 ACP, Clip Fed, Spur Cocking Piece, Flared Grip, *Curio*	**160.00**	**205.00**	**200.00**
☐ **Model 1917,** .380 ACP, Clip Fed, Spur Cocking Piece, Flared Grip, *Curio*	**190.00**	**240.00**	**235.00**
☐ **Military Model,** .45 ACP, Clip Fed, Original, *Curio*	**2800.00**	**3950.00**	**3750.00**
☐ **Military Model,** .45 ACP, Clip Fed, Surplus, Reblue, *Curio*	**1825.00**	**2925.00**	**2750.00**
☐ **.25 ACP,** Clip Fed, Blue, *Curio*	**3750.00**	**4950.00**	**4750.00**
HANDGUN, SINGLESHOT			
☐ **Model 101,** .22 L.R.R.F., Western Style, Single Action, Swing-Out Cylinder, *Modern*	**80.00**	**130.00**	**125.00**
RIFLE, BOLT ACTION			
☐ **Model 10,** .22 L.R.R.F., Target Sights, (Anschutz), *Modern*	**95.00**	**150.00**	**140.00**
☐ **Model 110,** Magnum Calibers, *Add* **$15.00**			
☐ **Model 110,** Various Calibers, Open Rear Sight, Checkered Stock, *Modern*	**135.00**	**180.00**	**170.00**
☐ **Model 110-B,** Various Calibers, Open Rear Sight, *Modern*	**150.00**	**200.00**	**190.00**
☐ **Model 110-BL,** Various Calibers, Open Rear Sight, Left-Hand, *Modern*	**160.00**	**225.00**	**210.00**
☐ **Model 110-C,** Various Calibers, Clip Fed, Open Rear Sight, *Modern*	**170.00**	**260.00**	**230.00**
☐ **Model 110-CL,** Various Calibers, Clip Fed, Open Rear Sight, Left-Hand, *Modern*	**175.00**	**275.00**	**240.00**
☐ **Model 110-E,** Various Calibers, Open Rear Sight, *Modern*	**135.00**	**180.00**	**170.00**
☐ **Model 110-EL,** Various Calibers, Open Rear Sight, Left-Hand, *Modern*	**145.00**	**185.00**	**175.00**
☐ **Model 110-ES,** Various Calibers, Internal Box Mag, Scope, *Modern*	**289.00**	**300.00**	**300.00**
☐ **Model 110-M,** Various Calibers, Open Rear Sight, Monte Carlo Stock, Checkered Stock, Magnum Action, *Modern*	**160.00**	**210.00**	**200.00**

	V.G.	Exc.	Prior Year Exc. Value
☐ **Model 110-MC,** Various Calibers, Open Rear Sight, Monte Carlo Stock, Checkered Stock, *Modern*	135.00	180.00	170.00
☐ **Model 110-MCL,** Various Calibers, Open Rear Sight, Monte Carlo Stock, Checkered Stock, Left-Hand, *Modern*	140.00	185.00	175.00
☐ **Model 110-ML,** Various Calibers, Open Rear Sight, Monte Carlo Stock, Checkered Stock, Magnum Action, Left-Hand, *Modern*	170.00	220.00	210.00
☐ **Model 110-P,** Various Calibers, Open Rear Sight, Fancy Wood, Monte Carlo Stock, Fancy Checkering, Sling Swivels, *Modern*	270.00	345.00	335.00
☐ **Model 110-PE,** Various Calibers, Engraved, Fancy Checkering, Fancy Wood, Sling Swivels, *Modern*	450.00	580.00	565.00
☐ **Model 110-PEL,** Various Calibers, Engraved, Fancy Checkering, Fancy Wood, Sling Swivels, Left-Hand, *Modern*	450.00	580.00	565.00
☐ **Model 110-PL,** Various Calibers, Fancy Wood, Monte Carlo Stock, Fancy Checkering, Sling Swivels, Left-Hand, *Modern*	290.00	390.00	370.00
☐ **Model 110-S Silhouette Rifle,** .308 Winchester and 7mm-08 Remington, Free Floating Barrel, Monte Carlo Stock, *Modern*	349.95	360.00	360.00
☐ **Model 110-V Varmint,** Various Calibers, 26" Heavy Barrel, *Modern*	349.95	360.00	360.00
☐ **Model 111,** Various Calibers, Clip Fed, Monte Carlo Stock, Checkered Stock, *Modern*	175.00	235.00	230.00
☐ **Model 112-V,** Various Calibers, Singleshot, no Sights, *Modern*	170.00	230.00	220.00
☐ **Model 1407,** Sights Only, *Add* **$55.00-$85.00**			
☐ **Model 1407 "I.S.U.",** .22 L.R.R.F., Heavy Barrel, no Sights, (Anschutz), *Modern*	330.00	460.00	440.00
☐ **Model 1407-L "I.S.U.",** .22 L.R.R.F., Heavy Barrel, no Sights, Left-Hand, (Anschutz), *Modern*	350.00	480.00	465.00
☐ **Model 1408,** .22 L.R.R.F., Heavy Barrel, no Sights, (Anschutz), *Modern*	255.00	380.00	365.00
☐ **Model 1408-ED,** .22 L.R.R.F., Heavy Barrel, no Sights, (Anschutz), *Modern*	370.00	480.00	465.00
☐ **Model 1408-L,** .22 L.R.R.F., Heavy Barrel, no Sights, Left-Hand, (Anschutz), *Modern*	255.00	375.00	360.00
☐ **Model 1411,** Sights Only, *Add* **$55.00-$80.00**			
☐ **Model 1411 "Prone",** .22 L.R.R.F., Heavy Barrel, no Sights, (Anschutz), *Modern*	360.00	500.00	485.00
☐ **Model 1411-L "Prone",** .22 L.R.R.F., Heavy Barrel, no Sights, Left-Hand, (Anschutz), *Modern*	375.00	500.00	500.00
☐ **Model 1413,** .22 L.R.R.F., Sights Only, *Add* **$55.00-$80.00**			
☐ **Model 1413 "Match",** .22 L.R.R.F., Heavy Barrel, no Sights, (Anschutz), *Modern*	540.00	680.00	665.00
☐ **Model 1413-L "Match",** .22 L.R.R.F., Heavy Barrel, No Sights, Left-Hand, (Anschutz), *Modern*	595.00	740.00	720.00
☐ **Model 1418,** .22 L.R.R.F., Clip Fed, Mannlicher, Fancy Checkering, (Anschutz), *Modern*	245.00	345.00	335.00
☐ **Model 1432,** .22 Hornet, Sporting Rifle, Clip Fed, Fancy Checkering, (Anschutz), *Modern*	360.00	480.00	465.00

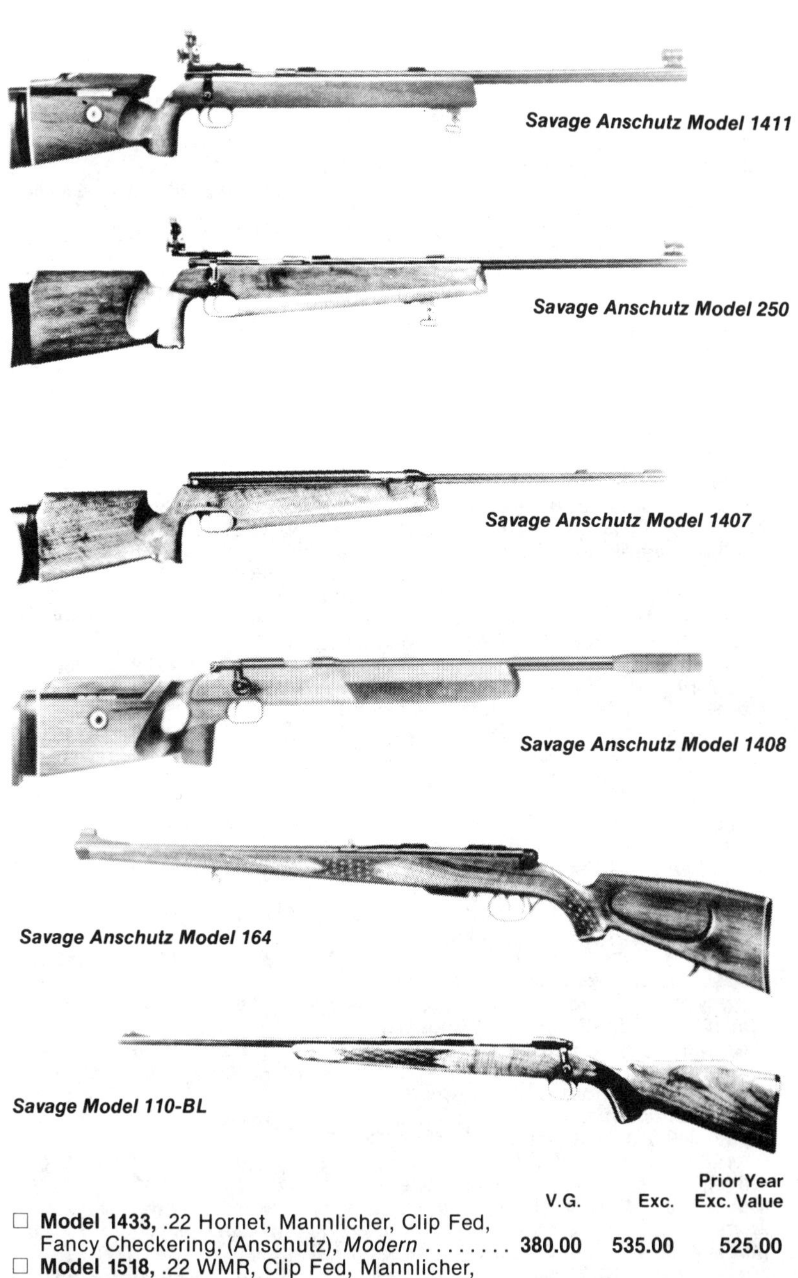

Savage Anschutz Model 1411

Savage Anschutz Model 250

Savage Anschutz Model 1407

Savage Anschutz Model 1408

Savage Anschutz Model 164

Savage Model 110-BL

	V.G.	Exc.	Prior Year Exc. Value
☐ **Model 1433,** .22 Hornet, Mannlicher, Clip Fed, Fancy Checkering, (Anschutz), *Modern*	380.00	535.00	525.00
☐ **Model 1518,** .22 WMR, Clip Fed, Mannlicher, Fancy Checkering, (Anschutz), *Modern*	255.00	370.00	360.00
☐ **Model 1533,** .222 Rem., Mannlicher, Clip Fed, Fancy Checkering, (Anschutz), *Modern*	380.00	510.00	500.00

	V.G.	Exc.	Prior Year Exc. Value
☐ **Model 164,** .22 L.R.R.F., Sporting Rifle, Clip Fed, Checkered Stock, (Anschutz), *Modern*	180.00	260.00	255.00
☐ **Model 164-M,** .22 WMR, Sporting Rifle, Clip Fed, Checkered Stock, (Anschutz), *Modern*	180.00	260.00	255.00
☐ **Model 19-H,** .22 Hornet, 5 Shot Clip, Peep Sights, *Modern*	200.00	285.00	280.00
☐ **Model 19-L,** .22 L.R.R.F., 5 Shot Clip, Lyman Sights, *Modern*	145.00	205.00	195.00
☐ **Model 19-M,** .22 L.R.R.F., 5 Shot Clip, Heavy Barrel, *Modern*	150.00	215.00	210.00
☐ **Model 19-N.R.A.,** .22 L.R.R.F., 5 Shot Clip, Full-Stocked, Peep Sights, *Modern*	130.00	185.00	170.00
☐ **Model 19-Speed Lock,** .22 L.R.R.F., 5 Shot Clip, Peep Sights, *Modern*	130.00	190.00	175.00
☐ **Model 1904,** .22 L.R.R.F., Singleshot, Takedown, *Modern*	43.00	68.00	65.00
☐ **Model 1904-Special,** .22 L.R.R.F., Singleshot, Takedown, Fancy Wood, *Modern*	70.00	100.00	95.00
☐ **Model 1905,** .22 L.R.R.F., Target, Singleshot, Takedown, Swiss Buttplate, *Modern*	53.00	85.00	80.00
☐ **Model 1905-B,** .22 L.R.R.F., *Modern*	42.00	62.00	60.00
☐ **Model 1905-Special,** .22 L.R.R.F, Fancy Wood, *Modern*	90.00	140.00	135.00
☐ **Model 1911,** .22 Short R.F., Target, Singleshot, Takedown, *Modern*	48.00	70.00	65.00
☐ **Model 20,** Various Calibers, Open Rear Sight, *Modern*	170.00	245.00	235.00
☐ **Model 20,** Various Calibers, Peep Sights, *Modern*	195.00	270.00	260.00
☐ **Model 23A,** .22 L.R.R.F., 5 Shot Clip, Open Rear Sight, *Modern*	115.00	150.00	145.00
☐ **Model 23AA,** .22 L.R.R.F, 5 Shot Clip, Open Rear Sight, Monte Carlo Stock, *Modern*	115.00	155.00	150.00
☐ **Model 23B,** .25-20 WCF, 5 Shot Clip, Open Rear Sight, Monte Carlo Stock, *Modern*	135.00	180.00	175.00
☐ **Model 23C,** .32-20 WCF, 5 Shot Clip, Open Rear Sight, Monte Carlo Stock, *Modern*	135.00	180.00	175.00
☐ **Model 23D,** .22 Hornet, 5 Shot Clip, Open Rear Sight, Monte Carlo Stock, *Modern*	190.00	255.00	250.00
☐ **Model 3,** .22 L.R.R.F., Singleshot, Takedown, Open Rear Sight, *Modern*	32.00	47.00	45.00
☐ **Model 3-S,** .22 L.R.R.F., Singleshot, Takedown, Peep Sights, *Modern*	37.00	53.00	50.00
☐ **Model 3-ST,** .22 L.R.R.F., Singleshot, Takedown, Peep Sights, Sling Swivels, *Modern*	37.00	58.00	55.00
☐ **Model 340,** Various Calibers, Clip Fed, *Modern*	90.00	140.00	135.00
☐ **Model 340-C,** Various Calibers, Clip Fed, Carbine, *Modern*	90.00	140.00	135.00
☐ **Model 340-S Deluxe,** Various Calibers, Clip Fed, Peep Sights, *Modern*	100.00	145.00	140.00
☐ **Model 342,** .22 Hornet, Clip Fed, *Modern*	120.00	160.00	155.00
☐ **Model 342-S,** .22 Hornet, Clip Fed, Peep Sights, *Modern*	100.00	155.00	150.00
☐ **Model 4,** .22 L.R.R.F., 5 Shot Clip, Takedown, *Modern*	42.00	65.00	60.00
☐ **Model 4-M,** .22 WMR, 5 Shot Clip, Takedown, *Modern*	48.00	80.00	75.00

	V.G.	Exc.	Prior Year Exc. Value
☐ **Model 35,** .22 L.R.R.F., Clip Fed, *Modern*	40.00	60.00	60.00
☐ **Model 35-M,** .22 W.R.M., Clip Fed, *Modern*	45.00	65.00	65.00
☐ **Model 36,** .22 L.R.R.F., Singleshot, *Modern*	40.00	55.00	55.00
☐ **Model 4-S,** .22 L.R.R.F., 5 Shot Clip, Takedown, Peep Sights, *Modern*	48.00	70.00	65.00
☐ **Model 40,** Various Calibers, Open Rear Sight, *Modern*	165.00	235.00	225.00
☐ **Model 45 Super,** Various Calibers, Peep Sights, Checkered Stock, *Modern*	185.00	260.00	250.00
☐ **Model 5,** .22 L.R.R.F., Tube Feed, Takedown, Open Rear Sight, *Modern*	48.00	75.00	70.00
☐ **Model 5-S,** .22 L.R.R.F., Tube Feed, Takedown, Peep Sights, *Modern*	48.00	75.00	70.00
☐ **Model 54,** .22 L.R.R.F., Sporting Rifle, Clip Fed, Fancy Checkering, (Anschutz), *Modern*	280.00	385.00	375.00
☐ **Model 54-M,** .22 WMR, Sporting Rifle, Clip Fed, Fancy Checkering, (Anschutz), *Modern*	300.00	400.00	390.00
☐ **Model 63,** .22 L.R.R.F., Singleshot, Open Rear Sight, *Modern*	32.00	47.00	45.00
☐ **Model 63-K,** .22 L.R.R.F, Singleshot, Open Rear Sight, *Modern*	32.00	47.00	45.00
☐ **Model 63-M,** .22 WMR, Singleshot, Open Rear Sight, *Modern*	37.00	60.00	55.00
☐ **Model 64,** .22 L.R.R.F., Sights Only, *Add* **$30.00-$55.00**			
☐ **Model 64,** .22 L.R.R.F., Heavy Barrel, no Sights, (Anschutz), *Modern*	160.00	225.00	220.00
☐ **Model 64-CS,** .22 L.R.R.F., Heavy Barrel, no Sights, Lightweight, (Anschutz), *Modern*	180.00	255.00	250.00
☐ **Model 64-CSL,** .22 L.R.R.F, Heavy Barrel, no Sights, Left-Hand, Lightweight, (Anschutz), *Modern*	190.00	270.00	265.00
☐ **Model 64-L,** .22 L.R.R.F., Heavy Barrel, no Sights, Left-Hand, (Anschutz), *Modern*	170.00	230.00	225.00
☐ **Model 64-S,** .22 L.R.R.F., Heavy Barrel, no Sights, (Anschutz), *Modern*	195.00	270.00	265.00
☐ **Model 64-SL,** .22 L.R.R.F., Heavy Barrel, no Sights, Left-Hand, (Anschutz), *Modern*	220.00	280.00	275.00
☐ **Model 65-M,** .22 WMR, Clip Fed, Open Rear Sight, *Modern*	53.00	80.00	75.00
☐ **Model 73,** .22 L.R.R.F., Singleshot, *Modern*	32.00	48.00	45.00
☐ **Model 73-Y Boys,** .22 L.R.R.F., Singleshot, *Modern*	32.00	48.00	45.00

RIFLE, LEVER ACTION

	V.G.	Exc.	Prior Year Exc. Value
☐ **Model 1892,** .30-40 Krag, Hammerless, Rotary Magazine, Military, *Antique*	920.00	1475.00	1450.00
☐ **Model 1895,** .303 Savage, Hammerless, Rotary Magazine, Open Rear Sight, *Antique*	510.00	750.00	725.00
☐ **Model 1899,** .30-30 Win., Hammerless, Rotary Magazine, Full-Stocked, Military, *Modern*	745.00	1325.00	1300.00
☐ **Model 1899,** Various Calibers, Hammerless, Rotary Magazine, Open Rear Sight, *Modern*	190.00	275.00	260.00
☐ **Model 1899 A2,** Various Calibers, Hammerless, Rotary Magazine, Checkered Stock, *Modern*	190.00	290.00	275.00
☐ **Model 1899 AB,** Various Calibers, Light Engraving, Checkered Stock, Hammerless, Rotary Magazine, *Modern*	360.00	465.00	445.00

	V.G.	Exc.	Prior Year Exc. Value
☐ **Model 1899 BC,** Various Calibers, Light Engraving, Checkered Stock, Hammerless, Rotary Magazine, *Modern*	320.00	415.00	400.00
☐ **Model 1899 Excelsior,** Various Calibers, Light Engraving, Checkered Stock, Featherweight, Hammerless, Rotary Magazine, *Modern*	500.00	710.00	695.00
☐ **Model 1899 Leader,** Various Calibers, Engraved, Checkered Stock, Hammerless, Rotary Magazine, *Modern*	475.00	695.00	675.00
☐ **Model 1899 Monarch,** Various Calibers, Fancy Engraving, Fancy Checkering, Ornate, Hammerless, Rotary Magazine, *Modern*	2000.00	2850.00	2800.00
☐ **Model 1899 Premier,** Various Calibers, Fancy Engraving, Fancy Checkering, Takedown, Hammerless, Rotary Magazine, *Modern*	1300.00	1735.00	1700.00
☐ **Model 1899 Rival,** Various Calibers, Fancy Engraving, Fancy Checkering, Hammerless, Rotary Magazine, *Modern*	1025.00	1580.00	1550.00
☐ **Model 1899 Victor,** Various Calibers, Engraved, Fancy Checkering, Hammerless, Rotary Magazine, *Modern*	690.00	975.00	950.00
☐ **Model 89,** .22 L.R.R.F., Singleshot, Open Rear Sight, *Modern*	37.00	60.00	55.00
☐ **Model 99,** for Extra Barrel, *Add* **$75.00-$110.00**			
☐ **Model 99 E,** Various Calibers, Solid Frame, Carbine, Hammerless, Rotary Magazine, *Modern*	160.00	230.00	220.00
☐ **Model 99-1895 Anniversary,** .308 Win., Octagon Barrel, Hammerless, Rotary Magazine, *Modern*	220.00	285.00	275.00
☐ **Model 99-358,** .358 Win., Solid Frame, Hammerless, Rotary Magazine, *Modern*	175.00	250.00	245.00
☐ **Model 99-A,** Various Calibers, Solid Frame, Hammerless, Rotary Magazine, *Modern*	180.00	240.00	235.00
☐ **Model 99-B,** Various Calibers, Takedown, Hammerless, Rotary Magazine, *Modern*	195.00	295.00	285.00
☐ **Model 99-C,** Various Calibers, Clip Fed, Solid Frame, Featherweight, Hammerless, *Modern*	180.00	250.00	245.00
☐ **Model 99-CD,** Various Calibers, Hammerless, Clip Fed, Solid Frame, Monte Carlo Stock, *Modern*	200.00	275.00	265.00
☐ **Model 99-DE,** Various Calibers, Solid Frame, Monte Carlo Stock, Light Engraving, Hammerless, Rotary Magazine, *Modern*	260.00	330.00	325.00
☐ **Model 99-DL,** Various Calibers, Solid Frame, Monte Carlo Stock, Hammerless, Rotary Magazine, *Modern*	180.00	240.00	235.00
☐ **Model 99-E,** Various Calibers, Solid Frame, Hammerless, Rotary Magazine, *Modern*	170.00	220.00	215.00
☐ **Model 99-EG,** Various Calibers, Takedown, Checkered Stock, Hammerless, Rotary Magazine, *Modern*	175.00	230.00	225.00
☐ **Model 99-F,** Various Calibers, Featherweight, Takedown, Hammerless, Rotary Magazine, *Modern*	215.00	280.00	275.00
☐ **Model 99-F,** Various Calibers, Solid Frame, Featherweight, Hammerless, Rotary Magazine, *Modern*	170.00	230.00	225.00

	V.G.	Exc.	Prior Year Exc. Value
☐ **Model 99-G,** Various Calibers, Takedown, Checkered Stock, Hammerless, Rotary Magazine, *Modern*	185.00	250.00	245.00
☐ **Model 99-H,** Various Calibers, Carbine, Solid Frame, Hammerless, Rotary Magazine, *Modern*	170.00	230.00	225.00
☐ **Model 99-K,** Various Calibers, Takedown, Light Engraving, Checkered Stock, Hammerless, Rotary Magazine, *Modern*	560.00	850.00	825.00
☐ **Model 99-PE,** Various Calibers, Solid Frame, Monte Carlo Stock, Engraved, Hammerless, Rotary Magazine, *Modern*	490.00	750.00	720.00
☐ **Model 99-R,** Various Calibers, Solid Frame, Checkered Stock, Pre-War, Hammerless, Rotary Magazine, *Modern*	310.00	445.00	435.00
☐ **Model 99-R,** Various Calibers, Solid Frame, Checkered Stock, Hammerless, Rotary Magazine, *Modern*	180.00	235.00	230.00
☐ **Model 99-RS,** Various Calibers, Solid Frame, Peep Sights, Pre-War, Hammerless, Rotary Magazine, *Modern*	250.00	355.00	350.00
☐ **Model 99-RS,** Various Calibers, Solid Frame, Peep Sights, Hammerless, Rotary Magazine, *Modern*	190.00	250.00	245.00
☐ **Model 99-T,** Various Calibers, Solid Frame, Featherweight, Hammerless, Rotary Magazine, *Modern*	225.00	320.00	310.00
RIFLE, SEMI-AUTOMATIC			
☐ **Model 1912,** .22 L.R.R.F., Half-Octagon Barrel, Takedown, Clip Fed, *Curio*	140.00	225.00	210.00
☐ **Model 6,** .22 L.R.R.F., Takedown, Tube Feed, Open Rear Sight, *Modern*	60.00	80.00	75.00
☐ **Model 6-S,** .22 L.R.R.F., Takedown, Tube Feed, Peep Sights, *Modern*	60.00	85.00	80.00
☐ **Model 60,** .22 L.R.R.F., Monte Carlo Stock, Checkered Stock, Tube Feed, *Modern*	65.00	90.00	85.00
☐ **Model 7,** .22 L.R.R.F., 5 Shot Clip, Takedown, Open Rear Sight, *Modern*	53.00	70.00	65.00
☐ **Model 7-S,** .22 L.R.R.F., 5 Shot Clip, Takedown, Open Rear Sight, *Modern*	53.00	80.00	75.00
☐ **Model 80,** .22 L.R.R.F., Tube Feed, *Modern*	48.00	65.00	60.00
☐ **Model 88,** .22 L.R.R.F., Tube Feed, *Modern*	53.00	75.00	70.00
☐ **Model 90,** .22 L.R.R.F., Carbine, Tube Feed, *Modern*	53.00	80.00	75.00
☐ **Model 987 Stevens Rimfire,** .22 Autoloader, Tubular Mag. 15 Rounds, Walnut Stock, *Modern*	100.00	115.00	110.00
☐ **Model 987-T Stevens Rimfire,** .22 Autoloader, Tubular Mag. 15 Rounds, 4x Scope and Mount, *Modern*	110.00	125.00	120.00
RIFLE, SINGLESHOT			
☐ **Model 219,** Various Calibers, Hammerless, Top Break, Open Rear Sight, *Modern*	60.00	80.00	75.00
☐ **Model 219L,** Various Calibers, Hammerless, Top Break, Open Rear Sight, Side Lever, *Modern*	60.00	80.00	75.00
☐ **Model 221,** .30-30 Win., Hammerless, Top Break, Extra Shotgun Barrel, *Modern*	65.00	95.00	90.00

	V.G.	Exc.	Prior Year Exc. Value
☐ **Model 222,** .30-30 Win., Hammerless, Top Break, Extra Shotgun Barrel, *Modern*	65.00	100.00	95.00
☐ **Model 223,** .30-30 Win., Hammerless, Top Break, Extra Shotgun Barrel, *Modern*	70.00	100.00	95.00
☐ **Model 227,** .30-30 Win., Hammerless, Top Break, Extra Shotgun Barrel, *Modern*	70.00	100.00	95.00
☐ **Model 228,** .30-30 Win., Hammerless, Top Break, Extra Shotgun Barrel, *Modern*	70.00	100.00	95.00
☐ **Model 229,** .30-30 Win., Hammerless, Top Break, Extra Shotgun Barrel, *Modern*	70.00	100.00	95.00
☐ **Model 71 Stevens Favorite,** .22 L.R.R.F., Lever Action, Falling Block, Favorite, *Modern*	90.00	145.00	140.00
☐ **Model 72,** .22 L.R.R.F., Lever Action, Falling Block, *Modern*	65.00	90.00	85.00
☐ **Model 89 Stevens Rimfire,** .22 L.R.R.F., Lever Action, 18″ Barrel, Sporting Sights, *Modern*	89.95	100.00	100.00
RIFLE, SLIDE ACTION			
☐ **Model 170,** Various Calibers, Open Rear Sight, *Modern*	120.00	155.00	150.00
☐ **Model 170-C,** .30-30 Win., Carbine, Open Rear Sight, *Modern*	105.00	145.00	140.00
☐ **Model 1903,** .22 L.R.R.F., Hammerless, Clip Fed, Octagon Barrel, *Modern*	80.00	130.00	125.00
☐ **Model 1903-EF,** .22 L.R.R.F., Hammerless, Clip Fed, Octagon Barrel, Fancy Wood, Engraved, *Modern*	380.00	510.00	500.00
☐ **Model 1903-Expert,** .22 L.R.R.F., Hammerless, Clip Fed, Octagon Barrel, Checkered Stock, Light Engraving, *Modern*	180.00	270.00	260.00
☐ **Model 1909,** .22 L.R.R.F., Half-Octagon Barrel, Takedown, Clip Fed, *Modern*	85.00	135.00	130.00
☐ **Model 1914,** .22 L.R.R.F., Half-Octagon Barrel, Takedown, Tube Feed, *Modern*	125.00	160.00	155.00
☐ **Model 1914-E.F.,** .22 L.R.R.F., Half-Octagon Barrel, Takedown, Tube Feed, Fancy Engraving, *Modern*	495.00	650.00	625.00
☐ **Model 1914-Expert,** .22 L.R.R.F., Half-Octagon Barrel, Takedown, Tube Feed, Light Engraving, *Modern*	335.00	465.00	445.00
☐ **Model 1914-Gold Medal,** .22 L.R.R.F., Half-Octagon Barrel, Takedown, Tube Feed, Checkered Stock, Light Engraving, *Modern*	220.00	295.00	285.00
☐ **Model 25,** .22 L.R.R.F., Tube Feed, Octagon Barrel, Open Rear Sight, Monte Carlo Stock, *Modern*	95.00	135.00	130.00
☐ **Model 29,** .22 L.R.R.F., Tube Feed, Octagon Barrel, Open Rear Sight, Monte Carlo Stock, *Modern*	130.00	195.00	185.00
☐ **Model 29,** .22 L.R.R.F., Tube Feed, Round Barrel, Open Rear Sight, *Modern*	120.00	150.00	145.00
☐ **Model 29-G,** .22 Short R.F., Tube Feed, *Modern*	125.00	160.00	155.00
SHOTGUN, BOLT ACTION			
☐ **Model 58,** .410 Ga., Singleshot, *Modern*	43.00	70.00	65.00
SHOTGUN, DOUBLE BARREL, OVER-UNDER			
☐ **Model 242,** .410 Ga., Hammer, Single Trigger, *Modern*	95.00	135.00	130.00

Savage Model 99-C

Savage Model 24

Savage Model 30

Savage Model 170

Savage Model 30 Slug

Savage Fox Model B

Savage Model 94-Y

Savage Model 333

	V.G.	Exc.	Prior Year Exc. Value
☐ **Model 330,** 12 and 20 Gauges, Hammerless, Single Selective Trigger, *Modern*	290.00	380.00	370.00
☐ **Model 330,** 12 and 20 Gauges, Hammerless, Extra Shotgun Barrel, Cased, *Modern*	360.00	460.00	450.00
☐ **Model 333,** 12 and 20 Gauges, Hammerless, Vent Rib, Single Selective Trigger, *Modern*	360.00	460.00	450.00
☐ **Model 333-T,** 12 Ga., Hammerless, Vent Rib, Trap Grade, Single Selective Trigger, *Modern*	330.00	445.00	435.00
☐ **Model 420,** Various Gauges, Hammerless, Takedown, Double Trigger, *Modern*	195.00	260.00	250.00
☐ **Model 420,** Various Gauges, Hammerless, Takedown, Single Trigger, *Modern*	240.00	320.00	310.00
☐ **Model 430,** Various Gauges, Hammerless, Takedown, Checkered Stock, Recoil Pad, Double Trigger, *Modern*	225.00	300.00	290.00
☐ **Model 430,** Various Gauges, Hammerless, Takedown, Checkered Stock, Recoil Pad, Single Trigger, *Modern*	265.00	360.00	350.00
☐ **Model 440,** 12 Ga., Hammerless, Vent Rib, Single Selective Trigger, Checkered Stock, *Modern*	180.00	255.00	250.00
☐ **Model 440-B,** 20 Ga., Hammerless, Vent Rib, Checkered Stock, *Modern*	205.00	300.00	290.00
☐ **Model 444,** 12 Ga., Hammerless, Vent Rib, Single Selective Trigger, Checkered Stock, Selective Ejector, *Modern*	230.00	310.00	300.00
☐ **Model 444-T,** 12 Ga., Hammerless, Trap Grade, *Modern*	230.00	310.00	300.00
RIFLE/SHOTGUN COMBINATION			
☐ **Model 24 Field Combo,** .22 L.R. Top Barrel, 4 10 Bore or 20 Gauge Bottom Barrel, Walnut Stock, *Modern*	169.50	180.00	175.00
☐ **Model 24-C Combo Gun, Camper's Break Action,** .22 L.R. Top Barrel, 20 Gauge Bottom Barrel, *Modern*	189.50	215.00	210.00
☐ **Model 24-CS Camper/Survival Combo Gun, Break Action,** .22 L.R. Top Barrel, 20 Gauge Bottom Barrel, Pistol Grip, Satin Nickel, *Modern*	219.50	230.00	230.00
☐ **Model 24-D Combo Gun,** .22 L.R. Top Barrel, 20 Gauge Bottom Barrel, Folding Rear Sight, *Modern*	210.00	220.00	220.00
☐ **Model 24-V Combo Gun, Break Action,** .22 Hornet Top Barrel, 20 Gauge Bottom Barrel, Monte Carlo Stock, *Modern*	242.00	250.00	250.00
☐ **Model 24-VS Camper/Survival Combo Gun, Break Action,** .357 Magnum Top Barrel, 20 Gauge Bottom Barrel, Pistol Grip, Satin Nickel, *Modern*	262.00	270.00	270.00
SHOTGUN, DOUBLE BARREL, SIDE-BY-SIDE			
☐ **Model B Fox,** Various Gauges, Hammerless, Vent Rib, Double Trigger, *Modern*	175.00	230.00	225.00
☐ **Model B-SE Fox,** Various Gauges, Hammerless, Vent Rib, Selective Ejector, Single Trigger *Modern*	190.00	270.00	260.00

	V.G.	Exc.	Prior Year Exc. Value
SHOTGUN, SEMI-AUTOMATIC			
☐ **Model 720,** 12 Ga., Tube Feed, Checkered Stock, Plain Barrel, *Modern*	115.00	150.00	145.00
☐ **Model 720-P,** 12 Ga., Checkered Stock, Adjustable Choke, *Modern*	125.00	160.00	155.00
☐ **Model 720-R,** 12 Ga., Riot Gun, *Modern*	105.00	150.00	145.00
☐ **Model 721,** 12 Ga., Tube Feed, Checkered Stock, Raised Matted Rib, *Modern*	145.00	180.00	175.00
☐ **Model 722,** 12 Ga., Tube Feed, Checkered Stock, Vent Rib, *Modern*	160.00	200.00	195.00
☐ **Model 723,** 16 Ga., Tube Feed, Checkered Stock, Plain Barrel, *Modern*	105.00	150.00	145.00
☐ **Model 724,** 16 Ga., Tube Feed, Checkered Stock, Raised Matted Rib, *Modern*	115.00	155.00	150.00
☐ **Model 725,** 16 Ga., Tube Feed, Checkered Stock, Vent Rib, *Modern*	115.00	155.00	150.00
☐ **Model 726,** 12 and 16 Gauges, 3 Shot, Checkered Stock, Plain Barrel, *Modern*	115.00	150.00	145.00
☐ **Model 727,** 12 and 16 Gauges, 3 Shot, Checkered Stock, Raised Matted Rib, *Modern*	125.00	160.00	155.00
☐ **Model 728,** 12 and 16 Gauges, 3 Shot, Checkered Stock, Vent Rib, *Modern*	130.00	170.00	165.00
☐ **Model 740-C,** 12 and 16 Gauges, Skeet Grade, *Modern*	155.00	200.00	195.00
☐ **Model 745,** 12 Ga., Lightweight, *Modern*	140.00	180.00	175.00
☐ **Model 750,** 12 Ga., *Modern*	155.00	200.00	195.00
☐ **Model 750-AC,** 12 Ga., Adjustable Choke, *Modern*	155.00	200.00	195.00
☐ **Model 750-SC,** 12 Ga., Adjustable Choke, *Modern*	165.00	205.00	200.00
☐ **Model 755,** 12 and 16 Gauges, *Modern*	135.00	165.00	160.00
☐ **Model 755-SC,** 12 and 16 Gauges, Adjustable Choke, *Modern*	140.00	180.00	175.00
☐ **Model 775,** 12 and 16 Gauges, Lightweight, *Modern*	145.00	190.00	185.00
☐ **Model 775-SC,** 12 and 16 Gauges, Adjustable Choke, Lightweight, *Modern*	150.00	190.00	185.00
SHOTGUN, SINGLESHOT			
☐ **Model 220,** Various Gauges, Hammerless, Takedown, *Modern*	37.00	52.00	50.00
☐ **Model 220-AC,** Various Gauges, Hammerless, Takedown, Adjustable Choke, *Modern*	43.00	60.00	55.00
☐ **Model 220-P,** Various Gauges, Hammerless, Takedown, Adjustable Choke, *Modern*	48.00	70.00	65.00
☐ **Model 94,** Various Gauges, Hammer, Takedown, *Modern*	88.50	105.00	100.00
☐ **Model 94-C,** Various Gauges, Hammer, Takedown, *Modern*	43.00	70.00	60.00
☐ **Model 94-Y Youth,** Various Gauges, Hammer, Takedown, *Modern*	43.00	65.00	55.00
☐ **Model 9478,** Various Gauges, Hammer, Auto Ejection, 42″ to 52″ Overall, *Modern*	84.95	100.00	95.00

	V.G.	Exc.	Prior Year Exc. Value
SHOTGUN, SLIDE ACTION			
☐ **Model 67,** 12 or 20 Gauge, Tubular Mag, Hammerless, Walnut Stock, *Modern*	181.50	190.00	190.00
☐ **Model 67-T Stevens,** 12 or 20 Gauge, Three Choke Tubes, 28″ Barrel, *Modern*	189.50	200.00	200.00
☐ **Model 67-VR Stevens,** 12 Gauge, 4 Shot Tubular, Vent Ribs, *Modern*	191.50	200.00	200.00
☐ **Model 69-N Guard Gun,** 12 Gauge, 7 Shot Tubular Mag., 18¼″ Cylinder Bore, Nickel, *Modern*	258.00	265.00	265.00
☐ **Model 69-R Guard Gun,** 12 Gauge, 5 Shot Tubular Mag., 20″ Cylinder Bore, *Modern*	185.50	200.00	200.00
☐ **Model 69-RXL Guard Gun,** 12 Gauge, 7 Shot Tubular Mag, 18¼″ Cylinder Bore, *Modern*	185.50	200.00	200.00
☐ **Model 21-A,** 12 Ga., Hammerless, Takedown, *Modern*	115.00	150.00	145.00
☐ **Model 21-B,** 12 Ga., Hammerless, Takedown, Raised Matted Rib, *Modern*	120.00	155.00	150.00
☐ **Model 21-C,** 12 Ga., Hammerless, Takedown, Riot Gun, *Modern*	100.00	140.00	135.00
☐ **Model 21-D,** 12 Ga., Hammerless, Takedown, Trap Grade, *Modern*	170.00	235.00	225.00
☐ **Model 21-E,** 12 Ga., Hammerless, Takedown, Fancy Wood, Fancy Checkering, Vent Rib, *Modern*	205.00	285.00	275.00
☐ **Model 28-A,** 12 Ga., Hammerless, Takedown, *Modern*	115.00	150.00	145.00
☐ **Model 28-B,** 12 Ga., Hammerless, Takedown, Raised Matted Rib, *Modern*	120.00	155.00	150.00
☐ **Model 28-C,** 12 Ga., Hammerless, Takedown, Riot Gun, *Modern*	100.00	145.00	140.00
☐ **Model 28-D,** 12 Ga., Hammerless, Takedown, Trap Grade, *Modern*	170.00	235.00	225.00
☐ **Model 28-S,** 12 Ga., Hammerless, Takedown, Fancy Checkering, *Modern*	155.00	200.00	195.00
☐ **Model 30,** For Vent Rib, *Add* **$15.00-$20.00**			
☐ **Model 30,** Various Gauges, Hammerless, Solid Frame, *Modern*	90.00	130.00	125.00
☐ **Model 30-AC,** Various Gauges, Hammerless, Solid Frame, Adjustable Choke, *Modern*	90.00	130.00	125.00
☐ **Model 30-ACL,** Various Gauges, Hammerless, Solid Frame, Left-Hand, Adjustable Choke, *Modern*	100.00	140.00	135.00
☐ **Model 30-D,** Various Gauges, Hammerless, Solid Frame, Light Engraving, Recoil Pad, *Modern*	115.00	155.00	150.00
☐ **Model 30-L,** Various Gauges, Hammerless, Solid Frame, Left-Hand, *Modern*	100.00	135.00	130.00
☐ **Model 30-Slug,** 12 Ga., Hammerless, Solid Frame, *Modern*	100.00	140.00	135.00

	V.G.	Exc.	Prior Year Exc. Value
☐ **Model 30-T,** 12 Ga., Hammerless, Solid Frame, Monte Carlo Stock, Recoil Pad, Vent Rib, *Modern*	120.00	160.00	155.00

SANTA BARBARA

Santa Barbara of America, Inc. of Irving, Tx. on Mauser actions made in La Caruna, Spain.

RIFLE, BOLT ACTION

☐ **Sporter**, Various Calibers, Custom Made, Medium Quality, *Modern*	90.00	135.00	130.00
☐ **Sporter**, Various Calibers, Custom Made, High Quality, *Modern*	130.00	185.00	180.00

SCHALL & CO.

Hartford, Conn.

HANDGUN, MANUAL REPEATER

☐ **.22 L.R.R.F.**, Target Pistol, Clip Fed, *Curio*	290.00	400.00	365.00

SCHEANER, WM.

Reading, Pa. 1779-1790. See Kentucky Rifles.

SCHILLING, V. CHARLES

Suhl, Germany. Also see Bergmann, German Military.

RIFLE, BOLT ACTION

☐ **Model 88 Sporter**, Various Calibers, Checkered Stock, *Curio*	235.00	325.00	325.00

SCHMIDT, ERNST

Suhl, Germany.

RIFLE, SINGLESHOT

☐ **8mm Roth-Steyr**, Schutzen Rifle, Engraved, Set Trigger, Takedown, Octagon Barrel, *Modern*	550.00	800.00	775.00

SCHMIDT, HERBERT

Ostheim/Rhon, West Germany.

HANDGUN, REVOLVER

☐ **Liberty 11**, .22 L.R.R.F., Double Action, Swing-Out Cylinder, Blue, *Modern*	25.00	40.00	40.00
☐ **Texas Scout**, .22 L.R.R.F., Western Style, Blue, *Modern*	25.00	40.00	40.00

SCHMIDT & HABERMANN

Suhl, Germany, 1920-1940.

COMBINATION WEAPON, OVER-UNDER

☐ **Various Calibers**, Pre-WW2, Engraved, Checkered Stock, *Modern*	475.00	700.00	675.00

SCHOUBOE

Dansk Rekylriffel Syndikat, Copenhagen, Denmark 1902-1917.

	V.G.	Exc.	Prior Year Exc. Value
HANDGUN, SEMI-AUTOMATIC			
☐ **Model 1903**, .32 ACP, Clip Fed, Blue, *Curio*	2,300.00	3,650.00	3,500.00
☐ **Model 1902/07**, 11.35mm Sch., *Curio*	3,500.00	4,750.00	4,500.00
☐ **Model 1902/10**, 11.35mm Sch., *Curio*	3,500.00	4,750.00	4,500.00
☐ **Model 1902/10**, 11.35mm Sch., with Holster Stock, *Curio*	4,750.00	6,200.00	6,000.00

SCHULTZ & LARSEN

Otterup, Denmark.

	V.G.	Exc.	Prior Year Exc. Value
HANDGUN, SINGLESHOT			
Free Pistol, .22 L.R.R.F., Bolt Action, Target Trigger, Target Sights, *Modern*	200.00	295.00	295.00
RIFLE, BOLT ACTION			
☐ **Model 47**, .22 L.R.R.F., Target Rifle, Thumbhole Stock, Adjustable Trigger, Singleshot, *Modern*	350.00	485.00	475.00
☐ **M54**, Various Calibers, *Modern*	475.00	665.00	650.00
☐ **M54J**, Various Calibers, *Modern*	400.00	575.00	575.00
☐ **Model 61**, .22 L.R.R.F., Target Rifle, Thumbhole Stock, Adjustable Trigger, Singleshot, *Modern*	325.00	450.00	450.00
☐ **Model 62**, Various Calibers, Target Rifle, Thumbhole Stock, Adjustable Trigger, Singleshot, *Modern*	375.00	525.00	525.00
☐ **Model 65DL**, Various Calibers, Sporting Rifle, Checkered Stock, Adjustable Trigger, no Sights, Repeater, *Modern*	325.00	450.00	450.00
☐ **Model 68DL**, .458 Win. Mag., Sporting Rifle, Checkered Stock, Adjustable Trigger, no Sights, Repeater, *Modern*	475.00	675.00	675.00
☐ **Model 68DL**, Various Calibers, Sporting Rifle, Checkered Stock, Adjustable Trigger, no Sights, Repeater, *Modern*	400.00	550.00	550.00

SCHUTZEN RIFLES, UNKNOWN MAKER

	V.G.	Exc.	Prior Year Exc. Value
RIFLE, SINGLESHOT			
☐ **Aydt System**, Various Calibers, Dropping Block, Plain Tyrol Stock, Light Engraving, Target Sights, *Modern*	350.00	600.00	600.00
☐ **Aydt System**, Various Calibers, Dropping Block, Fancy Tyrol Stock, Fancy Engraving, Target Sights, *Modern*	575.00	900.00	900.00
☐ **Martini System**, Various Calibers, Dropping Block, Fancy Tyrol Stock, Fancy Engraving, Target Sights, *Modern*	525.00	835.00	825.00

SCHWARZLOSE

Andreas W. Schwarzlose, Berlin, Germany 1911-1927.

	V.G.	Exc.	Prior Year Exc. Value
HANDGUN, SEMI-AUTOMATIC			
☐ **Standardt**, 7.63mm Mauser, Clip Fed, Blue, *Curio*	2,000.00	2,975.00	2,850
☐ **M 1908 Pocket**, .32 ACP, Blow-Forward, Clip Fed, Grip Safety, *Curio*	325.00	475.00	475.00

Schwarzlose M1908 WAC

	V.G.	Exc.	Prior Year Exc. Value
☐ **M 1908 W.A.C. Pocket**, .32 ACP, Blow-Forward, Clip Fed, Grip Safety, *Curio*	300.00	450.00	450.00

SCOTT ARMS CO.
Probably Norwich Fall Pistol Co., c. 1880.

HANDGUN, REVOLVER

☐ **.32 Short R.F.**, 5 Shot, Spur Trigger, Solid Frame, Single Action, *Antique*	95.00	170.00	160.00

SCOTT, D.
Edinburgh, Scotland 1727-1745.

HANDGUN, FLINTLOCK

☐ **Queen Anne Type**, .59, Screw Barrel, Holster Pistol, Marked "Edinboro," *Antique*	950.00	1,575.00	1,500.00

SCOTT REVOLVER-RIFLE
Hopkins & Allen, c. 1880.

HANDGUN, REVOLVER

☐ **24½" Brass Barrel**, .38 Short R.F., 5 Shot, Spur Trigger, Solid Frame, Single Action, *Antique*	155.00	275.00	250.00

SCOUT
Made by Stevens.

SHOTGUN, DOUBLE BARREL, SIDE-BY-SIDE

☐ **Model 311**, Various Gauges, Hammerless, Steel Barrel, *Modern*	110.00	175.00	165.00

SCOUT
Made by Hood Firearms for Frankfurt Hardware of Milwaukee, Wisc., c. 1870.

HANDGUN, REVOLVER

☐ **.32 Short R.F.**, 5 Shot, Spur Trigger, Solid Frame, Single Action, *Antique*	90.00	165.00	160.00

S.E.A.M.
Fab. d'Armes de Soc. Espanola de Armas y Municiones, Eibar, Spain.

HANDGUN, SEMI-AUTOMATIC

☐ **Eibar Type**, .25 ACP, 13 Slide Grooves, Fair Quality, Clip Fed, Blue, *Modern*	85.00	125.00	120.00

	V.G.	Exc.	Prior Year Exc. Value
☐ **Eibar Type**, .25 ACP, 11 Slide Grooves, Good Quality, Clip Fed, Blue, *Modern*	110.00	155.00	145.00
☐ **Walther Type**, .25 ACP, Clip Fed, Blue, *Modern*	155.00	220.00	195.00

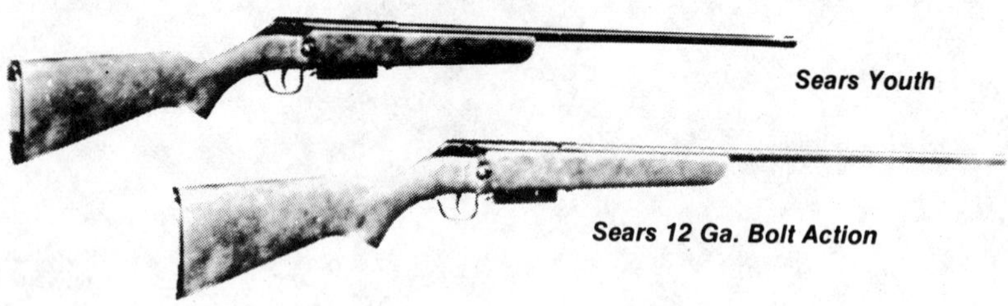
Sears Youth

Sears 12 Ga. Bolt Action

SEARS

Sears, Roebuck & Co., Chicago, Ill. Also see Ted Williams.

RIFLE, BOLT ACTION

☐ **Semi-Sporterized Mauser**, 8mm Mauser, Converted Military, *Modern*	80.00	125.00	115.00
☐ **Sporterized Mauser**, 8mm Mauser, Converted Military, Recoil Pad, *Modern*	85.00	135.00	125.00

SHOTGUN, BOLT ACTION

☐ **.410 Gauge**, Singleshot, Plain, *Modern*	25.00	40.00	35.00
☐ **.410 Gauge**, Clip Fed, Blue, Plain, *Modern*	30.00	45.00	45.00
☐ **12 or 20 Gauges**, Clip Fed, Blue, Plain, *Modern*	40.00	55.00	50.00
☐ **12 or 20 Gauges**, Clip Fed, Adjustable Choke, Blue, Plain, *Modern*	40.00	60.00	55.00

SHOTGUN, SINGLESHOT

☐ **Various Gauges**, Top Break, Plain, *Modern*	35.00	45.00	40.00
☐ **Youth**, 20 or .410 Gauges, Plain, *Modern*	35.00	45.00	40.00

SECRET SERVICE SPECIAL

Made for Fred Biffar, Chicago by Iver-Johnson and Meriden.

HANDGUN, REVOLVER

☐ **.32 S & W**, 5 Shot, Top Break, Hammerless, Double Action, *Modern*	80.00	130.00	125.00
☐ **.38 S & W**, 5 Shot, Top Break, Hammerless, Double Action, *Modern*	80.00	130.00	125.00

SECURITY INDUSTRIES OF AMERICA

Little Ferry, N.J.

HANDGUN, REVOLVER

☐ **Police Pocket**, .357 Magnum, Stainless Steel, 2" Barrel, Swing-Out Cylinder, Double Action, Spurless Hammer, *Modern*	120.00	170.00	165.00
☐ **Security Undercover**, .357 Magnum, Stainless Steel, 2½" Barrel, Swing-Out Cylinder, Double Action, *Modern*	115.00	165.00	160.00

SEDGLEY, R.F., INC.

Philadelphia, Pa. 1911-1938. Successor to Henry Kolb.

	V.G.	Exc.	Prior Year Exc. Value
HANDGUN, REVOLVER			
☐ **Baby Hammerless**, .22 L.R.R.F., Double Action, Folding Trigger, *Modern*	85.00	145.00	145.00
RIFLE, BOLT ACTION			
☐ **Springfield**, Various Calibers, Sporting Rifle, Lyman Sights, Checkered Stock, *Modern*	300.00	385.00	375.00
☐ **Springfield**, Various Calibers, Sporting Rifle, Lyman Sights, Checkered Stock, Left-Hand, *Modern*	340.00	435.00	425.00
☐ **Springfield**, Various Calibers, Sporting Rifle, Lyman Sights, Checkered Stock, Full-Stocked, *Modern*	375.00	500.00	500.00

Selecta Model 1919

SELECTA

Echave y Arizmendi, Eibar, Spain.

	V.G.	Exc.	Prior Year Exc. Value
HANDGUN, SEMI-AUTOMATIC			
☐ **Model 1918**, .25 ACP, Double Safety, Clip Fed, *Modern*	115.00	155.00	150.00
☐ **Model 1918**, .25 ACP, Triple Safety, Clip Fed, *Modern*	130.00	175.00	170.00
☐ **Model 1919**, .32 ACP, Double Safety, Clip Fed, *Modern*	125.00	170.00	165.00
☐ **Model 1919**, .32 ACP, Triple Safety, Clip Fed, *Modern*	145.00	190.00	180.00

SEMMERLING

Semmerling Corp., Newton, Mass.

	V.G.	Exc.	Prior Year Exc. Value
HANDGUN, MANUAL REPEATER			
☐ **LM-4**, .45 ACP, Double Action, Clip Fed, *Modern*	400.00	560.00	565.00

SHAKANOOSA ARMS MFG. CO.

1862-1864. See Confederate Military.

	V.G.	Exc.	Prior Year Exc. Value
RIFLE, PERCUSSION			
☐ **.58**, Military, Carbine, (C S A), *Antique*	1,275.00	1,800.00	1,750.00
☐ **.58**, Military, (C S A), *Antique*	950.00	1,325.00	1,300.00

SHARPE

English, 1670-1680.

	V.G.	Exc.	Prior Year Exc. Value
HANDGUN, FLINTLOCK			
☐ **Pair**, Pocket Pistol, Screw Barrel, Octagon, High Quality, *Antique*	1,850.00	3,250.00	3,200.00

SHARPS

Made by Shiloh Products, Farmingdale, N.Y.

	V.G.	Exc.	Prior Year Exc. Value
RIFLE, PERCUSSION			
☐ **Model 1859 New Model Cavalry Carbine**, .54, Reproduction, *Antique*	250.00	350.00	350.00
☐ **Model 1863 Cavalry Carbine**, .54, Reproduction, *Antique*	200.00	300.00	300.00
☐ **Model 1863 Sporting Rifle #3**, .54, Reproduction, *Antique*	235.00	350.00	350.00
☐ **Model 1863 Sporting Rifle #2**, .54, Reproduction, *Antique*	275.00	370.00	370.00
☐ **Model 1862 Robinson Confederate Cavalry Carbine**, .54, Reproduction, *Antique*	225.00	325.00	325.00
☐ **Model 1863 New Model Military Rifle**, .54, Reproduction, *Antique*	240.00	350.00	350.00
RIFLE, SINGLESHOT			
☐ **Model 1874 Military Rifle**, Various Calibers, Reproduction, *Modern*	250.00	385.00	380.00
☐ **Model 1874 Military Carbine**, Various Calibers, Reproduction, *Modern*	225.00	330.00	325.00
☐ **Model 1874 Hunter's Rifle**, Various Calibers, Reproduction, *Modern*	245.00	360.00	350.00
☐ **Model 1874 Business Rifle**, Various Calibers, Reproduction, *Modern*	250.00	360.00	350.00
☐ **Model 1874 Sporting Rifle #2**, Various Calibers, Reproduction, *Modern*	325.00	460.00	450.00
☐ **Model 1874 Sporting Rifle #3**, Various Calibers, Reproduction, *Modern*	250.00	380.00	375.00

Christian Sharps Patent Single Shot, .36 Caliber

SHARPS, CHRISTIAN

Mill Creek, Pa. 1848; moved to Hartford, Conn. in 1851 and became Sharps Rifle Mfg. Co., changing it's name to Sharps Rifle Co. in 1874, continuing operations until 1881. In 1854 formed C. Sharps & Co. in Philadelphia, Pa., became Sharps & Hankins in 1862, C. Sharps & Co. again in 1866, and continued until 1874.

	V.G.	Exc.	Prior Year Exc. Value
HANDGUN, MULTI-BARREL			
☐ **.22 R.F.**, Model 1, 4 Barreled Pistol, Frame to Muzzle Distance ⅛", *Antique*	265.00	390.00	375.00
☐ **.22 R.F.**, Model 1, 4 Barreled Pistol, Frame to Muzzle Distance ½", *Antique*	195.00	285.00	275.00
☐ **.22 R.F.**, Model 1, 4 Barreled Pistol, Frame to Muzzle Distance ¼", *Antique*	235.00	360.00	345.00
☐ **.22 R.F.**, Model 1, 4 Barreled Pistol, Frame to Muzzle Distance ¼", Iron Frame, *Antique*	340.00	480.00	465.00
☐ **.30 R.F.**, Model 2, 4 Barreled Pistol, Frame to Muzzle Distance ⅝", *Antique*	220.00	340.00	325.00
☐ **.30 R.F.**, Model 2, 4 Barreled Pistol, Frame to Muzzle Distance ¾", *Antique*	290.00	440.00	430.00
☐ **.32 R.F.**, Model 3, 4 Barreled Pistol, Mechanism in Frame, *Antique*	290.00	465.00	450.00
☐ **.32 R.F.**, Model 3, 4 Barreled Pistol, Mechanism on Hammer, *Antique*	260.00	375.00	365.00
☐ **.32 R.F. Bulldog**, Model 4, 4 Barreled Pistol, Screw Under Frame, *Antique*	260.00	375.00	365.00
☐ **.32 R.F. Bulldog**, Model 4, 4 Barreled Pistol, Pin on Side of Frame, *Antique*	290.00	440.00	425.00
HANDGUN, PERCUSSION			
☐ **Revolver**, .25, Tip-Up, 6 Shot, Blue, Spur Trigger, Single Action, *Antique*	525.00	895.00	875.00
☐ **Bryce Revolver**, .25, Tip-Up, 6 Shot, Blue, Spur Trigger, Single Action, *Antique*	575.00	975.00	950.00
HANDGUN, SINGLESHOT			
☐ **Small Frame,** Various Calibers, Single Action Dropping Block, Hammer, *Antique,*	1000.00	1800.00	1850.00
☐ **Medium Frame,** Various Calibers, Single Action, Dropping Block, Hammer, *Antique*	995.00	1975.00	1950.00
RIFLE, PERCUSSION			
☐ **1851 Carbine**, .52, Maynard Primer, *Antique*	1,450.00	2,650.00	2,500.00
☐ **1852 Carbine**, .52, Pellet Primer, *Antique*	625.00	895.00	875.00
☐ **1853 Carbine**, .52, Pellet Primer, *Antique*	645.00	975.00	950.00
☐ **1855 Carbine**, .52, Maynard Primer, *Antique*	795.00	1,550.00	1,500.00
☐ **1855 Rifle**, .52, Maynard Primer, *Antique*	1,300.00	1,975.00	1,950.00
☐ **1859 Carbine**, .52, Pellet Primer, *Antique*	640.00	995.00	995.00
☐ **1863 Carbine**, .52, Lawrence Cut-off, *Antique*	475.00	800.00	785.00
☐ **1863 Rifle**, .52, Lawrence Cut-off, *Antique*	975.00	1,550.00	1,500.00
RIFLE, SINGLESHOT			
☐ **1874 Sporting Rifle**, Various Calibers, Set Trigger, Target Sights, *Antique*	995.00	1,850.00	1,800.00
☐ **1874 Hunting Rifle**, Various Calibers, Open Sights, *Antique*	750.00	1,350.00	1,300.00
☐ **Long Range Rifle**, Various Calibers, Target Sights, *Antique*	1,800.00	2,900.00	2,850.00

SHARPSHOOTER

Hijos de Calixto Arrizabalaga, Eibar, Spain, c. 1920.

	V.G.	Exc.	Prior Year Exc. Value
HANDGUN, SEMI-AUTOMATIC			
☐ **"Sharp-Sooter"**, .25 ACP, Clip Fed, Hammer, Hinged Barrel, Blue, *Curio*	140.00	200.00	195.00
☐ **"Sharp-Sooter"**, .32 ACP, Clip Fed, Hammer, Hinged Barrel, Blue, *Curio*	160.00	230.00	225.00

	V.G.	Exc.	Prior Year Exc. Value
☐ **"Sharp-Sooter"**, .380 ACP, Clip Fed, Hammer, Hinged Barrel, Blue, *Curio*	195.00	290.00	280.00

SHATTUCK, C.S.

Hatfield, Mass. 1880-1890.

HANDGUN, REVOLVER

☐ **Lincoln/Garfield Grips**, Hard Rubber, *Add* **20%-30%**

	V.G.	Exc.	Prior Year Exc. Value
☐ **.22 R.F.**, Single Action, Spur Trigger, Swing-Out Cylinder, *Antique*	165.00	290.00	275.00
☐ **.32 R.F.**, Single Action, Spur Trigger, Swing-Out Cylinder, *Antique*	130.00	220.00	200.00
☐ **.38 R.F.**, Single Action, Spur Trigger, Swing-Out Cylinder, *Antique*	185.00	325.00	300.00
☐ **.41 R.F.**, Single Action, Spur Trigger, Swing-Out Cylinder, *Antique*	290.00	425.00	400.00

SHAW, JOHN

London, England, c. 1688.

HANDGUN, FLINTLOCK

	V.G.	Exc.	Prior Year Exc. Value
☐ **Holster Pistol**, Engraved, Steel Mounts, High Quality, *Antique*	1,450.00	2,200.00	2,100.00

SHELL, JOHN

Leslie County, Ky. 1810-1880. See Kentucky Rifles.

SHERIDEN

Racine, Wisc. 1953-1960.

HANDGUN, SINGLESHOT

	V.G.	Exc.	Prior Year Exc. Value
☐ **Knocabout**, .22 L.R.R.F., Tip-Up Barrel, Single Action, Hammer, Blue, *Modern*	100.00	155.00	145.00

SHILEN

Ennis, Tex.

RIFLE, BOLT ACTION

	V.G.	Exc.	Prior Year Exc. Value
☐ **DGA Sporter**, Various Calibers, Blind Magazine, Plain Stock, *Modern*	400.00	600.00	600.00
☐ **DGA Benchrest**, Various Calibers, Target Rifle, *Modern*	475.00	675.00	675.00
☐ **DGA Silhouette**, Various Calibers, Target Rifle, *Modern*	400.00	575.00	575.00
☐ **DGA Varmint**, Various Calibers, Heavy Barrel, *Modern*	400.00	600.00	600.00

SHORER, ANDREW

Northampton, Pa. 1775-1776. See Kentucky Rifles.

	V.G.	Exc.	Prior Year Exc. Value

SICKEL'S ARMS CO.

Belgium for Robert Sickels & Preston Co., Davenport, Iowa.

SHOTGUN, DOUBLE BARREL, SIDE-BY-SIDE

	V.G.	Exc.	Prior Year Exc. Value
☐ **Various Gauges**, Outside Hammers, Damascus Barrel, *Modern*	100.00	170.00	175.00
☐ **Various Gauges**, Hammerless, Steel Barrel, *Modern*	135.00	190.00	200.00
☐ **Various Gauges**, Hammerless, Damascus Barrel, *Modern*	100.00	170.00	175.00
☐ **Various Gauges**, Outside Hammers, Steel Barrel, *Modern*	125.00	185.00	190.00

SHOTGUN, SINGLESHOT

	V.G.	Exc.	Prior Year Exc. Value
☐ **Various Gauges**, Hammer, Steel Barrel, *Modern*	55.00	85.00	85.00

S.I.G.

Schweizerische Industrie Gesellschaft, Neuhausen, Switzerland since 1857.

AUTOMATIC WEAPON, ASSAULT RIFLE

	V.G.	Exc.	Prior Year Exc. Value
☐ **SIG 510**, .308 Win., Clip Fed, Bipod, *Class 3*	950.00	1,475.00	1,400.00

HANDGUN, SEMI-AUTOMATIC

	V.G.	Exc.	Prior Year Exc. Value
☐ **P210 Luxus**, Various Calibers, Clip Fed, Fancy Engraving, Gold Inlay, High-Polish Blue Finish, Carved Wood Grips, *Modern*	1,750.00	2,700.00	2,650.00
☐ **P210-1**, .22 L.R.R.F., Clip Fed, Blue, High-Polish Finish, Wood Grips, *Modern*	700.00	1,175.00	1,150.00
☐ **P210-1**, .30 Luger, Clip Fed, Blue, High-Polish Finish, Wood Grips, *Modern*	725.00	1,195.00	1,175.00
☐ **P210-1**, 9mm Luger, Clip Fed, Blue, High-Polish Finish, Wood Grips, *Modern*	725.00	1,195.00	1,175.00
☐ **P210-1**, .22 L.R.R.F., Conversion Unit Only *Modern*	375.00	525.00	500.00
☐ **P210-1**, Various Calibers, Clip Fed, High-Polish Finish, with 3 Caliber Conv. Units, Wood Grips, *Modern*	1,275.00	1,875.00	1,850.00
☐ **P210-2**, .30 Luger, Clip Fed, Blue, Plastic Stock, *Modern*	675.00	975.00	950.00
☐ **P210-2**, 9mm Luger, Clip Fed, Blue, Plastic Stock, *Modern*	650.00	925.00	900.00
☐ **P210-5**, .30 Luger, Clip Fed, Blue, Plastic Stock, Target Pistol, 6" Barrel, *Modern*	750.00	1,225.00	1,200.00
☐ **P210-5**, 9mm Luger, Clip Fed, Blue, Plastic Stock, Target Pistol, 6" Barrel, *Modern*	700.00	1,175.00	1,150.00
☐ **P210-6**, .30 Luger, Clip Fed, Blue, Plastic Stock, Target Pistol, 4¾" Barrel, *Modern*	675.00	1025.00	1,000.00
☐ **P210-6**, 9mm Luger, Clip Fed, Blue, Plastic Stock, Target Pistol, 4¾" Barrel, *Modern*	600.00	975.00	950.00
☐ **P 220 SIG-Sauer**, Various Calibers, Clip Fed, Double Action, Blue, *Modern*	300.00	425.00	425.00
☐ **P 225 SIG-Sauer**, 9mm Luger, Clip Fed, Double Action, Blue, *Modern*	260.00	375.00	375.00
☐ **P 230 SIG-Sauer**, 9mm Police, Clip Fed, Double Action, Blue, *Modern*	245.00	335.00	335.00
☐ **P 230 SIG-Sauer**, Various Calibers, Clip Fed, Double Action, Blue, *Modern*	200.00	300.00	300.00
☐ **SP 47/8**, 9mm Luger, Clip Fed, German Border Patrol, *Modern*	1,165.00	1,825.00	1,800.00

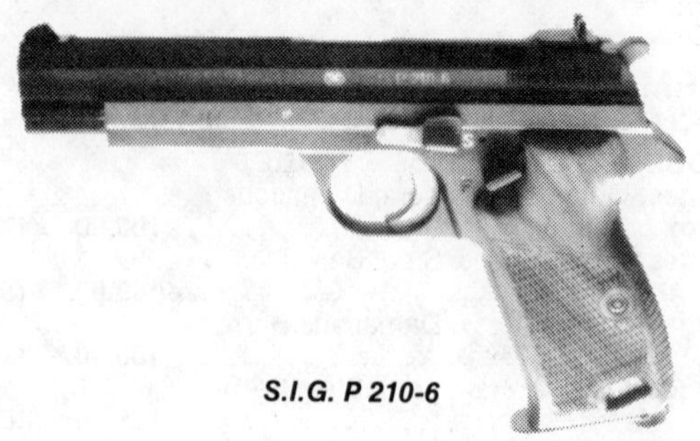

S.I.G. P 210-6

	V.G.	Exc.	Prior Year Exc. Value
☐ **SP 47/8**, 9mm Luger, Clip Fed, Swiss Military, *Modern*	1,675.00	2,550.00	2,500.00
RIFLE, SEMI-AUTOMATIC			
☐ **SIG AMT**, .308 Win., Clip Fed, Bipod, *Modern*	750.00	1,175.00	1,100.00
☐ **SIG STG-57**, 7.5 Swiss, Clip Fed, Bipod, *Modern*	775.00	1,250.00	1,200.00

SILE

Imported by Sile Distributers, N.Y.C., N.Y.

	V.G.	Exc.	Prior Year Exc. Value
HANDGUN, SEMI-AUTOMATIC			
☐ **Seecamp**, .25 ACP, Double Action, Clip Fed, Stainless Steel, *Modern*	85.00	135.00	130.00

SIMPLEX

Made in Belgium. Also see Bergmann.

	V.G.	Exc.	Prior Year Exc. Value
HANDGUN, SEMI-AUTOMATIC			
☐ **Simplex**, 8mm Bergmann, Blue, *Curio*	400.00	675.00	650.00

SIMSON & CO.

Waffenfabrik Simson & Co., Suhl, Germany 1910-1939. Also see Luger.

	V.G.	Exc.	Prior Year Exc. Value
HANDGUN, SEMI-AUTOMATIC			
☐ **Vest Pocket**, .25 ACP, Clip Fed, Blue, *Modern*	300.00	460.00	450.00
RIFLE, BOLT ACTION			
☐ **Precision Carbine**, 6mm Shot, Singleshot, Plain, *Modern*	35.00	50.00	50.00
☐ **Precision Carbine**, 9mm Shot, Singleshot, Plain, *Modern*	40.00	65.00	60.00
☐ **Model 1933**, .22 Extra Long, Singleshot, Checkered tock, Target Sights, *Modern*	70.00	100.00	95.00
☐ **Sportrifle #7**, .22 Extra Long, Singleshot, Checkered Stock, Target Sights, *Modern*	55.00	85.00	80.00
SHOTGUN, DOUBLE BARREL, OVER-UNDER			
☐ **Trap Grade**, 12 Ga., Automatic Ejectors, Checkered Stock, Engraved, Cocking Indicators, *Modern*	950.00	1,550.00	1,500.00
SHOTGUN, DOUBLE BARREL, SIDE-BY-SIDE			
☐ **Astora**, Various Calibers, Checkered Stock, Plain, *Modern*	200.00	325.00	300.00

	V.G.	Exc.	Prior Year Exc. Value
☐ **Magnum**, 12 Gauge 3″, Checkered Stock, Engraved, *Modern*	500.00	720.00	700.00
☐ **Monte Carlo**, 12 Ga., Checkered Stock, Fancy Engraving, Automatic Ejectors, Sidelock, *Modern*	900.00	1,550.00	1,500.00

SINGER

Arizmendi y Goenaga, Eibar, Spain.

HANDGUN, SEMI-AUTOMATIC

	V.G.	Exc.	Prior Year Exc. Value
☐ **.25 ACP**, Clip Fed, Blue, *Modern*	80.00	130.00	125.00
☐ **.32 ACP**, Clip Fed, Blue, *Modern*	90.00	140.00	135.00

SINGER

Frantisek Dusek, Opocno, Czechoslovakia.

HANDGUN, SEMI-AUTOMATIC

	V.G.	Exc.	Prior Year Exc. Value
☐ **Duo**, .25 ACP, Clip Fed, Blue, *Modern*	80.00	120.00	115.00

SJOGREN

Sweden.

SHOTGUN, SEMI-AUTOMATIC

	V.G.	Exc.	Prior Year Exc. Value
☐ **12 Ga.**, 5 Shot, Checkered Stock, Recoil Operated, *Curio*	300.00	425.00	400.00

SKB

Tokyo, Japan.

SHOTGUN, DOUBLE BARREL, OVER-UNDER

	V.G.	Exc.	Prior Year Exc. Value
☐ **Model 500**, 12 and 20 Gauges, Field Grade, Selective Ejector, Vent Rib, *Modern*	250.00	350.00	350.00
☐ **Model 500**, 12 Ga. Mag. 3″, Field Grade, Selective Ejector, Vent Rib, *Modern*	260.00	360.00	360.00
☐ **Model 600**, 12 Ga., Trap Grade, Selective Ejector, Vent Rib, *Modern*	360.00	460.00	460.00
☐ **Model 600**, 12 Ga., Trap Grade, Selective Ejector, Vent Rib, Monte Carlo Stock, *Modern*	360.00	460.00	460.00
☐ **Model 600**, 12 and 20 Gauges, Field Grade, Selective Ejector, Vent Rib, *Modern*	350.00	440.00	440.00
☐ **Model 600**, 12 and 20 Gauges, Skeet Grade, Selective Ejector, Vent Rib, *Modern*	360.00	460.00	460.00
☐ **Model 600**, 20 and .410 Gauges, Skeet Grade, Selective Ejector, Vent Rib, *Modern*	360.00	470.00	470.00
☐ **Model 600 Combo Set**, Various Gauges, Skeet Grade, Selective Ejector, Vent Rib, Cased, *Modern*	800.00	1,100.00	1,100.00
☐ **Model 680 English**, 12 and 20 Gauges, Field Grade, Selective Ejector, Vent Rib, *Modern*	370.00	460.00	460.00
☐ **Model 700**, 12 Ga., Trap Grade, Selective Ejector, Vent Rib, *Modern*	400.00	550.00	550.00
☐ **Model 700**, 12 Ga., Trap Grade, Selective Ejector, Vent Rib, Monte Carlo Stock, *Modern*	400.00	550.00	550.00
☐ **Model 700**, 12 and 20 Gauges, Skeet Grade, Selective Ejector, Vent Rib, *Modern*	400.00	550.00	550.00
☐ **Model 700 Combo Set**, Various Gauges, Skeet Grade, Selective Ejector, Vent Rib, Cased, *Modern*	900.00	1,450.00	1,450.00

	V.G.	Exc.	Prior Year Exc. Value
SHOTGUN, SEMI-AUTOMATIC			
☐ **900 Deluxe**, 12 and 20 Gauges, Vent Rib, *Modern*	150.00	180.00	180.00
☐ **900 XL**, 12 Ga., Trap Grade, *Modern*	170.00	225.00	225.00
☐ **900 XL**, 12 Ga., Trap Grade, Monte Carlo Stock, *Modern*	170.00	230.00	230.00
☐ **900 XL**, 12 and 20 Gauges, Skeet Grade, *Modern*	160.00	215.00	215.00
☐ **900 XL Deluxe**, 12 and 20 Gauges, Vent Rib, *Modern*	160.00	200.00	200.00
☐ **900 XL Slug**, 12 and 20 Gauges, Open Rear Sight, *Modern*	150.00	200.00	200.00

SLOANS

Importers, N.Y.C. Also see Charles Daly.

	V.G.	Exc.	Prior Year Exc. Value
SHOTGUN, DOUBLE BARREL, SIDE-BY-SIDE			
☐ **POS**, .410 Ga., Checkered Stock, Hammerless, Double Trigger, *Modern*	115.00	160.00	155.00
☐ **POS**, 10 Ga., 3½", Checkered Stock, Hammerless, Double Trigger, *Modern*	135.00	190.00	185.00
☐ **POS**, 12 and 20 Gauges, Checkered Stock, Hammerless, Double Trigger, *Modern*	100.00	155.00	150.00
☐ **POS Coach Gun**, 12 and 20 Gauges, Checkered Stock, Outside Hammers, Double Trigger, *Modern*	115.00	160.00	155.00

S-M CORP.

Sydney Manson, Alexandria, Va., c. 1953.

	V.G.	Exc.	Prior Year Exc. Value
HANDGUN, SEMI-AUTOMATIC			
☐ **Sporter**, .22 L.R.R.F., Blowback, *Modern*	90.00	135.00	125.00

SMITH & WESSON

Started in Norwich, Conn. in 1855 as Volcanic Repeating Arms Co. Reorganized at Springfield, Mass. as Smith & Wesson in 1857 (Volcanic Repeating Arms moved to New Haven, Conn. in 1856 and was purchased in 1857 by Winchester Repeating Arms Co.). Smith & Wesson at Springfield, Mass. to date. Also see U.S. Military.

	V.G.	Exc.	Prior Year Exc. Value
AUTOMATIC WEAPON, SUBMACHINE GUN			
☐ **Model 76,** 9mm Luger, Clip Fed, Commercial, *Class 3*	440.00	615.00	600.00
HANDGUN, REVOLVER			
☐ **.32 Double Action,** .32 S & W, 1st Model, Top Break, 5 Shot, Straight-Cut Sideplate, Rocker Cylinder Stop, *Antique*	950.00	1450.00	1400.00
☐ **.32 Double Action,** .32 S & W, 2nd Model, Top Break, 5 Shot, Irregularly-Cut Sideplate, Rocker Cylinder Stop, *Antique*	150.00	210.00	200.00
☐ **.32 Double Action,** .32 S & W, 3rd Model, Top Break, 5 Shot, Irregularly-Cut Sideplate, *Antique*	140.00	190.00	180.00
☐ **.32 Double Action,** .32 S & W, 4th Model, Round-Back Trigger Guard, Top Break, 5 Shot, Irregularly-Cut Sideplate, *Modern*	125.00	175.00	170.00

	V.G.	Exc.	Prior Year Exc. Value
☐ **.32 Double Action,** .32 S & W, 5th Model, Round-Back Trigger Guard, Top Break, 5 Shot, Irregularly-Cut Sideplate, Front Sight Forged on Barrel, *Modern*	125.00	175.00	170.00
☐ **.32 Hand Ejector,** .32 S & W Long, 1st Model, Solid Frame, Swing-Out Cylinder, Hammer Actuated Cylinder Stop, 6 Shot, *Modern*	330.00	495.00	485.00
☐ **.32 Hand Ejector,** .32 S & W Long, Solid Frame, Swing-Out Cylinder, 6 Shot, Target Sights, Double Action, *Modern*	675.00	1250.00	1200.00
☐ **.32 Hand Ejector 1903,** .32 S & W Long, Solid Frame, Swing-Out Cylinder, 6 Shot, Double Action, *Modern*	120.00	195.00	190.00
☐ **.32 Regulation Police,** .32 S & W Long, Solid Frame, Swing-Out Cylinder, 6 Shot, Double Action, *Modern*	125.00	185.00	175.00
☐ **.32 Safety Hammerless,** .32 S & W, 1st Model, Double Action, Top Break, 5 Shot, Push-Button Latch, *Modern*	165.00	280.00	265.00
☐ **.32 Safety Hammerless,** .32 S & W, 2nd Model, Double Action, Top Break, 5 Shot, T Latch, *Modern*	105.00	165.00	160.00
☐ **.32 Safety Hammerless,** .32 S & W, 3rd Model, Double Action, Top Break, 5 Shot, Over #170,000, *Modern*	105.00	175.00	170.00
☐ **.32 Single Action,** .32 S & W, Top Break, Spur Trigger, 5 Shot, *Antique*	290.00	395.00	375.00
☐ **.32 Single Action,** .32 S & W, 6″ or 8″ Barrel, *Add* **50%-75%**			
☐ **.32 Single Action,** .32 S & W, 10″ Barrel, *Add* **75%-100%**			
☐ **.38 D A Perfected,** .38 S & W, Solid Trigger Guard, Thumbpiece Hand-Ejector Action, Top Break, Double Action, *Modern*	205.00	330.00	325.00
☐ **.38 D A Perfected,** .38 S & W, made without Thumbpiece, Hand-Ejector Action, Top Break, Double Action, *Modern*	365.00	485.00	480.00
☐ **.38 Double Action,** .38 S & W, 1st Model, Straight-Cut Sideplate, Rocker Cylinder Stop, Double Action, Top Break, 5 Shot, *Antique*	490.00	700.00	685.00
☐ **.38 Double Action,** .38 S & W, 2nd Model, Irregularly-Cut Sideplate, Rocker Cylinder Stop, Double Action, Top Break, 5 Shot, *Antique*	140.00	210.00	200.00
☐ **.38 Double Action,** .38 S & W, 3rd Model, Irregularly-Cut Sideplate, Double Action, Top Break, 5 Shot, *Antique*	140.00	205.00	195.00
☐ **.38 Double Action,** .38 S & W, 4th Model, #'s 322,701-539,000, Double Action, Top Break, 5 Shot, *Modern*	100.00	175.00	170.00
☐ **.38 Double Action,** .38 S & W, 5th Model, #'s 539,001-554,077. Double Action, Top Break, 5 Shot, *Modern*	100.00	165.00	160.00
☐ **.38 Double Action,** .38 S & W, 4th Model, #'s 322,701-539,000, Double Action, Top Break, 5 Shot, Adjustable Sights, *Modern*	305.00	460.00	445.00

	V.G.	Exc.	Prior Year Exc. Value
☐ **.38 Double Action,** .38 S & W, 5th Model, #'s 539,001-554,077, Double Action, Top Break, 5 Shot, Adjustable Sights, *Modern*	300.00	400.00	390.00
☐ **.38 Hand Ejector,** .38 Long Colt, 1st Model, Solid Frame, Swing-Out Cylinder, no Cylinder-Pin Front-Lock, U.S. Army Model, *Modern*	415.00	710.00	695.00
☐ **.38 Hand Ejector,** .38 Long Colt, 1st Model, Solid Frame, Swing-Out Cylinder, no Cylinder-Pin Front-Lock, U.S. Navy Model, *Modern*	435.00	690.00	675.00
☐ **.38 Hand Ejector,** .38 Long Colt, 2nd Model, Solid Frame, Swing-Out Cylinder, U.S. Navy Model, *Modern*	410.00	665.00	650.00
☐ **.38 Hand Ejector,** .38 Special, 1st Model, Solid Frame, Swing-Out Cylinder, no Cylinder-Pin Front-Lock, *Modern*	225.00	360.00	350.00
☐ **.38 Hand Ejector,** .38 Special, 1st Model, Solid Frame, Swing-Out Cylinder, no Cylinder-Pin Front-Lock, Adjustable Sights, *Modern*	410.00	590.00	575.00
☐ **.38 Hand Ejector,** .38 Special, 2nd Model, Solid Frame, Swing-Out Cylinder, *Modern*	190.00	300.00	290.00
☐ **.38 Hand Ejector,** .38 Special, 2nd Model, Solid Frame, Swing-Out Cylinder, Adjustable Sights, *Modern*	400.00	565.00	550.00
☐ **.38 Hand Ejector 1902,** .38 Special, Military and Police, Solid Frame, Swing-Out Cylinder, Double Action, *Modern*	180.00	275.00	265.00
☐ **.38 Hand Ejector 1902,** .38 Special, Military and Police, Solid Frame, Swing-Out Cylinder, Double Action, Adjustable Sights, *Modern*	335.00	465.00	450.00
☐ **.38 Hand Ejector 1905,** .38 Special, Military and Police, Solid Frame, Swing-Out Cylinder, Double Action, *Modern*	160.00	260.00	250.00
☐ **.38 Hand Ejector 1905,** .38 Special, Military and Police, Solid Frame, Swing-Out Cylinder, Double Action, Adjustable Sights, *Modern*	330.00	465.00	450.00
☐ **.38 Safety Hammerless,** .38 S & W, 1st Model-Button Latch, Release on Left Topstrap, Top Break, Double Action, *Antique*	250.00	375.00	365.00
☐ **.38 Safety Hammerless,** .38 S & W, 2nd Model-Button Latch, Release on Top of Frame, Top Break, Double Action, *Antique*	190.00	280.00	275.00
☐ **.38 Safety Hammerless,** .38 S & W, 3rd Model-Button Latch, Release on Rear Topstrap, Top Break, Double Action, *Antique*	160.00	240.00	235.00
☐ **.38 Safety Hammerless,** .38 S & W, 4th Model T-Shaped Latch, Top Break, Double Action, *Modern*	130.00	230.00	220.00
☐ **.38 Safety Hammerless,** .38 S & W, 5th Model T-Shaped Latch, Top Break, Double Action, Front Sight Forged on Barrel, *Modern*	125.00	210.00	200.00
☐ **.38 Single Action,** .38 S & W, 1st Model, Baby Russian, Top Break, Spur Trigger, *Antique*	240.00	360.00	345.00
☐ **.38 Single Action,** .38 S & W, 2nd Model, Top Break, Spur Trigger, Short Ejector Housing, *Antique*	170.00	250.00	240.00
☐ **.38 Single Action,** .38 S & W, 3rd Model, Top Break, with Trigger Guard, *Modern*	400.00	600.00	575.00

	V.G.	Exc.	Prior Year Exc. Value
☐ **.38 Single Action,** .38 S & W, 3rd Model, Top Break, with Trigger Guard, with Extra Single-Shot Barrel, *Modern*	650.00	900.00	885.00
☐ **.38 Single Action,** .38 S & W, Mexican Model, Top Break, Spur Trigger, 5 Shot, *Modern*	1150.00	1700.00	1650.00
☐ **.38 Win. Double Action,** .38-40 WCF, Top Break, *Modern*	675.00	1025.00	995.00
☐ **.44 Double Action,** for Target Sights, *Add* **20%-30%**			
☐ **.44 Double Action,** .44 Russian, 1st Model, Top Break, 6 Shot, *Antique*	420.00	550.00	525.00
☐ **.44 Double Action,** .44 Russian, Wesson Favorite, 6 Shot, Lightweight, Top Break, *Antique*	1150.00	1700.00	1650.00
☐ **.44 Double Action Frontier,** for Target Sights, *Add* **20%-30%**			
☐ **.44 Double Action Frontier,** .44-40 WCF, Top Break, 6 Shot, *Antique*	525.00	725.00	675.00
☐ **.44 Hand Ejector,** Calibers other than .44 Spec., *Add* **15%-25%**			
☐ **.44 Hand Ejector,** 1st Model, for Target Sights, *Add* **20%-30%**			
☐ **.44 Hand Ejector,** Calibers other than .44 Spec., *Add* **15%-25%**			
☐ **.44 Hand Ejector,** 2nd Model, for Target Sights, *Add* **20%-30%**			
☐ **.44 Hand Ejector,** 3rd Model, for Target Sights, *Add* **20%-30%**			
☐ **.44 Hand Ejector,** .44 Special, 1st Model, Triple-Lock, Solid Frame, Swing-Out Cylinder, New Century, *Modern*	490.00	750.00	725.00
☐ **.44 Hand Ejector,** .44 Special, 2nd Model, Un-Shrouded Ejector Rod, Solid Frame, Swing-Out Cylinder, *Modern*	350.00	490.00	475.00
☐ **.44 Hand Ejector,** .44 Special, 3rd Model, Shrouded Ejector Rod, Solid Frame, Swing-Out Cylinder, *Modern*	300.00	440.00	425.00
☐ **.455 MK II Hand Ejector,** Solid Frame, Swing-Out Cylinder, Double Action, Military, *Modern*	260.00	465.00	450.00
☐ **22/32 Bekeart Model,** .22 L.R.R.F., #'s 138,220-139,275, Target Pistol, Double Action, Adjustable Sights, 6″ Barrel, *Modern*	410.00	575.00	550.00

S & W Model 10

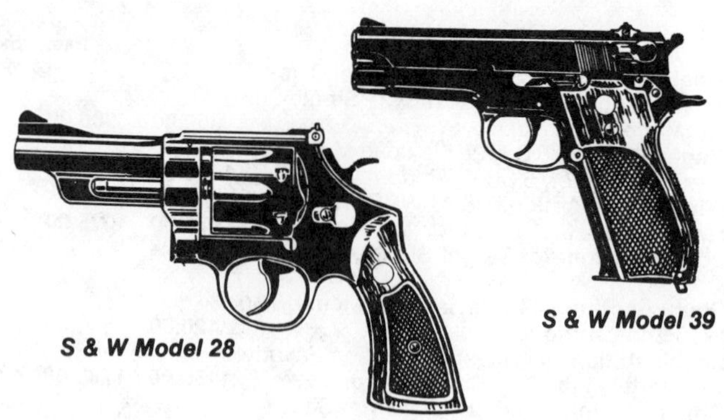

S & W Model 39

S & W Model 28

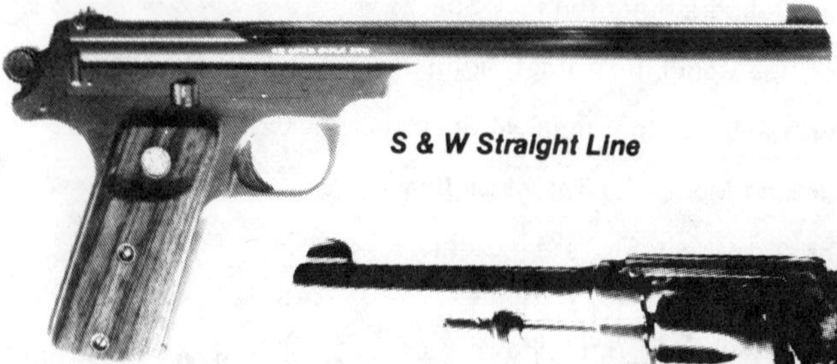

S & W Straight Line

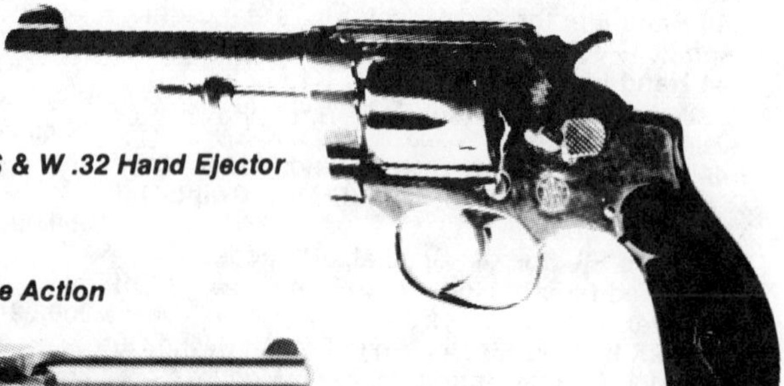

S & W .32 Hand Ejector

S & W .38 Double Action

S & W .38 Hand Ejector 1st Model

	V.G.	Exc.	Prior Year Exc. Value
☐ **22/32 Kit Gun,** .22 L.R.R.F., Early Model, Double Action, Adjustable Sights, 4″ Barrel, *Modern*	170.00	270.00	250.00
☐ **32/20 Hand Ejector,** .32-20 WCF, 1st Model, Solid Frame, Swing-Out Cylinder, 6 Shot, no Cylinder-Pin Front-Lock, *Modern*	270.00	410.00	385.00
☐ **32/20 Hand Ejector 1902,** .32-20 WCF, 2nd Model, Solid Frame, Swing-Out Cylinder, 6 Shot, *Modern*	225.00	340.00	325.00
☐ **32/20 Hand Ejector 1902,** .32-20 WCF, 2nd Model, Solid Frame, Swing-Out Cylinder, 6 Shot, Adjustable Sights, *Modern*	350.00	490.00	475.00
☐ **32/20 Hand Ejector 1905,** .32-20 WCF, Solid Frame, Swing-Out Cylinder, 6 Shot, Adjustable Sights, *Modern*	300.00	435.00	425.00
☐ **32/20 Hand Ejector 1905,** .32-20 WCF, Solid Frame, Swing-Out Cylinder, 6 Shot, *Modern*	195.00	310.00	295.00
☐ **38/200 British,** .38 S & W, Military & Police, Solid Frame, Swing-Out Cylinder, Double Action, Military, *Modern*	130.00	200.00	195.00
☐ **First Model Schofield,** .45 S & W, Top Break, Single Action, Military, *Antique*	950.00	1600.00	1500.00
☐ **First Model Schofield,** .45 S & W, Top Break, Single Action, Commercial, *Antique*	1600.00	2450.00	2300.00
☐ **First Model Schofield,** .45 S & W, Wells Fargo, Top Break, Single Action, *Antique*	1125.00	1425.00	1250.00
☐ **K-22 Hand Ejector,** .22 L.R.R.F., 1st Model, Double Action, Adjustable Sights, 6″ Barrel, *Modern*	185.00	275.00	260.00
☐ **K-22 Masterpiece,** .22 L.R.R.F., 2nd Model K-22 Hand Ejector, Speed Lock Action, Double Action, Adjustable Sights, 6″ Barrel, *Modern*	295.00	440.00	425.00
☐ **K-32 Hand Ejector,** .32 S & W Long, 1st Model, Pre-War, 6 Shot, Adjustable Sights, Target Pistol, *Modern*	430.00	595.00	575.00
☐ **K-32 Hand Ejector,** .32 S & W Long, 2nd Model, Post-War, 6 Shot, Adjustable Sights, Target Pistol, *Modern*	170.00	250.00	250.00
☐ **Model #1,** .22 Short R.F., 1st Issue, Tip-Up, Spur Trigger, 7 Shot, *Antique*	2000.00	2750.00	2700.00
☐ **Model #1,** .22 Short R.F., 2nd Issue, Tip-Up, Spur Trigger, 7 Shot, *Antique*	900.00	1500.00	1350.00
☐ **Model #1,** .22 Short R.F., 3rd Issue, Tip-Up, Spur Trigger, 7 Shot, *Antique*	575.00	950.00	850.00
☐ **Model #1½,** .32 Short R.F., 1st Issue, Tip-Up, Spur Trigger, 5 Shot, Non-Fluted Cylinder, *Antique*	230.00	375.00	360.00
☐ **Model #1½,** .32 Short R.F., 2nd Issue, Tip-Up, Spur Trigger, 5 Shot, Fluted Cylinder, *Antique*	210.00	360.00	350.00
☐ **Model #2 Old Army,** .32 Long R.F., Tip-Up, Spur Trigger, 6 Shot, *Antique*	350.00	475.00	465.00
☐ **Model #3 American,** .44 Henry, 1st Model, Single Action, Top Break, 6 Shot, *Antique*	1175.00	1750.00	1700.00
☐ **Model #3 American,** .44 Henry, 2nd Model, #'s 8,000-32,800, Single Action, Top Break, 6 Shot, *Antique*	950.00	1575.00	1500.00
☐ **Model #3 American,** .44 S & W, 1st Model, Single Action, Top Break, 6 Shot, *Antique*	720.00	985.00	945.00

	V.G.	Exc.	Prior Year Exc. Value
☐ **Model #3 American,** .44 S & W, 2nd Model, #'s 8,000-32,800, Single Action, Top Break, 6 Shot, *Antique*	625.00	880.00	835.00
☐ **Model #3 Frontier,** .44-40 WCF, Single Action, Top Break, 6 Shot, *Antique*	850.00	1250.00	1200.00
☐ **Model #3 New Model,** Calibers other than .44 Russian, *Add* **40%-60%**			
☐ **Model #3 New Model,** .44 Russian, Australian Police with Shoulder Stock, *Add* **200%-225%**			
☐ **Model #3 New Model,** .44 Russian, Single Action, Top Break, 6 Shot, *Antique*	550.00	720.00	695.00
☐ **Model #3 New Model,** .44 Russian Japanese Navy Issue, *Add* **30%-45%**			
☐ **Model #3 New Model,** .44 Russian, Australian Police with Shoulder Stock, *Add* **200%-225%**			
☐ **Model #3 New Model,** .44 Russian, Argentine Model, *Add* **25%-35%**			
☐ **Model #3 New Model,** .44 S & W, Turkish Model, *Add* **15%-25%**			
☐ **Model #3 New Model,** Various Calibers, Calibers other than .44 Russian, *Add* **40%-60%**			
☐ **Model #3 Russian,** .44 Russian, 1st Model, Single Action, Top Break, 6 Shot, Military, *Antique*	685.00	900.00	850.00
☐ **Model #3 Russian,** .44 Russian, 2nd Model, Finger-Rest Trigger Guard, Single Action, Top Break, 6 Shot, *Antique*	500.00	800.00	775.00
☐ **Model #3 Russian,** .44 Russian, 2nd Model, Finger-Rest Trigger Guard, Single Action, Top Break, with Shoulder Stock, *Antique*	935.00	1400.00	1375.00
☐ **Model #3 Russian,** .44 Russian, 3rd Model, Front Sight Forged on Barrel, Single Action, Top Break, 6 Shot, *Antique*	720.00	925.00	875.00
☐ **Model #3 Target,** .32-44 S & W, .38-44 S & W, New Model #3, Single Action, Top Break, *Modern*	535.00	750.00	725.00
☐ **Target Models,** For Target Hammer, Target Trigger, Target Stocks, *Add* **$30.00-$40.00**			
☐ **Target Models,** For Target Hammer, Target Trigger, Target Stocks, *Add* **$30.00-$45.00**			
☐ **Model 10,** .38 Special, Double Action, Blue, Various Barrel Lengths, Swing-Out Cylinder, *Modern*	135.00	175.00	170.00
☐ **Model 10,** .38 Special, Double Action, Swing-Out Cylinder, 4″ Barrel, Heavy Barrel, Blue, *Modern*	145.00	185.00	180.00
☐ **Model 10,** .38 Special, Double Action, Swing-Out Cylinder, 4″ Barrel, Heavy Barrel, Nickel Plated, *Modern*	150.00	190.00	185.00
☐ **Model 10,** .38 Special, Double Action, Swing-Out Cylinder, Various Barrel Lengths, Nickel Plated, *Modern*	140.00	180.00	175.00
☐ **Model 11,** .38 S & W, Double Action, Swing-Out Cylinder, *Modern*	240.00	350.00	325.00
☐ **Model 12,** .38 Special, Double Action, Swing-Out Cylinder, Various Barrel Lengths, Blue, *Modern*	155.00	220.00	215.00
☐ **Model 12,** .38 Special, Double Action, Swing-Out Cylinder, Various Barrel Lengths, Nickel Plated, *Modern*	180.00	235.00	230.00

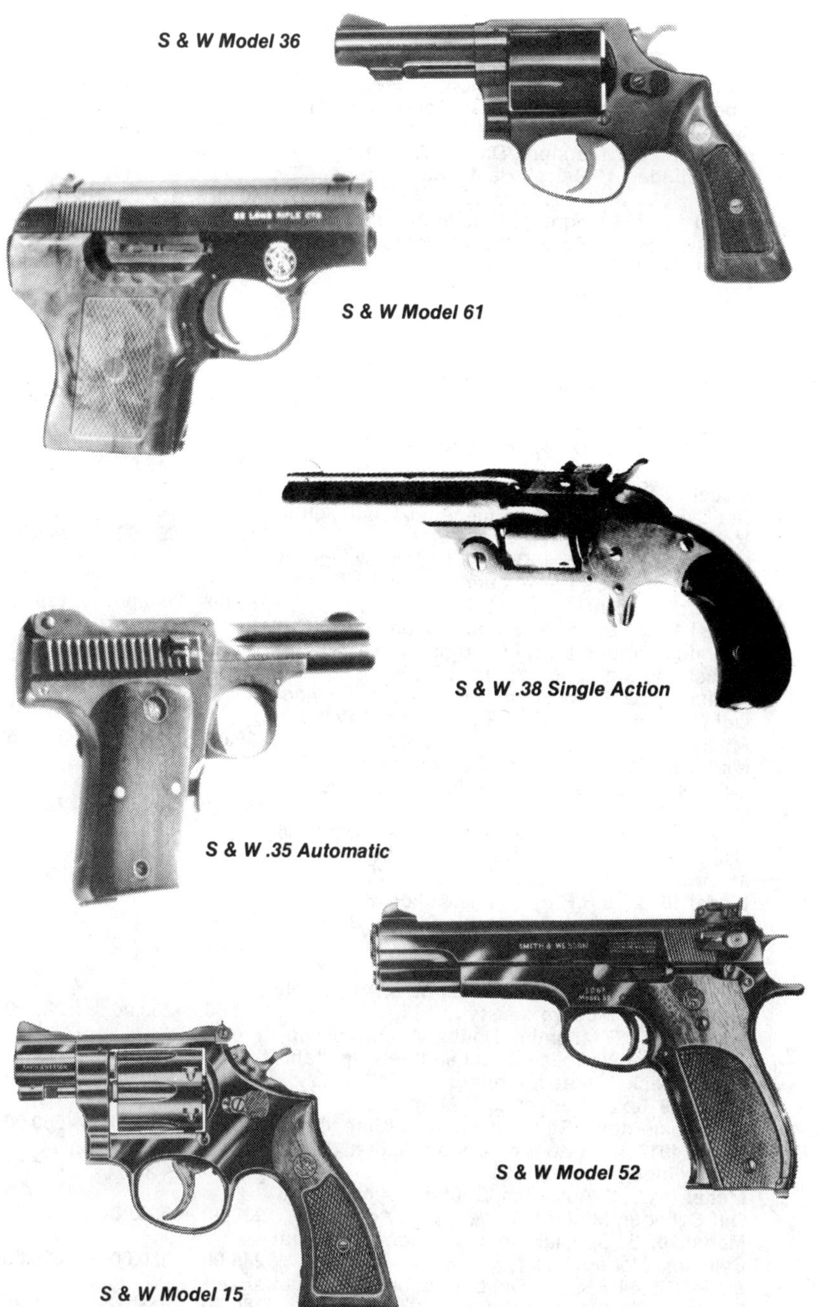

S & W Model 36

S & W Model 61

S & W .38 Single Action

S & W .35 Automatic

S & W Model 52

S & W Model 15

	V.G.	Exc.	Prior Year Exc. Value
☐ **Model 12 USAF,** .38 Special, Double Action, Swing-Out Cylinder, Lightweight, *Modern*	275.00	410.00	395.00
☐ **Model "13" Army,** .38 Special, Double Action, Swing-Out Cylinder, Lightweight, *Modern*	360.00	500.00	485.00
☐ **Model 13,** .357 Magnum, Double Action, Swing-Out Cylinder, 4" Barrel, Heavy Barrel, Blue, *Modern*	140.00	185.00	180.00
☐ **Model 13,** .357 Magnum, Double Action, Swing-Out Cylinder, 4" Barrel, Nickel Plated, Heavy Barrel, *Modern*	150.00	195.00	190.00
☐ **Model 14,** .38 Special, Double Action, Swing-Out Cylinder, 6" Barrel, Blue, Adjustable Sights, *Modern*	160.00	220.00	210.00
☐ **Model 14,** .38 Special, Double Action, Swing-Out Cylinder, 8⅜" Barrel, Blue, Adjustable Sights, *Modern*	170.00	225.00	215.00
☐ **Model 14 SA,** .38 Special, Single Action, Swing-Out Cylinder, 6" Barrel, Blue, Adjustable Sights, *Modern*	180.00	245.00	230.00
☐ **Model 14 SA,** .38 Special, Single Action, Swing-Out Cylinder, 8⅜" Barrel, Blue, Adjustable Sights, *Modern*	185.00	260.00	240.00
☐ **Model 15,** .38 Special, Double Action, Swing-Out Cylinder, Various Barrel Lengths, Blue, Adjustable Sights, *Modern*	150.00	190.00	185.00
☐ **Model 15,** .38 Special, Double Action, Swing-Out Cylinder, Various Barrel Lengths, Nickel Plated, Adjustable Sights, *Modern*	160.00	200.00	195.00
☐ **Model 16,** .32 S & W Long, Double Action, Swing-Out Cylinder, Adjustable Sights, Target Pistol, *Modern*	250.00	385.00	370.00
☐ **Model 17,** .22 L.R.R.F., Double Action, Swing-Out Cylinder, 6" Barrel, Adjustable Sights, Blue, *Modern*	165.00	230.00	220.00
☐ **Model 17,** .22 L.R.R.F., Double Action, Swing-Out Cylinder, 8⅜" Barrel, Adjustable Sights, Blue, *Modern*	180.00	240.00	230.00
☐ **Model 18,** .22 L.R.R.F., Double Action, Swing-Out Cylinder, 4" Barrel, Adjustable Sights, Blue, *Modern*	145.00	225.00	220.00
☐ **Model 19,** .357 Magnum, Double Action, Swing-Out Cylinder, Various Barrel Lengths, Adjustable Sights, Blue, *Modern*	180.00	235.00	225.00
☐ **Model 19,** .357 Magnum, Double Action, Swing-Out Cylinder, Various Barrel Lengths, Adjustable Sights, Nickel Plated, *Modern*	180.00	240.00	230.00
☐ **Model 19 Texas Ranger,** .357 Magnum, Commemorative, Blue, Cased, with Knife, *Curio*	390.00	560.00	550.00
☐ **Model 1917,** .45 Auto-Rim, Double Action, Swing-Out Cylinder, *Modern*	335.00	460.00	445.00
☐ **Model 1917,** .45 Auto-Rim, Double Action, Swing-Out Cylinder, Military, *Modern*	235.00	350.00	325.00
☐ **Model 20,** .38 Special, Double Action, Swing-Out Cylinder, *Modern*	245.00	380.00	365.00
☐ **Model 21,** .44 Special, Double Action, Swing-Out Cylinder, Various Barrel Lengths, *Modern*	380.00	515.00	495.00

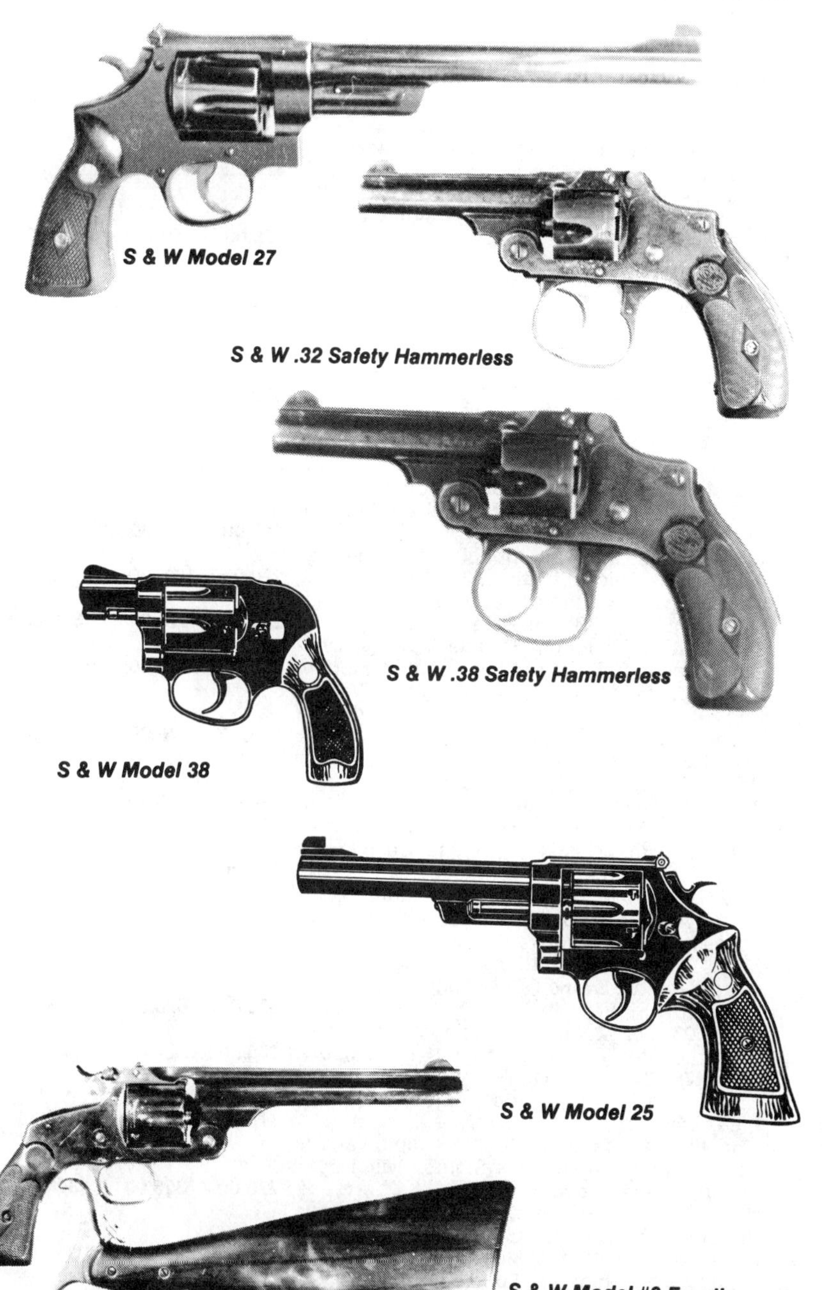

S & W Model 27

S & W .32 Safety Hammerless

S & W .38 Safety Hammerless

S & W Model 38

S & W Model 25

S & W Model #3 Frontier

	V.G.	Exc.	Prior Year Exc. Value
☐ **Model 22,** .45 Auto-Rim, Double Action, Swing-Out Cylinder, *Modern*	235.00	370.00	365.00
☐ **Model 23,** .38 Special, Double Action, Swing-Out Cylinder, Adjustable Sights, Target Pistol, *Modern*	325.00	465.00	465.00
☐ **Model 24,** .44 Special, Double Action, Swing-Out Cylinder, Various Barrel Lengths, Adjustable Sights, *Modern*	325.00	450.00	445.00
☐ **Model 25,** .45 Auto-Rim, Double Action, Swing-Out Cylinder, Target Pistol, Blue, Cased with Accessories, *Modern*	245.00	350.00	340.00
☐ **Model 25,** .45 Auto-Rim, Double Action, Swing-Out Cylinder, Target Pistol, Blue, *Modern*	220.00	300.00	300.00
☐ **Model 26,** .45 Auto-Rim, Double Action, Swing-Out Cylinder, *Modern*	350.00	500.00	500.00
☐ **Model 27,** .357 Magnum, Double Action, Swing-Out Cylinder, Pre-War, Adjustable Sights, *Modern*	370.00	550.00	550.00
☐ **Model 27,** .357 Magnum, Double Action, Swing-Out Cylinder, Various Barrel Lengths, Adjustable Sights, Blue, *Modern*	215.00	305.00	300.00
☐ **Model 27,** .357 Magnum, Double Action, Swing-Out Cylinder, Nickel Plated, *Modern*	220.00	315.00	310.00
☐ **Model 27,** .357 Magnum, Double Action, Swing-Out Cylinder, 8⅜" Barrel, Blue, *Modern*	230.00	310.00	310.00
☐ **Model 27,** .357 Magnum, Double Action, Swing-Out Cylinder, 8⅜" Barrel, Nickel Plated, *Modern*	230.00	310.00	310.00
☐ **Model 27,** .357 Magnum, Double Action, Various Barrel Lengths, Adjustable Sights, Cased with Accessories, Blue, *Modern*	245.00	340.00	340.00
☐ **Model 27,** .357 Magnum, Double Action, 8⅜" Barrel, Adjustable Sights, Cased with Accessories, Nickel Plated, *Modern*	255.00	345.00	345.00
☐ **Model 27,** .357 Magnum, Double Action, Various Barrel Lengths, Adjustable Sights, Cased with Accessories, Nickel Plated, *Modern*	245.00	340.00	340.00
☐ **Model 27,** .357 Magnum, Double Action, 8⅜" Barrel, Adjustable Sights, Cased with Accessories, Blue, *Modern*	255.00	350.00	350.00
☐ **Model 27 with Registration,** .357 Magnum, Double Action, Swing-Out Cylinder, Pre-War, Adjustable Sights, *Modern*	575.00	875.00	875.00
☐ **Model 28,** .357 Magnum, Double Action, Various Barrel Lengths, Adjustable Sights, Blue, *Modern*	165.00	225.00	220.00
☐ **Model 28,** .357 Magnum, Double Action, Various Barrel Lengths, Target Grips, Adjustable Sights, Blue, *Modern*	175.00	225.00	225.00
☐ **Model 29,** .44 Magnum, Double Action, Various Barrel Lengths, Adjustable Sights, Swing-Out Cylinder, Blue, *Modern*	270.00	355.00	350.00
☐ **Model 29,** .44 Magnum, Double Action, Various Barrel Lengths, Adjustable Sights, Swing-Out Cylinder, Nickel Plated, *Modern*	280.00	365.00	360.00
☐ **Model 29,** .44 Magnum, Double Action, 8⅜" Barrel, Adjustable Sights, Swing-Out Cylinder, Blue, *Modern*	300.00	380.00	375.00

	V.G.	Exc.	Prior Year Exc. Value
☐ **Model 29,** .44 Magnum, Double Action, 8⅜" Barrel, Adjustable Sights, Swing-Out Cylinder, Nickel Plated, *Modern*	300.00	370.00	380.00
☐ **Model 29,** .44 Magnum, Double Action, Various Barrel Lengths, Adjustable Sights, Cased with Accessories, Blue, *Modern*	290.00	365.00	375.00
☐ **Model 29,** .44 Magnum, Double Action, Various Barrel Lengths, Adjustable Sights, Cased with Accessories, Nickel Plated, *Modern*	300.00	375.00	380.00
☐ **Model 29,** .44 Magnum, Double Action, 8⅜" Barrel, Adjustable Sights, Cased with Accessories, Blue, *Modern*	310.00	385.00	390.00
☐ **Model 29,** .44 Magnum, Double Action, 8⅜" Barrel, Adjustable Sights, Cased with Accessories, Nickel Plated, *Modern*	315.00	375.00	395.00
☐ **Model 30,** .32 S & W Long, Double Action, Swing-Out Cylinder, *Modern*	170.00	270.00	270.00
☐ **Model 31,** .32 S & W Long, Double Action, Swing-Out Cylinder, Various Barrel Lengths, Nickel Plated, *Modern*	145.00	200.00	200.00
☐ **Model 31,** .32 S & W Long, Double Action, Swing-Out Cylinder, Various Barrel Lengths, Blue, *Modern*	135.00	195.00	190.00
☐ **Model 32,** .38 S & W, Double Action, Swing-Out Cylinder, 2" Barrel, *Modern*	155.00	245.00	240.00
☐ **Model 33,** .38 S & W, Double Action, Swing-Out Cylinder, *Modern*	175.00	255.00	250.00
☐ **Model 34,** .22 L.R.R.F., Double Action, Swing-Out Cylinder, Various Barrel Lengths, Adjustable Sights, Blue, *Modern*	160.00	205.00	200.00
☐ **Model 34,** .22 L.R.R.F., Double Action, Swing-Out Cylinder, Various Barrel Lengths, Adjustable Sights, Nickel Plated, *Modern*	170.00	210.00	210.00
☐ **Model 35,** .22 L.R.R.F., Double Action, Swing-Out Cylinder, Target Pistol, Adjustable Sights, *Modern*	230.00	330.00	325.00
☐ **Model 36,** .38 Special, Double Action, Swing-Out Cylinder, Various Barrel Lengths, Blue, *Modern*	140.00	190.00	190.00
☐ **Model 36,** .38 Special, Double Action, Swing-Out Cylinder, Various Barrel Lengths, Nickel Plated, *Modern*	155.00	210.00	210.00
☐ **Model 36,** .38 Special, Double Action, Swing-Out Cylinder 3" Barrel, Heavy Barrel, Blue, *Modern*	135.00	195.00	190.00
☐ **Model 36,** .38 Special, Double Action, Swing-Out Cylinder, 3" Barrel, Heavy Barrel, Nickel Plated, *Modern*	145.00	205.00	200.00
☐ **Model 37,** .38 Special, Double Action, Swing-Out Cylinder, Various Barrel Lengths, Lightweight, Blue, *Modern*	145.00	205.00	200.00
☐ **Model 37,** .38 Special, Double Action, Swing-Out Cylinder, Various Barrel Lengths, Lightweight, Nickel Plated, *Modern*	155.00	215.00	210.00
☐ **Model 38,** .38 Special, Swing-Out Cylinder, 2" Barrel, Hammer Shroud, Nickel Plated, Double Action, *Modern*	170.00	230.00	230.00

	V.G.	Exc.	Prior Year Exc. Value
☐ **Model 38,** .38 Special, Double Action, Swing-Out Cylinder, 2″ Barrel, Hammer Shroud, Blue, *Modern*	165.00	225.00	220.00
☐ **Model 40,** .38 Special, Double Action, Swing-Out Cylinder, Hammerless, *Modern*	270.00	385.00	380.00
☐ **Model 42,** .38 Special, Double Action, Swing-Out Cylinder, Hammerless, Lightweight, *Modern*	325.00	495.00	485.00
☐ **Mldel 43,** .22 L.R.R.F., Double Action, Swing-Out Cylinder, Adjustable Sights, Lightweight, *Modern*	315.00	440.00	420.00
☐ **Model 45,** .22 L.R.R.F., Double-Action, Swing-Out Cylinder, Commercial, *Modern*	510.00	800.00	775.00
☐ **Model 45 USPO,** .22 L.R.R.F., Double Action, Swing-Out Cylinder, *Modern*	435.00	600.00	575.00
☐ **Model 48,** .22 WMR, Double Action, Swing-Out Cylinder, Various Barrel Lengths, Blue, Adjustable Sights, *Modern*	165.00	230.00	225.00
☐ **Model 48,** .22 WMR, Double Action, Swing-Out Cylinder, 8⅜″ Barrel, Blue, Adjustable Sights, *Modern*	175.00	230.00	230.00
☐ **Model 49,** .38 Special, Double Action, Swing-Out Cylinder, 2″ Barrel, Hammer Shroud, Nickel Plated, *Modern*	170.00	235.00	230.00
☐ **Model 49,** .38 Special, Double Action, Swing-Out Cylinder, 2″ Barrel, Hammer Shroud, Blue, *Modern*	155.00	215.00	210.00
☐ **Model 50,** .38 Special, Double Action, Swing-Out Cylinder, Adjustable Sights, *Modern*	475.00	765.00	750.00
☐ **Model 51,** .22LR/.22 WMR Combo, Double Action, Swing-Out Cylinder, Adjustable Sights, *Modern*	375.00	515.00	500.00
☐ **Model 51,** .22 WMR, Double Action, Swing-Out Cylinder, Adjustable Sights, *Modern*	315.00	450.00	425.00
☐ **Model 53,** .22 Rem. Jet, Double Action, Swing-Out Cylinder, Adjustable Sights, *Modern*	450.00	650.00	625.00
☐ **Model 53,** .22 Rem. Jet, Double Action, Swing-Out Cylinder, Adjustable Sights, Extra Cylinder, *Modern*	520.00	700.00	675.00
☐ **Model 56,** .38 Special, Double Action, Swing-Out Cylinder, 2″ Barrel, Adjustable Sights, *Modern*	600.00	875.00	850.00
☐ **Model 57,** .41 Magnum, Double Action, Swing-Out Cylinder, Various Barrel Lengths, Blue, Adjustable Sights, *Modern*	220.00	295.00	300.00
☐ **Model 57,** .41 Magnum, Double Action, Swing-Out Cylinder, Various Barrel Lengths, Nickel Plated, Adjustable Sights, *Modern*	220.00	295.00	300.00
☐ **Model 57,** .41 Magnum, Double Action, Swing-Out Cylinder, 8⅜″ Barrel, Blue, Adjustable Sights, *Modern*	225.00	305.00	310.00
☐ **Model 57,** .41 Magnum, Double Action, Swing-Out Cylinder, 8⅜″ Barrel, Nickel Plated, Adjustable Sights, *Modern*	225.00	305.00	310.00
☐ **Model 57,** .41 Magnum, Double Action, Swing-Out Cylinder, Various Barrel Lengths, Blue, Cased with Accessories, *Modern*	240.00	320.00	330.00

	V.G.	Exc.	Prior Year Exc. Value
☐ **Model 57,** .41 Magnum, Double Action, Swing-Out Cylinder, Various Barrel Lengths, Nickel Plated, Cased with Accessories, *Modern*	250.00	340.00	340.00
☐ **Model 57,** .41 Magnum, Double Action, Swing-Out Cylinder, 8⅜″ Barrel, Blue, Cased with Accessories, *Modern*	250.00	340.00	340.00
☐ **Model 57,** .41 Magnum, Double Action, Swing-Out Cylinder, 8⅜″ Barrel, Blue, Cased with Accessories, *Modern*	250.00	340.00	340.00
☐ **Model 58,** .41 Magnum, Double Action, Swing-Out Cylinder, 4″ Barrel, Blue, *Modern*	215.00	310.00	310.00
☐ **Model 58,** .41 Magnum, Double Action, Swing-Out Cylinder, 4″ Barrel, Nickel Plated, *Modern*	235.00	335.00	330.00
☐ **Model 60,** .38 Special, Double Action, Swing-Out Cylinder, Stainless Steel, Adjustable Sights, *Modern*	665.00	925.00	900.00
☐ **Model 60,** .38 Special, Double Action, Swing-Out Cylinder, Stainless Steel, 2″ Barrel, *Modern*	190.00	260.00	250.00
☐ **Model 60,** .38 Special, Double Action, Swing-Out Cylinder, Early High Polish Stainless Steel, 2″ Barrel, *Modern*	245.00	365.00	350.00
☐ **Model 63,** .22 L.R.R.F., Double Action, Swing-Out Cylinder, Stainless Steel, 4″ Barrel, Adjustable Sights, *Modern*	180.00	235.00	230.00
☐ **Model 64,** .38 Special, Double Action, Swing-Out Cylinder, Stainless Steel, Various Barrel Lengths, *Modern*	145.00	195.00	190.00
☐ **Model 65,** .357 Magnum, Double Action, Swing-Out Cylinder, Stainless Steel, 4″ Barrel, Heavy Barrel, *Modern*	170.00	225.00	220.00
☐ **Model 66,** .357 Magnum, Double Action, Swing-Out Cylinder, Stainless Steel, 2½″ Barrel, *Modern*	190.00	240.00	250.00
☐ **Model 66,** .357 Magnum, Double Action, Swing-Out Cylinder, Stainless Steel, Various Barrel Lengths, *Modern*	170.00	230.00	235.00
☐ **Model 67,** .38 Special, Double Action, Swing-Out Cylinder, Stainless Steel, 4″ Barrel, *Modern*	160.00	220.00	225.00
☐ **Model 547,** 9mm Luger, Double Action, Swing-Out Cylinder, Blue, *Modern*	160.00	215.00	220.00
☐ **Model 581,** .357 Magnum, Double Action, Swing-Out Cylinder, Blue, *Modern*	150.00	185.00	190.00
☐ **Model 581,** .357 Magnum, Double Action, Swing-Out Cylinder, Nickel, *Modern*	155.00	190.00	195.00
☐ **Model 586,** .357 Magnum, Double Action, Swing-Out Cylinder, Blue, Adjustable Sights, *Modern*	185.00	235.00	240.00
☐ **Model 586,** .357 Magnum, Double Action, Swing-Out Cylinder, Nickel, Adjustable Sights, *Modern*	185.00	245.00	250.00
☐ **Model 629,** .44 Magnum, Double Action, Swing-Out Cylinder, Stainless Steel, Adjustable Sights, *Modern*	320.00	430.00	435.00
☐ **Model 629,** .44 Magnum, Double Action, Swing-Out Cylinder, 8⅜″ Barrel, Stainless Steel, Adjustable Sights, *Modern*	320.00	440.00	450.00
☐ **Model 649 Bodyguard,** .38 Special, J Frame, 5 Shot, Stainless Steel, *Modern*	300.00	326.50	—
☐ **Model 650,** .22 W.M.R., Double Action, Swing-Out Cylinder, Stainless Steel, *Modern*	180.00	225.00	225.00

	V.G.	Exc.	Prior Year Exc. Value
☐ **Model 651,** .22 W.M.R., Double Action, Swing-Out Cylinder, Stainless Steel, Adjustable Sights, *Modern*	190.00	240.00	240.00
☐ **Model 681,** .357 Magnum, Double Action, Swing-Out Cylinder, Stainless Steel, *Modern*	165.00	205.00	210.00
☐ **Model 686,** .357 Magnum, Double Action, Swing-Out Cylinder, Stainless Steel, Adjustable Sights, *Modern*	180.00	250.00	250.00
☐ **Model M Hand Ejector,** .22 Long R.F., 1st Model Ladysmith, Solid Frame, Swing-Out Cylinder, Double Action, *Curio*	575.00	810.00	795.00
☐ **Model M Hand Ejector,** .22 Long R.F., 2nd Model Ladysmith, Solid Frame, Swing-Out Cylinder, Double Action, *Curio*	490.00	675.00	665.00
☐ **Model M Hand Ejector,** .22 Long R.F., 3rd Model Ladysmith, Solid Frame, Swing-Out Cylinder, Double Action, *Curio*	430.00	640.00	625.00
☐ **Model M Hand Ejector,** .22 Long R.F., 3rd Model Ladysmith, Solid Frame, Swing-Out Cylinder, Double Action, Adjustable Sights, *Curio*	675.00	915.00	895.00
☐ **Second Model Schofield,** .45 S & W, Knurled Latch, Top Break, Single Action, Military, *Antique*	950.00	1350.00	1300.00
☐ **Second Model Schofield,** .45 S & W. Knurled Latch, Top Break, Single Action, Commercial, *Antique*	1050.00	1750.00	1700.00
☐ **Second Model Schofield,** .45 S & W, Wells Fargo, Knurled Latch, Top Break, Single Action, *Antique*	925.00	1285.00	1250.00
☐ **Victory,** .38 Special Military & Police, Solid Frame, Swing-Out Cylinder, Double Action, Military, *Modern*	130.00	200.00	185.00
HANDGUN, SEMI-AUTOMATIC			
☐ **.32 ACP,** Blue, *Curio*	700.00	1200.00	1150.00
☐ **.32 ACP,** Nickel Plated, *Curio*	800.00	1350.00	1350.00
☐ **.35 S & W Automatic,** Blue, *Curio*	450.00	550.00	525.00
☐ **.35 S & W Automatic,** Nickel Plated, *Curio*	475.00	650.00	625.00
☐ **Model 39,** 9mm Luger, Double Action, Steel Frame, *Curio*	835.00	1250.00	1300.00
☐ **Model 39,** 9mm Luger, Double Action, Steel Frame, *Curio*	835.00	1250.00	1300.00
☐ **Model 39,** 9mm Luger, Double Action, Blue, *Modern*	195.00	270.00	260.00
☐ **Model 39-1,** .38 AMU, Double Action, *Curio*	1250.00	2500.00	2000.00
☐ **Model 41,** .22 L.R.R.F., Various Barrel Lengths, *Modern*	200.00	285.00	280.00
☐ **Model 41-1,** .22 Short R.F., Various Barrel Lengths, *Modern*	265.00	350.00	350.00
☐ **Model 44,** 9mm Luger, Single Action, *Modern*	1400.00	2600.00	2200.00
☐ **Model 46,** .22 L.R.R.F., Various Barrel Lengths, *Modern*	250.00	345.00	345.00
☐ **Model 52,** .38 Special, Blue, *Modern*	320.00	425.00	425.00
☐ **Model 59,** 9mm Luger, Double Action, Blue, *Modern*	210.00	290.00	285.00
☐ **Model 59,** 9mm Luger, Double Action, Nickel Plated, *Modern*	250.00	330.00	325.00

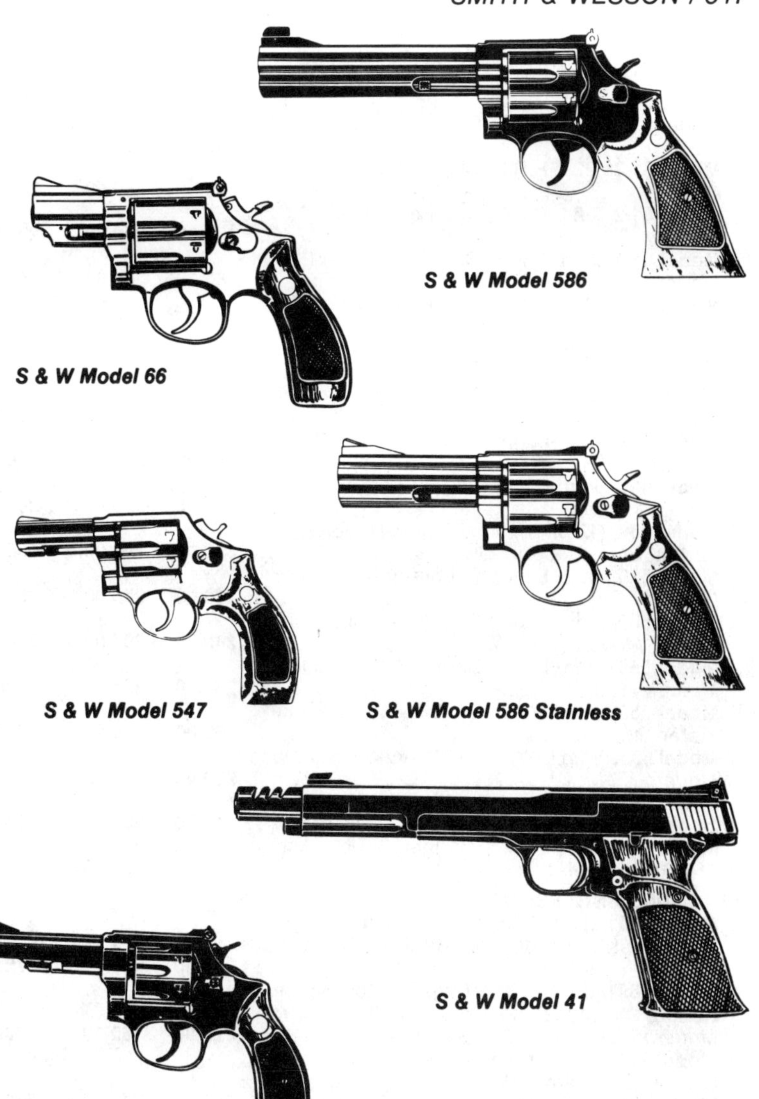

S & W Model 586

S & W Model 66

S & W Model 547

S & W Model 586 Stainless

S & W Model 41

S & W Model 34

	V.G.	Exc.	Prior Year Exc. Value
☐ **Model 61-1,** .22 L.R.R.F., Clip Fed, Nickel Plated, *Modern*	175.00	260.00	250.00
☐ **Model 61-1,** .22 L.R.R.F., Clip Fed, Blue, *Modern*	160.00	230.00	225.00
☐ **Model 61-2,** .22 L.R.R.F., Clip Fed, Nickel Plated, *Modern*	180.00	260.00	240.00
☐ **Model 61-2,** .22 L.R.R.F., Clip Fed, Blue, *Modern*	175.00	250.00	225.00
☐ **Model 61-3,** .22 L.R.R.F., Clip Fed, Nickel Plated, *Modern*	180.00	260.00	240.00
☐ **Model 61-3,** .22 L.R.R.F., Clip Fed, Blue, *Modern*	155.00	235.00	225.00
☐ **Model 439,** 9mm Luger, Double Action, Blue, *Modern*	200.00	270.00	280.00
☐ **Model 439,** 9mm Luger, Double Action, Nickel Plated, *Modern*	240.00	290.00	300.00
☐ **Model 459,** 9mm Luger, Double Action, Blue, *Modern*	240.00	330.00	340.00
☐ **Model 459,** 9mm Luger, Double Action, Nickel Plated, *Modern*	290.00	380.00	365.00
☐ **Model 469,** (12 Shot), 9mm Luger, Double Action, Blue, *Modern*	390.00	400.00	400.00
☐ **Model 539,** 9mm Luger, Double Action, Blue, *Modern*	220.00	285.00	290.00
☐ **Model 539,** 9mm Luger, Double Action, Nickel Plated, *Modern*	240.00	300.00	310.00
☐ **Model 559,** 9mm Luger, Double Action, Blue, *Modern*	235.00	325.00	340.00
☐ **Model 559,** 9mm Luger, Double Action, Nickel Plated, *Modern*	260.00	350.00	365.00
☐ **Model 639,** 9mm Luger, Double Action, Stainless, *Modern*	230.00	300.00	300.00
☐ **Model 659,** 9mm Luger, Double Action, Stainless, *Modern*	240.00	325.00	325.00
☐ **Model 669 (12 Shot),** 9mm Luger, Double Action, Stainless Steel, *Modern*	410.00	439.00	—
HANDGUN, SINGLESHOT			
☐ **Model 1891,** .22 L.R.R.F., Target Pistol, Single Action, 1st Model, Various Barrel Lengths, *Antique*	250.00	385.00	375.00
☐ **Model 1891,** .22 L.R.R.F., Target Pistol, Single Action, 2nd Model, no Hand or Cylinder Stop, *Modern*	225.00	350.00	340.00
☐ **Model 1891 Set,** Various Calibers, Extra Cylinder, Extra Barrel, Target Pistol, Single Action, 1st Model, *Antique*	560.00	770.00	750.00
☐ **Perfected,** .22 L.R.R.F., Double Action, Top Break, Target Pistol, *Modern*	260.00	375.00	365.00
☐ **Perfected Olympic,** .22 L.R.R.F., Double Action, Top Break, Tight Bore and Chamber, Target Pistol, *Modern*	475.00	660.00	640.00
☐ **Straight Line,** .22 L.R.R.F., Cased, *Curio*	700.00	1175.00	1100.00
RIFLE, BOLT ACTION			
☐ **Model 125 Deluxe,** Various Calibers, Monte Carlo Stock, *Modern*	150.00	200.00	195.00
☐ **Model 125 STD,** Various Calibers, Monte Carlo Stock, *Modern*	135.00	175.00	170.00

	V.G.	Exc.	Prior Year Exc. Value
☐ **Model 1500,** Various Calibers, Monte Carlo Stock, Checkered Stock, *Modern*	180.00	235.00	250.00
☐ **Model 1500 Deluxe,** Various Calibers, Monte Carlo Stock, Checkered Stock, *Modern*	190.00	265.00	285.00
☐ **Model 1500 Magnum,** Various Calibers, Monte Carlo Stock, Checkered Stock, *Modern*	170.00	255.00	275.00
☐ **Model 1500 Varmint,** Various Calibers, Monte Carlo Stock, Checkered Stock, Heavy Barrel, *Modern*	210.00	280.00	300.00
☐ **Model 1700 Classic,** Various Calibers, Monte Carlo Stock, Checkered Stock, Clip Fed, *Modern*	190.00	300.00	320.00
☐ **Model A,** Various Calibers, Monte Carlo Stock, Checkered Stock, *Modern*	190.00	280.00	300.00
☐ **Model B,** Various Calibers, Monte Carlo Stock, Checkered Stock, *Modern*	175.00	250.00	275.00
☐ **Model C,** Various Calibers, Sporting Rifle, Checkered Stock, *Modern*	175.00	250.00	275.00
☐ **Model D,** Various Calibers, Mannlicher, Checkered Stock, *Modern*	195.00	280.00	300.00
☐ **Model E,** Various Calibers, Monte Carlo Stock, Mannlicher, *Modern*	205.00	295.00	320.00
RIFLE, REVOLVER			
☐ **Model 320,** .320 S & W Rifle, Single Action, Top Break, 6 Shot, Adjustable Sights, Cased with Accessories, *Antique*	2500.00	3875.00	3500.00
RIFLE, SEMI-AUTOMATIC			
☐ **Light Rifle,** MK I, 9mm Luger, Clip Fed, Carbine, *Curio*	1300.00	1800.00	2000.00
☐ **Light Rifle MK II,** 9mm Luger, Clip Fed, Carbine, *Curio*	1900.00	2500.00	2650.00
SHOTGUN, SEMI-AUTOMATIC			
☐ **Model 1000 Field,** 12 Ga., Vent Rib, *Modern*	245.00	360.00	325.00
☐ **Model 1000 Field,** 12 Ga., 3″, Vent Rib, *Modern*	245.00	385.00	350.00
☐ **Model 1000 Slug,** 12 Ga., Open Sights, *Modern*	230.00	385.00	350.00
☐ **Model 1000 Skeet,** 12 Ga., Vent Rib, *Modern*	265.00	390.00	375.00
SHOTGUN, SLIDE ACTION			
☐ **Model 916 Eastfield,** Various Gauges, Plain Barrel, *Modern*	90.00	140.00	150.00
☐ **Model 916 Eastfield,** Various Gauges, Plain Barrel, Recoil Pad, *Modern*	90.00	130.00	135.00
☐ **Model 3000 Field,** 12 Ga. 3″, Vent Rib, *Modern*	145.00	235.00	250.00
☐ **Model 3000 Slug,** 12 Ga. 3″, Open Sights, *Modern*	145.00	235.00	250.00
☐ **Model 3000 Police,** 12 Ga., Open Sights, *Modern*	135.00	215.00	230.00
☐ **Model 3000 Police,** 12 Ga., Open Sights, Folding Stock, *Modern*	170.00	255.00	270.00

S & W Model 1000

SMITH, ANTHONY

Northampton, Pa., 1770-1779. See Kentucky Rifles and Pistols.

SMITH, L.C. GUN CO.

Syracuse, N.Y., 1877-1890, in 1890 became Hunter Arms, and in 1948 became a division of Marlin.

SHOTGUN, DOUBLE BARREL, SIDE-BY-SIDE

	V.G.	Exc.	Prior Year Exc. Value
☐ **Crown Grade**, Various Calibers, Sidelock, Single Selective Trigger, Automatic Ejector, Fancy Engraving, Fancy Checkering, *Modern*	2,700.00	3,800.00	3,750.00
☐ **Crown Grade**, Various Calibers, Sidelock, Double Trigger, Automatic Ejector, Fancy Engraving, Fancy Checkering, *Modern*	2,450.00	3,500.00	3,400.00
☐ **Field Grade**, Various Calibers, Sidelock, Double Trigger, Checkered Stock, Light Engraving, *Modern*	500.00	745.00	725.00
☐ **Field Grade**, Various Calibers, Sidelock, Double Trigger, Automatic Ejector, Checkered Stock, Light Engraving, *Modern*	450.00	690.00	675.00
☐ **Field Grade**, Various Calibers, Sidelock, Single Trigger, Checkered Stock, Light Engraving, *Modern*	475.00	725.00	700.00
☐ **Field Grade**, Various Calibers, Sidelock, Single Trigger, Automatic Ejector, Checkered Stock, Light Engraving, *Modern*	475.00	695.00	675.00
☐ **Ideal Grade**, Various Calibers, Sidelock, Double Trigger, Checkered Stock, Engraved, *Modern*	475.00	695.00	675.00
☐ **Ideal Grade**, Various Calibers, Sidelock, Double Trigger, Automatic Ejector, Checkered Stock, Engraved, *Modern*	500.00	845.00	825.00
☐ **Ideal Grade**, Various Calibers, Sidelock, Single Selective Trigger, Checkered Stock, Engraved, *Modern*	700.00	1,200.00	1,150.00
☐ **Ideal Grade**, Various Calibers, Sidelock, Single Selective Trigger, Automatic Ejector, Engraved, Checkered Stock, *Modern*	775.00	1,250.00	1,200.00
☐ **Marlin Deluxe**, 12 Ga., Double Trigger, Checkered Stock, Vent Rib, *Modern*	400.00	545.00	525.00
☐ **Marlin Field**, 12 Ga., Double Trigger, Checkered Stock, *Modern*	275.00	440.00	425.00
☐ **Monogram Grade**, Various Calibers, Sidelock, Single Selective Trigger, Automatic Ejector, Fancy Engraving, Fancy Checkering, *Modern*	4,250.00	6,600.00	6,500.00
☐ **Olympic Grade**, Various Calibers, Sidelock, Single Selective Trigger, Automatic Ejector, Engraved, Checkered Stock, *Modern*	700.00	975.00	950.00
☐ **Premier Grade**, Various Calibers, Sidelock, Single Selective Trigger, Automatic Ejector, Fancy Engraving, Fancy Checkering, *Modern*	7,500.00	11,500.00	11,500.00
☐ **Skeet Grade**, Various Calibers, Sidelock, Single Selective Trigger, Automatic Ejector, Engraved, Checkered Stock, *Modern*	750.00	1,175.00	1,150.00
☐ **Skeet Grade**, Various Calibers, Sidelock, Single Trigger, Automatic Ejector, Engraved, Checkered Stock, *Modern*	675.00	995.00	975.00

	V.G.	Exc.	Prior Year Exc. Value
☐ **Specialty Grade**, Various Calibers, Sidelock, Double Trigger, Engraved, Checkered Stock, *Modern*	775.00	1,250.00	1,200.00
☐ **Specialty Grade**, Various Calibers, Sidelock, Single Selective Trigger, Automatic Ejector, Engraved, Checkered Stock, *Modern*	850.00	1,265.00	1,225.00
☐ **Trap Grade**, 12 Ga., Sidelock, Single Selective Trigger, Automatic Ejector, Engraved, Checkered Stock, *Modern*	775.00	1,185.00	1,150.00

SHOTGUN, SINGLESHOT

	V.G.	Exc.	Prior Year Exc. Value
☐ **Crown Grade**, 12 Ga., Trap Grade, Vent Rib, Automatic Ejector, Fancy Engraving, Fancy Checkering, *Modern*	2,000.00	2,800.00	2,750.00
☐ **Olympic Grade**, 12 Ga., Trap Grade, Vent Rib, Automatic Ejector, Engraved, Fancy Checkering, *Modern*	775.00	1,250.00	1,200.00
☐ **Specialty Grade**, 12 Ga., Trap Grade, Vent Rib, Automatic Ejector, Engraved, Fancy Checkering, *Modern*	1,200.00	1,700.00	1,650.00

L.C. Smith Field Grade

SMITH, OTIS A.

Middlefield & Rockfall, Conn. 1873-1890.

HANDGUN, REVOLVER

	V.G.	Exc.	Prior Year Exc. Value
☐ **.22 Short R.F.**, 7 Shot, Spur Trigger, Solid Frame, Single Action, *Antique*	90.00	165.00	160.00
☐ **.32 S & W**, 5 Shot, Single Action, Top Break, Spur Trigger, *Antique*	85.00	140.00	135.00
☐ **.32 Short R.F.**, 5 Shot, Spur Trigger, Solid Frame, Single Action, *Antique*	90.00	165.00	160.00
☐ **.38 Short R.F.**, 5 Shot, Spur Trigger, Solid Frame, Single Action, *Antique*	95.00	175.00	170.00
☐ **.41 Short R.F.**, 5 Shot, Spur Trigger, Solid Frame, Single Action, *Antique*	120.00	200.00	195.00

SMITH, STOEFFEL

Pa. 1790-1800. See Kentucky Rifles and Pistols.

SMITH, THOMAS

London, England, c. 1850.

RIFLE, PERCUSSION

	V.G.	Exc.	Prior Year Exc. Value
☐ **16 Ga.**, Smoothbore, Anson-Deeley Lock, Octagon Barrel, Fancy Wood, Cased with Accessories, *Antique*	2,000.00	3,000.00	2,950.00

SMITH, WM.

England

HANDGUN, SEMI-AUTOMATIC

	V.G.	Exc.	Prior Year Exc. Value
☐ **Pocket**, .25 ACP, Clip Fed, 1906 Browning Type, *Modern*	325.00	435.00	425.00

SMOKER

Made by Johnson Bye & Co. 1875-1884.

	V.G.	Exc.	Prior Year Exc. Value
HANDGUN, REVOLVER			
☐ **#1**, .22 Short R.F., 7 Shot, Spur Trigger, Solid Frame, Single Action, *Antique*	90.00	165.00	160.00
☐ **#2**, .32 Short R.F., 5 Shot, Spur Trigger, Solid Frame, Single Action, *Antique*	95.00	170.00	170.00
☐ **#3**, .38 Short R.F., 5 Shot, Spur Trigger, Solid Frame, Single Action, *Antique*	95.00	170.00	170.00
☐ **#4**, .41 Short R.F., 5 Shot, Spur Trigger, Solid Frame, Single Action, *Antique*	120.00	200.00	195.00

SNAPHAUNCE, UNKNOWN MAKER

	V.G.	Exc.	Prior Year Exc. Value
HANDGUN, SNAPHAUNCE			
☐ **.45 Italian Early 1700's**, Holster Pistol, Half-Octagon Barrel, Engraved, Carved, High Quality, Furiture, *Antique*	2,000.00	2,500.00	2,500.00
☐ **Early 1800's Small**, Plain, *Antique*	600.00	1,000.00	1,000.00
☐ **English Late 1500's**, Ovoid Pommel, Engraved, Gold Damascened, High Quality, *Antique*	9,750.00	20,000.00	20,000.00
☐ **Italian Early 1700's**, Medium Quality, Brass Furniture, Plain, *Antique*	750.00	1,000.00	1,000.00
☐ **Italian 1700's**, High Quality, Belt Pistol, Light Ornamentation, *Antique*	1,800.00	2,800.00	2,800.00
RIFLE, SNAPHAUNCE			
☐ **Arabian**, .59, Ornate, Inlaid with Silver, Ivory buttstock Inlays, *Antique*	400.00	600.00	600.00
☐ **Italian Mid-1600's**, Half-Octagon Barrel, Carved, Engraved, Silver Inlay, Steel Furniture, Ornate, *Antique*	6,000.00	10,000.00	10,000.00

SODIA, FRANZ

Ferlach, Austria

	V.G.	Exc.	Prior Year Exc. Value
COMBINATION WEAPON, MULTI-BARREL			
☐ **Bochdrilling**, Various Calibers, Fancy Wood, Fancy Checkering, Fancy Engraving, *Antique*	2,300.00	3,750.00	3,750.00
☐ **Doppelbuchse**, Various Calibers, Fancy Wood, Fancy Checkering, Fancy Engraving, *Antique*	1,700.00	2,800.00	2,750.00
☐ **Over-Under Rifle**, Various Calibers, Fancy Wood, Fancy Checkering, Fancy Engraving, *Antique*	1,600.00	2,450.00	2,400.00

SOLER

Ripoll, Spain, c. 1625.

	V.G.	Exc.	Prior Year Exc. Value
HANDGUN, WHEEL-LOCK			
☐ **Enclosed Mid-1600's**, Ball Pommel, Ornate, *Antique*	7,000.00	12,500.00	12,500.00

SOUTHERN ARMS CO.

Made by Crescent for H. & D. Folsom, N.Y.C.

	V.G.	Exc.	Prior Year Exc. Value
SHOTGUN, DOUBLE BARREL, SIDE-BY-SIDE			
☐ **Various Gauges**, Outside Hammers, Damascus Barrel, *Modern*	100.00	170.00	175.00

	V.G.	Exc.	Prior Year Exc. Value
☐ **Various Gauges**, Hammerless, Steel Barrel, *Modern*	135.00	190.00	200.00
☐ **Various Gauges**, Hammerless, Damascus Barrel, *Modern*	100.00	170.00	175.00
☐ **Various Gauges**, Outside Hammers, Steel Barrel, *Modern*	125.00	185.00	190.00
SHOTGUN, SINGLESHOT			
☐ **Various Gauges**, Hammer, Steel Barrel, *Modern*	55.00	85.00	85.00

SPAARMAN, ANDREAS

Berlin, Germany, c. 1680.

RIFLE, FLINTLOCK			
☐ **.72**, Jaeger, Octagon Barrel, Swamped, Rifled, Iron Mounts, Ornate, Set Trigger, *Antique*	3,000.00	4,000.00	3,950.00

SPANISH MILITARY

Also see Astra, Star.

AUTOMATIC WEAPON, SUBMACHINE GUN			
☐ **Star Z-63,** 9mm Luger, Clip Fed, *Class 3*	500.00	775.00	775.00
HANDGUN, SEMI-AUTOMATIC			
☐ **Jo-Lo-Ar,** 9mm Bergmann, Clip Fed, Military, Hammer, *Curio*	110.00	150.00	235.00
☐ **M1913-16 Campo-Giro,** 9mm Bergmann, Clip Fed, Military, *Curio*	120.00	170.00	265.00
RIFLE, BOLT ACTION			
☐ **Destroyer,** 9mm Bayard Long, Clip Fed, Carbine, *Modern*	60.00	95.00	150.00
☐ **M98 La Caruna,** 8mm Mauser, Military, *Curio*	50.00	75.00	130.00
RIFLE, SEMI-AUTOMATIC			
☐ **CETME Sport,** .308 Win., Clip Fed, *Modern*	220.00	380.00	450.00

Spanish Military M1913-16

Spanish Military Model 400

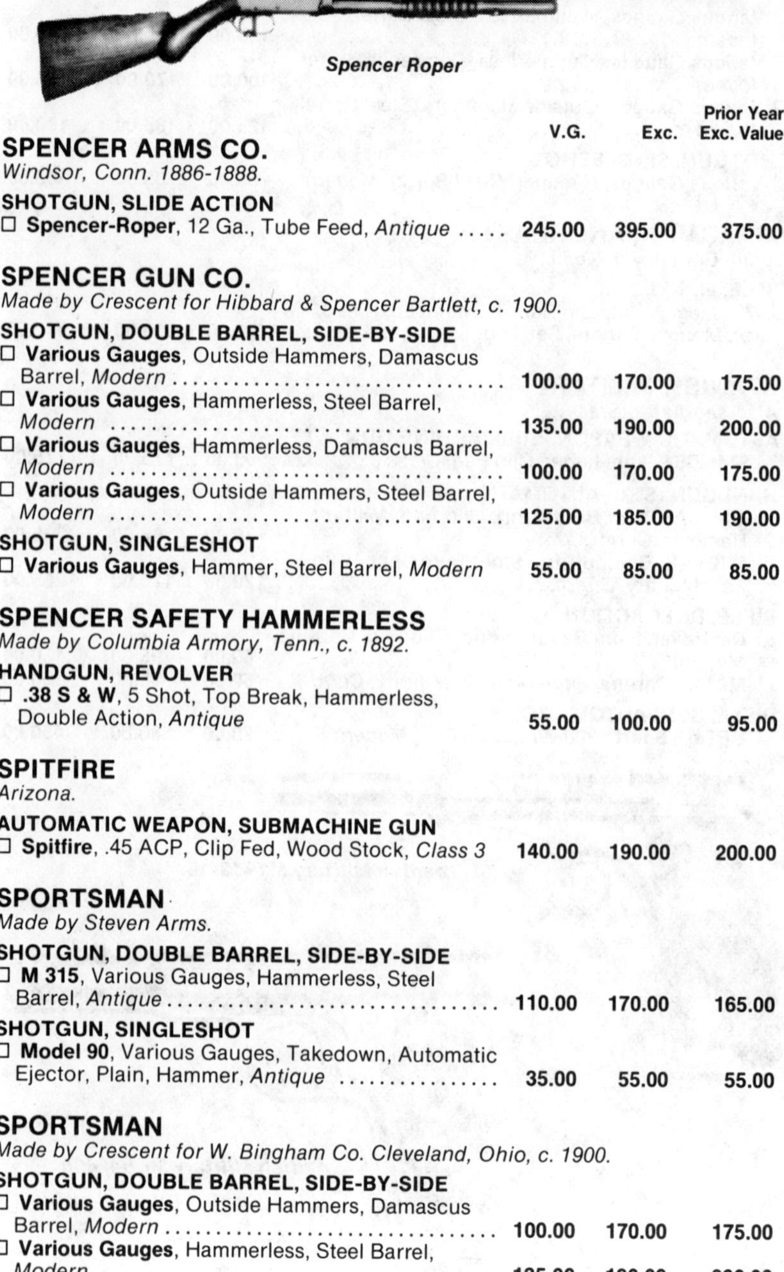

Spencer Roper

SPENCER ARMS CO.

Windsor, Conn. 1886-1888.

	V.G.	Exc.	Prior Year Exc. Value
SHOTGUN, SLIDE ACTION			
☐ **Spencer-Roper**, 12 Ga., Tube Feed, *Antique*	245.00	395.00	375.00

SPENCER GUN CO.

Made by Crescent for Hibbard & Spencer Bartlett, c. 1900.

	V.G.	Exc.	Prior Year Exc. Value
SHOTGUN, DOUBLE BARREL, SIDE-BY-SIDE			
☐ **Various Gauges**, Outside Hammers, Damascus Barrel, *Modern*	100.00	170.00	175.00
☐ **Various Gauges**, Hammerless, Steel Barrel, *Modern*	135.00	190.00	200.00
☐ **Various Gauges**, Hammerless, Damascus Barrel, *Modern*	100.00	170.00	175.00
☐ **Various Gauges**, Outside Hammers, Steel Barrel, *Modern*	125.00	185.00	190.00
SHOTGUN, SINGLESHOT			
☐ **Various Gauges**, Hammer, Steel Barrel, *Modern*	55.00	85.00	85.00

SPENCER SAFETY HAMMERLESS

Made by Columbia Armory, Tenn., c. 1892.

	V.G.	Exc.	Prior Year Exc. Value
HANDGUN, REVOLVER			
☐ **.38 S & W**, 5 Shot, Top Break, Hammerless, Double Action, *Antique*	55.00	100.00	95.00

SPITFIRE

Arizona.

	V.G.	Exc.	Prior Year Exc. Value
AUTOMATIC WEAPON, SUBMACHINE GUN			
☐ **Spitfire**, .45 ACP, Clip Fed, Wood Stock, *Class 3*	140.00	190.00	200.00

SPORTSMAN

Made by Steven Arms.

	V.G.	Exc.	Prior Year Exc. Value
SHOTGUN, DOUBLE BARREL, SIDE-BY-SIDE			
☐ **M 315**, Various Gauges, Hammerless, Steel Barrel, *Antique*	110.00	170.00	165.00
SHOTGUN, SINGLESHOT			
☐ **Model 90**, Various Gauges, Takedown, Automatic Ejector, Plain, Hammer, *Antique*	35.00	55.00	55.00

SPORTSMAN

Made by Crescent for W. Bingham Co. Cleveland, Ohio, c. 1900.

	V.G.	Exc.	Prior Year Exc. Value
SHOTGUN, DOUBLE BARREL, SIDE-BY-SIDE			
☐ **Various Gauges**, Outside Hammers, Damascus Barrel, *Modern*	100.00	170.00	175.00
☐ **Various Gauges**, Hammerless, Steel Barrel, *Modern*	135.00	190.00	200.00

	V.G.	Exc.	Prior Year Exc. Value
☐ **Various Gauges**, Hammerless, Damascus Barrel, *Modern*	100.00	170.00	175.00
☐ **Various Gauges**, Outside Hammers, Steel Barrel, *Modern*	125.00	185.00	190.00
SHOTGUN, SINGLESHOT			
☐ **Various Gauges**, Hammer, Steel Barrel, *Modern*	55.00	85.00	85.00

SPRINGFIELD ARMORY

Geneseo, Ill.

AUTOMATIC WEAPON, ASSAULT RIFLE			
☐ **M1A**, .308 Win., Clip Fed, Silencer, *Class 3*	750.00	1,000.00	1,000.00
☐ **M1A (M-14)**, .308 Win., Clip Fed, Commercial, *Class 3*	525.00	650.00	650.00
RIFLE, SEMI-AUTOMATIC			
☐ **M1A Super Match**, .308 Win., Clip Fed, Version of M-14, Heavy Barrel, *Modern*	475.00	675.00	675.00
☐ **M1A Match**, .308 Win., Clip Fed, Version of M-14, *Modern*	400.00	600.00	600.00
☐ **M1A Standard**, .308 Win., Clip Fed, Version of M-14, *Modern*	375.00	545.00	525.00
☐ **M1A Standard**, .308 Win., Clip Fed, Version of M-14, Folding Stock, *Modern*	425.00	585.00	575.00

SPRINGFIELD ARMS

Made by Crescent, c. 1900.

SHOTGUN, DOUBLE BARREL, SIDE-BY-SIDE			
☐ **Various Gauges**, Outside Hammers, Damascus Barrel, *Modern*	100.00	170.00	175.00
☐ **Various Gauges**, Hammerless, Steel Barrel, *Modern*	135.00	190.00	200.00
☐ **Various Gauges**, Hammerless, Damascus Barrel, *Modern*	100.00	170.00	175.00
☐ **Various Gauges**, Outside Hammers, Steel Barrel, *Modern*	125.00	185.00	190.00
SHOTGUN, SINGLESHOT			
☐ **Various Gauges**, Hammer, Steel Barrel, *Modern*	55.00	85.00	85.00

SPY

Made by Norwich Falls Pistol Co., c. 1880.

HANDGUN, REVOLVER			
☐ **.22 Short R.F.**, 7 Shot, Spur Trigger, Solid Frame, Single Action, *Antique*	95.00	165.00	160.00

SQUARE DEAL

Made by Crescent for Stratton-Warren Hdw. Co., Memphis, Tenn.

SHOTGUN, DOUBLE BARREL, SIDE-BY-SIDE			
☐ **Various Gauges**, Outside Hammers, Damascus Barrel, *Modern*	100.00	170.00	175.00
☐ **Various Gauges**, Hammerless, Steel Barrel, *Modern*	135.00	190.00	200.00
☐ **Various Gauges**, Hammerless, Damascus Barrel, *Modern*	100.00	170.00	175.00

	V.G.	Exc.	Prior Year Exc. Value
☐ **Various Gauges**, Outside Hammers, Steel Barrel, *Modern*	125.00	185.00	190.00
SHOTGUN, SINGLESHOT			
☐ **Various Gauges**, Hammer, Steel Barrel, *Modern*	55.00	85.00	85.00

SQUIBMAN

Made by Squires, Bingham, Makati, Phillipines.

	V.G.	Exc.	Prior Year Exc. Value
HANDGUN, REVOLVER			
☐ **Model 100 D**, .38 Spec., Double Action, Blue, Swing-Out Cylinder, Vent Rib, *Modern*	100.00	140.00	140.00
☐ **Model 100 DC**, .38 Spec., Double Action, Blue, Swing-Out Cylinder, *Modern*	80.00	125.00	125.00
☐ **Thunder Chief**, .38 Spec., Double Action, Blue, Swing-Out Cylinder, Vent Rib, Heavy Barrel, *Modern*	120.00	160.00	160.00
RIFLE, SEMI-AUTOMATIC			
☐ **Auto**, .22 L.R.R.F., Clip Fed, Shell Deflector, Flash Hider, *Modern*	40.00	60.00	55.00

SQUIRES BINGHAM

Makati, Phillipines.

	V.G.	Exc.	Prior Year Exc. Value
HANDGUN, REVOLVER			
☐ **M 100-D**, .22LR/.22 WMR Combo, Double Action, Solid Frame, Swing-Out Cylinder, Adjustable Sights, *Modern*	60.00	80.00	85.00
RIFLE, BOLT ACTION			
☐ **M 14D**, .22 L.R.R.F., Clip Fed, Checkered Stock, *Modern*	35.00	55.00	55.00
☐ **M 15**, .22 WMR, Clip Fed, Checkered Stock, *Modern*	55.00	75.00	75.00
RIFLE, SEMI-AUTOMATIC			
☐ **M-16**, .22 L.R.R.F., Clip Fed, Flash Hider, *Modern*	45.00	70.00	65.00
☐ **M20D**, .22 L.R.R.F., Clip Fed, Checkered Stock, *Modern*	45.00	65.00	65.00
SHOTGUN, SLIDE ACTION			
☐ **M 30/28**, 12 Ga., Plain, *Modern*	70.00	120.00	115.00

STAGGS-BILT

Staggs Enterprises, Phoenix, Ariz., c. 1970.

	V.G.	Exc.	Prior Year Exc. Value
COMBINATION WEAPON, OVER-UNDER			
☐ **20 Ga./.30-30**, Top Break, Hammerless, Double Triggers, Top Break, *Modern*	75.00	115.00	110.00

STANDARD ARMS CO.

Wilmington, Del., 1909-1911.

	V.G.	Exc.	Prior Year Exc. Value
RIFLE, SEMI-AUTOMATIC			
☐ **Model G**, Various Calibers, Takedown, Tube Feed, Hammerless, *Curio*	200.00	350.00	320.00
RIFLE, SLIDE ACTION			
☐ **Model M**, Various Calibers, Takedown, Tube Feed, Hammerless, *Curio*	175.00	265.00	250.00

	V.G.	Exc.	Prior Year Exc. Value

STANLEY
Belgium, c. 1900.

SHOTGUN, DOUBLE BARREL, SIDE-BY-SIDE

	V.G.	Exc.	Prior Year Exc. Value
☐ **Various Gauges**, Outside Hammers, Damascus Barrel, *Modern*	100.00	170.00	175.00
☐ **Various Gauges**, Hammerless, Steel Barrel, *Modern*	135.00	190.00	200.00
☐ **Various Gauges**, Hammerless, Damascus Barrel, *Modern*	100.00	170.00	175.00
☐ **Various Gauges**, Outside Hammers, Steel Barrel, *Modern*	125.00	185.00	190.00

SHOTGUN, SINGLESHOT

	V.G.	Exc.	Prior Year Exc. Value
☐ **Various Gauges**, Hammer, Steel Barrel, *Modern*	55.00	85.00	85.00

STANTON
London, England, c. 1778.

HANDGUN, FLINTLOCK

	V.G.	Exc.	Prior Year Exc. Value
☐ **.55 Officers**, Belt Pistol, Screw Barrel, Box Lock, Brass, *Antique*	950.00	1,750.00	1,700.00

Star Model A

Star Model 1 .32

STAR
Made by Bonifacio Echeverria, Eibar, Spain 1911 to date.

AUTOMATIC WEAPON, MACHINE-PISTOL

	V.G.	Exc.	Prior Year Exc. Value
☐ **Model MD**, .45 ACP, Clip Fed, Holster Stock, *Class 3*	650.00	875.00	850.00
☐ **Model MD**, 7.63 Mauser, Clip Fed, Holster Stock, *Class 3*	550.00	775.00	750.00
☐ **Model MD**, 9mm Luger, Clip Fed, Holster Stock, *Class 3*	650.00	825.00	800.00

AUTOMATIC WEAPON, SUBMACHINE GUN

	V.G.	Exc.	Prior Year Exc. Value
☐ **Model Z-45**, 9mm Luger, Clip Fed, Folding Stock, *Class 3*	400.00	550.00	525.00
☐ **Model Z-62**, 9mm Luger, Clip Fed, Folding Stock, *Class 3*	450.00	600.00	575.00
☐ **Model Z-63**, 9mm Luger, Clip Fed, Folding Stock, *Class 3*	525.00	700.00	675.00

HANDGUN, SEMI-AUTOMATIC	V.G.	Exc.	Prior Year Exc. Value
☐ **Model A**, .25 ACP, Clip Fed, *Modern*	140.00	195.00	190.00
☐ **Model A**, .38 ACP, Clip Fed, *Modern*	95.00	140.00	145.00
☐ **Model A**, .45 ACP, Clip Fed, Early Model, Adjustable Sights, Various Barrel Lengths, *Modern*	145.00	195.00	195.00
☐ **Model A**, 7.63 Mauser, Clip Fed, Early Model, Adjustable Sights, Various Barrel Lengths, Stock Lug, *Modern*	900.00	1,350.00	1,300.00
☐ **Model A**, 9mm Bergmann, Clip Fed, Early Model, Adjustable Sights, Various Barrel Lengths, *Modern*	125.00	160.00	165.00
☐ **Model A**, Various Calibers, Holster Stock, *Add* **$150.00-$250.00**			
☐ **Model AS**, .38 Super, Clip Fed, *Modern*	125.00	160.00	165.00
☐ **Model B**, 9mm Luger, Clip Fed, *Modern*	125.00	160.00	165.00
☐ **Model B**, 9mm Luger, Clip Fed, Early Model, Various Barrel Lengths, *Modern*	125.00	160.00	165.00
☐ **Model BKM**, 9mm Luger, Clip Fed, Lightweight, *Modern*	150.00	200.00	200.00
☐ **Model BKS-Starlight**, 9mm Luger, Clip Fed, Lightweight, *Modern*	175.00	225.00	225.00
☐ **Model BM**, 9mm Luger, Clip Fed, Steel Frame, *Modern*	150.00	200.00	200.00
☐ **Model C**, 9mm Bayard Long, Clip Fed, 8 Shot, *Modern*	120.00	160.00	160.00
☐ **Model C O**, .25 ACP, Clip Fed, *Modern*	110.00	150.00	150.00
☐ **Model C U**, .25 ACP, Clip Fed, Lightweight, *Modern*	85.00	125.00	125.00
☐ **Model D**, .380 ACP, Clip Fed, 6 Shot, *Modern*	115.00	150.00	150.00
☐ **Model D**, .380 ACP, Clip Fed, 15 Shot Clip, *Modern*	130.00	170.00	170.00
☐ **Model DK**, .380 ACP, Clip Fed, Lightweight, *Modern*	110.00	145.00	145.00
☐ **Model E Vest Pocket**, .25 ACP, Clip Fed, *Modern*	110.00	145.00	140.00
☐ **Model F**, .22 L.R.R.F., Clip Fed, *Modern*	90.00	135.00	135.00
☐ **Model F R S**, .22 L.R.R.F., Clip Fed, Target Pistol, Adjustable Sights, *Modern*	80.00	130.00	130.00
☐ **Model F T B**, .22 L.R.R.F., Clip Fed, Target Pistol, *Modern*	80.00	115.00	115.00
☐ **Model F-Olympic**, .22 Short R.F., Clip Fed, Target Pistol, *Modern*	135.00	175.00	175.00
☐ **Model F-Sport**, .22 L.R.R.F., Clip Fed, 6" Barrel, *Modern*	80.00	120.00	120.00
☐ **Model FR**, .22 L.R.R.F., Clip Fed, *Modern*	95.00	135.00	135.00
☐ **Model H**, .32 ACP, Clip Fed, 7 Shot, *Modern*	100.00	135.00	135.00
☐ **Model HF**, .22 L.R.R.F., Clip Fed, *Modern*	135.00	180.00	180.00
☐ **Model HN**, .380 ACP, Clip Fed, *Modern*	110.00	145.00	145.00
☐ **Model I**, .32 ACP, Clip Fed, 9 Shot, *Modern*	110.00	135.00	135.00
☐ **Model Lancer**, .22 L.R.R.F., Clip Fed, Lightweight, *Modern*	100.00	145.00	145.00
☐ **Model M**, .38 ACP, Clip Fed, *Modern*	100.00	135.00	135.00
☐ **Model Militar**, 9mm, Clip Fed, *Modern*	135.00	170.00	170.00
☐ **Model MMS**, 7.63 Mauser, Clip Fed, Stock Lug, *Modern*	675.00	1,000.00	1,000.00

	V.G.	Exc.	Prior Year Exc. Value
☐ **Model NZ**, .25 ACP, Clip Fed, *Modern*	325.00	435.00	425.00
☐ **Model 1**, .25 ACP, Clip Fed, *Modern*	185.00	250.00	250.00
☐ **Model 1**, .32 ACP, Clip Fed, *Mo, .380 ACP, Clip Fed, Modern*	185.00	250.00	250.00
☐ **Model P**, .45 ACP, Clip Fed, *Modern*	130.00	160.00	160.00
☐ **Model PD**, .45 ACP, Clip Fed, *Modern*	160.00	240.00	240.00
☐ **Model S**, .380 ACP, Clip Fed, *Modern*	95.00	135.00	135.00
☐ **Model S I**,Modern	110.00	145.00	
☐ **Model Militar**, 9mm, Clip Fed, *Modern*	135.00	175.00	175.00
☐ **Model NZ**, .25 ACP, Clip Fed, *Modern*	325.00	425.00	425.00
☐ **Model 1**, .25 ACP, Clip Fed, *Modern*	180.00	240.00	240.00
☐ **Model 1**, .32 ACP, Clip Fed, *Modern*	85.00	120.00	120.00
☐ **Model 28**, .9mm Luger, Clip Fed, *Modern*	250.00	365.00	—
☐ **Model SM**, .380 ACP, Clip Fed, *Modern*	95.00	130.00	130.00
☐ **Model Starfire**, .380 ACP, Clip Fed, Lightweight, *Modern*	95.00	135.00	135.00
☐ **Model Starlet**, .25 ACP, Clip Fed, Lightweight, *Modern*	80.00	120.00	120.00
☐ **Model Super A**, .38 ACP, Clip Fed, *Modern*	120.00	165.00	165.00
☐ **Model Super B**, 9mm Luger, Clip Fed, *Modern*	115.00	160.00	160.00
☐ **Model Super M**, .38 Super, Clip Fed, *Modern*	115.00	160.00	160.00
☐ **Model Super P**, .45 ACP, Clip Fed, *Modern*	135.00	185.00	185.00
☐ **Model Super S**, .380 ACP, Clip Fed, *Modern*	110.00	145.00	145.00
☐ **Model Super S I**, .32 ACP, Clip Fed, *Modern*	90.00	135.00	135.00
RIFLE, SINGLESHOT			
☐ **Rolling Block,** Various Calibers, Carbine, *Modern*	110.00	155.00	155.00

STAR GAUGE

Spain, Imported by Interarms.

	V.G.	Exc.	Prior Year Exc. Value
SHOTGUN, DOUBLE BARREL, SIDE-BY-SIDE			
☐ **12 and 20 Gauges**, Checkered Stock, Adjustable Choke, Double Trigger, *Modern*	150.00	220.00	225.00

STARR ARMS CO.

Yonkers and Binghamton, N.Y. 1860-1868

	V.G.	Exc.	Prior Year Exc. Value
HANDGUN, PERCUSSION			
☐ **1858 Navy**, .36, Revolver, 6 Shot, 6" Barrel, Double Action, *Antique*	400.00	675.00	650.00
☐ **1858 Army**, .44, Revolver, 6 Shot, 6" Barrel, Double Action, *Antique*	300.00	500.00	485.00
☐ **1863 Army**, .44, Revolver, 6 Shot, 6" Barrel, Double Action, *Antique*	375.00	600.00	585.00
RIFLE, PERCUSSION			
☐ **Carbine**, .54, Underlever, *Antique*	450.00	695.00	675.00
RIFLE, SINGLESHOT			
☐ **Carbine**, .52 R.F., Underlever, *Antique*	500.00	825.00	800.00

STATE ARMS CO.

Made by Crescent for J.H. Lau & Co., c. 1900.

	V.G.	Exc.	Prior Year Exc. Value
SHOTGUN, DOUBLE BARREL, SIDE-BY-SIDE			
☐ **Various Gauges**, Outside Hammers, Damascus Barrel, *Modern*	100.00	170.00	175.00

	V.G.	Exc.	Prior Year Exc. Value
☐ **Various Gauges**, Hammerless, Steel Barrel, *Modern*	135.00	190.00	200.00
☐ **Various Gauges**, Hammerless, Damascus Barrel, *Modern*	100.00	170.00	175.00
☐ **Various Gauges**, Outside Hammers, Steel Barrel, *Modern*	125.00	185.00	190.00

SHOTGUN, SINGLESHOT

☐ **Various Gauges**, Hammer, Steel Barrel, *Modern*	55.00	85.00	85.00

STEIGLEDER, ERNST

Suhl & Berlin, Germany 1921-1935.

RIFLE, DOUBLE BARREL, SIDE-BY-SIDE

☐ **Various Calibers**, Box Lock, Engraved, Checkered Stock, Color Case Hardened Frame, *Modern*	1,850.00	2,650.00	2,600.00

STENDA

Stenda Werke Waffenfabrik, Suhl, Germany, c. 1920.

HANDGUN, SEMI-AUTOMATIC

☐ **.32 ACP**, Blue, Clip Fed, *Modern*	145.00	210.00	195.00

STERLING ARMS CORP.

Gasport and Lockport, N.Y.

HANDGUN, SEMI-AUTOMATIC

☐ **#283 Target 300**, .22 L.R.R.F., Hammer, Adjustable Sights, Various Barrel Lengths, *Modern*	85.00	130.00	125.00
☐ **#284 Target 300 L**, .22 L.R.R.F., Hammer, Adjustable Sights, Tapered Barrel, *Modern*	85.00	130.00	125.00
☐ **#285 Huskey**, .22 L.R.R.F., Hammer, Heavy Barrel, *Modern*	75.00	120.00	115.00
☐ **#286 Trapper**, .22 L.R.R.F., Hammer, Tapered Barrel, *Modern*	75.00	120.00	115.00
☐ **Model 300B**, .25 ACP, Blue, *Modern*	55.00	80.00	80.00
☐ **Model 300N**, .25 ACP, Nickel Plated, *Modern*	60.00	85.00	85.00
☐ **Model 300S**, .25 ACP, Stainless Steel, *Modern*	60.00	95.00	95.00
☐ **Model 302B**, .22 L.R.R.F., Blue, *Modern*	55.00	80.00	80.00
☐ **Model 302N**, .22 L.R.R.F., Nickel Plated, *Modern*	60.00	85.00	85.00
☐ **Model 302S**, .22 L.R.R.F., Stainless Steel, *Modern*	65.00	95.00	95.00
☐ **Model 400B**, .380 ACP, Blue, Clip Fed, *Modern*	95.00	145.00	145.00
☐ **Model 400N**, .380 ACP, Nickel Plated, Clip Fed, *Modern*	100.00	150.00	150.00
☐ **Model 400S**, .380 ACP, Stainless Steel, Clip Fed, *Modern*	135.00	175.00	175.00
☐ **Model 402**, .22 L.R.R.F., Blue, Clip Fed, *Modern*	75.00	110.00	110.00
☐ **Model 402**, .22 L.R.R.F., Nickel Plated, Clip Fed, *Modern*	75.00	110.00	110.00
☐ **Model 402 MkII**, .32 ACP, Blue, Clip Fed, *Modern*	95.00	145.00	145.00
☐ **Model 402 MkIIS**, .32 ACP, Stainless Steel, Clip Fed, *Modern*	135.00	175.00	175.00

Sterling PPL

	V.G.	Exc.	Prior Year Exc. Value
☐ **Model 450**, .45 ACP, Clip Fed, Double Action, Adjustable Sights, Blue, *Modern*	175.00	265.00	250.00
☐ **Model PPL**, .380 ACP, Short Barrel, Clip Fed, *Modern*	110.00	150.00	145.00
RIFLE, SINGLESHOT			
☐ **Backpacker**, .22 L.R.R.F., Takedown, *Modern*	25.00	35.00	35.00

STERLING ARMS CORP.

Made by Crescent for H. & D. Folsom, c. 1900.

SHOTGUN, DOUBLE BARREL, SIDE-BY-SIDE			
☐ **Various Gauges**, Outside Hammers, Damascus Barrel, *Modern*	100.00	170.00	175.00
☐ **Various Gauges**, Hammerless, Steel Barrel, *Modern*	135.00	190.00	200.00
☐ **Various Gauges**, Hammerless, Damascus Barrel, *Modern*	100.00	170.00	175.00
☐ **Various Gauges**, Outside Hammers, Steel Barrel, *Modern*	125.00	185.00	190.00
SHOTGUN, SINGLESHOT			
☐ **Various Gauges**, Hammer, Steel Barrel, *Modern*	55.00	85.00	85.00

STERLING REVOLVERS

Maker unknown, c. 1880.

HANDGUN, REVOLVER			
☐ **.22 Short R.F.**, 7 Shot, Spur Trigger, Solid Frame, Single Action, *Antique*	90.00	165.00	160.00
☐ **.32 Short R.F.**, 5 Shot, Spur Trigger, Solid Frame, Single Action, *Antique*	95.00	170.00	170.00

STEVENS, J. ARMS & TOOL CO.

Chicopee Falls, Mass. 1864-1886. Became J. Stevens Arms & Tools Co. in 1886, absorbed Page-Lewis Arms Co., Davis-Warner Arms Co., and Crescent Firearms Co. in 1926. Became a subsidiary of Savage in 1936.

COMBINATION WEAPON, OVER-UNDER			
☐ **Model 22-410,** .22-.410 Ga., Hammer, Plastic Stock, *Modern*	55.00	85.00	85.00
☐ **Model 22-410,** .22-.410 Ga., Hammer, Wood Stock, *Modern*	65.00	95.00	95.00
HANDGUN, SINGLESHOT			
☐ **1888 #1,** Various Calibers, Tip-Up, Octagon Barrel, Open Rear Sight, *Antique*	95.00	155.00	150.00

	V.G.	Exc.	Prior Year Exc. Value
☐ **1888 #2 "Gallery",** .22 L.R.R.F., Tip-Up, Octagon Barrel, Open Rear Sight, *Antique*	115.00	150.00	145.00
☐ **1888 #3 "Combined Sight",** Various Calibers, Tip-Up, Octagon Barrel, *Antique*	125.00	165.00	160.00
☐ **1888 #4 "Combined Sight",** .22 L.R.R.F., Tip-Up, Octagon Barrel, *Antique*	120.00	155.00	150.00
☐ **1888 #5 "Expert",** Various Calibers, Tip-Up, Half Octagon Barrel, *Antique*	125.00	165.00	160.00
☐ **1894 "New Ideal",** Various Calibers, Level Action, Falling Block, Vernier Sights, *Antique*	220.00	315.00	300.00
☐ **Model 23 "Sure-Shot",** .22 L.R.R.F., Side-Swing Barrel, Hammer, *Antique*	85.00	120.00	115.00
☐ **Model 34 "Hunters Pet",** Various Rimfires, Tip-Up, Octagon Barrel, with Shoulder Stock, *Curio*	300.00	440.00	395.00
☐ **Model 39 New Model Pocket Shotgun,** Various Calibers, Tip-Up, Smoothbore, with Shoulder Stock, *Class 3*	115.00	160.00	155.00
☐ **Model 40 New Model Pocket Rifle,** Various Calibers, Tip-Up, with Shoulder Stock, *Curio*	295.00	405.00	390.00
☐ **Model 42 Reliable Pocket Rifle,** .22 L.R.R.F., Tip-Up, with Shoulder Stock, *Curio*	190.00	275.00	265.00
☐ **Model "Offhand",** .410 Ga., Tip-Up, *Class 3*	190.00	275.00	265.00
☐ **Model 10,** .22 L.R.R.F., Tip-Up, Target, Various Barrel Lengths, *Modern*	95.00	150.00	145.00
☐ **Model 34 "Hunters Pet",** Various Rimfires, Tip-Up, Half-Octagon Barrel, with Shoulder Stock, Vernier Sights, *Curio*	345.00	450.00	425.00
☐ **Model 35 "Offhand",** .22 L.R.R.F., Tip-Up, Target, Various Barrel Lengths, *Modern*	220.00	310.00	295.00
☐ **Model 35 "Offhand",** .22 L.R.R.F., Tip-Up, Target, Ivory Grips, Various Barrel Lengths, *Modern*	250.00	365.00	345.00
☐ **Model 35 Autoshot,** .410 Ga., Tip-Up, Various Barrel Lengths, *Class 3*	185.00	260.00	245.00
☐ **Model 37 "Gould",** Various Calibers, Tip-Up, *Modern*	200.00	285.00	275.00
☐ **Model 38 "Conlin",** .22 L.R.R.F., Tip-Up, *Modern*	250.00	350.00	335.00
☐ **Model 41,** .22 L.R.R.F., Tip-Up, Pocket Pistol, *Modern*	120.00	155.00	150.00
☐ **Model 43 "Diamond",** .22 L.R.R.F., Tip-Up, Spur Trigger, 6″ Barrel, Octagon Barrel, *Modern*	130.00	180.00	175.00
☐ **Model 43 "Diamond",** .22 L.R.R.F., Tip-Up, Spur Trigger, 10″ Barrel, Octagon Barrel, *Modern*	140.00	190.00	185.00
☐ **Model 43 "Diamond",** .22 L.R.R.F., Tip-Up, Spur Trigger, 6″ Barrel, Globe Sights, *Modern*	150.00	200.00	195.00
☐ **Model 43 "Diamond",** .22 L.R.R.F., Tip-Up, Spur Trigger, 10″ Barrel, Globe Sights, *Modern*	180.00	245.00	235.00

RIFLE, BOLT ACTION

	V.G.	Exc.	Prior Year Exc. Value
☐ **Model 053 Buckhorn,** Various Rimfires, Singleshot, Peep Sights, *Modern*	40.00	55.00	55.00
☐ **Model 056 Buckhorn,** .22 L.R.R.F., 5 Shot Clip, Peep Sights, *Modern*	55.00	80.00	75.00
☐ **Model 066 Buckhorn,** .22 L.R.R.F., Tube Feed, Peep Sights, *Modern*	55.00	80.00	75.00
☐ **Model 083,** .22 L.R.R.F., Singleshot, Peep Sights, Takedown, *Modern*	38.00	60.00	55.00

	V.G.	Exc.	Prior Year Exc. Value
☐ **Model 084,** .22 L.R.R.F., 5 Shot Clip, Peep Sights, Takedown, *Modern*	42.00	65.00	60.00
☐ **Model 086,** .22 L.R.R.F., Tube Feed, Takedown, Peep Sights, *Modern*	53.00	75.00	70.00
☐ **Model 15,** .22 L.R.R.F., Singleshot, (Springfield), *Modern*	32.00	48.00	45.00
☐ **Model 15Y,** .22 L.R.R.F., Singleshot, *Modern*	32.00	48.00	45.00
☐ **Model 322,** .22 Hornet, Clip Fed, Carbine, Open Rear Sight, *Modern*	85.00	130.00	125.00
☐ **Model 322-S,** .22 Hornet, Clip Fed, Carbine, Peep Sights, *Modern*	90.00	135.00	130.00
☐ **Model 325,** .30-30 Win., Clip Fed, Carbine, Open Rear Sight, *Modern*	85.00	130.00	125.00
☐ **Model 325-S,** .30-30 Win., Clip Fed, Carbine, Peep Sights, *Modern*	90.00	135.00	130.00
☐ **Model 416,** .22 L.R.R.F., 5 Shot Clip, Peep Sights, Target Stock, *Modern*	125.00	195.00	185.00
☐ **Model 419,** .22 L.R.R.F., Singleshot, Peep Sights, *Modern*	48.00	85.00	80.00
☐ **Model 48,** .22 L.R.R.F., Singleshot, Takedown, *Modern*	32.00	48.00	45.00
☐ **Model 49,** .22 L.R.R.F., Singleshot, Takedown, *Modern*	32.00	48.00	45.00
☐ **Model 50,** .22 L.R.R.F., Singleshot, Takedown, *Modern*	32.00	48.00	45.00
☐ **Model 51,** .22 L.R.R.F., Singleshot, Takedown, *Modern*	32.00	48.00	45.00
☐ **Model 52,** .22 L.R.R.F., Singleshot, Takedown, *Modern*	37.00	55.00	50.00
☐ **Model 53,** .22 L.R.R.F., Singleshot, Takedown, *Modern*	37.00	55.00	50.00
☐ **Model 56 Buckhorn,** .22 L.R.R.F., 5 Shot Clip, Open Rear Sight, *Modern*	42.00	65.00	60.00
☐ **Model 65 "Little Krag",** .22 L.R.R.F., Singleshot, Takedown, *Modern*	115.00	165.00	160.00
☐ **Model 66 Buckhorn,** .22 L.R.R.F., Tube Feed, Open Rear Sight, *Modern*	42.00	60.00	55.00
☐ **Model 82,** .22 L.R.R.F., Singleshot, Peep Sights, (Springfield), *Modern*	32.00	48.00	45.00
☐ **Model 83,** .22 L.R.R.F., Singleshot, Open Rear Sight, Takedown, *Modern*	27.00	42.00	40.00
☐ **Model 84,** .22 L.R.R.F., 5 Shot Clip, Open Rear Sight, Takedown, *Modern*	37.00	60.00	55.00
☐ **Model 86,** .22 L.R.R.F., Tube Feed, Takedown, Open Rear Sight, *Modern*	48.00	70.00	65.00
RIFLE, LEVER ACTION			
☐ **Model 425,** Various Calibers, Hammer, *Curio*	160.00	230.00	225.00
☐ **Model 430,** Various Calibers, Hammer, Checkered Stock, *Curio*	180.00	280.00	275.00
☐ **Model 435,** Various Calibers, Hammer, Light Engraving, Fancy Checkering, *Curio*	265.00	395.00	385.00
☐ **Model 440,** Various Calibers, Hammer, Fancy Checkering, Fancy Engraving, Fancy Wood, *Curio*	585.00	885.00	875.00

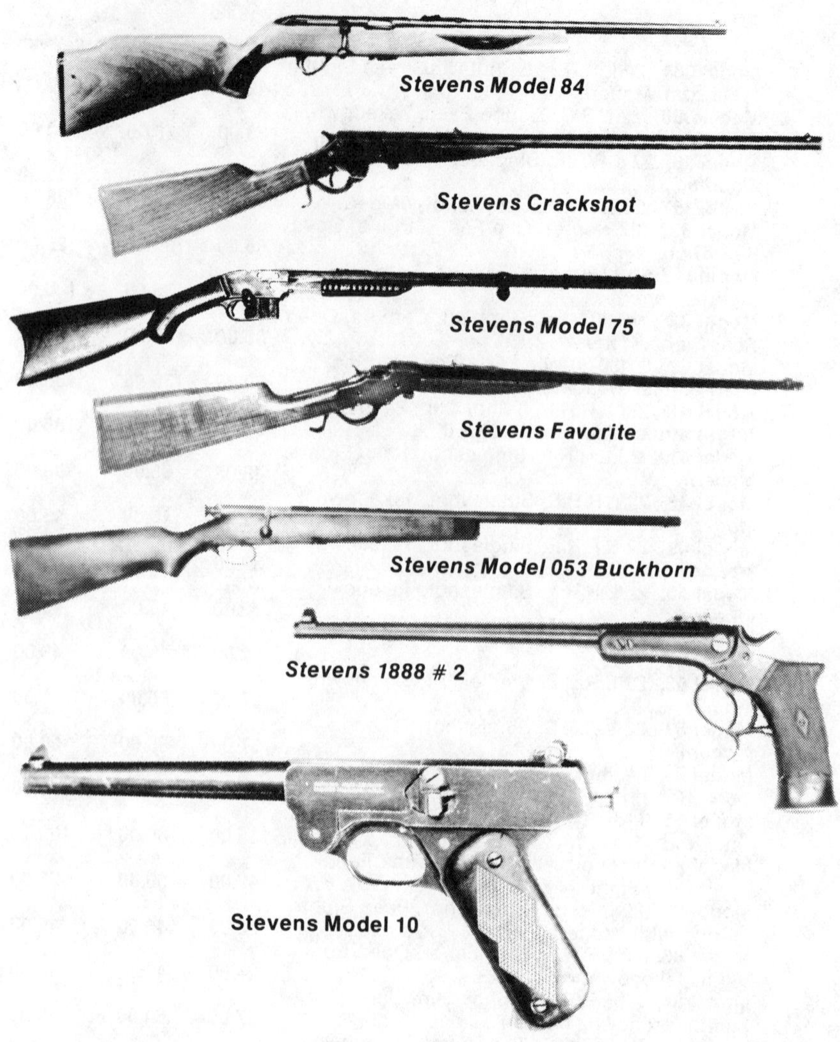
Stevens Model 84

Stevens Crackshot

Stevens Model 75

Stevens Favorite

Stevens Model 053 Buckhorn

Stevens 1888 # 2

Stevens Model 10

RIFLE, SEMI-AUTOMATIC	V.G.	Exc.	Prior Year Exc. Value
☐ **Model 057 Buckhorn,** .22 L.R.R.F., 5 Shot Clip, Peep Sights, *Modern*	60.00	85.00	80.00
☐ **Model 076 Buckhorn,** .22 L.R.R.F., Peep Sights, Tube Feed, *Modern*	60.00	85.00	80.00
☐ **Model 085 Springfield,** .22 L.R.R.F., 5 Shot Clip, Peep Sights, *Modern*	60.00	85.00	80.00
☐ **Model 57 Buckhorn,** .22 L.R.R.F., 5 Shot Clip, Open Rear Sight, *Modern*	55.00	80.00	75.00

	V.G.	Exc.	Prior Year Exc. Value
☐ **Model 76 Buckhorn,** .22 L.R.R.F., Open Rear Sight, Tube Feed, *Modern*	60.00	85.00	80.00
☐ **Model 85 Springfield,** .22 L.R.R.F., 5 Shot Clip, Open Rear Sight, *Modern*	60.00	85.00	80.00
☐ **Model 87,** .22 L.R.R.F., Tube Feed, Open Rear Sight, *Modern*	60.00	85.00	80.00
☐ **Model 87-S,** .22 L.R.R.F., Peep Sights, Tube Feed, *Modern*	60.00	85.00	80.00
☐ **Model 87K Scout,** .22 L.R.R.F., Tube Feed, Open Rear Sight, Carbine, *Modern*	60.00	85.00	80.00
RIFLE, SINGLESHOT			
☐ **1888 #10 "Range",** Various Calibers, Tip-Up, Half-Octagon Barrel, Fancy Wood, Vernier Sights, *Antique*	180.00	245.00	235.00
☐ **1888 #11 "Ladies",** Various Calibers, Tip-Up, Half-Octagon Barrel, Open Rear Sight, *Antique*	140.00	180.00	170.00
☐ **1888 #12 "Ladies",** Various Calibers, Tip-Up, Half-Octagon Barrel, Open Rear Sight, Fancy Wood, *Antique*	180.00	275.00	260.00
☐ **1888 #13 "Ladies",** Various Calibers, Tip-Up, Half-Octagon Barrel, Vernier Sights, *Antique*	175.00	245.00	235.00
☐ **1888 #14 "Ladies",** Various Calibers, Tip-Up, Half-Octagon Barrel, Vernier Sights, Fancy Wood, *Antique*	230.00	300.00	285.00
☐ **1888 #15 "Crack Shot",** Various Calibers, Tip-Up, Half-Octagon Barrel, Peep Sights, *Antique*	180.00	230.00	220.00
☐ **1888 #16 "Crack Shot",** Various Calibers, Tip-Up, Half-Octagon Barrel, Peep Sights, Fancy Wood, *Antique*	190.00	245.00	240.00
☐ **1888 #6 "Expert",** Various Calibers, Tip-Up, Half-Octagon Barrel, Fancy Wood, *Antique*	145.00	205.00	195.00
☐ **1888 #7 "Premier",** Various Calibers, Tip-Up, Half-Octagon Barrel, Globe Sights, *Antique*	140.00	185.00	180.00
☐ **1888 #8 "Premier",** Various Calibers, Tip-Up, Half-Octagon Barrel, Fancy Wood, Globe Sights, *Antique*	170.00	230.00	220.00
☐ **1888 #9 "Range",** Various Calibers, Tip-Up, Half-Octagon Barrel, Vernier Sights, *Antique*	155.00	195.00	190.00
☐ **Model 101 Featherweight,** .44-40 WCF, Lever Action, Tip-Up, Smoothbore, Takedown, Half-Octagon Barrel, *Modern*	120.00	160.00	155.00
☐ **Model 101,** with Extra 22 Barrel, .44-40 WCF, Lever Action, Tip-Up, Smoothbore, Takedown, Half-Octagon Barrel, *Modern*	170.00	230.00	225.00
☐ **Model 11 "Ladies",** Various Rimfires, Tip-Up, Open Rear Sight, *Modern*	125.00	180.00	170.00
☐ **Model 12 "Marksman",** Various Rimfires, Hammer, Lever Action, Tip-Up, *Modern*	95.00	145.00	135.00
☐ **Model 13 "Ladies",** Various Rimfires, Tip-Up Vernier Sights, *Modern*	140.00	185.00	175.00
☐ **Model 14 "Little Scout",** .22 L.R.R.F., Hammer, Rolling Block, *Curio*	105.00	165.00	155.00
☐ **Model 14½ "Little Scout",** .22 L.R.R.F., Hammer, Rolling Block, *Modern*	85.00	130.00	125.00
☐ **Model 15 "Maynard Jr.",** .22 L.R.R.F., Lever Action, Tip-Up, *Modern*	85.00	130.00	125.00

	V.G.	Exc.	Prior Year Exc. Value
☐ **Model 15½ "Maynard Jr.",** .22 L.R.R.F., Lever Action, Tip-Up, *Modern*	85.00	135.00	130.00
☐ **Model 17,** Various Rimfires, Lever Action, Takedown, Favorite, Open Rear Sight, *Modern*	95.00	150.00	145.00
☐ **Model 18,** Various Rimfires, Lever Action, Takedown, Favorite, Vernier Sights, *Modern*	110.00	165.00	160.00
☐ **Model 19,** Various Rimfires, Lever Action, Takedown, Favorite, Lyman Sights, *Modern*	100.00	160.00	155.00
☐ **Model 2,** Various Rimfires, Tip-Up, Open Rear Sight, *Modern*	155.00	240.00	220.00
☐ **Model 20,** Various Rimfires, Lever Action, Takedown, Favorite, Smoothbore, *Curio*	85.00	130.00	125.00
☐ **Model 26,** Crack-Shot, Various Rimfires, Lever Action, Takedown, Open Rear Sight, *Curio*	85.00	140.00	135.00
☐ **Model 26½,** Various Rimfires, Lever Action, Takedown, Smoothbore, *Modern*	95.00	140.00	135.00
☐ **Model 27,** Various Rimfires, Lever Action, Takedown, Favorite, Octagon Barrel, Open Rear Sight, *Modern*	120.00	160.00	155.00
☐ **Model 28,** Various Rimfires, Lever Action, Takedown, Favorite, Octagon Barrel, Vernier Sights, *Modern*	125.00	170.00	165.00
☐ **Model 29,** Various Rimfires, Lever Action, Takedown, Favorite, Octagon Barrel, Lyman Sights, *Modern*	125.00	170.00	165.00
☐ **Model 404,** .22 L.R.R.F., Hammer, Falling Block, Target Sights, Full-Stocked, *Modern*	375.00	480.00	475.00
☐ **Model 414 "Armory",** .22 L.R.R.F., Lever Action, Lyman Sights, *Modern*	225.00	330.00	325.00
☐ **Model 417½,** Various Calibers, Lever Action, Walnut Hill, *Modern*	325.00	430.00	425.00
☐ **Model 417-0,** Various Calibers, Lever Action, Walnut Hill, *Modern*	330.00	430.00	425.00
☐ **Model 417-1,** Various Calibers, Lever Action, Lyman Sights, Walnut Hill, *Modern*	325.00	430.00	425.00
☐ **Model 417-2,** Various Calibers, Lever Action, Vernier Sights, Walnut Hill, *Modern*	345.00	460.00	450.00
☐ **Model 417-3,** Various Calibers, Lever Action, no Sights, Walnut Hill, *Modern*	325.00	430.00	425.00
☐ **Model 418,** .22 L.R.R.F., Lever Action, Takedown, Walnut Hill. *Modern*	195.00	285.00	280.00
☐ **Model 418½,** Various Rimfires, Lever Action, Takedown, Walnut Hill, *Modern*	190.00	275.00	270.00
☐ **Model 44 "Ideal",** Various Calibers, Lever Action, Rolling Block, *Modern*	230.00	330.00	325.00
☐ **Model 44½ "Ideal",** Various Calibers, Lever Action, Falling Block, *Modern*	325.00	405.00	400.00
☐ **Model 49 "Ideal",** Various Calibers, Walnut Hill, Lever Action, Falling Block, Engraved, Fancy Checkering, *Modern*	590.00	865.00	850.00
☐ **Model 5,** Various Rimfires, Tip-Up, Vernier Sights, *Modern*	165.00	230.00	225.00
☐ **Model 51 "Pope",** Various Calibers, Schutzen Rifle, Lever Action, Falling Block, Engraved, Fancy Checkering, *Modern*	615.00	810.00	800.00

	V.G.	Exc.	Prior Year Exc. Value
☐ **Model 52 "Pope, Jr.",** Various Calibers, Schutzen Rifle, Lever Action, Falling Block, Engraved, Fancy Checkering, *Modern*	565.00	785.00	775.00
☐ **Model 54 "Pope",** Various Calibers, Schutzen Rifle, Lever Action, Falling Block, Fancy Engraving, Fancy Checkering, *Modern*	670.00	915.00	900.00
☐ **Model 56 "Pope Ladies",** Various Calibers, Schutzen Rifle, Lever Action, Falling Block, Fancy Checkering, *Modern*	310.00	430.00	425.00
☐ **Model 7 "Swiss Butt",** Various Rimfires, Tip-Up, Vernier Sights, *Modern*	170.00	250.00	245.00
RIFLE, SLIDE ACTION			
☐ **Model 70,** .22 L.R.R.F., Hammer, Solid Frame, *Modern*	125.00	175.00	170.00
☐ **Model 71,** .22 L.R.R.F., Hammer, Solid Frame, *Modern*	130.00	190.00	185.00
☐ **Model 75,** .22 L.R.R.F., Tube Feed, Hammerless, *Modern*	130.00	205.00	200.00
☐ **Model 80,** Various Rimfires, Tube Feed, Takedown, *Modern*	120.00	160.00	155.00
SHOTGUN, BOLT ACTION			
☐ **Model 237,** 20 Ga., Takedown, Singleshot, (Springfield), *Modern*	32.00	48.00	45.00
☐ **Model 258,** 20 Ga., Takedown, Clip Fed, *Modern*	47.00	70.00	65.00
☐ **Model 37,** .410 Ga., Takedown, Singleshot, (Springfield), *Modern*	37.00	55.00	50.00
☐ **Model 38,** .410 Ga., Takedown, Clip Fed, (Springfield), *Modern*	37.00	60.00	55.00
☐ **Model 39,** .410 Ga., Takedown, Tube Feed, (Springfield), *Modern*	43.00	60.00	55.00
☐ **Model 58,** .410 Ga., Takedown, Clip Fed, *Modern*	43.00	60.00	55.00
☐ **Model 59,** .410 Ga., Takedown, Tube Feed, *Modern*	48.00	70.00	65.00
SHOTGUN, DOUBLE BARREL, OVER-UNDER			
☐ **Model 240,** .410 Ga., Hammer, Plastic Stock, *Modern*	130.00	175.00	170.00
☐ **Model 240,** .410 Ga., Hammer, Wood Stock, *Modern*	140.00	180.00	175.00
SHOTGUN, DOUBLE BARREL, SIDE-BY-SIDE			
☐ **M 315,** Various Gauges, Hammerless, Steel Barrel, *Modern*	130.00	185.00	180.00
☐ **Model 215,** 12 and 16 Gauges, Outside Hammers, Steel Barrel, *Modern*	105.00	175.00	170.00
☐ **Model 235,** Various Gauges, Outside Hammers, Checkered Stock, Steel Barrel, *Modern*	115.00	170.00	165.00
☐ **Model 250,** Various Gauges, Outside Hammers, Checkered Stock, Steel Barrel, *Modern*	115.00	170.00	165.00
☐ **Model 255,** 12 and 16 Gauges, Outside Hammers, Checkered Stock, Steel Barrel, *Modern*	115.00	170.00	165.00
☐ **Model 260 "Twist",** Various Gauges, Outside Hammers, Checkered Stock, Damascus Barrel, *Modern*	100.00	155.00	150.00

	V.G.	Exc.	Prior Year Exc. Value
☐ **Model 265 "Krupp",** 12 and 16 Gauges, Outside Hammers, Checkered Stock, Steel Barrel, *Modern*	115.00	170.00	165.00
☐ **Model 270 "Nitro",** Various Gauges, Outside Hammers, Checkered Stock, Damascus Barrel, *Modern*	125.00	175.00	170.00
☐ **Model 311,** Various Gauges, Hammerless, Steel Barrel, *Modern*	140.00	200.00	195.00
☐ **Model 311-R Guard Gun,** 12 or 20 Gauge, Double Trigger, 18½" Cylinder Bore, Solid Rib, *Modern*	262.50	280.00	275.00
☐ **Model 311 ST,** Various Gauges, Hammerless, Steel Barrel, Single Trigger, *Modern*	150.00	205.00	200.00
☐ **Model 3151,** Various Gauges, Hammerless, Recoil Pad, Front and Rear Bead Sights, *Modern*	130.00	190.00	185.00
☐ **Model 330,** Various Gauges, Hammerless, Checkered Stock, *Modern*	120.00	170.00	165.00
☐ **Model 335,** 12 and 16 Gauges, Hammerless, Steel Barrel, Checkered Stock, Double Trigger, *Modern*	130.00	175.00	170.00
☐ **Model 345,** 20 Ga., Hammerless, Checkered Stock, Steel Barrel, Double Trigger, *Modern*	130.00	175.00	170.00
☐ **Model 355,** 12 and 16 Gauges, Hammerless, Steel Barrel, Checkered Stock, Double Trigger, *Modern*	115.00	170.00	165.00
☐ **Model 365 "Krupp",** 12 and 16 Gauges, Hammerless, Checkered Stock, Steel Barrel, Double Trigger, *Modern*	130.00	185.00	180.00
☐ **Model 375 "Krupp",** 12 and 16 Gauges, Hammerless, Light Engraving, Fancy Checkering, Double Trigger, Steel Barrel, *Modern*	140.00	195.00	190.00
☐ **Model 385 "Krupp",** 12 and 16 Gauges, Hammerless, Fancy Checkering, Fancy Engraving, Double Trigger, Steel Barrel, *Modern*	175.00	230.00	225.00
☐ **Model 515,** Various Gauges, Hammerless, *Modern*	105.00	150.00	145.00
☐ **Model 5151,** Various Gauges, Hammerless, Steel Barrel, *Modern*	130.00	170.00	165.00
☐ **Model 530,** Various Gauges, Hammerless, Steel Barrel, Double Trigger, *Modern*	115.00	165.00	160.00
☐ **Model 530 ST,** Various Gauges, Hammerless, Steel Barrel, Single Trigger, *Modern*	140.00	200.00	195.00
☐ **Model 530M,** Various Gauges, Hammerless, Plastic Stock, *Modern*	100.00	140.00	135.00
SHOTGUN, PUMP			
☐ **Model 520,** 12 Ga., Takedown, *Modern*	100.00	150.00	145.00
☐ **Model 620,** Various Gauges, Takedown, *Modern*	95.00	145.00	140.00
SHOTGUN, SEMI-AUTOMATIC			
☐ **Model 124,** 12 Ga., Plastic Stock, *Modern*	78.00	125.00	120.00
SHOTGUN, SINGLESHOT			
☐ **Various Gauges,** Hammer, Automatic Ejector, *Modern*	47.00	70.00	65.00

	V.G.	Exc.	Prior Year Exc. Value
☐ **Various Gauges,** Hammer, Automatic Ejector, Raised Matted Rib, *Modern*	53.00	80.00	75.00
☐ **1888 "New Style",** Various Gauges, Tip-Up, Hammer, Damascus Barrel, *Antique*	180.00	240.00	235.00
☐ **Model 100,** Various Gauges, Selective Ejector, Hammer, *Modern*	37.00	60.00	55.00
☐ **Model 102,** .410 Ga., Hammer, Featherweight, *Modern*	32.00	47.00	45.00
☐ **Model 102,** 24, 28 and 32 Gauges, Hammer, Featherweight, *Modern*	37.00	53.00	50.00
☐ **Model 104,** .410 Ga., Hammer, Featherweight, Automatic Ejector, *Modern*	43.00	53.00	50.00
☐ **Model 104,** 24, 28 and 32 Gauges, Hammer, Automatic Ejector, Featherweight, *Modern*	53.00	67.00	65.00
☐ **Model 105,** 20 Ga., Hammer, *Modern*	37.00	50.00	45.00
☐ **Model 105,** 28 Ga., Hammer, *Modern*	37.00	55.00	50.00
☐ **Model 106,** .410 Ga. 2½", Hammer, *Modern*	32.00	45.00	40.00
☐ **Model 106,** .44-40 WCF, Hammer, Smoothbore, *Modern*	43.00	60.00	55.00
☐ **Model 106,** .32 Ga., Hammer, *Modern*	32.00	50.00	45.00
☐ **Model 107,** Various Gauges, Hammer, Automatic Ejector, *Modern*	45.00	60.00	55.00
☐ **Model 108,** .410 Ga. 2½", Hammer, Automatic Ejector, *Modern*	33.00	50.00	45.00
☐ **Model 108,** .44-40 WCF, Hammer, Automatic Ejector, Smoothbore, *Modern*	42.00	70.00	60.00
☐ **Model 108,** 32 Ga., Hammer, Automatic Ejector, *Modern*	38.00	55.00	50.00
☐ **Model 110,** Various Gauges, Selective Ejector, Checkered Stock, Hammer, *Modern*	37.00	55.00	50.00
☐ **Model 120,** Various Gauges, Selective Ejector, Fancy Checkering, Hammer, *Modern*	43.00	60.00	55.00
☐ **Model 125 Ladies,** 20 Ga., Automatic Ejector, Hammer, *Modern*	43.00	60.00	55.00
☐ **Model 125 Ladies,** .28 Ga., Automatic Ejector, Hammer, *Modern*	48.00	70.00	65.00
☐ **Model 140,** Various Gauges, Selective Ejector, Hammerless, Checkered Stock, *Modern*	47.00	70.00	65.00
☐ **Model 160,** Various Gauges, Hammer, *Modern*	32.00	48.00	45.00
☐ **Model 165,** Various Gauges, Automatic Ejector, Hammer, *Modern*	32.00	48.00	45.00
☐ **Model 170,** Various Gauges, Automatic Ejector, Hammer, Checkered Stock, *Modern*	37.00	48.00	45.00
☐ **Model 180,** Various Gauges, Hammerless, Automatic Ejector, Checkered Stock, Round Barrel, *Modern*	57.00	90.00	85.00
☐ **Model 182,** 12 Ga., Hammerless, Automatic Ejector, Light Engraving, Checkered Stock, Trap Grade, *Modern*	80.00	125.00	120.00
☐ **Model 185,** For Damascus Barrel, *Deduct* **25%**			
☐ **Model 185,** For 16 or 20 Gauge, *Add* **20%**			
☐ **Model 185,** 12 Ga., Hammerless, Automatic Ejector, Checkered Stock, Half-Octagon Barrel, *Modern*	100.00	140.00	135.00
☐ **Model 190,** For Damascus Barrel, *Deduct* **25%**			
☐ **Model 190,** For 16 or 20 Gauge, *Add* **20%**			

	V.G.	Exc.	Prior Year Exc. Value
☐ **Model 190,** 12 Ga., Hammerless, Automatic Ejector, Fancy Checkering, Light Engraving, Half-Octagon Barrel, *Modern*	125.00	170.00	165.00
☐ **Model 195,** For Damascus Barrel, *Deduct* **25%**			
☐ **Model 195,** For 16 or 20 Gauge, *Add* **20%**			
☐ **Model 195,** 12 Ga., Hammerless, Automatic Ejector, Fancy Checkering, Fancy Engraving, Half-Octagon Barrel, *Modern*	200.00	285.00	275.00
☐ **Model 89 Dreadnaught,** Various Gauges, Hammer, *Modern*	50.00	67.00	65.00
☐ **Model 90,** Various Gauges, Takedown, Automatic Ejector, Plain, Hammer, *Modern*	40.00	58.00	55.00
☐ **Model 93,** 12 and 16 Gauges, Hammer, *Modern*	37.00	52.00	50.00
☐ **Model 94,** Various Gauges, Takedown, Automatic Ejector, Plain, Hammer, *Modern*	37.00	52.00	50.00
☐ **Model 944,** .410 Ga., Hammer, Automatic Ejector, (Springfield), *Modern*	37.00	52.00	50.00
☐ **Model 94A,** Various Gauges, Hammer, Automatic Ejector, *Modern*	37.00	52.00	50.00
☐ **Model 94C,** Various Gauges, Hammer, Automatic Ejector, *Modern*	37.00	52.00	50.00
☐ **Model 95,** 12 and 16 Gauges, *Modern*	40.00	57.00	55.00
☐ **Model 958,** .410 Ga., Automatic Ejector, Hammer, *Modern*	37.00	52.00	50.00
☐ **Model 958,** 32 Ga., Automatic Ejector, Hammer, *Modern*	48.00	68.00	65.00
☐ **Model 97,** 12 and 16 Gauges, Hammer, Automatic Ejector, *Modern*	37.00	47.00	45.00
☐ **Model 970,** 12 Ga., Hammer, Automatic Ejector, Checkered Stock, Half-Octagon Barrel, *Modern*	47.00	58.00	55.00
SHOTGUN, SLIDE ACTION			
☐ **Model 520,** 12 Ga., Takedown, *Modern*	115.00	160.00	150.00
☐ **Model 522,** 12 Ga., Trap Grade, Takedown, Raised Matted Rib, *Modern*	112.00	155.00	150.00
☐ **Model 621,** Various Gauges, Hammerless, Checkered Stock, Raised Matted Rib, Takedown, *Modern*	115.00	160.00	155.00
☐ **Model 620,** Various Gauges, Takedown, *Modern*	115.00	150.00	145.00
☐ **Model 67,** Various Gauges, Hammerless, Solid Frame, (Springfield), *Modern*	90.00	125.00	120.00
☐ **Model 67-VR,** Various Gauges, Hammerless, Solid Frame, Vent Rib, (Springfield), *Modern*	100.00	140.00	135.00
☐ **Model 77,** For Vent Rib, *Add* **$10.00-$15.00**			
☐ **Model 77,** 12 and 16 Gauges, Hammerless, Solid Frame, *Modern*	120.00	160.00	155.00
☐ **Model 77,** Various Gauges, Hammerless, Solid Frame, *Modern*	95.00	140.00	135.00
☐ **Model 77 S C,** 12 and 16 Gauges, Hammerless, Solid Frame, Recoil Pad, Adjustable Choke, *Modern*	130.00	170.00	165.00
☐ **Model 77-AC,** Various Gauges, Hammerless, Solid Frame, Adjustable Choke, *Modern*	90.00	135.00	130.00
☐ **Model 77-M,** 12 Ga., Hammerless, Solid Frame, Adjustable Choke, *Modern*	95.00	140.00	135.00
☐ **Model 820,** 12 Ga., Hammerless, Solid Frame, *Modern*	90.00	130.00	125.00

STEVENS, JAMES

SHOTGUN, PERCUSSION

	V.G.	Exc.	Prior Year Exc. Value
□ **14 Ga.**, Double Barrel, Side by Side, Engraved, Light Ornamentation, *Antique*	375.00	550.00	550.00

STEYR

Since 1963 in Steyr, Austria as Werndl Co.; in 1869 became Oesterreichische Waffenfabrik Gesellschaft; after WW I became Steyr Werke; in 1934 became Steyr-Daimler-Puch. Also see German Military, Austrian Military, Mannlicher-Schoenauer.

AUTOMATIC WEAPON, SUBMACHINE GUN

	V.G.	Exc.	Prior Year Exc. Value
□ **MP Solothurn 34,** 9mm Mauser, Clip Fed, *Class 3*	850.00	1325.00	1325.00

HANDGUN, SEMI-AUTOMATIC

	V.G.	Exc.	Prior Year Exc. Value
□ **Model 1901 Mannlicher,** 7.63mm Mannlicher, Commercial, *Curio*	400.00	675.00	675.00
□ **Model 1905 Mannlicher,** 7.63mm Mannlicher, Military, *Curio*	250.00	390.00	390.00
□ **Model 1908,** .32 ACP, Clip Fed, Tip-Up, *Modern*	125.00	175.00	175.00
□ **Model 1909,** .25 ACP, Clip Fed, Tip-Up, *Modern*	100.00	155.00	155.00
□ **Model 1909,** .32 ACP, Clip Fed, Tip-Up, *Modern*	115.00	165.00	165.00
□ **Model 1911,** 9mm Steyr, Commercial, *Curio*	320.00	435.00	435.00
□ **Model 1912,** 9mm Luger, Nazi-Proofed, Military, *Curio*	200.00	320.00	400.00
□ **Model 1912,** 9mm Steyr, Military, *Curio*	120.00	210.00	275.00
□ **Model 1912 Roumanian,** 9mm Steyr, Military, *Curio*	150.00	270.00	325.00
□ **Model GB,** 9mm Luger, Clip Fed, Double Action, *Modern*	265.00	365.00	365.00
□ **Model SP,** .32 ACP, Clip Fed, Double Action, *Modern*	185.00	300.00	300.00
□ **Solothurn,** .32 ACP, Clip Fed, *Modern*	130.00	190.00	190.00

STOCK, FRANZ

Franz Stock Maschinen u. Werkbaufabrik, Berlin, Germany 1920-1940.

HANDGUN, SEMI-AUTOMATIC

	V.G.	Exc.	Prior Year Exc. Value
□ **.22 L.R.R.F.**, Clip Fed, *Modern*	160.00	235.00	225.00
□ **.25 ACP**, Clip Fed, *Modern*	155.00	220.00	200.00
□ **.32 ACP**, Clip Fed, *Modern*	165.00	230.00	220.00

Steyr Model 1909

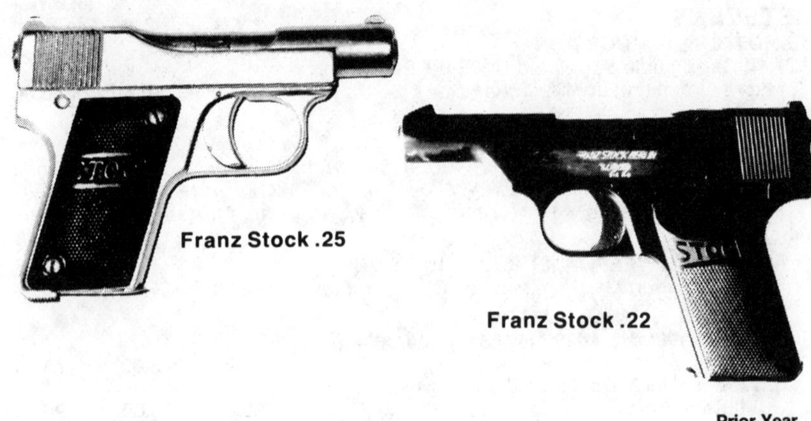

Franz Stock .25

Franz Stock .22

	V.G.	Exc.	Prior Year Exc. Value
STOCKMAN, HANS			
Dresden, Germany 1590-1621.			
HANDGUN, WHEEL-LOCK			
☐ **Pair**, Holster Pistol, Pear Pommel, Horn Inlays, Light Ornamentation, *Antique*	9,000.00	15000.00	15000.00
STOEGER, A.F.			
Stoeger Arms Corp., N.Y.C., now in South Hackensack, N.J. Also see Luger.			
COMBINATION WEAPON, OVER-UNDER			
☐ **Model 290**, Various Calibers, Blitz System, Box Lock, Double Triggers, Engraved, Checkered Stock, *Modern*	800.00	1,200.00	1,200.00
COMBINATION WEAPON, DRILLING			
☐ **Model 259**, 3 Calibers, Side Barrel, Box Lock, Double Triggers, Checkered Stock, *Modern*	950.00	1,500.00	1,500.00
☐ **Model 297**, Various Calibers, 2 Rifle Barrels, Box Lock, Double Triggers, Engraved, Checkered Stock, *Modern*	975.00	1,600.00	1,600.00
☐ **Model 300**, Vierling, 4 Barrels, Box Lock, Double Triggers, Checkered Stock, *Modern*	1,250.00	2,000.00	2,000.00
SHOTGUN, DOUBLE BARREL, SIDE-BY-SIDE			
☐ **Victor Special**, 12 Ga., Checkered Stock, Double Triggers, *Modern*	120.00	180.00	175.00
SHOTGUN, SINGLESHOT			
☐ **Model 27 Trap**, 12 Ga., Engraved, Vent Rib, Checkered Stock, Recoil Pad, *Modern*	500.00	725.00	750.00
STOSEL			
Retolaza Hermanos, Eibar, Spain.			
HANDGUN, SEMI-AUTOMATIC			
☐ **Model 1913**, .25 ACP, Clip Fed, *Modern*	90.00	140.00	135.00

	V.G.	Exc.	Prior Year Exc. Value

STUART, JOHAN

Edinburgh, Scotland 1701-1750.

HANDGUN, SNAPHAUNCE

	V.G.	Exc.	Prior Year Exc. Value
☐ **All Steel Highland**, Engraved, Scroll Butt, Ball Trigger, *Antique*	7,000.00	10,000.00	10,000.00

SULLIVAN ARMS CO.

Made by Crescent for Sullivan Hardware, Anderson, S.C., c. 1900.

SHOTGUN, DOUBLE BARREL, SIDE-BY-SIDE

	V.G.	Exc.	Prior Year Exc. Value
☐ **Various Gauges**, Outside Hammers, Damascus Barrel, *Modern*	100.00	170.00	175.00
☐ **Various Gauges**, Hammerless, Steel Barrel, *Modern*	135.00	190.00	200.00
☐ **Various Gauges**, Hammerless, Damascus Barrel, *Modern*	100.00	170.00	175.00
☐ **Various Gauges**, Outside Hammers, Steel Barrel, *Modern*	125.00	185.00	190.00

SHOTGUN, SINGLESHOT

	V.G.	Exc.	Prior Year Exc. Value
☐ **Various Gauges**, Hammer, Steel Barrel, *Modern*	55.00	85.00	85.00

SUPER DREADNAUGHT

Made by Stevens Arms.

SHOTGUN, SINGLESHOT

	V.G.	Exc.	Prior Year Exc. Value
☐ **Model 89 Dreadnaught**, Various Gauges, Hammer, *Modern*	45.00	65.00	60.00

SUPER RANGE GOOSE

Made by Stevens Arms.

RIFLE, SEMI-AUTOMATIC

	V.G.	Exc.	Prior Year Exc. Value
☐ **Model 85 Springfield**, .22 L.R.R.F., 5 Shot Clip, Open Rear Sight, *Modern*	45.00	65.00	65.00

SUTHERLAND, JAMES

Edinburgh, Scotland, c. 1790.

HANDGUN, FLINTLOCK

	V.G.	Exc.	Prior Year Exc. Value
☐ **.50**, all Steel, Engraved, Ram's Horn Butt, *Antique*	1,750.00	2,600.00	2,500.00

SUTHERLAND, RAMSEY

London and Birmingham, England, 1790-1827.

HANDGUN, FLINTLOCK

	V.G.	Exc.	Prior Year Exc. Value
☐ **.67**, George III, Calvary Pistol, Military, Tapered Round Barrel, Brass Furniture, *Antique*	775.00	1,200.00	1,150.00

RIFLE, FLINTLOCK

	V.G.	Exc.	Prior Year Exc. Value
☐ **.75**, 3rd Model Brown Bess, Musket, Military, *Antique*	950.00	1,500.00	1,500.00

SVENDSON

E. Svendson, Itasca, Ill., c. 1965.

HANDGUN, MANUAL REPEATER

	V.G.	Exc.	Prior Year Exc. Value
☐ **Four Aces**, .22 Short, Four Barrels, Derringer, Spur Trigger, *Modern*	45.00	65.00	65.00

	V.G.	Exc.	Prior Year Exc. Value

SWAMP ANGEL

Made by Forehand & Wadsworth, Worcester, Mass., c. 1871.

HANDGUN, REVOLVER

	V.G.	Exc.	Prior Year Exc. Value
☐ **.41 Short R.F.**, 5 Shot, Spur Trigger, Solid Frame, Single Action, *Antique*	120.00	195.00	195.00

SWEDISH MILITARY

HANDGUN, REVOLVER

	V.G.	Exc.	Prior Year Exc. Value
☐ **M1887 Husqvarna**, 7.5mm, Double Action, Blue, *Antique*	145.00	220.00	195.00

RIFLE, SINGLESHOT

	V.G.	Exc.	Prior Year Exc. Value
☐ **M1867/89 Remington**, 8mm, Full Stock, *Antique*	240.00	325.00	320.00

RIFLE, BOLT ACTION

	V.G.	Exc.	Prior Year Exc. Value
☐ **M1896 Mauser**, 6.5 x 55mm, Gustav, *Curio*	135.00	200.00	200.00

SWEITZER, DANIEL & CO.

Lancaster, Pa. 1808-1814. See Kentucky Rifles.

SWIFT

Made by Iver Johnson, Fitchburg, Mass. 1890-1900.

HANDGUN, REVOLVER

	V.G.	Exc.	Prior Year Exc. Value
☐ **.38 S & W**, 5 Shot, Top Break, Hammerless, Double Action, *Curio*	55.00	95.00	95.00
☐ **.38 S & W**, 5 Shot, Double Action, Top Break, *Curio*	45.00	95.00	95.00

SWISS MILITARY

AUTOMATIC WEAPON, SUBMACHINE GUN

	V.G.	Exc.	Prior Year Exc. Value
☐ **MP Solothurn 34**, 9mm Mauser, Clip Fed, *Class 3*	850.00	1,350.00	1,300.00

HANDGUN, REVOLVER

	V.G.	Exc.	Prior Year Exc. Value
☐ **M1872 Swiss Ordnance**, 10.4mm R.F., Double Action, Blue, Military, *Antique*	535.00	800.00	750.00
☐ **M1872/78 Swiss Ordnance**, 10.4mm C.F., Double Action, Blue, Military, *Antique*	300.00	450.00	400.00
☐ **M1882 Swiss Ordnance**, 7.5mm, Double Action, Blue, Military, *Antique*	125.00	185.00	165.00
☐ **M1882 Swiss Ordnance**, 7.5mm, Double Action, Blue, Military, With Holster Stock and All Leather, *Antique*	900.00	1,500.00	1,500.00

RIFLE, BOLT ACTION

	V.G.	Exc.	Prior Year Exc. Value
☐ **Vetterli,** Carbine, .41 Swiss R.F., Tube Feed, Military, *Antique*	285.00	400.00	400.00
☐ **Vetterli,** Bern 1878, .41 Swiss R.F., Tube Feed, Military, *Antique*	120.00	170.00	165.00
☐ **Vetterli,** Bern 1878/81, .41 Swiss R.F., Tube Feed, Military, *Antique*	120.00	180.00	170.00
☐ **M 1889,** 7.5 x 55 Swiss, Military, *Modern*	125.00	175.00	165.00
☐ **M 1889/1900,** 7.5 x 55 Swiss, Short Rifle, *Curio*	275.00	420.00	600.00
☐ **M 1893,** 7.5 x 55 Swiss, Military, *Curio*	275.00	420.00	600.00
☐ **M1911 Schmidt Rubin,** 7.5 x 55 Swiss, Clip Fed, Military, *Curio*	60.00	110.00	150.00

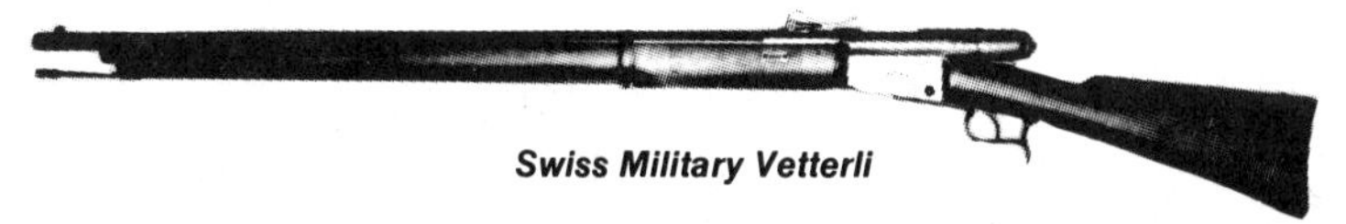
Swiss Military Vetterli

	V.G.	Exc.	Prior Year Exc. Value
☐ **M1911 Schmidt Rubin,** 7.5 x 55 Swiss, Clip Fed, Carbine, Military, *Curio*	70.00	125.00	160.00
RIFLE, PERCUSSION			
☐ **Federal Rifle,** .41 Caliber, Full Stocked, *Antique*	475.00	795.00	775.00

T.A.C.

Trocaola, Aranzabal y Cia., Eibar, Spain.

HANDGUN, REVOLVER			
☐ **Modelo Militar**, .44 Spec., S & W Triple Lock Copy, Double Action, Blue, *Modern*	155.00	225.00	225.00
☐ **OP No. 2 Mk.I**, .455 Eley, British Military, Double Action, Top Break, *Curio*	110.00	160.00	160.00
☐ **S & W Frontier Copy**, .44 American, Double Action, Break Top, Blue, *Modern*	90.00	135.00	135.00
☐ **S & W M&P Copy**, .38 Spec., Double Action, Blue, *Modern*	55.00	90.00	85.00

TALLARES

Tallares Armas Livianas Argentinas, Punta Alta, Argentina.

HANDGUN, SEMI-AUTOMATIC			
☐ **T.A.L.A.**, .22 L.R.R.F., Clip Fed, *Modern*	80.00	130.00	125.00

TANARMI

Made in Italy, Imported by Excam.

HANDGUN, REVOLVER			
☐ **E-15**, For Chrome, *Add* **$5.00**			
☐ **E-15**, .22LR/.22 WMR Combo, Single Action, Western Style, *Modern*	25.00	40.00	40.00
☐ **E-15**, .22 L.R.R.F., Single Action, Western Style, *Modern*	20.00	30.00	30.00
☐ **TA-22**, For Chrome, *Add* **$5.00**			
☐ **TA-22**, .22LR/.22 WMR Combo, Single Action, Western Style, Brass Grip Frame, *Modern*	40.00	60.00	60.00
☐ **TA-22**, .22 L.R.R.F., Single Action, Western Style, Brass Grip Frame, *Modern*	30.00	45.00	45.00
☐ **TA-76**, For Chrome, *Add* **$5.00**			
☐ **TA-76**, .22LR/.22 WMR Combo, Single Action, Western Style, *Modern*	30.00	45.00	45.00
☐ **TA-76**, .22 L.R.R.F., Single Action, Western Style, *Modern*	25.00	35.00	35.00

TANKE

Maker unknown.

HANDGUN, SEMI-AUTOMATIC			
☐ **.25 ACP**, Clip Fed, *Modern*	80.00	125.00	120.00

TANNER

Andrae Tanner, Werkstatte fur Praszisionswaffen, Fulenbach, Switzerland.

	V.G.	Exc.	Prior Year Exc. Value
RIFLE, BOLT ACTION			
☐ **Standard UIT**, .308 Win., Singleshot, Target Rifle, Monte Carlo Target Stock, *Modern*	875.00	1,300.00	1,300.00
☐ **Standard UIT**, .308 Win., Repeater, Target Rifle, Monte Carlo Target Stock, *Modern*	900.00	1,350.00	1,350.00
☐ **300m Match**, .308 Win., Offhand Target Rifle, Target Stock, Palm Rest, *Modern*	900.00	1,500.00	1,500.00
☐ **50m Match**, .22 L.R.R.F., Offhand Target Rifle, Target Stock, Palm Rest, *Modern*	675.00	1,000.00	1,000.00
☐ **Hunting Match**, Various Calibers, Checkered Monte Carlo Stock, Singleshot, *Modern*	800.00	1,200.00	1,200.00

TANQUE

Ojanguran y Vidosa, Eibar, Spain, c. 1930.

	V.G.	Exc.	Prior Year Exc. Value
HANDGUN, SEMI-AUTOMATIC			
☐ **.25 ACP**, Clip Fed, *Modern*	115.00	160.00	155.00

TARGA

Guiseppi Tanfoglio, Gardone Val Trompia, Italy, imported by Excam.

	V.G.	Exc.	Prior Year Exc. Value
HANDGUN, SEMI-AUTOMATIC			
☐ **Chrome Plating** For All Models *Add* **$5.00**			
☐ **GT22B**, .22 L.R.R.F., Clip Fed, Blue, *Modern*	65.00	90.00	90.00
☐ **GT32C**, .22 L.R.R.F., Clip Fed, Blue, *Modern*	65.00	95.00	95.00
☐ **GT27**, .25 ACP, Clip Fed, Blue, *Modern*	30.00	40.00	40.00
☐ **GT380B**, .380 ACP, Clip Fed, Blue, *Modern*	65.00	110.00	110.00
☐ **GT380BE**, .380 ACP, Clip Fed, Engraved, Blue, *Modern*	95.00	140.00	140.00
☐ **GT380XE**, .380 ACP, Clip Fed, *Modern*	95.00	140.00	140.00
☐ **GT32XEB**, .32 ACP, Clip Fed, *Modern*	85.00	125.00	125.00

T.A.R.N.

Swift Rifle Co., London, England, c. 1943.

	V.G.	Exc.	Prior Year Exc. Value
HANDGUN, SEMI-AUTOMATIC			
☐ **Polish Air Force**, 9mm Luger, Clip Fed, Blue, *Curio*	2,500.00	3,800.00	3,750.00

TAURUS

Forjas Taurus S.A., Porto Alegre, Brazil.

	V.G.	Exc.	Prior Year Exc. Value
HANDGUN, REVOLVER			
☐ **Model 65**, .38 Special, Solid Frame, Swing-Out Cylinder, Double Action, *Modern*	80.00	125.00	120.00
☐ **Model 66**, .38 Special, Solid Frame, Swing-Out Cylinder, Double Action, Adjustable Sights, *Modern*	90.00	135.00	135.00
☐ **Model 73**, .32 S & W Long, Solid Frame, Swing-Out Cylinder, Double Action, Fixed Sights, *Modern*	55.00	95.00	90.00
☐ **Model 74**, .32 S & W Long, Solid Frame, Swing-Out Cylinder, Double Action, Adjustable Sights, *Modern*	60.00	95.00	95.00
☐ **Model 80**, .38 Special, Solid Frame, Swing-Out Cylinder, Double Action, *Modern*	75.00	115.00	115.00

	V.G.	Exc.	Prior Year Exc. Value
☐ **Model 82**, .38 Special, Solid Frame, Swing-Out Cylinder, Double Action, Heavy Barrel, *Modern* ..	70.00	110.00	110.00
☐ **Model 83**, .38 Special, Solid Frame, Swing-Out Cylinder, Double Action, Adjustable Sights, *Modern* ...	80.00	120.00	120.00
☐ **Model 84**, .38 Special, Solid Frame, Swing-Out Cylinder, Double Action, Adjustable Sights, *Modern* ...	80.00	120.00	120.00
☐ **Model 85**, .38 Special, Solid Frame, Swing-Out Cylinder, Double Action, 3" Barrel, *Modern*	70.00	110.00	110.00
☐ **Model 86**, .38 Special, Solid Frame, Swing-Out Cylinder, Double Action, Adjustable Sights, 6" Barrel, *Modern* ...	85.00	130.00	130.00
☐ **Model 94**, .22 L.R.R.F., Solid Frame, Swing-Out Cylinder, Double Action, Adjustable Sights, *Modern* ...	90.00	135.00	130.00
☐ **Model 96**, .22 L.R.R.F., Solid Frame, Swing-Out Cylinder, Double Action, Adjustable Sights, 6" Barrel, *Modern* ...	85.00	125.00	120.00
HANDGUN, SEMI-AUTOMATIC			
☐ **PT-92**, 9mm Luger, Clip Fed, Blue, Double Action, *Modern* ...	165.00	225.00	225.00
☐ **PT-99**, 9mm Luger, Clip Fed, Blue, Double Action, *Modern* ...	195.00	285.00	285.00

T.D.E.

El Monte, Calif. Also see Auto-Mag.

	V.G.	Exc.	Prior Year Exc. Value
HANDGUN, SEMI-AUTOMATIC			
☐ **Backup**, .380 ACP, Stainless Steel, *Modern*	135.00	175.00	180.00

TED WILLIAMS

Trade name of Sears Roebuck, also see Sears.

	V.G.	Exc.	Prior Year Exc. Value
RIFLE, BOLT ACTION			
☐ **Model 52703**, .22 L.R.R.F., Singleshot, Plain, *Modern* ...	25.00	40.00	40.00
☐ **Model 52774**, .22 L.R.R.F., Clip Fed, Plain, *Modern* ...	35.00	55.00	55.00
☐ **Model 53**, Various Calibers, Checkered Stock, *Modern* ...	120.00	155.00	155.00
RIFLE, LEVER ACTION			
☐ **Model 120**, .30-30 Win., Carbine, *Modern*	60.00	80.00	80.00
RIFLE, SEMI-AUTOMATIC			
☐ **Model 34**, .22 L.R.R.F., *Modern* ...	35.00	55.00	55.00
☐ **Model 34**, .22 L.R.R.F., Carbine, *Modern*	35.00	55.00	55.00
☐ **Model 3T**, .22 L.R.R.F., Checkered Stock, *Modern*	65.00	85.00	85.00
☐ **Model 52811**, .22 L.R.R.F., Plain, Tube Feed, Takedown, *Modern* ...	45.00	60.00	60.00
☐ **Model 52814**, .22 L.R.R.F., Checkered Stock, Clip Fed, Takedown, *Modern* ...	75.00	115.00	115.00
SHOTGUN, BOLT ACTION			
☐ **Model 51106**, 12 or 20 Gauges, Clip Fed, Adjustable Choke, *Modern* ...	45.00	60.00	55.00
☐ **Model 51142**, .410 Gauge, Clip Fed, *Modern*	40.00	50.00	45.00

	V.G.	Exc.	Prior Year Exc. Value
SHOTGUN, DOUBLE BARREL, OVER-UNDER			
☐ **Model Laurona**, 12 Ga., Checkered Stock, Light Engraving, Double Trigger, Vent Rib, *Modern*	240.00	325.00	325.00
☐ **Model Zoli**, 12 Ga., Checkered Stock, Light Engraving, Double Trigger, Vent Rib, Automatic Ejector, *Modern*	150.00	275.00	275.00
☐ **Model Zoli**, 12 and 20 Gauges, Checkered Stock, Light Engraving, Double Trigger, Vent Rib, *Modern*	200.00	280.00	280.00
SHOTGUN, DOUBLE BARREL, SIDE-BY-SIDE			
☐ **Model 51226**, 12 and 20 Gauges, Plain, Double Trigger, *Modern*	80.00	125.00	125.00
☐ **Model Laurona**, 12 and 20 Gauges, Checkered Stock, Light Engraving, Hammerless, *Modern*	115.00	155.00	155.00
SHOTGUN, SEMI-AUTOMATIC			
☐ **Model 300**, 12 Ga., Plain, *Modern*	115.00	155.00	150.00
☐ **Model 300**, 12 and 20 Gauges, Checkered Stock, Vent Rib, Adjustable Choke, *Modern*	135.00	175.00	175.00
☐ **Model 300**, 12 and 20 Gauges, Checkered Stock, Vent Rib, *Modern*	125.00	170.00	165.00
SHOTGUN, SINGLESHOT			
☐ **Model 5108**, Various Gauges, Plain, *Modern*	35.00	45.00	45.00
SHOTGUN, SLIDE ACTION			
☐ **Model 200**, 12 and 20 Gauges, Checkered Stock, Vent Rib, Adjustable Choke, *Modern*	125.00	155.00	155.00
☐ **Model 200**, 12 and 20 Gauges, Checkered Stock, Vent Rib, *Modern*	110.00	140.00	140.00
☐ **Model 200**, 12 and 20 Gauges, Plain, *Modern*	80.00	115.00	110.00
☐ **Model 200**, 12 and 20 Gauges, Checkered Stock, Plain Barrel, *Modern*	90.00	125.00	125.00
☐ **Model 51454**, .410 Ga., Plain, *Modern*	65.00	100.00	95.00

TEN STAR

Belgium, c. 1900.

	V.G.	Exc.	Prior Year Exc. Value
SHOTGUN, DOUBLE BARREL, SIDE-BY-SIDE			
☐ **Various Gauges**, Outside Hammers, Damascus Barrel, *Modern*	100.00	170.00	175.00
☐ **Various Gauges**, Hammerless, Steel Barrel, *Modern*	135.00	190.00	200.00
☐ **Various Gauges**, Hammerless, Damascus Barrel, *Modern*	100.00	170.00	175.00
☐ **Various Gauges**, Outside Hammers, Steel Barrel, *Modern*	125.00	185.00	190.00
SHOTGUN, SINGLESHOT			
☐ **Various Gauges**, Hammer, Steel Barrel, *Modern*	55.00	85.00	85.00

TERRIBLE

Hijos de Calixto Arrizabalaga, Eibar, Spain, c. 1930.

	V.G.	Exc.	Prior Year Exc. Value
HANDGUN, SEMI-AUTOMATIC			
☐ **.25 ACP**, Clip Fed, Blue *Modern*	85.00	130.00	125.00

TERRIER

Made by J. Rupertus, Philadelphia, Pa. Sold by Tryon Bros., c. 1880.

	V.G.	Exc.	Prior Year Exc. Value
HANDGUN, REVOLVER			
☐ **.22 Short R.F.**, 7 Shot, Spur Trigger, Solid Frame, Single Action, *Antique*	90.00	165.00	160.00
☐ **.32 Short R.F.**, 5 Shot, Spur Trigger, Solid Frame, Single Action, *Antique*	95.00	170.00	170.00
☐ **.38 Short R.F.**, 5 Shot, Spur Trigger, Solid Frame, Single Action, *Antique*	95.00	170.00	170.00
☐ **.41 Short R.F.**, 5 Shot, Spur Trigger, Solid Frame, Single Action, *Antique*	120.00	195.00	195.00

TERROR

Made by Forehand & Wadsworth, c. 1870.

	V.G.	Exc.	Prior Year Exc. Value
HANDGUN, REVOLVER			
☐ **.32 Short R.F.**, 5 or 6 Shot, Spur Trigger, Solid Frame, Single Action, *Antique*	90.00	165.00	160.00

TEUF-TEUF

Arizmendi y Goenaga, Eibar, Spain, c. 1912.

	V.G.	Exc.	Prior Year Exc. Value
HANDGUN, SEMI-AUTOMATIC			
☐ **.25 ACP**, Clip Fed, Blue, *Curio*	85.00	130.00	125.00

TEUF-TEUF

Unknown Belgian maker, c. 1907.

	V.G.	Exc.	Prior Year Exc. Value
HANDGUN, SEMI-AUTOMATIC			
☐ **.25 ACP**, Clip Fed, Blue, *Curio*	120.00	160.00	155.00

TEXAS RANGER

Made by Stevens Arms.

	V.G.	Exc.	Prior Year Exc. Value
SHOTGUN, SINGLESHOT			
☐ **Model 95**, 12 and 16 Gauges, *Modern*	35.00	50.00	50.00

THAMES ARMS CO.

Norwich, Conn., c. 1907.

	V.G.	Exc.	Prior Year Exc. Value
HANDGUN, REVOLVER			
☐ **.22 L.R.R.F.**, 7 Shot, Double Action, Top Break, *Curio*	60.00	110.00	95.00
☐ **.32 S & W**, 5 Shot, Double Action, Top Break, *Curio*	55.00	100.00	95.00
☐ **.38 S & W**, 5 Shot, Double Action, Top Break, *Curio*	55.00	100.00	95.00

THAYER, ROBERTSON & CARY

Norwich, Conn., c. 1907.

	V.G.	Exc.	Prior Year Exc. Value
HANDGUN, REVOLVER			
☐ **.32 S & W**, 5 Shot, Double Action, Top Break, *Curio*	45.00	95.00	95.00
☐ **.38 S & W**, 5 Shot, Double Action, Top Break, *Curio*	45.00	95.00	95.00

THOMPSON

Developed by Auto-Ordnance, invented by Gen. John T. Thompson, made by various companies. Also see Numrich Arms.

Thompson M1928

	V.G.	Exc.	Prior Year Exc. Value
AUTOMATIC WEAPON, SUBMACHINE GUN			
☐ **M1**, .45 ACP, Clip Fed, with Compensator, Military, Plain Barrel, *Class 3*	600.00	900.00	900.00
☐ **M1921A**, .45 ACP, Early Model, Clip Fed, without Compensator, Lyman Sights, Curio, *Class 3*	2,000.00	2,500.00	2,500.00
☐ **M1921AC**, .45 ACP, Early Model, Clip Fed, with Compensator, Lyman Sights, Curio, *Class 3*	2,300.00	2,850.00	2,800.00
☐ **M1921AC**, .45 ACP, Early Model, Clip Fed, with Compensator, Cased with Accessories, Curio, *Class 3*	3,400.00	4,000.00	4,000.00
☐ **M1921AC**, .45 ACP, Early Model, Clip Fed, with Compensator, Metric Lyman Sights, Curio, *Class 3*	2,800.00	3,550.00	3,500.00
☐ **M1928 (Numrich)**, .45 ACP, Clip Fed, with Compensator, Lyman Sights, *Class 3*	400.00	500.00	500.00
☐ **M1928 Navy**, .45 ACP, Clip Fed, with Compensator, Lyman Sights, Finned Barrel, *Class 3*	1,900.00	2,400.00	2,400.00
☐ **M1928 Navy**, .45 ACP, Clip Fed, with Compensator, Lyman Sights, Finned Barrel, British Proofs, *Class 3*	2,300.00	2,700.00	2,750.00
☐ **M1928 Navy**, .45 ACP, Clip Fed, with Compensator, Lyman Sights, Finned Barrel, Cased with Accessories, *Class 3*	2,500.00	3,100.00	3,000.00
☐ **M1928A1 (AO)**, .45 ACP, Clip Fed, with Compensator, Adjustable Sights, Finned Barrel, Military, *Class 3*	1,200.00	1,650.00	1,600.00
☐ **M1928A1 (AO)**, .45 ACP, Clip Fed, with Compensator, Military, Plain Barrel, *Class 3*	800.00	1,100.00	1,100.00
☐ **M1928A1 (S)**, .45 ACP, Clip Fed, with Compensator, Lyman Sights, *Class 3*	1,000.00	1,400.00	1,400.00
☐ **M1A1**, .45 ACP, Clip Fed, with Compensator, Military, Plain Barrel, *Class 3*	550.00	875.00	850.00
HANDGUN, SEMI-AUTOMATIC			
☐ **Model 27A5**, .45 ACP, Clip Fed, Finned Barrel, Adjustable Sights, with Compensator, (Numrich), *Modern*	175.00	275.00	265.00
RIFLE, SEMI-AUTOMATIC			
☐ **M1927**, .45 ACP, Clip Fed, with Compensator, Short Barreled Rifle, Lyman Sights, Curio, *Class 3*	4,000.00	5,000.00	5,000.00
☐ **Model 27A1**, .45 ACP, Clip Fed, without Compensator, (Numrich), *Modern*	275.00	350.00	350.00
☐ **Model 27A1**, .45 ACP, Clip Fed, without Compensator, Cased with Accessories, (Numrich), *Modern*	225.00	325.00	325.00
☐ **Model 27A1 Deluxe**, .45 ACP, Clip Fed, Finned Barrel, Adjustable Sights, with Compensator, (Numrich), *Modern*	225.00	315.00	315.00

	V.G.	Exc.	Prior Year Exc. Value
☐ **Model 27A3**, .22 L.R.R.F., Clip Fed, Finned Barrel, Adjustable Sights, with Compensator, (Numrich), *Modern*	275.00	350.00	350.00

THOMPSON, SAMUEL

Columbus, Ohio 1820-1822. See Kentucky Rifles.

THOMPSON/CENTER

Rochester, N.H.

HANDGUN, SINGLESHOT

	V.G.	Exc.	Prior Year Exc. Value
☐ **Contender**, Various Calibers, Adjustable Sights, Rifle Conversion Kit with Buttstock, Long Barrel, Not Factory, *Modern*	245.00	325.00	325.00
☐ **Contender**, Various Calibers, Adjustable Sights, *Modern*	145.00	190.00	190.00
☐ **Contender**, Various Calibers, Adjustable Sights, Vent Rib, *Modern*	150.00	200.00	200.00
☐ **Contender**, Various Calibers, Adjustable Sights, Heavy Barrel, *Modern*	145.00	190.00	190.00
☐ **Contender**, Various Calibers, Adjustable Sights, Super 14" Barrel, *Modern*	155.00	215.00	215.00
☐ **Contender**, Various Calibers, Heavy Barrel, no Sights, *Modern*	145.00	195.00	195.00

RIFLE, FLINTLOCK

	V.G.	Exc.	Prior Year Exc. Value
☐ **.45 Hawken**, Set Trigger, Octagon Barrel, with Accessories, Reproduction, *Antique*	165.00	220.00	220.00
☐ **.45 Hawken**, Set Trigger, Octagon Barrel, Reproduction, *Antique*	155.00	210.00	210.00
☐ **.50 Hawken**, Set Trigger, Octagon Barrel, with Accessories, Reproduction, *Antique*	165.00	220.00	220.00
☐ **.50 Hawken**, Set Trigger, Octagon Barrel, Reproduction, *Antique*	155.00	210.00	210.00
☐ **Hawken Cougar**, .45 and .50 Caliber Caplock, Stainless Furniture, Reproduction, *Antique*	270.00	300.00	—

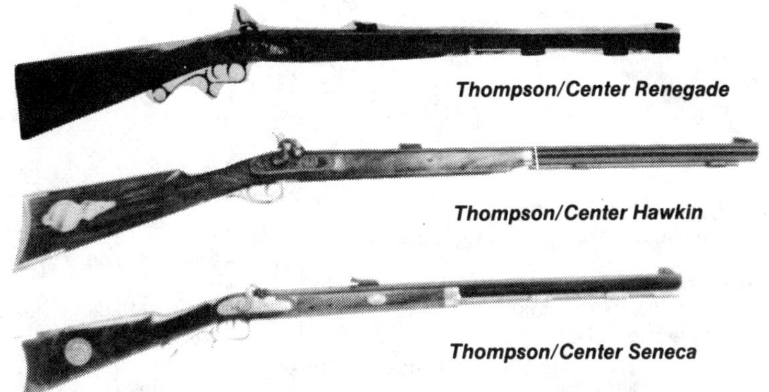

Thompson/Center Renegade

Thompson/Center Hawkin

Thompson/Center Seneca

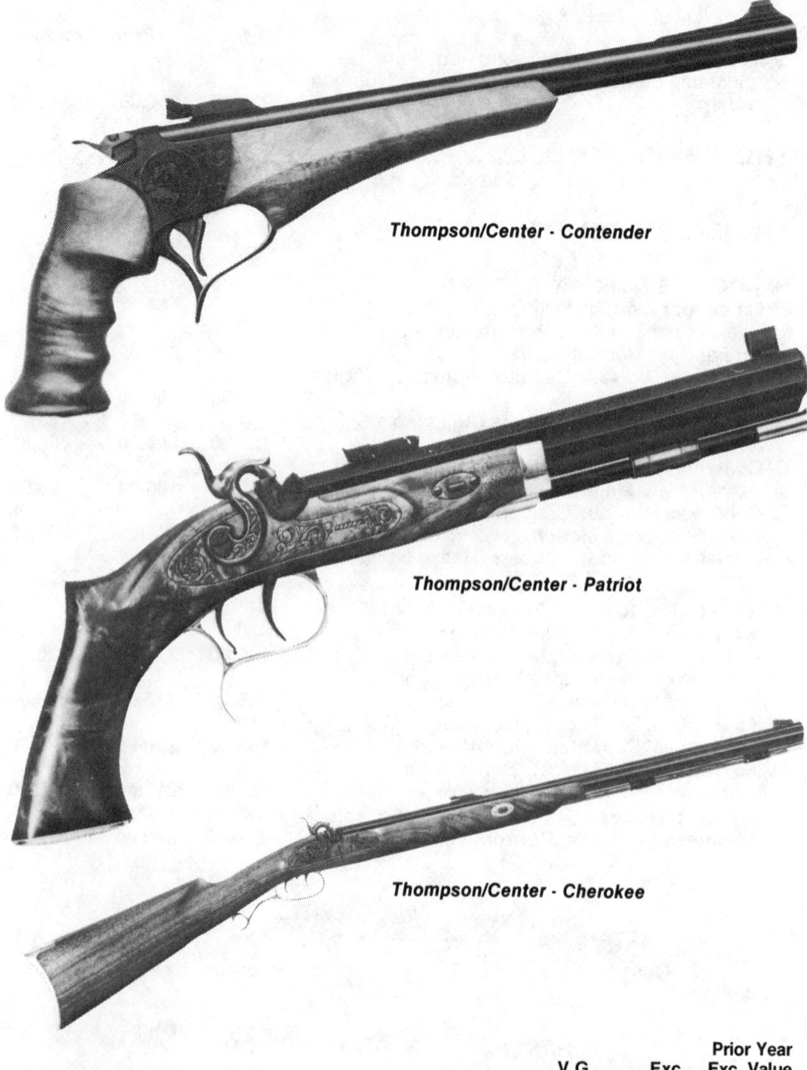

Thompson/Center - Contender

Thompson/Center - Patriot

Thompson/Center - Cherokee

	V.G.	Exc.	Prior Year Exc. Value
HANDGUN, PERCUSSION			
☐ **.45 Patriot**, Set Trigger, Octagon Barrel, Reproduction, *Antique*	85.00	130.00	130.00
☐ **.45 Patriot**, Set Trigger, Octagon Barrel, with Accessories, Reproduction, *Antique*	90.00	145.00	145.00
RIFLE, PERCUSSION			
☐ **Cherokee,** .32 or .45 Caliber, Brass Furniture, 24" Barrel, *Modern*	225.00	250.00	—
☐ **.36 Seneca,** Set Trigger, Octagon Barrel, with Accessories, Reproduction, *Antique*	160.00	210.00	210.00

	V.G.	Exc.	Prior Year Exc. Value
☐ **.36 Seneca,** Set Trigger, Octagon Barrel, Reproduction, *Antique*	150.00	200.00	200.00
☐ **.45 Hawken,** Set Trigger, Octagon Barrel, with Accessories, Reproduction, *Antique*	160.00	210.00	210.00
☐ **.45 Hawken,** Set Trigger, Octagon Barrel, Reproduction, *Antique*	150.00	200.00	200.00
☐ **.45 Seneca,** Set Trigger, Octagon Barrel, with Accessories, Reproduction, *Antique*	160.00	210.00	210.00
☐ **.45 Seneca,** Set Trigger, Octagon Barrel, Reproduction, *Antique*	150.00	200.00	200.00
☐ **.50 Hawken,** Set Trigger, Octagon Barrel, with Accessories, Reproduction, *Antique*	160.00	210.00	210.00
☐ **.50 Hawken,** Set Trigger, Octagon Barrel, Reproduction, *Antique*	150.00	200.00	200.00
☐ **.54 Renegade,** Set Trigger, Octagon Barrel, with Accessories, Reproduction, *Antique*	130.00	165.00	165.00
☐ **.54 Renegade,** Set Trigger, Octagon Barrel, Reproduction, *Antique*	120.00	150.00	150.00
RIFLE, SINGLESHOT			
☐ **TCR83 Sports Rifle,** Various Calibers, Interchangeable Barrels, Adjustable Double Set Triggers, *Modern*	425.00	475.00	—

THREE-BARREL GUN CO.

Moundsville, W. Va., 1906-1908, also at Wheeling, W. Va. as Royal Gun Co. and as Hollenbeck Gun Co.

COMBINATION WEAPON, DRILLING			
☐ **Various Calibers**, Damascus Barrel, *Antique*	675.00	1,100.00	995.00

THUNDER

Martin Bascaran, Eibar, Spain, made for Alberdi, Teleria y Cia. 1912-1919.

HANDGUN, SEMI-AUTOMATIC			
☐ **M 1919**, .25 ACP, Clip Fed, *Curio*	80.00	125.00	120.00

TIGER

Maker Unknown, c. 1880.

HANDGUN, REVOLVER			
☐ **#2**, .32 Short R.F., 5 Shot, Spur Trigger, Solid Frame, Single Action, *Antique*	90.00	165.00	160.00

TIGER

Made by Crescent for J.H. Hill Co. Nashville, Tenn., c. 1900.

SHOTGUN, DOUBLE BARREL, SIDE-BY-SIDE			
☐ **Various Gauges**, Outside Hammers, Damascus Barrel, *Modern*	100.00	170.00	175.00
☐ **Various Gauges**, Outside Hammers, Steel Barrel, *Modern*	125.00	185.00	190.00
SHOTGUN, SINGLESHOT			
☐ **Various Gauges**, Hammer, Steel Barrel, *Modern*	55.00	85.00	85.00

	V.G.	Exc.	Prior Year Exc. Value

TIKKA
Oy Tikkakoski AB, Tikkakoski, Finland.

RIFLE, BOLT ACTION

	V.G.	Exc.	Prior Year Exc. Value
☐ **Model 55 Standard**, Various Calibers, Clip Fed, Checkered Stock, *Modern*	185.00	280.00	275.00
☐ **Model 55 Sporter**, Various Calibers, Clip Fed, Checkered Stock, Heavy Barrel, *Modern*	220.00	300.00	295.00
☐ **Model 55 Deluxe**, Various Calibers, Clip Fed, Checkered Stock, *Modern*	220.00	300.00	295.00
☐ **Model 65 Standard**, Various Calibers, Clip Fed, Checkered Stock, *Modern*	185.00	280.00	275.00
☐ **Model 65 Sporter**, Various Calibers, Clip Fed, Checkered Stock, Target Rifle, Heavy Barrel, *Modern*	300.00	400.00	390.00
☐ **Model 65 Deluxe**, Various Calibers, Clip Fed, Checkered Stock, *Modern*	220.00	300.00	295.00

TINDALL & DUTTON
London, England 1790-1820.

HANDGUN, FLINTLOCK

	V.G.	Exc.	Prior Year Exc. Value
☐ **Pocket Pistol**, Various Calibers, Boxlock, *Antique*	325.00	450.00	425.00

TINGLE MFG. CO.
Shelbyville, Ind.

HANDGUN, PERCUSSION

	V.G.	Exc.	Prior Year Exc. Value
☐ **Model 1960 Target**, Octagon Barrel, Rifled, Reproduction, *Antique*	95.00	140.00	135.00

RIFLE, PERCUSSION

	V.G.	Exc.	Prior Year Exc. Value
☐ **Model 1962 Target**, Octagon Barrel, Brass Furniture, Rifled, Reproduction, *Antique*	145.00	200.00	195.00

SHOTGUN, PERCUSSION

	V.G.	Exc.	Prior Year Exc. Value
☐ **Model 1960**, 10 or 12 Gauges, Vent Rib, Double Barrel, Over-Under, Reproduction, *Antique*	150.00	215.00	210.00

TIPPING & LAWDEN
Birmingham, England, c. 1875.

HANDGUN, REVOLVER

	V.G.	Exc.	Prior Year Exc. Value
☐ **Thomas Patent**, .450, Solid Farme, Double Action, *Antique*	300.00	425.00	425.00

HANDGUN, MANUAL REPEATER

	V.G.	Exc.	Prior Year Exc. Value
☐ **Sharps Derringer**, Various Calibers, 4 Barrels, Spur Trigger, Cased with Accessories, *Antique*	425.00	675.00	675.00

TITAN
Guiseppi Tanfoglio, Gardone Val Trompia, Italy. Also see F.I.E.

HANDGUN, SEMI-AUTOMATIC

	V.G.	Exc.	Prior Year Exc. Value
☐ **Vest Pocket**, .25 ACP, Clip Fed, Hammer, *Modern*	45.00	60.00	60.00

TITAN
Retoloza Hermanos, Eibar, Spain, c. 1900.

	V.G.	Exc.	Prior Year Exc. Value
HANDGUN, SEMI-AUTOMATIC			
☐ **M 1913**, .25 ACP, Clip Fed, *Curio*	80.00	125.00	120.00

TITANIC

Retoloza Hermanos, Eibar, Spain, c. 1900.

	V.G.	Exc.	Prior Year Exc. Value
HANDGUN, SEMI-AUTOMATIC			
☐ **M 1913**, .25 ACP, Clip Fed, *Curio*	80.00	125.00	120.00
☐ **M 1914**, .32 ACP, Clip Fed, *Curio*	95.00	140.00	135.00

TOMPKINS

Varsity Mfg. Co., Springfield, Mass., c. 1947.

	V.G.	Exc.	Prior Year Exc. Value
HANDGUN, SINGLESHOT			
☐ **Target**, .22 L.R.R.F., Full Stock, *Modern*	145.00	220.00	210.00

TOWER'S POLICE SAFETY

Made by Hopkins & Allen, Norwich, Conn. c. 1875

	V.G.	Exc.	Prior Year Exc. Value
HANDGUN, REVOLVER			
☐ **.38 Short R.F.**, 5 Shot, Spur Trigger, Solid Frame, Single Action, *Antique*	95.00	170.00	170.00

TRADEWINDS, INC.

Tacoma, Wash., also see HVA.

	V.G.	Exc.	Prior Year Exc. Value
RIFLE, BOLT ACTION			
☐ **Husky (Early)**, Various Calibers, Checkered Stock, Monte Carlo Stock, *Modern*	225.00	325.00	325.00
☐ **Husky M-5000**, Various Calibers, Checkered Stock, Clip Fed, *Modern*	130.00	195.00	190.00
☐ **Husqvarna**, Various Calibers, Checkered Stock, Monte Carlo Stock, Lightweight, *Modern*	300.00	425.00	425.00
☐ **Husqvarna**, Various Calibers, Checkered Stock, Monte Carlo Stock, Lightweight, Full-Stocked, *Modern*	325.00	450.00	450.00
☐ **Husqvarna Crown Grade**, Various Calibers, Checkered Stock, Monte Carlo Stock, *Modern*	325.00	475.00	475.00
☐ **Husqvarna Imperial**, Various Calibers, Checkered Stock, Monte Carlo Stock, Lightweight, *Modern*	300.00	425.00	425.00
☐ **Husqvarna Imperial Custom**, Various Calibers, Checkered Stock, Monte Carlo Stock, *Modern*	300.00	425.00	425.00
☐ **Husqvarna Presentation**, Various Calibers, Checkered Stock, Monte Carlo Stock, *Modern*	425.00	600.00	600.00
☐ **Model 1998**, .222 Rem., no Sights, Heavy Barrel, Target Stock, *Modern*	265.00	375.00	375.00
☐ **Model 600K**, Various Calibers, Clip Fed, no Sights, Heavy Barrel, Set Trigger, *Modern*	170.00	250.00	250.00
☐ **Model 600S**, Various Calibers, Clip Fed, Heavy Barrel, Octagon Barrel, *Modern*	160.00	220.00	210.00
RIFLE, SEMI-AUTOMATIC			
☐ **Model 260A**, .22 L.R.R.F., 5 Shot Clip, Checkered Stock, *Modern*	85.00	140.00	135.00
SHOTGUN, DOUBLE BARREL, OVER-UNDER			
☐ **Gold Shadow Indy**, 12 Ga., Field Grade, Engraved, Fancy Checkering, Automatic Ejector, Vent Rib, *Modern*	1,000.00	1,400.00	1,400.00

	V.G.	Exc.	Prior Year Exc. Value
☐ **Gold Shadow Indy**, 12 Ga., Skeet Grade, Engraved, Fancy Checkering, Automatic Ejector, Vent Rib, *Modern*	1,000.00	1,400.00	1,400.00
☐ **Gold Shadow Indy**, 12 Ga., Trap Grade, Engraved, Fancy Checkering, Automatic Ejector, Vent Rib, *Modern*	1,000.00	1,400.00	1,400.00
☐ **Shadow Indy**, 12 Ga., Field Grade, Automatic Ejector, Vent Rib, Checkered Stock, *Modern*	325.00	425.00	425.00
☐ **Shadow Indy**, 12 Ga., Skeet Grade, Automatic Ejector, Vent Rib, Checkered Stock, *Modern*	325.00	425.00	425.00
☐ **Shadow Indy**, 12 Ga., Trap Grade, Automatic Ejector, Vent Rib, Checkered Stock, *Modern*	325.00	425.00	425.00
☐ **Shadow-7**, 12 Ga., Field Grade, Automatic Ejector, Vent Rib, *Modern*	200.00	300.00	300.00
☐ **Shadow-7**, 12 Ga., Skeet Grade, Automatic Ejector, Vent Rib, *Modern*	200.00	300.00	300.00
☐ **Shadow-7**, 12 Ga., Trap Grade, Automatic Ejector, Vent Rib, *Modern*	200.00	300.00	300.00
SHOTGUN, DOUBLE BARREL, SIDE-BY-SIDE			
☐ **Model G-1032**, 10 Ga. 3½", Checkered Stock, *Modern*	140.00	165.00	160.00
☐ **Model G-1228**, 12 Ga. Mag. 3", Checkered Stock, *Modern*	130.00	170.00	165.00
☐ **Model G-2028**, 20 Ga. Mag., Checkered Stock, *Modern*	130.00	170.00	165.00
SHOTGUN, SEMI-AUTOMATIC			
☐ **Model D-200**, 12 Ga., Field Grade, Vent Rib, Engraved, *Modern*	155.00	200.00	200.00
☐ **Model H-150**, 12 Ga., Field Grade, *Modern*	125.00	160.00	160.00
☐ **Model H-170**, 12 Ga., Field Grade, Vent Rib, *Modern*	140.00	180.00	180.00
☐ **Model T-220**, 12 Ga., Trap Grade, Vent Rib, Engraved, *Modern*	155.00	200.00	200.00
SHOTGUN, SINGLESHOT			
☐ **Model M50**, 10 Ga., 3½" Barrel, Checkered Stock, *Modern*	85.00	120.00	120.00

TRAMPS TERROR

Made by Hoods Firearms Co. Norwich, Conn., c. 1870.

	V.G.	Exc.	Prior Year Exc. Value
HANDGUN, REVOLVER			
☐ **.22 Short R.F.**, 7 Shot, Spur Trigger, Solid Frame, Single Action, *Antique*	90.00	160.00	160.00

TRIOMPH

Apaolozo Hermanos, Eibar, Spain.

	V.G.	Exc.	Prior Year Exc. Value
HANDGUN, SEMI-AUTOMATIC			
☐ **.25 ACP**, Clip Fed, Blue, *Modern*	85.00	125.00	120.00

TRIUMPH

Made by Stevens Arms.

	V.G.	Exc.	Prior Year Exc. Value
SHOTGUN, DOUBLE BARREL, SIDE-BY-SIDE			
☐ **Model 311**, Various Gauges, Hammerless, Steel Barrel, *Modern*	95.00	170.00	165.00

	V.G.	Exc.	Prior Year Exc. Value

TRUE BLUE
Made by Norwich Falls Pistols Co., c. 1880.

HANDGUN, REVOLVER

☐ **.32 Short R.F.**, 5 Shot, Spur Trigger, Solid Frame, Single Action, *Antique*	95.00	170.00	165.00

TRUST
Fab. d'Armes de Guerre de Grande Precision, Eibar, Spain.

HANDGUN, SEMI-AUTOMATIC

☐ **.25 ACP**, Clip Fed, Blue, *Modern*	85.00	125.00	120.00
☐ **.32 ACP**, Clip Fed, Blue, *Modern*	95.00	140.00	135.00

TRUST SUPRA
Fab. d'Armes de Guerre de Grande Precision, Eibar, Spain.

HANDGUN, SEMI-AUTOMATIC

☐ **.25 ACP**, Clip Fed, Blue, *Modern*	85.00	125.00	120.00

TUE-TUE
C.F. Galand, Liege, Belgium and Paris, France.

HANDGUN, REVOLVER

☐ **Velo Dog**, Various Calibers, Double Action, Hammerless, *Curio*	85.00	135.00	135.00

TURBIAUX
J.E. Turbiaux, Paris, France, c. 1885.

HANDGUN, MANUAL REPEATER

☐ **Le Protector**, Various Calibers, Palm Pistol, *Antique*	375.00	550.00	500.00

TURNER
Dublin, c. 1820.

HANDGUN, FLINTLOCK

☐ **.62**, Double Barrel, Pocket Pistol, Platinum Furniture, Plain, *Antique*	875.00	1,500.00	1,500.00

TURNER & ROSS
Made by Hood Firearms, Norwich, Conn., c. 1875.

HANDGUN, REVOLVER

☐ **.22 Short R.F.**, 7 Shot, Spur Trigger, Solid Frame, Single Action, *Antique*	95.00	165.00	160.00

TWIGG
London, England 1760-1813.

HANDGUN, FLINTLOCK

☐ **.58**, Pair, Belt Pistol, Flared, Octagon Barrel, Cased with Accessories, Plain, *Antique*	2,500.00	3,400.00	3,350.00

TYCOON
Made by Johnson-Bye, Worcester, Mass. 1873-1887.

HANDGUN, REVOLVER	V.G.	Exc.	Prior Year Exc. Value
☐ **#1**, .22 Short R.F., 7 Shot, Spur Trigger, Solid Frame, Single Action, *Antique*	95.00	165.00	160.00
☐ **#2**, .32 Short R.F., 5 Shot, Spur Trigger, Solid Frame, Single Action, *Antique*	145.00	195.00	190.00
☐ **#3**, .38 Short R.F., 5 Shot, Spur Trigger, Solid Frame, Single Action, *Antique*	95.00	165.00	160.00
☐ **#4**, .41 Short R.F., 5 Shot, Spur Trigger, Solid Frame, Single Action, *Antique*	105.00	145.00	140.00
☐ **#5**, .44 Short R.F., 5 Shot, Spur Trigger, Solid Frame, Single Action, *Antique*	150.00	225.00	225.00

TYROL

Made in Belgium for Tyrol Sport Arms, Englewood, Colo., c. 1963.

RIFLE, BOLT ACTION

☐ **Model DCM**, Various Calibers, Mannlicher Style, Checkered Stock, Recoil Pad, *Modern*	165.00	225.00	225.00
☐ **Model DC**, Various Calibers, Mannlicher Style, Checkered Stock, *Modern*	150.00	200.00	200.00
☐ **Model DM**, Various Calibers, Checkered Stock, *Modern*	135.00	180.00	175.00

UHLINGER, W.L. & CO.

Philadelphia, Pa., c. 1880.

HANDGUN, REVOLVER

☐ **.22 R.F.**, 7 Shot, Spur Trigger, Solid Frame, Single Action, *Antique*	145.00	225.00	225.00
☐ **.32 Short R.F.**, 6 Shot, Spur Trigger, Solid Frame, Single Action, *Antique*	165.00	275.00	275.00

U.M.C. ARMS CO.

Probably Norwich Arms Co., c. 1880.

HANDGUN, REVOLVER

☐ **.32 Short R.F.**, 5 Shot, Spur Trigger, Solid Frame, Single Action, *Antique*	95.00	165.00	160.00

UNION

Fab. Francaise.

HANDGUN, SEMI-AUTOMATIC

☐ **.32 ACP**, Ruby Style, Clip Fed, *Modern*	135.00	190.00	185.00
☐ **.32 ACP**, Ruby Style, with Horseshoe Magazine, *Modern*	600.00	850.00	850.00

UNION

France, M. Seytres.

HANDGUN, SEMI-AUTOMATIC

☐ **.25 ACP**, Clip Fed, Long Grip, *Modern*	75.00	125.00	120.00
☐ **.32 ACP**, Clip Fed, Long Grip, *Modern*	75.00	125.00	120.00

UNION

Unceta y Cia., Guernica, Spain 1924-1931.

HANDGUN, SEMI-AUTOMATIC

☐ **Mod I**, .25 ACP, Clip Fed, *Modern*	95.00	145.00	140.00

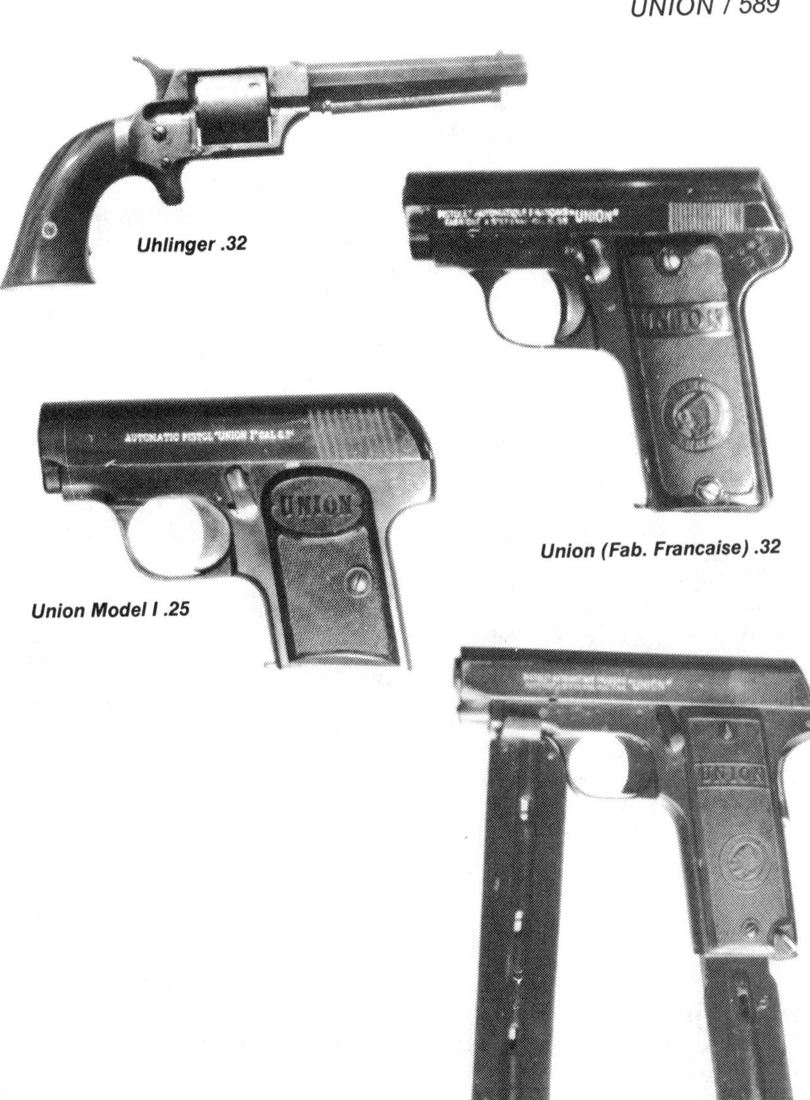

Uhlinger .32

Union (Fab. Francaise) .32

Union Model I .25

Union (Fab. Francaise) with Horseshoe

	V.G.	Exc.	Prior Year Exc. Value
☐ **Model II**, .25 ACP, Clip Fed, *Modern*	95.00	140.00	135.00
☐ **Model III**, .32 ACP, Clip Fed, *Modern*	115.00	160.00	155.00
☐ **Model IV**, .32 ACP, Clip Fed, *Modern*	115.00	160.00	155.00

UNION FIREARMS CO.

Toledo, Ohio, c. 1910.

HANDGUN, SEMI-AUTOMATIC, REVOLVER

	V.G.	Exc.	Prior Year Exc. Value
☐ **Lefever Patent**, .32 S & W, 5 Shot, Top Break, *Curio*	525.00	875.00	875.00
☐ **Reifgraber Patent**, .32 S & W, 8 Shot, *Curio*	600.00	950.00	950.00

UNION JACK

Made by Hood Firearms Norwich, Conn., c. 1880.

HANDGUN, REVOLVER

	V.G.	Exc.	Prior Year Exc. Value
☐ **.22 Short R.F.**, 7 Shot, Spur Trigger, Solid Frame, Single Action, *Antique*	95.00	165.00	160.00
☐ **.32 Short R.F.**, 5 Shot, Spur Trigger, Solid Frame, Single Action, *Antique*	95.00	170.00	170.00

UNION REVOLVER

Maker unknown, c. 1880.

HANDGUN, REVOLVER

	V.G.	Exc.	Prior Year Exc. Value
☐ **.22 Short R.F.**, 7 Shot, Spur Trigger, Solid Frame, Single Action, *Antique*	95.00	165.00	160.00
☐ **.32 Short R.F.**, 5 Shot, Spur Trigger, Solid Frame, Single Action, *Antique*	95.00	170.00	170.00

UNIQUE

Made by C.S. Shattuck, c. 1880.

HANDGUN, REVOLVER

	V.G.	Exc.	Prior Year Exc. Value
☐ **.32 Short R.F.**, 5 Shot, Spur Trigger, Solid Frame, Single Action, *Antique*	95.00	190.00	190.00
☐ **.38 Short R.F.**, 5 Shot, Spur Trigger, Solid Frame, Single Action, *Antique*	95.00	190.00	190.00

HANDGUN, REPEATER

	V.G.	Exc.	Prior Year Exc. Value
☐ **Shattuck Palm Pistol**, Various Calibers, 4 Shot, *Curio*	375.00	600.00	600.00

UNIQUE

Mre. d'Armes de Pyrenees, Hendaye, France, 1923 to date.

HANDGUN, SEMI-AUTOMATIC

	V.G.	Exc.	Prior Year Exc. Value
☐ **Kriegsmodell**, .32 ACP, Clip Fed, Magazine Disconnect, 9 Shot, Nazi-Proofed, Hammer, *Curio*	165.00	245.00	245.00
☐ **Model 10**, .25 ACP, Clip Fed, Magazine Disconnect, *Modern*	80.00	125.00	125.00
☐ **Model 11**, .25 ACP, Clip Fed, Magazine Disconnect, Grip Safety, Cartridge Indicator, *Modern*	110.00	150.00	150.00
☐ **Model 12**, .25 ACP, Clip Fed, Magazine Disconnect, Grip Safety, *Modern*	90.00	135.00	130.00
☐ **Model 13**, .25 ACP, Clip Fed, Magazine Disconnect, Grip Safety, 7 Shot, *Modern*	85.00	130.00	125.00

	V.G.	Exc.	Prior Year Exc. Value
☐ **Model 14**, .25 ACP, Clip Fed, Magazine Disconnect, Grip Safety, 9 Shot, *Modern*	90.00	135.00	130.00
☐ **Model 15**, .32 ACP, Clip Fed, Magazine Disconnect, 6 Shot, *Modern*	80.00	125.00	120.00
☐ **Model 16**, .32 ACP, Clip Fed, Magazine Disconnect, 7 Shot, *Modern*	80.00	125.00	120.00
☐ **Model 17**, .32 ACP, Clip Fed, Magazine Disconnect, 9 Shot, Nazi-Proofed, *Curio*	145.00	200.00	200.00
☐ **Model 17**, .32 ACP, Clip Fed, Magazine Disconnect, 9 Shot, *Modern*	90.00	135.00	130.00
☐ **Model 18**, .32 ACP, Clip Fed, Magazine Disconnect, 6 Shot, *Modern*	90.00	135.00	130.00
☐ **Model 19**, .32 ACP, Clip Fed, Magazine Disconnect, 7 Shot, *Modern*	85.00	130.00	125.00
☐ **Model 20**, .32 ACP, Clip Fed, Magazine Disconnect, 9 Shot, *Modern*	110.00	145.00	145.00
☐ **Model 21**, .380 ACP, Clip Fed, Magazine Disconnect, 6 Shot, *Modern*	110.00	145.00	145.00
☐ **Model 51**, .32 ACP, Clip Fed, Magazine Disconnect, 9 Shot, *Modern*	70.00	125.00	125.00
☐ **Model 51**, .380 ACP, Clip Fed, Magazine Disconnect, 6 Shot, *Modern*	70.00	130.00	125.00
☐ **Model 52**, .22 L.R.R.F., Clip Fed, Hammer, Various Barrel Lengths, *Modern*	75.00	120.00	115.00
☐ **Model 540**, .32 ACP, Clip Fed, Magazine Disconnect, 9 Shot, *Modern*	70.00	125.00	125.00
☐ **Model 550**, .380 ACP, Clip Fed, Magazine Disconnect, 6 Shot, *Modern*	70.00	125.00	125.00
☐ **Model C**, .32 ACP, Clip Fed, 9 Shot, Hammer, *Modern*	75.00	115.00	110.00
☐ **Model D-1**, .22 L.R.R.F., Clip Fed, Hammer, 3" Barrel, *Modern*	70.00	110.00	100.00
☐ **Model D-2**, .22 L.R.R.F., Clip Fed, Hammer, Adjustable Sights, 4" Barrel, *Modern*	85.00	125.00	120.00
☐ **Model D-3**, .22 L.R.R.F., Clip Fed, Hammer, Adjustable Sights, 8" Barrel, *Modern*	80.00	135.00	130.00
☐ **Model D-4**, .22 L.R.R.F., Clip Fed, Hammer, Muzzle Brake, Adjustable Sights, 9½" Barrel, *Modern*	95.00	155.00	155.00
☐ **Model D-6**, .22 L.R.R.F., Clip Fed, Hammer, Adjustable Sights, 6" Barrel, *Modern*	85.00	125.00	120.00
☐ **Model E-1**, .22 Short R.F., Clip Fed, Hammer, 3" Barrel, *Modern*	60.00	90.00	85.00
☐ **Model E-2**, .22 Short R.F., Clip Fed, Hammer, Adjustable Sights, 4" Barrel, *Modern*	85.00	125.00	120.00
☐ **Model E-3**, .22 Short R.F., Clip Fed, Hammer, Adjustable Sights, 8" Barrel, *Modern*	85.00	125.00	120.00
☐ **Model E-4**, .22 Short R.F., Clip Fed, Hammer, Muzzle Brake, Adjustable Sights, 9½" Barrel, *Modern*	95.00	150.00	150.00
☐ **Model F**, .380 ACP, Clip Fed, 8 Shot, Hammer, *Modern*	80.00	130.00	125.00
☐ **Model L (Corsair)**, .22 L.R.R.F., Clip Fed, Hammer, Lightweight, *Modern*	75.00	120.00	120.00
☐ **Model L (Corsair)**, .22 L.R.R.F., Clip Fed, Hammer, *Modern*	80.00	120.00	120.00

Unique Model L

	V.G.	Exc.	Prior Year Exc. Value
☐ **Model L (Corsair)**, .32 ACP, Clip Fed, Hammer, Lightweight, *Modern*	70.00	120.00	110.00
☐ **Model L (Corsair)**, .32 ACP, Clip Fed, Hammer, *Modern*	70.00	120.00	110.00
☐ **Model L (Corsair)**, .380 ACP, Clip Fed, Hammer, Lightweight, *Modern*	80.00	125.00	125.00
☐ **Model L (Corsair)**, .380 ACP, Clip Fed, Hammer, *Modern*	90.00	135.00	130.00
☐ **Model Mikros**, .25 ACP, Clip Fed, Magazine Disconnect, 6 Shot, *Modern*	80.00	125.00	120.00
☐ **Model RD (Ranger)**, .22 L.R.R.F., Clip Fed, Hammer, *Modern*	55.00	75.00	70.00
☐ **Model RD (Ranger)**, .22 L.R.R.F., Clip Fed, Muzzle Brake, Hammer, *Modern*	65.00	90.00	85.00
☐ **Model DES/69**, .22 L.R.R.F., Clip Fed, Target Pistol, *Modern*	225.00	325.00	325.00
☐ **Model DES/VO**, .22 L.R.R.F., Clip Fed, Rapid Fire Target Pistol, *Modern*	250.00	350.00	350.00
☐ **Model DES/VO 79**, .22 L.R.R.F., Clip Fed, Rapid Fire Target Pistol, Gas Ports, *Modern*	300.00	400.00	400.00
RIFLE, BOLT ACTION			
☐ **Dioptra 4131**, .22 W.M.R., Checkered Stock, Open Sights, *Modern*	200.00	300.00	300.00
☐ **Dioptra 3121**, .22 L.R.R.F., Checkered Stock, Open Sights, *Modern*	175.00	225.00	225.00
☐ **Dioptra 3121**, .22 L.R.R.F., Checkered Stock, Target Sights, *Modern*	200.00	300.00	300.00
☐ **Model T-66**, .22 L.R.R.F., Target Stock, Target Sights, Singleshot, *Modern*	300.00	400.00	400.00
☐ **Audax**, .22 L.R.R.F., Checkered Stock, Open Sights, *Modern*	110.00	150.00	150.00

UNITED STATES ARMS

Riverhead, N.Y., distributed by Mossberg.

HANDGUN, REVOLVER

	V.G.	Exc.	Prior Year Exc. Value
☐ **Abilene**, .44 Magnum, Single Action, Western Style, Adjustable Sights, *Modern*	135.00	190.00	185.00
☐ **Abilene**, .44 Magnum, Stainless Steel, Single Action, Western Style, Adjustable Sights, *Modern*	145.00	200.00	200.00

	V.G.	Exc.	Prior Year Exc. Value
☐ **Abilene**, .44 Magnum, Stainless Steel, Single Action, Western Style, 10" Barrel, Adjustable Sights, *Modern*	165.00	225.00	225.00
☐ **Abilene**, Various Calibers, Single Action, Western Style, Adjustable Sights, *Modern*	125.00	180.00	175.00
☐ **Abilene**, Various Calibers, Single Action, Western Style, Adjustable Sights, Stainless Steel, *Modern*	145.00	200.00	200.00

UNIVERSAL

Made by Hopkins & Allen, Norwich, Conn., c. 1890.

HANDGUN, REVOLVER

	V.G.	Exc.	Prior Year Exc. Value
☐ **.32 S & W, 5 Shot**, Double Action, Solid Frame, *Curio*	45.00	80.00	75.00

UNIVERSAL

Hialeah, Fla., Now owned by Iver Johnson - Jax

HANDGUN, SEMI-AUTOMATIC

	V.G.	Exc.	Prior Year Exc. Value
☐ **Model 3000 Enforcer**, .30 Carbine, Clip Fed, *Modern*	130.00	170.00	175.00
☐ **Model 3005 Enforcer**, .30 Carbine, Clip Fed, Nickel Plated, *Modern*	145.00	180.00	185.00
☐ **Model 3010 Enforcer**, .30 Carbine, Clip Fed, Gold Plated, *Modern*	150.00	185.00	190.00

RIFLE, SEMI-AUTOMATIC

	V.G.	Exc.	Prior Year Exc. Value
☐ **Model 1001**, .30 Carbine, Carbine, Clip Fed, *Modern*	85.00	130.00	125.00
☐ **Model 1002**, .30 Carbine, Carbine, Clip Fed, Bayonet Lug, *Modern*	90.00	135.00	130.00
☐ **Model 1003**, .30 Carbine, Carbine, Clip Fed, Walnut Stock, *Modern*	85.00	125.00	120.00
☐ **Model 1004**, .30 Carbine, Carbine, Clip Fed, Scope Mounted, *Modern*	95.00	135.00	130.00
☐ **Model 1010**, .30 Carbine, Carbine, Clip Fed, Nickel Plated, *Modern*	120.00	135.00	160.00
☐ **Model 1011 Deluxe**, .30 Carbine, Carbine, Clip Fed, Nickel Plated, Monte Carlo Stock, *Modern*	125.00	170.00	170.00
☐ **Model 1015**, .30 Carbine, Carbine, Clip Fed, Gold Plated, *Modern*	125.00	170.00	170.00
☐ **Model 1016 Deluxe**, .30 Carbine, Carbine, Clip Fed, Gold Plated, Monte Carlo Stock, *Modern*	140.00	180.00	180.00
☐ **Model 1025 Ferret**, .256 Win. Mag., Carbine, Clip Fed, Sporting Rifle, *Modern*	115.00	150.00	150.00
☐ **Model 1025 Ferret**, .30 Carbine, Carbine, Clip Fed, Sporting Rifle, *Modern*	110.00	145.00	145.00
☐ **Model 1941 Field Commander**, .30 Carbine, Carbine, Clip Fed, Fancy Wood, *Modern*	110.00	150.00	150.00

RIFLE, SLIDE ACTION

	V.G.	Exc.	Prior Year Exc. Value
☐ **Vulcan 440**, .44 Magnum, Clip Fed, Sporting Rifle, Open Rear Sight, *Modern*	125.00	160.00	160.00

SHOTGUN, DOUBLE BARREL, OVER-UNDER

	V.G.	Exc.	Prior Year Exc. Value
☐ **Baikal 1J-27**, 12 Ga., Double Trigger, Vent Rib, Engraved, Checkered Stock, *Modern*	150.00	200.00	200.00
☐ **Baikal 1J-27**, 12 Ga., Double Trigger, Vent Rib, Engraved, Checkered Stock, Automatic Ejector, *Modern*	160.00	220.00	220.00

	V.G.	Exc.	Prior Year Exc. Value
SHOTGUN, SINGLESHOT			
☐ **Model 7212**, 12 Ga., Trap Grade, Vent Rib, Engraved, Checkered Stock, Monte Carlo Stock, *Modern*	475.00	600.00	600.00
☐ **Model IJ18**, 12 Ga., Hammerless, *Modern*	30.00	45.00	40.00

UNWIN & ROGERS

Yorkshire, England, c. 1850.

HANDGUN, PERCUSSION			
☐ **Knife Pistol** with Ramrod and Mould, Cased with Accessories, *Antique*	750.00	1,100.00	1,000.00

U.S. ARMS CO.

Brooklyn, N.Y. 1874-1878.

HANDGUN, REVOLVER			
☐ **.22 Short R.F.**, 7 Shot, Spur Trigger, Solid Frame, Single Action, *Antique*	90.00	165.00	160.00
☐ **.32 Short R.F.**, 5 Shot, Spur Trigger, Solid Frame, Single Action, *Antique*	95.00	170.00	170.00
☐ **.38 Short R.F.**, 5 Shot, Spur Trigger, Solid Frame, Single Action, *Antique*	95.00	170.00	170.00
☐ **.41 Short R.F.**, 5 Shot, Spur Trigger, Solid Frame, Single Action, *Antique*	120.00	195.00	195.00

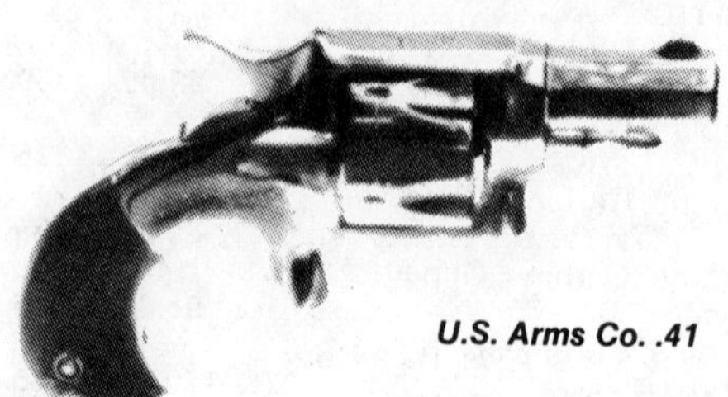

U.S. Arms Co. .41

U.S. ARMS CO.

Made by Crescent for H & D Folsom, c. 1900.

SHOTGUN, DOUBLE BARREL, SIDE-BY-SIDE			
☐ **Various Gauges**, Outside Hammers, Damascus Barrel, *Modern*	100.00	170.00	175.00
☐ **Various Gauges**, Hammerless, Steel Barrel, *Modern*	135.00	190.00	200.00
☐ **Various Gauges**, Hammerless, Damascus Barrel, *Modern*	100.00	170.00	175.00
☐ **Various Gauges**, Outside Hammers, Steel Barrel, *Modern*	125.00	185.00	190.00
SHOTGUN, SINGLESHOT			
☐ **Various Gauges**, Hammer, Steel Barrel, *Modern*	55.00	85.00	85.00

U.S. MILITARY

AUTOMATIC WEAPON, SUBMACHINE GUN

	V.G.	Exc.	Prior Year Exc. Value
☐ **M2**, .30 Carbine, Clip Fed, Military, Carbine, *Class 3*	325.00	450.00	425.00
☐ **M3**, 9mm Luger, Clip Fed, Military, *Class 3*	465.00	700.00	675.00
☐ **M3 Grease Gun**, .45 ACP, Clip Fed, Military, Silencer, *Class 3*	700.00	975.00	975.00
☐ **M3A1 Grease Gun**, .45 ACP, Clip Fed, Military, Flash Hider, *Class 3*	550.00	825.00	800.00
☐ **M50 Reising**, .45 ACP, Clip Fed, Wood Stock, Military, *Class 3*	170.00	250.00	225.00
☐ **M50 Reising**, .45 ACP, Clip Fed, Wood Stock, Military, Cased with Accessories, *Class 3*	225.00	345.00	325.00
☐ **M55 Reising**, .45 ACP, Clip Fed, Folding Stock, Military, *Class 3*	225.00	335.00	325.00
☐ **XM177E2**, .223 Rem., Clip Fed, Folding Stock, Silencer, Short Rifle, Military, *Class 3*	1,200.00	1,900.00	1,850.00

HANDGUN, FLINTLOCK

	V.G.	Exc.	Prior Year Exc. Value
☐ **.54 M1805 (06),** Singleshot, Smoothbore, Brass Mounts, Dated 1806, *Antique*	3700.00	7600.00	6500.00
☐ **.54 M1805 (06),** Singleshot, Smoothbore, Brass Mounts, Dated 1807, *Antique*	1300.00	2300.00	2150.00
☐ **.54 M1805 (06),** Singleshot, Smoothbore, Brass Mounts, Dated 1808, *Antique*	1350.00	2000.00	1950.00
☐ **.54 M1807-8,** Singleshot, Smoothbore, Brass Mounts, Various Contractors, *Antique*	2500.00	3500.00	3500.00
☐ **.54 M1816,** Singleshot, Smoothbore, S North Army, Brass Furniture, *Antique*	450.00	750.00	725.00
☐ **.54 M1819,** Singleshot, Smoothbore, S North Army, Iron Mounts, *Antique*	650.00	975.00	950.00
☐ **.54 M1826,** Singleshot, Smoothbore, S North Army, Iron Mounts, *Antique*	750.00	1250.00	1200.00
☐ **.54 M1836,** Singleshot, Smoothbore, R Johnson Army, Iron Mounts, *Antique*	575.00	840.00	825.00
☐ **.64 M1808,** Singleshot, Smoothbore, S North Army, Brass Furniture, *Antique*	1350.00	1850.00	1800.00
☐ **.69 M1799,** Singleshot, North & Cheney, Brass Furniture, Brass Frame, *Antique*	10000.00	18000.00	18000.00
☐ **.69 M1811,** Singleshot, Smoothbore, S North Army, Brass Furniture, *Antique*	1375.00	2200.00	2150.00
☐ **.69 M1817 (18),** Singleshot, Smoothbore, Springfield, Iron Mounts, *Antique*	1700.00	2550.00	2500.00

HANDGUN, PERCUSSION

	V.G.	Exc.	Prior Year Exc. Value
☐ **.54 M1836**, Singleshot, Smoothbore, Gedney Conversion from Flintlock, Iron Mounts, *Antique*	675.00	995.00	975.00
☐ **.54 M1842 Aston**, Singleshot, Smoothbore, Brass Mounts, *Antique*	425.00	575.00	550.00
☐ **.54 M1842 Johnson**, Singleshot, Smoothbore, Brass Mounts, *Antique*	425.00	575.00	550.00
☐ **.54 M1843 Deringer Army**, Singleshot, Smoothbore, Brass Mounts, *Antique*	425.00	750.00	725.00
☐ **.54 M1843 Deringer Army**, Singleshot, Rifled, Brass Mounts, *Antique*	700.00	995.00	975.00
☐ **.54 M1843 Deringer Navy**, Singleshot, Smoothbore, Brass Mounts, *Antique*	650.00	875.00	875.00

	V.G.	Exc.	Prior Year Exc. Value
HANDGUN, SINGLESHOT			
☐ **Liberator**, .45 ACP, Military, *Curio*	150.00	200.00	225.00
☐ **Liberator**, .45 ACP, Silencer, Military, *Class 3*	300.00	375.00	375.00
RIFLE, BOLT ACTION			
☐ **M1871 Ward-Burton**, .50 C.F., Iron Mountings, Rifle, *Antique*	500.00	835.00	800.00
☐ **M1871 Ward-Burton**, .50 C.F., Iron Mountings, Carbine, *Antique*	600.00	975.00	950.00
☐ **M1882 Chaffee-Reese**, 45-70, Rifle, *Antique*	500.00	825.00	800.00
☐ **M1892/6 Krag**, .30-40 Krag, Rifle, *Antique*	240.00	375.00	375.00
☐ **M1895 Lee Straight Pull**, 6mm Lee Navy, Musket, *Antique*	550.00	800.00	800.00
☐ **M1896 Krag**, .30-40 Krag, Rifle, *Antique*	275.00	400.00	400.00
☐ **M1896 Krag**, .30-40 Krag, Cadet, *Antique*	1,375.00	2,000.00	2,000.00
☐ **M1896 Krag**, .30-40 Krag, Carbine, *Antique*	375.00	550.00	550.00
☐ **M1898 Krag**, .30-40 Krag, Carbine, *Curio*	475.00	775.00	775.00
☐ **M1898 Krag**, .30-40 Krag, Rifle, *Curio*	200.00	350.00	350.00
☐ **M1899 Krag**, .30-40 Krag, Carbine, *Curio*	250.00	400.00	400.00
☐ **M1903**, .30-06 Springfield, Machined Parts, *Modern*	200.00	325.00	325.00
☐ **M1903/5**, 30-03 Springfield, *Curio*	650.00	1,100.00	1,100.00
☐ **M1903/5**, 30-06 Springfield, *Curio*	200.00	350.00	350.00
☐ **M1903/7**, 30-06 Springfield, Early Receivers, *Curio*	350.00	600.00	600.00
☐ **M1903/WWI**, 30-06 Springfield, *Curio*	300.00	450.00	450.00
☐ **M1903/Postwar**, 30-06 Springfield, *Curio*	250.00	375.00	375.00
☐ **M1903 National Match**, .30-06 Springfield, Target Rifle, *Curio*	500.00	725.00	700.00
☐ **M1903A1**, .30-06 Springfield, Parkerized, Checkered Butt, Machined Parts, *Curio*	190.00	270.00	250.00
☐ **M1903A1 National Match**, .30-06 Springfield, Target Rifle, *Curio*	450.00	675.00	650.00
☐ **M1903A3**, .30-06 Springfield, Stamped Parts, *Curio*	160.00	240.00	225.00
☐ **M1903A4 Sniper**, .30-06 Springfield, Scope Mounts, *Curio*	650.00	995.00	975.00
☐ **M1917 Eddystone**, .30-06 Springfield, *Curio*	165.00	220.00	200.00
☐ **M1917 Remington**, .30-06 Springfield, *Curio*	170.00	235.00	220.00
☐ **M1917 Winchester**, .30-06 Springfield, *Curio*	165.00	250.00	235.00
☐ **M1922 Trainer**, .22 L.R.R.F., Target Rifle, *Curio*	600.00	975.00	950.00
☐ **M1922M2 Trainer**, .22 L.R.R.F., Target Rifle, *Curio*	420.00	595.00	575.00
☐ **M40-XB Sniper (Rem.)**, .308 Win., Heavy Barrel, Scope Mounted, Silencer, *Class 3*	600.00	875.00	875.00
RIFLE, FLINTLOCK			
☐ **.52**, M1819 Hall, Rifled, Breech Loader, 32½" Barrel, 3 Bands, *Antique*	1,650.00	2,650.00	2,600.00
☐ **.52**, M1819 Hall Whitney, Rifled, Breech Loader, 32½" Barrel, 3 Bands, *Antique*	1,450.00	2,550.00	2,500.00
☐ **.54**, M1803 Harper's Ferry, Rifled, 32½" Barrel, *Antique*	1,400.00	2,300.00	2,250.00
☐ **.54**, M1807 Springfield, Indian, Carbine, 27¾" Barrel, *Antique*	1,400.00	2,300.00	2,300.00
☐ **.54**, M1814 Ghriskey, Rifled, 36" Barrel, *Antique*	1,400.00	2,500.00	2,500.00

	V.G.	Exc.	Prior Year Exc. Value
RIFLE, PERCUSSION			
☐ **.57**, M1841 U.S., Cadet Musket, 40" Barrel, 2 Bands, *Antique*	700.00	1,150.00	1,150.00
☐ **.57**, M1851 U.S., Cadet Musket, Rifled, 40" Barrel, 2 Bands, *Antique*	700.00	1,200.00	1,200.00
☐ **.57**, M1851 U.S., Cadet Musket, Smoothbore, 40" Barrel, 2 Bands, *Antique*	650.00	1,100.00	1,100.00
☐ **.58 Lindner**, Breech Loader, Carbine, Rising Block, *Antique*	675.00	1,150.00	1,150.00
☐ **.58**, M1841 Contract, Rifled, 33" Barrel, 2 Bands, (Mississippi Rifle), *Antique*	600.00	965.00	950.00
☐ **.58**, M1855 U.S., Rifled, 40" Barrel, 3 Bands, with Tape Priming System, *Antique*	900.00	1,500.00	1,550.00
☐ **.58**, M1855 U.S., Carbine, Rifled, 22" Barrel, 1 Band, with Tape Priming System, *Antique*	950.00	1,700.00	1,700.00
☐ **.64**, M1833 Hall-North, Rifled, Breech Loader, Carbine, 26⅛" Barrel, 2 Bands, *Antique*	800.00	1,475.00	1,450.00
☐ **.69**, M1842 U.S., Musket, 42" Barrel, 3 Bands, *Antique*	525.00	765.00	750.00
☐ **.69**, M1842 U.S., Musket, 42" Barrel, 3 Bands, *Antique*	550.00	800.00	800.00
☐ **.69**, M1847 Artillery, Musketoon, 26" Barrel, 2 Bands, Steel Furniture, *Antique*	600.00	950.00	950.00
☐ **.69**, M1847 Cavalry, Musketoon, 26" Barrel, 2 Bands, Brass Furniture, *Antique*	550.00	800.00	800.00
☐ **.69**, M1847 Sappers, Musketoon, 26" Barrel, 2 Bands, Bayonet Stud on Right Side, *Antique*	850.00	1,400.00	1,400.00
☐ **M 1864 Training Rifle**, Military, Wood Barrel, *Antique*	70.00	135.00	125.00
RIFLE, SEMI-AUTOMATIC			
☐ **M1941 Johnson**, 30-06 Springfield, Military, *Curio*	325.00	500.00	475.00
☐ **M-1 Carbine Inland**, .30 Carbine, Clip Fed, *Curio*	175.00	300.00	275.00
☐ **M-1 Carbine Nat. Postal Meter**, .30 Carbine, Clip Fed, *Curio*	475.00	725.00	700.00
☐ **M-1 Carbine Rochester**, .30 Carbine, Clip Fed, *Curio*	900.00	1,550.00	1,400.00
☐ **M-1 Carbine Commercial Control**, .30 Carbine, Clip Fed, *Curio*	945.00	1,600.00	1,450.00
☐ **M-1 Carbine Irwin-Pedersen**, .30 Carbine, Clip Fed, *Curio*	475.00	725.00	700.00
☐ **M-1 Carbine Un-Quality**, .30 Carbine, Clip Fed, *Curio*	475.00	725.00	700.00
☐ **M-1 Carbine Quality Hdw.**, .30 Carbine, Clip Fed, *Curio*	525.00	835.00	800.00
☐ **M-1 Carbine Winchester**, .30 Carbine, Clip Fed, *Curio*	250.00	385.00	365.00
☐ **M-1 Garand**, .30-06 Springfield, Military, *Curio*	525.00	850.00	800.00
☐ **M-1 Garand National Match**, .30-06 Springfield, Military, Target Sights, Target Trigger, Target Barrel, *Curio*	700.00	1,050.00	975.00
☐ **M-1 Garand Winchester**, .30-06 Springfield, *Curio*	675.00	950.00	925.00
☐ **M-180**, .22 L.R.R.F., Carbine, 177 Round Drum Magazine, *Modern*	255.00	325.00	325.00
☐ **M-1A1 Carbine**, .30 Carbine, Clip Fed, Folding Stock, *Modern*	350.00	500.00	475.00

U.S. REVOLVER CO.

MADE BY IVER JOHNSON

	V.G.	Exc.	Prior Year Exc. Value
☐ **.32 S & W**, 5 Shot, Double Action, Solid Frame, *Modern*	45.00	85.00	80.00
☐ **.32 S & W**, 5 Shot, Top Break, Hammerless, Double Action, *Modern*	55.00	95.00	95.00
☐ **.32 S & W**, 5 Shot, Double Action, Top Break, *Modern*	45.00	95.00	95.00
☐ **.32 Short R.F.**, 5 Shot, Spur Trigger, Solid Frame, Single Action, *Antique*	90.00	165.00	160.00
☐ **.38 S & W**, 5 Shot, Double Action, Solid Frame, *Modern*	45.00	75.00	70.00
☐ **.38 S & W**, 5 Shot, Top Break, Hammerless, Double Action, *Modern*	55.00	100.00	95.00
☐ **.38 S & W**, 5 Shot, Double Action, Top Break, *Modern*	55.00	100.00	95.00

VALIANT

Made by Stevens Arms for Spear & Co., Pittsburgh, Pa.

RIFLE, BOLT ACTION

	V.G.	Exc.	Prior Year Exc. Value
☐ **Model 51**, .22 L.R.R.F., Singleshot, Takedown, *Modern*	30.00	45.00	40.00

VALMET

Valmet Oy, Tourula Works, Jyvaskyla, Finland.

AUTOMATIC WEAPON, ASSAULT RIFLE

	V.G.	Exc.	Prior Year Exc. Value
☐ **M78 LMG**, .308 Win., Clip Fed, Bipod, *Class 3*	700.00	1,100.00	1,100.00
☐ **Model 718S**, .223 Rem., Clip Fed, Commercial, *Class 3*	450.00	670.00	650.00

RIFLE, SEMI-AUTOMATIC

	V.G.	Exc.	Prior Year Exc. Value
☐ **M78 HV**, .223 Rem., Clip Fed, Bipod, *Modern*	700.00	1,100.00	1,100.00
☐ **M78 Standard**, .308 Win., Clip Fed, Bipod, *Modern*	700.00	1,100.00	1,100.00
☐ **M-62S**, 7.62 x 39 Russian, Clip Fed, AK-47 Type, Sporting Version of Military Rifle, *Modern*	550.00	795.00	775.00
☐ **M-72S**, .223 Rem., Clip Fed, AK-47 Type, Sporting Version of Military Rifle, *Modern*	475.00	700.00	700.00

VALOR ARMS

Importers Miami, Fla.

HANDGUN, REVOLVER

	V.G.	Exc.	Prior Year Exc. Value
☐ **.22 L.R.R.F.**, Double Action, Lightweight, *Modern*	15.00	25.00	25.00
☐ **.32 S & W**, Double Action, Lightweight, *Modern*	15.00	25.00	25.00

VANDERFRIFT, ISAAC AND JEREMIAH

Philadelphia, Pa. 1809-1815. See Kentucky Rifles and Pistols.

VEGA

Sacramento, Calif.

HANDGUN, SEMI-AUTOMATIC

	V.G.	Exc.	Prior Year Exc. Value
☐ **Vega 1911a1**, .45 ACP, Stainless Steel, Clip Fed, *Modern*	220.00	325.00	295.00

	V.G.	Exc.	Prior Year Exc. Value

VELO DOG

Various makers, c. 1900.

HANDGUN, REVOLVER

	V.G.	Exc.	Prior Year Exc. Value
☐ **5mm Velo Dog**, Hammerless, Folding Trigger, *Curio*	70.00	100.00	100.00
☐ **5mm Velo Dog**, Hammer, Folding Trigger, *Curio*	60.00	95.00	90.00
☐ **5mm Velo Dog**, Hammerless, Trigger Guard, *Curio*	60.00	95.00	90.00
☐ **.25 ACP**, Hammerless, Folding Trigger, *Curio*	70.00	110.00	100.00
☐ **.25 ACP**, Hammer, Folding Trigger, *Curio*	70.00	110.00	100.00

VENCEDOR

San Martin y Cia., Eibar, Spain.

HANDGUN, SEMI-AUTOMATIC

	V.G.	Exc.	Prior Year Exc. Value
☐ **.25 ACP**, Clip Fed, Blue, *Modern*	85.00	125.00	120.00
☐ **.35 ACP**, Clip Fed, Blue, *Modern*	95.00	140.00	135.00

VENTURA IMPORTS (CONTENTO)

Seal Beach, Calif. Also see Bertuzzi and Piotti.

SHOTGUN, DOUBLE BARREL, OVER-UNDER

	V.G.	Exc.	Prior Year Exc. Value
☐ **MK-1 Contento**, 12 Ga., Field Grade, Automatic Ejector, Single Selective Trigger, Engraved, Checkered Stock, *Modern*	325.00	465.00	450.00
☐ **MK-2 Contento**, 12 Ga., Field Grade, Automatic Ejector, Single Selective Trigger, Engraved, Checkered Stock, *Modern*	450.00	675.00	650.00
☐ **MK-2 Contento**, 12 Ga., Trap Grade, with Extra Single Trap Barrel, Engraved, Checkered Stock, *Modern*	750.00	1,150.00	1,100.00
☐ **MK-2 Luxe Contento**, 12 Ga., Field Grade, Automatic Ejector, Single Selective Trigger, Engraved, Checkered Stock, *Modern*	625.00	825.00	800.00
☐ **MK-2 Luxe Contento**, 12 Ga., Trap Grade, with Extra Single Trap Barrel, Engraved, Checkered Stock, *Modern*	950.00	1,350.00	1,300.00
☐ **MK-3 Contento**, 12 Ga., Field Grade, Automatic Ejector, Single Selective Trigger, Engraved, Checkered Stock, *Modern*	750.00	1,050.00	1,000.00
☐ **MK-3 Contento**, 12 Ga., Trap Grade, with Extra Single Trap Barrel, Engraved, Checkered Stock, *Modern*	1,200.00	1,750.00	1,700.00
☐ **MK-3 Luxe Contento**, 12 Ga., Field Grade, Automatic Ejector, Single Selective Trigger, Engraved, Checkered Stock, *Modern*	950.00	1,350.00	1,300.00
☐ **MK-3 Luxe Contento**, 12 Ga., Trap Grade, with Extra Single Trap Barrel, Engraved, Checkered Stock, *Modern*	1,450.00	2,100.00	2,000.00
☐ **Nettuno Contento**, 12 Ga., Field Grade, Automatic Ejector, Single Selective Trigger, Engraved, Checkered Stock, *Modern*	250.00	395.00	375.00

SHOTGUN, DOUBLE BARREL, SIDE-BY-SIDE

	V.G.	Exc.	Prior Year Exc. Value
☐ **Ventura Model 51**, 12 and 20 Gauges, Boxlock, Checkered Stock, *Modern*	250.00	395.00	375.00
☐ **Ventura Model 62 Standard**, 12 and 20 Gauges, Sidelock, Checkered Stock, Engraved, *Modern*	475.00	725.00	700.00

	V.G.	Exc.	Prior Year Exc. Value
☐ **Ventura Model 64 Standard**, 12 and 20 Gauges, Sidelock, Checkered Stock, Engraved, *Modern*	475.00	725.00	700.00

VENUS
Tomas de Urizar y Cia., Eibar, Spain.

HANDGUN, SEMI-AUTOMATIC

	V.G.	Exc.	Prior Year Exc. Value
☐ **.32 ACP**, Clip Fed, *Modern*	95.00	135.00	125.00

VENUS
Venus Waffenwerk Oskar Will, Zella Mehlis, Germany, c. 1912.

HANDGUN, SEMI-AUTOMATIC

	V.G.	Exc.	Prior Year Exc. Value
☐ **.32 ACP**, Target Pistol, Hammerless, Blue, *Curio*	325.00	565.00	540.00

VERNEY-CARRON
St. Etienne, France

HANDGUN, SEMI-AUTOMATIC

	V.G.	Exc.	Prior Year Exc. Value
☐ **.25 ACP**, Clip Fed, Blue, *Modern*	125.00	165.00	

SHOTGUN, DOUBLE BARREL, OVER-UNDER

	V.G.	Exc.	Prior Year Exc. Value
☐ **Field Grade**, 12 Ga., Automatic Ejectors, Checkered Stock, Engraved, *Modern*	450.00	695.00	675.00

VESTA
Hijos de A. Echeverra, Eibar, Spain.

HANDGUN, SEMI-AUTOMATIC

	V.G.	Exc.	Prior Year Exc. Value
☐ **Pocket**, .32 ACP, Clip Fed, Long Grip, *Modern*	85.00	130.00	125.00
☐ **Vest Pocket**, .25 ACP, Clip Fed, *Modern*	80.00	125.00	120.00

VETERAN
Made by Norwich Falls Pistol Co., c. 1880.

HANDGUN, REVOLVER

	V.G.	Exc.	Prior Year Exc. Value
☐ **.32 Short R.F.**, 5 Shot, Spur Trigger, Solid Frame, Single Action, *Antique*	90.00	165.00	160.00

VETO
Unknown maker, c. 1880.

HANDGUN, REVOLVER

	V.G.	Exc.	Prior Year Exc. Value
☐ **.32 Short R.F.**, 5 Shot, Spur Trigger, Solid Frame, Single Action, *Antique*	90.00	165.00	160.00

VICI
Unknown Belgian maker.

HANDGUN, SEMI-AUTOMATIC

	V.G.	Exc.	Prior Year Exc. Value
☐ **.25 ACP**, Clip Fed, *Modern*	90.00	130.00	125.00

VICTOR
Made by Crescent, c. 1900.

SHOTGUN, DOUBLE BARREL, SIDE-BY-SIDE

	V.G.	Exc.	Prior Year Exc. Value
☐ **Various Gauges**, Outside Hammers, Damascus Barrel, *Modern*	100.00	170.00	175.00
☐ **Various Gauges**, Hammerless, Steel Barrel, *Modern*	135.00	190.00	200.00

Vesta

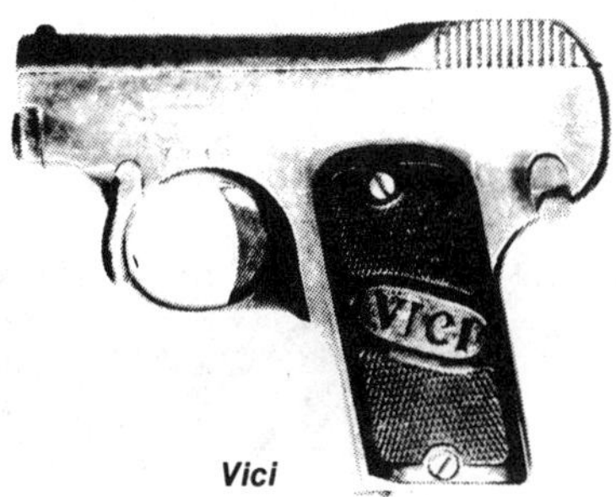
Vici

	V.G.	Exc.	Prior Year Exc. Value
☐ **Various Gauges**, Hammerless, Damascus Barrel, *Modern*	100.00	170.00	175.00
☐ **Various Gauges**, Outside Hammers, Steel Barrel, *Modern*	125.00	185.00	190.00

SHOTGUN, SINGLESHOT

	V.G.	Exc.	Prior Year Exc. Value
☐ **Various Gauges**, Hammer, Steel Barrel, *Modern*	55.00	85.00	85.00

VICTOR

Francisco Arizmendi, Eibar, Spain, c. 1916.

HANDGUN, SEMI-AUTOMATIC

	V.G.	Exc.	Prior Year Exc. Value
☐ **.25 ACP**, Clip Fed, Blue, *Curio*	85.00	125.00	120.00
☐ **.32 ACP**, Clip Fed, Blue, *Curio*	95.00	140.00	135.00

VICTOR #1

Made by Harrington & Richardson, c. 1876.

HANDGUN, REVOLVER

	V.G.	Exc.	Prior Year Exc. Value
☐ **.32 S & W**, 5 Shot, Single Action, Solid Frame, *Antique*	55.00	95.00	95.00
☐ **#1**, .22 Short R.F., 7 Shot, Spur Trigger, Solid Frame, Single Action, *Antique*	90.00	165.00	160.00
☐ **#2**, .32 Short R.F., 5 Shot, Spur Trigger, Solid Frame, Single Action, *Antique*	90.00	165.00	160.00

VICTOR SPECIAL

Made by Crescent for Hibbard-Spencer-Bartlett Co., c. 1900.

SHOTGUN, DOUBLE BARREL, SIDE-BY-SIDE

	V.G.	Exc.	Prior Year Exc. Value
☐ **Various Gauges**, Hammerless, Damascus Barrel, *Modern*	100.00	170.00	175.00
☐ **Various Gauges**, Outside Hammers, Steel Barrel, *Modern*	125.00	185.00	190.00

SHOTGUN, SINGLESHOT

	V.G.	Exc.	Prior Year Exc. Value
☐ **Various Gauges**, Hammer, Steel Barrel, *Modern*	55.00	85.00	85.00

VICTORIA

Made by Hood Firearms, c. 1875.

HANDGUN, REVOLVER

	V.G.	Exc.	Prior Year Exc. Value
☐ **.32 Short R.F.**, 5 Shot, Spur Trigger, Solid Frame, Single Action, *Antique*	90.00	165.00	160.00

	V.G.	Exc.	Prior Year Exc. Value

VICTORIA

Spain, Esperanza y Unceta, c. 1900.

HANDGUN, SEMI-AUTOMATIC

	V.G.	Exc.	Prior Year Exc. Value
☐ **M1911**, .32 ACP, Clip Fed, *Modern*	95.00	145.00	130.00
☐ **.25 ACP**, Clip Fed, *Modern*	90.00	125.00	120.00

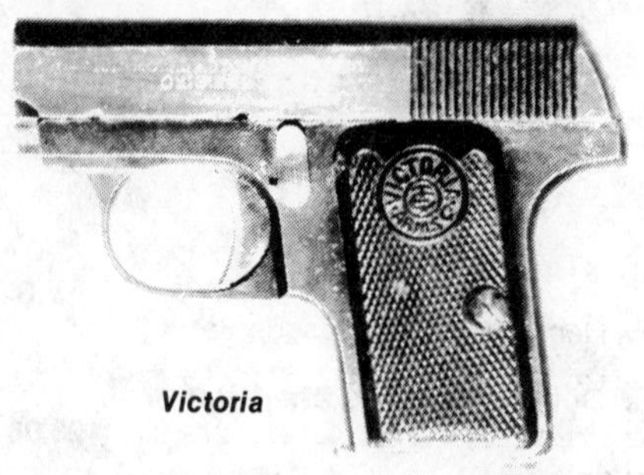

Victoria

VICTORY

M. Zulaica y Cia., Eibar, Spain.

HANDGUN, SEMI-AUTOMATIC

	V.G.	Exc.	Prior Year Exc. Value
☐ **.25 ACP**, Clip Fed, *Modern*	115.00	150.00	140.00

VILAR

Spain, unknown maker 1920-1938.

HANDGUN, SEMI-AUTOMATIC

	V.G.	Exc.	Prior Year Exc. Value
☐ **Pocket**, .32 ACP, Clip Fed, Long Grip, *Modern*	85.00	125.00	120.00

VINCITOR

M. Zulaica y Cia., Eibar, Spain.

HANDGUN, SEMI-AUTOMATIC

	V.G.	Exc.	Prior Year Exc. Value
☐ **Model 1914**, .25 ACP, Clip Fed, Blue, *Curio*	95.00	150.00	140.00
☐ **Model 14 No. 2**, .32 ACP, Clip Fed, Blue, *Curio*	115.00	160.00	150.00

VINDEX

Mre. d'Armes des Pyrenees, Hendaye, France.

HANDGUN, SEMI-AUTOMATIC

	V.G.	Exc.	Prior Year Exc. Value
☐ **.32 ACP**, Clip Fed, Blue, *Modern*	75.00	120.00	110.00

VIRGINIA ARMS CO.

Made by Crescent for Virginia-Caroline Co., c. 1900.

SHOTGUN, DOUBLE BARREL, SIDE-BY-SIDE

	V.G.	Exc.	Prior Year Exc. Value
☐ **Various Gauges**, Outside Hammers, Damascus Barrel, *Modern*	100.00	170.00	175.00
☐ **Various Gauges**, Hammerless, Steel Barrel, *Modern*	135.00	190.00	200.00
☐ **Various Gauges**, Hammerless, Damascus Barrel, *Modern*	100.00	170.00	175.00
☐ **Various Gauges**, Outside Hammers, Steel Barrel, *Modern*	125.00	185.00	190.00

	V.G.	Exc.	Prior Year Exc. Value
SHOTGUN, SINGLESHOT			
☐ **Various Gauges**, Hammer, Steel Barrel, *Modern*	55.00	85.00	85.00

VIRGINIAN

Made by Interarms, Alexandria, Va.

	V.G.	Exc.	Prior Year Exc. Value
HANDGUN, REVOLVER			
☐ **Dragoon, Buntline**, Various Calibers, Single Action, Western Style, Target Sights, Blue, *Modern*	140.00	190.00	185.00
☐ **Dragoon, Deputy**, Various Calibers, Single Action, Western Style, Fixed Sights, Blue, *Modern*	140.00	180.00	175.00
☐ **Dragoon, Deputy**, Various Calibers, Single Action, Western Style, Fixed Sights, Stainless Steel, *Modern*	140.00	180.00	175.00
☐ **Dragoon, Silhouette**, .44 Magnum, Single Action, Western Style, Target Sights, Stainless Steel, *Modern*	160.00	235.00	225.00
☐ **Dragoon, Standard**, Various Calibers, Single Action, Western Style, Target Sights, Blue, *Modern*	140.00	190.00	185.00
☐ **Dragoon, Standard**, Various Calibers, Single Action, Western Style, Target Sights, Stainless Steel, *Modern*	145.00	200.00	195.00
☐ **Dragoon, Engraved**, Various Calibers, Single Action, Western Style, Target Sights, Blue, *Modern*	225.00	360.00	350.00
☐ **Dragoon, Engraved**, Various Calibers, Single Action, Western Style, Target Sights, Stainless Steel, *Modern*	250.00	385.00	375.00

VOERE

Voere GmbH, Vohrenbach, West Germany.

	V.G.	Exc.	Prior Year Exc. Value
RIFLE, BOLT ACTION			
☐ **Model 3145 DJV**, .223 Rem., Match Rifle, Target Stock, *Modern*	300.00	465.00	450.00
☐ **Model 2145**, .308 Win., Match Rifle, Target Stock, *Modern*	450.00	665.00	650.00
☐ **Premier Mauser**, Various Calibers, Sporting Rifle, Checkered Stock, Recoil Pad, Open Rear Sight, *Modern*	145.00	200.00	195.00
☐ **Shikar**, Various Calibers, Sporting Rifle, Fancy Checkering, Fancy Wood, Recoil Pad, no Sights, *Modern*	275.00	385.00	375.00
☐ **Titan-Menor**, Various Calibers, Sporting Rifle, Checkered Stock, Recoil Pad, Open Rear Sight, *Modern*	200.00	285.00	275.00

VOERE

Voere Tiroler Jagd u. Sportwaffenfabrik, Kufstein, Austria.

	V.G.	Exc.	Prior Year Exc. Value
RIFLE, BOLT ACTION			
☐ **Model 2155**, Various Calibers, Sporting Rifle, Checkered Stock, Open Rear Sight, *Modern*	185.00	235.00	225.00

	V.G.	Exc.	Prior Year Exc. Value
☐ **Model 2165/1**, Various Calibers, Sporting Rifle, Checkered Stock, Recoil Pad, Open Rear Sight, *Modern*	320.00	425.00	400.00

VITE
Echave y Arizmendi, Eibar, Spain, c. 1913.

HANDGUN, SEMI-AUTOMATIC

	V.G.	Exc.	Prior Year Exc. Value
☐ **Model 1912**, .25 ACP, Clip Fed, Blue, *Curio*	80.00	125.00	120.00
☐ **Model 1915**, .32 ACP, Clip Fed, Blue, *Curio*	85.00	130.00	125.00

VOLUNTEER
Made by Stevens Arms for Belknap Hardware Co., Louisville, Ky.

SHOTGUN, SINGLESHOT

	V.G.	Exc.	Prior Year Exc. Value
☐ **Model 94**, Various Gauges, Takedown, Automatic Ejector, Plain, Hammer, *Modern*	40.00	65.00	60.00

VULCAN ARMS CO.
Made by Crescent, c. 1900.

SHOTGUN, DOUBLE BARREL, SIDE-BY-SIDE

	V.G.	Exc.	Prior Year Exc. Value
☐ **Various Gauges**, Outside Hammers, Damascus Barrel, *Modern*	100.00	170.00	175.00
☐ **Various Gauges**, Hammerless, Steel Barrel, *Modern*	135.00	190.00	200.00
☐ **Various Gauges**, Hammerless, Damascus Barrel, *Modern*	100.00	170.00	175.00
☐ **Various Gauges**, Outside Hammers, Steel Barrel, *Modern*	125.00	185.00	190.00

SHOTGUN, SINGLESHOT

	V.G.	Exc.	Prior Year Exc. Value
☐ **Various Gauges**, Hammer, Steel Barrel, *Modern*	55.00	85.00	85.00

WAFFENFABRIK BERN
Eidgenosssische Waffenfabrik, Bern, Switzerland. Also see Swiss Military.

RIFLE, BOLT ACTION

	V.G.	Exc.	Prior Year Exc. Value
☐ **Model 31**, 7.5mm Swiss, Military Style, *Modern*	450.00	650.00	600.00
☐ **Model 31 Target**, 7.5mm Swiss, Military Style, Match Rifle, Target Sights, *Modern*	550.00	825.00	775.00

WALDMAN
Arizmendi Y Goenaga, Eibar, Spain.

HANDGUN, SEMI-AUTOMATIC

	V.G.	Exc.	Prior Year Exc. Value
☐ **.25 ACP**, Clip Fed, *Curio*	85.00	130.00	125.00
☐ **.32 ACP**, Clip Fed, *Curio*	95.00	145.00	140.00

WALMAN
F. Arizmendi Y Goenaga, Eibar, Spain.

HANDGUN, SEMI-AUTOMATIC

	V.G.	Exc.	Prior Year Exc. Value
☐ **.25 ACP**, Clip Fed, *Curio*	85.00	130.00	125.00
☐ **.32 ACP**, Clip Fed, *Curio*	95.00	145.00	140.00
☐ **.380 ACP**, Clip Fed, *Curio*	150.00	220.00	200.00

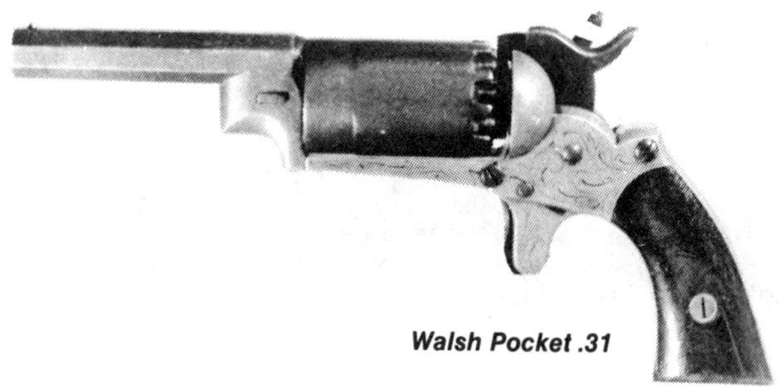
Walsh Pocket .31

WALSH FIREARMS CO.

N.Y.C., c. 1860.

	V.G.	Exc.	Prior Year Exc. Value
HANDGUN, PERCUSSION			
☐ **Navy**, .36, Revolver, 12 Shot, Double-Charge Cylinder, *Antique*	1,250.00	2,000.00	2,000.00
☐ **Pocket**, .31, Revolver, 12 Shot, Double-Charge Cylinder, *Antique*	450.00	650.00	650.00

WALSH, JAMES

Philadelphia, Pa. 1775-1779. See Kentucky Rifles and Pistols and U.S. Military.

WALTHER

First started in 1886 by Carl Walther in Zella Mehlis, Germany. After his death in 1915 the firm was operated by his sons Fritz, George, and Erich, and after WWII moved to Ulm/Donau, West Germany. Also see German Military, Manurhin.

	V.G.	Exc.	Prior Year Exc. Value
HANDGUN, PERCUSSION			
☐ **Model CP-2 C02,** .177 Caliber, Blue, Single Shot, *Modern*	600.00	700.00	700.00
☐ **Model FP Free Pistol,** .22 LR, Blue, Single Shot, *Modern*	650.00	750.00	750.00
☐ **Model LP-3,** .177 Caliber, Blue, Single Shot, *Modern*	350.00	400.00	400.00
HANDGUN, SEMI-AUTOMATIC			
☐ **Model 1,** .25 ACP, Blue, *Curio*	185.00	300.00	325.00
☐ **Model 2,** .25 ACP, Pop-Up Rear Sight, Blue, *Curio*	400.00	725.00	775.00
☐ **Model 3,** .32 ACP, Blue, *Curio*	425.00	675.00	700.00
☐ **Model 3/4,** .32 ACP, Takedown Lever, Blue, *Curio*	170.00	300.00	320.00
☐ **Model 4,** .32 ACP, Blue, *Curio*	150.00	230.00	250.00
☐ **Model 5/2,** .25 ACP, no Sights, Blue, *Curio*	150.00	225.00	245.00
☐ **Model 5,** .25 ACP, Solid Rib, Blue, *Curio*	155.00	230.00	250.00
☐ **Model 6,** 9mm Luger, Blue, *Curio*	810.00	1400.00	1475.00
☐ **Model 7,** .25 ACP, Blue, *Curio*	215.00	350.00	365.00
☐ **Model 8,** .25 ACP, Blue, *Modern*	170.00	275.00	290.00
☐ **Model 8,** .25 ACP, Blue, Lightweight, *Modern*	260.00	400.00	420.00
☐ **Model 9,** .25 ACP, Blue, *Modern*	200.00	280.00	300.00
☐ **Model GSP,** .22 L.R.R.F., 5 Shot Clip, Target Pistol, *Modern*	450.00	675.00	700.00
☐ **Model GSP C,** .22 Short, 5 Shot Clip, Target Pistol, *Modern*	530.00	750.00	775.00

	V.G.	Exc.	Prior Year Exc. Value
☐ **Model GSP C,** .22 Short, 5 Shot Clip, Target Pistol, with .22 L.R. Conversion Kit, *Modern*	800.00	1300.00	1300.00
☐ **Model HP,** .30 Luger, Single Action, *Modern*	3650.00	5000.00	5000.00
☐ **Model HP,** .30 Luger, Single Action, Wood Grips, *Modern*	3800.00	5500.00	5500.00
☐ **Model HP,** Commercial Finish, 9mm Luger, Double Action, Lightweight, *Modern*	2500.00	3650.00	3650.00
☐ **Olympia Rapid Fire,** .22 L.R.R.F., Target Pistol, *Modern*	495.00	750.00	750.00
☐ **Olympia Sport,** .22 L.R.R.F., Target Pistol, *Modern*	395.00	625.00	625.00
☐ **Model OSP,** .22 Short, Blue, Five Rounds Capacity, *Modern*	925.00	1050.00	1050.00
☐ **P .38,** 9mm Luger, Double Action, Military, *Modern*	350.00	525.00	525.00
☐ **P .38 (Current),** .22 L.R.R.F., Double Action, *Modern*	395.00	525.00	525.00
☐ **P-38 (Current),** .30 Luger, Double Action, Blue, *Modern*	340.00	475.00	475.00
☐ **P .38 (Current),** 9mm Luger, Double Action, *Modern*	320.00	450.00	450.00
☐ **P .38 "480",** 9mm Luger, Double Action, Military, *Curio*	420.00	650.00	875.00
☐ **P .38 1st, Model Zero Series,** 9mm Luger, Double Action, *Modern*	825.00	1400.00	1400.00
☐ **P .38 2nd, Model Zero Series,** 9mm Luger, Double Action, Military, *Curio*	635.00	950.00	1200.00
☐ **P .38 3rd, Model Zero Series,** 9mm Luger, Double Action, Military, *Curio*	410.00	630.00	995.00
☐ **P .38 ac No Date,** 9mm Luger, Double Action, Military, *Curio*	520.00	775.00	1100.00
☐ **P .38 ac-45 Zero Series,** 9mm Luger, Double Action, Military, *Curio*	275.00	450.00	625.00
☐ **P .38 ac-40,** 9mm Luger, Double Action, Military, *Curio*	310.00	490.00	590.00
☐ **P .38 ac-41,** 9mm Luger, Double Action, Military, *Curio*	300.00	480.00	600.00
☐ **P .38 ac-41 Military Finish,** 9mm Luger, Double Action, Military, *Curio*	250.00	360.00	495.00
☐ **P .38 ac-42,** 9mm Luger, Double Action, Military, *Curio*	190.00	295.00	435.00
☐ **P .38 Double Action,** .22 L.R., Blue, Eight Rounds Capacity, *Modern*	690.00	790.00	790.00
☐ **P .38 Double Action,** 9mm Para, Blue, Eight Rounds, *Modern*	650.00	750.00	790.00
☐ **P .38 ac-43 Double Line,** 9mm Luger, Double Action, Military, *Modern*	285.00	425.00	425.00
☐ **P .38 ac-43 Police,** 9mm Luger, Double Action, Military, *Modern*	725.00	1100.00	1100.00
☐ **P .38 ac-43 Single Line,** 9mm Luger, Double Action, Military, *Curio*	195.00	300.00	485.00
☐ **P .38 ac-43 WaA135,** 9mm Luger, Double Action, Military, *Curio*	210.00	310.00	480.00
☐ **P .38 ac-44,** 9mm Luger, Double Action, Military, *Curio*	195.00	290.00	435.00

	V.G.	Exc.	Prior Year Exc. Value
☐ **P .38 ac-44 Police,** 9mm Luger, Double Action, Military, *Curio*	530.00	800.00	1050.00
☐ **P .38 ac-44 WaA140,** 9mm Luger, Double Action, Military, *Curio*	260.00	385.00	475.00
☐ **P .38 ac-45,** 9mm Luger, Double Action, Military, *Curio*	200.00	305.00	420.00
☐ **P .38 ac-45 Mismatch,** 9mm Luger, Double Action, Military, *Curio*	205.00	315.00	445.00
☐ **P .38 byf-42,** 9mm Luger, Double Action, Military, *Curio*	280.00	400.00	575.00
☐ **P .38 byf-43,** 9mm Luger, Double Action, Military, *Curio*	205.00	320.00	450.00
☐ **P .38 byf-43 Police,** 9mm Luger, Double Action, Military, *Modern*	500.00	770.00	1000.00
☐ **P .38 byf-44,** 9mm Luger, Double Action, Military, *Curio*	220.00	340.00	450.00
☐ **P .38 byf-44 Police F Dual T,** 9mm Luger, Double Action, Military, *Modern*	575.00	850.00	850.00
☐ **P .38 byf-44 Police L Dual T,** 9mm Luger, Double Action, Military, *Modern*	900.00	1500.00	1500.00
☐ **P .38 byf-44 Police L,** 9mm Luger, Double Action, Military, *Modern*	700.00	1000.00	1000.00
☐ **P .38 cyq,** 9mm Luger, Double Action, Military, *Curio*	215.00	320.00	450.00
☐ **P .38 cyq 1945,** 9mm Luger, Double Action, Military, *Curio*	245.00	375.00	475.00
☐ **P .38 cyq Zero Series,** 9mm Luger, Double Action, Military, *Curio*	230.00	360.00	475.00
☐ **P .38 svw-45,** 9mm Luger, Double Action, Military, *Curio*	195.00	305.00	550.00
☐ **P .38 svw-45 French,** 9mm Luger, Double Action, Military, *Modern*	450.00	620.00	620.00
☐ **P .38 svw-45 Police,** 9mm Luger, Double Action, Military, *Modern*	900.00	1300.00	1300.00
☐ **P .38 svw-46,** 9mm Luger, Double Action, Military, *Modern*	500.00	750.00	750.00
☐ **P .38k,** 9mm Luger, Double Action, Short Barrel, *Modern*	395.00	475.00	475.00
☐ **P .38-IV (P .4),** 9mm Luger, Double Action, *Modern*	395.00	475.00	475.00
☐ **P .5,** 9mm Luger, Interarms, Double Action, Blue, *Modern*	495.00	700.00	700.00
☐ **P220 Sig Sauer,** 9mm Para, Double Action, *Modern*	585.00	675.00	675.00
☐ **P220 Sig Sauer,** .38 Super, Double Action, Blue, *Modern*	585.00	675.00	675.00
☐ **P220 Sig Sauer,** .45 ACP, Double Action, Blue, *Modern*	585.00	675.00	675.00
☐ **P225 Sig Sauer,** 9mm Para, Double Action, Blue, *Modern*	615.00	715.00	715.00
☐ **P226 Sig Sauer,** 9mm Para, Double Action, Blue, *Modern*	645.00	745.00	745.00
☐ **P230 Sig Sauer,** .380 ACP, Double Action, Blue, *Modern*	445.00	510.00	510.00
☐ **P230 Sig Sauer,** .380 ACP, Double Action, Stainless, *Modern*	495.00	550.00	550.00

	V.G.	Exc.	Prior Year Exc. Value
☐ **PP,** .22 L.R.R.F., Double Action, Pre-War, Commercial, Nickel Plated, *Curio*	300.00	435.00	550.00
☐ **PP,** .22 L.R.R.F., Double Action, Pre-War, Commercial, Nickel Plated, Nazi-Proofed, *Curio*	290.00	425.00	550.00
☐ **PP,** .22 L.R.R.F., Double Action, Pre-War, Commercial, High-Polish Finish, *Modern*	280.00	400.00	485.00
☐ **PP,** .22 L.R.R.F., Double Action, Pre-War, Commercial, High-Polish Finish, Nazi-Proofed, *Modern*	290.00	410.00	500.00
☐ **PP,** .22 L.R.R.F., Double Action, Lightweight, *Modern*	375.00	500.00	500.00
☐ **PP,** .25 ACP, Double Action, Pre-War, Commercial, High-Polish Finish, *Curio*	750.00	1175.00	1600.00
☐ **PP,** .32 ACP, Double Action, Pre-War, Commercial, Lightweight, High-Polish Finish, *Curio*	365.00	510.00	650.00
☐ **PP,** .32 ACP, Double Action, Pre-War, Nazi-Proofed, Lightweight, High-Polish Finish, *Curio*	365.00	510.00	625.00
☐ **PP,** .32 ACP, Double Action, Pre-War, Nazi-Proofed, Lightweight, *Curio*	280.00	400.00	550.00
☐ **PP,** .32 ACP, Double Action, Pre-War, Commercial, Nickel Plated, *Curio*	280.00	400.00	550.00
☐ **PP,** .32 ACP, Double Action, Pre-War, Commercial, Nickel Plated, Nazi-Proofed, *Curio*	280.00	400.00	550.00
☐ **PP,** .32 ACP, Double Action, Pre-War, Commercial, High-Polish Finish, *Modern*	200.00	320.00	425.00
☐ **PP,** .32 ACP, Double Action, Pre-War, Commercial, High-Polish Finish, Nazi-Proofed, *Modern*	205.00	335.00	435.00

Walther Sig Sauer P226

Walther Sig Sauer P230

	V.G.	Exc.	Prior Year Exc. Value
☐ **PP,** .32 ACP, Double Action, Pre-War, Commercial, Nazi-Proofed, *Modern*	220.00	340.00	400.00
☐ **PP,** .32 ACP, Double Action, Lightweight, *Curio*	300.00	430.00	500.00
☐ **PP,** .380 ACP, Double Action, Pre-War, Commercial, High-Polish Finish, *Modern*	315.00	440.00	500.00
☐ **PP,** .380 ACP, Double Action, Pre-War, Commercial, High-Polish Finish, Nazi-Proofed, *Modern*	330.00	450.00	535.00
☐ **PP,** .380 ACP, Double Action, Pre-War, Commercial, Nickel Plated, *Curio*	600.00	920.00	1100.00
☐ **PP,** .380 ACP, Double Action, Pre-War, Commercial, Nickel Plated, Nazi-Proofed, *Curio*	575.00	875.00	1000.00
☐ **PP,** .380 ACP, Double Action, Lightweight, *Modern*	375.00	550.00	550.00
☐ **PP "Nairobi",** .32 ACP, Double Action, Pre-War, High-Polish Finish, *Curio*	480.00	700.00	850.00
☐ **PP (Current),** .22 L.R.R.F., Double Action, *Modern*	325.00	415.00	415.00
☐ **PP (Current),** .32 ACP, Double Action, Blue, *Modern*	295.00	385.00	385.00
☐ **PP (Current),** .380 ACP, Double Action, Blue, *Modern*	300.00	410.00	410.00
☐ **PP (Early) 90 Degree Safety,** .32 ACP, Double Action, Pre-War, Commercial, High-Polish Finish, *Modern*	285.00	410.00	550.00
☐ **PP (Early) Bottom Magazine Release,** .380 ACP, Double Action, Pre-War, Commercial, High-Polish Finish, *Curio*	725.00	1175.00	1550.00
☐ **PP AC,** .380 ACP, Double Action, Pre-War, Nazi-Proofed, *Modern*	450.00	675.00	800.00
☐ **PP AC Police F,** .32 ACP, Double Action, Pre-War, Nazi-Proofed, *Curio*	270.00	380.00	450.00
☐ **PP AC Waffenamt,** .32 ACP, Double Action, Pre-War, Nazi-Proofed, *Curio*	270.00	400.00	475.00
☐ **PP Bottom Magazine Release,** .32 ACP, Double Action, Pre-War, Commercial, High-Polish Finish, *Curio*	320.00	480.00	575.00
☐ **PP Bottom Magazine Release,** .32 ACP, Double Action, Pre-War, Commercial, High-Polish Finish, Lightweight, *Curio*	320.00	480.00	550.00
☐ **PP Czech,** .32 ACP, Double Action, Pre-War, Commercial, High-Polish Finish, *Curio*	530.00	700.00	875.00
☐ **PP Mark II "Manurhin",** .22 L.R.R.F., Double Action, High-Polish Finish, Blue, *Curio*	300.00	435.00	550.00
☐ **PP Mark II "Manurhin",** .32 ACP, Double Action, High-Polish Finish, Blue, *Curio*	250.00	365.00	450.00
☐ **PP Mark II "Manurhin",** .380 ACP, Double Action, High-Polish Finish, Blue, *Curio*	265.00	390.00	475.00
☐ **PP NSKK,** .32 ACP, Double Action, Pre-War, High-Polish Finish, Nazi-Proofed, *Curio*	650.00	950.00	1200.00
☐ **PP PDM,** .32 ACP, Double Action, Pre-War, High-Polish Finish, *Curio*	350.00	495.00	625.00
☐ **PP Persian,** .380 ACP, Double Action, Pre-War, Commercial, High-Polish Finish, *Curio*	1100.00	1700.00	2200.00
☐ **PP Police C,** .32 ACP, Double Action, Pre-War, High-Polish Finish, Nazi-Proofed, *Curio*	300.00	440.00	500.00

	V.G.	Exc.	Prior Year Exc. Value
☐ **PP Police C,** .32 ACP, Double Action, Pre-War, Nazi-Proofed, *Curio*	240.00	365.00	475.00
☐ **PP Police F,** .32 ACP, Double Action, Pre-War, Nazi-Proofed, *Curio*	220.00	330.00	425.00
☐ **PP Presentation,** Double Action, Lightweight, *Modern*	575.00	800.00	800.00
☐ **PP RFV,** .32 ACP, Double Action, Pre-War, High-Polish, *Curio*	380.00	520.00	600.00
☐ **PP RFV,** .32 ACP, Double Action, Pre-War, Nazi-Proofed, *Curio*	330.00	460.00	550.00
☐ **PP RJ,** .32 ACP, Double Action, Pre-War, High-Polish Finish, *Curio*	340.00	470.00	550.00
☐ **PP SS,** .22 L.R.R.F., Double Action, Pre-War, High-Polish Finish, *Curio*	565.00	735.00	900.00
☐ **PP SA,** .32 ACP, Double Action, Pre-War, High-Polish Finish, *Curio*	435.00	620.00	800.00
☐ **PP Stoeger,** .32 ACP, Double Action, Pre-War, High-Polish Finish, *Curio*	360.00	510.00	675.00
☐ **PP Super,** 9 x 18mm, Clip Fed, Blue, *Modern*	335.00	475.00	475.00
☐ **PP Verchromt,** .32 ACP, Double Action, Pre-War, Commercial, *Curio*	480.00	675.00	835.00
☐ **PP Verchromt,** .380 ACP, Double Action, Pre-War, Commercial, *Curio*	550.00	725.00	1100.00
☐ **PP with Lanyard Loop,** .32 ACP, Double Action, Pre-War, Commercial, High-Polish Finish, Nazi-Proofed, *Modern*	335.00	465.00	550.00
☐ **PP Waffenamt,** .32 ACP, Double Action, Pre-War, High-Polish Finish, Nazi-Proofed, *Curio*	265.00	380.00	475.00
☐ **PP Waffenamt,** .32 ACP, Double Action, Pre-War, Nazi-Proofed, *Curio*	250.00	360.00	450.00
☐ **PP Waffenamt,** .380 ACP, Double Action, Pre-War, High-Polish Finish, Nazi-Proofed, *Curio*	370.00	535.00	625.00
☐ **PPK,** .22 L.R.R.F., Double Action, Pre-War, Commercial, Nickel Plated, *Curio*	410.00	580.00	675.00
☐ **PPK,** .22 L.R.R.F., Double Action, Pre-War, Commercial, Nickel Plated, Nazi-Proofed, *Curio*	360.00	530.00	630.00
☐ **PPK,** .22 L.R.R.F., Double Action, Pre-War, Commercial, High-Polish Finish, *Modern*	320.00	470.00	550.00
☐ **PPK,** .22 L.R.R.F., Double Action, Pre-War, Commercial, High-Polish Finish, Nazi-Proofed, *Modern*	335.00	515.00	625.00
☐ **PPK,** .22 L.R.R.F., Double Action, Post-War, *Modern*	295.00	395.00	395.00
☐ **PPK,** .22 L.R.R.F., Double Action, Lightweight, Post-War, *Modern*	425.00	565.00	565.00
☐ **PPK,** .25 ACP, Double Action, Pre-War, Commercial, High-Polish Finish, *Curio*	950.00	1475.00	1800.00
☐ **PPK,** .32 ACP, Double Action, Pre-War, Commercial, Nickel Plated, *Curio*	350.00	480.00	620.00
☐ **PPK,** .32 ACP, Double Action, Pre-War, Commercial, Nazi-Proofed, Nickel Plated, *Curio*	350.00	480.00	620.00
☐ **PPK,** .32 ACP, Double Action, Pre-War, Commercial, Lightweight, High-Polish Finish, *Curio*	380.00	540.00	635.00
☐ **PPK,** .32 ACP, Double Action, Pre-War, Nazi-Proofed, Lightweight, High-Polish Finish, *Curio*	380.00	540.00	650.00

	V.G.	Exc.	Prior Year Exc. Value
☐ **PPK,** .32 ACP, Double Action, Pre-War, Nazi-Proofed, Lightweight, *Curio*	285.00	415.00	550.00
☐ **PPK,** .32 ACP, Double Action, Pre-War, Commercial, High-Polish Finish, *Modern*	260.00	390.00	500.00
☐ **PPK,** .32 ACP, Double Action, Pre-War, Commercial, High-Polish Finish, Nazi-Proofed, *Modern*	270.00	415.00	525.00
☐ **PPK,** .32 ACP, Double Action, Pre-War, Commercial, Nazi-Proofed, *Modern*	250.00	375.00	500.00
☐ **PPK,** .32 ACP, Double Action, Post-War, *Modern*	250.00	325.00	325.00
☐ **PPK,** .32 ACP, Double Action, Lightweight, Post-War, *Modern*	400.00	575.00	575.00
☐ **PPK,** .380 ACP, Double Action, Pre-War, Commercial, Nickel Plated, *Curio*	725.00	1000.00	1250.00
☐ **PPK,** .380 ACP, Double Action, Pre-War, Commercial, Nickel Plated, Nazi-Proofed, *Curio*	725.00	1250.00	1500.00
☐ **PPK,** .380 ACP, Double Action, Pre-War, Commercial, High-Polish Finish, *Modern*	530.00	720.00	925.00
☐ **PPK,** .380 ACP, Double Action, Pre-War, Commercial, High-Polish Finish, Nazi-Proofed, *Modern*	610.00	925.00	1200.00
☐ **PPK,** .380 ACP, Double Action, Post-War, *Modern*	360.00	485.00	485.00
☐ **PPK,** .380 ACP, Double Action, Lightweight, Post-War, *Modern*	395.00	575.00	575.00
☐ **PPK "Nairobi",** .32 ACP, Double Action, Pre-War, High-Polish Finish, *Curio*	535.00	815.00	1100.00
☐ **PPK (Early) 90 Degree Safety,** .32 ACP, Double Action, Pre-War, Commercial, High-Polish Finish, *Modern*	290.00	410.00	550.00
☐ **PPK (Early) Bottom Magazine Release,** .380 ACP, Double Action, Pre-War, Commercial, High-Polish Finish, *Curio*	725.00	1150.00	1475.00
☐ **PPK Czech,** .32 ACP, Double Action, Pre-War, Commercial, High-Polish Finish, *Curio*	635.00	950.00	1050.00
☐ **PPK DRP,** .32 ACP, Double Action, Pre-War, High-Polish Finish, *Curio*	410.00	590.00	700.00
☐ **PPK DRP,** .32 ACP, Double Action, Pre-War, High-Polish Finish, Nickel Plated, *Curio*	520.00	700.00	885.00
☐ **PPK Mark II "Manurhin",** .22 L.R.R.F., Double Action, High-Polish Finish, Blue, *Curio*	440.00	620.00	725.00
☐ **PPK Mark II "Manurhin",** .22 L.R.R.F., Double Action, High-Polish Finish, Blue, Lightweight, *Curio*	510.00	715.00	850.00
☐ **PPK Mark II "Manurhin",** .32 ACP, Double Action, High-Polish Finish, Blue, *Curio*	380.00	530.00	635.00
☐ **PPK Mark II "Manurhin",** .32 ACP, Double Action, High-Polish Finish, Blue, Lightweight, *Curio*	435.00	650.00	750.00
☐ **PPK Mark II "Manurhin,** .380 ACP, Double Action, High-Polish Finish, Blue, *Curio*	410.00	625.00	675.00
☐ **PPK Mark II "Manurhin",** .380 ACP, Double Action, High-Polish Finish, Blue, Lightweight, *Curio*	450.00	695.00	750.00
☐ **PPK Model PP,** .32 ACP, Double Action, Pre-War, Commercial, High-Polish Finish, *Curio*	1075.00	1500.00	1700.00
☐ **PPK Party Leader,** .32 ACP, Double Action, Pre-War, High-Polish Finish, *Curio*	850.00	1375.00	1500.00

	V.G.	Exc.	Prior Year Exc. Value
☐ **PPK PDM,** .32 ACP, Double Action, Pre-War, High-Polish Finish, Lightweight, *Curio*	650.00	975.00	1250.00
☐ **PPK Police C,** .32 ACP, Double Action, Pre-War, High-Polish Finish, Nazi-Proofed, *Curio*	360.00	490.00	575.00
☐ **PPK Police C,** .32 ACP, Double Action, Pre-War, Nazi-Proofed, *Curio*	315.00	450.00	550.00
☐ **PPK Police F,** .32 ACP, Double Action, Pre-War, Nazi-Proofed, *Curio*	290.00	430.00	525.00
☐ **PPK RFV,** .32 ACP, Double Action, Pre-War, High-Polish Finish, *Curio*	490.00	680.00	900.00
☐ **PPK RZM,** .32 ACP, Double Action, Pre-War, High-Polish Finish, *Curio*	400.00	565.00	675.00
☐ **PPK RZM,** .32 ACP, Double Action, Pre-War, High-Polish Finish, Nickel Plated, *Curio*	535.00	730.00	975.00
☐ **PPK Stoeger,** .32 ACP, Double Action, Pre-War, High-Polish Finish, *Curio*	475.00	650.00	850.00
☐ **PPK Verchromt,** .32 ACP, Double Action, Pre-War, Commercial, *Curio*	600.00	825.00	950.00
☐ **PPK Verchromt,** .32 ACP, Double Action, Pre-War, Commercial, Lightweight, *Curio*	1025.00	1600.00	1800.00
☐ **PPK Verchromt,** .380 ACP, Double Action, Pre-War, Commercial, *Curio*	720.00	1085.00	1350.00
☐ **PPK Waffenamt,** .32 ACP, Double Action, Pre-War, High-Polish Finish, Nazi-Proofed, *Curio*	390.00	585.00	675.00
☐ **PPK Waffenamt,** .32 ACP, Double Action, Pre-War, Nazi-Proofed, *Curio*	310.00	465.00	550.00
☐ **PPK Waffenamt,** .380 ACP, Double Action, Pre-War, High-Polish Finish, Nazi-Proofed, *Curio*	725.00	1225.00	1400.00
☐ **PPKS (Current),** .22 L.R.R.F., Double Action, *Modern*	245.00	365.00	365.00
☐ **PPKS (Current),** .32 ACP, Double Action, Blue, *Modern*	300.00	410.00	410.00
☐ **PPKS (Current),** .380 ACP, Double Action, Blue, *Modern*	300.00	410.00	410.00
☐ **Self-Loading,** .22 L.R.R.F., Target Pistol, *Modern*	365.00	495.00	495.00
☐ **TPH,** .22 L.R.R.F., Double Action, Clip Fed, *Modern*	325.00	475.00	475.00
☐ **PPK/S Double Action,** .380 ACP, Stainless Steel, Seven Rounds Capacity, *Modern*	499.00	515.00	515.00
☐ **PPK/S Double Action,** .380 ACP, Blue, Seven Rounds Capacity, *Modern*	459.00	470.00	470.00
RIFLE, BOLT ACTION			
☐ **Model B,** Various Calibers, Checkered Stock, Mauser Action, Set Triggers, *Modern*	225.00	350.00	350.00
☐ **GX-1 Match,** .22 L.R.R.F., Singleshot, Target Stock, with Accessories, *Modern*	675.00	900.00	900.00
☐ **KKJ,** .22 Hornet, 5 Shot Clip, Open Rear Sight, Checkered Stock, *Modern*	340.00	450.00	450.00
☐ **KKJ,** .22 Hornet, 5 Shot Clip, Open Rear Sight, Checkered Stock, Set Trigger, *Modern*	360.00	465.00	465.00
☐ **KKJ,** .22 L.R.R.F., 5 Shot Clip, Open Rear Sight, Checkered Stock, *Modern*	275.00	385.00	385.00
☐ **KKJ,** .22 L.R.R.F., 5 Shot Clip, Open Rear Sight, Checkered Stock, Set Trigger, *Modern*	310.00	495.00	495.00

	V.G.	Exc.	Prior Year Exc. Value
☐ **KKJ,** .22 WMR, 5 Shot Clip, Open Rear Sight, Checkered Stock, *Modern*	295.00	375.00	370.00
☐ **KKJ,** .22 WMR, 5 Shot Clip, Open Rear Sight, Checkered Stock, Set Trigger, *Modern*	320.00	400.00	400.00
☐ **KKJ International Match,** .22 L.R.R.F., Singleshot, Target Stock, with Accessories, *Modern*	500.00	695.00	695.00
☐ **Model GX-1,** .22 L.R., Singleshot, Blue, *Modern*	1150.00	1200.00	1200.00
☐ **KK/MS Silhouette,** .22 L.R., Singleshot, Blue, *Modern*	700.00	725.00	725.00
☐ **Model KKW,** .22 L.R.R.F., Pre-WW2, Singleshot, Tangent Sights, Military Style Stock, *Modern*	320.00	460.00	525.00
☐ **Model LGR,** .177 Caliber, Singleshot, Blue, *Modern*	625.00	650.00	650.00
☐ **Model LGR Match,** .177 Caliber, Singleshot, Blue, *Modern*	700.00	725.00	725.00
☐ **Model LGR Running Boar,** .177 Caliber, Singleshot, Blue, *Modern*	650.00	675.00	675.00
☐ **Running Boar,** .22 L.R., Singleshot, Blue, *Modern*	750.00	775.00	775.00
☐ **U.I.T.-E. Universal Match,** .22 L.R., Singleshot, Blue, *Modern*	1150.00	1200.00	1200.00
☐ **Model V,** Singleshot, Sporting Rifle, Open Rear Sight, *Modern*	275.00	365.00	365.00
☐ **Model V "Meisterbushse",** Singleshot, Pistol-Grip Stock, Target Sights, *Modern*	290.00	385.00	385.00
☐ **Moving Target,** .22 L.R.R.F., Singleshot, Target Stock, with Accessories, *Modern*	525.00	690.00	690.00
☐ **Olympic,** .22 L.R.R.F., Singleshot, Target Stock, with Accessories, *Modern*	400.00	565.00	565.00
☐ **Prone "400",** .22 L.R.R.F., Singleshot, Target Stock, with Accessories, *Modern*	375.00	485.00	485.00
☐ **UIT Match,** .22 L.R.R.F., Singleshot, Target Stock, with Accessories, *Modern*	550.00	750.00	750.00
☐ **UIT Super,** .22 L.R.R.F., Singleshot, Target Stock, with Accessories, *Modern*	500.00	665.00	665.00
RIFLE, SEMI-AUTOMATIC			
☐ **Model 1,** Clip Fed, Carbine, *Modern*	175.00	285.00	285.00
☐ **Model 2,** .22 L.R.R.F., Clip Fed, *Modern*	175.00	285.00	285.00
SHOTGUN, DOUBLE BARREL, SIDE-BY-SIDE			
☐ **Model S.F.,** 12 or 16 Gauges, Checkered Stock, Cheekpiece, Double Triggers, Sling Swivels, *Modern*	275.00	400.00	400.00
☐ **Model S.F. D.,** 12 or 16 Gauges, Checkered Stock, Cheekpiece, Double Triggers, Sling Swivels, *Modern*	325.00	500.00	500.00

WAMO

Wamo Mfg. Co., San Gabriel, Calif.

HANDGUN, SINGLESHOT			
☐ **Powermaster**, .22 L.R.R.F., Target Pistol, *Modern*	75.00	120.00	115.00

	V.G.	Exc.	Prior Year Exc. Value

WARNANT

L. & J. Warnant Freres, Hognee, Belgium.

HANDGUN, SEMI-AUTOMATIC

	V.G.	Exc.	Prior Year Exc. Value
☐ **.25 ACP**, Clip Fed, Blue, *Curio*	140.00	200.00	200.00

HANDGUN, REVOLVER

	V.G.	Exc.	Prior Year Exc. Value
☐ **.32 S & W**, Double Action, Folding Trigger, Break Top, *Curio*	50.00	85.00	80.00
☐ **.38 S & W**, Double Action, Folding Trigger, Break Top, *Curio*	50.00	85.00	80.00

HANDGUN, SINGLESHOT

	V.G.	Exc.	Prior Year Exc. Value
☐ **Traff**, 6mm R.F., Spur Trigger, Parlor Pistol, *Curio*	30.00	55.00	55.00
☐ **Traff**, 9mm R.F., Spur Trigger, Parlor Pistol, *Curio*	35.00	60.00	60.00

RIFLE, SINGLESHOT

	V.G.	Exc.	Prior Year Exc. Value
☐ **Amelung**, Various Rimfires, Plain, Parlor Rifle, *Curio*	35.00	50.00	50.00
☐ **Amelung**, Various Rimfires, Checkered Stock, Set Triggers, , Parlor Rifle, *Curio*	65.00	85.00	85.00

WARNER

Warner Arms Corp., Brooklyn, N.Y., formed about 1912, moved to Norwich, Mass. in 1913, and in 1917 merged and became Davis-Warner Arms Corp., Assonet, Mass., out of business about 1919. Also see Schwarzlose.

SEMI-AUTOMATIC

	V.G.	Exc.	Prior Year Exc. Value
☐ **Infallable**, .32 ACP, Clip Fed, *Modern*	155.00	215.00	195.00
☐ **The Infallable**, .32 ACP, Clip Fed, *Modern*	165.00	235.00	220.00

WARREN ARMS CORP.

Belgium, c. 1900.

SHOTGUN, DOUBLE BARREL, SIDE-BY-SIDE

	V.G.	Exc.	Prior Year Exc. Value
☐ **Various Gauges**, Outside Hammers, Damascus Barrel, *Modern*	100.00	170.00	175.00
☐ **Various Gauges**, Hammerless, Steel Barrel, *Modern*	135.00	190.00	200.00
☐ **Various Gauges**, Hammerless, Damascus Barrel, *Modern*	100.00	170.00	175.00
☐ **Various Gauges**, Outside Hammers, Steel Barrel, *Modern*	125.00	185.00	190.00

SHOTGUN, SINGLESHOT

	V.G.	Exc.	Prior Year Exc. Value
☐ **Various Gauges**, Hammer, Steel Barrel, *Modern*	55.00	85.00	85.00

WATSON BROS.

London, England 1885-1931.

RIFLE, BOLT ACTION

	V.G.	Exc.	Prior Year Exc. Value
☐ **.303 British**, Express Sights, Sporting Rifle, Checkered Stock, *Modern*	440.00	675.00	650.00

RIFLE, DOUBLE BARREL, SIDE-BY-SIDE

	V.G.	Exc.	Prior Year Exc. Value
☐ **.450/.400 N.E. 3"**, Double Trigger, Recoil Pad, Plain, Cased, *Modern*	2,750.00	3,800.00	3,750.00

WATTERS, JOHN

Carlisle, Pa. 1778-1785. See Kentucky Rifles.

WEATHERBY'S, INC.

South Gate, Calif.

	V.G.	Exc.	Prior Year Exc. Value
HANDGUN, SINGLESHOT			
☐ **Mk. V Silhouette**, Various Calibers, Thumbhole Target Stock, Target Sights, *Modern*	400.00	600.00	600.00
RIFLE, BOLT ACTION			
☐ **For German Manufacture** *Add* **30%-50%**			
☐ **Deluxe**, .378 Wby. Mag., Magnum, Checkered Stock, *Modern*	300.00	400.00	400.00
☐ **Deluxe**, Various Calibers, Checkered Stock, *Modern*	200.00	285.00	275.00
☐ **Deluxe**, Various Calibers, Magnum, Checkered Stock, *Modern*	225.00	365.00	350.00
☐ **Mark V**, .378 Wby. Mag., Checkered Stock, *Modern*	395.00	490.00	475.00
☐ **Mark V**, .460 Wby. Mag., Checkered Stock, *Modern*	475.00	590.00	575.00
☐ **Mark V**, Various Calibers, Varmint, Checkered Stock, *Modern*	300.00	415.00	400.00

Weatherby Mk.V

	V.G.	Exc.	Prior Year Exc. Value
☐ **Mark V**, Various Calibers, Checkered Stock, *Modern*	300.00	415.00	400.00
☐ **Mark V Crown Custom,** Various Calibers, 24″ or 26″ Barrel, Right Hand Only, *Modern*	2,581.50	2,600.00	—
☐ **Mark V Fibermark,** Various Calibers, Fiberglass, Right Hand Only, *Modern*	869.00	880.00	—
☐ **Mark V Lazermark,** Various Calibers, Carved Stock (Carved With Laser Beam), *Modern*	874.00	1,208.00	—
☐ **Vanguard,** Various Calibers, Checkered Stock, *Modern*	225.00	320.00	300.00
RIFLE, SEMI-AUTOMATIC			
☐ **Mark XXII,** .22 L.R.R.F., Clip Fed, Checkered Stock, *Modern*	150.00	210.00	200.00
☐ **Mark XXII,** .22 L.R.R.F., Tube Feed, Checkered Stock, *Modern*	180.00	250.00	235.00
☐ **Model M-82,** Various Gauges, Gas Operated, Various Barrel Lengths, *Modern*	429.00	440.00	—
SHOTGUN, DOUBLE BARREL, OVER-UNDER			
☐ **Athena Skeet Grade,** 12 Gauge, Single Selective Trigger, 26″ Barrels, *Modern*	1,159.00	1,200.00	—
☐ **Athena Trap Grade,** 12 Gauge, Single Selective Trigger, 30″ Barrels, *Modern*	1,169.00	1,200.00	—
☐ **Orion Field Grade,** 12 Gauge, Single Selective Trigger, 26″ or 28″ Barrel, *Modern*	769.00	790.00	—

Weatherby Athena O/U Shotgun

	V.G.	Exc.	Prior Year Exc. Value
☐ **Orion 20 Field Grade,** 20 Gauge, Single Selective Trigger, 26" or 28" Barrel, *Modern*	769.00	700.00	—
☐ **Orion Skeet Grade,** 12 Gauge, Single Selective Trigger, 26" Barrel, *Modern*	809.00	825.00	—
☐ **Orion Trap Grade,** 12 Gauge, Single Selective Trigger, 30" or 32" Barrel, *Modern*	819.00	825.00	
☐ **Regency,** 12 Gauge, Trap Grade, Vent Rib, Checkered Stock, Engraved, Single Selective Trigger, *Modern*	575.00	700.00	700.00
☐ **Regency,** Field Grade, 12 and 20 Gauges, Vent Rib, Checkered Stock, Engraved, Single Selective Trigger, *Modern*	550.00	675.00	675.00
SHOTGUN, SEMI-AUTOMATIC			
☐ **Centurion,** 12 Gauge, Field Grade, Vent Rib, Checkered Stock, *Modern*	160.00	225.00	220.00
☐ **Centurion,** 12 Gauge Trap Grade, Checkered Stock, Vent Rib, *Modern*	185.00	250.00	245.00
☐ **Centurion Deluxe,** 12 Gauge, Checkered Stock, Vent Rib, Light Engraving, Fancy Wood, *Modern*	210.00	270.00	265.00
SHOTGUN, SLIDE ACTION			
☐ **Model M-92,** 12 Gauge, Vent Rib, Three Shell Mag, *Modern*	339.00	350.00	—
☐ **Patrician,** 12 Gauge, Field Grade, Checkered Stock, Vent Rib, *Modern*	135.00	195.00	190.00
☐ **Patrician,** 12 Gauge, Trap Grade, Checkered Stock, Vent Rib, *Modern*	155.00	225.00	220.00
☐ **Patrician,** Deluxe, 12 Gauge, Checkered Stock, Light Engraving, Fancy Wood, Vent Rib, *Modern*	185.00	235.00	230.00

WEAVER, CRYPRET

Pa., c. 1818. *See Kentucky Rifles.*

WEBLEY & SCOTT

Located in Birmingham, England operating as P. Webley & Son, 1860-1897; Webley & Scott Revolver & Arms Co.. 1898-1906; Webley & Scott since 1906.

	V.G.	Exc.	Prior Year Exc. Value
HANDGUN, REVOLVER			
☐ **#1**, .577 Eley, Solid Frame, Double Action, Blue, *Curio*	115.00	170.00	160.00
☐ **British Bulldog**, Various Calibers, Solid Frame, Double Action, *Curio*	85.00	140.00	135.00
☐ **Tower Bulldog**, Various Calibers, Solid Frame, Double Action, *Curio*	80.00	130.00	120.00
☐ **Webley Kaufmann**, .45 Colt, Top Break, Square-Butt, Commercial, *Antique*	350.00	475.00	450.00

	V.G.	Exc.	Prior Year Exc. Value
☐ **Webley Mk 1**, .455 Revolver Mk 1, Top Break, Round Butt, Military, *Antique*	170.00	235.00	225.00
☐ **Webley Mk 1***, .455 Revolver Mk 1, Top Break, Round Butt, Military, *Antique*	165.00	225.00	200.00
☐ **Webley Mk 1** Navy**, .455 Revolver Mk 1, Top Break, Round Butt, Military, *Modern*	150.00	210.00	190.00
☐ **Webley Mk 2**, .455 Revolver Mk 1, Top Break, Round Butt, Military, *Antique*	165.00	225.00	220.00
☐ **Webley Mk 2***, .455 Revolver Mk 1, Top Break, Round Butt, Military, *Curio*	165.00	230.00	220.00
☐ **Webley Mk 2****, .455 Revolver Mk 1, Top Break, Round Butt, Military, *Curio*	165.00	230.00	220.00
☐ **Webley Mk 3**, .455 Revolver Mk 1, Top Break, Round Butt, Military, *Curio*	175.00	255.00	245.00
☐ **Webley Mk 4**, .455 Revolver Mk 1, Top Break, Round Butt, Military, *Curio*	165.00	230.00	220.00
☐ **Webley Mk 5**, .455 Revolver Mk 1, Top Break, Round Butt, Military, *Curio*	175.00	250.00	245.00
☐ **Webley Mk 6**, .455 Revolver Mk 1, Top Break, Square-Butt, Military, *Curio*	145.00	220.00	200.00
☐ **Webley Mk 6**, Detachable Buttstock Only	180.00	275.00	225.00
☐ **Webley Mk III M & P**, .38 S & W, Top Break, Square-Butt, Commercial, *Modern*	95.00	170.00	165.00
☐ **Webley Mk IV**, .22 L.R.R.F., Top Break, Square-Butt, Commercial, *Modern*	165.00	235.00	225.00
☐ **Webley Mk IV**, .38 S & W, Top Break, Square-Butt, Military, *Curio*	125.00	175.00	175.00
☐ **Webley R I C**, .455 Revolver Mk 1, Solid Frame, Square-Butt, Commercial, *Antique*	95.00	155.00	145.00
☐ **Webley-Green**, .455 Revolver Mk 1, Top Break, Square-Butt, Commercial, Target Pistol, *Antique*	270.00	390.00	375.00
☐ **Webley-Green**, .476 Enfield Mk 3, Top Break, Square-Butt, Commercial, Target Pistol, *Antique*	320.00	465.00	450.00
HANDGUN, SEMI-AUTOMATIC			
☐ **Model 1904**, .455 Webley Auto., Clip Fed, Grip Safety, Hammer, *Curio*	575.00	800.00	775.00
☐ **Model 1906**, .25 ACP, Clip Fed, Hammer, *Modern*	145.00	200.00	195.00
☐ **Model 1909**, .32 ACP, Clip Fed, Hammerless, *Modern*	195.00	325.00	295.00
☐ **Model 1909**, .25 ACP, Clip Fed, Hammerless, *Modern*	180.00	275.00	250.00
☐ **Model 1909 M & P**, 9mm Browning Long, Clip Fed, Hammer, *Curio*	335.00	450.00	425.00
☐ **Model 1909 M & P**, 9mm Browning Long, South African Police, Clip Fed, Hammer, *Curio*	435.00	650.00	625.00
☐ **Model 1910**, .38 ACP, Clip Fed, Hammerless, *Curio*	280.00	425.00	395.00
☐ **Model 1911 Metro Police**, .32 ACP, Clip Fed, Hammer, *Modern*	170.00	255.00	245.00
☐ **Model 1911 Metro Police**, .380 ACP, Clip Fed, Hammer, *Modern*	215.00	325.00	310.00
☐ **Model 1913**, .38 ACP, Clip Fed, Hammerless, *Curio*	275.00	420.00	395.00
☐ **Model 1913 Mk 1**, .455 Webley Auto., Clip Fed, Grip Safety, Military, Hammer, *Curio*	295.00	445.00	425.00
☐ **Model 1913 Mk 1 #2**, .455 Webley Auto., Clip Fed, Grip Safety, Adjustable Sights, Hammer, *Curio*	575.00	875.00	850.00

	V.G.	Exc.	Prior Year Exc. Value
SHOTGUN, DOUBLE BARREL, SIDE-BY-SIDE			
☐ **Model 700**, 12 and 20 Gauges, Box Lock, Hammerless, Checkered Stock, Light Engraving, Single Trigger, *Modern*	350.00	500.00	500.00
☐ **Model 701**, 12 and 20 Gauges, Box Lock, Hammerless, Checkered Stock, Fancy Engraving, Double Trigger, *Modern*	600.00	800.00	800.00
☐ **Model 701**, 12 and 20 Gauges, Box Lock, Hammerless, Checkered Stock, Fancy Engraving, Single Trigger, *Modern*	650.00	850.00	850.00
☐ **Model 702**, 12 and 20 Gauges, Box Lock, Hammerless, Checkered Stock, Engraved, Double Trigger *Modern*	425.00	600.00	600.00
☐ **Model 702**, 12 and 20 Gauges, Box Lock, Hammerless, Checkered Stock, Engraved, Single Trigger, *Modern*	475.00	650.00	650.00

WELSHANTZ, DAVID

York, Pa. 1780-1783. See Kentucky Rifles, U.S. Military.

WELSHANTZ, JACOB

York, Pa. 1777-1792. See Kentucky Rifles, U.S. Military.

WELSHANTZ, JOSEPH

York, Pa. 1779-1783. See Kentucky Rifles, U.S. Military.

WESSON & HARRINGTON

Worcester, Mass. 1871-1874. Succeeded by Harrington and Richardson

	V.G.	Exc.	Prior Year Exc. Value
HANDGUN, REVOLVER			
☐ **.22 Short R.F.**, 7 Shot, Spur Trigger, Solid Frame, Single Action, *Antique*	95.00	170.00	160.00
☐ **.32 Short R.F.**, 5 Shot, Spur Trigger, Solid Frame, Single Action, *Antique*	95.00	170.00	160.00
☐ **.38 Short R.F.**, 5 Shot, Spur Trigger, Solid Frame, Single Action, *Antique*	95.00	185.00	180.00

WESSON, FRANK

Worcester, Mass. 1854 to 1865. 1865-1875 at Springfield, Mass. Also see U.S. Military, Wesson & Harrington, Harrington & Richardson.

	V.G.	Exc.	Prior Year Exc. Value
HANDGUN, SINGLESHOT			
☐ **Model 1859**, .22 Short, Tip-Up Barrel, Spur Trigger, *Antique*	145.00	215.00	200.00
☐ **Model 1862**, .22 Short, Tip-Up Barrel, Spur Trigger, *Antique*	125.00	180.00	170.00
☐ **Model 1859**, .30 R.F., Tip-Up Barrel, Spur Trigger, *Antique*	145.00	215.00	200.00
☐ **Model 1862**, .30 R.F., Tip-Up Barrel, Spur Trigger, *Antique*	145.00	215.00	200.00
☐ **Model 1859**, .32 R.F., Tip-Up Barrel, Spur Trigger, *Antique*	145.00	215.00	200.00
☐ **Model 1862**, .32 R.F., Tip-Up Barrel, Spur Trigger, *Antique*	145.00	215.00	200.00

	V.G.	Exc.	Prior Year Exc. Value
☐ **Model 1862 Pocket Rifle**, Various Calibers, Medium Frame, Spur Trigger, Target Sights, Detachable Stock, *Antique*	190.00	320.00	300.00
☐ **Model 1870 Pocket Rifle**, .22 Short, Small Frame, Spur Trigger, Target Sights, Detachable Stock, *Antique*	220.00	370.00	350.00
☐ **Model 1870 Pocket Rifle**, Various Calibers, Medium Frame, Spur Trigger, Target Sights, Detachable Stock, *Antique*	185.00	315.00	300.00
☐ **Model 1870 Pocket Rifle**, Various Calibers, Large Frame, Spur Trigger, Target Sights, Detachable Stock, *Antique*	425.00	575.00	550.00
HANDGUN, DOUBLE BARREL, OVER-UNDER			
☐ **Vest Pocket**, .22 Short, Twist Barrel, Spur Trigger, *Antique*	335.00	525.00	500.00
☐ **Vest Pocket**, .32 Short, Twist Barrel, Spur Trigger, *Antique*	220.00	365.00	350.00
☐ **Vest Pocket**, .41 Short, Twist Barrel, Spur Trigger, with Knife, *Antique*	425.00	675.00	650.00
RIFLE, SINGLESHOT			
☐ **.32 Long R.F.**, Double Trigger, Tip-Up, *Antique*	370.00	500.00	475.00

WESTERN ARMS CO.

	V.G.	Exc.	Prior Year Exc. Value
HANDGUN, REVOLVER			
☐ **.32 Long R.F.**, 5 Shot, Folding Trigger, Double Action, *Antique*	55.00	95.00	95.00

WESTERN FIELD

Trade name for Montgomery Ward.

	V.G.	Exc.	Prior Year Exc. Value
RIFLE, BOLT ACTION			
☐ **Model 56 Buckhorn**, .22 L.R.R.F., 5 Shot Clip, Open Rear Sight, *Modern*	35.00	55.00	55.00
☐ **Model 724**, .30-06 Springfield, Checkered Stock, Full-Stocked, *Modern*	130.00	175.00	170.00
☐ **Model 732**, .30-06 Springfield, Checkered Stock, Recoil Pad, *Modern*	135.00	180.00	175.00
☐ **Model 734**, 7mm Rem. Mag., Checkered Stock, Recoil Pad, *Modern*	140.00	190.00	190.00
☐ **Model 765**, .30-06 Springfield, Checkered Stock, *Modern*	115.00	150.00	150.00
☐ **Model 770**, Various Calibers, Checkered Stock, Sling Swivels, *Modern*	135.00	175.00	175.00
☐ **Model 78**, Various Calibers, Checkered Stock, Sling Swivels, *Modern*	135.00	175.00	175.00
☐ **Model 780**, Various Calibers, Checkered Stock, Sling Swivels, *Modern*	125.00	160.00	160.00
☐ **Model 815**, .22 L.R.R.F., Singleshot, *Modern*	20.00	30.00	25.00
☐ **Model 822**, .22 WMR, Clip Fed, *Modern*	35.00	55.00	55.00
☐ **Model 83**, .22 L.R.R.F., Singleshot, Open Rear Sight, Takedown, *Modern*	20.00	40.00	40.00
☐ **Model 830**, .22 L.R.R.F., Clip Fed, *Modern*	30.00	45.00	45.00
☐ **Model 832**, .22 L.R.R.F., Clip Fed, Checkered Stock, *Modern*	30.00	45.00	45.00
☐ **Model 84**, .22 L.R.R.F., 5 Shot Clip, Open Rear Sight, Takedown, *Modern*	30.00	45.00	45.00

	V.G.	Exc.	Prior Year Exc. Value
☐ **Model 840**, .22 W.M.R., Clip Fed, *Modern*	40.00	55.00	55.00
☐ **Model 842**, .22 L.R.R.F., Tube Feed, *Modern*	35.00	45.00	45.00
☐ **Model 852**, .22 L.R.R.F., Clip Fed, *Modern*	35.00	45.00	45.00
☐ **Model 86**, .22 L.R.R.F., Tube Feed, Takedown, Open Rear Sight, *Modern*	35.00	55.00	55.00
RIFLE, LEVER ACTION			
☐ **Model 72**, .30-30 Win., Pistol-Grip Stock, Plain, Tube Feed, *Modern*	75.00	120.00	115.00
☐ **Model 72C**, .30-30 Win., Straight Grip, Plain, Tube Feed, *Modern*	75.00	120.00	115.00
☐ **Model 79**, .30-30 Win., Pistol-Grip Stock, Plain, Tube Feed, *Modern*	75.00	125.00	120.00
☐ **Model 865**, .22 L.R.R.F., Tube Feed, Sling Swivels, *Modern*	45.00	70.00	65.00
☐ **Model 895**, .22 L.R.R.F., Tube Feed, Carbine, *Modern*	40.00	70.00	65.00
RIFLE, SEMI-AUTOMATIC			
☐ **Model 808**, .22 L.R.R.F., Tube Feed, *Modern*	35.00	55.00	50.00
☐ **Model 828**, .22 L.R.R.F., Clip Fed, Checkered Stock, *Modern*	40.00	60.00	55.00
☐ **Model 836**, .22 L.R.R.F., Tube Feed, *Modern*	40.00	60.00	55.00
☐ **Model 846**, .22 L.R.R.F., Tube Feed, *Modern*	40.00	60.00	55.00
☐ **Model 850**, .22 L.R.R.F., Clip Fed, *Modern*	40.00	60.00	55.00
☐ **Model 880**, .22 L.R.R.F., Tube Feed, *Modern*	35.00	55.00	50.00
☐ **Model M-1**, .30 Carbine, Clip Fed, *Modern*	90.00	145.00	135.00
SHOTGUN, BOLT ACTION			
☐ **Model 150**, .410 Ga., Clip Fed, *Modern*	35.00	55.00	55.00
☐ **Model 172-5**, 12 and 20 Gauges, Magnum, Clip Fed, Adjustable Choke, *Modern*	45.00	60.00	60.00
SHOTGUN, DOUBLE BARREL, SIDE-BY-SIDE			
☐ **12 and 20 Gauges**, Single Trigger, Hammerless, Checkered Stock, *Modern*	110.00	155.00	150.00
☐ **Various Gauges**, Hammerless, Plain, *Modern*	80.00	130.00	125.00
☐ **Long-Range**, Various Gauges, Double Trigger, Hammerless, *Modern*	120.00	170.00	165.00
☐ **Long-Range**, Various Gauges, Single Trigger, Hammerless, *Modern*	140.00	195.00	195.00
☐ **Model 330**, Various Gauges, Hammerless, Checkered Stock, *Modern*	95.00	155.00	155.00
☐ **Model 5151**, Various Gauges, Hammerless, Steel Barrel, *Modern*	95.00	155.00	155.00
SHOTGUN, SEMI-AUTOMATIC			
☐ **Model 600**, 12 Ga., Takedown, Plain Barrel, Checkered Stock, *Modern*	95.00	140.00	135.00
☐ **Model 600**, 12 Ga., Takedown, Vent Rib, Checkered Stock, *Modern*	115.00	155.00	150.00
SHOTGUN, SINGLESHOT			
☐ **Model 100**, Various Gauges, Hammerless, Adjustable Choke, *Modern*	35.00	50.00	50.00
☐ **Trap**, 12 Ga., Hammer, Solid Rib, Checkered Stock, *Modern*	55.00	85.00	85.00
SHOTGUN, SLIDE ACTION			
☐ **Model 500**, .410 Ga., Plain, Takedown, *Modern*	85.00	130.00	125.00

	V.G.	Exc.	Prior Year Exc. Value
☐ **Model 502**, .410 Ga., Checkered Stock, Light Engraving, Takedown, Vent Rib, *Modern*	95.00	135.00	130.00
☐ **Model 520**, 12 Ga., Takedown, *Modern*	90.00	135.00	135.00
☐ **Model 550**, 12 and 20 Gauges, Checkered Stock, Light Engraving, Vent Rib, Takedown, *Modern*	100.00	135.00	135.00
☐ **Model 550**, 12 and 20 Gauges, Checkered Stock, Light Engraving, Vent Rib, Takedown, Adjustable Choke, *Modern*	115.00	150.00	150.00
☐ **Model 550**, 12 and 20 Gauges, Plain, Takedown, *Modern*	95.00	130.00	125.00
☐ **Model 620**, Various Gauges, Takedown, *Modern*	95.00	145.00	145.00

WESTLEY RICHARDS

London, England, Since 1812.

RIFLE, BOLT ACTION

	V.G.	Exc.	Prior Year Exc. Value
☐ **Best Quality**, Various Calibers, Express Sights, Fancy Wood, Fancy Checkering, Repeater, *Modern*	1,500.00	2,400.00	2,300.00

RIFLE, DOUBLE BARREL, OVER-UNDER

	V.G.	Exc.	Prior Year Exc. Value
☐ **Ovundo**, 12 Ga., Ventilated Barrels, Vent Rib, Single Selective Trigger, Extra Barrel, Detachable Side Lock, *Modern*	10,000.00	15,500.00	15,500.00

RIFLE, DOUBLE BARREL, SIDE-BY-SIDE

	V.G.	Exc.	Prior Year Exc. Value
☐ **Best Quality**, Various Calibers, Box Lock, Double Trigger, Fancy Engraving, Fancy Checkering, Express Sights, *Modern*	3,750.00	6,000.00	6,000.00
☐ **Best Quality**, Various Calibers, Sidelock, Double Trigger, Fancy Engraving, Fancy Checkering, Express Sights, *Modern*	9,500.00	13,500.00	13,500.00

SHOTGUN, DOUBLE BARREL, OVER-UNDER

	V.G.	Exc.	Prior Year Exc. Value
☐ **Ovundo**, 12 Ga., Sidelock, Single Selective Trigger, Selective Ejector, Fancy Engraving, Fancy Checkering, *Modern*	9,750.00	17,500.00	17,500.00

SHOTGUN, DOUBLE BARREL, SIDE-BY-SIDE

	V.G.	Exc.	Prior Year Exc. Value
☐ **10 Ga. Pinfire**, Engraved, Carbine, *Antique*	450.00	700.00	700.00
☐ **Best Quality**, Various Gauges, Sidelock, Hammerless, Fancy Engraving, Fancy Checkering, Double Trigger, *Modern*	7,500.00	11,500.00	11,000.00
☐ **Best Quality**, Various Gauges, Sidelock, Hammerless, Fancy Engraving, Fancy Checkering, Single Selective Trigger, *Modern*	8,000.00	13,500.00	13,000.00
☐ **Best Quality**, Various Gauges, Box Lock, Hammerless, Fancy Engraving, Fancy Checkering, Double Trigger, *Modern*	5,500.00	8,900.00	8,500.00
☐ **Best Quality**, Various Gauges, Box Lock, Hammerless, Fancy Engraving, Fancy Checkering, Single Selective Trigger, *Modern*	6,000.00	10,000.00	9,500.00
☐ **Best**, Pigeon, 12 Ga. Mag. 3", Sidelock, Hammerless, Fancy Engraving, Fancy Checkering, Double Trigger, *Modern*	11,500.00	18,000.00	18,000.00
☐ **Best**, Pigeon, 12 Ga. Mag. 3", Sidelock, Hammerless, Fancy Engraving, Fancy Checkering, Single Selective Trigger, *Modern*	13,500.00	19,000.00	19,000.00

	V.G.	Exc.	Prior Year Exc. Value
☐ **Deluxe Quality**, Various Gauges, Sidelock, Hammerless, Fancy Engraving, Fancy Checkering, Double Trigger, *Modern*	8,500.00	12,000.00	12,000.00
☐ **Deluxe Quality**, Various Gauges, Sidelock, Hammerless, Fancy Engraving, Fancy Checkering, Single Selective Trigger, *Modern*	9,000.00	13,000.00	13,000.00
☐ **Deluxe Quality**, Various Gauges, Box Lock, Hammerless, Fancy Engraving, Fancy Checkering, Double Trigger, *Modern*	5,500.00	7,800.00	7,750.00
☐ **Deluxe Quality**, Various Gauges, Box Lock, Hammerless, Fancy Engraving, Fancy Checkering, Single Selective Trigger, *Modern*	6,500.00	8,600.00	8,500.00
☐ **Model E**, Various Gauges, Box Lock, Hammerless, Engraved, Double Trigger, Selective Ejector, *Modern*	3,500.00	5,000.00	5,000.00
☐ **Model E**, Various Gauges, Box Lock, Hammerless, Engraved, Double Trigger, *Modern*	2,800.00	3,800.00	3,750.00
☐ **Model E Pigeon**, 12 Ga. Mag. 3", Box Lock, Hammerless, Engraved, Double Trigger, Selective Ejector, *Modern*	4,000.00	5,500.00	5,500.00
☐ **Model E Pigeon**, 12 Ga. Mag 3", Box Lock, Hammerless, Engraved, Double Trigger, *Modern*	3,300.00	4,300.00	4,250.00
SHOTGUN, SINGLESHOT			
☐ **12 Ga.**, Trap Grade, Vent Rib, Fancy Engraving, Fancy Checkering, Hammerless, *Modern*	5,500.00	8,000.00	8,000.00
☐ **12 Ga.**, Vent Rib, Plain, Monte Carlo Stock, Trap Grade, *Modern*	1,800.00	2,700.00	2,600.00

WESTON, EDWARD

Sussex, England 1800-1835.

	V.G.	Exc.	Prior Year Exc. Value
HANDGUN, FLINTLOCK			
☐ **.67**, Pair, Duelling Pistols, Octagon Barrel, Silver Furniture, Plain, *Antique*	1,600.00	2,600.00	2,575.00

WHEEL-LOCK, UNKNOWN MAKER

	V.G.	Exc.	Prior Year Exc. Value
COMBINATION WEAPON, PISTOL			
☐ **German**, 1500's War-Hammer, All Metal, *Antique*	9,000.00	15,000.00	15,000.00
HANDGUN, WHEEL-LOCK			
☐ **Augsburg**, Late 1500's, Ball Pommel, Engraved, Ornate, *Antique*	14,000.00	20,000.00	20,000.00
☐ **Brescian**, Mid-1600's, Military, Fish-Tail Butt, Plain, *Antique*	1,500.00	2,600.00	2,500.00
☐ **Embellished Original**, Ornate, *Antique*	2,500.00	3,550.00	3,500.00
☐ **Enclosed Lock German**, Mid-1600's, Engraved, Holster Pistol, *Antique*	3,000.00	3,800.00	3,750.00
☐ **Enclosed Lock**, Late 1600's, Military, Plain, *Antique*	1,500.0	2,500.00	2,500.00
☐ **English**, Mid-1600's, Ornate, *Antique*	14,000.00	20,000.00	20,000.00
☐ **English**, Mid-1600's, Military, Holster Pistol, Plain, *Antique*	1,500.00	2,500.00	2,500.00
☐ **French**, Early 1600's, Military, Silver Inlay, *Antique*	2,500.00	3,600.00	3,500.00
☐ **German**, 1600, Dagger-Handle Butt, Military, Plain, *Antique*	2,000.00	2,800.00	2,750.00

	V.G.	Exc.	Prior Year Exc. Value
☐ **German**, Late 1500's, Carved, Horn Inlays, Ball Pommel, Flattened, *Antique*	12,500.00	18,000.00	18,000.00
☐ **German**, Mid-1500's, Horn Inlays, Dagger-Handle Butt, Gold and Silver Damascened, Ornate, *Antique*	35,000.00	55,000.00	55,000.00
☐ **German**, Mid-1600's, Military, Fish-Tail Butt, Plain, *Antique*	1,250.00	2,000.00	2,000.00
☐ **German Puffer**, Late 1500's, Horn Inlays, Ball Pommel, *Antique*	6,000.00	10,000.00	10,000.00
☐ **German Style**, Reproduction, Engraved, Inlays, High Quality, *Antique*	1,400.00	2,000.00	1,950.00
☐ **Italian**, 1500's, Dagger-Handle, External Mechanism, *Antique*	9,000.00	16,500.00	16,500.00
☐ **Late 1500's Odd Butt**, all Metal, Engraved, Ornate, *Antique*	7,000.00	10,000.00	10,000.00
☐ **Old Reproduction**, High Quality, *Antique*	1,200.00	1,800.00	1,800.00
☐ **Pair Brescian**, Mid-1600's, Inlays, Engraved, Ornate, Fish-Tail Butt, *Antique*	18,000.00	25,000.00	25,000.00
☐ **Pair Dutch**, Mid-1600's, Holster Pistol, Gold Damascened, Inlays, Ornate, *Antique*	18,000.00	25,000.00	25,000.00
☐ **Pair Saxon**, Late 1500's, Ball Pommel, Medium Ornamentation, *Antique*	14,000.00	20,000.00	20,000.00
☐ **Pair Saxon**, Late 1500's, Ball Pommel, Light Ornamentation, *Antique*	9,000.00	15,000.00	15,000.00
☐ **Pair Saxon**, Late 1500's, Ball Pommel, Inlays, Engraved, *Antique*	24,000.00	30,000.00	30,000.00
☐ **Saxon**, Double Barrel, Over-Under, Inlays, Ornate, Ball Pommel, *Antique*	24,000.00	30,000.00	30,000.00
☐ **Saxon**, Dated 1579, Horn Inlays, Engraved, Ball Pommel, *Antique*	6,000.00	10,000.00	10,000.00
☐ **Saxon**, Late 1500's, Ball Pommel, Checkered Stock, Military, Plain, *Antique*	4,000.00	6,000.00	6,000.00
RIFLE, WHEEL-LOCK			
☐ **Brandenburg 1620**, Cavalry Rifle, Military, *Antique*	5,500.00	8,000.00	8,000.00

WHIPPET

Made by Stevens Arms

	V.G.	Exc.	Prior Year Exc. Value
SHOTGUN, SINGLESHOT			
☐ **Model 94A**, Various Gauges, Hammer, Automatic Ejector, *Modern*	35.00	55.00	55.00

WHITE POWDER WONDER

Made by Stevens Arms.

	V.G.	Exc.	Prior Year Exc. Value
SHOTGUN, SINGLESHOT			
☐ **Model 90**, Various Gauges, Takedown, Automatic Ejector, Plain, Hammer, *Modern*	35.00	55.00	55.00

WHITE, ROLLIN, ARMS CO.

Hartford, Conn. 1849-1858; Lowell, Mass. 1864-1892.

	V.G.	Exc.	Prior Year Exc. Value
HANDGUN, REVOLVER			
☐ **.22 Short R.F.,** 7 Shot, Spur Trigger, Tip-Up, *Antique*	175.00	290.00	275.00
HANDGUN, SINGLESHOT			
☐ **SS Pocket,** .32 Cal., no Trigger Guard, *Antique*	160.00	260.00	240.00

Rollin White Single Shot Pocket Pistol, .32 Caliber

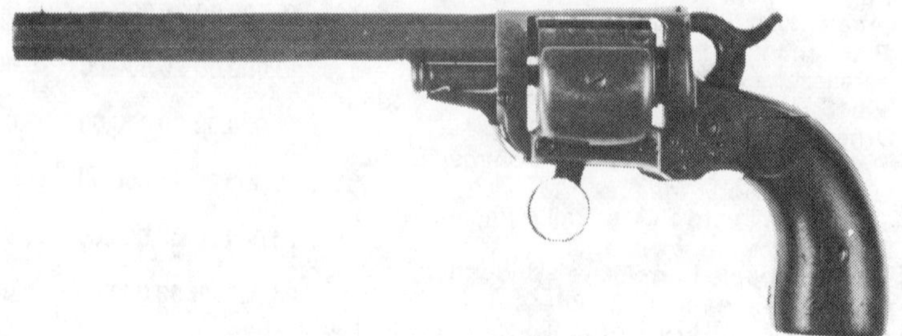

Whitney Beals Standard Revolver, .31 Caliber

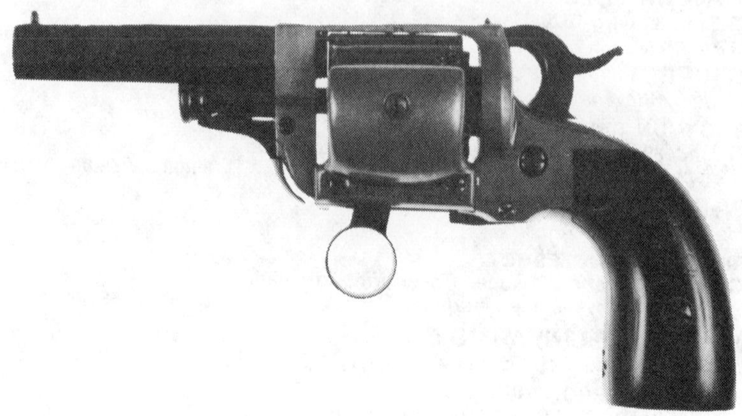

Whitney Beals Walking Beam Pocket Revolver, .31 Caliber

	V.G.	Exc.	Prior Year Exc. Value

WHITE STAR

Maker unknown, c. 1880.

HANDGUN, REVOLVER

	V.G.	Exc.	Prior Year Exc. Value
☐ **.32 Short R.F.**, 5 Shot, Spur Trigger, Solid Frame, Single Action, *Antique*	90.00	165.00	160.00

HANDGUN, REVOLVER

	V.G.	Exc.	Prior Year Exc. Value
☐ **.32 Short R.F.**, 5 Shot, Spur Trigger, Solid Frame, Single Action, *Antique*	95.00	170.00	170.00

WHITNEY ARMS CO.

New Haven, Conn. 1866-1876, also see U.S. Military.

HANDGUN, PERCUSSION

	V.G.	Exc.	Prior Year Exc. Value
☐ **Hooded Cylinder,** .28, 6 Shot, Hammer, *Antique*	750.00	1450.00	1400.00
☐ **Whitney-Beals,** .31, Ring Trigger, 7 Shot, *Antique*	200.00	525.00	425.00
☐ **Whitney-Beals Walking Beam Pocket Revolver,** .31, 6 Shot, *Antique*	775.00	1600.00	1525.00
☐ **Navy,** .36, 6 Shot, Colt 1851 Type, *Antique*	420.00	800.00	800.00
☐ **Whitney Navy,** .36, 6 Shot, Single Action, Hammer, *Antique*	295.00	425.00	400.00
☐ **Pocket Model,** .31, 5 Shot, Single Action, *Antique*	175.00	285.00	275.00
☐ **New Pocket Model,** .28, 6 Shot, Single Action, *Antique*	275.00	420.00	400.00

HANDGUN, REVOLVER

	V.G.	Exc.	Prior Year Exc. Value
☐ **.22 Short R.F.**, 7 Shot, Spur Trigger, Solid Frame, Single Action, *Antique*	90.00	165.00	160.00
☐ **.38 Short R.F.**, 5 Shot, Spur Trigger, Solid Frame, Single Action, *Antique*	90.00	165.00	160.00
☐ **.32 Short R.F.**, 5 or 6 Shots, Spur Trigger, Solid Frame, Single Action, *Antique*	95.00	170.00	170.00

RIFLE, SINGLESHOT

	V.G.	Exc.	Prior Year Exc. Value
☐ **Whitney-Howard**, .44 R.F., Carbine, Lever Action, *Antique*	200.00	395.00	375.00
☐ **Whitney-Howard**, .44 R.F., Rifle, Lever Action, *Antique*	310.00	465.00	450.00
☐ **Phoenix**, Various Calibers, Carbine, Hammer, *Antique*	415.00	725.00	700.00
☐ **Phoenix**, Various Calibers, Rifle, Hammer, *Antique*	220.00	365.00	350.00
☐ **Rolling Block**, Various Calibers, Carbine, *Antique*	350.00	500.00	500.00
☐ **Rolling Block**, Various Calibers, Rifle, *Antique*	225.00	350.00	

RIFLE, LEVER ACTION

	V.G.	Exc.	Prior Year Exc. Value
☐ **Kennedy**, Various Calibers, Tube Feed, Plain, *Antique*	300.00	575.00	550.00
☐ **Model 1886**, Various Calibers, Tube Feed, Plain, *Antique*	500.00	875.00	850.00

SHOTGUN, DOUBLE BARREL, SIDE-BY-SIDE

	V.G.	Exc.	Prior Year Exc. Value
☐ **12 Ga.**, Damascus Barrel, Outside Hammers, *Antique*	175.00	320.00	300.00

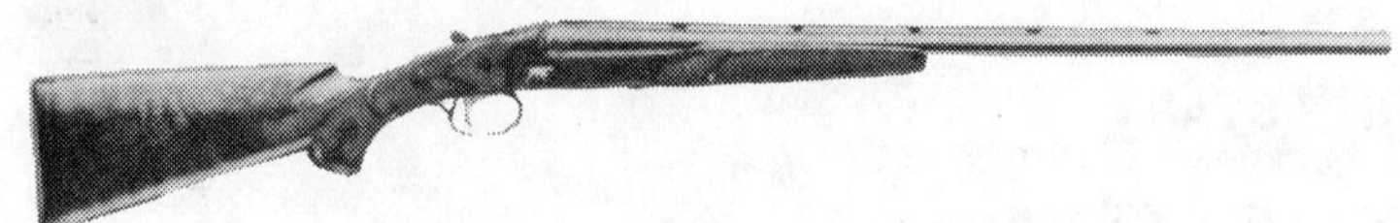

Winchester M21 Grand American

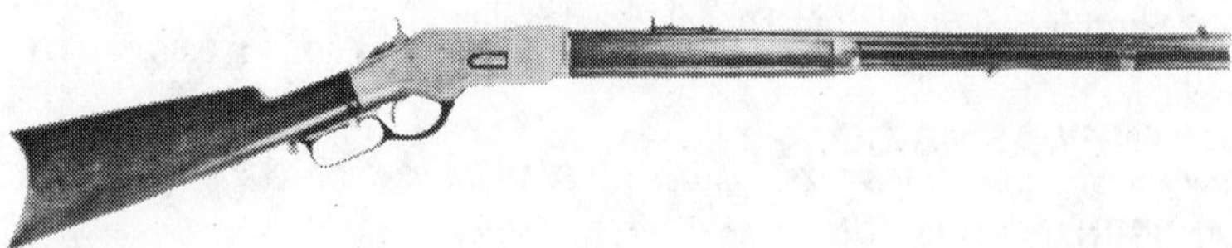

Winchester M1866

Winchester M1873

Winchester Big Bore 94XTR

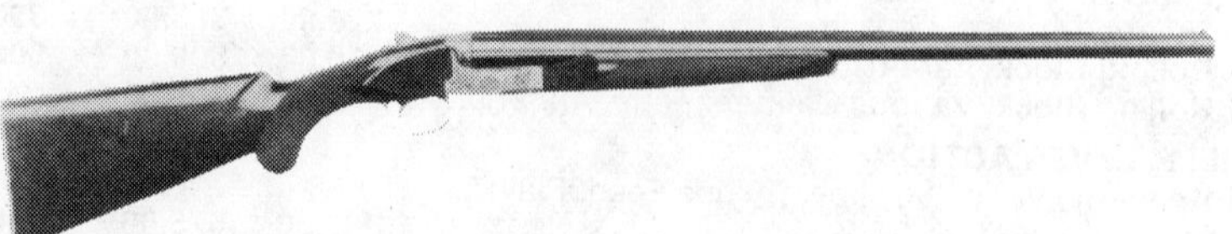

Winchester Model 23 Pigeon Grade XTR Field Gun

Winchester M1400

	V.G.	Exc.	Prior Year Exc. Value
WHITNEY FIREARMS CO.			
Hartford, Conn. 1955-1962			
HANDGUN, SINGLESHOT			
☐ **Wolverine**, .22 L.R.R.F., Blue, *Modern*	90.00	135.00	130.00
WHITNEYVILLE ARMORY			
See Whitney Arms Co.			
WHITWORTH			
Made in England, imported by Interarms.			
RIFLE, BOLT ACTION			
☐ **Express**, Various Calibers, Checkered Stock, *Modern*	275.00	400.00	400.00
WICHITA ENGINEERING & SUPPLY			
Wichita, Kans.			
HANDGUN, SINGLESHOT			
☐ **Classic**, Various Calibers, Singleshot, Target, *Modern*	625.00	900.00	750.00
☐ **Silhouette Pistol**, Various Calibers, Bolt Action, *Modern*	370.00	500.00	400.00
RIFLE, BOLT ACTION			
☐ **Magnum**, Various Calibers, Repeater, Stainless Steel, *Modern*	900.00	1,450.00	1,250.00
☐ **Magnum**, Various Calibers, Singleshot, Stainless Steel, *Modern*	800.00	1,350.00	1,250.00
☐ **Varmint**, Various Calibers, Repeater, Target, *Modern*	525.00	700.00	600.00
☐ **Classic**, Various Calibers, Singleshot, Target, *Modern*	625.00	900.00	750.00
☐ **Classic**, Various Calibers, Repeater, *Modern*	700.00	975.00	750.00
WICKLIFFE			
Triple-S Development, Wickliffe, Ohio.			
RIFLE, SINGLESHOT			
☐ **Stinger Standard**, Various Calibers, Falling Block, *Modern*	180.00	260.00	250.00
☐ **Stinger Deluxe**, Various Calibers, Falling Block, *Modern*	220.00	310.00	300.00
☐ **'76 Standard**, Various Calibers, Falling Block, *Modern*	180.00	260.00	250.00
☐ **'76 Deluxe**, Various Calibers, Falling Block, *Modern*	220.00	310.00	300.00
Traditional, Various Calibers, Falling Block, *Modern*	180.00	260.00	250.00
WIDE AWAKE			
Made by Hood Fire Arms, Norwich, Conn., c. 1875.			
HANDGUN, REVOLVER			
☐ **.32 Short R.F.**, 5 Shot, Spur Trigger, Solid Frame, Single Action, *Antique*	90.00	165.00	160.00
WILKINSON ARMS			
South El Monte, Calif., c. 1976.			
HANDGUN, SEMI-AUTOMATIC			
☐ **Diane**, .25 ACP, Clip Fed, Blue, *Modern*	115.00	160.00	150.00

WILKINSON ARMS
Parma, Ind.

	V.G.	Exc.	Prior Year Exc. Value
HANDGUN, SEMI-AUTOMATIC			
☐ **Linda**, 9mm Luger, Clip Fed, Blue, *Modern*	200.00	300.00	300.00

WILKINSON ARMS CO.
Made in Belgium for Richmond Hardware Co. Richmond, Va., c. 1900.

	V.G.	Exc.	Prior Year Exc. Value
SHOTGUN, DOUBLE BARREL, SIDE-BY-SIDE			
☐ **Various Gauges**, Outside Hammers, Damascus Barrel, *Modern*	100.00	170.00	175.00
☐ **Various Gauges**, Hammerless, Steel Barrel, *Modern*	135.00	190.00	200.00
☐ **Various Gauges**, Hammerless, Damascus Barrel, *Modern*	100.00	170.00	175.00
☐ **Various Gauges**, Outside Hammers, Steel Barrel, *Modern*	125.00	185.00	190.00
SHOTGUN, SINGLESHOT			
☐ **Various Gauges**, Hammer, Steel Barrel, *Modern*	55.00	85.00	85.00

WILLIAMS, FREDERICK
Birmingham, England 1893-1929.

	V.G.	Exc.	Prior Year Exc. Value
SHOTGUN, DOUBLE BARREL, SIDE-BY-SIDE			
☐ **12 Ga.**, Damascus Barrel, Outside Hammers, Checkered Stock, Engraved, *Antique*	300.00	465.00	450.00

WILLIAMSON, DAVID
Brooklyn, N.Y. and Greenville, N.J. 1864-1874. Also see Moore's Patent Firearms Co.

	V.G.	Exc.	Prior Year Exc. Value
HANDGUN, SINGLESHOT			
☐ **.41 Short R.F.**, Derringer, Nickel Plated, *Antique*	195.00	300.00	300.00

WILLIS, RICHARD
Lancaster, Pa., c. 1776. See Kentucky Rifles and Pistols.

WILMONT ARMS CO.
Belgium, c. 1900.

	V.G.	Exc.	Prior Year Exc. Value
SHOTGUN, DOUBLE BARREL, SIDE-BY-SIDE			
☐ **Various Gauges**, Outside Hammers, Damascus Barrel, *Modern*	100.00	170.00	175.00
☐ **Various Gauges**, Hammerless, Steel Barrel, *Modern*	135.00	190.00	200.00
☐ **Various Gauges**, Hammerless, Damascus Barrel, *Modern*	100.00	170.00	175.00
☐ **Various Gauges**, Outside Hammers, Steel Barrel, *Modern*	125.00	185.00	190.00
SHOTGUN, SINGLESHOT			
☐ **Various Gauges**, Hammer, Steel Barrel, *Modern*	55.00	85.00	85.00

WILSON, R.
London, England 1720-1750.

	V.G.	Exc.	Prior Year Exc. Value
SHOTGUN, FLINTLOCK			
☐ **Fowling**, 9 Ga., Queen Anne Style, Half-Stock, *Antique*	900.00	1,600.00	1,500.00

WILTSHIRE ARMS CO.

Belgium, c. 1900.

	V.G.	Exc.	Prior Year Exc. Value
SHOTGUN, DOUBLE BARREL, SIDE-BY-SIDE			
☐ **Various Gauges**, Outside Hammers, Damascus Barrel, *Modern*	100.00	170.00	175.00
☐ **Various Gauges**, Hammerless, Steel Barrel, *Modern*	135.00	190.00	200.00
☐ **Various Gauges**, Hammerless, Damascus Barrel, *Modern*	100.00	170.00	175.00
☐ **Various Gauges**, Outside Hammers, Steel Barrel, *Modern*	125.00	185.00	190.00
SHOTGUN, SINGLESHOT			
☐ **Various Gauges**, Hammer, Steel Barrel, *Modern*	55.00	85.00	85.00

WINCHESTER REPEATING ARMS CO.

New Haven, Conn. 1866 to date. In 1857 Oliver Winchester reorganized the Volcanic Repeating Arms Co. into the New Haven Arms Co., and it became Winchester Repeating Arms Co. in 1866. In 1869 Winchester absorbed Fogerty Repeating Rifle Co., and the American Rifle Co. In 1870 it acquired The Spencer Repeating Arms Co. and AdironDack Arms Co. in 1874. In 1881 was purchased by U.S. Repeating Arms Co. Also see U.S. Military.

☐ **For Custom Features,** *Add* **50%-100%**
☐ **For Special Sights,** *Add* **25%-50%**

	V.G.	Exc.	Prior Year Exc. Value
AUTOMATIC WEAPON, ASSAULT RIFLE			
☐ **M-1 Garand (Win),** .30-06 Springfield, Clip Fed, Experimental, *Class 3*	6025.00	9450.00	9300.00
☐ **M1918 BAR,** .30-06 Springfield, Clip Fed, Bipod, Modern, *Class 3*	1775.00	2725.00	2700.00
AUTOMATIC WEAPON, SUBMACHINE GUN			
☐ **M-2,** .30 Carbine, Clip Fed, Military, *Class 3*	500.00	800.00	750.00
RIFLE, BOLT ACTION			
☐ **Hotchkiss,** .40-65 Win., Sporting Rifle, *Antique*	800.00	1150.00	1100.00
☐ **Hotchkiss 1st Model Fancy,** .45-70 Government, Sporting Rifle, *Antique*	575.00	900.00	875.00
☐ **Hotchkiss 1st Model Fancy,** .45-70 Government, Sporting Rifle, *Antique*	575.00	900.00	875.00
☐ **Hotchkiss 1st Model,** .45-70 Government, Military, Rifle, *Antique*	410.00	650.00	625.00
☐ **Hotchkiss 1st Model,** .45-70 Government, Military, Carbine, *Antique*	430.00	695.00	670.00
☐ **Hotchkiss 1st Model,** .45-70 Government, Sporting Rifle, *Antique*	475.00	750.00	720.00
☐ **Hotchkiss 2nd Model,** .45-70 Government, Military, Rifle, *Antique*	475.00	750.00	720.00
☐ **Hotchkiss 2nd Model,** .45-70 Government, Sporting Rifle, *Antique*	575.00	850.00	825.00
☐ **Hotchkiss 3rd Model,** .45-70 Government, Military, Rifle, *Antique*	375.00	725.00	700.00
☐ **Hotchkiss 3rd Model,** .45-70 Government, Military, Carbine, *Antique*	500.00	840.00	820.00
☐ **Hotchkiss 3rd Model,** .45-70 Government, Sporting Rifle, *Antique*	565.00	935.00	900.00
☐ **Lee Straight-Pull,** 6mm Lee Navy, Musket, *Antique*	485.00	650.00	625.00

	V.G.	Exc.	Prior Year Exc. Value
☐ **Lee Straight-Pull,** 6mm Lee Navy, Sporting Rifle, *Antique*	510.00	760.00	750.00
☐ **M121,** .22 L.R.R.F., Singleshot, *Modern*	42.00	58.00	55.00
☐ **M121-Y,** .22 L.R.R.F., Singleshot, *Modern*	42.00	58.00	55.00
☐ **M121 Deluxe,** .22 L.R.R.F., Singleshot, *Modern*	48.00	70.00	65.00
☐ **M131,** .22 L.R.R.F., Clip Fed, Open Rear Sight, *Modern*	57.00	85.00	80.00
☐ **M135,** .22 WMR, Clip Fed, *Modern*	70.00	95.00	90.00
☐ **M141,** .22 WMR, Tube Feed, *Modern*	57.00	80.00	75.00
☐ **M145,** .22 WMR, Tube Feed, *Modern*	68.00	90.00	85.00
☐ **M1900,** .22 Long R.F., Singleshot, *Modern*	75.00	125.00	120.00
☐ **M1902,** Various Rimfires, Singleshot, *Curio*	90.00	160.00	155.00
☐ **M1904,** Various Rimfires, Singleshot, *Curio*	90.00	160.00	155.00
☐ **Thumb Trigger,** .22 L.R.R.F., Singleshot, *Curio*	165.00	240.00	235.00
☐ **M43,** Various Calibers, Sporting Rifle, *Modern*	160.00	275.00	265.00
☐ **M43 Special Grade,** Various Calibers, *Modern*	190.00	330.00	325.00
☐ **M47,** .22 L.R.R.F., Singleshot, *Modern*	63.00	100.00	95.00
☐ **M52,** .22 L.R.R.F., Heavy Barrel, *Modern*	245.00	400.00	395.00
☐ **M52 Slow-Lock,** .22 L.R.R.F., *Modern*	190.00	290.00	275.00
☐ **M52 Speed-Lock,** .22 L.R.R.F., *Modern*	240.00	330.00	325.00
☐ **M52 Sporting,** .22 L.R.R.F., Rifle, *Modern*	565.00	860.00	845.00
☐ **M52-B,** .22 L.R.R.F., *Modern*	230.00	350.00	345.00
☐ **M52-B,** .22 L.R.R.F., Heavy Barrel, *Modern*	260.00	400.00	395.00
☐ **M52-B,** .22 L.R.R.F., Bull Gun, *Modern*	280.00	450.00	445.00
☐ **M52-B,** .22 L.R.R.F., Sporting Rifle, *Modern*	535.00	825.00	800.00
☐ **M52-C,** .22 L.R.R.F., *Modern*	225.00	330.00	325.00
☐ **M52-C,** .22 L.R.R.F., Standard Barrel, *Modern*	230.00	350.00	340.00
☐ **M52-C,** .22 L.R.R.F., Bull Gun, *Modern*	310.00	470.00	450.00
☐ **M52-D,** .22 L.R.R.F., *Modern*	285.00	470.00	450.00
☐ **M52 International,** .22 L.R.R.F., *Modern*	490.00	750.00	725.00
☐ **M52 International Prone,** .22 L.R.R.F., *Modern*	400.00	565.00	550.00
☐ **M54,** .270 Win., Carbine, *Curio*	465.00	750.00	725.00
☐ **M54,** .30-06 Springfield, Sniper Rifle, *Modern*	395.00	600.00	575.00
☐ **M54,** Various Calibers, Carbine, *Modern*	310.00	550.00	520.00
☐ **M54,** Various Calibers, Sporting Rifle, *Modern*	330.00	550.00	520.00
☐ **M54 Match,** Various Calibers, Sniper Rifle, *Modern*	440.00	700.00	675.00
☐ **M54 National Match,** Various Calibers, *Modern*	385.00	525.00	520.00
☐ **M54 Super Grade,** Various Calibers, *Modern*	385.00	580.00	570.00
☐ **M54 Target,** Various Calibers, *Modern*	360.00	565.00	550.00
☐ **M56,** .22 L.R.R.F., Sporting Rifle, Clip Fed, *Modern*	90.00	165.00	165.00
☐ **M57,** Various Rimfires, Target, *Modern*	320.00	430.00	425.00
☐ **M58,** .22 L.R.R.F., Singleshot, *Modern*	85.00	135.00	130.00
☐ **M59,** .22 L.R.R.F., Singleshot, *Modern*	95.00	160.00	155.00
☐ **M60,** .22 L.R.R.F., Singleshot, *Modern*	85.00	135.00	130.00
☐ **M60-A,** .22 L.R.R.F., Target, Singleshot, *Modern*	130.00	170.00	165.00
☐ **M67,** Various Rimfires, Singleshot, *Modern*	75.00	110.00	100.00
☐ **M67 Boy's Rifle,** Various Rimfires, Singleshot, *Modern*	63.00	100.00	95.00
☐ **M68,** Various Rimfires, Singleshot, *Modern*	85.00	125.00	120.00
☐ **M69,** .22 L.R.R.F., Clip Fed, *Modern*	100.00	150.00	145.00
☐ **M69 Match,** .22 L.R.R.F., Clip Fed, *Modern*	120.00	175.00	170.00
☐ **M69 Target,** .22 L.R.R.F., Clip Fed, *Modern*	115.00	160.00	150.00
☐ **M70 Action Only,** Various Calibers, Pre'64, *Modern*	195.00	275.00	265.00
☐ **M70,** For Pre-War, *Add* **25%-50%**			

	V.G.	Exc.	Prior Year Exc. Value
☐ **M70,** For Mint Unfired, Pre'64, *Add* **50%-100%**			
☐ **M70 African,** .458 Win. Mag., Pre'64, *Modern*	685.00	950.00	945.00
☐ **M70 Alaskan,** Various Calibers, Pre'64, Checkered Stock, *Modern*	520.00	700.00	695.00
☐ **M70 Barreled Action Only,** Various Calibers, Pre'64, Checkered Stock, *Modern*	300.00	435.00	425.00
☐ **M70 Bull Gun,** Various Calibers, Pre'64, Checkered Stock, *Modern*	610.00	825.00	800.00
☐ **M70 Carbine,** Various Calibers, Pre'64, Checkered Stock, *Modern*	565.00	800.00	775.00
☐ **M70 Featherweight Sporter Grade,** Various Calibers, Pre'64, Checkered Stock, *Modern*	565.00	800.00	775.00
☐ **M70 Featherweight Sporter Grade,** Various Calibers, Pre'64, Checkered Stock, *Modern*	565.00	800.00	775.00
☐ **M70 Featherweight,** Various Calibers, Pre'64, Checkered Stock, *Modern*	470.00	690.00	675.00
☐ **M70 National Match,** .30-06 Springfield, Pre'64, *Modern*	565.00	825.00	800.00
☐ **M70 Target,** Various Calibers, Pre'64, Checkered Stock, *Modern*	580.00	900.00	875.00
☐ **M70 Varmint,** Various Calibers, Pre'64, Checkered Stock, *Modern*	490.00	715.00	700.00
☐ **M70 Westerner,** Various Calibers, Pre'64, Checkered Stock, *Modern*	465.00	690.00	675.00
☐ **Model 70,** Various Calibers, Post '64, Checkered Stock, Open Rear Sight, Magnum Action, *Modern*	170.00	250.00	245.00
☐ **Model 70 African,** .458 Win. Mag., Post '64, Checkered Stock, Open Rear Sight, Magnum Action, *Modern*	260.00	365.00	350.00
☐ **Model 70 International Match,** .308 Win., Post '64, Checkered Stock, Target Stock, *Modern*	320.00	475.00	450.00
☐ **Model 70 Standard,** Various Calibers, Post '64, Checkered Stock, Open Rear Sight, *Modern*	145.00	210.00	200.00
☐ **Model 70 Target,** Various Calibers, Post '64, Checkered Stock, Target Stock, *Modern*	230.00	350.00	340.00
☐ **Model 70 Varmint,** Various Calibers, Post '64, Checkered Stock, Heavy Barrel, *Modern*	170.00	225.00	220.00
☐ **Model 70A,** Various Calibers, Post '64, Magnum Action, *Modern*	150.00	250.00	240.00
☐ **Model 70A Police,** Various Calibers, Post '64, *Modern*	145.00	210.00	200.00
☐ **Model 70A Standard,** Various Calibers, Post '64, *Modern*	135.00	190.00	185.00
☐ **M70 Super Grade,** Various Calibers, Pre'64, *Modern*	565.00	835.00	825.00
☐ **Model 70XTR Featherweight,** Various Calibers, No Sights, *Modern*	275.00	365.00	350.00
☐ **Model 70XTR Featherweight,** Various Calibers, with Sights, *Modern*	300.00	400.00	380.00
☐ **Model 70XTR Sporter,** Various Calibers, *Modern*	225.00	325.00	310.00
☐ **Model 70XTR Super Express Magnum,** .375 H&H, *Modern*	360.00	500.00	485.00
☐ **Model 70XTR Super Express Magnum,** .458 Win., *Modern*	380.00	525.00	500.00
☐ **Model 70XTR Varmint,** Various Calibers, *Modern*	225.00	320.00	300.00
☐ **Model 70XTR Westerner,** Various Calibers, No Scope, *Modern*	180.00	275.00	265.00

	V.G.	Exc.	Prior Year Exc. Value
☐ **M72,** .22 L.R.R.F., Tube Feed, *Modern*	95.00	140.00	135.00
☐ **M75,** .22 L.R.R.F., Sporting Rifle, Clip Fed, *Modern*	200.00	290.00	285.00
☐ **M75 Target,** .22 L.R.R.F., Clip Fed, *Modern*	170.00	260.00	250.00
☐ **M99 Thumb Trigger,** Various Rimfires, Singleshot, *Modern*	180.00	350.00	335.00
☐ **Model 52 I.M.,** .22 L.R.R.F., Post '64, Heavy Barrel, Target Stock, *Modern*	395.00	580.00	565.00
☐ **Model 52 I.M.I.S.U.,** .22 L.R.R.F., Post '64, Heavy Barrel, Target Stock, *Modern*	430.00	635.00	620.00
☐ **Model 52 I.M. Kenyon,** .22 L.R.R.F., Post '64, Heavy Barrel, Target Stock, *Modern*	430.00	575.00	570.00
☐ **Model 52 International Prone,** .22 L.R.R.F., Post '64, Heavy Barrel, Target Stock, *Modern*	310.00	440.00	435.00
☐ **Model 52D,** .22 L.R.R.F., Post '64, Heavy Barrel, Target Stock, *Modern*	180.00	290.00	285.00
☐ **Model 670,** Various Calibers, Post '64, Scope Mounted, *Modern*	125.00	180.00	175.00
RIFLE, DOUBLE BARREL, SIDE-BY-SIDE			
☐ **Model 21,** .405 Win., Checkered Stock, Fancy Wood, *Modern*	7750.00	12900.00	12750.00
RIFLE, LEVER ACTION			
☐ **Henry,** .44 Henry, Brass Frame, Rifle, *Antique*	4000.00	6575.00	6300.00
☐ **Henry,** .44 Henry, Brass Frame, Military, Rifle, *Antique*	4200.00	7000.00	6800.00
☐ **Henry,** .44 Henry, Iron Frame, Rifle, *Antique*	5500.00	8500.00	8300.00
☐ **M 88,** Various Calibers, Clip Fed, Checkered Stock, Open Rear Sight, *Modern*	175.00	290.00	290.00
☐ **M1866,** .44 Henry, Musket, *Antique*	1150.00	1850.00	1800.00
☐ **M1866,** .44 Henry, Rifle, *Antique*	1300.00	2075.00	2000.00
☐ **M1866,** .44 Henry, Carbine, *Antique*	975.00	1700.00	1650.00
☐ **M1866 Improved Henry,** .44 Henry, Carbine, *Antique*	1000.00	1850.00	1800.00
☐ **M1866 Improved Henry,** .44 Henry, Rifle, *Antique*	1400.00	2250.00	2100.00
☐ **M1873,** Various Calibers, Rifle, *Modern*	650.00	1300.00	1300.00
☐ **M1873,** Various Calibers, Musket, *Modern*	750.00	1500.00	1500.00
☐ **M1873,** Various Calibers, Carbine, *Modern*	600.00	1150.00	1150.00
☐ **M1873 1 of 1,000,** Various Calibers, Rifle, *Antique*	6000.00	12000.00	12000.00
☐ **M1873,** For Deluxe, *Add* **$350.00-$500.00**			
☐ **M1873,** For Extra Fancy Deluxe, *Add* **$2,000.00-$5,000.00**			
☐ **M1873 Special,** under #525,299, Various Calibers, Sporting Rifle, *Antique*	1000.00	1850.00	1800.00
☐ **M1873 Special,** Various Calibers, Sporting Rifle, *Modern*	775.00	1650.00	1650.00
☐ **M1873,** under #525,299, Various Calibers, Musket, *Antique*	900.00	1500.00	1450.00
☐ **M1873,** under #525,299, Various Calibers, Carbine, *Antique*	745.00	1290.00	1250.00
☐ **M1873,** under #525,299, Various Calibers, Rifle, *Antique*	935.00	1475.00	1450.00
☐ **M1876,** Various Calibers, Carbine, *Antique*	850.00	1575.00	1550.00
☐ **M1876,** Various Calibers, Octagon Barrel, Rifle, *Antique*	725.00	1485.00	1350.00
☐ **M1876,** Various Calibers, Round Barrel, Rifle, *Antique*	725.00	1250.00	1200.00

	V.G.	Exc.	Prior Year Exc. Value
☐ **M1876,** Various Calibers, Musket, *Antique*	1475.00	2400.00	2300.00
☐ **M1876,** For Deluxe, *Add* **$400.00-$550.00**			
☐ **M1876,** For Extra Fancy Deluxe, *Add* **$2,000.00-$5,000.00**			
☐ **M1876 RCMP,** Various Calibers, Carbine, *Antique*	1000.00	1650.00	1575.00
☐ **M1886,** Various Calibers, Rifle, *Modern*	410.00	700.00	675.00
☐ **M1886,** Various Calibers, Carbine, *Modern*	620.00	925.00	900.00
☐ **M1886,** Various Calibers, Musket, *Modern*	675.00	1000.00	975.00
☐ **M1886,** For Deluxe, *Add* **$200.00-$400.00**			
☐ **M1886,** For Extra Fancy Deluxe, *Add* **$1,500.00-$3,500.00**			
☐ **M1886,** uner #118,443, Various Calibers, Musket, *Antique*	725.00	1250.00	1200.00
☐ **M1886,** under #118,443, Various Calibers, Rifle, *Antique*	500.00	825.00	800.00
☐ **M1886,** under #118,443, Various Calibers, Carbine, *Antique*	700.00	1200.00	1150.00
☐ **M150,** .22 L.R.R.F., Tube Feed, *Modern*	70.00	95.00	90.00
☐ **M250,** .22 L.R.R.F., Tube Feed, *Modern*	70.00	100.00	95.00
☐ **M250 Deluxe,** .22 L.R.R.F., Tube Feed, *Modern*	75.00	115.00	110.00
☐ **M255,** .22 WMR, Tube Feed, *Modern*	75.00	105.00	100.00
☐ **M255 Deluxe,** .22 WMR, Tube Feed, *Modern*	90.00	130.00	125.00
☐ **M53,** Various Calibers, *Modern*	440.00	750.00	700.00
☐ **M55,** Various Calibers, *Modern*	400.00	700.00	675.00
☐ **M64,** .219 Zipper, Pre'64, *Modern*	425.00	590.00	565.00
☐ **M64,** .30-30 Win., Late Model, *Modern*	130.00	220.00	210.00
☐ **M64,** Various Calibers, Pre'64, *Modern*	350.00	470.00	450.00
☐ **M64 Deer Rifle,** Various Calibers, Pre'64, *Modern*	380.00	510.00	495.00
☐ **M65,** .218 Bee, *Modern*	625.00	900.00	875.00
☐ **M65,** Various Calibers, *Modern*	390.00	590.00	565.00
☐ **M71,** .348 Win., Tube Feed, *Modern*	365.00	535.00	525.00
☐ **M71 Special,** .348 Win., Tube Feed, *Modern*	500.00	680.00	665.00
☐ **M92,** Various Calibers, Rifle, *Modern*	390.00	500.00	485.00
☐ **M92,** Various Calibers, Carbine, *Modern*	485.00	610.00	585.00
☐ **M92,** Various Calibers, Musket, *Modern*	525.00	750.00	725.00
☐ **M92,** For Takedown, *Add* **$150.00-$275.00**			
☐ **M92,** under #103316, Various Calibers, Rifle, *Antique*	425.00	600.00	575.00
☐ **M92,** under #103316, Various Calibers, Carbine, *Antique*	475.00	690.00	665.00
☐ **M92,** under #103316, Various Calibers, Musket, *Antique*	550.00	850.00	825.00
☐ **M94,** .30-30 Win., Carbine, Late Model, *Modern*	100.00	150.00	145.00
☐ **M94,** .44 Magnum, Carbine, *Modern*	175.00	300.00	290.00
☐ **M94,** Various Calibers, Carbine, Pre'64, *Modern*	290.00	460.00	445.00
☐ **M94,** Various Calibers, Carbine, Pre-War, *Modern*	330.00	530.00	515.00
☐ **M94,** Various Calibers, Rifle, Pre-War, *Modern*	370.00	590.00	565.00
☐ **M94,** Various Calibers, Rifle, Takedown, Pre-War, *Modern*	440.00	685.00	665.00
☐ **M94 Alaska Centennial,** .30-30 Win., Commemorative, Carbine, *Curio*	875.00	1475.00	1450.00
☐ **M94 Antique,** .30-30 Win., Carbine, *Modern*	70.00	115.00	110.00
☐ **Antlered Game,** .30-30 Win., Commemorative, *Modern*	310.00	430.00	425.00
☐ **M94 Bicentennial,** .30-30 Win., Commemorative, *Curio*	465.00	700.00	695.00

	V.G.	Exc.	Prior Year Exc. Value
☐ **M94 Buffalo Bill 1 of 300,** .30-30 Win., Commemorative, Rifle, *Curio*	835.00	1400.00	1450.00
☐ **M94 Buffalo Bill,** .30-30 Win., Commemorative, Rifle, *Curio*	190.00	270.00	290.00
☐ **M94 Buffalo Bill,** .30-30 Win., Commemorative, Carbine, *Curio*	190.00	270.00	290.00
☐ **M94 Buffalo Bill Set,** .30-30 Win., Commemorative, *Curio*	465.00	610.00	625.00
☐ **M94 Canadian Centennial,** .30-30 Win., Commemorative, Rifle, *Curio*	190.00	275.00	290.00
☐ **M94 Canadian Centennial,** .30-30 Win., Commemorative, Carbine, *Curio*	190.00	275.00	290.00
☐ **M94 Canadian Centennial Set,** .30-30 Win., Commemorative, *Curio*	435.00	615.00	635.00
☐ **M94 Centennial 66,** .30-30 Win., Commemorative, Rifle, *Curio*	215.00	340.00	365.00
☐ **M94 Centennial 66,** .30-30 Win., Commemorative, Carbine, *Curio*	215.00	330.00	350.00
☐ **M94 Centennial 66 Set,** .30-30 Win., Commemorative, *Curio*	500.00	690.00	750.00
☐ **M94 Classic,** .30-30 Win., Carbine, *Modern*	115.00	185.00	200.00
☐ **M94 Classic,** .30-30 Win., Rifle, *Modern*	115.00	185.00	200.00
☐ **M94 Cowboy 1 of 300,** .30-30 Win., Commemorative, Carbine, *Curio*	900.00	1700.00	1735.00
☐ **M94 Cowboy,** .30-30 Win., Commemorative, Carbine, *Curio*	275.00	400.00	425.00
☐ **M94 Deluxe,** Various Calibers, Pre-War, *Modern*	700.00	1000.00	1000.00
☐ **Duke,** .32-40 Win., Commemorative, *Modern*	1420.00	2000.00	2250.00
☐ **M94 Golden Spike,** .30-30 Win., Commemorative, Carbine, *Curio*	215.00	300.00	325.00
☐ **M94 Illinois,** .30-30 Win., Commemorative, Carbine, *Curio*	190.00	265.00	295.00
☐ **John Wayne,** .32-40 Win., Commemorative, *Modern*	435.00	580.00	600.00
☐ **M94 Klondike,** .30-30 Win., Commemorative, *Curio*	285.00	400.00	425.00
☐ **Legendary Frontiersman,** .38-55 Win., Commemorative, *Modern*	285.00	400.00	425.00
☐ **Legendary Lawman,** .30-30 Win., Commemorative, *Modern*	285.00	400.00	425.00
☐ **Limited Edition I,** .30-30 Win., Commemorative, *Modern*	930.00	1675.00	1750.00
☐ **Limited Edition II,** .30-30 Win., Commemorative, *Modern*	930.00	1675.00	1750.00
☐ **M94 Lone Star,** .30-30 Win., Commemorative, Rifle, *Curio*	225.00	330.00	350.00
☐ **M94 Lone Star,** .30-30 Win., Commemorative, Carbine, *Curio*	225.00	330.00	350.00
☐ **M94 Lone Star Set,** .30-30 Win., Commemorative, *Curio*	520.00	725.00	750.00
☐ **M94 Nebraska Centennial,** .30-30 Win., Commemorative, Carbine, *Curio*	715.00	1200.00	1250.00
☐ **M94 NRA,** .30-30 Win., Commemorative, Musket, *Curio*	190.00	280.00	295.00
☐ **M94 NRA,** .30-30 Win., Commemorative, Rifle, *Curio*	190.00	270.00	295.00

	V.G.	Exc.	Prior Year Exc. Value
☐ **M94 NRA Set,** .30-30 Win., Commemorative, *Curio*	450.00	600.00	625.00
☐ **Oliver Winchester,** .38-55 Win., Commemorative, *Modern*	380.00	500.00	525.00
☐ **M94 RCMP,** .30-30 Win., Commemorative, *Curio*	380.00	615.00	650.00
☐ **M94 Texas Ranger,** .30-30 Win., Commemorative, *Curio*	380.00	500.00	525.00
☐ **M94 Theodore Roosevelt,** .30-30 Win., Commemorative, Rifle, *Curio*	215.00	310.00	325.00
☐ **M94 Theodore Roosevelt,** .30-30 Win., Commemorative, Carbine, *Curio*	215.00	310.00	325.00
☐ **M94 Theodore Roosevelt Set,** .30-30 Win., Commemorative, *Curio*	500.00	675.00	700.00
☐ **U.S. Border Patrol,** .30-30 Win., Commemorative, *Modern*	650.00	900.00	950.00
☐ **Wells Fargo,** .30-30 Win., Commemorative, *Modern*	430.00	580.00	595.00
☐ **M94 Wyoming Diamond Jubilee,** .30-30 Win., Commemorative, Carbine, *Curio*	800.00	1375.00	1450.00
☐ **M94,** under #50,000 Various Calibers, Carbine, *Antique*	415.00	600.00	575.00
☐ **M94,** under #50,000, Various Calibers, Rifle, *Antique*	435.00	675.00	650.00
☐ **M94XTR,** .30-30 Win., *Modern*	135.00	185.00	180.00
☐ **M94 Standard,** .30-30 Win., *Modern*	125.00	175.00	170.00
☐ **M94 Antique,** .30-30 Win., *Modern*	135.00	185.00	180.00
☐ **M94 Trapper,** .30-30 Win., *Modern*	125.00	170.00	165.00
☐ **M94XTR Big Bore,** .375 Win., *Modern*	150.00	210.00	200.00
☐ **M95,** Various Calibers, Rifle, *Modern*	490.00	700.00	675.00
☐ **M95,** Various Calibers, Carbine, *Modern*	600.00	820.00	795.00
☐ **M95,** Various Calibers, Musket, *Modern*	610.00	900.00	875.00
☐ **M95,** For Takedown, *Add* **$100.00-$200.00**			
☐ **M95,** under #19,477, Various Calibers, Rifle, *Antique*	570.00	900.00	875.00
☐ **M95,** under #19,477, Various Calibers, Carbine, *Antique*	710.00	1050.00	1000.00
☐ **Model 9422,** .22 L.R.R.F., Tube Feed, *Modern*	120.00	170.00	165.00
☐ **Model 9422M,** .22 WMR, Tube Feed, *Modern*	130.00	185.00	180.00
☐ **Model 9422XTR,** .22 L.R.R.F., Tube Feed, *Modern*	140.00	210.00	200.00
☐ **Model 9422MXTR,** .22 WMR, Tube Feed, *Modern*	170.00	230.00	220.00

RIFLE, SEMI-AUTOMATIC

	V.G.	Exc.	Prior Year Exc. Value
☐ **M100,** Various Calibers, Clip Fed, *Modern*	235.00	395.00	380.00
☐ **M100,** Various Calibers, Clip Fed, Carbine, *Modern*	240.00	380.00	375.00
☐ **M1903,** .22 Win. Auto R.F., Tube Feed, *Modern*	200.00	330.00	325.00
☐ **M1905,** Various Calibers, Clip Fed, *Modern*	350.00	560.00	540.00
☐ **M1907,** .351 Win. Self-Loading, Clip Fed, *Modern*	300.00	460.00	450.00
☐ **M1907 Police,** .351 Win. Self-Loading, Clip Fed, *Modern*	335.00	515.00	495.00
☐ **M1910,** .401 Win. Self-Loading, Clip Fed, *Modern*	310.00	465.00	450.00
☐ **M190,** .22 L.R.R.F., Tube Feed, *Modern*	47.00	70.00	65.00
☐ **M190 Deluxe,** .22 L.R.R.F., Tube Feed, *Modern*	52.00	80.00	75.00
☐ **M290,** .22 L.R.R.F., Tube Feed, *Modern*	58.00	90.00	85.00

	V.G.	Exc.	Prior Year Exc. Value
☐ **M290,** .22 L.R.R.F., Tube Feed, Checkered Stock, *Modern*	63.00	100.00	95.00
☐ **M290 Deluxe,** .22 L.R.R.F., Tube Feed, Monte Carlo Stock, *Modern*	75.00	105.00	100.00
☐ **M490 Deluxe,** .22 L.R.R.F., Clip Fed, Monte Carlo Stock, *Modern*	170.00	265.00	250.00
☐ **M55 Automatic,** .22 L.R.R.F., *Modern*	95.00	150.00	145.00
☐ **M63,** .22 L.R.R.F., Tube Feed, *Modern*	325.00	450.00	440.00
☐ **M74,** .22 L.R.R.F., Clip Fed, *Modern*	120.00	190.00	185.00
☐ **M77,** .22 L.R.R.F., Clip Fed, *Modern*	80.00	125.00	120.00
☐ **M77,** .22 L.R.R.F., Tube Feed, *Modern*	80.00	125.00	120.00
RIFLE, SINGLESHOT			
☐ **Model 310,** .22 L.R.R.F., Bolt Action, *Modern*	50.00	80.00	75.00
☐ **High-Wall,** Various Calibers, Sporting Rifle, *Curio*	375.00	590.00	550.00
☐ **High-Wall,** Various Calibers, Sporting Rifle, Takedown, *Curio*	530.00	750.00	700.00
☐ **High-Wall,** Various Calibers, Schutzen Rifle, Takedown, *Curio*	1075.00	1700.00	1650.00
☐ **High-Wall,** Various Calibers, Schutzen Rifle, *Curio*	925.00	1300.00	1250.00
☐ **Low-Wall,** .22 Long R.F., Musket, *Curio*	275.00	390.00	375.00
☐ **Low-Wall,** Various Calibers, Sporting Rifle, *Curio*	300.00	410.00	385.00
☐ **Winder,** .22 Long R.F., Musket, Takedown, *Curio*	370.00	525.00	500.00
☐ **Winder,** .22 Long R.F., Musket, *Curio*	310.00	450.00	425.00
RIFLE, SLIDE ACTION			
☐ **M1890,** Various Rimfires, *Modern*	240.00	360.00	350.00
☐ **M1890,** Various Rimfires, Solid Frame, *Curio*	265.00	375.00	365.00
☐ **M1890,** under #64,521, Various Rimfires, *Antique*	300.00	450.00	425.00
☐ **M1906,** .22 L.R.R.F., Tube Feed, Hammer, *Modern*	260.00	400.00	390.00
☐ **M270,** .22 L.R.R.F., Tube Feed, *Modern*	65.00	95.00	90.00
☐ **M270 Deluxe,** .22 L.R.R.F., Tube Feed, *Modern*	80.00	120.00	115.00
☐ **M275,** .22 WMR, Tube Feed, *Modern*	75.00	105.00	100.00
☐ **M275 Deluxe,** .22 WMR, Tube Feed, *Modern*	90.00	135.00	130.00
☐ **M61,** .22 L.R.R.F., Tube Feed, *Modern*	265.00	400.00	385.00
☐ **M61,** Various Rimfires, Tube Feed, Octagon Barrel, *Modern*	330.00	465.00	450.00
☐ **M61 Magnum,** .22 WMR, Tube Feed, *Modern*	330.00	485.00	470.00
☐ **M62,** .22 L.R.R.F., Tube Feed, Hammer, *Modern*	270.00	400.00	390.00
☐ **M62 Gallery,** .22 Short R.F., Tube Feed, Hammer, *Modern*	290.00	435.00	420.00
SHOTGUN, BOLT ACTION			
☐ **Model 36,** 9mm Shotshell, Takedown, Singleshot, *Curio*	150.00	235.00	225.00
☐ **Model 41,** .410 Ga., Takedown, Singleshot, *Modern*	140.00	225.00	220.00
☐ **Model 41,** .410 Ga., Takedown, Singleshot, Checkered Stock, *Modern*	155.00	260.00	250.00
SHOTGUN, DOUBLE BARREL, OVER-UNDER			
☐ **Model 101,** 12 Ga., Trap Grade, Monte Carlo Stock, Single Trigger, Automatic Ejector, Engraved, *Modern*	600.00	790.00	775.00
☐ **Model 101,** 12 Ga., Trap Grade, Single Trigger, Automatic Ejector, Checkered Stock, Engraved, *Modern*	600.00	790.00	775.00

	V.G.	Exc.	Prior Year Exc. Value
☐ **Model 101,** 12 Ga. Mag. 3″, Vent Rib, Single Trigger, Automatic Ejector, Checkered Stock, Engraved, *Modern*	565.00	775.00	725.00
☐ **Model 101,** Various Gauges, Skeet Grade, Single Trigger, Automatic Ejector, Checkered Stock, Engraved, *Modern*	585.00	790.00	775.00
☐ **Model 101,** Various Gauges, Featherweight, Single Trigger, Automatic Ejector, Checkered Stock, Engraved, *Modern*	585.00	790.00	775.00
☐ **Model 101 3 Ga. Set,** Various Gauges, Skeet Grade, Single Trigger, Automatic Ejector, Checkered Stock, Engraved, *Modern*	1120.00	1750.00	1700.00
☐ **Model 101,** 12 Ga., Field Grade, Single Trigger, Automatic Ejector, Engraved, *Modern*	535.00	775.00	750.00
☐ **Model 101 Pigeon,** 12 Ga., Trap Grade, Single Trigger, Automatic Ejector, Engraved, *Modern*	535.00	775.00	750.00
☐ **Model 101 Pigeon,** 12 Ga., Trap Grade, Monte Carlo Stock, Single Trigger, Automatic Ejector, Engraved, *Modern*	535.00	775.00	750.00
☐ **Model 101 Pigeon,** 12 and 20 Gauges, Skeet Grade, Checkered Stock, Single Trigger, Automatic Ejector, Engraved, *Modern*	600.00	850.00	825.00
☐ **Model 101 Magnum,** 12 Ga. 3″, Single Trigger, Automatic Ejector, Engraved, *Modern*	600.00	795.00	775.00
☐ **Model 96,** 12 Ga., Trap Grade, Checkered Stock, Vent Rib, *Modern*	430.00	610.00	595.00
☐ **Model 96,** 12 Ga., Trap Grade, Monte Carlo Stock, Vent Rib, *Modern*	430.00	610.00	595.00
☐ **Model 96,** 12 and 20 Gauges, Field Grade, Checkered Stock, Vent Rib, *Modern*	400.00	595.00	585.00
☐ **Model 96,** 12 and 20 Gauges, Skeet Grade, Checkered Stock, Vent Rib, *Modern*	415.00	610.00	590.00
☐ **Xpert,** 12 Ga., Trap Grade, Checkered Stock, Vent Rib, *Modern*	425.00	615.00	595.00
☐ **Xpert,** 12 Ga., Trap Grade, Monte Carlo Stock, Vent Rib, *Modern*	425.00	615.00	595.00
☐ **Xpert,** 12 and 20 Gauges, Field Grade, Checkered Stock, Vent Rib, *Modern*	400.00	595.00	580.00
☐ **Xpert,** 12 and 20 Gauges, Skeet Grade, Checkered Stock, Vent Rib, *Modern*	420.00	615.00	590.00
SHOTGUN, DOUBLE BARREL, SIDE-BY-SIDE			
☐ **Model 21,** For Extra Barrels, *Add* **25%-30%**			
☐ **Model 21,** For Vent Rib, *Add* **$350.00-$400.00**			
☐ **Model 21,** 410 Ga., Checkered Stock, Fancy Wood, *Modern*	4500.00	7500.00	7500.00
☐ **Model 21,** 12 Ga., Trap Grade, Hammerless, Single Selective Trigger, Selective Ejector, Vent Rib, *Modern*	2900.00	4250.00	4250.00
☐ **Model 21,** 12 Ga., Trap Grade, Hammerless, Single Selective Trigger, Selective Ejector, Raised Matted Rib, *Modern*	2700.00	4000.00	4000.00
☐ **Model 21,** 12 and 16 Gauges, Skeet Grade, Hammerless, Single Selective Trigger, Selective Ejector, Vent Rib, *Modern*	2800.00	4000.00	4000.00
☐ **Model 21,** 12 and 16 Gauges, Skeet Grade, Hammerless, Single Selective Trigger, Selective Ejector, Raised Matted Rib, *Modern*	2900.00	4250.00	4250.00

	V.G.	Exc.	Prior Year Exc. Value
☐ **Model 21,** 12 and 16 Gauges, Field Grade, Double Trigger, Automatic Ejector, Hammerless, *Modern*	2250.00	3400.00	3400.00
☐ **Model 21,** 12 and 16 Gauges, Field Grade, Double Trigger, Automatic Ejector, Hammerless, *Modern*	2450.00	3550.00	3550.00
☐ **Model 21,** 12 and 16 Gauges, Field Grade, Single Selective Trigger, Automatic Ejector, Hammerless, *Modern*	2450.00	3700.00	3700.00
☐ **Model 21,** 12 and 16 Gauges, Field Grade, Single Selective Trigger, Selective Ejector, Hammerless, *Modern*	2500.00	3700.00	3700.00
☐ **Model 21,** 20 Ga., Skeet Grade, Hammerless, Single Selective Trigger, Selective Ejector, Vent Rib, *Modern*	2950.00	4550.00	4550.00
☐ **Model 21,** 20 Ga., Skeet Grade, Hammerless, Single Selective Trigger, Selective Ejector, Raised Matted Rib, *Modern*	2800.00	4300.00	4300.00
☐ **Model 21,** 20 Ga., Field Grade, Double Trigger, Automatic Ejector, Hammerless, *Modern*	2500.00	3700.00	3700.00
☐ **Model 21,** 20 Ga., Field Grade, Double Trigger, Selective Ejector, Hammerless, *Modern*	2650.00	3900.00	3900.00
☐ **Model 21,** 20 Ga., Field Grade, Single Selective Trigger, Automatic Ejector, Hammerless, *Modern*	2700.00	4000.00	4000.00
☐ **Model 21,** 20 Ga., Field Grade, Single Selective Trigger, Selective Ejector, Hammerless, *Modern*	2900.00	4100.00	4100.00
☐ **Model 21 Custom,** 12 Ga., Hammerless, Single Selective Trigger, Selective Ejector, Fancy Engraving, Fancy Checkering, *Modern*	4500.00	6000.00	6000.00
☐ **Model 21 Custom,** 20 Ga., Hammerless, Single Selective Trigger, Selective Ejector, Fancy Checkering, Fancy Engraving, *Modern*	4750.00	6750.00	6750.00
☐ **Model 21 Duck,** 12 Ga. Mag. 3″, Hammerless, Single Selective Trigger, Selective Ejector, Raised Matted Rib, *Modern*	2000.00	3900.00	3900.00
☐ **Model 21 Duck,** 12 Ga. Mag. 3″, Hammerless, Single Selective Trigger, Selective Ejector, Vent Rib, *Modern*	2500.00	3950.00	3950.00
☐ **Model 21 Grand American,** 12 Ga., Hammerless, Single Selective Trigger, Selective Ejector, Fancy Engraving, Fancy Checkering, *Modern*	6500.00	9750.00	9750.00
☐ **Model 21 Grand American,** 20 Ga., Hammerless, Single Selective Trigger, Selective Ejector, Fancy Checkering, Fancy Engraving, *Modern*	7000.00	10500.00	10500.00
☐ **Model 21 Pigeon,** 12 Ga., Hammerless, Single Selective Trigger, Selective Ejector, Fancy Engraving, Fancy Checkering, *Modern*	4500.00	6250.00	6250.00
☐ **Model 21 Pigeon,** 12 Ga., Hammerless, Single Selective Trigger, Selective Ejector, Fancy Engraving, Fancy Checkering, *Modern*	4800.00	7000.00	7000.00
☐ **Model 23 English,** 12 or 20 Gauges, Hammerless, Single Trigger, Selective Ejector, Fancy Checkering, Engraved, *Modern*	615.00	865.00	865.00
☐ **Model 23 Pigeon,** 12 or 20 Gauges, Hammerless, Single Trigger, Selective Ejector, Engraved, Fancy Checkering, *Modern*	560.00	825.00	825.00
☐ **Model 23 Grand European,** 12 Ga., Hammerless, Single Selective Trigger, Selective Ejector, Fancy Engraving, Fancy Checkering, *Modern*	775.00	1250.00	1250.00

	V.G.	Exc.	Prior Year Exc. Value
☐ **Model 24,** Various Gauges, Double Trigger, Automatic Ejector, *Modern*	255.00	350.00	345.00
SHOTGUN, LEVER ACTION			
☐ **M 1887,** Various Gauges, *Antique*	410.00	565.00	500.00
☐ **M 1887,** Deluxe Grade, Various Gauges, *Antique*	435.00	615.00	585.00
☐ **M 1901,** 10 Ga., 2⅞, Tube Feed, Damascus Barrel, *Curio*	350.00	500.00	480.00
☐ **M 1887,** 10 Ga., 2⅞, Tube Feed, Checkered Stock, Damascus Barrel, *Curio*	385.00	535.00	520.00
☐ **M 1887,** 10 Ga., 2⅞, Tube Feed, Plain, *Curio*	350.00	460.00	435.00
☐ **M 1887,** 12 Ga. Damascus Barrel, Checkered Stock, Tube Feed, *Curio*	435.00	600.00	540.00
☐ **M 1887,** 12 Ga., Tube Feed, Plain, *Curio*	380.00	500.00	465.00
☐ **M 1887,** under #64842, 10 Ga., 2⅞, Tube Feed, Plain, *Antique*	400.00	510.00	475.00
☐ **M 1887,** under #64842, 12 Ga., Tube Feed, Plain, *Antique*	415.00	535.00	495.00
☐ **M 1887,** under #64842, Tube Feed, Damascus Barrel, Checkered Stock, *Antique*	500.00	625.00	585.00
☐ **1901,** 10 Ga., 2⅞, Tube Feed, Plain, *Curio*	375.00	580.00	545.00
SHOTGUN, SEMI-AUTOMATIC			
☐ **Model 1400 Trap,** 12 Ga., Vent Rib, *Modern*	185.00	270.00	260.00
☐ **Model 1400 Trap,** 12 Ga., Monte Carlo Stock, Vent Rib, *Modern*	205.00	295.00	280.00
☐ **Model 1400 Trap,** 12 Ga., Vent Rib, Recoil Reducer, *Modern*	225.00	325.00	315.00
☐ **Model 1400 Skeet,** 12 and 20 Gauges, Vent Rib, *Modern*	185.00	270.00	260.00
☐ **Model 1400 Deer,** 12 Ga., Open Sights, Slug Gun, *Modern*	170.00	235.00	230.00
☐ **Model 1400 Field,** 12 and 20 Gauges, Winchoke, *Modern*	155.00	220.00	215.00
☐ **Model 1400 Field,** 12 and 20 Gauges, Winchoke, Vent Rib, *Modern*	170.00	235.00	230.00
☐ **Model 1400 Mk. II Trap,** 12 Ga., Vent Rib, *Modern*	185.00	275.00	260.00
☐ **Model 1400 Mk. II Trap,** 12 Ga., Monte Carlo Stock, Vent Rib, *Modern*	205.00	295.00	280.00
☐ **Model 1400 Mk. II Trap,** 12 Ga., Vent Rib, Recoil Reducer, *Modern*	225.00	330.00	315.00
☐ **Model 1400 Mk. II Skeet,** 12 and 20 Gauges, Vent Rib, *Modern*	185.00	275.00	260.00
☐ **Model 1400 Mk. II Deer,** 12 Ga., Open Sights, Slug Gun, *Modern*	170.00	235.00	230.00
☐ **Model 1400 Mk. II Field,** 12 and 20 Gauges, Winchoke, *Modern*	155.00	220.00	215.00
☐ **Model 1400 Mk. II Field,** 12 and 20 Gauges, Winchoke, Vent Rib, *Modern*	170.00	245.00	235.00
☐ **Model 1500,** 12 or 20 Gauges, Field Grade, Plain, *Modern*	215.00	295.00	290.00
☐ **Model 1500,** 12 or 20 Gauges, Field Grade, Vent Rib, *Modern*	230.00	320.00	315.00
☐ **Model 1911,** 12 Ga., Takedown, Plain, *Modern*	250.00	340.00	335.00
☐ **Model 1911,** 12 Ga., Takedown, Checkered Stock, *Modern*	275.00	410.00	400.00
☐ **Model 40,** 12 Ga., Takedown, Field Grade, *Modern*	240.00	350.00	340.00

	V.G.	Exc.	Prior Year Exc. Value
☐ **Model 40,** 12 Ga., Takedown, Skeet Grade, Adjustable Choke, *Modern*	290.00	400.00	390.00
☐ **Model 50,** 12 Ga., Trap Grade, Vent Rib, Monte Carlo Stock, *Modern*	350.00	485.00	470.00
☐ **Model 50,** 12 and 20 Gauges, Field Grade, Plain Barrel, Checkered Stock, *Modern*	225.00	300.00	295.00
☐ **Model 50,** 12 and 20 Gauges, Field Grade, Vent Rib, Checkered Stock, *Modern*	235.00	335.00	320.00
☐ **Model 50,** 12 and 20 Gauges, Skeet Grade, Vent Rib, Checkered Stock, *Modern*	310.00	450.00	440.00
SHOTGUN, SINGLESHOT			
☐ **Model 101,** 12 Ga., Trap Grade, Vent Rib, *Modern*	375.00	490.00	475.00
☐ **Model 20,** .410 Ga., 2⅛", Takedown, Hammer, Checkered Stock, *Modern*	175.00	270.00	265.00
☐ **Model 37,** For Red Letter, *Add* **25%-40%**			
☐ **Model 37,** .410 Ga., Takedown, Automatic Ejector, Plain Barrel, *Modern*	100.00	140.00	135.00
☐ **Model 37,** 12 Ga., Takedown, Automatic Ejector, Plain Barrel, *Modern*	85.00	125.00	120.00
☐ **Model 37,** 16 Ga., Takedown, Automatic Ejector, Plain Barrel, *Modern*	75.00	115.00	110.00
☐ **Model 37,** 20 Ga., Takedown, Automatic Ejector, Plain Barrel, *Modern*	90.00	135.00	130.00
☐ **Model 37,** 28 Ga., Takedown, Automatic Ejector, Plain Barrel, *Modern*	115.00	165.00	160.00
☐ **Model 37A,** Various Gauges, *Modern*	53.00	75.00	70.00
☐ **Model 37A Youth,** Various Gauges, *Modern*	53.00	75.00	70.00
☐ **Model 37 Youth,** Takedown, Automatic Ejector, Plain Barrel, *Modern*	48.00	70.00	65.00
☐ **High Wall,** 20 Ga., Falling Block, Plain, *Curio*	450.00	730.00	700.00
SHOTGUN, SLIDE ACTION			
☐ **Model 12,** 12 Ga., Pre'64, Takedown, Trap Grade, Raised Matted Rib, *Modern*	495.00	750.00	725.00
☐ **Model 12,** 12 Ga., Pre'64, Takedown, Trap Grade, Vent Rib, *Modern*	550.00	830.00	800.00
☐ **Model 12,** 12 Ga., Pre'64, Takedown, Trap Grade, Vent Rib, Monte Carlo Stock, *Modern*	600.00	875.00	850.00
☐ **Model 12,** 12 Ga., Pre-War, Takedown, Vent Rib, *Modern*	490.00	575.00	550.00
☐ **Model 12,** 12 Ga., Pre-War, Takedown, Riot Gun, *Modern*	265.00	420.00	400.00
☐ **Model 12,** 12 Ga., Post '64, Trap Grade, Checkered Stock, *Modern*	435.00	575.00	550.00
☐ **Model 12,** 12 Ga., Post '64, Trap Gun, Monte Carlo Stock, *Modern*	435.00	575.00	550.00
☐ **Model 12,** Various Gauges, Pre'64, Takedown, Skeet Grade, Raised Matted Rib, *Modern*	435.00	700.00	675.00
☐ **Model 12,** Various Gauges, Pre'64, Takedown, Skeet Grade, Vent Rib, *Modern*	490.00	750.00	730.00
☐ **Model 12,** Various Gauges, Pre'64, Takedown, Skeet Grade, Plain Barrel, *Modern*	410.00	675.00	650.00
☐ **Model 12,** Various Gauges, Pre'64, Takedown, Skeet Grade, Plain Barrel, Adjustable Choke, *Modern*	435.00	710.00	680.00
☐ **Model 12,** Various Gauges, Pre'64, Takedown, Raised Matted Rib, *Modern*	435.00	645.00	625.00

	V.G.	Exc.	Prior Year Exc. Value
☐ **Model 12,** Featherweight, Various Gauges, Pre'64, Takedown, *Modern*	410.00	625.00	600.00
☐ **Model 12,** Heavy Duck, 12 Ga. Mag. 3″, Pre'64, Takedown, Vent Rib, *Modern*	420.00	675.00	650.00
☐ **Model 12,** Heavy Duck, 12 Ga. Mag. 3″, Pre'64, Takedown, Raised Matted Rib, *Modern*	430.00	650.00	625.00
☐ **Model 12,** Pigeon Grade, 12 Ga., Pre'64, Takedown, Trap Grade, Vent Rib, *Modern*	850.00	1350.00	1300.00
☐ **Model 12,** Pigeon Grade, 12 Ga., Pre'64, Takedown, Trap Grade, Raised Matted Rib, *Modern*	800.00	1200.00	1150.00
☐ **Model 12,** Pigeon Grade, 12 Ga., Various Gauges, Pre'64, Takedown, Skeet Grade, Raised Matted Rib, *Modern*	670.00	1075.00	1025.00
☐ **Model 12,** Pigeon Grade, Various Gauges, Pre'64, Takedown, Skeet Grade, Vent Rib, *Modern*	790.00	1175.00	1150.00
☐ **Model 12,** Pigeon Grade, Various Gauges, Pre'64, Takedown, Skeet Grade, Plain Barrel, Adjustable Choke, *Modern*	615.00	975.00	940.00
☐ **Model 12,** Pigeon Grade, Various Gauges, Pre'64, Takedown, Field Grade, Plain Barrel, *Modern*	615.00	920.00	900.00
☐ **Model 12,** Pigeon Grade, Various Gauges, Pre'64, Takedown, Field Grade, Vent Rib, *Modern*	670.00	1000.00	965.00
☐ **Model 12,** Standard, Various Gauges, Pre'64, Takedown, *Modern*	390.00	565.00	535.00
☐ **Model 12,** Super Pigeon, 12 Ga., Post'64, Takedown, Vent Rib, Engraved, Checkered Stock, *Modern*	1275.00	2100.00	2000.00
☐ **Model 1200,** For Recoil Reducer, *Add* **$35.00-$50.00**			
☐ **Model 1200 Field,** 12 and 20 Gauges, Adjustable Choke, *Modern*	130.00	170.00	165.00
☐ **Model 1200 Field,** 12 and 20 Gauges, Adjustable Choke, Vent Rib, *Modern*	135.00	175.00	170.00
☐ **Model 1200 Field,** 12 and 20 Gauges, *Modern*	115.00	150.00	145.00
☐ **Model 1200 Field,** 12 and 20 Gauges, Vent Rib, *Modern*	125.00	160.00	155.00
☐ **Model 1200 Field,** 12 Ga. Mag. 3″, *Modern*	130.00	170.00	165.00
☐ **Model 1200 Field,** 12 Ga. Mag. 3″, Vent Rib, *Modern*	140.00	180.00	175.00
☐ **Model 1200 Deer,** 12 Ga., Open Sights, *Modern*	130.00	175.00	170.00
☐ **Model 1200 Riot,** 12 Ga., *Modern*	115.00	160.00	155.00
☐ **Model 1200 Defender,** 12 Ga., *Modern*	125.00	165.00	160.00
☐ **Model 1200 Police,** 12 Ga., *Modern*	175.00	265.00	250.00
☐ **Model 1200 Stainless,** 12 Ga., *Modern*	175.00	270.00	255.00
☐ **Model 1300,** 12 or 20 Gauges, Plain Barrel, *Modern*	145.00	195.00	190.00
☐ **Model 1300,** 12 or 20 Gauges, Vent Rib, *Modern*	160.00	215.00	210.00
☐ **Model 1300,** 12 or 20 Gauges, Plain Barrel, Winchoke, *Modern*	165.00	230.00	225.00
☐ **Model 1300,** 12 or 20 Gauges, Vent Rib, Winchoke, *Modern*	180.00	265.00	250.00
☐ **Model 1300 Deer,** 12 Ga., Open Sights, *Modern*	175.00	240.00	235.00
☐ **Model 25,** 12 Ga., Solid Frame, Plain Barrel, *Modern*	180.00	265.00	250.00
☐ **Model 25,** 12 Ga., Solid Frame, Riot Gun, *Modern*	165.00	230.00	225.00

	V.G.	Exc.	Prior Year Exc. Value
☐ **Model 42,** .410 Ga., Field Grade, Takedown, *Modern*	485.00	685.00	675.00
☐ **Model 42,** .410 Ga., Field Grade, Takedown, Raised Matted Rib, *Modern*	540.00	735.00	725.00
☐ **Model 42,** .410 Ga., Skeet Grade, Takedown, Raised Matted Rib, *Modern*	635.00	865.00	850.00
☐ **Model 42 Deluxe,** .410 Ga., Takedown, Vent Rib, Fancy Checkering, Fancy Wood, *Modern*	690.00	975.00	950.00
☐ **Model 97,** 12 Ga., Solid Frame, Plain, *Modern*	190.00	260.00	250.00
☐ **Model 97,** 12 Ga., Takedown, Plain, *Modern*	230.00	330.00	315.00
☐ **Model 97,** 12 Ga., Takedown, Riot Gun, *Modern*	270.00	365.00	350.00
☐ **Model 97,** 12 Ga., Solid Frame, Riot Gun, *Modern*	230.00	320.00	315.00
☐ **Model 97,** 16 Ga., Solid Frame, Plain, *Modern*	165.00	235.00	225.00
☐ **Model 97,** 16 Ga., Takedown, Plain, *Modern*	185.00	265.00	250.00
☐ **Model 97 Pigeon,** 12 Ga., Takedown, Checkered, *Modern*	750.00	1175.00	1150.00
☐ **Model 97 Tournament,** 12 Ga., Takedown, Checkered Stock, *Modern*	500.00	735.00	725.00
☐ **Model 97 Trap,** 12 Ga., Takedown, Checkered Stock, *Modern*	415.00	580.00	565.00
☐ **Model 97 Trench,** 12 Ga., Solid Frame, Riot Gun, Military, *Curio*	335.00	460.00	450.00
☐ **Model 97 Trench,** 12 Ga., Solid Frame, Riot Gun, Military, with Bayonet, *Curio*	395.00	535.00	525.00

WINFIELD ARMS CO.

Made by Norwich Falls Pistol Co., c. 1880.

HANDGUN, REVOLVER

	V.G.	Exc.	Prior Year Exc. Value
☐ **.32 Short R.F.**, 5 Shot, Spur Trigger, Solid Frame, Single Action, *Antique*	95.00	165.00	160.00

WINFIELD ARMS CO.

Made by Crescent, c. 1900.

SHOTGUN, DOUBLE BARREL, SIDE-BY-SIDE

	V.G.	Exc.	Prior Year Exc. Value
☐ **Various Gauges**, Outside Hammers, Damascus Barrel, *Modern*	100.00	170.00	175.00
☐ **Various Gauges**, Hammerless, Steel Barrel, *Modern*	135.00	190.00	200.00
☐ **Various Gauges**, Hammerless, Damascus Barrel, *Modern*	100.00	170.00	175.00
☐ **Various Gauges**, Outside Hammers, Steel Barrel, *Modern*	125.00	185.00	190.00

SHOTGUN, SINGLESHOT

	V.G.	Exc.	Prior Year Exc. Value
☐ **Various Gauges**, Hammer, Steel Barrel, *Modern*	55.00	85.00	85.00

WINGERT, RICHARD

Lancaster, Pa. 1775-1777. See Kentucky Rifles, U.S. Military.

WINOCA ARMS CO.

Made by Crescent for Jacobi Hardware Co., Philadelphia, Pa.

SHOTGUN, DOUBLE BARREL, SIDE-BY-SIDE

	V.G.	Exc.	Prior Year Exc. Value
☐ **Various Gauges**, Outside Hammers, Damascus Barrel, *Modern*	100.00	170.00	175.00

	V.G.	Exc.	Prior Year Exc. Value
☐ **Various Gauges**, Hammerless, Steel Barrel, *Modern*	135.00	190.00	200.00
☐ **Various Gauges**, Hammerless, Damascus Barrel, *Modern*	100.00	170.00	175.00
☐ **Various Gauges**, Outside Hammers, Steel Barrel, *Modern*	125.00	185.00	190.00
SHOTGUN, SINGLESHOT			
☐ **Various Gauges**, Hammer, Steel Barrel, *Modern*	55.00	85.00	85.00

WINSLOW ARMS CO.

Established in Venice, Fla. about 1962, moved to Osprey, Fla. about 1976, and is now in Camden, S.C.

	V.G.	Exc.	Prior Year Exc. Value
RIFLE, BOLT ACTION			
☐ **For Left-Hand Act,** *Add $50.00-$70.00*			
☐ **Crown**, Various Calibers, Carved, Fancy Wood, Inlays, *Modern*	750.00	1,125.00	1,100.00
☐ **Emperor**, Various Calibers, Carved, Fancy Engraving, Ornate, Fancy Wood, Inlays, *Modern*	3,850.00	5,000.00	5,000.00
☐ **Imperial**, Various Calibers, Carved, Engraved, Fancy Wood, Inlays, *Modern*	2,100.00	2,800.00	2,800.00
☐ **Regal**, Various Calibers, Fancy Checkering, Inlays, *Modern*	395.00	550.00	525.00
☐ **Regent**, Various Calibers, Inlays, Carved, Fancy Wood, *Modern*	475.00	675.00	650.00
☐ **Regimental**, Various Calibers, Carved, Inlays, *Modern*	550.00	850.00	825.00
☐ **Royal**, Various Calibers, Carved, Fancy Wood, Inlays, *Modern*	950.00	1,450.00	1,400.00
☐ **Varmint**, Various Calibers, Fancy Checkering, Inlays, *Modern*	490.00	695.00	675.00
SHOTGUN, DOUBLE BARREL, OVER-UNDER			
☐ **Hammerless**, 12 and 20 Gauges, Single Trigger, Checkered Stock, Inlays, *Modern*	600.00	950.00	925.00
SHOTGUN, DOUBLE BARREL, SIDE-BY-SIDE			
☐ **Hammerless**, 12 Ga., Single Trigger, Checkered Stock, Inlays, *Modern*	520.00	750.00	725.00

WITHERS, MICHAEL

Lancaster, Pa. 1774-1805. See Kentucky Rifles, U.S. Military.

WITTES HDW. CO.

Made by Stevens Arms.

	V.G.	Exc.	Prior Year Exc. Value
SHOTGUN, DOUBLE BARREL, SIDE-BY-SIDE			
☐ **Model 311**, Various Gauges, Hammerless, Steel Barrel, *Modern*	115.00	175.00	165.00
SHOTGUN, SINGLESHOT			
☐ **Model 90**, Various Gauges, Takedown, Automatic Ejector, Plain, Hammer, *Modern*	40.00	60.00	55.00
☐ **Model 94**, Various Gauges, Takedown, Automatic Ejector, Plain, Hammer, *Modern*	40.00	60.00	55.00

WOGDON

London, England & Dublin, Ireland 1760-1797.

	V.G.	Exc.	Prior Year Exc. Value
HANDGUN, FLINTLOCK			
☐ **.56**, Officers, Holster Pistol, Flared, Octagon Barrel, Steel Furniture, Engraved, High Quality, *Antique*	1,695.00	2,900.00	2,750.00

WOLF

Spain, c. 1900.

HANDGUN, SEMI-AUTOMATIC			
☐ **.25 ACP**, Clip Fed, *Modern*	95.00	135.00	125.00

WOLF, A.W.

Suhl, Germany, c. 1930.

SHOTGUN, DOUBLE BARREL, SIDE-BY-SIDE			
☐ **12 Ga.**, Engraved, Platinium Inlays, Ivory Inlays, Ornate, Cased, *Modern*	5,200.00	6,800.00	6,750.00

WOLFHEIMER, PHILIP

Lancaster, Pa., c. 1774. See Kentucky Rifles.

WOLVERINE ARMS CO.

Made by Crescent for Fletcher Hardware Co., c. 1900.

SHOTGUN, DOUBLE BARREL, SIDE-BY-SIDE			
☐ **Various Gauges**, Outside Hammers, Damascus Barrel, *Modern*	100.00	170.00	175.00
☐ **Various Gauges**, Hammerless, Steel Barrel, *Modern*	135.00	190.00	200.00
☐ **Various Gauges**, Hammerless, Damascus Barrel, *Modern*	100.00	170.00	175.00
☐ **Various Gauges**, Outside Hammers, Steel Barrel, *Modern*	125.00	185.00	190.00
SHOTGUN, SINGLESHOT			
☐ **Various Gauges**, Hammer, Steel Barrel, *Modern*	55.00	85.00	85.00

WOODWARD, JAMES & SONS

London, England.

SHOTGUN, DOUBLE BARREL, OVER-UNDER			
☐ **Best Quality**, Various Gauges, Sidelock, Automatic Ejector, Double Trigger, Fancy Engraving, Fancy Checkering, *Modern*	10,000.00	15,000.00	15,000.00
☐ **Best Quality**, Various Gauges, Sidelock, Automatic Ejector, Single Trigger, Fancy Engraving, Fancy Checkering, *Modern*	11,000.00	17,000.00	17,000.00
SHOTGUN, DOUBLE BARREL, SIDE-BY-SIDE			
☐ **Best Quality**, Various Gauges, Sidelock, Automatic Ejector, Double Trigger, Fancy Engraving, Fancy Checkering, *Modern*	8,500.00	12,000.00	12,000.00
☐ **Best Quality**, Various Gauges, Sidelock, Automatic Ejector, Single Trigger, Fancy Engraving, Fancy Checkering, *Modern*	9,000.00	13,500.00	13,500.00
SHOTGUN, SINGLESHOT			
☐ **12 Ga.**, Trap Grade, Vent Rib, Hammerless, Fancy Engraving, Fancy Checkering, *Modern*	8,000.00	14,000.00	14,000.00

	V.G.	Exc.	Prior Year Exc. Value
WORTHINGTON ARMS			
Made by Stevens Arms.			
SHOTGUN, DOUBLE BARREL, SIDE-BY-SIDE			
☐ **M 315**, Various Gauges, Hammerless, Steel Barrel, *Modern*	115.00	175.00	165.00
☐ **Model 215**, 12 and 16 Gauges, Outside Hammers, Steel Barrel, *Modern*	110.00	165.00	160.00
WORTHINGTON ARMS CO.			
Made by Crescent for Geo. Worthington Co., Cleveland, Ohio.			
SHOTGUN, DOUBLE BARREL, SIDE-BY-SIDE			
☐ **Various Gauges**, Outside Hammers, Damascus Barrel, *Modern*	100.00	170.00	175.00
☐ **Various Gauges**, Hammerless, Steel Barrel, *Modern*	135.00	190.00	200.00
☐ **Various Gauges**, Hammerless, Damascus Barrel, *Modern*	100.00	170.00	175.00
☐ **Various Gauges**, Outside Hammers, Steel Barrel, *Modern*	125.00	185.00	190.00
SHOTGUN, SINGLESHOT			
☐ **Various Gauges**, Hammer, Steel Barrel, *Modern*	55.00	85.00	85.00
WORTHINGTON, GEORGE			
Made by Stevens Arms.			
SHOTGUN, DOUBLE BARREL, SIDE-BY-SIDE			
☐ **M 315**, Various Gauges, Hammerless, Steel Barrel, *Modern*	95.00	165.00	160.00
☐ **Model 215**, 12 and 16 Gauges, Outside Hammers, Steel Barrel, *Modern*	90.00	160.00	155.00
☐ **Model 311**, Various Gauges, Hammerless, Steel Barrel, *Modern*	110.00	170.00	165.00
WUETHRICH			
W. Wuethrich, Werkzeugbau, Lutzelfluh, Switzerland.			
RIFLE, SINGLESHOT			
☐ **Falling Block**, Various Calibers, Engraved, Fancy Wood, Scope Mounted, *Modern*	875.00	1,250.00	1,250.00
YATO			
Hamada Arsenal, Japan.			
HANDGUN, SEMI-AUTOMATIC			
☐ **Yato**, .32 ACP, Clip Fed, Pre-War, *Curio*	1,850.00	3,000.00	2,950.00
☐ **Yato**, .32 ACP, Clip Fed, Military, *Curio*	1,350.00	2,200.00	2,150.00
YDEAL			
Made by Francisco Arizmendi, Eibar, Spain.			
HANDGUN, SEMI-AUTOMATIC			
☐ **.25 ACP**, Clip Fed, Blue, *Modern*	95.00	135.00	125.00
☐ **.32 ACP**, Clip Fed, Blue, *Modern*	100.00	145.00	140.00

	V.G.	Exc.	Prior Year Exc. Value

YOU BET
Made by Hopkins & Allen, c. 1880.

HANDGUN, REVOLVER

	V.G.	Exc.	Prior Year Exc. Value
☐ **.22 Short R.F.**, 7 Shot, Spur Trigger, Solid Frame, Single Action, *Antique*	**95.00**	**165.00**	**160.00**

YOUNG AMERICA
See Harrington & Richardson Arms Co.

YOUNG, HENRY
Easton, Pa. 1774-1780. See Kentucky Rifles.

YOUNG, JOHN
Easton, Pa. 1775-1788. See Kentucky Rifles, U.S. Military.

Z
Ceska Zbrojovka, Prague, Czechoslovakia.

HANDGUN, SEMI-AUTOMATIC

	V.G.	Exc.	Prior Year Exc. Value
☐ **Vest Pocket**, .25 ACP, Clip Fed, *Modern*	**85.00**	**125.00**	**120.00**

Z-B

AUTOMATIC WEAPON, LIGHT MACHINE GUN

	V.G.	Exc.	Prior Year Exc. Value
☐ **VZ-26**, 8mm Mauser, Finned Barrel, Clip Fed, Bipod, *Class 3*	**2,150.00**	**2,950.00**	**2,950.00**

ZABALA
Zabala Hermanos, Eibar, Spain.

SHOTGUN, DOUBLE BARREL, SIDE-BY-SIDE

	V.G.	Exc.	Prior Year Exc. Value
☐ **12 Ga.**, Boxlock, Chackered Stock, Double Triggers, *Modern*	**115.00**	**170.00**	**165.00**

ZANOTTI
Ravenna, Italy.

HANDGUN, FLINTLOCK

	V.G.	Exc.	Prior Year Exc. Value
☐ **Brescia Style**, .50, Carved Stock, Engraved, Reproduction, *Antique*	**75.00**	**130.00**	**125.00**

ZARAGOZA
Zaragoza, Mexico.

HANDGUN, SEMI-AUTOMATIC

	V.G.	Exc.	Prior Year Exc. Value
☐ **Corla, Type 1**, .22 L.R.R.F., Colt System, Clip Fed, Blue, *Modern*	**525.00**	**650.00**	**600.00**
☐ **Corla, Type 2**, .22 L.R.R.F., Clip Fed, Blue, *Modern*	**325.00**	**450.00**	**400.00**

ZASTAVA
Zavodi Crvena Zastava, Kragujevac, Yugoslavia. Also see Mark X.

HANDGUN, SEMI-AUTOMATIC

	V.G.	Exc.	Prior Year Exc. Value
☐ **Model 65**, 9mm Luger, Clip Fed, Blue, *Modern*	**175.00**	**250.00**	**240.00**
☐ **Model 67**, .32 ACP, Clip Fed, Blue, *Modern*	**90.00**	**140.00**	**135.00**

	V.G.	Exc.	Prior Year Exc. Value

ZEHNA
Made by E. Zehner Waffenfabrik, Suhl, Germany 1919-1928.

HANDGUN, SEMI-AUTOMATIC

	V.G.	Exc.	Prior Year Exc. Value
□ **Vest Pocket**, .25 ACP, Under #5,000, Clip Fed, Blue, *Curio*	175.00	265.00	250.00
□ **Vest Pocket**, .25 ACP, Clip Fed, Blue, *Curio*	215.00	300.00	285.00

ZEPHYR
Tradename of A.F. Stoeger.

SHOTGUN, DOUBLE BARREL, SIDE-BY-SIDE

	V.G.	Exc.	Prior Year Exc. Value
□ **Woodlander II**, Various Gauges, Checkered Stock, Boxlock, Double Triggers, Light Engraving, *Modern*	160.00	220.00	200.00
□ **Sterlingworth II**, Various Gauges, Checkered Stock, Sidelock, Double Triggers, Light Engraving, *Modern*	225.00	320.00	300.00

ZOLI, ANGELO
Brescia, Italy.

RIFLE, PERCUSSION

	V.G.	Exc.	Prior Year Exc. Value
□ **.50 Hawkin**, Brass Furniture, Reproduction, *Antique*	110.00	155.00	150.00

SHOTGUN, DOUBLE BARREL, OVER-UNDER

	V.G.	Exc.	Prior Year Exc. Value
□ **Angel**, 12 Ga., Trap Grade, Single Selective Trigger, Engraved, Checkered Stock, *Modern*	360.00	465.00	450.00
□ **Angel**, 12 and 20 Gauges, Field Grade, Single Selective Trigger, Engraved, Checkered Stock, *Modern*	335.00	420.00	400.00
□ **Condor**, 12 Ga., Trap Grade, Single Selective Trigger, Engraved, Checkered Stock, *Modern*	320.00	390.00	375.00
□ **Condor**, 12 and 20 Gauges, Single Selective Trigger, Field Grade, Checkered Stock, Engraved, *Modern*	285.00	365.00	350.00
□ **Monte Carlo**, 12 Ga., Trap Grade, Single Selective Trigger, Engraved, Checkered Stock, *Modern*	440.00	545.00	525.00
□ **Monte Carlo**, 12 and 20 Gauges, Field Grade, Single Selective Trigger, Engraved, Checkered Stock, *Modern*	415.00	520.00	500.00

ZOLI, ANTONIO
Gardone, V.T., Italy.

SHOTGUN, DOUBLE BARREL, OVER-UNDER

	V.G.	Exc.	Prior Year Exc. Value
□ **Golden Snipe**, 12 Ga., Trap Grade, Single Trigger, Automatic Ejector, Engraved, Checkered Stock, *Modern*	325.00	445.00	425.00
□ **Golden Snipe**, 12 and 20 Gauges, Vent Rib, Single Trigger, Automatic Ejector, Engraved, Checkered Stock, *Modern*	290.00	385.00	370.00
□ **Golden Snipe**, 12 and 20 Gauges, Skeet Grade, Single Trigger, Automatic Ejector, Engraved, Checkered Stock, *Modern*	325.00	450.00	425.00
□ **Silver Snipe**, 12 Ga., Trap Grade, Single Trigger, Vent Rib, Engraved, Checkered Stock, *Modern*	270.00	365.00	350.00

	V.G.	Exc.	Prior Year Exc. Value
☐ **Silver Snipe**, 12 and 20 Gauges, Vent Rib, Single Trigger, Engraved, Checkered Stock, *Modern*	**240.00**	**335.00**	**320.00**
☐ **Silver Snipe**, 12 and 20 Gauges, Skeet Grade, Single Trigger, Vent Rib, Engraved, Checkered Stock, *Modern*	**270.00**	**365.00**	**350.00**
SHOTGUN, DOUBLE BARREL, SIDE-BY-SIDE			
☐ **Silver Hawk**, 12 and 20 Gauges, Double Trigger, Engraved, Checkered Stock, *Modern*	**250.00**	**345.00**	**325.00**

ZONDA

Hispano Argentina Fab. de Automiviles, Buenos Aires, Argentina.

	V.G.	Exc.	Prior Year Exc. Value
HANDGUN, SINGLESHOT			
☐ **.22 L.R.R.F.**, Blue, *Modern*	**195.00**	**275.00**	**275.00**

ZULAICA

M. Zulaica y Cia., Eibar, Spain.

	V.G.	Exc.	Prior Year Exc. Value
HANDGUN, SEMI-AUTOMATIC			
☐ **.32 ACP**, Clip Fed, Blue, Military, *Curio*	**125.00**	**160.00**	**135.00**
AUTOMATIC REVOLVER			
☐ **.22 L.R.R.F.**, Zig-Zag Cylinder, Blue, *Curio*	**575.00**	**900.00**	**800.00**

CARTRIDGE PRICES

The newcomers joining the swelling ranks of cartridge collectors have made prices in this specialized field quite volatile because of increased demand. This trend will continue for the foreseeable future.

The prices shown are based on the average value of a single cartridge with (unless otherwise noted) a common headstamp ranging from very good to excellent condition. Rare headstamps, unusual bullets, scarce case construction, will add to the value of the item. On common cartridges, empty cases are worth about **20%** to **25%** of the value shown; with rare calibers the empties should bring about **75%** to **80%** of the price of the loaded round. Dummies and blanks are worth about the same as the value shown. Full boxes of ammunition of common type should earn a discount of **15%** to **20%** per cartridge, whereas full boxes of rare ammo will command a premium because of the collectability of the box itself.

	V.G.	Exc.	Prior Year Exc. Value
☐ **.145 Alton Jones,** *Modern*	2.75	4.00	3.00
☐ **.17 Alton Jones,** *Modern*	1.40	2.25	1.75
☐ **.17 Rem.**, Jacketed Bullet, *Modern*	.60	.80	.65
☐ **.218 Bee**, Various Makers, *Modern*	.60	.80	.65
☐ **.219 Zipper**, Various Makers, *Modern*	.85	1.20	1.00
☐ **.22 BB Cap R.F.**, Lead Bullet *Antique*	.15	.25	.20
☐ **.22 CB Cap R.F.**, Lead Bullet *Antique*	.15	.25	.20
☐ **.22 CB Cap R.F.**, Two Piece Case, *Antique*	.20	.35	.30
☐ **.22 Extra Long R.F.**, Various Makers, *Curio*	.85	1.35	1.10
☐ **.22 Hi-Power**, Various Makers, *Modern*	.80	1.25	1.00
☐ **.22 Hornet**, Various Makers, *Modern*	.50	.75	.60
☐ **.22 L.R.R.F.**, Various Makers, *Modern*	.05	.10	.10
☐ **.22 L.R.R.F.**, Shotshell, Various Makers, *Modern*	.10	.15	.15
☐ **.22 L.R.R.F.**, Brass Case Russian, *Antique*	.35	.50	.45
☐ **.22 L.R.R.F.**, Brass Case Austrian, *Antique*	.25	.45	.40
☐ **.22 L.R.R.F.**, British Raised K, *Antique*	2.60	3.25	3.00
☐ **.22 L.R.R.F.**, Wadcutter, *Modern*	.35	.50	.45
☐ **.22 L.R.R.F.**, Tracer, U.M.C., *Modern*	.55	.85	.70
☐ **.22 L.R.R.F.**, Tracer, Gevelot, *Modern*	.20	.30	.25
☐ **.22 L.R.R.F.**, Devastator, *Modern*	.15	.25	.25
☐ **.22 L.R.R.F.**, U.M.C., "S & W Long", *Modern*	3.45	4.85	4.50
☐ **.22 Long R.F.**, Various Makers, *Modern*	.04	.09	.08
☐ **.22 Long R.F.**, Lead Bullet *Antique*	.15	.25	.25
☐ **.22 Maynard Extra Long**, Various Makers, *Curio*	.95	1.75	1.50
☐ **.22 Newton**, Soft Point Bullet, *Modern*	9.50	15.00	14.00
☐ **.22 Rem. Auto. R.F.**, Various Makers, *Modern*	.30	.45	.45
☐ **.22 Rem. Jet**, Jacketed Bullet, *Modern*	.40	.65	.50
☐ **.22 Short R.F.**, Various Makers, *Modern*	.03	.05	.05
☐ **.22 Short R.F.**, Blank, Various Makers, *Modern*	.05	.10	.10
☐ **.22 Short R.F.**, Copper Case Raised "U", *Antique*	2.75	3.45	3.25
☐ **.22 Short R.F.**, Copper Case Raised "H", *Antique*	2.35	2.95	2.75
☐ **.22 Short R.F.**, Lead Bullet *Antique*	.15	.25	.25
☐ **.22 WCF**, Various Makers, *Modern*	.55	.75	.75
☐ **.22 Win. Auto. R.F.**, Various Makers, *Modern*	.25	.35	.35
☐ **.22 WMR**, Various Makers, *Modern*	.10	.17	.15
☐ **.22 WMR**, Shotshell, Various Makers, *Modern*	.15	.25	.20
☐ **.22 WRF**, Various Makers, *Modern*	.10	.17	.15
☐ **.22-15-60 Stevens**, Lead Bullet *Curio*	2.95	4.00	3.50
☐ **.22-3000 G & H**, Soft Point Bullet, *Modern*	1.75	2.35	2.00

	V.G.	Exc.	Prior Year Exc. Value
☐ **.220 Swift**, Various Makers, *Modern*	.80	1.20	.95
☐ **.221 Rem. Fireball**, Various Makers, *Modern*	.45	.65	.55
☐ **.222 Rem.**, Various Makers, *Modern*	.45	.65	.55
☐ **.222 Rem. Mag.**, Various Makers, *Modern*	.40	.55	.50
☐ **.22-250**, Various Makers, *Modern*	.50	.70	.60
☐ **.223 Rem.**, Various Makers, *Modern*	.45	.60	.50
☐ **.223 Rem.**, Military, Various Makers, *Modern*	.30	.50	.40
☐ **.223 Armalite**, Experimental, *Modern*	3.95	5.25	4.75
☐ **.224 Wby.**, Varmintmaster, *Modern*	.85	1.25	1.00
☐ **.224 Win.**, Experemental, *Modern*	3.25	4.50	4.00
☐ **.224 Win.**, E2 Ball WCC 58, *Modern*	4.65	6.25	6.00
☐ **.225 Win.**, Various Makers, *Modern*	.45	.65	.55
☐ **.230 Long**, Various Makers, *Modern*	1.30	1.65	1.50
☐ **.230 Short**, Various Makers, *Modern*	.75	1.00	.90
☐ **.236 U.S. Navy Rimless**, *Modern*	5.25	8.00	7.00
☐ **.236 U.S. Navy Rimmed**, *Modern*	3.50	5.50	5.00
☐ **.240 Belted N.E.**, Jacketed Bullet, *Modern*	.90	1.50	1.25
☐ **.240 Flanged N.E.**, Various Makers, *Modern*	2.50	3.00	2.75
☐ **.240 Wby. Mag.**, *Modern*	.90	1.35	1.20
☐ **.242 Rimless N.E.**, Various Makers, *Modern*	3.50	5.00	4.75
☐ **.243 Win.**, Various Makers, *Modern*	.50	.75	.65
☐ **.244 H & H Mag.**, Jacketed Bullet, *Modern*	3.25	4.80	4.50
☐ **.244 Halger Mag.**, Various Makers, *Modern*	21.00	27.00	25.00
☐ **.244 Rem.**, Various Makers, *Modern*	.80	1.10	.95
☐ **.246 Purdey**, Soft Point Bullet, *Modern*	2.95	4.00	3.75
☐ **.247 Wby. Mag.**, *Modern*	.95	1.45	1.30
☐ **.25 ACP**, Various Makers, *Modern*	.20	.35	.30
☐ **.25 L.F.**, Various Makers, #50 Allen, *Curio*	3.65	4.75	4.50
☐ **.25 Rem.**, Various Makers, *Modern*	.90	1.25	1.15
☐ **.25 Short R.F.**, Lead Bullet *Antique*	.30	.45	.40
☐ **.25 Stevens R.F.**, Wood Shotshell Bullet, *Modern*	.80	1.25	1.00
☐ **.25 Stevens Short R.F.**, Various Makers, *Modern*	.30	.45	.40
☐ **.25 Stevens Long R.F.**, Various Makers, *Modern*	.30	.40	.35
☐ **.25-06 Rem.**, Various Makers, *Modern*	.55	.75	.65
☐ **.25-20 WCF**, Lead Bullet, Various Makers, *Modern*	.35	.45	.40
☐ **.25-20 WCF**, Jacketed Bullet, Various Makers, *Modern*	.35	.50	.45
☐ **.25-21**, Jacketed Bullet, *Curio*	3.40	4.25	4.00
☐ **.25-25**, Various Makers, *Modern*	3.25	4.00	3.75
☐ **.25-35 WCF**, Various Makers, *Modern*	.55	.85	.75
☐ **.25-36**, Jacketed Bullet, *Curio*	1.90	2.45	2.25
☐ **.250 Savage**, Various Makers, *Modern*	.55	.80	.70
☐ **.255 Rook**, Various Makers, *Curio*	.85	1.35	1.20
☐ **.256 Gibbs Mag.**, Various Makers, *Modern*	3.75	5.00	4.75
☐ **.256 Newton**, Soft Point Bullet, *Modern*	1.85	2.25	2.00
☐ **.256 Win. Mag.**, Various Makers, *Modern*	.45	.65	.55
☐ **.257 Roberts**, Various Makers, *Modern*	.45	.75	.65
☐ **.257 Wby. Mag.**, *Modern*	.95	1.40	1.30
☐ **.26 BSA**, Soft Point Bullet, *Modern*	3.35	4.25	4.00
☐ **.264 Win. Mag.**, Various Makers, *Modern*	.55	.80	.70
☐ **.267 Rem. R.F.**, Experimental, *Curio*	7.95	10.25	9.75
☐ **.270 Wby. Mag.**, *Modern*	.85	1.30	1.20
☐ **.270 Win.**, Various Makers, *Modern*	.55	.80	.70
☐ **.270 Win.**, Flare Cartridge, Various Makers, *Modern*	1.75	2.40	2.25
☐ **.275 Flanged Mag.**, Various Makers, *Modern*	1.65	2.25	2.00

	V.G.	Exc.	Prior Year Exc. Value
☐ **.275 H & H Mag.**, Various Makers, *Modern*	3.45	4.25	4.00
☐ **.275 Rigby**, Various Makers, *Modern*	2.85	3.75	3.50
☐ **.276 Pederson**, Various Makers, Miliary, *Curio*	2.40	3.25	3.00
☐ **.276 Garand**, Military, Experimental, *Curio*	2.45	3.25	3.00
☐ **.276 Enfield**, Various Makers, Miliary, *Modern*	5.95	8.25	8.00
☐ **.28 Cup Primed Cartridge**, Various Makers, *Curio*	8.50	10.25	9.75
☐ **.28-30-120 Stevens**, Lead Bullet, *Curio*	3.45	4.50	4.25
☐ **.280 Flanged N.E.**, Various Makers, *Modern*	3.35	4.25	4.00
☐ **.280 Halgar Mag.**, Various Makers, *Modern*	3.75	4.65	4.50
☐ **.280 Jeffery**, Various Makers, *Modern*	4.75	6.00	5.75
☐ **.280 Rem.**, Various Makers, *Modern*	.50	.75	.65
☐ **.280 Ross**, Various Makers, *Modern*	2.25	3.65	3.50
☐ **.280/30 Experimental**, Various Makers, Miliary, *Modern*	6.95	9.50	9.00
☐ **.284 Win.**, Various Makers, *Modern*	.50	.75	.65
☐ **.295 Rook**, Various Makers, *Modern*	.70	1.15	.95
☐ **.297/.230 Morris**, Various Makers, *Modern*	.70	1.10	.95
☐ **.297/.230 Morris Short**, Various Makers, *Modern*	.60	1.00	.90
☐ **.297/.250 Rook**, Various Makers, *Modern*	.70	1.15	.95
☐ **.297 R. F. Revolver**, Various Makers, *Modern*	3.10	4.25	4.00
☐ **.30 Carbine**, Various Makers, *Modern*	.35	.55	.45
☐ **.30 Carbine**, Various Makers, Military, *Modern*	.25	.45	.35
☐ **.30 Cup Primed Cartridge**, Various Makers, *Curio*	6.25	7.75	7.50
☐ **.30 H & H Super Mag. Flanged**, Various Makers, *Modern*	2.50	3.75	3.50
☐ **.30 Long R.F.**, Merwin Cone Base, *Antique*	23.50	29.00	27.50
☐ **.30 Long R.F.**, Various Makers, *Antique*	1.60	2.25	2.00
☐ **.30 Luger**, Various Makers, *Modern*	.35	.55	.45
☐ **.30 Newton**, Soft Point Bullet, *Modern*	2.00	3.00	2.75
☐ **.30 Pederson**, Various Makers, Military, *Modern*	2.35	3.25	3.00
☐ **.30 Rem.**, Various Makers, *Modern*	.50	.75	.65
☐ **.30 Short R.F.**, Various Makers, *Curio*	3.25	4.25	3.90
☐ **.30-03 Springfield**, Various Makers, *Curio*	1.60	2.25	2.00
☐ **.30-06 Springfield**, Various Makers, *Modern*	.50	.80	.65
☐ **.30-06 Springfield**, Various Makers, Military, *Modern*	.25	.45	.35
☐ **.30-06 Springfield**, Accelerator, *Modern*	.55	.90	.75
☐ **.30-06 Springfield**, Flare Cartridge, Various Makers, *Modern*	1.75	2.50	2.25
☐ **.30-30 Wesson**, Lead Bullet, *Curio*	19.50	27.25	26.00
☐ **.30-30 Win.**, Various Makers, *Modern*	.40	.65	.50
☐ **.30-30 Win.**, Bicentennial, Various Makers, *Modern*	.50	.75	.65
☐ **.30-30 Win.**, Flare Cartridge, Various Makers, *Modern*	1.70	2.50	2.25
☐ **.30-40 Krag**, Various Makers, *Modern*	.50	.80	.65
☐ **.300 AMU Mag.**, Various Makers, Military, *Modern*	2.20	3.00	2.75
☐ **.300 Hoffman Mag.**, Soft Point Bullet, *Modern*	2.70	3.75	3.50
☐ **.300 H & H Mag.**, Various Makers, *Modern*	.75	1.10	.95
☐ **.300 Rook**, Various Makers, *Modern*	.90	1.35	1.20
☐ **.300 Savage**, Various Makers, *Modern*	.55	.80	.65
☐ **.300 Sherwood**, Various Makers, *Modern*	1.85	3.00	2.75
☐ **.300 Wby. Mag.**, *Modern*	.90	1.40	1.20
☐ **.300 Win. Mag.**, Various Makers, *Modern*	.75	1.10	.90
☐ **.303/.22**, Soft Point Bullet, *Modern*	6.95	9.00	8.50
☐ **.303 British**, Various Makers, *Modern*	.50	.80	.65

	V.G.	Exc.	Prior Year Exc. Value
☐ **.303 Lewis Rimless**, Various Makers, Military, *Modern*	3.75	4.80	4.50
☐ **.303 Mag.**, Various Makers, *Modern*	3.25	4.25	4.00
☐ **.303 Savage**, Various Makers, *Modern*	.55	.80	.65
☐ **.305 Rook**, Various Makers, *Modern*	1.35	2.00	1.75
☐ **.308 Norma Mag.**, Various Makers, *Modern*	1.25	1.55	1.40
☐ **.308 Win.**, Various Makers, *Modern*	.55	.80	.65
☐ **.308 Win.**, Various Makers, Military, *Modern*	.35	.50	.40
☐ **.308 Win.**, Flare Cartridge, Various Makers, *Modern*	1.75	2.50	2.25
☐ **.31 Eley R.F.**, Lead Bullet, Dished Base, *Modern*	9.75	15.00	14.00
☐ **.31 Crispin**, Patent Ignition, *Antique*	130.00	165.00	150.00
☐ **.31 Milbank**, Patent Ignition, *Antique*	43.25	57.50	55.00
☐ **.31 Theur**, Patent Ignition, *Antique*	9.25	14.30	13.00
☐ **.31 Volcanic**, Patent Ignition, *Antique*	11.00	16.50	15.00
☐ **.310 Cadet**, Various Makers, *Modern*	.95	1.75	1.50
☐ **.318 Rimless N.E.**, Various Makers, *Modern*	1.35	1.95	1.75
☐ **.32 ACP**, Various Makers, *Modern*	.25	.45	.35
☐ **.32 Ballard Extra Long**, Lead Bullet, *Curio*	.95	1.50	1.35
☐ **.32 Colt New Police**, Various Makers, *Modern*	.25	.45	.35
☐ **.32 Extra Long R.F.**, Various Makers, *Curio*	5.00	7.00	6.50
☐ **.32 Extra Short R.F.**, Lead Bullet, *Antique*	.65	1.10	.95
☐ **.32 Ideal**, Lead Bullet, *Curio*	.85	1.50	1.25
☐ **.32 Teat-Fire Cartridge**, Various Makers, *Curio*	2.95	3.75	3.50
☐ **.32 L.F.**, Various Makers, #52 Allen, *Curio*	5.90	7.85	7.50
☐ **.32 Long Colt**, Various Makers, *Modern*	.25	.40	.30
☐ **.32 Long R.F.**, Various Makers, *Modern*	6.25	8.00	7.50
☐ **.32 Long R.F.**, Shotshell, *Curio*	.30	.55	.45
☐ **.32 Long Rifle**, Lead Bullet, *Antique*	3.50	4.75	4.50
☐ **.32 Rem.**, Various Makers, *Modern*	.50	.80	.65
☐ **.32 Rem. Rimless**, Various Makers, *Modern*	.60	.90	.75
☐ **.32 S & W**, Various Makers, *Modern*	.20	.35	.30
☐ **.32 S & W**, Shotshell, Various Makers, *Modern*	.20	.35	.25
☐ **.32 S & W**, Blank Cartridge, Various Makers, *Modern*	.15	.25	.25
☐ **.32 S & W Long**, Various Makers, *Modern*	.20	.35	.30
☐ **.32 Short Colt**, Various Makers, *Modern*	.20	.35	.30
☐ **.32 Short R.F.**, Various Makers, *Modern*	.25	.40	.35
☐ **.32 Win. Self-Loading**, Various Makers, *Modern*	.50	.80	.65
☐ **.32 Win. Special**, Various Makers, *Modern*	.50	.80	.65
☐ **.32-20 WCF**, Lead Bullet, Various Makers, *Modern*	.55	.90	.70
☐ **.32-20 WCF**, Jacketed Bullet, Various Makers, *Modern*	.85	1.30	1.10
☐ **.32-30 Rem.**, Lead Bullet, *Curio*	3.75	4.65	4.30
☐ **.32-35 Stevens & Maynard**, Lead Bullet, *Curio*	3.75	4.50	4.25
☐ **.32-40 Bullard**, Lead Bullet, *Curio*	2.20	3.00	2.75
☐ **.32-40 Rem.**, Lead Bullet, *Curio*	1.95	3.00	2.65
☐ **.32-40 WCF**, Various Makers, *Modern*	.50	.80	.55
☐ **.320 Rook**, Various Makers, *Modern*	.60	1.10	.95
☐ **.320 Extra Long Rifle**, Various Makers, *Modern*	1.85	2.75	2.50
☐ **.322 Swift**, Various Makers, *Modern*	4.75	6.00	5.50
☐ **.33 BSA**, Soft Point Bullet, *Modern*	3.00	4.00	3.75
☐ **.33 Win.**, Soft Point Bullet, *Modern*	1.20	1.75	1.55
☐ **.333 Flanged N.E.**, Various Makers, *Modern*	3.25	4.80	4.50
☐ **.333 Rimless N.E.**, Various Makers, *Modern*	3.25	4.90	4.50
☐ **.338 Win. Mag.**, Various Makers, *Modern*	.70	1.20	1.00

	V.G.	Exc.	Prior Year Exc. Value
☐ **.340 Wby. Mag.**, *Modern*	.95	1.45	1.30
☐ **.340 R.F. Revolver**, Various Makers, *Modern*	1.85	2.75	2.50
☐ **.348 Win.**, Various Makers, *Modern*	.95	1.40	1.20
☐ **.35 Allen R.F.**, Lead Bullet, *Curio*	11.00	15.00	14.00
☐ **.35 Newton**, Soft Point Bullet, *Modern*	3.35	4.25	4.00
☐ **.35 Rem.**, Various Makers, *Modern*	.50	.80	.65
☐ **.35 S & W Auto.**, Jacketed Bullet, *Curio*	.70	1.20	1.00
☐ **.35 Win.**, Various Makers, *Modern*	2.25	3.25	3.00
☐ **.35 Win. Self-Loading**, Various Makers, *Modern*	.50	.80	.65
☐ **.35-30 Maynard**, Lead Bullet, with Riveted Head, *Curio*	8.25	13.00	12.00
☐ **.35-30 Maynard**, Lead Bullet, without Riveted Head, *Curio*	5.25	7.00	6.50
☐ **.35-40 Maynard**, Various Makers, *Curio*	8.95	13.50	12.00
☐ **.350 Rem. Mag.**, Various Makers, *Modern*	.85	1.30	1.10
☐ **.350 Rigby**, Various Makers, *Modern*	3.00	4.00	3.75
☐ **.351 Win. Self-Loading**, Various Makers, *Modern*	1.25	2.10	1.80
☐ **.357 Magnum**, Lead Bullet, Various Makers, *Modern*	.30	.50	.40
☐ **.357 Magnum**, Jacketed Bullet, Various Makers, *Modern*	.30	.50	.40
☐ **.358 Norma Mag.**, Various Makers, *Modern*	.95	1.40	1.25
☐ **.358 Win.**, Various Makers, *Modern*	.65	1.15	.90
☐ **.36 L. F.**, #56 Allen, Various Makers, *Curio*	5.75	7.50	7.00
☐ **.36 Crispin**, Patent Ignition, *Antique*	147.50	200.00	195.00
☐ **.36 Theur Navy**, Patent Ignition, *Antique*	9.50	15.50	14.00
☐ **.360 #5 Rook**, Various Makers, *Modern*	8.50	13.50	12.00
☐ **.360 N.E.**, Various Makers, *Modern*	1.20	2.00	1.75
☐ **.360 N.E. #2**, Various Makers, *Curio*	2.00	3.00	2.75
☐ **.369 Purdey**, Soft Point Bullet, *Curio*	5.50	7.00	6.50
☐ **.370 Flanged**, Various Makers, *Modern*	1.25	2.00	1.85
☐ **.375 Flanged Mag. N.E.**, Various Makers, *Modern*	2.10	3.00	2.75
☐ **.375 Flanged N.E.**, Various Makers, *Modern*	2.60	3.65	3.25
☐ **.375 H & H Mag.**, Various Makers, *Modern*	1.00	1.60	1.40
☐ **.375 Rimless N.E. 2¼"**, Various Makers, *Curio*	.95	1.50	1.30
☐ **.375/.303 Axite**, Various Makers, *Curio*	1.95	2.85	2.50
☐ **.378 Wby. Mag.**, *Modern*	2.20	3.25	3.00
☐ **.38 ACP**, Various Makers, *Modern*	.25	.40	.35
☐ **.38 AMU**, Various Makers, Military, *Modern*	.40	.70	.55
☐ **.38 Ballard Extra Long**, Lead Bullet, *Curio*	1.25	2.00	1.75
☐ **.38 Extra Long R.F.**, Lead Bullet, *Curio*	4.25	5.50	5.00
☐ **.38 Long CF**, Lead Bullet, *Curio*	.50	.80	.65
☐ **.38 Long Colt**, Various Makers, *Modern*	.30	.50	.40
☐ **.38 Long R.F.**, Various Makers, *Curio*	2.75	4.25	3.75
☐ **.38 S & W**, Various Makers, *Modern*	.25	.45	.35
☐ **.38 S & W**, Blank Cartridge, Various Makers, *Modern*	.15	.30	.25
☐ **.38 Short R.F.**, Various Makers, *Modern*	2.60	3.75	3.50
☐ **.38 Short R.F.**, Shotshell, *Curio*	.35	.60	.50
☐ **.38 Short Colt**, Various Makers, *Modern*	.20	.30	.25
☐ **.38 Special**, Lead Bullet, Various Makers, *Modern*	.25	.40	.35
☐ **.38 Special**, Flare Cartridge, Various Makers, *Modern*	1.60	2.25	2.00
☐ **.38 Special**, Sub-Velocity Ammo, Various Makers, *Modern*	.15	.30	.20
☐ **.38 Special**, Shotshell, Various Makers, *Modern*	.25	.40	.35
☐ **.38 Special**, Blank Cartridge, Various Makers, *Modern*	.15	.25	.25

	V.G.	Exc.	Prior Year Exc. Value
☐ **.38 Special**, Tracer, Military, *Modern*	.30	.55	.45
☐ **.38 Super**, Various Makers, *Modern*	.25	.45	.35
☐ **.38-40 Rem. Hepburn**, Various Makers, *Curio*	2.50	3.80	3.50
☐ **.38-40 WCF**, Various Makers, *Modern*	.50	.75	.60
☐ **.38-44**, Various Makers, *Modern*	.30	.45	.35
☐ **.38-45 Bullard**, Lead Bullet, *Curio*	4.50	5.75	5.25
☐ **.38-50 Ballard**, Lead Bullet, *Curio*	4.75	5.80	5.50
☐ **.38-50 Maynard**, Various Makers, *Curio*	8.75	13.50	12.00
☐ **.38-50 Rem. Hepburn**, Lead Bullet, *Curio*	2.75	3.65	3.25
☐ **.38-55 Win. & Ballard**, Various Makers, *Modern*	.95	1.60	1.40
☐ **.38-56 Win.**, Lead Bullet, *Curio*	2.00	3.00	2.75
☐ **.38-72 Win.**, Lead Bullet, *Curio*	3.30	4.20	3.75
☐ **.38-90 Win. Express**, Lead Bullet, *Curio*	5.75	7.25	6.75
☐ **.380 ACP**, Various Makers, *Modern*	.25	.45	.35
☐ **.380 Revolver**, Various Makers, Military, *Modern*	.40	.60	.50
☐ **.380 Revolver**, Shotshell, *Modern*	.70	1.15	.95
☐ **.40-40 Maynard**, Lead Bullet, *Curio*	9.25	13.00	11.50
☐ **.40-50 Sharps (Necked)**, Lead Bullet, *Curio*	4.50	5.75	5.00
☐ **.40-50 Sharps (Straight)**, Lead Bullet, *Curio*	3.50	4.65	4.25
☐ **.40-60 Marlin**, Various Makers, *Curio*	7.00	14.00	12.00
☐ **.40-60 Maynard**, Lead Bullet, *Curio*	13.00	19.00	17.00
☐ **.40-60 Win.**, Various Makers, *Modern*	2.95	4.00	3.50
☐ **.40-63 Ballard**, Lead Bullet, *Antique*	6.50	8.00	7.25
☐ **.40-65 Win.**, Lead Bullet, *Curio*	1.95	2.80	2.50
☐ **.40-70 Ballard**, Lead Bullet, *Curio*	3.25	4.65	4.25
☐ **.40-70 Maynard**, Lead Bullet, *Curio*	14.00	20.50	18.00
☐ **.40-70 Peabody "What Cheer"**, Lead Bullet, *Curio*	24.00	33.00	29.00
☐ **.40-70 Rem.**, Lead Bullet, *Curio*	3.85	5.00	4.50
☐ **.40-70 Sharps (Necked)**, Various Makers, *Curio*	4.75	6.00	5.50
☐ **.40-70 Sharps (Straight)**, Various Makers, *Curio*	4.00	5.50	5.00
☐ **.40-70 Win.**, Lead Bullet, *Antique*	3.50	4.50	4.00
☐ **.40-72 Win.**, Various Makers, *Modern*	1.75	2.85	2.50
☐ **.40-75 Bullard**, Lead Bullet, *Curio*	5.50	7.00	6.50
☐ **.40-82 Win.**, Various Makers, *Modern*	2.25	3.25	2.75
☐ **.40-82 Win.**, Shotshell, Various Makers, *Modern*	3.95	5.00	4.50
☐ **.40-85 Ballard**, Lead Bullet, *Curio*	5.00	6.75	6.00
☐ **.40-90 Ballard**, Lead Bullet, *Curio*	5.95	8.00	7.00
☐ **.40-90 Peabody "What Cheer"**, Lead Bullet, *Curio*	47.50	60.00	58.00
☐ **.40-90 Sharps (Necked)**, Various Makers, *Curio*	4.75	7.25	6.75
☐ **.40-90 Sharps (Straight)**, Lead Bullet, *Curio*	9.25	13.00	11.50
☐ **.40-110 Win.**, Lead Bullet, *Curio*	17.50	25.00	21.50
☐ **.400 Nitro 3"**, Various Makers, *Modern*	5.75	7.25	6.75
☐ **.400/.350 Rigby Flanged**, Various Makers, *Modern*	3.00	4.25	3.75
☐ **.400/.360 Purdey Flanged**, Various Makers, *Curio*	3.25	4.25	3.75
☐ **.400/.375 H & H**, Various Makers, *Modern*	3.30	4.25	3.75
☐ **.401 Herter Mag.**, Various Makers, *Modern*	.70	1.30	1.10
☐ **.401 Win. Self-Loading**, Various Makers, *Modern*	.95	1.50	1.30
☐ **.404 N.E.**, Various Makers, *Modern*	2.95	4.00	3.50
☐ **.405 Win.**, Jacketed Bullet, *Modern*	1.30	1.75	1.50
☐ **.41 Long Colt**, Wood Shotshell Bullet, *Modern*	1.30	1.80	1.55
☐ **.41 Long Colt**, Various Makers, *Modern*	.45	.80	.60
☐ **.41 Long R.F.**, Various Makers, *Curio*	3.70	5.00	4.50
☐ **.41 Short C. F.**, Lead Bullet, *Modern*	.30	.55	.40
☐ **.41 Magnum**, Jacketed Bullet, Various Makers, *Modern*	.35	.55	.45
☐ **.41 Magnum**, Lead Bullet, Various Makers, *Modern*	.30	.50	.40

	V.G.	Exc.	Prior Year Exc. Value
☐ **.41 Short R.F.**, Various Makers, *Modern*	2.20	3.25	2.80
☐ **.41 Swiss R.F.**, Various Makers, *Modern*	1.50	2.65	2.25
☐ **.41 Swiss R.F.**, Kynoch with Raised "C", *Antique*	3.75	5.00	4.50
☐ **.41 Volcanic**, Patent Ignition, *Antique*	14.50	21.00	19.00
☐ **416 Ribgy**, Soft Point Bullet, *Modern*	4.00	5.25	4.75
☐ **.42 Allen R.F.**, Lead Bullet, *Antique*	3.20	4.25	3.75
☐ **.42 Cup Primed Cartridge**, Various Makers, *Curio*	7.00	9.25	8.50
☐ **.425 Westley Richards Mag.**, Various Makers, *Modern*	3.70	4.65	4.25
☐ **.44 AMP**, Various Makers, *Modern*	.75	1.20	1.00
☐ **.44 Bulldog**, Lead Bullet, *Antique*	.45	.80	.60
☐ **.44 Colt**, Various Makers, *Modern*	.60	1.10	.85
☐ **.44 Crispin**, Patent Ignition, *Antique*	145.00	175.00	175.00
☐ **.44 Evans Short**, Various Makers, *Curio*	4.70	6.50	6.00
☐ **.44 Extra Long Ballard**, Lead Bullet, *Curio*	7.80	10.50	9.50
☐ **.44 Henry R.F.**, Blank Cartridge, *Curio*	3.70	5.00	4.50
☐ **.44 Henry R.F.**, Lead Bullet, *Curio*	2.20	3.25	2.75
☐ **.44 L.F.**, #58 Allen, Various Makers, *Curio*	14.00	20.00	18.00
☐ **.44 Long R.F.**, Various Makers, *Curio*	4.25	6.00	5.50
☐ **.44 Russian**, Lead Bullet, *Modern*	.65	1.10	.85
☐ **.44 S & W**, Various Makers, *Modern*	.25	.45	.35
☐ **.44 S & W**, Sub-Velocity Ammo, Various Makers, *Modern*	.15	.30	.25
☐ **.44 Magnum**, Various Makers, *Modern*	.40	.75	.55
☐ **.44 Magnum**, Shotshell, Various Makers, *Modern*	.40	.75	.55
☐ **.44 Short R.F.**, Lead Bullet, *Curio*	.85	1.45	1.25
☐ **.44 Short R.F.**, Blank Cartridge, *Antique*	.30	.55	.40
☐ **.44 Theur**, Patent Ignition, *Antique*	17.50	24.00	22.00
☐ **.44 Webley**, Blank Cartridge, *Curio*	.45	.70	.50
☐ **.44-100 Ballard**, Lead Bullet, *Curio*	9.75	15.50	14.00
☐ **.44-100 Wesson**, Lead Bullet, *Curio*	2.75	4.00	3.50
☐ **.44-40 WCF**, Various Makers, *Modern*	.50	.80	.65
☐ **.44-40 WCF**, Shotshell, Various Makers, *Modern*	.75	1.10	.95
☐ **.44-60 Sharps**, Lead Bullet, *Curio*	4.20	5.25	4.75
☐ **.44-60 Win.**, Lead Bullet, *Curio*	2.50	3.65	3.25
☐ **.44-70 Maynard**, Lead Bullet, *Curio*	33.00	46.00	45.00
☐ **.44-75 Ballard Everlasting**, Lead Bullet, *Curio*	2.70	4.00	3.50
☐ **.44-77 Sharps & Rem.**, Lead Bullet, *Curio*	4.95	6.25	5.75
☐ **.44-90 Rem.**, Lead Bullet, *Curio*	8.00	10.75	9.50
☐ **.44-90 Rem. Special**, Various Makers, *Curio*	16.00	22.50	20.00
☐ **.44-90 Sharps**, Various Makers, *Curio*	7.75	10.00	9.00
☐ **.44-95 Peabody "What Cheer"**, Lead Bullet, *Curio*	29.00	37.50	34.00
☐ **.440 Eley R.F.**, Lead Bullet, no Headstamp, *Modern*	.55	.90	.75
☐ **.442 Eley R.F.**, Lead Bullet, no Headstamp, *Modern*	.65	1.15	.90
☐ **.444 Marlin**, Various Makers, *Modern*	.60	.90	.70
☐ **.45 ACP**, Various Makers, *Modern*	.30	.50	.40
☐ **.45 ACP**, Military, Tracer, *Modern*	.55	.90	.70
☐ **.45 Auto-Rim**, Various Makers, *Modern*	.30	.50	.40
☐ **.45 Colt**, Various Makers, *Modern*	.30	.50	.40
☐ **.45 Colt**, Wood Shotshell Bullet, *Modern*	1.65	2.25	2.00
☐ **.45 Danish R.F.**, Lead Bullet, no Headstamp, *Modern*	15.00	21.00	19.00
☐ **.45 S & W**, Various Makers, *Modern*	2.20	3.25	2.75
☐ **.45 Teat-Fire Cartridge**, Various Makers, *Curio*	46.50	.57.50	55.00
☐ **.45 Webley**, Lead Bullet, *Modern*	.70	1.20	.95

	V.G.	Exc.	Prior Year Exc. Value
☐ **.45-100 Ballard**, Various Makers, *Curio*	8.50	13.00	11.00
☐ **.45-100 Sharps**, Lead Bullet, *Curio*	14.00	20.00	17.00
☐ **.45-125 Win.**, Lead Bullet, *Curio*	19.00	26.50	24.00
☐ **.45-50 Peabody**, Lead Bullet, *Curio*	14.00	19.50	17.00
☐ **.45-60 Win.**, Lead Bullet, *Curio*	2.00	3.00	2.25
☐ **.45-70 Marlin**, Various Makers, *Modern*	4.45	5.50	5.00
☐ **.45-70 Government**, Various Makers, *Modern*	.50	.80	.65
☐ **.45-70 Van Choate**, Lead Bullet, *Curio*	27.00	35.00	35.00
☐ **.45-75 Sharps**, Lead Bullet, (Rigby), *Curio*	8.00	14.00	12.00
☐ **.45-75 Sharps**, Lead Bullet, *Curio*	7.25	10.00	9.00
☐ **.45-75 Win.**, Various Makers, *Modern*	1.75	2.90	2.50
☐ **.45-80 Sharpshooter**, Various Makers, *Curio*	1.90	3.00	2.50
☐ **.45-85 Marlin**, Various Makers, *Modern*	4.75	6.00	5.50
☐ **.45-85 Win.**, Lead Bullet, *Curio*	4.25	5.50	5.00
☐ **.45-90 Win.**, Lead Bullet, *Curio*	2.70	3.65	3.25
☐ **.45-90 Win.**, Jacketed Bullet, *Curio*	3.20	4.25	3.80
☐ **.450 Gatling**, Various Makers, *Modern*	4.75	6.00	5.50
☐ **.450 #2 N.E. 3½"**, Various Makers, *Modern*	7.25	1.75	9.50
☐ **.450 Long Revolver**, Various Makers, *Curio*	1.45	2.25	1.75
☐ **.450 N.E. 3¼"**, Various Makers, New Make, *Modern*			
.450 N.E.	3.95	5.00	4.50
☐ **.450 N.E. 3¼"**, Various Makers, *Curio*	4.95	6.50	6.00
☐ **.450 Revolver**, Various Makers, *Curio*	.75	1.25	.95
☐ **.450 #1 Carbine**, Various Makers, *Modern*	4.25	5.65	5.25
☐ **.450 Rigby Match 2.4"**, Soft Point Bullet, *Modern*	3.25	4.50	4.00
☐ **.450/.400 BPE**, Various Makers, *Modern*	3.25	4.25	3.75
☐ **.450/.400 Mag. N.E. 3¼"**, Various Makers, *Modern*	4.25	5.90	5.50
☐ **.450/.400 N.E. 3"**, Various Makers, *Modern*	4.00	5.00	4.50
☐ **.454 Casull Mag.**, Various Makers, *Modern*	.45	.90	.65
☐ **.455 Revolver Mk 1**, Jacketed Bullet, Military, *Modern*	.50	.80	.65
☐ **.455 Webley Mk 2**, Various Makers, *Modern*	.60	1.10	.85
☐ **.458 Win. Mag.**, Various Makers, Full Jacketed Bullet, *Modern*	1.70	2.25	2.00
☐ **.458 Win. Mag.**, Soft Point Bullet, Various Makers, *Modern*	.95	1.50	1.35
☐ **.46 Extra Long R.F.**, Various Makers, *Curio*	16.00	22.00	20.00
☐ **.46 Extra Short R.F.**, Lead Bullet, *Curio*	20.00	27.50	25.00
☐ **.46 Long R.F.**, Lead Bullet, *Antique*	2.65	3.90	3.50
☐ **.46 Remington & Ballard**, Lead Bullet, *Curio*	5.25	7.25	6.75
☐ **.46 Short R.F.**, Various Makers, *Curio*	5.25	7.00	6.50
☐ **.460 Wby. Mag.**, *Modern*	1.75	2.65	2.20
☐ **.470 N.E.**, Various Makers, *Modern*	4.25	5.50	5.00
☐ **.475 #2 N.E.**, Various Makers, *Modern*	6.45	8.00	7.50
☐ **.475 N.E.**, Various Makers, *Modern*	5.75	7.75	7.00
☐ **.476 N.E.**, Soft Point Bullet, *Modern*	5.75	7.75	7.00
☐ **5-in-One**, Blank Cartridge, Various Makers, *Modern*	.50	.70	.60
☐ **.50 BMG**, Various Makers, Military, *Modern*	.95	1.80	1.55
☐ **.50 Rem.**, Various Makers, *Curio*	2.60	3.85	3.50
☐ **.50 Rem. Navy R.F.**, Various Makers, *Curio*	22.00	28.00	25.00
☐ **.50 U.S. Carbine**, Various Makers, *Curio*	3.95	5.75	5.00
☐ **.50-100 Win.**, Various Makers, *Curio*	5.00	7.50	7.00
☐ **.50-110 Win.**, Lead Bullet, *Curio*	3.75	5.25	5.00
☐ **.50-115 Bullard**, Lead Bullet, *Curio*	5.50	7.25	7.00
☐ **.50-140 Sharps**, Lead Bullet, *Curio*	35.00	48.50	45.00
☐ **.50-140 Win. Express**, Lead Bullet, *Curio*	87.50	125.00	120.00

	V.G.	Exc.	Prior Year Exc. Value
☐ **.50-50 Maynard**, Lead Bullet, *Curio*	5.50	7.25	6.75
☐ **.50-70 Government R.F.**, Various Makers, *Curio*	32.00	38.00	35.00
☐ **.50-70 Musket**, New Make, Various Makers, *Modern*	1.60	2.25	1.75
☐ **.50-70 Musket**, Various Makers, *Curio*	9.75	15.00	13.00
☐ **.50-70 Musket**, Shotshell, Various Makers, *Modern*	5.25	7.50	7.00
☐ **.50-90 Sharps**, Lead Bullet, *Curio*	15.00	22.50	20.00
☐ **.50-90 Win.**, Various Makers, *Curio*	2.75	4.00	3.50
☐ **.500 #2 Express**, Soft Point Bullet, *Modern*	4.25	6.00	5.50
☐ **.500 Jeffery**, Various Maker, *Modern*	13.00	20.00	18.00
☐ **.500 Irish Constabulary Revolver**, Various Makers, *Modern*	18.50	24.50	22.00
☐ **.500 N.E. 3″**, Various Makers, *Modern*	3.75	5.25	4.75
☐ **.500 Nitro BPE**, Various Makers, *Curio*	6.75	9.25	8.50
☐ **.500/.450 #1 Express**, Various Makers, *Modern*	3.75	5.50	5.00
☐ **.500/.450 #2 Musket**, Various Makers, *Modern*	3.00	4.25	4.00
☐ **.500/.450 Mag. N.E. 3¼″**, Various Makers, *Modern*	7.00	9.25	8.75
☐ **.500/.465 N.E.**, Various Makers, *Modern*	4.70	6.00	5.50
☐ **.505 Gibbs**, Lead Bullet, *Modern*	6.70	8.50	8.00
☐ **.52-70 Sharps R.F.**, Lead Bullet, *Curio*	31.50	40.00	38.00
☐ **.54 Ballard R.F.**, Lead Bullet, *Curio*	36.00	48.50	45.00
☐ **.55-100 Maynard**, Lead Bullet, *Curio*	33.50	45.00	42.00
☐ **.56-46 Spencer R.F.**, Various Makers, *Curio*	22.00	30.00	27.50
☐ **.56-50 Spencer R.F.**, WRA, Commercial, *Antique*	1.95	3.00	2.50
☐ **.56-52 Spencer R.F.**, Various Makers, *Curio*	3.25	4.45	4.00
☐ **.56-52 Spencer R.F.**, Shotshell, Various Makers, *Curio*	18.50	23.75	22.50
☐ **.56-56 Spencer R.F.**, Various Makers, *Antique*	5.50	7.25	6.75
☐ **.577 N.E. 2¾″**, Various Makers, *Modern*	6.00	9.25	8.75
☐ **.577 N.E. 3″**, Various Makers, *Modern*	7.00	10.25	9.75
☐ **.577 Snyder**, Various Makers, *Modern*	4.25	6.00	5.75
☐ **.577 Snyder**, Shotshell, Various Makers, *Modern*	5.25	7.25	6.75
☐ **.577/.450 Martini-Henry**, Various Makers, *Modern*	4.75	6.00	5.50
☐ **.577/.500 3⅛″**, Various Makers, *Modern*	5.65	7.50	7.00
☐ **.58 Berdan**, Various Makers, *Curio*	4.75	6.90	6.50
☐ **.58 Gatling R.F.**, Lead Bullet, *Curio*	23.00	30.00	28.50
☐ **.58 Joslyn Carbine R.F.**, Various Makers, *Curio*	28.00	37.50	35.00
☐ **.58 Mont Storm R.F.**, Various Makers, *Curio*	34.00	45.00	42.00
☐ **.58 U.S. Musket**, Lead Bullet, *Curio*	12.00	20.00	18.00
☐ **.600 N.E.**, Lead Bullet, *Curio*	22.00	31.00	28.00
☐ **.70-150 Win.**, Cartridge Board Dummy, *Curio*	120.00	150.00	140.00
☐ **2mm Rimfire**, Blank Cartridge, *Modern*	.10	.20	.15
☐ **2mm Rimfire**, Lead Bullet, *Modern*	.30	.45	.40
☐ **2.7mm Kolibri**, Jacketed Bullet, *Curio*	12.00	16.50	15.00
☐ **3mm Kolibri**, Various Makers, *Curio*	12.50	18.50	16.00
☐ **4mm R.F.**, Lead Bullet, *Antique*	.15	.25	.20
☐ **4.25mm Liliput**, Jacketed Bullet, *Curio*	4.95	7.00	6.50
☐ **5.5mm Soemmerda**, Various Makers, *Modern*	2.95	4.00	3.50
☐ **5.5mm Velo Dog**, Lead Bullet, *Curio*	.45	.80	.65
☐ **5.6 x 33 Rook**, Various Makers, *Modern*	1.25	1.85	1.60
☐ **5.6 x 35R Vierling**, Various Makers, *Modern*	.55	1.10	.80
☐ **5.6 x 50R Mag.**, Various Makers, *Modern*	.95	1.45	1.30
☐ **5.6 x 50 Mag.**, Various Makers, *Modern*	.95	1.45	1.30
☐ **5.6 x 52R**, Various Makers, *Modern*	.75	1.10	.95
☐ **5.6 x 57**, Various Makers, *Modern*	.95	1.45	1.30

	V.G.	Exc.	Prior Year Exc. Value
☐ **5.6 x 61 Vom Hofe Express**, Soft Point Bullet, *Modern*	3.95	5.00	4.75
☐ **5.6 x 57R**, Various Makers, *Modern*	.95	1.55	1.40
☐ **5.6 x 61R Vom Hofe Express**, Various Makers, *Modern*	3.65	5.00	4.50
☐ **5.7mm Target Pistol**, Various Makers, *Modern*	3.70	4.65	4.25
☐ **5.75mm Velo-Dog**, Various Makers, *Modern*	.95	1.40	1.25
☐ **5.75mm Velo-Dog Short**, Various Makers, *Modern*	1.95	2.95	2.50
☐ **5mm Bergmann**, Various Makers, *Curio*	6.75	9.50	9.00
☐ **5mm Bergmann**, Grooved, Various Makers, *Curio*	4.95	7.00	6.50
☐ **5mm Brun**, Various Makers, *Modern*	10.00	18.00	15.00
☐ **5mm Clement**, Soft Point Bullet, *Curio*	3.50	4.75	4.50
☐ **5mm French Revolver**, Various Makers, *Modern*	.65	1.00	.80
☐ **5mm Pickert**, Various Makers, *Modern*	12.00	19.00	17.50
☐ **5mm Rem. RFM**, Jacketed Bullet, *Modern*	.15	.25	.25
☐ **6 x 58 Forster**, Various Makers, *Curio*	6.50	9.00	8.75
☐ **6 x 58R Forster**, Various Makers, *Curio*	3.35	4.45	4.20
☐ **6.35mm Pickert**, Various Makers, *Modern*	4.25	5.75	5.50
☐ **6.5 x 48R Sauer**, Various Makers, *Curio*	2.20	3.00	2.75
☐ **6.5 x 52 Mannlicher-Carcano**, Various Makers, *Modern*	.65	.90	.80
☐ **6.5 x 54 M.S.**, Various Makers, *Modern*	1.15	1.65	1.40
☐ **6.5 x 54 Mauser**, Soft Point Bullet, *Modern*	2.20	3.00	2.75
☐ **6.5 x 55 Swedish**, Various Makers, *Modern*	.65	1.00	.80
☐ **6.5 x 57**, Various Makers, *Modern*	.95	1.50	1.35
☐ **6.5 x 57R**, Various Makers, *Modern*	.95	1.50	1.35
☐ **6.5 x 58 Vergueiro**, Various Makers, Military, *Modern*	4.50	5.75	5.50
☐ **6.5mm Dutch**, Various Makers, Military, *Modern*	.15	.25	.20
☐ **6.5 x 58R Sauer**, Jacketed Bullet, *Modern*	1.90	3.00	2.75
☐ **6.5mm Jap**, Various Makers, *Modern*	.65	.95	.80
☐ **6.5 x 68 Schuler**, Various Makers, *Modern*	1.25	1.90	1.70
☐ **6.5 x 68R**, Various Makers, *Modern*	1.70	2.50	2.25
☐ **6.5mm Bergmann**, Various Makers, *Curio*	8.00	12.00	11.00
☐ **6.5mm Bergmann Grooved**, Various Makers, *Curio*	5.85	7.35	7.00
☐ **6.50mm Mannlicher**, Various Makers, *Modern*	4.75	6.75	6.50
☐ **6.8mm Gasser**, Various Makers, *Modern*	4.50	6.00	5.75
☐ **6.8mm Schulhof**, Various Makers, *Modern*	2.85	3.95	3.75
☐ **6mm Lee Navy**, Various Makers, Military, *Modern*	2.25	3.25	3.00
☐ **6mm Loron**, Patent Ignition, *Antique*	3.50	4.50	4.25
☐ **6mm Flobert**, 2 Piece Case, *Antique*	.40	.70	.55
☐ **6mm Merveilleux**, Various Makers, *Modern*	1.85	2.75	2.50
☐ **6mm Protector**, Various Makers, *Modern*	1.25	2.00	1.80
☐ **6mm Rem.**, Various Makers, *Modern*	.50	.80	.65
☐ **6.5mm Reg. Mag.**, Various Makers, *Modern*	.75	1.20	1.00
☐ **7 x 57R**, Various Makers, *Modern*	.85	1.35	1.20
☐ **7 x 61 Norma**, Various Makers, *Modern*	.85	1.40	1.25
☐ **7 x 64 Brenneke**, Various Makers, *Modern*	.95	1.60	1.45
☐ **7 x 64**, Various Makers, *Modern*	.95	1.60	1.40
☐ **7 x 65R**, Various Makers, *Modern*	.95	1.65	1.45
☐ **7 x 72R**, Various Makers, *Modern*	2.65	3.75	3.50
☐ **7 x 72R**, Dummy Cartridge, *Curio*	2.60	3.50	3.25
☐ **7 x 73 Vom Hofe**, Soft Point Bullet, *Modern*	7.95	9.95	9.50
☐ **7.25mm Adler**, Various Makers, *Modern*	68.50	95.00	90.00
☐ **7.35mm Carcano**, Various Makers, Military, *Modern*	.15	.25	.20

	V.G.	Exc.	Prior Year Exc. Value
☐ **7.5 x 54 MAS**, Various Makers, Military, *Modern*	.15	.25	.25
☐ **7.5 x 55 Swiss**, Military, *Modern*	.70	1.00	.90
☐ **7.5mm Swedish Nagent**, Various Makers, *Modern*	.65	1.00	.85
☐ **7.5mm Swiss Nagent**, *Modern*	.75	1.15	.95
☐ **7.6mm Mauser Revolver**, Various Makers, *Modern*	5.95	9.00	8.50
☐ **7.62 x 39 Russian**, Various Makers, Military, *Modern*	.35	.60	.45
☐ **7.62 x 39 Russian**, Various Makers, *Modern*	.50	.85	.65
☐ **7.62 x 54R Russian**, Various Makers, *Modern*	.70	.95	.80
☐ **7.62mm Nagent**, Various Makers, Military, *Modern*	1.60	2.25	1.95
☐ **7.62mm Tokarev**, Various Makers, Military, *Modern*	.45	.80	.60
☐ **7.63 Mannlicher**, Various Makers, Military, *Modern*	.15	.25	.25
☐ **7.63 Mauser**, Various Makers, *Modern*	.20	.35	.30
☐ **7.65 Borchardt**, Various Makers, *Modern*	2.65	3.50	3.25
☐ **7.65mm Francotte**, Various Makers, *Modern*	19.00	27.50	25.00
☐ **7.65mm Glisenti**, Various Makers, *Modern*	77.50	100.00	95.00
☐ **7.65mm Pickert**, Various Makers, *Modern*	3.65	4.75	4.50
☐ **7.65 Roth-Sauer**, Various Makers, *Curio*	2.70	4.00	3.75
☐ **7.65 x 53 Mauser**, Military, *Modern*	.60	.90	.75
☐ **7.65 Argentine**, Various Makers, *Modern*	.70	.95	.80
☐ **7.65 Argentine Navy Match**, Military, *Curio*	26.50	38.00	35.00
☐ **7.7mm Jap**, Various Makers, *Modern*	.60	.95	.80
☐ **7.7mm Bittner**, Various Makers, *Modern*	27.50	34.00	32.50
☐ **7.8mm Bergmann #5**, Various Makers, *Modern*	5.25	7.80	7.50
☐ **7.92 x 33 Kurz**, Various Makers, Military, *Modern*	.85	1.40	1.25
☐ **7mm Baer**, Various Makers, *Modern*	1.90	2.75	2.50
☐ **7mm Charola**, Various Makers, *Modern*	5.60	6.75	6.50
☐ **7mm Flobert**, Lead Bullet, *Antique*	.50	.65	.50
☐ **7mm French Revolver**, Various Makers, *Modern*	1.00	1.70	1.55
☐ **7mm H & H**, Soft Point Bullet, *Modern*	1.80	2.75	2.50
☐ **7mm Mauser**, Various Makers, *Modern*	.55	.80	.65
☐ **7mm Mauser**, Various Makers, Military, *Modern*	.25	.40	.35
☐ **7mm Nambu**, Various Makers, *Curio*	6.25	8.85	8.50
☐ **7mm Rem. Mag.**, Various Makers, *Modern*	.75	1.10	.90
☐ **7mm Rem. Mag.**, Various Makers, Flare Cartridge, *Modern*	1.75	2.40	2.25
☐ **7mm Rigby Mag.**, Soft Point Bullet, *Modern*	2.45	3.25	3.00
☐ **7mm Target Pistol**, Various Makers, *Modern*	1.95	2.65	2.50
☐ **7mm Vom Hofe S.E.**, Various Makers, *Modern*	7.25	8.75	8.50
☐ **7mm Wby. Mag.**, *Modern*	.95	1.40	1.20
☐ **8 x 48R Sauer**, Various Makers, *Curio*	3.60	4.75	4.50
☐ **8 x 50R Lebel**, Various Makers, Military, *Modern*	.25	.40	.35
☐ **8 x 50R Mannlicher**, Various Makers, *Modern*	1.80	2.65	2.50
☐ **8 x 51 Mauser**, Various Makers, *Curio*	1.10	1.55	1.35
☐ **8 x 51R Mauser**, Various Makers, *Curio*	4.85	6.80	6.50
☐ **8 x 56R Mannlicher**, Various Makers, Military, *Modern*	4.95	6.25	6.00
☐ **8 x 56R Kropatschek**, Various Makers, Military, *Curio*	.35	.50	.40
☐ **8 x 57 Jrs**, Various Makers, *Modern*	.95	1.40	1.25
☐ **8 x 57S**, Various Makers, *Modern*	.70	.95	.85
☐ **8 x 58R Krag**, Jacketed Bullet, Military, *Modern*	2.65	3.55	3.25
☐ **8 x 58R Saver**, Various Makers, *Curio*	3.35	4.25	4.00
☐ **8 x 60 Mauser**, Various Makers, *Modern*	1.90	2.75	2.50

	V.G.	Exc.	Prior Year Exc. Value
☐ **8 x 60S**, Various Makers, *Modern*	1.40	1.90	1.70
☐ **8 x 64 Brenneke**, Various Makers, *Modern*	1.60	2.25	2.00
☐ **8 x 68S**, Various Makers, *Modern*	1.25	1.75	1.55
☐ **8 x 75**, Various Makers, *Curio*	3.65	4.50	4.25
☐ **8 x 75R**, Various Makers, *Curio*	2.85	4.00	3.75
☐ **8.1 x 72R**, Lead Bullet, *Modern*	2.95	3.70	3.45
☐ **8.15 x 46R**, Lead Bullet, *Modern*	.95	1.35	1.20
☐ **8.15 x 46R**, Soft Point Bullet, *Modern*	1.60	2.25	2.00
☐ **8mm Bergmann #4**, Various Makers, *Modern*	9.75	16.00	14.00
☐ **8mm Bergmann-Simplex**, Various Makers, *Modern*	1.90	2.75	2.50
☐ **8mm Dormus**, Various Makers, *Modern*	12.95	21.50	16.00
☐ **8mm Gaulois**, Various Makers, *Curio*	.95	1.45	1.30
☐ **8mm Lebel Revolver**, Various Makers, Military, *Modern*	.55	.80	.65
☐ **8mm Lebel Revolver**, Various Makers, *Modern*	1.10	1.70	1.50
☐ **8mm Kromar**, Various Makers, *Modern*	34.00	46.50	45.00
☐ **8mm Mauser**, Various Makers, *Modern*	.55	.80	.65
☐ **8mm Mitrailleuse**, Various Makers, *Modern*	1.10	1.55	1.35
☐ **8mm Nambu**, Various Makers, Military, *Modern*	1.45	3.80	3.50
☐ **8mm Pieper Revolver**, Lead Bullet, *Modern*	1.20	1.70	1.50
☐ **8mm Protector**, Various Makers, *Modern*	.95	1.40	1.25
☐ **8mm Rast-Gasser**, Various Makers, *Modern*	1.25	1.70	1.50
☐ **8mm Schulhof**, Various Makers, *Modern*	4.75	6.80	6.50
☐ **8mm Steyr Revolver**, Various Makers, *Modern*	45.00	65.00	65.00
☐ **8mm Roth-Steyr**, Various Makers, *Modern*	.95	1.70	1.50
☐ **9 x 56 M.S.**, Soft Point Bullet, *Modern*	.90	1.35	1.20
☐ **9 x 63**, Various Makers, *Modern*	2.90	3.75	3.50
☐ **9.3 x 53R Swiss**, Lead Bullet, *Curio*	.95	1.40	1.25
☐ **9.3 x 57**, Various Makers, *Modern*	1.05	1.45	1.30
☐ **9.3 x 57R**, Various Makers, *Modern*	3.65	4.75	4.50
☐ **9.3 x 62 Mauser**, Various Makers, *Modern*	1.35	1.80	1.65
☐ **9.3 x 64 Brenneke**, Various Makers, *Modern*	1.65	2.25	2.00
☐ **9.3 x 72R**, Various Makers, *Modern*	1.65	2.25	2.00
☐ **9.3 x 74R**, Various Makers, *Modern*	1.75	2.35	2.10
☐ **9.3 x 82R**, Lead Bullet, *Modern*	2.25	3.00	2.75
☐ **9.3 x 82R**, Soft Point Bullet, *Modern*	2.65	3.45	3.25
☐ **9.4mm Dutch Rev.**, Various Makers, *Modern*	2.65	3.75	3.50
☐ **9.5 x 57 M.S.**, Various Makers, *Modern*	1.40	2.25	1.90
☐ **9.5 x 60R Turkish**, Lead Bullet, *Modern*	21.50	30.00	28.00
☐ **9mm Bayard Long**, Various Makers, Military, *Modern*	.35	.50	.40
☐ **9mm Borchardt**, Various Makers, *Modern*	60.00	75.00	75.00
☐ **9mm Browning Long**, Various Makers, *Modern*	.95	1.65	1.50
☐ **9mm Devisme**, Patent Ignition, *Antique*	8.50	14.00	12.00
☐ **9mm Devisme**, *Modern*	1.60	2.25	1.95
☐ **9mm Danish Ronge**, Lead Bullet, *Modern*	.55	.90	.75
☐ **9mm Flobert**, Lead Bullet, *Antique*	.35	.55	.55
☐ **9mm Campo Giro**, Various Makers, *Modern*	12.50	18.00	17.00
☐ **9mm Gasser-Kropatschek Rev.**, Various Makers, *Modern*	3.65	4.75	4.50
☐ **9mm Glisenti**, Various Makers, *Modern*	.95	1.65	1.50
☐ **9mm Bergmann**, Jacketed Bullet, Military, *Modern*	.30	.45	.40
☐ **9mm Luger**, Various Makers, *Modern*	.30	.50	.40
☐ **9mm Luger**, Various Makers, Military, *Modern*	.25	.40	.35
☐ **9mm**, Lead Bullet, *Modern*	4.75	5.65	5.50

	V.G.	Exc.	Prior Year Exc. Value
☐ **9mm Makarov**, Jacketed Bullet, Military, *Modern*	11.00	16.50	15.00
☐ **9mm Mauser**, Various Makers, *Modern*	.90	1.35	1.20
☐ **9mm Nagent**, Various Makers, *Modern*	1.65	2.45	2.20
☐ **9mm Salvo Squeeze Bore**, Various Makers, *Curio*	16.00	24.00	23.00
☐ **9mm Steyr**, Various Makers, Military, *Modern*	.65	1.00	.85
☐ **10mm Hirst Auto Pistol**, Various Makers, *Modern*	17.00	25.00	23.00
☐ **10mm Soerabaja**, Lead Bullet, *Antique*	3.25	4.25	4.00
☐ **10,15 x 61R Jarmann**, Paper-Patched, Lead Bullet, *Curio*	4.25	5.80	5.50
☐ **10.3 x 65R Baenziger**, Soft Point Bullet, *Modern*	3.45	5.00	4.75
☐ **10.4 Italian Revolver**, Military, *Modern*	1.25	2.00	1.70
☐ **10.4mm Swiss Ordnance Rev.**, Various Makers, *Modern*	2.95	4.00	3.75
☐ **10.4 x 47R Italian Vetterli**, Jacketed Bullet, *Modern*	.90	1.30	1.10
☐ **10.6mm Schulhof**, Various Makers, *Modern*	1.75	2.45	2.25
☐ **10.6mm Spanish Ordnance Rev.**, Various Makers, *Modern*	1.35	2.00	1.75
☐ **10.75 x 58R Berdan**, Military, Various Makers, *Curio*	1.40	2.00	1.75
☐ **10.75 x 68 Mauser**, Various Makers, *Modern*	1.65	2.25	2.00
☐ **10.75 x 73**, Various Makers, *Modern*	1.85	2.45	2.25
☐ **19.8mm Montenegrin Rev.**, Various Makers, *Modern*	12.00	18.50	16.00
☐ **11 x 59R Gras**, Jacketed Bullet, *Curio*	1.10	1.75	1.50
☐ **11 x 59R Gras**, Lead Bullet, *Curio*	1.40	2.10	1.80
☐ **11.15 x 58R Werndl**, Lead Bullet, *Modern*	4.75	6.00	5.75
☐ **11.15 x 60R Mauser**, Lead Bullet, *Modern*	4.25	5.25	5.00
☐ **11.15 x 65R**, Lead Bullet, *Modern*	2.90	3.75	3.50
☐ **11.2mm Gasser**, Various Makers, *Modern*	7.25	9.00	8.50
☐ **11.43 x 50R Egyptian**, Various Makers, *Modern*	1.95	3.00	2.75
☐ **11.43 x 50R Egyptian**, Wood Shotshell Bullet, *Modern*	3.25	4.00	3.75
☐ **11.5 x 57R Spanish**, Various Makers, *Modern*	2.90	4.00	3.75
☐ **11.5mm Montenegrin-Gasser**, Various Makers, *Modern*	6.75	9.25	8.75
☐ **11.5mm Werder**, Various Makers, *Modern*	5.90	8.25	8.00
☐ **11mm Danish Ordnance Rev.**, Various Makers, *Modern*	26.00	33.00	30.00
☐ **11mm Chassepot**, Patent Ignition, *Antique*	4.95	6.25	6.00
☐ **11mm Devisme**, Patent Ignition, *Antique*	9.50	14.00	12.00
☐ **11mm French Ordnance**, Various Makers, *Curio*	.75	1.25	1.10
☐ **11mm German Service**, Various Makers, *Curio*	1.05	1.90	1.65
☐ **11mm Loran**, Patent Ignition, *Antique*	2.95	3.75	3.50
☐ **11mm Mannlicher**, Military, Paper-Patched Lead Bullet, *Curio*	.40	.55	.45
☐ **11mm Rapnael**, Patent Ignition, Outside Primed, *Antique*	18.50	30.00	25.00
☐ **11mm Rapnael**, Patent Ignition, Inside Primed, *Antique*	26.00	39.00	35.00
☐ **12.7 Russian M.G.**, Various Makers, Military, *Modern*	.65	1.00	.75
☐ **15mm French Rev.**, Various Makers, *Modern*	12.00	17.50	16.00
☐ **4 Ga.**, Various Makers, Paper Case,.Shotshell, *Modern*	3.25	4.25	4.00
☐ **8 Ga.**, Various Makers, Paper Case, Shotshell, *Modern*	2.95	4.00	3.75

The New Balancing Act in the Business of Higher Education

Edited by

Robert Clark

North Carolina State University, USA

and

Madeleine d'Ambrosio

TIAA-CREF Institute, USA

Edward Elgar

Cheltenham, UK • Northampton, MA, USA

Published by
Edward Elgar Publishing Limited
Glensanda House
Montpellier Parade
Cheltenham
Glos GL50 1UA
UK

Edward Elgar Publishing, Inc.
136 West Street
Suite 202
Northampton
Massachusetts 01060
USA

A catalogue record for this book is available from the British Library

Library of Congress Cataloging in Publication Data

The new balancing act in the business of higher education / edited by Robert Clark, Madeleine d'Ambrosio.
p. cm.
Includes bibliographical references and index.
1. Education, Higher—United States—Finance. 2. Universities and colleges—United States—Business management. I. Clark, Robert Louis, 1949– II. d'Ambrosio, Madeleine, 1950–
LB2342.N373 2006
378.1′06–dc22 2006008414

ISBN-13: 978 1 84542 731 3
ISBN-10: 1 84542 731 9

Printed and bound in Great Britain by MPG Books Ltd, Bodmin, Cornwall

Contents

Contributors

Michael F. Adams President, University of Georgia

Herbert M. Allison, Jr. Chairman, President and Chief Executive Officer of TIAA; President and Chief Executive Officer of CREF

David W. Breneman University Professor and Dean, Newton and Rita Meyers Professor of Economics of Education, Curry School of Education, University of Virginia; TIAA-CREF Institute Fellow

Robert H. Bruininks President, University of Minnesota

Robert L. Clark Professor of Economics and Professor of Business Management, North Carolina State University; TIAA-CREF Institute Fellow

Allan R. Cohen Edward A. Madden Professor and Director of Corporate Entrepreneurship, Babson College; TIAA-CREF Institute Fellow

Madeleine B. d'Ambrosio Vice President and Executive Director, TIAA-CREF Institute

Ronald G. Ehrenberg Irving M. Ives Professor of Industrial and Labor Relations and Economics, Cornell University; Director of the Cornell Higher Education Research Institute; TIAA-CREF Institute Fellow

Kermit L. Hall President, University at Albany, State University of New York

James C. Hearn Professor of Public Policy and Higher Education, Vanderbilt University; TIAA-CREF Institute Fellow

Stanley O. Ikenberry Regent Professor and President Emeritus, University of Illinois; Past President and CEO at the American Council on Education; President of TIAA and CREF Boards of Overseers

William E. Kirwan Chancellor, University System of Maryland

H. Lane Kneedler Partner, Reed Smith LLP

David A. Longanecker Executive Director, Western Interstate Commission for Higher Education

Benjamin F. Quillian Senior Vice President, Business and Operations, American Council on Education

John Edward Sexton President, New York University

Kenneth A. Shaw Chancellor Emeritus and University Professor, Syracuse University; TIAA-CREF Institute Fellow

Cathy A. Trower Co-Principal Investigator and Research Associate, Graduate School of Education, Harvard University; TIAA-CREF Institute Fellow

Robert W. Wagner PhD candidate, State University of New York at Albany

Foreword

Herbert M. Allison, Jr.

Can American colleges and universities remain the world's best institutions of higher education? Can they continue to provide access to all students, regardless of income, race and gender, and a quality learning experience for the leaders of tomorrow? These are among the difficult questions facing our nation's institutions of higher education today.

At TIAA-CREF we have a long history of working with higher education, our core market, to address such challenges. Our partnership with academic leaders enables us to develop services and solutions in response to the evolving needs of institutions and those of their employees. Acting as a bridge between higher education and our company, the TIAA-CREF Institute generates research and information on financial security and higher education issues, and shares knowledge through its Series on Higher Education, which includes books, DVDs, conferences, webcasts and other forums. This volume, part of the TIAA-CREF Institute Series on Higher Education, is one example of its output.

In November 2005 the Institute convened 'The New Balancing Act in the Business of Higher Education', a major national conference of college and university leaders to exchange ideas on two critical issues at the forefront of higher education economics. First, how do universities continue to hire and retain the best faculty in an adverse economic environment? Increased reliance on contract faculty and lessened dependence on tenure-track faculty at American universities is a trend that seems to be driven by the lower cost of contract faculty and the greater teaching demands placed on them. Campus leaders and scholars examine such emerging employment patterns in this book.

Second, revenue sources have changed substantially for American colleges and universities. Uncertain returns on endowments, slow economic growth, reductions in state appropriations and overall limited governmental funding have forced many higher education institutions to increase tuition charges, reduce spending and reconsider resource allocation decisions. This volume includes important insights into how they are coping with these challenges.

Finally, this book offers some of the conference's discussions on principles for change and how academic leaders confronted with difficult choices can successfully implement fundamental change at their institutions.

As a respected and longstanding partner to higher education, TIAA-CREF has fostered ongoing dialogue with thought leaders and decision makers in this field. This book reflects that dialogue, including input from more than a hundred individuals who participated in the conference. TIAA-CREF is proud to explore issues of strategic importance to higher education and to TIAA-CREF, alongside the very people we aim to serve. The future of higher education is intertwined with the future of TIAA-CREF and together we can help ensure the continued vitality of America's colleges and universities.

INTRODUCTION

1. Walking the financial tightrope: balancing costs and revenues with commitment to mission

Robert L. Clark and Madeleine B. d'Ambrosio

BALANCING THE COUNTERWEIGHTS IN THE ACADEMIC MARKET PLACE

Virtually all colleges and universities are facing the twin challenges of revenue enhancement and cost containment. The new balancing act in higher education requires innovative policies to increase revenues but to do so in a manner that does not deny access to students from low-income households. The decline in traditional revenue sources, such as state appropriations, has caused many institutions to raise tuition charges in an effort to maintain total revenues. Thus, part of the balancing act necessitates a careful assessment of needed revenues, the cost of providing quality education, and the net price that students must pay to attend the universities of their choice. To maintain access, greater emphasis and concern has been placed on need-based financial aid, even as there is pressure to provide broad-based merit aid to qualified students to offset the increasing price of higher education.

To attract public and private funds, colleges and universities must prove themselves to be good stewards of their resources. Efficiency and accountability have entered the lexicon of higher education, and academic leaders must balance the need for adequate resources to achieve their teaching, research and service missions with the bottom line. Traditional management methods are now inadequate and universities are recognizing the need to partner with their stakeholders as they walk the tightrope of cost containment and quality education. Examples of major changes in management and pricing policies include the move to greater operational autonomy by three Virginia universities, the use of vouchers for state residents to attend colleges and universities in Colorado, and Miami of Ohio's adoption of equal tuition charges for both in-state and out-of state students, coupled with the establishment of scholarships for Ohio residents.

College budgets are dominated by the compensation for faculty and staff. In response to adverse economic conditions, universities have traditionally reduced faculty size and left positions unfilled, thus increasing class size and reducing course offerings. Recently, there has been a significant shift by many institutions toward the utilization of more part-time and contract faculty and reduced reliance on tenure-track faculty. Generally, contingent faculty teach more classes and are paid less than tenure-track faculty. In addition, they are often not provided employee benefits such as health insurance and pension plans. Thus, more contingent faculty typically means lower cost per student credit hour of instruction. But students may receive a very different educational experience when they are taught by contingent instructors instead of tenure-track faculty. As utilization of tenure-track faculty declines, there will be less research at the institution. Furthermore, contingent faculty tend to have less long-term commitment to the university, so the level of service to and governance of the institution may decline. The balancing of these factors will determine whether institutions of higher education in the United States continue to be the world leaders in graduate education and research and whether American undergraduates are encouraged to seek graduate degrees and careers in research.

The challenge to American higher education in the global market is clearly shown by graduation and employment data. In 2000, Asian universities produced 1.2 million graduates in science and engineering while European universities produced 850 000. In contrast, the US produced 500 000 new graduates in these fields (Kirwan, Chapter 4). National comparisons are equally striking. The United States now lags behind the United Kingdom, South Korea, Germany, Australia, Singapore, Japan, Canada and France in the percentage of 24-year-olds who have degrees in science and engineering (Ikenberry, Chapter 2).

The fraction of PhD degrees granted by US universities that go to American citizens and permanent residents has been declining for the past three decades. In 1974, non-US citizens with temporary visas received 11 per cent of all doctoral degrees from American universities. The proportion of PhD degrees being awarded to such individuals had risen to 29 per cent by 2004. The trends are even more dramatic in the areas of science and engineering. Ehrenberg (Chapter 8) reports that 38 per cent of PhD degrees awarded by US universities in the physical sciences now go to foreign students and foreign students receive 55 per cent of all doctorate degrees in engineering.

Recognizing the challenges facing higher education is not enough. Developing and implementing solutions is required. Achieving fundamental change at universities often has proven to be difficult. Identifying key principles that facilitate real change in the management structure of colleges and

universities is essential. Knowing the elements of successful change will help academic leaders in their balancing act. This volume consists of 15 chapters that focus on the new balancing act in the business of higher education. The chapters include analyzes of the major national trends affecting higher education and case studies focusing on how some institutions have walked the financial tightrope and balanced the challenges. The authors are prominent thought leaders in higher education, including university presidents and chancellors and leading researchers on the business of higher education. What do we learn from their thoughtful examinations of these issues?

In Chapter 2, Stanley Ikenberry provides a clear assessment of many of the major challenges facing higher education today. He argues that the social compact between higher education and the American people is no longer in place and that the United States is adrift on higher education policy. One manifestation of this is the decline in state appropriations for higher education. Between 1977 and 2002, state funding for higher education declined from $8.50 per $1000 in personal income to $7.00. The ensuing higher tuition rates have continued to push the price of a college degree up faster than the general rate of inflation in the US. This reduction in state support is due in part to the increasing requirements of other mandated expenditures such as those associated with an aging population, that is, Medicare and pensions, and the need to provide health care for low-income families through Medicaid. However, the most recent data show an increase in state appropriations averaging 5.3 per cent for 2005–06 compared with the previous year.

Ikenberry questions whether colleges and universities are still contributing to upward mobility across generations and reducing the income inequality among American households. He notes that children from families in the top income quartile have a 75 per cent chance of going to college but only 10 per cent of young people from households in the lowest income quartile are attending college. Given economic trends, Ikenberry does not believe that higher education will return to the days of low tuition charges. Thus, universities must make better use of financial aid if a higher proportion of low-income students is to attend colleges and universities in the future. He challenges academic leaders to develop policies to moderate the differences in attendance rates by income level.

Further, Ikenberry notes that other countries are catching up to the quality of education provided by US institutions. In addition, enrollments in other countries are surging forward while the college attendance rate in the US is stagnant. He presents evidence that the relative number of graduate students in the US is declining, especially in the areas of science, technology and engineering. By comparison, growth in education in Asian countries such as China and Korea is increasing rapidly.

In this context, Ikenberry argues that colleges and universities must once again partner with the American people and reestablish the trust that Americans have historically placed in higher education. A central component for many academic leaders on this tightrope is what it means to be a 'public' institution. This balancing act requires improving the image of higher education, containing costs and raising new revenues but still providing access to all qualified students. By reviewing the current landscape of higher education, Ikenberry defines the challenges and questions that are addressed in the following chapters. Is higher education in the US in a state of crisis that will mark the end of American preeminence in educational quality and academic research? Or can academic administrators make the difficult decisions that result in another century of greater access to high-quality education? The balancing act is defined; now how do academic leaders move American higher education forward?

THE BALANCING ACT, PART ONE: ENHANCING REVENUES WHILE REDUCING COSTS

The challenges associated with shifting revenue streams are examined in the next five chapters. In Chapter 3, James Hearn reviews recent trends in revenue sources. He points out that colleges and universities are quite diverse and have different options and opportunities to generate new revenues. One balancing act that every institution faces is to utilize its assets and reputation to appeal to stakeholders to adequately fund the university. Revenue options include research partnerships with industry, patents, sale of university items, donations and endowments, tuition charges, state appropriations and government grants. Hearn notes that in 2000 tuition charges and fees and government appropriations accounted for only half of total revenues at public four-year institutions. Thus, other fund raising activities were required to generate the remaining half of the funds needed to run these institutions of higher education.

Hearn's historical review notes that universities have long been in the business of raising money from these activities. The challenge confronting many public institutions is how to balance the need for state revenues with the restrictions of state regulations. As the proportion of state appropriations in the total university budget declines, the demand for fewer restrictions and more autonomy grows. Hearn believes that increased reliance on market factors for revenues is inevitable but that appropriate responses mean that this can be done without abandoning core academic values. One approach has been to charge differential tuition for courses by discipline and degree level. These higher prices can reflect demand for popular majors

and the cost of providing certain courses. In response to the pressure to raise funds with diminishing allocations from state appropriations, public colleges and universities have considered many options to generate new sources of revenue and to attempt to reduce operating costs. The stories of higher education in two states are presented in Chapters 4 and 5.

William Kirwan, in Chapter 4, describes what he perceives as a funding crisis facing higher education. Kirwan states that the crisis is either a wake-up call for our nation or a harbinger of our worst nightmare. The nation's responses to the current problems will determine whether we achieve an appropriate balance of increasing revenues and reducing costs, access to all qualified students and a continued commitment to quality, and a use of the market to augment revenues without losing sight of fundamental academic values.

Nationwide, Kirwan believes that America is developing an education deficit in relation to the demands of our economy and in comparison with other industrialized nations. Only a few years ago, the US was the global leader in high school completion rates and in the college participation rates among high school graduates. Today, America ranks fifth among industrialized nations in high school completion rates and seventh in college participation rates. Finally, the US is the only industrialized nation with a declining college participation rate. Determining the causes of these changes and developing policies to offset the declines is essential if American universities are to remain worldwide leaders. To reestablish higher education in the US, academic leaders must work with stakeholders to choose appropriate policies.

Kirwan addresses several aspects of the new balancing act in higher education and how the University System of Maryland has been moving ahead in this challenging environment. At Maryland he developed an approach to the funding crisis which he titled Effectiveness and Efficiency. This policy required that all of the campuses in the system demonstrate that they were cutting costs and increasing teaching loads for tenure-track faculty. The policies mandated that the average faculty teaching load for tenure-track faculty be increased by 10 per cent, and the number of hours for any university degree was capped at 120 credit hours. Kirwan states that, in his view, just being more efficient will not alleviate the financial crisis. Working with the state legislature, results from the Effectiveness and Efficiency plan helped to persuade the state to provide additional funding for the system. Thus, partnering with stakeholders is essential to develop a funding plan for the future.

Still tuition charges were rising at the University of Maryland. A review of financial aid policies indicated that low-income students were accumulating significantly more debt than the average student. This occurred as the

proportion of institutional financial aid awarded on the basis of need declined from 90 per cent in 1990 to 60 per cent today. The University developed new targets and aid policies to move toward a substantial reduction in the debt load that future students from low-income backgrounds will have upon graduation. Kirwan and the University System of Maryland have tried to walk the financial tightrope by reducing costs and partnering with key stakeholders while continuing to provide access to the citizens of Maryland.

In Chapter 5, David Breneman and Lane Kneedler discuss the emergence of a new relationship between the state of Virginia and three of its universities, the University of Virginia, Virginia Tech and the College of William & Mary. They begin by placing the decline in state appropriations for higher education in Virginia in the context of national trends. Funding for higher education was 17 per cent of Virginia's general fund budget in 1985 but had fallen to 10 per cent by 2004. As a result, state support as a share of the total budget of these universities declined. For example, state appropriations dropped from 35 per cent to only 13 per cent of the budget of the University of Virginia.

Over the past three years, these institutions have negotiated with the state government for greater autonomy over setting tuition rates and in their general operations. The objective was to remove them from the status of state agencies and to provide greater freedom from regulation. The negotiations were driven by the belief that state appropriations to the universities would not recover and that the universities must seek alternative funding sources in order to remain competitive. However, the universities did not seek to drop their public status and state funds remain an important, though diminished, source of revenue to each of the universities.

After three years of discussions, the Restructured Higher Education Financial and Administrative Operations Act of 2005 was enacted. The process produced a new set of goals for higher education in Virginia, standards for accountability to which the universities would be held, and financial incentives for those institutions to achieve their goals. Breneman and Kneedler provide a detailed review and assessment of the unique changes in higher education funding in Virginia. The details of the agreement and its implications provide important lessons for academic leaders and policy makers in other states. Chapter 5 also represents an important contribution to this volume through its discussion of the change process and how to achieve fundamental change in higher education, which is the theme of the last section of the book.

David Longanecker, in Chapter 6, presents an overview of the funding status of public education by state. He argues that the funding crisis is not as bad as many believe and that universities have a difficult time in

committing to major changes. He presents data showing that public funding for higher education has fluctuated greatly over the past 30 years; however, funding per student has actually increased over the past 30 years after adjusting for inflation. In Longanecker's view, the perception of a decline in funding is due to the decline in state appropriations to higher education as a percentage of the state government's budget and the decline in these appropriations as a percentage of the university's budget.

While Longanecker believes that public higher education has not faced a crisis in the past, the future does not look bright. He cites projections that indicate that every state faces a structural budget deficit in the next decade. Competing demands for public funds and limited increases in future revenues will make it more difficult for states to continue to fund higher education at current levels. Methods to solve the pending crisis include increasing productivity, cutting costs and enhancing revenues. Longanecker is not optimistic that real cost savings can be achieved. While he notes that universities have become very good at expanding their search for new resources, in general these new funds do not support the teaching mission of the university. Instead, funds are raised for research and new activities.

Challenges to public higher education vary substantially across the country. Longanecker presents projections of enrollments by states over the next 15 years. Some states are expecting declines in enrollment in excess of 10 per cent while others are anticipating growth in student populations of 25 per cent or greater. States with a sharp decline in enrollments can expect considerable decline in revenues from tuition charges and thus will have to balance reduced revenues with fewer students and the need to cut costs. Institutions expecting a growth in enrollments of 25 per cent or more will have to balance the increased student demands against a potential shortfall in resources necessary to maintain quality. The projections of differential growth in student population mean that developing a national policy toward higher education will be difficult. The challenges facing states with declining enrollments are very different from those confronting states whose student populations are expected to grow by more than 25 per cent over the next 15 years. As a result, states will need to assume the leadership in balancing revenues and costs.

In Chapter 7, Benjamin Quillian provides an excellent historical perspective on public funding of higher education in the United States. He describes the basis of the compact between federal, state and local governments with institutions of higher education beginning during President Jefferson's administration. He sees a strong and developing commitment by the federal government in the nineteenth century to providing access to a low-cost college education, as illustrated by the Morrill Act of 1862, the

Hatch Act of 1887 and the second Morrill Act of 1890. Support for higher education for the general population continued in the twentieth century with the GI Bill after World War II and the passage of the Higher Education Act in 1965. This support by the federal government, along with major funding by state governments, helped to stimulate an increase in the proportion of Americans with college degrees, which provided significant public and private returns.

Quillian notes that universities are now competing with other public interests such as those associated with an aging population, defense and the war on terror. Concern over rising costs, inefficiencies and the lack of accountability has weakened the social compact with higher education. In the current environment, academic leaders must strive to reestablish the public's faith and trust in higher education. They must refocus the nation's attention on the public benefits of higher education, which include a more educated electorate, a stimulus to national economic growth and the value of research. Colleges and universities must prove that they still provide access to all Americans and contribute to upward mobility, the reduction of poverty and the ending of discrimination. In sum, the higher education community must demonstrate its worth to society in order for it to maintain the historical commitment from the public.

THE BALANCING ACT, PART TWO: CHANGING FACULTY EMPLOYMENT PRACTICES WHILE ACHIEVING THE MISSION OF TEACHING, RESEARCH AND SERVICE

An important component of the new balancing act is how colleges and universities will decide on the optimal mix between tenure-track and contingent faculty and how institutions will balance the needs of the faculty of the future. Ronald Ehrenberg describes the increasing use of part-time and contract faculty and the reduced reliance on tenure-track faculty (see Chapter 8). Across the country, retiring tenured faculty are being replaced by contingent faculty. Ehrenberg reports that the proportion of faculty at two- and four-year colleges and universities represented by tenured and tenure-track faculty declined from 57 per cent in 1975 to only 35 per cent in 2003.

In general, the factor tipping the balance toward greater use of contingent faculty seems to be cost. Contingent faculty are typically paid less than tenure-track faculty, often do not receive important employee benefits, and teach more classes. Ehrenberg notes that salary differentials between public institutions and private institutions are growing. A related trend is the

widening of average faculty salaries across departments (for example, between English and Finance) and salary inversion within departments as new assistant professors are hired at salaries that exceed current faculty.

Ehrenberg describes potential adverse effects associated with the employment balance being tipped toward contingent faculty. Research by Ehrenberg and others points to less student learning, slower progress toward graduation, less research conducted by university faculty and less commitment by the faculty to the institution. Ehrenberg also discusses the importance of student access to research-oriented professors and how this often turns students on to research and leads them to consider graduate school. He argues that these adverse productivity effects are an important counterbalance to the lower cost of contingent faculty. Ehrenberg believes that balancing revenues and costs in this manner will alter the quality of higher education.

In Chapter 9 John Sexton objects to this conclusion. A hallmark of his tenure as President of New York University (NYU) has been the development of what he calls the common enterprise university. In this new paradigm for faculty composition, Sexton argues that there has been a disconnect between the research enterprise and the teaching enterprise of many of our leading universities. He believes that all faculty should teach but there can also be specialization in the common enterprise university. His idea for balancing the competing interests at research universities is to devote significant resources to the hiring of contingent faculty. However, contingent faculty at NYU are not low-paid, fill-in-when-needed faculty.

Sexton's plan for contingent faculty is to hire master teachers who will specialize in teaching but must also be respected in their field. He wants to utilize experts in the professions such as law, the arts and financial services to provide a different set of experiences for students. He is striving to make part-time faculty permanent members of the NYU faculty. They may be part-time, year-round, or full-time but part-year. They should be well respected in their fields and add to NYU's reputation. Some of these part-time faculty will be internationally prominent faculty at prestigious universities around the world; these faculty Sexton calls the global professors. Thus, Sexton promotes greater reliance on contingent faculty because of their positive effects on the university. These nationally and internationally prominent individuals may actually be more costly to NYU than tenure-track faculty, not less. An important issue in whether the common enterprise university can be a model for the future is whether this academic structure can only be successful in major urban areas like New York City. In less urban areas, colleges and universities will not have the same access to experts in professional fields who are so prevalent in New York City. As Sexton notes, each university has its own version of change and each

successful institution will shape its future through an explicit commitment to its own mission.

Kermit Hall and Robert Wagner examine the challenges of faculty employment practices at public universities in Chapter 10. They begin their analysis with an assessment of the state of the social contract on higher education. In particular, they focus on the different perspectives of academic leaders, public policy makers and the public at large. While academic leaders focus on the decline in the share of public dollars going to higher education, lawmakers note that total spending per student has risen. While those in the academy tout the public good aspects of a college education, the general impression of others concerns the private gains individuals receive from their college degrees. Finally, Hall and Wagner report that, while academic leaders and their organizations such as the American Council on Education argue that more funding is needed to retain competitiveness, the public seems more concerned about accountability and performance.

Hall and Wagner examine the implications for faculty of this environmental disconnect between the various stakeholders of American universities. They note two key developments that will affect faculty employment and compensation policies of the future: the continuing trend toward greater use of contingent faculty, and the increasing diversity of the population and student bodies of public universities. Human resource policies of institutions of higher education will help to determine how universities balance their changed funding status with the need to continue to provide a quality education. In particular, Hall and Wagner focus on developing policies that have flexibility, provide equity to all employees and promote efficiency. Employment and compensation policies must be appropriate for the more diverse faculty and student population of the future (see Chapter 11).

To assess the value of policies that achieve these goals, Hall and Wagner provide a brief overview of the employment policies of SAS, a software company that has received national attention for its innovative policies and working conditions that help them attract and retain high-quality employees. The employment policies of SAS offer flexible working conditions that can be tailored to the preferences of its employees. The policies are equitable and apply to all employees. And, in the view of James Goodnight, founder of SAS, they promote efficiency by treating people well and this enhances their job performance. Hall and Wagner then speculate on whether similar policies could work in the public university environment and whether they could apply to both tenure-track and contingent faculty.

Cathy Trower provides a much different assessment of the most important issues concerning faculty employment contracts in Chapter 11. She

notes the relative lack of female faculty and faculty of color in institutions of higher education and laments the lack of change in their representation at most campuses over time. The low levels of representation are especially common among tenure-track faculty and even more so among full professors. In contrast to the other authors who describe crises in higher education and the rapid changes to address these issues, Trower examines the compensation and working conditions of today's faculty and thinks universities move more like a glacier. She concludes that universities change very slowly, almost imperceptibly.

Trower argues that evaluation standards, promotional requirements and tenure standards have not changed much. Further, she argues that these methods of identifying meritorious performance were developed years ago and reflect the lifestyles of white men at that time. She questions whether these reward structures of our universities are appropriate for today's academic labor market. Trower argues that, to attract more women and faculty of color, universities must reconsider the academic career and rewards structure that was developed years ago in response to the lifestyles of a more homogeneous professorate. She proposes new criteria for identifying and promoting quality faculty that place higher value on teaching and service to the community and the institution and allow a more flexible lifestyle for faculty. She believes that such changes would attract more faculty from under-represented groups and enrich the academy.

THE BALANCING ACT, PART THREE: IMPLEMENTING CHANGE IN HIGHER EDUCATION WHILE WORKING WITH ALL STAKEHOLDERS

Kenneth Shaw presents in Chapter 12 a model of how fundamental change can be achieved at colleges and universities. He draws on the lessons he learned while Chancellor of Syracuse University. During his tenure, Syracuse faced a significant budgetary shortfall and Shaw was forced to walk the financial tightrope. To reduce the annual operating budget, he significantly reduced the number of faculty. The balancing act he confronted was how to reduce the university's labor costs while increasing the focus on the quality of undergraduate education and maintaining Syracuse's position as a research university.

In restructuring Syracuse, Shaw developed a series of basic principles that he believes are essential to achieving fundamental change. First, he notes that having a crisis really helps because it forces all stakeholders to focus on the issues. As one develops a plan of action, academic leaders must

consider the entire system and how its various parts are integrated. The change process must be driven by a commitment to the institution's mission and its core values and all aspects of the process should be transparent to all stakeholders. Resources must be allocated in accordance with the key goals or – as Shaw writes – walk the talk. He believes that it is important to benchmark other universities and borrow policies that have worked. To achieve the change goals, leaders must maintain their commitment to change and keep the pressure on the change process. Appropriate groups and key individuals should be involved in the process and they should be empowered to facilitate change. It is important to show immediate progress and continue to make improvements along the way to the final goals. Finally, Shaw notes the importance of continued commitment to the change process and the persistence needed to reach those final objectives.

In Chapter 13 Michael Adams describes how the University of Georgia has fundamentally altered its approach to capital budgeting. Through the use of innovative approaches to generating and managing new resources for enhancing the infrastructure of the Athens campus, the university was able to make significant improvements in its campus. In 1999 Adams established the University of Georgia Real Estate Foundation for the purpose of providing a mechanism that would allow the university to dramatically shorten the construction time for new buildings. The Real Estate Foundation allowed the university to develop a strategic capital and property acquisition plan in a fiscally responsible manner outside the limits imposed on the use of state funds. The use of the foundation also allowed Georgia to focus on erecting quality buildings that were architecturally pleasing.

Under Adams' leadership, the university also created the UGA Research Foundation, which manages an endowment that is helping to build research complexes on campus more swiftly. Rapid change and a remodeling of the university was achieved by involving relevant stakeholders in key decisions and by seeking and finding ways to move the university forward at a faster pace. Working together, the university was able to break out of the traditional financing model and achieve fundamental change.

Robert Bruininks describes in Chapter 14 how he led a change process that focused on changing the academic aspirations, directions and culture of the University of Minnesota. The chapter describes the change process at Minnesota and identifies key aspects needed for successful change. The first step was to organize a new strategic planning process. The planning committee was drawn from stakeholders throughout the university system in an effort to involve students, faculty, state leaders and the citizens of Minnesota in the effort to reshape the university. The university community engaged in this process through town-hall style meetings,

university-wide messages, and postings of the strategic plan on the web. Working with faculty leaders, the provost then presented the strategic planning and positioning process to three dozen groups and organizations inside and outside the university. The primary objective of the initiative was to improve academic quality and strengthen the top academic programs on all campuses of the university. The planning process recognized that the university must continue to diversify its connections and partnerships to generate new revenue sources even as it tried to reestablish its partnership with the state legislature.

Bruininks offers some lessons learned from leading the change effort. First, academic leaders must prepare the stakeholders for change and make a strong case for why change is needed. Second, buy-in must be obtained from faculty, staff, the Board of Regents and the community. Third, each component of the change process must have strong and visible leadership. Fourth, change is an integrated process and the institution should examine both its academic and its administrative operations. Fifth, the process must be transparent and the vision and objectives must be clearly communicated. Sixth, the change process must be centered on a plan of action which calls for timely and identifiable results. Finally, the entire process must include measurable goals and public accountability. Bruininks, along with Shaw and Adams, emphasizes that a clear and open communications policy is essential to achieving buy-in to the change process and, without the buy-in, successful change is unlikely.

In Chapter 15 Allan Cohen comments on some of the key points raised in the earlier chapters and how they define the need for change at institutions of higher education. The need for new sources of funds that offset cuts by state and federal governments has placed greater pressure on tuition charges. Higher tuition charges have intensified the race to attract students, which has caused universities to build fancier facilities and provide more and better amenities for students. Balancing these competing interests requires new policies in the use of funds, the search for funds, the organization of the institution and the ability to attract a diverse student body.

Cohen notes that 'at the heart of the educational enterprise is the behavior of the faculty'. To achieve its mission, a university must have a faculty that delivers quality teaching services, provides the level of research appropriate to the school's mission, and generates service activities essential to operation of the enterprise. Trower, in Chapter 11, described the slowness of change by faculty and in the management areas dominated by faculty decisions. Cohen picks up on this theme and argues that many individuals and faculty groups can block change but few are empowered to make it happen.

While many challenges exist, Cohen is hopeful that transforming change can occur. In fact, he argues that such change did occur at Babson College.

A comprehensive structural change at Babson led to a reorganization of curriculum at the undergraduate and graduate levels that has received national recognition. New faculty decision-making structures were implemented, along with the mandating of greater cooperation and flexibility in the development of courses and curriculum. These changes at Babson produced significant improvements in its programs, higher national rankings and the attraction of more qualified students. On the basis of his experiences in achieving real change at Babson, Cohen presents a simple model of the change process that emphasizes the state of the current problem, a vision for the future, support from stakeholders for change, and the methods of achieving change. It is clear that change is costly, but the balancing act requires a careful consideration of the cost of doing nothing compared with the cost of moving ahead to fundamentally alter the way the institution manages itself.

WALKING THE TIGHTROPE WHILE BALANCING COSTS, REVENUES AND COMMITMENT

American colleges and universities must attempt to balance the need to raise sufficient resources from various sources to build and maintain the faculties and facilities that are necessary to continue to provide the best undergraduate and graduate education in the world. This balancing act has become more difficult in recent years as the social compact between higher education and the American public has weakened and competing public interests draw resources away from institutions of higher education. This volume examines the steps of academic administrators on this tightrope and provides insights into the future of higher education in the United States.

As cost pressures have mounted, tuition charges and fees have been increased. The ever rising cost of a college degree threatens access to universities for many individuals from lower-income households. Many public institutions have been given greater authority in setting their own tuition rates and as a result have become more responsible for raising funds and ensuring access. This financial balancing act requires a rethinking of need-based versus merit-based financial aid. The following chapters show how difficult these decisions can be in today's environment, where institutions compete for students, faculty and revenues.

Lawmakers and the public generally are demanding more accountability from colleges and universities. Academic leaders must show that they are good stewards of their resources and that they are attempting to provide high-quality education at reasonable costs. Efficiency demands that the

academy reevaluates how it recruits and retains quality faculty and how the appropriate mix of contingent versus tenure-track faculty is determined. Faculty employment, evaluation and compensation policies must be revised so that universities can successfully walk this tightrope of competing financial and social demands. The chapters in this volume provide different opinions on the use of contingent faculty and their value to colleges and universities. The authors express concern over how to balance low-cost teaching of undergraduates with the quality of instruction and their exposure to research methodology and how to balance the need for a more diverse faculty with the existing methods of performance review. To remain the best educational system in the world, American colleges and universities must have the best faculty, compensate them appropriately and reward teaching, research and service.

The world is changing and institutions of higher education must also change. Successful change is a complicated process. It requires inspired leadership, buy-in from all stakeholders and a clear vision of the future. Chapters in this volume present models of change and provide guidance on how successful leaders balance the competing interests that are always present. Several authors describe the experiences of their institutions in creating the environment that is conducive to achieving successful change.

In summary, the challenges are great and at times the tightrope seems to be wavering instead of remaining taut. As academic leaders walk the tightrope, they must balance costs versus access, reform versus commitment to tradition, retaining world class faculty with cost containment and providing appealing facilities without shortchanging their teaching mission. The authors of this volume describe the challenges and provide methods of performing the balancing act and successfully walking the tightrope.

2. American higher education: the new balancing act

Stanley O. Ikenberry

'The New Balancing Act' aptly characterizes where America and its colleges and universities now stand: on a *tightrope*. The best description of the relationship between higher education and the American people came not from a higher education scholar but from a journalist, one of my favorite oracles, David Brooks, *New York Times* columnist. Recently, Brooks (2005) wrote about the Education Gap and captured my attention in the very first sentence when he wrote:

> Especially in these days after Katrina, everybody laments poverty and inequality. But what are you doing about it? For example, let's say you work at a university or a college. You are a cog in one of the great inequality producing machines this country has known. What are you doing to change that?

Brooks went on to observe that as the information age has matured, a new sort of stratification is setting in between those who have a college education and those without. To be sure, there is the growing economic gap, greater lifetime earnings, and better career prospects; consequently, Brooks (ibid.) has argued that 'economic stratification is translating into social stratification', with those who went to college functioning in workplaces, living in neighborhoods and congregating in other social milieus where almost everyone else has a similar background.

The balancing act, therefore, is not just between college and not, those who have good jobs and regular paychecks and those who don't, but also in divorce rates, health and illness, volunteerism, voter behavior, unemployment, crime and the consumption of social services. And, Brooks argues correctly, these social assets are passed down from generation to generation, shaping expectations, habits and abilities, ending up with the prospect of what he called 'a hereditary meritocratic class that reinforces itself generation after generation'. This, he said, is where America is failing most.

We are a lucky generation; America is a lucky nation. We have been lucky in our inheritance: a free democratic society, one that values education, and

universal free access to high school; and because of the Dartmouth case, the Morrill Act, the GI Bill, a baby boom, aid to students, a diverse system of finance and a sound national science policy, we have been stakeholders in an incredibly diverse and strong system of higher education in this country.

Our standard of living and our place in the world grow out of this so-called luck. America's competitive edge has come from our brain power, our human capital and the knowledge and skill of the American people. With 5 per cent of the world's population, the United States employs nearly one-third of the world's scientific and engineering researchers, accounts for a vastly disproportionate share of the world's GNP, and leads in patents, copyrights and Nobel prizes. The full impact of education on the quality of life in the United States is almost beyond comprehension.

And so it is ironic that, at the very moment a college education is more crucial than ever in the global knowledge economy and at a time when the economic and social challenges facing America are steeper than ever, this country seems adrift in its higher education policy. As we struggle to regain our balance on the tightrope, other countries have closed the gap and in many respects moved ahead. In a generation China has increased its college attendance rate from less than 2 per cent to nearly 20 per cent and is following an ambitious national policy to create some of the best universities and one of the most extensive higher education systems in the world. Even now, as the US produces some 70 000 engineers each year, 600 000 engineers walk the stage in China. Looking more broadly at the pool of scientists and engineers, America has fallen behind the UK, South Korea, Germany, Australia, Singapore, Ireland, Japan, Canada and France in the percentage of 24-year-olds with degrees.

From a global perspective much, if not all, of this is great news. More higher education, stronger colleges and universities around the globe mean more opportunity, a higher standard of living and the prospect of a wiser, safer, more humane global village. But these trends also tell us that what happens to American higher education has long-term ramifications for this country's future, our quality of life, the health of communities, the resilience of our democratic institutions and traditions, the adaptability and competitive strength of the economy, and our national security and place in the world. And so, in a very real sense, we do find ourselves in a *balancing act* with America's future perched on a precarious tightrope.

A recent Brookings study by Kane and Orszag (2003) documented a 25-year decline in higher education state appropriations per $1000 personal income, from $8.50 in 1977 to $7.00 in 2003, roughly a 20 per cent drop. The causes are many: other competing demands for state support and declining state revenues, to mention only two. One of the consequences,

however, has been a steep and unrelenting rise in college tuition charges, up again in 2005 more than average family income, at a rate faster than the GNP, and by all accounts the biggest threat to equality of access and the greatest single irritant to the American public.

Still, the gradual weakening of state support and the sluggish increases in federal support for need-based student aid have not come about as a result of any deliberate public policy. I do not know of a single governor or state legislature that made a deliberate conscious decision to disinvest in higher education. In fact, most governors and almost every United States president and Congress professes support for higher education and students who need it. And still young people in the top family income quartile have a 75 per cent chance of going to college, while the prospects of those in the lowest income quartile are less than 10 per cent.

This is the growing social stratification that should worry all Americans. The educational and cultural gap should signal that the tightrope is strained and the balance that will shape America's future for the next half-century is precarious.

Others have written about the social compact and the need to launch a national conversation that brings us together, thinking seriously about the future and exploring the implications for the roles played by colleges and universities.

Larry Faulkner, who at the time of writing (2005) is concluding his tenure as President of the University of Texas at Austin, recently commented on the social compact, asking the question, was it real, did it ever really exist?

> A compact is such a civilized idea. It evokes an atmosphere of amicability and trust . . . The real questions for today are whether one ever existed, whether *compact* is just a label for our wistfulness regarding a simpler era, and whether anything like a compact can be fashioned in our time. (Faulkner, 2005, pp. 16–21)

Recognizing these limits, however, Faulkner went on to say, 'there *was* something that we seem to have lost. There *was* an atmosphere of amicability and trust. The community interest *was* generally placed foremost. The players *were* mostly honorable . . .' So, he concludes, 'Let's call it a social compact.' Faulkner then outlined his understanding of the essential terms of this civilized idea, this social compact we seem to have lost; broad access, low tuition charges and fees, the primary role for the state in financing public higher education, and key clauses related to graduate education, research, donor support, public service and outreach.

More or less, those were indeed the planks of the mid-twentieth-century compact between higher education and the American people. Both the American public and its colleges need to acknowledge that simpler day is

gone. Public and independent higher education institutions have long since abandoned low or no tuition charge policies. Access and choice for students from low-and middle-income families is a growing concern. Other state mandates such as Medicaid and desires by politicians to cap and cut taxes have strained state budgets and pushed higher education funding lower on the state's priority list. And, as the many teaching, research and public service roles of universities and colleges have multiplied, accountability and the question of who is paying for what has become more confusing and opaque to the public.

In the absence of a compact, both society and higher education have come to rely more and more on the market to decide questions of mission and strategic direction, who will be admitted, what will be taught and where the societal interface will be. As others have observed, 'This compact now suffers from a slow but deeply concerning erosion – a slow weakening that is causing, in turn, erosion of the special nature of higher education' (Newman et al., 2004).

As academics, what responsibility do we share for addressing the new balancing act in the business of higher education? Or, as David Brooks phrased it, 'What are you going to do to change that?'

One's first impulse is to begin to think of what the planks in a new social compact might look like. All of us have candidates, but before those of us from the Ivory Tower write the new compact we need to find ourselves a partner – the American people. We need to open up a dialogue, to talk and, more importantly, to listen.

Over the last several months a coalition of nearly 100 higher education institutions and associations led by the American Council on Education has been underway to do just that. 'Solutions for our Future', as the initiative has come to be called, will give every college and university in the United States an opportunity to reach out to the public, to alumni and friends, community and civic leaders, labor unions and business groups, neighborhoods, policy makers, the media, parents and students, Rotary Clubs and churches, talking not about us, not about higher education's future, but about our future, the nation's future and the opportunities and the challenges we face.

Colleges and universities do not and will not solve the world's problems. Still, we prepare the people who ultimately will help solve the problems and we teach the people who will shape and change the world. The American public does value what we do, but they see what we do in highly individualistic terms: better careers and more money for the individuals who attend. Hidden from view are the broader social benefits: stronger communities, healthier families and lives, a more civil society, a better informed and a more engaged democracy, a more adaptable, innovative and competitive

economy, a more sophisticated understanding of other nations and cultures, and a greater capacity to craft meaningful solutions for whatever challenges an uncertain future may bring.

Higher education's role in this conversation is to do a better job of telling the public what colleges and universities in this country are all about and to engage in a genuine dialogue, listening to the hopes and dreams of those we serve, to their aspirations and frustrations, and exploring the ramifications for higher education in all our varied forms.

My point is this. As we worry about the continued weakening of the social compact and the new balancing act in the business of higher education, the essential first step is to talk with and listen to the American public in new, more attentive ways. As a community we can do that and we must get about it, campus by campus, state by state, coast to coast.

What should be the essential components of a new social compact? Larry Faulkner suggested the need to help the public understand better what academic institutions actually do and our contributions to the common good: rebuilding public trust; embracing accountability, not just accepting it grudgingly; working with public leaders to strengthen college access for low- and middle-income students; addressing our cost structure; and making the link between public investment and public benefit more transparent.

On the cost front, the Lumina Foundation has offered the higher education community a good platform to at least begin to think in new ways about costs. We all understand how to cut budgets, having had to do that more times than we care to remember. What we do not do well, however, is cut actual operating *costs*. Yet access, choice, quality and virtually every other element on any social compact list is going to turn on the ability to better manage costs and increase the financial stability of the higher education enterprise. For the foreseeable future and for virtually all institutions except the unimaginably wealthy, better academic quality and wider and more equitable access to higher education will only come from greater efficiency and lower operating costs.

As we reflect on the social compact and the balance between higher education and society, one question that needs special attention by public higher education is: what does it mean to be *public?* Historically the terms *state* and *public* have been used interchangeably, and as financial support from the state has diminished the language of privatization has emerged. Graham Spanier was quoted recently discussing what he called 'public higher education's slow slide toward privatization' (Dillon, 2005).

The essence of being public lies in a fidelity to the broader societal public good, a commitment independent institutions share alongside their public counterparts. As a community, however, we cannot make that fidelity

meaningful, we cannot make it operational until we engage with the American people on campuses, in communities and states, on the farms and in the cities, in the boardrooms and labs, through television and print media, over the Internet – wherever we need to go to make the connection and start the conversation.

The devastation of Hurricane Katrina and its aftermath remind us all of how important the social fabric of this country is. The people who will rebuild New Orleans and other towns and cities, deal with the environmental and psychological damage, design the stronger levees and develop the better strategies for the future – the architects and scientists, the urban planners and engineers, the social workers and civic leaders, the physicians and the teachers – will be the graduates of America's colleges and universities.

Jack Welch, former General Electric CEO, has talked about 'the Five Stages of Crisis-management'. His five stages are not particularly novel: denial of the crisis, containment, shame mongering, and bloodletting. But then, he said, there was a fifth and final stage, 'the crisis gets fixed'. Let's hope he's right!

REFERENCES

Brooks, D. (2005), 'The Education Gap', *The New York Times*, (25 September), section 4, 11.

Dillon, S. (2005), 'At public universities, warning of privatization', *The New York Times*, (16 October), section 1, 12.

Faulkner, L.R. (2005), 'The Changing Relationship between Higher Education and the States', paper presented at the 87th Annual Meeting of the American Council on Education, Washington, DC, 13 February 2005, pp. 16–21.

Kane, T. and P. Orszag (2003), *Funding Restrictions at Public Universities: Effects and Policy Implications*, Washington, DC: Brookings Institution, September.

Newman, F., L. Coutourier and J. Scurry (2004), *The Future of Higher Education: Rhetoric, Reality, and the Risks of the Market*, San Francisco, CA: Jossey-Bass, pp. 213–23.

PART I

Enhancing revenues at colleges and universities

3. Enhancing institutional revenues: constraints, possibilities and the question of values

James C. Hearn

It would be very wrongheaded to assert that colleges and universities were until recent years somehow above the unruly fray of commerce. High-minded notions of the public good, with the accompaniment of guidance and support by governmental and spiritual organizations, have indeed long been elements in higher education, and of learning more generally, but the first of the modern universities were market-driven in the most basic, foundational sense (Kerr, 1993).[1] The organizational form of the modern university, now largely taken for granted, originated not from the highest reaches of government and church, with the inevitable accompaniment of lofty rhetoric, but rather from old-fashioned demand at 'the ground level'. In these early exemplars, adequate revenues from paying customers were essential for survival.

Perhaps inevitably, this simple, ground-level marketplace came to be supplanted by larger forces. Church and state gradually came to be more intimately involved in subsidizing the emerging institutions. In the US especially, other actors also became financially involved. Largesse from businesses, charitable organizations, alumni and friends enabled institutions to persist, prosper, and also to price low, despite rising costs.

Through the 1800s, these diverse non-tuition revenues were directed toward supporting the costs of teaching and learning, that is, the heart of these early collegiate operations. Revenue complexity grew further in the late 1800s and into the 1900s, however, as external research contracts, university hospitals, museums and athletics each began to involve new campus activities and provide additional sources of funding. By the 1970s, institutional revenues were far more diverse than a century earlier, and observers were noting the advantages of variety. Economist and college president Howard Bowen (1980) observed that leaders continually seek funding growth because they operate under a 'revenue theory of cost': new revenues are always being sought in order to pursue excellence, prestige and influence. Because there is

no limit to what might be spent in pursuit of those goals, institutions will always raise and spend all the money they can. Bowen's analysis echoed that of some of his contemporaries: 'a workable twentieth-century definition of institutional autonomy [is] the absence of dependence upon a single or narrow base of support' (Babbidge and Rosenzweig, 1962).

For contemporary institutions, the point is more salient than ever. The financial complexity of the enterprise is greater than ever (Winston, 1999). Economic downturn and political change have squeezed revenues from governments (Hovey, 1999; Toutkoushian, 2001; Schmidt, 2004). Students' acceptance of rising prices has somewhat offset this trend, but not entirely, and legislators and the public resist sustained, significant rises. In public institutions, policy makers seem to be asking the impossible, expecting improvements and expansion when only maintenance of effort seems financially in reach (Clark, 1998) and gaps have emerged in spending relative to private institutions (Alexander, 2003; Immerwahr, 2002). Making matters worse, labor, construction, plant maintenance and health-care costs have risen dramatically, lessening the likelihood of significant overall cost containment.

Clearly the context demands new funding sources, and institutions appear to be responding. By the fall of 2000, tuition and fees and government appropriations were accounting for only about half of all revenues in public four-year institutions, and auxiliary enterprises, hospitals and non-degree-oriented educational activities were accounting for a quarter (24.9 per cent) of all revenues (Knapp et al., 2002), a pattern notably different from earlier years. Indeed, in public institutions, revenue mixes are beginning to resemble those of private institutions and it is becoming appropriate to label much of public higher education 'state-assisted' rather than state-supported. Even in private four-year institutions, tuition charges and fees accounted for only about one-fourth (24.4 per cent) of all revenues in 2000 (ibid.).[2] Thus, institutions increasingly appear to be accepting the potential benefits of diversifying revenues (Ehrenberg, 2000; Breneman, 1997; Clark, 2002). The more difficult issue is not whether to diversify, but rather how. In the best case, institutional leaders can develop educationally valuable revenue-generating activities integral to campus values and missions. Less edifying are defensive pursuits that simply help institutions survive under austere conditions. Most troubling, of course, are new activities that may threaten core, cherished academic values.

NEW REVENUE STREAMS

Instructional initiatives, research and analysis initiatives, pricing initiatives, reforms in financial decision-making and management, human

resource initiatives, franchising, licensing, sponsorship and partnering arrangements with third parties, initiatives in auxiliary enterprises, facilities and real estate, and development office initiatives are all aspects of diversifying institutional revenue streams worthy of attention and review here.

Instructional Initiatives

New providers, new markets and new technologies are changing the grounds on which faculty and institutions make academic decisions, and sometimes can even endanger the financial resilience of institutions' core academic programming (Eckel, 2003). Whether these developments pose threats or opportunities varies by context (Davies, 2001), but, whichever the case, many institutions have been responding aggressively, targeting such new instructional markets as corporate learners, professional enhancement learners, degree-completion adult learners, pre-college (K-12) learners, remediation and test-preparation learners, and recreational learners (Sekera et al., 1999; Oblinger et al., 2001; Levine, 2000a; Kerr, 2002). Summer courses, short courses, online courses, credentialing programs in areas demanded by the labor force (such as information technology, education, nursing) and offerings abroad (for example, see Primary Research Group, 1997; Hinchcliff, 2000; Wills, 2005) are among the items being offered to specialized market niches at specialized prices. Often, such offerings are provided with funding by states or in concert with corporate sponsors or for-profit subsidiaries.

For Levine (2000a), the 'sweet spot' for mainstream higher education's financial survival is combining 'brick' and 'click': offering learning opportunities both online and through a traditional physical campus. Critics suggest that the sweet spot will be illusive. Collis (2002) suggests that, for non-elite institutions without superior 'brands', online education may in fact be a losing proposition (a prediction supported by the very visible failures of several major, highly touted distributed learning initiatives (Oblinger et al., 2001; Hitt and Hartman, 2002). Collis also predicts that online corporate training will be a larger and more profitable market than online academic education.

Partnerships can be an especially effective way to balance the risks in instructional innovations (Collis, 2002). Partnerships can provide needed human and financial capital, lessened risk and minimized brand exposure for generating revenues in distributed education, where early outlays for content development, technical infrastructure and marketing can be substantial (Katz et al., 2002).

Research and Analysis Initiatives

With support from enabling federal legislation, patents and licenses based in university research have risen markedly since the 1980s (Geiger, 2002; Press and Washburn, 2000; Blumenstyk, 2004), especially in such areas as computer technology, medicine and biotechnology (Wellman and Phipps, 2001; Etkowitz et al., 1998). Viewing potential returns from patents and licenses and facing rising financial pressures, many universities have reorganized and repackaged their research and analysis efforts (Feller, 1997; Karr and Kelley, 1996; Kozeracki, 1998; Thursby and Thursby, 2002; Lewis and Hearn, 2003). Specifically, research institutions have moved increasingly toward creating new organizations to generate revenues from research, including for-profit subsidiaries as well as units to nurture start-up firms via consulting and financial support (Leslie and Slaughter, 1997; Johnstone, 2002; Levine, 2000b). In addition, institutions have begun to provide products and fee-for-service offerings for off-campus parties (Wellman and Phipps, 2001; Geiger, 2002).

Overall, the evidence on mission, governance and cost-effectiveness effects for these efforts is quite mixed (Blumenstyk, 2003b). Experiences at Stanford, Berkeley and a few other elite institutions suggest that technology-transfer initiatives can pay off spectacularly when core expertise and energy are present (Clark, 1998; Geiger, 2002), but many initiatives fail to break even, much less return net revenue to their home institutions (Shane and Stuart, 2002; Powers, 2003). Similarly, the evidence for 'research parks' affiliated with campuses is quite mixed (Hebel, 2003a). This realization has prompted reconsideration, redirection and retrenchment of technology-transfer efforts (Feller, 1997; Press and Washburn, 2000; Geiger, 2002).[3] While academic research activity provides undeniable benefits to the public and institutions, its potential for increased financial returns remains ambiguous (Nicklin, 1992a; Mansfield, 1995).

Pricing Initiatives

While some institutions have taken the radical step of lowering prices for their instruction, the general trend in recent years has been toward steep rises in tuition charges and fees (Jaschik, 2005). These increases have been documented and discussed extensively, but two other trends have been less noticed: unbundling and differentiated instructional pricing.

Increasingly, undergraduate education charges have been unbundled into tuition fees and specific 'user fees' for technology, athletics and other services (Wellman and Phipps, 2001). This has allowed some institutions to increase revenues while restraining highly visible tuition charge rises.

The adoption of new user fees makes pricing and costing more transparent to students and families, and tying pricing to discrete 'objects' can also make institutional decision-making more informed and effective, but expanding user fees may or may not raise total or net revenues for an individual institution.

Another pricing approach of increasing institutional interest is tuition charge differentiation. Tuition charges may be varied by the offering unit, by the instructional or facilities costs associated with a particular course offering, by the timing of the offering, by the course level, by the physical location of the course, by the student's major field and degree level, by the number of credits being taken or previously accumulated by the student, and by student residency status (Yanikoski and Wilson, 1984; Wetzel, 1995). Tuition charges have long been differentiated for out-of-state students and for students in medicine and law, but institutions are now beginning to experiment with finer distinctions (for example, see Hebel, 2003b). The online education and distance education markets are prime grounds for such experimentation in tuition charges and fees (Collis, 2002, p. 190).

There is no guarantee that unbundling or tuition charge differentiation will generate additional revenues and, in particular, additional *net* revenues (that is, revenues remaining after offsetting costs, such as student-aid awards and tuition discounts; see McPherson and Schapiro, 1998; Johnstone, 2002). Econometric analysis of the responses of students and families to different prospective pricing and aid configurations can aid in projecting revenue effects of tuition-differentiation initiatives.

Reforms in Financial Decision Making and Management

Changes in investment approaches, debt strategies, financial operations and capital spending can improve institutional revenue streams.[4] Historically, colleges and universities have employed investment approaches that are conservative, compared with those of other major investors, and done well thereby (Morrell, 1997; Spitz, 1999), but some have recently become more aggressive, pursuing program trading and participation in foreign, arbitrage and options markets. These arenas require specialized expertise, legal charters and regulatory contexts, and limits to leaders' risk tolerance may deter such activities in many institutions (Geiger, 2002).

Several other financing innovations can facilitate new revenue generation. Institutions often rely on debt financing when initiating new projects (Standard and Poor, 2005), and revenue bonds (which are repaid out of future returns) can be more appropriate than general-obligation bonds when the acquisition of new revenue streams requires significant front-end investments and seed funding is unavailable. The risk in such instruments,

however, is that revenue streams may be uncertain for dramatically new initiatives (Wellman and Phipps, 2001). Residence halls, for example, have far more predictable returns than, say, an online-education launch.

The intelligent design of internal financial systems can also play a major role in revenue improvement. Revolving and incentive funds can be created to support teaching, research and improvements in physical plant (ibid.). Similarly, institutions can encourage entrepreneurial faculty behavior by adopting decentralized budgeting systems that distribute revenues directly to units that provide lucrative returns for the institution (Priest et al., 2002).

Human Resource Initiatives

Institutions can refine individual compensation and promotion processes to provide more explicit incentives (for example, salary bonuses) for revenue-generating activities by faculty (Hearn, 1999). Conversely, tightening institutional regulations concerning faculty consulting can help ensure that institutions fairly garner revenues associated with faculty work done directly or indirectly under institutional auspices.

Franchising, Licensing, Sponsorship, and other Partnering Arrangements with Third Parties

Collaborations with externally based partners can be fruitful for institutions (NASULGC, 1997). For example, alumni and other support organizations may be attracted to tours and camps, conferences, concert series, museum showings and athletic competitions. Vendor partners can potentially bring expert staffing as well as useful discounts and incentives to those activities, thus directly or indirectly raising net revenues (Wellman and Phipps, 2001).

Partnerships in instruction can take many forms, including online applications, campus-based portals, online procurement, online course delivery, supplemental content provision, online library services, online textbooks, advising and tutoring (see Katz et al., 2002). Many such partnerships focus on distributed learning and distance education (Levine, 2000a).

Sometimes, new revenues may be generated simply by exercising control over the ways third parties use university resources, including the ‘brand’. Colleges and universities were slow to realize the revenues potentially generated by enforcing legal rights over distinctive logos and emblems (Grassmuck, 1990), but most institutions now closely monitor sales of institutionally themed merchandise in the pursuit of potential revenues from sales.

The goal should be to establish close association between the use of university assets by others and the revenues gained by such use. For example, institutions strive to ensure that food and drink companies, athletic-gear manufacturers and others provide appropriate payments in exchange for exclusive rights to vend on campus, sell themed items or have their names and logos displayed prominently at university athletic events or on university facilities.[5] Such arrangements can be attractive to corporations and can generate substantial additional revenues (Wertz, 1997; Arnone, 2003).[6]

Initiatives in Auxiliary Enterprises, Facilities and Real Estate

Revenues from auxiliary units such as athletics departments, bookstores, hospitals and dining facilities quite often do not exceed costs (Nicklin, 1996; Geiger, 2002; Kirp, 2003; Zimbalist, 1999; Arnone, 2003). Upgrading athletic or dining facilities can sometimes increase corporate and consumer demand and thus revenues (Swanquist, 1999; Koger, 2001). Relatedly, outsourcing certain auxiliary services can bolster revenue generation (Davies, 2005).

Creating new auxiliary services can also pay off. Debit cards for purchasing on-campus products and services are increasingly familiar (see Nicklin, 1993), and many institutions are extending use of the cards to off-campus businesses willing to pay a fee for greater access to the spending power of the institution's students, faculty and staff. Debit-card programs encourage spending on campus, provide institutions interest income from funds deposited onto the card accounts and attract fees from outside businesses seeking student and faculty business.

Sometimes revenues are enhanced simply by new pricing for popular services and products. In major-revenue sports, many NCAA Division I institutions are raising prices for season tickets and 'priority seating', confident that the demand for such seating is sufficiently strong. Such price rises may be overt, but sometimes they are indirect, promising superior tickets to those making generous institutional or booster-club contributions. Increasingly, institutions are sending their formerly free alumni magazines only to those who have purchased alumni society memberships or provided gifts, and many such magazines are upgrading features and accepting paying advertisers. Also, alumni organizations within institutions are making arrangements to profit from formerly complimentary linkages to other services, including banking services and home and health insurance (Leder, 2002).

Institutions are also garnering additional revenues from classrooms, residence halls, recreational areas and undeveloped land (Kienle, 1997; Biddison

and Hier, 1998). These assets can be put to use for educational or recreational offerings, retirement communities, cooperative revenue-generating efforts with third parties or third-party leases; in addition, real estate can be sold, rented or used as collateral to secure financing for new entrepreneurial initiatives (for example, see Horwitz and Rolett, 1991; Nicklin, 1996; Wills, 2005).[7] Referring to his institution's decision to rent space to a cell phone company for transmission towers, one financial officer said, 'They install it. You forget about it, and you just get the checks each month' (June and Fain, 2005, p. A21).

Development Office Initiatives

Former SUNY Chancellor Bruce Johnstone (2002, p. 32) has wryly noted, 'No source of revenue is quite as benign and reliable as revenue from unrestricted endowment, once the institution has it.' Many institutions are aggressively expanding their pursuit of such funding (Hirsch, 1999; Strout, 2005), but the dramatic growth of the 1990s has ended (Blumenstyk, 2003a). Few colleges or universities have alumni willing and able to contribute sizable unrestricted funds and most institutions have to work hard to build a self-sustaining development effort. The costs of that effort, viewed comprehensively and objectively, can be daunting to leaders. An emphasis on private giving can also 'unbalance' institutions, tending to favor certain fields and certain aspects of institutional mission over others (Hirsch, 1999). Still, the willingness of alumni and other interested parties to support institutions financially cannot be ignored as a potential aid in difficult financial times.

MAKING DECISIONS ABOUT NEW REVENUE STREAMS

Returns from new enterprises can be non-financial as well as financial and can come in the short or long term. The generation of new *net returns* should nevertheless remain the ultimate goal of any revenue-diversification effort, not simply the generation of new revenues. New institutional funding that is fully offset by new, associated costs is acceptable only if there are non-financial returns of note *and* the new net costs are viewed as acceptable from an individual, institutional or public perspective. New revenues should be pursued only after thorough consideration of the associated costs, including the opportunity costs of forgoing other initiatives. Effective decision making should consider non-monetary factors that are distinctive to the institution's context. Below are some general considerations and guidelines.

Mission and Culture

Struggling liberal arts institutions may face dramatic internal strains if their most attractive new revenue opportunities emerge out of programming for working adults. This dilemma highlights the importance of values in the pursuit of new financial support. How a new revenue-seeking initiative fits with the pre-existing institutional context must be addressed (Tierney, 1999). Is the prospective activity effectively demanded by difficult conditions? If not, and if alternative choices are available, the acceptability of an initiative's likely threats to the institution's core mission and organizational culture must be seriously considered.

Strategic Analysis

Beyond mission and culture, institutions considering new revenue-oriented initiatives need to ascertain the substantive quality of an initiative, its short- and long-term financial prospects, the institution's comparative advantage over other existing and potential providers, the risk tolerance of all involved parties, the potential for collaboration with other organizations, the odds that high levels of potential demand may not translate into additional revenues at the margin, and organizational sustainability (Oblinger et al., 2001; Zemsky et al., 2001; Blustain et al., 1998; Katz et al., 2002).

Clearly, it is simplistic for institutions to think in terms of there being a single market for new services. The adult-student market is clearly distinctive from that for 'traditional' students, for example, (Levine, 2000a; Zemsky et al., 2005) and both are distinct from the market for high-school students seeking advanced academic preparation. Such distinctions in both buyers and selling units highlight the need for understanding the particulars of potential markets facing new initiatives. A strategic approach that speaks in generalities about 'the market' for a college's services is quite likely to fail.

Implementation

Entrepreneurially oriented institutional leaders often choose to restructure (Davies, 2001), but doing so raises a number of questions regarding implementation. Is restructuring necessary to success? Are new, buffering or spin-off organizations advisable?[8] Are new partnerships needed? Are relationships among existing stakeholders and constituents (for example, funders, government leaders, faculty, staff, students, families, the press) likely to be affected, and if so, how? Are additional structural changes necessary to address these transitions?

The research evidence suggests that effective implementation requires cultural and organizational conditions necessary to fuel and support entrepreneurial spirit (Leslie et al., 2002; Clark, 1998; Davies, 2001). Developing and sustaining a culture supportive of change requires leaders who are oriented to problem solving, operate on trust and with openness, are self-critical, are internally responsive and flexible, are thoughtful about staff-development priorities and budgets, are able to identify opportunistic, talented individuals with good ideas, are willing to be simultaneously calculating and daring, and are consultative with key stakeholders (Clark, 2002; Davies, 2001; Hirsch, 1999; Matkin, 1997; Newman and Couturier, 2001).

Perhaps the most frequent mistake institutions make in implementing new revenue-seeking efforts in the instructional arena is program cannibalization, that is, identifying a seemingly promising new academic market only to learn in the end that the new program simply draws students formerly enrolling in other programs on the same campus (Blustain et al., 1998). Other mistakes include failure to identify wants and needs of customers, failure to establish guidelines for program development, remaining committed to old-style pedagogy and curricular organization, ignoring or downplaying faculty and staff resistance, and assuming that simply providing the program will be enough, without efforts to market it (ibid.).

Incentives for departments, colleges, staff and line administrative units are all important for successful implementation, but the financial, professional and personal incentives for *individual* faculty merit special attention (Hearn et al., 1993; Hearn, 1996; Newman and Couturier, 2001). How should institutions structure faculty salaries and resource contexts to create incentives for new revenue generation? In-kind support, development funds, the offering of internal 'start-up' or venture capital pools, structured time for entrepreneurial activity, salary bonuses, and targeted salary and promotion criteria reflective of the entrepreneurial agenda are among the incentive ideas leaders might consider providing for faculty (Davies, 2001). It is also critical that potential faculty concern over threats to core missions and activities be forthrightly addressed (Johnstone, 2002), especially in the humanities and social science fields where entrepreneurialism may elicit the most anxiety (Clark, 2002; Campbell and Slaughter, 1999).

Implementation of major new initiatives also requires rethinking academic roles and structures. Should continuing and distance-education units be merged into traditional academic units (Barbulies and Callister, 2000)? Should institutions begin hiring more non-tenure-track faculty, especially in professional schools (Hearn and Anderson, 2001)? Such adaptations

may make sense but can raise internal tensions around faculty activity and reward systems (Tierney, 1999; Baldwin and Chronister, 2001).

Finances and Evaluation

Clearly, colleges and universities need to ensure that unambiguous, enforceable and appropriately structured contracts and control mechanisms are in place for all new revenue-seeking activities (Teitel, 1989; Johnstone, 2002). The dollars involved in these efforts are too precious for any other approach.

Similarly, systematic financial forecasting and analysis, including ongoing and tough-minded cost-effectiveness studies, are essential elements of new revenue-seeking initiatives (Caruthers and Wentworth, 1997; Day, 1997; Institute for Higher Education Policy and the National Education Association, 2000). Among leadership teams, a firm commitment to withdraw from failing enterprises should be established from the beginning, because the costs of maintaining a losing operation, especially in arenas not central to institutional mission, are substantial.

In many revenue initiatives, short-term losses can be offset by longer-term gains, and vice versa. For example, licensing some products and services as associated with the institution may offer short-term financial gain, but may undercut longer-term prospects by diminishing the value of the institution's 'brand' among funders or students (Kaludis and Stine, 2000). Conversely, in technology-based initiatives, development costs on the front end can be daunting, but prospects may be strong for net positive returns years after the initial investment is undertaken. In sum, time horizons can and should play a significant role in how initiatives are evaluated.

Leaders contemplating new initiatives may tend to be overoptimistic financially, making hard-nosed analysis by non-partisans essential (Nicklin, 1992b). Leaders may also tend to underplay the potential non-financial costs and benefits of initiatives. Feller (1997) notes, for example, that technology-transfer offices can serve faculty and promote regional economic development as well as generate additional revenues. Similarly, Tornatzky et al. (2002) found that business–university partnerships provide jobs for graduates and geographically marooned spouses of faculty and staff members, stimulate local research partnerships and encourage lifestyle amenities associated with the technology industry. None of these non-financial benefits is easily quantified, but each merits attention. Again, non-partisan analysis of all aspects of an effort, not just the financial, is essential.

CONCLUSION

Clark Kerr (1993, p. 56) referred to the naïveté of those who see higher education's current controversy over marketization as something new:

> The cherished academic view that higher education started out on the acropolis and was desecrated by descent into the agora led by ungodly commercial interests and scheming public officials and venal academic leaders is just not true. If anything, higher education started in the agora, the market, at the bottom of the hill and ascended to the acropolis at the top of the hill . . . Mostly it has lived in tension, at one and the same time at the bottom of the hill, at the top of the hill, and on the many pathways in between.

That tension continues. What is new, and constantly changing, are the approaches to dealing with it.

Recently, there have been proposals for public institutions to acquire greater autonomy from state authority at the expense of losing their regular supply of state funding. One observer titled his essay on the subject 'Give us liberty or give us revenue' (Fish, 2003). This challenge posed to public institutions reflects a larger dilemma facing all institutions. That is, the recent reform proposals simply aim to formalize a process already underway informally: as financially pressed governments disengage from their implicit contracts with higher-education institutions public and private, they and thus the citizenry at large must be prepared to accept institutions no longer so integrally tied to the will of the public. While institutions have not been 'bought and paid for', they have certainly at least paid close attention to their government sponsors and that attention may begin to wander. More profoundly, the citizenry and institutions alike have been participants in something philosophically grander than the individuals and the dollars involved. Now, though, revenue strains present the potential of directly and indirectly threatening those larger purposes.

There are no simple answers for institutions. Refusing on principle to seek new revenues makes little sense if institutional missions remain sound and if governments and other sponsors are unlikely to return to former funding levels. On the other hand, when pursuing new revenues, institutions must take care not to suggest to sponsors that public investment is becoming less necessary as new revenues are secured (Johnstone, 2002). Governmental commitment remains essential to higher education in a democratic society. What is more, aggressively pursuing new revenues may well mean confronting threats to the institution's core traditions and values (Bok, 2003; Johnstone, 2002). The push for more reliance on grants and contracts from external organizations, for example, can raise costs on campus, redistribute academic power, shift academic priorities and reduce

the sense of community (Slaughter and Leslie, 1997; Leslie et al., 2002). Doing business differently will not come easily to most institutions and, indeed, it *should not* come easily.

As I have noted elsewhere (Hearn, 2003), the pursuit of new revenues at its worst can be mindless and dispiriting. When ideas for new revenue streams are promising in a business sense but threatening in a cultural and organizational sense, and perhaps disserving the public good, the best choice for institutions may well be to ignore the financial appeal and walk away. But, for those rare ideas that are not only promising but also inspired and inspiring, wisdom almost certainly lies in moving forward.

The challenge lies in identifying danger. The risks to essential traditions and values in higher education may lie more in the cumulative effects of seemingly minor, necessary, and attractive adaptations than in obviously radical reforms (Breneman, 2002; Clark, 2002; Newman, 2000). Increasing marketization is probably inevitable in US higher education, but that inevitability does not warrant abandoning vigilance over core values that may be imperiled, such as those favoring faculty and institutional autonomy.

Most of us are familiar with the old folk warning concerning the frog in hot water: dropped into boiling water, a frog will promptly jump out, but, dropped into cool water that is being slowly heated to boiling, a frog may well end up being boiled to death. Of course, the consequences of marketization and revenue diversification are not nearly so dire for students, faculty or institutional leaders. Still, as the old tale warns us, careful scrutiny of one's emerging environment is always warranted.

ACKNOWLEDGMENTS

This essay revises and builds upon earlier work conducted under contract for the American Council of Education. The author gratefully acknowledges suggestions and feedback from Jacqueline King, Melanie Corrigan, Grady Bogue, Tim Caboni, John Davies, David Longanecker, Michael McLendon, Betty Price, King Alexander, Ed St John, Bob Clark and John Yeager, as well as research assistance by Kathryn Balink, Edmund Ford and Ying Liu.

NOTES

1. Historians generally agree that, by the twelfth century, students' and teachers' growing demands for independence from the control of the church and political leaders led to the founding of the two earliest universities (Perkins, 1973). In Italy an emerging guild of students responded to the dominance of the Catholic Church over what and how they

learned by establishing the University of Bologna. These renegade students used their funds to hire tutors at market-rate wages to instruct them in both canon and civil law, unconstrained by the dictates of the Church. In Paris, faculty with similar motivations established the University of Paris and soon met with a ready demand from students disaffected by traditional structures for learning.

2. It should be noted, however, that this proportion was unusually low, in part because of unusually high returns from investments that year (31.5 per cent of revenues).
3. Traditionally, technology transfer provides returns only when patents and licenses are activated and successful (Geiger, 2002). Therefore, some institutions accept equity holdings in return for their technology transfers to industry (Feller, 1997): because such holdings may be sold, they can represent institutions' only hope for shorter-term returns on frontier technology.
4. For example, some institutions have adopted unitized investment pools, which pool funds from multiple sources and are managed under a consistent investment approach.
5. A striking recent example: the indoor stadium at Boise State University was renamed 'Taco Bell Arena', prompting a local observer to question whether the university was 'thinking outside the bun or inside the wallet' (Karlin-Resnick, 2004, p. A7).
6. Outsourcing may also be viewed as a way to seek new revenues, in that such arrangements can trade one form of revenue gathering (the term-by-term garnering of funds from individual students, for example) for another form of revenue gathering (term-by-term payments from third parties).
7. The history of Stanford University (see http://www.stanford.edu/home/stanford/history/lands.html) is often cited as the model use of real estate, but there are numerous other success stories.
8. For example, a separate full-service technology corporation might take responsibility for business aspects of the commercialization of intellectual property, while a university-owned investment company might manage funds generated by non-traditional activities and donation campaigns.

REFERENCES

Alexander, F.K. (2003), 'Comparative study of state tax effort and the role of federal government policy in shaping revenue reliance patterns', in F.K. Alexander and R.G. Ehrenberg (eds), *Maximizing Revenue in Higher Education*, (New Directions for Institutional Research, 119), San Francisco: Jossey-Bass, pp. 13–26.

Arnone, M. (2003), 'IRS ruling on naming rights for facilities may jeopardize status of some tax-exempt bonds', *Chronicle of Higher Education*, (18 April), A30.

Babbidge, H.D. and R. Rosenzweig (1962), *The Federal Interest in Higher Education*, New York: McGraw-Hill.

Baldwin, R.G. and J.L. Chronister (2001), *Teaching without Tenure: Policies and Practices for a New Era*, Baltimore: Johns Hopkins Press.

Barbulies, N.C. and T.A. Callister (2000), 'Universities in transition: the promise and challenge of new technologies', *Teachers College Record*, **102** (2), 271–93.

Biddison, G. and T. Hier (1998), 'Wringing dollars out of campus space', *Facilities Manager*, **14** (6), 18–23.

Blumenstyk, G. (2003a), 'Donations to colleges decline for the first time since 1988', *Chronicle of Higher Education*, (21 March), A29–30.

Blumenstyk, G. (2003b), 'Deflated deals', *Chronicle of Higher Education*, (9 May), A27–8.

Blumenstyk, G. (2004), 'Colleges seek a record number of patents', *Chronicle of Higher Education*, (3 December), A27.

Blustain, H., P. Goldstein and G. Lozier (1998), 'Assessing the new competitive landscape', *CAUSE/EFFECT*, **21** (3), 19–27.

Bok, D. (2003), *Universities in the Marketplace: the Commercialization of Higher Education*, Princeton, NJ: Princeton University Press.

Bowen, H.H. (1980), *The Costs of Higher Education: How Much Colleges and Universities Spend Per Student and How Much Should They Spend?*, San Francisco, CA: Jossey-Bass.

Breneman, D.W. (1997), 'The "privatization" of public universities: mistake or model?', *Chronicle of Higher Education*, (14 June), B4–5.

Breneman, D.W. (2002), 'For colleges, this is not just another recession', *Chronicle of Higher Education*, (14 June), B7–9.

Campbell, T.I.D. and S. Slaughter (1999), 'Faculty and administrators' attitudes toward potential conflicts of interest, commitment, and equity in university–industry relationships', *Journal of Higher Education*, **70** (3), 309–52.

Caruthers, J.K. and C.L. Wentworth (1997), 'Methods and techniques of revenue forecasting', in D.T. Layzell (ed.), *Forecasting and Managing Enrollment and Revenue: an Overview of Current Trends, Issues, and Methods*, (New Directions for Institutional Research, 93), San Francisco, CA: Jossey-Bass, pp. 81–93.

Clark, B.R. (1998), *Creating Entrepreneurial Universities: Organizational Pathways of Transformation*, Oxford, UK: Pergamon for the IAU Press.

Clark, B.R. (2002), 'University transformation: primary pathways to university autonomy and achievement', in S.J. Brint (ed.), *The Future of the City of Intellect: the Changing American University*, Palo Alto, CA: Stanford University Press, pp. 322–42.

Collis, D.J. (2002), 'New business models for higher education', in S.J. Brint (ed.), *The Future of the City of Intellect: the Changing American University*, Palo Alto, CA: Stanford University Press, pp. 181–202.

Davies, J.L. (2001), 'The emergence of entrepreneurial cultures in European universities', *Higher Education Management*, **13** (2), 25–43.

Davies, P. (2005), 'Outsourcing can make sense, but proceed with caution', *Chronicle of Higher Education*, **51** (21), B20.

Day, J.H. (1997), 'Enrollment forecasting and revenue implications for private colleges and universities', in D.T. Layzell (ed.), *Forecasting and Managing Enrollment and Revenue: an Overview of Current Trends, Issues, and Methods*, (New Directions for Institutional Research, 93), San Francisco, CA: Jossey-Bass, pp. 51–65.

Eckel, P.D. (2003), 'Capitalizing on the curriculum: the challenges of curricular joint ventures', *American Behavioral Scientist*, **46** (7), 865–82.

Ehrenberg, R.G. (2000), 'Financial forecasts for the next decade', *The Presidency*, (Spring), 30–34.

Etkowitz, H., A. Websterand and P. Healy (eds) (1998), *Capitalizing Knowledge: New Intersections of Industry and Academia*, Albany, NY: SUNY Press.

Feller, I. (1997), 'Technology transfer from universities', in J.C. Smart (ed.), *Higher Education: Handbook of Theory and Research*, **XII**, New York, NY: Agathon Press, pp. 1–42.

Fish, S. (2003), 'Give us liberty or give us revenue', *Chronicle of Higher Education*, **50** (10), C4.

Geiger, R.L. (2002), 'The American university at the beginning of the twenty-first century: signposts on the path to privatization', in R.M. Adams (ed.), *Trends in American and German Higher Education*, Cambridge, MA: American Academy of Arts and Sciences, pp. 33–84.

Grassmuck, K. (1990), 'Colleges fight bootleggers as sales boom for goods that bear logos and emblems', *Chronicle of Higher Education*, 21 February, A32–3.

Hearn, J.C. (1996), 'Transforming higher education: an organizational perspective', *Innovative Higher Education*, **21** (2), 141–54.

Hearn, J.C. (1999), 'Pay and performance in the university: an examination of faculty salaries', *Review of Higher Education*, **22** (4), 391–410.

Hearn, J.C. (2003), *Diversifying Campus Revenue Streams: Opportunities and Risks*, report for the American Council on Education series, 'Informed Practice: Syntheses of Higher Education Research for Campus Leaders', (July), Washington, DC: American Council on Education.

Hearn, J.C. and M.S. Anderson (2001), 'Clinical faculty in schools of education: using staff differentiation to address disparate goals', in W. Tierney (ed.), *Faculty Work in Schools of Education: Rethinking Roles and Rewards for the 21st Century*, Albany, NY: SUNY Press, pp. 125–49.

Hearn, J.C., R. Clugston and R. Heydinger (1993), 'Five years of strategic environmental assessment efforts at a research university: a case study of an organizational innovation', *Innovative Higher Education*, **18** (1), 7–36.

Hebel, S. (2003a), 'If you build it, they will come', *Chronicle of Higher Education*, (7 February), A16–19.

Hebel, S. (2003b), 'Same classroom, different price: colleges debate ways to vary tuition among students and increase revenue', *Chronicle of Higher Education*, **50** (4), A10.

Hinchcliff, J. (2000), 'The globalization of education', paper presented at the Technological Education and National Development Conference held in Abu Dhabi, United Arab Emirates, April, ED447296.

Hirsch, Werner Z. (1999), 'Financing universities through nontraditional revenue sources: opportunities and threats', in W.Z. Hirsch and L.E. Weber (eds), *Challenges Facing Higher Education at the Millennium*, (American Council on Education series on higher education), Phoenix, AZ: Oryx Press, pp. 75–84.

Hitt, J.C. and J.L. Hartman (2002), *Distributed Learning: New Challenges and Opportunities for Institutional Leadership*, Washington, DC: American Council on Education, Center for Policy Analysis.

Horwitz, M.D. and R.L Rolett (1991), 'Retirement communities: a financially rewarding educational approach', *Business Officer*, **24** (January), 33–5.

Hovey, H.A. (1999), *State Spending for Higher Education in the Next Decade: the Battle to Sustain Current Support*, Washington, DC: National Center for Public Policy and Higher Education.

Immerwahr, J. (2002), *Meeting the Competition: College and University Presidents, Faculty, and State Legislators View the New Competitive Academic Arena*, a report by Public Agenda for the Futures Project: Policy for Higher Education in a Changing World, Providence, RI: Brown University.

Institute for Higher Education Policy and the National Education Association (2000), *Benchmarks for Success in Internet-based Distance Education*, Washington, DC: Institute for Higher Education Policy.

Jaschik, S. (2005), 'Cutting tuition, increasing revenue', *Inside Higher Education*, (11 July), available at http://insidehighered.com/news/2005/07/11/tuition.

Johnstone, D.B. (2002), 'Challenges of financial austerity: imperatives and limitations of revenue diversification in higher education', *Welsh Journal of Education*, **11** (1), 18–36.

June, A.W. and P. Fain (2005), 'Dorm renovation and competition draw attention at business officers' meeting', *Chronicle of Higher Education*, (22 July), A21.

Kaludis, G. and G. Stine (2000), 'From managing expenditures to managing costs: strategic management for information technology', in M.J Finkelstein, C. Frances, F.I. Jewett and B.W. Scholz, *Dollars, Distance, and Online Education: the New Economics of College Teaching and Learning*, Phoenix, AZ: Oryx Press and the American Council on Education, pp. 256–68.

Karlin-Resnick, J. (2004), 'Blueprints: a look at a campus building that is generating discussion', *Chronicle of Higher Education*, (9 July), A7.

Karr, S. and R.V. Kelley (1996), 'Attracting new sources of research funding', in D.W. Breneman (ed.), *Strategies for Promoting Excellence in a Time of Scarce Resources*, (New Directions for Higher Education, 94), San Francisco, CA: Jossey-Bass, pp. 33–4.

Katz, R.N., E.M. Ferrara and Ian S. Napier (2002), *Partnerships in Distributed Education*, Washington, DC: American Council on Education, Center for Policy Analysis.

Kerr, C. (1993), *Troubled times for American higher education: the 1990s and beyond*, Albany, NY: SUNY Press.

Kerr, C. (2002), 'Shock wave II: an introduction to the twenty-first century', in S.J. Brint (ed.), *The Future of the City of Intellect: the Changing American University*, Palo Alto: Stanford University Press, pp. 1–19.

Kienle, J. (1997), 'Facilities that help pay for themselves', *Planning for Higher Education*, **26** (1), 14–17.

Kirp, D.L. (2003), *Shakespeare, Einstein, and the Bottom Line: the Marketing of Higher Education*, Cambridge, MA: Harvard University Press.

Knapp, L.G., J.E. Kelly, R.W. Whitmore, S. Wu, L.M. Gallego and S.G. Broyles (2002), 'Enrollment in postsecondary institutions, Fall 2000 and financial statistics, fiscal year 2000', *Education Statistics Quarterly*, **4** (4), NCES publication 2002–212, available at http://nces.ed.gov/programs/quarterly/vol_4/4_4/q4_6. asp.

Koger, D. (2001), 'Expanding sports facilities', *American School and University*, **73** (11), 48–51.

Kozeracki, C. (1998), 'Institutional entrepreneurship in higher education', *CELCEE Digest*, (98–5), Kansas City, MO: Center for Entrepreneurial Leadership; Ewing Marion Kauffman Foundation.

Leder, M. (2002), 'Your alma mater wants to become your bank', *The New York Times*, (25 August), 8.

Leslie, L.L., R.L. Oaxaca and G. Rhoades (2002), 'Revenue flux and university behavior', in D.M. Priest, W.E. Becker, D. Hossler and E.P. St John (eds), *Incentive-based Budgeting Systems in Public Universities*, Cheltenham, UK and Northampton, MA: Edward Elgar, pp. 55–91.

Leslie, L.L. and S.A. Slaughter (1997), 'The development and current status of market mechanisms in United States post-secondary education', *Higher Education Policy*, **10** (3–4), 239–52.

Levine, A. (2000a), 'Restructuring higher education to meet the demands of a new century', 22nd annual Pullias address presented at the University of Southern California, Los Angeles, CA, 1 July.

Levine, A. (2000b), 'The soul of a new university', *The New York Times*, (20 March), A25.

Lewis, D.R. and J.C. Hearn (eds) (2003), *The Public Research University: Serving the Public Good in New Times*, Lanham, MD: University Press of America.

Mansfield, E. (1995), 'Academic research underlying industrial innovations: sources, characteristics, and funding', *The Review of Economics and Statistics*, (February), 55–65.

Matkin, G.W. (1997), *Organizing University Economic Development: Lessons from Continuing Education and Technology Transfer*, (New Directions for Higher Education, 97), San Francisco, CA: Jossey-Bass.

McPherson, M.S. and M.O. Schapiro (1998), *The Student Aid Game: Meeting Need and Rewarding Talent in American Higher Education*, Princeton, NJ: Princeton University Press.

Morrell, L.R. (1997), 'Success in investing: integrating spending policy with asset allocation strategy', *Business Officer*, (30), 38–42.

National Association of State Universities and Land-Grant Colleges (NASULGC) (1997), *Value Added: the Economic Impact of Public Universities*, Washington, DC: National Association of State Universities and Land-Grant Colleges.

Newman, F. (2000), 'Saving higher education's soul', *Change*, (September/October), 16–23.

Newman, F. and L.K. Couturier (2001), 'The new competitive arena: market forces invade the academy', *Change*, (September/October), 11–17.

Nicklin, J.L. (1992a), 'Many institutions conduct research for companies for a fee, but others assail the practice', *Chronicle of Higher Education*, (19 February), A29–30.

Nicklin, J.L. (1992b), 'Discipline-minded president credited with reviving Northwestern', *Chronicle of Higher Education*, (3 June), A29.

Nicklin, J.L. (1993), 'Colleges seeking new sources of revenue herald creation of the cashless campus', *Chronicle of Higher Education*, (3 February), A29.

Nicklin, J.L. (1996), 'Finding the green on the fairway', *Chronicle of Higher Education*, (5 July), A37–8.

Oblinger, D.G., C.A. Barone and B.L. Hawkins (2001), *Distributed Education and Its Challenges: an Overview*, Washington, DC: American Council on Education and EDUCAUSE.

Perkins, J.A. (1973), 'Organization and functions of the university', in J.A. Perkins (ed.), *The University as an Organization*, New York, NY: McGraw-Hill, pp. 3–14.

Powers, J.B. (2003), 'Commercializing academic research: resource effects on performance of university technology transfer', *Journal of Higher Education*, **74** (1), 26–50.

Press, E. and J. Washburn (2000), 'The kept university', *Atlantic Monthly*, **285** (3), 39–54.

Priest, D.M., W.E. Becker, D. Hossler and E.P. St John (eds) (2002), *Incentive-based Budgeting Systems in Public Universities*, Cheltenham, UK and Northampton, MA: Edward Elgar.

Primary Research Group (1997), *Forecasting College and University Revenues*, New York: Primary Research Group.

Schmidt, P. (2004), 'College leaders ask states for new sources of money', *Chronicle of Higher Education*, **50** (18), A20.

Sekera, J., B. Baran and S. Teegarden (1999), *California Community Colleges and Economic Development: Options and Opportunities*, Sacramento, CA: Economic Development Coordination Network (EDNet), California Community Colleges, Office of the Chancellor.

Shane, S. and T. Stuart (2002), 'Organizational endowments and the performance of university start-ups', *Management Science*, **48** (1), 154–70.

Slaughter, S. and Leslie, L.L. (1997), *Academic Capitalism*, Baltimore and London: The Johns Hopkins University Press.

Spitz, W.T. (1999), 'Investment policies for college and university endowments', in L. Lapovsky and M.P. McKeown-Moak (eds), *Roles and Responsibilities of the Chief Financial Officer*, (New Directions for Higher Education, 107), San Francisco, CA: Jossey-Bass, pp. 51–60.

Standard and Poor (2005), *Fiscal 2004 Ratios for Colleges and Universities*, New York, NY: Standard and Poor Corporation.

Strout, E. (2005), 'Building a fund-raising culture, one college at a time', *Chronicle of Higher Education*, **51** (22), A25.

Swanquist, B. (1999), 'A new trend in dining design', *College Planning and Design*, **2** (45), 34–6.

Teitel, L. (1989), 'Managing the new frontier between colleges and companies', in D.T. Seymour (ed.), *Maximizing Opportunities through External Relationships*, (New Directions for Higher Education, 68), San Francisco, CA: Jossey-Bass, pp. 43–64.

Thursby, J. G. and M.C. Thursby (2002), *Who's Selling the Ivory Tower? Sources of Growth in University Licensing*, (NBER Working Paper No. 7718), Cambridge, MA: National Bureau of Economic Research.

Tierney, W.G. (ed.) (1999), *Faculty Productivity: Facts, Fictions, and Issues*, New York: Falmer.

Tornatzky, L.G, P.G. Waugsman and D.O. Gray (2002), *Innovation U.: New University Roles in a Knowledge Economy*, a report of the Southern Technology Council and the Southern Growth Policies Board, Research Triangle Park, NC: Southern Growth Policies Board.

Toutkoushian, R.K. (2001), 'Trends in revenues and expenditures for public and private higher education', in M.B. Paulsen and J.C. Smart (eds), *The Finance of Higher Education: Theory, Research, Policy, and Practice*, New York, NY: Agathon Press, pp. 11–38.

Wellman, J. and Phipps, R. (2001), *Funding the 'Infostructure': A Guide to Financing Technology Infrastructure in Higher Education*, report for the Lumina Foundation for Education, Indianapolis, IN: Lumina Foundation for Education.

Wertz, R.D. (1997), 'Big business on campus: examining the bottom line', *Educational Record*, **78** (1), 19–24.

Wetzel, James N. (1995), 'The effect of tuition differentials on student enrollment patterns and university revenues. Final report', final report of an FIPSE-sponsored project, Richmond, VA: Virginia Commonwealth University, ED414833.

Wills, E. (2005), 'Campuses for hire', *Chronicle of Higher Education*, (5 August), A6.

Winston, G.C. (1999), 'Subsidies, hierarchy, and peers: the awkward economics of higher education', *Journal of Economic Perspectives*, **13** (1), 13–36.

Yanikoski, R.A. and R.F. Wilson (1984), 'Differential pricing of undergraduate education', *Journal of Higher Education*, **55** (6), 735–50.

Zemsky, R., S. Shaman and D.B. Shapiro (2001), '*Higher Education as Competitive Enterprise: When Markets Matter*', (New Directions for Institutional Research, 111), San Francisco, CA: Jossey-Bass.

Zemsky, R., G.R. Wegner and W.F. Massy (2005), *Remaking the American University*, Piscataway, NJ: Rutgers University Press.

Zimbalist, A. (1999), *Unpaid Professionals: Commercialization and Conflict in Big-Time College Sports*, Princeton, NJ: Princeton University Press.

4. Higher education: meeting today's challenges and regaining the public's trust

William E. Kirwan

The necessity for colleges and universities to increase revenues in the current adverse economic environment is extraordinarily important, not just for our nation's colleges and universities but for our nation as well. It is interesting to note that I recently participated in a national summit on college costs sponsored by the Lumina Foundation,[1] while in this chapter I focus on the issue of raising revenues. These are, of course, two components of the same equation. However, you cannot talk about one without addressing the other. So in this analysis, I address both, as well as a third issue: reestablishing higher education as a national priority for public investment.

Why are we so concerned about the costs and funding of higher education? The answer is obvious. Probably most of us would agree that our nation is in the early stages of a national crisis on higher education, a crisis not primarily about quality but one of access and affordability. Someone at the Lumina conference said that 'a crisis is a terrible thing to waste'. Our expectation must be that all these meetings and discussions begin to gel into innovative solutions to our current challenges.

Tom Friedman of the *New York Times* was the keynote speaker at the Lumina conference. From my perspective, Friedman's most recent work, *The World is Flat*, should be required reading for all. It is either a wake-up call for our nation or it is the harbinger of our worst nightmare for the decades ahead. It all depends on how our nation responds to the issues raised in this book. What the book and many other reports document is that for the first time since the beginning of the twentieth century, perhaps for the first time in our nation's history, we are developing an education deficit in relation to the rest of the industrialized world. There are warning signals that, if not addressed, could lead to the demise of the US as the world's leader in knowledge creation and dissemination, particularly in science and technology. If this were to happen in this era of the knowledge

economy, it would surely mean our demise as the world's economic superpower.

A few decades ago, we were the leader in high school completion rates and in the college participation rates of our high school graduates. Today we rank fifth among industrialized nations in high school completion rates and seventh in post-secondary participation rates. In fact, we are the only industrialized nation with a declining college participation rate. Our middle and high school students rank near the bottom among all industrialized nations in maths and science achievement.

A piece of data that I find especially alarming is the following: Take 100 8th graders today and ask how many will have a college degree in ten years. Given current completion and participation rates along the way, the answer is 18. What, I ask you, will the other 82 students be doing in the America of 2015?

Our educational deficit does not stop at the K-12 level. As I noted, we simply are not producing scientists and engineers at a rate to keep pace with the demands of our economy or with the rest of the world. In 2000, Asian universities produced 1.2 million graduates in science and engineering. European universities produced 850 000. The US produced 500 000 (National Science Board, 2004).

In an economy that puts a premium on a skilled workforce, creativity and innovation, these trends – if unchecked – do not bode well for our global competitiveness and economic security in the decades ahead.

Clearly, the most important challenge we in higher education face is funding. We all know that adequate funding is the sine qua non of quality higher education. Attracting the best faculty in competition with the private sector and – increasingly – universities in other countries, developing state-of-the-art facilities with cutting-edge technology, supporting the best and brightest academic talent, expanding capacity to serve more students and meeting the growing demand for financial aid, all require resources. Moreover, we have a self-imposed expectation and the larger society also expects us to pursue excellence. Building excellence and capacity come at a significant cost!

This is one of the reasons that raising revenues from non-state sources has become so important. We all see a greater emphasis placed on private fundraising and an expansion of the role and importance of foundations. The University System of Maryland Foundation, for example, is gearing up for an aggressive $1.5 billion-plus campaign.

At the institutional level, individual campuses are stressing academic research and development efforts tied to technology transfer and to building stronger collaboration with the private sector in the hope of building new sources of funding. Campuses are also offering a growing roster of

'short courses' and even renting out facilities in order to generate additional revenue.

Certainly, when such actions are undertaken without compromising the integrity of the university, they are good things. There are, however, pitfalls, unintended consequences and ethical issues in some of these 'entrepreneurial' revenue-generating efforts. Therefore, they should be entered into only after comprehensive policies have been developed that protect the openness of university based research and educational offerings.

Done correctly, these revenue-generating efforts are positive, not just for the additional funding they provide but also because they demonstrate to the body politic that the higher education community is willing to be more entrepreneurial and seek non-traditional sources of funding. There is an essential point, however. In many, if not most cases, such revenue is restricted and must be used for a specific purpose. Thus, these funds are generally not available in a fungible manner to support an institution's core educational programs. Moreover, except for a relatively small fraction of the nation's more elite universities, these sources of funds will not be available in the magnitude necessary to make a substantial dent in the decline in the rate of public investment or the rise in tuition rates.

By all means, to whatever extent possible, systems and institutions should look to secure non-state revenue sources. But we cannot put forth the notion that such funding is a 'substitute' for adequate public funding. Such revenue can complement public funding and enhance our ability to achieve our mission and goals, but it cannot effectively replace growth in traditional funding sources.

Clearly, what we are facing is not growing public investment in higher education. We are instead witnessing a systemic and sustained disinvestment in higher education at the federal, state and local levels. And this is certainly more than a short-term trend. Consider that in the mid-to-late 1970s, as a nation, we invested more than $10 for every $1000 of personal income in higher education. Today that investment stands at about $6 for every $1000 of personal income (Postsecondary Education Opportunity, 2005). That is a 40 per cent decline in the rate of investment.

Unfortunately, the disinvestment trend has accelerated in recent years owing to rising health-care and energy costs and mandated spending for primary and secondary education. Higher education, which is usually the largest discretionary item in most state budgets, has borne the brunt of recent cuts. For example, in Maryland, from 1990 to the present – in constant dollars – state support for higher education has dropped from almost $7900 per student to less that $5700 per student. Even counting last year's increase in state support (more about that later), that is a reduction in state investment of almost 28 per cent in less than 15 years.

Moreover, the cuts to higher education could not have come at a worse time, because the children of the baby boomers – the baby boom echo – are beginning to reach college age. In many states demand is expected to rise significantly over the next half-dozen years. We in Maryland, for example, anticipate a 20 per cent increase in high school graduates by 2012. And the increased demand will come disproportionately from low-income students who would be the first in their families to go to college. Cost will be a huge factor for them. Already we are seeing the impact of cost on access. The Secretary of Education's Advisory Committee on Financial Aid reported recently that 250 000 college-capable students did not attend college last year because they could not afford it.

The public disinvestment in higher education is one of the great ironies of our times. Ask parents of almost any child in America today and the odds are extremely high they will say they want their son or daughter to get a college degree. In my 41 years in higher education, there has never been a time when the general public has had such a collective desire for our product. Yet when legislative bodies act, higher education is cut or underfunded. How can this be?

For one thing, we do not have a common language and message that applies across the various sectors of higher education and resonates with the public. In fact, we are sending very confusing and mixed messages. On the one hand, we cry poverty. But, in the same breath, we boast of the huge growth in our research expenditures, or our latest multi-million dollar gift, or how little of our budget now comes from the state, or how students are beating down the doors to attend our institutions, or our latest top ranking by some publication, or how much our graduates will earn with our degrees.

At some of our institutions, athletics programs generate tens of millions of dollars and coaches earn what most would describe as exorbitant salaries. Faculty teaching loads at many institutions seem unrealistic to the public and classrooms and offices are empty by noon on most Fridays. Is it any wonder that many see us – at least relatively speaking – as fat and happy? Of course, we know that the auxiliary revenue of research grants or athletics programs cannot be used to expand and/or reduce the cost of our education programs. But can we really expect the public to analyze our various messages and make the subtle distinctions between arcane topics like restricted and unrestricted funds? Is it any wonder that when legislators are faced with the choice of funding us or other strapped programs, like K-12 education or public safety, that have state funds as their sole source of revenue, we come up on the short end of the stick?

Besides cursing our fate and wringing our hands, what should we in higher education be doing about this situation? What actions should we be taking to address the enormous challenges facing our institutions and to

better meet our responsibilities to our communities and our nation? What steps can we take to rebuild public support for our mission? Some of the answers to these questions are presented in the chapters in this volume.

I would like to offer three things I believe we must collectively do *in addition to* an aggressive push to secure alternative sources of revenue.

First, we in higher education must address the way we administer and distribute financial aid. In 1990 about 90 per cent of all financial aid was distributed on the basis of need. Today only about 60 per cent is awarded according to need. That is a huge shift in funding. Sadly, a high percentage of the merit aid goes to students from middle- and upper-middle-class families at the expense of aid for truly needy low-income families. The situation has become so bad that we are at risk of destroying the American dream of upward mobility and creating a permanent economic underclass. Indeed, a student from a family in the upper quartile of income today has more than an 80 per cent chance of getting a college degree, whereas a student from a family in the lowest quartile of income has only about a 7 per cent chance of getting a degree. In today's world, where a college degree leads to almost double the income of those with only a high school degree, can we really claim that higher education offers an equitable ladder of opportunity?

We recently conducted a study within the University System of Maryland to determine the debt load of our graduates. To our dismay, we learned that, as in most other institutions, our poorest students were graduating with the most debt, 25 per cent above the average debt load in our case. That is not what was intended when financial aid programs were created several decades ago. Armed with this information, our Board of Regents adopted a new financial aid policy which mandates, among other things, that by the year 2008–09 our lowest-income students must graduate with debt burdens that are 25 per cent below the average or less. This will require a huge shift in our distribution of financial aid from merit-based to need-based programs. I hope other universities will follow our lead in this matter.

The second thing we in higher education must do is make a much more serious commitment to controlling the costs of our operations. It sounds almost trite to say that. But, if we are honest with ourselves, I think we would agree that cutting costs is not in our personal or institutional DNA. We operate under a model where educational expenditures at colleges and universities across the country are rising by about 4.5 per cent to 5 per cent annually. In a nation with an entrenched 3 per cent inflation rate, this is not sustainable long term, no matter what our source of revenue. That is one reason we need to get more focused on cost containment. Another is that, in my view, we have little hope of regaining public support for increased investment unless we are seen as more effective stewards of public funds. We live in a world that has become accustomed to cost reductions and

efficiencies. While we represent a fundamentally different kind of enterprise and should not be compared with the private sector in this regard, we cannot ignore the environment in which the rest of the world operates.

To address this issue in Maryland, the USM Board of Regents, its presidents and I launched an effort two years ago that we call our Effectiveness and Efficiency (E&E) initiative. It consists of a systematic examination and reengineering of all our academic and administrative processes, aimed at finding ways we can reduce costs and create savings to better support our priorities. With the E&E initiative we have, among other things, increased faculty teaching loads by 10 per cent on average across the system; limited to 120 the number of credits required for most degrees; required that, on average, students will earn at least 10 per cent of their credits outside the classroom, through faculty approved advance placement exams, study abroad programs and internships; expanded greatly our on-line educational offerings; created two-plus-two articulation agreements with community colleges to ensure seamless transfer to four-year degrees at lower cost to students; leveraged our power as a system to drive down prices and negotiate better product, service and energy contracts for all 13 campuses; and consolidated back-office operations rather than have duplicate operations on all 13 campuses. Through these and other E&E efforts we have documented savings to the base budget in excess of $40 million over the past two years.

We issued a report on our efforts to the Governor and the General Assembly. The rigor and impact of our efforts have so impressed our Governor and Legislature that they have rewarded us with a 6.2 per cent increase in state funding for this fiscal year. With the pledge that we will continue our effectiveness and efficiency efforts, we have been promised a similar increase for the next fiscal year. Our E&E efforts also resulted in several positive newspaper articles across the state.

To complement the cost savings and cost-avoidance of our E&E initiative, we are also expanding cost-effective alternatives for course and program delivery.

The University System of Maryland is fortunate to be home to the University of Maryland University College, arguably the leader in the development of online education. With over 140 000 course registrations, UMUC has the largest number of online enrollments in the world. One of UMUC's great strengths is its ability to respond quickly to the needs of the students online, any time, anywhere. It will soon be the largest university in our system not just by head count but in full-time equivalent (FTE) students.

UMUC has entered into a remarkable agreement with community colleges in Maryland. Under this agreement, a community college and UMUC can guarantee students enrolling in the community college that if they complete the two-year college prep curriculum, they can complete a four-year

degree from UMUC drawing upon UMUC's online and on-site course delivery capabilities.

We are exploring other innovative, cost effective approaches. A few years ago, the USM established a single facility in a highly populated region of our state with no four-year school, public or private. Seven separate USM institutions have come together in this location – under one roof – to deliver low-cost access to a range of different USM programs, selected to meet high student demand, in areas such as biosciences, information sciences, business, nursing and education. A local community college provides the lower division course work and each of the participating institutions provides regular faculty and academic support services to the center. Students earn their degrees from the institution offering their particular programs. This model has been so successful and well-received that we have in fact replicated it in a different region of the state.

Between UMUC, its partnerships with the community colleges, and our educational centers, we anticipate that we can accommodate approximately 50 per cent of the state's projected enrollment growth – and at a lower cost to the students and the state than would be incurred to educate these students at a traditional campus. This will be a huge boost in our efforts to both serve the needs of the state and protect the quality of our existing campuses.

The fact is, however, we in higher education cannot simply 'manage' our way out of reduced public support and growing enrollment. Without adequate support – including most especially state support – higher education will face two options: we can maintain quality by continuing to raise tuition charges at a very high rate, closing the door to higher education for thousands of students who represent our future workforce; or we can keep tuition charges modest to allow for affordable access, putting higher education on the path to mediocrity.

Given that neither of these options is acceptable, I come to my third and final point: we must make it clear to all concerned that we cannot address our challenges just by being more efficient. Important as it is to demonstrate our commitment to access and to holding down costs and making substantially more need-based aid available, our nation will not prosper in the decades ahead if we do not also convince the body politic that we need and deserve greater investment of public funds.

We must seek out enlightened third-party advocates who understand what is at stake and are willing to help carry our message to the general public. Obviously, it will be easier to recruit such people if they are convinced we are serious about holding down cost increases.

The American Council of Education has launched just such an initiative, which will include some impressive corporate partners, dedicated full-page ads in prestigious newspapers and free TV spots on a major network.

However, all politics is local. It will not be enough to have a national campaign on the importance of reinvesting in higher education. We must launch efforts state by state as well.

In Maryland we have pulled together every two-year, four-year public and four-year private institution and members of the private sector into a single statewide effort to get a unified message out. Imagine the entire spectrum of higher education joining with representatives of the private sector in a unified front, presenting a coherent message – unheard of, at least in Maryland. We will be holding listening tours, workshops and other events to highlight the broad public benefits of higher education.

At both the state and national levels we must collectively work to find more effective ways to remind the public that the entrepreneurs who create jobs in the knowledge economy and the highly skilled workers who fill them come from higher education. The teachers who educate our children from grade school through high school come from higher education. The doctors and nurses who provide our health care come from higher education. The medical and technological innovations that improve our lives every single day come from higher education. The breakthroughs in security matters that will better protect our nation and the world come from higher education.

Higher education raises incomes and lowers poverty; creates opportunities and solves problems; reduces barriers and elevates civic engagement. Higher education changes the lives of the people who will change the world. For these reasons, higher education is the quintessential common good.

These are the reasons why we must – as a nation – ensure access for all qualified students to a high-quality higher education. Doing that is our best hope, one might say our only hope, for building a bright future for America.

NOTE

1. Lumina 2005 Invitational Summit, 'College Costs: Making Opportunity Affordable', 2 November 2005, Washington, DC.

REFERENCES

National Science Board (2004), 'Science and engineering indicators 2004', Arlington, VA: National Science Foundation, Division of Science Resources Statistics, available at http://www.nsf.gov/statistics/seind04/.

Postsecondary Education Opportunity (2005), 'State Tax fund appropriations for higher education for FY1961 to FY2005', *Postsecondary Education Opportunity Research Newsletter*, **151** (January), available at http://www.postsecondary.org/rl/rl_02.asp.

5. Negotiating a new relationship with the state: the Virginia experience

David W. Breneman and H. Lane Kneedler

The focus of this volume is budgetary austerity in higher education and the various responses that institutions and governments are making to this new reality. As Stanley Ikenberry suggests in Chapter 2, the social compact regarding the purpose of public support for colleges and universities that marked the post-World War II decades seems to have come to an end, replaced by a period of policy drift and budget cutting at both the state and federal levels of government. David Kirp (2003) highlights the growing forms of market-based behavior that have arisen in response to budget shortfalls, including attempts at privatization, differential tuition among fields of study, distance learning and for-profit subsidiaries that provide support for core non-profit activities. Colleges and universities have also sought increased revenue from sharply rising tuitions and private fund-raising, cost savings in the form of increased numbers of adjunct, non-tenure-track faculty, and cost postponement in the form of deferred maintenance.

For public colleges and universities, however, the most significant change in the past decade has been the declining share of support provided by state government, the focus of this chapter. The Commonwealth of Virginia provides a particularly instructive case study of how one state and its public institutions have negotiated a new relationship in the light of changing budgetary realities. The lessons learned from that experience are developed here in some detail. We begin, however, with basic data on the tidal shifts that have occurred in state support, both nationally and in Virginia.

SHIFTING PATTERNS OF STATE SUPPORT

As noted earlier, higher education experienced substantial public and private investment in the post-World War II era, initially through the GI Bill and its support for returning veterans, and through growth in federally funded basic research, often linked to defense concerns of the Cold War. The National Defense Education Act of 1958 encouraged further student enrollments, and

the surging numbers of students from the baby boom generation prompted massive state investment in public universities and community colleges. The Higher Education Act of 1965 and the Education Amendments of 1972 created federal grant and loan programs that helped millions of students pay their college bills. To many in higher education these were the Golden Years, as state, federal and private funds flowed freely to expand the system and to move higher education from an elite to a mass phenomenon. In retrospect, such growth could not have been expected to continue indefinitely and indeed by the early 1980s the tide had begun to turn.

Kane et al. (2003) provide two measures of this change: state appropriations for higher education as a share of state outlays declined from 7.3 per cent in 1977 to 5.3 per cent in 2000, and state appropriations as a share of public university revenue fell from a peak of about 50 per cent in 1979 to about 36 per cent in 2000. Their analysis indicates that the rapid growth of state Medicaid expenditures has crowded out funds that might otherwise have gone to higher education. More recently, the National Conference of State Legislatures reports that between fiscal years (FY) 2002 and 2004, higher education was the only major function of state government that experienced large cuts in state funding.[1] Lyall and Sell (2006) provide extensive data and analyzes on financial trends in public higher education, highlighting particularly the dilemmas faced by the less selective and less prestigious regional state universities that do not have the pricing power or fund-raising opportunities that the more selective campuses enjoy. While the precise pattern of shifting support varies across the 50 states, the general trend since 1980 has been one of sharp cuts to higher education budgets during recessions, with funding often not fully recovered when the economy improves (State Higher Education Executive Officers, 2004, p. 21).

Breneman (2004) described efforts being made in seven states (Colorado, Florida, Oregon, South Carolina, Texas, Virginia and Washington) to cope with the volatile nature of state support. While the states differ in approach, the common themes are efforts on the part of institutions to gain control over tuition charge setting and deregulation from state control over various administrative functions. The Association of Governing Boards (2004) has provided further information on such state efforts. Each of the studies mentioned here helps to explain why efforts are underway to define and negotiate new ways for public universities to relate to state government.[2]

VIRGINIA AS A CASE STUDY

Virginia has 15 four-year public institutions of higher education, one two-year junior college and 23 two-year community colleges. These 39

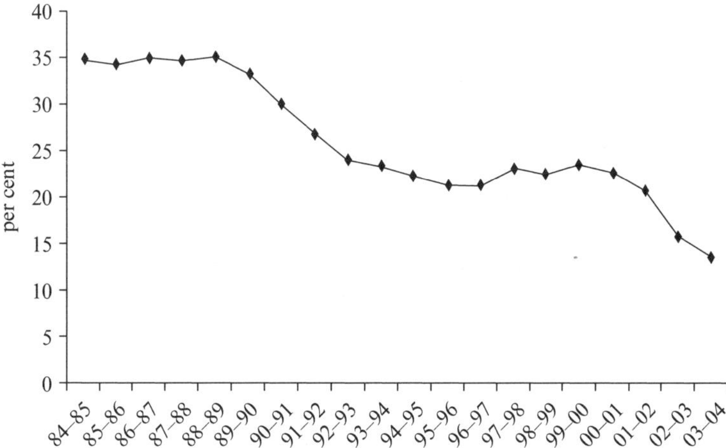

Source: Budget office, University of Virginia.

Figure 5.1 University of Virginia Academic Division Budget: percentage funded from state appropriations

institutions are coordinated, but not controlled, by the State Council of Higher Education for Virginia (SCHEV), an 11-member council supported by an executive director and staff.

The trends discussed above are clearly evident in Virginia, where new legislation restructuring the relationship between public colleges and universities and the state is farther advanced than in virtually any other state. As such, there is much to be learned from examining the Virginia experience, beginning with a brief discussion of the financial context that prompted the legislation recently passed and signed into law.[3]

In 1985 funding for higher education represented 17 per cent of the state's general fund budget; by 2004 this figure had dropped to 10 per cent, while other main functions of state government remained stable as a share or, in the case of Medicaid, increased significantly, bearing out the analysis of Kane et al. noted earlier. Indeed, while higher education's share dropped 7 percentage points, Medicaid's share increased from 5 to 12 per cent, a gain of 7 percentage points. Over this 20-year span state support as a share of the University of Virginia's Academic Division Budget dropped from 35 per cent to slightly more than 13 per cent (see Figure 5.1). Looking at actual dollars rather than percentage shares, the highest general fund appropriation to the University of Virginia was in FY 1990 approximately $170 million; by FY 2004 that figure had fallen to just over $100 million (see Figure 5.2).

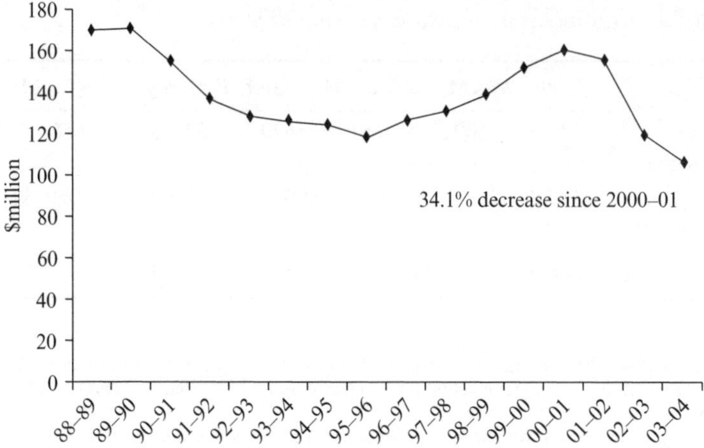

Source: State council of Higher Education for Virginia (SCHEV).

Figure 5.2 State appropriations to University of Virginia: inflation-adjusted general fund appropriations for educational and general programs (E&G)

While institutions in many states regained funding lost in the early 1990s, Virginia institutions clearly did not. As a result, the resources per in-state student at three Virginia universities (the College of William & Mary, Virginia Polytechnic Institute and State University ('Virginia Tech') and the University of Virginia) were far behind those of major competitors, such as the University of Maryland, the University of California at Berkeley, the University of North Carolina at Chapel Hill and the University of Michigan (see Table 5.1). The stark nature of the funding gap shown in Table 5.1 served to motivate these three Virginia universities to propose legislation making them what were initially labeled 'Commonwealth Chartered Universities and Colleges' or 'chartered institutions', removing them from the status of state agencies and providing greater freedom from regulation and from tuition charge controls imposed by the state. The basic argument was that Virginia's public universities would cease being competitive for top faculty and students and research grants if radical steps were not taken to alter their circumstances.

The issue of tuition charge control was prompted by the erratic nature of governmentally imposed tuition charge freezes and rollbacks during the 1990s (see Figure 5.3). Note that by FY 2004 actual tuition charges had returned to the path of FY 1996 tuition charges inflated by the CPI, with the gap between the two lines measuring the lost revenue caused by freezes

Table 5.1 Resources per in-state student, 2002–03

	Tech	W&M	U.Va.	Maryland	Berkeley[1]	UNC	Michigan
In-state tuition charge[2]	$3936	$5092	$5169	$5670	$3695	$3856	$7485
State appropriation	$7900	$8192	$9748[3]	$16 909	$22 309	$22 484	$19 213
Total funding	$11 836	$13 284	$14 917	$22 579	$26 004	$26 340	$26 698

Notes:
1. Data for 2002–2003 are not available for Berkeley. These figures represent 2001–02 data.
2. 'In-state tuition charge' represents tuition charge and all required fees (E&G and non-E&G).
3. U.Va. state appropriation per in-state student for 2003–04 has decreased to $8802.

Source: Institutional data and Grapevine (Center for the Study of Education Policy, Illinois State University).

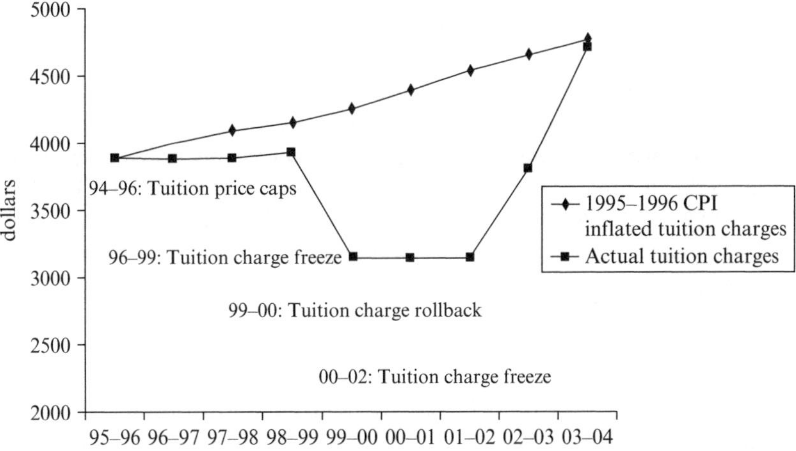

Note: Includes tuition charges and E&G fees. Does not include non-E&G fees. 1998–99 Increase represents $45 E&G technology fee.

Source: Budget Office, University of Virginia.

Figure 5.3 Undergraduate in-state tuition charges, 1995–96: tuition charges inflated using CPI vs. actual tuition charges

and rollbacks. The combination of unpredictable and volatile tuition revenue (Figure 5.3) and unpredictable and volatile state appropriations (Figure 5.2) also helped to motivate the move toward a restructured relationship with the state.

These historic data help to explain the proposal by the University of Virginia, Virginia Tech and the College of William & Mary to restructure their relationship with the state, but only if one assumes that the leadership of the institutions has given up hope of regaining the level of support received in earlier years. What has happened in Virginia and is happening in many other states is that university leaders are concluding that they must find alternative sources of revenue and new relationships with state government in an environment in which state support, while still vital, will not regain its earlier dominant role. This is a political and economic judgment that may be wrong, but it is widely shared among leaders of public colleges and universities and they are acting on that belief. It is worth noting, however, that in Virginia no reference was made by these three universities to their proposal being a form of 'privatization', nor was any attempt made to drop the word 'public' from the university descriptions. While diminished relative to earlier years, state support remains essential to the financial well-being of public universities and could not feasibly be replaced by unrestricted endowments or (for most institutions) by increased tuition revenues. Nonetheless, the stage was set by 2003 for these three universities to move forward with their proposal for a new partnership between the Commonwealth and higher education. The next section describes the process and outcome of that effort.

VIRGINIA'S APPROPRIATION PROCESS AND HIGHER EDUCATION FUNDING FORMULAE

Public institutions of higher education in Virginia are funded through a combination of state tax dollars and revenues from state bonds (state general funds) and tuition charges, fees, research funds and revenues from auxiliary enterprises (non-general funds). Many public universities in the state also have access – in greatly varying degrees – to private funds raised through affiliated foundations. Under the Constitution of Virginia, because public institutions of higher education are state agencies, all their funds are 'revenues of the Commonwealth' that must be appropriated by the legislature. Thus even their non-general funds, such as tuition charges and fees, are not retained by the institution but must be deposited with the state and then appropriated by the legislature. The state has no formal control over private foundation funds.

As noted above, since the early 1990s public institutions of higher education in Virginia have experienced significant volatility and unpredictability in their state appropriations. The problem has resulted from a combination of inadequate state general fund appropriations and restrictions on permissible tuition charge increases. Healthy increases in general fund and tuition charge appropriations in the late 1980s were followed by periods of general fund reductions and tuition charge caps and freezes, including a 20 per cent roll-back in tuition charges. Over the past three years, however, incremental increases in tuition charges have brought the institutions back to about where they were for tuition revenues prior to the tuition charge caps and freezes and budget cuts, but have still left them significantly behind in general funds. All of this volatility has resulted in a significant and increasing deficit in funding for higher education. Even with the infusion of approximately $175 million in general funds in 2005, the total deficit for higher education funding in Virginia now stands at approximately $377 million, of which $206 million is in general funds.

Although it does not appear anywhere in the Code of Virginia or the biennial Appropriation Act, a concept labeled the 'cost of education' is used to describe the funding needs of Virginia's public institutions of higher education. This institution-specific calculation has three components: (1) 'base adequacy', which is the state's higher education funding formula, consisting primarily of amounts for faculty and staff salaries and operating expenses (capital expenses are considered separately); (2) additional funds to place faculty salaries at the 60th percentile of each institution's peer institutions, a group that is determined by SCHEV; and (3) the state funds necessary, in combination with institutional funds, to meet student financial aid needs.

Out-of-state students are expected to pay at least 100 per cent of the cost of their education. Although the state's goal is for in-state students to pay only 33 per cent of their cost of education, with the remaining 67 per cent coming from state general funds, the state has not been able to meet this goal. In practice, therefore, although it varies considerably from institution to institution, the funding split for in-state students is closer to 47 per cent from non-general funds, mainly tuition charges and fees, and only 53 per cent from general funds – considerably less than the state's goal.

GREATER OPERATIONAL AUTONOMY

At the same time that Virginia's public institutions of higher education were experiencing this very real pinch financially, they also felt significantly overburdened by what they perceived to be increasing bureaucratic red tape

and centralized control by administrative agencies in the state capital. Public universities in Virginia have argued for many years that they should not be governed in the same manner as other state agencies. Unlike many state agencies, for example, they are not located in the seat of government. In addition, they are not like the Department of Transportation or the Department of Corrections, which, while they have 'branches' in other parts of the state, are governed by a central state agency in Richmond. Over time, as many of Virginia's public universities have developed administrative expertise themselves, they have come to view central state agencies as duplicative, meddlesome, excessively bureaucratic and therefore, while this is perhaps overstated, unnecessary. Finally, public universities really are a different kind of state agency. They compete with public and private peers for their 'employees' (faculty and staff) and for their 'customers' (students) in a way that other state agencies do not.

Since the mid-1990s the legislature has responded by including in the biennial Appropriation Act a series of pilot projects and decentralization programs that have granted public institutions of higher education (sometimes all of them, sometimes only certain of them) additional operational flexibility in such areas as non-general fund capital projects, human resources, procurement and financial operations. But this flexibility fell short – generally far short – of operational autonomy and often still contained some form of 'prior approval' for that operational flexibility rather than 'post-audit' review of the institution's performance.

RESTRUCTURING HIGHER EDUCATION IN VIRGINIA

By the late 1990s the situation had reached a critical point where a number of institutions felt that the integrity and quality of their programs were being seriously threatened, and that once they began a descent (that some would say already had begun) they would lose good faculty and students and their reputations would suffer – perhaps irreparably – resulting in a downward spiral from which it would take decades to recover.

In response, three of these institutions – the University of Virginia, Virginia Tech and the College of William & Mary – decided to work together for the enactment of legislation that would grant them greater authority over the generation and expenditure of revenues and greater autonomy to operate their institutions free of central state agency control, by changing the paradigm for state oversight from one of 'pre-approval' permission to 'post-audit' review of their performance. The effort took over three years – internal work on a proposal, a legislative study of the issue,

expansion of the proposal to provide benefits to all public institutions of higher education in the state and not just the major research universities, the inclusion of a commitment by these institutions to meeting certain state goals determined by the Governor and legislature, and an in-depth consideration of the proposal by the 2005 Session of the Legislature.

The result was enactment of the Restructured Higher Education Financial and Administrative Operations Act of 2005 (the 'Restructuring Act'), Chapters 933 and 945 (two identical House and Senate acts) of the 2005 Virginia Acts of Assembly, codified primarily as Chapter 4.10 of Title 23 of the Code of Virginia. The two acts appear at http://leg1.state.va.us/cgi-bin/legp504.exec?051+ful+CHAP0933 and http://leg1.state.va.us/cgi-bin/legp504.exec?051+ful+CHAP0945. Descriptions of the legislation and the process leading up to its enactment can be found at the websites for the University of Virginia, www.virginia.edu/restructuring, Virginia Tech, www.vt.edu/restructuring, and the College of William & Mary, www.wm.edu/restructuring.

OVERVIEW OF THE RESTRUCTURING ACT

Level 1 (All Institutions) and Articulated State Goals

The Restructuring Act establishes a three-level approach to providing greater autonomy to public institutions of higher education in Virginia. What is commonly known as 'Level 1' provides all institutions with additional operational authority in exchange for a commitment to meet articulated state goals. This additional authority includes the disposition of surplus real and personal property; the use of operating, income and capital leases; institutional certification of small, women-owned and minority-owned (SWAM) businesses as part of meeting state SWAM requirements; an exemption from certain procurement reporting requirements; and permission to use certain previously restricted methods of procurement. In addition, all Level 1 institutions may receive the financial incentives and may apply for the additional Level 2 and Level 3 authority described below.

The newly articulated state goals for higher education, for which institution-specific benchmarks will be developed consistent with each institution's mission, are:

1. providing access for Virginia students, including under-represented populations, according to enrollment projections as agreed upon with SCHEV;
2. ensuring affordability regardless of individual or family income;

3. offering a broad range of programs and assessing regularly whether the institution is meeting state needs for graduates in particular shortage areas, including specific academic disciplines, professions and geographic regions;
4. ensuring that programs and courses maintain high academic standards;
5. improving student retention and graduation rates;
6. developing uniform articulation agreements with the community college system that provide additional opportunities for transfer admission, and offering dual enrollment programs with Virginia high schools;
7. contributing actively to efforts to stimulate economic development, especially in areas of low income or high unemployment;
8. increasing the level of externally funded research and facilitating the transfer of technology from university research centers to the private sector;
9. working actively and cooperatively with elementary and secondary schools and school divisions to improve student achievement and the skills of teachers and administrators;
10. preparing and submitting to SCHEV by 1 October 2005 a six-year plan that addresses the institution's academic, financial, and student enrollment plans for that period and that is updated every two years (six-year plans for the University of Virginia, Virginia Tech and the College of William & Mary can be found at their websites listed on p. 62);
11. conducting the institution's business affairs efficiently and economically.

All public institutions of higher education will be assessed annually by SCHEV, using performance criteria developed by SCHEV for the first ten goals, with input from the institutions, and approved or modified by the Governor. The criteria for the eleventh goal will be developed by the Governor. These performance criteria are then to be included in the Budget Bill submitted by the Governor to the legislature, considered by the legislature as part of the budget approval process, and implemented as contained in the enacted Appropriation Act.

If this annual assessment by SCHEV indicates that the institution has met these state goals for the fiscal year, the institution will receive certain financial incentives: (1) the interest the state has earned on the institution's tuition charges and fees and certain other non-general funds it has held that year; (2) any unexpended appropriations at the close of the fiscal year, which will be re-appropriated to the institution for the following fiscal year; and (3) a pro rata amount of the rebates due to the state on credit card

purchases of $5000 or less made during that fiscal year. Although unstated in the Restructuring Act, an institution that has failed to meet these state goals – particularly if that failure has occurred over several years – presumably not only would not receive these financial incentives but also would risk losing the additional operational authority granted in Level 1.

Level 2

'Level 2' permits an institution to negotiate a 'Memorandum of Understanding' with the Governor for additional authority in an operational area or areas to be designated by, and according to eligibility criteria to be developed by, the Governor and approved by the General Assembly as part of the budget process.

Level 3

Finally, 'Level 3' is reserved for institutions that have an AA or better rating from a national bond rating agency or can demonstrate successful past performance in the state's decentralization programs and pilot projects and in at least one Level 2 area of additional authority. An institution that wishes to be granted Level 3 autonomy must apply to the Governor and document that (1) it possesses the necessary administrative infrastructure, experience and expertise to implement Level 3 authority; (2) it is able to operate as a Level 3 institution without jeopardizing its financial integrity and stability; (3) it consistently meets the Governor's financial and administrative standards; and (4) it has adopted performance and accountability standards, in addition to the standards developed by SCHEV and the Governor and approved by the legislature, against which its implementation of Level 3 authority can be measured.

Once satisfied that the institution will be able to manage itself successfully, the Governor will authorize the appropriate cabinet secretaries to negotiate a 'management agreement' with the institution, under which the institution will be granted considerably greater operational autonomy in the areas of capital projects, leases, information technology, procurement of goods, services, insurance and construction, human resources (including the authority to have their own human resources systems and pay-for-performance), and finance and accounting. The Restructuring Act sets forth the maximum operational authority that may be granted to the institution in each operational area – which constitutes almost complete autonomy in that area – but leaves it to the Governor's Administration and the institution to negotiate how much additional autonomy is appropriate for that institution, subject to the legislative approval detailed below.

The Restructuring Act reiterates the prior authority of institutions to set their tuition charges and fees, and tuition charges and fees also may be addressed in the management agreement. A management agreement, however, is not a true 'contract' enforceable in court; it is the implementing document for a legislatively authorized program. Because one legislature may not constitutionally bind future legislatures to continue a government program, the Restructuring Act does not provide either a long-term guarantee of complete tuition charge 'autonomy' or absolute protection against later tuition charge and fee caps or freezes. Only an amendment to the state constitution could do that. But a management agreement may include an agreement to provide an annual 'sum sufficient' appropriation to an institution of its non-general funds based on its projected annual range of tuition charges and fees contained in its six-year plan required by state goal 10 above. A 'sum sufficient' appropriation is an estimated appropriation that permits the institution to receive whatever non-general funds it generates and not be bound by a specific appropriated non-general fund figure.

As a practical matter, therefore, when coupled with the statutorily reiterated authority of institutions to set their tuition charges and fees, the approach of the Restructuring Act provides institutions with much greater tuition charge authority and flexibility than they had previously. As with most government programs, 'university restructuring' in Virginia is likely to be continued as long as it is implemented reasonably and responsibly. Furthermore, once the new structure has been successfully implemented and has been in place for several years, it will be much more difficult for the state to reverse course.

Over the summer and fall of 2005 the University of Virginia, Virginia Tech and the College of William & Mary each successfully negotiated a management agreement with the Governor's administration. Executed agreements, which can be found on the institutions' websites listed above, were submitted to the legislature on 15 November 2005 and recommendtions for their approval were included in the biennial Budget Bill that the Governor submitted to the legislature in December 2005. The three management agreements will be considered by the 2006 Session of the Legislature and, if the recommendations for approval are included in the enacted 2006–08 Appropriation Act, the agreements will become effective on 1 July 2006.

TEN KEYS TO SUCCESS

There were several factors that were critical to the enactment of the 2005 Restructuring Act in Virginia. Some are obvious; others may not be. The

absence of any one of these factors would have made enactment of the legislation much more difficult and perhaps impossible. The absence of any two would have doomed the project.

1. A genuine multi-institution 'team' approach that focused on the amount of autonomy granted, not on the autonomy that was not granted The University of Virginia, Virginia Tech and the College of William & Mary are three preeminent public universities, both in Virginia and nationally. They often have understandable competing priorities, including annual funding from the legislature. Yet they also work well together on issues of common interest. This effort was no exception. The representatives from the three institutions – from the three presidents down – held together as a group even when there was enormous pressure, both from within the institutions and from outside, to break ranks. Without this uncompromising commitment to a common goal, the Restructuring Act would not have become a reality.

As the proposal proceeded through the legislative process and the management agreements were negotiated with the Governor and his administration, there was a natural tendency to focus not on how much autonomy had been granted, but on how much had not yet been granted or had been lost along the way. By the end of both the legislative process and the management agreement negotiation process, the disagreements generally were over the nuances of the proposal, not its core principles. And many of these final disagreements were resolved in favor of the institutions. Fortunately there were very perceptive and able representatives from each of the three institutions who continually focused on and reminded each other and the team, as well as their internal and external constituencies, how much had been achieved. Not only was this insight and wisdom reassuring internally, but without it the final negotiations and agreement on both the legislation and the management agreements would have been exceedingly more difficult and arguably impossible in some respects.

2. Support from the Governor and key legislators From the outset Governor Mark R. Warner, whose term ended in January 2006, signaled strong support for the restructuring of higher education. But it was not clear – at least in the beginning – how strongly he would support the approach advocated by the three institutions.

Unfortunately, just as headway was being made in the fall of 2003, a major battle with the legislature erupted over a tax reform proposal by the Governor to address a looming budget crisis that threatened to endanger the state's AAA bond rating – a battle that resulted in the most protracted legislative session in Virginia history (from early January to early June).

This unprecedented development temporarily diverted the attention of the Governor and his secretaries. Over the next year, however, support for the proposal from the Governor and his administration grew and the Governor once again signaled his strong support for the proposal as the 2005 legislative session approached.

Following that session, the Governor offered a substitute to address his concerns with the restructuring bills enacted by the legislature (in Virginia, governors may propose changes to bills passed by the legislature; they are considered when the legislature returns six weeks after a legislative session for its Reconvened, or so-called 'Veto', Session to consider a Governor's vetoes, amendments and substitutes). The substitute was adopted overwhelmingly – by a 35–2 vote (with three members not voting) in the Senate and a 79–17 vote (with four members not voting) in the House.

Because the initiative proposed greater autonomy for institutional financial and administrative operations and not 'education reform', strong support not only from the legislature's leadership but also from the two money committees was critical. The leadership in both houses and both money committee chairmen were supportive from the outset. The Speaker of the House was one of the earliest proponents of the proposal; his early support was critical, especially in the House. The Senate Finance Committee Chairman, who is also the President *pro tempore* of the Senate of Virginia, had been a leading advocate for higher education for many years. The House Appropriations Committee Chairman also had been very supportive of higher education and one of the Commonwealth's newer but influential universities is located in his district. Other key members of both committees also were quite supportive, especially during a 2004 legislative study of the proposal, as were several key members of both majority caucuses and both money committee staffs during critical points in the deliberations.

It was not clear how extensive the role of the two education committees would be. In the Senate, while the Finance Committee and its members were kept informed of the initiative both prior to and during the session, only the Education and Health Committee formally considered the legislation. Under the guidance and leadership of its chairman, the committee reported it to the floor unanimously. In the House, the Education Committee never considered the legislation; only the Appropriations Committee did.

3. Legislative and Executive Branch 'champions' As with any complex and controversial legislation, this initiative needed a 'champion' in each house, someone who was on the key committees and was willing to take the considerable time necessary to persuade his colleagues – individually, in

committee, and on the floor – to vote for the proposal. The institutions were very fortunate to identify two such individuals. One is a highly respected senator who is the Majority Floor Leader, a member of the Senate Finance Committee and a strong supporter of higher education and in whose district one of the three institutions is located. The second is a highly respected delegate who is a member of the House Appropriations Committee, a strong supporter of higher education and a key member of the House majority caucus. Both individuals did an extraordinary job in learning the nuances of the initiative, and in persuading their colleagues – many of whom were doubtful initially – to support the legislation. In many ways, the legislation was passed because members trusted these two distinguished legislators.

In the Executive Branch, in addition to the Governor, who was personally involved at various stages of the process, there were several other 'champions', particularly at the Cabinet level. The coordinator of the effort was the Secretary of Finance, who is highly respected and trusted by the legislature and devoted countless hours to the project. The Restructuring Act would not have been enacted without his untiring leadership.

4. A commitment to articulated state goals in exchange for additional autonomy There had been intermittent calls for years by both the Governor and the legislature for greater accountability by the state's public institutions of higher education in meeting the state's goals for higher education. No one had ever articulated those goals, however. The Governor and his Secretary of Finance, assisted by the Deputy Secretary (and later Secretary) of Education, crafted the 11 state goals described above – known as the state 'ask'. These goals were quickly embraced by key legislators. In retrospect it is clear that the Restructuring Act would not have been enacted without this requirement that public universities commit to meeting articulated state goals for higher education. It also is clear that this balance between the 'benefits' of greater autonomy and the 'burdens' of these commitments, if indeed they should be labeled as such, is appropriate.

State goals 3 (offering a broad range of programs) and 4 (ensuring that such programs and courses maintain high academic standards) are worthy of special note. At least initially, the Restructuring Act dealt almost exclusively with greater autonomy for financial and administrative operations. As consideration of the initiative continued, however, led by the Chairman of the Senate Finance Committee, the proposal was amended to include state goals that would require high standards for academic programs.

Because the performance criteria and benchmarks for these two academic goals will require the collection of data and the preparation of new reports by the academic side of the institutions, some on that side have

voiced concerns that the academic side has somehow been disadvantaged so that university administrators could obtain greater autonomy in their operations. Such conclusions are shortsighted. To the extent that the Restructuring Act will allow institutions to raise additional financial resources so that they can raise faculty salaries, provide additional research funds and facilities, provide additional student financial aid and better compensate staff, and to the extent that the additional autonomy makes the institutions more efficient, the academic side of the institutions clearly will benefit both directly and indirectly.

5. A stated willingness to be more accountable From the outset, the three institutions made it clear that they were not seeking to avoid state oversight but were merely seeking to change the paradigm for that oversight from a 'pre-approval' model to a 'post-audit' model. They therefore repeatedly emphasized that they intended to be fully accountable for the additional autonomy granted to them in whatever manner the Governor and legislature deemed appropriate. Thus, the Restructuring Act requires annual assessments by SCHEV and the state's Auditor of Public Accounts and a performance study by the legislature's Joint Legislative Audit and Review Commission.

6. An inclusive proposal The three institutions also recognized from the outset that they would not receive the necessary support from other public universities in the state, or from the legislature, if their proposal was in fact only for the three of them, or was perceived as such. Unfortunately, however, despite significant efforts by these three institutions, the proposal was viewed from the start as being both exclusive and elitist. Because it was designed to grant considerably greater autonomy in financial and administrative operations, the proposal was appropriate only for those institutions that had in place the necessary infrastructure to manage those operations successfully. But of Virginia's 39 public institutions of higher education, only a handful – probably no more than two or three in addition to the three original institutions – had, or in the reasonably foreseeable future could have, in place the necessary infrastructure to obtain the additional autonomy authorized in the original proposal. Even these two or three other institutions viewed that autonomy as being at least a year or two in the future for them.

The remaining institutions saw nothing in the original proposal for them. Indeed, the proposal only increased frustrations for some of these institutions, because they perceived that they too were suffering from bureaucratic central state agency red tape. Yet they all realized – probably accurately – that the state would not consider them as being capable of managing

themselves. They therefore viewed the proposal as exclusive and elitist: these three institutions, which already enjoyed many advantages that other public institutions of higher education in the state did not, would be cut free of the central state bureaucracy while other institutions would remain ensnarled in bureaucratic red tape.

The solution was quite simple. The then Chairman of the Council of Presidents, an informal group of the presidents of Virginia's public institutions of higher education – who happened to be the Chancellor of the Virginia Community College System – appointed a subgroup, which devised a new proposal that offered something for all institutions. The key was the three-level system described above, which provides some additional financial and administrative operational authority for *all* institutions and the opportunity for even more autonomy for those institutions that can demonstrate they can manage their own operations. The new proposal was endorsed by the Council, and received additional credibility when it was strongly supported not only by the Chancellor of the Virginia Community College System but also by the president of one of Virginia's two historically black public universities. With the endorsement of these institutions, it was much more difficult for the proposal to be portrayed as exclusive and elitist.

7. Openness to change as the process evolved In addition to amending the proposal to be more inclusive, the three institutions demonstrated a disciplined willingness to change the proposal in other ways. One example involved a change in terminology that at one point was important to the institutions. The original proposal established 'chartered institutions' that were not 'state agencies' but were separate 'political subdivisions'. The 'political subdivision' term was used because the institutions were seeking a way that their tuition charges and fees and other non-general funds could be retained by them and would not have to be appropriated by the legislature. As noted above, both the general funds and non-general funds of a 'state agency' are 'revenues of the Commonwealth', which constitutionally must be appropriated by the legislature. On the other hand, non-general funds of 'political subdivisions' such as state authorities and localities are not required to be appropriated. The term 'chartered institution' was used because the institutions did not want to be called a 'political subdivision' or an 'authority'. Since the College of William & Mary had been established by a charter from the King of England, the term 'chartered institution' initially was selected.

Unfortunately, both terms caused considerable confusion. 'Chartered' was viewed as elitist. To some it connoted something akin to elementary and secondary 'charter schools', which have been controversial in Virginia.

Others viewed it as a signal that the three institutions were separating themselves from the remainder of higher education in the Commonwealth. 'Chartered', especially when combined with the 'political subdivision' designation, was viewed by many as an effort by these three institutions to 'go private', which never was intended but which had the potential to cause significant political problems. Thus, 'chartered institutions' became simply 'covered institutions', meaning they were institutions covered and governed by the Level 3 provisions of the Restructuring Act.

A second example of this capacity for change involved a change in approach. The money committee staffs suggested a solution to the appropriation issue that gave rise to the 'political subdivision' designation. Their suggestion, which is included in the executed management agreements, was the more flexible 'sum sufficient' appropriation explained previously. On the basis of this proposed modification and the continued opposition to the 'political subdivision' designation, the three institutions dropped the designation and agreed to remain 'state agencies'.

8. *An independently calculated cap on tuition charge and fee increases*
Legislators feel a need to have control over increases in tuition charges and fees because they fear that, if institutional discretion is unfettered, the governing boards of these institutions – which in Virginia consist solely of gubernatorial appointments not necessarily related to a governor's four-year term[4] – will approve tuition charge and fee increases that are unacceptable to their constituents and therefore are politically unpalatable. In return, the institutions fear that politically imposed tuition charge caps will be unrelated to institutional needs and difficult to remove. What was needed for the proposal was an independently calculated, somewhat flexible, self-imposed cap.

Virginia's concept of the 'cost of education' for each institution provided just such a cap. As noted previously, the 'cost of education' is comprised of three factors: (1) base adequacy, (2) reaching the 60th percentile for faculty salaries, and (3) required need-based financial aid. The first two factors are the major components of the calculation and are determined by someone other than the institutions themselves. Thus the institutions' use of the 'cost of education' concept was intended to place an independently calculated but flexible cap on the total mix of general funds and tuition charges and fees and other non-general funds needed by each institution, with each institution having the authority to raise tuition charges and fees over a stated phase-in period (now six years) to close the gap of whatever the state was not able to provide in general funds. Early in the process, however, this cost of education concept was perceived by legislators and legislative staff as a statutory commitment to provide a certain level of general fund

appropriations to higher education – a goal that they knew they could not meet. Even though the three institutions intended quite the opposite, this perception was insurmountable.

The solution was the six-year plans described above as state goal 10 of the state's 11 articulated goals for higher education. As part of these plans, each institution sets forth in considerable detail its proposed funding needs over the next six years. Those needs include anticipated tuition charge and fee increases based on two scenarios – a 'worst case' scenario under which no additional state general funds are provided, and a 'better (not best) case' scenario that includes figures provided by SCHEV and the money committee staffs for certain anticipated state general fund increases. The result is the same as what the institutions initially proposed, but it is reached in a much more acceptable fashion. Institutional needs are still calculated using the 'cost of education' concept, tuition charges and fees are increased to narrow and finally eliminate the gap in state general funds so that institutions can fully fund their cost of education, and that increase is phased in over a six-year period.

9. Involvement of institutional staff in the preparation of the legislation and implementing procedures The three institutions were careful to involve key operational staff – who will implement the proposal – in both the development of the legislation and the negotiation of the management agreements. A working group with representatives from each of the three institutions was established in each operational area. These groups proposed most of what was originally included for each operational area in the legislation and they drafted the initial operational area policies that, after negotiations with the Governor, were eventually adopted by the Board of Visitors for each institution and were incorporated in, and attached as exhibits to, each executed management agreement. These groups were also regularly consulted as changes were made to both the legislation and the management agreements. Because of the speed with which both the legislative process and the negotiations often proceeded, it was not possible to consult with these working groups on all changes. While this consultation process, therefore, was not perfect, most members of the working groups have remarked that they felt included and that their views were heard.

10. Regular communications with institutional constituencies It was critical, of course, that the institutions communicated regularly with their internal constituencies (faculty, staff and students) and with their external constituencies (alumni, friends, donors and their local communities) throughout the process. Each of the three institutions took specific steps to do so. Communications occurred in various ways – open public meetings

with affected constituents, internal newsletters, external newsletters, institutional website communications, media reports and so on. This was not an easy task, especially for institutions as large and diverse as the University of Virginia and Virginia Tech. Unfortunately, as will occur in any large and complex institution, there were individuals in some constituent groups who did not feel that they were given the opportunity to participate in the process as much as they would have liked. This was particularly true of some employees who were fearful that the new autonomy, especially in human resources, would not be positive for university employees. The overwhelming majority of both internal and external constituents, however, appear to be informed, supportive and even enthusiastic about the initiative. On balance, therefore, given the immensity of the task, the three institutions, as well as Virginia's other institutions of higher education, did an admirable job of communicating with their various constituent groups.

CONCLUSION

As implementation of the Restructuring Act in Virginia has just begun, evaluation of its effects is premature.[5] Early criticisms of the initial proposal included a concern that low-income students would be priced out of higher education by the sharp tuition charge increases likely to follow, a concern that the less selective public universities and the two-year colleges would be unable to benefit from policies that accepted reduced levels of state support in exchange for deregulation, higher tuition charges and greater reliance on private fund-raising, and some concerns that staff would be disadvantaged by the greater freedom given to universities to set human resources policies. The first concern has been addressed to some degree by new financial aid programs such as the College of William & Mary's 'Gateway William and Mary', Virginia Tech's 'Funds for the Future' and University of Virginia's 'AccessUVa', which guarantee full financial aid with no loans for admitted students from low-income families.[6] The second concern was handled politically by admitting all public institutions to the restructuring plan, with the three levels defining different degrees of financial and managerial capability. The extent to which regional comprehensive institutions and two-year colleges will ultimately benefit from the provisions is one of the main issues for any subsequent evaluation. The third concern also appears largely to have been overcome, although a minority of staff continue to argue that the new arrangement will deprive employees of certain rights and guarantees, also an issue for future evaluation.

At this point, we conclude that the new legislation promises significant benefits to the universities and to the state and its citizens, but we also

acknowledge that complex legislation often contains surprises in the form of unintended consequences that only reveal themselves after the program has run for some years. We believe, therefore, that while those in other states can learn much from the restructuring process in Virginia and while we are encouraged by the potential for the new legislation, it is still too early to claim complete victory for a new financing model.

NOTES

1. Data provided by the National Conference of State Legislatures, Denver, CO.
2. As this paper was being written, an op-ed piece written by the president of Miami University in Ohio appeared in the *Washington Post* (30 December 2005, p. A27), arguing, 'With declining state support driving up tuition charges, the trend is absolutely clear. Public higher education is moving down the track toward privatization, and the train is not coming back.'
3. Data in this section were provided by the Office of the President, University of Virginia.
4. In Virginia, governors may serve only one four-year term at a time but may serve again after being out of office for four years or more. Since the mid-1960s, only one governor has served more than one four-year term – Mills Godwin, from 1966 to 1970 (as a Democrat) and from 1974 to 1978 (as a Republican).
5. One leading administrator at the University of Virginia has said that it will be five years before results are fairly clear.
6. Information about these financial aid programs can be found at http://www.wm.edu/financialaid/, http://www.finaid.vt.edu/forms/Funds_for_the_Future.pdf, and http://www.virginia.edu/accessuva/.

REFERENCES

Association of Governing Boards (2004), *Balancing Act: Public Higher Education in Transition*, Washington, DC: Association of Governing Boards.

Breneman, D.W. (2004), 'Are the States and Public Higher Education Striking a New Bargain?', Public Policy Paper Series No. 04-02, Washington, DC: Association of Governing Boards.

Kane, T.J., P.R. Orszag and D.L. Gunter (2003), *State Fiscal Constraints and Higher Education Spending: the Role of Medicaid and the Business Cycle*, Washington, DC: The Brookings Institution, April.

Kirp, D. (2003), *Shakespeare, Einstein and the Bottom Line: the Marketing of Higher Education*, Cambridge, MA: Harvard University Press.

Lyall, K.C. and K.R. Sell (2006), *The True Genius of America at Risk: Are We Losing our Public Universities to De Facto Privatization?*, ACE/Praeger Series on Higher Education.

State Higher Education Executive Officers (SHEEO) (2004), *State Higher Education Finance, FY 2003*, Denver, CO: SHEEO.

6. Money for something – but what?

David A. Longanecker

Two distinct themes permeate the other chapters of this book: first, the change-agenda theme, a reflection of the increasingly loud call to alter the way American higher education does business; and second, the revenue enhancement theme, which focuses on creative new ways to generate more money for this valuable enterprise. This twin focus comes as no surprise. Beyond the pages of this book, the demand for change and the need to increase revenue are realities that higher education deals with every day. But there is a peculiar disconnect in the ways we are dealing with and discussing these issues – a shying away from what needs to be done, a turning away from a critical part of our mission.

Take the issue of change: many agree that American higher education faces a crisis that demands a major overhaul, yet most of the reforms that are proposed today are incremental in nature. When it comes to enhancing revenue, there is a different problem: while excellent strategies are in place to support such worthy things as research, facilities and proprietary scholarships, there are relatively few that provide much money in support of higher education's core mission – educating students.

Herein lies the rub – a double one. We need to change US higher education in big ways, but we operate an industry that is more comfortable with modest change (and which, frankly, has been able to get away with only modest changes in the past). In addition, we need to imagine creative ways to sustain higher education's historic core reason for being – student education – yet our comfort zone, when it comes to raising revenue, lies elsewhere.

It is worth asking: is there a financial crisis in American higher education that warrants our current level of worry? And, if there is, can it be best addressed by attracting new revenues or by changing the way we do business? This chapter examines both of these questions.

IS THE FINANCIAL CRISIS REAL?

All of us who work in higher education know the mantra: 'Government no longer appreciates the value of higher education (woe is us).' According to

Notes:
1. Finance data are from Grapevine and reflect appropriations of state and local tax funds for operating expenses of higher education. Dollars adjusted with CPI-U.
2. FTE are from IPEDS as reported in the NCES *Digest of Education Statistics 2002*, Table 200, and reflect enrollment at all levels (undergraduate, graduate and first-professional) in degree-granting public 2-year and 4-year institutions.

Source: SHEEO, *State Higher Education Finance Survey*, 2003.

Figure 6.1 Educational appropriations per FTE, US fiscal 1980–2004

this scenario, both public and private higher education institutions are being forced to abandon activities that promote the public good in favor of those that curry favor with the gods of a market-based economy.

The problem is that much evidence simply contradicts this perception. Data from the State Higher Education Executive Officers demonstrate that state and local funding per student has actually increased over the past 30 years, after adjusting for inflation (see Figure 6.1). Certainly, public funding has fluctuated greatly during this period, generally peaking during times when the economy is strong and dropping off substantially when there is economic difficulty, but the researchers' so-called 'best fitting line' shows consistent growth over the last 30 years.

Nevertheless, within higher education the idea that public funding has dropped off substantially remains deeply entrenched. Five factors contribute to this misperception.

Higher education shares the wealth First, public support of higher education as a share of total public resources has clearly fallen off. States used to

allocate a much larger share of their resources to higher education than they do today. As states picked up additional areas of responsibility – indigent health care, for instance, and many others evolving from emerging public needs or mandated by the federal government – an increasing share of state dollars was dedicated to new services. In addition, demographic and societal changes created a greater demand for other services, such as corrections and elementary/secondary education. States increased taxes to support the increased demand for such services and, as a result, the share of the pool of all public revenues going to higher education declined. That decline triggered a wave of justifiable concern in higher education, but what we failed to recognize is that the *value* of the funding we were receiving was not declining over time. Our smaller share of a larger budget left us pretty much where we were in the old days.

Public funding's slice of the pie has shrunk On the flip side, public funding as a share of higher education's overall budget has also fallen – providing a second reason higher education believes public funding is in decline. Two factors account for this drop. First, the cost of providing higher education has increased over time – a natural consequence of our particular kind of enterprise. Because higher education is a labor-intensive enterprise with little opportunity for increasing productivity and because wages increase more rapidly than other goods and services that factor into inflation, our costs will rise more rapidly than inflation in general. What is more, we widen that gulf by helping to produce an educated workforce, which subsequently creates productivity gains in the rest of the economy and slows the pace of general inflation (but not ours). We have, in fact, codified this cost-spiraling conundrum by creating our own cost inflation indexes – the Halstead Higher Education Price Index (HEPI) and the SHEEO Higher Education Cost Adjustment (HECA). Many public policy makers, however, have difficulty buying our arguments, believing our super inflationary cost increases are more a function of inefficiencies within the system, along with a reluctance to adopt the productivity improvement models other industries have used.

The second reason the publicly supported slice of the higher education funding pie has shrunken is that higher education has entered new lines of business (and expanded old ones) that have little to do with its traditional instructional core function – which is what public funding supports. The revenue supporting these activities often comes from new sources and, when factored into the total finance equation, it has the effect of reducing instruction's share of the budget and also the publicly funded share. Thirty years ago, instruction (and the internally funded research that is imbedded within what we call instructional costs) represented 33 per cent of overall

higher education expenditures. Today instruction represents less than 30 per cent, with the rapid growth in research funding replacing a portion of the share that used to go to instruction. Indeed, this trend is even more rapid than reflected in these statistics because institutionally funded research, which is imbedded within the instructional budget, has also grown disproportionately, thus further eroding the share of dollars committed to instruction per se (NCES, 2004). In addition, institutionally supported financial aid, used to advance both access and enrollment-management objectives, has increased substantially. Auxiliary student activities and accouterments (comfort dorms, gourmet cafeterias, exercise facilities and so on) and intercollegiate athletics have also expanded on many campuses. While these activities have not necessarily diminished higher education's original instructional mission, they have without doubt increased its overall budget and reduced instruction's share of that budget – the publicly supported share.

Averages do not tell the whole story The third factor contributing to our misperception about the level of public support is that averages do not reflect the huge variation within higher education. In a number of states, higher education has seen substantial funding increases in real (inflation-adjusted) terms over the past few years, while in many others its support has declined (see Figure 6.2). Between 1991 and 2004, Missouri, Wyoming, Rhode Island, Maryland, Delaware, Alabama and Kentucky experienced increases of at least 20 per cent in total educational revenues per full-time-equivalent (FTE) student after adjusting for inflation, whereas New Mexico, South Carolina and Washington lost more than 20 per cent. Because those of us in higher education believe passionately in the value of what we do, we tend to think that what happened in the first seven states is as it should be and what happened in New Mexico, South Carolina and Washington is a travesty. Furthermore, because higher education is a growth-driven industry, we tend to see stability as equivalent to decline.

Our spin has become our truth Fourth, we have begun to believe in our own spin. Leaders in higher education feel it is their job to make the best case for increased public funding. They have a responsibility to be the best spokes-people for their enterprises, to garner enough resources not just to sustain but to enhance their institutions' efforts. So they make the most convincing case they can (and yes, it is spin), a case so convincing that they, and we, come to believe it. In this respect the leaders of US higher education exhibit the same habits of mind as the leaders of our states and our nation. They repeat the same line so often that it becomes their truth and ours (we tend to believe those who espouse what we want to believe anyway).

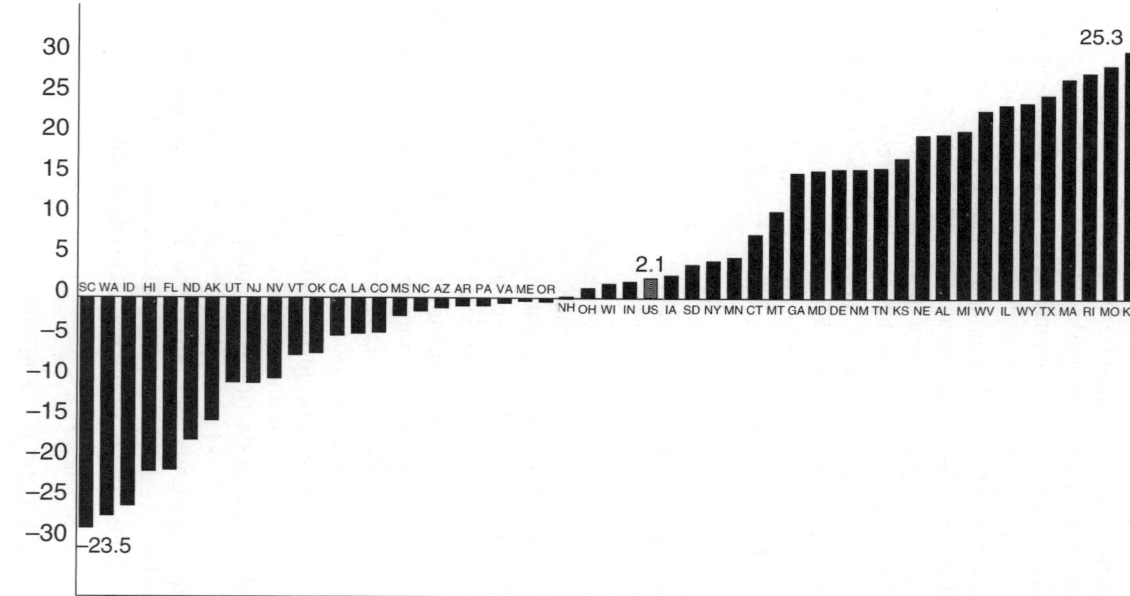

Notes: Total educational funding is the sum of educational appropriations plus net tuition charge revenue. Constant 2003 dollars adjusted by SHEEO HECA.

Source: SHEEO. *State Higher Education Finance Survey*, 2003.

Figure 6.2 Total educational funding per FTE, percentage change by state, FY 1991–2003

We are still in recovery The fifth and final reason why we believe public funding for higher education is dropping is that the last few years have been very hard on states and on higher education. Funding in the first few years of the new millennium dropped off precipitously, reaching the lowest level in the last 30 years, after adjusting for inflation (see Figure 6.2). There is legitimate concern that this downward trend, though short lived, could reflect a marked diminution of public support. Yet past trends and current data appear not to support this concern. After every other recessionary drop, public funding for higher education has rebounded – and preliminary data for FY 2005 indicate that public support increased substantially as state coffers began to refill.

In sum, it is not accurate to say we have a funding crisis today because of a diminution of public support. It is true that in some states higher education is struggling with a major loss of resources and in most states the economic decline of the last five years has taken a toll on many institutions' current operations. But US higher education is not in the throes of a funding crisis today. Tomorrow, however, may be a very different story.

A REAL CRISIS LOOMS

The future for US higher education does not look bright; in fact, it looks very ominous. Projections from the National Center for Higher Education Management Systems (NCHEMS) suggest that every state in the union will face a structural budget deficit by 2013, given current tax and revenue structures and the likely demand for public services (see Figure 6.3). Projections from the Western Interstate Commission for Higher Education (2003) indicate that higher education institutions in nearly one third of the states are likely to face substantial enrollment increases as the number of high school graduates grows over the next decade (see Figure 6.4).

These economic and demographic projections raise the serious possibility that public support, though it may not have fallen off substantially in the past, might well decline in the future. The drop, over time, in the share of public resources devoted to higher education in both federal and state budgets has left the enterprise vulnerable. And if the demand for other public services continues to grow, as it is projected to do, the likelihood that higher education will fare well in future budgets is doubtful.

SOLVING THE CRISIS I: CAN WE CUT ENOUGH?

There is much ado these days about cutting the costs and improving the productivity of US higher education. This was a major theme at the

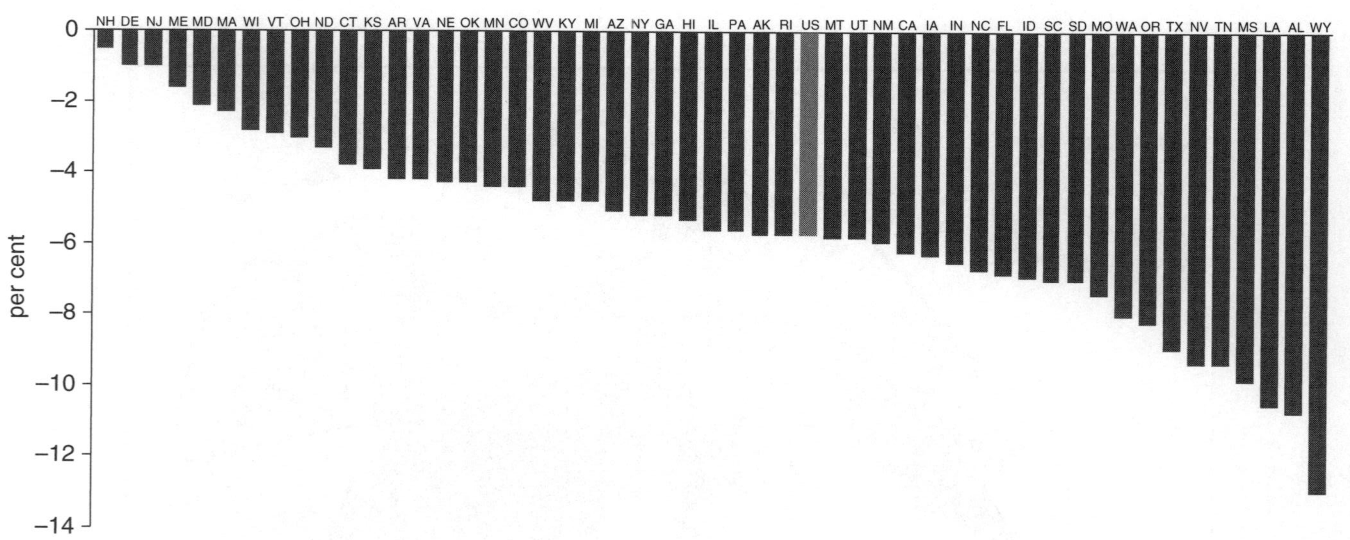

Source: National Center for Higher Education Management Systems.

Figure 6.3 State and local surplus or shortfall as a percentage of baseline revenues

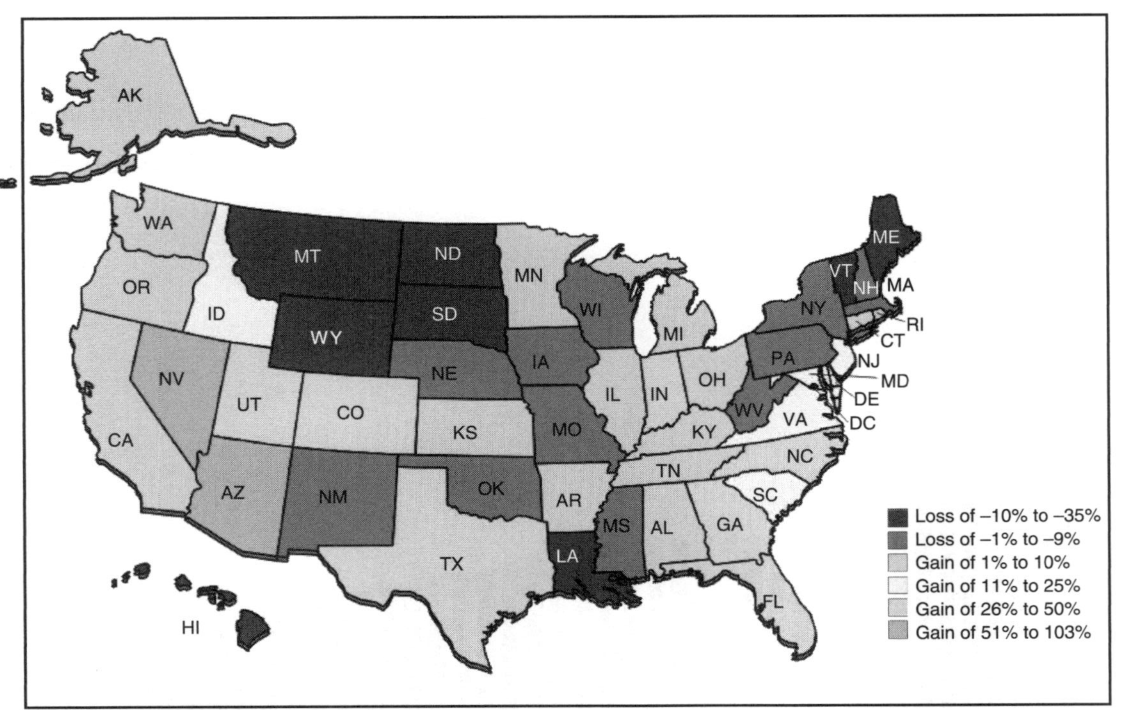

Source: Western Interstate Commission for Higher Education (2003).

Figure 6.4 *Percentage change in number of public and nonpublic high school graduates by state, 2001–02 (actual) and 2017–18 (projected)*

TIAA-CREF Institute 2005 conference, on which this book is based. Stan Ikenberry, in his introductory chapter, suggests that, while cost cutting is imperative, higher education does not seem to understand what that really means. He points out that we are quite good at cutting budgets when we must, but we do so without really cutting costs. We rarely work to lower the price tag of higher education by improving efficiency or boosting productivity. Instead, our method is often to defer costs (by not filling vacant faculty slots until funds return, for instance) or to shift them to a new revenue stream. Some universities do work at making every dollar go farther, of course: the University System of Maryland, discussed by William Kirwan in Chapter 4, is cutting costs by increasing faculty teaching productivity, amongst other things.

There are plenty of measures we can take to reduce our costs. Teaching costs can be lowered by assigning professors more courses or by implementing new pedagogical techniques, such as the course-redesign project developed by Carol Twigg and her colleagues at the Center for Academic Transformation. Remedial education costs can be reduced by working with state policy makers and the various national P/20 initiatives to assure that more students come to college prepared to perform. Time to degree – and overall educational costs – can be cut by giving college credit (and credit toward majors, where appropriate) for high school accelerated-learning courses and for proficiency demonstrated through course-equivalency exams. And the cost of goods and services that colleges and universities regularly buy can be lowered by participating in cooperative-purchasing collaboratives.

That is the good news. The bad news is that each of these strategies will contribute only marginally to improving the productivity of US higher education. Taken together, they might reduce costs by 10 per cent, plus or minus. And a 10 per cent improvement will not be enough in the future. As mentioned earlier, at least one third of our states will face enrollment increases that will exceed 10 per cent over the next decade – and some states face almost insuperable challenges. Nevada projects a potential enrollment increase in excess of 100 per cent; Arizona expects a boost of over 65 per cent; Colorado, Utah, Texas, Florida, Georgia, North Carolina and Indiana face a more than 25 per cent increase. And each of these ten states is expected to face a structural budget deficit during the same time period. In this environment, how can higher education as a public good be preserved with only a 10 per cent increase in productivity? It can not.

Therefore we must turn to more radical ways of improving productivity. We must shift more students to institutions where faculty focuses more on the scholarship of teaching than on the scholarship of research. We must reduce the breadth of the curriculum, at least at some of our institutions.

We must find ways to enhance student success, so that more of them earn degrees. We must reduce the costs of marketing our enterprise – costs that do little for our public mission but add substantially to our total costs. We may even need to develop a triage strategy, accepting the substantial research indicating that some of the students we seek to serve are beyond our abilities to teach. It makes little difference whether students cannot learn at the college level because their own recalcitrance has left them ill-prepared or because our educational system has failed them – it is foolish to expend public resources pretending they can learn and succeed in college if they truly cannot.

Adopting such radical approaches to productivity enhancement could reduce the cost of the enterprise substantially. And it can be and has been done: for example, the University of Virginia is recognized as an exceptional teaching and research university, yet it operates on three-fourths of the resources per student available to the University of Michigan. Radical approaches to cost cutting would radically change the nature of American higher education, however – and higher education is too proud of what it has accomplished to accept such changes comfortably. No wonder we face a collision between what is needed on the cost-cutting front and what will be deemed possible and acceptable by those within academe.

SOLVING THE CRISIS II: CAN WE MAKE ENOUGH?

Without doubt, American higher education has shown exceptional ingenuity in identifying, pursuing and generating new sources of revenue. Public institutions have substantially increased their endowment revenues and alumni giving. The University of Michigan, for example, has amassed an endowment of more than $2 billion, which yields $90 million to support the university's various missions annually. Research funding from federal, state and proprietary private sources has increased exponentially, with many institutions that traditionally had no research role now touting their research activities. Customized training, paid for by private-sector industry and often matched by state economic development funds, has become a major revenue source for community colleges and, more recently, public four-year institutions as well. Ferreting out new funding opportunities is a mainstay of many colleges' and universities' capital development.

Increasingly, state and federal government and governing boards have encouraged higher education to boost its reliance on nontraditional sources of revenue. The problem is that these new sources of revenue generally provide little new support for the core educational function of our colleges and universities – student instruction. Two revenue sources – state

appropriations and tuition – continue to be the only significant resources available for funding instruction.

Is this a problem? Is it not commendable if institutions diversify, seeking revenue from sources other than state and student support? That depends. If the activities supported by new funding are consistent with the overall mission of the institution, then seeking such funding is certainly appropriate.

But too often institutional focus and energy follow the money. Recently I shared a cab to the airport with a visionary leader of a regional university, whose mission is to serve the citizens of its state. Yet, during our cab ride together, I heard nothing about the state or the institution's role within it. Rather, I heard about the university's entrepreneurial and rapidly expanding new activities in China, which are providing substantial revenues to the institution – revenues that are allowing the university to invest more in its globalization efforts. No doubt, this new global mission is a positive thing for some of the institutions' students. But it was also clear that the revenues and energy of this new venture had captured the imagination of the university's president, leaving him not very engaged in or excited about the day-to-day mission of serving students within the state.

I present this example not to castigate this president, who is in fact a fine leader, but rather to highlight the seductive nature of new revenues. Intellectual energy often follows new money. Every leader wants to make a difference in the institution she or he leads. Doing more of the same does not seem like making a difference, while securing new funds to do new things does. Yet doing more of the same – educating our students well – is one of our most important roles. Unfortunately, following the money rarely leads us back to this essential task; instead, it usually leads away from it.

TUITION CHARGES AS A SOURCE OF REVENUE

As I stated above, within the public sector of higher education, only two revenue sources contribute substantially to our core mission of student learning – appropriations and tuition charges. Within the elite segment of private higher education, endowments contribute substantially to this mission; however, even here, this phenomenon is limited to a few institutions. (In the case of public institutions, the number who benefit is far fewer.) Since public resources will remain constrained for most if not all states for the foreseeable future, there is only one likely source available for covering increased costs in the future: tuition charges.

This is certainly not a new discovery. In recent years, virtually all of the increases in the net costs of public higher education have been covered by

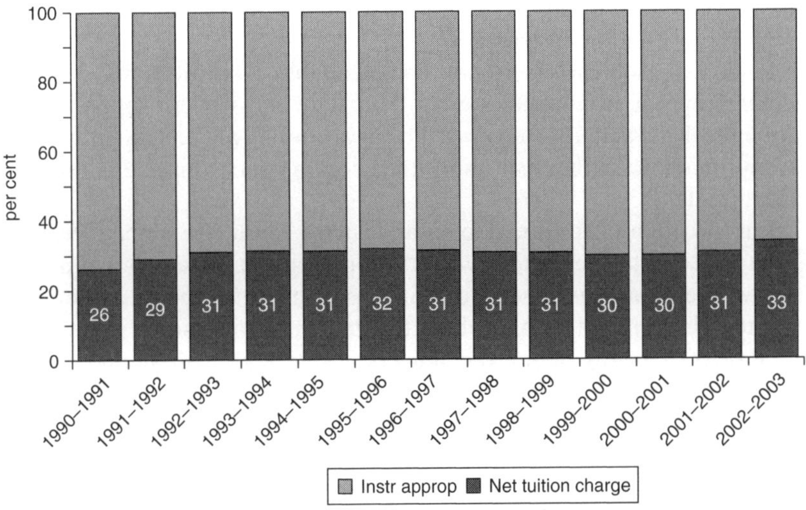

Source: SHEEO, 2005, p. 9.

Figure 6.5 Net tuition charge revenues as a percentage of public higher education total educational revenues, fiscal years 1991–2004

increases in tuition charges. Whereas tuition charges represented only 26.2 per cent of total educational revenues in public higher education in 1992, they represented 35.8 per cent in 2004 (see Figure 6.5). The average tuition charge in FY 2004 of $3187 represents a 38 per cent increase over 1992, after adjusting for inflation (see Figure 6.6).

The escalating price of public higher education raises two major policy issues. First, will tuition charges continue to be the major means of covering the rising cost of instruction? Those states that will see substantially higher numbers of students demanding a higher education will certainly garner additional tuition charges revenue from them, but the cost of educating large numbers of new students well will exceed today's $3187 average tuition charge. Since it is unlikely that many states will have the capacity or will to increase funding commensurate with the increase in demand, states and their institutions will probably face an uncomfortable choice: either increase tuition charges substantially to sustain broad access or limit enrollments, abandoning the long-held (but not sacrosanct) goal of broad educational access.

It is ironic that increasing price may well be the best option for preserving broad access. Yet research has consistently demonstrated that most students and their families are quite impervious, within reason, to the price

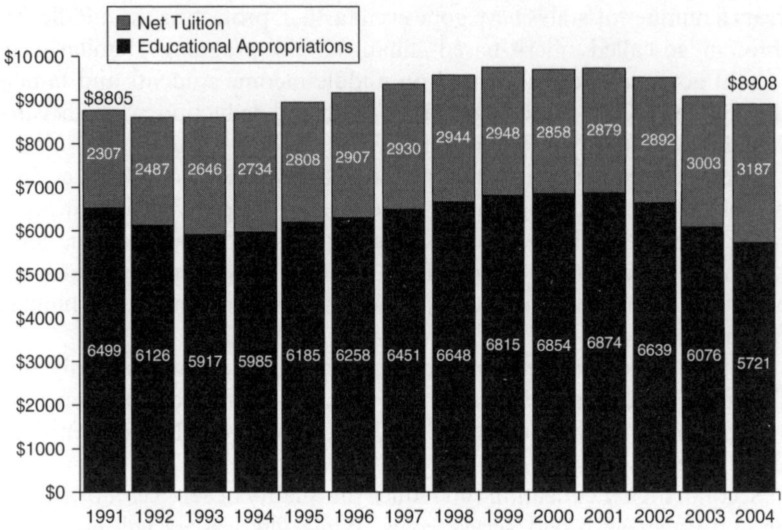

Source: SHEEO, *State Higher Education Finance Survey*, 2005, p. 6.

Figure 6.6 Total educational revenues from appropriations and tuition charges: constant 2004 dollars, using SHEEO Higher Education Cost Adjustment

of higher education, particularly within the public sector. Research from the 1970s originally demonstrated that the price elasticity of demand for higher education was nearly zero, except for low-income students. Yet low-income students can be protected from substantial price increases through targeted need-based financial aid. Thus, broad access can be preserved by increasing tuition charges and boosting highly targeted financial aid. Such a strategy would provide the revenues necessary to expand educational opportunities to meet demand and still protect financial access for all students.

But rational economic strategies often run counter to rational political strategies and such is the case with respect to increasing tuition charges. Recent concerns at the federal and state level have heightened scrutiny of increased tuition prices. While most politicians can appreciate the theoretical argument for a rational economic approach, they have difficulty abiding by the political ramifications. Most politicians are elected by middle-class voters, who enjoy the American tradition of low public-sector tuition charges and whose children generally go to college. Relatively few politicians are elected by low-income people, who tend to be less well represented in the voting public. Not surprisingly, politicians see substantial political salience in constraining tuition charge increases. Indeed, in recent

years a number of states have gone even farther, protecting the middle class through so-called ‘merit-based’ financial aid programs. Similarly, the federal government has focused on middle-income students and families through the HOPE tuition charge tax credit and deduction, which began in 1999 for taxes paid on 1998 income.

There is nothing wrong with attempting to hold the price of college down by controlling escalating tuition price levels. The problem is that, at the same time, states have been holding appropriations at previous levels, whether by necessity or choice. Thus institutions within those states have no capacity to generate the revenues necessary to serve increasing numbers of students.

In such a constrained environment, higher education has only three choices. The first is to become more efficient, so that current funds will support an increasing number of students. Significant efficiencies are possible but, as I said before, unlikely.

Second, higher education can reduce the quality of services it provides in order to achieve broad access goals. While few leaders will ever admit quality has declined on their watch, telltale signs suggest that quality is indeed eroding. One need only look at the progression and retention rates of students, particularly at-risk students, to see the ominous signs of declining quality.

Lastly, if improving efficiency or reducing quality proves insufficient or untenable, the only strategy left is to let access erode. The history and tradition of US higher education tend to drive institutions and states to this strategy. Many if not most US institutions of higher education strive to be more prestigious and the most common avenue to prestige is to become more selective; an environment in which demand for services exceeds supply provides a ripe opportunity to do just that. But when institutions become selective, some students get left out – and the students who are left out are precisely those who need public service and protection the most.

While I have focused here on the forces facing public higher education, in many respects the circumstances are no different for private higher education. While private higher education does not need to worry as much about public financial support, at least at the state level, it does face increasing difficulty in attracting students as the price of tuition continues to escalate. While it may be true, as research indicates, that only poor students make their decisions about whether to go to college based on college price, students’ choices about where to go to college are generally price sensitive.

Virtually all of the growth in American higher education in recent years has been in the lower-cost public sector, not in private higher education. (An exception to this is the for-profit sector, but it markets to a very limited segment of the student population.) Within the traditional private college

sector, market forces have become paramount, and marketing strategies have become the dominant components of institutional finance.

Yet, just as within the public sector, these finance strategies, while they can be quite effective for individual institutions, are quite expensive for the sector as a whole and counterproductive to its long-term viability. Tuition price discounting, for example, has become almost an imperative in the private college community. Yet it has created a perverse environment, where the advertised price of tuition seems unachievable for the unsophisticated lay consumer and where the sophisticated consumer believes there is no fixed price – everything is negotiable. This is simply not sound business policy for the long-term financial health of private colleges. But it is a cycle that will be hard to break.

MONEY FOR SOMETHING: A SUMMARY

This chapter has described how critical the present moment is to our ability to finance US higher education. Our institutions have managed to serve their students exceptionally well, in part because (despite our rhetoric) they have educated only a small portion of our population: today, less than one third of our young adults will receive a college degree. And higher education has also served the US well, proving to be an exceptional investment in human capital and creating the most productive workforce and research engine in the world.

Yet it is clear that, if we maintain the status quo, higher education will not continue to serve the country well in the future. Constrained public financial resources and increasing demands for the service, both from individuals and from our economy, are creating a financial conundrum: we can not pay for what we must provide.

This need not be a catastrophe, though. Various combinations of productivity improvements and revenue enhancements can be used to ensure that we continue to provide broad access to high-quality higher education for our citizens. We can substantially improve the productivity of our system by imposing discipline on institutional mission differentiation and redirecting students to institutions that focus on the scholarship of teaching. We can also improve productivity by adopting modern evidence-based improvements in the pedagogy of college teaching. And we can increase revenues through tailored tuition price increases, which occur in sync with financial aid increases.

What we cannot do, however, is to ignore the reality of the challenges ahead or dream up unrealistic schemes for solving the dilemma we face. Failing to seriously confront the collision between constrained resources

and increasing demand will lead to either reduced quality or reduced access, neither of which fits our current perception of what the US stands for. In higher education – public or private – we get what we pay for. If we pay for less, we will get less.

Certainly, substantial efficiencies can and should be achieved. But they can only be achieved with some incentives for change. None of the most significant partners – not students, nor faculty, nor the businesses that hire our graduates (or who hire graduates from elsewhere) nor public policy makers – will accept a change agenda without some positive stake in the outcome, without some quid pro quo.

Our challenge is to fashion an approach that respects the legitimate needs of each of these partners and still maintains access to high-quality higher education for all our citizens. Privatizing higher education, which seems to be the direction of much activity and rhetoric today, is not the answer; indeed it may be the problem. Market forces, though all the rage, do not address the public good very well. That is why we have governments to protect the public good. Preserving higher education as a public good will require sound public policy – new policy that is appropriate to a new age, perhaps, but public policy nonetheless.

REFERENCES

National Center for Education Statistics (NCES) (2004), *Digest of Educational Statistics 2004*, available at http://nces.ed.gov/programs/digest/d04/.

State Higher Education Executive Officers (SHEEO) (2005), *State Higher Education Finance, FY 2004*, available at www.sheeo.org/finance/shef05.pdf?bcsi_scan_B356EF9F3E6DB8D9=0&bcsi_scan_filename=shef05.pdf.

Western Interstate Commission for Higher Education (WICHE) (2003), *Knocking at the College Door: Projections of High School Graduates by State, Income, and Race/Ethnicity, 1988 to 2018*, Boulder, CO: WICHE.

7. Regaining the trust in higher education

Benjamin F. Quillian

INTRODUCTION

When I was young and growing up in a low-income community of a midwestern city, my parents often told me, 'Go to school and get a good education.' They had not had the opportunity to go to high school, but they believed that a 'good education' would prepare me to 'do better' than they had been able to do. That essentially meant obtaining a position with better working conditions and pay than the job my father had at the dry cleaning plant or that my mother had as a domestic worker. In their view, education would provide the necessary reading, writing and computational skills. They also thought the 'good education' would teach me to behave properly; that is, stay out of trouble with the law.

Although my first aspirations were to become a bus driver, my parents were hoping I would become a teacher – one of the few professional jobs then open to African-Americans. It is interesting to note that the local transit company would not hire African-Americans at the time, a fact that had eluded me. I just thought it would be 'cool' to drive a big red bus.

Encouraged by my parents I managed to stay out of trouble and do well in school. And as I grew older I did indeed aspire to become a teacher. Most of the colleges and universities in the area were far too expensive for me to attend, but the local teachers' college was supported by public funds. The tuition charge was only $70 per semester. With a little help from my parents and a few part-time jobs, I could afford to get that 'good education'. Four years later I graduated and began my career as an educator.

The story of how I was able to attend college illustrates a couple of important points. First, education was viewed by my family as something that would help me personally – the personal benefit. Even though teaching was considered an honorable and helping profession, it was attractive because it promised a better life. Second, my education was possible only because of the public funding that supported the local college. The public policy makers apparently recognized the importance of offering education

broadly in society – the public good. As discussed below, there was an arrangement or compact between the citizens and the government to educate the population. The compact was based on the belief that education was a significant underpinning of a democratic society. But now there is cause for concern, and the future is uncertain.

In these times of economic downturns, limited resources and tighter budgets, higher education must compete for resources with wars against terrorism, health care for an aging society, the criminal justice system, and infrastructure needs such as roads, bridges and levees. Higher education no longer enjoys the beyond reproach status it once enjoyed. 'College may be the ticket to the good life, but its benefits for democracy and culture no longer command top priority for the public purse' (Massy, 2003). The notion that education is a public good has eroded (Sosin, 2002), and our public policy makers now focus more on the quality of life it brings to its recipients – it is an 'investment in an individual's human capital that has limited spillovers. Therefore, it should be primarily financed by the individual' (Moskow, 2005). Such a view obviously fails to recognize the worth of broadly educating the citizenry in a democratic society. Many families simply cannot afford to finance a college education.

This chapter briefly examines the views on education held through the years by our policy makers, presents some of the reasons for a changing landscape, and sends a challenge to the greatest educational system in the world to move off its haunches and find the solutions necessary to avoid a crisis. The purpose is to call to action faculty and administrators who are willing to support the need for concerted transformational actions on a variety of fronts.

A BRIEF HISTORICAL PERSPECTIVE

In the eighteenth century, it was relatively easy to garner the political will to support higher education in the United States. If the people were to manage and govern their own affairs, universal education was needed (Cremin, 1980, p. 103). Education was viewed as the vehicle to improve the moral character of young people and prepare them to behave properly and assume the responsibilities of adulthood in a free society (Vine, 1997, p. 116). During the Jefferson administration, legislation was proposed that called for 'public primary schools, quasi-public grammar schools, a publicly controlled college (the College of William & Mary) and a great public reference library at Richmond' (ibid.). It was commonly believed that a literate people who had free access to information could responsibly manage their affairs. While African-Americans and Native Americans

were excluded from citizenship and education for the purpose of self-government, publicly supported colleges for the dominant majority began to take hold in several states (Cremin, 1980, p. 105). The prevailing notion of the time was that the government should provide direct assistance to schools and colleges (Robson, 1985, p. 227). 'Education, including higher education, was inextricably linked in the public mind with the preservation of republicanism. It was the state's duty to forge those links into indissoluble bonds' (ibid., p. 228). Higher education was valued for the benefits it rendered to the common good of the social order.

The young republic was highly dependent on agriculture, but American farming was inefficient and lacking in scientific knowledge and technology (Cremin, 1980, p. 337). As cities in the east began to grow and European markets opened up, farming began to move from growing crops to feed a family to commercial agriculture (ibid., p. 338). Commercial farming required greater efficiencies and an educational system that would lead to new farming methods. The Morrill Act of 1862, which gave education support directly from the government, fostered such a system most notably in the North and the West. The South, with family farms and the free labor of the slavery system, was less ready to embrace technology and a more rational system of agriculture (ibid., p. 342).

After the Civil War the country was reunited, but the war had left the North with a large debt and the South was insolvent (Williams, 1991, p. 40). The nation faced difficult financial times, which were exacerbated by the Panic of 1873 (ibid., p. 75). The legislators in the northern and southern states found it difficult to appropriate funds to the land-grant colleges (ibid., p. 40). As economic conditions began to improve, the federal government passed the Hatch Act in 1887 and the second Morrill Act in 1890. Such legislation enhanced agricultural education and provided general support to colleges and universities. As a result, the numbers of students pursuing baccalaureate degrees increased dramatically around the turn of the century (Williams, 1997, p. 268).

After World War I, colleges and universities in the United States made significant advances, particularly in conducting quality research and offering graduate studies. Even as the country fell into the Great Depression of the 1930s, philanthropic foundations and private industry provided assistance to colleges and universities. The complex social problems and economic challenges of the time gave patrons incentives to provide financial support to higher education. Research was deemed necessary to provide intelligent solutions (Geiger, 1997, p. 279). 'For the first time American universities could look to a regular, recurrent source of support for the direct expenses of conducting organized research' (ibid., p. 280).

The end of World War II brought dramatic changes to the face of higher education. The passage of the GI Bill (Servicemen's Readjustment Act) in 1944 sowed the seed for mass higher education in the United States on a scale no nation had ever seen (Ikenberry, 2001, p. 34). The GI Bill 'allowed unprecedented numbers and segments of the population to enjoy improved access to education, land (housing), and legal remedies' (Hyman, 1986, p. 65). It was in the interests of society to assist veterans returning home from World War II. Among other benefits the legislation subsidized tuition charges, fees and educational materials, as well as living expenses related to college attendance. By 1951 the government had spent approximately $14 billion providing benefits to veterans, and enrollment in higher education increased dramatically as eight million veterans received educational benefits (Schugurensky, 2005).

In 1965 Congress passed another major piece of legislation that greatly expanded the opportunities for citizens of the United States to receive a higher education: the Higher Education Act (HEA). HEA provides funding for student financial aid, services to help students graduate from high school and enter post-secondary education, direct aid to colleges and universities, and grants to improve teacher education programs at colleges and universities (Stedman, 2002, par. 3). As a result, there has been increasing participation in higher education, but the effectiveness of the programs for low-income and minority students remains an issue. 'Despite making substantial increases in enrollment, African-Americans and Hispanics continue to trail whites in the percentage of the college-age cohorts enrolled in college, commonly referred to as the college participation rate' (Harvey and Anderson, 2005).

As Congress now grapples with the reauthorization of the Higher Education Act, we see challenges to the traditional goals of expanding access to higher education. A key issue is couched in the term 'accountability'. Questions are being raised about the escalating price of a college education, which has grown at a more rapid rate than inflation and inflation-adjusted median incomes. The increases undoubtedly relate in part to the constraints that state budgets are experiencing and the reductions in funding for public higher education. The costs also track the high and ever-rising costs of technology and other tools now necessary to conduct quality teaching and research. Nevertheless, questions are being raised about the way colleges and universities conduct themselves and how they use the resources at their disposal. Recent studies tend to show that the public blames the high cost of tuition more on inefficiency and fiscal mismanagement than on reductions in governmental support (Immerwahr, 1999).

The public and policy makers no longer assume that colleges and universities are giving students the education they need to be productive

citizens. Whether students receive enough value for their experience and for their financial investment has been called into question. As a result, the individual planning to attend a college or university recognizes the personal benefits of attendance but is often uncomfortable with or unable to afford the price – even though most students do not pay the full 'sticker price'. Our policy makers see the greater good provided by a broadly educated citizenry, but question whether the resources going into higher education are being used most effectively.

THE NEED FOR JOINT EFFORTS

The nature of the 'social compact' is indeed changing. However, it is an oversimplification to suggest the reason for the change lies solely in the public's lack of understanding or policy makers' failure to recognize the importance of higher education both as a personal benefit and a public good. In fact, political leaders are reasonably knowledgeable about higher education, but their criticisms relate to student learning outcomes, affordability and what they perceive as inefficiency (Ruppert, 2001, pp. i, iv–vi, 35). The issues are complex and multi-faceted. Addressing the pertinacious problems will require a sensitivity to and respect for competing forces.

Downturns in the economy, post 9/11 safeguards, natural disasters, wars, health care, infrastructure maintenance, crime and punishment, the environment and education are but a few of the interrelated and competing demands faced by today's policy makers. In that context, it becomes a matter of priorities as defined by political interests. It will be necessary for the higher education community to establish more effective means to compete in the political arena and there will be a need for financial resources to make it happen. A key component will be giving the public the necessary tools to help influence the political agendas and the setting of priorities for the allocation of resources.

The American Council on Education has found that, although the population still views education positively, there are some concerns. The public does not fully understand the workings of higher education, the sources and uses of its funding and the various restrictions on the use of that funding. However, the public has a right to raise questions about rising costs, quality and the way resources are used. Educators should expect and be prepared to answer questions about the quality of the educational experience being given to students and the ability of our colleges and universities to equip students with the skills and values they will need to contribute in positive ways to our society. If the public are going to step forward and

exert the necessary political pressure to make higher education a priority, their questions will have to be answered.

Reestablishing the public's faith and trust in higher education will require a willingness on the part of educators, both administrators and faculty members, to examine the fundamental tenets of the academy to make sure they serve the intended purposes and fulfill the desired objectives. For example, the public will not understand that tenure is connected to academic freedom when academic freedom takes the form of 'sociopolitical evangelism' (Salerno, 2004, p. 9) and is unrelated to the knowledge base of the discipline being taught, and tenure takes on the meaning of being untouchable no matter what. This is not to suggest doing away with tenure or academic freedom. Rather, it is a call for educators to scrutinize the purposes of tenure and academic freedom and consider ways to curb abuse and maximize effectiveness.

The academic community has a tendency to shun terms like 'efficiency', 'speed', 'productivity', 'entrepreneurialism' and 'bottom line'. Yet, the public and our policy makers are calling for institutions of higher learning that can demonstrate such characteristics. If the academy expects to receive the trust it deserves and the resources it needs, it will have to learn how to become more efficient, be more productive, and recognize the need to embrace sound business practices in a way that preserves the integrity of the academic mission. On the other hand, the public and our policy makers need to understand that the pursuit of knowledge and the transmission of understandings are costly endeavors and cannot always be forced into a business model.

> Policy makers don't understand the economic behavior of universities, and the universities themselves know too little about their costs and the degree of cross subsidy among programs. Faculty lack needed understanding of education quality and how to produce it at optimal cost levels, they don't know how to measure it, and their incentive system doesn't reward efforts to improve. (Massy, 2003, p. 5)

The 'knowledge age' and an extraordinarily complex combination of social factors have brought to the fore the need to address the issue of quality and cost in higher education, as well as its priority status. The complexities of our times are placing pressure on policy makers, the general public, administrators and faculty members to do more than sometimes seems possible. Getting the job done will require a joint effort.

It is now necessary to put aside the tendency to point fingers. Politicians and the general public need to recognize higher education's importance to society, the contributions it makes and the significance of an educated population in the management of a free and democratic society. Policy

makers must also recognize that parts of society still face barriers like poverty and racial discrimination. Such barriers make it difficult and often impossible to succeed in educational settings. If the promise of education in this society is to be fulfilled, factors beyond the academy must be continually addressed.

The higher education community also has much to do. The academy must remain sensitive to and understanding of the competing demands that policy makers face. Sensitivity and understanding, however, should not suggest resignation. The academy must be persistent and make sure the competencies and contributions of post-secondary education are understood and rightfully supported by the public and policy makers. Making sure the public and policy makers understand and trust the academy will require a concerted effort to provide compelling evidence of both the personal benefits and the public good that higher education offers.

In addition, the academy must look critically at its own practices and traditions and embrace change that maintains stability of mission, improves the quality and controls the cost of the educational experience. Transformational change in the academy will require the collaborative efforts of accrediting agencies, governing boards, administrators and faculty members. Accrediting agencies must broaden their focus and look more intently at outcomes and the value added by the educational experience. They should look closely at the changes institutions are making to improve outcomes and increase the value. Governing boards should demand to see an agenda of change – change that relates directly to improving quality and outcomes and controlling costs. Administrators and faculty must identify the costs, develop outcome-based curricula and measure the impact of the changes on both costs and learning.

SUMMARY

Higher education is both a personal benefit and a public good. It is the responsibility of the public, policy makers and the higher education community to make sure the public good is fully recognized and supported. The public good was once taken for granted, and the public and policy makers had faith in the ability of educators to educate. Now, the situation is much more complex. Questions are being raised about cost, access, quality and the way resources are used. The ability of educators to equip students with the skills needed by our society is being challenged. The situation is complicated by economic downturns, limited resources, tighter budgets and competing priorities. Even the political and philosophical orientation of the faculties, the types of research being conducted, the structure of the

curriculum and the social atmosphere on campuses as portrayed in novels[1] have an impact on the public and policy makers.

Restoring the trust and returning higher education to its rightful place in the priorities of public support is daunting but achievable. There are four central issues to be confronted: the social compact in today's world; the pricing and quality of the educational experience; the diversification of the funding base; and the reexamination of the governance structure (Ikenberry, 2005, p. 8). As long as there is willingness for the public, policy makers and the higher education community to work cooperatively with mutual understanding and appreciation of varying points of view, the public good can be served. If the higher education community cannot adequately demonstrate its worth, this grand experiment in democracy will not be able to reach full potential.

NOTE

1. See, for example, Wolfe (2004).

REFERENCES

Cremin, L.A. (1980), *American Education: the National Experience, 1783–1876*, New York: Harper & Row.

Geiger, R.L. (1997), *Research, Graduate Education, and the Ecology of American Universities: an Interpretive History*, in H.S. Wechsler and L.F. Goodchild (eds) (1997), *The History of Higher Education*, 2nd edn, (ASHE Reader Series), Boston, MA: Simon & Schuster Custom Publishing.

Harvey, W.B. and E.L. Anderson (2005), *Minorities in Higher Education Twenty-First Annual Status Report*, Washington, DC: American Council on Education.

Hyman, H.M. (1986), *American Singularity: the 1787 Northwest Ordinance, the 1862 Homestead and Morrill Acts, and the 1944 G.I. Bill*, Athens, GA: The University of Georgia Press.

Ikenberry, S.O. (2001), 'Higher education and market forces', *USA Today*, **129** (2670).

Ikenberry, S.O. (2005), 'Higher ed: dangers of an unplanned future', *State Legislatures*, **31** (8), Denver, CO: accessed at http://proquest.umi.com/pqdweb?index=3&sid=1&srchmode=1&vinst=PROD&fmt=4&s.

Immerwahr, J. (1999), *Taking Responsibility: Leaders' Expectations of Higher Education*, a report by Public Agenda for the National Center for Public Policy and Higher Education, San Jose, CA: National Center for Public Policy and Higher Education, accessed at www.highereducation.org/reports/responsibility/responsibility.pdf.

Massy, William F. (2003), *Honoring the Trust: Quality and Cost Containment in Higher Education*, Bolton, MA: Anker Publishing Company.

Moskow, M.H. (2005), 'The future of higher education: higher education at a crossroad', speech given at a conference at the Federal Reserve Bank of

Chicago, Chicago, IL, 2 November 2005, accessed at www.chicagofed.org/news_and_conferences/speeches/2005_11_02_higher_ed.cfm.

Robson, D.W. (1985), *Educating Republicans: the College in the Era of the American Revolution, 1750–1800*, Westport, CT: Greenwood Press.

Ruppert, S.S. (2001), *Where We Go from Here: State Legislative Views on Higher Education in the New Millennium, Results of the 2001 Higher Education Issues Survey*, Littleton, CO: Educational Systems Research, National Education Association of the United States.

Salerno, S. (2004), 'Higher Edumacation', *The American Enterprise*, **15** (7).

Schugurensky, D. (2005), 'History of Education: Selected Moments of the 20th Century', work in progress, Department of Adult Education, Community Development and Counseling Psychology, The Ontario Institute for Studies in Education of the University of Toronto OISE/UT, available at http://fcis.oise.utoronto.ca/~daniel_schugurensky/assignment1/1944gibill.html.

Sosin, J. (2002), 'Higher education's role in serving the public good', paper presented at the Kellogg Forum on Higher Education for the Public Good, Ann Arbor, MI, October, (National Leadership Dialogue Series), available at www.kelloggforum.org/activities/national_summit.html#summit.

Stedman, J.B. (2002), 'Higher Education Act: Reauthorization Status and Issues', (updated 9 October), Washington, DC: US Department of State, Congressional Research Services, available at www.policyalmanac.org/education/archive/crs_higher_education.shtml.

Vine, P. (1997), 'The Social Function of Eighteenth Century Higher Education', H.S. Wechsler and L.F. Goodchild (eds), *The History of Higher Education*, 2nd edn, (ASHE Reader Series), Boston, MA: Simon & Schuster Custom Publishing.

Williams, R.L. (1991), *The Origins of Federal Support for Higher Education: George W. Atherton and the Land-Grant College Movement*, University Park, PA: The Pennsylvania State University Press.

Williams, R.L. (1997), *The Origins of Federal Support for Higher Education*, in H.S. Wechsler and L.F. Goodchild (eds), *The History of Higher Education*, 2nd edn, (ASHE Reader Series), Boston, MA: Simon & Schuster Custom Publishing,

Wolfe, T. (2004), *I am Charlotte Simmons*, New York: Farrar, Straus and Giroux.

PART II

Changing faculty employment practices

8. The changing nature of the faculty and faculty employment practices

Ronald G. Ehrenberg

INTRODUCTION

The nature of faculty employment practices at American colleges and universities is changing rapidly. So too is the gender, racial and ethnic composition of American faculty members. These changes, along with the growing importance and costs of scientific research, the increased commercialization of faculty research, the elimination of mandatory retirement for tenured faculty members and the growing costs of retiree health insurance, the growing salary differentials across universities and academic fields within a university, and the growth of collective bargaining for tenured and tenure-track faculty and graduate assistants at public universities and now adjuncts at private universities, have put enormous stresses on our nation's academic institutions and their leaders. The discussion that follows explains why.

THE GROWTH IN CONTINGENT FACULTY

During the last three decades there has been a significant growth in the share of faculty members at American colleges and universities who are employed in part-time or full-time non-tenure-track positions (Anderson, 2002; Baldwin and Chronister, 2001; Conley et al., 2004; Ehrenberg and Zhang, 2005a). In 1975 full-time tenured and tenure-track faculty members were 56.8 per cent of the faculty nationwide at America's 2-year and 4-year colleges and universities, while full-time non-tenure-track faculty and part-time faculty were 13 per cent and 30.2 per cent respectively. By 2003 full-time tenured and tenure-track faculty had fallen to 35.1 per cent, while the latter two categories had risen to 18.7 per cent and 46.3 per cent respectively (Curtis, 2005). This substitution of *contingent* or *contract* faculty for tenured and tenure-track faculty is at least partially due to the growing financial pressures faced by public and private higher education institutions, partially

due to the lower costs of hiring non-tenure-track faculty members and partially due to the increased flexibility that hiring such faculty members gives academic institutions in the face of uncertain economic times and the end of mandatory retirement for tenure-track faculty members (that took place in 1994) (Ehrenberg and Zhang, 2005a; Monks, 2004).

To give the reader a sense of the role that contingent faculty play at major American universities, Table 8.1 presents information on the distribution of faculty types at selected private universities during the academic year 2003–2004. That year less than 25 per cent of the faculty members were contingent faculty at Cornell and Rochester; however, 50 per cent or more of the faculty members were contingent faculty at Boston College, Brown, NYU and Tufts. At the latter set of institutions many of these contingent faculty members were part-time faculty.

Of course part-time faculty members teach fewer classes than full-time faculty members and it is interesting to ask what percentage of undergraduate credit hours at an academic institution are generated by contingent faculty. Such information is not readily available for private institutions, but data from the State University of New York system show that between the fall of 1992 and the fall of 2001 the percentage of undergraduate credit hours taught by faculty members with tenure or on tenure tracks at the four university centers fell from 81 per cent to 58.4 per cent, a decrease of over 22 percentage points (Ehrenberg and Klaff, 2003, Table 2).[1] Moreover,

Table 8.1 Numbers and percentages of faculty in different categories at selected private universities in 2003–2004[a]

Institution	Total faculty size	Tenured and tenure-track (percentage)	Full-time non-tenure track (percentage)	Part-time non-tenure track (percentage)
Boston College	1089	548 (50)	131 (12)	410 (38)
Brown	902	468 (52)	285 (32)	149 (17)
Cornell	1940	1477 (76)	348 (18)	115 (6)
NYU	5083	1292 (25)	630 (12)	3162 (62)
Rochester	591	465 (79)	100 (17)	26 (4)
Tufts	1036	359 (35)	275 (27)	402 (39)

Note: [a] Excluding medical college faculty.

Source: Report from the *ad hoc* Committee on Contract Faculty to the Provost and the Faculty Senate, Brandeis University (17 March 2005), Appendix Table A-2 (available at www.brandeis.edu/departments/provost/contract_faculty_comm.html). The data come from the 2003 IPEDs EAP Survey (available at http://nces.ed.gov/ipeds). The data are as reported by the institutions. Employees who do not have faculty status are excluded, as are graduate assistants.

between the fall of 1994 and the fall of 2004 the number of full-time faculty members at the four university centers (including those not on tenure tracks) fell by 251 from 4348 to 4097, while the number of part-time faculty members increased by 616 from 1283 to 1899 (Office of Institutional Research and Analysis, 2005). Given that the number of full-time equivalent students at the university centers increased from 62 179 to 72 571 during the period, it is clear that the instructional workload was being shifted onto the backs of part-time faculty.[2]

There are a number of reasons that the public and university leaders should be concerned about such shifts in who is teaching our undergraduate students.[3] First, while it would be delightful if we could substitute lower paid part-time and full-time non-tenure-track faculty for more costly tenure-track faculty and not influence the quality of education that undergraduate students receive, a growing body of research suggests that on balance there is a cost to students of this type of substitution. For example, Liang Zhang and I analyzed institutional level panel data from the *College Board* and other sources and found that increases in a 4-year institution's usage of part-time or full-time non-tenure-track faculty is associated, other factors held constant, with a decline in its students' graduation rates (Ehrenberg and Zhang, 2005b). Similarly, using a unique individual record data set for all students enrolled in 4-year public higher education institutions in Ohio, Bettinger and Long (forthcoming) found that students with adjunct-heavy course schedules in their first year of study are less likely to persist at the institution into the second year. Other factors held constant.

Why might such findings occur? After all, many non-tenure-track faculty are dedicated teachers and, without any research expectations placed on them, can devote themselves fully to teaching. However, full-time non-tenure-track faculty teaching loads are often higher than tenure-track faculty teaching loads, which may leave the former less, rather than more, time for individual students. Part-time faculty members, especially in urban areas, often must find employment at multiple institutions to make ends meet and have little time (and often no place) to meet students outside class. The full-time tenured and tenure-track faculty members, who may be more connected to their institution and more up to date on their department's curriculum, may also be better prepared to advise students.

The term contingent faculty is probably a misnomer, because many full-time non-tenure-track faculty are in fact quasi-permanent employees who have multi-year contracts and for whom there often is a career path. For example, at Cornell University lecturers typically have multi-year contracts and, after a period of service, can be promoted to the rank of senior lecturer. A number of research universities, including Duke, Emory and NYU, are experimenting with creating a more prestigious 'professor of practice'

career path in which faculty members who specialize in teaching are paid salaries much closer to the average tenure-track salaries in their fields than lecturers are paid, receive the same benefits as their tenure-track colleagues (but often not sabbaticals) and are employed on renewable long-term contracts (Fogg, 2004).

Whether such a two-tier system, with lower (but better than now) paid teaching faculty who have higher teaching loads than other faculty, will be a direction in which more universities will move is unclear. If they do so the financial savings to universities from substituting away from tenure-track faculty will be smaller than it currently is. To the extent that the undergraduate teaching at an institution is done by non-tenure-track faculty without research responsibilities, undergraduate students will miss out on one of the major reasons for coming to a research university – being exposed to great researchers and the research process. Indeed, if we view one of the important roles of research universities as encouraging undergraduate students to consider undertaking advanced study in the disciplines, the failure to involve our undergraduate students in research will reduce the flow of American college graduates into PhD programs (Ehrenberg, 2005a).

Indeed, the fraction of PhD degrees granted in the United States that go to American citizens and permanent residents has been declining for decades. In 1973 less than 10 per cent of PhDs went to temporary residents of the United States; by 2003 this had risen to 26 per cent. Virtually all of the increase in the total number of PhDs produced during the 30-year period has come from the growth in foreign PhD students; the number of American students receiving PhDs remained essentially flat in spite of large increases in the number of American college graduates. Moreover, in key science and engineering fields, the percentage of PhD degrees now granted to foreign students is much higher. In 2003 38 per cent of all the PhDs in the physical sciences and 55 per cent of all the PhDs in engineering granted by American colleges and universities went to foreign students (Hoffer et al., 2004, Table 2).

Part of the decline in the interest of American students in pursuing PhDs is undoubtedly due to the reduction in the likelihood that new PhDs will obtain tenure-track positions, because of the growing use of contingent faculty positions. Increasing time to degrees, coupled with the increasing need for multiple multi-year, relatively low-paid postdoctoral appointments in many science and engineering fields before tenure-track positions can be obtained, has also increased PhD students' discontent and led to the growing unionization of graduate students in public higher education.[4] So a new generation of PhDs will have very different attitudes towards collective bargaining from those of the older faculty whom they are replacing.

The lower salaries and benefits that contingent faculty receive has also led to a growing movement to have contingent faculty covered by collective

bargaining agreements. Although tenure-track faculty at private colleges and universities at which the faculty have managerial responsibilities are precluded from organizing under the National Labor Relations Board's (NLRB) *Yeshiva* decision in July 2002, NYU became the first major private university in the nation in which an adjunct-only union was certified as a bargaining agent by the NLRB (Smallwood, 2002). While the university has publicly painted the pay increases, health benefits, pension benefits and job security arrangements that were negotiated in the contract as a win-win situation, collective bargaining contracts constrain the freedom of university administrators to manage their institutions as they see fit.[5]

WHO WILL BE THE FACULTY OF THE FUTURE?

In 1973, 18 per cent of all new PhDs in the United States were female; by 2003 this percentage had risen to 45.3 per cent. The female share of PhDs has risen in all fields, even in traditionally male dominated fields such as the physical sciences and engineering (Hoffer et al., 2004, Table 7). However, in spite of the growing numbers of new female PhDs, females are under-represented on the faculty of most major American research universities, especially in the science and engineering fields, and are more likely to be found on the faculty of liberal arts colleges. For example, in economics, females represented 15 per cent of the tenured and tenure-track faculty at doctorate granting institutions but 27.7 per cent at liberal arts colleges (*Newsletter of the Committee on the Status of Women in the Economics Profession*, 2005, Tables 2 and 4).

The under-representation of female faculty at research universities may be due to a number of factors. It may represent female PhDs' preferences for teaching rather than research. It may represent perceptions by females that research universities are not hospitable environments for them. It may represent perceptions by females that there is more gender discrimination in hiring and promotion decisions at research universities or the actuality of more gender discrimination at research universities. Finally, it may represent the difficulty faced by female faculty members in combining families and careers at research universities.

A recent study suggests that family issues are an important component of the explanation (Mason and Goulden, 2004). This study analyzed data from the *Survey of Doctorate Recipients*, a large biennial national longitudinal study that follows the careers of about 160000 PhD recipients. It focused on the career histories of individuals who received PhDs between 1978 and 1984, started their careers at universities and were still working in academia 12 to 14 years later. It found that men who had children within

5 years of receiving their PhDs were 38 per cent more likely to have received tenure than their female counterparts who had children within 5 years of receiving their PhDs. While 70 per cent of the male faculty members who received tenure were married with children, only 44 per cent of female faculty members who received tenure were married with children; moreover female faculty members with tenure were twice as likely as male faculty members with tenure to be single. It also found that only one in three women who took a university job before having children ever became a mother during the period and that women who were married at the time they began their first academic jobs were more likely than their male counterparts to get divorced or separated.

Not surprisingly then, in an attempt to increase the attractiveness to both young female and male PhDs of faculty careers at research universities, a number of major universities have launched efforts to make their institutions more 'family friendly'. One notable example is the University of California system, which, with the help of the Alfred P. Sloan Foundation, has developed a set of policies that it calls 'The UC Family Friendly Edge' (University of California, 2005). These policies include:

1. a flexible part-time option for tenured and tenure-track faculty that can be used for up to five years as life-course needs arise
2. a guarantee to make high-quality child care available
3. a commitment to assist new faculty members with spousal/partner employment issues
4. a postdoctoral fellowship program to encourage PhDs who have taken time off from their careers for family reasons to reenter academia
5. instructing faculty committees that family-related gaps in résumés (such as those due to time off for childbirth and/or the postponing of tenure clocks for the same reason) should be discounted in hiring and tenure decisions
6. establishing summer camps and school-break child care for faculty children
7. establishing emergency backup child-care programs
8. establishing benefits for faculty who want to adopt children.

Key aspects of the UC policy include marketing it to potential new hires and building mechanism to ensure that all faculty members at the university, including department chairs, fully understand the policies. Other universities are involved in similar efforts. For example, Princeton has made it mandatory that all faculty members of either gender who have a new child (through birth or adoption) automatically get a year extension on their tenure clocks as a way of eliminating the concern of some female faculty

members that they would be stigmatized in their departments if they had to request such leave. Some institutions have adopted or are considering adopting a wider range of policies including providing funding for child care when faculty members are presenting papers at conferences, developing permanent part-time tenure-track positions, and addressing other family-related issues, such as the serious illness of a faculty member or a faculty member's family, elder care issues and support for faculty facing such problems. Their hope is that, by making their workplace more family friendly, universities will find it easier to attract and retain female faculty.

Their desire to attract and retain female faculty, especially in science and engineering fields, derives at least partially from the belief that if they provide same-gender role models more female students will major in science and engineering, go on to advanced study in these fields and, once enrolled in advanced study, persist to earn their degrees. Evidence to support these beliefs is in fact mixed.[6] Even if these hypotheses are correct, there is still the question of from where the resources will come to support the creation of these family-friendly policies. It is not an accident that the first research universities to develop them are our nation's wealthiest private and public institutions. It will be more difficult, for example, for universities that currently do not have enough resources to provide meaningful travel funds for their faculty to even dream about being able to provide funding for child care for faculty attending meetings.

In contrast to the large increase in the fraction of PhDs being awarded to American citizens and permanent residents that go to women, the fraction of PhDs being awarded to students from historically under-represented groups is still quite modest, especially in key science and engineering fields. For example, the percentages of American citizen doctoral degrees that went to members of under-represented groups (African-Americans, Hispanic Americans and Native Americans) in 2003 were 6.7 per cent, 8.5 per cent and 8.1 per cent in the physical science, engineering and life science fields respectively (Hoffer et al., 2004, Table 8). The small numbers of members of these groups in faculty positions in American universities is largely a pipeline problem and America's great research universities need to devote more effort to increase the flow of their undergraduate students from under-represented groups into PhD programs (Ehrenberg, 2004a).

INCREASING IMPORTANCE AND COST OF SCIENTIFIC RESEARCH

Advances in modern biology, advanced materials and information sciences, which together promise (and are beginning to deliver) improvements in

human welfare, have led to the growing importance of scientific and engineering research at universities. In spite of generous increases in external funding, the cost of research is increasingly being borne by academic institutions themselves and the start-up-cost packages necessary to attract top young scientists and engineers are now in the $500 000 area; the start-up-cost packages for senior scientists are often well over $1 000 000 (Ehrenberg et al., forthcoming). Public universities, more than private universities, indicate that they fund these start-up-cost packages at least partially by keeping faculty positions for scientists and engineers vacant until the salary savings provide the resources needed; this contributes to the growing use of contingent faculty for instructional purposes at public universities (Ehrenberg et al., 2003).

The growth in the demand for scientific research has led to a growth in the demand for scientific researchers that exceeds the growth in demand for faculty to teach science at universities. As a result, we have seen a tremendous expansion in the usage of research assistants, postdoctoral fellows, research associates and senior research associates at universities. At many universities individuals employed in these positions cannot be principle investigators on research grants and some universities are now experimenting with professorial titles (for example, Research Professor) to retain top non-teaching faculty and to allow them to pursue independent research grants. Individuals in these positions are typically not on tenure tracks, so all the issues that arise in terms of improving compensation and job security for contingent teaching faculty also arise here. The compensation of people in these positions is often very similar to the compensation of research faculty in medical colleges; the faculty members are expected to generate research funding to cover most or all of their salaries. How they are treated when their grant funding expires is a major issue in defining these types of appointment.

The growth of scientific enterprise in the US has been fueled by the growing number of foreign PhD students and foreign postdoctoral researchers in the United States. Changes in US policy since 9/11, coupled with the growth of graduate education and research enterprises in foreign countries, make it unclear whether the US can continue to count on attracting the same numbers of these talented foreign PhD students and postdoctoral researchers to our country in the years ahead (Ehrenberg, 2005b). This means that steps must be taken to increase the supply of American students going into PhD study and academic careers and to accomplish this will inevitably require increases in faculty compensation levels, which American colleges and universities will have to bear.

FACULTY COMPENSATION DIFFERENTIALS

Growing faculty salary differential across institutions, across fields within each institution and across faculty members in the same department, as well as growing compensation differences between faculty members who receive income from commercializing their research findings and those who do not, are a fact of life in American higher education. These trends create serious problems for leaders of our universities.

The financial problems faced by public higher education institutions have led to the average salaries of faculty at public doctoral universities falling substantially relative to the average faculty salary at private doctoral universities over the last three decades; this makes it harder for the public universities to recruit and retain top faculty (Ehrenberg, 2003). During periods of relatively modest faculty salary increases in public higher education, efforts by public universities to retain top faculty who have received job offers from other academic institutions contribute to growing salary differentials within departments. This creates strains on academic institutions; if the only way to generate salary increases is to search for an outside offer, faculty commitment to the institution goes down and faculty members' sense of shared purpose is also diminished.

This problem is exacerbated by a widening of salary differentials across fields, which reflects the growing importance of external nonacademic markets in faculty salary determination in higher education. Data from an annual salary survey by field for a set of doctoral-granting institutions (mainly public ones) that has been conducted by the Office of Institutional Research and Information Management at Oklahoma State University since 1974 illustrate the magnitude of this problem. In 2001–2002 the average salaries of new assistant professors in Business Management, Computer and Information Sciences, Economics, Engineering, and Law and Legal Studies were, respectively, 213.5, 169.7, 150.5, 147.1 and 168.2 per cent higher than the average salaries of assistant professors in English (Ehrenberg, 2004b, Table D). Faculty salary differentials by field are smaller at the full professor level and also vary across universities (ibid., Tables C and D). When the quality of the faculty in a field is higher, as measured by the National Research Council ratings of the field at an institution, other factors being held constant, average full professor salaries in the field are higher relative to average full professor salaries in English at the institution (Ehrenberg et al., forthcoming a). Wide and growing faculty salary differentials across fields also contribute to the loss of collegiality at the university.

In fields that are growing in importance and that have substantial nonacademic employment opportunities, the increase in the starting salary for new assistant professors that occurs between two years, which is

determined by market forces at the national level, is sometimes larger than the amount by which the resources of an institution permit the average salary for continuing assistant professors to increase. This leads to a form of salary inversion, with new faculty members earning more than faculty members with a number of years' experience at the institution. Such salary inversion creates incentives for experienced faculty members to look for other employment and also has a negative impact upon faculty morale.

So, too, do efforts to commercialize scientists research findings. The financial rewards from patenting research findings that lead to licensing agreements or the creation of start-up companies is potentially very large for both the university and the faculty member making a discovery.[7] Researchers are just beginning to sort out how these relationships affect academic culture and the relationships between faculty members in departments in which some faculty members earn large incomes from commercialization of their research findings but others earn none (Stephan and Ehrenberg, forthcoming).

MANDATORY RETIREMENT AND HEALTH INSURANCE ISSUES

The abolition of mandatory retirement for tenured faculty, effective from 1994, has fundamental implications for academia. Studies suggest that the abolition of mandatory retirement has had only a small impact on faculty members' retirement rate, with the largest impact coming at our nation's private research universities (Ashenfelter and Card, 2002; Ehrenberg et al., 2000). However, these studies were undertaken before the dramatic decline in the stock market in 2000; the values of the retirement accounts of many faculty members covered by defined contribution pension plans are barely at the same levels in 2005 that they were five years earlier. As a result, many senior faculty members' expectations about their retirement incomes are lower now than they were five years ago and this may induce some to postpone retirement.

Dramatic increases in health insurance costs are also leading some academic institutions to modify or reduce the generosity of their health insurance coverage for retirees, a trend that is occurring among American employers (Moon, 2005). Unlike pension benefits, which cannot be legally reduced once a faculty member retires, retiree health insurance programs can be altered after retirement (by negotiations if the health benefits are provided through collective bargaining contracts, unilaterally by the university otherwise). Moreover a large number of faculty are employed at academic institutions that do not provide any funding for retiree health

costs; a national survey undertaken by the American Association of University Professors in 2000 found that only 58 per cent of academic institutions contributed to the costs of their faculty retirees' health insurance (Ehrenberg, 2001). Uncertainty about who will pay for their health costs in retirement may well cause many faculty members to postpone their plans for retirement.

The postponement of retirement decision by faculty, as well as the uncertainty of when faculty will retire, imposes costs on academic institutions; new faculty hiring is slowed down and it is difficult to plan for faculty replacements. Academic institutions have altered their retirement programs to provide incentives for faculty to retire (buy-outs and so on) and provided other incentives for faculty to retire, such as opportunities for phased retirement and for retired faculty to teach on a part-time basis (Ehrenberg, 2001). Only recently, however, have they begun to confront the issue of retiree health insurance.

One innovative program has been developed by the Emeriti Consortium for Retirement Health Solutions, a nonprofit company that grew out of a project funded by the Andrew W. Mellon Foundation (Pulley, 2005).[8] The program combines tax advantages for academic employers and faculty members to contribute to a personal retiree health-care account for a faculty member using before-tax dollars. These funds are invested in selected mutual funds whose investment returns are not subject to personal income taxes. When a faculty member retires, he or she can make tax-free withdrawals from his or her account to cover the costs of Medicare supplemental insurance premiums and out-of-pocket medical expenses, including prescription-drug costs not covered by Medicare.[9]

As of August 2005, 29 academic institutions, primarily private liberal arts colleges, belonged to the consortium and were making contributions to these accounts for their older faculty members; many other institutions have expressed interest in participating in the program. Some participating institutions have their own retiree health insurance plans, but others do not. So another aspect of the program is the establishment of several health insurance options that provide supplementary health insurance coverage designed to supplement Medicare coverage. These programs were designed with faculty members' needs in mind and, by being open to faculty around the nation, can be offered at relatively low costs to individuals.

Recently public attention has been drawn to the difficulty that public and private employers in many industries nationwide are having in financing defined benefit pension plans. In large part these difficulties arise from low rates of stock market returns at the turn of the twenty-first century and, in some industries such as automotives, an increasing ratio of retirees to active employees. As a result, a number of employers are abandoning their

defined benefit plans (which can be done prior to participants retiring) and substituting defined contribution retirement accounts in an effort both to cap their liabilities for retirees' pension benefits and to increase the predictability of what their liabilities for future retirement benefits will be each year.

The Emeriti Consortium for Retirement Health Solutions program may lead to a similar thing occurring with respect to faculty retiree health-care coverage. Faculty at institutions that previously did not fund any retiree health insurance benefits will clearly be better off with such a program, and an institution's adopting it may lead its faculty members to retire earlier than otherwise would be the case. On the other hand, academic institutions that currently contribute to faculty retirees' health insurance costs may see participating in the Emeriti Consortium program as a way of limiting their future liabilities for retiree health-care costs, and they may substitute this defined contribution program for their own current retiree health insurance plan. Such a substitution might increase older faculty members' uncertainty about their future health-care costs and induce them to postpone their retirement dates. Academic administrators will have to think long and hard in the years ahead about the issue of health coverage for retired faculty members.

CONCLUDING REMARKS

As a former Cornell Vice President, I can attest that it is much easier to write about and conduct research on the problems that our nation's academic leaders face, owing to the changing nature of the faculty and faculty employment practices, than it is to actually deal with these problems. Academic leaders are often preoccupied with the short-run academic and financial challenges that they face, and may postpone thinking about the longer-term issues that I have raised. However, this would be a mistake; addressing these issues is essential to the well-being of the academic enterprise. Thoughtful leaders will understand this and devote attention to both thinking about them and designing creative solutions.

ACKNOWLEDGMENTS

The Cornell Higher Education Research Institute (CHERI) is supported by the Andrew W. Mellon Foundation, the Atlantic Philanthropies (USA) Inc. and the TIAA-CREF Institute and I am grateful to them for their support. However, the views expressed here are solely my own.

NOTES

1. The four university centers in the SUNY system are Albany, Binghamton, Buffalo and Stony Brook.
2. A number of the papers in Ehrenberg (forthcoming) present similar data on the growing use of part-time and full-time non-tenure-track faculty in other states' public universities.
3. Professional schools, both at the undergraduate and graduate levels, have long used adjunct faculty members who bring professional expertise to the classroom that their full-time academic colleagues may not have. My concern here is largely with undergraduate students and the substitution of contingent for other faculty in arts and science and other academic areas.
4. In 2005 collective bargaining for graduate assistants at private universities was effectively at least temporarily precluded by the NLRB in its New York University decision.
5. In November 2005 the New School became the first private university to guarantee job security to part-time faculty when it ratified a contract with the union representing its part-time faculty, who make up over 80 per cent of the teaching staff at the institution (Gravois, 2005).
6. Canes and Rosen (1995) found no evidence that the gender composition of departments at three selected academic institutions influenced female undergraduates choice of majors, while Rask and Bailey (2002) and Ashworth and Evans (2001) found that it did. More recently Bettinger and Long (2005) found that having a female faculty member in a class increased the likelihood that female college students would take additional classes in mathematics and geology, but they found no such relationship in engineering, physics and computer science. Finally, Neumark and Gardecki (1998) found that female graduate students in economics were more likely to complete their degrees when they had female mentors.
7. However, Ehrenberg et al. (forthcoming b) find that very few universities are actually making money on their commercialization activities.
8. See also the program's website, www.emertihealth.org, for details.
9. Fronstin and Yakoboski (2005) provide a broader discussion of such retiree medical account programs.

REFERENCES

Anderson, E.L. (2002), *The New Professoriate: Characteristics, Contributions and Compensation*, Washington, DC: American Council on Education.

Ashenfelter, O. and D. Card (2002), 'Did the elimination of mandatory retirement affect faculty retirement?', *American Economic Review*, **92** (September), 957–80.

Ashworth, J.L. and J.L. Evans (2001), 'Modeling student subject choice at secondary and tertiary level: a cross-section study', *Journal of Economic Education*, **32**, 311–22.

Baldwin, R.G. and J.L. Chronister (2001), *Teaching Without Tenure: Policies and Practices for a New Era*, Baltimore, MD: Johns Hopkins Press.

Bettinger, E.P. and B.T. Long (2005), 'Do faculty serve as role models? The impact of instructor gender on female students', *American Economic Association Papers and Proceedings*, **95** (May).

Bettinger, E.P. and B.T. Long (forthcoming), 'Help or hinder? Adjunct professors and student outcomes', in R.G. Ehrenberg (ed.), *What's Happening to Public Higher Education?*, Westport, CT: ACE Praeger Series on Higher Education.

Canes, B. and H. Rosen (1995), 'Following in her footsteps? Faculty gender composition and women's choice of college majors', *Industrial and Labor Relations Review*, **48** (April), 486–504.

Conley, V.M., D.W. Lesley and L.J. Zimbler (2004), *Part-time Instructional Faculty and Staff: Who They Are, What They Do, and What They Think*, Washington, DC: US Department of Education.

Curtis, J. (2005), *Trends in Faculty Status, 1975–2003*, Washington, DC: American Association of University Professors, available at http://www.aaup.org/research/facstattrends.htm.

Ehrenberg, R.G. (2001), 'Career's end: a survey of faculty retirement policies', *Academe*, **87** (July/August), 24–9.

Ehrenberg, R.G. (2003), 'Studying ourselves: the academic labor market', *Journal of Labor Economics*, **21** (April), 221–35.

Ehrenberg, R.G. (2004a), 'Two Different Worlds – Discussion', *American Economic Association Papers and Proceedings*, **94** (2).

Ehrenberg, R.G. (2004b), 'Don't blame faculty for high tuition: the Annual Report on the Economic Status of the Profession, 2003–2004', *Academe*, **90** (March/April), 20–31.

Ehrenberg, R.G. (2005a), 'Involving undergraduate students in research to encourage them to undertake PhD study in economics', *American Economic Association Papers and Proceedings*, **95** (May).

Ehrenberg, R.G. (2005b), 'Graduate education, innovation and the federal responsibility', *Communicator*, **38** (July), 1–8.

Ehrenberg, R.G. (ed.) (forthcoming), *What's Happening to Public Higher Education?*, Westport, CT: ACE/Praeger Series on Higher Education.

Ehrenberg, R.G. and D.B. Klaff (2003), 'Changes in faculty composition within the State University of New York System: 1985–2001', (Working Paper 38), Ithaca, NY: Cornell Higher Education Research Institute, available at www.ilr.cornell.edu/cheri.

Ehrenberg, R.G. and L. Zhang (2005a), 'The changing nature of faculty employment', in R. Clark and J. Ma (eds), *Recruitment, Retention and Retirement in Higher Education: Building and Managing the Faculty of the Future*, Cheltenham, UK and Northampton, MA: Edward Elgar, 32–52.

Ehrenberg, R.G. and L. Zhang (2005b), 'Do tenured and tenure-track faculty matter?', *Journal of Human Resources*, **40** (Summer), 647–59.

Ehrenberg, R.G., M. Matier, and P. Fontanella (2000), 'Cornell University confronts the end of mandatory retirement', in R. Clark and B. Hammond (eds), *To Retire or Not Retire: Retirement Policy and Practice in Higher Education*, Philadelphia, PA: University of Pennsylvania Press.

Ehrenberg, R.G., M.J. Rizzo and S.S. Condie (2003), 'Start-up costs in American research universities', (Working Paper 33), Ithaca, NY: Cornell Higher Education Research Institute, available at www.ilr.cornell.edu/cheri.

Ehrenberg, R.G., M. McGraw and J. Mrdjenovic (forthcoming a), 'Why do field differentials in average faculty salaries vary across universities?', *Economics of Education Review*.

Ehrenberg, R.G., M.J. Rizzo and G.H. Jakubson (forthcoming b), 'Who bears the growing cost of science at universities?', in P.E. Stephan and R.G. Ehrenberg (eds), *Science and the University*, Madison, WI: University of Wisconsin Press.

Fogg, P. (2004), 'For these professors, "practice" is perfect', *Chronicle of Higher Education*, **50** (16 April), A12.

Fronstin, P. and P. Yakoboski (2005), *Options and Alternatives to Fund Retiree Health Care Expenditures*, New York, NY: TIAA-CREF Institute.

Gravois, J. (2005), 'Both sides say agreement at the New School sets a gold standard for adjunct-faculty contracts', *Chronicle of Higher Education*, **51** (2 November).

Hoffer, T. et al. (2004), *Doctorate Recipients from United States Universities: Summary Report 2003*, Chicago, IL: NORC at the University of Chicago.

Mason, M.A. and M. Goulden (2004), 'Do babies matter? (Part II)', *Academe*, **90** (November/December), 11–15.

Monks, J.W. (2004), 'The relative earnings of contingent faculty in higher education', (Working Paper 59), Ithaca, NY: Cornell Higher Education Research Institute, available at www.ilr.cornell.edu/cheri.

Moon, M. (2005), 'Retiree health care: individuals picking up bigger tab', *Trends and Issues*, (1 July), New York: TIAA-CREF Institute.

Neumark, D. and R. Gardecki (1998), 'Women helping women? Role model and mentoring effects on female PhD students in economics', *Journal of Human Resources*, **33** (Winter), 220–46.

Newsletter of the Committee on the Status of Women in the Economics Profession, (2005), (Winter), Ithaca, NY: American Economic Association, Committee on the Status of Women in the Economics Profession, available at www.cswep.org.

Office of Institutional Research and Analysis (2005), *Trends in SUNY Employees, Fall 1994 Through Fall 2004*, Albany, NY: State University of New York System, available at www.sysadm.suny.edu/irdocs/employees/employees.htm.

Pulley, J.L. (2005), 'College group devises a new way to pay for retirees' Healthcare costs', *Chronicle of Higher Education*, **51** (3 June), A21.

Rask, K.N. and E.M. Bailey (2002), 'Are faculty role models? Evidence from major choice in an undergraduate institution', *Journal of Economic Education*, **33** (Spring), 99–124.

Smallwood, S. (2002), 'UAW will represent part-time faculty members at New York U.', *Chronicle of Higher Education*, **48** (19 July), A10.

Stephan, P.E. and R.G. Ehrenberg (eds) (forthcoming), *Science and the University*, Madison, WI: University of Wisconsin Press.

University of California (2005), *Faculty Family Friendly Edge: An Initiative for Tenure-Track Faculty at the University of California, Report*, available at http://ucfamilyedge.berkeley.edu.

9. The faculty of tomorrow's research universities

John Edward Sexton

INTRODUCTION

I am pleased to be a contributor to this volume because the themes that are examined in it are ones that have been my focus since I was installed as New York University's president three years ago. At that time I began to articulate a vision of what I call a common enterprise university. Key to that notion was the role of faculty in such a university and I have continued to elaborate on that fundamental issue ever since. This chapter provides me with an opportunity to share and deepen my reflections on the role of faculty seen primarily from the perspective of large urban research universities.

It is no surprise that the issues confronting my university and universities generally are the same issues that concern TIAA-CREF. As the principal retirement system for the nation's education, research and healthcare communities – including some 3200 current employees and over 9000 retirees of New York University (NYU) – TIAA-CREF and the TIAA-CREF Institute are deeply involved in our business and serve as our partners in addressing the challenges we face.

TIAA-CREF and NYU also share other similarities; we each trace our founding to immigrants to the United States who went on to achieve spectacular success in their chosen fields and lent their talent and treasure to the creation of institutions that have enabled millions of people over the years to realize their own dreams.

It was Albert Gallatin – of Swiss descent and Secretary of the Treasury for both Thomas Jefferson and James Madison – who founded NYU in 1831. He was on a special mission. He saw the great universities of the day, Oxford and Cambridge in England and the Ivy League in the United States, and recognized that they were built on a model of withdrawal from the world and service to the privileged in a bucolic setting. He rejected that model and saw great cities as potentially great centers of learning. With several other notable New Yorkers, he established New York University as

a place that would be 'fitted for all and graciously open to all', a university 'in and of the city'.

Similarly, TIAA-CREF was founded by someone born into a weaver's family in a little Scottish town. Andrew Carnegie came with his family to the United States in 1848. A giant of the industrial revolution, he was also a larger-than-life philanthropist who established the public library system across America, from sea to shining sea. In 1918 he was shocked to discover that many academics were destitute in retirement. Through the Carnegie Foundation for the Advancement of Teaching, he created the company that for almost a century has been a careful steward of the finances of our colleagues in the academy: TIAA-CREF.

AN ERA OF HYPERCHANGE

It is an undeniable reality that powerful forces – good and bad – are reshaping our society, our times and (inevitably) our universities. What we confront is not just change, but hyperchange – and, most importantly, hyperchange in the very province in which universities live and operate, the domain of knowledge and ideas. Today universities confront the collapse of traditional boundaries – in time, in space, in disciplines and in culture. And this collapse is compounded by the financial pressures – what this volume has captured in the phrase 'the new balancing act in the business of higher education'; we are witnessing a tectonic shift in the ground on which our universities stand.

Such hyperchange compels dramatic adaptation within higher education, rooted in serious reflection on the nature of who we are, what we do and how we do it. Research universities – those that operate at the frontier of knowledge – are at a critical threshold, and the chapters in this volume quite properly focus on the emerging paradigm shift in our understanding of the nature, needs and day-to-day operations of higher education.

In Chapter 8, Ron Ehrenberg lays out several of the economic and demographic dimensions of this period of change and challenge, and points to strategies of adaptation that some institutions may pursue to relieve the pressures upon them. I am fortunate to lead an institution that has not felt forced to tailor its strategic thinking to financial considerations alone. Nonetheless, you will see that the themes of my chapter press in many of the same directions as his; the difference is that mine are driven mainly by academic imperatives as we at NYU strive to position ourselves for the twenty-first century.

Each university will have its own version of change and each successful university will shape its future through an explicit articulation of mission.

Thus great universities are in a race, not against each other, but to reach their own distinct vision and ideals, and the journey will require us to apply to our study of institutional self the same principles of continuous, rigorous examination and inquiry that guide our academic research and dialogue.

THE RESEARCH UNIVERSITY

The research university is designed to provide the broadest, deepest and most immediate forum for conversation and criticism. We *both* observe and enforce the established norms of the disciplines *and* offer a rebuke to those who view those norms as beyond question.

Above all I reject the idea that changes in the business of higher education can or should mean a denigration of the central role of the research university; instead the changes have to be compatible with that role and if possible move it forward.

And what is that role? As one privileged to have studied with those who were creating the next version of the subjects they taught, I can attest to the magic that permeates such a learning environment. The foundation blocks of that environment are faculty whose research makes a difference in their fields and in the world and the infrastructure of support which their work requires. Only after setting and securing this foundation can we successfully integrate the process of educating our students with the imperative of advancing knowledge. This integration – an explicit connection of the great researchers to students at all levels – characterizes and nourishes the research university. The students who choose to study at a place like NYU expect to be engaged in a field, in a frame of mind, in a spirit of inquiry and in the excitement of the creative endeavor. And it is this aspect of the research university that justifies the presence of undergraduate students and the concomitant support of the research enterprise which their tuition charges provide.

In my view, the very notion of the research university refutes the false dichotomy, too often advanced, between research and teaching. Those familiar with our great research universities know that both in theory and in fact the greatest classroom professors often are the leading thinkers in their field.

But the high quality and status enjoyed by our research universities can be a source of complacency. Our great universities are so successful and so in demand and have been for so long that they may take for granted their value and continued existence; in other words, in a manner quite remarkably at odds with their core commitment to rigorous inquiry, they may fall into an unreflective view of their own excellence, one that is largely autobiographical and simply reifies their view of themselves.

Such complacency will be steadily more unsustainable in the face of mounting financial pressures, demographic changes and heightened scrutiny from outside the university's gates – both from the students and parents who are our consumers and from the government, which more and more assigns itself an oversight role. But complacency is not only increasingly impractical; it also represents a disconnect between the ideal and the reality – a disconnect which ultimately could jeopardize the very existence of the research university.

One version of this disconnect might be an unhealthy separation in our universities of the research enterprise from the teaching enterprise. In my view, this version of the disconnect is sufficiently widespread to engage our attention – manifesting itself, for example, in the tendency even at the finest research universities to entrust undergraduate teaching to part-time faculty. Today, at private research universities in the United States, at least one out of every three classes is taught by part-time faculty or graduate students. They can make an important contribution, but there is also a danger. Too often their greater part in the university enterprise has been accompanied by a reduced commitment to teaching for many senior faculty.

This is a troubling development, for, to be attractive to students and true to itself, the research university must ensure the connection between research and learning which is its justification. We must not create a set of incentives instilling and reinforcing a dichotomy in which faculty are not encouraged to view the teaching enterprise (including the undergraduate teaching enterprise) as a natural concomitant of the research enterprise and vice versa. We must be especially careful lest research come to be seen as the privilege and teaching undergraduates as a painful chore.

TOWARD A COMMON ENTERPRISE UNIVERSITY

The conventional wisdom among the public, encouraged by a set of popular books written largely by ideologues outside the university and with relatively little experience of it, is that professors in research universities are essentially underworked and overindulged producers of esoteric and even solipsistic tracts. The truth is quite the contrary. Notwithstanding the fact that work of the mind is neither linear nor standardized and thus not susceptible to clock punching, there is hard evidence that professors in higher education generally work on average 50 hours a week. And in research universities the number rises to 60 hours a week.

Of course, there are examples in elite universities of faculty who, even as they work very hard, view themselves simply as independent contractors and there are too many forces, both within and outside the research

university, that press against a sense of institutional loyalty. Thus, for example, as our celebrity culture has infiltrated the culture of the academy, the economy of rewards and recognition tends to push faculty members to seek compensation and satisfaction outside their university – and, indeed, sometimes to consider the university as honored by their affiliation. To faculty who adopt this view, tenure may be little more than a retainer, the university merely one of many clients.

Contributing to this attitude is a phenomenon that is otherwise powerfully positive: the advancement through the Internet and the communications revolution of a disciplinary community characterized by a continuing conversation unconfined by boundaries of campus, space or time. The result is that scholars may come to value their academic specialization and not their academic institution as their primary allegiance. The phenomenon is likely to accelerate as now unimagined technological advances offer faculty more absorbing and more meaningful membership in virtual academic communities that can literally span the globe.

In my view, the challenge is not to discourage faculty loyalty to disciplines or to stifle their ambition to have an effect in the wider world; rather the challenge is to produce an appreciation that one of the best tools for inquiry and insight is examining intellectual formulations not just with colleagues in the same discipline, wherever they are located, but with colleagues and even students in the same discipline and colleagues in other disciplines within a scholar's own university. Put another way, there is a richness to be found at home, sometimes discovered quite serendipitously, in the ordinary course of campus life, that can be invaluable to the scholar.

In the best of our universities faculty will be present – not just on the campus but of it. They will welcome and engage with colleagues of differing views and expertise. They will be even more available to mentor and advise students and to continue the classroom conversation outside class. And, in doing so, they will dedicate their time and energy not only to their graduate students but also to undergraduates. In all this and more, they will internalize the collective interest as part of their own interests and, in effect, embrace the notion of what I call the common enterprise university – a university characterized by collective faculty responsibility and full citizenship in an institution that is the central focus of their vocation as scholars.

There are clear moral grounds for this vision of the common enterprise university, but there are more utilitarian ones as well. The best faculty are ambitious with respect to what they want to accomplish personally in their teaching as well as in their research, but the wisest will realize that neither ambition can be achieved easily in a university comprised only of

independent contractors. For example, there are severe limits to what one can achieve in teaching class A if other faculty are not teaching powerful classes in B, C and D. And, with respect to research, an analogous point can be made: with the possible exception of a few intellectual geniuses, scholarship is inherently communal, both because it builds on what others have accomplished and because even the deepest insights can be improved by testing them with colleagues across a range of disciplines.

In addition, there is a second utilitarian, practical and inescapable argument for the common enterprise university, which arises from the harsh economic realities of our time. In the United States, and the Western world generally, the gulf between public esteem for higher education and public willingness to pay for it is wide and growing wider as public finances come under increasing pressure. At the same time, higher education faces rising costs for hiring the best faculty, stocking libraries with an expanding range of more expensive books and journals, and obtaining and sustaining the latest facilities in technology and the sciences. The explosion of new academic fields and curricular areas, from human genetics to cognitive sciences, yields great societal and academic benefits; but here too costs can soar. And, in traditional fields as well as new ones, as the great physicist Max Planck observed, each new advance in knowledge costs more than the one before. It is not only true that first come the easier questions, then the harder ones; it is concomitantly true that first come the less expensive questions and then the more expensive ones.

How then will we generate the resources to fulfill our mission? The answer again is found in the move to common enterprise with its emphasis on faculty engagement in the setting of priorities, the making of decisions in all parts of the university, and led by the faculty, a willingness to sacrifice for the collective good.

Surely, as a general proposition, the argument for a common enterprise faculty flows from enlightened self-interest. But, beyond that, the university I envision – the one I call the common enterprise university – will demand that faculty have deep in their souls an inclination to build community: a spirit that will display itself in different ways at different moments.

Let me offer just one example. In my view, the faculty of the common enterprise university will reverse conventional assumptions about seniority. They will understand that, with regard to institutional direction, senior faculty, even as they exercise authority, must view themselves as standing not just at a shaping point but at a listening point. In short, the generation in power must accept that one of their most crucial roles is to hear and heed the voices of the next generation of leaders. I recognize that this strategy for institutional continuity and organic, consensual evolution may not win ready acceptance from some who have climbed to the pinnacle. But the

world of hyperchange in which our universities and their faculties now function will mean that research and learning will often be shaped more decisively by scholars who are younger in years or experience. So the common enterprise university must resist a hierarchy that suppresses younger faculty and makes them wait their turn. Instead, such a university – in an iterative and progressive process – must foster an empowering intergenerational relationship across its faculty.

But, if a university demands so much of faculty, will it compromise its ability to secure the talent it seeks? The answer, based on my experience not just as a university president but as a law school dean, although perhaps counterintuitive, is that a social contract of obligation can make the common enterprise university irresistibly attractive to some of the finest scholars, because a good number of those who are drawn to the life of the mind derive satisfaction not merely from material rewards but from a strong sense of vocation. Many of the best, although concededly not all, are attracted powerfully and primarily to the excitement of unfettered inquiry, the serious and at times even playful exchange of ideas. They are likely to recognize the high value to them of building a stronger university, one committed to excellence and centered in a vibrant intellectual community.

THE COMMON ENTERPRISE FACULTY IN ACTION

The changes we are witnessing in the nature and composition of university faculty need not be regarded as simply a reflex reaction to economic realities. If that is all they are, they will devalue the research university. But in the context of the common enterprise university that I envision – animated as it is by a desire of each member of the faculty orchestra to produce (in cooperation with others) a symphony of discovery and learning – we can encourage the development of new kinds of players, with each addition enhancing our overall performance in some way.

Of course, every faculty member – from the most senior world-renowned scholar to the most junior adjunct – must embrace the importance of integrating knowledge creation with knowledge transmission and understand their place in the process. The principal responsibility for this integration lies with the tenured faculty, who have been chosen for their dual capacities in research and teaching – in effect making them the primary incarnation of the core purpose of the research university.

While I am unwilling at this stage to subscribe to a single formula for each member of the faculty, I am certain that the research faculty at our great universities must accept that undergraduate teaching is a vital part of their vocation. This is not to say that every tenured professor must teach

undergraduates every semester. Our aim must be a moving of the dial, a reweighing of the balance, so that every student will have contact not only with those who write the textbooks used in the classroom but also with those who are forging the ideas that will inform the next generation of those books. For the moment, I offer this as a possible benchmark: even in the first year students should be able to enroll in more than one class with an actively engaged scholar in the field, and by the senior year a majority of a student's courses ought to be taught by such professors.

My experience at NYU leads me to be optimistic about the willingness of even august academics to commit themselves to this. Some of our leading researchers, senior and junior alike, find it extremely rewarding to teach large introductory courses, ranging from economics to English literature. There are university professors at NYU who teach a freshman seminar. For twelve years I myself have done so – first, as Dean of the Law School and now as President of the University.

The tenured faculty is only part of the story, however. Important as they are and always will be, the tenured faculty increasingly will comprise only a segment – albeit the core segment – of the research university. Notwithstanding that every course, introductory or advanced, is an integral component of the educational mission of the university, the tenured faculty do not do all the teaching in the research university today, and, more importantly, they should not do it in the research university of tomorrow. Thus, at every university new types of faculty, many of whom are on full-time or even multi-year contracts, have proliferated – with the effect that important parts of the curriculum at today's universities are entrusted to faculty who are neither tenured nor on the tenure track.

As this important phenomenon has developed, however, too little (if any) thought has been given to the definition, role and rewards of the array of faculty who all carry significant responsibilities in the teaching enterprise. Even less attention has been paid to connecting the deployment of those faculty to the rationale of the research university. What results is a kind of unexamined, often accidental and incidental evolution of faculty functions, some of which is undeniably driven by financial pressures, which has brought to the research university a host of actors whose presence may be critical but who are frequently underappreciated and undervalued.

I will not pause here to review the taxonomy of titles that have blossomed in our research universities to designate these faculty – or to enumerate the variety of privileges, rights and worth attendant to each. Suffice it to say that at most research universities there are scores of such titles, and they have sprung up ad hoc. This in turn has generated increasingly stark divisions and valuations among segments of the faculty, with too many feeling they are second- or third-class citizens.

The proliferation in types of faculty may reflect fiscal realities; but, if we consider and shape their proper roles, they can enrich the intellectual life of the university in truly important ways. I will contend that, quite apart from financial considerations, we ought to embrace new forms of faculty in ways that bring value to the academic enterprise and, in many cases, bring a unique value which tenured faculty cannot provide.

I propose to discuss four broad categories of such faculty, primarily outside the tenure system. I will give each of these categories a name; I emphasize, however, that any connection between the name that I offer and the use of a similar term in the taxonomy of titles now existing in any university is purely coincidental, and I refuse to be limited in my exposition by any assumptions arising from the use of the title somewhere in the status quo.

First I will discuss what I call the master teacher – a category which will evoke existing forms of faculty on many campuses but which adds a new dimension to them. Next is what I call the global professor, then the adjunct (or part-time) professor and finally the cyber faculty. These four categories do not exhaust all of the categories outside the tenured faculty – for example, emeriti faculty, visiting faculty or faculty fellows. The four categories I treat are sufficient, however, to capture the principles of faculty deployment that I mean to advance here.

The Master Teacher

I define the ideal of the master teacher as someone chosen through a rigorous academic review process to join the faculty because he or she has been adjudged to be capable of conveying the most advanced stage of a discipline and appreciating the creative side of the venture, while possessing a particular ability in the classroom and a special dedication to the enterprise of teaching. The teaching professor causes students to think, to reason, to question and ask the right questions, to push beyond conventional assumptions, and to reach higher than they might have reached on their own; the teaching professor will instill in students a desire to understand the subject and to see the beauty of linking that subject to others. He or she will be capable of appreciating and participating in the research enterprise; but he or she will have chosen to tilt the personal mix of research and teaching more dramatically in the direction of teaching than would be appropriate for one seeking tenure. The teaching professor will dedicate a full professional life to the university as an active participant in the institution and a premier participant in the education of students. The teaching professor will not be given the lifetime position we associate with tenure, but the possibility of

remaining with the institution for a whole professional career will be very real.

It is my claim that teaching professors will be and ought to be key players in the symphony – in other words, even in a world unrestrained by considerations of time and resources, the tenured faculty ought not to cover every course.

In part, this view is derived from a principle of comparative advantage applied to the enterprise of undergraduate education in our research universities. Simply put, although the importance of exposing undergraduates to those who are engaged in advanced research cannot be overstated, it would be a misallocation of aggregate faculty time to carry that principle to the extreme that every course were taught by such persons. Moreover, as undergraduate education at our universities moves – quite felicitously, in my view – in the direction of increasing the time devoted to student contact outside class, whether to continue the classroom conversation or to provide career and personal counseling, the kind of time and devotion I associate with the teaching professor – the master teacher – will become more and more important. And, finally, incorporating into the enterprise a set of actors singularly devoted to the development of pedagogies to integrate research and teaching is bound to be beneficial.

The Global Professor

In addition to the teaching professor, I propose another relatively new but increasingly important category of faculty, the global professor. By this I mean a distinguished academic from outside the United States who, if not willing to move here permanently, is willing on a long-term continuing basis to commit a portion of the year – two or three months – to the research university. Global professors engage in collaborative research with others on the faculty, teach courses on a compressed schedule, and make themselves available to the university's students throughout the year – whether they are students studying abroad or drawing on the resources of cyberspace.

Global faculty add perspective and dimension – both inside disciplines, which may manifest themselves differently in different cultural contexts, and in a more general sense, because they bring their conceptions of reality and the richness of their own values into the wider university conversation. As the pace of globalization accelerates and the value of integrating perspectives other than our own is accepted in disciplines or professions that have not already embraced it, the university will enlist an increasing number of global professors.

The Adjunct Faculty

At the same time, the common enterprise university will value and valorize adjunct faculty who truly can make distinctive contributions. In my lexicon, an adjunct professor is someone selected because he or she, while forswearing a full-time academic life, comes into the classroom as an exemplar of the application of knowledge creation in the world outside the gates. His or her commitment to the university may be less intense or less consuming, since the commitment in both directions is less than full-time.

But consider the advantage of such adjuncts at a university like NYU. Blessed by our location we are able to draw on the unparalleled pool of talent in the world's capital city. To bring that breadth of experience and expertise to our students is not an expedient measure; it adds another layer of richness and depth to a liberal education.

I would argue that the impact of adjuncts on campus cannot be captured in a simple statistic: the category itself tends to obscure a broad range of activities, from teaching introductory language courses to offering novel and interesting insights from the best of practitioners who are willing not only to convey but also to reflect on their own work. A pie chart of faculty categories cannot tell us what individual faculty members are contributing to students and to the university itself. Adjuncts can offer students exposure to knowledge, experience and insight from creative and professional careers that have changed society and even the very disciplines we teach and study. A Spike Lee can be an extraordinary gift to film students. And what law student would not want to learn from someone like Marty Lipton, who has changed the face of corporate law?

Not every adjunct will be as famous as these, and no one should teach in the classroom who is not competent to do so. But it would be shortsighted and dogmatic to deny the special qualities that adjunct faculty can bring – whether they are celebrated movie directors, public officials, journalists, social workers who know how theory works in practice, newly-minted PhDs or more experienced ones who are exposing students to introductory concepts and theories in their fields.

Clearly, adjunct faculty play a different role in the common enterprise university. They are not constantly present; the opportunities for serendipitous engagement with other faculty and with students outside the classroom will be rarer; their participation in the wider academic dialogue will be intermittent. But in contexts where such costs are outweighed by the benefits of the rich experiences or the depth of knowledge they can bring to the university, adjunct professors can offer much that we should prize.

Cyber Faculty

The final form of faculty that I will discuss is inspired by the enormous possibilities affecting both research and teaching that are opened up by the continuing advances in technology. Gradually, if sometimes grudgingly, we are letting technology transform the way we think, teach and learn in the research university. And the truth of the matter is that all faculty will have to be expert in new technologies. As new generations of students take technology more and more for granted, they will demand faculty who deal with technology as readily and deftly as they do. Students who were apparently born with a mouse in their hands will themselves become faculty. In brief, I think that all faculty will, within a generation or two, be acting like cyber faculty, even if much of their teaching is done face to face and on-site. This involves more than just technical capacities. Just as there will be great research in pedagogy that will be brought to bear in teaching, so there will be a whole wisdom that will integrate technologies into research and teaching that will not be known to the domestic computer user and will require more than the traditional IT department provides.

But, thus far, the response of universities has been bifurcated. Some have created new technology ventures to produce digitized versions of instructional materials, with the aim of delivering high-quality content to what were assumed to be vast untapped markets of prospective students. Other institutions of higher education have pursued an electronic infrastructure, which enables the traditional faculty and students to work more efficiently within the traditional modalities. I believe that both responses, while useful, only represent early waves of much more dramatic innovations essential to realizing the full potential of technology for teaching and learning in the new research university.

So, at least for a significant transition period, I believe it is necessary to create a group of faculty whom I call cyber faculty, a set of new actors within the university charged with linking the coming waves of technological innovation with the challenges and aspirations of higher education. Cyber faculty will have quadruple-powered capacity: first, a level of technological sophistication well beyond what we associate with all but a few of today's faculty and possibly even beyond what we will associate with many of tomorrow's faculty; second, an unusually creative appetite for deconstructing traditional teaching and research and reconceptualizing them; third, an advanced competence in a substantive and traditional academic discipline; fourth, and most important, an unusual talent to inspire collaboration among contributors with diverse expertise in innovation.

The cyber faculty will be viewed as full faculty colleagues with a specific mandate within the academic enterprise to integrate research and teaching

into the new world of scholarly cyberspace. This is very different from what we typically find today in our IT service organizations, our libraries or our centers for teaching excellence, where talented and dedicated people are not nuanced in their engagement with the material – only intermittently collaborative with the knowledge creators, and then often purely as facilitators.

The creation of a cyber faculty will require an investment of resources, but one that is essential to enhance and speed the integration of technology into what universities do. True, some faculty, already masters of technology, have brought it into their work; however, far from demonstrating that cyber faculty are unnecessary (at least for an interim period), what has already been achieved by some faculty provides tantalizing evidence of the potential technology offers for all. We are already witnessing signs of this at NYU, where individuals are demonstrating the importance of this new category. Some are at work in collaborations of scholars and practitioners to create new technological infrastructure and new multimedia contents for transformative approaches to learning. A team of faculty at the School of Medicine has created Surgical Interactive Multimedia Modules, which combine rich media-enhanced lectures, annotated imaging studies, pathology data and digitized video footage of both animated and real surgical procedures. With these modules, a student in the surgery clerkship can pursue multiple lines of inquiry, interacting online, with the story of a patient – from presentation to treatment and follow-up. Students thus gain self-paced exposure to information and problem-solving experiences not available in the classroom or even in the hospital setting. Faculty can focus more on guiding the students' engagement in learning because they need less class time to transmit information. Inspired by this experiment, the Medical School is now launching a collaborative effort to apply the same approach to other areas of the curriculum.

Conceivably, some cyber faculty will never enter a traditional classroom, and hence will not be evaluated on their capacity for traditional teaching. Instead, their performance will be normed on their ability to create in their colleagues and in the life of the university an actuation of the technological revolution, the effects of which have only begun to be felt in the research and learning process.

CONCLUSION

So, not just in response to new financial pressures but also in response to the new imperatives of hyperchange in the world of knowledge, we must encourage, draw on, respect and reward an appropriate blend of the array of faculty actors I have described here. This will be a foundation of the new

research university, creating a culture of institutional citizenship that honors equality of voice and the role of all members of the community.

I have argued that many of the best of the faculty of today will embrace this vision and not reject it as just abstract theory. And I have asserted that universities will invite and evoke that response by adding another element to our traditional criteria for faculty – not just excellence in scholarship and quality of teaching but also a dedication to the university community. I have acknowledged that some potential faculty will be allergic to this ideal; but, for many, the very demand will appeal to their higher and more aspirational conception of themselves, will raise the standard of their ambitions and affect every aspect of what they do. For them the mutual obligations of the social compact will be a positive and even irresistibly powerful magnet.

For NYU and other great research universities the common enterprise ideal is the best and, in the end, the only way that, facing the realities of today, we can fulfill our mission for the faculty, students and society of the twenty-first century. Each institution will find its own path. But I am convinced that the guiding principles are the same: self-reflection, but not self-absorption, at the institutional and individual level; respect for the rigor of scholarship, but equal respect for the vocation and variety of teaching; the cultivation of the autonomy of the individual mind and creative spirit, coupled with the integration of every mind and talent into a community of learning. In my view this is the research university of the future, rooted in enduring principles but ready to encompass and enhance the best possibilities of this transformed and transformative era.

10. Of canaries, storms and Dickens: finding balance for faculty in public higher education

Kermit L. Hall and Robert W. Wagner

THE NEW ENVIRONMENT FOR AMERICAN PUBLIC HIGHER EDUCATION

The challenges facing American public higher education beg for unique, path-breaking solutions. Globalization, technological change, uneven and uncertain funding, increasing demands for greater access by more diverse groups and rising expectations about the performance and accountability of universities are part of the story. The American experience is far from unique. In 1998 the World Conference on Higher Education released its declaration citing many of these pressures as well as the employability of graduates, the efficiency of operations, and, most notably, the future status of faculty and staff. Students of American higher education, including Ronald G. Ehrenberg (forthcoming, p. 1), have described these developments as a 'perfect storm'. As Ehrenberg notes, since the early 1980s taxpayers have clamored for state income tax cuts, driven in part by the impact of Ronald Reagan's federal tax cutting revolution, which reduced the value of state income tax deductions on federal income tax returns (ibid., pp. 1–2). Faculties sit in the eye of that storm.

The story, however, is more complicated than merely tax cutting, a point driven home by David Longanecker (2004), who has turned to a different figure of speech to describe the situation as 'A Tale of Two Pities'. According to Longanecker, the leaders of higher education, on the one hand, and governors and state legislators, on the other, are increasingly like ships passing in the night (ibid., pp. 13, 24). They view essentially the same set of circumstances in radically different ways. Kane and Orszag (2003, p. 5) have given statistical credibility to Longanecker's provocative analysis.

Higher education leaders, including national organizations such as the American Council on Education (ACE), complain that public officials do not love them any more (Longanecker, 2004, p. 2). They claim that the

share of public dollars going into colleges and universities has gone down and that the priority they enjoyed from the 1950s through the 1970s has shifted elsewhere, notably to crime control, K-12 education, and, most recently, health care (ibid., p. 5). State legislators and governors, however, respond that higher education does not understand either what has happened or the problems they face. Lawmakers emphasize the point that over the past three decades total appropriations per student have actually gone up, as has spending on Pell grants. And leaders in several high growth states, such as California, Texas, Florida and North Carolina, insist that they have driven additional dollars into their higher education systems to take account of that growth. State leaders everywhere also protest that college and university presidents neither understand nor appreciate that the growth of entitlement programs, such as Medicaid, often leave them with little budgetary flexibility.

This 'Tale of Two Pities' demonstrates that the social contract between public higher education and the states has withered over the last quarter century. Increasingly, as Mark Yudof (2002, p. B24) has written, public higher education, which was once viewed as a public good, has become a private good in which individuals, not society as a whole, reap the fullest benefit. In many instances, moreover, the rationale for public higher education has increasingly become one of driving economic development rather than producing an educated public. This has thrust higher education administrators into new contexts, required leaders to search for innovative solutions, and applied new pressures to professors at public universities.

While groups such as ACE insist that the rapid increases in tuition charges are more than justified in order to maintain quality and international competitiveness, the public has responded with increasing skepticism (Hebel, 2003, p. A14). Critics claim professors teach too little and conduct research too much. Evidence of such concerns is clear in the growing calls to make public universities and their faculties more accountable and performance driven, just as has happened in the K-12 arena with *No Child Left Behind*. In September 2005 President George W. Bush's Secretary of Education, Margaret Spellings, announced the formation of a national commission to develop a 'strategy' for higher education (Field, 2005a, p. A29).

Spellings' position is simple in its statement but complex in its impact, especially as it relates to careers of faculty. America's colleges and universities will not remain the best in the world, according to Spellings, unless they become more efficient, more accessible, and more accountable to parents, students and taxpayers. A majority of commission members have insisted already that the status quo is unacceptable. The invited speakers who have appeared before the commission have been unsparing in their criticism of academe, calling colleges and their faculties complacent,

resistant to change and sometimes downright lazy. As the commission's chairman, Charles Miller, put it, 'We would not be here if there were not a lot of things to question' (Field, 2005b).

THE IMPLICATIONS FOR FACULTY

These demands come at a time when public higher education faces an increasing challenge to recruit and retain the best faculty (see Chapter 8). Recent studies, for example, make clear the significant gap between what faculty at public and private institutions earn. Full professors at public institutions earn on average about 20 per cent less than their counterparts at private universities. While it is true that faculty salaries have gone up, a report by the American Association of University Professors (AAUP, 2004) indicates that, when adjusted for inflation over the last decade, public university faculty salaries have actually declined slightly.

The consequences of the 'Tale of Two Pities' appears also in the changing nature of the professoriate. Take one example, contingent faculty. Both full-time and part-time faculty in non-tenure-track positions fall into this category, as do term-faculty, adjunct professors, visiting professors and lecturers (Baldwin and Chronister, 2001, p. 3). On the one hand, tenured faculty enjoy long-term job security and significant benefits such as paid sabbaticals (conditions of work that prompt protest from some public officials as being over-generous). In contrast, contingent faculty have limited contracts and thus limited job security, with one-year appointments being the norm. Most colleges and universities hire full-time non-tenure-track faculty to teach lower division undergraduate courses, though many 4-year colleges will allow non-tenure-track faculty to teach both upper and lower division courses. Baldwin and Chronister (ibid., p. 5) found that some institutions hire full-time non-tenure-track faculty to fulfill teaching duties and clinical or field supervision or administrative work. Rarely do universities expect non-tenure-track staff to do the same amount of research, teaching and service as tenured faculty. Colleges also employ full-time non-tenure faculty as specialists in certain curricula or fields, especially professional schools; colleges foster continuity in academic programs by relying more on full-time non-tenure faculty and less on part-time faculty (Gappa, 1996, p. 141).

The hiring of full-time and part-time faculty in non-tenure-track positions has been a growing and significant trend in higher education for more than a decade (Holub, 2003, p. 1). The pattern has become pervasive, while the social contract that has traditionally sustained public higher education has eroded. The issues associated with contingent faculty are legion and the

question they pose is whether such faculty represents the canary in the coal mine of higher education. Are these developments sounding an alarm about more basic changes in the structure of the workforce? The lack of job security posed by term contracts, obstacles to academic freedom and diminished opportunities for student learning are cited as some of the main concerns. Academic freedom, the right of faculty to freely express and publish their ideas without fear of reprisal, is a core value in higher education. Without the security that tenure provides, many worry that contingent faculty will not express unpopular, challenging or even innovative ideas (Gappa, 1996, p. 144). There is also a belief that as the numbers of contingent faculty increase the broad rights of regular faculty will become increasingly tenuous (ibid.). Then there are the students, whose academic and career fates are shaped by the faculty that teach them. Some critics complain that contingent faculty, especially part-timers who are paid by each course and not by office hours, have neither the time nor the motivation to mentor students outside class or to become involved in student activities. Since contingent faculty are mainly employed to teach undergraduate lower division courses, Benjamin (2002, p. 4) argues that 'such over-reliance particularly disadvantages the less-well-prepared entering and lower-division students in the non-elite institutions who need more substantial faculty attention'. And the rise of increasing numbers of non-tenured positions may also threaten one of the most treasured aspects of the academy, collegiality, because of growing inequities in job security, status, pay and benefits between tenured and contract faculty. The system of shared governance seems under attack as well, since contract faculty are often either barred or marginalized from governance activities. In short, morale may be diminished in this new environment in which faculty are pressed to be more productive (and accountable) with shrinking resources. The AAUP (2005), responding to what it perceives as a threat to quality in higher education, has recommended that universities cap instruction by non-tenured employees to 15 per cent (25 per cent per department).

There seems little doubt that contingent faculty will remain a central and growing feature of American public higher education. The issue is not whether they will continue but how their interest in job security and appropriate pay will be balanced against the need for quality student learning.

The rise of contingent faculty is only one manifestation of how this new Dickensian era is re-shaping faculty lives. Morrison (2003) outlines four demographic changes that are affecting higher education: ethnicity, increasing enrollments, age demography and increasing retirees. First, the proportions of historically under-represented racial and ethnic groups are growing much faster than their numbers in faculty ranks. Statistics show that by the end of the current century whites will make up less than half the

population of America, yet the numbers of faculty from historically under-represented groups is growing only incrementally. If students are to be taught by faculty members who come from backgrounds like their own, there will have to be considerable change in faculty recruitment (Nasser, 2000). Second, the demand for post-secondary education is on the rise, especially from groups that have been historically under-represented. The National Center for Education Statistics (NCES, 2003) notes that between 2000 and 2013 the number of 18–24-year-olds in America will increase by 19 per cent in higher education enrollment (18 per cent in public institutions and 20 per cent in private institutions). Age will also ignite change. The NCES shows that between 2000 and 2014 higher education enrollees between the ages of 18 and 24 will increase by 16 per cent, while enrollees over the age of 35 will increase by 5 per cent (ibid.). Third, as Morrison (2003) explains, 'the graying of the population is also reflected in the graying of the workforce, a workforce that needs continuing education to remain viable'. Related to age demographics is a fourth challenge to higher education: the number of retirees. The number of Americans 55 years or older will increase from 59 million in 2001 to 85 million by 2015 and the faculty of public institutions will be graying along with the rest of the population (National Census Bureau, 2002).

These developments, of course, are not unique to the public higher education sector. They also apply to corporations, especially the traditional Goliaths of American business, such as General Motors and Ford (Birnbaum and Freeman, 2005). Whether public or private the implications of national demographic and employment fluctuations strike at the core of the twenty-first century human resource dilemma. Taken together, then, these developments drive home the basic point that teaching at a public university is not what it used to be. To make the professoriate more attractive and responsive in the era of greater accountability, measured performance and limited resources, there will need to be change.

HOW WE TREAT OUR EMPLOYEES

New demands require new measures and to that end we might take note of what is happening in the private sector where similar pressures are operating. Attracting qualified employees, retaining them and making them more productive is a tall order. Yet examples from the private-sector knowledge industry suggest a way forward.

Take Jim Goodnight and his software company, SAS. Like institutions of higher learning, SAS depends on talented people to keep business thriving. SAS, which is located in Cary, NC, regularly ranks among the best

employers in the United States (Levering and Moskowitz, 2005). That status reflects a commitment to its employees, a commitment that public universities might well heed. What distinguishes SAS is its talent for blending principles of flexibility, equity and efficiency to create a dynamic work environment.

SAS provides its employees (all of them, not just the programmers and software developers) office massages, a state-of-the-art gym, a gourmet cafeteria, on-site child and health care, professional counseling, flexible work rules and incentives for performance. These and other benefits go to day-care workers, landscapers and food service people. Moreover, rather than out-source jobs, SAS keeps them in-house, doing so in the belief that it will get better quality work from people who feel they are part of the company. All employees receive the same profit-sharing and health care. The only benefits that vary are bonuses, salaries, promotions and raises. These are based on merit, just as universities claim theirs to be. All of SAS's benefits extend to part-time as well as full-time employees.

The result is a privately held corporation that seeks to improve its bottom line by strengthening the morale of its employees and implementing innovative solutions. And SAS managers have the proof to justify their decisions: voluntary turnover is under 3 per cent a year. By keeping its turnover so low compared with other software companies, SAS has undoubtedly been able to save more money than it spends. 'You either are going to spend your money on headhunters and training,' Goodnight notes, 'or you could spend it taking care of the people you have' (Kirby, 2003, p. E1).

The example of SAS, of course, cannot be fully replicated across all of public higher education. Indeed, it is not even replicated across all private, for-profit corporations. Admittedly, some state legislators are likely to balk at the idea of office massages for employees. Still, the broadly progressive nature of SAS's approach to its employees is a reminder of what is required to recruit and retain quality employees in three areas: flexibility, equity and efficiency.

Flexibility

The changes underway in higher education are bound to affect the *who*, *what*, and *how* of the faculty's important tasks, of which teaching is one of the most significant. For the *who* of teaching, university leaders must recognize that as age, ethnic and gender demographics reshape higher education, higher education must respond in flexible ways. The key questions are not whether diversity is a good thing or whether it will occur; demographic trends are to some extent overwhelming ideological differences. The nation is headed towards a much more diverse student population and almost

certainly a much more diverse faculty. Scholarship is replete with studies that show the benefits of diversity in higher education, but the emphasis should also be on *how* to manage such diversity (Smith, 2000). There is considerable evidence that students from historically under-represented backgrounds will benefit from faculty drawn from those same backgrounds (Antonio, 2003). Change is already on the way. Less than two decades ago, white males made up 90 per cent of all full-time faculty. Today, women represent 38 per cent of full-time faculty (ACE, 2005b).

Ethnicity and age demographics will demand modifications to the *what* of teaching, as curriculum and human resource policies adapt to the burgeoning diversity of students and faculty alike. Technological advancements have and will continue to change *how* higher education delivers knowledge. New and promising technological teaching methods may well offer the opportunity to deliver more higher learning to populations not otherwise accessible through the traditional forms of delivery. While not the 'magic bullet' that Van Dusen (1998, p. 59) heralds in his analysis of technologically-delivered education, its 'just-in-time' qualities do mean that potentially more students can be accommodated. To do so, however, faculty will have to learn new pedagogical and delivery skills.

Despite the concerns with contingent faculty, there remain issues and opportunities for improving the lot of tenure-track faculty. Remaining also are compelling structural barriers to change. For example, tenure is a fact of business life; despite the on-again, off-again clamor for reform, it is unlikely to go away. There are issues surrounding promotion policies, probationary periods during pre-tenure years, and a lack of flexibility in employment options for retirement age faculty. Administrators are well-acquainted with roadblocks in the tenure process: ambiguous and contradictory criteria, conflicting messages between institutional rhetoric and actual reward structure, conflict between promotion and tenure processes and personal responsibilities, and structural barriers for women and people of color (ACE, 2005b). Scholars are calling for increased awareness of these problems, a national dialogue to address specific tenure-track issues, and manageable approaches to assist universities in implementing flexible solutions (ibid.).

Administrators would do well to consider flexible employment options for their full-time faculty members, whether on or off the tenure track. For example, there are work/life issues whose solutions respond to many of the significant changes in higher education. Flexibility in paid-leave policies, in response to pregnancy, family care and emergencies, is one strategy. The University of California system, faced with a surge in enrollments and a sizeable new round of faculty hires over the next decade, has taken a page from Goodnight's book in seeking to hire the best and brightest scholars to

its ranks (University of California, 2005). The UC Faculty Family Friendly Edge program is designed to assist tenure-track faculty, pre- and post-tenure, in achieving simultaneously satisfying and productive career and family experiences. The idea is to not let them become the enemies of one another. And the goal is to make the University of California an employer that takes account of the realities of a twenty-first century workforce, including a greater number of women entering the academy, more families with two spouses working and patterns of professional development different from those in the past.

Plans like those adopted by UC will help to ameliorate the pressing needs arising from gender and age diversity. As universities benefit from a stronger presence of women in their workforces, pregnancy and child-care needs threaten to slow progress or even prohibit women's inclusion. Scholars have examined the tension that still exists in higher education faculties between work, family and home roles. Too many women consider temporary leave for childbirth or family care to be detrimental to their careers and they opt for part-time or full-time, non-tenure-track positions. Interestingly, scholars have discovered that 55 per cent of women prefer full-time, non-tenure-track positions (Perna, 2001, p. 604). The choices almost certainly reflect the too-often inflexible options presently available to women in the higher education workforce. As the UC program demonstrates, inflexibility could be alleviated by active-service modifications that permit temporarily reduced workloads or leave without the loss of status. Also, administrators should consider policies that allow the tenure clock to stop, while extending probationary periods following childbirth or adoption (ACE, 2005b).

Flexible approaches can also make a difference in other ways. For example, higher education administrators who conduct post-tenure reviews to accommodate shifts in professional values and priorities and create and appoint integral institutional committees to address needed reform learn that administrative flexibility is a work in progress (ACE, 2005b). Flexible approaches must bear the stamp of being deliberate and consensual. Administrators who are too flexible or who apply change simply for the sake of change threaten to weaken institutional safeguards that protect employees and provide valuable stability. Nonetheless, administrations need flexible solutions when confronted with change or they risk institutional atrophy.

Equity

Equity in higher education administration, with all its connotations, is an essential principle. As with flexibility, administrators face problems of equity in the *who*, *what*, and *how* of higher education faculty employment.

To return to the issue of contingent faculty, universities today face a much greater issue of how to accommodate such faculty than they did only a few years ago. The *Chronicle of Higher Education* (2005, p. A8) reports that degree-granting institutions hired 60 000 more contingent faculty members in 2003 than they did in 2001. If you subscribe to the notion that a higher ratio of tenure to non-tenure-track positions is detrimental to the quality of higher education, this demonstrates flexibility run amok. If, however, employing contingent faculty represents one tool in a kit of instruments to respond to new challenges (like reduced funding and growing enrollments), then such faculty positions may in fact be helpful.

The accelerating rise in the 1990s of contingent faculty spawned profound issues of equity. Decreasing government appropriations and other funding sources during the 1980s and 1990s forced higher education administrators to look 'outside' their lists of traditional financial providers (NCES, 1997). Finding alternative funding sources was not enough, however. Since instructional costs represented the greatest single expenditure of higher education institutions, with by far the largest part consisting of faculty salaries, changes in faculty profiles could mean substantial savings for weary budget administrators. Consequently, as early as 1992, 42 per cent of higher education instructors were employed part-time (an increase of nearly 122 000 from 1987); meanwhile full-time instructors were becoming less satisfied with their increasing workloads (ibid.).

Necessity and desperation are unsteady guides to the best institutional decision making. As the *who* of faculty and students changed, so did the challenges faced by higher education administrators. Frequently, the *what* will appear as a logical solution (even flexible), but it poses its own inherent roadblocks. As a case in point, administrators are accused of using contingent faculty to limit the number of tenure-track positions at their institutions. Certainly the rise of contingent faculties was brought to bear during a budget crisis, but some feel state budgets are not entirely to blame (Todd, 2004, p. 17). Such a path of action makes sense in light of the fact that contingent faculty cost 33 per cent of an average tenure-track position (Schneider, 2004, p. 18). The cold numbers indicate significant cost savings to an institution by employing contingent instructors.

Such a scheme, however, may not be equitable for either the students or the contingent faculty teaching them. For example, from a student perspective, more contingent faculty members might be viewed as a threat to their higher education experience. Despite budget deficits and the presence of contingent faculty, students still deserve instructors (full- or part-time) able to offer quality teaching, student advising and counseling and innovative curricula. Administrators must weigh the effects that the bottom line will have on their most valuable asset, the students. Interestingly, some for-profit

institutions like the University of Phoenix (2005) market their contingent faculty as essential to their education paradigm. Part-time faculty who are also professionals in their fields of instruction offer students a more 'practical' or 'applied' education experience. Therefore the hiring of contingent faculty may well produce a more grounded educational experience, based on the careers of their instructors, than would otherwise be the case.

Several organizations have published recommendations (the *how*) for higher education administrators to direct toward contingent faculty. In an echo of SAS's approach, the American Federation of Teachers (AFT, 2002, p. 7) suggests fairness and equity standards for part-time faculty. They begin with recommendations for equitable compensation: part-time/adjunct teachers should be paid a salary proportionate to full-time, tenured faculty of the same qualifications for doing the same work. This includes pro-rated sick-leave and holiday pay, proportionate healthcare and retirement benefits, and even unemployment insurance when they are not on the institution's payroll. The AFT also recommends equitable employment standards, including a more professional and credible hiring process, job security after a probationary and evaluation period, freedom to design their own courses, and the right to develop a form of seniority and be considered a preference for full-time hiring (ibid., p. 9).

There is much work to be done to ensure equity in contingent faculty policies. Doing so, however, makes excellent sense in light of the simple fact that the morale and well-being of these faculty are essential to the success of the institutions that employ them. As Goodnight has reminded us, treating people well is the best way to enhance their performance.

The need for equity is important in another way. There is evidence that, from a student perspective, the use of contingent faculty may not be detrimental to the learning process. Toutkoushian and Bellas (2003), for example, empirically showed that most contingent faculty members are satisfied with their employment arrangements. Even though there are disproportionately more women than men as contingent faculty their employment seems to fill a need they have in their professional and personal lives. The positive findings underscore how important it is for institutions to develop equitable solutions that give more appropriate rewards and recognition to contingent faculty. Health benefits and equality of pay between men and women are two important recommendations (ibid., p. 192).

Equity in the treatment of all faculty is important in another way. A more diverse student body will benefit from a more representative and diverse faculty (Gater, 2005). Also, recognizing that women earn nearly half of the PhDs awarded today, while an increasingly significant number of elderly people rely on their children for their care, means work and life issues are (or soon will be) at the forefront of employee-related needs (NCES, 2005a).

The UC model is equitable because it is flexible. To address the problem of many women faculty members encountering difficulty reentering tenure-track positions after being out of the professoriate, the UC programs offer several different approaches, all of which emphasize equity. For example, equitable solutions to gender and family matters can include better paid-leave policies, a variety of workload options, and facilitating the movement into, out of and back into the tenure track.

Achieving equity in faculty employment practices requires an administrative revolution that balances the realities of demographic and social change with the academy's traditional emphasis on quality-tested peer review. Fortuitously, the reality of limited institutional funds opens the door to alternative employment practices. However, if institutions are to keep the best people, higher education employees, like SAS's employees, will expect the best and fairest treatment. Flexible options abound to address even the most sensitive employment challenges. Unfortunately, the threat of inequity seems never to have been as apparent in higher education as it does today.

Efficiency

The increasingly stringent public funding of higher education is likely to persist. The old adage, 'do more with less', seems eerily appropriate when describing higher education, even in the face of the reality that the ambitions of faculty and administrators always run beyond the available resources. However, perhaps it would be more effective to urge administrators to 'do *better* with less'. Considering the fiscal deprivations that higher education faces with increasing regularity, it would serve administrators little if their flexible and equitable options resulted in institutional inefficiency.

The SAS model suggests that efficiency, equity and flexibility are reinforcing rather than conflicting ideals. Efficiency means to act or produce effectively with a minimum amount of waste, expense and effort, along with a high ratio of output per unit of input. As the rising chorus of demands for greater accountability reminds us, efficiency is no longer either administratively or politically taboo. The *who* and the *how* are especially important to a dialogue of efficiency in higher education. The *who* addresses the question: is it possible for administrators to make more efficient human resource policies, rooted in career socialization and career completion? And can administrators find meaningful ways to enhance faculty productivity? The *how* focuses on the innovative tools increasingly at administrators' disposal to make higher education instruction more efficient.

A rising number of retirees combined with growing enrollments in many states will generate a new wave of hiring. How we handle not only the hiring

process but also the end-of-career issues for colleagues will become increasingly important, as a matter of both equity and efficiency. That means better policies and programs dealing with the front-end, middle and back-end of academic careers. At a time of scarce resources it might make sense, on first impression, to write off the fate of retirees. Doing so, however, would be a mistake, both for the former faculty and for the institution. Faculty members who feel secure in their status after leaving the full-time ranks are more likely to be productive when they are fully engaged.

At the front-end of careers, new faculty should be socialized in their responsibilities. Administrators should consider developing (or improving) faculty orientations designed to define professional responsibilities and expectations in an initial environment of support. New faculty members, eager to begin their jobs, should leave an orientation with a strong sense that their university strives to support them. And universities, for their part, should treat orientation as an on-going rather than a one-time, usually one-day, process. University and departmental handbooks, updated regularly, offer *when-needed* reminders or clarifications of institutional policies and reminders of administrative support. New faculty members will also benefit from effective mentoring and support networks. The American Council on Education (ACE, 2005b, p. 10) recommends offering incentives to faculty members to develop 'more collegial environments', for guiding, collaborating with and mentoring colleagues.

Effective mid-career policies will add efficiency by enhancing faculty productivity. First, in some instances, administrators should tackle the difficult task of teaching loads. One approach is to ask colleagues with less productive research careers to teach more hours, while offering more productive researchers fewer student contact hours. Such a scheme, however, often means that the best researchers have less access to students, especially undergraduate students. Still, it is difficult for an overworked or overwhelmed faculty member to perform efficiently either as a teacher or a researcher. Institutional research leaves can also be valuable aids to productivity. Such leaves not only encourage scholarship but also allow a faculty member to devote themselves full-time to research activities. In addition to research leaves, administrators can create an environment that encourages interdisciplinary research. Faculty members can be reminded that some of the best scholarship in higher education is taking place at their own institution. Research grants provide the necessary funding to undergird research leaves and research collaboration. In the areas of mathematics, science, engineering and social sciences the National Science Foundation alone funds approximately 11 000 research, education and training projects a year (NSF, 2005). Administrators would also do well to provide their faculties institutional research grant support – to teach

faculty members the ins and outs of grant writing and research. Such practices help new and mid-career faculty members maintain positions on the cutting edge of scholarship and improve morale and job satisfaction. The valuable resources that administrators need to implement such solutions are frequently already part of their institution. It takes an administration cued into its faculty to recognize and tap into the existing pool of talent.

Faculty members can also be more efficient in their careers and more equitably treated if they have confidence in the back-end career decisions they will need to make. Administrators should consider developing phased retirement programs which would allow professors to continue teaching and conducting research on a part-time basis (for a limited number of years) in return for the understanding that at the end of that period they will leave the faculty. Such a scheme makes it possible to plan for new hires while treating departing colleagues with dignity informed by flexibility. And retired faculty need to know that, if they wish, they can provide valuable support to new faculty and engage new students. At the University at Albany, for example, emeritus faculty participate as leaders of a semester-long, university-wide discussion on common books. Using retired faculty in this way strengthens the intellectual community, pays appropriate homage to the years of experience that colleagues develop and acknowledges that there are different ways to contribute to the institution at different times in a career (ACE, 2005b, p. 11). Similarly, a faculty emeritus center can give retiring colleagues the hope of staying in contact with their university while having a place to work.

Technological innovations provide promising opportunities to produce a more efficient learning environment, for both the students and the faculty. Technology is permeating the very heart of higher education's mission. While hardly the magic bullet it was represented to be a decade ago, technology remains an important way of increasing faculty productivity and extending the impact of higher education to new audiences. Consider the Sloan Consortium's (2005) report that over 1.6 million students took at least one online course in fall 2002 and this will grow at a rate of 20 per cent per annum. The new technologies make it possible for busy, place-bound learners and others to make the best use of their time. Technology's impact is far from reaching its peak, not just on students but also on faculty.

The logical use of technology in higher education is to reach the greatest number of students in the most efficient way possible. Online courses, electronic reading reserves, online worksite programs and even electronic discussion boards broaden higher education's reach to the homes, job-sites and personal computers of a variety of post-secondary students. Van Dusen (1998, p. 64) found that fewer than half of US colleges and universities have a strategic plan for technology and fewer than a third have

a financial plan. Technology plans should be viewed as faculty-use plans, not just documents about what software and hardware to adopt. In fact, most of the existing technology plans are short on how to better use the human capital required to make a success of the new learning strategies. Without such planning, it will be impossible to ascertain what technology can and cannot do and what its true costs are, both financial and professional. Before the question of affordability can be answered, these issues must be resolved.

The implications of technology for faculty employment practices are provocative. A few brief examples will suffice. Technology has given human resource personnel efficient ways to communicate with and instruct their higher education faculty compatriots. Likewise, faculties have more efficient ways to communicate with each other – facilitating a more close-knit institutional community. E-mail has become ubiquitous; students now expect instructors to respond to queries that come outside the classroom and office hours. In theory, such communication should drive greater productivity and, ironically, bring student and faculty members closer together. Also, new faculty members and retirees are able to stay 'in tune' with the day-to-day administrative network of ideas, policies and events. Technology makes employment and communication available to a more diverse faculty – removing the barriers of disability, for example.

Efficiency is only as good as it is weighed against the other essential principles of flexibility and equity. For example, when technological solutions are provided for only full-time, tenure-track faculty members it does little to support the growing number of contingent instructors teaching at universities. Limiting the benefits afforded to contingent instructors or constraining tenure-track options might be the most fiscally efficient way to administer higher education, but is not the most equitable and, in the SAS sense, it is also not efficient in general. Flexible human resource policies might seem to be expensive perks to administrators, but companies like SAS prove how efficient employees can be when administrators invest in meeting their needs.

CONCLUSION

Seeking balance in the treatment of faculty will require, as the SAS model tantalizingly suggests, more than business as usual. As the new age of accountability in higher education emerges, one of the important, but not exclusive, measures of its performance should be its ability to nourish the human capital represented in the faculty. The task is to fashion an environment in which bright, talented, committed and diverse individuals can

flourish, whether part- or full-time. An environment marked by flexibility and equity can also be, as the SAS example reminds us, an efficient environment. The UC Family Friendly programs offer a way forward. Such an approach seems more rather then less important in an age when higher education commentators openly invoke Dickensian and atmospheric metaphors. Rebuilding the social contract for public higher education means that taking care of the people in the institutions is the first, not the last, step in restoring balance amidst the turmoil of unrelenting change.

REFERENCES

AFT Higher Education (2002), *Fairness and Equity: Blue Print for Quality*, available at www.aft.org/pubs-reports/higher_ed/standards_pt_adjunct.pdf, visited 25 November 2005.

American Association of University Professors (AAUP) (2004), *Don't Blame Faculty for High Tuition: the Annual Report of the Economic Status of the Profession*, available at www.aaup.org/surveys/zrep.htm, visited 12 December 2005.

American Association of University Professors (AAUP) (2005), *Background Facts on Contingent Faculty*, available at www.aaup.org/Issues/part-time/Ptfacts.htm, visited 23 November 2005.

American Council on Education (ACE) (2005a), *An Agenda for Excellence: Creating Flexibility in Tenure-Track Faculty Careers – Executive Summary*, available at www.acenet.edu/bookstore/pdf/2005_tenure_flex_summary.pdf, visited 23 November 2005.

American Council on Education (ACE) (2005b), *Creating Options: Models for Flexible Faculty Career Pathways*, available at www.acenet.edu/AM/Template.cfm?Section=OWHE&Template=/CM/HTMLDisplay.cfm&ContentID=5663, visited 23 November 2005.

Antonio, A. (2003), 'Diverse student bodies, diverse faculties', *Academe*, **89** (6), 14–17.

Baldwin, R.G. and J.L. Chronister (2001), *Teaching Without Tenure: Policies and Practices for a New Era*, Baltimore, MD and London, UK: Johns Hopkins University Press.

Benjamin, E. (2002), 'How over reliance on contingent appointments diminishes faculty involvement in student learning', *Peer Review*, **5** (1), 4–11.

Birnbaum, J.H. and S. Freeman (2005), 'Automakers are lining up aid, but just don't call it a bailout', *The Washington Post*, (4 December), A1.

Chronicle of Higher Education (2005), 'More faculty jobs go to part-timers', *Chronicle of Higher Education*, **51** (39).

Ehrenberg, R.G. (forthcoming), 'The perfect storm and the privatization of public higher education', *Change*.

Field, K. (2005a), 'Education-Department panel will develop a "National Strategy" for Higher Education', *Chronicle of Higher Education*, (30 September), A29.

Field, K. (2005b), 'Federal Panel on Higher Education appears likely to call for testing of college students', *Chronicle of Higher Education*, (9 December), available at http://chronicle.com/daily/2005/12/2005120902n.htm.

Gappa, J.M. (1996), 'Off the tenure track: six models for full-time, nontenurable appointment', *New Pathways: Faculty Careers and Employment for the 21st*

Century, Inquiry 10, Washington, DC: American Association for Higher Education.

Gater, L. (2005), 'Human capital: diverse faculty reflects diverse world', *University Business*, (March), available at www.universitybusiness.com/page.cfm?p=750, visited 25 November 2005.

Hebel, S. (2003), 'Public colleges emphasize research, but the public wants a focus on students', *Chronicle of Higher Education*, (2 May), A14.

Holub, T. (2003), *Contract Faculty in Higher Education. ERIC Digest*, Washington, DC: ERIC Clearing House on Higher Education, ED482556, available at www.eric.ed.gov/ERICDocs/data/ericdocs 2/content_storage_01/0000000b/80/2a/3b/06.pdf, visited 3 December 2005.

Kane, T.J. and P.R. Orszag, (2003), *Funding Restrictions at Public Universities: Effects and Policy Implications*, Brookings Institution working paper, (September), Washington, DC: Brookings Institution.

Kirby, C. (2003), 'Jim Goodnight: private company pampers workers', *San Francisco Chronicle*, (19 May), E1.

Levering, R. and M. Moskowitz (2005), 'The 100 best companies to work for', *Fortune*, **51** (2), 61–90.

Longanecker, D. (2004), 'A Tale of Two Pities: the story of public support for higher education in the Pacific Northwest and the US', presentation given at the Annual Conference of the Pacific Northwest Association for Institutional Research and Planning, Western Interstate Commission on Higher Education, 14 October, available at www.wiche.edu/PPT/BC-PNAIRP-TaleofTwoPities-10-04.pdf, visited 12 December 2005.

Morrison, J.L. (2003), 'U.S. Higher Education in Transition', *On the Horizon*, **11** (1), 6–10, available at http://horizon.unc.edu/courses/papers/InTransition.asp, visited 23 November 2005.

Nasser, H.E. (2000), 'Census predicts ethnic face of nation in 100 years', *USA Today*, (13 January), News section, 3A.

National Census Bureau (2002), *National Population Projections, Summary Files*, Washington, DC: US Census Bureau, Population Division, Population Projections Branch, available at www.census.gov/population/www/projections/natsum-T3.html, visited 22 November 2005.

National Center for Education Statistics (NCES) (1997), *Statistical Analysis Report: Instructional Faculty and Staff in Higher Education Institutions: Fall 1987 and Fall 1992*, Washington, DC: US Government Printing Office, US Department of Education, National Center for Education Statistics, available at http://nces.ed.gov/pubs 97/web/97470.asp, visited 23 November 2005.

National Center for Education Statistics (NCES) (2003), 'Section 2: Enrollment in degree granting institutions', *Projection of Education Statistics to 2013*, Washington, DC: US Government Printing Office, US Department of Education, National Center for Education Statistics, available at http://nces.ed.gov/programs/projections/ch_2.asp, visited 22 November 2005.

National Center for Education Statistics (NCES) (2005a), 'Indicator 25: degrees conferred', *Youth Indicators, 2005: Trends in the Well-being of American Youth*, Washington, DC: US Government Printing Office, US Department of Education, National Center for Education Statistics, available at http://nces.ed.gov/programs/youthindicators/Indicators.asp?PubPageNumber=25, visited 25 November 2005.

National Center for Education Statistics (NCES) (2005b), *Projections of Education Statistics to 2014*, Washington, DC: US Government Printing Office, US Department of Education, available at http://nces.ed.gov/pubs 2005/2005074.pdf, visited 22 November 2005.

National Science Foundation (NSF) (2005), 'About funding', available at www.nsf.gov/funding/aboutfunding.jsp, visited 23 November 2005.

Parsad, B. and D. Glover (2002), 'Tenure status of post secondary instructional faculty and staff: 1992–1998', *Education Statistics Quarterly*, **4** (3), National Center For Education Statistics, US Department of Education, available at http://nces.ed.gov/programs/quarterly/vol_4/4_3/4_7.asp, visited 3 December 2005.

Perna, Laura W. (2001), 'The relationship between family responsibilities and employment status among college and university faculty', *Journal of Higher Education*, **72** (5), 584–611.

Schneider, J.M. (2004), 'Employing adjunct faculty from an HR perspective', *Phi Kappa Phi Forum*, **84** (4), 18.

Sloan Consortium (2005), *Sizing the Opportunity: the Quality and Extent of Online Education in the United States, 2002 and 2003*, available at www.sloan-c.org/resources/overview.asp, visited on 25 November 2005.

Smith, D.G. (2000), 'How to diversify the faculty', *Academe Online*, **86** (5), available at www.aaup.org/publications/Academe/2000/00so/SO00Smit.htm, visited 23 November 2005.

Todd, J.G. (2004), 'Adjunct faculty: a crisis of justice in higher education', *Phi Kappa Phi Forum*, **84** (4), 17–18.

Toutkoushian, R.K. and M.L. Bellas (2003), 'The effects of part-time employment and gender on faculty earnings and satisfaction: evidence from the NSOPF: 93', *Journal of Higher Education*, **74** (2), 172–95.

University of California (2005), *Faculty Family Friendly Edge: an Initiative for Tenure-Track Faculty at the University of California, Report*, February, available at http://ucfamilyedge.berkeley.edu/ucfamilyedge.pdf.

University of Phoenix (2005), 'About us – our faculty', available at www.phoenix.edu/about_us/our_faculty/, visited 23 November 2005.

Van Dusen, Gerald C. (1998), 'Technology: higher education's magic bullet', *NEA Higher Education Journal*, (Spring), available at www2.nea.org/he/heta98/s98pg59.pdf, visited 23 November 2005, 59–67.

World Conference on Higher Education (1998), *World Declaration on Higher Education for the Twenty-First Century: Vision and Action*, 9 October, available at www.unesco.org/education/educprog/wche/declaration_eng.htm.

Yudof, M. (2002), 'Is the public research university dead?', *Chronicle of Higher Education*, (11 January), B24, available at http://chronicle.com/weekly/v48/i18/18b02401.htm.

11. Socrates, Thoreau and the status quo

Cathy A. Trower

The three primary themes of this volume are enhancing revenues, evolving faculty contracts and implementing change. The authors use an assortment of metaphors to describe the current state of higher education, from Stan Ikenberry's tightrope, on which administrators are trying to balance student access with issues of tuition charges and cost control, to David Kirp's inner tube heading down a class five river, with regard to new technologies, to James Hearn's frog in a pot of water heated up so slowly that it does not realize that it is boiling until it is too late, with regard to incremental change toward becoming commercial enterprises. In my assessment, a more appropriate metaphor might be a glacier: universities do move, but they move so slowly that change is almost imperceptible; they move only of their own accord and en masse; and they pursue the path of least resistance.

The authors of the various chapters are all over the map as to whether or not there is a 'crisis' in higher education and they cover a lot of ground in terms of possible responses. David Kirp has described the 'problematic successes' of colleges that have transformed themselves through technology or by adopting a business model; problematic because, while there is a place for the market, 'the market must be kept in its place' (economist Arthur Okun) and, presumably, because

> embedded in the very idea of the university . . . the university at its truest and best – are values that the market does not honor: the belief in a community of scholars and not a confederacy of self-seekers; in the idea of openness and not ownership; in the professor as a pursuer of truth and not an entrepreneur; in the student as an acolyte whose preferences are to be formed, not a consumer whose preferences are to be satisfied. (Kirp, 2003, p. 7)

And yet the downside of a community of scholars shut off from market forces is insularity; the flipside of autonomy is isolation. Without the market, where is accountability? 'Academic freedom is a widely shared value; academic duty, which ought to count for as much, is mysterious' (Kennedy, 1997, p. 2).

The topic of revenues and spending is examined in many of the chapters. James Hearn (Chapter 3), citing economist and college president, Howard Bowen, points out that

> leaders continually seek funding growth because they operate under a 'revenue theory of cost': new revenues are always being sought in order to pursue excellence, prestige, and influence. Because there is no limit to what might be spent in pursuit of those goals, institutions will always raise and spend all the money that they can.

Authors lament (Ehrenberg) or support (Sexton) the use of adjunct and full-time non-tenure-stream faculty. Ehrenberg effectively argues that substituting these non-traditional faculty for tenure-track and tenured faculty has enormous costs in terms of student interest in doctoral work (Ehrenberg, 2005) and retention, which may not be offset by lower salaries and benefits (see Chapter 8).

Sexton, on the other hand, as president of NYU – a 'university in and of the city' – writes that this institution would be remiss if it did *not* employ large numbers of adjuncts, given the depth and breadth of expertise in the NYC area, NYU's mission and its students. Sexton suggests that the academy should rethink how it distributes shame and honor. He comes close, at least to my mind, to stabbing (but not slaying) the sacred tenure cow, although that may not have been his intent. Sexton (2004) carefully highlighted the role of the tenured faculty at research universities, as well as 'five broad categories of faculty, by and large outside the tenure system' (university teachers, arts professors, adjunct faculty, global professors and cyber faculty), and concluded thus:

> In short, we must encourage, draw on, respect and reward an appropriate blend of faculty actors . . . This will be a foundation of the new research university, creating a culture of institutional citizenship that honors equality of voice and the role of all members of the community. The notion of faculty governance, which will characterize this university, does not entail faculty literally running the institution and goes far beyond mere consultation. It entails instead meaningful inclusion of all faculty in a discussion of institutional priorities, conducted in a way that enables them to balance the variables and complexities of decision making. It entails a commitment by university leadership to conference ideas with faculty in a transparent process that empowers them to participate meaningfully in shaping both aspirations and strategies.

Throughout this volume, authors address the necessity of involving the faculty in conversations about strategy, new revenue sources, cost control, access and productivity, but producing real and lasting change will be enormously difficult, for reasons I shall now address.

Let us turn this discussion on its head for a moment. What would have had to happen for the following to be the central questions that are addressed in this volume?

- Why are the faculty so obsessed with student performance that their research is lagging?
- Why will faculty not allow the administration to wrest control of advising and turn it over to a central office?
- How do we get the best faculty out of the classroom and into the lab?
- How can we interest tenured professors in teaching something other than large, introductory courses to freshmen?
- Why are most of the tenured professors, especially in science, maths, technology and engineering, white women and persons of color? What happened to all the white men?
- How can we get the faculty senate to focus on the details of its own welfare rather than the keys to a successful undergraduate education?

What would have had to happen is for the academy to have done a 180° turn. If these were the questions, we would not recognize this enterprise. We are as likely to see the day when these questions are addressed as we are to see pigs fly, and for good reason.

If these were the questions the academy was addressing, would you be of a mind that the academy was a much better place than it is today? Would there be any market advantage in behaving differently?

We know that most faculty at research universities do not take a great deal of interest in undergraduate education, prefer to conduct research rather than to advise students, yearn for the lab over the classroom and favor teaching small, graduate courses over large, introductory ones. We know that the numbers of women and minorities in the tenured ranks at the most prestigious universities are stagnant at best, and virtually nonexistent at worst. We know the agendas for most faculty meetings are apt to be focused inward rather than out, and to cover minutiae affecting the faculty themselves rather than cost control, finding new revenue streams or institutional strategy.

It does not take any deep, penetrating insight to say that excellence in undergraduate education, diversity, equity and cost control are important priorities to pursue, or to acknowledge that our colleges and universities are facing vast changes. In late October 2005, I read that 'Harvard . . . is facing unprecedented change and new challenges brought about by the growth of interdisciplinary fields, the explosion of information technology, the desire of students and faculty to engage globally, and a spate of new government regulations' (*Harvard University Gazette*, 2005, p. 3).

And yet, I ask you, are any of these really unexpected or completely unpredictable? Why do we almost always seem to be reactive rather than proactive? Presumably, some really smart people work at Harvard who had to have seen these things coming. Why the apparent shock about the fact that the 'intellectual landscape is being redefined'? One answer is that we are structured in a way that practically ensures business as usual. We have structured intentional continuity.

Universities are mired in the status quo because of an entrenched culture where it is nearly impossible to do business differently and a market that says, 'Why would you want to?' I have four primary points that, I believe, lie behind status quo maintenance and that make me less than optimistic about the academy's ability to respond to a changed environment:

1. Tenure shields faculty from the vicissitudes of the marketplace.
2. Shared governance shields faculty from leadership.
3. Decisions happen by accretion because of decentralization and loose coupling.
4. The market is saying that nothing is wrong.

Those who may want change – 'intentional leaders' (Shaw, 2005) who want to lead – and those who may be in the best position to carry out the work of the new university in the global community in the twenty-first century – junior faculty – have little power.

Why is change the exception in the academy? We have deeply held rules, beliefs and values embedded in the culture of the dominant coalition, which wishes to preserve its power base at almost any cost and operates largely in its own best interest, with little understanding of, or interest in, the university writ large.

> Men have become the tools of their tools. (Henry David Thoreau)

What are the rules that govern our faculty and, thus, our institutions? *Tenure*. We have institutionalized a promotion, tenure and reward structure designed by and for white men of a bygone era that perpetuates the status quo because it favors basic over applied research and research over teaching and community service, uses peer review methods proven to be fraught with cronyism and even bias (or, if you prefer, 'cognitive errors') (Moody, 2005) and ensures allegiance to disciplines by supporting narrow research within disciplines over that which crosses boundaries, conformity over innovation, and solo over collaborative work. In the minds of the dominant coalition, there is and always has been a 'right' way to

conduct research, the 'right' methods and even the 'right' journals in which to publish results.

Many tenured, senior faculty are loath to teach and provide service, and for good reason. 'Senior professors in great demand often insist on modest teaching loads. Their reputation, their bankable asset, depends on what they write, not how they teach' (Kirp, 2003, p. 69). The way we train doctoral students and socialize junior faculty feeds this mentality. Kennedy (1997, p. 30) highlighted the issue for doctoral students:

> Too often, little attention is given to the teaching responsibilities that doctoral students will have later . . . Faculty members-in-training receive little or no preparation for the range of personal and professional challenges they will face as practicing members of the professoriate. The vast majority of academic doctorates are produced in fewer than one hundred 'research universities', but 90 per cent of them will teach in several thousand institutions that are quite different from the places in which they were trained.

Regarding junior faculty, Kennedy noted, 'Young faculty, whether as candidates for junior positions or as aspirants at the tenure bar, are regularly urged to concentrate on research and, if necessary, skimp on teaching' (ibid.). The late Ernest Boyer, former Vice President of the Carnegie Foundation for the Advancement of Teaching, said, 'Winning the campus distinguished teaching award is the kiss of death when it comes time for tenure'. This relationship made headlines in The Tech at MIT in the early 1990s when the Baker Teaching Award was announced and several winners of the award who were assistant professors were denied tenure. The lack of rewards for teaching excellence is also described as 'Teaching excellence is a perishable commodity', in medical schools by Aron et al. (2000, p. 1) on the basis of an empirical study.

In the relentless quest for individual and institutional prestige there is, naturally, a relative indifference to efficiency as any component of strategy (and even to strategy, for that matter). 'Not only research but most activities in the university are carried out by individuals working on their own . . . The work of the university is left almost entirely in individual hands' (Damrosch, 1995, p. 57). This may be why William T. Foster, then president of Reed College, said, 'The progress of this institution . . . will be directly proportional to the death rate of the [tenured] faculty' (quoted in Birnbaum, 2004, p. 60), and a tenured professor at a major research university recently quipped during a retreat on the strategic plan, 'I and every one of my tenured colleagues *is* a strategic plan!'

> Let him that would move the world first move himself. (Socrates)

My second point is that *shared governance* shields faculty from unilateral, centralized decision making. Presidents have little power to control, move, or change institutions; so do deans and chairs. 'There are too many stakeholders who can block change, and almost no one who can legitimately drive it' (Cohen, 2003, personal copy, p. 16).

Highly decentralized authority is the norm (Damrosch, 1995, p. 59). Academic institutions have been described as organized anarchies, whereby we discover preferences through action more often than we act on the basis of preferences, we learn more often by trial and error and the residue of learning from the accidents of past experiences, imitation and the inventions born of necessity, and we have fluid participation in decision-making arenas (Cohen and March, 1974).

In organized anarchies, decision making through shared governance happens according to a garbage can model where 'issues just keep getting thrown in' and the 'weightiest tend to sink out of sight, and only the most insistently recycled or lightest matters receive any actual attention'. Further, the 'items that do end up on top tend to get mixed together in unpredictable ways' (Damrosch, 1995, p. 59, quoting from Cohen et al., 1972).

> Faculties are . . . composed largely of people who like problems, perhaps even more than solutions, and even to the point of actively seeking them where they have not been recognized. Indeed, some of these individuals positively dislike solutions, preferring the deeper existential absurdity of the problem itself. (Adams, 1988, p. 11)

> The tendency for nothing ever to get decided on a campus reflects the extreme diffusion of authority within the system. With little or no direction coming from the top, the university bureaucracy really works as an antibureaucracy, whose ideal is to allow the greatest possible number of individuals to pursue their own private interests with the least possible interaction. (Damrosch, 1995, p. 59)

All too often, in practice, shared governance is just another term for 'death by faculty senate'. Increased institutional size and complexity, the division of faculty into departments and committees, the presence of external funding and control agencies that bypass and weaken institutional administration combine in such a way that 'individuals and groups lose their ability to affect their institution through the implementation of positive or constructive programs, [so] they increasingly tend to assert their influence and status by acting as veto blocs, thus increasing institutional conservatism' (Birnbaum, 1988, p. 15). When all is said and done, it is in senate committee that we can kill most ideas to do things differently, in part because 'The status quo is the only solution that cannot be vetoed' (Kerr, 1982, p. 30).

This leads to my third point: *decentralization and loose coupling*. If decisions are made, they are more often than not made by accretion and so are not really decisions for which anyone can be held responsible. I wrote a piece (Trower, 2003) about the huge increase in part-time and non-tenure-track faculty, where I surmised that there was no central decision to reduce the percentage of tenured faculty on any given campus to 25 per cent and expand the other lines accordingly. But nor has any president or any faculty said, 'This far and no further' or, 'Henceforth, all introductory courses will be taught by senior, tenured faculty. Too much research is being conducted here and undergraduate education is being neglected.'

> . . . the larger institution may become an academic holding company, presiding over a federation of quasi-autonomous subunits. Unable to influence the larger institution, faculty retreat into the small subunit for which they feel affinity and from which they can defend their influence and status. (Birnbaum, 1988, p. 17)

This further perpetuates status quo maintenance.

Another characteristic of our organized anarchy academic institutions is loose coupling, meaning that connections between organizational subsystems (for example, academic departments, schools) are infrequent, circumscribed, unimportant and slow to respond (Weick, 1976). Loose coupling makes it difficult to discard bad ideas or disseminate good ones throughout an institution, repair defective systems, coordinate activities and use administrative functions to effect change (Birnbaum, 1988, p. 42).

Finally, there really is *no market pressure* to do anything differently. In a nutshell, there is no crisis. In every industry, there are rule makers, rule takers and rule breakers (Hamel and Prahalad, 1994). Rule makers are well served by preserving the status quo. To the extent that there is a market, it responds most favorably to the rule makers. In the main, money flows to the rule makers.

Rule takers are not in an advantaged position. These are the Ivy League 'wannabes' who follow the rules of the rule makers and systematically try to catch the present market leaders (for example, climb in the *US News & World Report* rankings, experience mission creep as teaching institutions attempt to mimic research universities, the amenities arms race), but never succeed in catching them. These institutions practice institutional isomorphism (DiMaggio and Powell, 1991), whereby organizations strive to resemble others with the same set of circumstances. However, 'A lot of time lost in benchmarking does not solve the problem. What is profitable is to be a rule breaker, and reinvent the industry' (Hamel, 1996). In academe, for the most part, rule breakers (for example, the University of Phoenix) are the worst off in terms of the dominant coalition's entrenched rules; they

are the lowest in the food chain (in the market, however, they are eating our lunch!).

On the faculty, those with tenure are the rule makers, probationary faculty are the rule takers and there are no rule breakers. There are only the unloved, underpaid and untenured – the part-time and non-tenure-track faculty – who have to play by an entirely different set of rules if they want to play at all.

Yet we constantly remind ourselves that this is a collegial 'community of scholars'. And the fact is that it is this collegium that chooses to do business this way. It is very difficult for leaders to overturn any of this by saying that we are disserving undergraduates or persons of color or women in science or early career faculty with young children.

We could look at the Harvard President Summers situation as a case in point. Apparently Mr Summers was hired to bring Harvard into the twenty-first century; he was meant to be a catalyst for change. And so he asked a lot of questions of the faculty. Those questions, in part, were said to have driven out Cornel West; several other prominent African-American scholars left thereafter. Earlier Summers had angered many with his remarks about innate differences between men and women in science. He angered Native Americans in a speech prior to that. The faculty voted no confidence, but the corporation is backing Summers, who apologized profusely and seems to have all but faded into the woodwork. Despite the controversy, people are not leaving Harvard in droves. The endowment stands at nearly $26 billion. Harvard had record enrollments this year. Harvard is still recruiting outstanding faculty. This can only happen in the academy, where markets function quite differently from those in the private sector.

> To appreciate the sheer strangeness of his [Summers'] situation, imagine the reaction of the CEO of a business firm, and his board of directors, if after the CEO criticized one of the firm's executives for absenteeism, ascribed the under representation of women in the firm's executive ranks to preferences rather than discrimination, dealt in peremptory fashion with the firm's employees, and refused to share decision-making powers with them, was threatened with a vote of no confidence by the employees. He and his board would tell them to go jump in the lake. (Becker, 2005)

Would not transformational change require a much deeper cultural change, to reward structures, to tenure, yes, but also, much deeper, to whether or not the faculty should be the primary architects of the terms and conditions of their own employment?

Faculty determine process, criteria and standards because that has worked in the past. It has been exceedingly difficult to get to issues of the numbers of full-time non-tenure-track or part-time faculty and the effects

on undergraduate retention and success. The faculty do not – and, apparently, will not – 'own' this problem. As Kirp (2003, p. 86) wrote, the 'professors who unhesitatingly protest the working conditions of janitors in LA and picket companies like Nike for their treatment of pieceworkers in Indonesia have generally been mute about the plight of these not-quite members of the academy'.

Can you construct a circumstance under which the faculty would take responsibility for improving graduation rates or student retention? The same faculty who see themselves as the owner of the promotion and tenure process are unlikely to say that they are the owner of inadequate undergraduate education. You could probably get a few people organized around that but not many. Can you construct a circumstance under which the faculty would say, 'No more part-time and non-tenure-track faculty. We will teach those classes'?

The trade-off for having a highly democratic institution is that, in the absence of market induced crises, you have to accept this. If you believe there is a crisis, it is self-imposed, and, to reiterate President Kermit Hall's point, can something twenty years in the making appropriately be called a 'crisis'? Students certainly are not asking, 'How many of your faculty are full-time versus part-time, non-tenure-track versus tenured?' and their parents are not saying, 'Our children will not attend your university unless you guarantee they will be taught by tenured faculty.'

Imagine an institution that has unquestionably solved most of these problems. It has a 100 per cent graduation rate and a dedicated full-time faculty committed to undergraduate education. You have Williams College. It already exists and it is doing really well. There is high student satisfaction and there are manageable costs. But what if it could be said that the greatest learning gains were made at Coe College in Cedar Rapids, Iowa? In addition, students graduate from Coe with full preparedness to work in a diverse environment. What percentage of market share would Coe College grab from institutions higher than them in the marketplace? Would faculty migrate to Cedar Rapids to be part of all that?

When all is said and done, as I look around, what is really remarkable is what has stayed the same, not what has changed.

Imagine that a faculty member who died in 1950 came back in 2005. What would he find astonishing? Very little. He would not say he did not recognize this enterprise. The rules of the game would not have changed so much that he would not recognize the game. The tenured faculty are still in their labs or teaching boutique classes. The most prestigious institutions are still the most prestigious. The faculty at these institutions is still comprised mostly of white males. And many of the same issues are probably still in play at faculty meetings.

The dominant coalition is saying that this works, and there is little market evidence to the contrary. There are no conspicuous failures. Students are still flocking to our doors. Faculty are still signing on. The numbers of women and faculty of color are not that different after 35 years of Affirmative Action, because the dominant coalition on any given campus cannot conceptualize, let alone implement, an appointment, promotion, tenure and reward system that is constructed for a new workforce – one that is demographically different, yes, but, perhaps even more importantly, one that has different values, beliefs and preferences.

For 200 years, no one really challenged the fact that women did not vote, because it worked. For 200 years, no one really challenged the fact that women did the domestic work and men worked outside the home, because it worked.

The academy is blessedly free of crises and, thus, continues on its tried and true course of intentional continuity. In the words of Frederick Rudolph, formerly Professor of History at Williams College:

> Assemble a cluster of professors in a county town, surround them with scenic grandeur, cut them off from the world beyond, and they will not have much trouble congratulating themselves into curricular torpor. Let someone knock on the door with a vision of change, he will discover that access is blocked by those within the gate. Let him argue on behalf of some perceived need or desire of students, and he will discover his mistake: The institution is really not for the students, after all, but for the professors. (Birnbaum, 2004, p. 62)

The academy has intentional continuity that has, thus far, served it well. In fact,

> . . . nearly every aspect of the university has a long product life cycle and is associated with a high 'regret function.' The immediate consequence is that it is difficult to envision a new or radically altered condition, and the eventual result is a set of policies and practices that favor the present state of affairs over any possible future. It is a portrait of conservatism, perhaps of senescence. (Kennedy, 1997, p. 272)

> It is never too late to give up your prejudices. (Henry David Thoreau)

Difficult as it is, I do envision a future academic enterprise:

- that reinvents itself;
- where rule makers become rule breakers and where rule breakers succeed;
- that spends more time creating its future than defending its past (Hamel and Valikangas, 2003, p. 54).

- where, if tenure is preserved, it may be earned not only through research but also by excellence in teaching and by being actively involved in the community – by making a difference;
- where shared governance means that everyone on campus with a stake in this enterprise works together, continually, to improve what we do, to periodically look backward together to see what worked well and what did not and discuss why, and to look forward to construct a better future;
- where leaders – among the faculty, the study body, the board, the alumni and the administration – can actually lead, dare I say, intentionally;
- that is authentic; it rewards what it says it values and its leaders and faculty at all levels mirror the rich diversity of our world.

In the words of inventor Buckminster Fuller, 'You never change things by fighting the existing reality. To change something, build a new model that makes the existing model obsolete.' Perhaps it is time for a new model.

REFERENCES

Adams, H. (1988), *The Academic Tribes*, 2nd edn, Urbana, IL: University of Illinois Press.

Aron, D.C., J.N. Aucott and K.K. Papp (2000), 'Teaching awards and reduced departmental longevity: kiss of death or kiss goodbye? What happens to excellent clinical teachers in a research intensive medical school', *Medical Education Online*, **5** (3), available at www.med-ed-online.org.

Becker, G. (2005), 'The Summers controversy and university governance', *The Becker-Posner Blog*, (27 February), available at www.becker-posner-blog.com.

Birnbaum, R. (1988), *How Colleges Work: the Cybernetics of Academic Organization and Leadership*, San Francisco, CA: Jossey-Bass Publishers.

Birnbaum, R. (2004), *Speaking of Higher Education*, Westport, CT: Greenwood Publishing Group.

Cohen, A.R. (2003), 'Transformational change at Babson College: notes from the firing line', *The Academy of Management Learning and Education Journal*, **2** (2), 155–80.

Cohen, M.D. and J.G. March (1974), *Leadership and Ambiguity: the American College President*, Boston, MA: Harvard Business School Press.

Cohen, M.D., J.G. March and J. Olsen (1972), 'A garbage can model of organizational choice', *Administrative Science Quarterly*, (17), 1–25.

Damrosch, D. (1995), *We Scholars: Changing the Culture of the University*, Cambridge, MA: Harvard University Press.

DiMaggio, P.J. and W.W. Powell (1991), 'The iron cage revisited: institutional isomorphism and collective rationality in organizational fields', in W.W. Powell and P.J. DiMaggio (eds), *The New Institutionalism in Organizational Analysis*, Chicago, IL: University of Chicago Press, pp. 63–82.

Ehrenberg, R.G. (2005), 'Involving undergraduates in research to encourage them to undertake Ph.D. study in economics', *Perspectives on Research and Teaching in Economics*, **95** (2), 1884–8.

Hamel, G. (1996), 'Jorge Nascimento Rodriguez with Gary Hamel, 1996', interview, available at http://gurusonline.tv/uk/conteudos/hamel.asp.

Hamel, G. and C.K. Prahalad (1994), *Competing for the Future*, Boston, MA: Harvard Business School Press.

Hamel, G. and L. Valikangas (2003), 'The quest for resilience', *Harvard Business Review*, **81** (9), 52–63.

Harvard University Gazette (2005), Cambridge, MA: Harvard News Office, 20 October.

Kennedy, D. (1997), *Academic Duty*, Cambridge, MA: Harvard University Press.

Kerr, C. (1982), 'Postscript 1982', *Change*, (October), 23–31.

Kirp, D.L. (2003), *Shakespeare, Einstein, and the Bottom Line: the Marketing of Higher Education*, Cambridge, MA: Harvard University Press.

Moody, J.A. (2005), 'Rising above cognitive errors: guidelines for search, tenure review, and other evaluation committees', self-published paper available at www.DiversityOnCampus.com.

Sexton, J. (2004), 'The common enterprise university and the teaching mission', available at www.nyu.edu/about/sexton-teachingmission04.html.

Shaw, K.A. (2005), *The Intentional Leader*, Syracuse, NY: Syracuse University Press.

Trower, C. (2003), 'Whither the traditional faculty?', *Trusteeship*, **11** (1), 34–5.

Weick, K.E. (1976), 'Educational organizations as loosely coupled systems', *Administrative Science Quarterly*, (21), 1–19.

PART III

Implementing change at colleges and universities

12. Institutional change: the why and the how

Kenneth A. Shaw

'Often a new program is just another management fad in an endless series of such fads. A model of change doesn't correspond to reality. This is why so many fail' (Duck, 2000).

> Three words come to mind when I think of the [police] chief: Chain of command. If the chief were beside me while I choked on a gumball, he would walk to his office and call the Deputy Chief of Support Services. The DCSS would inform the major in charge of the Criminal Investigation Section to alert the Captain of the Investigative Services Division. The Captain would inform the Lieutenant in charge of the Crime against Persons Unit, and the Lieutenant would send a Sergeant from homicide to Heimlich my corpse. (Kerley, 2004)

What does Perry, a middle-level executive at a national consulting firm, say about change? The following is an excerpt of an interview that I conducted with Perry, who prefers to remain anonymous.

Perry, in your experience, what are the most important things to know about effecting change?

1. You need strong estimating skills – that is, you need to be able, through data and experience, to determine if the change is going to be worth it.
2. While a long-term vision is important, you need short-term goals that can be realized.
3. You need a change agent – a leader who is behind the project 'come hell or high water', a person who removes obstacles so that momentum is maintained.

Perry, when change efforts fail, what is usually the cause?

1. Having a thousand ideas, but no focus or follow-through.
2. Not rewarding those responsible for implementing change.
3. Leaders who show ambivalence – they are not behind the project, 'come hell or high water'.

I begin this chapter with quotes from others to remind you that institutional change is extremely complex. It requires sophistication, the ability to *do* leadership and the ability to deal with two important questions: why change and how? In the following sections, I begin by stating some general observations about leadership and change, moving from there to the question of why. Then I tell a brief story, which leads to the important 'how' issue.

OBSERVATIONS ABOUT CHANGE

I have the following observations about the change process that I formed during my years as an academic leader.

Not all change is good While the change or perish mantra may be true in many cases, Abrahamson (2004) reminds us that organizations can perish because they change. Maybe change is not what was needed.

Is this the right time for change? Will the culture reinforce the change needed? Is this the right change to push at this time?

Technology is only a tool to use in making change happen It is not the be-all and end-all. We must use this tool wisely and strategically; we cannot make the mistake of believing that technology is the sole reason for the change or the sole tool to be used in making change happen.

Too often leaders press for wholesale, transforming change when important, lasting change around the margins is what is needed A good example is what happens with the short shelf life of too many superintendents of urban public schools. A new person is appointed; soon after, she announces a program to correct all the ills in the school system. The basics of the new program are usually spelled out under a very catchy acronym that is soon forgotten when the leader flames out or moves to a bigger job just a few years later. Was there not anything the previous leader did that should be preserved and enhanced? Could previous accomplishments have been built on while the problematic issues were given more attention? A leader who wants to make a lasting impact builds on what is working while also focusing on what is not.

We generally underestimate the degree of change needed in our institutions This may seem to contradict the last two observations, but I do not think so. Let us look at three ways to describe institutions and the change dimension.

First, there are institutions that merely need to improve incrementally to stay at the top of their game. As long as there is careful monitoring of the external environment and continuous improvement of what is working, things go well. Of course, the big danger here is complacency. The saga of the big three US automakers is a lesson in the danger of believing one's own PR rather than keeping pace with changes in the public's needs and desires.

Then there are those organizations that are losing ground or are barely keeping pace with their competitors. Continuous improvement alone will not be enough. Major change is needed.

And thirdly there are those institutions that require transformational change to maintain viability. Institutions in serious financial crisis, where their very existence depends on positive, effective change, do not have the luxury of incremental improvement or in change efforts that fall short of transformation.

Most universities fall somewhere between the second and third situation. I believe that most of us make the mistake of underestimating what we need to do. If we are tempted to think we are one of the fortunate ones that can get by with just continuous improvement, we probably should be thinking about major change. If we think we are in the second category, it is quite possible that what is needed comes closer to transformation. And if our need is for true transformation, we must get moving! Low-balling our analysis of what is needed is a serious mistake, leading to even greater challenges in the future.

Change is also about emotions In another publication (Shaw, 1991), I observed that universities and other social institutions go through a grieving process when they are dealing with change, analogous to what individuals feel when they confront their own death or that of a loved one. Ross (1969) and others have defined the stages of grief as denial, anger, bargaining, depression and acceptance.

Institutions and their members must deal not only with the objective issues at hand but also with the emotions surrounding them, and often they are very significant. Many change efforts fail because leaders neglect the affect that goes with major change. They misinterpret denial as institutional stupidity and anger as directed to them personally. Change is laden with heavy emotion because people are giving something up for the unknown. Successful leaders never ignore the feelings, often strong feelings, that accompany change.

Change requires leadership And it requires people 'doing leadership', not just talking about it. Warren Bennis – scholar, advisor to four US presidents and internationally acknowledged expert on the subject of

leadership – believes he was not particularly good at 'doing leadership'. When he was the president of the University of Cincinnati in the 1970s, he had an epiphany. There was, he discovered, a real difference between being a leader and 'doing leadership', and he knew that he was not happy doing it. 'I wanted to be a university president', he said, 'but I didn't want to do it' (Bennis, 1993, p. 81).

Luckily for those who care very much about leadership, Bennis changed his course and went on to become one of the foremost thinkers and writers in this field in the past 25 years. He was right. Being and doing are very different things. I believe that in higher education there is no dearth of grand ideas about how to make change. Rather we suffer from an inability or unwillingness to do those things that are required to make things better. Leadership, then, is about the doing.[1]

Those leading change must be trusted Robert House and colleagues (2004) have conducted studies of leadership characteristics in 62 countries. In all these cultures trust was one of the prime attributes of effective leaders. When we think of trust, we, of course, think of people who are honest, honor their commitments and are compassionate. But trust also involves believing that our leaders know what they are doing – that they have the competence to lead us through change. Failure in change efforts can often be traced to the fact that those in the institutions simply do not trust their leaders.

Change requires more than the generation of new ideas to meet today's and tomorrow's challenges Let us distinguish between innovation and invention. Often we use the terms interchangeably and, I believe, inappropriately. An inventor comes up with something new and creative – something worthy of the label 'unique'. Certainly Thomas Edison and Henry Ford were creative geniuses, inventors.

Innovation is something else. Innovators take ideas – perhaps new ones, perhaps old, perhaps a combination of new and old, perhaps someone else's from somewhere else – and make them happen in the real world. Often an innovator's creativity comes from finding ways to make an existing organizational structure amenable to new approaches to change. As innovators take great ideas and find creative, sophisticated ways of making them work in the real world, they 'do leadership'; they make change.

Those of us in higher education do not suffer from a shortage of invention – new ideas. Rather, the change process gets bogged down because our commitment to implementation and our leadership skills are lacking. It will be those institutions with the organizational savvy, determination and persistence to make things happen which will see the greatest change.

Institutions that get caught in denial, anger and self-pity have convinced themselves that 'no one else is called upon to do so much' Objectively, of course, we know this is not true. How does the displaced autoworker who cannot find a job even at one-half his previous salary feel, or the programmer whose job has been moved offshore or the doctor forced to contend with rising expectations but at no extra cost? In truth, to date, the change required of our institutions of higher education and the people in them, even for those with major budgetary problems, pales by comparison with what is going on elsewhere in society. Effective leaders help people get past this feeling that they and their institutions are the only ones dealing with change.

WHY CHANGE?

Change is all around us, on both an individual and an institutional level. Young children seem to have the ability to use technology as if their DNA is wired that way. On a personal level, I am teaching this fall, and it was soon apparent that, without the ability to effectively use the Web, PowerPoint and Blackboard, I would be at a real disadvantage teaching today's eco-boomers. And institutionally, of course, higher education has seen enormous change brought about not only by technology but also by other changes in our environment.

We would all benefit by spending time with the directors of college and university libraries. In a few short years, they have had to adjust to Google's entry into the library picture and to undergraduate libraries becoming 'information commons' which Managan (2005, p. A27) sees as 'a growing trend of colleges and universities around the country'. One librarian described what is happening as a 'digital tsunami' – likening it to the enormous change that occurred when the printing press replaced the handwritten manuscript.

So, change is all around us. In most cases, the 'why' question can be answered simply by saying we have no choice. But we do have a choice as to what we change and how we go about it. Knowing that over two-thirds of institutional change efforts end in failure should give us motivation to want to 'do' change the right way. This leads to my story, which is followed by a set of principles dealing with institutional change.

THE SYRACUSE STORY

As was true for many good, selective – though not highly selective – private institutions in the late 1980s, Syracuse was hit by the double whammy of

a demographic downturn in the numbers of college-bound students at a time of great economic uncertainty. We had some difficult decisions to make. Would we try to compete for a greater share of the decreasing cohort of 18-year-olds projected through the 1990s? Or should we enroll fewer students and thus ensure that we kept quality high?

We chose to allow undergraduate enrollments to fall by more than 2500 students. Naturally there had to be a corresponding decrease in the numbers of faculty and staff. Not easy. All told, by 1999 we had cut in excess of $60 million from our base budget and become smaller not only in our student body but also by 165 fewer faculty members and 400 fewer staff. We did this without disenfranchising the tenured faculty and without gutting our complement of outstanding tenure-track young faculty. But that is another story for another time. This is a story about how Syracuse University underwent a transformational change.

The process began in 1992 with a $60 million cut phased in over five years, followed by another $6 million cut, which we euphemistically referred to as fine-tuning. And we crafted a new vision for the future: to be the nation's leading student-centered research university. We decided that this was an opportunity for renewal, for transformation, understanding that cutting budgets alone would not make us better.

We made the cuts strategically rather than across the board. For example, the academic side absorbed a 17 per cent cut while administrative services sustained a 22 per cent cut. And within each academic area priorities were set and followed, such that some programs received budget add-ons while others were trimmed. One program in particular experienced more than a 30 per cent reduction in its operating funding.

But, as I said, we did not stop with budget cuts. Rather, we used this situation as an opportunity to become a better place – an opportunity for both renewal and transformation. That transformation will never be complete – we have created a new set of challenges for the new chancellor to deal with, but the momentum we started will not stop.

When the restructuring program was announced in 1992, we launched 33 initiatives for improvement. Three or four of them did not work out, but most did, including an improved faculty reward system, the integration of undergraduate research and teaching, the improvement of advising, a much stronger first-year experience, the promotion of active learning, the blending of liberal arts and professional studies, improvements in retention, enhanced services through a quality improvement program, and numerous unanticipated but welcomed spin-offs that occurred in the spirit of the student-centered research university enterprise.

I am very proud of our results. Each year at the annual meeting of our Trustees, I would present what I call the dashboard indicators of the

institution's well-being. The indicators that I presented in May of 2004 showed that over the 13-year period of my tenure – from 1991 to 2004 – we acquired a more diverse faculty and witnessed a 90 per cent increase in high school students coming from the top 10 per cent of the class. There was a two-thirds improvement in our two-year attrition rate and an improvement in our six-year graduation rate from around 70 per cent to over 81 per cent.

Alumni responded by supporting the successful Commitment to Learning fund drive to the tune of over $370 million – and over $700 million over the entire 13 years of my tenure. During that time Syracuse earned the Hesburgh Award for Innovation in Faculty Development and awards for academic advising, among others.[2]

Today Syracuse is a much better university. *Change* magazine had this to say: 'Today Syracuse is down the road toward its becoming the nation's leading student-centered research university. It can serve as a model for institutional change and leadership in the cause of undergraduate reform.'

So, there has been a transformation – not everything worked, and we have not finished yet – but we learned a lot, lessons I will now pass on to you.

Having a crisis really helps Ours was not quite a crisis, but it was a serious challenge. Had we done nothing, we would have found ourselves with a crisis – serious financial difficulties and no plan to work our way through them. We knew we had to do something, since 85 per cent of our operating budget came from tuition charges and the auxiliary services that serve our students. We had to cut our budget and we had to be a student-centered place in more than just rhetoric.

I note that recently the University of Wisconsin System has been dealing with its budget challenges. One of its consultants said, 'This isn't something that the System can muddle through. Budget reductions can't be based on "everything is going to be OK" principles because that will deteriorate student learning and decrease student access to faculty.' The Wisconsin Regents discussed a plan for trying to ensure quality while taking a huge hit to the System budget.

Perhaps you do not have that kind of crisis. This is for you to decide. Do you have a crisis? A challenge? Or maybe just a small problem that you believe will go away. You had better be thinking about it.

Think about the entire system and its interrelatedness Any substantive change in an institution has implications far beyond the area directly impacted. The National Association of College and University Business Officers (NACUBO), under the leadership of Jay Morley, is engaged in a project to build organizational capacity (BOC) by attending to the most

important and interrelated institutional elements when change is needed.[3] BOC identifies eight such elements: mission/vision/goals, systems, policies and practices, structure, processes, infrastructure, governance and culture. If all or most of the elements are not addressed, change often has a short life. In SU's case, the budget cuts would not have had legitimacy if we had not involved our entire governance system – internal and external. Our efforts to be more student-centered would not have worked if we had not instituted changes in the faculty evaluation system. We could not have advised students better had we not attended to the processes that were being used. Whether there are eight such elements, more or less, is not the issue. Rather, it is essential to recognize that change involves attending to the interrelated parts, if it is to have a lasting impact.

Be transparent At Syracuse we opened our books to everyone, which was unique for a private institution. In fact the news spread nationally when the *New York Times* published an article about our financial difficulties. It did not hurt our enrollment, although many felt it would.

The materials we released showed how we spent our money and where, which schools and colleges were bringing in more money than they spent, and which were not doing well. And some truly were not doing well. At that time a good dean was expected to stay within the budget given; there was very little consideration of matching income brought in with expenses.

All of this openness gave us the credibility to move forward. Some felt we had billions of dollars in reserve and hence no problem. Showing our reserves solved that issue. Others thought we were broke and headed for financial ruin. Showing everything helped people understand that that was far from the case – that as a matter of fact we were poised to spend money to save money if that made sense (and it did and we did).

Focus on the institution's mission, vision and core values Change does not come out of nowhere – it has to be grounded in what the institution represents. At Syracuse we used our values, mission and a new vision statement to direct our energies. We stressed core values – quality, caring, diversity, innovation and service – repeatedly during the first few years of restructuring. Our mission statement was revised to state that together we would promote learning through teaching, research, scholarship, creative accomplishment and service. That, too, was frequently repeated. And we crafted a new vision for the future – to be the nation's leading student-centered research university. Students soon picked up on the acronym (SCRU). These three, the values, mission and vision, guided our efforts. It is essential to know and to articulate mission, vision and values.

Improve services to students and the learning community quickly We did this through a quality improvement program, which involved every staff member. It proved to be far more complex than necessary, but in the end services improved greatly. We learned the importance of focusing on our 'customer'. We had to ask ourselves who our customers are, what their needs are, and how best to meet them. The biggest gain from this enterprise was getting groups from all over the campus to work together through the training process. I will not say it has taken hold a hundred per cent, but I will say that services greatly improved, as did morale.

Expand learning opportunities for students outside class We know that students spend more time outside class than in. Therefore we developed 29 residential and non-residential learning communities for our beginning students.

Of course, student services and academic affairs must work together to make out-of-class learning experiences happen. Under the newly revised orientation program, the schools and colleges now require summer reading from their students. We also created a Center for Public and Community Service that now oversees 500 000 plus hours per year of student volunteer time and over 40 academic courses that have a service-learning component. The university also imposed additional fees to support academic department organizations, leadership development, outdoor education, arts, community cultural events and the like to provide wholesome, academic-related activities out of class.

Walk the talk As we were cutting budgets, we spent $2 million over three years on improving teaching. Faculty projects to enhance teaching at the lower-division level were given priority. That carries over to today, with a variety of these kinds of projects being funded through the University Vision Fund administered by the Vice Chancellor and Provost.

In the early 1990s Syracuse received a gift of about $5 million. That money was unrestricted. We chose to use it to emphasize the importance of teaching by creating the Meredith Professors. These are singular honors for professors whose excellence as teachers sets them apart. Since two are appointed each year and serve a three-year term, there are six Meredith Professors at any one time. Each receives $22 000 as a salary add-on for those three years, plus $10 000 in funds for professional development for them and their departments. We walked the talk.

Borrow from others Remember, the goal is innovation not invention. It is all right to borrow good ideas from your peers; actually it is all right to borrow from those below you in the pecking order. Some very great ideas

come from institutions that you do not feel are as distinguished as yours. Focus on the strength of the ideas and how they can be adapted rather than on who is doing it.

Keep the pressure on Complacency is always tempting. I like to describe Syracuse as a place that is dissatisfied – it has done a lot but knows it must do even more with scarce resources. This creates a healthy dissatisfaction, which results in the constant pressure to get better.

To enhance the academic enterprise, our Board of Trustees allowed us to take $5 million a year beyond the norm from the endowment for academic improvements. This money is not given out across the board. Under the leadership of the Provost, an academic plan was developed which focuses on four areas of emphasis – information management and technology, environmental systems and quality, citizenship and social transformation and collaborative design – all interdisciplinary programs requiring high levels of collaboration and cooperation. That plan also calls for continuing to improve the undergraduate learning environment.

Give people the tools for change Too often we misinterpret people's resistance to change as their being opposed to everything. In fact, people can deal with even enormous change if their fears are allayed and they are given the reasons and the tools for change. We confronted people's fears by reminding them that, once the cuts were made, if we committed a hundred per cent to our vision, things would get much better. And they did. And, while cutting budgets we also spent millions of dollars on curricular reform, quality improvement programs, and reinforcing our in-house programs for staff. We defined ourselves as a learning community where all were expected to learn. People did buy into the program; the university continues to provide resources for faculty and staff to continue growing.

Use triage in dealing with resistance to change There are three types of people when it comes to change: (1) those who will support the change if it can be shown that it is in the best interest of the institution, (2) those who are on the fence waiting to decide whether the change is going to succeed, and (3) those who resist regardless of the value of the change proposed. It is better to spend more of your time shoring up the committed and encouraging the fence sitters. Trying to woo the strongly opposed diverts your energies and raises questions about your true commitment from those who would support if things were handled correctly. While we did not have very many people in the third category, we did not give them much of our time either.

Show immediate progress While it is important to have long-term and middle-range goals, more is needed. We did frequent updates through our various news organizations to show that things were progressing – that our efforts were paying off. This gives people pride and creates the momentum necessary to sustain the effort.

Involve the people During the time before the announcement of our restructuring plan and afterward, thousands of people were involved. The University Senate and its committees developed over 90 policy recommendations for me to consider. Open forums were held to encourage new ideas. A preliminary plan was released to give the university community an opportunity to comment; hundreds did. During the implementation phase, all staff received quality improvement training and many faculty and administrators were deeply involved in making the 33 initiatives successful. We were engaged and busy.

Persist In my observations and study of leadership I have noticed that very little attention is given to persistence. We read and hear much about charisma, about transforming leaders, about the personal characteristics of leaders, about the environmental influences that impact on what leaders can and cannot do, but little is said about what I believe is highly under-rated – the importance of persistence.

I have seen effective leaders who had dandruff on their suits and halting speech but who somehow remained standing after everyone else had gone home. Similarly, institutional change requires more than just a chancellor and provost being persistent. It requires people believing in the cause and being willing to dedicate their time and talents to it. It requires people willing to stay the day, to not give up, to persist.

CONCLUSION

I began my discussion with a series of observations about change and the change process. On the basis of these observations, I then examined the reasons why leaders strive for change. During my tenure as Chancellor of Syracuse University, I developed my own principles of change. During this time, Syracuse faced significant financial challenges. Confronting these challenges required change, difficult change. This chapter describes our efforts to change the university for the better while alleviating the financial crisis. I have tried to generalize the steps that we took to achieve successful change at Syracuse into a set of principles that can be applied in other settings.

NOTES

1. To learn more about doing leadership, see Shaw (2005).
2. The Hesburgh Award is presented annually by the TIAA-CREF Institute and the American Council on Education. The TIAA-CREF Hesburgh Award recognizes exceptional programs designed to enhance undergraduate teaching and learning. Named in honor of Theodore M. Hesburgh, CSC, President Emeritus of the University of Notre Dame and former member of the TIAA and CREF Boards of Overseers, this award seeks to strengthen the teaching tradition at America's undergraduate colleges and universities by acknowledging that an energized faculty is the key to educational excellence. Syracuse University won the award in 1996.
3. For more information on the BOC initiative, see 'Building organizational capacity', at www.nacubo.org, accessed July 2004.

REFERENCES

Abrahamson, E. (2004), 'Moving change', Harvard Business School Case Study.

Bennis, W. (1993), *An Invented Life*, Reading, MA: Addison-Wesley, 81.

Duck, J.D. (2000), *Harvard Business Review*, (July/August).

House, R. et al. (2004), *Cultural Leadership and Organization: the Global Study of 62 Countries*, Thousand Oaks, CA: Sage.

Kerley, J. (2004), *The Hundredth Man*, New York: Penguin Group.

Managan, K.S. (2005), 'Packing up the books', *Chronicle of Higher Education*, **51** (43), A27.

Ross, E.K. (1969), *On Death and Dying*, New York: Macmillan.

Shaw, K.A. (1991), *The Successful President: Buzzwords on Leadership*, Phoenix, AZ: Oryx Press.

Shaw, K.A. (2005), *The Intentional Leade*r, Syracuse, NY: Syracuse University Press.

13. Effecting institutional change through innovative capital financing

Michael F. Adams

A great deal of external, visible, physical plant change has taken place at the University of Georgia over the past nine years. Many people do not understand what has taken place in the state of Georgia and at the University of Georgia, the first state-chartered public university in America. This backdrop has in many ways made our on-campus constituents tired of change.

The University of Georgia is an institution in what is now the ninth-largest state in America, whereas 15 years ago the state of Georgia was grouped among those southern states trying to find industrial might and economic opportunity for the future. Along with California and Florida, Georgia has been one of the fastest-growing states in the nation over the last ten years. The University of Georgia has grown from 25 000 to 35 000 students in a period of less than 15 years, going from what was a better-than-average, open admission, public flagship university to what is now – according to grades and board scores – one of the most competitive public universities in America. Admission is routinely denied to fifth- and sixth-generation applicants in a rapidly changing environment where the social dimension remains tied to change coming out of the racial politics of the 1960s and 1970s. Today the state is enjoying a time of dramatic growth, particularly in the northern arc of Atlanta, with a high-tech business and economic environment that rivals those in many other parts of the United States. A great deal of this change was already in motion when I arrived almost ten years ago.

In fiscal year 2001 the University of Georgia received $421 million from the state in a budget of about $1.2 billion, or 41 per cent of its budget. Today, the total budget is approximately $1.4 billion, with that growth largely fueled by an explosion in research, but UGA receives about $20 million less from the state than five years ago, for a total state contribution of about 31 per cent. These changes reflect national trends. Georgia was actually very late coming into the recession of 2002 and 2003 and has been

late coming out of it; happily, for fiscal year 2006 the budget is back to where it was several years ago.

The major theme of the change that has been implemented at the University of Georgia is straightforward: to become the kind of institution envisioned in our strategic plan – to be not only one of America's best publics but also certainly one of the best universities in America – will require a campus-wide commitment to excellence. When I arrived in 1997, a considerable level of complacency existed. Most of the senior administrators had been in their jobs for many years and were nearing retirement. The members of the University System Board of Regents, when they hired me, told me they wanted new blood, new plans and new visibility. They told me they wanted a change agent and they got one, for good or ill, depending upon whom you ask. They wanted me serving on national boards; they wanted me speaking at higher education conferences; they wanted to raise the visibility of a rapidly changing institution.

Michelangelo said, 'The greater danger for most of us is not that our aim is too high and we miss it, but that it is too low and we reach it.' And, frankly, there had been some of that in the history of UGA. My predecessor, Dr Charles Knapp, deserves a great deal of credit for beginning the process of change, but after a ten-year period as president he had decided to move on to other ventures. The challenge that remained was one of overcoming complacency in a traditionally conservative southern state, and there are two ways of overcoming complacency. One may be characterized by the old joke that 'the beatings will continue until morale improves'. The other is to offer a clear vision of benefits to the affected parties in order to secure buy-in, and we have tried to follow the latter approach.

When I arrived at the University of Georgia, we were facing very serious physical plant challenges. In 1997 the UGA campus was like many others: some quite good Georgian architecture and some excellent historic structures, one of which dates to 1806 and was built by a great gentleman, Josiah Meigs, who started the University of Georgia and modeled Old College on Connecticut Hall at Yale, where he had taught. Like many other institutions, the University of Georgia also built some of the worst buildings in history, particularly during the 1960s and 1970s. They are characterized by poor architecture, poor utility and high upkeep. These are ugly square boxes with flat roofs and few redeeming aesthetic qualities.

Georgians love North Campus, the oldest section of campus and the equal of any in the country, I believe, for its sheer beauty and architectural charm. Moore College is the home of the Honors Program. Meigs Hall is home to the Institute for Higher Education, and Phi Kappa Hall is the traditional home of one of the university's debating societies. We have taken special care of this part of the campus. It tugs at the heart strings of most

of our alumni and it has been easy to raise the money to do the kind of renovation that has been needed there. Historic buildings like Candler Hall, Meigs Hall, Phi Kappa Hall, Moore College, the Administration Building (which was the university's first stand-alone library and home of the Georgia Museum of Art for many years) all exemplify the ongoing effort to renovate and preserve the university's valuable old structures.

South Campus has been quite different. This is a large area of campus, over 600 acres with north, south, east, west and central precincts. UGA's campus grew southward in the 1960s and '70s, driven largely by a rapidly developing science complex. As it grew, however, the character of North Campus was discarded for a style that is modern and postmodern in the worst sense of those terms. We hired the Ayers/Saint/Gross firm from Baltimore, the master-planning consultants for the University of Virginia and Emory University, which we thought were two of the best campuses in the South, to help us develop a master plan and a full set of design standards for any campus facility.

Meanwhile, the faculty was wondering where all this money would be coming from and how it would impact on everyone's compensation. The consultants worked closely with the Office of University Architects, the Physical Plant and the senior administration, holding forums to gather input from the entire campus community. We indicated that we would be moving the parking decks to the periphery of the campus; that you could not park next to your building any more; and that dramatic design changes were on the horizon. The campus was going to be more pedestrian-friendly and energy-efficient, and we were going to build things in an entirely different way.

Achieving the goals of the master plan required two things: a set of design standards and an entirely new set of funding mechanisms that differed from the way the University of Georgia had done business in the past. There is a fine line between having buildings that all look alike and having a set of meaningful design standards that bring continuity to a campus. The master plan says that a building at UGA built in the Georgian style would look as if it belongs at the University of Georgia, and it would also address long-neglected core infrastructure issues that most large universities have not handled very effectively. Danny Sniff, the campus's chief architect, has a very good presentation entitled 'Why does it cost so much to construct a building at the University of Georgia?' As Mr Sniff states, the first factor is quite simply a commitment to the quality of construction. Developers around the campus build apartments more cheaply than we build residence halls, but we do not want to build cheaply (and, in the short term, they do). Developers also build office space and dining facilities more cheaply than we do. The issue of site selection is key, of course. We are

bound by the existing limits of the campus and often must build on very tight sites, limiting the 'lay down' space needed for construction equipment and, by extension, increasing costs and lengthening timelines. The academic calendar also impacts on costs by necessitating aggressive and tight construction schedules with multiple shifts and night and weekend work.

A commitment to quality guides choices at all stages of the building process. All utilities are underground now. Mechanical systems and their enclosures are tastefully screened and all service access points are hidden. We exceed engineering codes in every aspect of construction; we use hard pipe conduit larger than that required by code and larger than flexible metal conduit. We require brick exteriors, even on taller structures; we require sloped roofs, slate and standing seam only. We require precast concrete for cornices and other details, for both aesthetic and maintenance reasons. Many of the systems are designed to be linked rather than to function alone. We use concrete structural frames rather than steel, although a building can go up more quickly with steel, which is the choice of most private developers today.

With this commitment to quality in the master plan comes a concomitant acknowledgement that quality costs more than conventional construction. There are always tradeoffs between having the maximum space available in the building, which is usually desired by the faculty and other administrators, and ensuring quality and long-term viability. A school or college at the University of Georgia that wants to maintain a certain level of quality cannot simply build the biggest box possible. Quality may mean less space, but it also means less maintenance and longer usage. Senior administrators must become involved in adjudicating those kinds of decisions.

One of the toughest construction decisions I made came early in my career at Georgia. I cut 30 000 square feet out of our signature Student Learning Center in order to maintain quality and meet the guidelines on required materials like brick and granite and marble, rather than wallboard and sideboard, which would have allowed the full building to have been built. The Student Learning Center is a three-story classroom and electronic library space in the center of the campus. It has become the academic heart of the University of Georgia, visited by people from 47 states, in use at all hours and well received by students and faculty. It also symbolically espouses this new quality standard, both intellectually and physically, and an adherence to a set of design standards that ensures long-term viability.

There were additional battles regarding the design of one of the university's most important research facilities, the Complex Carbohydrate Research Center. The desire again from the faculty was for as much laboratory space as possible. Some, frankly, said they cared very little about the

aesthetics of the building. By the time we designed the Paul D. Coverdell Center for Biomedical and Health Sciences, however, which is scheduled to open this year, the campus culture had begun to change. This building is a twenty-first-century center for biomedical and health research and represents the kind of planned, careful design process that will propel us physically into the future. Both the interior and exterior spaces blend form and function in an aesthetically pleasing way. Over time the impact of the master plan, with green space and quality construction, had begun to shift the campus mindset about what quality change in the physical plant really means.

In that vein, every campus should develop a firm set of guidelines for construction standards. Once the guidelines are in place and the entire community has devoted at least some level of adherence to them, it is amazing how many issues down the road can be solved when plans or proposals do not meet the original agreed-upon design standards. It is also critically important to get buy-in from a campus in the early stages of this kind of physical change; otherwise people will react negatively to the changes to a place that they know very well, believing that the place in its present condition looks the best it could ever look.

We undertook two early projects that, while not major parts of the master plan in terms of facilities, demonstrated the principles of the master plan in a very visible way, and in a way that had a positive impact on people's lives. These projects were controversial at the start, but once completed they helped build credibility for the entire plan. The first was the conversion of a Herty Drive parking lot into Herty Field. Herty Drive is an access point into North Campus from downtown Athens, which lies immediately across the street on the northern edge of campus. In 1997 Herty Drive included a 139-space parking lot, pure asphalt that was ringed by some of our most historic buildings. Historically, this area was the site of UGA's first football game, in the 1890s, versus Auburn. A parking lot was clearly out of place there. One of the tenets of the master plan is an expansion of green space, so we proposed that the parking lot be restored as the original Herty Field. The immediate response was not very positive, especially from those 139 people, most of whom were administrators who were parking in the heart of North Campus every day. Today, however, Herty Field is one of the most popular spots on campus. Given Georgia's climate, students, faculty and staff are out on the field almost every day of the year. The use is profound. The Terry College of Business sponsors a weekly concert series in the spring and fall; a fountain serves as an informal meeting spot; people read, play Frisbee and nap throughout the day. Herty Field today looks like the campus spots that we all feature in our recruitment literature.

Similarly, as part of a project to improve the South Campus infrastructure to support the Coverdell Building, D.W. Brooks Drive, which was named for one of the university's largest benefactors and is the main access point into South Campus, was converted into a lawn and pedestrian mall. The reaction was predictable. Brooks Drive's associated parking was used by thousands of UGA faculty and staff and students every day. But the site was ugly, barren and uninviting and surrounded by those 1960s and 1970s buildings. What is there now is just as attractive as North Campus and has become a popular site for departmental and school and college receptions and special events.

We have employed multiple creative funding sources on these and other projects, almost a billion dollars' worth in the past nine years, using a mix of private funds, some public funding and some bonded indebtedness. When possible, in cash-rich areas like athletics, those funds have helped pay down indebtedness, resulting in increased future flexibility from a bonding standpoint. Georgia's state construction process can take up to ten years from the approval of a building to actual facility completion. The University System Board of Regents maintains a capital construction projects priority list, submitting three to five projects each year to the legislature for funding and adding others to the bottom of the list. Currently the Regents' list contains a $600 million backlog in System-wide unfunded projects, with about $130 million of that at the University of Georgia: a $40 million expansion of the College of Pharmacy building; a new special collections library, $36 million; and a College of Veterinary Medicine teaching hospital, almost $70 million. We need those facilities today, but we could expect them in four or six or eight years with legislative funding. We realized that we simply could not wait for the state to meet such pressing facility needs.

In 1999 the University of Georgia Real Estate Foundation was created specifically for the purpose of providing a mechanism for meeting these needs faster. The Real Estate Foundation has a board of three university people and eight of the best developers in the state of Georgia. It provides a funding vehicle for the university to address strategic capital and property acquisition through a fiscally responsible debt structure by taking advantage of some of the most favorable bond market conditions in the history of the United States. Since its inception the University of Georgia Real Estate Foundation has helped finance more than $200 million in campus facilities. They include the Complex Carbohydrate Research Center, where some of the most sophisticated research on cancer causes in the country is taking place; the Coverdell Center for Biomedical and Health Sciences, now a $42 million project; East Campus Village Housing, the first new housing built on the campus since 1968, at $72 million; the East

Campus Commons Dining Hall, $17 million; expanded studio space for the School of Art and the College of Environment and Design, $4 million; and two new parking decks at $17 million each. In finding money for these facilities during a time of shrinking state support and a Regents' policy of funding only purely academic facilities through state funds, the Real Estate Foundation has been cited as one of the most innovative entities in the country. What follows are two examples of how the Foundation has helped meet campus needs.

The Paul D. Coverdell Center for Biomedical and Health Sciences is the centerpiece of a growing research program at UGA and is perhaps the single most creative financing arrangement we have managed to date. Many lawyers were kept busy in the process of arranging the financing of this facility. Paul Coverdell represented Georgia in the US Senate from 1993 until he died of a stroke in July 2000. He was one of those moderate senators held in high esteem by colleagues in both parties and we were soon engaged in a conversation with two UGA alumni, Senators Zell Miller of Georgia and Phil Gramm of Texas, about an appropriate memorial. A proposal for a $40 million biomedical facility to be named for Senator Coverdell was developed in about three weeks. Congress, at the urging of these Georgia alumni, appropriated $10 million for the memorial. Governor Roy Barnes of Georgia, who was close to Senator Coverdell although of a different political party, agreed to match the federal commitment with $10 million in state money. The university pledged to raise the remaining $20 million and in about a seven-day period we had gone from nothing to a $40 million commitment.

To keep all the local, state and federal lawyers happy, we actually had to condominiumize the air rights of the building to help assess and regularize who owned what part of the facility for the terms of amortization. We partnered with the local economic development authority and the local housing authority to issue bonds to finance some of the construction. While there is no direct monetary benefit for these local agencies, which had never engaged in a project like this before, they recognized that a healthy, vibrant and forward-moving University of Georgia is critical to the economic well-being of the entirety of North Georgia. Some indebtedness will be paid off by leveraging indirect cost recovery dollars generated by additional research; in short, the building will pay its own way, with the university receiving a $40 million building for only $20 million of its own money. This financing arrangement is allowing the University of Georgia to meet immediately a pressing need for biomedical research facilities that would have taken at least ten years to meet if the proposal had gone through the normal state process. We broke ground for the Coverdell building in January 2003 and moved into it in November 2005. It is a 135 000-square-foot-area with

wet labs, 30 procedure rooms, six chemical hood rooms and space for 275 scientists, staff and graduate students. In total, it is a project that met all of the design standards and moved from conception to completion in just over two years. Such an accomplishment would have been unthinkable even five years ago.

Similarly, the UGA Real Estate Foundation was the vehicle for the financing and construction of a new home for the Complex Carbohydrate Research Center, one of the university's most successful research programs. The CCRC was recruited to Georgia in 1985 from the University of Colorado with its team of 16 faculty and support staff. It now houses approximately 300 scientists, working on major health concerns from cancer to Parkinson's disease to diabetes in a 140 000-square-foot building. The Real Estate Foundation actually owns title for this facility and leases it back to the university, as that was the most cost-effective way to do it. The payments are generated by additional indirect cost recovery, and the building is designed to look like some of the early mills that shared the Oconee River location of the current CCRC.

The UGA Research Foundation, another cooperative organization, manages an endowment that is helping us build to completion an animal health research center, a bio-safety Level III facility. This is another joint state–federal initiative that will allow our researchers, in concert with Atlanta's Centers for Disease Control and Prevention, to analyze tissue samples of all animal-borne diseases in the southeastern United States. If there is an outbreak of West Nile virus or bird flu in the United States, this facility will be ground zero, along with our adjacent veterinary and pharmacy schools. For this structure, the state provided $25 million, the university $15 million, with an additional $15 million coming from UGA's external support. Again, the payback mechanism is similar to those above.

We have done the same sort of thing, but usually with more cash, in the athletics area. We have done some refinancing under the lower, favorable rates that have been available for the past four to five years. We paid down a great deal of long-term indebtedness, which improved the entire cash flow process at the university and, importantly, strengthened the future bonding position. Among the facilities that have been added in athletics are new skyboxes, which immediately paid their own way; an upper deck in Sanford Stadium, taking capacity to almost 95 000; and a women's athletics complex with softball and soccer fields. Work is beginning now on an additional $30 million practice facility for men's and women's basketball and women's gymnastics.

Faced with cutbacks in state funding, limits on the types of construction for which public funding can be used, and growing demand for a variety of campus facilities, the University of Georgia has taken the initiative to meet

those needs through aggressive and innovative funding mechanisms. It is this kind of entrepreneurial spirit, now better understood by on-campus constituents, that has helped the faculty as well as the administration take great pride in the fact that change can happen in two or three years, rather than only in ten- or twelve-year increments. Paul Young, the former dean of architecture at Ohio State, has said that the academic quality of a place is often reflected in the architectural standards of a place and that learning does take place best in an environment which is conducive to it. The quality of the learning environment speaks symbolically of the quality of a place and it is not accidental that quality places look like quality places. A healthy change agent with supportive buy-in by key constituencies, coupled with creative financing, can lead to change in the learning environment that will enhance research, improve instruction and increase commitment to public service. That is what has been achieved collectively through creative change at the University of Georgia.

14. Implementing renewal and change

Robert H. Bruininks

In Chapter 13, Michael Adams has addressed the major capital changes at the University of Georgia, where the construction of some new buildings meant the destruction of parking lots. That reminded me of how Clark Kerr, the late president of the University of California System, once described a university as a loose association of individual scholars 'held together by a common grievance over parking' (Kerr, [1963] 2001, p. 15). As President Adams has addressed the challenges faced in revitalizing a campus's capital infrastructure, in this chapter I address change in the academic aspirations, directions and culture of the University of Minnesota.

I believe the British author John Galsworthy got it right when he said, 'If you do not think about the future, you cannot have one' (1928 [2004], Part II, Chapter 6). In my judgment, these times require thinking in a self-conscious way about the future of higher education and the future of our institutions – and our responsibility to shape that future. Daniel Seymour (1995, p. xix) wrote: 'Sailing a ship across the Pacific is no different from organizing a college or university for performance improvement. In both instances, it is immensely helpful if we can come to some agreement on which way to aim the pointy end.' So I am going to address the special challenges today in 'aiming the pointy end' of our institutions, and I am going to start by describing the context – a context that may be familiar to anyone in public higher education today – that was the setting for the University of Minnesota's strategic plan and the very ambitious positioning effort that we are pursuing at the present time.

THE CONTEXT FOR CHANGE AT MINNESOTA

I was asked to assume the presidency of the University of Minnesota on an interim basis in the summer of 2002, when Mark Yudof left the post to become Chancellor of the University of Texas System. At that time, Minnesota's projected revenue shortfall was about $2.5 billion dollars over the next two fiscal years. By November, when I was officially asked to take

the presidency on a more permanent basis, that amount had nearly doubled. I was haunted by a comment that H. Ross Perot allegedly made when running for president: 'A vision without resources just could be an hallucination.' (I also said to myself, on numerous occasions, that I might have picked a better time to assume the presidency!)

On a per capita basis, Minnesota's problem was on the scale of the contemporaneous state shortfall that faced California. It was enormous. To compound matters, we had our governor's unprecedented pledge not to raise taxes, a pledge that no previous governor had ever taken under similar circumstances. Whenever we had had a crisis like this in the past, the solution had been both to increase state taxes and reduce expenditures.

The University of Minnesota sustained a 15 per cent cut to its two-year budget in 2003 – the largest at that time, to my knowledge, given to any public college or university campus in the United States, even in a period of cuts and retrenchments in state budgets around the country.

We decided to use the challenges we faced to help establish the case for change and undertake a very ambitious strategic planning and positioning process. We began formally in the summer of 2004, at a retreat of the University's Board of Regents, and by the next spring we had put a plan on the table for the Board of Regents to review and ratify, followed quickly by a set of 40 recommendations to position the University for a strong future.

The University of Minnesota is similar to the University of Georgia: it is the state's major land grant and research university. With 53 000 students, our Twin Cities Campus is the second largest in the United States this academic year, but we also have three other campuses, plus research stations and extension offices throughout the state of Minnesota. And we have one of the broadest ranges of academic fields in any university across the world. So it is a fairly large and complex place, making 'aiming the pointy end' all the more challenging.

MAKING THE CASE FOR CHANGE

Although Minnesota is really only at the beginning of this exciting adventure, I think there are points worth noting about how we have navigated this process of change so far. There are remarkable similarities between our process and what Kenneth Shaw and Michael Adams have described in Chapters 12 and 13. I think they would agree that in most of our universities, in most of our experiences, we spend too little time making the case for change and preparing people for change.

The typical route in changing and positioning institutions of higher education is to appoint a committee. Then the committee creates a strategic

plan; you argue about the strategic plan; and it ends up being mostly an academic exercise, largely because the community that you are dealing with is not sufficiently engaged to actually reflect on the process of change and act upon it.

At the University of Minnesota we understood that, to have any chance of succeeding, we would need our entire community to understand the context – to help create a sense of urgency, to use the terminology of John P. Kotter.[1] It is absolutely critical to engage all of the relevant communities in the conversation at the very front end of the process and to spend time preparing the people who comprise your organization.

One area where I believe we did a very thorough job was in engaging our external communities. For example, I sought an audience with the Minnesota Business Partnership, which is made up of the CEOs of the 100 largest corporations in Minnesota. I made the case that the University of Minnesota was their most important asset when it came to competing in the global economy. That led to them inviting me to join their organization, and later their executive committee. It also led to my involvement with something called the Itasca Group, an informal group of civic and business leaders, which was formed to call attention to issues related to the future of our state, the region and the regional economy. The Itasca Group named the University of Minnesota as one of its chief priorities and asked the CEO of 3M to lead a study of the future of the University of Minnesota and its connections to Minnesota's private sector. There were also two other studies that looked at the university and higher education in Minnesota, one commissioned by the Legislature and one commissioned by Governor Tim Pawlenty through a local civic group called the Citizens' League.

Each of these situations involved in-depth conversation about the future of the University of Minnesota, and in each instance we helped create a broader awareness of the university's role in the state and the context and challenges it faced. It was not all about asking for increased state and private support or lamenting state budget cuts. The point was that we made a public commitment to improve the university's direction and performance and its connections to the needs and interests of Minnesota. We really wanted the university not only to be positioned as the cornerstone of the state's economy and its future but also to be perceived as a force for change and innovation. In short, we wanted the university community and our external community to feel a sense of urgency to reform the University of Minnesota.

We did engage opinion leaders and the public, but public relations alone was not going to be enough for us to regain a somewhat eroded public trust. Most people in our state do not believe that universities – or any large

organizations, for that matter – are capable of reforming themselves and, truthfully, our university had a reputation as particularly set in its ways. So we undertook some very visible reform initiatives.

One of these initiatives had to do with reforming the service culture of our business operations at the University of Minnesota. I kept making the point publicly that I wanted the university to be known as much for the quality of its service and management as it is for the quality of its academic programs. That notion resonated very deeply with the business and civic leaders in our state.

We started what we call an Office of Service and Continuous Improvement. It reports directly to my office and is designed to inject a lot of innovation into our administrative practices. For instance, we spend approximately $110 million on utility costs just to stay warm in Minnesota during the winter. I believed we had to figure out a way to drive down those costs, and we were able to do that through new conservation practices, the purchasing of energy futures and many other small improvements. In fact we drove down energy costs per gross square foot even while putting newer, more energy-intensive facilities online.

We reorganized the University of Minnesota Extension Service, bringing it out of 92 county-based offices into 18 regional centers and creating a stronger connection between local communities and research at the University of Minnesota. We improved the student experience, connected with key constituencies, streamlined university operations and strengthened our connections to Minnesota communities. At the same time, I decided that we ought to bring the football program out of the Metrodome, a downtown professional sports complex, and back to the University of Minnesota.

All of these initiatives were our way, in this early stage, of making the case for change in a very deliberate and self-conscious way. We knew we were going to launch a strategic plan and positioning exercise, but we did not just spring it on people; we tried to create the case for change, prepared for it and tried to prepare others as well.

ENGAGING LEADERSHIP IN THE CHANGE PROCESS

We gave special attention to engaging our system of governance and oversight. As a student of these processes at the University of Minnesota and of organizational change and development more generally, I had noticed that many previous attempts at transformative change had failed at the University of Minnesota because people lobbied the Board of Regents to

change its mind on one aspect or another of an overall plan, which would often end up unraveling the entire plan. So, engaging the board was an essential priority.

After a year of discussion regarding the budget challenge and important trends in higher education, we formally brought the need for strategic positioning to the board's summer retreat in 2004. They embraced it so thoroughly that they decided to make it the centerpiece of their annual work plan and I heard the board chair say the other day, regarding strategic planning and positioning, 'We demanded that the president do this. We asked the president to do this.' And, as much as I would like to take some credit for moving this process forward, I was glad to hear the board's feeling of ownership. They really made the plan their own, chartering it in the early fall of 2004. At that time, I appointed a working group of university faculty and administrators under the leadership of Tom Sullivan, Senior Academic Vice President and Provost, to develop an initial strategic positioning document that would evolve, given the input of the public and the university community and the oversight of the board.

Our Board of Regents is highly engaged and takes issues of oversight very seriously, meeting nearly every month of the year for a day and a half. So, over a two-year period, we put together special work sessions where my administrative team and I met with all 12 board members and examined the broad trends affecting higher education generally and the University of Minnesota in particular – the demographic challenges, economic challenges, and so on. At the same time, my administration and I engaged on a regular basis in some very deep and probing conversations about the intellectual future of the university with our Faculty Consultative Committee.

CONTINUING ENGAGEMENT

The engagement of our governance system was not just in the launch but for the duration of the entire process. How did that work? I have already mentioned that in the summer of 2004 the Board of Regents affirmed the need for planning and the need to position the university in a new way. In September we brought them our vision of what the strategic planning process would look like and we asked them whether our strategy addressed the appropriate questions and issues. In October we brought to them for review the values and planning principles for evaluating programs and setting priorities. At the board's November meeting, we brought in the state economist and the state demographer to talk about how changing demographics and financial trends were likely to affect state priorities and needs.

Our Provost, Tom Sullivan, addressed the major trends in the direction and organization of higher education. We talked about financing the future of the university in December, looking at its revenues, its expenses and the possibilities for being more creative in the future. And, as I indicated, these work sessions have become a regular part of the work plan of the board going forward.

At the same time, we also engaged the public in an ongoing conversation. So, as the board and the university community were deeply engaged in these issues, we went out to the general public, talking to business leaders, talking to civic leaders, talking to legislators, all by way of keeping them not just informed but engaged in this process on an ongoing basis.

PUTTING EVERYTHING ON THE TABLE

It was important to me that this process be broad enough in scope to actually address the challenges we faced. One of my favorite expressions comes from the naturalist John Muir, who once remarked that everything in the universe is connected to everything else. Often, when we think about strategic planning and higher education today, there is a tendency to think only about academic priorities, interdisciplinary programs or the education of students. All of these are important elements of strategic planning, but we thought it was important to also look at the service and management side of the University of Minnesota, because, while there are roughly 3500 tenure-track faculty members at the university, there are about 15 000 other employees who support the work of those faculty members and the university across Minnesota. So, if you examine the academic programs of the University of Minnesota without looking at the rest of the institution, you have misalignment rather than alignment. In this process, we set out to look at everything, academic and non-academic, to take this as a systemic challenge and responsibility.

On the basis of the evolving mission, values, evaluation criteria and action strategies, in January 2005 I appointed two task forces to create recommendations that would support these elements of our planning process. One task force, made up of academic leaders and headed by Provost Tom Sullivan, was charged with developing recommendations for academic improvements and priorities, and another, headed by Vice President for University Service, Kathleen O'Brien, and Executive Associate Vice Provost, Al Sullivan, was asked to develop recommendations to improve the university's service culture and administrative management.

MAINTAINING TRANSPARENCY AND COMMUNICATING THE VISION

From the beginning, we adopted a clear and transparent process. People who oppose some of the recommendations and ideas might disagree, but, as Shaw has pointed out in Chapter 12, when you make changes and decisions, when you set priorities, it is a very emotional process in our institutions.

Given the goal of engaging the broad university community in the process of transforming the university, it was essential that our process be open, transparent and information- and communication-rich, as was Shaw's at Syracuse University. The strategic positioning work group held university-wide town hall meetings in November and took input via the strategic positioning website.

As I have mentioned, in January 2005, just a few months after launching the strategic planning process, the strategic planning working group came forward with a strategic positioning report that, using the regents' input, outlined the university's mission, aspirations, criteria for decisions and action strategies going forward. (I think this might have been a record time for a planning process at a college or university.)

In late March the two academic and administrative task forces came forward with more than 40 recommendations for transforming the University of Minnesota. The recommendations for the re-design of the university included the integration of three colleges into other colleges as well as major recommendations for reforming the education of our students and the competitiveness of our research, and the way we conduct our service, our business and our administrative operations.

From February to June 2005, we held consultations with at least 17 governance and advisory groups, 6 major student groups, 8 collegiate campus units, the board and more than half a dozen community groups, including elected officials. Our administration sent regular letters and e-mails to update the entire university community on the progress of our process, and we continued to take input on the draft report and later the draft recommendations on the strategic planning website.

And the discussion about change pervaded our joint governance structure. The University Senate, which I usually preside over, conducted an animated two-hour debate in which the faculty took over. They asked me to sit down and listen (a rare event at the University of Minnesota!) and they actually conducted this debate, which was one of the most marvelous discussions about the future of the University of Minnesota that I had ever experienced in my 37 years there. And then the Senate voted 120 to 3 in support of the strategic plan and positioning process, with its extensive recommendations for reform. I thought that was an unbelievable event. The

chair of the Board of Regents agreed and told me later that he doubted the University Senate would vote to support a 25 per cent increase in its own salary by a vote of 120 to 3!

For me, this was an important time to 'communicate the change vision', to use Kotter's language, and I attended many of the consultation sessions listed above and conducted more than 20 interviews about strategic planning with newspaper editorial boards and reporters from all types of media (Kotter, 1996, pp. 85–100); I even went on Governor Tim Pawlenty's weekly radio talk show to present the plan and its recommendations.

What was amazing to me in this process – because universities have been characterized, from time to time, as being the places on the planet where all changes are resisted as a matter of principle – is how quickly the campus community and the citizens of Minnesota embraced this effort. And they embraced it not just with a simple majority but very affirmatively.

Frankly, I think we underestimate the hunger of the university communities that we represent for the kind of change this book addresses. We talk about complacency, often at great length. But we do not often celebrate the kind of resources, the kind of ingenuity that our colleagues bring to their work each and every day. And many of them are too humble to express the sense of adventure and commitment that would create a better future for our institutions. The Board of Regents reflected this excitement. After reviewing the strategic positioning report, called 'Advancing the public good', in February, the Regents endorsed it unanimously at their March meeting. After extensive consultations in March and April, I presented a slightly modified version of the recommendations put forward by the two task forces in a document called 'Transforming the University' to the board in May and they approved it by a vote of 11–1 in June.

MOVING FROM PLANNING TO ACTION

To my mind, strategic planning without action is probably an empty exercise. To help ensure we could move quickly from ideas to action, we incorporated action strategies that were within the initial strategic plan, the precursors to the sweeping recommendations that went to the board in May–June 2005. Once the board accepted the recommendations for change, we created an implementation framework that is aggressive in its time frame and its scope.

I was heartened that, when we sent out a call for volunteers to work on 34 proposed task forces, nearly 600 people responded for 300 slots. That is a clear indication of a pent-up demand for change and the desire to be a part of a successful enterprise.

Some of these 34 task forces are charged with implementing specific recommendations, be they college consolidations or administrative improvements, and others are taking a closer look at how the university can best meet the future in broad areas such as internationalization, the education of our students, the support of research and the structure of our programs in science, technology and health.

Critical to our work was the creation of a task force charged with metrics and measurement, in order to help us clarify our aspirations and assess whether we are making progress toward achieving them. I believe great organizations measure what they value. This task force is helping us monitor the implementation and impact of our strategic planning recommended actions. An important aspect of the renewal process in our institutions is the achievement of agreement on measures and processes that will be needed to guide internal reform and public accountability. At the University of Minnesota, that discussion is underway, but by no means concluded.

LESSONS LEARNED

Keeping this process moving, and broadening it as we have, has required a great deal of time and effort on the part of staff and leadership in the central administration. But I believe this investment of effort is key to maintaining momentum and excitement around these ideas and aspirations. While we are still quite 'in process', I can offer some lessons learned from our experience thus far:

- Prepare and make the case for change. Do it as thoughtfully and deliberately as the process itself, highlighting long-term trends in programs, resources and demography, with attention to both internal and external audiences.
- Charter the process. If you do not get the buy-in and engagement of governance at the front end, you are likely to pay dearly at the tail end. For us this meant careful work with faculty and staff leadership groups, internal and external constituencies and the university's Board of Regents.
- Establish strong, visible leadership at all levels of the institution to drive the planning and change processes.
- Address both the academic and the administrative side of your operations. If you spend $2.5 billion a year as we do at the University of Minnesota, you have to take a close look at your service and management practices. They support and sustain the excellence of our academic programs.

- Use transparent processes, with ample opportunity for input from the university community and the broader community.
- Communicate your vision and recommended actions broadly, both within and outside the institution, and be prepared to defend them vigorously.
- Develop a plan of action as part of the strategic planning and positioning process. It is not enough to put the plan on the table. You have to move quickly, without hesitation, from the affirmation of a plan to an action strategy. As one of my friends from the banking industry puts it, you have to develop the plan, you have to work the plan and that is what it is all about.
- Create a measurement, assessment and public accountability system to track how well you are doing and the progress you are making. Doing so is, to my mind, essential to sustaining the renewal process over the long term.

With so much time, effort and expense at stake, the question that Kenneth Shaw raises in Chapter 12 must be faced squarely: is this change worth the cost? I think it clearly is. I often think of Washington Irving (1824 [2004], p. 7), who wrote, 'There is certain relief in change . . . As I have often found in traveling in a stagecoach, that it is often a comfort to shift one's position, and be bruised in a new place.' Change can be rough and tumble, and it can be bruising. At the risk of mixing my transportation metaphors, change is usually well worth the cost if you can find broad agreement on your institutional direction – on where to aim the pointy end.

ACKNOWLEDGMENTS

Dan Gilchrist and Eve Wolf in the Office of the President at the University of Minnesota contributed research and other assistance for this chapter. The author would like to thank the University of Minnesota's Board of Regents, senior administrative officers, Faculty Consultative Committee and University Senate for their help and leadership in strategic planning and positioning.

NOTE

1. I have found Kotter's (1996, p. 21) eight stages of transformational change, the first of which is 'establishing a sense of urgency', to be a useful framing device for understanding planning and positioning. Kotter's work was used extensively in workshops and discussions during the university's process.

REFERENCES

Galsworthy, J. ([1928] 2004), *Swan Song*, Adelaide, AU: eBooks@Adelaide, web ed., accessed on 30 November 2005 at http://etext.library.adelaide.edu.au/g/galsworthy/john/swan/

Irving, W. ([1824] 2004), *Tales of a Traveler*, Whitefish, MT: Kessinger Publishing.

Kerr, C. ([1963] 2001), *The Uses of the University*, 5th edn, Cambridge, MA: Harvard University Press.

Kotter, J.P. (1996), *Leading Change*, Cambridge, MA: Harvard Business School Press.

Seymour, D. (1995), *Once Upon a Campus*, Phoenix, AZ: American Council on Education/Oryx Press.

15. Observations and reflections on organizational change

Allan R. Cohen

The chapters in this volume can be seen as an urgent plea for change in the world of colleges and universities – both in their relationships to external environments and within the institutions themselves. In Chapter 2 Stanley Ikenberry provides an overview of the competitive challenges faced by the US economy and the crisis likely to result if public support for higher education continues to weaken. Authors discuss the need for the base costs of education to be reduced so that students outside the top income quintile can still afford a college degree. Ideas for revenue enhancement and cost cutting are offered by James Hearn, William Kirwan, David Breneman, Benjamin Quillian and David Longanecker. The need for change in dealing with external constituencies and forces is manifest in their analyzes.

Particularly compelling is the discussion in earlier chapters about the competitive race for attracting students by means of fancier facilities and amenities only loosely connected with the learning context, and the impact on costs and tuition charges. This problem of the commons can only be addressed collectively – a dim prospect without a champion who can gain attention and perhaps government pressure. As state and federal support diminishes, there is greater need to attract tuition dollars, making it hard for individual institutions to get off the runaway train of competitive spending.

Arguments for controlling costs, possibly through cooperative buying arrangements (such as the Boston Consortium, which has 13 colleges and universities collaborating on purchasing, training and other services), all make sense, but implementation will require a new, collaborative attitude among already pressured administrators. I have seen how hard it can be to get such collaboration going, for reasons of pride, 'not invented here' attitudes or snobbery, traditions that die hard and short-sighted managers. Nevertheless, as the theme of the book suggests, a new balance between economic imperatives and institutional autonomy will have to be found.

Some of the changes discussed, however, demonstrate that it is possible to alter the usual ways of doing business. Michael Adams, of the

University of Georgia, in Chapter 13, describes how clever policies of working with the multiple stakeholders and creative financing could enable the massive building and renovation of the physical arrangements on campus in a timely manner. Careful planning can change how space is used and can create conditions for better research. But, while we can embrace the proposition that sound minds develop in sound buildings, educational reform still needs to capture the hearts and minds of faculty, not just gain their compliance. Teaching and learning cannot be done well by people who are just going through the motions or who think that information transmission is higher education. We need to prepare people for an increasingly complex and interdependent world, where thinking and problem-solving are the prime outcomes of education. This was one of the implicit messages contained in David Kirp's (2004) analysis of the glories and limitations he found in his wanderings through the groves of academia in the US.

At the heart of the educational enterprise is the behavior of the faculty, those charged with delivering the education that justifies the existence of educational institutions. The creation of knowledge certainly matters and the country is in a dangerous position without the resources to fund it or the continuing interest of current and potential researchers – by no means assured, given the reduced number of those going into the sciences and engineering. But students need to learn and faculty behavior is central to that.

As I see it, the real challenge is in moving faculty. It isn't just a joke that it is easier to move a graveyard than change faculty and curriculum. Universities are designed for inertia, as Cathy Trower eloquently states in Chapter 11. Many different individuals and groups can derail any proposal, yet almost no one is considered to be legitimate to declare a direction or meaningful policy. Structurally, there are too many people in the act and traditions of egalitarianism give everyone, and therefore no one, a voice. As my colleagues and I (Cohen et al., 2005) wrote:

> In fact, [academic institutions] suffer from an *overload of many forms of participation* (on the academic side anyway), and structural and cultural barriers to action on all the ideas. Academics seldom are willing to delegate to colleagues anything on which they have a strong opinion – whenever they decide to get involved. So decisions get stalled or revisited, initiatives start without widespread support and just trickle along, many individuals and groups can say no, but almost no one is legitimized to say yes, or to insist on it against (loud) minority opposition. OD [Organization Development] was partly developed to counter the top-down, directive traditions of industry in the 50s and 60s, so it takes for granted that there is in place an enabling authority system that must be democratized to get the best ideas and most commitment. It wasn't really designed for the extraordinarily decentralized structures of academia.

In that context, changes to employment practices, as outlined by Ron Ehrenberg (Chapter 8), discussed by Kermit Hall (Chapter 10) and modeled by John Sexton's powerful use of a visionary story to recruit, motivate and compensate faculty differently (Chapter 9), are certainly useful. Sexton's plea that we change the way we shame and honor faculty, and not let tenure be the way of defining status, offers one potent way of energizing behavioral change – and requires change skills that are in short supply.

The challenge, then, is to figure out how to lead change in our own institutions. Change is needed for the sake of educational improvements, but also to improve our public image. Unless we reform ourselves, we are not likely to dent the public view of higher education as a bastion of privileged, self-serving and expensive elites who do not care about the worries of ordinary citizens. By demonstrating that they are competent at the 'tough stuff', like managing costs, successful change agents can gain credibility with those who have a narrow view of what matters and then gain latitude to do more creative change work. That is how I interpret the success of Jack Welch, the former CEO of General Electric, whom *Fortune* named as the best manager of the twentieth century. He spent several years buying and selling businesses, reducing staff from 400 000 to 200 000 and raising it back to 300 000, thus earning the nickname 'Neutron Jack'. This gave him credibility with the GE board and allowed him to tackle the 'software' of business: culture, talent development, confidence, risk-taking and entrepreneurial behavior in a huge organization.[1]

Even schemes to raise more money so that we can institute new programs, while probably necessary and sometimes extremely valuable, can be a lever for other changes – or a sidetrack. We have to keep in mind the warning of Dave Longanecker (Chapter 6): 'New spending from new revenue is good, but it can divert from the core teaching mission.' Revenue enhancement has to help us carry out the core educational mission, not be an end in itself.

Reforming the core educational mission, however, brings us back to faculty and their role in the educational experiences of students. Unlike some of my colleagues in higher education, I do not directly equate good research with good teaching or good education. It is not just that some good researchers are neither interested nor effective in their teaching role, but that not all teaching-centered faculty are creating effective learning either or are teaching what they should. Effective education is always about more than information transmission (written or otherwise recorded material does that reasonably well); it involves learning fundamental skills and meta-skills of thinking, communicating, problem-finding as well as problem-solving, living with and embracing ambiguity and uncertainty, learning how to learn and keep on learning, and how to understand one's

own goals and efforts in larger contexts. Subject matter is only the ground on which this can take place. Educational reforms that fail to encourage these kinds of learning do not go far enough.

For the purposes of this chapter, I will not address in any detail another difficulty in faculty behavior: far too much 'research' is trivial, aimed at publication in journals read by only a handful of narrow specialists and not particularly helpful to society. Social benefits, however, are precisely the justification for research activity at universities, especially those publicly funded. Fortunately, Cathy Trower (Chapter 11) does an excellent job of skewering the misplaced efforts of many faculty members and the structural reasons why meaningful change is so difficult.

While I agree with her diagnosis, I am more optimistic about the possibility of moving what I like to call 'the last Mandarins' – full-time, tenure-track faculty members. (I include pre-tenured faculty because, even when they identify with behavior that is needed for educational reform, they fear that they will not receive tenure if they do not play the current game. I have never forgotten the young faculty candidate from Wharton who told us that, when he won a teaching award there in his first year, two senior faculty members told him he was lucky, 'because by the time you come up for tenure, no one will remember this'.)

Despite the forces for deep resistance, then, I believe that at least some important change is possible in some contexts. I am encouraged by the incredible accomplishments of John Sexton (Chapter 9) at NYU and Robert Bruininks (Chapter 14) at the University of Minnesota, and the hard-earned wisdom about change provided by Kenneth Shaw (Chapter 12), but also by my own experiences at Babson College. Over a number of years, we accomplished transformational changes in curriculum, classroom practice, learning outcomes and institutional standing.

Because I have written about this elsewhere (Cohen, 2003; Cohen et al., 2005), I will only summarize what we managed: we changed tiers, moving from a decent regional player to national rankings in all our programs (undergraduate, MBA and executive education). Moving up is a mixed blessing, however, since we now compete for students and faculty with business schools that are part of large universities with huge endowments, places like Harvard Business School, The Tuck School at Dartmouth, Wharton at the University of Pennsylvania, and at the undergraduate level with outstanding (and well-endowed) liberal arts colleges such as Bates, Bowdoin and the little Ivies. Our undergraduate program reforms won TIAA-CREF's Hesburgh prize and a Pew award, and our integrated curriculum at the graduate level has been a model for other business schools.[2]

In that curriculum, for example, the first year of the full-time MBA eliminated 13 separate discipline courses (the standard assortment) and replaced

them with four integrated modules. Faculty address the same material from various perspectives; students engage in a year-long consulting project with a mentor company; student teams work in an unfamiliar art form to learn about creativity and present their products to the community. It still is not easy to get faculty to design and deliver together a curriculum that consistently provides global and entrepreneurial skills, fosters teamwork and ethical awareness, and integrates all knowledge and skills, but I think we have done it. The undergraduate curriculum made similar changes, identifying core competences and building classroom and field experiences around them.

To accomplish these radical changes, we had to reform our decision-making processes. We agreed that to compete we needed to become faster and more flexible, so we delegated decentralized decision making to small, elected bodies for undergraduate and for graduate programs, with five faculty at large, two students and the respective dean empowered to make curriculum decisions. We charged each group with studying the external environment and adapting the curriculum to sustain suitability, and turned the old decision making on its head: the burden of proof now is on the dissenters, not on the advocates of change. Although there is a 'fail-safe' mechanism that allows dissenting faculty to initiate a plenary discussion that could trigger an overriding vote, in a dozen years that has only happened once, and the dissenter was defeated by a 93–7 vote. There is still considerable participation in curriculum decisions, through open hearings and departmental discussions, but faculty with good ideas no longer assume that they will be defeated in the glacial and log-rolling politics of the past, and therefore they can make serious proposals that are investigated, modified when necessary and implemented.

In the process we have attracted far superior students and many talented faculty, despite the intense demands created by integrated teaching and higher research expectations. We also reengineered and utilized Total Quality methods for many of our administrative processes, reducing costs yet providing much better service to students.

The resulting increase in rankings, student quality, student satisfaction, fund raising and employer attraction have reinforced the general directions we moved in, though I would be remiss if I did not admit that, without vigilance and administrative effort, there is constant temptation for faculty to slide back toward the stovepipes of traditional disciplines. The narrow academic training of PhD programs and the marketplace for researchers, decried by Trower, sustain the siren song for younger faculty, even those who love what we have created but fear for their marketability if they do not receive tenure or want to move elsewhere. Although we are forced to compete against more elite schools and universities now, so far we have managed to sustain the changes we made.

ORGANIZING LEARNING ABOUT CHANGE WITH THE CHANGE FORMULA

As a way of summarizing what has been said in this book and what has to happen to lead change, I suggest use of a change formula that was developed by management consultant David Gleicher and modified according to my experiences and training. The formula is:

$$C = f(D \times V \times S \times P) > Co,$$

that is, change is a function of the product of dissatisfaction with status quo, times vision of the ideal future state, times support, times pathways for accomplishing the change; all greater than the cost of the change.

The formula is written as an equation because all the terms inside the parentheses are multiplied by each other and, if any one of them is zero, the whole result drops to zero and change does not happen. In my career I have seen change fail when any one of the four elements is not present. Grand visions have gone nowhere because key players liked the status quo or the visionary had no idea how to put in place the necessary processes. Change agents with wonderful tools could not get traction because they were not tied to a meaningful vision. I will explain more about each term and connect back to other chapters in this volume.

Managing Dissatisfaction with the Status Quo

Although dissatisfaction is necessary to get us ready for change, we know from learning theory that moderate dissatisfaction or tension is best. Too much dissatisfaction, and people tend to freeze (as in maths anxiety); too little, and they see no need to be bothered.

If faculty are as self-satisfied as Trower (Chapter 11), Kirp (2004) and others say, it is necessary to show them enough about external dangers to raise their dissatisfaction, making them a bit more tense. This may appear counter-intuitive, since managers have been bombarded with the idea that they should try to make everyone happy, but it is necessary. For example, when I was Academic Vice President at Babson and we were discussing the need for curricular and other changes, I realized that many faculty members were not convinced that being good enough was not good enough. As a result, I deliberately talked in every faculty meeting for two years about competitive threats and we did surveys of employers to show how poorly some companies regarded our graduates. Deans did the same. Some faculty were puzzled or annoyed, but we needed more discomfort with the status quo or, as the industry metaphor goes, a 'burning platform'.

As Shaw advises, 'Having a crisis is a good thing', and Kirp quipped, 'A crisis is a terrible thing to waste.'[3] It needs to be used as a motivator.

Similarly, sometimes it is necessary to slow down to get tension into the moderate zone. After we really got rolling at Babson, for example, in response to my sense that we had so many initiatives going that people were feeling overwhelmed and again resisting, I made one overhead with our core vision at the center, and all the initiatives and activities linked to it, to demonstrate that there was coherence to all the efforts. As organized information often can do, it seemed to help people relax a bit and allow for more movement.

Vision

It will come as no surprise that articulating a powerful vision of the future desired state is a critical part of serious change efforts that require others to cooperate. Many of the authors in this volume, including Bruininks, Adams and Shaw, mentioned this in one fashion or another; John Sexton talked about it as having 'a story', and Fritz Fleischmann reminded us that 'everyone wants to be part of something great'.[4] This is exceedingly tricky in the academic world, however.

For one thing, there is almost as much cynicism among academics as among business people about lofty vision statements that are created, posted, included in the institution's literature and then completely ignored. No one wants to get excited about some grand purpose and then discover that he or she is all alone waving arms and shouting. And it is not easy to find genuine common vision among the many colleges, programs and departments in a large university. It is far easier to say that vision is important than to decide which one is inspirational in that context, concrete enough to be understood, broad enough to cover the gamut of activities and viable enough to be credible as an aspirational statement.[5] Far too many vision statements are not worth the cost of printing them.

Furthermore, the idiosyncratic way that authority works in academia makes it especially hard for senior administrators to take the lead in establishing a vision. You cannot get too far ahead of where the faculty are or the very attempt will create resistance. Faculty members do not like to be told what to do or what to aim for. On the other hand, most faculty complain about 'lack of vision or leadership' in their leaders, so they, like all humans, have a desire for direction. Thoughtful timing can help us overcome this impasse: allowing a great deal of wallowing in the territory, and then coming in with an articulation that pulls together many ideas and shows participants how higher-order agreement is possible. Given the daily stresses under which educational leaders labor, the ability to lift concrete ideas to a higher level of abstraction is no mean feat.

Of course, it is not nearly enough to articulate a compelling vision; as Shaw (Chapter 12) points out, you have to walk the talk and follow up consistently or the elegant phrases become empty words and generate cynicism. In fact, not only does the leader have to behave consistently with the vision to make it real, but many policies and practices have to be aligned and executed consistently in order to make the vision stick.

John Sexton (Chapter 9) mentions his experiences at St Francis College in Brooklyn, which reminded me of work I did with the College of the Holy Cross in Worcester, Massachusetts. In one draft of a possible vision statement, Holy Cross said it wanted to be 'the pre-eminent liberal arts college that in the Jesuit tradition educates men and women for intellectual and moral leadership'. But it took a great deal of discussion to figure out what that meant and who would be the relevant competitors. Should Holy Cross be competing with Boston College and Gonzaga, or with any outstanding liberal arts college such as Amherst, Williams, Wesleyan or Swarthmore that claims to develop leaders? And what would it mean for athletic teams, residence halls, classroom pedagogy, curriculum and so on? Taken seriously, a vision can stimulate transformation of all aspects of an organization, which is certainly not easy.

A variation of this need is that vision becomes relevant to leaders at all levels of the organization. The institution's larger vision does not always specify what the physics or history department will become, how the financial aid office will be run or how student affairs relates to students. Leadership implies change, so each leader needs to articulate a vision for his or her unit and live it.

Although different visions or aspirations will appeal to different faculty groups and individuals, very few faculty members do not care about student learning or how students perceive them. No one wants to be disrespected. It is not impossible to unite faculty in a common cause that includes learning, though I admit that some faculty members can disguise this quite well.

Support

Even brilliant visions will not be realized if the key stakeholders are not supportive or at least neutral. Figuring out how to influence them is central to producing change. There are great examples of this from Adams at Georgia (Chapter 13) and Bruininks at Minnesota (Chapter 14); both leaders identified critical stakeholders, in and outside the university, and used everything from creative financing to allowing widespread participation in order to win necessary support. One important suggestion is to chart all possible stakeholders in advance, so that no important ones pop

up to create havoc unexpectedly. President Adams discovered late that students wanted a voice in the campus and building designs, which fortunately did not end his building program, but might have been anticipated. Shaw (Chapter 12) has several good suggestions in this realm, including transparency, quick wins, providing the tools needed to implement the changes and triaging which stakeholders to cater to and which just to be nice to.

My own advice is to embrace resisters, for two reasons: sometimes they actually know things that are useful, and by listening carefully you reduce secondary resistance. They may still disagree, but do not become furious and retaliatory for feeling cut out.

I immodestly suggest that the model of influence without authority that I developed with David Bradford, based on reciprocity and exchange, can be a useful guide for dealing with difficult stakeholders (Cohen and Bradford, 2005). The basic idea is that you have to determine what 'currencies' stakeholders value and find ways to give them some of what they value for what you want. The chance to believe in a compelling vision, for example, may be enough to get some stakeholders to play, though others may prefer status, recognition, resources – especially those controlled by the individual, freedom (a faculty favorite) or an infinite host of other things. Most individuals and groups send many messages about what they value (and why they resist), but eager change agents sometimes are so busy insisting on how wonderful their change is that they never hear what it would take to gain cooperation.

Pathways and Procedures

Even with the right kind of moderate dissatisfaction, a well-articulated vision and support from key stakeholders, change is unlikely to take hold if no one knows how to get there from here. If, for example, you want to pursue the cross-disciplinary grail but the faculty do not know how to share the classroom, cannot make curriculum decisions as a team and have no integrated teaching materials, your worthy goal may elude you.

To sustain a new direction, eventually everything about the way an institution is run should align with the strategy and vision. As discussed in other chapters, in order to sustain innovation, recruiting, hiring and retention, rewards and incentives, administrative systems, information systems and the like need to be at least consistent with the intended changes. Even physical facilities may have to be altered to support the changes. At Babson we had to make over 200 changes to support systems in order to implement our new MBA curriculum, ranging from when residences had to be ready to accommodate an earlier fall start, to how we distributed materials, assignments and a complicated new class schedule to students, to when the

bookstore would be open. And when undergraduate reforms were implemented, some of these had to be changed again.

Cost of Change

There is no free lunch. In addition to the enormous amount of time and effort required, meaningful changes will incur many costs. Some good people will be deskilled and have to spend a long time learning new ways to be effective. Some will lose power or status. Others will have social connections broken, which is seldom discussed but drives a lot of behavior in the academic world. Just try to get people to change their office locations or reassign their favorite janitor to another building, and see the resistance!

As John Sexton suggests, some faculty members may have to go, if they cannot go along with the new way, whatever that is. In fact, if some faculty do not decide that they would rather be at a place that is more to their liking, the changes and all the supporting arrangements have probably not gone far enough. There is ample diversity among institutions for many of those who want some other direction and policies to find another home, though not everyone is mobile or adaptable. And not all of those who do not accept the changed direction or practices will decide to leave; they will exercise their faculty prerogative to complain mightily. (Although I am observing at a distance, I suspect that Larry Summers' troubles at Harvard are connected with his mandate to alter some traditional practices there and not just with his remarks on women and science. As Shaw mentions, change involves emotions.)

Courage Needed

That leads to a final point. Change in any organization is never easy and it requires true courage of those who lead it. It takes courage to make some people uncomfortable, to commit to a vision even though we can never be certain it is the right one, to drive changes against opposition and yet find the heart and patience to listen to our critics and adjust plans accordingly.

It is important to be a good person, and critical to be a trusted one, but, if academic leaders only care about being liked and approved of, they are looking for love in the wrong places. More likely than not, you can achieve 'beloved' status only after the battles are over and the new ways have taken root. The coming crises in higher education, so aptly diagnosed in this volume, require all our courage to lead necessary changes and to bear the personal consequences. More power to us all.

NOTES

1. For a discussion of Welch's accomplishments, see A.R. Cohen and D.L. Bradford (2002), 'Power and Influence', in S. Chowdhury (ed.), *Organization 21C: Someday We'll All Lead This Way*, a Financial Times Prentice Hall book, Saddle River, NJ: Pearson Education Inc., pp. 193–211.
2. Babson won the Hesburgh Award in 2002. This award is given by the American Council of Education in conjunction with TIAA-CREF to recognize exceptional programs designed to enhance undergraduate teaching and learning. Babson won the Pew Award in 1997. The Pew Award is given for the renewal of undergraduate education and recognized the development and initial implementation of a new integrated undergraduate curriculum.
3. In David Kirp's presentation at 'The New Balancing Act in the Business of Higher Education', a conference sponsored by the TIAA-CREF Institute, 3 November 2005.
4. Comment by Fritz Fleischmann, Dean of Faculty at Babson College, at 'The New Balancing Act in the Business of Higher Education', a conference sponsored by the TIAA-CREF Institute, 3 November 2005.
5. For further discussion of vision, see Vaill, P.B. (with Cohen, A.R.) (2003), 'Visionary Leadership', in Allan R. Cohen (ed.), *The Portable MBA in Management*, 2nd edn, New York, NY: Wiley, pp. 17–47.

REFERENCES

Cohen, A.R. (2003), 'Transformational change at Babson College; notes from the firing line', *Academy of Management Learning and Education*, **2** (2), 154–80.

Cohen, A.R and D.L. Bradford (2005), *Influence without Authority*, 2nd edn, New York: John Wiley & Sons.

Cohen, A.R., M. Fetters and F. Fleischmann (2005), 'Major change at Babson College, curricular and administrative, planned and otherwise', *Advances in Developing Human Resources*, **7** (3), 324–37.

Kirp, D.L. (2004), *Shakespeare, Einstein and the Bottom Line: The Marketing of Higher Education*, Cambridge, MA: Harvard University Press.

Index

ACKNOWLEDGMENTS

The prices listed in this guide were gathered from dealers, collectors, auctions, and ads in collectors' publications. They were then computer sorted and double-checked to ensure maximum reliability.

Sherry Rich of Browning
Bill Mrock & Chuck Lanham of the B.A.T.F.
Tim Pancurak of Thompson-Center
Nadine Ljutic of Ljutic Industries
Jim Casillo and Fred Paddock of Navy Arms
Vicky Barton of Universal
Fred Karp of Sears, Roebuck & Co.
Brian Herrick of Hi Standard
Charley Gara of Charter Arms
Nolen Jackson of Wichita Engineering & Supply
Sharon Cunningham of Dixie Gun Works
Pat Bogush of Colt
Chris Graziano of Ruger
Judy Schroepfer of Kreighoff
Jinny Sundius of Marlin
Bob Greenleaf of Savage
Fred Hill of Dan Wesson
Bob Magee of Interarms
Ron Vogel of F.I.E.
Allen Fire Arms Co.
Boyd Davis of E.M.F.
V. Fresi & A. Seidel of Mauser-Werke
C. Ledoux of ManuFrance
Jennings Firearms
Beeman, Inc.
Rick Kenny of Stoeger Industries
J.P. Sauer & Sohn GmbH
John Hanson of Magnum Research, Inc.
Dynamit Nobel of America
Peter Hoffman of Carl Walther GmbH
Bob Saunders of American Derringer Corp.
Jay Hostetter of Praegers Gun Shop, Orlando, FL
Astra-Unceta y Cia.
Vincenzo Bernardelli
Dan Coonan of Coonan Arms, Inc.
Charles Meyers and Gary Rathman of the Florida Regional Crime Lab
Linda Lassotta of Heckler & Koch
Dot Ferreira of Remington
Jan Herriott of Detonics
Tol Cherry of Cherry's
Nancy Damone of Mossberg
Deanna McDermott of U.S. Repeating Arms
Frederich Hege of Hege Waffen
Bruce Hacker of Ventura Imports
Debbie Dean of Weatherby's
I.W. Walentiny of Tradewinds
Marian Partridge of Ithaca
Sy Wiley of Randall Firearms
John Hill of Webley & Scott
Tom Barness of Manurhin
John Leek of Sterling Arms Corp.
Ilan Shalev of I.M.I.
Marc Bauer of Action Arms Ltd.
Ira Trast of Auto Ordnance
George Numrich of Numrich Arms
Sig Himmelmann of United Sporting Arms
Bill Clede & June Sears of Smith & Wesson
Iver Johnson
Raven Arms
R.G. Industries
Guy Lepeintre
Syd Rachwal
David Rachwal
Peter Potter
Alvin Snaper
Col. Mel Pfankuche
Bill Drollinger
Chuck L. Doire of Healdsburg, CA